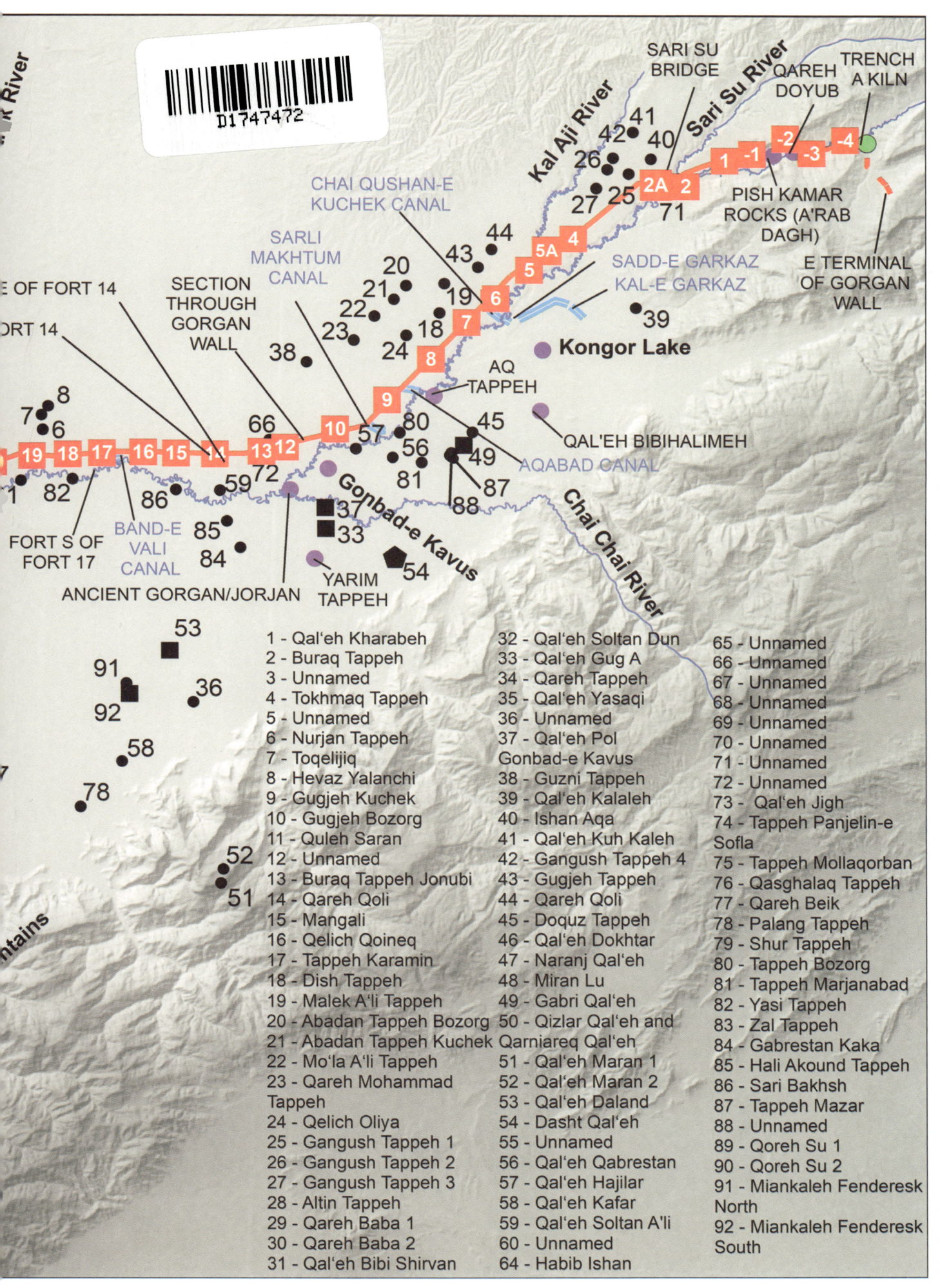

ANCIENT ARMS RACE:
ANTIQUITY'S LARGEST FORTRESSES
AND SASANIAN MILITARY NETWORKS OF
NORTHERN IRAN

ANCIENT ARMS RACE: ANTIQUITY'S LARGEST FORTRESSES AND SASANIAN MILITARY NETWORKS OF NORTHERN IRAN

A JOINT FIELDWORK PROJECT BY THE IRANIAN CENTER FOR ARCHAEOLOGICAL RESEARCH, THE RESEARCH INSTITUTE OF CULTURAL HERITAGE AND TOURISM AND THE UNIVERSITY OF EDINBURGH (2014–2016)

BRITISH INSTITUTE OF PERSIAN STUDIES ARCHAEOLOGICAL MONOGRAPHS SERIES VII, VOLUME 1

Generously supported by the European Research Council Persia and its Neighbours Project, the Iranian Center for Archaeological Research, the Iranian Cultural Heritage, Handcraft and Tourism Organization, the Ministry of Cultural Heritage, Tourism and Handcraft and the Research Institute of Cultural Heritage and Tourism.

EBERHARD W. SAUER, JEBRAEL NOKANDEH AND HAMID OMRANI REKAVANDI

With contributions by

C. RICHARD BATES, CATHY M. BATT, CARLO G. CERETI, MARIA DAGHMEHCHI, KRISTEN HOPPER, MEYSAM LABBAF-KHANIKI, SUZANNE A.G. LEROY, MARJAN MASHKOUR, MAHDI MOUSAVINIA, MOHAMMADREZA NEMATI, BARDIA SHABANI, LYUDMILA SHUMILOVSKIKH, MARTINA ASTOLFI, MOHAMMADAMIN EMAMI, MOHAMMAD ARMAN ERSHADI, ROYA KHAZAELI, EVE MACDONALD, FIONA A. MOWAT, DAVIT NASKIDASHVILI, TIM PENN, SETH M.N. PRIESTMAN, ESMAIL SAFARI TAMAK, ST JOHN SIMPSON, RILEY SNYDER, HOSSEIN TOFIGHIAN, GHORBAN ALI ABBASI, SOLMAZ AMIRI, BAYGELDI ARTEGHI, MOHAMMAD BAGHER BAYATI, IAN BAILIFF, MARTIN R. BATES, FARAHNAZ BAYAT NEJAD, FELIX BITTMANN, MOHAMMAD MEHDI BORHANI, FRANCESCO CAPUTO, LANA CHOLOGAURI, HOMA FATHI, ANA GABUNIA, DAVID GAGOSHIDZE, DAVID P. GREENWOOD, MARC HEISE, MARYAM HOSSEIN-ZADEH, EMANUELE E. INTAGLIATA, MAHDI JAHED, JULIAN JANSEN VAN RENSBURG, FRIEDERIKE JÜRCKE, KOBA KOBERIDZE, DAN LAWRENCE, MAJID MAHMOUDI, MOHADDESEH MANSOURI RAZI, KOUROSH MOHAMMADKHANI, MARZIEH MOSLEHI, ALI NANKALI, CLAUDIA NUNES CALDEIRA, SILVIA PERINI, GRAHAM PHILIP, PRZEMYSŁAW POLAKIEWICZ, GABRIELE PUSCHNIGG, MAHSHAH ALLAH RAHMANI, ANDREA RICCI, ALIREZA SALARI, LISA SNAPE, BRIGITTE TALON, LYNN WELTON, ROGER AINSLIE, MARYAM AJAMHOSSEINI, ALIYEH AMIRINEZHAD, ZAHRA ASGHARI, SANAZ BEIZAEE DOOST, FRANÇOISE CHALIÉ, HOSSEIN DAVOUDI, KARYNE DEBUE, FRANÇOIS DEMORY, MORTEZA HASSANI, MONA HOSSEINDUSHT, TEHREEM KAINAAT, BEHROUZ KARIMI SHAHRAKI, FATEMEH KHAJAVI, HAEEDEH LALEH, MASUMEH MADANIPOUR, MOHADESSEH MALEKAN, MEGHDAD MIRMOUSAVI, MILAD MIRMOUSAVI, ANAHITA MITTERTRAINER, SOROUSH MOHAMMADKHANI, AZADEH MOHASEB, NAHID NAZIFI, HADI OMRANI, DANIELA PAETZOLD, CATRIONA PICKARD, MADIEH POURBAKHT, VALENTIN RADU, MOHAMMAD REZA RAHIMI, MAJID RAMZANI FARD, ARIANIT A. REKA, ANTOINE RUCHONNET, SAHAR SHAFAZADE, MOHAMMAD TAGHI MALEKA, HAMED TAHMASEBIFAR AND DAVOUD TAJI

Published in the United Kingdom in 2022 by
OXBOW BOOKS
The Old Music Hall, 106–108 Cowley Road, Oxford, OX4 1JE

and in the United States by
OXBOW BOOKS
1950 Lawrence Road, Havertown, PA 19083

© Oxbow Books and the individual authors 2022

Hardcover Edition: ISBN 978-1-78925-462-4
Digital Edition: ISBN 978-1-78925-463-1 (epub)

A CIP record for this book is available from the British Library

Library of Congress Control Number: 2022932389

All rights reserved. No part of this book may be reproduced or transmitted in any form or by any means, electronic or mechanical including photocopying, recording or by any information storage and retrieval system, without permission from the publisher in writing.

Printed in Malta by Melita Press

Typeset by Frabjous Books, UK

For a complete list of Oxbow titles, please contact:

UNITED KINGDOM
Oxbow Books
Telephone (01865) 241249
Email: oxbow@oxbowbooks.com
www.oxbowbooks.com

UNITED STATES OF AMERICA
Oxbow Books
Telephone (610) 853-9131, Fax (610) 853-9146
Email: queries@casemateacademic.com
www.casemateacademic.com/oxbow

Oxbow Books is part of the Casemate Group

Front cover: Gabri Qal'eh: a Sasanian fortress of the fourth or early fifth century, surviving as a city for approximately a thousand years beyond its foundation (top), the mega-fortress of Qal'eh Iraj erected in the early fifth century (centre right), Fort 9 on the Great Wall of Gorgan built probably in the mid- to later fifth century (centre left) and the fertile Gorgan Plain and the Alborz Mountains (bottom). Drone images by Davit Naskidashvili and the joint project.

Back cover: Fort 4 (top left), Fort 5 (bottom left), Fort 9 (top right) and Fort 20 (bottom right) on the canal-lined Great Wall of Gorgan (always on the left). Drone images by Davit Naskidashvili and the joint project.

Endpapers (front): Map of the Gorgan Plain with the sites and monuments explored (2005–2016) and other significant places. Only parts of the easternmost section of the Gorgan Wall are clearly traceable, and it is therefore marked via a discontinuous line. Numbered sites are Gorgan Wall Survey (GWS) sites. 61–63 are not plotted, as they correspond to GWS-83, GWS-73 and the slopes west of the Sari Su Bridge respectively. (Map by Kristen Hopper; base imagery: SRTM 30 m/90 m available from the USGS.)

Endpapers (back): Location of sites and monuments excavated and surveyed in Iran, from the Tehran Plain to Khorasan. Digital elevation model data are captured at intervals. The Caspian Sea is currently at c. -28 m, the highest point within the area of the map (Mount Damavand) rises to c. 5,671 m height. (Map by Kristen Hopper; base imagery: SRTM 90 m available from the USGS.)

Contents

Volume 1

Acknowledgements — xvi

Section A: Preliminaries

Chapter 1. Introduction — 3
    1.1. An ancient arms race – shaping world history to the present day? — 3
    1.2. Scope and context of the project — 5

Section B: Terrestrial excavations and survey

Chapter 2. Sasanian landscapes of the Gorgan Plain: new insights from remote sensing and field survey — 11
    Kristen Hopper, Hamid Omrani Rekavandi, Andrea Ricci, Lynn Welton, Dan Lawrence and Graham Philip
    2.1. Introduction — 11
    2.2. The Gorgan Wall Survey 2014–2016 — 11
    2.3. Sasanian site types: geometric fortified sites — 11
        2.3.1. Geometric fortified enclosures over 6 ha — 14
        2.3.2. Geometric fortified enclosures of 2–6 ha — 16
        2.3.3. Geometric enclosures of 1 ha or less — 18
    2.4. Sasanian rural settlements: intensive survey at GWS-79 — 18
    2.5. Investigations of features in the vicinity of Gorgan Wall Forts — 20
    2.6. Hydrological features associated with the Gorgan Wall and geometric fortified sites — 21
    2.7. Conclusion — 22

Chapter 3. The Gorgan Wall — 27
    3.1. Introduction — 27
    3.2. The Gorgan Wall Bridge and a Sasanian reservoir between Forts 2A and 2 — 29
        3.2.1. Sasanian hydraulic installations in the Sari Su River Valley — 29
        3.2.2. A new section of the Gorgan Wall, discovered by geophysical and pedestrian survey, leading towards a bridge — 30
        3.2.3. The Gorgan Wall Bridge (Trench b) — 34
        3.2.4. Bridge design — 49
        3.2.5. Protecting the bridge from erosion — 52
        3.2.6. Alluvial deposits and circumstantial evidence for a Sasanian barrage and reservoir in the Sari Su River — 55
        3.2.7. Chronology — 63
        3.2.8. The purpose of the reservoir — 66
        3.2.9. Brick robbing and sedimentation in post-Sasanian times — 68
    3.3. Drone survey of the Gorgan Wall — 70

Chapter 4. Forts on the Gorgan Wall — 75
    4.1. Fort 2 — 75
        4.1.1. Introduction — 75
        4.1.2. Remote, pedestrian, magnetometer and topographical survey of Fort 2 — 76

4.1.2.1. The fort defences	76
4.1.2.2. Interior occupation	80
4.1.2.3. Results	82
4.1.3. Excavation of an interval tower of Fort 2 (Trench c)	82
4.1.4. The barracks in Fort 2 (Trench d)	84
4.1.4.1. Introduction	84
4.1.4.2. Construction and layout of the barracks, phase 1 (Trench d)	85
4.1.4.2.1. The original barracks	85
4.1.4.2.2. Attempted quantification of mud-bricks needed for barracks construction	88
4.1.4.2.3. Barracks extension via annexes	89
4.1.4.3. Chronology of barracks construction and occupation in Trench d	99
4.1.4.4. The history of occupation of the barrack rooms	106
4.1.4.4.1. The original barracks: rows 2 and 3	106
4.1.4.4.1.1. The western row of rooms (2) in the original barracks	106
4.1.4.4.1.2. The eastern row of rooms (3) in the original barracks	111
4.1.4.4.1.3. Characteristics of the original barracks (rows 2 and 3)	116
4.1.4.4.2. The western annexe: rows 0 and 1	116
4.1.4.4.2.1. The eastern row of rooms (1) in the western annexe	116
4.1.4.4.2.2. The western row of rooms (0) in the western annexe	129
4.1.4.4.3. The eastern annexe: rows 4 and 5	136
4.1.4.4.3.1. The western row of rooms (4) in the eastern annexe	136
4.1.4.4.3.2. The eastern row of rooms (5) in the eastern annexe	141
4.1.4.4.4. The area outdoors to the west of the barracks	152
4.1.4.4.5. The area outdoors to the east of the barracks	153
4.1.4.5. Life in Sasanian barracks on the Gorgan Wall	155
4.1.4.5.1. Heating and cooking in Sasanian barracks	155
4.1.4.5.2. Food storage	161
4.1.4.5.2.1. Storage pits	161
4.1.4.5.2.2. Storage vessels and possible reforms in provisioning the army	163
4.1.4.5.3. Finds distribution over space and time	165
4.1.4.6. The chronology of Fort 2's occupation (Trench d)	167
4.1.4.6.1. The start of occupation	167
4.1.4.6.2. The end of occupation	170
4.1.4.6.3. Occupation density over time	172
4.2. Barracks in Fort 15	173
4.3. Barracks in Fort 25	173
4.4. Barracks in Fort 26	175
4.5. Geophysical survey at a compound on the north side of the Great Wall: GWS-65 near Fort 28	178
4.6. Remote survey of forts along the Great Wall	178
4.6.1. Introduction	178
4.6.2. Satellite survey	179
4.6.3. Drone survey	179
Chapter 5. The Tammisheh Wall and associated forts	**203**
5.1. Introduction	203
5.2. Underwater survey of a submerged fort	204
5.3. Remote survey of the Tammisheh Wall	209
Chapter 6. Post-Sasanian barriers	**211**
6.1. The Jar-e Kulbad Earthwork: a basic clone of the Tammisheh Wall, decisive in modern warfare	211
6.2. The Forud Wall near Kalat in Khorasan	214
Meysam Labbaf-Khaniki, Eberhard W. Sauer, Kristen Hopper, Davit Naskidashvili, Bardia Shabani and David Gagoshidze	
6.2.1. The Forud Wall	214
6.2.2. The Arg-e Forud	216

	6.2.3. Pedestrian and aerial survey of the Forud Wall	219
	6.2.4. A sondage within the Arg-e Forud (Trench j)	225
	6.2.5. A sondage within a watchtower on the Forud Wall (Trench k)	231
	6.2.6. The date, historical context and function of the barriers around Kalat	234
6.3.	The valley of Landar	237
	Meysam Labbaf-Khaniki and Kristen Hopper	
6.4.	Walls, towers and a fort or caravanserai at Mozdouran	242
	Meysam Labbaf-Khaniki, Kristen Hopper and Eberhard W. Sauer	

Chapter 7. Hinterland forts 249
    7.1. Forts on the Gorgan Plain 249
    7.2. Buraq Tappeh 253
        7.2.1. Buraq Tappeh: siting and research potential of a strategic guard-post 253
        7.2.2. Geophysical survey 255
        7.2.3. Aerial and pedestrian survey 258
        7.2.4. A sondage at Buraq Tappeh (Trench g) 260
            7.2.4.1. Introduction 260
            7.2.4.2. Fort construction and the architecture of interior buildings 261
            7.2.4.3. Early occupation within the fort 268
            7.2.4.4. Levelling and living on higher ground 269
            7.2.4.5. Oven construction 269
            7.2.4.6. A new fireplace as a focus for domestic activities 270
            7.2.4.7. Temporary site abandonment and decay? 271
            7.2.4.8. Reoccupation with a reduced garrison living nearby? 271
            7.2.4.9. Latest occupation and renewed oven construction 272
            7.2.4.10. Disturbed horizons above the abandoned fort 272
            7.2.4.11. Garrison size 273
            7.2.4.12. History and chronology of Buraq Tappeh's occupation 277
    7.3. Habib Ishan: a hinterland fortification with a corner citadel? 278
    7.4. Forts on the Old Gorgan River: parts of a Sasanian defensive network? The purpose
        of the Sasanian forts south of the Great Wall 280

Chapter 8. Campaign bases 287
    8.1. Introduction 287
    8.2. Qal'eh Pol Gonbad-e Kavus: the largest Sasanian fortress on the Gorgan Plain 287
        8.2.1. Introduction and comparative analysis of Qal'eh Pol Gonbad-e Kavus and
            other campaign bases 287
        8.2.2. The towered and gated walls 292
        8.2.3. The moat 294
        8.2.4. Surface scatter of finds 295
        8.2.5. Geophysical survey 296
        8.2.6. A section through the defences (Trench a) 297
        8.2.7. The stratigraphy of the ditch system 298
        8.2.8. The earliest ditches (1–4) 299
        8.2.9. The fifth ditch 304
        8.2.10. The sixth ditch 308
        8.2.11. The seventh ditch 311
        8.2.12. The Sasanian-era topsoil and land surface 311
        8.2.13. The wall 312
        8.2.14. Dimensions of the defences in phase 1 315
        8.2.15. The modern field boundary ditches 320
        8.2.16. The date of Qal'eh Pol Gonbad-e Kavus 320
    8.3. Gabri Qal'eh: from Sasanian campaign base to Ilkhanid town 325
        8.3.1. Introduction and topographical survey 325
        8.3.2. Geophysical survey 333
        8.3.3. A busy bazaar street in a medieval town (Trench e) 334
        8.3.4. The causewayed access to Sasanian and medieval Gabri Qal'eh (Trench f) 338

	8.3.5. Gabri Qal'eh's origins and significance	343
8.4.	Qal'eh Kharabeh	345
	8.4.1. Geophysical survey	345
	8.4.2. Drone survey	345
	8.4.3. Recalibration of radiocarbon samples	345
8.5.	Campaign bases on the Gorgan Plain	346

Chapter 9. Qal'eh Iraj: a campaign base/command centre of the army's northern division? 357
Mahdi Mousavinia, Mohammadreza Nemati and Eberhard W. Sauer
    9.1. Introduction 357
    9.2. Excavations within the south-eastern gate 359
        9.2.1. The first field seasons 359
        9.2.2. Dating the fortress: excavations within the south-eastern gateway in 2016 361
        9.2.2.1. Excavations in the gateway (Trench h) 361
        9.2.2.2. A side chamber of the south-eastern gate (Trench i) 367
    9.3. Geophysical survey 373
        9.3.1. Introduction 373
        9.3.2. Site A 373
        9.3.3. Sites B–D 374
    9.4. New insights into the fortress's history of occupation: excavations on the southern fortress walls in 2017 377
        9.4.1. Introduction 377
        9.4.2. Trench F128 377
        9.4.3. Trench F129 378
        9.4.4. Trench G129 379
        9.4.5. Discussion 379
    9.5. The chronology of Qal'eh Iraj 381
    9.6. Qal'eh Iraj: nerve centre of northern Persia's defensive network? 382

Chapter 10. A Sasanian city: fire temple, brick pillar avenues and residential quarters: geophysical and aerial surveys at Dasht Qal'eh 387
    10.1. Introduction 387
    10.2. Remote surveys 388
    10.3. A fire temple 389
    10.4. Roads and residential quarters 392
    10.5. The region's capital? 398

Section C: Marine survey

Chapter 11. Discovering unknown sections of the Great Wall of Gorgan near the shores of the Caspian Sea 405
C. Richard Bates, Martin R. Bates and Hamid Omrani Rekavandi
    11.1. Introduction 405
    11.2. Aims of the survey 405
    11.3. Methodology 405
    11.4. Results 406
        11.4.1. Survey results near the westernmost known location of the Gorgan Wall and the associated ditch (section 1) 406
        11.4.2. Geophysical survey of remains of the Gorgan Wall and its associated ditch exposed in an irrigation trench 409
        11.4.3. Survey results (section 2) 410
        11.4.4. Survey results (section 3) 410
    11.5. A bathymetric and sub-bottom investigation in the Caspian Sea across the alignment of the Gorgan Wall 411
        11.5.1. Introduction 411
        11.5.2. Sidescan sonar 412
        11.5.3. Sub-bottom profiling 412
        11.5.4. Results 413
    11.6. Discussion 413

| Contents | ix |

Chapter 12. A bathymetric and sub-bottom investigation of the Tammisheh Wall's northernmost section
        submerged in the Caspian Sea   415
   C. Richard Bates, Hamid Omrani Rekavandi and Hossein Tofighian
   12.1. Introduction   415
   12.2. Aims of the survey   416
   12.3. Methodology   416
   12.4. Results   417
      12.4.1. The site   417
      12.4.2. Seafloor bathymetry   417
      12.4.3. Sidescan sonar   417
      12.4.4. Sub-bottom profiling   417
   12.5. Discussion   423

Chapter 13. Palaeoenvironments at the Caspian terminals of the Gorgan and the Tammisheh Walls   425
   Suzanne A.G. Leroy, François Demory, Françoise Chalié, Martin Bates, C. Richard Bates,
   Hamid Omrani Rekavandi, Eberhard W. Sauer and Paula J. Reimer
   13.1. Setting and aims   425
   13.2. Previous palynological studies   425
   13.3. Material and methods   425
      13.3.1. Fieldwork and core description   425
      13.3.2. Magnetic susceptibility   426
      13.3.3. Palynology   427
      13.3.4. Radiocarbon dating   427
   13.4. Results   428
      13.4.1. Western end of the Gorgan Wall   428
      13.4.2. The vicinity of the northern end of the Tammisheh Wall   432
   13.5. Interpretation   436
      13.5.1. Western terminal of the Gorgan Wall   436
      13.5.2. The vicinity of the northern terminal of the Tammisheh Wall   437
   13.6. Caspian Sea level changes from pre-Sasanian to early modern times   438
      13.6.1. The era preceding wall construction   438
      13.6.2. Sasanian-period walls and the lowstand of the Caspian Sea   438
      13.6.3. From the late Sasanian era to the Early Middle Ages   438
      13.6.4. Medieval and Little Ice Age flooding   439
   13.7. The coastal environment in Sasanian times   439
      13.7.1. The Gorgan Wall west of the S2-V3 sequence   439
      13.7.2. Vegetation at the time of the walls and later   439
   13.8. Conclusion   440

Title, Contents and Dedication in Persian   458

Volume 2

Acknowledgements   xvi

Section D: Specialist contributions: written documents, finds, building materials, biological and environmental evidence and scientific dating

Chapter 14. Ostraca and bullae from Qal'eh Iraj	461
Carlo G. Cereti, Mohammadreza Nemati and Mahdi Mousavinia	
14.1. Introduction	461
14.2. Catalogue	462
14.3. Conclusion	472
Chapter 15. Comparative studies of the Sasanian ceramics from forts on the Great Wall of Gorgan and fortifications in its hinterland	475
Maria Daghmehchi, Seth M.N. Priestman, Gabriele Puschnigg, Jebrael Nokandeh,	
Emanuele E. Intagliata, Hamid Omrani Rekavandi and Eberhard W. Sauer	
15.1. Preliminaries	475
15.1.1. Abstract	475
15.1.2. Introduction	475
15.2. Material and methods	476
15.3. Classification	478
15.3.1. Physical characterisation of the Sasanian period ceramics	478
15.3.2. Firing groups of the ceramics	479
15.3.3. Petrographic characterisation of the ceramics	480
15.3.3.1. Coarse wares (western part of the Gorgan Wall and Buraq Tappeh)	481
15.3.3.2. Coarse wares (eastern part of the Gorgan Wall, Fort 2)	487
15.3.4. Typological characterisation of the ceramics	497
15.3.4.1. Medium closed form	497
15.3.4.1.1. Neckless jars	497
15.3.4.1.2. Coarse fabric neckless jars	499
15.3.4.1.3. Trefoil-mouthed jugs	500
15.3.4.2. Large closed forms	501
15.3.4.2.1. One-handled jars with narrow tall straight necks	501
15.3.4.2.2. Storage jars	501
15.3.4.2.3. Cooking pots	503
15.3.4.3. Small open forms	505
15.3.4.3.1. Bowls	505
15.3.5. Alternative quantitative method	506
15.4. Sites explored	507
15.4.1. Sari Su Bridge (Trench b)	507
Emanuele E. Intagliata	
15.4.2. Fort 2 (Trenches c and d; eastern part of the Great Wall of Gorgan)	508
15.4.2.1. Materials and methods	508
15.4.2.2. Ceramic assemblages from the barrack rooms (Trench d): a clue to their function over space and time	510
15.4.2.3. Changes in the ceramic assemblage from the barrack rooms (Trench d) over time	515
15.4.2.4. Results and discussion	518
15.4.3. Buraq Tappeh (Trench g)	534
15.4.4. Qa'leh Pol Gonbad-e Kavus (Trench a)	539
Emanuele E. Intagliata	
15.4.5. Gabri Qal'eh (Trenches e and f)	540
15.4.6. Qal'eh Iraj	542
15.5. Comparative studies	542
15.5.1. Contemporary ceramics from forts on the Gorgan Wall and the fortifications in its hinterland	542
15.5.2. Contemporary ceramics from neighbouring regions	548

15.6. Conclusion	549
15.7. Chemical and vibrational spectroscopic analyses of similar types of vessels from forts on the Great Wall of Gorgan and fortifications in its hinterland	551

Maria Daghmehchi, Behrouz Karimi Shahraki, Hadi Omrani, Masumeh Madanipour, Arianit A. Reka, Jebrael Nokandeh, Hamid Omrani Rekavandi, Mohammadamin Emami and Eberhard W. Sauer

15.7.1. Introduction	551
15.7.1.1. Outline	551
15.7.1.2. Background	551
15.7.2. Materials and methods	552
15.7.3. Petrographic characterisation	553
15.7.4. Chemical compositions of mineral grains and clayey paste	554
15.7.4.1. Chemical analysis	559
15.7.4.2. FTIR analysis	559
15.7.4.3. TGA-DTA and XRD analyses	563
15.7.5. Conclusion	570
15.8. Appendix: pottery from the 2017 season at Qal'eh Iraj	570

Mohammadreza Nemati and Mahdi Mousavinia

Chapter 16. Glass — 577
Fiona Anne Mowat and Tim Penn

16.1. Introduction	577
16.2. Assemblage overview	577
16.3. Fabric classes	577
16.3.1. Blue-green	577
16.3.2. Blue	582
16.3.3. Green	583
16.3.4. Yellow, amber and brown	583
16.3.5. Opaque fabrics	584
16.3.6. Colourless fabrics	584
16.3.7. Indeterminate fabrics	585
16.4. Securely dated vessels	586
16.5. Findspots and distribution	587

Chapter 17. Vessel glass: an archaeometric approach — 591
Mohammadamin Emami and Farahnaz Bayat Nejad

17.1. Introduction	591
17.2. Materials and methods	591
17.2.1. Analytical methods	591
17.2.1.1. Wavelength X-ray fluorescence (WXRF)	591
17.2.1.2. Scanning electron microscopy (SEM)	592
17.2.1.3. Simultaneous thermal analysis (STA)	592
17.2.2. The sample	592
17.3. Results and discussion	592
17.3.1. WXRF analysis of bulk chemical composition	592
17.3.2. Microstructural analysis through scanning electron microscopy (SEM)	593
17.3.3. Simultaneous thermal analysis (STA)	596
17.4. Conclusion	598

Chapter 18. Small objects and other finds — 601
Eberhard W. Sauer, St John Simpson, Mahdi Jahed, Mohaddeseh Mansouri Razi, Marzieh Moslehi, Mohammadreza Nemati, Jebrael Nokandeh, Hamid Omrani Rekavandi, Tim Penn and Alireza Salari

18.1. Introduction	601
18.2. Weapons	601
18.3. Tools	605
18.3.1. Knives and other personal implements	605
18.3.2. Whetstones	607

	18.3.3. Grinding stones	608
	18.3.4. Metal vessels	608
	18.3.5. Textile production	609
18.4.	Beads	615
	Tim Penn	
	18.4.1. Introduction, materials, style and chronology	615
	18.4.2. Spatial distribution, chronology and significance	617
18.5.	Other items of personal adornment, dress and furniture fittings	619
18.6.	Building materials	624
18.7.	Coins	625
18.8.	Miscellaneous objects, slag and metal debris	628
18.9.	Prehistoric stone tools	634

Chapter 19. Lime mortars from the Gorgan Wall Bridge over the Sari Su River — 641
Martina Astolfi and Riley Snyder

- 19.1. Introduction — 641
- 19.2. Materials and methods — 641
  - 19.2.1. The samples — 641
  - 19.2.2. Petrographic analyses of polished sections — 643
  - 19.2.3. XRF analysis — 644
- 19.3. Discussion — 644
- 19.4. Conclusion — 645

Chapter 20. Archaeozoology of Sasanian and Islamic sites from the Gorgan Wall to the Tehran Plain — 647
Marjan Mashkour, Roya Khazaeli, Solmaz Amiri, Homa Fathi, Sanaz Beizaee Doost, Azadeh Mohaseb, Karyne Debue, Valentin Radu, Hossein Davoudi, Antoine Ruchonnet, Haeedeh Laleh, Jebrael Nokandeh, Hamid Omrani Rekavandi, Mohammadreza Nemati and Eberhard W. Sauer

- 20.1. Introduction — 647
- 20.2. Material and methods — 647
  - 20.2.1. Quantification and taphonomy — 647
  - 20.2.2. Biometry — 648
  - 20.2.3. Demographic analysis — 650
- 20.3. Consumption practices and animal use at Sasanian and later sites from the Gorgan to the Tehran Plain — 650
  - 20.3.1. Fort 2 — 650
  - 20.3.2. The Gorgan Wall Bridge over the Sari Su River — 658
  - 20.3.3. Gabri Qal'eh — 658
  - 20.3.4. Qal'eh Pol Gonbad-e Kavus — 659
  - 20.3.5. Buraq Tappeh — 661
  - 20.3.6. Qal'eh Iraj — 661
- 20.4. Species represented — 661
  - 20.4.1. The morphology of sheep, goat and cattle populations — 661
    - 20.4.1.1. Introduction — 661
    - 20.4.1.2. Sheep — 664
    - 20.4.1.3. Goats — 665
    - 20.4.1.4. Cattle — 665
  - 20.4.2. Suids and their status at Fort 2 — 665
  - 20.4.3. Equid remains — 668
    - 20.4.3.1. Teeth — 668
    - 20.4.3.2. Metacarpals and radius — 669
    - 20.4.3.3. Horse remains: potential evidence for cavalry at Fort 2? — 670
  - 20.4.4. Bird remains — 671
  - 20.4.5. Fish remains — 672
    Valentin Radu, Marjan Mashkour and Eberhard W. Sauer
- 20.5. The age at death of sheep and goats — 675
- 20.6. Craft activities — 676

20.7. Conclusion	676
20.8. Appendices	678
20.8.1. Appendix 1: Measurements	678
20.8.1.1. Appendix 1.1: Measurements for *Ovis* (sheep)	678
20.8.1.2. Appendix 1.2: Measurements for *Capra* (goat)	681
20.8.1.3. Appendix 1.3: Measurements for Caprini (sheep/goat)	684
20.8.1.4. Appendix 1.4: Measurements for *Bos* (cattle)	684
20.8.1.5. Appendix 1.5: Measurements for *Sus scrofa* (pig/boar)	688
20.8.1.6. Appendix 1.6: Measurements for Equidae (equids)	690
20.8.2. Appendix 2: Comparative sites	691
20.8.3. Appendix 3: Statistical test for suid teeth	694
20.8.4. Appendix 4: Caprini (sheep/goat) tooth age attribution	694
Chapter 21. Palaeoenvironment	**699**
Lyudmila Shumilovskikh, Felix Bittmann, Brigitte Talon, Daniela Paetzold and Catriona Pickard	
21.1. Woodland use: the evidence from anthracological analysis	699
Lyudmila Shumilovskikh and Brigitte Talon	
21.1.1. Introduction	699
21.1.2. Materials and methods	699
21.1.3. Results	699
21.1.3.1. Introduction	699
21.1.3.2. Fort 2 (Trench d)	700
21.1.3.3. Buraq Tappeh (Trench g)	700
21.1.3.4. Qal'eh Iraj (Trench i)	700
21.1.3.5. Forud Wall (Trench k)	703
21.1.4. Discussion	703
21.1.5. Conclusion	705
21.2. Archaeobotanical studies on the Gorgan Plain	705
Lyudmila Shumilovskikh, Felix Bittmann and Daniela Paetzold	
21.2.1. Introduction	705
21.2.2. Materials and methods	705
21.2.3. Results and discussion	713
21.2.3.1. Qal'eh Pol Gonbad-e Kavus (Trench a)	713
21.2.3.2. Gorgan Wall Bridge over the Sari Su River (Trench b)	713
21.2.3.3. Fort 2 (Trench d)	716
21.2.3.4. Gabri Qal'eh (Trench e)	718
21.2.3.5. Gabri Qal'eh (Trench f)	718
21.2.3.6. Buraq Tappeh (Trench g)	718
21.2.3.7. Qal'eh Iraj (Trench i)	718
21.2.3.8. Forud Wall (Trench k)	719
21.3. Vegetation history of the Gorgan Plain: the evidence from palynological analysis at Lake Kongor	719
Lyudmila Shumilovskikh	
21.3.1. Introduction	719
21.3.2. Geographical setting	720
21.3.3. Palaeoecological records from Kongor	720
21.3.4. Human impact, climate and landscape change	721
21.3.4.1. Climate	721
21.3.4.2. Forest cover	722
21.3.4.3. Agriculture and arboriculture	723
21.3.4.4. Pasture	723
21.3.4.5. Fire	724
21.4. Molluscs	725
Catriona Pickard and Lyudmila Shumilovskikh	
Chapter 22. Archaeomagnetic studies of features excavated along the Gorgan Wall	**727**
Cathy M. Batt, David P. Greenwood and Tehreem Kainaat	
22.1. Abstract	727
22.2. Introduction	727

22.3. Background	728
22.4. Archaeomagnetic sampling in the field	729
22.4.1. Qal'eh Pol Gonbad-e Kavus	729
22.4.2. Sari Su Valley: alluvial deposits	729
22.4.3. Sari Su Valley: stream channels	730
22.4.4. Fort 2: oven d.010	730
22.4.5. Fort 2: oven d.114	730
22.4.6. Fort 2: oven d.169	731
22.5. Archaeomagnetic measurements	731
22.5.1. Sample preparation	731
22.5.2. Measurement procedures	732
22.6. Results	732
22.6.1. Sediments	732
22.6.2. Fired materials	733
22.7. Interpretation of the archaeomagnetic results and comparison with the global geomagnetic field model	733
22.8. Previous archaeomagnetic studies in the region	735
22.9. Summary and conclusion	736
22.10. Further work	737
Chapter 23. Luminescence dating and micromorphological assessment	**739**
Lisa Snape and Ian Bailiff	
23.1. Introduction	739
23.1.1. Samples	739
23.1.2. OSL background	740
23.2. Methodology	740
23.2.1. Field sampling	740
23.2.2. OSL measurements	741
23.2.3. Micromorphology	741
23.3. Results	741
23.3.1. OSL Age	741
23.3.2. Micromorphology	742
23.4. Discussion	742

Section E: History

Chapter 24. New light on Sasanian military infrastructure	**747**
24.1. Introduction	747
24.2. Flexible strategies: distribution of different types of defences	747
24.3. Learning from the past, adopting provincial traditions: the ancient world's largest fortresses, inspired by Central Asian architecture	752
24.4. Evolution of the ancient world's grandest fortification programme	755
24.5. Sasanian and Roman troop numbers and capabilities	760
24.6. An ancient arms race	765
24.7. Royal control of imperial defence	768
24.8. Purpose and effectiveness of fortifying the empire	770
24.9. The Sasanian army's legacy	780
24.10. *Pax Sasanica*	781

Section F: Conclusion and bibliography

Conclusion	793
Acknowledgements	793
Preliminaries	793
Terrestrial excavations and survey	793
Marine survey	796
Written documents, finds, building materials, biological and environmental evidence and scientific dating	796
History	799
Bibliography	803
Title, Contents, Dedication, Acknowledgements and Conclusion in Persian	880

We dedicate this book to the late Professor Tony Wilkinson in fond memory of his vital contribution to the project from 2005 to 2014.

Figs 1–2: Tony Wilkinson on Qal'eh Maran in 2007.

Acknowledgements

We are most grateful to the Iranian Cultural Heritage, Handcraft and Tourism Organization (ICHHTO), especially to Sayed Mohammed Beheshti, the director of the Research Institute of Cultural Heritage and Tourism (RICHT), Dr Behruz Omrani, the deputy for research of the RICHT, Dr Hamideh Choubak, the director of the Iranian Center for Archaeological Research (ICAR), Jalil Golshan, the vice-director of the RICHT, and Monir Kholghi, the head of the international section of the RICHT, for their kind support of our joint project without which it could not have taken place.

We are indebted to the European Research Council for its generous and fundamental financial support via the 'Persia and its Neighbours' project. We are very grateful for the help by colleagues at Edinburgh University for the 2014 season, notably Hugh Edmiston, Lindsay Hampton, Professor Alvin Jackson, Hamish MacAndrew, Professor Dorothy Miell, Jennifer Mills, Angela Noble and Dr Ulrike Roth. We also very grateful to Dr Valérie Andrieu-Ponel, Dr Warwick Ball, Kevin Bryant, Professor Pierfrancesco Callieri, Professor Ewen Cameron, Dr Morteza Djamali, Dr Morteza Fattahi, Anna Gibbons, Michael Hogg, Dr Amin Nazifi, Brian Pacey, Dr Philippe Ponel, James Ratcliffe, Dr Joanne Rowland and Keith Tracey for crucial support on practical and academic matters. Numerous colleagues, notably Dr Vesta Sarkhosh Curtis, Dr John Curtis, Dr Hassan Fazeli and the late Dr Massoud Azarnoush, offered essential support for the fundamental first phase of our fieldwork (2005–2009) and their kind help is acknowledged in our previous report.[1] Mohadesseh Mansouri Razi accomplished all the beautiful and accurate drawings of the artefacts recovered. Maryam Hossein-Zadeh and her team drew most of the detailed plans and sections of the features excavated and other team members were also involved in such graphic documentation. Our conservator, Marzieh Moslehi, restored our finds. Mohammad Bagher Bayati directed the topographical surveys. Plans and sections were later further edited, e.g. to produce phase plans. Dr Silvia Perini and Dr Emanuele Intagliata not only were invaluable key members of the team, but also digitised, jointly with Graeme Erskine, the hand-drawn plans and sections. We are grateful to the Oriental Institute of the University of Chicago, notably Dr Kiersten Neumann and Susan Allison, for their kind permission to reproduce the earliest aerial photograph ever taken of Gabri Qal'eh. The research leading to chapter 14 in this volume was accomplished with the support of the PRIN research project 2017PR34CS 'Eranshahr: uomo, ambiente e società nell'Iran arsacide e sasanide. Testimonianze scritte, cultura materiale e società da Arsace a Yazdegard III. Tre casi studio: Pars, Pahlaw e Khuzestan'.

Maria Daghmehchi and her co-authors would like to thank Mohaddeseh Mansouri Razi, Zahra Asghari, Alieh Amirinezhad, Alireza Salari Barkuei and Maryam Ajamhosseini for their invaluable assistance throughout our studies of the ceramics for chapter 15. We are very grateful to Mohaddeseh Mansouri Razi for her beautiful drawings of the ceramics and Mohadeseh Qanbari for taking photographs of the ceramics that were subjected to experimental analyses. We are indebted to Dr Hamed Rezaee from the Department of Geology, Golestan University, and Dr Abbas Ghaderi and Mir Amir Salahi from the Department of Geology, Ferdowsi University of Mashhad, for allowing us to use the geology laboratory for petrographic studies of the Gorgan Wall ceramics. Our research was financially supported by RICHT (Iran, Golestan, Gorgan Wall project). The SEM-EDS analysis was conducted at Razi Metallurgy Center. EPMA, FTIR, XRD, ICP-OES and TGA-DTA analyses were carried out

Fig. 3: Team members posing for purposes of scale in the stepped section (Trench a) through the massive moat around Qal'eh Pol Gonbad-e Kavus in 2014.

at Iran Mineral Processing Research Center (IMPRC). Petrography was analysed in the geology laboratory at Golestan University and Ferdowsi University of Mashhad. Anahita Mittertrainer and Kristen Hopper provided support for the ceramic studies, notably in 2014 and 2015.

We would like to thank our skilled boatmen, Hassan and Davoud Taji, the technician from the Iranian National Institute of Oceanography, Naser Ghasemi Ebtehaj, our drivers, Mohammad Taha Asgari, Mohammad Taghi Maleka, Ali Naroii and Mohammad Paghe, our housekeepers, Siavash Ghasemabadi, Masoud Mirmousavi and Milad Mirmousavi, and our dedicated workmen, too numerous to list. Colleagues at the Cultural Heritage, Handcraft and Tourism Organization of Golestan Province (CHTOG)), notably Reza Ghasemabadi, and its security staff, notably Mohammad Shahi Poudineh, Mohammad Taha Asgari, Mahshah Allah Rahmani, Rahim Soleimani, Safar Gholi Soleimani, Shir Mohammad Niyazi, Rahim Tavkoli and Abdullah Kishmili, provided crucial logistical support. We are also indebted to colleagues at the Great Wall of Gorgan Cultural Heritage Base, especially to Mohammad Taghi Maleka. We are particularly grateful to our Iranian and international team and regret that our group photos (Figs 3–5) only feature some of those who have made this project a success.

We are very grateful to Dr Cameron Petrie and colleagues at Oxbow, notably Jessica Hawxwell, Mette Bundgaard, Dr Julie Gardiner, Felicity Goldsack, Declan Ingram and Sarah Stamp, for their kind editorial efforts. Our diligent copy editor, Linda Fisher, has thoroughly checked all chapters and has saved us from numerous imperfections. Dr James Howard-Johnston reviewed the volume and offered invaluable observations, not just on the historical context, but also on the function of archaeological structures, such as the possible benefits of the reservoir in protecting the Gorgan Wall Bridge from erosion. We are also grateful to a second anonymous reviewer for further important advice. Needless to stress that any remaining errors and structural imperfections remain our own responsibility. Maria Daghmehchi kindly translated the cover, the table of contents, the acknowledgements and the conclusion into Persian, and Omolbanin Ghafoori, of the National Museum of Iran, edited the Persian version. We are also very grateful to Dr Vesta Sarkhosh Curtis for her advice and support.

Most of all are we indebted to the late Professor Tony Wilkinson, the Co-PI on our project. Without his

Fig. 4: Team members in Trench d in Fort 2 on the Great Wall of Gorgan with large storage vessels in situ *in 2015.*

Fig. 5: Team members at the excavation base in 2016.

crucial contribution, our previous research project on the Great Wall of Gorgan or the 'Persia and its Neighbours' project may never have received the green light, and they certainly would have been far less successful. Tony still offered every support for the 2014 season and his departure on 25 December 2014 has been an irreplaceable loss.

Notes

1   Sauer *et al.* 2013, xiv–xvi.

SECTION A

Preliminaries

1

Introduction

1.1. An ancient arms race – shaping world history to the present day?

Midnight, 26/27 June AD 363, headquarters of the Roman invasion army near Samarra:[1] the Roman emperor Julian lies dying, fatally wounded in enemy territory, following an unsuccessful invasion of Persian Mesopotamia. His army, deprived of supplies, suffering from hunger, diminished in strength and unable to capture the heavily defended Sasanian cities of Ctesiphon and Coche, is in a precarious situation. Julian had evidently seriously underestimated Sasanian military and organisational capabilities.[2] Arguably, it was the desperate plight of his army, attacked whilst already on retreat, that had inspired the emperor's high-risk strategy of fighting on the frontline where he suffered his fatal injury. Never again should a non-Christian rule over the Roman Empire.

Forced into a humiliating peace treaty, ceding the cities of Nisibis, Singara and other Near Eastern possessions to Persia, Julian's successor Jovian is forced to return to Roman territory. Had Julian not failed to see the signs of rising Persian military might, had he focused on internal affairs rather than an expedition doomed to defeat, might this have changed the course of world history? Had Rome's last pagan ruler, instead of embarking on a suicide mission against Persia in his early thirties, enjoyed a long reign and secured succession by an emperor sharing his faith – would Christianity ever have become the dominant religion in the west?

AD 603–651: over twenty years of Persian onslaught on Rome[3] are followed by a successful Romano-Turkish counteroffensive. A peace treaty of AD 630 restores the status quo.[4] Exhausted through prolonged warfare, the late antique world's major powers suffer heavily when Arab forces attack, annihilating the Sasanian Empire and reducing the Roman Empire to a regional power. Had confidence[5] in his empire's formidable military apparatus not inspired Khusro II to invade Rome, had more attention been paid to Persia's southern defences, might the Sasanian and Roman Empires have been able to withstand the emerging Caliphate and might they have remained the dominant players in the Mediterranean and Near Eastern World far beyond the mid-seventh century?

These questions may be unanswerable, but there is no question that the Sasanian army has shaped world history far beyond Persia and the late antique era. How Christianity and Islam became world religions and how the political landscape of Europe and the Near East was transformed beyond recognition at the transition of antiquity and the Middle Ages cannot be fully understood without an appreciation of the military capabilities of Sasanian Persia. And it is archaeology that has in recent years transformed our understanding of what made the Sasanian Empire a military superpower, able to withstand invasion and launch expeditions into the heartlands of its imperial rival.

The word 'arms race' in the title requires an explanation. Applied in particular to the confrontation between NATO and the Eastern Bloc during the Cold War, but also to the build-up of German and British military forces on the eve of the First World War, is it a valid concept in our particular historic setting one-and-a-half millennia before? Various definitions of the phenomenon have been offered, and we cite here just two. Writing at the height of the Cold War, Colin S. Gray argues that the following four factors must be present for the assertion that there is an 'arms race':

(1) There must be two or more parties, conscious of their antagonism.
(2) They must structure their armed forces with attention to the probable effectiveness of the forces in combat with, or as a deterrent to, the other arms race participants.

(3) They must compete in terms of quantity (men, weapons) and/or quality (men, weapons, organization, doctrine, deployment).

(4) There must be rapid increases in quantity and/or improvements in quality.[6]

Some 40 years later, Sam Perlo-Freeman offers a more concise definition of a military 'arms race':

> An arms race may be defined as a pattern of competitive acquisition of military capability between two or more countries. The term *arms race* is often used quite loosely to refer to any military buildup or spending increases by a group of countries. This definition requires that there be a competitive nature to this buildup, often reflecting an adversarial relationship.[7]

That there was often an antagonistic or adversarial relationship between Persia and Rome, as well as between them and some of their neighbours, notably those in the north, can hardly be disputed. That attention was paid to effectiveness is not in doubt either, as shown by numerous developments, e.g. a trend to create higher walls and stronger defences, more systematic efforts to block potential invasion routes via mountain passes etc., and we will argue that the Sasanian system often indeed proved effective in deterring invasion, limiting damage when it occurred or achieving victory. That there was competition in terms of the size of armies and the quality of military hardware and architecture is clear too. The late Roman army reportedly reached high six-digit numbers of soldiers. If true, it was at times numerically larger than it had been under the early and high empire. One wonders, however, if qualitatively there was in some respects not rather the opposite trend. In the light of the discovery of numerous Sasanian compounds, the largest ones capable of housing several tens of thousands of men each, one cannot doubt that the Sasanian army reached substantial six-digit numbers too.[8] Competition existed also in terms of building impregnable strongholds in border territories, such as fortress cities.[9]

As to 'rapid increases in quantity and/or improvements in quality' or 'military buildup or spending increases', that applies undoubtedly to the late Sasanian military infrastructure project that dwarfs all earlier Near Eastern defensive installations as well as those of the contemporary late Roman world – perhaps even those of the early Roman Empire. Hundreds of kilometres of barrier walls were erected, many of them lined by forts. Not only is the longest fort-lined barrier (the Great Wall of Gorgan) Sasanian, the largest military fortresses in the ancient world we know are also Sasanian: Qal'eh Iraj (175 ha) and a probable further massive Sasanian campaign base (210 ha) recently discovered by Dr Anthony Comfort on satellite imagery at Ghobal on the western frontiers[10] (leaving aside only thinly occupied hilltop refuges and an enigmatic, over 16 km² large, fortress at Zadiyan in modern Afghanistan that may well be Sasanian as well)[11] are of greater dimensions than any other non-urban fortresses in the ancient world. The probably Sasanian siege camp at Hatra (a 184 ha large camp situated within an even larger 285 ha enclosure that formed the outer ring of defence) is also the greatest installation of its kind; the largest certain Roman camps do not even reach half its size.[12]

A caveat must be offered, too: whilst the late Roman army reportedly increased in numbers and fort walls in strength, in terms of overall scale of known military installations, one cannot escape the impression that there was a reduction in the late Roman World in comparison with the early empire. Furthermore, much of Persian and Roman defensive efforts were not directed against each other, but against other adversaries, notably those in the north. The 'arms race' between Rome and Persia and their respective northern enemies was an unequal one. Our Mediterranean and Near Eastern great powers possessed capabilities in building fortifications and military barriers that were unmatched by any of their northern neighbours, though interestingly we witness a technology transfer from south to north in defensive architecture, notably geometric fortifications. Northerners, however, often possessed highly effective mobile forces and were engaged in what one may metaphorically compare with a gladiatorial combat between differently armed fighters, yet both in their different ways effective. Overall, we feel that the concept of an arms race is a useful one to describe developments in the late antique world. Notwithstanding the cited significant differences between the arms race in Late Antiquity and those of the twentieth century, there is much common ground. As in the run-up to the World Wars and during the Cold War, there was massive and, in the Near East, unprecedented investment in military infrastructure.

The significance of this arms race goes far beyond a competition. Even in critical situations (e.g. the Hephthalite success of AD 484) effective defences limited loss of territory and assets – thus paving the way to recovery in the long term. No system will be effective for all parties involved, and none is foolproof. Indeed, it might be argued that the Western Roman Empire's failure to engage in an effective arms race with its enemies and to maintain its military capabilities (though unquestionably correlated with economic, demographic and other developments) was one of the main reasons for its eventual annihilation. Military investment could make the difference between the survival of major power blocs or their disappearance from the world stage. Whilst this may seem self-evident, it is astonishing how often modern scholars doubt that some of the largest and most sophisticated military construction projects served any rational purpose beyond the symbolic.

The arms race phenomenon explains rapid Roman territorial losses to its northern neighbours in the west as well as Persia's resilience in the east. Yet, scholars have often failed to see the reasons why northerners conquered much of Roman Europe and temporarily even North Africa, but failed to make permanent inroads into Persia. In part, this is a result of over-reliance on Mediterranean-centric textual evidence (not without selectively distrusting statements on large troop numbers deployed or the effectiveness of fortifications). Roman authors' western focus and bias have led to frequent modern assumptions that the late antique Persian army lagged far behind its better-known Roman counterpart in troop numbers and organisational and technical capabilities. Military successes of the Huns in the west have inspired scholars to believe in similar power imbalances in the east – with both Rome and Persia being at the mercy of their northern neighbours.[13] The archaeological evidence that has now emerged redresses the balance. An appreciation of the nature and strength of Persia's defences, enabling it to launch successful offensive operations from a secure base – in comparison with the capabilities of its neighbours – explains why it proved unconquerable from the north. An appreciation of its Achilles heel in the south is crucial for understanding and contextualising the Arab conquest and subsequent developments that have shaped the course of world history to the present day: the transformation of the ancient world order and the rise of world religions.

1.2. Scope and context of the project

Between 2005 and 2009 a joint team from the Iranian Cultural Heritage, Handcraft and Tourism Organization and the Universities of Edinburgh and Durham and further partner organisations explored the Gorgan and Tammisheh Walls in northern Iran and archaeological sites, canal systems and landscapes in their vicinity. These five seasons have been fully published,[14] but a brief summary is offered here to provide the context for our more recent work. Using scientific techniques, we were able to date these major frontier walls to the fifth or early sixth century AD (with a fifth-century construction being easier to reconcile with historical developments). It emerged that there were military-style accommodation blocks in the associated forts. The Gorgan Wall remained occupied to the early or mid-seventh century, whilst the Tammisheh Wall reportedly retained its function for centuries beyond. Heavily fortified geometric campaign bases in the hinterland, c. 40 ha each being the most common size, were explored too. One of them could be shown to be filled with neatly arranged temporary accommodation, probably for a large mobile military force, and to date to the fifth or early sixth century too, and the same is likely to apply to several compounds of similar plan. Scientific dating also allowed us to assign the foundation of the 3 km² large city of Dasht Qal'eh to the same or a similar era as the long walls and campaign bases. Landscape survey shed light on how water was channelled to the Gorgan Wall and on settlement patterns nearby, notably the earlier expansion of settlement into the steppe. Yet, it was in the fifth to sixth centuries that the largest and most ambitious monuments were erected. This remarkable burst of activity in Late Antiquity is probably related to the strategic significance of this fertile frontier zone, reflected in a series of major armed conflicts in the area.

In the five and a half years following the last season of the first phase (April to May 2009), no joint research on the ground took place, except for visits to the Great Wall and Forts 2, 2A, 5 and 28, the Jar-e Kulbad linear barrier and two large fortified compounds (GWS-55 and GWS-61 = GWS-83) in January 2013. After this long break, we were able to resume joint fieldwork for three seasons (from 9 November to 6 December 2014, from 15 October to 10 December 2015 and from 25 September to 2 November 2016), thanks to the kind and generous support of the European Research Council, via the 'Persia and its Neighbours' project, and the Iranian Cultural Heritage, Handcraft and Tourism Organization. This was followed by a brief finds study season at Gorgan and Tehran from 15 to 23 December 2018. Whilst the 2014–2016 seasons have yielded significant new results, they are inevitably also following in some respects in the footsteps of the previous project (2005–2009), and our results and working hypotheses then are essential for contextualising our results now.[15]

Whilst this book is mainly focused on the research carried out jointly by our Iranian and international team within the framework of our ERC project, it would have made little sense to present the results of fieldwork from 2014 to 2016 in isolation and to exclude relevant and important work at the sites studied before and since this short period. This applies particularly to Qal'eh Iraj.[16] We have been privileged to be able to work on this pivotal site and to obtain firm scientific dating for early activity within Persia's largest pre-modern military fortress during a brief joint fieldwork season in 2016. It cannot be understood, however, without the pioneering research accomplished by Dr Mohammadreza Nemati and Dr Mahdi Mousavinia before and since. We are thus delighted that it has been possible to include a report on their excavations in 2017 as well as on the ostraca and bullae discovered earlier by Dr Nemati's team within the same gateway where we subsequently excavated in 2016. These provide fascinating and unparalleled insights into administration and written culture at a Sasanian military site. They have been deciphered and studied by Professor Carlo G. Cereti who participated as the epigraphist in the project.

Geographically, our focus is on the area covered by our fieldwork in northern Iran, i.e. from the Tehran Plain in the west to Khorasan in the east, with a particular emphasis on the Gorgan Plain. Our 'Persia and its Neighbours' project also encompassed excavations and surveys in modern Georgia[17] and Oman,[18] which have contributed greatly to our understanding of Sasanian defensive infrastructure on an imperial scale, but they have been published separately. It is our aim, however, not to present our findings as isolated regional case studies, but to explore what our new evidence contributes to our understanding of the late antique world, notably the military strategy and infrastructure of Persia in comparison with the military capabilities of its western and northern neighbours. We therefore also discuss other relevant Sasanian fortifications, including those in the Caucasus and the north of the Arabian Peninsula. There is little to be gained, however, by any attempt to cover them in detail. As we have carried out no excavations or surveys on the Persian Gulf, in Mesopotamia, along the Batman River, in the Mughan Steppe, in most of Transcaucasia (with the cited exception of Dariali Gorge), in the Empire's north-eastern and south-eastern frontier territories and on strongholds all over its interior, there is no new evidence at our disposal. Little would be gained by extensive repetition of the results of other projects that are already in the public domain and that we know less well, but this should not imply that we consider them less relevant. To systematically describe, map and analyse the published defensive monuments all over the Sasanian Empire, let alone the late antique world as a whole, would furthermore take years or decades, whilst a superficial summary would be of little benefit to the reader. That fortifications in these vast territories are only discussed selectively should not imply that they are of lesser relevance than those we have been privileged to explore, only that time and resources forced us to be selective and to concentrate on familiar territory and new evidence. We focus on our own fieldwork also, as it is our duty to make our new evidence available to the scholarly community.

For similar reasons, there is little emphasis on weapons and armour, recruitment and training, generalship, naval operations, siege warfare and battle tactics. Comprehensive coverage, in depth and detail, of a topic as multi-faceted and complex as the arms race in Late Antiquity, or even just the multi-layered defences of the Sasanian Empire, is impossible to achieve. Yet, our fieldwork has focused on the arguably most heavily fortified frontier zone of the ancient world, on some of the largest fortifications of their kind and/or the first examples explored in detail. We feel that these case studies make a major contribution to late antique military history, shed much new light on strategies and capabilities and justify the title of the study. It is, however, an exploration as to what our new evidence contributes to our understanding of the arms race in Late Antiquity.[19] It does not and cannot do justice to all aspects of this phenomenon all over the ancient world. Our aim is to present the results of our fieldwork in their proper historical context, not to produce a general historical study with fieldwork cited only in so far as relevant.

We have also gained insights into urban life at Gabri Qal'eh in the thirteenth to fourteenth centuries[20] and have explored two linear barriers likely erected in the sixteenth to eighteenth centuries.[21] It is the duty of field archaeologists to publish the results of their excavations and surveys and not just those concerning the era at the heart of a study. Yet the results of our medieval and post-medieval work are far from irrelevant for the themes explored in this volume. Late medieval life at a Sasanian-built fortress, heavily occupied a millennium after construction, is a telling testimony for the foresight and lasting legacy of Sasanian imperial strategists and architects. Barriers built over a thousand years after the Great Wall of Gorgan and the Wall of Tammisheh provide vital clues as to the much-debated purpose and efficacy of such monuments. Impressive as the two post-medieval linear defences were for their time, they are dwarfed by some of their much earlier Sasanian counterparts and help us to appreciate the exceptional nature and dimensions of monuments erected at the climax of the late antique arms race. If the Sasanian era is chronologically at the heart of this monograph, it is only in the *longue durée* that the success and failure of similar and different defensive strategies can be evaluated. If northern Iran is geographically at the heart of this monograph, the new evidence is pivotal for understanding the capabilities of competing empires in an interconnected late antique world much more broadly.

September 2021

Notes

1. See Ammianus Marcellinus 23.3–25.9; Libanius, *Orationes* 18.204–82; Zosimus 3.12–33; cf. Dodgeon and Lieu 1991, 231–74 on further sources for the war. See Den Boeft *et al.* 2005, 61, 75–76 and Northedge 2007, 49 on the location of Julian's fatal injury.
2. See Edwell 2013, 847–48 and 2020, 237–38, 253 for a similar assessment; cf. Frendo 2012 on Julian's military miscalculations; see also Bringmann 2004, 187–89; Harrel 2016 and McLynn 2020.
3. The term 'Rome' and/or 'Roman Empire' is used in this volume for the successor state(s) of the Roman Empire, i.e. the Western and Eastern Roman Empire, as long as both existed, and the Eastern Roman or 'Byzantine' Empire thereafter. 'Rome' epitomised the major western power even long after the city had ceased to be its centre. It was the lasting legacy of Rome that determined how people in the Eastern Roman Empire self-identified (at least as far as the literate elite is concerned), despite the eternal city no longer being the imperial capital and only intermittently still part of the empire: see Sauer 2017b, xv; Sauer *et al.* 2020a, 12; Sauer and Pitskhelauri 2018, 279 no. 27.
4. Howard-Johnston 2021, 355.
5. We are conscious of the fact that this hypothesis has attracted criticism (Benfey 2020, 183), as well as support (Jackson Bonner 2020b, 121, cf. 267), but make no excuses for the view that confidence in military strength has often led rulers and generals to imprudent decisions, defeat, loss of territory and even the end of empires. Examples, from antiquity to Modernity, e.g. during the Napoleonic and the World Wars, are too numerous to list – even if

theoreticians may find it difficult to accept that simple errors of judgement can sometimes change the course of world history.
6   Gray 1971, 41; see also Sheehan 1983, 9–10. Interesting in this context is the study by Vern L. Bullough (1963, especially 56–58, 66–67) who argues, evidently seeing parallels to his own time, that 'successful deterrence' between the 'two powers' of Rome and Persia resulted in 'a "cold war" relationship' from AD 363 until AD 502. This involved construction of fortifications and mutual influence, notably in the methods of warfare. EWS is grateful to the students in his 'Ancient Superpowers' honours course for having drawn the latter article to his attention.
7   Perlo-Freeman 2011; see also *id.* 2018. We are grateful to the audience of the Mediterranean Archaeology Seminar Series at Edinburgh University on 27 January 2020 for their thoughts on the appropriateness of the title.
8   See chapter 24.5; cf. Sauer *et al.* 2013, 613–16.
9   Crow 2007; 2017a; Rizos 2017b, *passim*.
10 Dr Anthony Comfort, personal information 12 February 2020. See Comfort 2021 and chapter 8.2.1 for further details.
11 See discussion in Nemati *et al.* 2019/2020 with further sources; see now also Ball *et al.* 2019, 386–90; Ball 2019, 453 no. 2281.
12 Hauser and Tucker 2009; Sauer *et al.* 2017, 250–51. See also chapter 24.2 on Hatra and the large camps at Dura-Europos and for a brief discussion whether the latter are Persian or Roman.
13 See chapter 24.8.
14 Sauer *et al.* 2013; see also Hopper 2009; Mashkour *et al.* 2017; Nokandeh *et al.* 2006; Omrani Rekavandi and Sauer 2013; Omrani Rekavandi *et al.* 2006; 2007a; 2007b; 2008a; 2008b; 2008c; 2009; 2010; 2011; 2017; Sauer and Omrani Rekavandi 2013; Sauer *et al.* 2009; 2015a; 2020e.
15 The final report of the previous season (Sauer *et al.* 2013) is cited frequently to save space by not repeating in detail what is already in the public domain. The results of the 2014–2016 seasons are fully covered in this report; see, however, also the following publications for supplementary information and illustrative material, notably on the landscape survey: Hopper 2017a; 2017b; Hopper and Omrani Rekavandi 2020; Hopper *et al.* 2022; Naskidashvili *et al.* 2019; Nemati *et al.* 2019/2020; Nokandeh and Sauer 2018; Nokandeh *et al.* 2016; 2017; Sauer *et al.* 2017; 2018; 2019; 2020d; 2020e; 2021b; Shumilovskikh *et al.* 2016a; 2016b; 2017a; 2021.
16 Chapters 9 and 14; see also Mousavinia and Nemati 2016; Nemati *et al.* 2019/2020.
17 Sauer *et al.* 2020a; 2020b; see also Mashkour *et al.* 2017; Naskidashvili *et al.* 2019; Sauer and Naskidashvili 2018; Sauer and Pitskhelauri 2018; Sauer *et al.* 2015b; 2016; 2017; 2020c; 2020d; 2021a.
18 Al-Jahwari *et al.* 2018; Dabrowski *et al.* 2021; Priestman *et al.* 2022.
19 The term 'Late Antiquity' is defined here as the period from the late third to the mid-seventh centuries. Most of the monuments explored during our project were erected in the fourth to sixth centuries, construction arguably peaked in the fifth century, but occupation mostly continued at least into the sixth and often to the first half of the seventh century. See Sauer *et al.* 2020a, 12 for a discussion and definition of the term.
20 See chapter 8.3.
21 See chapter 6; see also Labbaf-Khaniki *et al.* 2019; 2020.

SECTION B

TERRESTRIAL EXCAVATIONS AND SURVEY

2

Sasanian landscapes of the Gorgan Plain: new insights from remote sensing and field survey

Kristen Hopper, Hamid Omrani Rekavandi, Andrea Ricci, Lynn Welton, Dan Lawrence and Graham Philip

2.1. Introduction

The Gorgan Plain contains a large number of archaeological sites and features representing occupation in the region from the Palaeolithic to the modern period.[1] Due to the fundamental work undertaken by our landscape team, and in particular the late Tony Wilkinson, between 2005 and 2009, we have a good understanding of some elements of the Sasanian-period landscape, especially military infrastructure and water management systems.[2] However, there is a noteworthy gap in our knowledge relating to the overall settlement pattern in this period; specifically, information about villages, towns and cities of the region is still sketchy. Our recent research has sought to redress this through new fieldwork and ceramic analyses, and the examination of modern and historical satellite imagery, unpublished legacy data and previously published surveys undertaken since the late nineteenth century.[3] The complete results of this comprehensive study will be presented in a separate volume focusing on long-term settlement patterns in the context of imperial landscapes.[4] Here we present a summary of the results of our recent fieldwork with a particular focus on new insights regarding settlement and land use in the Sasanian period.

2.2. The Gorgan Wall Survey 2014–2016

Between 2014 and 2016, the landscape team documented 35 sites (Fig. 2.1; Table 2.1).[5] The activities we undertook fell into several categories:

– Site visits and surface collections from geometric fortified enclosures identified on CORONA imagery.

– Site visits and surface collections from sites with occupation potentially dating between the Late Iron Age and the Sasanian period.[6]

– Intensive surface collections, and off-site transects, at and around sites with possible Sasanian activity.

– Investigations of possible canal features associated with either the Gorgan Wall or geometric fortified enclosures dated to the Sasanian period.

Table 2.1 lists all the sites visited (or revisited) in the 2014–2016 survey along with a brief description and periods of occupation identified during survey. We recorded the dimensions of each site as defined by the extent of the mounding and/or artefact scatter and collected a grab sample of representative artefacts. We subdivided each site into spatially defined units for surface collection (i.e. the tops and sides of prominent mounds were recorded separately, as were any outlying mounds). We undertook intensive surveys at GWS-4, GWS-15 and GWS-79. All three sites had evidence for possible Sasanian occupation. The former two were located north of the Gorgan Wall, while the latter one was located much closer to the Alborz foothills. Our goal was to confirm Sasanian occupation and develop a better understanding of site occupation area by period. Off-site areas surrounding GWS-25, GWS-60, GWS-79, GWS-86 were also investigated through transect survey.

2.3. Sasanian site types: geometric fortified sites

A working morphological typology of site forms commonly found on the Gorgan Plain was developed during the Gorgan Wall Survey 2005–2009.[7] Several site morphologies, such as geometric fortified enclosures, are associated with the Sasanian period. These include the urban site of Dasht Qal'eh (GWS-54), which is enclosed within ramparts and contains a dense patterning of internal features,[8] and the forts lining the lowland section of the Gorgan Wall, which generally cover between c. 1

Table 2.1: List of GWS sites surveyed in 2014–2016. All coordinates are in UTM zone 40N. A question mark after the period name in 'Dating' indicates that there is uncertainty in the assessment. See Fig. 2.1 for the location of the listed sites.

GWS no.	Name	Dating of surface finds	Brief description and notes	Coordinates
4	Tokhmaq Tappeh	Iron III; Iron IV?; Parthian; early-mid-Sasanian?; late Sasanian?; Islamic	Detailed re-collection of previously recorded site.[1]	E 259074, N 4115591
15	Mangali	Iron III; Parthian; early Sasanian	Detailed re-collection of previously recorded site.[2]	E 272482, N 4115339
25	Gangush Tappeh 1	Bronze Age?; Iron III; Parthian; early Sasanian?; Islamic	Previously recorded site.[3] Re-collection on main tappeh, and off-site transects. Pottery from tappeh and transects appears consistent; very few diagnostic pieces were recovered.	E 365385, N 4152386
37	Qalʻeh Pol Gonbad	Islamic	Re-collection of previously recorded site.[4]	E 337324, N 4120502
49	Gabri Qalʻeh	Early Sasanian?; Islamic	Re-collection of the tappeh and interior of the enclosure.[5]	E 350088, N 4126456
55	Unnamed	Parthian–early Sasanian; Islamic	Large geometric fortified enclosures, with central mound. Smaller rectilinear enclosures in the south-east and north-west corners of the larger enclosure.[6]	E 285124, N 4104072
59	Qalʻeh Sultan Ali	Parthian; early Sasanian(?); Islamic	Large mound and qalʻeh with an attached geometric fortified enclosure.[7]	E 327698, N 4121815
60	Unnamed	Chalcolithic; Bronze Age; Iron III?; early Sasanian?; Islamic	Large tappeh or qalʻeh with an attached geometric fortified enclosure.[8]	E 278053, N 4085834
64	Habib Ishan	Parthian?; Islamic	Square fortified mound, with a square corner citadel.[9]	E 292125, N 4112953
65	Unnamed	Iron III?; late Sasanian; Islamic	Immediately north of Fort 28 and the Gorgan Wall. Possible square anomaly on CORONA. In the field marked by a concentration of artefacts and in-situ bricks in a modern irrigation ditch.	E 274250, N 4111225
66	Unnamed	Bronze Age (MBA–LBA?); Iron III?; Islamic	Tappeh complex, part covered by modern village. Approximately 650 m north of Forts 12 and 13.	E 332152, N 412646
67	Unnamed	Bronze Age?; Iron III?; Islamic	Tappeh	E 265724, N 4114204
68	Unnamed	Islamic	Tappeh	E 258495, N 4114367
69	Unnamed	Iron III	Tappeh complex	E 267536, N 4116270
70	Unnamed	Parthian; early Sasanian?; Islamic	Tappeh	E 257847, N 4106998
71	Unnamed	No lab assessment of ceramics; field spot date: late Iron Age/Parthian	Tappeh	E 369412, N 4151382
72	Unnamed	Iron III?; Iron IV; Parthian; Islamic	Tappeh	E 332437, N 4125969
73	Qalʻeh Jigh (same as GWS-62)	Chalcolithic; Bronze Age (EBA? MBA/LBA?); Iron III; Iron IV?; Parthian; early-mid-Sasanian?; late Sasanian?; Islamic	Central qalʻeh surrounded by low outer mounds. On satellite imagery a possible large geometric fortified enclosure was visible;[10] however, no evidence for this located in the field. Irrigation ditches along the same alignment appear relatively modern.	E 277059, N 4093734
74	Tappeh Panjelin Sofla	Chalcolithic; Bronze Age; Parthian; Sasanian; Islamic	Qalʻeh with outer mounding	E 280840, N 4084179
75	Tappeh Mollaqorban or Migurban	Iron III; Parthian; Sasanian; Islamic	Tappeh	E 282010, N 4084283
76	Qasghalaq Tappeh	Parthian; early Sasanian; late Sasanian?; Islamic	Tappeh complex	E 268839, N 4105130
77	Qareh Beik	Iron IV?; Parthian?; (early and late) Sasanian?; Islamic	Tappeh	E 305130, N 4093253

Table 2.1: (Continued)

GWS no.	Name	Dating of surface finds	Brief description and notes	Coordinates
78	Palang Tappeh	Iron III; Parthian; late Sasanian; Islamic	Tappeh	E 314710, N 4091687
79	Shur Tappeh	Parthian; (early–late) Sasanian; Islamic	Prominent multi-level tappeh; small lower mound c. 120 m to the south-east.	E 304631, N 4100437
80	Tappeh Bozorg	Bronze Age; Iron III; Islamic?	Tappeh	E 344150, N 4127785
81	Tappeh Marjanabad	Chalcolithic; Bronze Age; Sasanian–Islamic?	Tappeh	E 346266, N 4124938
82	Yasi Tappeh	Iron III?; Parthian; (early–late) Sasanian?	Tappeh	E 313972, N 4123237
83	Zal Tappeh (same as GWS-61)	Chalcolithic; Bronze Age; Islamic	Tappeh surrounded by a possible large geometric fortified enclosure.[11] We found no trace of the square enclosure in the field.	E 259712, N 4087422
84	Gabrestan Kaka	Bronze Age?; Iron III; Iron IV?; Parthian; Islamic	Tappeh complex	E 329837, N 4116377
85	Hali Akound Tappeh	Iron III?; Parthian?; early Sasanian?; late Sasanian; Islamic?	Tappeh surrounded by depression and possible rampart.	E 328215, N 4119243
86	Sari Bakhsh	Iron III; Parthian; early–mid-Sasanian; late Sasanian; Islamic	Tappeh complex	E 323592, N 4122263
87	Tappeh Mazar	Iron III?; Parthian; Islamic	Tappeh complex	E 348881, N 4125618
88	Unnamed	Chalcolithic; Bronze Age (EBA?); Iron III; Parthian; Islamic	Tappeh	E 348876, N 4125934
89	Qoreh Su 1	Sasanian–Islamic?	Tappeh	E 245039, N 4107967
90	Qoreh Su 2	Islamic	Upper crescent-shaped mound, abutted by a cemetery.	E 245301, N 4107079
91	Miankaleh Fenderesk North	Chalcolithic; Bronze Age; Islamic	Tappeh complex	E 318956, N 4103643
92	Miankaleh Fenderesk South	No samples located	Large geometric fortified enclosure	E 319233, N 4102622

[1] Wilkinson et al. 2013, 113; Sauer et al. 2013, 361–65.
[2] Wilkinson et al. 2013, 116.
[3] Wilkinson et al. 2013, 119.
[4] Wilkinson et al. 2013, 89 fig. 3:70, 122; Sauer et al. 2013, 358–60; see also chapter 8.2.
[5] Wilkinson et al. 2013, 46 fig. 3:20, 124; Sauer et al. 2013, 364–68; see also chapter 8.3.
[6] Wilkinson et al. 2013, 88 fig. 3:69, 125; Sauer et al. 2013, 369–70; see also chapter 8.5.
[7] Wilkinson et al. 2013, 95 fig. 3:75, 125.
[8] Wilkinson et al. 2013, 96 fig. 3:76, 125.
[9] See also chapter 7.3.
[10] Wilkinson et al. 2013, 93, 98 fig. 3:78, 128–29.
[11] Wilkinson et al. 2013, 93, 97 fig. 3:77, 128.

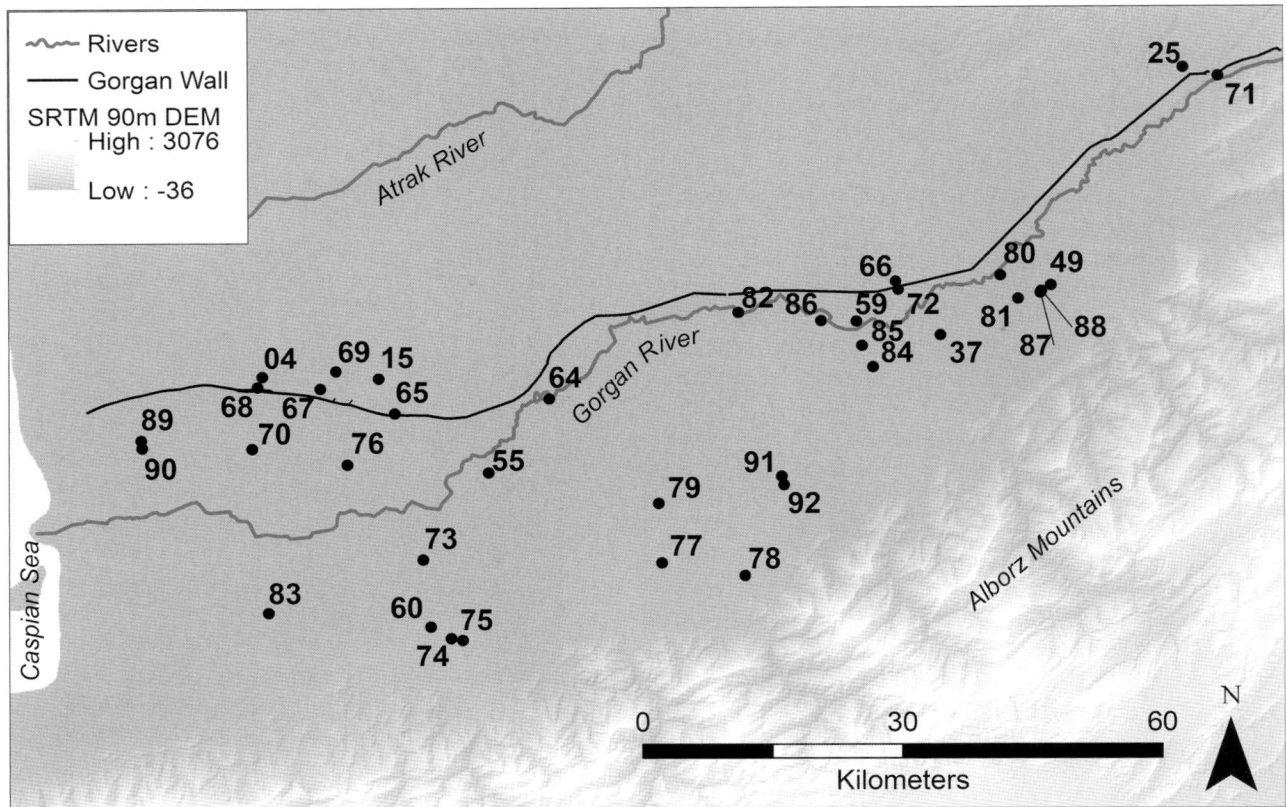

Fig. 2.1: Sites investigated in the 2014–2016 seasons. Numbers indicate Gorgan Wall Survey (GWS) site numbers (Imagery SRTM 90 m DEM, available from the USGS).

and 8 ha (with an average of 3 ha) including the moat and any outer settlements (and thus differing from the intramural dimensions of forts that are cited elsewhere in the report).[9] Also numerous are large geometric fortified enclosures with few to no discernible internal features, which are typically located at considerable distances to the south of the wall (Fig. 2.2). These sites have been interpreted as Sasanian campaign bases, but could have served numerous functions following military campaigns.[10]

There is a strong but not exclusive association between geometric fortified enclosures with a minimum of internal features, and Sasanian occupation.[11] Furthermore, data on Sasanian site types from neighbouring regions indicate a strong correlation between geometric fortified enclosures (of varying sizes and multiple functions) and Sasanian-period occupation.[12] To explore this association, we produced a list of all sites with morphologies consistent with a Sasanian date (geometric/rectilinear enclosures) documented in the Gorgan Plain Survey Database;[13] this included site morphology observed on the CORONA imagery taken in 1969,[14] or described by various published surveys, as rectilinear, rectangular, square or geometric, in combination with site feature such as qal'ehs, ramparts and enclosures.[15] We have divided these features into three size categories: over 6 ha, between 2 and 6 ha and 1 ha or less, and were able to visit several in the field. Our observations are presented in the following sections by size category. The database ID number is used to refer to the sites that were located on satellite imagery only and were not visited in the field and therefore do not have a GWS number.[16]

2.3.1. Geometric fortified enclosures over 6 ha

The largest rectangular enclosure detected on the CORONA imagery, GWS-92 (c. 77 ha with its defences and c. 63 ha internal area), was located approximately 4.5 km to the south-west of Qal'eh Daland (GWS-53) (Fig. 2.3; Endpapers, front). To our knowledge, no record of this site exists in any other survey. The site sits between two streams flowing down from the Alborz Mountains towards the Gorgan River. These channels (along with their relict incarnations) have eroded out parts of both the east and west sides of the enclosure. On the east side, a dark linear feature following the outer edge of the enclosure may represent a ditch or moat that would have surrounded the site. Regularly spaced mounds around the exterior of the enclosure resemble those visible on the CORONA imagery of similar enclosures, such as Qal'eh Gug A (GWS-33) and Qal'eh Daland (GWS-53); these were interpreted as representing projecting towers (Fig. 2.3).[17] Like Qal'eh Daland (GWS-53) and Qal'eh Pol

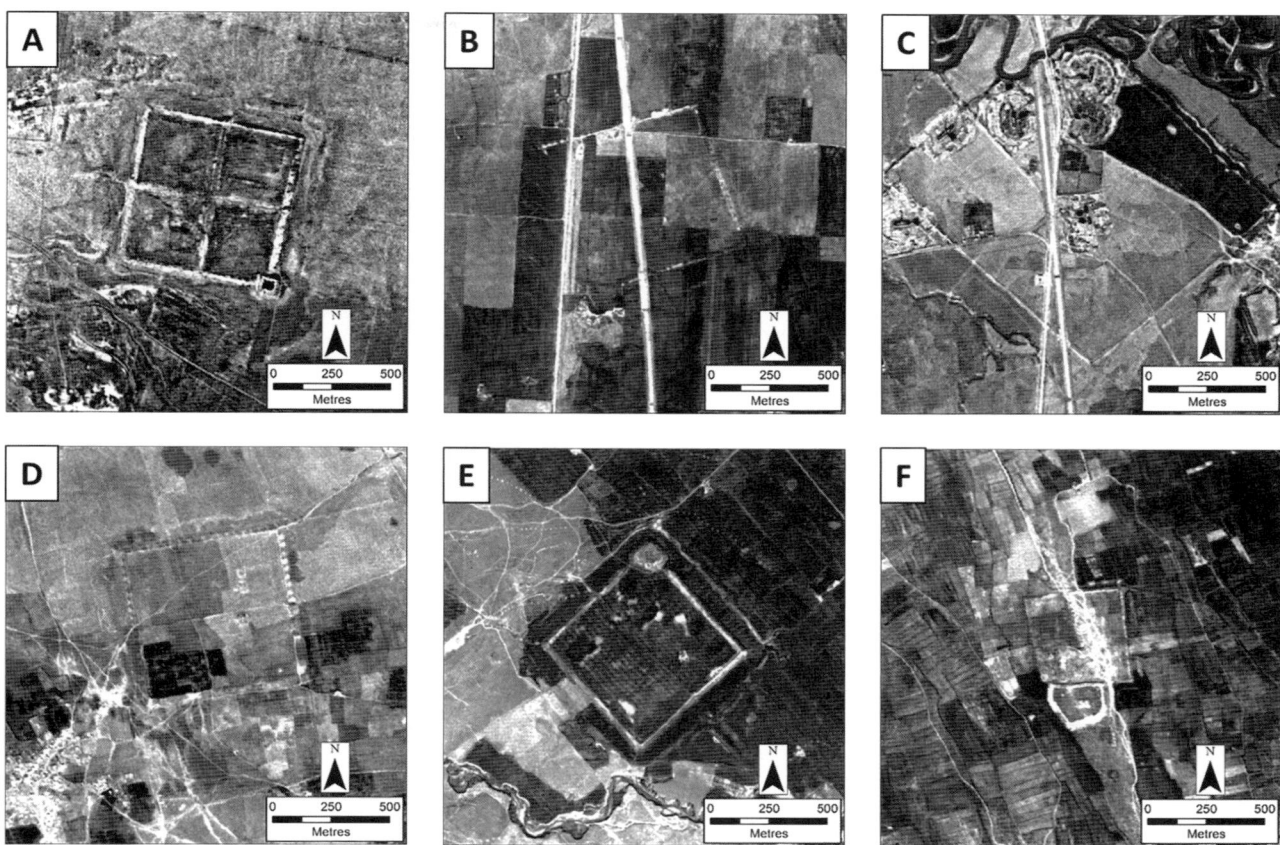

Fig. 2.2: A) GWS-1; B) GWS-33; C) GWS-37; D) GWS-53; E) GWS-49; F) GWS-35. See Endpapers, front, for the location of these sites (CORONA imagery taken on 6 October 1969, available from the USGS).

Gonbad-e Kavus (GWS-37), it appears to lack a corner citadel or any internal features. The shape of the site (rectangular rather than square) marks it out from the other examples listed above, and it is larger than Qal'eh Daland (GWS-53), Qal'eh Kharabeh (GWS-1), Qal'eh Gug A (GWS-33) and Gabri Qal'eh (GWS-49), but still smaller than the proposed campaign base of Qal'eh Pol Gonbad-e Kavus (GWS-37) (see Figs 2.2 and 2.3). Its morphological similarity to other sites, such as Qal'eh Daland (GWS-53), may suggest that it represents a further example of the 'campaign base' site type. In our field visit, we were unable to locate any trace of the ramparts. Destroyed by modern agriculture and building activities, the site is not visible on the ground; the village of Miankaleh Fenderesk and a modern dam/reservoir cover part of the site area (Fig. 2.4). We did not find any ceramics within the area of the former structure.

GWS-55 consists of a large parallelogram-shaped enclosure with a central qal'eh, and an internal square enclosure in the north-west corner, and is clearly visible on CORONA images and in aerial photographs from the 1930s[18] (Fig. 2.5). There is also a small square enclosure in the south-east corner of the large external enclosure. The only part of the site that is still visible in the field is a section of the east wall of the smaller enclosure. We also located an area of subtle mounding immediately west of the location of where the qal'eh was visible on the CORONA image (Fig. 2.5). This may be the remains of the ploughed-out lower mounds surrounding the central qal'eh. Based on field observations and inspection of recent high-resolution imagery, ploughing and agricultural activities have been the cause of most of the damage (Fig. 2.6). The majority of the diagnostic ceramics came from the central area of mounding (perhaps the former qal'eh and its surrounding mounds), and consisted of red ware jar forms suggesting Parthian or early Sasanian activity. Smaller quantities of Islamic glazed wares were also present. No traces of late Sasanian ceramics equivalent to those unearthed during excavations at Qal'eh Kharabeh or Fort 4 were located here.[19]

A further four sites, previously identified on the CORONA imagery, were also investigated in the field because they appeared to consist of geometric enclosures, or tappehs/qal'ehs with attached geometric enclosures. These are GWS-59, GWS-60, GWS-73 (formerly GWS-62) and GWS-83 (formerly GWS-61) (see Fig. 2.1 and Table 2.1). The geometric enclosures at GWS-59 and GWS-60 were still partly visible in the field, and ceramics

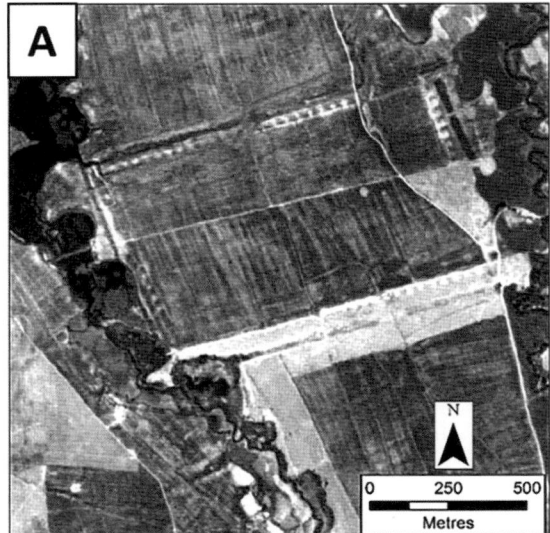 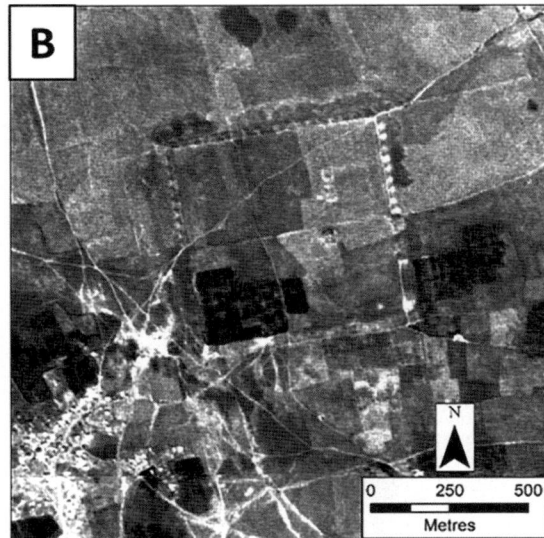

Fig. 2.3: A) The site of GWS-92, a large geometric fortified enclosure, and B) the site of Qal'eh Daland (GWS-53). Ramparts are visible on both structures (CORONA imagery taken on 6 October 1969, available from the USGS).

Fig. 2.4: No traces of GWS-92 are visible on this image from 2 August 2017 on Google Earth. It was likely destroyed by ploughing and modern construction (Image © Maxar Technologies 2020).

indicated possible early Sasanian wares, though there is much stronger evidence for Parthian and Islamic wares, respectively. At GWS-73 and GWS-83, however, we were unable to confirm the presence of preserved geometric enclosures, though surface ceramics suggest that Sasanian settlement is likely at GWS-73.

2.3.2. Geometric fortified enclosures of 2–6 ha

A handful of the rectilinear enclosures identified on the CORONA imagery measured between 2 and 6 ha (Table 2.2 and Fig. 2.7). Previously, it was suggested that several of these sites served as forts during the Sasanian period.[20] The majority have only been identified on imagery and therefore no dating information is available (Table 2.2). One of these sites (GWS-64), however, was visited in the field in 2014.

GWS-64, known as Habib Ishan, is composed of an approximately square mound measuring c. 200 × 180 m on the CORONA image (Fig. 2.7.C). A square citadel measuring c. 80 × 70 m is located in the south-east corner of the mound and is surrounded by a ditch.[21] The material from GWS-64 dates almost exclusively to the Islamic period, and includes a significant amount of ceramic roof tiles. Analyses of the glazed wares suggest a date in the tenth–eleventh centuries AD (though some wares could suggest activity ranging between the ninth–thirteenth centuries AD).[22] In the initial assessment, unglazed ware types similar to those associated with the Sasanian period were noted on the citadel, but none of the form types appeared to be directly comparable with the known Sasanian vessel types, suggesting an earlier or later date for the site based on the recovered ceramics. The pottery collected within the square enclosure also contains unglazed ware of types similar to those associated with Sasanian occupation, but again, there are almost no direct parallels with the forms recorded at previously excavated Sasanian sites. Kitchen ware is very recognisable because of the great quantity of grit visible on the surface of the pottery, but it is not of the cooking ware types that are usually associated with the Sasanian period (WIGTEM or MIGTEM).[23] While red ware body sherds with combed decoration could date to the late Sasanian period, this decoration type likely continued into the Islamic period, so these do not necessarily by themselves suggest a late Sasanian occupation. Furthermore, some red ware jar forms are similar to those from Tureng Tappeh Level VIIC and support a date in the Islamic period.[24]

Overall, the material from this site combines to suggest intensive occupation in the tenth–eleventh centuries AD, particularly in the Samanid period.²⁵ The frequency of fine wares at the site may suggest that the site did not have a solely military purpose at the time (though some fine wares would likely be found in a military context). Instead, although the architectural plan may relate to a defensive structure, the occupation at the site may have been largely residential, similar to other *qasr* type settlements of the Islamic period. The glazed wares suggest that the site did not have direct connections to the west, and therefore that the primary external influences were filtered through

Fig. 2.5: GWS-55. The red dotted lines indicate the areas that were visible during the 2016 field visit. The outer ramparts of the site have been completely or almost completely destroyed (CORONA imagery taken on 6 October 1969, available from the USGS).

Fig. 2.6: A Google Earth image of GWS-55 taken on 24 June 2016 (Image © 2020 CNES/Airbus).

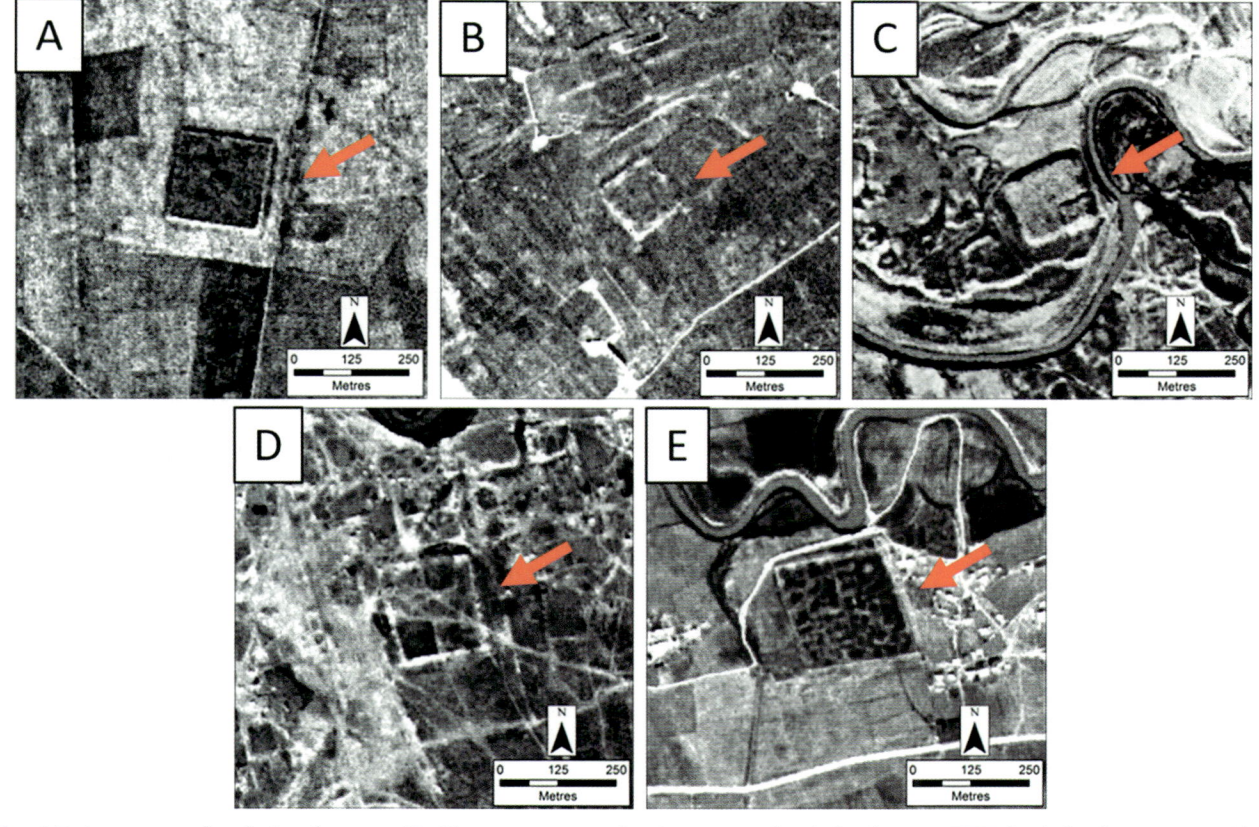

Fig. 2.7: A geometric fortified enclosures of 2–6 ha in size pictured at the same scale. A) database ID TJW_3; B) database ID KH_196; C) GWS-64 (Habib Ishan); D) database ID KH_5; E) GWS-57 (Qal'eh Hajilar). See Figs 2.1 and 2.19 for the location of these sites (CORONA imagery taken on 6 October 1969, available from the USGS).

Table 2.2: Geometric fortified enclosures between 2 and 6 ha. All coordinates in UTM Zone 40 N. See Figs 2.1 and 2.19 for their location.

Site	Size	Dating	Comments	Coordinates
Unnamed Square Enclosure (database ID TJW_3)	c. 4.5 ha	Unknown[1]	Briefly visited in an earlier phase of the project and noted as a possible fort.[2] Its size is similar to many of the forts lining the Gorgan Wall, and its close proximity to the wall (c. 450 m south of it), and Fort 14 and a small fort north of Fort 14 and the Gorgan Wall (Fig. 2.8.I), may suggest a relationship with one or the other of these features (Fig. 2.7.A).	E 328451, N 4125073
Unnamed Square Enclosure (database ID KH_196)	c. 2 ha	Unknown	Not visited in the field. Located c. 800 m to the N–NW of the citadel at Gabri Qal'eh (GWS-49). Its proximity to the likely Sasanian campaign base may suggest a relationship, although Gabri Qal'eh (GWS-49) continued to have significant occupation until the Ilkhanid period (Fig. 2.7.B).[3]	E 349935, N 4127650
Habib Ishan GWS-64	c. 3 ha	Islamic	See description in text (Fig. 2.7.C).[4]	E 292132, N 4112949
Unnamed Square Enclosure (database ID KH_5)	c. 4 ha	Unknown	Not visited in the field. Located immediately south of the Gorgan River to the east of Gonbad-e Kavus, and c. 5 km south of the Gorgan Wall within a palimpsest of archaic field systems and other features of unknown date (Fig. 2.7.D).	E 327934, N 4120404
Qal'eh Hajilar (GWS-57)	c. 6 ha	Islamic?	Not re-visited in the field. Located immediately south of the Gorgan River, and c. 2 km south of the Gorgan Wall. Despite its proximity to the wall, Qal'eh Hajilar (GWS-57) differs slightly in morphology in that 'the distinct internal patterning of buildings and walls within the interior of the fort suggests that this may be a rather late, post-Gorgan wall structure' (Fig. 2.7.E).[5]	E 340166, N 4126149

[1] The small fort north of Fort 14 (Fig. 2.8.I), may have been constructed or reoccupied in the Islamic period. Wilkinson *et al.* (2013, 99, 131 no. 228) observed some bricks similar to those from the Gorgan Wall and some probably Islamic bricks, as well as middle Islamic pottery.
[2] Tony Wilkinson and Hamid Omrani Rekavandi visited the site in an earlier phase of the project, but no dating evidence was collected.
[3] See also chapter 8.3.
[4] See also chapter 7.3.
[5] Wilkinson *et al.* 2013, 125, cf. 83, 91 fig. 3:72.

Nishapur and Samarkand. To conclude, known Sasanian ware types are present (although not in large quantity), but on balance the assemblage suggests that it is more likely that this site was occupied primarily in the Islamic period.

2.3.3. Geometric enclosures of 1 ha or less

There was no opportunity to visit any of the geometric enclosures that measured c. 1 ha or less in area (Figs 2.8 and 2.19) during our surveys in 2014–2016 and there is therefore no associated dating information. Unlike almost all other known geometric enclosures in the plain, several examples in this size category were located to the north of the Gorgan River and Wall. These, in particular, may have been associated with route systems in use from at least the Islamic period.[26] However, without further evidence it is difficult to speculate on the dating of these features.

2.4. Sasanian rural settlements: intensive survey at GWS-79

Our knowledge of site types associated with occupation in the Sasanian period beyond large rectilinear enclosures and fortifications is poor.[27] Examples of small single qal'ehs or prominent mounds that can be confidently dated to the Sasanian period include Buraq Tappeh (GWS-2, c. 0.5 ha, a small fort),[28] Tureng Tappeh, a prominent qal'eh-like mound with occupation dating back thousands of years,[29] and possibly Qal'eh Qabrestan (GWS-56), also interpreted as a possible Sasanian fort based on its morphology (Fig. 2.9).[30] However, these site morphologies are just as often associated with other chronological periods.

During the recent survey we targeted several tappeh sites that had been dated to the Sasanian period based on other published survey material.[31] The identification of likely Sasanian ceramics and a Sasanian coin from the

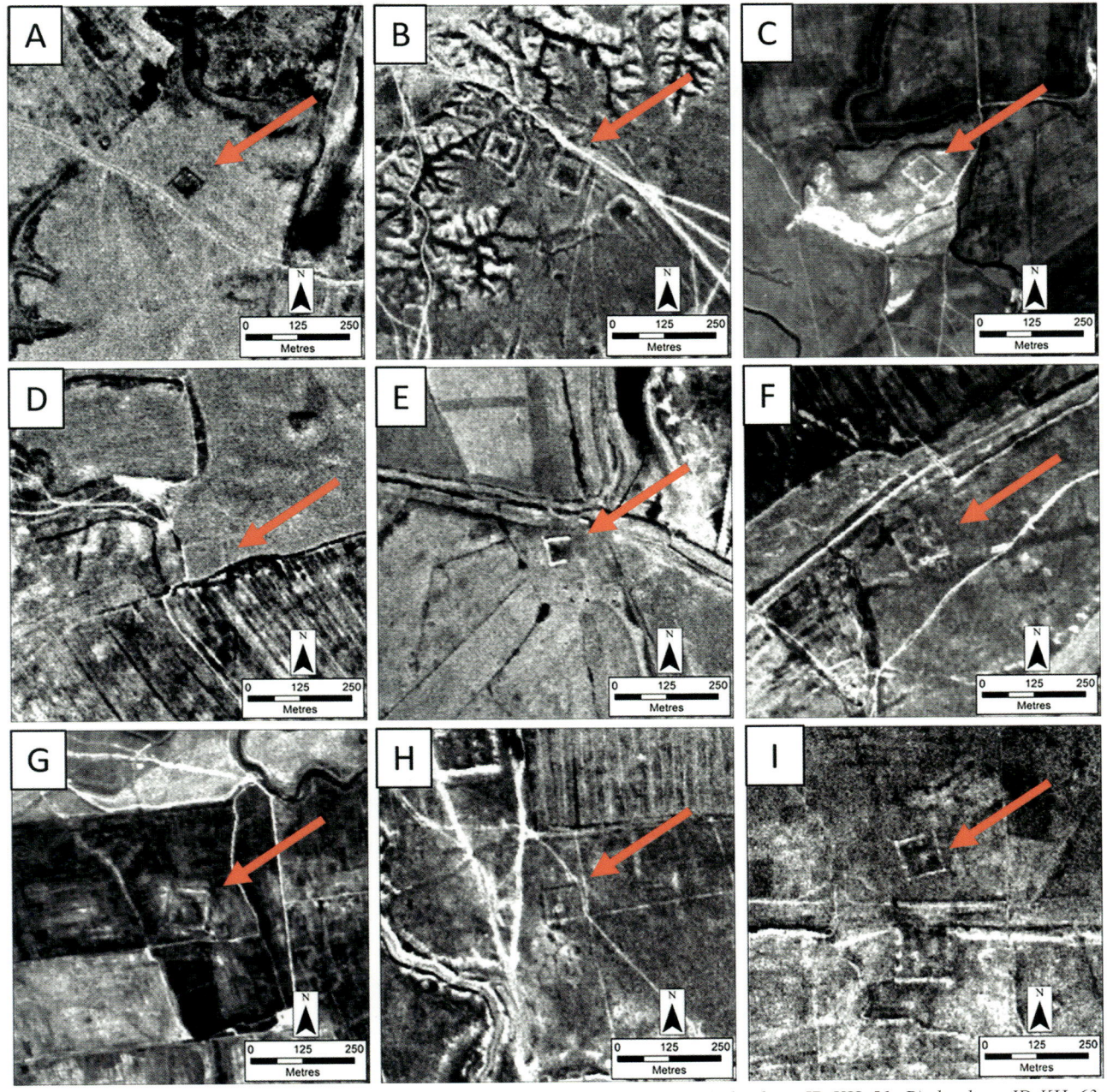

Fig. 2.8: Geometric enclosures of 1 ha or less in size pictured at the same scale. A) database ID KH_51; B) database ID KH_63; C) database ID KH_74; D) database ID KIA_13; E) database ID KIA_7; F) database ID KH_11; G) database ID KH_93; H) database ID KIA_28; I) Fort 14A, north of Fort 14. See Fig. 2.19 for the location of these sites (CORONA imagery taken on 6 October 1969, available from the USGS).

surface at GWS-79 in our own field visit prompted us to undertake a more intensive survey at this multi-period site. GWS-79 consists of a prominent tappeh with a lower terrace and a second lower tappeh located approximately 200 m to the east (Fig. 2.10). A continuous scatter of pottery was present between the prominent tappeh and the lower tappeh. A considerable amount of glass was found at the site.[32]

We defined a 340 m (west–east) × 140 m (north–south) survey area that covered the area of the prominent tappeh and the lower tappeh to the east. We collected surface material from 5 × 5 m square collection areas, 15 m apart (i.e. there was a distance of 15 m between the edge of one square and the edge of the next) (Fig. 2.11). Our goal was not only to determine occupied area by period, but to detect activity areas within the site. The survey was

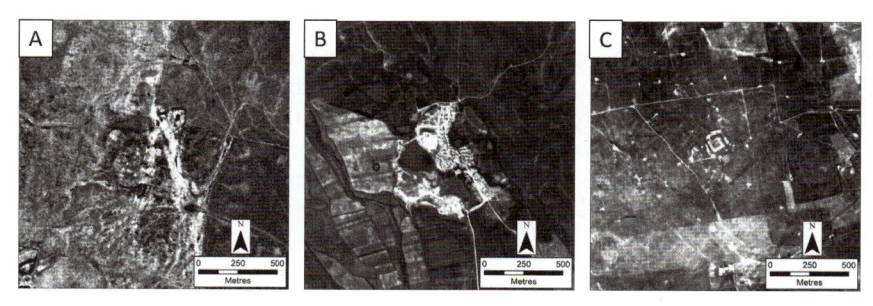

Fig. 2.9: Two small qal'eh sites with Sasanian or possible Sasanian occupation pictured at the same scale. A) GWS-2 and GWS-13; B) Tureng Tappeh; C) GWS-56. See Endpapers, front, for the location of these sites (CORONA imagery taken on 6 October 1969, available from the USGS).

small in scale due to the limited time and staff resources available for this activity. Pottery from both the prominent tappeh and the lower tappeh is consistent with occupation in the Parthian, Sasanian (both early and late) and Islamic periods. Occupied area by period, however, could not be broken down, as most of the sherds recovered were red wares attributable to all periods from at least the Iron Age to the Islamic era. Even so, GWS-79 appears to represent a small relatively long-lived rural settlement.

2.5. Investigations of features in the vicinity of Gorgan Wall Forts

Satellite remote sensing and previous fieldwork suggested that extramural settlement was present around a number of Gorgan Wall Forts.[33] Circumstantial evidence also indicated that there may have been a major crossing point of the Gorgan Wall between Forts 12 and 13.[34] Therefore, we selected the surroundings of Forts 2, 12, 13, 16, 18 and 28 for further investigation. While no evidence was found to validate our theories about extramural settlement or a crossing point of the wall, we were able to identify a number of previously unrecorded archaeological sites: GWS-65, GWS-66, GWS-71 and GWS-72 (see Table 2.1).

Of these sites, GWS-65, located immediately north of the wall and Fort 28, is the most relevant to our discussion of the Sasanian landscape (see Figs 2.1 and 2.12). Abundant artefacts were found along, immediately around and on the upcast banks of a modern canal cut (approximately 80 to 100 cm deep), which runs north–south, starting a few metres north of the Gorgan Wall. Whole bricks measuring c. 42–43 × 42–43 × 10 cm and large brick fragments are scattered over the same area. Two joining fragments of an iron knife were also found in the upcast of the canal. Seven fired bricks lie horizontally *in situ* in the western section of the canal cut (Fig. 2.13). Due to destruction by modern agriculture, it was impossible to determine the extent of the site, and no mound or tappeh was present. However, a possible rectilinear feature is visible near this location on the CORONA imagery and

Fig. 2.10: GWS-79 overview (photo by Kristen Hopper/Andrea Ricci).

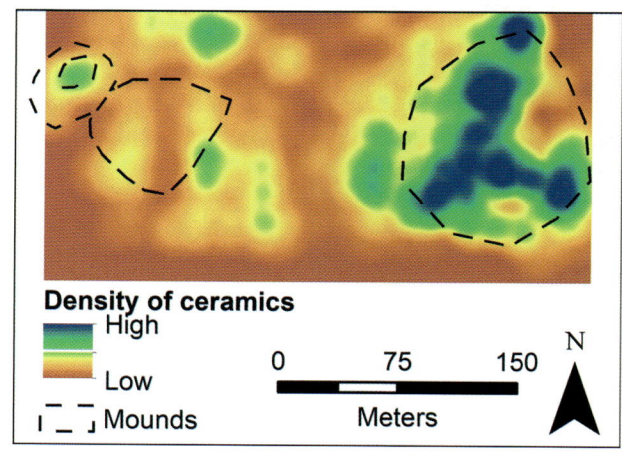

Fig. 2.11: A visualisation showing the density of ceramics documented in sampling survey at GWS-79 using Kernel density analysis. The density of surface ceramics was highest over the lower mound (the eastern mound). Kernel density analysis calculates the density of features in a neighbourhood around a point. In this case, the value of each point is the amount of pottery collected within a 5 m² collection area (spaced 15 m apart, edge to edge). The resulting raster image shows the density of point features around each cell. In this case, cells with a high density are blue, while cells with a low density are red. In this case we used an output cell size of 1 m, and a search radius of 25 m. (See Wheatley and Gillings 2002, 166–67 and Conolly and Lake 2006, 166 for uses of Kernel Density estimates in archaeology.)

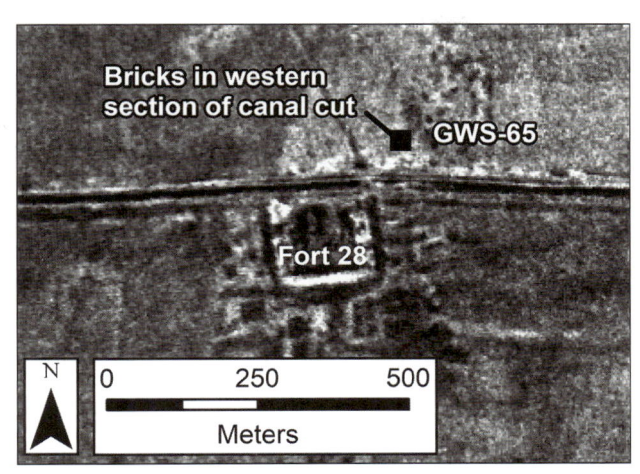

Fig. 2.12: Fort 28 and site GWS-65 mapped on CORONA imagery. Notice the possible rectangular shape in the area where site GWS-65 is located (CORONA imagery taken on 6 October 1969, available from the USGS).

Fig. 2.13: The western section of the canal cut showing seven bricks in situ *at GWS-65 (photo by Andrea Ricci).*

the *in-situ* bricks are located on the southern edge of this feature. A magnetometer survey was carried out at the site, but revealed no features beyond what was visible on the satellite imagery, except for detecting a possible oval feature in the interior, potentially a burial enclosure.[35] The pottery recovered indicates a date in the late Sasanian and Islamic periods, though one jar recovered appears to represent a form common in the Iron III period. The function of the site is unknown, but its possible rectangular shape and spatial and temporal proximity suggest it is related to activity on the Gorgan Wall.

2.6. Hydrological features associated with the Gorgan Wall and geometric fortified sites

In a previous publication, we suggested that the water supply for the Sasanian site of Qal'eh Kharabeh (GWS-1) may have come via a water collection point attached to a section of the South Canal (a pre-Sasanian canal probably reused in the Sasanian period).[36] If so, this reused portion of the South Canal may also have supplied water to other sites along the wall's course such as Qizlar Qal'eh (GWS-50), and Tokhmaq Tappeh (GWS-4). This hypothesis was supported by the identification of a possible canal feature on the CORONA imagery that we decided to verify in the field.

Approximately 200 m to the west of the estimated junction between the South Canal and this newly documented canal feature, we identified a linear depression (waypoint 279 on Fig. 2.14). Beyond this point, the feature was difficult to trace until approximately 2.5 km further west, where a shallow linear depression was again visible on the projected orientation (waypoint 281 on Fig. 2.14). This feature continued for c. 1.5 km until we were directly south of the eastern parts of the site of Qizlar Qal'eh (GWS-50). A possible continuation of this canal is again visible from c. 6 km to the west of GWS-50, but is disrupted by later irrigation features. In short, it is difficult to confirm our hypothesis, but it remains a possibility.

At Gabri Qal'eh (GWS-49) a possible raised canal or roadway was located on the CORONA satellite imagery. It extends from the north-west ramparts and crosses the ditch surrounding the site (Fig. 2.15). On the ground, we located this raised feature, which runs in a north-west to south-east direction for at least 70 m. Excavation of the feature, however, suggests it is more likely to have functioned as a causeway entering the site.[37] The water supply for the ditch surrounding the site probably came from a canal feature leading to and connecting with the ditch outside the south-east rampart (Fig. 2.15).

We also investigated a possible canal feature associated with the site of Qal'eh Pol Gonbad-e Kavus (GWS-37) (Fig. 2.16). This is suggested by a linear feature that appears to cross the large, roughly rectangular enclosure from north-west to south-east and is visible on the CORONA imagery. In the field, we explored the location where, according to the CORONA imagery, the linear feature should have met the river (that is, to the north-west of Qal'eh Pol Gonbad-e Kavus). However, due to erosion by the river, no evidence for a canal was found here. Near to where the feature is cut by the modern highway, however, the ground level had been lowered through commercial activities and modern development, leaving an exposed section (Fig. 2.17). Within the c. 2.5 m high section, an approximately 10 m wide area contained gravel layers, sand lenses and pottery that may represent successive fills of a canal, but our observations were far from conclusive.[38] We had more success in attempting to trace the feature where it met the south-east rampart of the site at a right angle. A raised bank, possibly representing the east bank of the canal, was located (Fig. 2.18).

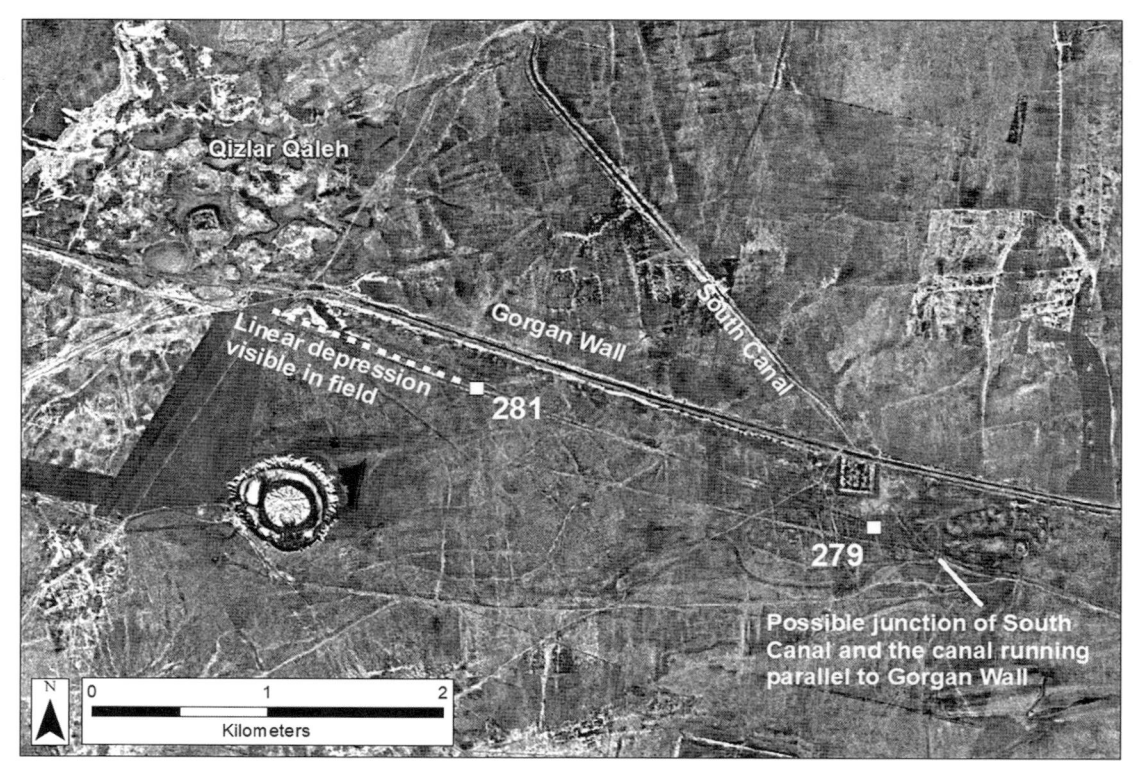

Fig. 2.14: Features documented in field investigations of a possible canal located south of the Gorgan Wall (CORONA imagery taken on 6 October 1969, available from the USGS).

2.7. Conclusion

Our recent fieldwork has identified further examples of the large geometric enclosures that appear to be a key feature of Sasanian imperial military infrastructure. The scale of these enclosures reinforces the fact that significant investment was put into defending the Gorgan region. GWS-55, GWS-59, GWS-60, GWS-73, GWS-83 and GWS-92 were all targeted because they consisted of a geometric enclosure, or a mound or mounds with an attached geometric enclosure visible on the CORONA imagery. Of these, the central mounded area at GWS-55 was definitely occupied in the early Sasanian period; GWS-59, GWS-60 and GWS-73 may also have been occupied in this phase, though it is not clear whether GWS-73 belongs to this morphological category. GWS-92, while producing no ceramic evidence, shows strong morphological similarities to known Sasanian 'campaign bases' (see Fig. 2.19 for the location of, and dating evidence for, these sites).

Furthermore, we also identified a likely late Sasanian fortified mound at GWS-85 (Fig. 2.20) c. 2 km south of the Gorgan River. Roughly rectangular in shape, and measuring c. 45 m (north–south), by 30 m (west–east), and 8 m high, the tappeh appears to be right in the centre of an outer square rampart-enclosed compound (of c. 200 × 200 m), surrounded by a depression (a moat?). A central gap, c. 40 m across, along the southern side of

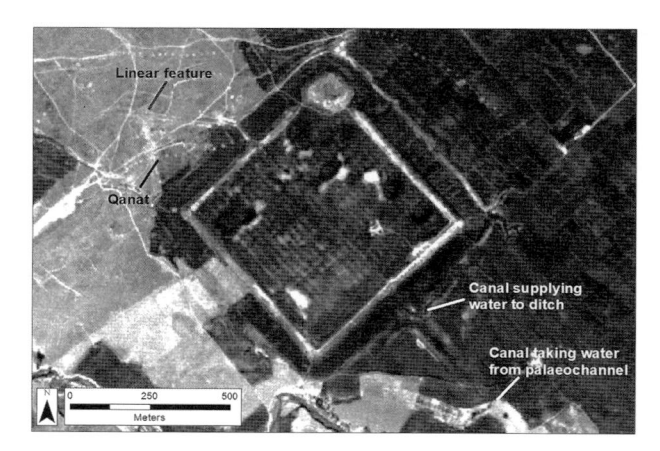

Fig. 2.15: Overview of a possible canal, and route features associated with Gabri Qal'eh (CORONA imagery taken on 6 October 1969, available from the USGS).

the possible ramparts of an outer enclosure was apparent and may represent a gate (Fig. 2.21). While the tappeh was occupied as early as the Iron III period, it was most clearly in use contemporary with the Gorgan Wall. Its morphology and possible location on the approaches to the river suggest that it was a fortification.

There was much stronger evidence for early, as opposed to late, Sasanian activity to the north and immediately

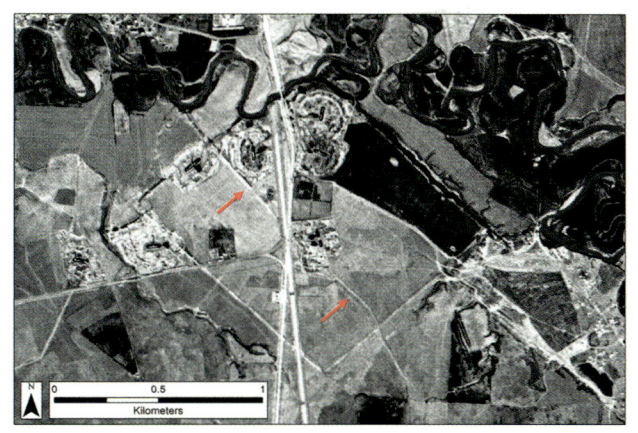

Fig. 2.16: The site of Qal'eh Pol Gonbad-e Kavus. The red arrows indicate the location of a possible canal feature (CORONA imagery taken on 6 October 1969, available from the USGS).

Fig. 2.17: The possible location of a former canal running through Qal'eh Pol Gonbad-e Kavus. The land surface has been lowered considerably since the 1960s.

Fig. 2.18: Location of field investigations at Qal'eh Pol Gonbad-e Kavus on imagery dated to 22 January 2020 on Google Earth (Image © 2020 Maxar Technologies).

south of the Gorgan Wall in the western part of the plain, with the exception of GWS-65. This site, based on its ceramic assemblage, appears to be roughly contemporary with the wall. Its location, along with its possible rectilinear morphology visible on the CORONA imagery, suggests it is also likely to have had a military function.

We also identified several sites that likely represent examples of Sasanian-period rural settlements. GWS-79, for example, appears to be a long-lived habitation site extending all the way through the Sasanian period (and was also occupied earlier and later). Further investigation of this and similar sites may reveal important information about Sasanian domestic activities and related pottery assemblages.

The evidence presented here, coupled with the results of the earlier phase of the project, suggests that significant effort was put into the construction and maintenance of defensive infrastructure and related water management systems by the Sasanian imperial apparatus. However, the same level of engagement with the organisation (or reorganisation) of the rural landscape does not appear to have occurred. This raises interesting questions

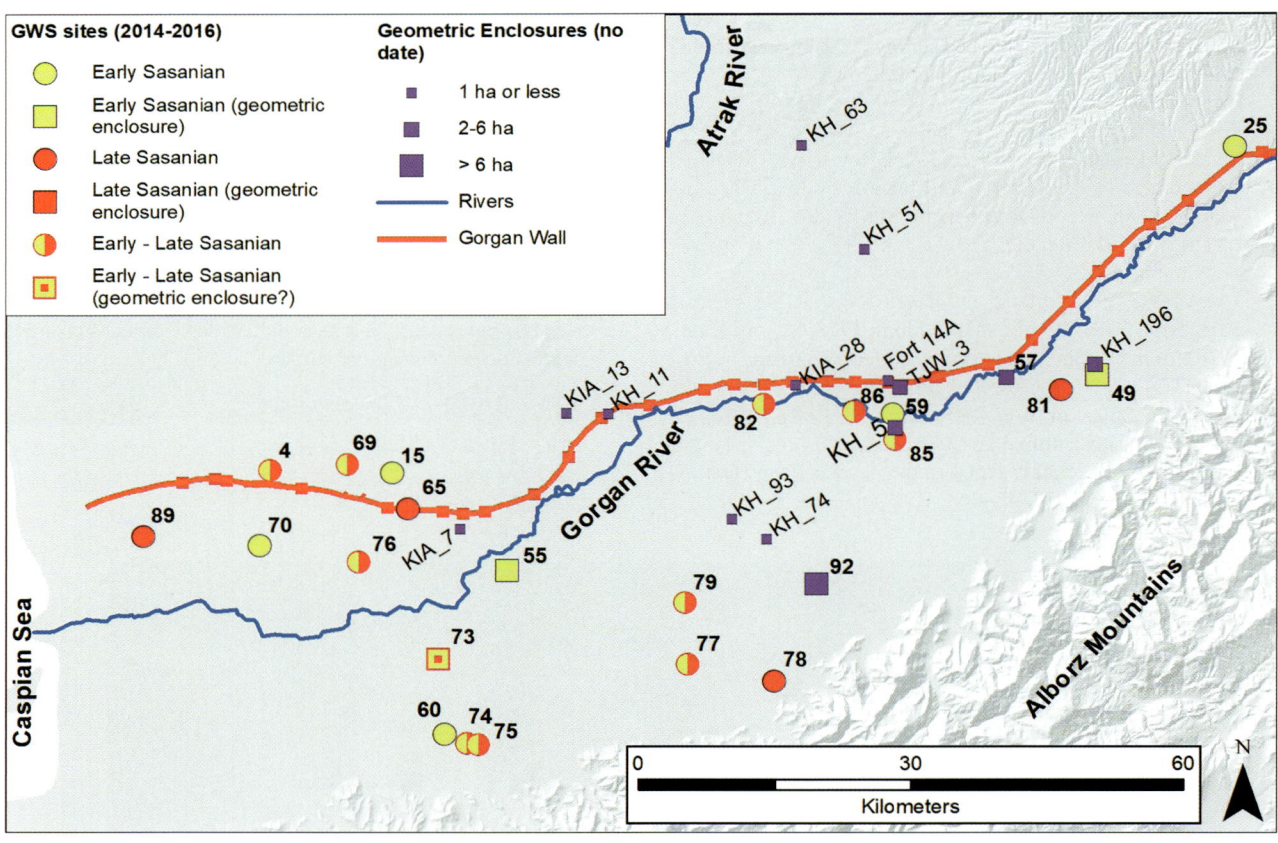

Fig. 2.19: A map indicating the location of sites identified in the 2014–2016 survey that had ceramics that were classified as indicating 'maybe', 'probable' or 'definite' early or late Sasanian occupation (in yellow and red, respectively). A selection of geometric enclosures identified on satellite imagery, but with no independent dating, are also indicated (in purple). (Base map SRTM 90 m DEM, available from the USGS.)

Fig. 2.20: The site of GWS-85 looking NW towards (photo by Kristen Hopper/Andrea Ricci).

Fig. 2.21: Looking south from the top of the tappeh (GWS-85) across the shallow depression and towards the gap in the outer ramparts (photo by Kristen Hopper/Andrea Ricci).

regarding how the Sasanian imperial court viewed the Gorgan Plain, the longevity of local practices and the relationships between imperial plans, local elite and non-elite communities that we will explore more fully in a forthcoming publication.[39]

Notes

1. Hopper 2017b.
2. Wilkinson *et al.* 2013.

3 See Hopper 2017b; a full discussion of this data derived from remote sensing, published surveys and the recent field evidence will appear in Hopper *et al.* 2022.
4 Hopper *et al.* 2022.
5 The field survey was led by Hamid Omrani Rekavandi, Kristen Hopper, and Andrea Ricci, who were assisted by members of the Gorgan Wall team including Maryam Ajamhosseini, Maria Daghmehchi, Marc Heise, Emanuele Intagliata, Friederike Jürcke, Abdullah Kishmili, Mohammad Paghe, Silvia Perini and Bardia Shabani.
6 These were selected from published sources (i.e. Abbasi 2011; Arne 1945; Kiani 1982b; Shiomi 1978; Shiomi *et al.* 1976), from examination of survey collections (made by the ICHHTO) undertaken by Seth Priestman and Habibollah Rezaee in 2009, or from those identified on CORONA imagery. Those identified on CORONA shared morphology similar to those reliably dated to the periods of interest.
7 Wilkinson *et al.* 2013, 43–46.
8 See chapter 10.
9 See also chapter 4.
10 See chapter 8 and Sauer *et al.* 2013, 303–81; these sites might also potentially have served as defensible refuges, or focal points for other activities outside of military campaigns.
11 For example, the Islamic-period site of Aq Qal'eh (c. 88 ha) has a similar morphology. See also chapters 7.1 and 24.9 on similarities between Sasanian and Islamic-era geometric foundations.
12 Alizadeh 2011; Trinkaus 1983; Venco Ricciardi 1981a.
13 See Hopper 2017b; Hopper *et al.* 2022.
14 CORONA KH-4A, mission 1052, acquired on 6 October 1969.
15 Aq Qal'eh is not included in this analysis because of its clearly Islamic date.
16 This refers to the database of sites and features located on the CORONA imagery and presented in Hopper 2017b, which will be discussed in further detail in Hopper *et al.* 2022.
17 Sauer *et al.* 2013, 324; see also chapter 8.
18 See Schmidt 1940, pl. 68.
19 See also chapter 8.5 on this site and a further field visit in 2013 that revealed possible traces of the westernmost part of the north wall of the large enclosure.
20 Sauer *et al.* 2013, 305-10 with fig. 12:2; Wilkinson *et al.* 2013, 83, 91 fig. 3:72.
21 See also chapter 7.3; note that these dimensions refer to the entire mounds, not just the intramural area.
22 See Hopper *et al.* 2022 for complete details of the ceramic analysis and parallels.
23 See chapter 15 and Priestman 2013, 458–59.
24 Gardin 1987, pl. 72.
25 See Hopper *et al.* 2022 for a complete description of Islamic wares located during the survey.
26 See Hopper 2017a.
27 See Priestman 2013, 526 fig. 18:39 for a map of previously known sites with Sasanian ceramics.
28 See chapter 7.2.
29 Boucharlat and Lecomte 1987.
30 Sauer *et al.* 2013, 305 fig. 12:2, 306, 309–10, 360; Wilkinson *et al.* 2013, 83, 90 fig. 3:71, 125. Interestingly, while no site description is provided, pottery from the site illustrated by Kiani 1982b, 64, 74 fig. 56 includes incised red wares that he attributes to the Sasanian period. This category has proven generally comparable to the REDPLI ware type in the excavated Qal'eh Kharabeh (GWS-1) and Fort 4 ceramic assemblages, though Kiani's illustrated examples from this particular site provide no exact parallels (Priestman 2013, 528). Incised red wares also continue into the Islamic period at Tureng Tappeh (Gardin 1987, 123–24).
31 Abbasi 2011; Arne 1945; Kiani 1982b; Shiomi 1978; Shiomi *et al.* 1976.
32 See chapters 16–17 on the glass finds.
33 Wilkinson *et al.* 2013, 82 table 3:4.
34 Hopper 2017a, 133–40; Sauer *et al.* 2013, 20 no. 12; see also chapter 4.6.3.
35 See chapters 4.5 and 4.6.3.
36 Wilkinson *et al.* 2013, 80.
37 See chapter 8.3.4.
38 See also chapter 8.2.1.
39 See Hopper *et al.* 2022.

3

The Gorgan Wall

3.1. Introduction

Whilst our fieldwork in 2014–2016 ranged from Qal'eh Iraj on the Tehran Plain to Mozdouran in Khorasan, some 800 km apart as the crow flies, the two, in terms of architecture exposed, most prolific trenches were just 700 m apart: Trenches b and d. The former exposed the remains of a monumental bridge on which the Gorgan Wall crossed the Sari Su River, the latter, parts of the barracks within Fort 2. There is enough major new evidence for both, forts on the Gorgan Wall and wall architecture, to merit two separate chapters, notably as remote surveys added important new information also on forts and parts of the Great Wall far away from these large trenches. Unlike our fieldwork in 2005–2009, we excavated no brick kilns during the second phase of the joint project (2014–2016). Dr Jebrael Nokandeh and the ICHHTO excavated, however, a further kiln in 2012 west of Fort 28 and to the south of the Gorgan Wall, after prior geophysical survey, in advance of railway construction across the Great Wall. This survey also detected a second kiln, c. 80 m west (centre to centre) of the one excavated.[1] A further brick kiln plus a possible second kiln were also detected by geophysical survey in the Sari Su River Valley.[2] These discoveries have yielded no significant new insights into kiln architecture or even spacing as, due to deep burial under alluvial sediments, we cannot be sure that all kilns in the area surveyed in the Sari Su River Valley were detected. There is thus not enough new information on kilns to merit a separate chapter as in the previous report. In order to facilitate comparison with radiocarbon dates cited elsewhere in the report, we have, however, recalibrated the radiocarbon samples from kiln fuel from the first phase of the project using the 2020 version of the OxCal programme, confirming that the kilns

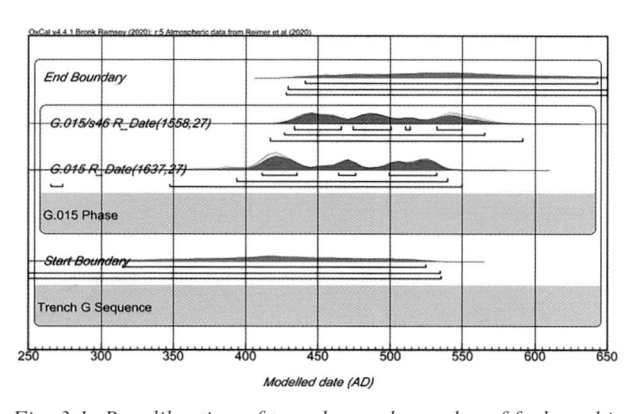

Fig. 3.1: Recalibration of two charcoal samples of fuel used in the kiln in Trench G west of Fort 30. One sample (G.015) dates at 95.4% probability to c. AD 376–539 (modelled date: 394–540), the other (G.015/s46), to c. AD 430–573 (modelled date: 427–565).

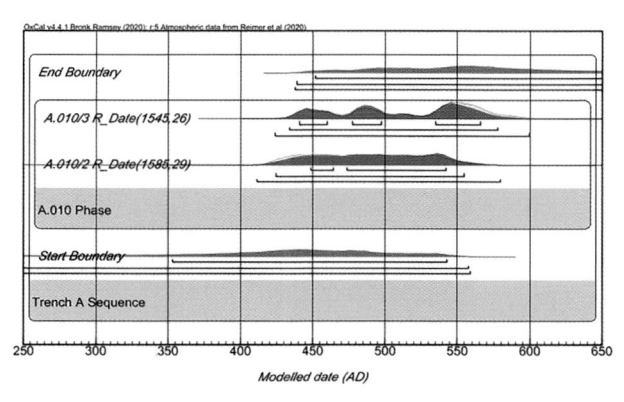

Fig. 3.2: Recalibration of two charcoal samples of fuel used in the kiln in Trench A on the eastern extension of the Great Wall. One sample (A.010/2) dates at 95.4% probability to c. AD 420–550 (modelled date: 424–555), the other (A.010/3), to c. AD 433–591 (modelled date: 433–577).

were in use between the AD 420s and c. 540 in the west (Trench G kiln)[3] and between the AD 420s and 550s in the east (Trench A kiln);[4] historically the first half of this period seems more likely than the second, notably as far as the lowland section of the Great Wall is concerned. Recalibration of a bone from the canal along the Gorgan Wall at Trench B[5] has increased the likelihood of this sample being late, i.e. dating to the last two thirds of the sixth or the early seventh century, a time when the garrison of adjacent Fort 9 evidently had abandoned their previous reluctance to deposit rubbish in the canal/ditch. To judge by further finds at higher levels, the fort continued to be occupied for some time beyond.

If we have little to add to our work on brick kiln design, fieldwork in the second phase of the joint project has yielded significant new insights on how river crossings were secured, notably on how the Gorgan Wall crossed one of the few northern tributaries to the Gorgan River, the

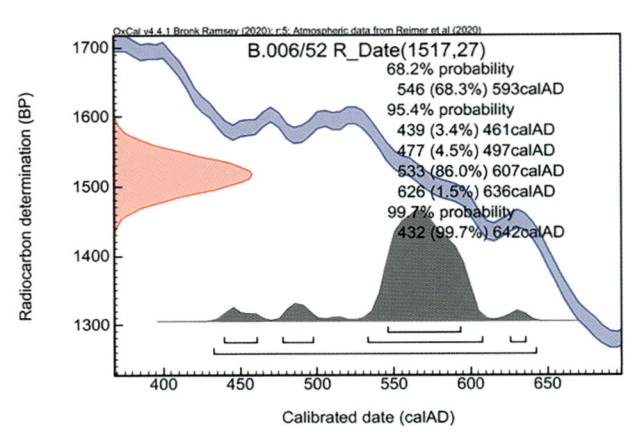

Fig. 3.3: Recalibration of a bone sample from the fill of the canal along the Gorgan Wall next to Fort 9 in Trench B. The sample (B.006/52) dates at 95.4% probability to c. AD 439–636 (93.9%: 439–607; 90.5%: 477–607; 86.0%: 533–607).

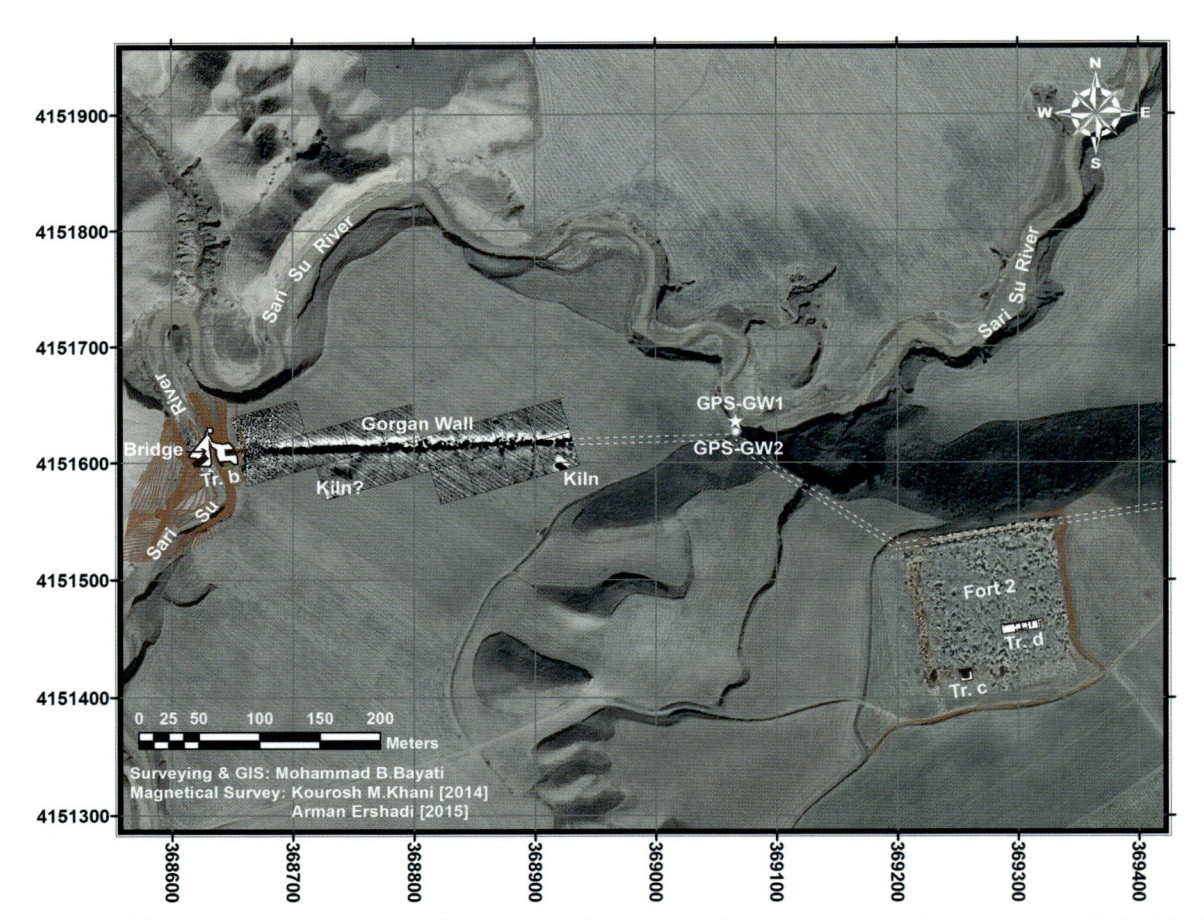

Fig. 3.4: Plan of the excavations and geophysical and topographical surveys between Fort 2 and the bridge across the Sari Su River by Mohammad Bagher Bayati et al. Note that the brick structure, almost certainly part of the Gorgan Wall, exposed in the western loess cliff framing the Sari Su River Valley north-west of Fort 2, has been recorded by GPS. GPS-GW2 (concentric circle symbol) has been taken on top of the cliff and is likely to be more reliable than GPS-GW1 (star symbol). Bearing in mind that there is a possible error of a few metres, it appears that the Gorgan Wall, traced further west via magnetometer survey, runs in a (perfectly or almost) straight alignment over some 420 m from the Sari Su Bridge to the cliffs below Fort 2.

Sari Su. Buried deep under substantial alluvial deposits, excavations here have unearthed the by far highest and best-preserved section of the Great Wall found to date. The Gorgan Wall Bridge over the Sari Su is the main focus of this chapter on the Gorgan Wall and its architecture. It will also present new aerial imagery for the second major river crossing (over the Kal Aji River), the Sadd-e Garkaz Aqueduct, channelling water into the canal lining the Great Wall and the topography of the wall's eastern terminal. The forts on the Gorgan Wall, notably new evidence on their interior plan and history and nature of occupation, will be covered in a separate chapter.[6]

Our introductory chapter on the Gorgan Wall is also the appropriate place to acknowledge and correct at the outset a significant factual error concerning the length of the Great Wall, unnoticed for far too long. According to the late Mohammad Yusef Kiani, the lowland section of the Gorgan Wall measured 175 km,[7] a figure accepted by other scholars, e.g. Martin Charlesworth whose important research on the eastern extension to the wall added a further 15 km,[8] and us. Kiani's length estimate refers to the section from the Pishkamar Rocks (at or very near Fort 1) to the westernmost point known then, 4 km west of Fort 33.[9] One of Kiani's maps implies a possible continuation to a point c. 7.5 km west of Fort 33,[10] another even c. 12 km beyond this westernmost known fort.[11] Yet, Kiani's own figures for distances between key points only add up to a distance of 141.450 km from Pishkamar to the point 4 km west of Fort 33.[12] Even assuming Kiani's estimate relates to the westernmost hypothetical point near Gomish Tappeh, some 12 km beyond the fort, the distance from Pishkamar would just be c. 150 km, not 175 km. Checking the distances independently, our own estimate now implies that the wall ran for c. 144 km from Pishkamar to Fort 33, c. 148 km to the point 4 km west of Fort 33 and c. 155 km to the westernmost point now found by Richard Bates et al.[13] The eastern extension beyond the Pishkamar Rocks was, based on measurements by Kristen Hopper,[14] 16.7 km long. The total length of the Great Wall known to date, i.e. of the eastern extension plus the section from Fort -1 on the Pishkamar Rocks to the westernmost point known now, thus adds up to a little over 170 km (or to c. 175 km if one also counts the 3.5 km gap protected by natural cliffs between these two sections), not to some 200 km, as we had assumed before. This should not be seen as criticism of the late Kiani's pioneering work on mapping the wall. It is rather a criticism of ourselves for not having checked before the accuracy of the estimate. Neither does this downward correction much diminish the impressiveness of the building project.[15] It is likely that the wall runs for several kilometres further west to the Sasanian-era shoreline or even into the Caspian Sea, but even a little over 170 km would be very impressive, and it is still by some margin the longest fort-lined barrier of the late antique world.[16] The at least 12 km long Tammisheh Wall (or c. 14 km in total, if one adds the section of the associated ditch/canal that continues beyond the southern terminal of the wall)[17] is not included in this figure.

3.2. The Gorgan Wall Bridge and a Sasanian reservoir between Forts 2A and 2

3.2.1. Sasanian hydraulic installations in the Sari Su River Valley

The Gorgan Wall's location north of the Gorgan River is not fortuitous, but offered three major advantages:

1 The river was within the protective bounds of the linear barrier, securing permanent access to its water as well as the fields and pastures on both banks of the river.

2 There are far fewer tributaries on the right bank of the river. Each river crossing formed a potential weak point, as during episodes of heavy rain swollen streams could have undermined and washed away segments of wall, whilst in drier conditions stream beds, impossible to seal off hermetically, may have provided enemy forces or lawless elements with loopholes in the wall, facilitating unauthorised entry or exit. Building the wall on the bank with fewer streams crossings to negotiate, and lesser quantities of flowing water to be channelled through openings in the barrier, facilitated construction and reduced the risk of flood damage and trespass by northerners.

3 The River Gorgan itself would not have formed an impermeable barrier. Only a wall north of the river could have secured all the land south. This is true even considering that in the past the river reportedly carried much more water than today, and crossing it reportedly often involved a risk to life.[18] Yet at normal times, the river would not have been wide enough to form an unsurmountable obstacle to well-organised enemies or larger raiding parties, capable of constructing a makeshift bridge, rafts or securing a ford. Any unauthorised attempts at crossing the Gorgan River would have been further facilitated at times of drought and low water. And the river's meandering course in places would have made it difficult to patrol the banks effectively.

Whilst the wall's chosen route north of the Gorgan River crossed few streams, they could not be bypassed altogether. One of the most prominent crossing points was located between Forts 2 and 2A. The principal duties of the garrisons of this pair of forts, both in elevated positions ideal for area surveillance – and in unusually close proximity just some 900 m apart (centre to centre) – undoubtedly included keeping a watchful eye on the Sari Su River in between. A brick structure running into the stream, discovered by Hamid Omrani Rekavandi and

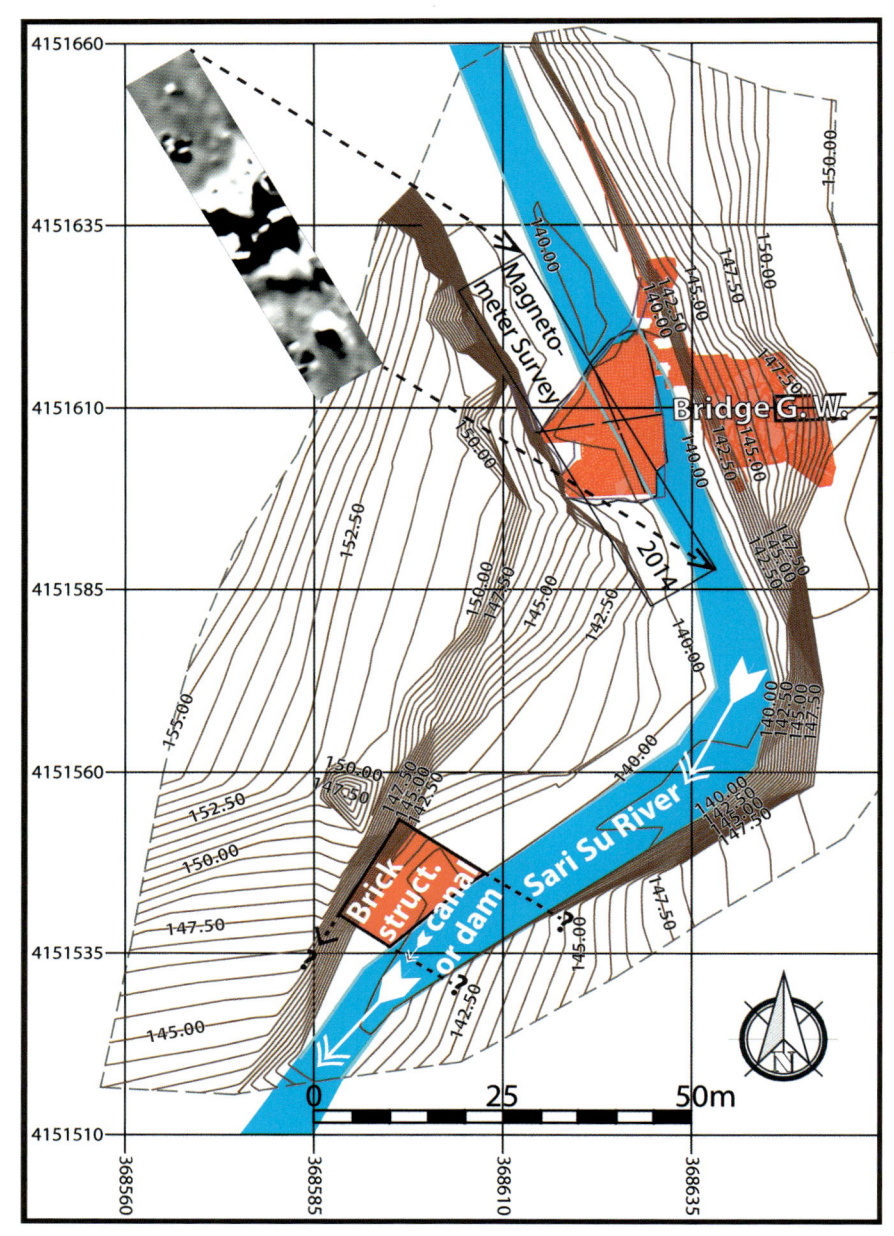

Fig. 3.5: Topographical survey in the Sari Su Valley by Mohammad Bagher Bayati, showing also the location of the 2014 magnetometer survey and the remains of the bridge revealed by subsequent excavations (2014–2015). G.W. is the Gorgan Wall, the edges of the excavated section are marked with solid and the projected continuation with dotted lines. Note that the topographical survey was conducted prior to the excavations when much of the bridge was still buried under many metres of alluvial sediments. A second substantial brick structure downstream, just at the point where the valley widens and the southernmost point where the river could easily have been dammed, has not been excavated and its location is approximate only. Remains of this feature (perhaps the lining of a canal or potentially a dam) are only visible on the river's western bank, and its postulated continuation may have been partially or completely washed away and/or buried under sediments. Excavation or geophysical survey would be needed to establish whether or not some of its lower courses survive under the river bed or on its eastern bank.

first explored by him and the late Tony Wilkinson, proved crucial in guarding the river crossing.[19] As recognised by them, the wall splits here into two branches, and the brick feature is close to the alignment of the southern (and probably original) branch.

3.2.2. A new section of the Gorgan Wall, discovered by geophysical and pedestrian survey, leading towards a bridge[20]

In 2014, the western side of this brick structure was first geophysically examined, and it produced a very strong

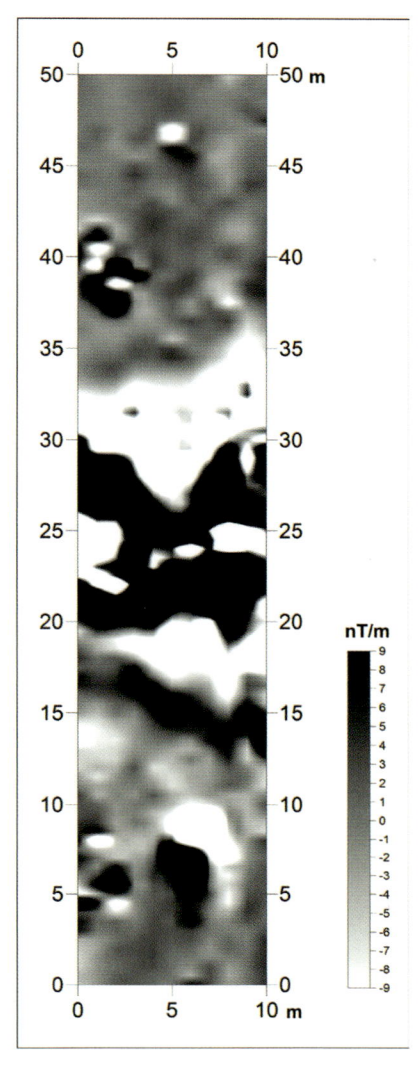

Fig. 3.6: Magnetometer survey of the structure (centre of the plot) in the Sari Su River Valley, subsequently shown to form part of a bridge, by Kourosh Mohammadkhani and Soroush Mohammadkhani. (North: top of the plot; south: bottom of the plot; see Fig. 3.5 for the location of the survey.)

magnetic anomaly. Subsequently, it was excavated west of the river; unearthing of the eastern side had to wait until 2015. Its function was unknown in 2014, notably as it was only in the subsequent season that we were able to detect the remains of the Gorgan Wall between Forts 2 and 2A. Initially, we thought it was part of a dam. Subsequent excavation and survey established that the upstream brick structure was a bridge on which the Gorgan Wall crossed the Sari Su River. There is, however, evidence for a Sasanian dam and canal further downstream.[21] The purpose of these structures only becomes apparent, if we evaluate their location in relation to the Gorgan Wall, and we therefore present the new evidence for the course of the wall first.

Until 2015, there had been no firm evidence for the Gorgan Wall between Forts 2 and 2A beyond the section leading from Fort 2 down to the edge of the Sari Su River Valley. On the map produced by Kiani's team, there is a half-kilometre gap in the wall north-west of this point.[22] There is also no trace of wall here on satellite imagery. Our own pedestrian survey revealed a fairly dense brick concentration[23] on top of a steep loess cliff at the edge of the Sari Su River Valley north-west of Fort 2, coinciding with the terminal point of this section of wall on Kiani's map. We failed to detect any continuation of this brick scatter towards Trench b. Nor is there any other evidence for the wall's course or existence on the large arable field between the cliff-top brick concentration and Trench b.[24] If the wall ran from Fort 2 right to the edge of a steep loess cliff, it would have been impossible to bypass the barrier at this point or further east. Did the brick concentration perhaps mark a terminal point of a section of the Great Wall, and was there perhaps indeed a gap of several hundred metres in the Gorgan Wall between Forts 2 and 2A?

Magnetometer survey in December 2015 decisively proved that there was no such gap. Whilst this discovery post-dates our excavations, it is best presented at the outset, as it will enable the reader to appreciate how the excavated monument functioned as a part of the defensive barrier. The geophysical survey revealed that the central wall within the eastern brick abutment in Trench b is in direct continuation of the Great Wall of Gorgan (Fig. 3.10). The latter could be traced as far as surveyed very clearly (i.e. for another 280 m beyond the eastern edge of Trench b). Mahshah Allah Rahmani found a wall preserved to a height of at least six courses exposed in the loess cliffs of the Sari Su River north-west of Fort 2 (Figs 3.11–3.12).[25] This is in alignment with the Gorgan Wall detected by magnetometer survey (Fig. 3.4) and, whilst there was no time to continue the survey to the terminal, we may conclude that the wall runs in a straight alignment across the river bend over some 420 m. Near the cliff-top above the wall's river-side terminal, there is the above-cited scatter of Gorgan Wall brick fragments on the surface, and some brick is also visible in a nearby erosion tunnel. It must be near this point that the newly discovered west–east section of the Great Wall joins the previously known section leading up to Fort 2. It would have been risky to build a heavy brick structure at the edge of an unstable loess cliff, and one wonders if the cliff edge may have been a little further from edge of the wall in antiquity. The corner exposed on the cliff face has straight edges on both sides without any obvious trace of bricks having fallen out and lost to erosion (Figs 3.11–3.12). It is therefore possible that this might have been part of a real terminus or the corner point or an associated structure, such as a tower, on the unscalable loess cliffs.

The survey also revealed in the south-easternmost grid (Figs 3.4 and 3.7–3.10) part of a strong magnetic anomaly that appears to be of rectangular shape. This strikingly resembles, in dimensions and shape, brick kilns detected

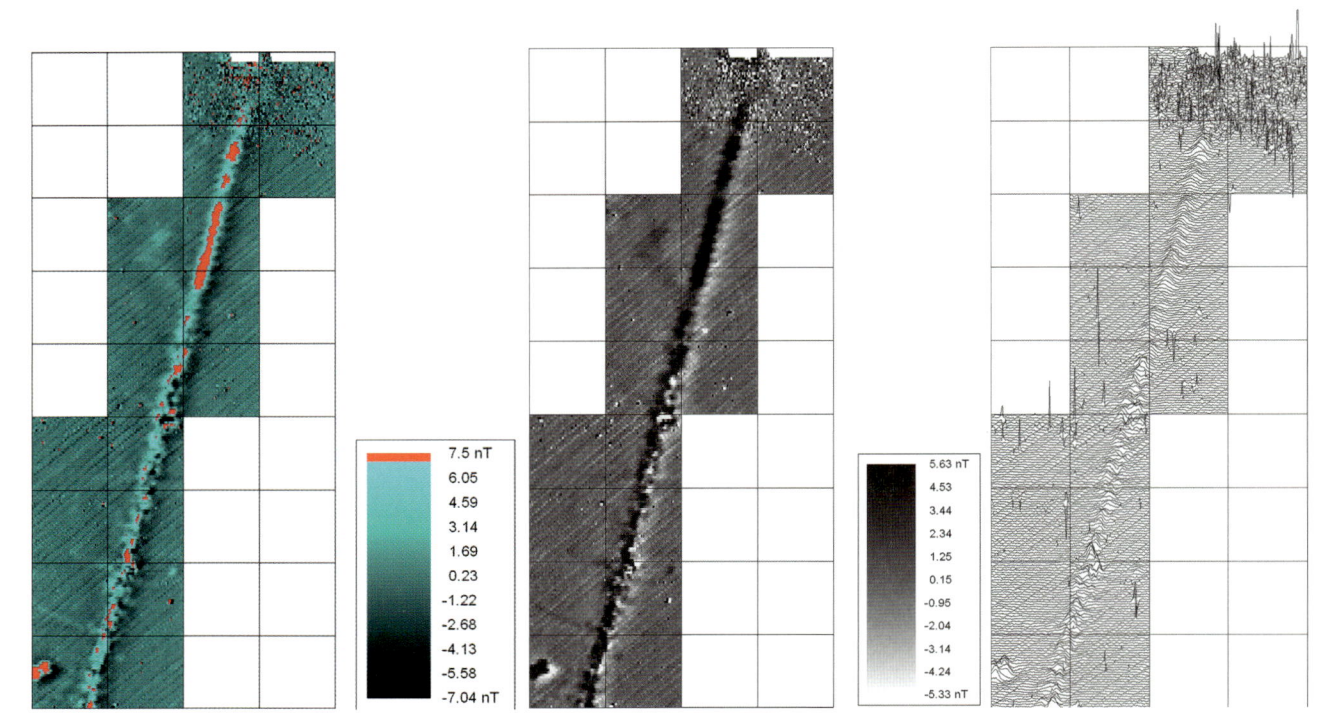

Figs 3.7, 3.8 and 3.9: Colour, black and white and trace plots of the geophysical survey of the Great Wall of Gorgan from the east edge of Trench b (top) towards Fort 2, by the joint team, notably Mohammad Arman Ershadi. Processed by him and Roger Ainslie of Abingdon Archaeological Geophysics. Each grid measures 30 × 30 m. (See Figs 3.4 and 3.10 for the location of the survey.)

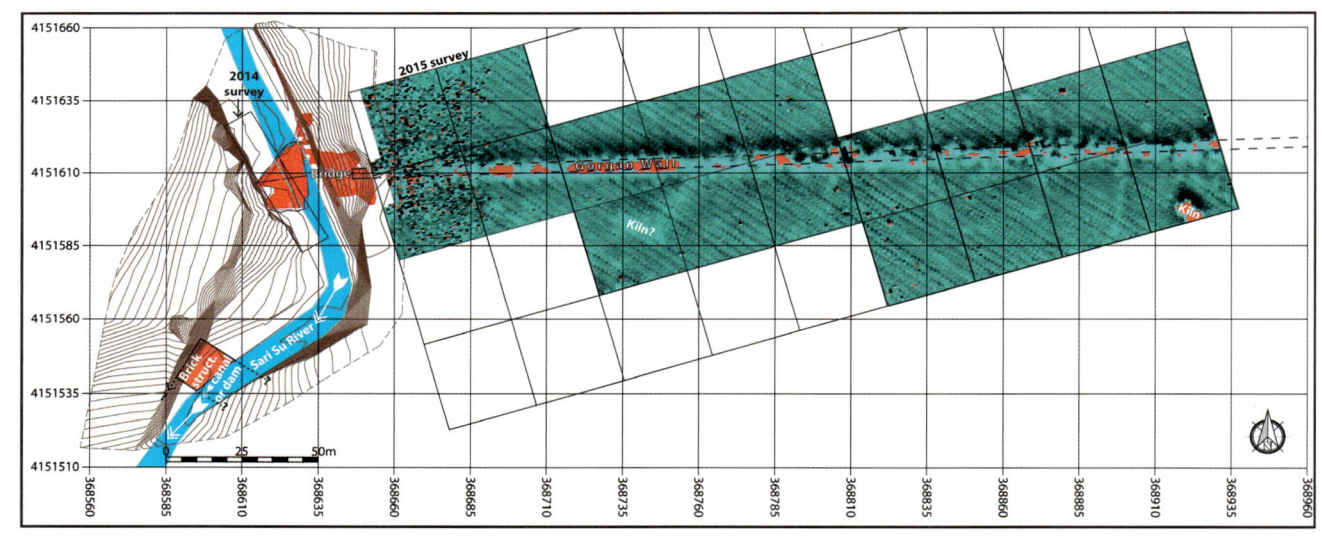

Fig. 3.10: Location of the magnetometer surveys of 2014 and 2015, the former detecting a strong magnetic anomaly, subsequently shown to be a bridge abutment, the latter the Great Wall east of Trench b. The plot revealed that the central wall of the eastern bridge abutment is a continuation of the Gorgan Wall and that the bridge itself is part of the barrier.

elsewhere on the Gorgan Wall. Its close vicinity to the wall adds strength to this interpretation. Its orientation, at an oblique angle to the wall, is unusual. Kilns elsewhere tended to be at a right angle or parallel to the Gorgan and Tammisheh Walls, although the kiln explored in Trench A is at a slightly oblique angle too.[26] Some 185 m further west, there is another rectangular anomaly that might be another kiln, although it is far less distinct and appears to be linked to the wall by a line at a right angle to the rectangular feature. Whether it is a kiln, perhaps with a brick scatter towards the wall, or some other L-shaped feature is hard to tell. If it is a kiln, the distance of 185 m would be the greatest yet observed between two kilns along the wall on flat terrain. Perhaps the distance was indeed unusually high here or perhaps some kilns are buried too deeply under alluvial sediments for detection. It is worth noting too that there are no bricks on the surface of the field, with the exception only of the area where it terminates in the east. The wall's remains thus seem to be buried beneath the modern plough horizon. The wall itself, built of strongly magnetic fired bricks, is nonetheless clearly detectable. The detection of just a single kiln or two could be the result of the wall surviving to greater height and being nearer to the surface or its robber trench being full of brick debris – or, indeed, fewer kilns being used when building this section of the wall.[27]

In the westernmost 20–25 m of the survey, there appears to be a linear high magnetic anomaly in alignment with the much crisper and better-defined anomaly further east (Figs 3.4, 3.7–3.10). In this area, the survey generally shows little beyond a dense and wide scatter of magnetic

Fig. 3.11: (left) Exposed part of the Gorgan Wall in the Sari Su Canyon to the north-west of Fort 2. The scale measures 4 × 50 cm.

Fig. 3.12: (below) Location of the above section of the Gorgan Wall. It is likely that the terminus of this branch of the wall would have been near this point already in antiquity. The high vertical loess cliffs would have made it very difficult to bypass this cliff-top wall terminal, north-west of Fort 2. Note the erosion tunnel on the left.

Fig. 3.13: Geophysical and pedestrian survey established that the Gorgan Wall ran from Fort 2 (on the terrace, background right) to its bridge crossing over the Sari Su River (foreground).

material. This may be the result of mechanical excavations in 2015 moving upcast onto the westernmost grids of the survey area. The magnetic debris in the upcast could easily mask any buried archaeology. The area could be cleaned from debris and resurveyed. Little, however, is likely to be gained from such an exercise, as there is no serious doubt that the wall ran towards Trench b and that the structure exposed in the trench is in alignment with the Great Wall.

3.2.3. The Gorgan Wall Bridge (Trench b)[28]

During our field season, in autumn 2014, an opportunity arose to explore the then enigmatic brick structure, later proven to be a bridge. The initial geophysical survey summarised above revealed a large and very strong positive magnetic anomaly in the area of the brick structure. Subsequent excavations proved that this structure indeed extended well beyond what had been exposed before. It established that what the survey had detected were parts of the western brick-built bridge abutment.

Aided by a comparatively low water table at the outset, excavations of a large Trench (b) succeeded in unearthing considerably more of this feature than had been visible when described previously.[29] Excavation here was far from easy and necessitated diverting the stream east of the trench into an underground pipe channel. Repeated blockage of the piped diversion, notably when the stream was swollen following rain, led to flooding within the trench and the need to repeatedly drain and clean the trench, requiring strenuous efforts of a large number of impressively industrious workmen.

Whilst most of our work in the first season focused on the right (western) bank of the river, evidence emerged already in 2014 to suggest that the feature covered the width of the valley, being preserved under the bed of the modern stream as well as extending to both of its banks. The structure rises to much greater heights towards the edges of the valley than in the centre. No doubt, already in antiquity the stream bed was in a similar location to the modern stream channel, so that the bridge opening would have been in the area where the river still flows today. The partial destruction of the abutments was probably the result of them having been affected by riverine erosion during episodes of flooding, as well as the demolition of easily accessible parts of the monument by local people in need of building material.

Whilst excavations in 2014 had unearthed a substantial brick structure to the west of the Sari Su River, but only traces of a brick platform on the opposite shore, more of this had been exposed by fluvial erosion at the start of the 2015 season. We first excavated the overburden manually. In the course of these earthmoving operations it became clear that the structure extended deep into the loess cliff. Manual excavation of the substantial and largely sterile overburden would have been excessively slow and labour-intensive, not easy to conduct safely and not likely to yield much, if any, evidence on the site's history. Much of the sediment covering the brick structure was thus excavated by machine, whilst the *in-situ* masonry underneath was uncovered and cleaned by hand.

The entire structure exposed in Trench b (Fig. 3.14), measured some 40 m west–east (and reached from one edge of the steep-sided river valley to the other), by up to 33 m north–south. The highest surviving wall (b.002) on top of the brick platform (b.003) west of the river is roughly parallel to the north-western edge of the platform b.003, but at a c. 38–39-degree angle to its southern edge. The narrow wall itself is only three and a half to four bricks wide (c. 1.53 m near its western terminal), less than the Great Wall which is normally five courses (just over 2 m) wide. In Trench b, the Gorgan Wall (b.290) is even wider, some 2.30 m in its upper courses and 3 m and more at foundation levels, perhaps to give it additional stability to withstand possible flooding; the wall in the valley had deeper foundation, and it would have been higher than away from the river, if its crest was level. As excavations in the second season established, the width of wall b.002 corresponds to that of a narrow wall, which forms part of the wider northern wall (b.288) of the eastern bridge abutment (b.156). Wall b.002 may have formed the south-east side of the western abutment of the bridge. This narrow wall is preserved up to a height of 1.80 m (15 courses) at its highest point above platform b.003. There are at least another ten courses of foundation platform underneath (of 1.21 m height), reaching down to c. 138.84 m or even deeper. Counting both, the overall height of the wall thus adds up to at least 3.01 m (25 courses). This is just the minimum height, as the foundations could reach deeper, not to mention substantial later robbing of the wall's upper courses, suggesting that it was much higher. If we assume that the wall reached the upper edge of the escarpment on the right bank of the

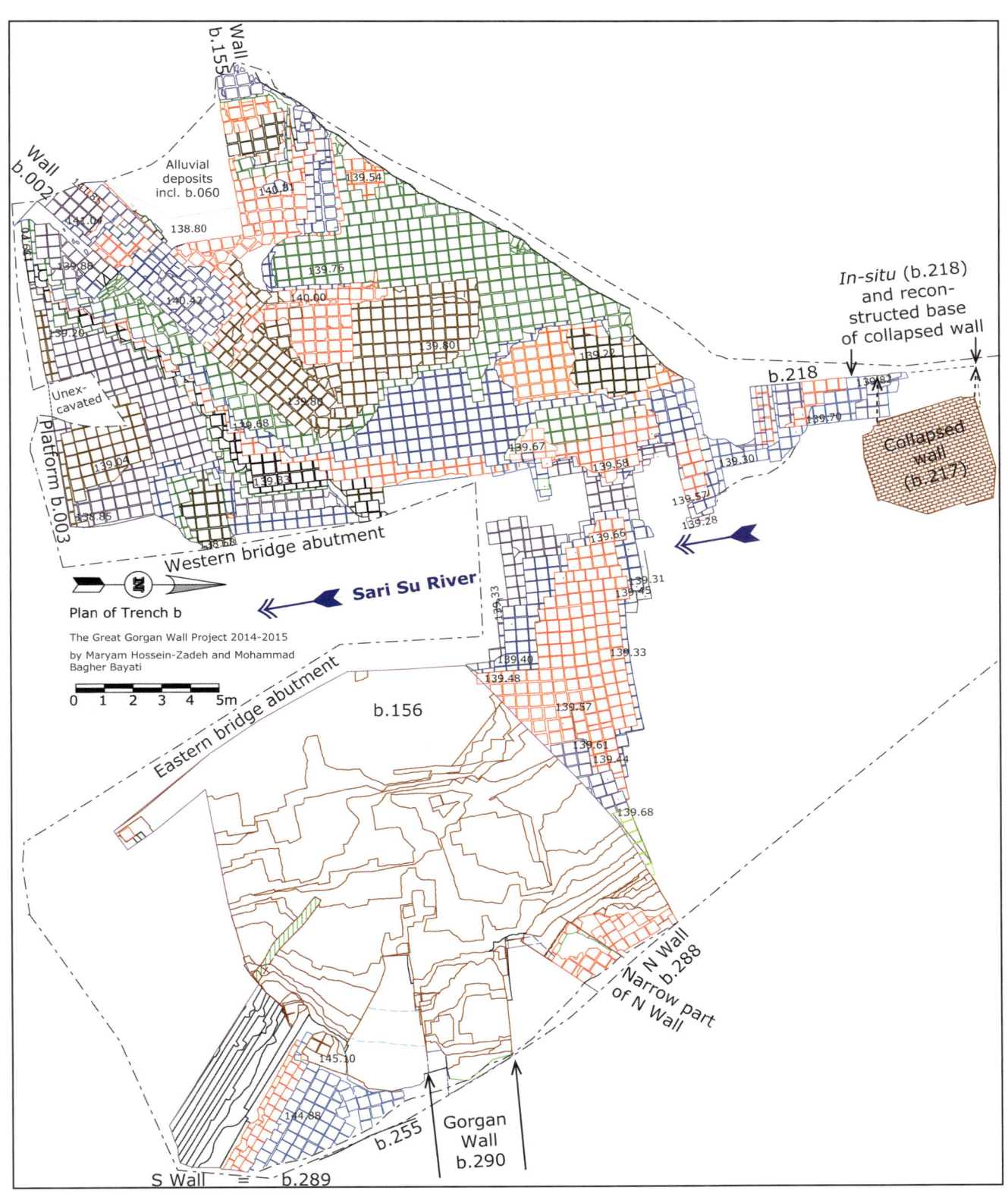

Fig. 3.14: Plan of Trench b, with the western and eastern bridge abutments and the collapsed wall b.217 (the latter in antiquity standing on the west bank of the Sari Su River), by Mohammad Bagher Bayati, Maryam Hossein-Zadeh et al. Most of the western abutment was excavated in 2014, the collapsed wall and most of the eastern abutment were excavated in 2015. The river made it impossible to excavate extensively on both banks simultaneously, as the water had to be diverted away from the excavations. Note that colours are used, purely as a visual aid, to make the different overlapping courses of brick stand out more clearly; colours do not represent specific elevations or different structures. The trench extended beyond the plan in the north; the northernmost corner was c. three metres north of the right edge of the plan. There were no structures in the northernmost part of the trench: see Figs 3.27 and 3.64–3.65 for later stream channels in the area and Fig. 3.22 for an aerial view of the extent of the excavations in 2015.

Fig. 3.15: The western abutment of the Gorgan Wall Bridge at a narrow section of the valley, seen from the south in 2014. Note the stepped section (section 6) through alluvial sediments (middle-ground, centre–right).

Fig. 3.16: View of the western bridge abutment from the west in 2014. Note the stepped section (section 6) through alluvial sediments (background, left).

river (which is at a similar level to the top of the north and south walls of the eastern bridge abutment) and that this was of a similar elevation in antiquity as it is now, then the wall would have been over 3 m higher, measuring more than 6 m from top to bottom, similar to the much better preserved abutment on the opposite bank.

The Gorgan Wall itself may be represented by wall b.155, which is wider but less well preserved than wall b.002. It is in a similar, but not in an identical, alignment to the Great Wall (b.290) further east, and it is possible that the wall bends slightly to the south. Alternatively, b.155 may be just part of the western bridge abutment, with the Great Wall once built on top and no longer preserved here. We do not know if the Gorgan Wall continued beyond the western edge of Trench b. The eastern terminal of the southern branch of the bifurcating wall, as far as traceable, is some 400 m west of the bridge, the northern

Fig. 3.17: (left) Work-in-progress in 2014 at wall b.002 (left), with fired brick fragments at the bottom of a robber trench (right) and the space underneath, to the right/north-west of this wall, filled with alluvial layers. (See also Fig. 3.43.)

Fig. 3.18: (below) Walls b.002 (centre, foreground to left, background) and b.155 (behind the total station, centre, background) built on top of the stepped platform b.003, the steps in the foreground lining the river.

Fig. 3.19: Fort 2A towered above the very steep loess cliffs (background, left to centre). The eastern bridge abutment is in the foreground, right.

branch, some 200 m NNW.[30] Has the missing link between the western bridge abutment and the southern branch of the Gorgan Wall been robbed or erased or covered by landslides? More probably, as the terrain is very steep here, there was a gap in the wall on the right/western bank of the Sari Su River. It is also possible that it took an unknown circuitous route, bypassing the most difficult terrain, as extremely steep and unstable loess cliffs would have made it hard to construct a continuous wall joining up with the southern branch of Gorgan Wall. It would have been no easier to build a wall leading up to Fort 2A on the northern branch, and a wall may not have been required here. The extremely steep loess cliffs between the bridge and Fort 2A would have been hard to scale even in dry conditions – and exceptionally slippery and dangerous when wet. Any attempted ascent of the steep slopes, notably if there were guards armed with missiles or bricks on the cliff-top, would have been a suicide mission. It is possible that there was a gap in the wall and that the steep slopes between the bridge and Fort 2A (Figs 3.19–3.21 and 4.97) would have formed a natural barrier.[31]

The brick platform (b.003) was built on top of sterile soft brown, reddish brown and yellowish brown clay (b.005, b.006 = b.046 and b.042), probably pre-Sasanian alluvial deposits. Between walls b.002 and b.155 there is no brick paving. Wall b.002 has deeper foundations, of at least ten courses, the base of the wall b.155 in the north is at least two courses higher, the base of the platform (b.003) in between is at least three courses higher than that of b.002. Excavations in 2015 established that also on the opposite bank there were wedge-shaped voids between the walls of the eastern bridge abutment. The bridge abutments were evidently not solid throughout. Initially, the void between walls b.002 and b.155 appears to have been empty.[32]

We found a large brick fragment between walls b.002 and b.155 at the same level as the third course from the bottom of the deepest wall (b.002) (i.e. just underneath the base of platform b.003), proving that layers at least from this elevation upwards must post-date bridge construction. The surface at the time of bridge construction, or the bottom of the foundation trench, must have been at this level or below. As there was no obvious trace of a cut for the foundation or for a cleaning trench, deposit b.055 in the gap between the walls (Fig. 3.43) seems to have built up against the brick walls. The bottom deposits accumulating between the walls, b.061 on top, soft mid-greyish brown clayey silt, and b.060 below, soft

Fig. 3.20: View from the Fort 2A area down to the Sari Su Bridge.

Fig. 3.21: Close-up of the steep slopes beneath Fort 2A which would have made any ascent here virtually impossible.

Fig. 3.22: Aerial view of the 2015 excavations of the bridge on 29 November 2015 (drone image by Hassan Sohouri). Note that at this stage much of the 2014 excavations had been reburied under alluvial sediments, with only the tall wall b.002 and parts of platform b.003 in the modern river-bed remaining visible.

Fig. 3.23: View of parts of the western bridge pier in the foreground and the eastern pier in the background. Fort 2 is on the plateau in the background, right.

Fig. 3.24: The eastern bridge abutment. (The red and white segments of the scales measure 50 cm each.)

dark grey sandy clay, contained no finds and were first considered to be natural soil. B.060, however, yielded seeds of c. AD 426–567 (Table 3.3), clearly proving that this is an early alluvial deposit building up perhaps at the time of the construction of the Gorgan Wall. This is the only clay deposit from the sondage, and one wonders if it may have been washed in prior to completion of the construction works.

Just as its counterpart on the western bank of the Sari Su, all structures on the opposite bank were built of typical Gorgan Wall bricks and employed strong waterproof mortar.[33] They form a substantial abutment,[34] evidently designed to withstand water pressure. The eastern abutment (b.156) was much better preserved than its western counterpart. A 3.50 m long wall running from the south-west of the abutment to the south-east (Figs 3.14 and 3.22–3.25) will have been designed to divert stream water from the foundations of the abutment and to prevent it from being undermined by riverine erosion. In the centre of the valley, the upper parts of the abutment have evidently not been preserved, in part robbed where exposed (as on the opposite shore), in part perhaps also damaged and washed away by floods.

Three massive brick walls rested on this platform (Fig. 3.14). The northern wall (b.288) is 4 m wide at the north-eastern edge of Trench b and widens to 5 m, 3 m

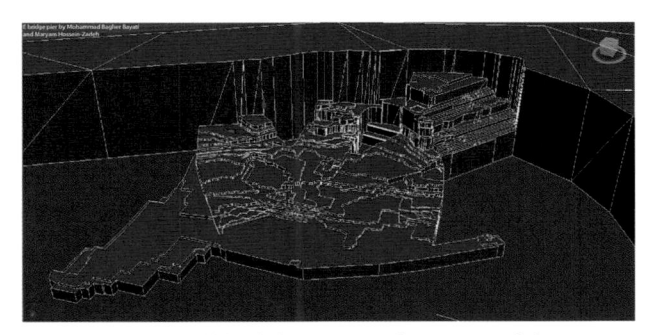

Fig. 3.25: 3D-model of the preserved remains of the eastern bridge abutment by Mohammad Bagher Bayati and Maryam Hossein-Zadeh. Note that the model does not show structures visible in or near the profile only. It thus underrepresents the elevation of the Gorgan Wall in the centre and the north face of the abutment (left).

WSW away from the profile. It is preserved to a height of c. 6.14 m (c. 138.60–144.74 m); its north face, to a height of c. 6.04 m (c. 138.60–144.64 m).[35] Its south-east side is formed by a wall, three and a half bricks (1.55 m) wide (similar in dimensions to walls b.002 and b.218 on the opposite bank). The latter narrow wall is built on top of the northern wall and thus considered part of it, rather than a separate wall. The northern wall is near vertical

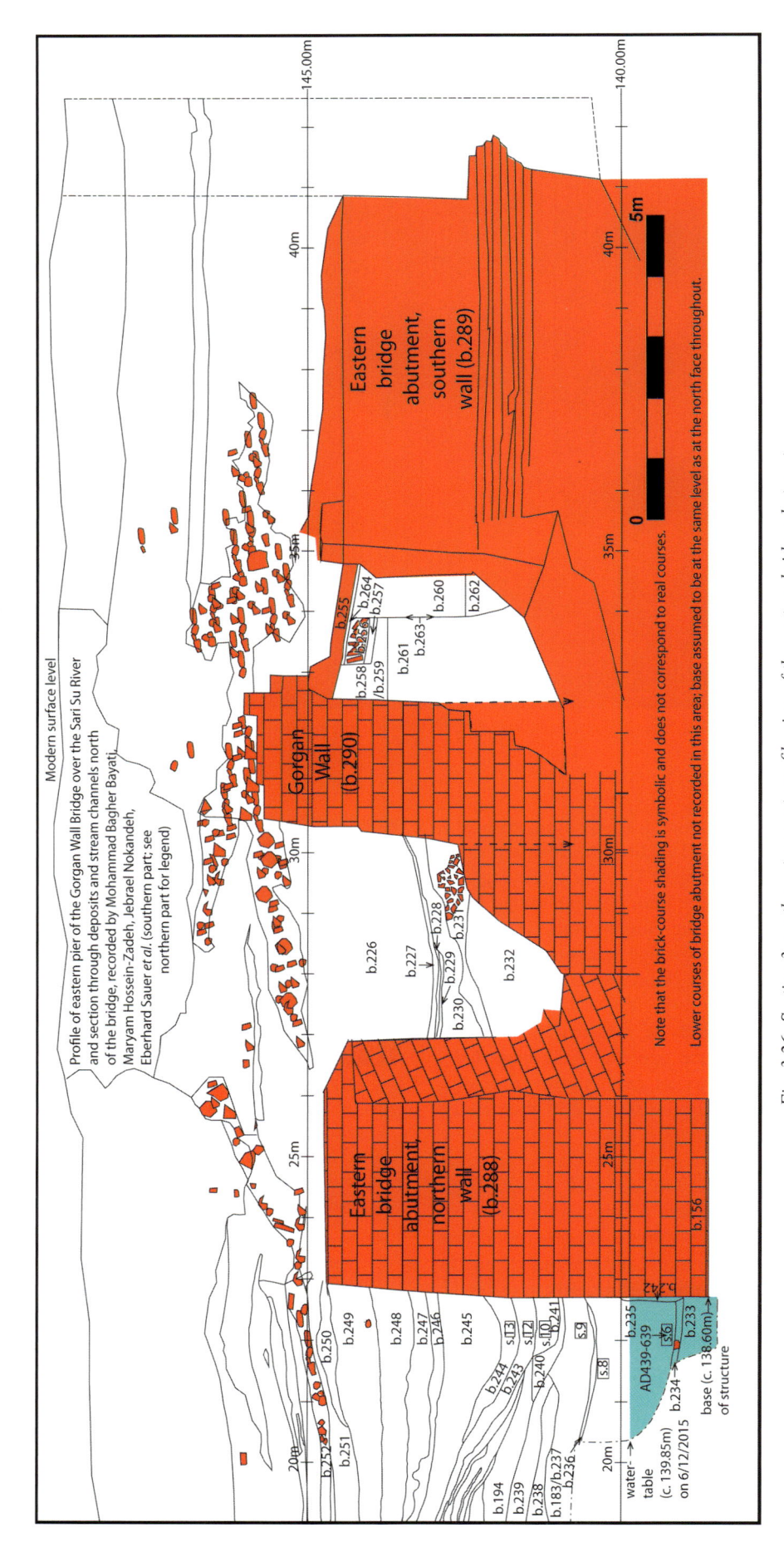

Fig. 3.26: Section 3, south-eastern part: profile view of the eastern bridge abutment.

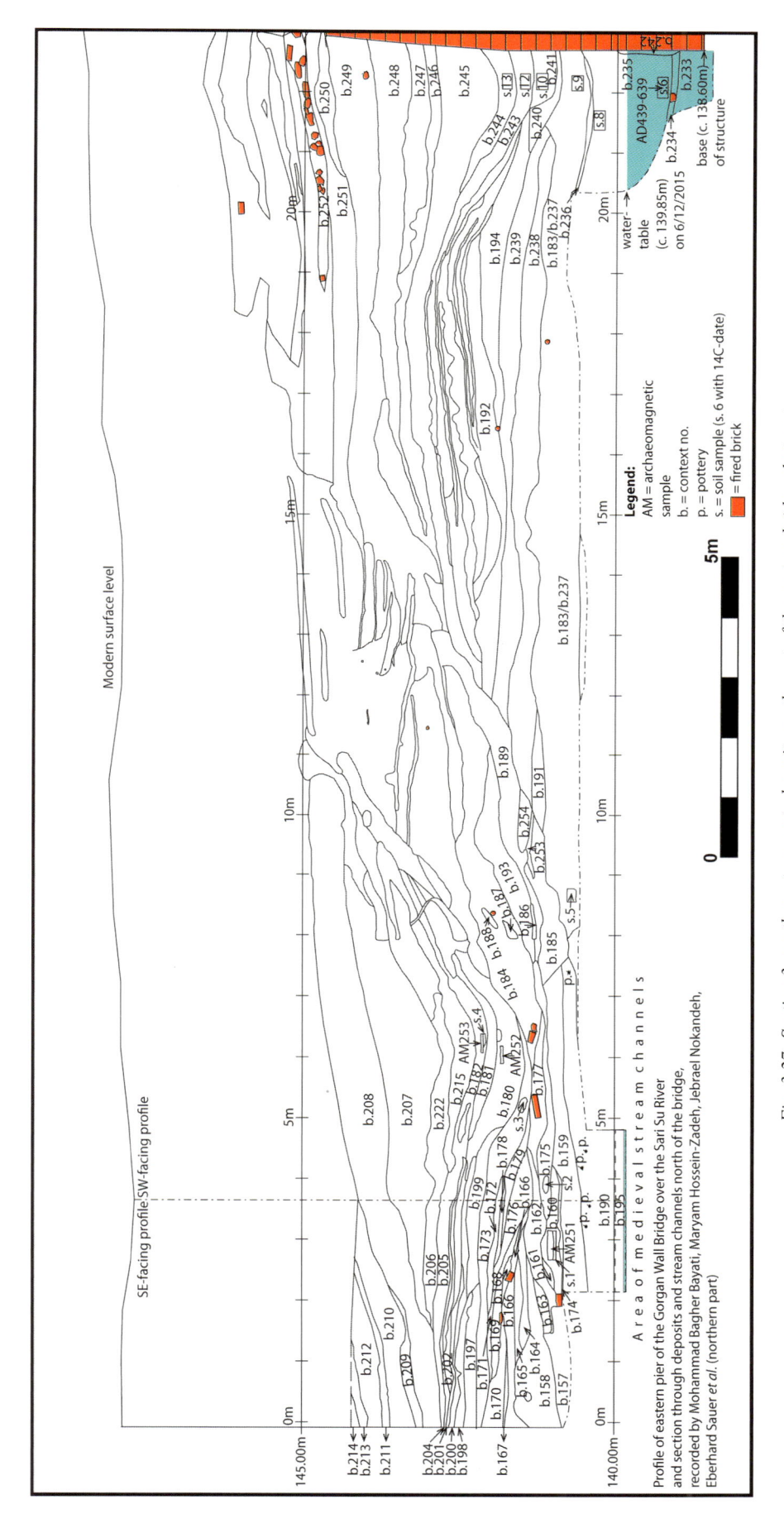

Fig. 3.27: Section 3, north-western part: deposits north-west of the eastern bridge abutment.

Fig. 3.28: The middle wall (b.290) on the eastern bridge abutment is part of the Great Wall of Gorgan.

and forms the north side of the abutment. We may assume that it once extended to the westernmost point of the abutment, forming the north side of this massive structure. It faced the upstream/enemy side of the structure and was probably designed to withstand water pressure and to be difficult to scale.

The middle wall is in direct alignment with the Gorgan Wall, as established towards the end of the 2015 season via geophysical survey.[36] Its upper section is five to five and a half bricks (c. 2.24–2.38 m) wide, which more or less matches the Great Wall's normal width of five bricks. The middle wall is unquestionably part of the Great Wall and the structure as a whole must be a bridge on which the wall crossed the Sari Su River. Its highest point is between c. 146 m and 146.16 m (depending on whether the highest preserved horizontal brick is the highest course or debris fallen on top), c. 1.26–1.42 m higher than the northern, and c. 0.80–0.96 m higher than the southern wall. The overall height of the preserved brick abutment with the Gorgan Wall built on top thus amounts to c. 7.40–7.56 m.

At approximately 7.50 m in height, this is by a long margin the highest preserved part of the Great Wall found to date. It is worth noting that there is nothing to suggest that the irregular and uneven top represents the original crest of the wall. The abundance of bricks in layers above suggests that the top of the wall has been unsystematically demolished, and partial collapse is possible too. Indeed, much of the brick collapse layers are clearly associated with the middle wall and are separated by layers of soil from the northern and southern walls (Figs 3.24, 3.26 and 3.29). This suggests that the demolition/collapse of the middle wall accounts for the dense brick concentration in the upper levels of section 3. The middle wall must once have been much taller than the southern and northern walls of the eastern bridge abutments and must have remained standing until other parts of the bridge abutment had been buried under sediments. How much higher the Great Wall may once have risen is impossible to tell.

Was there a wall-walk on top of the Gorgan Wall or the northern wall or both or neither? A wall-walk on top of the northern wall may have been advantageous, to prevent a dead angle out of sight and reach for archers/guardians on top of the central Great Wall behind. There is, however, no evidence for a parapet on top of the north wall, nor is there evidence for an associated collapse layer – suggesting that there either was no parapet here or that it has been systematically demolished at an early stage. The former seems more likely than the latter, bearing in mind that there may have been no dead angle in front of the north wall for archers stationed on the Gorgan Wall right in the centre of the bridge. Furthermore, the northern wall may not have risen much, if at all, over the top of the slope at the time. Soldiers would have been much safer behind a parapet on top of the Gorgan Wall than in an exposed position north of the defensive barrier and on the lower northern wall, potentially accessible from the east. There is no way of proving, of course, if the demolished/collapsed section of the central wall, the Gorgan Wall, boasted a parapet. Considering that it would not have required much building material, but would have greatly strengthened the defensive capabilities of the wall bridge and the deterrent effect on any would-be attackers, we think it is a near certainty that there was a wall-walk on the Great Wall, including its crossing over the Sari Su River. Sceptics of the hypothesis that ancient long walls were ever designed to serve as fighting/observation/missile-launch platforms will undoubtedly come to different conclusions.

Is our section a reliable guide to the construction of the Great Wall elsewhere? The base of the bridge will, of course, have been at a much lower level than the base of the wall away from the banks of the river. Indeed, the highest recorded point of the Gorgan Wall (b.290) may have been as much as 7.50 m above the base of the bridge (Fig. 3.26), but perhaps as little as 1.50 m above the natural ground at the time (assuming the top of deposit b.258 represents the surface at the time of wall construction). The wall and the bridge abutments had evidently been cut into the natural slope to reduce the risk of fluvial erosion undermining the structure, and it is hard to establish

Fig. 3.29: The northern and middle wall with brick collapse layer (b.252) on top. (As usual, each red and white segment of the scales is 50 cm long.)

even a minimum height of the Great Wall based on our excavations of the Gorgan Wall Bridge. It is, however, worth noting that the Gorgan Wall's north face in Trench b exceeded 5 m in height, as far as preserved (and reached c. 7.50 m if its foundations were at the same level as those of the north wall). Prior to collapse and/or demolition, the wall will undoubtedly have risen several metres more. Excavation (or perhaps ground-penetrating radar) further east should be able to trace the base of the wall east of the bridge and its preserved minimum height, but is not likely to enable us to reconstruct its original elevation. What the excavations, however, have demonstrated is that such brick structures could rise to a height of well over 7 m at the very least. Admittedly, the bridge employed strong mortar as opposed to mere mud mortar where the Gorgan Wall was built on dry land. But lime mortar will have been employed to compensate for greater exposure to water rather than necessarily to enable construction to greater height. We may conclude that Trench b has demonstrated that the Great Wall rose to substantial height where it crossed the Sari Su River, evidence for the Sasanian builders' ability to construct a tall wall and their intention to create a monument that could withstand water pressure and attack. It seems inconceivable that so much effort would have been invested to secure the river crossing, if the wall elsewhere had been of low elevation and an easy obstacle to overcome.

The abutment's southern wall (b.289) rests on a stepped foundation. The actual wall on top is three and a half bricks (c. 1.48 m) wide. Three and a half bricks, corresponding to c. 5 feet, seems a common width for walls of the bridge abutments, though a few walls are much wider. It abuts the Gorgan Wall on the downstream side and would have added much to its stability (Fig. 3.14). Like the pier's northern wall, it is much better preserved close to the eastern trench edge and heavily robbed and/or affected by flood damage towards the centre of the valley. Its highest *in-situ* brick is at 145.20 m, c. 6.60 m above the base of the north wall. There was no time to excavate the south wall to its foundations.

There were triangular spaces between the Gorgan Wall (b.290) in the centre of the structure, and the northern (b.288) and southern walls (b.289) on either side of it (Fig. 3.14). Leaving natural soil between the walls or filling the gaps with soil saved building material, and a solid core would not necessarily have improved the structure's stability. An examination of the deposits (b.226–b.232, top to bottom: Fig. 3.26) between the north (b.288) and middle

Fig. 3.30: Brick paving (b.255) between the middle and southern wall.

(b.290) walls suggests that these are post-Sasanian. Most consist of redeposited loess with brick fragments (b.226, b.228, b.230 and b.232). Two bands of soft mid-yellowish brown silty clay (b.227 and b.229) appear to be the result of flooding. A brick collapse layer (b.231), densest and highest next to the middle wall (b.290), appears to have resulted from a partial collapse or destruction of the latter at an early stage. Most of the middle wall, i.e. the Gorgan Wall, however, probably remained standing until much later, when a substantial collapse layer of Gorgan Wall bricks (b.225 = b.252) built up over the walls (Figs 3.26 and 3.29). Sloping away from the middle wall, the demolition or collapse of the upper courses of the Gorgan Wall will have caused it.

This sequence of deposits between the middle and the northern wall suggests that the void between the two walls was open and not filled with sediments until after the abandonment of the structure. This would match a similar observation on the western bank of the Sari Su where we also found early alluvial deposits between walls b.002 and b.155. These spaces may initially have been largely above the water level, except perhaps for periods of extreme flooding. Later, a postulated reservoir would have raised the water table substantially.

The deposits between the middle (b.290) and the south wall (b.289) seem to be natural in part. The middle wall (b.290), i.e. the Gorgan Wall, may have been cut into natural soil (b.261) here (Fig. 3.26). Deposits b.258 and b.259 are more difficult to interpret, as b.258, closer to the Gorgan Wall, contained a few small brick fragments, suggesting it either post-dates wall construction or that animal burrows account for their redeposition in a natural deposit. A construction trench (b.263 filled with b.262 and b.260) for the south wall, also cutting natural soil, survived. The latter construction trench also cut construction-related deposits: firm mid-yellowish brown clay with small brick fragments (b.257) and very soft mid-yellowish brown clay with an estimated 70% of large brick fragments (b.256). This observation indicates that the southern wall (b.289) was built after the Great Wall (b.290), but as much brick will have been used and broken during construction works, the gap in time need not have been long, and we cannot tell if it was days or decades. The walls may well have been cut into the natural ground on the slopes. On top of the natural and the construction trench for the southern wall, a paving of Gorgan Wall bricks, three courses thick (b.255), bedded on a thin band of soft mid-brown clay with c. 5% brick fragments (b.264), only preserved on the slope side, linked the middle and the southern wall (Figs 3.26 and 3.30). This paving may form the top of the bridge abutment and led perhaps to the actual bridge crossing. Whilst we do not know how much higher the Gorgan Wall originally was, the substantial layers of bricks above (with most probably taken away as building material), suggest that it was several metres higher and that paving b.255, perhaps just above the natural ground at the time, is far too low for the wall-walk of the Gorgan Wall. If so, we do not know if the bridge could have been crossed at one or two levels: the hypothetical wall-walk at a higher level, a crossing at the level of paving b.255 south of the wall or both.

To the north of the bridge, roughly in the axis of symmetry between its western and eastern abutment, we found a wall (b.217) fallen from west to east (Figs 3.14, 3.31–3.34). The base of the fallen wall matches exactly a wall (b.218) west of it, proving that the southern part of the fallen wall had once rested on the preserved wall. The fallen wall (b.217) was preserved to a height of c. 3.80 m (32 courses) excluding a thirty-third bottom course which overlaps with the foundations (b.218) of eight courses (0.94 m). Only one brick of the highest course of the fallen wall remained *in situ*. The total preserved height of the wall, counting the overlapping course only once, is thus c. 4.74 m (40 courses). Its maximum length is 4.67 m (at the thirteenth course from the top). The 33 courses include one course (the twelfth from the top) consisting exclusively of clay as far as exposed. Whether there was a recess here (for timber?), and bricks are deeper inside, is unknown. If there were no bricks at all, it would suggest that the wall was not intended to withstand water at this level. The mortar employed seemed softer than that used in the bridge abutments further south, but this must be a result of more extensive water exposure over the past one-and-a-half millennia rather than any differences in quality.[37] The wall was three and a half courses (1.48 m) wide, matching the width of its base wall (b.218) of 1.48–1.54 m, which is also three and a half courses wide. Wall b.218 was eight courses high at its deepest point in the south, but only two courses in the north (originally probably three, as one course at the top seems to have been lost). Its base was at 138.88 m, c. 1 foot higher than that of the northern face of the eastern bridge abutment

Fig. 3.31: The collapsed wall (b.217) north of the bridge.

Fig. 3.32: The collapsed wall (b.217) north of the bridge with its bottom courses (b.218 in the foreground) in situ.

Fig. 3.33: Close-up of the matching section. (Each segment of the small scales measures 10 cm.)

(c. 138.60 m). The difference may be due to the eastern bridge abutment being higher and heavier, designed to withstand greater water pressure and located further downstream than the wall lining the western bank of the Sari Su. It is, however, at a similar level to the lowest (or lowest traced) course of wall b.002 (c. 138.84 m) which forms part of the same bridge abutment. More fieldwork is needed to establish if these measurements

Fig. 3.34: The collapsed wall (b.217) seen from the north. (Each segment of the scales measures 50 cm.)

are representative for the western and eastern bridge abutments and whether or not the foundations of the eastern abutment were indeed deeper. Assuming the five bottom courses of wall b.218 were underground, the wall would have stood 35 courses (c. 4.15 m high). The whole wall appears to have been built on, or cut into, natural soil. To the east of the fallen wall (b.217), we found a deposit of 90% coarse sand in a matrix of brownish grey clayey silt (b.223), perhaps deposits associated with a flash flood that undermined the wall. The wall is abutted by alluvial layers also in the west, soft mid-brownish grey clay (b.221) containing large Sasanian fired brick fragments. These may be riverine deposits accumulating in the aftermath of the postulated flood by water flowing at a slower speed. It appears that it was flood-water rather than a landslide that caused the wall to collapse. By contrast, in the north the fallen wall (b.217) was abutted by natural loess (b.220), perhaps indicating that it had been built against a natural slope here. The wall's width of three and a half bricks, c. 1.50 m on average, matches that of wall b.002, framing the western abutment further south, as well the width of walls forming the edge of the bridge abutment on the opposite side. It seems likely it was part of the western abutment and may have followed the edge of the natural slope. If so, the abutment's shape differed from the eastern abutment and was perhaps influenced by the natural slope at the time. It is also possible that the wall was designed to prevent enemies from potentially bypassing the bridge after having waded through the river upstream. It may have secured the western bank of the Sari Su on the approaches to Fort 2A. The above observations suggest that it did not continue further north. Wall b.218 continues, however, for a further 3.50 m south. Perhaps the north part of the wall collapsed early and was covered in sediments whilst the southern part remained standing until demolished by local people in need of bricks for construction works.

The north-western edge of the brick platform (b.003) on the right (west) bank of the river is at a c. 45-degree angle to its east side, the latter facing the river. Perhaps the edge of the western slope of the valley was at the time indeed at the north-western edge of the platform, adding strength to our hypothesis that wall b.218 was perhaps also built against a natural slope. If so, the natural slope from the west end of wall b.155 to the south end of wall b.218 ran from south-west to north-east before turning a corner and continuing in a south–north alignment (Fig. 3.14). Erosion will have transformed the loess slopes framing the valley over the past one-and-a-half millennia, even if the Sari Su's course at the time of bridge-construction must have been very close to its current alignment.

Fig. 3.35: At this narrow point, the Sari Su Valley could easily be bridged by a single arch.

Fig. 3.36: Roman single-arched bridge over the River Chabinas in Commagene.

3.2.4. Bridge design

Much of the upstanding elements of the installation have fallen prey to brick robbing and others will have collapsed. Whilst it is thus difficult to reconstruct the monument, its location alone provides decisive clues as to its function. Its design points clearly to it being a bridge. It is certain, in the light of the geophysical survey, that it formed part of the Gorgan Wall.

The height of the preserved walls of the abutments provides us with the likely minimum height of the bridge. Polygonal abutments, of trapezium to D-shape,[38] are not uncommon in ancient bridges, intended to protect the bridge and the bank of the river from riverine erosion. The bridge appears to have had only a single arch, spanning the gap between the two abutments, not dissimilar perhaps to the Severan bridge over the River Chabinas in Commagene (modern south-east Turkey), if differing distinctly in function and, probably, design of the upper sections.[39]

The western bridge abutment is harder to reconstruct than its eastern counterpart. Only the bottom courses of a probable central wall (b.155), north of b.002, are preserved, running parallel to the southern edge of the platform (b.003). Assuming they are indeed the lower courses of a wall, they suggest that this wall was of similar width to the Gorgan Wall east of the river. This postulated wall is, however, not in a perfect alignment with the Gorgan Wall (b.290) east of the river (Fig. 3.14). We do not know whether b.155 is part of Great Wall (bending south, to be more resistant to pressure from floodwater from the north?) or part of the western bridge abutment or just part of a stepped platform at its base. If the alignments of b.290 and b.155 represent those of the bridge, then they would have joined at a slight angle. This would not be unique; the Sasanian bridge at Gondeshapur also consists of two straight sections joining at an angle (Fig. 3.37).[40] Perhaps b.155 represents the lower courses of a once tall central wall, joining up with b.290. Walls b.002 and b.289 probably formed the southern walls of

Fig. 3.37: Whilst of a very different design (on top of a siphon tunnel and with multiple arches) and much longer than the Sari Su Bridge, the Sasanian bridge at Gondeshapur also employs mortar. It consists of two straight sections joining at an angle (centre), which may also be true for the bridge over the Sari Su River (if the alignments of walls b.290 and b.155 represent those of the bridge and the Gorgan Wall).

the two bridge abutments; there is, however, no evidence for an even roughly symmetrical arrangement in the north. The prominent north wall (b.288) of the eastern abutment has no preserved equivalent in the west. Perhaps there was once a third wall to the north of b.155 destroyed through brick-robbing. If so, this hypothetical third wall may, with walls b.002 and b.155, have formed a similar arrow-shaped arrangement as the three walls (b.288, b.289 and b.290) of the eastern bridge abutment. That the angles between the central and southern walls are similar in both abutments, c. 34–38 degrees in the east and 38–39 degrees in the west, may strengthen this hypothesis. Even if there were once three walls in an arrow-shaped arrangement on top of both bridge abutments, they are not symmetrical: the Gorgan Wall (b.290) is clearly in the centre of the eastern abutment, but it points in a different direction to b.155. The southern wall (b.289) of the eastern abutment is much wider at the base than its postulated counterpart in the west (b.002). Wall b.218 raises further questions. If this framed the western bridge abutment, its shape would have differed markedly from the eastern abutment. More probably, wall b.218 secured the north-western approaches to the bridge as well as to Fort 2A and no equivalent was needed in the east. Wall b.218 may also have protected the western bridge pier from riverine erosion. There is not enough symmetry to reconstruct the bridge with confidence, though it seems likely that b.290 bent slightly to the south to join up with b.155, both being broadly in the centre of the opposite abutments (even if too little is preserved of the western abutment to prove it). If b.155 should be part of the Great Wall bending south, then there are two possibilities: either it terminated nearby at the edge of the high loess cliff, or it potentially curved south.

The bridge abutments, certainly the well-preserved parts of the eastern abutment, would have been difficult to scale, though perhaps a little easier on the south side than the near vertical north face; any enemies, of course, would have had to make their way first through the arch of the bridge to reach the south. We can only speculate how the lost upper sections of bridge were designed, but one is tempted to think that the Sasanian engineers would have wished the bridge to be defensible and not just a pedestrian crossing point over the stream. A hypothetical portcullis or a permanent wooden palisade or iron or brick-pillar grid in the gate opening, for example, would have made it impossible to walk through the arch, following the stream bed. Any group attempting to remove such an obstacle would have been in a vulnerable position at the valley bottom and an easy target for archers positioned on the bridge barrier or the top of the loess cliffs. A probable walkway on the Gorgan Wall, protected by a parapet, on top of the bridge and on either side of the stream could have been manned by soldiers when required. One might also imagine that the garrison of Fort 2A, commanding the high western slope, may have been in a position to target any enemy force approaching the wall along the riverbed with arrows or even basic missiles (e.g. brick fragments or a collection of stones). Admittedly, this is hypothetical. Only the lower courses of the structure survived in the centre of the valley, and there is no concrete evidence for or against the existence of a parapet, or the concrete strategies employed to defend this weak point in the Gorgan Wall. What seems certain is that the bridge could have been designed quite easily as an effective defensive obstacle. And it seems unlikely, if so much labour was invested in building a wall, securing it with forts and, where possible, using terrain for defensive advantage, that the architects would have avoided a little extra effort in securing one of the few weak points in the system.

For the Hadrian's Wall bridges, it has been argued that there probably would have been no permanent railings

Fig. 3.38: Only one pier is preserved of the Sasanian Mihr-Narseh Bridge near Gur/Ardashir Khurrah. Like the bridge over the Sari Su, it employed lime-mortar and was located in a narrow gorge (of the Tang-e Ab).

within the bridge arches, as a build-up of debris could have jeopardised the stability of the bridges. Such an argument against the existence of any railings within the arch would be less strong in the case of the Sari Su Bridge, as there would have been less driftwood in the treeless environment of the Sari Su. Furthermore, considering the normally low water levels in the river, it would not have been difficult to remove any debris. Even for Hadrian's Wall, Paul Bidwell and Neil Holbrook consider the possibility that there may have been temporary barriers within the arches during times of low water in summer. They argue persuasively that there was likely to be a parapet and intensive surveillance to prevent trespass and that the bridge guardians might have discharged javelins, arrows and throwing-stones from an elevated position on the bridge or associated towers against any intruders or attackers. Like their counterparts on the Gorgan Wall, the bridges on Hadrian's Wall tend to be within sight of forts, fortlets and/or towers.[41]

Why was the bridge so massive? Its remote location meant that few, other than the wall's guardians, local peasants and potential would-be trespassers would have seen it – not a place where any propagandistic statement would have reached a large audience. Defensive considerations have already been cited. One wonders whether it was also designed to withstand potential natural disasters. The stream could, of course, swell after heavy rain and alluvial erosion was a factor to be reckoned with. For similar reasons, much effort was devoted to make the bridges on Hadrian's Wall strong enough to withstand flash flooding.[42] It is worth noting that there are high loess cliff on the right (west) bank of the river north of the Sari Su Bridge. Massive landslides were a danger to be taken into account, and the substantial loess deposits over the bridge could easily be in part the result of such events. A little further upstream, the cliffs were much higher and the bridge was probably deliberately built out

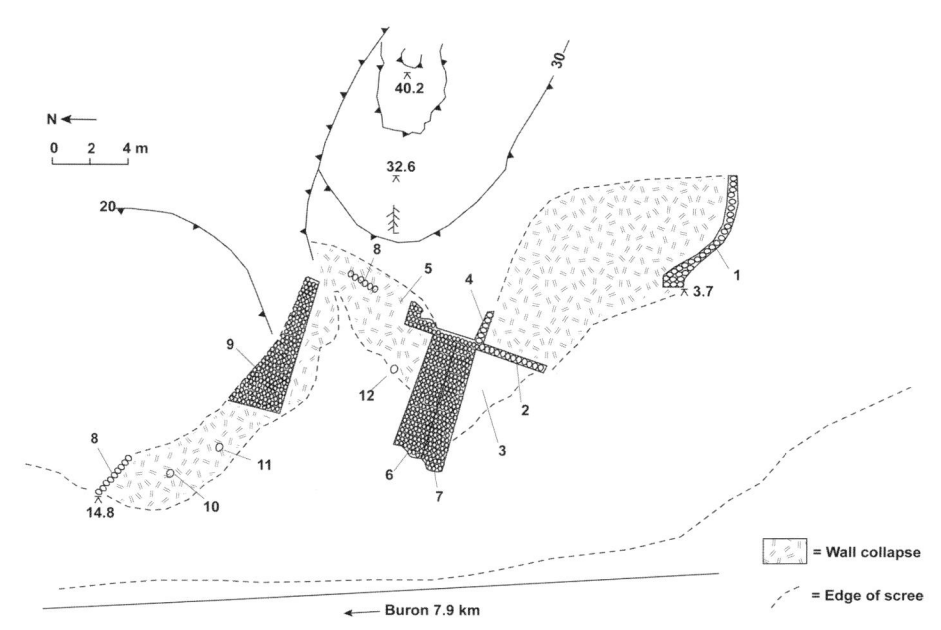

Fig. 3.39: Plan of the Kasar Wall (after Kuznetsov 1990, 183 fig. 38), employing mortar and a masonry style that resembles Sasanian walls at Dariali Fort. Key: 1: Southern face of the platform; 2: Western face of the platform; 3: Accumulation of cultural material; 4: Edge of an aperture (an embrasure?); 5: Collapsed masonry; 6: Wall B; 7: Wall A; 8: Wall fragments; 9: Wall C; 10–12: Cavities of rotted beam structures.

of the zone of greatest danger where it could easily have been buried or destroyed. Yet a landslide further upstream posed a risk as well, as it could have resulted in a natural dam being created. Was the bridge perhaps intended to be strong enough to withstand a flood-wave likely to be unleashed on the bridge when such a natural bank burst?

Our Sasanian bridge differs markedly from most of its southern counterparts where often much wider river valleys had to be negotiated and where there was no need for defensive walls to negotiate rivers. Instead of the multiple piers that are typical for Sasanian bridges elsewhere,[43] there may have been no more than two abutments in case of the narrow Sari Su Valley. The use of waterproof lime mortar in our bridge finds parallels in other Sasanian bridges.[44] A narrow brick bridge also appears to have formed part of the Sadd-e Garkaz aqueduct, and its collapsed remains were still visible when Clement Augustus de Bode visited the monument in 1841.[45] Whilst known Sasanian bridges are a rarity in northern Persia, we can be sure that there were many more, destroyed through brick robbing, buried under alluvial sediments or built of non-durable materials, such as timber.[46] We postulate elsewhere that the Sasanian fort of Buraq Tappeh may have guarded a bridge over the Old Gorgan River and that there may well have been several bridges over this river under military control.[47]

Was the bridge not just a defensive installation, but also a heavily frequented piece of traffic infrastructure – or was it used mainly or exclusively by military patrols? There are no hollow ways leading towards the bridge, but these could easily have been buried by hill-wash since. Whilst the slope on the river's right bank is steep and very slippery when wet, there must have been tracks linking the feature with Fort 2A just as there are tracks to link the river with nearby villages today. It seems doubtful, however, pedestrians or herds of domestic animals would have required a bridge to make it across the Sari Su. It would have been safe and easy for them to wade through this small river, even when swollen by rainwater (unless at times when it formed a reservoir, and even then it could have been crossed effortlessly downstream of the dam). Of course, water levels in antiquity may not have been identical to those today, but there is no obvious reason why they should have greatly exceeded those observed at present. Evidence for Sari Su River water being used to feed a probable late Sasanian canal is worth noting too in this context.[48] Yet, the canal could only have been much deeper than the shallow river is today, if weirs regulated water-flow and these could then have been used as pedestrian crossing points. We may conclude that it seems unlikely that the bridge's primary function was facilitation of traffic – nor can we even be sure that it would have been wide enough for this purpose.

In all probability, the bridge over the Sari Su served predominantly or exclusively military purposes. Defensive barrier-wall bridges were not be unique to any one frontier, but have been built also elsewhere in Sasanian Persia's vast realm. The Sasanian Ghilghilchay Wall crossed the Ghilghilchay River on a bridge built, like the Sari Su Bridge, of fired bricks and lime mortar.[49] There are three

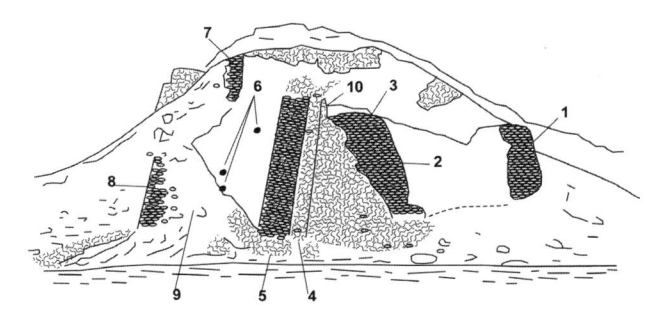

Fig. 3.40: The Kasar Wall (after Kuznetsov 1990, 184 fig. 39) seen in profile from the south-west. Its sloping walls, to increase stability (and withstand water pressure during floods?), resemble those of the Gorgan Wall Bridge over the Sari Su River, also employing strong mortar: perhaps the Kasar Wall was a gorge-blocking Sasanian gated bridge barrier on the approaches to the Mamison Pass? Key: 1: Southern (rounded) face of the platform; 2: Western face of the platform; 3: Cavity of rotted plank; 4: Defensive wall A; 5: Defensive wall B; 6: Cavities of rotted beam structures; 7: Collapsed masonry and face of the wall, directed against the north; 8: Defensive wall C; 9: Remains of the material to fill the space between the walls; 10: Edge of a destroyed aperture. There is no scale, but the plan (Fig. 3.39) will give an idea of dimensions.

or four further mortared bridge barriers blocking narrow valleys in the northern Caucasus. They are discussed in more detail in the context of our research into Sasanian Persia's Caucasian defences,[50] but are also of particular interest in the context of the Gorgan Wall Bridge over the Sari Su. We will focus here only on the one that is published in some detail, the Kasar Wall. Its sloping walls may also have been built to withstand water pressure. Built of stone (in plentiful supply in the Caucasus), it unsurprisingly does not employ bricks, but, like the Gorgan Wall Bridge bricks, these are bonded by strong mortar. If, it seems, not well preserved, there were traces of breastwork, adding strength to Russian archaeologists' persuasive interpretation of the monument as defensive. The location, blocking a narrow passage in the Ardon Gorge (in modern North Ossetia, Russia) certainly adds much strength to a defensive interpretation. An eighteenth-century report attests that an arch, whether for a gate next to the river or spanning the water course, was still standing then. The Kasar Wall controls the northern approaches to the Mamison Pass, a little over 50 km west of Dariali Gorge with its prominent Sasanian defensive barriers. Whilst the Kasar Wall is not securely dated, Sasanian defensive efforts in the area and the lack of known examples for solid mortar barriers or bridges from the Middle Ages in the central Caucasus suggest it is Sasanian too.[51] Also worth noting are the remnants of a probable mortared bridge pier, employing large square bricks (perhaps Sasanian, in so far as it is possible to base a judgement on old photographic evidence), at Kalat in Khorasan. Located in a narrow gorge that formed the only viable access route to a natural fortress, and succeeded by a heavily guarded later bridge at the same point, this may be a further bridge barrier of possible Sasanian origins.[52] Even disregarding the potential parallel in Khorasan, it seems certain that there were bridge barriers on the Ghilghilchay and Gorgan Walls and probably also in the central Caucasus. They are not unique to one region, just as Sasanian barracks forts, linear barriers and campaign bases are also found in a variety of frontier zones. The empire's engineers built defensible bridge barriers of broadly similar design in the Gorgan Plain, as they did elsewhere – proof of significant involvement of central planning in the empire's defences, rather than a laissez-faire approach leaving such matters in local hands.

3.2.5. Protecting the bridge from erosion

The build-up of substantial alluvial deposits immediately to the south of wall b.002 (described below) suggests that there has been no soil bank here – further evidence to suggest that the structure was indeed a bridge and not a dam.[53]

Examination of the right river bank yielded circumstantial evidence for measures taken to protect the bridge. One notices courses of mud-brick on top of a probable erosion channel (b.041), cutting natural soil.[54] The upper northern side of this erosion channel survives to the present day (Figs 3.41–3.43). The lowest three deposits within its fill (b.033, b.034 and b.035) are devoid of finds and their composition, soft to very soft light-yellowish brown clayey silt and silty clay, with some iron staining in the upper two deposits, is consistent will loess washed down the hill at a time of little if any human activity. B.036 is the earliest deposit within the fill to contain brick fragments and, whilst small, they provide strong circumstantial evidence to suggest that the light brownish yellow clay was washed down the channel not before the time when the Gorgan Wall and the associated brick structure in the Sari Su River Valley were built or under construction. Interestingly, the next layer (b.037) provides evidence for an increased speed of waterborne erosion: within the deposit six thin bands of light-brown clayey silt, just 5 mm thick on average, were observed in a matrix of very soft mid-yellowish brown sandy clay. Each heavy downpour appears to have washed down material, quite possibly as a result of a reduced plant cover on the slope. Perhaps this was the time when Fort 2A was already occupied, leading to increased human traffic and probably sheep grazing in its surroundings. Subsequently, a series of deposits (from b.039 to b.072) appear to have accumulated rapidly, pointing to increased human activity and accelerated erosion.[55] On top of b.072, one sees clearly several courses of mud-brick (b.071, b.070, b.069 and b.068) in the profile. B.067 above, sloping at a similar gradient to the mud-brick below (perhaps as a result of subsidence within the channel) and of the same material (soft

Fig. 3.41: The loess landscape is prone to heavy erosion today as well as in antiquity. To the right of the vertical scale there may be traces of a blocked erosion channel. Tunnel erosion (right) is ubiquitous in the area.

Fig. 3.42: The mud-brick blockage of the probable erosion channel. (Each red and weight segment of the scales is 10 cm long.)

mid-yellowish brown clayey silt) is likely to be decayed mud-brick too. If so, the mud-brick wall or blockage survives to a height of up to 1.50 m.

If we are right in thinking that b.036 dates to the time when the Gorgan Wall and the hydraulic installation in Trench b were constructed or shortly after and that the mud-brick blockage was built when this installation was still in use (and before the creation of a reservoir would have made such a structure of sun-dried bricks obsolete), then the sequence makes perfect sense: the erosion channel was natural, but erosion accelerated massively as a result of the construction and occupation of a Sasanian Fort (2A) on top of the slope and, probably, intensive use of nearby land. Approximately 2 m of sediments (b.036 to b.072) built up in the channel within a short period of time. To reduce the risk that water and mud, washed down the channel, would undermine walls or create substantial soil deposits north of the bridge, the natural erosion channel was blocked. The blockage also prevented potential hostile forces from trying to ascend the erosion channel, if scalable, and to occupy high ground overlooking the bridge. No dwelling would have been built in an erosion channel and its elaborate blockage must have been intended to protect the bridge in Trench b and perhaps also to plug a potential pedestrian route from the river valley to the top of the loess cliff. The deposits above (b.075, b.066 and b.065) may be related to a Sasanian reservoir and are discussed in the next section. The earliest robber trench was subsequently cut through this sequence (Fig. 3.43).

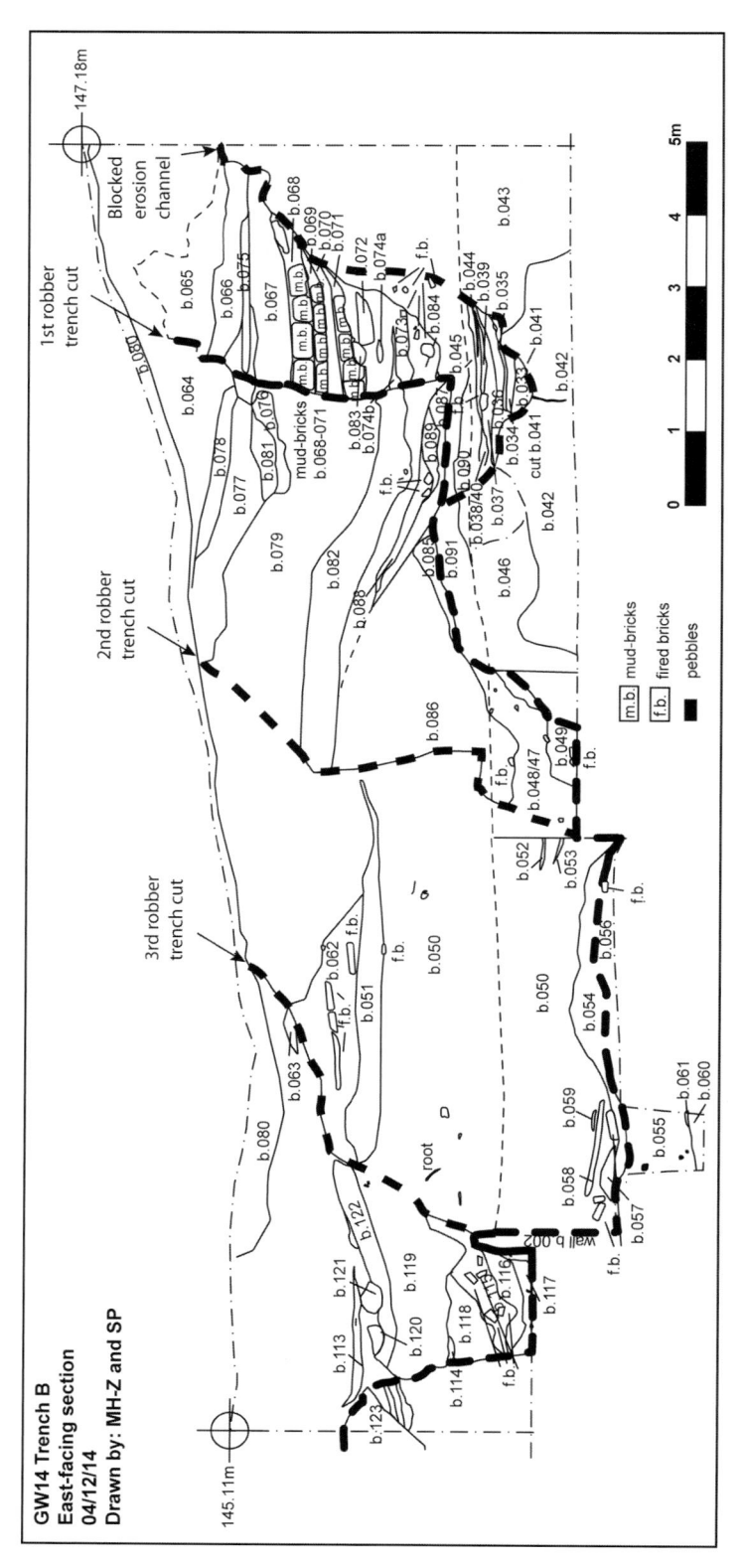

Fig. 3.43: Trench b, section 1, drawn by Maryam Hossein-Zadeh and Silvia Perini.

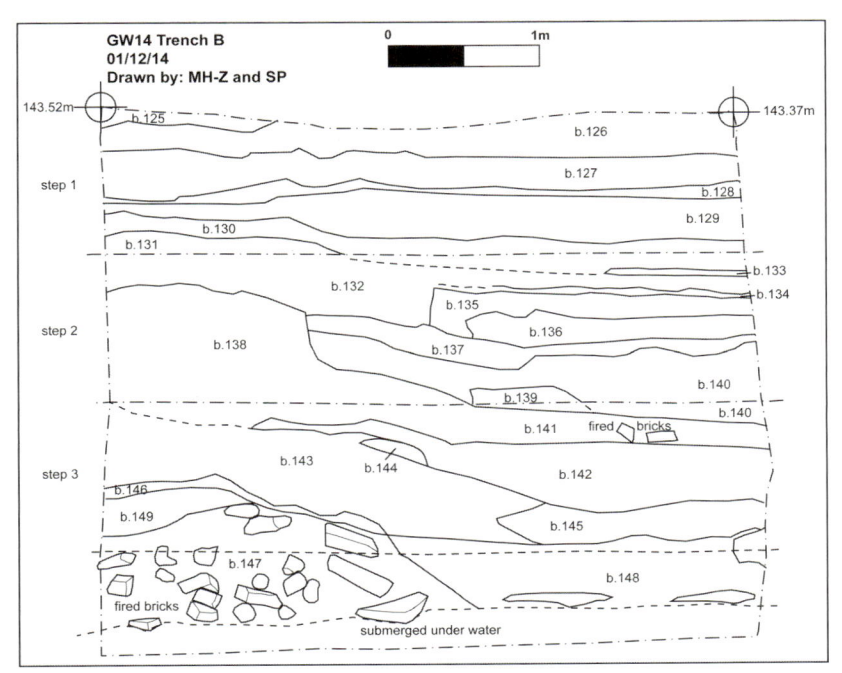

Fig. 3.44: Trench b, section 6, through alluvial sediments above the centre of the platform, drawn by Maryam Hossein-Zadeh and Silvia Perini.

3.2.6. Alluvial deposits and circumstantial evidence for a Sasanian barrage and reservoir in the Sari Su River

Initially, we thought that our brick structure at a narrow point in the valley, employing, unlike the Gorgan Wall, strong white, lime-based and probably waterproof mortar,[56] was part of a barrage, with a second later one being further downstream. Its architecture and location in alignment with the Gorgan Wall, however, show now clearly that it was a bridge and not part of a dam. Yet, we were probably right in thinking that there was a barrage damming the river further downstream. Alluvial layers both upstream and downstream of the bridge provide circumstantial evidence for our postulated reservoir.

We observed and recorded alluvial deposits at a range of locations within the trench. Centrally in the valley, we excavated in 2014 a stepped section (section 6)[57] through the alluvial sediments on top of the brick platform on the eastern bank of the current course of the Sari Su River. Immediately above the preserved brick platform (b.003) of the bridge, there was a layer (b.147), with broken brick fragments as well as complete bricks. This brick collapse layer is overlain and abutted by alluvial sediments: soft brownish and blueish grey clay (b.148 and b.149) (Figs 3.44–3.45). This suggests that the brick-built bridge may have been damaged as a result of flooding that may have led to the collapse of parts of the brick abutments and the probable arched superstructure once connecting them. The quantity of bricks is small, suggesting that the bulk was recycled as building material by local people and in part perhaps washed a little further downstream by the river.

Fig. 3.45: Trench b, section 6, through alluvial sediments overlying the centre of the platform.

Brick-robbing does not appear to have been conducted very systematically or it may have been done at a time when alluvial deposits already covered and concealed parts of the heap of bricks, to judge by complete bricks having been left behind. Unsurprisingly, flooding and sedimentation continued and most deposits higher up in the section are alluvial too, consisting of clay,[58] sandy clay[59] or sand,[60] those with more sand pointing to faster water flow. Just two layers were silt,[61] probably washed-in loess. Many of the successive deposits contain iron stains, a sign of waterlogged conditions, many, brick fragments and b.127, plastic, indicating that this deposit and those above are modern. The combined depth of deposits is substantially lower than at the edges of the valley and the active river may have caused greater disturbance.

Fig. 3.46: Section 2: in the south, brick platform b.003 (foreground) is overlain by, and the brick wall b.002 (right) abutted by, a substantial sequence of alluvial layers (left).

More significant insights into the chronology and significance of the substantial build-up of alluvial deposits emerged from sections at the edges of the valley, which were largely undisturbed by recent activity. In 2014, we encountered a sequence of alluvial layers downstream and on top of the southern part of brick platform b.003. Cleaning the section revealed that the alluvial layers abut the southern face of wall b.002 and slope away from the wall and towards the centre of the valley. Except for the bottom part of the lowest deposit (b.007) in the sequence, they all overlie the brick platform (b.003), proving clearly that their formation post-dates bridge construction. Subsequent radiocarbon dating established that they are indeed late Sasanian.[62] The thick build-up of alluvial sediments here points to a deep pool of water south of wall b.002, existing over a long period of time. The lowest deposit (b.007), soft mid-grey clay, contained the odd charcoal fleck. A charcoal-rich deposit (b.008) above, of soft dark-grey clay, points to intensified human activity nearby. Subsequently, approximately 0.5 m of sterile mid-greyish brown clay (b.004) accumulated, followed by the gradual build-up of 14 further alluvial deposits.[63] The approximately 2.50 m deep sequence up to this point (b.007 to b.022) appears to have built up within a reservoir. The clayey nature of most deposits is indicative of waterlogged conditions, as is iron-staining. Grey colour suggests stable conditions, whilst a brownish hue or silt components mark periods when more humus was washed in; a yellowish hue or sand component will have been caused by natural soil being washed into the reservoir. Most deposits are largely or completely sterile, but more frequent charcoal in b.008 and b.017 point to two phases of increased human activity in the vicinity.

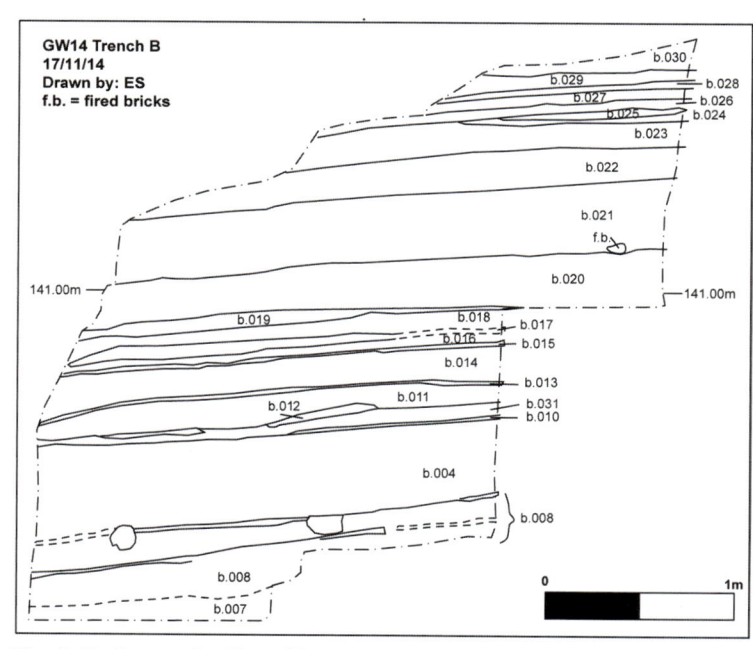

Fig. 3.47: Section 2: alluvial layers south of wall b.002, north-facing profile.

3. The Gorgan Wall

Table 3.1: Section 4: the north-facing profile, south of the eastern bridge abutment.

Context	Top E (left)	Top W (right)	Soil
b.286	144.35	144.35	firm mid-yellowish brown clayey silt
b.285	143.22	143.20	soft mid-brownish yellow clayey silt
b.284	143.16	143.14	firm mid-yellowish brown clayey silt
b.283	143.01	143.06	soft mid-brownish yellow clayey silt
b.282	142.93	142.90	firm mid-yellowish brown clayey silt
b.281	142.87	142.88	soft mid-brownish yellow clayey silt
b.280	142.81	142.77	firm mid-yellowish brown clay
b.279	142.74	142.71	soft mid-brownish yellow clayey silt
b.278	142.67	142.65	firm mid-yellowish brown clay
b.277	142.59	142.60	soft mid-yellowish brown clayey silt
b.276	142.19	142.13	firm mid-yellowish brown clay
b.275	142.12	142.06	very soft mid-brown clayey silt
b.274	142.00	141.98	soft mid-yellowish brown clay
b.273	141.94	141.93	very soft mid-yellowish brown clayey silt, light iron-staining
b.272	141.88	141.87	firm mid-yellowish brown clay, light iron-staining
b.271	141.80	141.78	soft mid-brownish yellow clayey silt
b.270	141.74	141.69	firm mid-yellowish brown clay, iron-stained
b.269	141.57	141.53	soft mid-brownish yellow silty clay, iron-stained
b.268	141.52	141.47	firm mid-yellowish brown clay
b.267	141.34	141.27	firm mid-greyish brown clay, heavily iron-stained
b.266	141.22	141.17	soft mid-yellowish brown clay
b.265	140.98	140.98	soft mid-blueish grey clay, iron-stained
base	140.50	140.50	n/a

Fig. 3.48: Section 4: the north-facing profile, south of the eastern bridge abutment. The horizontal scale is at 142.24 m height.

B.022 is the last deposit thought to have built up within standing water, whilst the composition of the soil horizons above suggests that loess accumulated on what was now dry land, washed down from the slopes above: eight recognisable horizons (b.023–b.030) of soft to very soft yellow, brownish yellow or brown clayey silt.

To the south-east of the bridge, we found in 2015 a similar build-up of alluvial layers. A 1.50 m wide part of the north-facing section south-east of the bridge was cleaned and documented (Figs 3.48–3.49 and Table 3.1). At the bottom of the sequence, all deposits up to b.270, disregarding a thin band of iron-stained soft mid-brownish

Fig. 3.49: Location of section 4 south of the eastern bridge abutment (right).

Fig. 3.50: The sediments on the north side of the eastern bridge abutment.

Fig. 3.51: Close-up of the alluvial sediments.

yellow silty clay (b.269), consist of pure clay. They tend to slope from east to west, i.e. towards the centre of the valley. These deposits probably formed at the base of the postulated reservoir. The yellowish-brown colour of b.268 and b.270, the highest of these alluvial deposits, suggests an increased rate of erosion. Above, there is a deep sequence (b.271 to b.286) of soil horizons which will have built up after the reservoir had dried up, even if there still appear to have been periods of standing water when clay deposits accumulated. Deposits with a higher silt content, and often eroded brown humus, represent periods of increased erosion, alternating with more inorganic clayey deposits. Except for charcoal flecks in b.265, we spotted no finds in section 4, but it is worth noting that we only cleaned and recorded the profile and took no samples. The absence of brick fragments may be the result of the section being more than 4 m from the nearest brick wall and probably all deposits forming after bridge construction and prior to demolition, in slow-flowing or stagnant water or at times of slow natural sedimentation. The top of b.270 and b.022 are at a similar level at the two opposite sides of the valley. This suggests, despite the lack of positive dating evidence from the eastern section, that these two deposits are contemporary and that they are the latest alluvial deposits before the reservoir dried up.

A deep alluvial sequence also emerged when we cleaned west-facing section 3 (Figs 3.26–3.27 and 3.50–3.51), north of the eastern bridge abutment, and excavated a sondage down to its foundations.[64] The northern wall (b.288) of the eastern bridge abutment

3. The Gorgan Wall

Table 3.2: Top of alluvial deposits, likely to be associated with the reservoir.

Section	2: SW of bridge	4: SE of bridge	3: NE of bridge
Top of reservoir deposits	141.80 m	141.74 m	141.40 m
Highest reservoir deposit	b.022	b.270	b.241
Combined depth of reservoir deposits	≥2.58 m	>1.24 m	2.27 m

Fig. 3.52: The Sari Su ('Yellow Water') River, swollen by rainwater on 5 December 2015, carries a heavy sediment load, accounting for the substantial build-up of alluvial deposits.

(b.156), reaching down to c. 138.60 m (c. 1.25 m below the water table on 6 December 2015), was cut about 0.5 m deep into natural sterile mid-brownish grey clay with c. 90% of poorly sorted natural river pebbles (b.233). Only the top 10–12 cm (b.234) of these river pebbles were washed in after construction, as shown by a large chunk of fired brick that will have fallen on the ground during construction works. Above, alluvial clay deposits, attesting slower sedimentation, start at c. 139.13 m. First c. 1.30 m of soft mid-brownish grey clay (b.235) built up. This substantial mass of fine-grained sediments contained charcoal, including one sample dated to c. AD 439–639,[65] i.e. the time of the construction or subsequent occupation of the Gorgan Wall (or, at an 88.0% probability, AD 533–639, the time of the later reservoir). A band of soft mid-brownish grey clayey silt (b.236) above is suggestive of some erosion, before further substantial alluvial deposits accumulated (b.237–b.241).[66] Overall the alluvial deposits, excluding b.234 as deposited at times of faster currents, reach a combined depth of c. 2.27 m (from c. 139.13–141.40 m), evidence for a deep pool of sediment-rich water. It is worth comparing the top of the alluvial layers likely to be associated with the reservoir in the relevant sections (Table 3.2).

All deep alluvial deposits described above will have formed at the base of the same reservoir extending from somewhere downstream of the bridge through its postulated arch to its northern side and undoubtedly well beyond. Minor differences in maximum elevation are easily explained, as we have seen in our sections that the reservoir deposits tend to be higher towards the edge of the valley and lower towards the centre. Water will have flowed faster in the centre and slower at the edges, accounting for the differential speed of sedimentation.

Fig. 3.53: Trench b with location of the sondage (section 5) into alluvial layers upstream (right, middle ground, with two team members working at this section).

The sedimentation rate may have been higher closer to the actual barrage further south and lower further north. The pool of water is likely to have been much deeper than the sediments at its base. Their depth of over 2 m is remarkable and suggests that water was deep, perhaps up to 6 or 7 m at some early stage, the approximate difference in elevation between the platform and the postulated dam (as far as preserved) downstream, and that the reservoir will have been maintained for a considerable period of time.

Potentially significant in this context is a small segment of the northern parts of section 1 (Fig. 3.43) not obscured by later robber trenches. On top of the blocked erosion channel described in the previous sub-chapter,[67] we found a sequence of alluvial deposits: soft mid-yellowish brown clay (b.075), soft mid-yellowish brown silty clay (b.066) and soft mid-greyish brown sandy clay (b.065). They may represent material building up at the sides of the late reservoir mixed with washed-in loess. The base of b.075 is at c. 144.93 m and whilst observation high up on the profile was not easy, the alluvial deposits seem to be at least 0.5 m thick. They are thus at a much higher level than the alluvial deposits in sections 2, 3 and 4, thought to be associated with a late Sasanian reservoir. If, however, water was very deep and penetrated into erosion channels at the edge of the valley, it would be logical for alluvial layers to be deposited at a much higher level than in deep water at the centre of the pool. If we are right in thinking that these deposits accumulated in the same reservoir as those in sections 2, 3 and 4 (and there is no absolute proof), water must have risen at some stage to well over 145.50 m height – more than 6 m higher than the base of the alluvial sequence, as far as excavated, in section 3 (c. 139.13 m).

One observes a substantial build-up of alluvial deposits not just immediately downstream of b.002, but also upstream of the brick feature (b.003), where such water-borne deposits were exposed at the western slope of the valley. We cleaned these and excavated a sondage, 38 m NNW of the northern edge of wall b.002, in 2014. Well over 2 m of fine-grained alluvial sediments point to a body of stagnant or slow-flowing water here, existing for a considerable period of time.[68] We observed no brick flecks nor any finds in any of the deposits in the sequence. A charcoal sample from b.101 yielded a radiocarbon date probably pre-dating 45000 BC (Table 3.3). This deposit was, in absolute terms, more than 1 m above the highest of the Sasanian-era reservoir

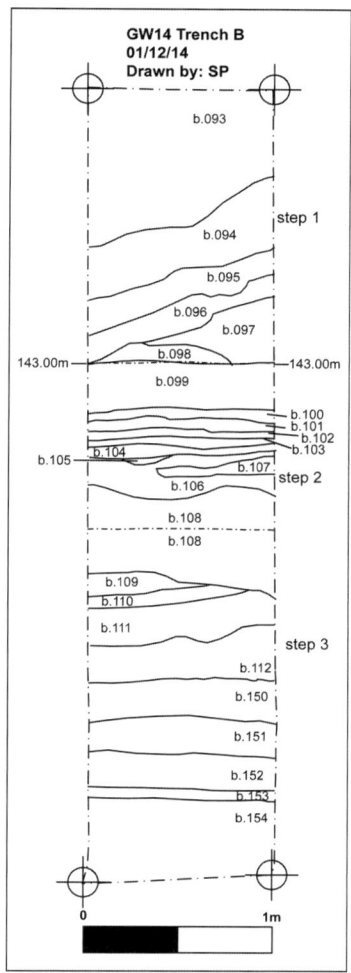

Fig. 3.54: Section 5: sondage into alluvial layers (of geological age) upstream, drawn by Silvia Perini. Note that this sondage has been assigned to Trench b, but is outside the area that has been systematically excavated.

deposits a little further downstream in sections 2, 3 and 4 (though below those in the erosion channel in section 1). It appears that the entire sequence, including the alluvial layers, is of geological age and was located beyond the western edge of the valley and reservoir. If of no direct significance for the Sasanian era, it is clear from this section that the valley at this point extended no further west in recent millennia than it does today. It is interesting to note, of course, that also in the area of Trench b, no Sasanian-era reservoir deposits survive north-west of the bridge. It seems that in the area from wall b.155 to section 5, riverine erosion in past millennia cut into the natural slope, moving the western edge of the valley a little further to the west.

Whilst the latter section (5), through geological layers, proves alluvial sedimentation perhaps tens of thousands of years ago, the substantial alluvial deposits in three sections near the bridge, two of them (2 and 3) firmly and independently dated to the late Sasanian era and two of them (2 and 4) south of the bridge, provide circumstantial evidence for a Sasanian dam downstream of the bridge. Where was it? Some 55–75 m SSW from western bridge abutment wall b.002, there is much broken brick, as well as courses of complete bricks *in situ*, visible, exposed on the right slope of the valley (Figs 3.5 and 3.55–3.56). Whilst we did not have the time to excavate this feature, we observed that it employs Gorgan Wall-type bricks and mortar. In addition to masonry *in situ*, there is also a significant quantity of brick debris nearby. There is little doubt that it is also a Sasanian construction, built to withstand water pressure. The uppermost brick courses *in situ* exposed at the edge of the river are at a height of c. 144.51–144.92 m, reaching higher than the north wall of the eastern bridge abutment, though not quite as high as the middle and south walls. The valley was narrow here, but its steep sides are today some 6 m high. This would have been an ideal point to dam the river, thus creating a huge reservoir. It is possible that this was part of a barrage. Alternatively, and perhaps more probably, it may have been the lining of a canal. Strong support for the latter hypothesis is provided by the discovery of a similar masonry structure (WP 731) parallel to the river some 660 m SSW, interpreted as a canal wall to protect the canal from riverine erosion.[69] The valley is wider at this point, so that it would have involved more effort to dam the river at this point. Furthermore, as it seems improbable that there would have been two dams just a few hundred metres apart, an interpretation of both features as the lining of the same canal seems more plausible than two similar barrages 660 m apart. If so, the dam must have been between the bridge and the brick structure (55–75 m SSW of wall b.002) discovered in 2013. In this area, the valley reaches one of its narrowest points, and it would have been easy to block it with a dam. Such a dam, perhaps completely destroyed and washed away by the river since, could have raised the water level higher than any hypothetical barrage further south. It is also possible that the monument 55–75 m SSW of wall b.002 represents the remains of a barrage with an associated canal inlet. It is almost certain that the monument was a hydraulic feature, but without excavation it is hard to be sure what its precise function was. The build-up of alluvial layers to the south of the bridge is any case only conceivable if the river had been dammed for some time and further downstream.

That creating a reservoir would have been comparatively easy became dramatically clear when on 22 November 2014 our piped diversion got blocked and the stream, swollen by overnight rain, created an impressive reservoir upstream from our trench (Fig. 3.57). A low earth dam, consisting of sacks of soil piled up upstream of Trench b, had created this huge reservoir in the river within hours, whilst also flooding the trench, demonstrating powerfully

Fig. 3.55: Exposed Sasanian brick masonry downstream of Trench b (c. 55–75 m SSW of wall b.002) on 12 January 2013 (see Fig. 3.5 for the location of this brick structure).

Fig. 3.56: Close-up view of the brick masonry downstream of Trench b.

Fig. 3.57: A reservoir created by the blocked Sari Su River on 22 November 2014.

how rapidly a reservoir can be created even if there is little water in the small stream – as well as the vulnerability of barrages. Our makeshift dam was, of course, of far lesser dimensions than its likely predecessor and so will have been the reservoir. Whilst on dry days even in autumn and winter the Sari Su is a small stream that can easily be crossed, local residents confirm that it does not run dry in summer. Assuming this was also the case in the Sasanian era, a reservoir would constantly have been replenished with water. The top of the preserved parts of the bridge were at a higher level than the top of the brick structure/postulated canal inlet or dam downstream. We may be sure that the Gorgan Wall and the walkway(s) on the bridge were still above water even after the creation of the reservoir.

3.2.7. Chronology

Whilst Trench b was one of our largest trenches, it was one of the least prolific in terms of finds other than building material. This is unsurprising. We found no occupation layers anywhere and the deposits excavated formed mostly during later alluviation and sedimentation. Other than bricks, there was not a single well-stratified artefact from the entire trench. Survey above Trench b yielded typical Gorgan Wall-era pottery, perhaps in part related to occupation of Fort 2A above. By contrast, on top of the brick monument in Trench b, notably in the immediate vicinity of the current riverbed, we found a much wider spectrum of pottery, including prehistoric pieces.[70] Evidently, the highly abraded pottery has been deposited here by the river and is associated with modern finds, all found embedded in a matrix of alluvial deposits, clay and rounded river pebbles. We also discovered a prehistoric flint blade, a grinding stone and a whetstone, the former two from unstratified layers, the latter from a deposit (b.006) into which the brick platform had been cut and thus probably earlier, but by how much is impossible to tell.[71] We do not know when any of these items had been lost, though of course typology excludes a recent manufacture for any of them. For lighter and/or abraded finds, we also cannot be sure if they had been used or discarded in the area of Trench b or perhaps upstream and washed downstream and/or slid down the steep slopes. The finds provide unsurprising evidence for a range of activities from prehistory to modern times in the valley or on its slopes. The absence of stratified Sasanian-era portable objects is no doubt the result of no Sasanian occupation levels surviving and any items lost by those guarding or using the bridge having been washed away by the river.

Table 3.3: Radiocarbon and archaeomagnetic dates of samples from Trench b; a.s.l. = above sea level (absolute heights approximate only, but exact in relative terms). Dates with question mark and in square brackets are considered unreliable.[72] Note that in the text, in this and subsequent chapters, we refer to dates at 95.4% confidence, unless otherwise specified. Where models were attempted, we normally refer to the modelled dates at the same confidence range. We considered marking unmodelled calibrated dates with 'cal', but have implemented this only in chapter 13 where exclusively unmodelled dates are cited. As there does not appear to be a commonly used abbreviation for modelled dates, we felt it would cause confusion to create our own. Radiocarbon dates cited in chapters other than 13 are normally marked with 'c.' (= circa), as there is of course an almost 5% probability that the real date could be outside the cited range. This abbreviation is used for both modelled and unmodelled dates, but the former tend to be cited, if available. The relevant tables will always allow the reader to verify what the modelled and unmodelled dates were for all cited samples, and we felt there was no need to duplicate this information in the text.

Context and sample no.	Location	Laboratory no.	Sample description	Date	Calibrated date at 95.4% confidence	Comments
b.182	N of E bridge abutment, above b.180 (c. 142.13–142.34 m a.s.l.)	AM253	Sediment	n/a	[AD 223–351?]	Archaeomagnetic dates incompatible with stratigraphy (probably medieval river channels and all above redeposited 5th-century fired brick)
b.180	N of E bridge abutment, above b.160 (c. 141.81–141.85 m a.s.l.)	AM252	Sediment	n/a	[AD 222–375?]	
b.160	N of E bridge abutment, below b.180 (c. 140.98–141.08 m a.s.l.)	AM251	Sediment	n/a	[AD 208–347?]	
b.008/s110	S of W bridge abutment, above b.007 (40–60 cm above b.003 = c. 139.62–139.82 m a.s.l.)	SUERC-60038	*Sueda maritima* seed	1516 ± 26 BP	AD 440–636 → modelled date: 550–634 (93.8%: 550–609)	d13C = -25.8
b.008/s118	S of W bridge abutment, above b.007 (c. 139.67 m a.s.l.)	SUERC-60042	Thorns or prickles	1465 ± 30 BP	AD 562–648 → modelled date: 561–640	d13C = -26.3
b.008/s115	S of W bridge abutment, above b.007 (relative sequence of b.008 samples cannot be established)	AM237	Sediment	n/a	[222 BC–AD 125, AD 388–403?] AD 519–649 [AD 1717–1810?]	AD 519–649 overlaps with ¹⁴C dates
b.007/s76–77&81	S of W bridge abutment, below b.008 (0–20 cm above b.003 = c. 139.22–139.42 m a.s.l.)	SUERC-60037	*Heliotropium* sp. seeds	1496 ± 29 BP	AD 541–642 → modelled date: 542–601	d13C = -25.1
b.235/s6	N of E bridge abutment (c. 139.21–139.36 m a.s.l.)	Poz 2-80699	*Heliotropium* sp. seeds	1513 ± 29 BP	AD 439–639 (92.1%: 477–639; 88.0%: 533–639; 84.2%: 533–610)	d13C = -21.0
b.060/s159–161	Space between walls b.002 and b.155	SUERC-60036	*Medico* sp. seeds	1566 ± 29 BP	AD 426–567	d13C = -28.2
b.101/s5	N of W bridge abutment, above b.108	Poz-71967	*Juniperus* sp.	⁻47000 BP	⁻45000 BC	n/a
b.108	N of W bridge abutment, below b.101	AM238	Sediment	n/a	[1000–882 BC, AD 281–313, 363–552 1086–1361, 1829–1990?]	Date must be geological and before the period covered by the calibration data set.

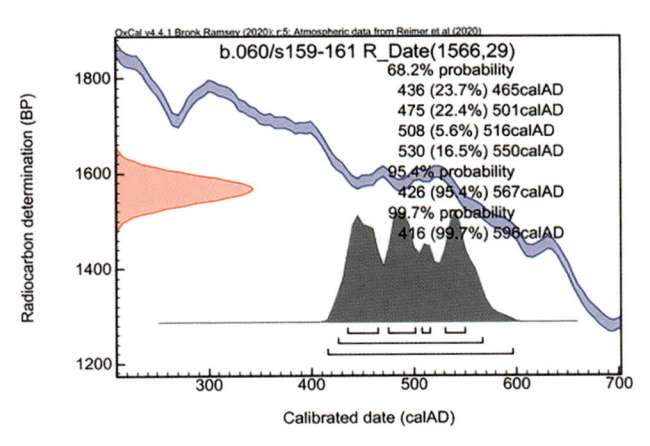

Fig. 3.58: Radiocarbon sample from an early alluvial layer, between walls b.002 and b.155, next to the western bridge abutment. (See Table 3.3 for further details.)

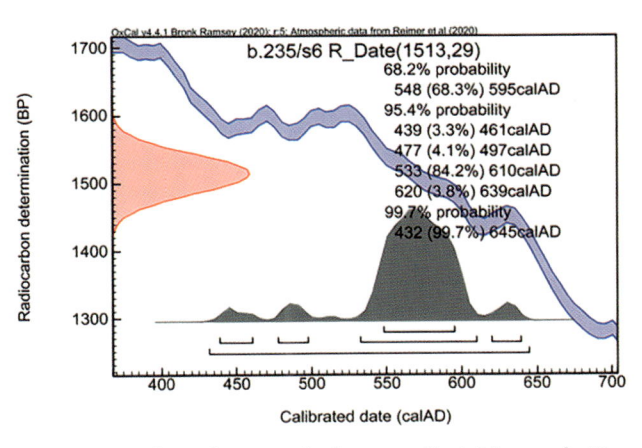

Fig. 3.59: Radiocarbon sample from an alluvial layer, abutting the north side of the eastern bridge abutment in section 3. (See Table 3.3 for further details.)

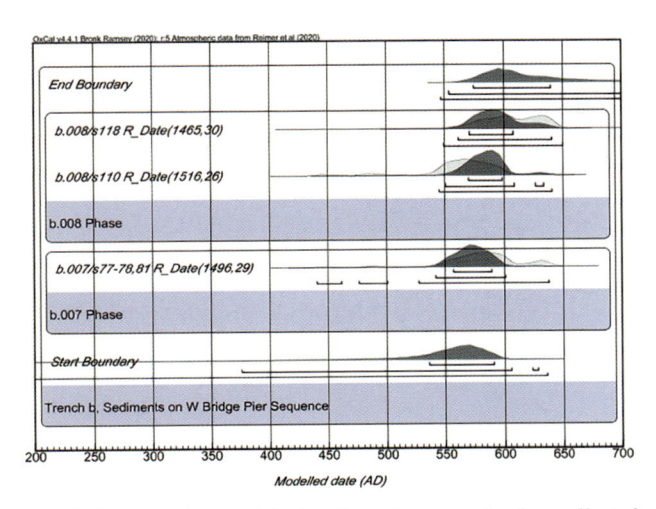

Fig. 3.60: Bayesian model of radiocarbon samples from alluvial layers in section 2, downstream of the western bridge abutment. (See Table 3.3 for further details.)

If there is no artefactual evidence for the date of construction works or the duration of maintenance of the bridge, there was no question as to its approximate chronology, even prior to obtaining independent scientific dates for deposits associated with the hydraulic features. Built exclusively of the typical Gorgan Wall-style bricks, with not even a single specimen of a different type coming to light, we may be confident that the monument in Trench b dates to the time of large-scale manufacture of these bricks and the same era as the Gorgan Wall itself. Later monuments reusing Gorgan Wall bricks tend to contain a much higher proportion of broken bricks and normally consist of a patchwork of bricks of a wide variety of dimensions – not to mention that there was no obvious motive for building a bridge at this point after the Great Wall had been abandoned.

Radiocarbon dates have confirmed what was to be expected, i.e. that associated deposits are contemporary to the occupation of the Gorgan Wall, as Table 3.3 demonstrates.

The sample from b.060, the deposit at the base of the alluvial sequence filling the space between walls b.002 and b.155 (Fig. 3.43), may stratigraphically be the earliest from the trench (excluding the sample of geological age from b.101). Dating to c. AD 426–567, it is also conceivably the earliest in absolute terms and is certainly the earliest in terms of median date. Whilst, due to the plateau in the radiocarbon calibration curve at the time, we cannot exclude that it could be generations earlier or later than the Gorgan Wall, it is perfectly compatible with our assumption that the bridge is part of, and contemporary to, the Great Wall.

Whilst it is unsurprising that a bridge on the Gorgan Wall is likely to be contemporary to this barrier, these findings are of significance for the history of Sasanian engineering. Tabari and Ferdowsi attest the employment of Roman prisoners of war in building a long dam/bridge at Shushtar, following their capture in AD 260, often cited as evidence of technology transfer from west to east.[73] Some two centuries later, at a time of peace with Rome, Sasanian engineers were perfectly capable of building similar monuments quite independently. The Sasanian Ghilghilchay Wall, whether contemporary with the Gorgan Wall, slightly earlier or, as has been proposed, slightly later also boasted a bridge built of bricks and lime mortar.[74] However great or small the role of captured Romans was in early Sasanian construction projects of this kind, by the fifth century certainly there was no longer a technology gap.

By contrast, the three dated samples downstream of b.002 are all likely to be later than that from b.060. The stratigraphically lowest and earliest, from b.007

immediately on top of the brick platform (i.e. within 0–20 cm of its surface) dates to c. AD 542–601. One of the two samples from b.008, the deposit above, is of the mid-sixth to early or mid-seventh century; the other, whilst it could be as early as AD 440, may well be no earlier than AD 550 and no later than the early seventh century, based on our modelling. The archaeomagnetic sample from b.008 also dates to the sixth or the first half of the seventh century (AD 519–649). On the opposite bank and upstream of the bridge, we processed a further sample (b.235/s6), which is potentially as early as the late AD 430s or as late as the 630s. There is, however, an 84.2% probability of the date falling between AD 533 and AD 610 and a roughly nine in ten chance of it dating to the sixth or early to mid-seventh century. Whilst it is not impossible that the dam could have been built at the same time as the bridge, it seems much more probable that the reservoir was not in existence until the sixth century. The radiocarbon dates thus suggest that the original bridge may well have been built and put into operation at the same time as the Great Wall, i.e. probably in the fifth century. It was, however, only in the sixth century that a dam was built downstream of b.002, resulting in the build-up of a large and deep reservoir. The *terminus post quem* of c. AD 561 for a radiocarbon sample from more than 2 m below the top of the alluvial layers suggests that the artificial lake did not run dry until the following century at the earliest. The reservoir may well have lasted until the end of the Sasanian era or beyond, whether the barrage or weir was deliberately decommissioned or not. More probably, nature took its course; perhaps the river eventually broke through the artificial barrier or the natural loess cliffs on either side of it.

3.2.8. The purpose of the reservoir

Why was effort invested in damming the waters of the Sari Su River? Archaeobotanical analysis by Lyudmila Shumilovskikh has shown that fig trees were growing at the edges of the water pool. Black mulberry and grapevine may have been cultivated, too, though the evidence is more ambiguous.[75] Perhaps there were orchards and gardens on the shores of the reservoir, enriching the diet and quality of life of the guardians of the wall, their families or the local civilian population in the area. Surplus water channelled into a canal could also have been put to good use and could have been employed for irrigation. Hamid Omrani Rekavandi, Tony Wilkinson and Kourosh Roustaei observed, as noted above, segments of a canal further downstream.[76] It is possible that this canal was supplied with water from the reservoir. Perhaps water could also have powered mills, as amply attested for other parts of the Sasanian Empire. A huge millstone at Dasht Qal'eh[77] suggests that water power may have been used in the Gorgan Plain too. Could the water have been raised in the postulated reservoir, to feed an elevated canal, ideal to power mills and/or irrigate fields? Until there is more concrete evidence it may be best not to speculate any further, but it is safe to conclude that the creation of reservoirs to feed canals was far from unprecedented. Dams for water management were widely employed in Sasanian Iran, and to a lesser extent already before, notably under the Achaemenid Empire,[78] as well as in the Islamic era later.[79] It is possible that Sari Su River water was channelled into a canal on the right bank of the valley. At Shushtar, Dezful, Pa-ye Pol and Ahvaz similar techniques were applied in the Sasanian era, and dams were used to raise the water table, thus enabling regular water supply to canals.[80] In southern Arabia, two locks channelling off water at a diagonal angle to that of the main water course have been explored at Ma'rib. These locks appear to have been repeatedly rebuilt and modified, from before the sixth century BC to the sixth century AD (when Yemen eventually became part of the Sasanian Empire), the diagonal branches it seems not yet precisely dated.[81] There is a strong possibility that the Sari Su reservoir also fed a canal. Yet, the postulated reservoir need not have been created exclusively or mainly to water fig trees and other plants on its shores or to channel water to irrigate fields further downstream. Alternatively, could its primary purpose have been defensive, even if surplus water was put to good use?

A reservoir would have been helped to protect the bridge from riverine erosion. Notably during episodes of flooding, there was a risk that the river might undermine parts of the structure or even break through the loess cliffs abutting it. Accumulation of alluvial sediments upstream would have gradually weakened the defences and/or necessitated constant maintenance. The sudden collapse of a loess cliff upstream could have created a ramp, potentially enabling enemy forces to scale or bypass the bridge barrier. A dam downstream and a large reservoir engulfing the bridge abutments would have prevented any flash-floods or fast-flowing water from reaching the structure, thus reducing erosion. Whilst sediments continued to build up upstream, they did so in deep water – out of sight and out of reach of any assailants. Judging by the later date of the reservoir, it was perhaps a result of observing the effects of riverine erosion over time which led eventually to the decision to create the reservoir.

But perhaps the creation of the reservoir had even more ambitious aims than to reduce erosion and prevent it from damaging or weakening the bridge barrier. Could the reservoir itself have functioned as a defensive obstacle? Or would there have been no need for this, the high loess cliffs on the left bank of the Sari Su (Figs 3.11–3.12, 3.57, 3.61–3.63) perhaps forming a sufficient natural defensive barrier on the northern approaches to the wall? This seems unlikely. There is a section of the valley, between Forts 2A and 2, where the river can easily be crossed from both sides of the valley, and we managed to do so repeatedly without even getting wet feet or having to negotiate any steep slopes. Despite massive cliffs in places, it would have been easy for any small raiding parties or enemy armies to cross the river at points in between, probably even during episodic floods. Whilst this is a dynamic landscape, with deep crack-lines forming in the loess cliffs, sections of them constantly eroding and collapsing, and new cliffs forming, there is nothing to suggest that there would have been a continuous cliff in antiquity or that it would have been any more difficult to cross the valley at the time than it is now.

Whilst there was no continuous natural high cliff, the wall would have formed an obstacle, and the garrisons of Forts 2 and 2A would have been able to spot any unauthorised approaches during daylight hours, but not necessarily in the dark. The bridge, even if defended, may have been permeable and a possible weak point in the system, especially as we cannot be sure how its, probably arched, crossing was guarded and secured. A later barrage, perhaps filled with water up to 6 or 7 m high, would have created a reservoir of sufficient depth that it would have required barges to enable a mounted army to cross and even to approach the Gorgan Wall and the associated brick-built bridge.

Under the eastern terminal of the section of the Great Wall north-west of Fort 2, there is a high vertical loess cliff (Figs 3.11–3.12 and 3.63) – showing that it would have been nearly impossible to ascend and attack here. Whilst the landscape will have changed, it is not likely that there was no steep cliff at this bend in the river in antiquity. Creating a deep reservoir in the river would have created an additional significant obstacle between Forts 2 and 2A, both protected by towering loess cliffs. The water-filled valley and the loess cliffs on the left bank of the river would have formed a formidable obstacle. To judge by our radiocarbon dates, this reservoir seems to post-date the construction of the Gorgan Wall and may be part of an attempt to strengthen it in the sixth century.

The Sasanian Empire appears to have used deep water as a defensive obstacle – a strategy that was far from unique. Not only will the deep canal along most sections of the Gorgan Wall have made it much harder to venture across,[82] substantial water courses also served as defensive obstacles elsewhere, as James Howard-Johnston has persuasively postulated for Mesopotamia.[83] In AD 363, Julian's invasion army repeatedly encountered impregnable fortifications protected by river or canal water.[84] On at least one occasion, the Persians deliberately flooded a stretch of land in central Mesopotamia with canal/reservoir water to impede the invaders' advance.[85] Our hypothesis that the Sari Su was dammed to create a reservoir of multiple functions, including the creation of a defensive obstacle between Forts 2A and 2, seems very attractive. The reservoir and its northern approaches could easily have been monitored from Forts 2 and 2A and archers dispatched in case of any attempt at unauthorised crossing. Such a venture would have taken much more time and entailed far greater challenges and risks than

Fig. 3.61: A high loess cliff on the left bank of the Sari Su River upstream from Trench b.

Fig. 3.62: Further upstream towards Fort 2, the Sari Su River can easily be crossed (in the middle ground).

Fig. 3.63: Beneath the brick concentration near Fort 2 there is a vertical loess cliff. (The Sari Su River Valley under Fort 2 is in the foreground. A part of the Great Wall is preserved near the top of the loess cliff ahead, as also shown on Figs 3.11–3.12.)

riding or running across an ankle-deep stream. An enemy force attempting to swim or paddle across a reservoir would have been an easy target for archers. Bringing across horses would have been no mean task. The wall

Fig. 3.64: Medieval stream channels c. 16–20 m north-west of the north face of the eastern abutment of the Sasanian bridge (compare Fig. 3.27).

Fig. 3.66: The Gorgan Wall, following the right (south-west) upper edge of the stream channel (centre) terminates in the east at the rock cliffs in the background.

Fig. 3.65: Location of medieval stream channels north of the Sasanian bridge. The two team members standing next to each other take samples from deposits b.180 and b.182; b.160 is to the right of the three figures on the left (compare Fig. 3.27).

and monumental bridge to the south of the reservoir would have formed a second line of defence and any trespassers would have been trapped between the Gorgan Wall ahead and the reservoir behind. This is not to imply that any such hostile engagement will necessarily ever have taken place here. The reservoir may have transformed a potential weak link of the barrier into one of the most impermeable parts of the defensive chain. If deep water between Forts 2A and 2 should have deterred any would-be attackers, it will have served its purpose, even if the barrier's effectiveness at this point was never put to the test.

3.2.9. Brick robbing and sedimentation in post-Sasanian times

Like all of the Gorgan Wall, the bridge lost its function once this great barrier was abandoned. Heavy sedimentation in the river valley buried significant parts of the structure before it could be demolished by locals in search of bricks for building – unlike most other parts of the wall. Its more accessible parts have, however, not been spared from robbing nor was it invulnerable to flooding and erosion, damaging and perhaps washing away parts of the bridge, the dam and the brick-lined canal. The probably early collapse of wall b.217 has already been summarised above.[86] In this section, we will focus on what our excavations have revealed about the later history of the landscape around the ruin and its partial demolition.

On top of the clayey deposits (b.235–b.241), we observed a myriad of bands of soft mid-yellowish brown and brownish yellow clayey silt, with the odd lens of sand (Fig. 3.27). Most of them are devoid of artefacts. They represent natural erosion over a millennium or more, with phases of more loess and less humus accumulating and vice versa accounting for the colour variations. Due to the absence of artefacts and the scarcity of organic matter, these deposits are undated and little would be gained by detailed description. More significant is a sequence of post-Sasanian stream beds, centred some 16–20 m north-west of the northern edge of the eastern bridge abutment. Clay deposits point to flowing or stagnant water and there was a small quantity of broken brick and undiagnostic pot sherds from their fill. The examination of water-plant and ostracod remains from b.173 by Lyudmila Shumilovskikh *et al.* suggest stagnant or slow-flowing water; perhaps it was part of an oxbow lake, a former meander of the Sari Su, but not the main channel of the river.[87] It seems likely that the successive channel deposits (b.160, b.175, b.173, b.180 and b.182) represent the beds of such side-channels over a period of time. Archaeomagnetic dating of some of these successive stream bed/oxbow lake deposits (b.160, b.180 and b.182) suggest a date in the third or fourth century for all three (Table 3.3 and Fig. 3.27),[88] but as there is redeposited Gorgan Wall brick underneath, a date prior to the fifth century seems impossible. Stratigraphy suggests that they are significantly later and

Fig. 3.67: The Gorgan Wall, marked by a broad band of robber pits, led right to the edge of the Kal Aji River (foreground), probably crossed via a bridge similar to that excavated on the banks of the Sari Su. Fort 5 (middle-ground), towering over this vulnerable point, abuts the canal-lined continuation of the Great Wall (right) on the plateau.

Fig. 3.68: The c. 20 m-high Sadd-e Garkaz, a Sasanian aqueduct crossing the Gorgan River Valley on a massive earth dam (middle-ground, right, to foreground, left), was supplied with water from the fertile Gorgan Plain (background, right).

Fig. 3.69: The Sadd-e Garkaz aqueduct (foreground, right, to middle-ground, left) channelled water across the Gorgan River, via a (no longer preserved) brick bridge, into a canal (middle-ground to background, left). This canal fed the main canal along the Great Wall, reaching it between Forts 6 and 7.

all post-date the late Sasanian reservoir having dried up. The date of the successive channels, if we disregard the archaeomagnetic dates, is unknown, but the elevation of the deposits and the gradual build-up of soil suggest that the stream beds/oxbow lakes are several centuries later than the bridge and the earliest and latest may be a few centuries apart. Their depth of burial beyond the modern surface and the lack of any modern finds, however, also suggest that they are not modern and may be tentatively assigned to the Middle Ages, i.e. the later first and/or early to mid-second millennium.

Burial of the eastern bridge abutment under sediments explains why so much of it survives. The western bridge abutment was more intensely robbed out, with only the brick foundation and some of the courses of the walls built upon it remaining. Least is preserved near the current course of the stream as a result of flood damage and brick-robbing. The clearest evidence for deliberate demolition emerged from the west of the trench. One can see the robber trenches clearly in the profile (Fig. 3.43), widening at the top, suggesting that the walls had once reached to or beyond the current surface at the top of the loess cliff. It is hard to establish the date of robbing, but it is possible that the most recent phase occurred within living memory.[89] Whilst context boundaries were often diffuse, a result no doubt of the main component of many of them being redeposited loess, there appear to be at least three phases of robbing. The combined width of these robber trenches is approximately 15 m or more and, varying from place to place, they reach a depth of up 5.20 m below the modern surface. Robbing clearly targeted major walls, notably b.002 and b.155, but extended beyond them in the north, perhaps to create a working platform that facilitated lifting bricks to the surface. The successive robber trenches are filled by a multitude of deposits. Little would be gained by a detailed description of all of them, but it is worth noting that, unsurprisingly, many of them contain fragments of Sasanian brick. Brick fragments are most frequent towards the bottom of the robber trenches, where any broken or discarded fragments would naturally have accumulated, and less so in their middle and upper fills, the latter containing much material gradually washed down the natural slopes and thus unsurprisingly virtually devoid of other artefacts.

3.3. Drone survey of the Gorgan Wall

As part of our project, and on the initiative of Davit Naskidashvili who took all the photos guided by Iranian members, drone photographs were taken of all well-preserved forts on the Great Wall. Due to time constraints, it was not possible to record all sections of the Gorgan Wall between forts. The forts are discussed in the next chapter,[90] but three locations surveyed are more appropriately covered in this section, as they focus on the wall and associated structures rather than forts. Indeed, they provide visual evidence for other river crossings and the use of natural defensive obstacles – important parallels for contextualising the results of our excavations in the Sari Su River Valley.

Aerial imagery powerfully demonstrated how the landscape was used for defensive advantage, not just in the Sari Su Valley, but also elsewhere, notably in the easternmost section of the Gorgan Wall. Here, the wall follows the upper edge of a deep stream channel, which forms a natural defensive ditch, before terminating (at least as far as securely traced so far) at an overhanging rock cliff (Fig. 3.66).[91]

Between Forts 5A and 5, the Gorgan Wall crossed the Kal Aji River (Fig. 3.67), a potential weak point, similar to the Sari Su River crossing. As in the case of the Sari Su, care was taken not to leave a gap in the wall. An alignment of robber pits indicates that the Great Wall led right to the edge of the river. We may assume that it crossed the river via a bridge, similar to the one exposed in Trench b in the Sari Su River Valley.[92]

A brick bridge also existed where the Sadd-e Garkaz aqueduct channelled water across the Gorgan River (Figs 3.68–3.69). Its collapsed remains, still visible in the 1840s, have now disappeared, but the aqueduct south-east of the river and the canal north-west of it are still prominent landscape features. There must have been several such aqueducts to supply all sections of the canals along the lowland portion of the Great Wall with water.[93] The one surviving aqueduct powerfully demonstrates the scale of the task of channelling water into the steppes north of the river. Without canal water, the hundreds of millions of large bricks needed for wall and fort construction could not have been made. It would have been impossible to build the Great Wall without such advanced hydraulic engineering.

Notes

1. See Nokandeh 2014. The kiln is centred on UTM 40S E 0273869, N 4111009. Preservation was similar to the kiln excavated near Fort 30 (Sauer *et al.* 2013, 145–49) and the lower part of the firing chamber and the crossbars were still preserved.
2. See chapter 3.2.2.
3. Sauer *et al.* 2013, 145–49.
4. Sauer *et al.* 2013, 133–44.
5. Sauer *et al.* 2013, 163–73.
6. See chapter 4.
7. Kiani 1982b, 14, cf. Kiani 1982a, 73 providing an even higher estimate of 'more than 180 km'.
8. Charlesworth 1987.
9. Kiani 1982b, 15 fig. 9, cf. fig. 8b.
10. Kiani 1982b, fig. 8b.
11. Kiani 1982b, General Map.
12. Kiani 1982b, 15 fig. 9.
13. See chapter 11.
14. Personal information by Kristen Hopper, 23 June 2020. We are also grateful to Kristen Hopper for checking and confirming the revised estimate for the length of the lowland section and the wall as a whole.
15. For a visual idea of the scale of the construction project, see now also the impressive reconstruction drawings by Rezaeian 2014, 19, 186–203 that provide an excellent idea of the likely magnitude of Fort 4 and adjacent sections of the Great Wall in three dimensions. Note that there would have been a moat around this fort and many others, so the efforts in building the fort-lined wall would have been even greater. Inevitably, any reconstruction will involve debatable details, but Rezaeian ought to be congratulated on the first visualisation of the magnitude of a fort on the Gorgan Wall.
16. The correction of the length estimate may, however, require us to reduce our estimate of the number of bricks needed to build the wall (maybe over 170 million, depending on how much further the wall runs to the west, as opposed to 210 million as postulated before: Sauer *et al.* 2013, 144 table 4:2). As, however, the height of the wall is unknown and as the model does not make any allowance for associated features, such as towers, such estimates can never provide more than an idea of magnitude. CORONA images sometimes show the wall as a dotted line, e.g. in the sections near Fort 10, implying that there may have been more or less regularly spaced towers on the wall (as there were on the Ghilghilchay Wall: Aliev *et al.* 2006; Gadjiev 2017a), but the phenomenon has not as yet been systematically investigated or examined on the ground. The significance of these dots is not easy to explain, as normally only mud-brick towers are visible as collapse mounds, though other explanations (e.g. a line of robber pits) are possible. The same is true for brick kilns. We had assumed 3,000–7,000 based on a hypothetical combined length of c. 250 km for the Gorgan and Tammisheh Walls, then assumed to be linked (Sauer *et al.* 2015a, 327). Yet, even the minimum combined length of the two walls (assuming, as before, a spacing of 37–86 m) still suggests there were at least c. 2,000–5,000 kilns. One wonders if the slightly larger bricks used in the central and eastern (and later?) section of the Gorgan Wall, as opposed to the slightly smaller bricks in the (earlier?) western section and the Tammisheh Wall (Sauer *et al.* 2013, 174, 248 table 7:1, 594) reflect a desire to speed up construction work and/or further enhance the stability of the wall.
17. See chapters 5, 12 and 13; Jansen Van Rensburg *et al.* 2013; Sauer *et al.* 2013, 252–72.
18. See more detailed discussion in chapter 7.2.1; cf. Mustawfi 18 = trans. Le Strange 1919, 206; cf. Hopper 2017a, 132; Le Strange 1905, 376–77.
19. Wilkinson *et al.* 2013, 60–63 with figs 3:37–3:41: WP 438. WP stands for waypoint.
20. Carried out by Mohammad Arman Ershadi and Mohammad Taghi Maleka. Results processed by Roger Ainslie and Mohammad Arman Ershadi.
21. See chapter 3.2.6.
22. Kiani 1982b, fig. 1.
23. Centred on UTM 40S 0369056, 4151626, at c. 148 m OD.
24. The survey was led by Hamid Omrani Rekavandi and Andrea Ricci. It is worth noting that there is an area of soil discoloration thought to represent a brick kiln and quite a number of Sasanian bricks on the slope below Fort 2.

25 At UTM 40S 0369067, 4151627.
26 Sauer *et al.* 2013, 133–55, 223–27, 244–51, 684 pl. 6:11.
27 It is hard to imagine that the water table was high enough to impede brick production.
28 Excavations directed by Dr Jebrael Nokandeh, who initiated excavation of this important feature, Hamid Omrani Rekavandi and Eberhard Sauer and supervised by Meghdad Mirmousavi, Mahshah Allah Rahmani and Silvia Perini, with key involvement of other team members and workmen. Kourosh Mohammadkhani carried out a magnetometer survey, and Mohammad Bagher Bayati a topographical survey of the installation and its surroundings. Maryam Hossein-Zadeh and Mohammad Bagher Bayati accomplished a detailed and accurate plan, whilst Silvia Perini, Mohammad Bagher Bayati and Marc Heise recorded sections.
29 Wilkinson *et al.* 2013, 60–62 with figs 3:37–3:39.
30 Kiani 1982b, fig. 1; Wilkinson *et al.* 2013, 60 fig. 3:37 (note that the scale of the latter figure is not quite correct).
31 See chapter 4.6.3, with Fig. 4.97, for an image of the terrain between the bridge and Fort 2A.
32 On top, there was soft mid-brownish clayey silt (b.055), with a more or less horizontal upper boundary – as opposed to alluvial layers to the south of b.002, which slope down, away from the wall (b.002) and towards the centre of the valley. Not just horizontal layering, but also the composition of the deposit, provides clues as to the possible history of the hydraulic feature. We noticed a high proportion of large river pebbles in the upper section of the deposit (b.055), but no pebbles in the lower section (the bottom 50 cm of b.055). Perhaps this indicates that the void was not hermetically sealed and that flood water and sediments were washed in: initially fine-grained sediments, perhaps when water-flow was slow or the inlet high enough above the river bed to prevent stones from being washed in; later, rapid water-flow may have washed in large pebbles perhaps during episodes of flooding. That the deposit was clayey silt rather than pure clay also allows for the possibility that this is redeposited material. Our observations are tentative as the sondage reached well under the water table, impeding recording. Charcoal confined to the lower part of b.055 indicates human activity nearby.
33 See chapter 19.
34 An elderly visitor told the team on 26 October 2015 that a similarly monumental structure had been visible on the opposite side (i.e. the right bank/west side) of the river, but was buried as a result of a mountain collapsing (a landslide)? Yet, nobody else seems to remember this postulated massive landslide.
35 Note that we spotted and corrected a small error (of, on average, c. 40 cm too low) in some total-station elevation measurements in 2015 in the text, tables and the drawings. Whilst we are reasonably confident that the elevation figures are now reliable, in terms of relative height, it cannot be excluded that the odd inaccuracy has been overlooked.
36 See chapter 3.2.2.
37 See chapter 19.
38 E.g. Bidwell and Holbrook 1989, *passim*; Gazzola 1963, 146 no. 202, 177 no. 261, 178 no. 265.
39 Dörner 1987, 57–58, 70–71, 160–61; Mitford 2018, 47–49, 107–11, pl. 2; O'Connor 1993, 127–29.
40 Adams and Hansen 1968, 59–63 with fig. 2.
41 Bidwell and Holbrook 1989, *passim*, especially 134–35; Morgan 2015, especially 48–50.
42 Morgan 2015, especially 48–49; Bidwell and Holbrook 1989.
43 E.g. Adams and Hansen 1968, fig. 1, pp. 59–63; Graadt van Roggen 1905; Huff 1990; Kleiss 1976b, 136–39 with figs 6–7, pls 27.1–2, 28.1; 2015, 157–59, 162–64; Reuther 1938, 570–72; cf. Pope 1938b, pls 261A–262B; Safar 1974; cf. Altaweel *et al.* 2012, 16; Bier 1988; O'Connor 1993, 130; Ghirshman 1971, 30, pl. IX; Huff 1974, 157, 175 fig. 14.
44 Huff 1990; cf. chapter 19.
45 Bode 1849, 404–06; cf. Sauer *et al.* 2013, 637–38, 645–46 nos 90–91. The Sadd-e Garkaz bears some resemblance to the dam at Nehavand (Kleiss 1976b, 139–40 with fig. 8, pl. 28.2). See also Figs 3.68–3.69.
46 Fiey 1967, 11; Huff 1990.
47 See chapter 7.
48 See chapter 3.2.6 and Wilkinson *et al.* 2013, 60–63.
49 Aliev *et al.* 2006, 173.
50 See Sauer *et al.* 2020b, 888–90.
51 Kuznetsov 1990, 121–26, 182–86 figs 37–41, 192 fig. 47; Albegova 2010, especially 37; Albegova and Vereshchinskii-Babailov 2010, 133, pls between pp. 128/129. We are very grateful to Professor Dmitry S. Korobov for having drawn our attention, at a workshop at Oxford organised by Dr Irina Shingiray, to this wall, its possible Sasanian origins and its mortar construction (resembling the late antique walls in Dariali Gorge), as well as to Nick Evans who alerted us to Albegova's work on an earlier occasion. See Vakhusht'i (ed. and trans. Brosset 1842, 444–45; cf. Kuznetsov 1990, 121) for the eighteenth-century testimony. We are grateful to Lana Chologauri for confirming that Vakhusht'i clearly states that the gate employed mortar, but that it is ambiguous as to whether the arch spanned the river or was next to the river. See Sauer *et al.* 2020b, 890, 923 no. 269 for further discussion.
52 See chapter 6.2.1.
53 We considered the possibility that a triangular projection south-east of wall b.002, and at a c. 45-degree-angle to the wall (Figs 3.14 and 3.18), was the foundation of a buttress. Masonry barrages are often abutted by buttresses downstream or by earth banks downstream, as well as sometimes upstream, to counterbalance water pressure and prevent dams from bursting or collapsing: e.g. the Roman dam at Böget in Asia, consisting of a 2.50 m wide wall with earth dams on both sides: Garbrecht 1991, 98 Fig. 9. The Harbaqa dam in Syria is provided with buttresses: Calvet and Geyer 1992, 84–85 figs 44–45. See also Baratte *et al.* 2014, *passim*; Hodge 2000. In the light of the 2015 excavations, it seems, however, clear that we are dealing with a bridge. Whilst any soil bank could easily have been washed away, the distance between the two abutments is too great to allow for their interpretation as dam. A buttress, however, would also have enhanced the stability of a bridge.
54 A natural alluvial deposit of soft yellowish brown clay (b.042), what appears to be a mixture of alluvial deposition and hill-wash (b.091, soft mid-reddish brown sandy clay) and loess (b.043, mid-yellowish grey clayey silt).
55 Soft mid-brownish grey sandy clay with brick fragments (b.039) and soft mid-yellowish to mid-greyish brown sandy

silt and sandy clay (b.038 = b.040), the sand component pointing to accelerated water-flow, probably built up in the wake of further human interference with the natural vegetation. B.044, mid-yellowish brown clayey silt, and b.045, mid-yellowish brown clay, represent more fine-grained deposits, following the gradient of the valley, the latter probably an alluvial deposit. Erosion appears to have continued at a rapid pace, and soft mid-yellowish brown sandy clay with brick fragments of up to 13 cm diameter (b.084), soft yellowish brown silty clay (b.073) with lenses of iron-stained soft mid-yellowish brown silty sand (b.074a and b) and very soft reddish brown clayey silt (b.072) successively built up.

56 See chapter 19.
57 Note that sections have been numbered solely to facilitate cross-referencing; the sequence is arbitrary and does not reflect the relative date of excavation or recording or any other chronological or spatial sequence.
58 From bottom to top: b.145, b.139 and b.131.
59 B.143, b.142, b.141, b.138, b.140, b.137, b.135, b.134, b.132, b. 133, b.130, b.128, b.127 and b. 126.
60 B.146 and b.144.
61 B.136 and b.129.
62 See chapter 3.2.7, with Table 3.3.
63 The sequence is as follows: a thin band of dark grey clay (b.010) with some charcoal, mid-grey clay with iron-staining and charcoal (b.031), a band of loose mid-brownish yellow coarse sand (b.012), soft mid-brown clay (b.011), a band of very soft mid-yellowish brown clayey silt (b.013), yellowish-brown clayey silt (b.014), mid-reddish grey clay (b.015), soft mid-yellowish grey clay (b.016), soft mid-yellowish grey clay with frequent charcoal inclusions (b.017), soft iron-stained mid-yellowish grey clay with some fragments of charcoal (b.018), very soft mid-yellowish grey silt (b.019), soft mid-grey clay with intensive iron-staining (b.020), soft mid-grey clay with occasional iron staining (b.021) and soft mid-brownish yellow clayey silt, again with intensive iron-staining (b.022).
64 There was much disturbance through robber trenches and, probably, riverine erosion upstream of the western abutment (section 1: Fig. 3.43), which is likely to explain the absence of a similar alluvial sequence in this area, leaving aside the early alluvial deposits between walls b.003 and b.155 and later deposits b.075, b.066 and b.065.
65 See Table 3.3.
66 Soft mid-brownish grey clay (b.237), soft to firm mid-brownish yellow grey clay (b.238), soft to firm mid-yellowish brown clay (b.239), soft mid-brownish yellow clay (b.240) and soft mid-yellow clay (b.241).
67 See chapter 3.2.5.
68 It is worth noting that the base of the alluvial deposits has not been reached in this sondage. The lowest deposit within the sondage, iron-stained soft mid-brownish grey clay (b.154) has yielded a minute quantity of charcoal from a floated soil sample. Flotation of a c. 10 litre sample by Lyudmila Shumilovskikh yielded a small quantity of charcoal (see chapter 21, Table 21.3). Above, there is a sequence of deposits, some more clayey and alluvial, others more silty or sandy and evidently containing a higher contents of washed-in soil, some with visible charcoal flecks and others without: soft mid-yellowish brown silt with charcoal (b.153), soft mid-greyish brown sandy silt (b.152), soft mid-greyish brown silty clay with charcoal (b.151), soft mid-brownish grey sandy clay (b.150), soft brownish grey sandy clay (b.112), iron-stained soft mid-yellowish grey clay with charcoal (b.111), soft mid-yellowish grey sandy silt (b.110), soft mid-brownish grey clay (b.109), iron-stained soft mid-brownish grey soft clay with charcoal (b.108), soft mid-yellowish grey sandy silt (b.106) with a lens of iron-stained soft mid-brownish grey sandy silt (b.107), soft mid-yellowish grey sandy silt (b.105), soft mid-yellowish grey clay (b.104) and soft mid-yellowish sandy clay (b.103). B.102, soft mid-brownish grey clay, is the highest horizontal clay deposit and suggests that there was standing water at the time. The three deposits (b.101, b.100 and b.099) above are more silty and sandy, but still form thin horizontal bands, suggesting that the pool of water was drying up: soft mid-yellowish grey clayey silt with charcoal (b.101), soft mid-yellowish grey silty sand (b.100) and soft greyish brown silty sand (b.099). None of the uppermost six deposits (b.098 to b.093), whilst clayey, are layered horizontally, and they will have built up as a result of waterborne erosion.
69 Wilkinson *et al.* 2013, 62, cf. 60–63, with figs 3:37, 3:40–3:41; note that the scale on fig. 3:37 is not quite correct; see Wilkinson *et al.* 2013, 128 for the location of WP731; see also Google Earth.
70 Survey by Emanuele Intagliata, Silvia Perini and other members of our team; pottery identified by Emanuele Intagliata, Jebrael Nokandeh, Hamid Omrani Rekavandi and Silvia Perini.
71 See chapters 18.3.2–18.3.3 and 18.9. See also chapter 20.3.2 for poorly stratified equid and goat bones from alluvial layer b.143.
72 Radiocarbon dates kindly supplied by the Scottish Universities Environmental Research Centre (SUERC) and Poznan Radiocarbon Laboratory. Further samples were submitted but proved undatable. Plant remains identified by Dr Lyudmila Shumilovskikh (cf. chapter 21). For archaeomagnetic dates, see chapter 22.
73 Tabari 1.827 = trans. Bosworth 1999, 29–30; Ferdowsi, *Shahnama* C.1420 = ed. and trans. Mohl 1866, 392–95 = trans. Warner and Warner 1912, 298–99; cf. Farrokh 2015, 91–92; Favro 2019; Huff 1990; Maresca 2019, 211–12, 220; Shukurov 2019, 65.
74 Aliev *et al.* 2006, 173; see also Henning 1954; Maresca 2019, 212; Miri 2012, 106; and Mittertrainer 2020, 94, 126–29 on Sasanian bridge construction in the fifth century, and Tabari 1.897 = trans. Bosworth 1999, 157 on the rebuilding of Sasanian bridges in the sixth century.
75 See chapter 21.2.3.2.
76 Wilkinson *et al.* 2013, 60–63. In 2014, our landscape team, led by Hamid Omrani Rekavandi and Andrea Ricci, was able to confirm the existence of this canal.
77 Sauer *et al.* 2013, 388 with fig. 13:4; see Hartnell 2014, 195 with fig. 4 for animal- and water-powered mills near Istakhr; cf. Rahimi-Laridjani 1988, 239.
78 Alizadeh *et al.* 2004, 78–79; Graadt van Roggen 1905; Hartung and Kuros 1987, 231–32, 237–38, 245–52; Huff 1990; Kleiss 2015, 157–60, 162–64; Planhol 1989; Schnitter 1987, 11–13; Vogel 1987, 50.

79 E.g. Garbrecht 1987, *passim*; Hartung and Kuros 1987, 239–44; 253–74; Kleiss 1993a, 235–38; 2015, 221–30; Schnitter 1987, 14–17; Wilkinson 2009a, 64 fig. 59, 67 fig. 62.
80 Dieulafoy 1889, 105–12, pls X–XIII; Graadt van Roggen 1905, 174–207; Hartung and Kuros 1987, 238, 245–50; Maresca 2019, 212–14, 221–22 figs 4–5; Stein 1940, 171–74; Wenke 1977, 134, 137–38, pl. III; cf. Adams and Hansen 1968, 59–61. See also Kleiss 1993b, 142–45, pls 36.2–38.2 and 2015, 159–60, 164 on the Band-e Bahman dam thought to be late Sasanian or early Islamic. Such techniques were widely applied in Late Antiquity and in arid territories within the Roman Empire rivers were also dammed to feed canals: e.g. Calvet and Geyer 1992, *passim*.
81 Darles *et al.* 2014; Mouton and Schiettecatte 2014, 135–37; Robin 2012, 267–84; Russo 2018.
82 See Sauer *et al.* 2013, 163–73.
83 Howard-Johnston 1995, 188–91; 2014, especially 148; 2021, 313, 316; cf. Comfort and Marciak 2018, 117–18; Daryaee 2017, 398; Sauer *et al.* 2017, 259; Theophanes Confessor, *Chronographia* AM 6118 = ed. Boor 1883, 321, 324–25 = trans. Mango and Scott 1997, 451, 453.
84 See Ammianus Marcellinus 24.2.1–2 (cf. Den Boeft *et al.* 2002, 29–33), Libanius, *Orationes* 18.219 and Zosimus 3.15.1–2 on impregnable Persian fortifications on islands in the Euphrates (cf. Dabrowa 2007, 239; Edwell 2020, 223–27, 253; Gregory and Kennedy 1985a, 146–55; 1985b, 403–04; McLynn 2020, 300–02; Morley 2016, 19; Rosen 2006, 352–53) and Zosimus 3.17.4 on a canal used to enhance urban defences. See also Ammianus Marcellinus 24.8.2 (cf. Den Boeft *et al.* 2002, 227) on raging swollen streams causing great difficulties to Julian's army and Libanius, *Orationes* 18.232–34 and Zosimus 3.16.1–2 on canals impeding progress.
85 Ammianus Marcellinus 24.3.10–11 (cf. Den Boeft *et al.* 2002, 89–93; Edwell 2020, 224, 227; McLynn 2020, 303–04; Rosen 2006, 354); Libanius, *Orationes* 18.222–27; Zosimus 3.19.3–4; cf. Kettenhofen 2011, 244–45.
86 See chapter 3.2.3.
87 See chapter 21.2.3.2.
88 See chapter 22.
89 An old man living locally told Dr Jebrael Nokandeh that he had seen the wall survive much to a much higher level. There is no evidence from our sections for very recent robbing, but this may have focused on parts of the monument elsewhere.
90 See chapter 4.6.
91 Omrani Rekavandi *et al.* 2008c, 15; Sauer *et al.* 2013, 14–15, 674 pl. 2:2; Wilkinson *et al.* 2013, 64–68.
92 Sauer *et al.* 2013, 220–21, 685 pl. 6:10; cf. chapter 4.6.3.
93 Sauer *et al.* 2013, 637–38; Wilkinson *et al.* 2013, 69–80.

4

Forts on the Gorgan Wall

4.1. Fort 2

4.1.1. Introduction

Geophysical survey in 2006 in Fort 4, followed by excavations in the same year and in 2007, has for the first time revealed the plan of barracks in a fort on the Great Wall, as well as providing insights into its occupation and chronology. Yet limited time enabled us to excavate no more than the corners of two adjacent rooms in Trench H in 2006, followed by excavation of a larger plot between two barracks (Trench J) in 2006–2007. To gain a better understanding of the architecture and nature of occupation, it seemed essential to excavate a range of rooms completely. We could have returned to Fort 4, but there would have been no certainty then that the results were representative for the forts on the Gorgan Wall as a whole. We decided therefore to focus on another fort and eventually opted for Fort 2. Our choice was based on the following criteria:

- Unlike Fort 4, the largest fort on the wall covering some 5.5 ha and containing eight barracks, Fort 2

Fig. 4.1: Fort 2 overlooking the Sari Su River Valley. Drone image by Davit Naskidashvili and the joint project.

belongs to the smallest and most common category of forts on the lowland section of the Great Wall, with just two barracks. It thus represents a different category of fort.

- It seemed fairly well preserved, with two distinct parallel long mounds on either side of a central hollow way, undoubtedly two barracks flanking a central road.

- Unlike some other forts, there were no known modern graves, that would have damaged archaeological structures and impeded fieldwork, on the fort platform.

- It overlooks the Sari Su River Valley and controlled (with Fort 2A) this river crossing and offered wide views over the surrounding landscape, suggesting that it was a strategically significant place.

It thus seemed an ideal site to explore, differing in size and location from the best-known installation on the wall, Fort 4 with its eight barracks at a mid-point between river crossings. The fort and its surroundings have been surveyed by Hamid Omrani Rekavandi and Tony Wilkinson in 2007.[1] It was visited by Mohammad Arman Ershadi, Jebrael Nokandeh, Hamid Omrani Rekavandi, Bardia Shabani and Eberhard Sauer on 12 January 2013. Fieldwork took place over three successive seasons, in 2014, 2015 and 2016.

4.1.2. Remote, pedestrian, magnetometer and topographical survey of Fort 2

4.1.2.1. The fort defences

Not only the barracks, but also the regularly spaced towers are visible on the ground as hillocks along the west, south and east sides of the fort (Fig. 4.8). The 1969 CORONA image (Fig. 4.2) is similarly clear: there are two long mounds in the interior, four distinct interval towers (including the two towers flanking the gate) in

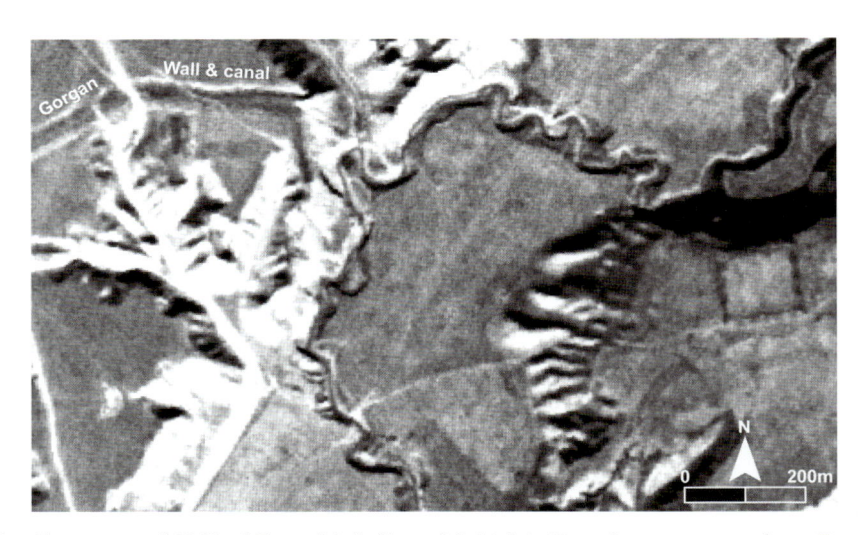

Fig. 4.2: CORONA Satellite image of 1969 of Forts 2A (left), and 2 (right). Note the tower mounds on Fort 2's walls and the two oblong mounds/barracks in the interior (Courtesy of the USGS).

Fig. 4.3: Google Earth Image of 19 March 2012 of Forts 2 (right) and 2A (dotted with robber pits, left) (Image © DigitalGlobe).

the south, three each on the west and east sides and distinct corner towers in the south-west and the south-east. Twelve tower mounds in total are thus visible, not counting bulges at the intersection between the western and eastern fort walls and the Great Wall (perhaps just modern access ramps for machinery, but more probably, as explored below, corner towers damaged by machinery where the fort abuts the Great Wall). In the light of their symmetrical arrangement, we may assume that these are all towers, excluding solely any further towers on the (as always) robbed-out Great Wall.

A complete magnetometer survey of Fort 2 and its surroundings was carried out by Dr Kourosh Mohammadkhani and Soroush Mohammadkhani.[2] The survey (Figs 4.4–4.5) revealed clearly the towers of the fort on the south side and, less distinctly but still discernibly, on the west and east sides. In the south-west, there is a strong anomaly which is likely to mark the position of a corner tower; in the south-east there is a much fainter anomaly which, whilst indistinct, is of the right size and location for another corner tower. Average spacing between interim towers, and between interim and corner towers, appears to be c. 28–29 m centre to centre on average on the west and east sides (marginally less than the 30–31 m at Fort 4[3]), c. 25–26 m on the south side and that between the towers flanking the south gate approximately half this distance. Narrow spacing of gate towers is characteristic for forts on the Gorgan Wall as well as some Sasanian campaign bases (though perhaps not for the earliest campaign bases).[4] The interim and gate towers of Fort 2 were projecting U-shaped towers of some 7 m diameter. The frequent spacing of towers at c. 28–31 m intervals (centre to centre), though occasionally less, may suggest that the aim was to position them at neat distances of c. 100 feet – as quite common in Sasanian architecture.[5] The narrow distance (edge to edge) of c. 21–24 m, in some cases just 18 m, between towers (and probably under 6 m between gate towers) ensured furthermore that no approaching enemy could evade the most effective 'firing' range of archers stationed on the towers.[6] At the mid-point between two towers, an assailant was no more than 40 feet at most from either tower and was at risk of being simultaneously targeted from the left, right and multiple angles by bowmen on the towers and the fort walls in front.

On the outside, the towers are defined by a distinct white line, approximately 1 to 2 m wide. One notices that these lines are not continuous, but dotted. The darker (more magnetic?) gaps in the dotted line are some 2 m apart. Do these white U-shaped lines represent the outer mud-brick wall? Dr Christophe Benech suggested to us that surveying on a slope could explain such an interrupted line.[7] Excavations add strength to his hypothesis that U-shaped dotted white lines follow slopes; in Trench c, they extend beyond the edge of the tower, showing that they are not outer walls. On the inside of the towers one finds dark, i.e. more magnetic, anomalies of semi-circular shape. Excavation so far suggests that only a solid core of mud-brick appears to survive.[8] When dried in the sun, the mud-brick will have acquired magnetic properties, and this may account for the towers being more magnetic than the surrounding areas.

As in all forts surveyed to date, by far the strongest anomaly is formed by the Great Wall itself. Built of fired

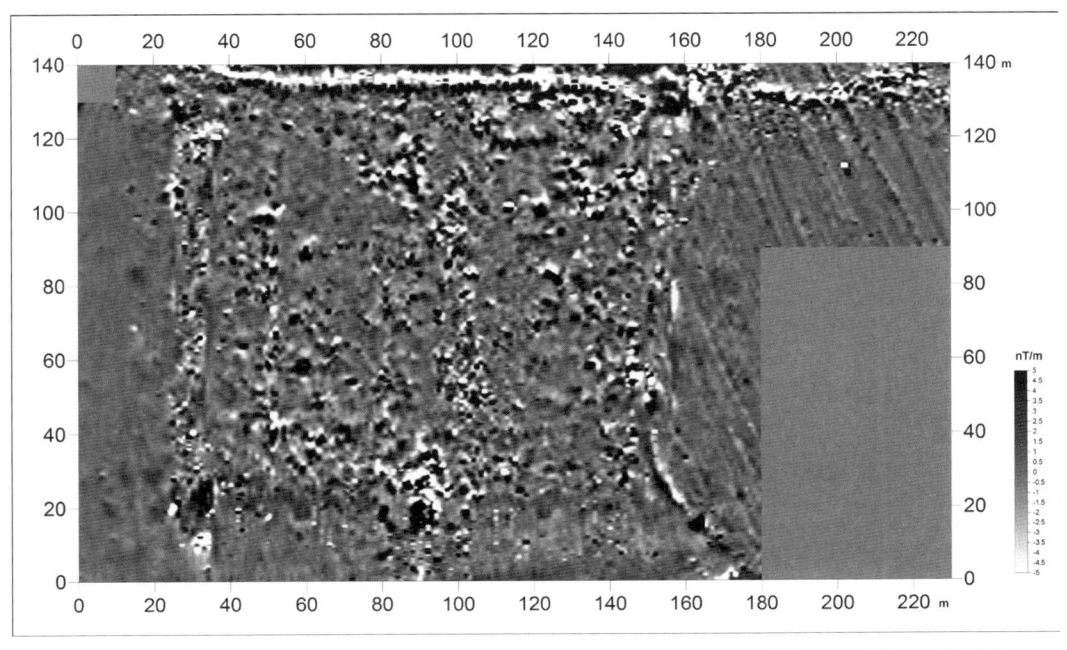

Fig. 4.4: Magnetometer survey of Fort 2 and its surroundings by Dr Kourosh Mohammadkhani and Soroush Mohammadkhani.

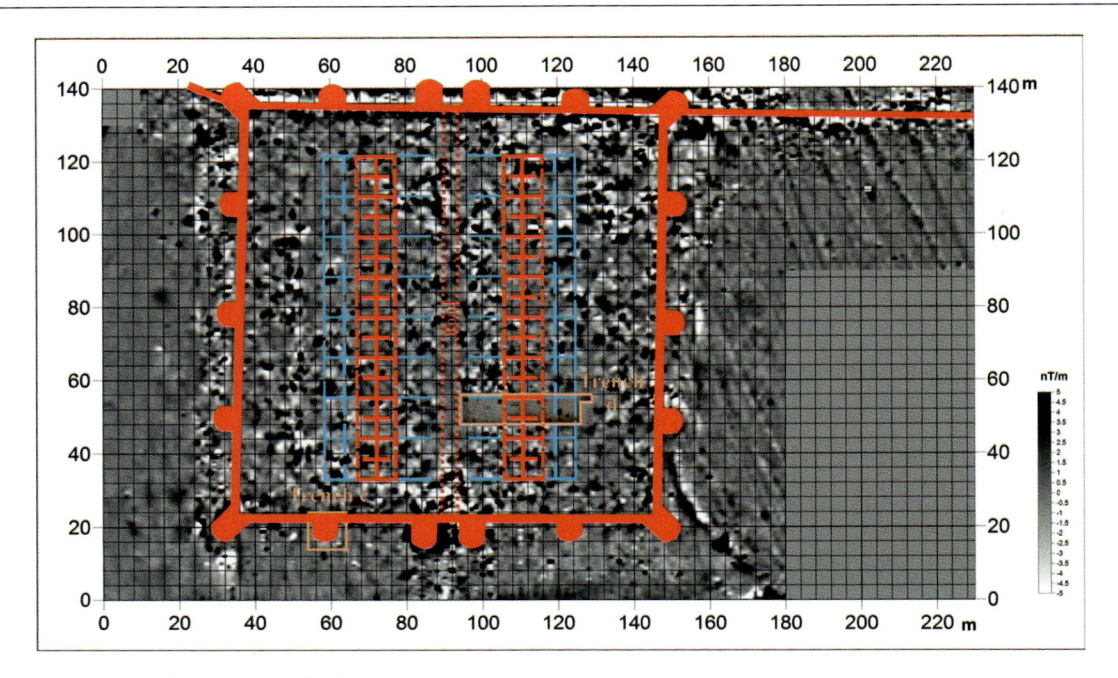

Fig. 4.5: Interpretative plot. Note that the fort defences and towers showed up clearly, were selectively explored via Trench c and are almost certainly correct, though the exact location and dimensions of features could differ by a metre or two here and there. There are potential faint traces of corner bastions in the north-west and north-east (top left and right), but these may be heavily disturbed through modern access ramps. Corner towers, as well as hypothetical interim towers along the Great Wall, have been plotted based on the assumption of a symmetrical arrangement. The location of the barracks (in red) and the later annexes (in blue) is based largely on our excavations in Trench d and satellite imagery showing that they were arranged symmetrically (as was also the case at other forts on the wall). The barracks did not show up clearly in the magnetometer plot, even if there is clearly much magnetic material in and around these buildings plus the odd line marking a mud-brick wall.

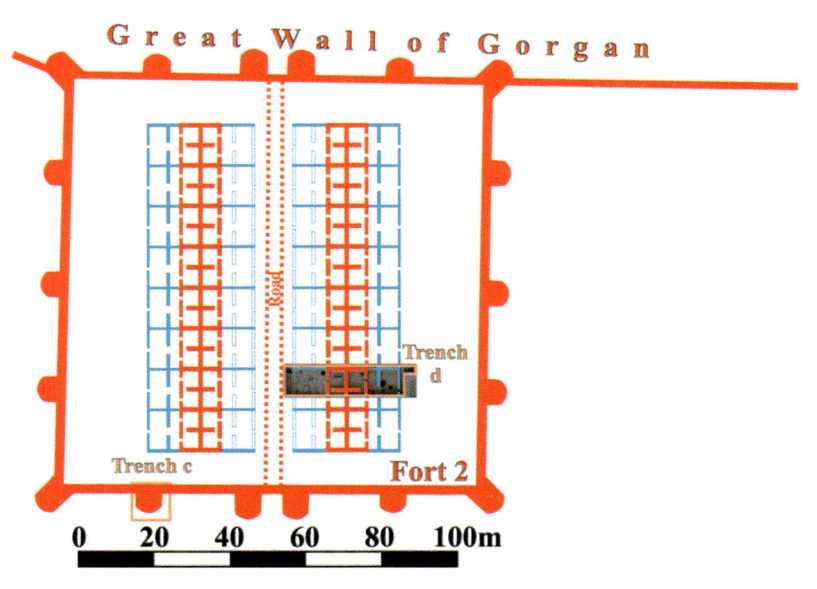

Fig. 4.6: Interpretative plot without geophysical survey. Hypothetical towers on the side of the Great Wall were probably built of fired bricks and have therefore been completely robbed out. There might be traces of the north-west and north-east corner bastions (here assumed to be at a 135-degree angle to the sides of the fort) in the magnetometer survey, satellite imagery and topography, but they are obscured by modern access ramps for agricultural machinery. Note that it is also possible that they were aligned at a right angle or parallel to the Great Wall. No towers are plotted on the Great Wall away from the fort, as we lack information on location and spacing.

Fig. 4.7: Fort 2 with its towers in the west (top) and east (bottom) showing up as distinct hillocks, overlooking the Sari Su River Valley in the north (right). Drone image by Davit Naskidashvili and the joint project.

bricks and subsequently robbed out, one sees the usual myriad of red brick fragments on the ground, which account for the strong and irregular band of magnetic material. Unsurprisingly, there are no traces of towers on the Great Wall. This is probably the result of systematic robbing to the foundations. It seems a near certainty that the enemy side of the forts on the Gorgan Wall would have been provided with towers, too, for defence and surveillance. Interestingly, however, there are traces of the fort platform bulging out in the fort's north-east corner and, less clearly, in its north-west corner in topography, aerial imagery and magnetometer survey (Figs 4.2–4.7, 4.9). This may be circumstantial evidence for the existence of projecting towers at the points where the fort abuts the Great Wall.

The evidence is clearer in the case of Fort 7 where one observes prominent U-shaped bulges at the points where this fort abuts the Gorgan Wall (Fig. 4.102). Both bulges, like the alignment of the Great Wall, are covered in robber pits, suggesting that Fort 7 once had projecting U-shaped corner towers, built of fired bricks, on the side facing the enemy. The north-eastern bastion appears to have been at a c. 135° angle to the fort platform (to judge by the area covered in robber trenches on top of the bulge), whereas the angle of south-western bulge is harder to determine (oblique to parallel to the Great Wall). The Gorgan Wall between these two corner bastions at Fort 7 was heavily robbed, but it is impossible to identify the location of any interim towers on the basis of pit distribution.[9]

The lack of clear evidence for forts having interval towers on the side of the Great Wall, as opposed to all well-preserved forts demonstrably boasting towers on the three other sides, is unquestionably the result of different building materials having been used: un-robbed mud-bricks, decayed and transformed into earth mounds, as opposed to robbed-out reusable fired bricks. For similar reasons, no traces of a gate would necessarily survive, if there had been one in the north. We thus cannot be sure whether or not there was a gate here, but there are three arguments to suggest that there was little, if any, traffic in and out of Fort 2's north side:

– The high magnetic anomaly following the robber trench along the Great Wall runs through without any obvious gap or change in width.

– The fort faced a steep slope on this side, at the base of which there would have been a large water reservoir in the sixth to seventh centuries.[10] Anybody wishing to advance in a northerly direction would have faced significant obstacles, especially in the later phases of occupation.

– There is no evidence of a hollow way on the approaches to the fort's north walls on the satellite

Fig. 4.8: The tower mounds on the west and east sides of Fort 2 are also distinctly visible from a terrestrial perspective: view of the fort's west side, looking south.

images or on the ground, suggesting that there at least never was heavy traffic through a hypothetical gate. (Admittedly, there is also no trace of an access route on the southern approaches to the fort, which must have seen much traffic, but where, unlike in the uncultivable slope in the north, ploughing may have erased or masked any remnants of routeways.)

Whilst there is little doubt that there were towers on the side of the Great Wall, we do not know whether there were six, two corner towers, two interval towers and two towers flanking a gate (as on the opposite side), or maybe just five, two corner and three interval towers, but no gate. The former seems more likely, as Sasanian military compounds in the Gorgan Plain tend to be remarkably, if not perfectly, symmetrical. Whilst, indeed, no major traffic route is likely to have led up the steep slope on the fort's north side, a gate would have been advantageous and would have facilitated access to the stream or reservoir north of the fort. It seems probable that there was a gate symmetrical to that on the opposite side, but also possible that there was no more than a postern gate or none at all. In the former case, the fort would have had 18 towers in total, in the latter only 17.

As usual, the disintegrated mud-brick architecture of the fort has created a platform. The plan of the fort resembled a square. Its interior measured c. 108–109 m (west–east) by c. 109–111 m (north–south), i.e. c. 1.2 ha, excluding the (c. 2.50 m wide) walls and the projecting towers. Patches of high magnetic anomalies all around the edges and slopes probably represent material fallen off the fort platform or the collapsed fort walls. This is not unique to Fort 2. A higher concentration of high magnetic anomalies along the three fort walls away from the Great Wall has also been observed at Forts 4,[11] 9[12] and 16.[13] Forts 1 and 5 failed to yield clear evidence for the use of magnetic material in the walls other than the Great Wall, but it is hard to tell whether this was the result of the lower quality of the survey (in the case of Fort 1) or its limited extent (in the case of Fort 5) or real absence.[14] The west, east and south walls of Fort 2, whilst built mainly of sun-dried bricks, may have employed some fired bricks, even if much more sparingly than the solid Great Wall. It is possible that fired bricks were used for the most vulnerable rain-exposed parts of the outer walls, notably the parapet, at Fort 2 and other Sasanian forts on the Gorgan Plain.

4.1.2.2. Interior occupation

Patches of high magnetic anomalies are also evident in the interior of the fort. These probably represent a scatter of bricks and maybe other ceramic material. Features of clear geometric shape are far and few between. A circular high magnetic anomaly of c. 8 m diameter near the mid-point of the platform (centred on c. 90 m east and 74 m north in the geophysics grid: Figs 4.4–4.5) may have been caused by debris accumulating in a silted-up ring ditch around a post-Sasanian burial mound (as also observed in Fort 4).[15] Some other less distinct features may represent other burial monuments or possible pits ploughed flat, but are too uncertain to merit discussion.

Any such features, and most notably the brick scatter, mask any mud-brick architecture underneath. Whilst CORONA and Google Earth satellite images show clearly that there were two barrack mounds, symmetrically arranged on both sides of a central road, unmistakable traces failed to emerge during geophysical survey. There are possible discontinuous north–south-aligned white lines, of similar width and low magnetic properties to those alongside the outer walls of the projecting towers, but they are far less distinct. One such line is c. 115–117 m east, visible from c. 53–111 m north (Figs 4.4–4.5). Recognised and attributed to the eastern

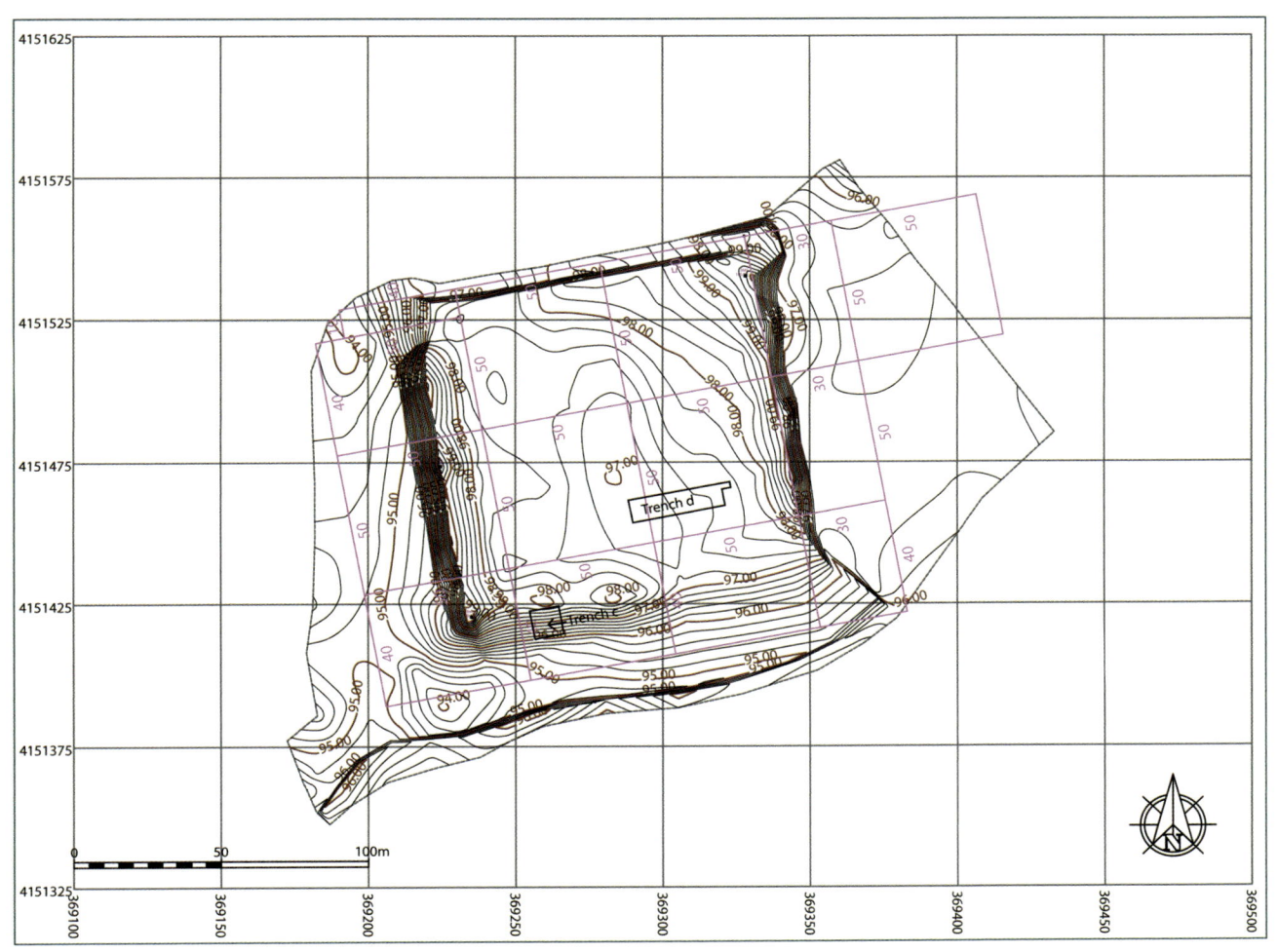

Fig. 4.9: Topographical survey of Fort 2 by Mohammad Bagher Bayati in 2014, featuring the geophysics grids as well as our trenches. (Trench d was plotted onto the plan later.) Note that the heights relate to a benchmark for the 2014 season set an arbitrary level of 100 m. They are valid for Trench c. For Trench d, excavated in 2015–2016, a new benchmark was set up: 100 m in 2015–2016 corresponds to c. 97.30 m in 2014. It has not been possible to link these benchmarks to the sea level, but they will enable the reader to establish the relative elevation of finds and structures at Fort 2.

barrack block prior to excavation (even if we had been unable to predict correctly which of the parallel north–south walls it represented), Trench d proved subsequently that the eastern wall of the main barrack block (in red on Fig. 4.5) indeed follows this line. This linear anomaly showed up as a dashed rather than a continuous line, the interruptions marking in part disturbances and in part door openings. The segments of this dashed line and gaps between are too faint to inspire confidence that our interpretation is sufficiently accurate, and we have therefore decided not plot them on our plans. There is no clear evidence of the middle wall or any west–east-running walls branching off it. Even more guesswork is involved in any attempt to find traces of the western barrack block on the plot. Whilst there are possible north–south lines also west of the road, they are even less clearly defined, and it is uncertain whether or not they are related to the western barracks. The collapse mound visible on satellite imagery leaves, however, no doubt that there was a second long building west of the road, parallel to its counterpart on the opposite side. Not even the central hollow way, whilst still clearly visible, is easy to make out. The central road and the approximate area of the barrack blocks appear to show on average lower magnetic readings than the land in between and around the inner edges of the fort (though the pattern is far from clear and uniform) – perhaps reflecting, as suggested by excavations in Fort 4, that magnetic debris were preferentially discarded outdoors. Other activities which could have contributed to heat-induced magnetisation of the soil, notably baking and cooking, probably took place both outdoors and indoors. (And our subsequent excavations in Trench d certainly unearthed multiple ovens and fireplaces within the barracks.[16])

Fig. 4.10: The projecting mud-brick tower in Trench c. Each red and white segment of the scales measures 50 cm.

A topographical survey of the fort and its surroundings (Fig. 4.9) was carried out by Mohammad Bagher Bayati. It shows the contours of the fort platform clearly, but the central road is marked only by an indistinct depression in the central and southern parts of the platform. Some of the towers are also traceable, but others are not visible all, and neither can we discern the barracks. This is probably a result of them having been almost ploughed flat (even if still visible as very shallow long mounds today) and the limited number of points measured in.

4.1.2.3. Results

Our surveys revealed no significant new insights into the interior layout of forts on the Gorgan Wall, but they mark a milestone in detecting a Sasanian fort's defensive architecture. Previously, we had to rely on visual inspection, topographical survey or satellite imagery to detect towers, and satellite images often fail to reveal the towers of forts even where these are still visible on the ground (as opposed to towers of campaign bases which are often more easily detectable). Drone images in low sunlight more often show tower mounds distinctly, e.g. at Forts 2, 4, 14, 27 and 30.[17] Whilst these survey techniques often allowed us to establish number and spacing of towers, none of them could reveal the exact dimensions and architecture of individual towers. The late Mohammad Kiani has excavated one tower of similar dimensions at Fort 13.[18] This is the first time that geophysical survey has revealed towers on a Gorgan Wall fort, and it has done so in remarkable detail and clarity. Topography facilitated this breakthrough: the gentle slopes of Fort 2, unlike the steep slopes of Fort 4, could be surveyed. Yet, despite its even gentler slopes, our magnetometer survey at Fort 16 failed to detect any towers.[19] The success is in part at least the result of the skills of the survey team, notably Dr Kourosh Mohammadkhani, in part perhaps also the result of ground conditions and preservation that can vary greatly from site to site.

4.1.3. Excavation of an interval tower of Fort 2 (Trench c)

One of the interval towers (the western interval tower on the fort's south side: Figs 4.4–4.6) was explored via excavation (Trench c), directed by Esmail Safari Tamak in 2014.[20] We found a projecting U-shaped tower whose dimension (c. 7 m wide and projecting by c. 5.50 m beyond the outer face of the fort wall) matched that indicated by prior survey. The fort's outer wall was also within the limits of the trench. No bricks were observed in the northernmost 20 cm of the trench,

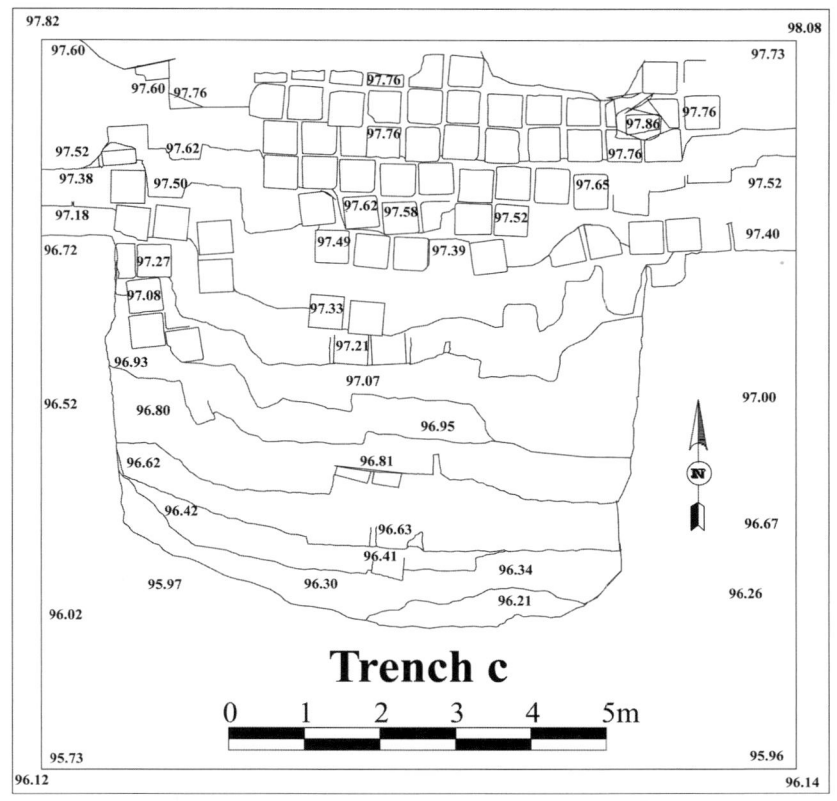

Fig. 4.11: Plan of Trench c by Maryam Hossein-Zadeh.

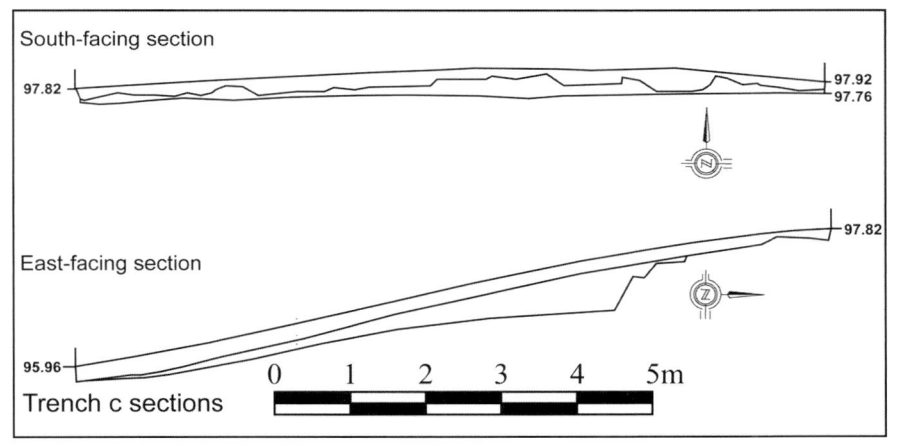

Fig. 4.12: Sections of Trench c by Maryam Hossein-Zadeh.

suggesting that we found the wall's northern edge. If so, it was c. 2.60 m wide, but without further excavation we cannot exclude that it could have been wider and that bricks in the northernmost part of the trench were not recognised or preserved only at a deeper level. Tureng Tappeh's outer walls were of a similar width, measuring some 2.20–3.00 m across.[21] This wall and the U-shaped tower were built, as we had correctly surmised, of mud-brick. These bricks varied in dimensions and shape; most of them were square and measured 42–45 cm across;

unusually, there was also a rectangular brick of c. 38 × 45 cm size. The tower had a solid core. It is likely that there would have been one or more habitable storey(s) above. All mud-bricks appear to be *in situ* and are part of the solid foundations. Whilst no occupation layers survive within the tower, we found a blue glass bead (c.002/8) to the west of the tower.[22] There is no way of telling whether this was lost by an occupant of the tower, a person on patrol outside or perhaps even an outsider, e.g. during any maintenance operations.

4.1.4. The barracks in Fort 2 (Trench d)

4.1.4.1. Introduction[23]

Prior to 2015, Sasanian barracks on the Great Wall of Gorgan have been explored via excavations only once, in Fort 4 in 2006. It is, of course, possible that some of the mud-brick features unearthed in the excavations of the late Mohammad Kiani in Fort 13[24] might belong to barracks, but the published evidence does not allow us to identify any as such. In Fort 2, as pointed out above, the geophysical survey revealed no more than possible traces of barrack walls, but the satellite imagery features two unmistakable barrack mounds in typical symmetry on both sides of the central road. Trench d, laid out at a right angle to the long axis of the eastern barracks, was intended to explore the layout, chronology and nature of occupation of this building, with a view of comparing and contrasting the results to those achieved in Trench H in Fort 4. How standardised or varied was the design of Sasanian barracks on the Great Wall? Were they all built and occupied at a similar time – or were there any major differences?

Trench d was first marked out in the 2014 season, but there was no time even to start with the excavations until the next season in 2015. Initially, it measured 12 × 2 m, was subsequently extended, first by 6 m to the west and then by another 6 m as well as by 6 m to the south in the westernmost 10 m. By the end of the 2015 season, it measured 24 m west to east and 8 m north to south in the western 10 m and 2 m in the eastern 14 m, giving it a total size of 108 m².[25] It was further extended in 2016, in order to explore a complete row of rooms across a narrow section of a barrack block. Eventually, it measured 34 m west to east and 8 m north to south in the western 31 m and 2 m north to south in the eastern 3 m, increasing its total size to 254 m².[26]

In contrast to Fort 4 (Trench H), where the mud-brick walls of the barracks still stood over 3 m high, the walls survived to a height of only approximately 1 m maximum in Trench d. We cannot, of course, be certain that preservation all across Fort 2 is similar to Trench d, but the lay of the land suggests that there is probably no significant variation. The platform of Fort 2 is of much lower elevation over the natural terrain in the south and east than that of Fort 4. This may in part be the result of topography. Fort 4 is located in flat terrain, and a water supply canal led past its western side and supplied the canal along the Great Wall, as well as probably the massive moat around the fort, with water. The upcast of the moat provided plenty of material for mud-brick production and raising the surface sufficiently to prevent any intramural flooding. By contrast, Fort 2 occupied the top of a naturally well-defended and well-drained hill, with a particularly steep escarpment in the north, overlooking the deeply incised Sari Su River. It would have been impossible and unnecessary to surround it with a permanently water-filled moat. No clear traces of a ditch survive to the west and east of the fort, nor of course along the escarpment in the north, whilst there is a linear depression in the south, probably indeed representing a silted-up (dry?) ditch. The track/hollow way following it is likely to be a secondary feature. On the CORONA image (Fig. 4.2), the ditch/hollow way in the south is distinctly visible, but no more than faint traces of potential ditches are detectable in the west and east. The lesser quantity of upcast may have resulted in a lesser platform, even if the lesser quantity of upcast could in theory have been supplemented by soil extraction pits.

We do not know for certain whether Fort 2's defences and internal buildings were of lesser elevation than those of Fort 4, even if it is clear that their preserved walls and collapse mounds are of far lower elevation. Wind and waterborne erosion may have swept away more sediments on the hilltop than in the plain, but is unlikely to account solely for the substantial difference in platform elevation between the two forts. The lesser elevation of Fort 2 may be a result of fewer mud-bricks having been employed per given area and/or lesser intramural disposal of debris. The two barracks certainly survive as mounds, evidence for collapsed mud-brick architecture surviving *in situ* (as also proven by excavations in Trench d), even if flattened through recent ploughing. Modern agriculture has also damaged the south side of the fort, now forming a gentle slope, where the gate and towers have been ploughed almost flat (even if, as shown by Trench c, still surviving below the surface). Furthermore, as we will see, in the late phases of occupation (4.1–5), we find storage jars in pits cut into walls and eventually even fireplaces overlying walls. This suggests that parts of the walls were already demolished in antiquity and the bricks perhaps reused elsewhere. This may have involved partial demolition and narrowing of walls, during the building's later phase of occupation. It may in part account for the poorer preservation of the barracks in Fort 2. That the hilltop fort was safe from flooding is likely to explain not just the absence of prominent ditches on the outside, but also the poor preservation of buildings on the inside. Unlike Fort 4, lined by canals and surrounded by a water-filled moat, there was no need to raise the surface within Fort 2 by quite so much as in Fort 4 to keep floors dry. The walls at Fort 4 are abutted by deposits of over 3 m height, much of them levelling horizons and not just the collapsed upper storey of the barracks. They are thus preserved to this level, whereas those at Fort 2 are abutted and protected by lesser amounts of soil and therefore not preserved to the same height. The walls of the original barracks in Forts 2 and 4 were of almost identical width (normally c. 1.20–1.25 m), and it is perfectly possible, indeed likely, that they once rose to a similar height.

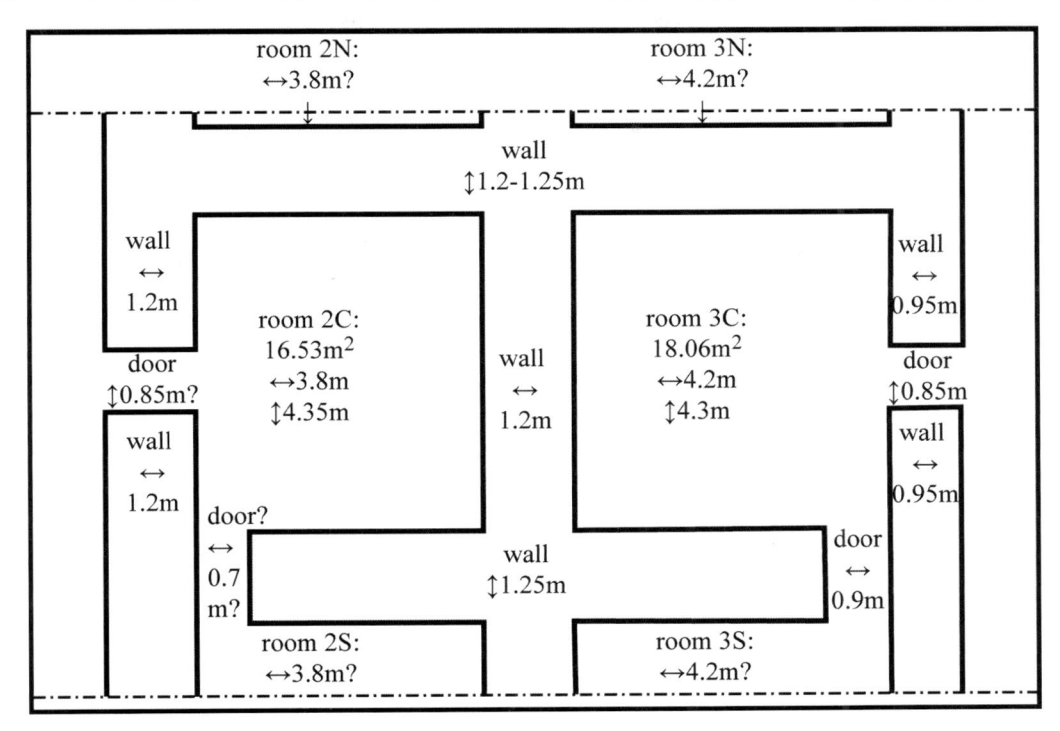

Fig. 4.13: Schematic plan of the original barracks, as far as exposed, in Trench d, assuming the original doorway of room 2C was of the same width as that of room 3C. Approximate dimensions are rounded to the nearest 5 cm. (Note that there is a minor difference in the width of some walls to the models presented below, which assume that in the original barracks all west–east walls were 1.20 m wide and all rooms had a north–south extent of 4.35 m. This makes little difference in terms of indoor space and the amount of bricks needed in construction. Models, based on the assumption of multiple small irregularities, would have been unnecessarily complex and confusing and would perhaps have conveyed a wrong sense of greater accuracy.)

4.1.4.2. Construction and layout of the barracks, phase 1 (Trench d)

4.1.4.2.1. THE ORIGINAL BARRACKS

Attributing structures and occupation layers to consecutive phases was not easy, due to deposits displaying little clear variation in colour, composition or inclusions, as is typical for this semi-arid environment. Furthermore, unlike Trench H in Fort 4, where the floor surface was raised by c. 1.50 m, there is no evidence for similarly substantial artificial levelling, nor for much organic occupation levels building up indoors during the building's active period of use. In Fort 4's barracks we similarly found no evidence for intensive rubbish deposition indoors; there was the odd lost or discarded item, such as two lamps, as well as a moderate quantity of material embedded in levelling deposits, but no indication that organic debris was allowed to build up inside. By contrast, the quantity of bones and pottery discarded in Trench J was much greater. Much or all of the area of Trench J was outdoors, though it is possible that parts of the trench in the north-east and perhaps also south-west were later covered with lightly built annexes. Outdoor deposition of debris (in Trench J) may have been the reason why it was eventually necessary to raise the floor indoors (in Trench H), so as to prevent mud, water and rubbish from being washed in.[27] The well-drained hilltop location of the smaller Fort 2, and perhaps a lesser intensity of intramural rubbish deposition in general, may have been the reason why there is no evidence for any similarly substantial levelling deposits within Trench d. Like their fellow soldiers (plus family members?) in Fort 4, those in Fort 2 appear to have been tidy, and the relative scarcity of finds need not indicate a short occupation or lesser occupation density.

Detecting successive phases was not easy, but features cutting earlier walls provide unmistakable clues to relative chronology. The sequence is, however, not always clear, and some features could belong to more than one phase. There is no evidence for any human activity prior to the construction of the barracks, other than redeposited prehistoric stone tools pre-dating the fort by millennia.[28] Whilst many individual mud-bricks could be clearly identified, the wall joints were not sufficiently well preserved to allow us to tell which wall abutted which other wall or whether bricks were interlocking. Being closer to the modern surface, plant roots and bioturbation appear to have caused greater damage to the walls in Fort 2 and the upper sections of their counterparts in Fort 4 than the lower parts of Fort 4's tall walls.

Despite all these caveats, it seems clear that mud-brick walls at Fort 2 belong to at least two different phases. The walls of rows 2 and 3 appear to have been built first. They are mostly 1.20 m (± 5 cm) wide, corresponding to two-and-a-half mud-bricks with joints of mud mortar in between. This applies to the wall separating these two rows as well as the western wall of row 2 and the walls dividing the rooms that were fully excavated (2C and 3C) from those north (2N and 3N) and south (2S and 3S). The eastern wall of row 3, however, forms an exception, measuring only c. 0.95 m across, i.e. two mud-bricks or one and two half-bricks with mud-mortar joints. In every other respect, this wall is similar to the other walls in rows 2 and 3: they are all rectilinear, well-built, consist of sun-baked mud-bricks only and their base is at a similar elevation (at c. 98.20 m site height). If, as appears to be the case, the original barracks only consisted of two rows of rooms (2 and 3), the western wall of row 2 and the eastern wall of row 3 would have formed the original outer walls of the building. Why the eastern wall was a little thinner than all other walls is unknown. It is interesting to note, however, that the internal width of room 3C was c. 4.20 m, that of room 2C just 3.80 m. Room 3C was 40 cm (c. one brick without joint) wider than room 2C, whilst its outer wall was 25 cm thinner. Perhaps wall width was reduced to increase indoor living space. More probably, the architects never had the ambition that the dimensions of all walls and rooms matched exactly, as neither rooms nor outer walls nor the two combined are perfectly symmetrical. So long as the rooms were large enough to house each group of fort occupants and the building stable and sufficiently rectilinear to make good use of the space, the workforce may have been free to proceed in whichever way seemed most efficient to them.

There was no door connecting rooms 2C and 3C, nor did we find any doorways in the northern walls of rooms 2C and 3C. A 1.10 m wide gap in brick bench d.059 on the east side of room 2C does not appear to mark the location of a door, as we observed mud-bricks in the division wall and as there was no gap in brick bench d.124 in room 3C (e.g. Fig. 4.16).[29] By contrast, there was a c. 0.90 m wide doorway connecting rooms 3C and 3S. Considering the small area explored and the poor preservation of mud-bricks, we can neither be sure whether the doorway between rooms 3C and 3S was original or cut into an originally continuous wall – nor whether doorways in division walls followed a symmetrical or a random pattern. Interestingly, we also failed to find any positive evidence for mud-bricks in the westernmost 90 cm of the alignment of the wall dividing room 2C and 2S, except for one at an odd angle that is likely to belong a later phase or may just represent random debris. Brick bench d.059 appears to come to a terminal 70 cm before reaching the south-west corner of room 2C. Both observations mirror the wall dividing rooms 3C and 3S terminating 90 cm before reaching the south-east corner of room 3C as well as the brick ledge d.124 also terminating at some distance from the corner (90 cm in room 3C). These observations suggest that there was also a doorway connecting rooms 2C and 2S of 70–90 cm width. Regrettably, there was no opportunity to test this during fieldwork, but it should be possible in future to check whether or not there was a door between rooms 2C and 2S, as there certainly was between their counterparts in row 3. It is thus tempting to think that the larger annexe rooms in the west (0CS and 1CS) formed a unit with the connected pair of rooms 2C and 2S; similarly, the annexe rooms in the east (4CS and 5CS) and rooms 3C and 3S in the original barracks may have mirrored this arrangement and formed another interconnected unit of rooms.

Our reconstruction (Figs 4.5–4.6, 4.15) is based on the assumptions that all doorways in the barracks in Trench d were found and that all doorways in the barracks followed a symmetrical pattern. We furthermore assume that there were indeed connecting doors in both rows 2 and 3. This is no more than a hypothesis and, for this reason, it is best to refrain from speculating what presence or absence of doorways in connecting walls may reveal about use and function of rooms. It is possible that each room in the original barracks (2C, 3C, 2N, 3N, 2S and 3S within our trench, as well as all other unexcavated rooms) formed a separate unit, each probably housing a group of soldiers plus perhaps family members. It is also possible that some groups occupied more than one room and/or that some of the rooms served other purposes than housing.

Most walls in the solidly-built original barracks (i.e. rows 2 and 3) of Fort 2 were as wide as those of the barracks in Fort 4. The latter (even if affected by bioturbation in the top section) survived to c. 3.30 m height and produced a massive collapse mound, making it highly probable that they were at least two storeys high. It is possible that in Fort 2 there was also a second storey above the ground-floor rooms, plus perhaps a loft – potentially more than doubling the floor space. Alternatively, the barracks may have been just a single storey high. Even allowing for the possibility that the barracks in Fort 2 were of lesser height than those in Fort 4 and that there was no or less upstairs storage or accommodation, after addition of the annexes there would have been plenty of space. It seems more likely, however, that there was a degree of standardisation in the height of buildings and that also the original barracks in Fort 2 once rose to two storeys plus perhaps a loft; the less regularly built, and mostly thinner, annexe walls point perhaps to rows 0, 1, 4 and 5 being just one storey high. Fort 2 may have been more heavily affected by windborne erosion than Fort 4, with parts of the crumbling walls after abandonment literally blown away on the windswept plateau – but more research is required to decide whether the lesser height of preserved walls and of the collapse mound in Fort 2 (as opposed to Fort 4) reflect modern preservation or, less probably, ancient reality.

Table 4.1: Comparison of the original barracks in Forts 2, 4, 15, 25 and 26, excluding annexes. Only rooms in Fort 2 have been excavated completely, whilst proposed dimensions in Fort 4 are based in part on geophysics and those for barrack rooms in Forts 15, 25 and 26, solely on drone and satellite images.[30] There is a margin of error in the estimates for the latter four.

Fort	Fort 2	Fort 4	Fort 15	Fort 25	Fort 26
Rows of rooms	2	2	2	2	2
Rooms per row and total per barracks (excl. poss. 2nd storey and poss. loft)	c. 16 × 2 = 32	c. 24 × 2 = 48	c. 20–24 × 2 = 40–48	c. 25–28 × 2 = 50–56	c. 16 × 2 = 32
Average room size, internal	c. 17.30 m^2	c. 22.32 m^2	c. 16.60 m^2	c. 19.10 m^2	c. 19.24 m^2
Combined indoor floor space of all rooms per barracks (excl. poss. 2nd storey and poss. loft)	c. 554 m^2	c. 1,071 m^2	c. 664–797 m^2	c. 955–1,069 m^2	c. 616 m^2
Total width of barracks	11.35 m	c. 16 m	c. 11–12 m	c. 15 m	c. 14 m
Length of barracks	c. 90 m	c. 116 m	c. 110–130 m	c. 115–128 m	c. 80 m
Number of barracks in fort	2	8	4	4	2
Doors in outside walls in each room	yes	yes	yes	?	?
Doors in long division wall	no	no	?	?	no?
Doors/windows in short division walls	present (2?), width 0.90 m	present (≥1), width 0.45 m	?	?	?
Width of walls	0.95–1.25 m, mostly c. 1.20 m	1.20 m	? (1.20 m assumed)	? (1.20 m assumed)	? (1.20 m assumed)

The eastern doorway of room 3C is well preserved, measuring just 0.85 m in width. Its counterpart in the west of room 2C appears to have been heavily damaged when parts of the western wall of room 2C were demolished to create additional space for storage vessels. Traces of the northern edge of the western access doorway to room 2C were tentatively identified next to storage jar 1, and its terminal appears to be in alignment with its counterpart in 3C. In the south, only possible remnants of a north–south wall survived next to jar 7.[31] We assume that originally there was a doorway of the same width (0.85 m) as that in the east wall of room 3C in the west wall of room 2C and that it was widened substantially prior to the insertion of storage jar 7 (e.g. Fig. 4.18). Yet this postulated demolition of c. 1.50 m of the western wall of room 2C is hypothetical. No clear traces of this 1.50 m stretch were found, implying that it was completely demolished or, potentially, that the doorway here had been much wider from the start. As the barracks were otherwise broadly symmetrical (even if not perfectly so), it seems more likely that the original outer doorways in the barracks were all of a similar width. Furthermore, narrow doorways provided better insulation, keeping out the heat in summer and the cold on chilly and wet autumn, winter and spring days. Such insulation would have been important, particularly prior to the construction of the annexes. Afterwards, the western entrance of room 2C would no longer have led to the outside, but to an indoor buffer zone.

The rooms in Trench d are the only complete rooms ever excavated in Sasanian barracks on the Gorgan Wall. How typical are they, and how much or little may other barracks have differed? In Fort 4, we only excavated parts of two rooms. Whilst mud-brick walls proved to be of a similar width (1.20 m) to their Fort 2 counterparts, the internal dimensions of rooms appear to have differed, estimated at c. 3.60 × 6.20 m each (based on the results of the magnetometer survey, but not verified via excavations).[32] The quality of the survey in Fort 4[33] gives us confidence, however, that the estimate is close to the truth and the rooms in the barracks in Fort 4 were indeed larger than those in Fort 2. There may well be a small error in the estimate, but it cannot be far from the truth.

It is also clear from the survey that each room in the barracks in Fort 4 had a separate entrance from the outside, whilst there were no detectable doorways in the long wall separating the two rows. Geophysical survey also failed to reveal traces of doorways in the shorter division walls between the rooms in each long row,[34] but we found a window or narrow door in the division wall in Trench H in Fort 4 via excavation. It was only half the width of the doorway in the division wall between rooms 3C and 3S in Trench d in Fort 2 and in a different position within the wall.[35] Whilst there were evidently differences in the layout of the barracks in Forts 2 and 4, it appears that in both cases rooms or room units were accessed from the two opposite long sides of the barracks and that a central door-less long wall separated the buildings into two halves.

Interestingly, the original barracks in Fort 2 were architecturally strikingly similar to those in Fort 4, but no simple clones. Whether or not there was a difference in elevation, they differed in width, length and number of rooms. Each of the original barracks in Fort 4 provided an estimated one and a half times as many rooms, of roughly twice as much indoor living and/or storage space as their counterparts in Fort 2 combined, assuming both contained the same number of storeys. Perhaps the eight barracks in Fort 4 were designed for not just four times the number of occupants than the two in Fort 2, but six or even eight times the number. It should be noted that there is a lower level of accuracy in our estimates of room dimensions in Fort 4 than in room number. If the barracks were 15 m wide (instead of the 16 m estimated based on the magnetometer plot), this would reduce the area of each room by 1.8 m².

Aerial survey revealed the plan of barracks also in Forts 15, 25 and 26. The evidence, which will be presented in detail below,[36] is important to contextualise the results of our excavations and surveys at Forts 2 and 4. The barracks in the small Forts 2 and 26 were clearly shorter than those in the larger Forts 4, 15 and 25, both in terms of length (c. 80–90 m as opposed to c. 110–130 m) and room number (an estimated 16 × 2 as opposed c. 20–25 × 2). Whatever the precise dimensions, there is little doubt that the combined ground-floor space in the eight original barracks in Fort 4 exceeded that in the two buildings in Fort 2 at least sixfold, and probably eightfold. The original barracks in Fort 25 may have had similar dimensions to those in Fort 4. It ought to be stressed, however, that this is uncertain, as their width (of c. 15 m) can be much more securely measured than their length and number of rows (c. 115–128 m and 25–28 rows?).[37] Also the original Fort 15 barracks, whilst perhaps no wider than those in Fort 2, were clearly longer and provided more space. (We will explore below[38] how much the later addition of annexes may have increased the amount of indoor space in absolute and in relative terms when comparing long barracks in large forts with shorter barracks in smaller forts.) Future research may reveal whether the number of rooms in the original barracks does or does not follow a neat numerical system. Table 4.1 allows for the possibility that in all instances the number of rooms is divisible by eight. As the precise length of barracks and number of rooms is not known for certain in any of the forts (though our estimates are likely to be close to the truth), it is no more than an unproven working hypothesis that this multiplier might have been applied – potentially reflecting how rooms in barracks, or military units occupying them, were subdivided.

4.1.4.2.2. Attempted quantification of mud-bricks needed for barracks construction

The Sasanian mud-bricks in Trench d tended to be square, but they were often halved. They varied in size, some measured 40 × 40 cm and some 45 × 45 cm; 42 × 42 cm appeared to be the most common size. Thickness, perhaps c. 10 cm or up to 12 cm, was harder to discern, mainly because there will have been mud mortar between courses of bricks. In places, they were in neat alignment, in places there were broken pieces in odd alignments. Considerable numbers of mud-bricks would have been needed to construct the barracks in the forts on the Great Wall. Whilst precision is impossible to achieve, our models (Tables 4.2 and 4.3) may provide an idea of magnitude.

Needless to stress that many of the variables in our models are based on estimates, but they are likely to provide us with an approximate idea of magnitude. Roughly seven million sun-baked square mud-bricks of c. 42–45 cm diameter in layers of c. 16 cm height, allowing for mud mortar used as a bonding agent, may have been needed to construct the original two-room wide barracks in the known forts on the Great Wall. This estimate does not include the bricks needed for the later annexes to the barracks that may have almost tripled the width of the buildings; the annexes tended to have thinner, less well-built and probably lower walls. The walls of the later annexes of the eastern barrack block in Fort 2 covered an estimated 402.46 m² (Table 4.5). Assuming they rose to c. 2.40 m height, half that of the original barracks, almost 966 m³ of mud-bricks (corresponding to just over 26,000 bricks plus mud mortar) would have been required for the annexes to this building. These estimates refer to just one of Fort 2's two barracks. They suggest that a little less than half the quantity of bricks was needed for building the annexes than had been required for erecting the original barracks. The annexes in Fort 2 were probably smaller than those of the barracks in large forts. Assuming all barracks on forts on the Great Wall were provided with annexes and the relative dimensions of buildings and quantities of bricks needed were similar, perhaps the total number of bricks required for barracks and annexes in all known forts combined may have risen by about half or just under. If so, maybe around ten million large mud-bricks were needed to build the barracks and their annexes in all known forts on the Gorgan Wall. The estimate makes no allowance for the outer walls and projecting towers, requiring almost certainly a substantially greater number of bricks.[39]

Even all barracks, fort walls and projecting towers combined (but excluding hinterland fortifications) probably did not require as many bricks as the Great Wall itself. The latter may have contained almost two hundred million fired bricks of almost similar size to the sun-baked mud-bricks, if over 170 km long, five bricks wide (not counting a much more substantial earth bank behind) and an estimated 80 courses (c. 9 m) high.[40] This is not an unlikely height estimate, considering that the Sasanian Ghilghilchay Wall (built of mud-bricks not worth robbing) survives to 7 m height after exposure to wind and weather for one and a half millennia, with one of the eroded tower mounds still rising to a height of as much as 10 m today.[41] On the likely assumption that there were projecting towers on the Great Wall,[42] an additional allowance ought to be made for the fired bricks needed. We may conclude that

Table 4.2: Estimated number of bricks needed for building the barracks in Forts 2 and 4.

Fort 2 Wall	Length[1]	Width[2]	Height[3]	No.	Volume[4]	No. of bricks[5]
Central	90.00	1.20	4.80	1	518.40	14,063
West (minus 16 door openings of 0.85 m)	76.40	1.20	4.80	1	440.06	11,938
East (minus 16 door openings of 0.85 m)	76.40	0.95	4.80	1	348.38	9,451
Doorless interim walls	8.00	1.20	4.80	9	414.72	11,250
Interim walls with doors	6.40	1.20	4.80	8	294.91	8,000
Total per barracks, excluding later annexes	n/a	n/a	n/a	n/a	2,016.48	54,701
2 barracks combined, excluding later annexes	n/a	n/a	n/a	n/a	4,032.96	109,401
Fort 4 Wall	Length	Width	Height	No.	Volume	No. of bricks
Central	116.00	1.20	4.80	1	668.16	18,125
West and east (minus 24 door openings of 0.85 m)	95.60	1.20	4.80	2	1,101.31	29,875
Doorless interim walls	12.40	1.20	4.80	13	928.51	25,188
Interim walls with doors (estimated)	10.80	1.20	4.80	12	746.50	20,250
Total per barracks, excluding later annexes	n/a	n/a	n/a	n/a	3,444.48	93,438
8 barracks combined, excluding later annexes	n/a	n/a	n/a	n/a	27,555.84	747,500

[1] Approximate measurements in metres. Note that the numbers are not always neatly divisible by brick or half-brick length, incl. mud mortar (c. 0.48 and 0.24 m respectively), but as this is only a model and mud mortar joints may have varied in width, it is better to base estimates on measured dimensions than rounding them to multiples of mud-bricks.
[2] Approximate measurements in metres etc., as in the case of length estimates.
[3] Height estimated, assuming there were two storeys with a flat roof (though a pitched roof would perhaps have been more rain-resistant). No additional allowance has been made for building material for ceilings and interim floors. The assumption that there were two storeys is based on excavations in Fort 4; the estimate that one storey was c. 2.40 m high is based on excavations in Dariali Fort (Sauer *et al.* 2020a, 25–28).
[4] Approximate volume in cubic metres.
[5] Assumed to be 48 × 48 × 16 cm for a brick plus mud mortar (disregarding that the ratio of joints to bricks would have been lower across the short side of a wall and higher on the long side). Estimate based on excavations of barracks in Forts 2 and 4.

Table 4.3: Estimated number of bricks needed for building the original barracks in Forts 1 to 33 on the Gorgan Wall.[43]

Bricks required	Number
Average bricks required per two-row barracks (assumed to be the average between those in Forts 2 and 4, excluding annexes).	74,069
Total bricks for an estimated 92 barracks in the forts on Gorgan Wall, excl. likely additional forts W of Fort 33 and hinterland forts, but including some forts whose interior housing is not preserved (see Table 4.33).	6,814,349

the efforts involved in producing the sun-baked bricks for the barracks, towers and walls of all the forts on the Great Wall were massive. They were dwarfed, however, by the time and workforce required for the (much more labour-intensive) production of the more numerous fired bricks for the Great Wall itself. More modelling is required to gain an idea of the scale of labour needed to dig the canals and build the hinterland fortresses.

4.1.4.2.3. BARRACKS EXTENSION VIA ANNEXES
Geophysical survey, partially corroborated by excavation, indicates that each of the Fort 4 barracks consisted of two parallel rows of rooms, each of which was accessible via a door opening from the outside. Including their c. 1.20 m wide walls, the barracks in Fort 4 reached an overall width of c. 16 m, based on our initial interpretation.[44] Geophysical survey in Fort 2 was far less successful in

Table 4.4: Rows of rooms in the barracks in Trench d, from west to east. Measurements are in metres, rounded to the nearest 0.05 m. Eastings for the W and E side of each feature relate to the western edge of the 2016 trench; 'double' refers to (probably) twice the north–south extent of a 'single' room (not to single and two-person occupancy; all rooms probably sheltered small groups unless used for storage, cooking or other activities).

Feature	Wall 0(?)	Row 0	Wall 1(?)	Row 1	Wall 2	Row 2	Wall 3	Row 3	Wall 4	Row 4	Wall 5	Row 5	Wall 6
Phasing		Western annexe				Original barracks					Eastern annexe		
Row W–E width	-	wide	-	narrow	-	wide	-	wide	-	narrow	-	wide	-
Room N–S category	-	double?	-	double?	-	single	-	single	-	double	-	double	-
Width	1.00	4.05	1.15	2.70	1.20	3.80	1.20	4.20	0.95	2.25	1.10	4.45	0.75
W side	1.50	2.50	6.55	7.70	10.40	11.60	15.40	16.60	20.80	21.75	24.00	25.10	29.55
E side	2.50	6.55	7.70	10.40	11.60	15.40	16.60	20.80	21.75	24.00	25.10	29.55	30.30
Rooms in trench	-	0N 0CS	-	1N? 1CS	-	2N? 2C 2S	-	3N? 3C 3S	-	4N 4CS	-	5N 5CS	-

tracing barracks walls than in Fort 4, but excavation has demonstrated that the barracks were eventually extended to, probably, six rows, two added in the east and two in the west.

The postulated two rows of rooms in the west failed to produce more than faint and fragmentary traces of possible north–south walls, but the west–east-running mud-brick wall separating rooms 2C and 3C from the northern range (rooms 2N and 3N), clearly runs further west for another c. 8.90 m. It is narrower here (c. 0.80 m/ one-and-a-half mud-bricks plus joint wide), and its base appeared to be c. 20 cm above that of the mud-brick walls in rows 2 and 3. It seems plausible therefore to suggest that it formed an annexe to the original barracks rather than being contemporary. Whilst north–south room divisions in the west are somewhat speculative, there is no doubt that the wall was part of a roofed building, as it is hard to see the purpose of an open-air wall leaning onto an existing building, not to mention that rain would soon have reduced any mud-brick wall exposed to the elements to a heap of soil. The discovery of a lamp in room 0CS[45] provides further circumstantial evidence that this was probably an indoor area (even if outdoor use and/ or deposition of lamps is also possible).

There were remnants of a possible north–south decayed mud-brick or rammed-earth wall, some 1.15 m wide, c. 2.70–3.85 m west of the western face of the western wall of row 2. An edge of a further possible north–south mud-brick wall of c. 1 m width was observed branching off the western terminal of the west–east wall and forming the western wall of row 0 and the building. Both observations are tentative at best; if correct, there would be two further rows of rooms west of row 2: row 1, 2.70 m wide and row 0, c. 4.05 m wide. Two further indications point to the existence of these room divisions:

- The extent of the brick-paved area in postulated room 0CS and the area filled with storage vessels in postulated room 1CS (Figs 4.18 and 4.19) suggest that there was a clear division in the use of space at least in the later phases of occupation.

- The postulated division of the western annexe into a wide outer row 0 and a narrow inner row 1 would be broadly symmetrical to the eastern annexe, and it seems that Sasanian fort design often followed, more or less, the laws of symmetry.

It should be noted that the rows were first numbered in 2015 when our trench did not extend to row 0 in the west. Considering that the two north–south walls (separating row 0 from row 1 and row 0 from the outdoor area west) are not proven beyond doubt, not to mention the possible confusion it may have caused to relabel rows 0–5 to 1–6, it was decided to keep the numbering system for the rows explored already in 2015 (i.e. 1–5) and to label the additional likely row in the west 0. The six rows fall into the following groups: 0–1 form the postulated western annexes, 2–3 the original barracks and 4–5 the eastern annexes.

There is no doubt as to the annexes in the east. Rows 4 and 5 were separated by a mud-brick wall, and there was a further mud-brick wall at the east side of row 5. No further walls were found to the east of row 5, and the west–east wall separating the central from the northern range of rooms comes to a terminal at its T-junction with the north–south wall east of row 5. We may thus conclude that the latter formed the external wall of the building. The bases of both walls were, like that of the west–east wall in rows 0 and 1, c. 20 cm above that of the walls of rows 2 and 3. The outer wall, on the east side of row 5, employed, in addition to sun-dried mud-bricks, haphazardly fired bricks and was 70–80 cm (one and a half bricks) wide. A row of fired brick fragments lined the east side of the division wall between rows 4 and 5. Originally, it seems, it was just 0.40 m (one row of

Table 4.5: Estimated size (in square metres) and number of rooms in the eastern barracks. The values refer only to one of Fort 2's two barracks and exclude the area of a probable second storey in the original barracks. The model assumes a degree of symmetry and is based on the following estimated dimensions: width of all west–east walls in the original barracks: 1.20 m; width of internal west–east walls in the annexes: 0.70 m; width of outer west–east walls in the annexes: 0.95 m; internal north–south extent of all rooms in the original barracks: 4.35 m; internal north–south extent of all rooms in the annexes: 10.40 m; width of doorways of rows 0 and 5: 0.80 m; width of doorways of rows 1 and 4: 2.10 m; width of doorways of rows 2 and 3: 0.85 m; width of internal north–south doorways in row 2: 0.70 m; width of internal north–south doorways in row 3: 0.90 m; west–east extent of all rooms and walls: see previous table.

Row	0	1	2	3	4	5	Orig. E barracks	Annexes	Total (1-st. barr. + ann.)	Total (2-st. barr. + ann.)
Room size	42.12	28.08	16.53	18.27	23.40	46.28	see left	see left	n/a	n/a
Room no.	8	8	16	16	8	8	32	32	64	96
W–E door area	0.80	2.42	1.02	0.81	2.31	0.60	see left	see left	see left	see left
W–E door no.	8	8	16	16	8	8	32	32	64	96
N–S door area	0.00	0.00	0.84	1.08	0.00	0.00	see left	see left	see left	see left
N–S door no.	0	0	8	8	0	0	16	0	16	32
Total area (rooms)	336.96	224.64	264.48	292.32	187.20	370.24	556.80 (54.51%)	1,119.04 (71.25%)	1,675.84 (64.65%)	2,232.64 (61.79%)
Total area (doors)	6.40	19.32	23.04	21.56	18.48	4.80	44.60 (4.37%)	49.00 (3.12%)	93.60 (3.61%)	138.20 (3.82%)
Rooms and doors	343.36	243.96	287.52	313.88	205.68	375.04	601.40 (58.87%)	1,168.04 (74.37%)	1,769.44 (68.27%)	2,370.84 (65.61%)
Total area (walls)	111.14	102.54	216.48	203.62	95.82	92.96	420.10 (41.13%)	402.46 (25.63%)	822.56 (31.73%)	1,242.66 (34.39%)
Total area	454.50	346.50	504.00	517.50	301.50	468.00	1,021.50	1,570.50	2,592.00	3,613.50

mud-bricks) wide. Subsequently half a row of mud-bricks and then another full row of mud-bricks were added in the east, increasing its width to c. 1.10 m (two and a half mud-bricks). This was increased further to c. 1.40 m after a row of fired brick fragments had been added on the east side of the mud-brick wall. Despite the substantial width which the division wall between rows 4 and 5 eventually reached, it is clear that it was a makeshift construction that did not match the careful planning and execution of the walls of rows 2 and 3. Rows 4 and 5 are clearly later additions to the original barracks (rows 2 and 3).

Unlike the original barracks (rows 2 and 3), there was no division wall between a central and southern range of rooms in rows 4 and 5. The same is likely to be true for rows 0 and 1, but not proven, due to the poor preservation of walls here. The following observations suggest that rooms in rows 0 and 1 were, like their counterparts in rows 4 and 5, also of greater north–south extent than those in rows 2 and 3:

- Three ovens (d.028, d.030 and d.187) were in alignment with the division wall between the central rooms 2C and 3C and the southern rooms 2S and 3S (e.g. Fig. 4.18). This proves that there was no wall in the same alignment in rows 0 and 1, unless demolished prior to phase 3.

- The position of storage jars 8, 9 and 10 in room 1CS also proves that there was no division wall in row 1 in alignment with the wall between rooms 2C–3C and 2S–3S (Fig. 4.18) at the time.

- There is no gap in the later brick paving in room 0CS in the alignment of the division wall between rooms 2C–3C and 2S–3S (Fig. 4.19).

Even if late brick alignments d.014 and d.015 (e.g. Fig. 4.19) appear to subdivide room 1CS along a similar alignment as (though slightly south of) the wall between rooms 2C and 2S, there is no evidence that they succeed or

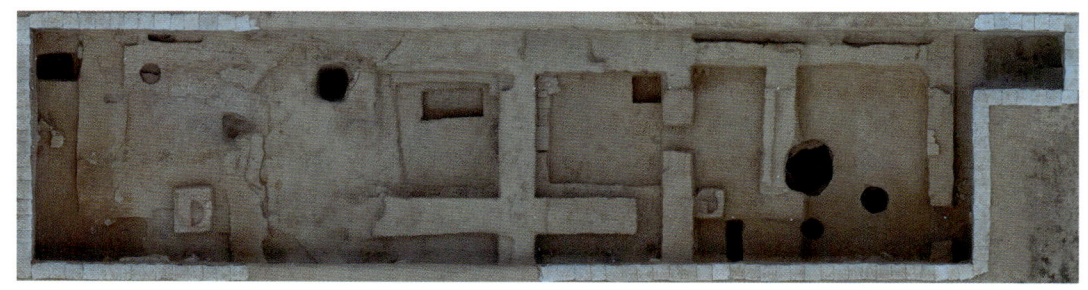

Fig. 4.14: Trench d, rectified photo at the end of the 2016 season by Eve MacDonald et al. (Note that the large round, oval or square pits, the latter with rounded corners, are storage pits; the small circular features, often half-sectioned, are ovens. Not all ovens are visible, as those on higher levels could not be preserved; the four rectangular cuts are sondages and no ancient features.)

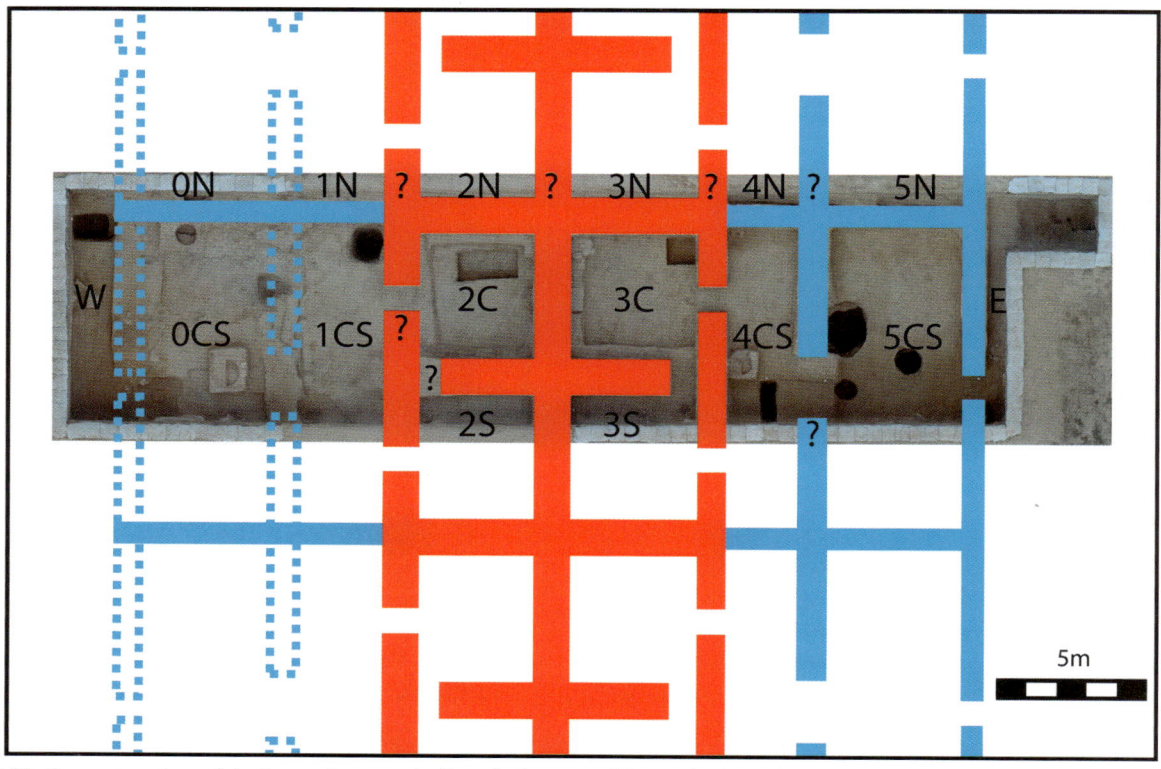

Fig. 4.15: Reconstruction of the barrack rooms in Trench d: original barracks (in red); annexes (in blue); filled features = certain walls (within the trench plus their hypothetical extent beyond trench borders, based on the assumption of a symmetrical arrangement); ?-symbol on a filled feature: likely but hypothetical continuation of certain walls within the trench; dotted features: hypothetical, poorly preserved and partially destroyed, walls. Rows of rooms are labelled west to east (0 to 5) and north to south (N = northern row in the trench; C = central row; CS = central to southern row; S = southern row). Rooms are labelled by location in relation to rows, e.g. 2C = room in row 2 in the central range. The outdoor areas are labelled W = western outdoor area; E = eastern outdoor area. (Very little of the northern row was within the trench and only parts of rooms 0N, 4N and 5N were excavated, whilst 1N, 2N and 3N are largely conjectural.) Note that the width of the doorway between rows 4 and 5 is hypothetical, as is the assumption that the western annexe was more or less a mirror image of the better-preserved and more solidly built eastern annexe. The doorway between rooms 2C and 2S is, unlike its excavated counterpart between rooms 3C and 3S, not proven either. Three observations, however, suggest it existed: (1) no bricks were observed in the area of the postulated doorway between 2C and 2S, (2) brick alignment/bench d.059 terminates 70 cm before reaching the south-west corner of the room and (3) a symmetrical arrangement with row 3 seems more likely than doorways being in random positions.

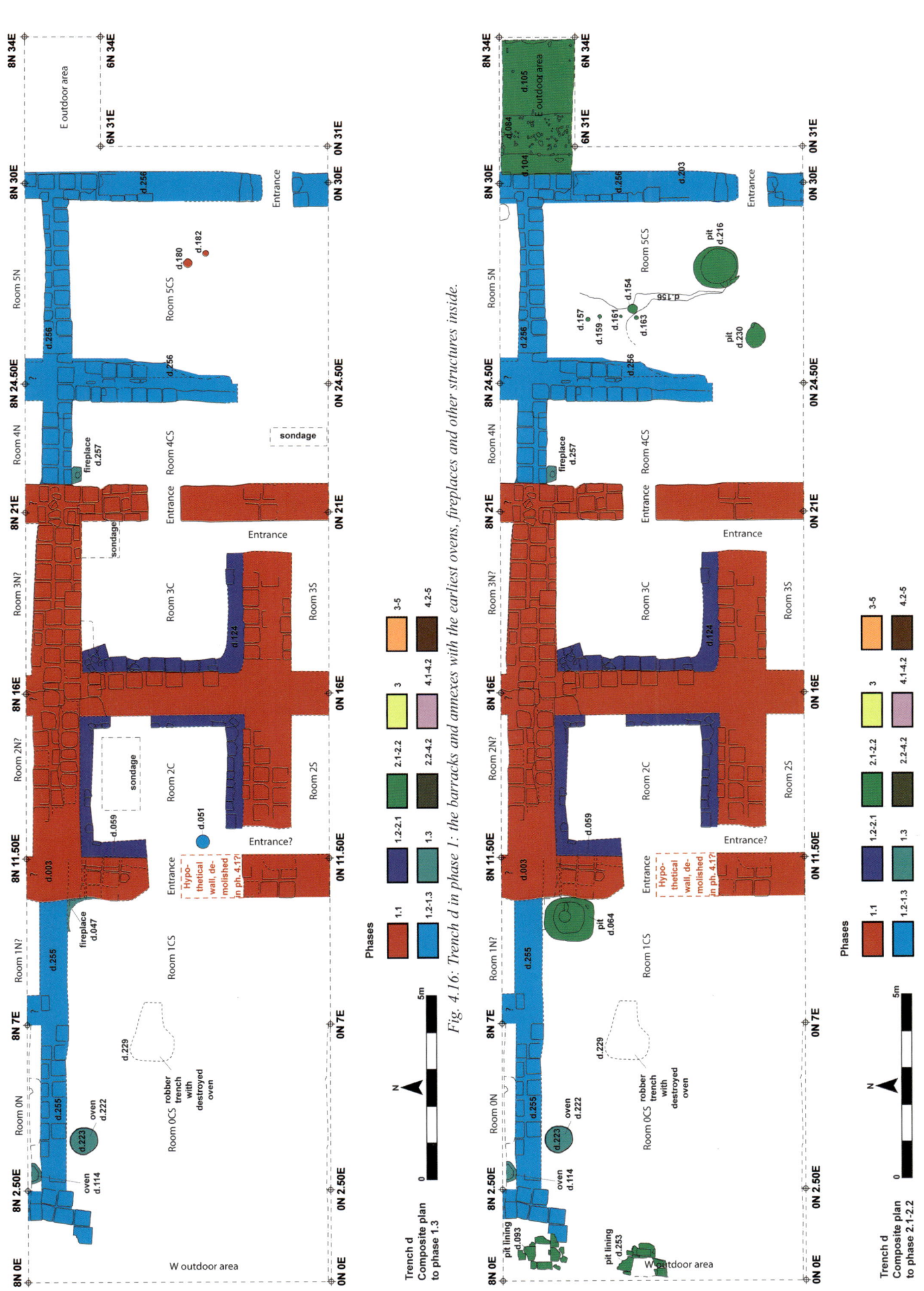

Fig. 4.16: Trench d in phase 1: the barracks and annexes with the earliest ovens, fireplaces and other structures inside.

Fig. 4.17: Trench d up to phase 2.2: the barracks and annexes with most of the storage pits added.

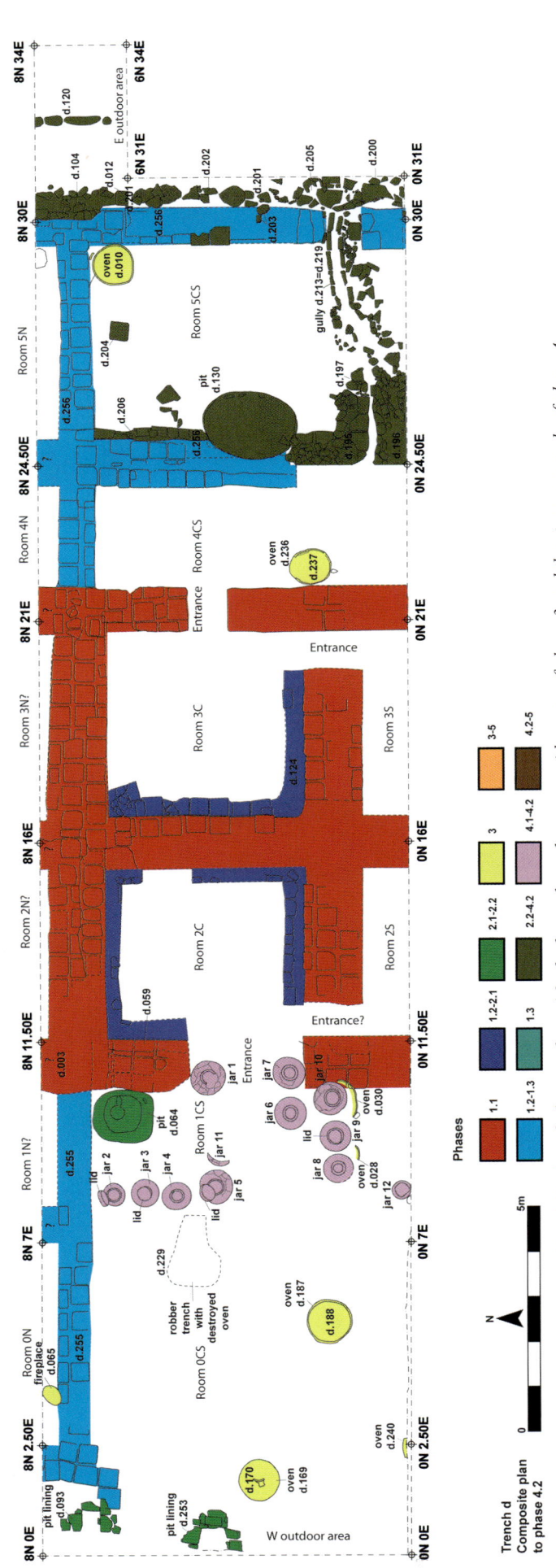

Fig. 4.18: Trench d up to phase 4.2: the barracks and annexes with ovens of phase 3 and the storage vessels of phase 4.

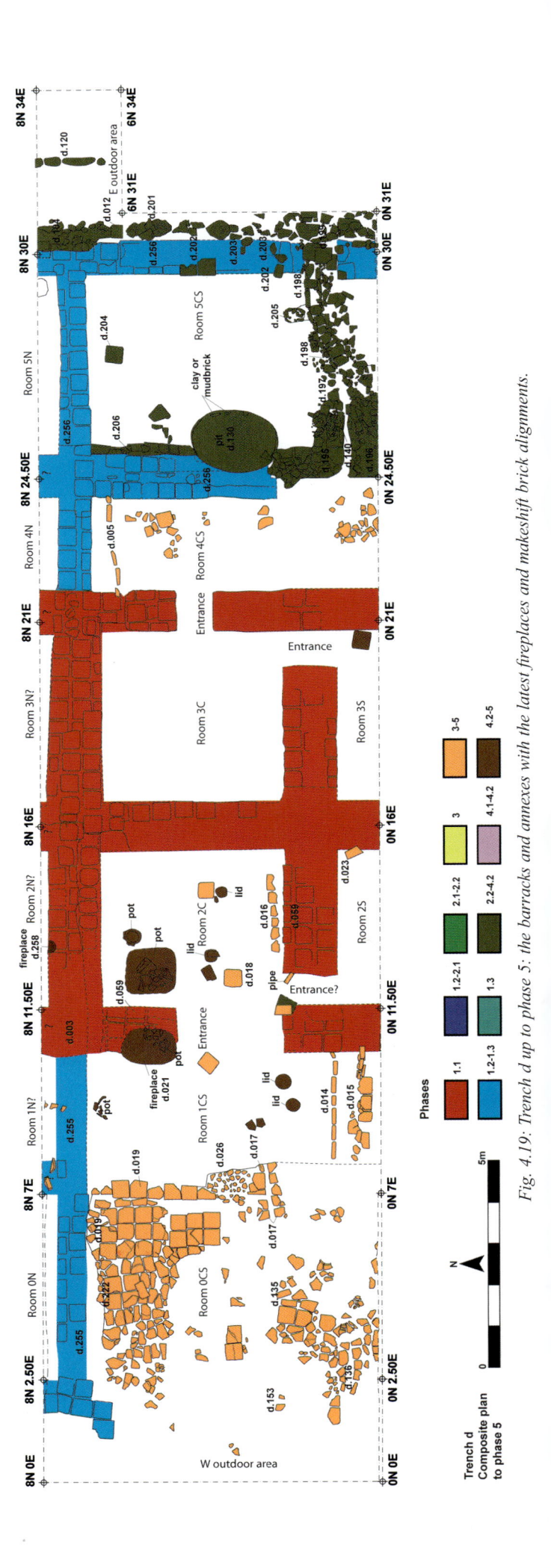

Fig. 4.19: Trench d up to phase 5: the barracks and annexes with the latest fireplaces and makeshift brick alignments.

line an earlier wall. If there were divisions at all between the central and southern range in rows 0 and 1, they appear to have been lightly built. By contrast, the wall separating the central from the northern range of rooms extended to the west, as well as to the east. We may conclude that the rooms in rows 4 and 5 (and probably also in rows 0 and 1) were probably twice the north–south extent of those in rows 2 and 3. In theory, they could, of course, have been even up to four room units wide. Further excavation is needed to decide whether the next west–east wall is in alignment with the southern walls of rooms 2S and 3S (as our reconstruction assumes), making rooms 0CS, 1CS, 4CS and 5CS twice as long as the rooms in rows 2 and 3, or whether it is elsewhere. Alternative possibilities include that rooms 0CS, 1CS, 4CS and 5CS extend to the southern end of the building, making them an estimated four room units wide, or that other division walls are not in alignment with the west–east walls of the original barracks. The door opening in the east of room 5CS – probably in alignment with the less well-preserved door in the division wall between rooms 4CS and 5CS – adds much strength to our hypothesis that these rooms were twice as long as those in rows 2 and 3. These door openings would be near the centre of rooms 4CS and 5CS if two room units long. If rooms 4CS and 5CS had been larger, the doors would not be anywhere near their axis of symmetry.

Do the greater size of rooms in the annexes (rows 4 and 5 and probably also 0 and 1) and the connecting doorway between rooms 3C and 3S (and the probable doorway between 2C and 2S) suggest that the occupants of an original barrack room did not possess allocated annexe rooms, but that these were shared? Alternatively, were there groups occupying a pair of barrack rooms plus additional space in the annexes? Perhaps, but it is worth remembering that a row of fired bricks (d.014) in room 1CS (with a parallel brick alignment, d.015, further south) is in alignment with the southern edge of the west–east wall dividing rooms 2C and 3C from 2S and 3S. These late features indicate that in the latest phase of occupation there was at least a basic screen or boundary feature that divided room 1CS into a northern (or central) and southern unit (1C and 1S). Alignments of upright bricks need not always be preserved, and we should also allow for the possibility that there were basic partitions consisting of organic materials, which have perished or been reused. Such basic divisions would have saved building material and time and at the same time would have increased indoor space. Brick alignments d.014 and d.015 may potentially attest that annexe rooms were subdivided not just in room 1CS, but more widely. It is also worth noting that we cannot be sure if the doorway between rooms 3C and 3S was an original feature or potentially cut into the wall at a later stage to increase the space available to the group of occupants. Whilst brick divisions d.014 and d.015 attest subdivision of a room roughly following the alignment of rows (central and southern), the doorway between rooms 3C and 3S shows that rows were not always strictly separated. The picture is complex, and we have to allow for more than one mode of division of space. The two most obvious possibilities are as follows:

1. Perhaps each western and eastern half-row was occupied and used by a separate group. In our trench, we would thus have the following six groups of rooms/room divisions 0N–1N–2N, 3N–4N–5N, 0C–1C–2C, 3C–4C–5C, 0S–1S–2S and 3S–4S–5S. In each 16 × 6-row barracks, there would have been 32 units of three rooms each and 64 in the two barracks in Fort 2 combined (not counting any rooms upstairs).

2. Alternatively, there may have been some shared space between adjacent half-rows: in our trench, the following larger units may have existed, if we assume that the basic brick alignments d.014 and d.015 marked no divisions: 0CS–1CS–2C/2S and 3C/3S–4CS–5CS. Rooms of the northern range may have been subdivided similarly, as shown in our reconstruction drawings (Figs 4.5–4.6, 4.15). In each 16 × 6-row barracks, there would have been just 16 units of two rooms plus two double-rooms each and 32 in the two barracks of Fort 2 combined.

We do not know which of the above models is correct. Whether model 1 or 2 is correct may have ramifications on group size. Numerical estimates are always fraught with difficulty but, assuming our previous estimate of a garrison of c. 500 occupying a compound the size of Fort 2 is plausible (leaving aside the question how many dependents may have been present),[46] the first model may imply 64 groups of eight each, the second model 32 groups of 16 each (in both cases adding up to a theoretical total of 512). We may be certain, of course, that the number of occupants fluctuated, e.g. as a result of disease and numerous other factors affecting local demography and/or recruitment. The size of room units and groups will have changed over time, and this will have affected the available space per person. Models as to the possible number of occupants of the fort, in comparison with the potential holding capacity of other forts, are presented below.[47]

Whilst clearly later and not built to the same standards as the original barracks, it seems clear that the annexes were no shanty huts built without much care. Several observations suggest that they were carefully planned:

- The west–east wall separating the central and northern range of rooms was extended to the west and east in a straight alignment.

- The north–south walls were parallel to those of the existing barracks.

- The eastern entrances to rooms 4CS and 5CS appear to be in alignment. (That of 4CS was much wider, perhaps as insulation was of lesser concern in the case of an internal room division, but it is also possible that it was originally as narrow as that of 5CS, but widened later.)

- The western and eastern annexes are symmetrical, even if not perfectly so: the western annexe (rows 0 and 1 combined) was 8.90 m wide, the eastern annexe (rows 4 and 5) 8.55 m – no massive difference, particularly as the precise dimensions of the western annexe cannot be measured as accurately as those of the better-preserved (and more solidly constructed) eastern annexe.

- Even row width follows a broadly symmetrical pattern: the inner rows (1 and 4) are narrow (row 1: 3.85 m with its postulated western wall or 2.70 m internally – row 4: 3.35 m with its eastern wall or 2.25 m internally); the outer rows were wider (row 0: 5.05 m with its, tentatively identified, western wall or 4.05 m internally – row 5: 5.20 m with its eastern wall or 4.45 m internally).

- It appears that different activities took place in different rows – possible evidence for systematic organisation. The provision of large storage jars, some in neat rows in the corridor-like row 1, may point to central planning. The absence of equivalent *in-situ* storage jars in its corridor-like counterpart (row 4), although there were fragments of broken storage jars from early and late levels in row 4, may be due to its greater distance to the road, making it more difficult to bring or collect heavy provisions. Almost 90% of both storage jars and cooking pots came from the annexes and only a little over 10% from the original barracks, as shown by Maria Daghmehchi *et al*.[48] – remarkable, even considering that the annexes covered a larger area and generally yielded more pottery. Vessel glass was found almost exclusively in rows 0 and 5, perhaps evidence for drinking and dining taking place in these more accessible areas or them being used for storage of such items.[49] Oven and fireplaces were also exclusively located in the annexes, except for the latest phase of occupation.[50] There was much more bone from all rows in the eastern barracks than from any row in the western half. Within the rows, most bone came from row 5 in the east and row 0 in the west, but still less from row 0 than from any of the eastern rows. As it would have been impractical to use ovens in the western half of the barracks for meals consumed in the eastern half without any connecting door, perhaps bone distribution reflects deposition more than consumption habits.[51] Overall, it seems that the different rows served different functions:

  - Accommodation in the centre.
  - Storage in the annexes, notably rows 1 and 5 (both provided with one or more storage pit(s) and the former with *in-situ* storage jars in phase 4).
  - Cooking and food preparation in rows 0, 4 and 5 (and 1, prior to its repurposing as a storage area).
  - Textile production (and perhaps other domestic work) in the later phases of occupation in rows 2, 3 and 5.[52]
  - The late patchy brick floor in row 0, easy to sweep clean, may have served as a special work area.

It appears that the use of space followed a system, rather than a free-for-all principle prevailing.

The eventual width of the barracks of c. 28.80 m (close to 29–30 m), and their length of c. 3 × 30 m, makes one wonder if its architects aimed at round multiples of a unit of measurement. One encounters dimensions of c. 28–30 m (roughly 100 feet) unusually often in Sasanian military architecture, e.g. in tower-spacing, dimensions of small forts etc. If admittedly there are also many forts whose dimensions are not multiples of, and/or whose towers are not spaced at intervals of 30 m ± 5% (centre to centre), our impression is that this dimension is found more often than is likely to happen in a random sample.[53] Fort 4's barracks being c. 116 m (i.e. 4 × 29 m) long would fit the pattern; it should be noted that these dimensions are based on our interpretation of the magnetometer survey and include a margin of error.[54] Worth noting too is that the original width of the Fort 2 barracks of c. 11.35 m, i.e. close to 40 feet/40% of the width after extension, may not be random either – though admittedly we do not have enough accurate measurements for the width of barracks to test whether or not there is a numerical pattern in barracks width that applies to Sasanian buildings of this type more broadly. A systematic study is required to ultimately prove or disprove the hypothesis that a measurement unit of 28–30 m played a role in barracks design and that the length of barracks may add up to 3 or 4 × 28–30 m and their width, after extension, sometimes to c. 28–30 m.

Were the width and length of the original barracks (and their annexes) and the final barracks perhaps designed to correspond to multiples of ten of a local foot, or an equivalent to the Attic foot (Table 4.6)?[55] One needs to bear in mind that the width of the western annexe, and as a result that of the extended barracks as a whole, could not be measured precisely. Assuming the original barracks were intended to be 40 times a local foot, the eastern annexe would be within 0.5% of 30 times the equivalent. Assuming (less plausibly) that the Attic foot was the intended unit of measurement, the deviation is greater (except for the western annexe whose dimensions are, however, not exactly known), but still under 5%. We may conclude that it is likely that the dimensions of the original barracks and annexes were intended to correspond

Table 4.6: Hypothetical units of measurement potentially used in barracks plan.

Fort 2 barracks components	Dimensions in m	Assumed equivalent in feet	Length of foot in cm	Deviation from hypothetical original barracks foot in %	Equivalent in Attic feet (c. 29.70 cm each)	Deviation from assumed value in %
W annexe (NB: dimensions only approximate)	8.90	30	29.67	4.55	29.97	-0.11
Original barracks	11.35	40	28.38	0.00	38.22	-4.46
E annexe	8.55	30	28.50	0.44	28.79	-4.04
Total (NB: dimensions only approximate)	28.80	100	28.80	1.50	96.97	-3.03

Table 4.7: Increase in extent of built-up space and available indoor space in Fort 2 after annexe construction (excl. possible loft). Note that the figures represent the likely minimum area covered by buildings. Excavations within the c. 57% of fort interior not covered by barracks and annexes are needed to test whether or not there may have been further lightly built structures, e.g. rooms lining the inside of the fort walls or any sheds in the interior. It seems unlikely, however, that there were additional free-standing buildings as tall and solid as the original barracks, as these should have produced detectable collapse mounds.

Buildings/area	Approx. area
Original barracks (surface area only, not counting possible 2nd storey)	2,043 m²
Barracks with annexes	5,184 m²
Fort interior (c. 108.50 m W–E × 110 m N–S)	11,935 m²
Percentage of fort interior covered by original barracks	17.12%
Percentage of fort interior covered by barracks with annexes	43.44%
Increase	**253.74%**
Indoor ground-floor area (excl. walls and doors), original barracks	1,113.60 m²
Indoor ground-floor area (excl. walls and doors), barracks with annexes	3,351.68 m²
Increase	**300.98%**
Indoor area, original barracks, if 2 storeys high	2,227.20 m²
Indoor area, 2-storey barracks with 1-storey annexes	4,465.28 m²
Increase	**200.49%**

to 40 plus twice 30, i.e. 100 feet. More barracks need to be excavated, however, to prove or disprove the hypothesis that multiples of ten feet feature prominently in Sasanian barracks design.

There is enough similarity between the western and eastern annexes in the excavated Fort 2 barracks to suggest that they were added as part of a single extension plan and probably built at a similar time. Systematic planning, architecture in rectilinear alignment and effective use of space all point to state-sponsored initiatives rather than those of a peasant community left to its own devices. One has the impression that the fort remained under military control throughout its occupation. Whether or not the proportion of non-combatant family members accommodated in the intramural area may have increased over time, there is no reason to think that the military garrison was replaced by civilian squatters.

No further fieldwork has been carried out in the extramural area. We do not know if low mounds to the south and north-east of Fort 2, tentatively identified as a possible outer settlement by the landscape survey team,[56] were indeed an area where family members and/or other camp-followers may have lived. It would be interesting to establish in future if these mounds are indeed collapsed mud-brick houses and, if so, whether these potential civilian dwellings were occupied simultaneously with the fort or whether they were partially or completely abandoned after annexe construction.

Whatever the precise purpose of annexe construction, there is no question that the addition of the annexes (rows 0, 1, 4 and 5) massively increased indoor space available for accommodation, storage and other activities. The original barracks were 11.35 m wide, the extended barracks 28.80 m, an increase to c. 250% of the original width (and size) of the building. More than 40% of the interior of the fort was now covered in barracks. Bearing in mind that the original barracks were solidly built and may well have risen to a height of two storeys, there is little doubt that the fort was intensively occupied. At ground-floor level, indoor space would have increased about threefold, bearing in mind that the annexes had, on average, thinner walls and fewer room divisions and leaned against the original thick-walled barracks. Even on the likely assumption that the original barracks were two storeys high and their annexes only a single storey, indoor space available to occupants would have doubled.

As we will see, there is no evidence for cooking and storage facilities in the original barracks, and we may assume that food was initially largely prepared outdoors (or perhaps upstairs). Food may have been kept partially indoors already prior to annexe construction (though there is no concrete evidence) and partially in outdoor storage pits. It is possible that the increase in indoor food storage after the construction of the annexes may in part be related to a taxation in kind system and/or storing a greater amount of provisions per occupant.[57] Overall it seems that, prior to phase 4.2 or 5, the original barracks (rows 2 and 3) never accommodated cooking facilities (at least not at ground-floor level) and fewer storage jars (probably too heavy when full for upstairs storage). We may assume that they served mainly as accommodation units. Cooking and storage facilities in the annexes suggest an, at least in part, different function. It is possible, even likely, that there would also have been additional accommodation in the annexes. It seems unlikely, however, with part of the space clearly used for catering and food storage, that the number of fort occupants grew by as much as the available indoor space.

In theory, there would have been space for two further narrow barracks between the fort walls and the two barracks lining the central road of Fort 2. There is, however, no trace of further longitudinal collapse mounds visible on any of the satellite and drone images or on the ground today. We may thus conclude that there was space for outdoor activities here and no more than two, very large and symmetrically arranged, buildings in the interior of the fort. We should note that, without trial trenches within the under 60% of postulated open space, we cannot exclude that there were further dwellings here, not to mention potential tents or yurts, though the absence of mounding suggests that any hypothetical buildings can only have been lightly constructed and single-storey.

There is as yet no evidence for or against the existence of rooms lining the inside of the outer walls at Fort 2 or other forts on the Gorgan Wall. The outer walls of forts on the Great Wall have often created substantial linear collapse mounds,[58] but we do not know whether these represent solely the remains of the defensive walls or perhaps also of a row of rooms leaning against the walls. Should there have been a row of (double-storey?) rooms all around the perimeter, as common in both Sasanian and contemporary late Roman fortifications,[59] with gaps perhaps only for the gateways, this would have greatly increased the amount of intramural indoor accommodation and storage space. It should be possible to establish the presence or absence of such casemates via excavations in future, and it is perhaps best to refrain from proposing models as to the potential additional floor space as long as we have no clear evidence for their existence.

Was it standard for Sasanian barracks to be eventually six rooms/almost 30 m wide, as our excavations in Fort 2 may imply – or just two rooms/10–16 m, as the geophysical survey in Fort 4 and the excavated barracks in Ain Sinu I[60] may suggest? Geophysical survey in Fort 16, whilst far from clear, seems to suggest that the two barracks in this fort were much wider than those detected in Fort 4.[61] In Fort 26, satellite imagery and observations on the ground similarly suggest that there were more than two rows of rooms and that the width of the barracks perhaps even exceeded 30 m. The traces of decayed walls in Fort 26 are also far from clear and do not allow us to draw certain conclusions as to the precise width of buildings or the number, size and arrangement of rooms. For the northern parts of the eastern barrack block in Fort 26, one could make a case, however tentatively, for six rows of rooms and an overall width of c. 34 m. Two north–south rows in the eastern barracks are particularly distinct and may well be the original barracks, the core building to which annexes were added later.[62] The large Fort 25 might have been filled even more densely with barracks and annexes.[63] Should this be true, the barracks in Fort 2 and Fort 26 had the same number of rows of rooms, but differed in width. Forts 2, 16 and 26 – unlike Fort 4 with its probable eight barracks – belong to the same category of fort with just two barracks arranged symmetrically on either side of a central road. Are our postulated six-row barracks typical for the smaller forts and were they perhaps more densely occupied than the bigger forts? As barracks in smaller forts did not reach the same length as those in bigger forts, were annexes perhaps intended to make sure that the widened shorter buildings contained a similar amount of space as their longer counterparts in the large forts? The latter hypotheses would make sense, if we assumed that each barrack building in a Gorgan Wall fort, whether long or short, accommodated members of a division of troops of identical numerical strength.

The existence of extensive annexes in large Fort 25[64] and re-examination of the Fort 4 magnetometer survey plot, however, casts doubt on the latter hypothesis. There may be traces on the latter, though far less distinct than those of the strikingly clear double-row barracks, of possible rows of additional rooms abutting them. These potential additional rows of rooms show up most clearly in the southern building east of the central road. If so, the barracks could have been some 30 m wide (similar to their counterparts in Fort 2).[65] The additional rows could be later and less well-constructed annexes. Excavation is needed to test whether or not annexes were also added to the Fort 4 barracks, if perhaps all barracks in all Gorgan Wall forts were provided with annexes and if these were of similar or variable dimensions. If the walls of the probable annexes in Fort 4 were similar in construction to those in Fort 2, i.e. being mostly of lesser width, often not preserved to the same height, generally of less regular and stable construction (and their walls, unlike those of the original barracks, perhaps not reaching the modern surface), it should come as no surprise that they are harder to detect by means of magnetometer survey. In the light of our excavations in Fort 2, it seems perfectly possible that the less distinct potential linear anomalies on either side of some of the Fort 4 barracks were indeed parallels to what we found at Fort 2: lightly built annexes, leaning against solidly constructed original barracks. This observation also sheds new light on our excavations at Trench J in Fort 4. A brick-paved area (J.005) reminds one of the patchy late brick floor in Fort 2's room 0CS. It would be in the right location for the outer row of a hypothetical two-row annexe on the south-west side of Fort 4's barrack block 8, notably if we assume that these postulated annexes matched those in Fort 2 in width (rather than the wider original barracks in Fort 4 having even wider or much narrower annexes). If so, not all rooms in this row were provided with brick paving, as paving extends less than 2 m into the trench from its north-eastern and north-western edge. Perhaps it was only the odd room in the outermost row that required a brick paving in Fort 4 (and perhaps the same was true for Fort 2 and other forts). It is also possible, though unproven, that some of the ovens in Trench J may have been in the entrance areas to annexes attached to barrack blocks 6 and 8. Gully J.009 was probably outdoors midway between the two barrack blocks. Storage pits J.033 and J.034, to judge by their location, could have been just outdoors – similar to Fort 2, where we also find two storage pits just to the west outside of the barracks. Admittedly, this is hypothetical, but it is worth noting that brick paving J.005 was only some 70 cm below the modern surface. It was only at a much deeper level that we could identify mud-bricks at Fort 4. Hypothetical thin mud-brick walls in the area of our potential annexes at such shallow depth would have been erased by bioturbation. Indeed, it is also possible that paving J.005 was on top of a single-storey annexe buried when the ground was raised substantially. If so, the question arises whether or not the annexe was rebuilt at a higher level and whether late paving J.005 was outdoors or indoors at the time.[66] If there were indeed substantial annexes at Fort 4, as there certainly were at Fort 25, annexe-building occurred at the largest fort on the wall, just as in its much smaller counterparts. Forts 4 and 25, just like Forts 2, 16 and 26 (and maybe most or all forts on the wall) may have been provided with enlarged wide barracks in a later phase.

The soil marks, visible on drone and satellite imagery of Fort 15, whilst clearly showing two barracks, have failed to produce unmistakable evidence for annexes; it is hard to tell whether some of the linear alignments visible on the drone imagery have been created exclusively by modern agricultural activities and or whether some of them might potentially be related to earlier annexe walls. As field boundaries and ploughing are parallel or perpendicular to archaeological features at Fort 15, modern and potentially ancient features are not always easy to tell apart. The evidence from Fort 15 neither proves the existence of annexes nor their absence, but it also suggests that any potential annexes were less solidly built than the original barracks.[67]

Whether or not most or even all forts on the Gorgan Wall were included in a programme of barracks extension, what seems certain is that barracks, even if the rooms within them were not of identical dimensions and layout, always appear to have been long, rectangular and broadly symmetrical structures. We may tentatively conclude that barracks, even after the addition of annexes, probably differed in size, and there was not necessarily a standardised ground-floor space for each building. Barracks were probably of similar dimension within any one fort, and they may have been of similar dimensions within any one fort type, e.g. the smaller two-barracks forts. More fieldwork is needed to establish how much barracks size differed between smaller and larger forts and what this may reveal about the numerical strength of the military divisions that occupied any one of these buildings (and whether or not it may have differed between different types of forts). Many other factors may account for variations in the size of buildings. It is possible, for example, that the amount of space available per occupant for living, indoor work and storage may have differed from fort to fort. Excavations and surveys have proven that there was extensive provision of indoor space in all forts on the Gorgan Wall (unless too poorly preserved for traces to remain), but we are not yet able to reconstruct the exact width (and ground-floor area) of buildings, with few exceptions, notably the barracks at Fort 2.

4.1.4.3. Chronology of barracks construction and occupation in Trench d

The large barracks prove that the Gorgan Wall forts were designed for permanent occupation. Excavations at Fort 2 have also shown that they were indeed intensively occupied for some time. Prior to exploring the history of the occupation of the barracks, row by row, it is necessary to explain the phasing and the evidence it is based upon. It is also important to detail the difficulties in establishing a precision-chronology and gauge the level of accuracy of our dating. This chapter focuses on methodology and a brief descriptive summary of the successive phases. The broader historical significance of the chronological developments observed is discussed in the concluding section of this chapter.[68]

Overall we processed 20 radiocarbon samples from Trench d (Table 4.8), only one of which was intrusive (belonging to a rodent burrowing in the Late Middle Ages into Sasanian layers); the remainder were all Sasanian.

Phasing, however, was not easy and impeded/not helped by the following factors.

- With the sole exception of the latest one or two of the 19 samples (excluding again the intrusive rodent sample), which are clearly later than some of the early samples, the unmodelled dates of all

Table 4.8: Radiocarbon and archaeomagnetic dates of samples from Trench d. Dates with a question mark and in square brackets are considered unreliable for dating the deposit, though in case of the rodent (marked in red on Fig. 4.22), the date is perfectly credible for the creature creating a burrow into a much older layer. In the case of archaeomagnetic dates where there tend to be multiple possibilities, date ranges that are compatible with the orientation of the samples but incompatible with the stratigraphy, are also marked as doubtful. (SH = site height in relation to a benchmarks for Trench d, set at an arbitrary height of 100 m.)[69]

Find no.	Location	Laboratory no.	Sample description	Date	Calibrated date at 95.4% confidence	Comments
d.004/16	27.80 m E, 6.80 m N, 99.00 m SH (room 5CS)	SUERC-65860	Bone: *Bos*, tibia, diaphysis	1456±21	AD 578–646 → modelled date: 561–636	d13C = -19.1
d.010	Oven in room 5CS	AM250	Burnt soil: Oven wall	n/a	[1000–885 BC?] AD 249–531 [AD 1096–1224, 1283–1332, 1833–1990?]	AD 249–531 in part compatible with ^{14}C dates
d.024/103	14.98 m E, 3.63 m N, 98.61 m SH (room 2C)	SUERC-65861	Bone: *Sus*, tooth, M3, inf., mandibular, complete	1501±25	AD 540–640 → modelled date: 545–635 (93.4%: 545–609)	d13C = -20.3
d.040/183	c. 9.37 m E, 1.65 m N, 98.25 m SH (fill of jar 9, room 1CS)	SUERC-65862	Bone: Rodent, femur, complete	524±21	[AD 1396–1440?]	d13C = -10.0 (intrusive)
d.041/205	c. 8.24 m E, 4.25 m N, 97.71 m SH (fill of jar 5, room 1CS)	SUERC-65869	Bone: *Sus*, phalanx 1, complete	1543±21	AD 435–591 → modelled date: 443–585 (90.3%: 476–585; 71.9%: 529–585)	d13C = -20.2
d.044/211	12.50 m E, 2.99 m N, 98.36 m SH (room 2C)	SUERC-65870	Bone: *Sus*, mandibular, P4, M1, complete	1534±21	AD 436–599 → modelled date: 440–595 (93.4%: 477–595; 88.4%: 530–595)	d13C = -19.6
d.045/251	7.74 m E, 2.89 m N, 98.28 m SH (room 1CS)	SUERC-65871	Bone: Caprini, calcaneus, PM	1561±21	AD 432–566 → modelled date: 432–551	d13C = -17.8
d.070/313	17.72 m E, 3.33 m N, 98.91 m SH (room 3C)	SUERC-71964	Bone: *Bos*, right humerus	1576±18	AD 430–548	d13C = -13.7
d.090/s3	Fill of pit d.064 (room 1CS)	SUERC-71965	Bone: Caprini, foetus, first phalanx	1566±18	AD 432–560 → modelled date: 441–560 (83.7%: 472–560)	d13C = -20.2
d.132/501	22.26 m E, 2.62 m N, 98.38 m SH (floor, room 4CS)	Poz-89932	Charred dicot herb	1511±26	AD 442–639 → modelled date: 484–635 (94.5%: 536–635; 93.4%: 536–608)	d13C = -24.7

(Continued)

Table 4.8: (Continued)

Find no.	Location	Laboratory no.	Sample description	Date	Calibrated date at 95.4% confidence	Comments
d.150/547	26.87 m E, 5.21 m N, 98.26 m SH (room 5CS)	SUERC-71966	Bone: *Sus*, right scapula	1584±18	AD 428–544 → modelled date: AD 447–542	d13C = -19.8
d.165/649	4.53 m E, 5.83 m N, 98.78 m SH (room 0CS)	SUERC-71972	Bone: *Bos*, tooth P3/P4 sup.	1535±18	AD 439–595 → modelled date: 544–594	d13C = -10.9
d.169	Oven in room 0CS/W outdoor area	AM272	Burnt soil: Oven wall	n/a	[1000–825 BC?] AD 418–520 [AD 1076–1379, 1900–1990?]	AD 418–520 in part compatible with ^{14}C dates
d.184/862	24.50 m E, 3.17 m N, 96.31 m SH (bottom fill of pit d.130, room 5CS)	SUERC-71973	Bone: Large mammal, long bone, medial	1536±18	AD 439–594 → modelled date: 548–591	d13C = -12.2
d.186/674	28.50 m E, 5.13 m N, 97.95 m SH (room 5C)	SUERC-71974	Bone: *Equus caballus* (horse)	1597±18	AD 423–539 → modelled date: AD 430–535	d13C = -18.9
d.214/789	28.40 m E, 1.42 m N, 98.27 m SH (fill of gully, room 5CS)	SUERC-71975	Bone: *Sus*, metapodial	1542±18	AD 436–591 → modelled date: 479–576 (90.4%: 527–576)	d13C = -19.2
d.223/s7	Fill of oven d.222 (room 0CS)	Poz-89870	Charred *Hordeum vulgare*, 2 seeds	1515±22	AD 482–632 → modelled date: 483–590 (94.2%: 534–590)	d13C = -21.2
d.226/739	27.57 m E, 1.97 m N, 96.63 m SH (bottom fill of pit d.216, room 5CS)	SUERC-71976	Bone: Medium mammal, cranium	1597±18	AD 423–539 → modelled date: 471–550	d13C = -14.8
d.233/756	25.60 m E, 1.38 m N, 97.88 m SH (bottom fill of pit d.230, room 5CS)	Poz-89871	Charred *Juglans* nut shell	1560±23	AD 432–568 → modelled date: 478–569	d13C = -27.3
d.239/797	28.07 m E, 1.06 m N, 98.31 m SH (room 5CS)	Poz-89872	Charred monocots	1519±22	AD 442–605 → modelled date: 532–584	d13C = -28.8
d.250/843	22.90 m E, 1.30 m N, 97.68 m SH (room 4CS)	SUERC-71982	Bone: Caprini, rib	1556±18	AD 433–570 → modelled date: 436–571 (83.1%: 474–571)	d13C = -18.4
d.252/854	0.42 m E, 6.70 m N, 97.60 m SH (fill of pit d.254, W outdoor area)	SUERC-71983	Bone: Large mammal, humerus	1583±18	AD 429–544	d13C = -16.9

- other radiocarbon samples overlap (at the 95.4% confidence range).

- There is no artefact chronology or other dating technique that enables us to distinguish between different phases of occupation (leaving aside Stone Age flint tools[70] attesting much earlier activity in the area, even if found redeposited in much later deposits).

- Deposits often contained few artefacts and little organic matter, making it difficult or impossible to identify distinct contemporary horizons in different parts of the trench. Indeed, colour and composition were so uniform that little would be gained by providing soil descriptions when discussing deposits. Soft or very soft light to mid-yellowish brown clayey silt, i.e. loess, forms almost always the principal component. (Trampled earth floors were of firmer composition, but identical colour.)

- The challenges of identifying layers, differing little in colour and composition, was exacerbated by mud-brick walls often confining layers to an individual room unit without any obvious clues as to what may chronologically correspond to them in the next room.

- Indeed, the mud-brick walls themselves are often of a very similar colour to the material abutting them, and mud-bricks were often hard or impossible to identify, notably in upper layers disturbed by bioturbation. As a result, door openings in mud-brick wall were often only clearly identified at a late stage, necessitating separate excavation of the deposits filling them. Even if it had been possible to securely identify doorways always immediately, the absence of layers standing out distinctly in terms of colour or composition would not have allowed us to follow a deposit from one room to the next.

- Whilst the relative elevation of layers, the base of structures and the top of pits in different rooms provides possible clues as to their relative age, there is no evidence that the speed of deposition in different rooms was identical. We cannot be sure that deposits at, brick structures built on, or pits cut from, a certain level in one room are contemporary to deposits or features of identical elevation in another room. We may, however, assume that the floor level of rooms was probably not below that of the contemporary land surface outdoors, as this would have resulted in surface water infiltrating during episodes of heavy or persistent rain. As there is no evidence of deposits suggestive of standing water within the barracks, we may assume that floors were well drained and at a similar or slightly higher level to outdoor areas, an observation that aids us in phasing.

- Where there are unmistakable signs for relative stratigraphy, e.g. storage vessel pits cutting mud-brick walls and/or ovens, such observations may be applicable to the room in question only and there may be no clear evidence as to which deposits and structures in other rooms may be contemporary.

Despite all these difficulties, we have tentatively assigned all deposits and structures to phases, but often have to allow for attribution to more than one phase or sub-phase. Some observations aid us with tentative phasing:

- Deposits sealed under floors must evidently be earlier – though not necessarily by much (phase 1.1 or 1.2).

- All compacted earth floors (phases 1.2–1.3) must have formed indoors, as outdoors, in wet conditions, no walking surface would have remained level. We may conclude that the trampled earth floors are all later than the mud-brick walls they abut. They probably formed as a result of indoor traffic immediately after or during construction, but will have been used and kept clean well beyond.

- There were similar trampled-earth floors in rows 2–5 (as well as in the doorway between rows 3 and 4), but none were found in rows 0–1. Those in rows 2–4 were at a similar level, that in row 5 roughly half a foot deeper. Whilst this does not prove contemporary creation, it suggests that the phase 1.2 floors of the original barracks (rows 2–3) were still in use when the eastern annexe was added (phases 1.2–1.3).

- It follows that the earliest deposits (phase 2.1) on top of the floors (phases 1.2–1.3) appear to be later than the addition of the annexes.

- A range of early ovens and fireplaces were found above the early floors (but none in the original barracks). They are all at a similar level, and it is tempting to think they are contemporary (phase 1.3). They are abutted and/or overlain by phase 2.1 deposits and must be earlier.

- On top of the trampled-earth floor level, and abutting the inside of the mud-brick walls in rows 2 and 3, we found ledges of fired and sun-baked bricks (phases 1.2–2.1). These could be a little earlier than, contemporary with or later than the phase 1.3 ovens.

- That the eastern annexe had floors at a similar and lower level to the main barracks and that there were no ovens or fireplaces in the original barracks (rows 2 and 3), with no evidence for preserved outdoor ovens or fireplaces from Trench d so far, may suggest that the annexes were added soon after the original barracks had been erected. Alternatively, if occupants cleared out rubbish, they may have occupied the original barracks for some time without any debris building up on the original earth floors. Cooking might have taken place in a hypothetical upper storey or in separate facilities outside the barracks. That the bases of the annexe walls appear to be some 20 cm higher and that their architecture differed greatly from the much more regular and solid original barracks may offer support for a few years or decades passing between the construction of the original barracks and that of the annexes.

- We cannot be sure how long it took for deposits on top of the earthen floors in rows 2–5 (and at equivalent levels in rows 0–1) to build up. No new trampled earth horizons formed, or were preserved, at a higher level. Whilst we subdivided phase 2 into lower, middle and upper horizons (phases 2.1, 2.2 and 2.3), these need not represent separate events and might all have formed in a short period of time – e.g. when a decision was taken to raise the floor, perhaps to prevent muddy water from flowing in from outdoors. There are no ovens or other structures at intermediate levels, which one might have expected had there been a significant gap in time between sub-phases 2.1 and 2.2 or between 2.2 and 2.3. A sample (d.044/211) from just above the clay floor in room 2C in the original barracks could be as early as c. AD 440 or as late as AD 595, but is with an over 88% probability later than AD 530. A sample (d.070/313) from 0.50 m above the floor in adjacent room 3C is not likely to be later than the AD 540s (suggesting that the sample from near the floor of room 2C is earlier than that). A sample (d.132/501) from the original floor in annexe room 4CS is likely to be no earlier than the 530s. Perhaps the barracks were kept clean for some time and then the floor raised no earlier than the middle third of the sixth century.

- The top of five storage pits appears to be at phase 2 levels, but it is hard to be sure precisely when the pits were cut. Most may potentially have been used until phase 4. At least four of them had been abandoned by or before the AD 560s (assuming the samples from their fill were not redeposited later), though the largest pit (d.130) is likely to have remained in use to the mid- or, more probably, later sixth century. The early filling of many of the pits does not necessarily prove that they had been created much earlier; probably cut from phase 2 levels, it is possible that the pits all date to the time from c. AD 530 onwards. It is, however, hard to be sure whether they were cut from phase 2 levels or, once the decision was made to raise the floor, the surface was raised around their edges. Their attribution to phase 2 or later should be considered tentative, and earlier origins are possible.

- On top of phase 2 deposits, seven ovens and one fireplace were created (in phase 3), though again none in the original barracks (rows 2–3). They are all at a similar level (except for an oven in row 5, probably a result of everything in row 5 being at a slightly lower level than in rows 0–4). It seems reasonable to propose that they replaced the ovens and fireplaces of phase 1.3 – and that the gap in time between the last use of the phase 1.3 ovens and the creation of the phase 3 ovens was short. If so, the absence of ovens or fireplaces in phase 2 may also point to the surface having been raised rapidly in a very short phase 2.

- Some phase 3 ovens were cut into or overlay earlier mud-brick walls, suggesting a major change in the use of space.

- A series of basic alignments of fired bricks (phases 3–4.2) are on top of phase 2.3 levels and may be contemporary to the phase 3 ovens. Even if they, or some of them, should be later, they are likely to pre-date the disuse of these cooking and heating facilities (perhaps with the exception of the decommissioned ovens in room 1CS).

- Pits, for a series of large storage vessels in row 1, were dug from a similar level (phase 4.1). These must be later than the ovens (or at least some of them) as they cut through oven walls in row 1. This proves that phase 3 ovens in row 1 were largely demolished prior to the insertion of the storage vessels. It does not prove that phase 3 ovens or fireplaces in other rows went out of use at the same time, and one is inclined to think that some of them will have functioned throughout phase 4 or beyond. Unlike areas used for domestic activities, heating will not have been required in a storeroom (i.e. room 1CS), nor would there have been much space for food preparation.

- After an unknown period of use, the storage vessels in room 1CS were filled with debris (phase 4.2).

- On top of the filled-up storage vessels and ovens, the latest preserved occupation level (phase 5) formed. No new structures, with the probable exception of one oven and one basic fireplace, can certainly be associated with this phase or phase 4.2, though it is possible that some phase 3 and 4 structures might still have been in use at the start of phase 5.

- The subsoil (phase 6) and topsoil (phase 7) contained no structures, but redeposited Sasanian-era material. It is possible that they may include the latest (disturbed) horizons.

With most samples yielding overlapping dates, it seemed worthwhile to attempt to create Bayesian models to refine dating, even if in the fifth- to early sixth-century plateau of the radiocarbon calibration curve this often adds little precision. To err on the side of caution, each of our models relates to one room only, and we did not attempt to create multi-room models.[71] Our latest sample, d.004/16, is likely to be stratigraphically later than all other samples from Trench d. As it is, however, just a few

Table 4.9: Phasing of Trench d. No precision-dating can be offered, due to most dates falling into the fifth- to sixth-century plateau in the radiocarbon calibration curve, but it is clear that no structures found in the trench can be earlier than the AD 420s at the earliest and none later than the seventh century at the latest. Even the attribution to centuries is tentative only, whilst it is clear that most traceable activity belongs to the sixth century, and a start in the fifth century seems likely.

Phase	Short description	Chronology
7	Topsoil	21st c.
6	Subsoil	7th–21st c., mostly prob. to mid-7th c.
5	Latest surviving occupation layer; latest basic fireplaces on top of partially demolished room partitions	mid–late 6th/early–mid-7th c.
4.2	Filling up of storage vessels; some ovens and pits may remain in use	c. 6th c.
4.1	Insertion and use of storage vessels; some ovens and pits prob. remain in use	c. 6th c.
3–4.2	Erection of late brick alignments along old mud-brick walls	c. 6th c.
3	Creation of later ovens and hearths, incl. one cut into earlier mud-brick wall	c. 6th c.
2.3	Higher deposits/raising of surface	c. 5th–6th c., prob. 6th c.
2.2	Mid deposits/raising of surface	c. 5th–6th c., prob. 6th c.
2.1	Earliest deposits on floors/raising of surface	c. 5th–6th c., prob. 6th c.
1.1–2.1	Earliest deposits to earliest post-floor levels	c. 5th–6th c.
1.3	Early ovens and fireplaces	c. 5th–6th c.
1.2–1.3	Annexe mud-brick walls and floors	c. 5th–6th c.
1.2	Earliest deposits and main barrack floors	c. 5th c.
1.1	Main mud-brick barrack walls	c. 5th c.
0	Geological	Ice Age

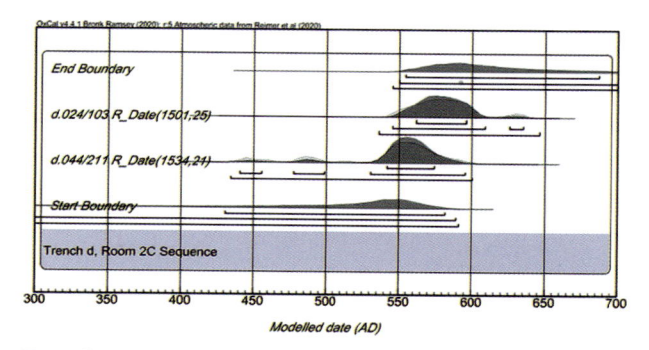

Fig. 4.20: Bayesian model of radiocarbon samples from room 2C, in the west of the original barracks, attesting activity in the sixth century (or potentially fifth to sixth/early seventh centuries) – in a room kept clean initially? Note that the lower sample is from just above the clay floor. Late occupation levels have not been sampled in this room.

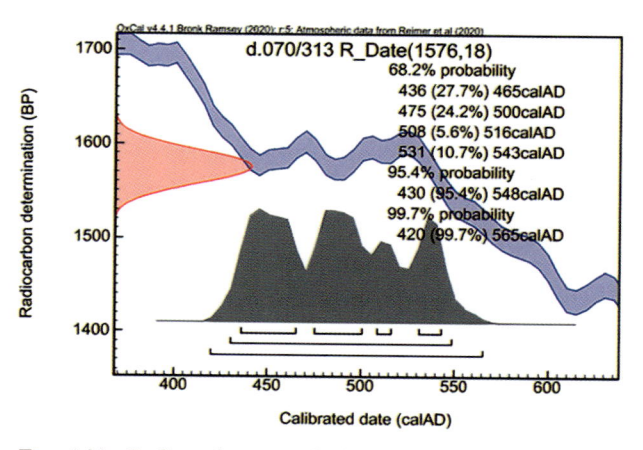

Fig. 4.21: Radiocarbon sample from room 3C, in the east of the original barracks. The sample of phases 3–5 is from half a metre above the original floor level in this room, suggesting that construction and original occupation started well before the latest likely date of the sample in the 540s.

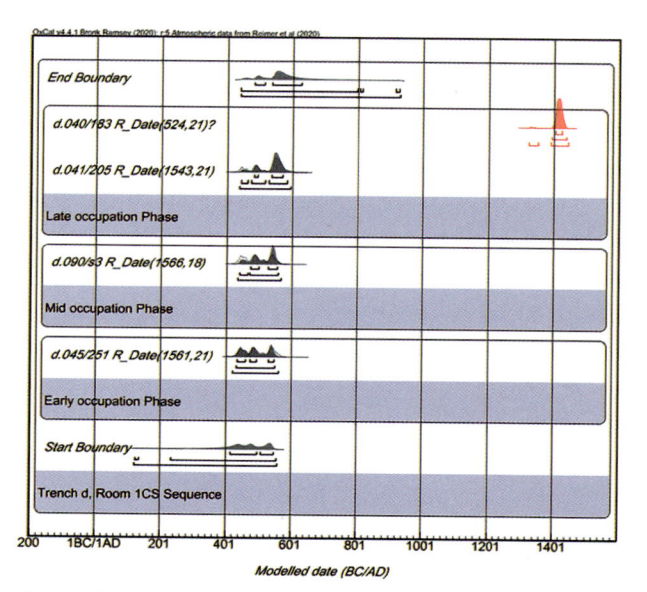

Fig. 4.22: Bayesian model of radiocarbon samples from room 1CS, in the east of the western annexe. Deposit d.045, most likely of the fifth or early sixth century, probably pre-dates the construction of the annexe. A bone sample from near the bottom of a storage pit (d.090 in pit d.064) attests (unless redeposited) that this had gone out of use before c. AD 560 at the latest. A further bone sample from the fill (d.041) of one of the big storage jars in situ, proves that this had also been filled up with debris no later than the 580s at the latest. A late medieval rodent sample (d.040/183) is evidently intrusive.

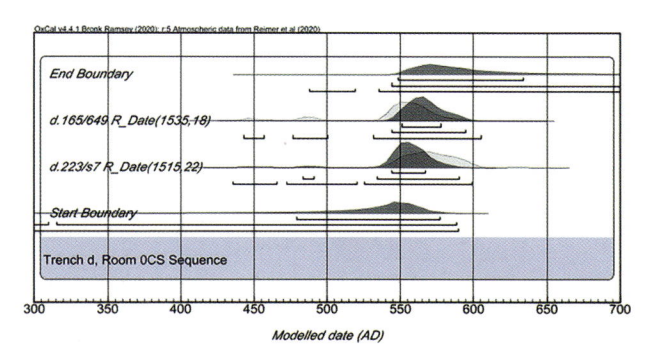

Fig. 4.23: Bayesian model of radiocarbon samples from room 0CS, in the west of the western annexe. Barley seeds from the fill (d.223) of a phase 1.3 oven (d.222) could date to the late fifth or sixth century, but a date in or after the AD 530s is much more likely and perhaps further circumstantial evidence for long use of early installations and tidiness. A bone sample (d.165/649) found 30 cm higher than the top of the oven is likely to date to the last two thirds of the sixth century.

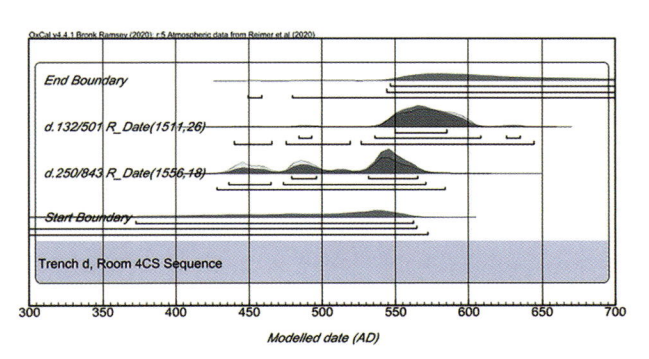

Fig. 4.24: Bayesian model of radiocarbon samples from room 4CS, in the west of the eastern annexe. A bone sample (d.250) of the fifth or sixth century from a probable material extraction pit is likely to have been discarded by occupants of the original barracks before the annexe was built. Charcoal from the original trampled earth floor (d.132) of the annexe could date to the fifth century, but is much more likely later than AD 530 – perhaps suggesting that it was not before the middle third of the sixth century that floor levels in the barracks were raised.

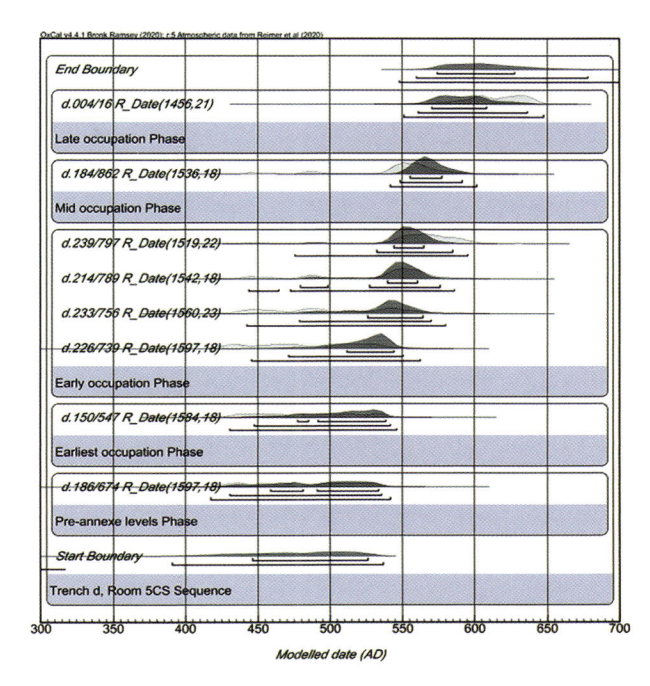

Fig. 4.25: Bayesian model of radiocarbon samples from room 5CS, in the east of the eastern annexe. A fifth- or early sixth-century bone from a horse is from a deposit (d.186) from under the floor of the annexe. Like the earliest samples from annexe room 1CS and 4CS, it probably pre-dates annexe construction, but post-dates the erection of the original barracks. The seven samples above could all date to the sixth century, though a fifth-century date for the earliest samples and an early seventh-century date for the latest sample is possible. It was in the sixth century that this annexe room was most heavily occupied and/or its occupants deposited occupation materials indoors or used them to raise floors. The deposits sampled include early occupation (d.150) within the annexe, a further occupation/levelling deposit (d.239) the secondary bottom fills of two storage pits (d.226 in pit d.216 and d.233 in pit d.230) and the fill (d.214) of a gully (d.213 = d.219). Pit d.216 appears to have been filled up by AD 550 at the latest or before, pit d.230 and the gully by the 560s and 570s at the very latest – and, of course, they might have been filled up decades earlier. A sample from the bottom fill (d.184) of the largest pit (d.130), that is likely to have replaced the two smaller earlier pits, probably dates to the 540s–590s – suggesting that this pit had gone out of use at some stage in the last two thirds of the sixth century. The latest sample, from a phase 5 deposit (d.004), attests continued occupation in the second half of the sixth or early seventh century.

Table 4.10: Finds from the interior of the fully excavated barracks room 2C, not listing deposits (or structures) without finds (or with archaeobotanical material and/or small fragments of objects from sieving or flotation).[72] Weights (in this table and the subsequent ones) are in grams and are based, for reasons of consistency and as the dataset is more complete, largely on those recorded after recovery rather than those recorded later by the finds specialists. Elevation (in metres) refers to arbitrary site height. Top and bottom elevations of deposits in this and subsequent tables are average values, and it should be noted that context/spit boundaries were not totally level and there are sometimes finds from above or below the height range indicated for the context in question. Note that some of the upper bulk deposits were allocated before the top of the walls were reached and room divisions recognised. Most of d.007 belongs to room 2C, but some is also from 2S and row 1 and the top of the walls in between. Overall, the table thus may over-represent the quantity of finds in room 2C.[73]

Room 2C deposits	Bottom	Top	Depth	Phase	Pottery	Bone	Other finds
d.007 (mainly in 2C)	98.73	99.12	0.39	2.3–5	72,053	12	Charcoal, 2 clay spindle whorls (44 g), copper alloy (7 g), glass (39 g) iron, incl. 2 nails (47 g) and slag (236 g)
d.024 and d.025	98.60	98.73	0.13	2.2	38,109	160	Charcoal and slag (96 g)
d.034	98.43	98.60	0.17	2.1	2,685	193	Iron (2 g)
d.044, d.049 and d.050 (floor, at c. 98.32–98.37)	98.32	98.43	0.11	1.2–2.1	255	117	Charcoal and flint blade (2 g)
d.053	98.18	98.32	0.14	1.2	66	0	Charcoal and whetstone (777 g)
Total					**113,168**	**482**	**Ratio, pot:bone: c. 235:1**
Up to phase 2.2					**41,115**	**470**	**Ratio, pot:bone: c. 87:1**

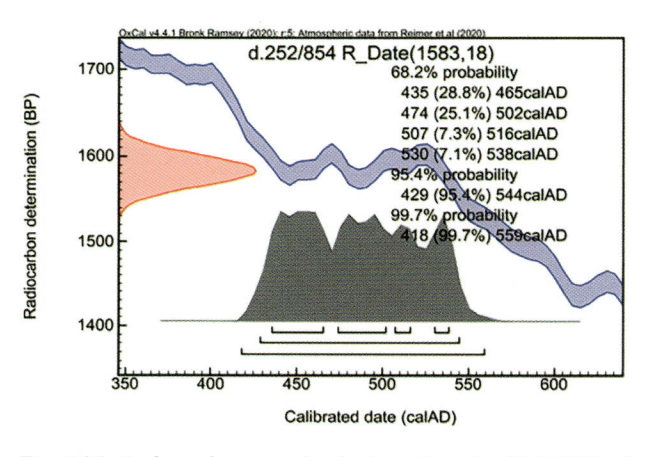

Fig. 4.26: Radiocarbon sample of a bone from the fill (d.252) of a partially excavated storage pit (d.254) in the western outdoor area, suggesting that this food storage facility had probably also been abandoned by the middle of the sixth century at the latest, or before. As with all single samples, one has to allow for the possibility of later redeposition, but it seems unlikely that those filling up disused features had easier access to old than recent material, though there may well be the occasional exception.

centimetres above other samples, it seemed safer only to use it for chronological modelling for the room unit in question (5CS).

4.1.4.4. The history of occupation of the barrack rooms

4.1.4.4.1. The original barracks: rows 2 and 3

We will first examine the occupation of the original barracks before exploring the western and eastern annexes and the outdoors areas. The mud-brick walls of the original complex were built on the surface at the time (at c. 98.20 m site height), and there was no evidence for any foundation trenches. The layout and phasing of the construction have already been discussed,[74] and this chapter focuses on the occupation within the rows of rooms (2 and 3) that constitute the original barracks, notably the two fully excavated rooms 2C and 3C.

4.1.4.4.1.1. The western row of rooms (2) in the original barracks

Inside room 2C, we found an early levelling deposit: soft mid-yellowish brown clayey silt (d.053), i.e. redeposited loess with a small quantity of pottery and charcoal as well as a whetstone (see Table 4.10 for quantities). A 2 × 1 m sondage into a deposit of identical composition (d.055) down to 97.71 m site height yielded no further finds, suggesting it is natural loess. The building had evidently been erected on virgin land. A clay floor (d.050) in room 2C, at 98.32–98.37 m site height, c. 2 cm thick, on top of the levelling deposits and a few centimetres above the base of the mud-brick walls (d.003) of c. 98.20 m, is likely to belong to the earliest occupation.

A round posthole (d.051, filled by d.052), centred on 11.95 m east and 3.35 m north, of 36 cm diameter and 24 cm depth (98.34 m down to 98.10 m site height), either cuts through floor d.050, or is abutted by this earthen floor and is evidently early. Located near the entrance to room 2C, but not within the actual doorway, its function is unclear. One wonders if it might have contained a post supporting the floor of an upper storey, perhaps to bridge a wide gap in the mud-brick walls in this corner of the room that may have supported such a floor elsewhere. There is, however, a strong possibility that the doorway was initially as narrow as that of room 3C and only widened later, after the annexes had been added. Perhaps the post supported a jamb or parts of the frame of an early narrow door, if it is perhaps a little further south-east than one would expect for a door-post.

There is much uncertainty also about the internal furnishing of rooms and the phasing of the little that was left behind. In room 2C, we found rows of fired bricks and fragments thereof with the odd fragment of sun-baked brick (d.059), just one course (c. 10 cm) high, lining the base of the mud-brick walls. Brick alignment d.059 was best preserved on the south side of the room and least well in the west. As the entrance was in the west, it may not have been continuous (even if it would have been easy to step over the ledge). We do not know whether d.059 was discontinuous from the start or whether gaps are the result of later selective removal. It appeared to overlie floor d.050 and was above the level of posthole d.051. It did not overlie this posthole and may have left a gap for it. The structure's purpose is unclear, but must be the same as that of a virtually identical feature (d.061 = d.124) in room 3C: it was too low and narrow for seating, a working surface or a shelf. There is no evidence that the bricks held some carpet or textile floor cover in place or that they supported a raised wooden floor above. The reuse of brick fragments may be an argument for a later modification rather than an original feature. It is certain that the brick alignments post-date the construction of the barracks and cannot be later than phase 2.1, when the floor was raised. In the early Sasanian Paykand fortifications, the inside walls of rooms were also lined by shallow benches, but they were about twice as wide (c. 0.80–1.00 m) as their counterparts in Fort 2. They are thought to have served as benches to sit on, whilst their narrow Fort 2 counterparts would not have provided comfortable seating. There were also fireplaces on the benches at Paykand,[75] whilst we found none on their counterparts in Fort 2. Perhaps they supported timber furnishings leaning against the wall, e.g. shelves or posts holding an interim floor in place.

Little material attributable to initial occupation survived within the barracks. It seems the rooms were initially kept clean, and neither rubbish nor debris were allowed to build up indoors, nor was the floor surface artificially raised. On top of the trampled earth floor d.050 and abutting brick alignment d.059, we found deposits of similar composition to those below. A noticeable difference was that they contained patches of blackish brown clayey silt (d.049) and extensive patches of very soft greyish brown silt (d.044), but little charcoal. Perhaps these are disintegrated cinders of fires employing dung fuel[76] embedded in levelling deposits. They provide circumstantial evidence for heating or cooking, even if there were no ovens or hearths or any trace of *in-situ* fire-reddened soil in room 2C. These deposits contained a moderate quantity of pottery and bone and are clearly the earliest horizons within the room above the trodden-earth floor (d.050).

The high loess component and a redeposited prehistoric (Mesolithic?) flint blade (d.044/216, at 98.33 m site height, i.e. from the interface between floor d.050 and deposit d.044) suggest that this horizon formed as a result of levelling rather than indoor dumping of organic debris. Bone and pot fragments suggest, however, that there was active occupation nearby at the time. A sample (d.044/211) from pig teeth (see Table 4.8) yielded a date of c. AD 440–595 (530–595 with an 88.4% probability). Found at 98.36 m, it was only just above the trodden-earth floor. Whilst it could in theory be redeposited, the sample belongs to the earliest in the stratigraphic sequence, suggesting the room was kept clean up to the 530s or so.

A further deposit (d.034 of phase 2.1), containing much more pottery than the deposits underneath (Table 4.10), but only a slightly higher quantity of bone, overlay the top of the brick alignment (d.059) and deposit d.044 within the room. Above, we found a further patch of possible cinders of a fire (d.025, phase 2.2). The quantity of pottery increased massively, to c. 38 kg, in d.024 above (phase 2.2), whilst the concentration of animal bone (Table 4.10) remained similar to that in the layers below. A pig tooth (d.024/103) from the bottom of this deposit (98.61 m) dates to c. AD 545–635, with an over 93% probability of the date falling before AD 610. This suggests that the floor may not have been raised before the middle of the sixth century.

The main bulk deposit associated with phases 2.3–5 was d.007 in the first and second rows of rooms. Overlying in part the mud-brick walls and assigned before the walls were found, this deposit spans more than one room unit, even if much of it was from the room 2C area. At a base level of 98.90 m and 98.93 m respectively, well above the bottom of d.007 (c. 98.68–98.77 m), we found two structures made of reused fired Gorgan Wall brick: brick pillar d.018 and brick alignment d.016. D.016 consisted of six fragments of bricks standing on edge, 41 cm tall and c. 1.90 m long. Its southern edge is c. 2.40 m north, parallel and close to the north edge of the southern wall of the room. The top of the preserved mud-brick wall is at 98.95 m, whereas the base of d.016 was at 98.90 m and its top at 99.31 m. The mud-brick wall still appears to have been standing at the time, but has been lost to erosion and possible robbing since. Bioturbation will have caused further damage. Structure d.016 clearly lines the south edge of the room and leans against the wall, proving that the original room division was still maintained at the time.

A similar alignment of bricks, parallel to the wall of a building in the Sasanian hilltop fort or settlement of Gird-î Qalrakh, has been interpreted as a support for a vertical loom placed against the wall.[77] As three spindle whorls were found in room 2C and a fourth in the area of the postulated corridor to room 2S, the three stratified ones all from later phases of occupation as well (Fig. 18.13; Tables 18.5 and 18.7), it is clear that textile production took place in the area. One wonders if brick alignment

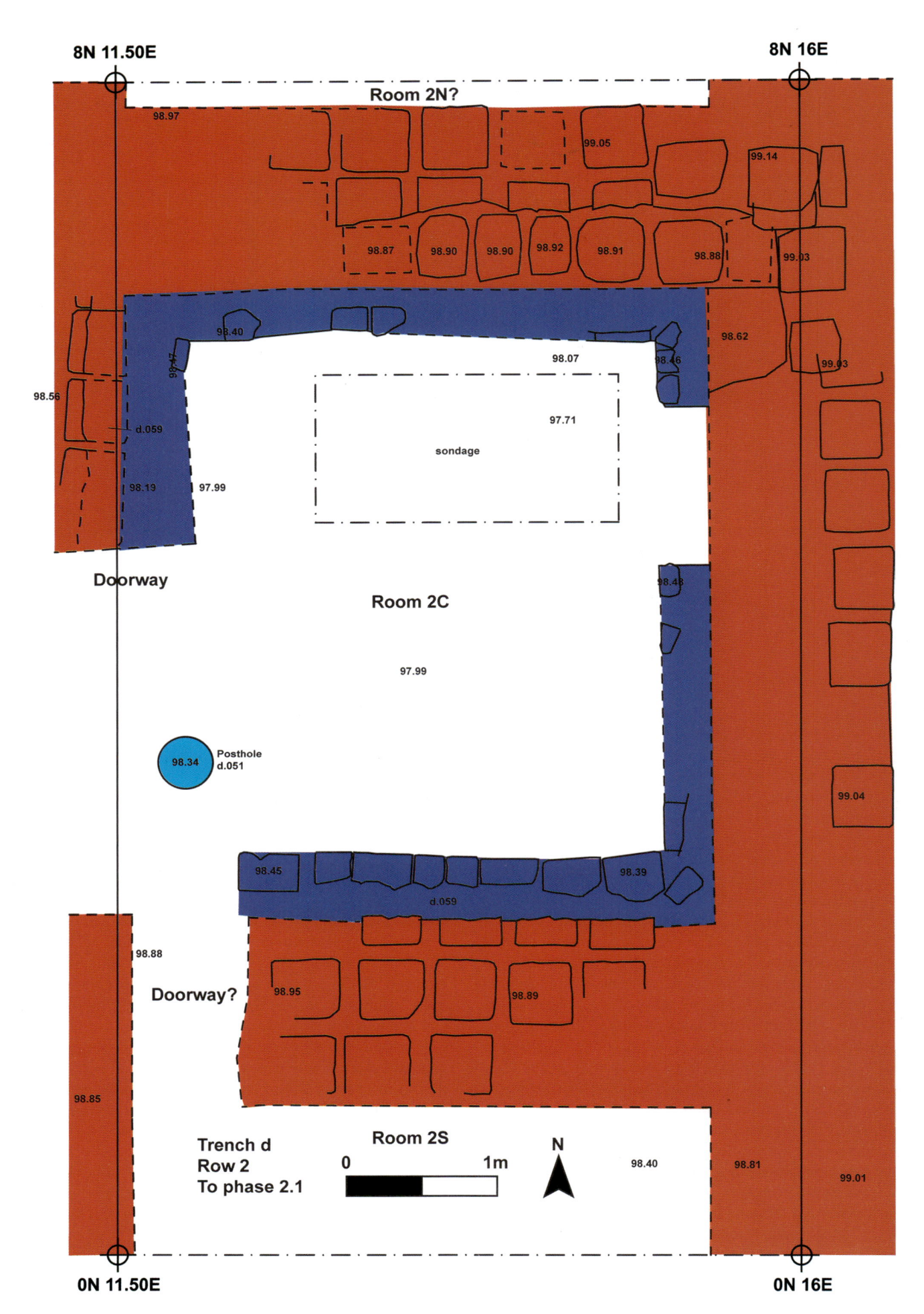

Fig. 4.27: Row 2: the western half of the original barracks in phase 1.

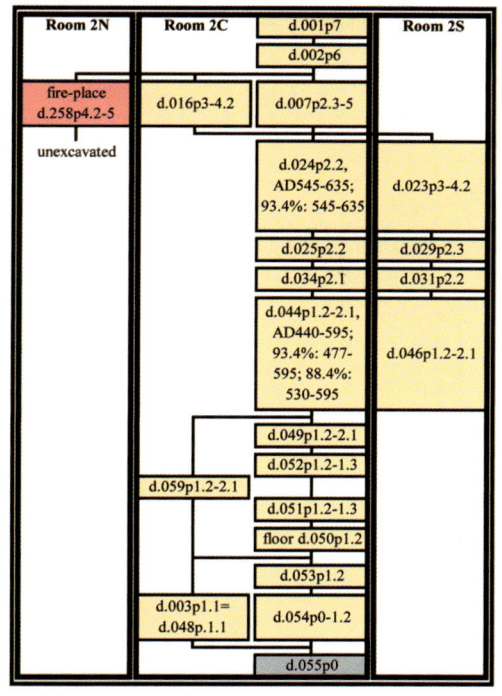

Fig. 4.28: Stratigraphic matrix for row 2. Colour code for this and other matrices: grey: natural (not always plotted); green: pits and deposits from within their fill; red: ovens and fireplaces; light brown: other deposits, structures and cuts. The matrix lists modelled radiocarbon dates. (For unmodelled dates, see Table 4.8.)

d.016 might also have supported a vertical loom, even if no loom-weights have come to light in this particular room. It is worth noting, however, that similar late brick alignments were also found in row 1 without any small finds pointing to textile production. And there had been low brick alignments lining the bases of walls in rooms 2C (d.059) and 3C (d.124) already in phase 1.2/2.1. As all implements used in textile production from Fort 2 belong to later phases, these low benches may have served a different function, unless one assumes that the looms were removed and all associated implements so systematically recovered that none was left behind. We may conclude that the brick alignments in the Fort 2 barracks were probably not mono-functional; that some of the late ones supported looms is at least a possibility.

A basic pillar (d.018) of phases 3–4.2, consisting of three flat fired bricks, the top and bottom brick complete, the middle a fragment (98.93–99.26 m elevation), near the western entrance to the room, will have supported a structure of unknown function. Perhaps it formed the base of a post or, more probably as neither very solid nor in the centre of a room, some table or other basic feature. It would be a futile exercise to try to establish what the purpose of each pile of bricks may have been. The use of bricks to stabilise the site guard's tent in 2015 (Fig. 4.31) is a telling testimony as to the multiple uses these heavy items can serve. What seems clear is that we see substantial modifications of the building at this late stage.

The upper parts of deposit d.007 abut the brick structures. The deposit contained over 72 kg of pottery, but little bone, as well as small quantities of glass, iron and slag. Significantly, there were three spindle whorls in this late deposit, two of them from room 2C and both from the northern half of the room. One of them (d.007/85) was found at 98.87 m, perhaps just before makeshift brick structures d.016 and d.018 were erected, one (d.007/69) at 99.01 m, i.e. perhaps lost after the last traceable structural alterations. A further unstratified spindle whorl (d.US/779) can probably also be attributed to room 2C, but we cannot be sure as to the time of loss. A probable iron knife (d.002/56) is a further item worth noting, coming from the subsoil above room 2C, but probably used by one of its latest occupants.[78]

Only the northernmost metre of room 2S was excavated, down to 98.28 m at the deepest point. The deposits inside (from bottom to top, d.046, d.031 and d.029) were fairly rich in pottery, yielding a combined total of over 5 kg of sherds, but far less so in bone (just 50 g combined). As in room 2C, there was much redeposited loess suggesting that, in addition to indoor deposition of finds, material was brought in to gradually raise surface levels. Near the north-east corner of the room, we found a basic pillar-like structure (d.023) made of two reused fired Gorgan Wall bricks on top of each other, at a level of 98.99–99.22 m. It is even more basic than its counterpart in room 2C consisting of three bricks (d.018). Evidently, the same makeshift structures as elsewhere in the building were erected at a late stage in room 2S. A spindle whorl (d.007/82) was found at 12.55 m east, 1.35 m north, 98.97 m site height, placing it on top of the preserved part of the division wall between rooms 2S and 2C. It does not seem likely that the item was embedded in a disintegrated mud-brick, as there is no evidence for the use of spindle whorls in the earliest phases of occupation, let alone during original construction of the barracks. Perhaps the upper sections of the wall were thinner or, more probably, there were niches in the wall, or it had been partially demolished then. Whilst about one foot north of the original northern edge of the room, the spindle whorl may attest that textile production also took place in room 2S. We found no evidence of a brick ledge along the walls as in rooms 2C and 3C (d.059 and d.061 = d.124), but as the preservation of this ledge was variable in these two rooms and could not be clearly shown to line all walls, this is no certain evidence of absence.

Little is known about room 2N, although its southern edge appears to be just within the trench, but none of the interior, except (as for the remainder of the trench) the overlying subsoil (d.002) and topsoil (d.001) have been excavated. We identified a small oven (d.258), probably of phases 4.2–5, on top of the division wall between rooms

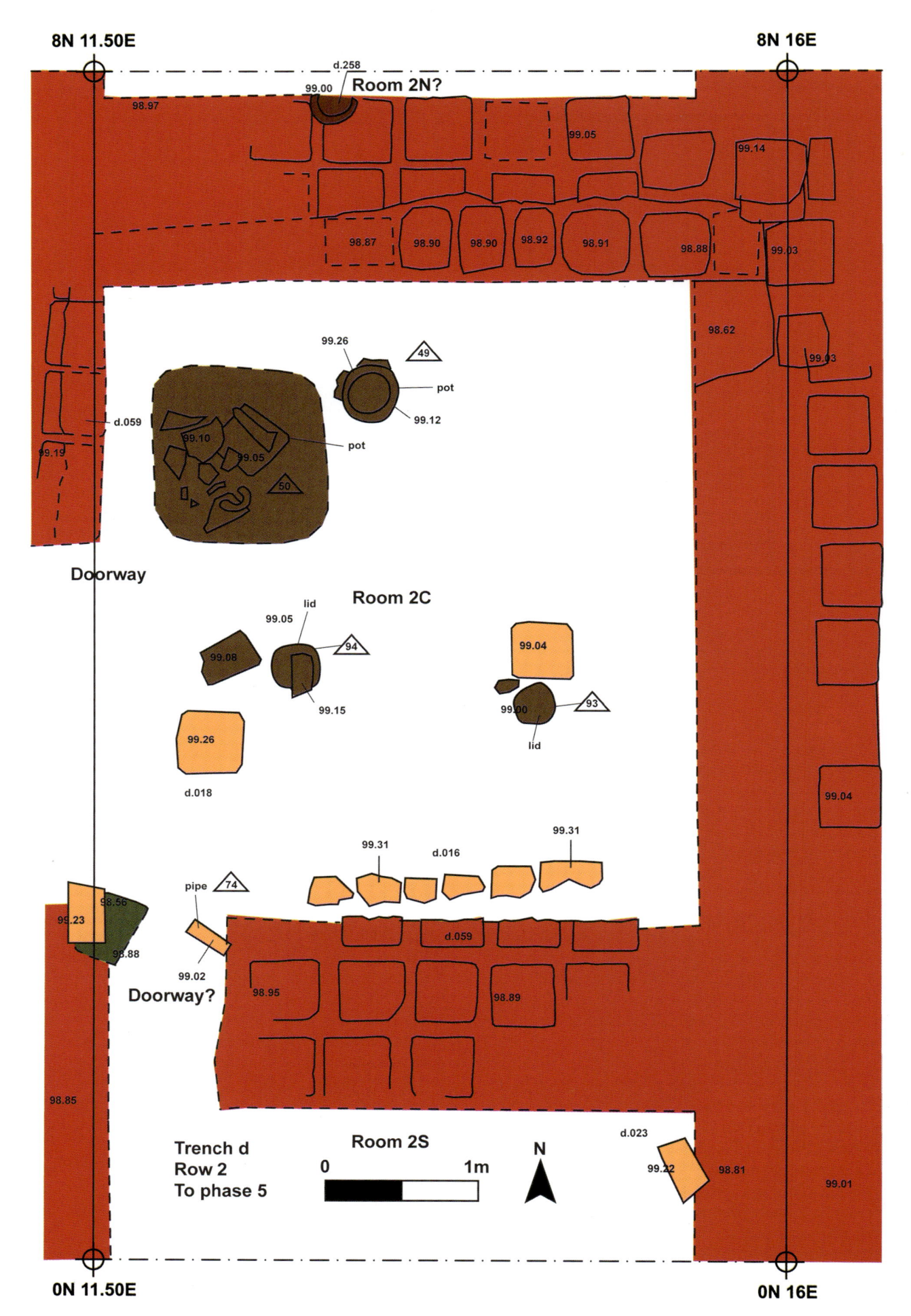

Fig. 4.29: Row 2: the western half of the original barracks in phases 3–5. Numbers in triangles refer to finds numbers.

Fig. 4.30: In the last phases of occupation various basic fired-brick structures, such as pillar d.018 (in the centre), were erected within the old mud-brick walls of rooms 2C (right) and 1CS (left). Note the large mud-bricks of the wall on the south side of room 2C (foreground, right), some of the large storage jars in room 1CS (top, left) and the late brick alignment d.014 subdividing room 1CS (left).

Fig. 4.31: This modern tent, with its porch and anchoring mechanisms, demonstrates that basic pillar-like structures made of reused Gorgan Wall bricks could have served a variety of functions, now as well as in antiquity.

Table 4.11: Finds from the interior of the northern edge of room 2S. Weights are in grams.

Room 2S deposits	Bottom	Top	Depth	Phase	Pottery	Bone	Other finds
d.007 (mainly in 2C)	98.82	99.12	0.30	2.3–5	?	?	1 clay spindle whorl (46 g)
d.029	98.72	98.82	0.10	2.3	2,545	3	Copper alloy sheet fragment (8 g)
d.031	98.63	98.72	0.09	2.2	1,007	36	Stone lid (10 g)
d.046	98.28	98.63	0.35	1.2–2.1	2,004	11	Copper alloy sheet fragments (3 g)
Total					5,556	50	Ratio, pot:bone: c. 111:1
Up to phase 2.2					3,011	47	Ratio, pot:bone: c. 64:1

2N and 2C, perhaps suggesting that also part of it had been demolished prior to complete abandonment. One wonders whether the evidence for finds and structures overlying the edge of internal walls is a sign of them having been reduced in width, or for the existence of niches in the non-preserved upper parts, rather than demolition. In Fort 4, there is no evidence for the upper sections of one barrack wall, excavated to its full width, getting narrower towards the top, even though they were preserved to a height of over 3 m. It was c. 1.20 m wide at all levels, but the barrack walls at Fort 4 demonstrably contained windows and perhaps also niches.[79]

4.1.4.4.1.2. THE EASTERN ROW OF ROOMS (3) IN THE ORIGINAL BARRACKS

Row 2 had been excavated in its entirety in 2015, but only the western and northern margins of room 3C, the southern edge of room 3N and the north-western corner of room 3S had been within our trench then. Extension of the trench in 2016 enabled us to explore row 3, the eastern counterpart of row 2, and we excavated room 3C completely as well as parts of room 3S. Unsurprisingly, room 3C was similar in design to its equivalent west (2C). There was also an earthen floor (d.085) on top of a levelling deposit (d.131). Both were of the usual soil colour, but the trampled earth floor (d.085) was of firmer composition. There were more pot sherds from d.131 than its equivalent (d.053) in 2C, as well as 18 g of bone; floor d.085 (of phases 1–2.1) yielded redeposited or trampled-in pot, as well as fragments of sun-baked and fired brick (as opposed to floor d.050 in room 2C being devoid of finds).

As in room 2C, there was a brick ledge (d.061 = d.124) on top of the earthen floor, lining the inside of the west and south walls in room 3C, whilst no traces of it were found in the north and east. It was one brick (c. 35/40–47 cm wide and c. 10 cm high) and consisted of fired and sun-baked mud-bricks and fragments thereof. Abutting and overlying the ledge, a deposit (d.082) rich in pottery and bone built up. The next layer (d.080) contained even more bone, though less pottery (Table 4.12). The uppermost deposit in room 3C (d.070) yielded significant quantities of pottery and bone as well. Overall, it is interesting to note that there was far more bone from room 3C than 2C, suggesting that use and/or disposal patterns differed substantially. Perhaps the picture is more complex than the two rooms serving as

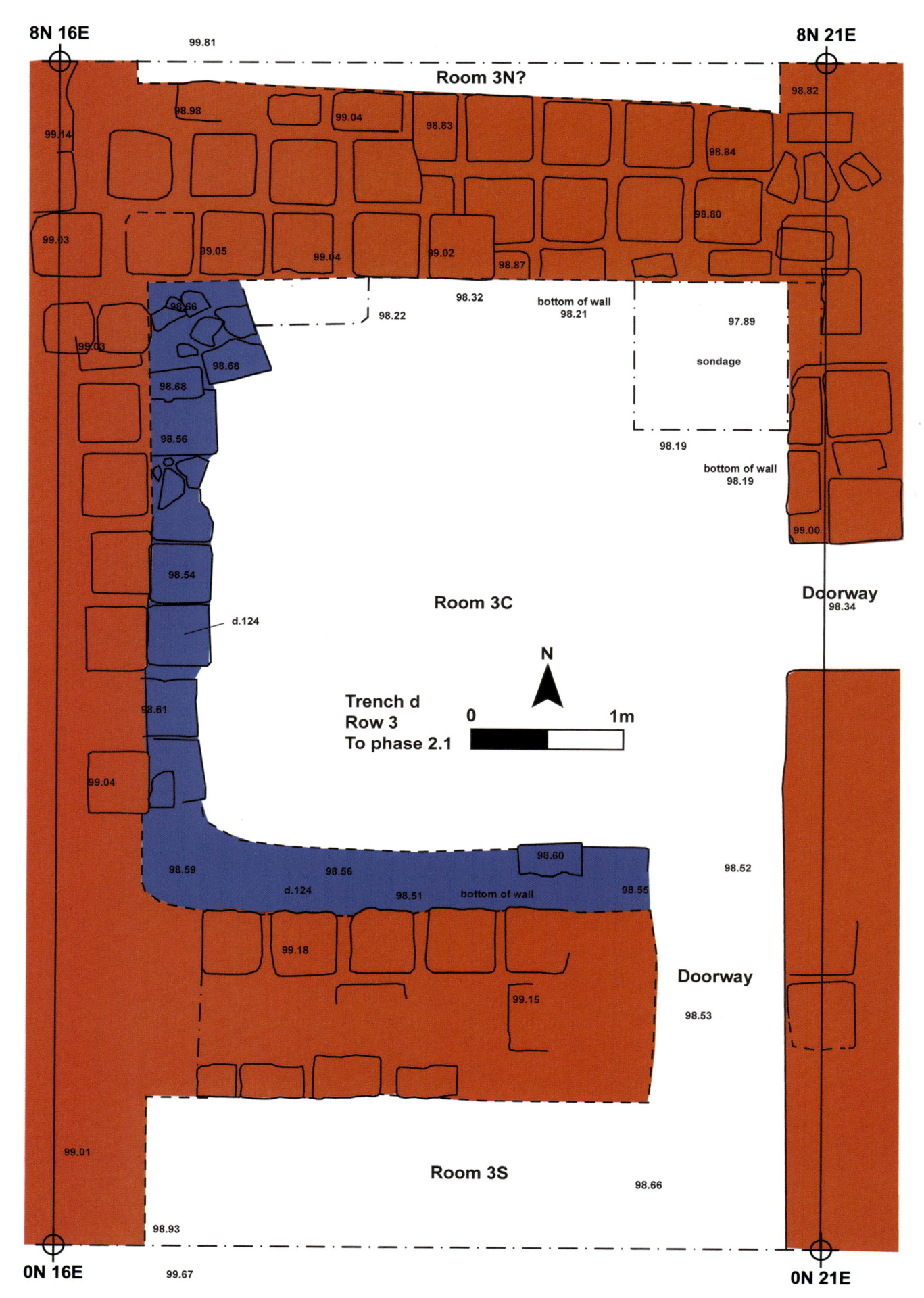

Fig. 4.32: Row 3: the eastern half of the original barracks in phase 1.

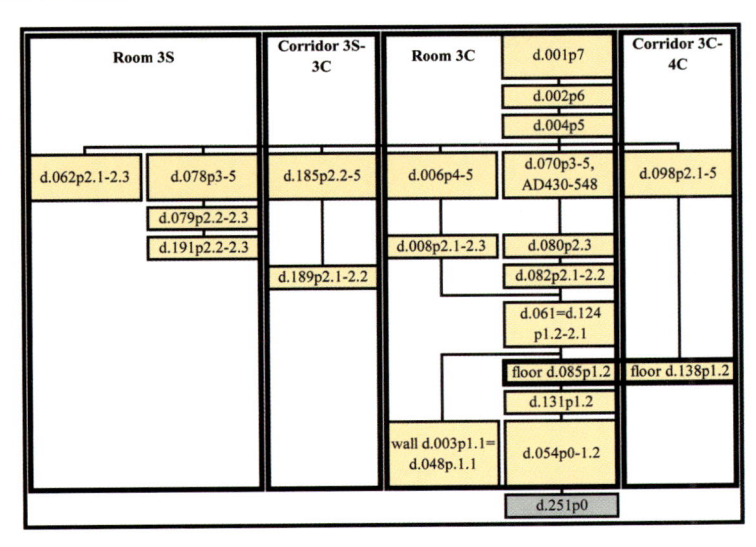

Fig. 4.33: Stratigraphic matrix for row 3.

Table 4.12: Finds from the interior of the fully excavated barrack room 3C. Weights are in grams. Note that some of the top bulk deposits were allocated before the top of the walls were reached and room divisions recognised. Deposit d.006 and d.008 have not been tabulated as they extend from rows 3 to 5 and 3 to 4 respectively and can no longer be neatly subdivided. Overall, the table may thus under-represent finds in room 3C (and over-represent those of 2C to which all of deposit d.007 has been allocated in the tables, even though some of it may belong to adjacent rooms). Up to phase 2.2, however, the quantity of finds in both rooms is reasonably reliable.

Room 3C deposits	Bottom	Top	Depth	Phase	Pottery	Bone	Other finds
d.070	98.91	99.15	0.24	3–5	13,525	2,104	Copper alloy sheet (1 g) and iron arrowhead (4 g)
d.080	98.74	98.91	0.17	2.3	7,390	2,590	n/a
d.082	98.41	98.74	0.33	2.1–2.2	16,235	1,578	Charcoal
d.085 (floor)	98.37	98.41	0.04	1.2	57	0	Charcoal
d.131	98.19	98.37	0.18	1.2	510	18	n/a
d.054	97.89	98.23	0.34	0–1.2	8	0	n/a
Total					37,725	6,290	Ratio, pot:bone: c. 6:1
Up to phase 2.2					16,810	1,596	Ratio, pot:bone: c. 11:1

accommodation for a small group of garrison members following similar cultural traditions. Yet, it is hard to establish the reasons for the difference: perhaps more food was consumed in room 3C than 2C or perhaps the two units differed in disposal of food remains; perhaps differences in group dynamics account for such behavioural differences, perhaps the assumption that the two rooms served as accommodation is mistaken and they were used for different activities. It also worth noting that the differences between the two rooms, with bone not only being more dominant at one stage of room 3C's occupation, but throughout the sequence, argue against the bulk of material being brought in from outside to raise the floor (unless consistently from a similar source – which seems improbable). Whilst soil may have been deposited to raise the floor on occasions, the actual pottery sherds and animal bones probably represent *in-situ* deposition.[80]

Very interesting is a radiocarbon sample from a cattle humerus (d.070/313) from d.070, the highest stratified deposit within room 3C. The sample itself was from the south-western quadrant of the room and 98.91 m site height, i.e. from the interface with deposit d.080 underneath. Found just 27 cm below the highest preserved point of the barrack mud-brick wall (at 99.18 m site height) and some 70 cm above their base and 50 cm above the original floor surface, the building will have been occupied for some time before deposition of the sample. Dating to c. AD 430–548, it suggests, unless redeposited, that all activity up to this point must be assigned to the 540s or before. Perhaps this 50–70 cm sequence formed rapidly, when the floor surface was raised, but it is impossible to reliably estimate the time it took for the deposits to build up. It should be borne in mind that AD 548 is the latest likely *terminus ante quem* (at 95.4% confidence), and it is possible that the real *terminus ante quem* could

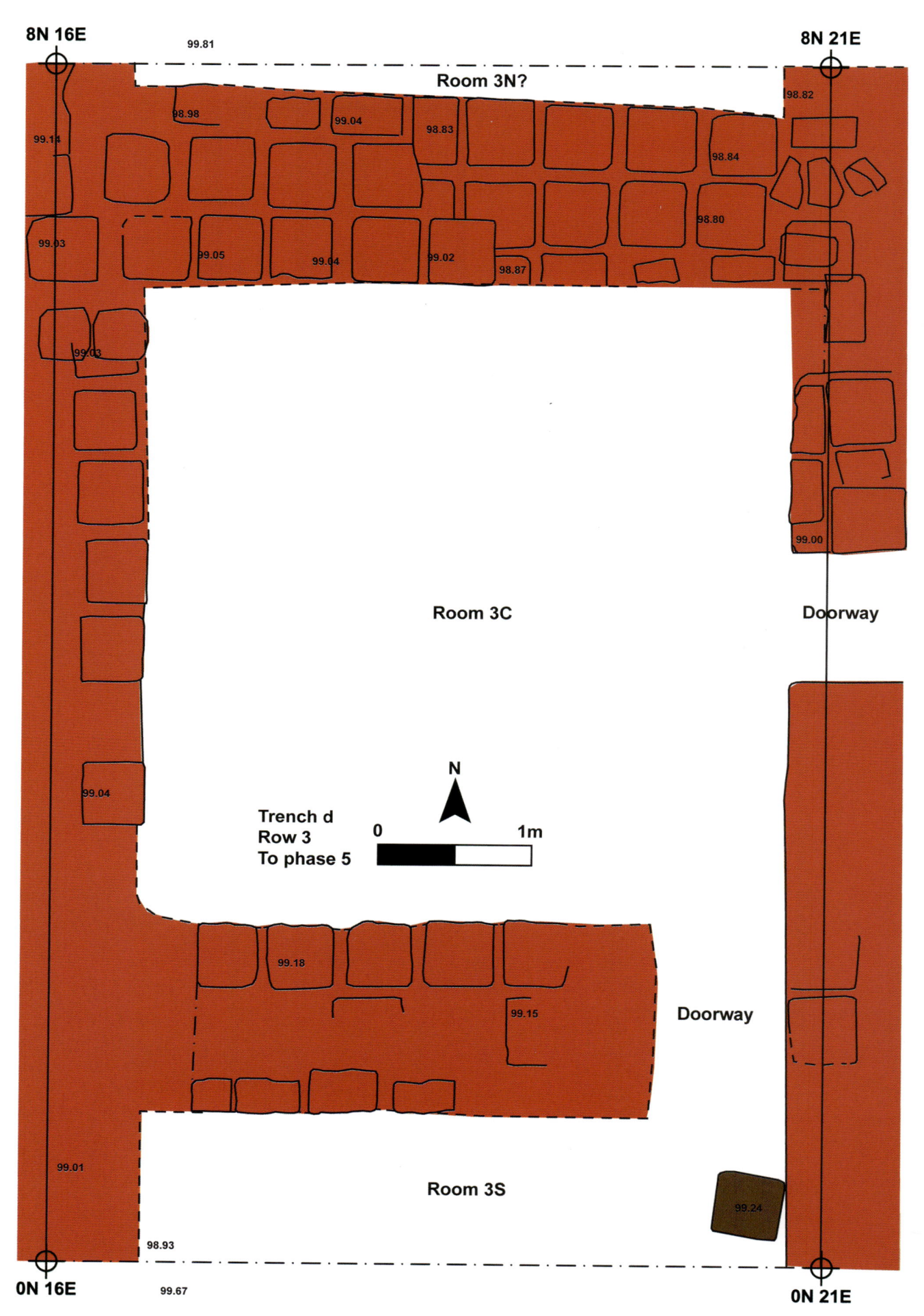

Fig. 4.34: Row 3: the eastern half of the original barracks in phases 3–5, remaining structurally virtually unchanged.

Table 4.13: Finds from the corridor connecting room 3C with the outdoor area/annexe room 4C. Weights are in grams.

Corridor 3C–4C deposit	Bottom	Top	Depth	Phase	Pottery	Bone	Other finds
d.098	98.41	99.05	0.64	2.1–5	1,083	1,225	n/a
Total					**1,083**	**1,225**	**Ratio, pot:bone: c. 1:1**

Table 4.14: Finds from the corridor connecting rooms 3C and 3S. Weights are in grams.

Corridor 3C–3S deposit	Bottom	Top	Depth	Phase	Pottery	Bone	Other finds
d.185	98.64	99.13	0.49	2.2–5	450	25	n/a
d.189	98.51	98.64	0.13	2.1–2.2	350	11	n/a
Total					**800**	**36**	**Ratio, pot:bone: c. 22:1**
Up to phase 2.2					**350**	**11**	**Ratio, pot:bone: c. 32:1**

Table 4.15: Finds from the interior of the northern edge of room 3S. Weights are in grams.

Room 3S deposits	Bottom	Top	Depth	Phase	Pottery	Bone	Other finds
d.078	98.91	99.13	0.22	3–5	566	0	n/a
d.079 and d.191	98.66	98.91	0.25	2.2–2.3	1,740	0	n/a
Total					**2,306**	**0**	

be a few decades earlier. The *terminus post quem* for the construction of the Gorgan Wall and its earliest occupation also falls within the radiocarbon calibration curve of the AD 420s–530s, as indicated by numerous samples.

Half a metre south of the sample and 3 cm higher, we found an iron arrowhead (d.070/309),[81] a weapon that may originally have been stored in the room. No doubt, there will have been many iron-tipped arrows in the arsenal of the garrison. The scarcity of metal in the assemblage is likely to reflect in part its value, resulting in high levels of ancient reuse, as well as low levels of loss even of small metal objects.

In the east, room 3C was connected via a doorway to annexe room 4C. Originally, it will have led to the outdoor area. At the bottom of the sequence within the doorway, we found sterile stiff mid-yellowish brown silty clay (d.138) with a top elevation of 98.41 m site height, evidently an earthen floor and the continuation of floor d.085, whose elevation is identical and whose composition is strikingly similar, leaving no doubt that d.085 and d.138 are part of the same floor. The trodden-earth floor continued into annexe room 4C (d.132, with a similar top elevation of 98.40 m), suggesting that the floor level was not raised in room 3C until the annexe room 4C had been added. The fill on top, which will have risen at the same speed as the surface in the interior of room 3C, contained, as usual, much redeposited loess and some pottery and bone.

In the south-east, a door opening connected room 3C with room 3S. This was only recognised late and excavated separately, but we may assume that deposits will have built up at a similar speed as in the two rooms it connected. Soil colour and composition followed the usual pattern, with redeposited loess evidently being the principal component.

As in row 2, little has been excavated of the southern and northern rooms and no major insights as to their layout and use can be offered. The northernmost metre of room 3S was within the trench. The room was of identical width to 3C. As we excavated the room only down to 98.66 m site height, we cannot tell whether or not the walls were lined with bricks (as in rooms 3C and 2C) as the top of the alignments (d.059 and d.061 = d.124) in these rooms was mostly below this level. Finds consisted exclusively of pottery.

The southernmost part of room 3N was within our trench, but has not been excavated. Its extent has been plotted tentatively, based on exposed parts of mud-brick walls and the assumption that the arrangement of rooms follows a symmetrical pattern.

4.1.4.4.1.3. Characteristics of the original barracks (rows 2 and 3)

Significant for the function of the rooms in rows 2 and 3 is not just what was found, but also what was absent. Unlike the annexes, there were no ovens or evidence for *in-situ* cooking. There was no storage pit in either room. Neither did we find any storage jars *in situ* in rows 2 and 3 of the barracks. (There were, however, fragments of storage jars from row 2, interestingly exclusively early and perhaps pre-dating the creation of storage facilities in the annexes.[82]) The latter observation seems less significant than the former two. We found ovens in all other rows (0, 1, 4 and 5), whereas storage jars *in situ* were placed exclusively in row 1. If the rooms in rows 2 and 3 mainly served as overnight bedrooms, then it made sense not to clutter them with cooking facilities or bulky storage jars. The absence of fireplaces for heating is still astonishing in an area that can get chilly and very wet from autumn to spring.[83] We observed possible cinders of fire, perhaps suggesting that there were heating facilities that have left no archaeological traces. Heating would have been essential for keeping the garrison in good health, for drying wet garments etc. Perhaps there was a fireplace upstairs, perhaps thick blankets were used to keep warm indoors. If the fort maintained its military purpose throughout its occupation, as it almost certainly did, then there must have been rooms to accommodate its guardians as well as their portable equipment in all phases. Rooms in rows 2 and 3, as far as excavated, probably served this purpose, lacking cooking and storage facilities at ground-floor level for most of their occupation. A late fireplace (phases 4.2–5) just to the south of room 2N on top of the (perhaps partially demolished) division wall to room 2C, or in a niche, forms the sole exception, perhaps indicating that there was more flexibility in the use of space towards the end of the occupation of the barracks.

This late fireplace may be the exception to prove the rule that the original barracks lacked storage and cooking facilities, at least at ground-floor level. The original barrack rooms (rows 2 and 3) seem to have served a similar purpose throughout their occupation. They were never transformed into storage rooms, kitchens or workshops. This is not to imply that the function of all rooms in these two rows within our trench (let alone the whole barracks) was uniform, unchanging and identical. That there was almost three times as much pottery from row 2 than from row 3, but only a twelfth of the quantity of bone, may point to variations in the types of activities taking place in the rooms or their occupants' habits and thoroughness in rubbish removal.[84]

4.1.4.4.2. THE WESTERN ANNEXE: ROWS 0 AND 1

As argued above, room units of roughly 30 feet each west and east of the original narrow barracks (with just two rows of rooms of c. 40 feet combined) are later annexes. The principal observations to support this hypothesis are as follows:

1. Internal and outer walls of rows 0–1 and 4–5 were less regularly built and, mostly, thinner than those of the original barracks (rows 2 and 3).

2. The base of the walls of the postulated annexes (e.g. on the north side of rows 0–1 and 4) appeared to be at a higher level, of c. 98.40 m site height, as opposed to c. 98.20 m in the original barracks (although courses of mud-bricks were often hard to identify and there is no absolute certainty that this was the real base).

3. Ovens and storage pits were invariably outside the original barracks (rows 2–3), with the sole exception of a late oven (d.258) within a niche in, or on top of, the (partially demolished?) division wall between rooms 2N and 2C.

4.1.4.4.2.1. The eastern row of rooms (1) in the western annexe

The western annexe covered rows 0 and 1, but initially the area would have been an open outdoor space between the central road and the eastern of Fort 2's two barracks. Stratigraphy indeed indicates that the earliest occupation horizon (d.045) in row 1 started to build up outdoors. Its base was at c. 98.18 m site height, i.e. at a similar level as the base of the walls of the original barracks, but below that of the annexe walls. The spit was c. 40 cm deep, and there was (unlike rows 2–4) no compacted floor at this or any other level, within room 1CS, nor was there a trampled earth floor anywhere in the western annexe, as far as we could observe. D.045 contained much more pottery than deposits at the same level within the adjacent room (2C) in the original barracks, but was, as were most deposits in the western half of the building and nearby outdoor areas, poor in bone, perhaps pointing to extramural disposal of food remains (and a greater level of intramural deposition of broken pot). The deposit also included patches of ashy material, probably cinders of fire.

The walls of row 1 were poorly preserved, but there is no doubt that the north side of room 1CS was lined by a mud-brick wall in identical alignment to the wall dividing rooms 2C and 3C from 2N and 3N. On the west side of row 1, there were faint traces of a possible north–south mud-brick or rammed earth wall, with a (later?) alignment of fired brick (d.019) and other fired brick structures (d.017 and d.026) on top (Fig. 4.49). Admittedly, the probable division between rows 1 and 0 is not proven and has therefore not been plotted onto most of the plans. We do not know its base level, whilst the base level of the clear west–east wall on the north side of room 1CS and 0CS was, as far as we could see, at c. 98.40 m site height.

It is hard to know how much later these walls are than the original barracks. The absence of fireplaces

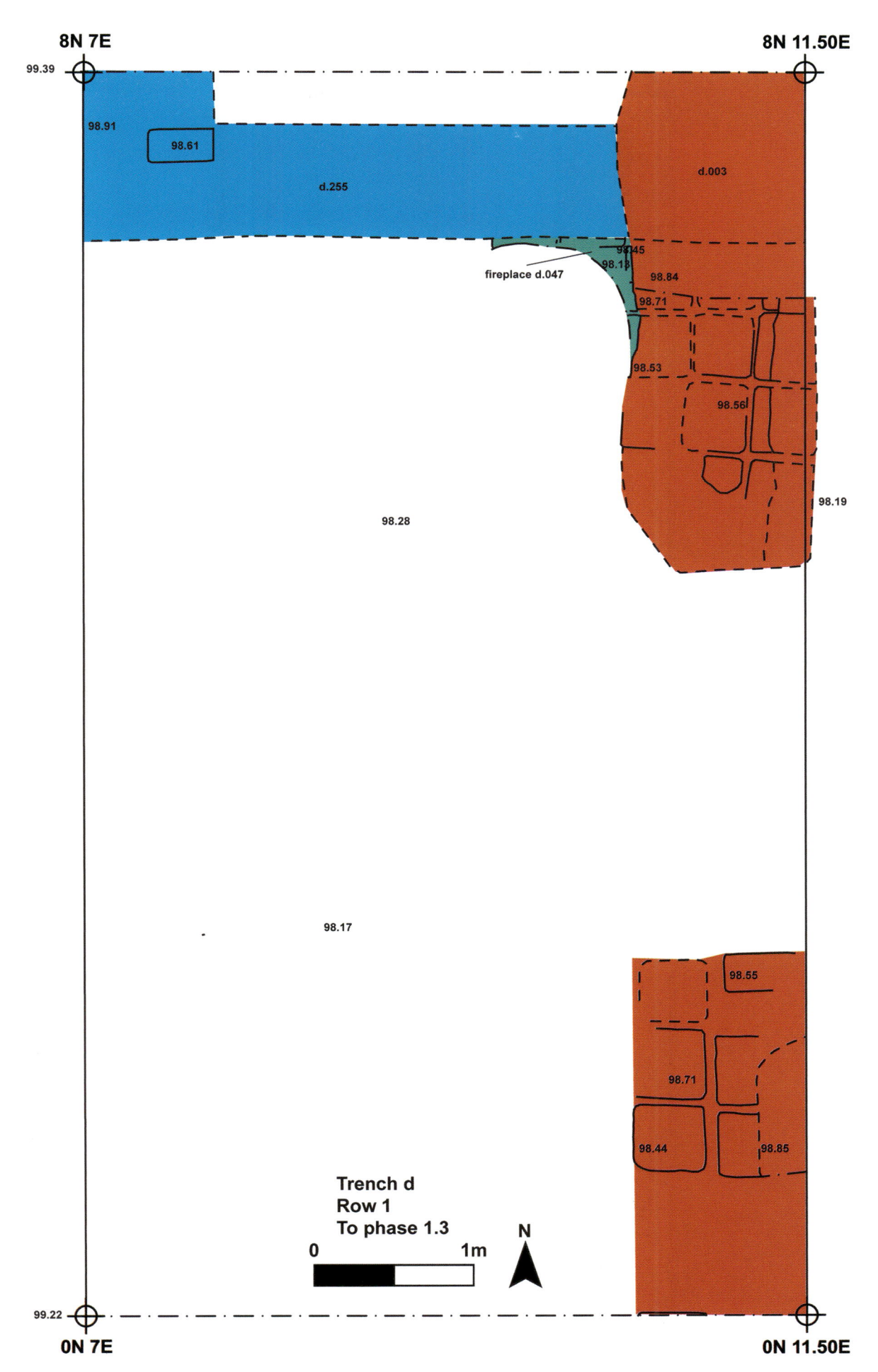

Fig. 4.35: Row 1 in the western annexe in phase 1.

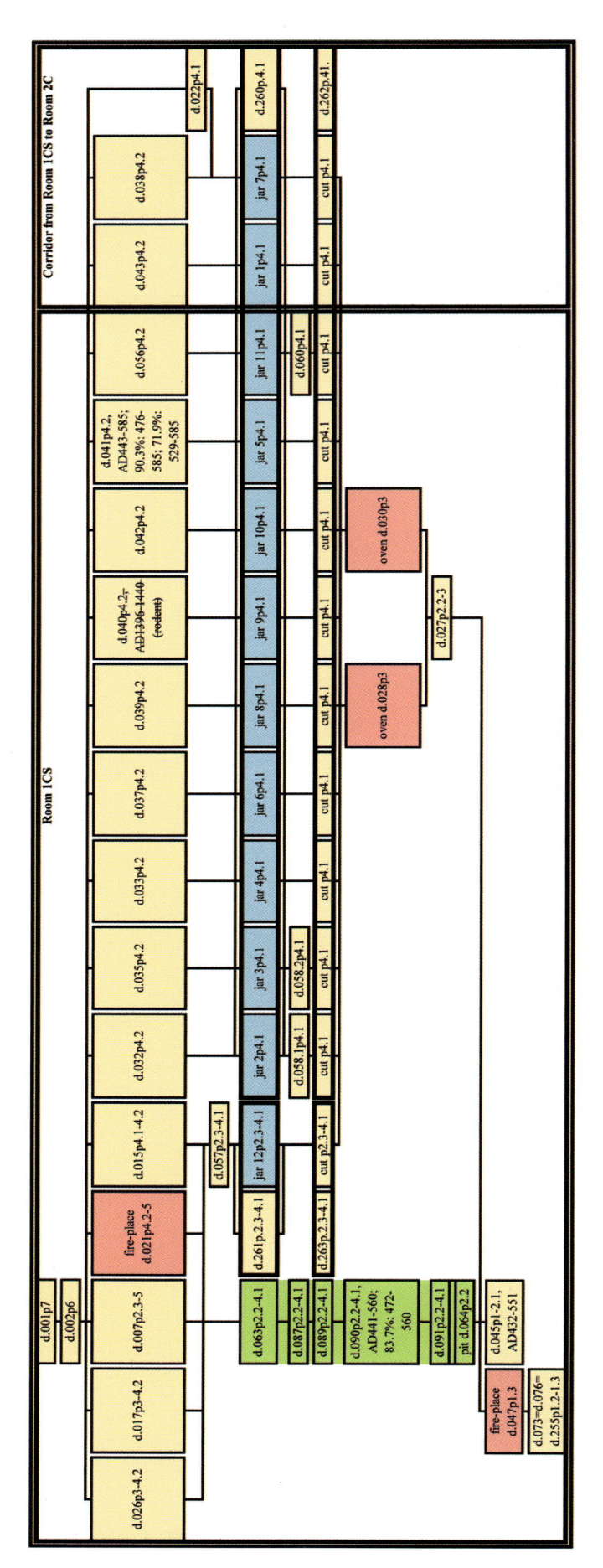

Fig. 4.36: Stratigraphic matrix for row 1. The matrix lists modelled radiocarbon dates. (For unmodelled dates, see Table 4.8.)

Table 4.16: Finds from within room 1CS.

Room 1CS deposits	Bottom	Top	Depth	Phase	Pottery	Bone	Other finds
d.043 (fill of jar 1)	98.09	98.99	0.90	4.2	0	0	NB: bone present, but <0.5 g
d.032 (fill of jar 2)	98.04	98.94	0.90	4.2	6	24	Charcoal and slag (1 g)
d.035 (fill of jar 3)	98.06	98.97	0.91	4.2	0	0	Charcoal
d.033 (fill of jar 4)	97.96	98.97	1.01	4.2	136	11	Charcoal and slag (11 g)
d.041 (fill of jar 5)	97.46	98.75	1.29	4.2	510	62	Charcoal and (intrusive?) rodent bone (1 g)
d.037 (fill of jar 6)	97.80	98.88	1.08	4.2	505	2	Charcoal and (intrusive?) rodent bone (1 g)
d.038 (fill of jar 7)	97.82	98.91	1.09	4.2	611	0	NB: bone present, but <0.5 g
d.039 (fill of jar 8)	97.85	98.89	1.04	4.2	4	0	NB: bone present, but <0.5 g
d.040 (fill of jar 9)	97.94	98.86	0.92	4.2	113	10	Charcoal and intrusive rodent bone (5 g)
d.042 (fill of jar 10)	97.84	98.84	1.00	4.2	57	0	n/a
d.260 (jars 1–11)	97.43	98.99	1.56	4.1	444,800	0	n/a
d.261 (jar 12)	98.02	98.58	0.56	2.3–4.1	14,660	0	n/a
d.027	98.58	98.88	0.30	2.2–3	6,833	0	Charcoal and slag (8 g)
d.063 (fill of pit d.064)	98.02	98.52	0.50	2.2–4.1	0	0	Copper alloy sheet bracelet fragments (4 g). NB: the pit was only securely identified after the top fill had been excavated and the bulk finds are thus tabulated under d.045.
d.087 (fill of pit d.064)	97.51	98.02	0.51	2.2–4.1	1,010	0	n/a
d.089 (fill of pit d.064)	97.18	97.51	0.33	2.2–4.1	1,322	20	Charcoal
d.090 (fill of pit d.064)	96.94	97.18	0.24	2.2–4.1	105	6	Charcoal
d.045	98.18	98.58	0.40	1.2–2.1	22,428	225	Charcoal and glass bead (1 g)
Total					493,100	360	Ratio, pot:bone: c. 1,370:1 (93:1, excl. 12 large storage jars)
Up to phase 2.2					22,428	225	Ratio, pot:bone: c. 100:1
Pit					2,437	26	Ratio, pot:bone: c. 94:1
Other deposits					490,663	334	Ratio, pot:bone: c. 1,469:1

and ovens in the original barracks makes one wonder if they were added soon. That the base of the annexe walls was c. 20 cm higher than that of the original barracks, on the other hand, may imply that at least some years, more probably decades, separated the construction of the original barracks (phase 1.1) and the annexes (phases 1.2–1.3). The complete change in building style may also suggest that the annexe walls were not built by the same generation who had erected the original barracks, even if there is no certainty of course that different factors (e.g. a desire to save material and efforts or to maximise indoor space) account for the change in style. The use of some annexe rooms for storage and as a workspace may have made solid walls and proper insulation a lesser priority than had been the case for the original barracks containing probably the garrison's principal living quarters.

What was the original function of room 1CS? In the north-east corner of the room, the mud-bricks of the walls were distinctly fire-reddened from c. 98.50–98.98 m site height, i.e. a level above the floor of adjacent room 2C.[85] This fireplace (d.047) is thus evidently later than the construction of the barracks in phase 1 and the western annexe, as the annexe wall on the north side of room 1CS was evidently exposed to fire. No certain remains of an associated fire-exposed floor survived, though its approximate extent has been tentatively plotted on Fig. 4.35, based largely on the extent of the adjacent distinctly fire-reddened walls. The base of the fireplace appears to have been at c. 98.50 m, but must have been largely destroyed when later a pit (d.064) was dug in the same corner, erasing all earlier horizons here. This fireplace clearly belongs to the original occupation of the room prior to pit digging, and was probably used for heating and/or

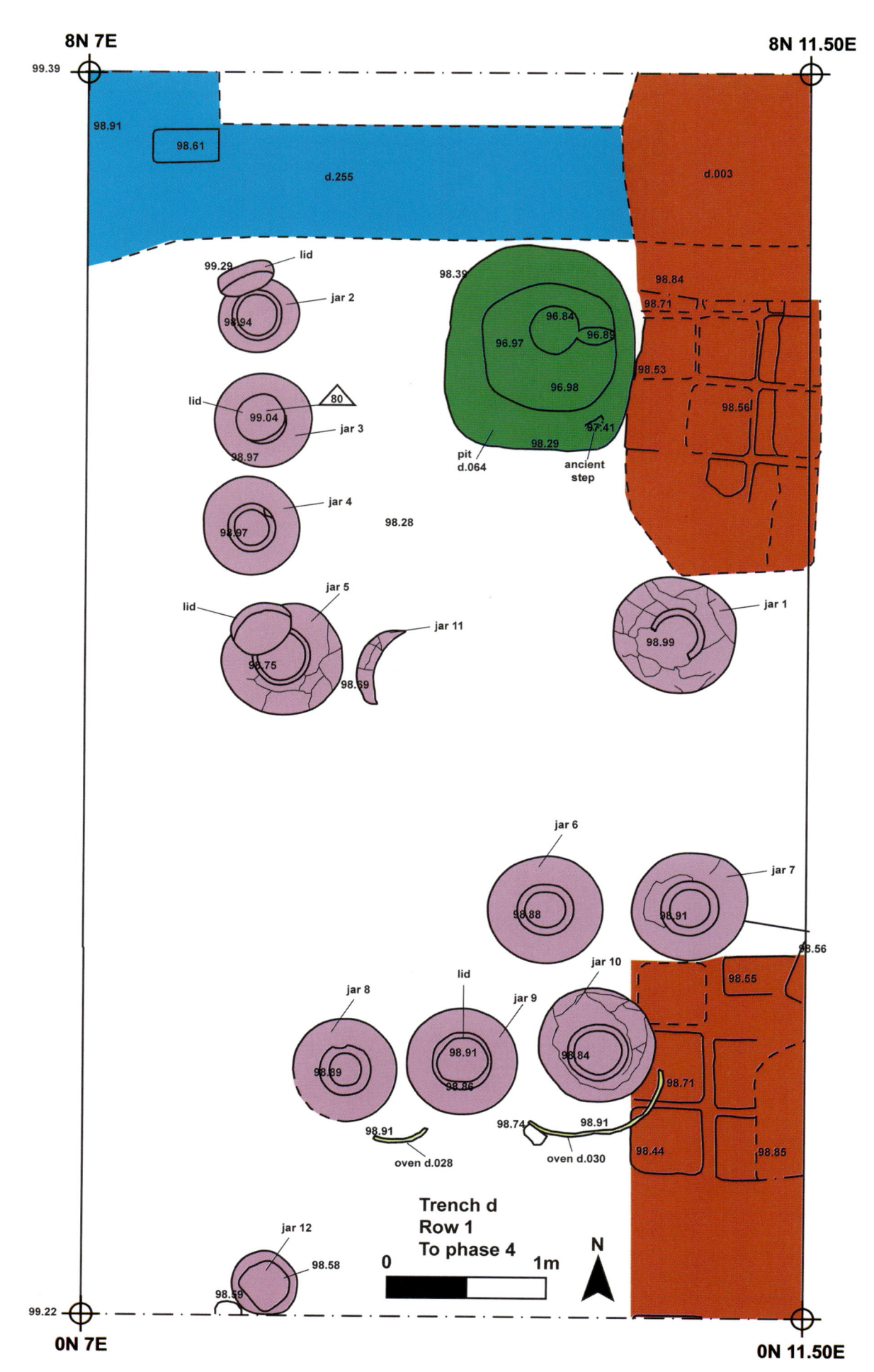

Fig. 4.37: Row 1 in the western annexe up to phase 4.

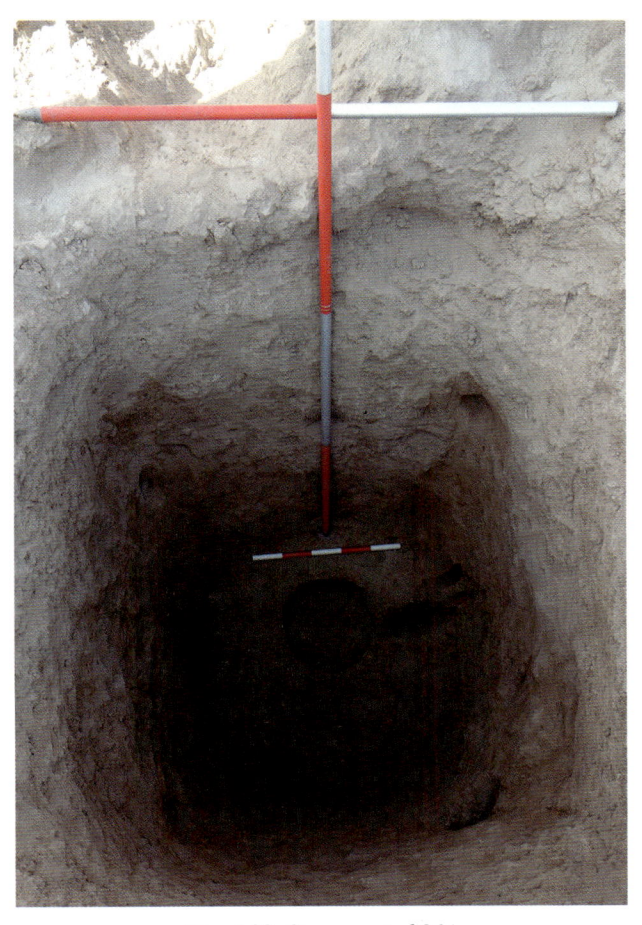

Fig. 4.38: Storage pit d.064.

pit was devoid of finds. Above, the pit contained a fair concentration of pottery and a small quantity of bones (see Table 4.16), but less towards the bottom (in spit d.090) than the two spits above (d.089 and d.087), even taking into account that spit d.090 was of lesser depth (and the shaft marginally narrower) and overall of smaller volume than the spits above. The pit's top fill (d.063, soft mid-yellowish brown clayey silt – evidently redeposited loess) was not initially recognised as such, being of identical colour and similar composition to d.045, and thus it was not possible to separate finds, except for copper alloy bracelet fragments (d.063/261)[86] whose three-dimensional position was recorded. The pit may have been filled up with debris once no longer needed. The pit's fill was soft, as opposed to the more compact natural loess underneath and at its sides. A small cavity in the pit wall (filled with soft soil, but cut into hard sediment) was probably an ancient step hole to enable access to, and exit from, the pit.

D.064 was evidently a storage pit.[87] It was of lesser volume and differed in shape from storage pits in Fort 4 as well as pit d.130 in Fort 2 (a shaft as opposed to the cited bell-shaped pits).[88] It is interesting to note that the two pits we found in Fort 4 (even if no statistically viable sample) were outside the original barracks and probably also outside their hypothetical annexes.[89] Pit d.064 clearly was dug after the annexe had been built, as it was cut through fireplace d.047 that had already caused heat-induced discoloration of both, a stretch of original barrack wall and a stretch of annexe wall. We do not know if the pit was sealed and for storage of grain over a longer period or for commodities that needed to be retrieved frequently. In the latter case, the presence of a storage pit may indicate that room 1CS was, or when the pit was dug was converted into, a store-room or a multi-purpose room. Its fill will post-date its use. Interestingly, it contains as little bone as most deposits in row 1. This is in sharp contrast to row 5 where both the fill of the three storage pits (and the two large ones in particular) and the occupation and levelling layers contain a much higher proportion of bones. Not even counting the 12 large storage vessels in room 1CS, the overall weight ratio of bone to pot is c. 1.1:98.9 in room 1CS (or 0.1:99.9 including them), as opposed to c. 24.1:75.9 in room 5CS. For the deposits filling pit d.064, it is also c. 1.1:98.9, as opposed to c. 27.2:72.8 for the three pits in 5CS.[90] In other words, there is consistently far less bone in room 1CS than in room 5CS deposits and the same holds true for the fill of pits. This suggests that the pits were not filled with material from a common source or from random sources, but that much of the finds in each pit will have been deposited by occupants of nearby rooms.

In a later phase, ovens (d.028 and d.030) were installed within room 1CS. As oven d.030 is cut into the earlier mud-brick wall of the original barracks (the western terminal of the wall dividing rooms 2C and 2S), it is not only certain to be later, but likely to be significantly later.

cooking. It should be remembered here that rooms in the original barracks (including probably 2C and 3C) will have functioned as accommodation/bedrooms, without any evidence for ovens or fireplaces at ground-floor level. The fireplace d.047 allows for the possibility that room 1CS was initially used as an additional occupation unit, a kitchen facility, a heated workspace or a multi-purpose room.

It was also in the north-eastern corner of room 1CS that we found a shaft (d.064), of a diameter of around 1 m (c. 1.10–1.40 m at the top). Whilst most of room 1CS was explored in the 2015 season, pit d.064 was only fully excavated in 2016. Cut from 98.52 m site height, it reached a maximum depth of 1.68 m (Fig. 4.84). The shaft was squarish with rounded corners. We encountered a round depression in the centre of, and a linear slot on the east side of, its otherwise flat base. The function of the round depression is unclear, perhaps for inserting a vessel of unknown material of which no traces remained. The linear slot of similarly uncertain function east of it reached almost the same depth (96.89 m) as the round depression (96.84 m) in the centre. The fill (d.091) of the small round depression at the very bottom of the

Evidently, it post-dates a reorganisation of the internal layout and use of space within the building. Oven d.030 clearly cuts at least two bricks of this west–east mud-brick wall. There was no preserved mud-brick wall, in continuation of that between rooms 2C and 2S, dividing room 1CS into a central and southern row. Yet, these two ovens would have blocked movement and may have abutted a makeshift division, in alignment with the southern edge of the wall between 2C and 2S. Both ovens had been cut into soil (d.027) from a top elevation of 98.91 m site height; their bottom elevation was at 98.69 m. Significantly, they are partially overlain by a west–east brick alignment d.014 (base elevation 98.94 m), probably functioning as a makeshift division of room 1CS into two smaller units (1C and 1S) in the latest traceable phase of occupation.

Storage facilities in row 1

Within room 1CS, we found 12 large storage jars dug into the ground, ten of which (nos 1–10) were complete. Of these, some were entirely unbroken and could be lifted in one piece, whilst others had cracked either already in Late Antiquity or perhaps more recently, under the weight of modern agricultural machinery. A series of solid ceramic lids were also found, some still covering vessels (i.e. jars 3 and 9), some next to vessel rims, some elsewhere in the trench. Jars 8, 9 and 10 could only have been placed into their respective position after ovens d.028 and d.030 had been largely destroyed and must belong to a later phase. The other storage vessels could in theory have been in place before and might be contemporary to the ovens. Much more probably, however, all storage vessels should be attributed to a later phase than the ovens. The top of the vessels (not counting broken jars 11 and 12) were between 98.75 m and 98.99 m site height, i.e. not of identical elevation, but all within 0.24 m. The vessels, however, may have been placed in pits cut into the ground from the top of d.045 whose top elevation (c. 98.58 m) corresponds roughly to the level at which vessels reached the greatest diameter. It is tempting to think that they all belong to a new phase after the decision had been taken to devote a significant part of the barracks to storing

Fig. 4.39: Jars 1 to 11, 3 and 9 still with their lids in situ, seen from the south. Note that jars 1 and 10 (right top and right bottom) were complete, but broken. The rims of oven d.030 and d.028 south of (below) jars 10, 9 and 8 are distinctly visible too. Late brick alignment d.015 (in the foreground) may have formed part of a makeshift subdivision of room 1CS.

Table 4.17: The in-situ storage jars in Trench d (Site heights refer to a benchmark for the trench set at an arbitrary height of 100 m. Top of vessel refers to vessel rims (except for jars 11 and 12 where the rim was no longer in situ), not the lids (where still in situ).

Jar	Find no.	Weight (in g)	Fill	Top of vessel	Bottom of vessel (internal)	Bottom of vessel impression
1	d.260/118/d.260/208	38,700	d.043	98.99	98.09	98.07
2	d.260/125	30,000	d.032	98.94	98.04	98.02
3	d.260/127	41,000	d.035	98.97	98.06	98.02
4	d.260/128	47,500	d.033	98.97	97.96	97.92
5	d.260/126/d.260/201	62,300	d.041	98.75	97.46	97.43
6	d.260/154	47,000	d.037	98.88	97.80	97.75
7	d.260/156	50,500	d.038	98.91	97.82	97.79
8	d.260/157	47,700	d.039	98.89	97.85	97.83
9	d.260/168	38,200	d.040	98.86	97.94	97.91
10	d.260/204	28,200	d.042	98.84	97.84	97.81
11	d.260/229	13,700	d.056	98.69	unrecorded	97.85
12	d.261/255	14,660	d.057	98.58	unrecorded	98.02

Fig. 4.40: *The jars seen from the west. Jars 1 and 10, already broken, could not be preserved* in situ. *In the north-east corner of the room and in front of the wall dividing rooms 1CS and 2C, there was a large storage pit (d.064), only partially excavated at this stage.*

Fig. 4.41: *The jars seen from the east.*

Fig. 4.42: The jars in the barracks seen from the north-east, with the substantial walls of room 2C in the foreground.

Fig. 4.43: Jar 10 with oven d.030 on the right.

Fig. 4.44: Jar 6 being lifted on 20 November 2015.

Fig. 4.45: Storage jars 2 to 4 seen from the west. Jar 3 (in the middle) retained its cover. Jar 2's lid (left) had been lifted at some late stage.

commodities. The jars differed in shape and volume, but were all of substantial size, from 0.92–1.32 m height. Jar 7 was protected by a substantial packing of coarse mid-yellowish grey coarse sand (d.022). The top of packing d.022 (at an elevation of 98.82 m) was just 9 cm below the rim of the jar. Perhaps the vessels were largely buried and the (liquid?) contents scooped out rather than the heavy full vessels lifted. The high surface level around jar 7 suggests that it was, or remained, in use until a late phase of occupation. Sand packing was also observed under jars 2, 3 and 11, whilst other jars appear to have been placed in pits cut into earlier deposits without such packing. The sand packing under jar 11 (d.060) showed greenish iron-staining, in contrast to the packing under jars 2 and 3 (d.058) and that around jar 7 (d.022). The iron-staining was probably a result of water infiltration; jar 11 had broken already in antiquity.

Jars 8, 9 and 10 were in a row that was parallel to a second and third row (the former consisting of jars 6 and 7, the latter, of jars 5, 11 and 1) – an observation that offers support for the assumption that they all belong to the same phase, though admittedly not proving it. It seems likely that parts of the mud-brick wall between rooms 1CS and 2C had been demolished to create space for jar 7, whereas the terminal of the wall north of jar 1 is in alignment with the north edge of the eastern doorway of room 3C, suggesting that jar 1 had been placed next to the original terminal of this wall. The 1 m wide corridor between jars 7 and 1 is in alignment with the postulated late western entrance (threshold d.026) to room 1CS. Care was evidently taken not to block access to the next room east (room 2C). The gap between jars 11 and 1 will similarly mark an access route to the northern part of the room. It is interesting to note that there were no storage vessels on top of pit d.064 nor south of it. If pit d.064 was still in use, it would have made sense to leave a gap between jars 11 and 1 to facilitate access. The eastern parts of jar 11 had been destroyed in antiquity, whether deliberately (e.g. to widen the access) or accidentally. Does this indicate that the pit remained in use and needed to remain accessible at the time when jars 1–5 were in use? The level of the cut, at 98.52 m, suggests that the pit was dug not too long after the construction of the western annexe but we cannot precision-date when it was filled up, not helped by most deposits being of identical colour and a lack of sufficiently precise artefact chronology to differentiate between phases. Radiocarbon samples, discussed above,[91] suggest that the pit had been filled up by or before c. AD 560 at the latest, the jars by the 580s, i.e. potentially at a similar time. Admittedly, the samples from the fill of the pit and one of the jars only provide *termini post quos* for them having been out of use. Yet, the cited indications for bone probably having come from a very local source within the room or nearby makes it unlikely that the bones represent dug-up old residual material. The packing of vessel 7 proves that in the area of the southern two rows the surface had been raised to one foot above the top of storage pit d.064, but surface levels must have been lower in the northern half of room 1CS, as the top of vessel 5 was at 98.75 m, below the level of the packing of jar 7. It seems likely that the pit and the storage vessels were all in use simultaneously.

Jar 12 was at a distinctly lower level (98.58 m) than all other jars. Even if we take into account that it had lost its rim, it is well below the level of the other vessels. It is also the smallest of the *in-situ* jars and the only one in the southern part of room 1CS. Whether it belongs to an earlier phase than the other vessels and/or broke and went out use before jars 1–11 were placed in room 1CS or whether space was used differently in the southern part (1S) of room 1CS is unknown.

It seems clear that room 1CS, or at least its northern part (1C), served now exclusively or almost exclusively as a store-room. Not only was much of the space taken up with storage vessels and a pit, but also evidence is lacking for other activities. The early fireplace (d.047) and the later ovens (d.028 and d.030) had evidently all been disused or deliberately demolished to make way for the storage jars and the pit. No heating or cooking appears to have taken place in room 1CS whilst the jars and the pit were in use, nor would there have been much space left. It is also worth noting that, unlike several other rooms, no spindle whorls and no positive evidence for textile production has come to light in this room or anywhere within the western annexe.

Is the position of the store-room within the building significant? It is tempting to explore a possible parallel in earlier Roman barracks design. In the Roman imperial army, each group of eight soldiers (*contubernium*) shared a tent in a marching camp and a room, and more often a double-room, in barracks. The front room of such an accommodation unit provided storage space for equipment, whilst soldiers mainly dwelt and slept in the back room.[92] Do we see a similar arrangement in the barracks in Fort 2 with store-rooms (e.g. 1CS) being in front of bedrooms (e.g. 2C)? Whilst it is tempting to draw such a parallel, there are major differences in design:

- Front room 1CS was used for storing commodities, as opposed to equipment in Roman barracks.

- There appears to have been a further room (0CS) in front of storage room 1CS, so that 1CS was positioned in the centre of the unit, as opposed to Roman barracks where the outermost rooms served storage purposes.

- It only appears to have been transformed into a storeroom at a later stage.

- There were at least five rows of rooms in the barracks, more probably six, allowing for units of at least three rooms each (or perhaps even four, e.g. 0CS, 1CS, 2C and 2S), separated by the door-less wall between rows 2 and 3; both units were accessed from each long side of the building. In Roman barracks, there was normally a maximum of two rooms available for each small group of soldiers.

- The arrangement of storage facilities in rows is not mirrored in the two halves of the building: whilst there is a narrow room (4CS) also in front of postulated bedroom 3C, there is no evidence for *in-situ* storage jars (though there were broken storage vessels also in row 4).[93] Storage pits occur in both annexes, but in unequal number and distribution: there was one large storage pit in row 1, but none in matching row 4; and there was no storage pit in row 0, but two large storage pits and a small one in matching row 5 (though not all in use at the same time). Perhaps ease of access to the central road was the reason for placing the vessels in a room near the road, rather than the back of the building. Differences between the western and eastern rooms in provision of storage facilities suggest that commodities stored were for communal use rather than solely for that of the occupants of adjacent rooms.

- It is likely (even if not proven for the Fort 2 buildings) that the solidly built original two-row barracks were two storeys high (and that living quarters were in part perhaps upstairs). Each unit in the barracks thus may

Fig. 4.46: Jars 2 to 5 (right to left) and broken jar 11 (foreground left). Jar 3 was still covered with its lid; those of jars 2 and 5 were found lifted. (Each red and each white segment of the scale is 10 cm long.)

have comprised four separate rooms (e.g. 0C, 1C and 2C plus a room above 2C) or even six separate rooms (e.g. 0CS, 1CS, 2C and 2S, plus one room each above 2C and 2S). Whichever of the models is correct, room units in Sasanian barracks differed substantially in room number and layout from Roman barracks.

We may conclude that similarities to Roman barracks were not close and reflect independent logical thinking rather than Roman influence. It makes sense to store heavy items closer to the entrance of a building rather than in the back room, minimising transport efforts and making it possible to gain access to supplies without the need to enter the postulated bedrooms behind. Similarly, food preparation in the front or middle rooms helped to avoid unnecessary disturbance and traffic in the sleeping quarters. Furthermore, the back-rooms (rows 2 and 3) would have been best insulated from the heat in summer and cold in winter, making them ideal bedrooms.

A key question is what commodities were once stored in the vessels. The fill of all 12 jars consisted of light to mid-yellowish brown clayey silt with a low concentration of finds – evidently redeposited occupation deposits, containing occupation debris, and much redeposited natural loess. In no case were there any visible traces of decayed organic matter, neither at the base of the vessels nor anywhere else. We may thus be certain that they did not contain grain or other staple foods or that they had all been emptied. One vessel (jar 3) was largely filled with water rather than soil, a result no doubt of its lid having remained in place, preventing it from silting up. Jar 9 was also still closed by its lid. Jars 2 and 5 had lids standing on one edge of the rim, perhaps moved in more recent times. The odd bone of domestic animals as well

Fig. 4.47: The imprint of storage jar 10 cuts an earlier mud-brick wall. (The scale measures, as usual, 2 × 50 cm.)

as rodent remains were found in the fill of vessels, all of which was carefully excavated. There was no noticeable concentration of bones or rodent remains at any particular level, neither the bottom of vessels nor elsewhere. Bones of domestic animals must evidently be part of redeposited soil. Did the same apply to the well-preserved rodent remains or might these animals have consumed the supplies? Radiocarbon dating of one (c. AD 1396–1440), from jar 9, proved that it was some 800–1000 years more recent than the fort's occupation. Evidently, the rodent did not consume the vessel's contents which, if not emptied, must have disintegrated centuries before. Neither is it likely to be part of redeposited soil, as the vessels will have filled up long before the late fourteenth or fifteenth century. The rodent (just as probably most of the other rodents found) simply dug a burrow that reached down

Fig. 4.48: Brick alignments d.014 (foreground) and d.015 (background) may have subdivided room 1CS.

into the silted-up vessel. Jar 9, whilst having retained its lid, still was full of sediments. The rodent evidently found a gap between lid and rim when excavating its burrow. The contents of the vessels were extensively sampled, most of it floated, and examination of the pollen by Lyudmila Shumilovskikh suggests that there may have been honey in jar 7.[94] Honey could have been a component of alcoholic drinks, such as mead. Oil would be more difficult to reconcile with these findings. Not all vessels need, of course, have been intended for the same product. Rooms full of large interred storage vessels in Mtskheta in Iberia have plausibly been interpreted as wine cellars, and similar jars are still used for wine storage today.[95] Water storage is also possible, notably in a hilltop fort, almost certainly too high for digging wells and without evidence for a cistern. Perhaps, however, drinking water would have been stored in cheaper and lighter containers, that could also have been transported uphill more easily, e.g. skins or wooden barrels.[96] And it would have been easier to keep water in such containers than to pour it into dug-in ceramic jars and scoop it out. Storage of wine or some other precious drinks seems more probable. If the contents of the vessels were liquid, it certainly would explain the absence of decayed organic matter – all the more so if partially or completely consumed prior to abandonment.

THE LAST PHASE OF OCCUPATION

Brick alignments are of particular interest for room 1CS. These basic structures are on a similar level to, or slightly higher level than, those attributed to phase 3. The main mud-brick walls were evidently still standing, as the alignments are often parallel to their edge or terminate at or near an edge of an earlier wall. Two such alignments (d.014 and d.015) may have divided room 1CS into two possible sub-units, 1C and 1S. Alignment d.015 runs broadly parallel to d.014 west–east within the interior of the room. The lower courses of d.015 overlie broken jar 12, evidently no longer in use in phase 4.2. Perhaps these two parallel alignments marked the edges of a rammed-earth wall or held a wooden screen in place. As alignment d.014 overlies oven d.028 (and runs along the very edge of oven d.030) and as d.015 overlies jar 12, they must be later, though some other alignments could be of a similar age to some phase 3 ovens or phase 4 jars. Contrary to their earlier counterparts in rooms 2C and 3C, the brick alignments do not line two or three walls of a room, but only parts of the odd wall here and there – or indeed subdivide rooms. It is possible that these makeshift features were erected unsystematically or that we only see parts of the picture; other walls may have been lined by vertical mud-bricks, that have not been preserved or recognised, or phase 4 brick alignment may have been partially robbed later.

An alignment of flat fired bricks (d.019), a probable paved brick doorway (d.026) and a brick-lined slot (d.017) on its southern side, perhaps intended to hold a pipe or one side of a timber doorframe, are probably of a similar date. No pipe was found in the slot, but it might have been removed or made of wood and disintegrated. A redeposited ceramic pipe (74/d.002), of c. 7 cm outer and 4 cm inner diameter, has been found in the trench, at a similar level to, and some 5 m east of, d.017, in the area of the postulated doorway between rooms 2C and 2S.[97] Whilst not *in situ*, it suggests that pipes may have been used to keep indoor areas dry. D.026 is in alignment with the (widened) entrance to the next room (2C) east (but not in alignment with any doorway in the well-preserved eastern half of the building), adding strength to its interpretation as a paved entrance to the room. A large Sasanian brick fragment (d.007/81), with a worn pivot hole of 10 cm diameter, was found redeposited upside down near the north-west corner of room 2C,[98] evidence for the use of fired bricks in doorframes. The eastern edge of an alignment of flat bricks (d.019) is in a similar north–south alignment to a possible decayed mud-brick wall further south dividing rooms 1CS and 0CS. Perhaps it indicates that parts of this postulated wall were no longer standing in phase 4. Except for d.015 over jar 12, none of the brick alignments appears to overlie a jar, and their bases are at 98.80–98.94 m site height, i.e. at a similar level to the top of the jars. Jars 1–11 may already have been filled with sediments at the time brick structures d.014, d.015, d.017, d.019 and d.026 were created or they may still have been in use. Whilst structures of fired brick are most easily recognisable, mud-bricks appear to have been reused too, and the odd mud-brick was found in the interior of rooms. Perhaps some were reused, like fired bricks, to create makeshift structures. It is possible that such building material became available in the wake of partial demolition of some of the walls.

At the interface between d.007 and the subsoil (d.002) there was an ovoid fire-reddened patch (d.021) at 99.03 m site height, c. 10.10–11.10 m east and 4.75–6.10 m north. It overlay part of the division wall between rooms 1CS

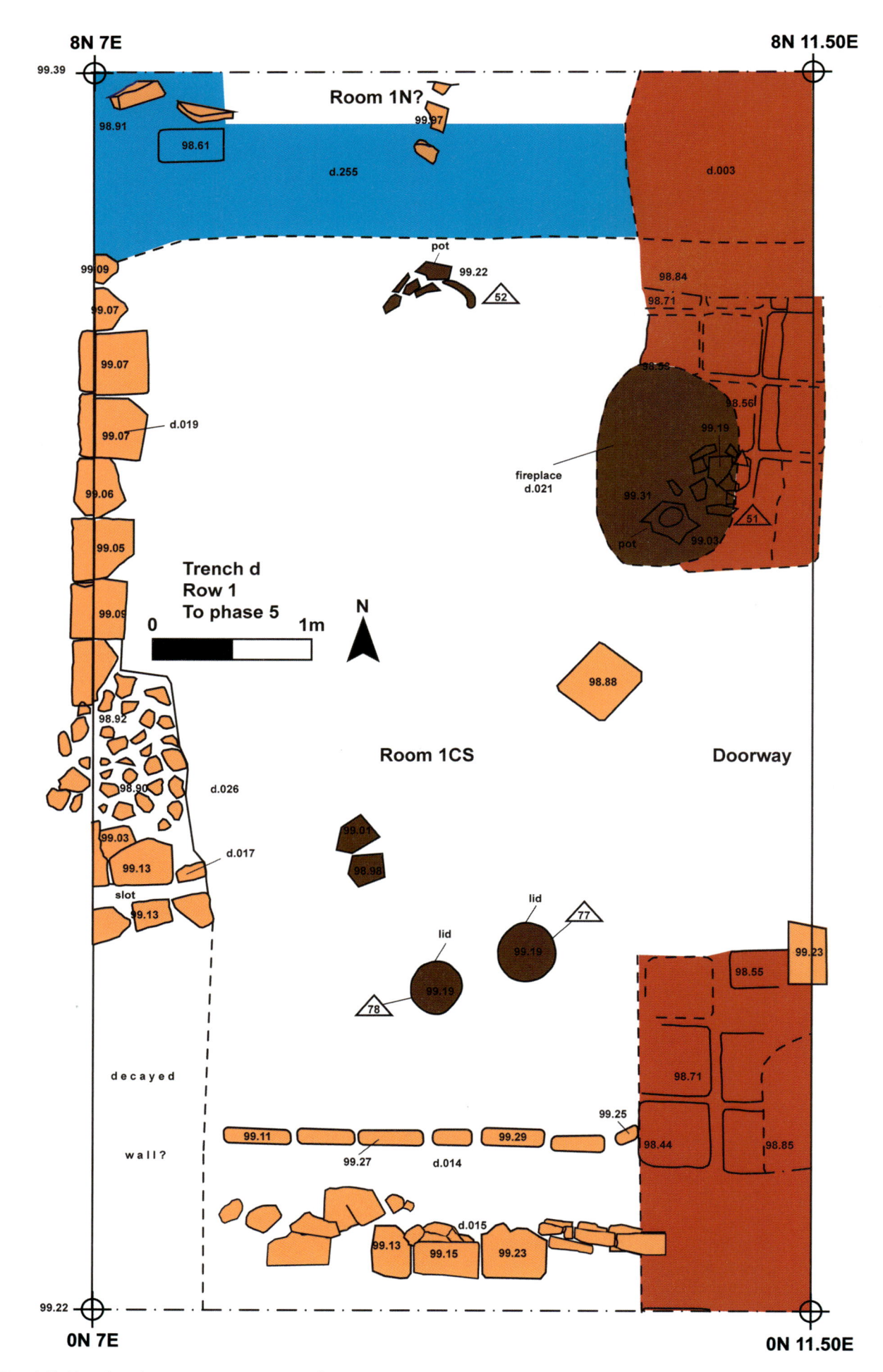

Fig. 4.49: Row 1 in the western annexe up to phase 5, with a late fireplace overlying an earlier wall, and redeposited lids of storage vessels. Brick alignments d.014 and d.015 may have subdivided room 1CS (with most of the southern part being outside Trench d). D.026 may be a paved doorway on top of potential traces of a decayed mud-brick or rammed earth wall (identified tentatively only and therefore not assigned to a particular phase or plotted onto earlier plans; perhaps of phases 1.2–1.3).

Fig. 4.50: Storage vessels of phase 4.1 and some makeshift brick structures of phases 3–5 in Trench d in 2015. Note the mud-bricks of the walls, including that on the north side of annexe room 1CS (foreground), showing up very clearly. Brick rows d.014 (background right, in alignment with the southern edge of the west–east wall separating rooms 2C and 2S, background centre) and d.015 (background right, behind d.014) suggest that room 1CS was subdivided into two units in, or until, a late phase of occupation.

and 2C (as phase 4.2–5 oven d.258 was on top of the division wall between 2N and 2C), suggesting that more of the mud-brick walls had been demolished at this late stage of occupation. That features of phases 3–5 were increasingly cut into earlier walls is a surprising finding (though one also has to allow for the possibility that some were positioned in niches in the walls which would not be preserved at this level). Perhaps it suggests that there were still many occupants in need of space and that not all division walls were needed to support the roof. The fire-reddened patch d.021 was at a higher level than the top of the storage vessels (though the top of the lifted lid of jar 2 was as high as 99.29 m), but did not overlie them. It is hard to tell if the storage vessels were still in use by the time fires were lit at fireplace d.021 on top of a demolished (or partially demolished) wall. Perhaps 1CS no longer served as a store-room at the time, but a domestic function, perhaps it served multiple purposes. A potential continued use of the storage vessels might explain why they remained intact. There is no evidence for post-Sasanian occupation, and we may assume that the finds from d.002 also still form part of the latest occupation.

Particularly interesting is a copper alloy fitting, featuring a palmette or a fir or pine tree (d.007/98), probably from phase 5, for which we have found no close parallel so far. It was found between jars 6 and 9, 2–4 cm above the rims,[99] suggesting that at the time the item was lost the vessels had already been filled up with debris and buried. It is worth noting that arguably the most unusual metal artefact found at Fort 2 was lost towards the end of occupation – suggesting that garrison members then still had access to refined metalwork, whether via barter trade, official supply or inheritance.

4.1.4.4.2.2. THE WESTERN ROW OF ROOMS (0) IN THE WESTERN ANNEXE

Of all six rows of rooms of the barracks, the westernmost (row 0) was least well preserved. It was only excavated in the 2016 season. When we arrived, we found that we had not been the first to dig in the area. Some damage has been caused by robber pits dug at the edges of our 2015 trench between the two seasons. One of these modern robber pits was a small tunnel dug under brick paving d.019 and extended c. 1.50 m to the west. A pervasive belief that there is hidden treasure to be found at archaeological sites, notably behind or under brick walls and pavements, will have motivated this modern enterprise. It was just one of several cases where our fieldwork inspired such private investigations.[100] This robber trench (d.229) is likely to have destroyed one oven, as parts of oven wall were found in the fill of the robber trench. The damage done by this particular modern tunnel was limited to roughly 1.50 m². Light construction rather than modern destruction meant that we know least about the westernmost row of rooms. Neither its western outer wall nor a wall separating it from row 1 is proven beyond doubt. Yet the mud-bricks of the wall marking the northern edge of postulated room 0CS could be clearly identified, and the wall was one and a half mud-bricks wide. There were traces of a wall, the probable western outer wall of the building, branching off it in the west. We assume, based on the rectilinear alignment of the west–east wall, that the construction of the western annexe, both of rows 0 and 1, occurred in a single phase (tentatively assigned to phases 1.2–1.3). The earliest deposits (notably d.243, d.215 and d.242, as well as probably most of d.210 and d.225) are likely to pre-date the construction of the annexe, but in the light of the poor preservation of the walls, it should be emphasised that there is no absolute certainty about the relative phasing. It is worth noting that the earlier deposits in the area of 0CS have also yielded a higher proportion of bone than the later ones – which may add strength to them representing deposition outdoors where rotting food remains would have caused less inconvenience than indoors.

Unlike row 1, there were no storage vessels and no storage pits in row 0. There were, however, a fair number of ovens, suggesting that this was an area of food preparation. Two of these appear to belong to the earliest phase of the annexe: oven d.222 in room 0CS and oven d.114 in room 0N. Both abut the west–east mud-brick wall dividing the two rooms, and d.114 was in the corner of the room, so as to cause as little obstruction as possible. These two ovens are at a similar level to the fireplace d.257 in room 4CS and fireplace (or oven?) d.047 in room 1CS (later largely erased by pit d.064), which was also placed in a corner. In the case of d.047, we know that it post-dates

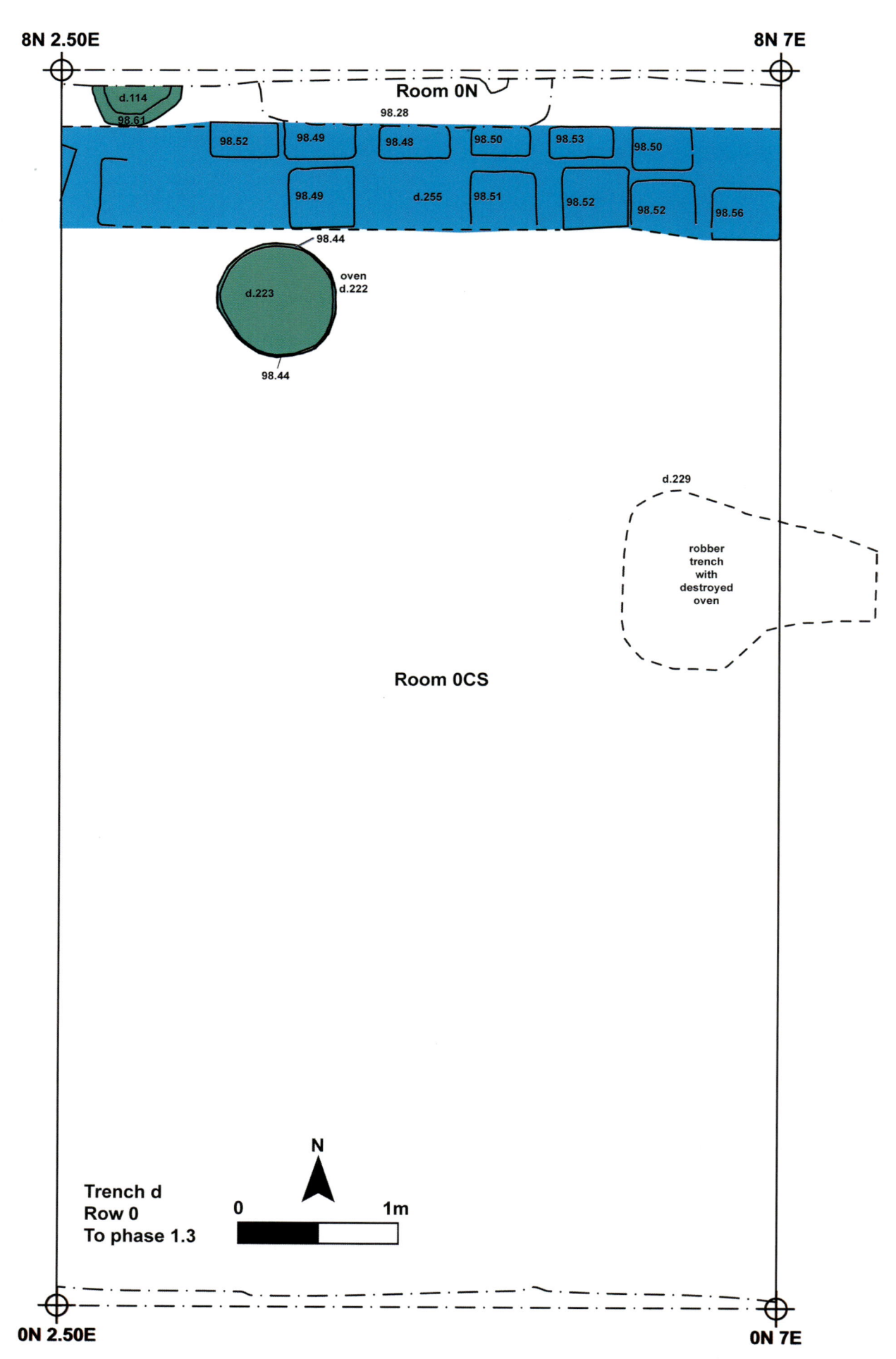

Fig. 4.51: Row 0 in the western annexe in phase 1.

Table 4.18: Finds from room unit 0CS. Note that the walls are poorly preserved or untraceable in the west and that it is a matter of judgement whether a part of the assemblage (d.069, d.088, d.142, d.153, d.169, d.174, d.192 and d.228 = d.235) should be attributed to indoor or outdoor areas. Weights are in grams.

Room 0CS deposits	Bottom	Top	Depth	Phase	Pottery	Bone	Other finds
d.142	98.90	99.01	0.11	3–5	12,280	0	Glass (106 g)
d.170 (fill of oven)	98.63	98.84	0.21	3	53	0	Iron object (4 g)
d.188 (fill of oven)	98.77	98.82	0.05	3	15	0	Charcoal
d.069	98.69	99.00	0.31	2.3–5	225	0	White plaster-like substance (45 g).
d.165	98.70	98.98	0.28	2.3–4.2	4,092	42	Charcoal and iron objects, incl. nail shaft fragment (11 g)
d.077	98.76	98.81	0.05	2.3	535	0	n/a
d.153	98.76	98.86	0.10	2.3	3,943	0	Glass and iron object (4 g)
d.174	98.63	98.76	0.13	2.2–2.3	4,124	34	Clay objects (52 g)
d.088	98.42	98.70	0.28	2.1–2.2	330	0	n/a
d.208	98.53	98.63	0.10	2.1–2.2	2,585	55	Flint working debris
d.192	98.49	98.60	0.11	2.1	7,628	427	Glass (6 g) and prehistoric stone axe (238 g)
d.245	98.38	98.51	0.13	2.1	0	30	n/a
d.221	98.45	98.54	0.09	1.2–2.1	2,153	51	n/a
d.228 = d.235	98.44	98.50	0.06	1.2–2.1	3,996	40	Charcoal and iron (9 g)
d.225	98.33	98.57	0.24	1.2–2.1	15,625	1,699	Charcoal, flint working debris (18 g) and iron blade(?) fragment (19 g)
d.223 (fill of oven)	98.33	98.49	0.16	1.3	0	>0	Charcoal [NB: 1 bone, not weighed]
d.210	98.37	98.49	0.12	1.2–1.3	1,778	282	Charcoal
d.242	98.36	98.44	0.08	1.1–1.3	613	0	n/a
d.215	98.18	98.38	0.20	1.1–1.3	1,700	141	Charcoal and slag (12 g)
d.243	98.18	98.36	0.18	1.1–1.3	335	9	n/a
Total					62,010	2,810	Ratio, pot:bone: c. 22:1
Up to phase 2.2 (incl. d.174)					40,867	2,768	Ratio, pot:bone: c. 15:1
Up to phase 1.3					4,426	432	Ratio, pot:bone: c. 10:1

Table 4.19: Finds from room unit 0N. Weights are in grams.

Room 0N deposits	Bottom	Top	Depth	Phase	Pottery	Bone	Other finds
d.066 = d.107	98.71	98.86	0.15	2.3	74	0	NB: bone present, but only 0.4 g
d.113	98.18	98.38	0.20	2.1–2.2	275	0	n/a
d.119	98.16	98.51	0.35	2.1	236	0	n/a
Total					585	0	
Up to phase 2.2					511	0	

annexe construction, as the walls in the north-east corner of room 1CS, where an annexe wall abutted the original barracks, were distinctly fire-reddened. We may assume that the same is true for ovens d.114 and d.222.

The fill (d.223) of oven d.222 yielded charred barley seeds, identified by Lyudmila Shumilovskikh,[101] further evidence to suggest that these ovens were used to bake bread and prepare meals. One barley seed was radiocarbon-dated and yielded a date of c. AD 483–590 (with a 94.2% probability of the date falling between AD 534 and 590). It is tempting to hypothesise that the oven was still in use during the reign of Khusro I

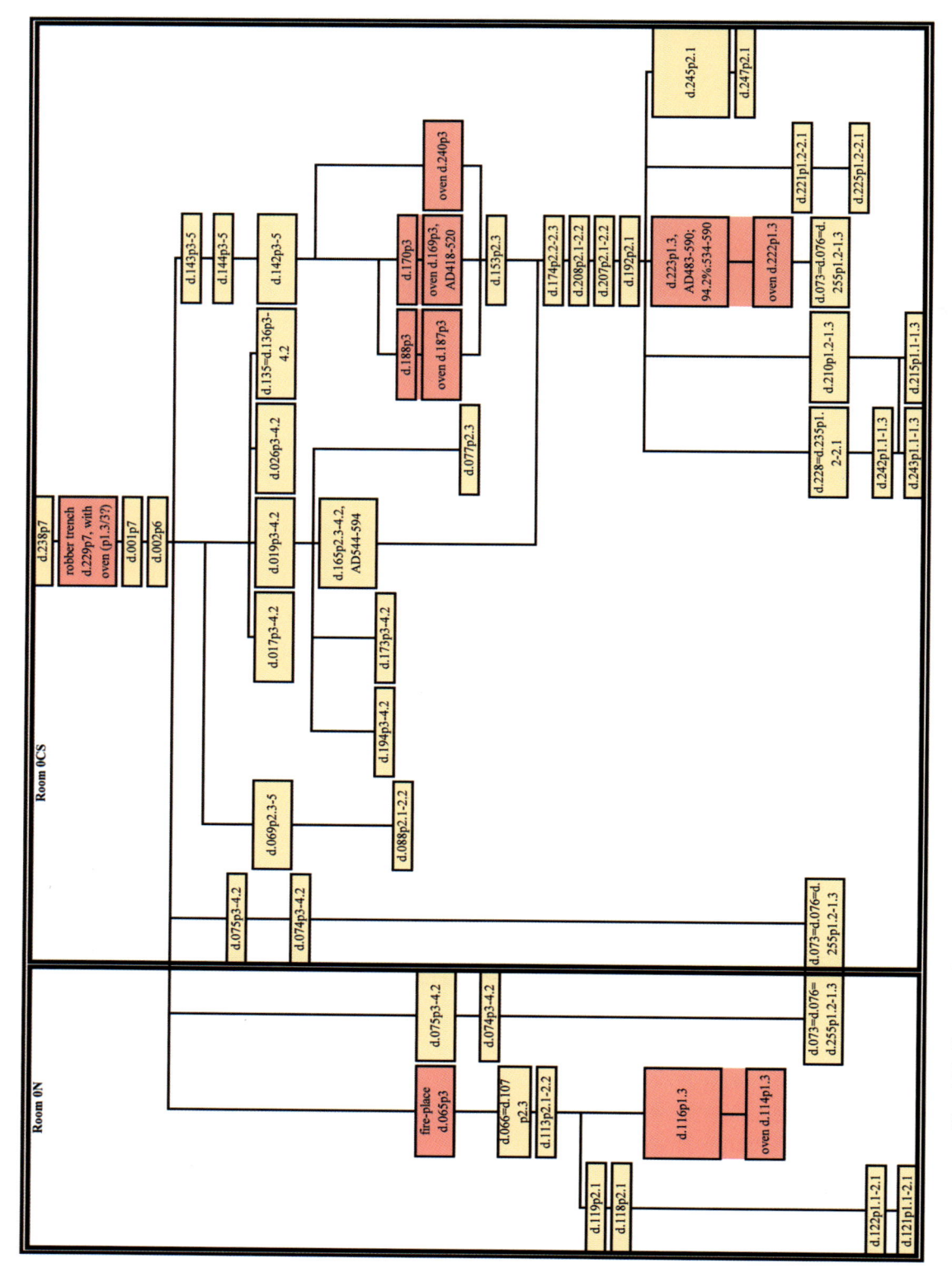

Fig. 4.52: Stratigraphic matrix for row 0. The matrix lists modelled radiocarbon dates. (For unmodelled dates, see Table 4.8.)

Fig. 4.53: Oven d.222, half-sectioned; north is on the left. This oven of the first phase, with typical fire-reddened walls, contained barley seeds. (Each red and white segment of the scales measures 10 cm.)

(AD 531–579), on the basis of this sample. Even if used for food preparation into the AD 530s or beyond, the oven could have been in use for some time, and the annexe itself could be earlier. The oven is stratigraphically clearly earlier than phase 3 oven d.169 (at the interface of room 0CS and the western outdoor area), suggesting that a date around the middle of the sixth century or before is more likely than a date in the second half of the century. The archaeomagnetic *terminus ante quem* of AD 520 for oven d.169 would rule out a date under the reign of Khusro I, if the archaeomagnetic dating should be accurate and reliable. Precision-dating is not easy in the fifth to early sixth century, and the annexe may have been constructed at any stage between the second half of the fifth century and the early sixth century. Judged by the radiocarbon sample, the earliest ovens may have remained in use until the 530s or so. Assuming that the annexe was at least a few years, more likely a few decades, later than the original barracks, a date around the mid-fifth century seems unlikely. Similarly, bearing in mind that the surface in the annexe rose by 30–50 cm before another set of ovens was built, some demolished and storage vessels installed in row 1, with further occupation at a later date, it seems improbable that the western annexe is much later than the early sixth century at the very latest.

In phases 2.1–2.3, the surface was raised by about one to one-and-a-half foot, and afterwards new ovens were installed in room 0CS. As no ovens anywhere in the trench are likely to belong to phases 2.1–2.3, these phases need not represent a long period of time; perhaps no more than a few days were needed to raise the surface in phase 2. The new ovens include d.187. It was probably intended to replace the then disused oven d.222, though it was of slightly larger dimensions and some 5 m south of d.222. Its fill (d.187) contained charcoal, including wood charcoal. Another oven (d.169), of similar dimensions and elevation to d.187, was found further west (Fig. 4.74). Its location is difficult to explain, as it is in alignment with the postulated western wall of the barracks, if correctly identified in the north-west corner of 0CS. It should be stressed that despite careful and repeated cleaning and spraying of the soil with water to reveal any potential subtle differences in colour, we were unable to trace any more of the postulated western wall of room 0CS, and the barracks as a whole, beyond the north-west corner. Whether the wall never existed, if there was a very wide entrance (and oven d.169 oddly located within), if it was demolished, if it did not follow a rectilinear alignment or if the western side of room 0CS was marked via some basic screen is unknown. Neither would much be gained by speculating how to explain the location of the oven in the light of so many unknown variables. What seems clear is that row 0 was the least solidly built and/or least well-preserved part of the building and oven d.169 was probably just within or just outside. The oven wall yielded an archaeomagnetic date of AD 418–520, an early sixth-century date perhaps being easiest to reconcile with the stratigraphy.[102] Considering that the oven, based on its elevation, belongs to phase 3, a date a few years or decades after AD 520 would be easier to reconcile with the stratigraphy, and it ought to be remembered that archaeomagnetic dating in the region is still a dating method in its early development. A further poorly preserved oven (d.240) at a similar level was only observed in section, in the southern part of unit 0CS. Most of this feature must have been beyond the limits of our trench. Of the little we were able to observe within our trench, only its western edge appears to survive, suggesting that it had been partially destroyed already in antiquity. All three ovens (d.169, d.187 and d.240) in room unit 0CS are at a similar elevation to ovens d.028 and d.030 in room 1CS, and they are probably contemporary. Ovens d.028 and d.030 in 1CS were partially demolished to make space for storage vessels. Oven d.240 appears to have been partially destroyed too, though for unknown reasons, whilst ovens d.169 and d.187 remained intact. It is tempting to think that a fireplace (d.065) in room 0N, also at a similar level, is contemporary to these five ovens (probably all of phase 3). A further oven appears to have been destroyed by treasure hunters digging the cited small tunnel (d.229) into the eastern part of room 0CS between the 2015 and 2016 field seasons, as suggested by fragments of oven wall from its fill. It is impossible to tell whether this oven belonged to the earlier or later phase, as the tunnel under paving d.019) erased all earlier archaeological layers and structures in this area. This oven was in the east of room 0CS and may have abutted the western side of the postulated wall dividing rooms 0CS and 1CS. (It seems improbable that the destroyed oven was in the area of the postulated wall, as the eastern half of the robber trench was narrower than the typical diameter of an oven; only the western half of the robber pit was wide enough that it could have erased an entire oven.)

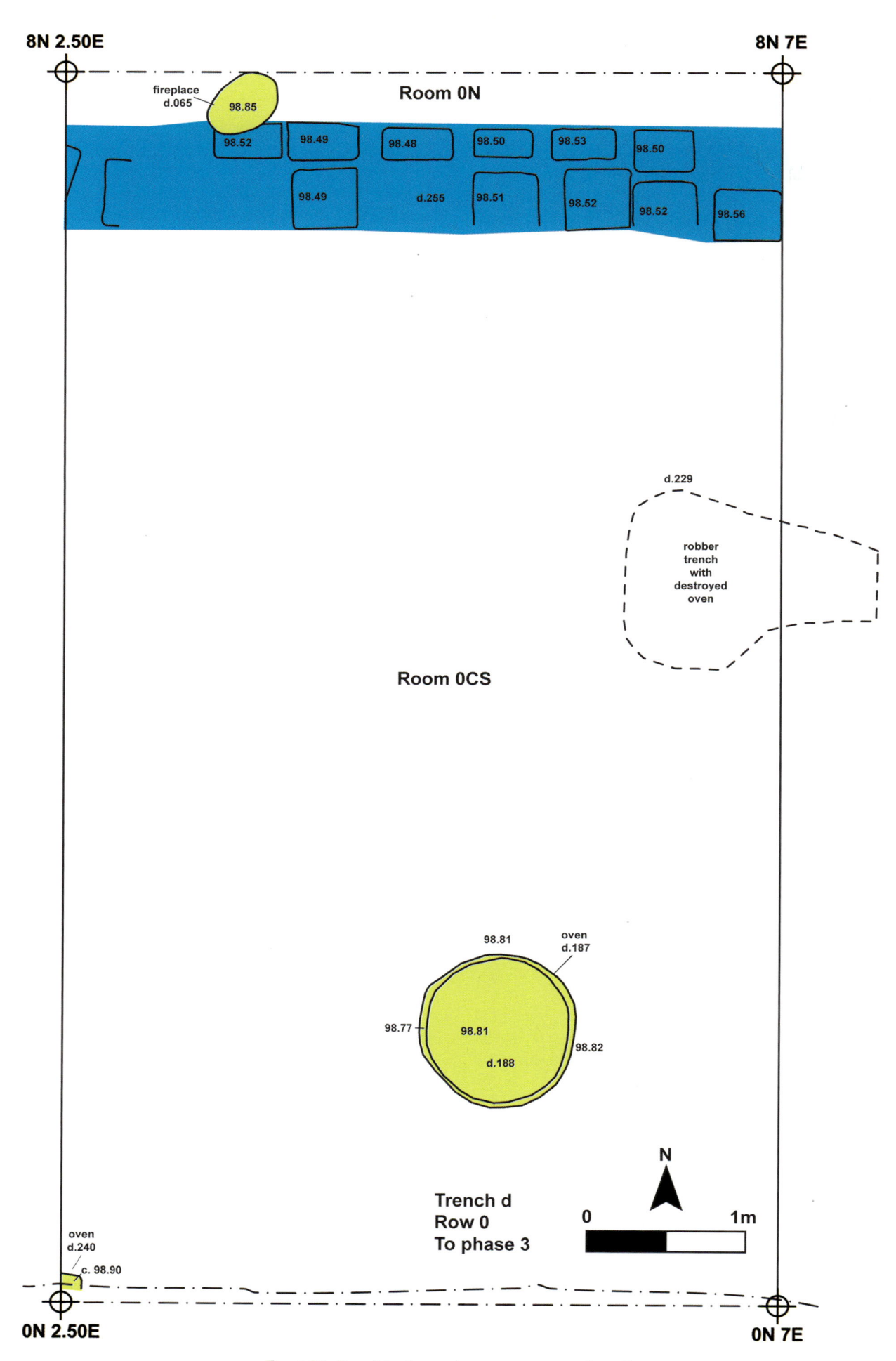

Fig. 4.54: Row 0 in the western annexe up to phase 3.

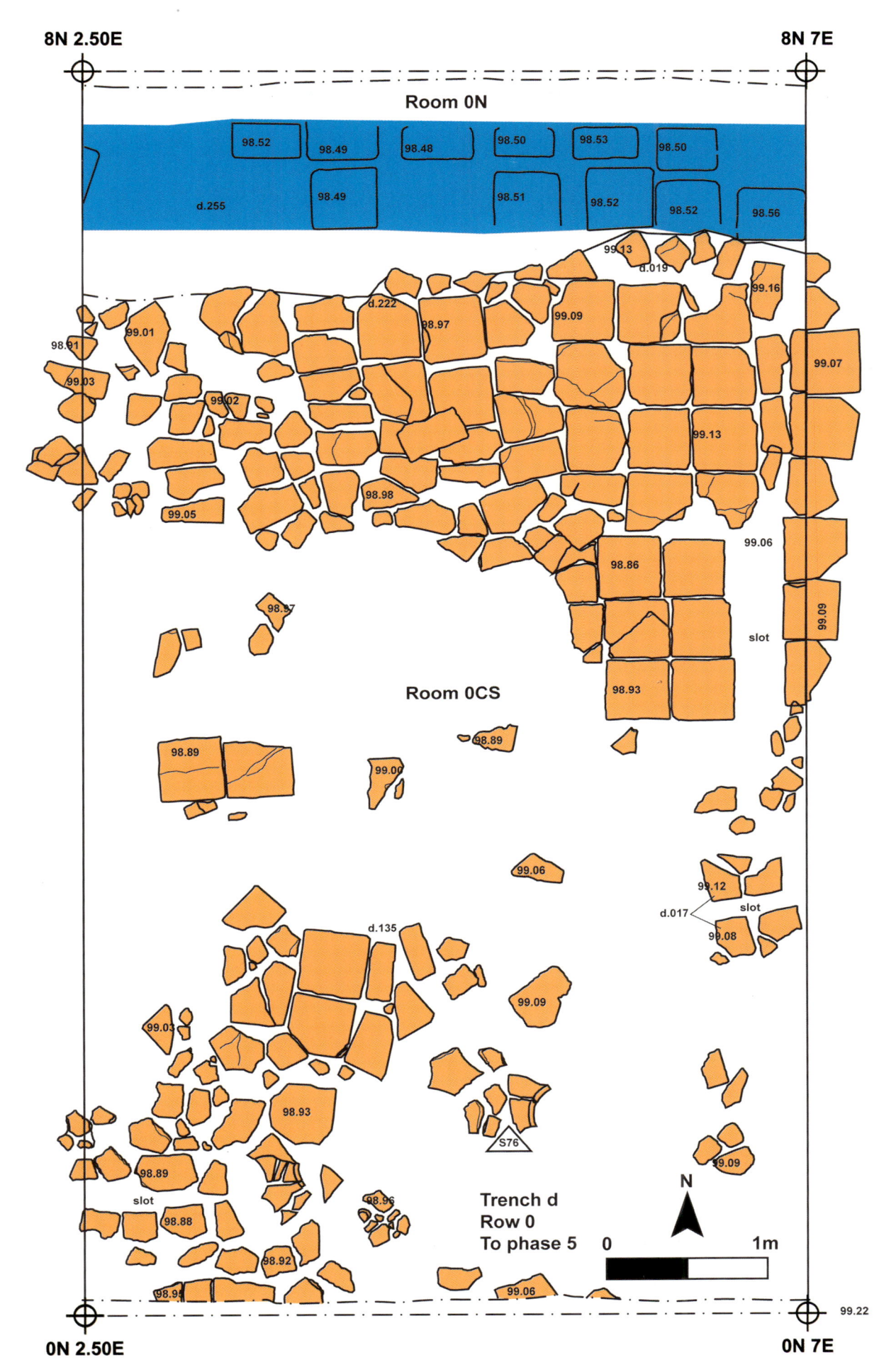

Fig. 4.55: Row 0 in the western annexe up to phase 5.

Fig. 4.56: The patchy paving made of fired bricks of room 0CS in the western annexe, with rows 1, 2 and 3 in the background.

Later, the surface of room 0CS was paved with reused fired Gorgan Wall bricks, including many broken fragments. The northern half of the room was paved fairly systematically, extending right to the western edge of room 1CS. In places, there were two layers of bricks on top of each other (d.173 and d.194 under d.019), within a matrix of stiff redeposited loess (d.165). The paving covered c. 0.50 m of deposits (notably d.192, d.174 and d.165) on top of oven d.222 and is evidently much later. The central and southern parts of 0CS were paved more haphazardly than the north, perhaps reflecting that the work surface or paved access route was only needed in parts of the room. It is also possible that there was not enough reusable brick to pave the entire room. A paved working surface (J.005), using re-employed Gorgan Wall bricks, has also been uncovered in Trench J in Fort 4 and it is possible that it could also have been within the outermost room of an annexe. It is, however, also possible that it was outdoors or on top of an earlier annexe buried when the surface in Fort 4 was raised substantially.[103]

We cannot be sure if there was a wall or screen between rooms 0CS and 1CS at this stage. Paving d.019 extended to and covered parts of the (partially demolished?) postulated division wall, in which we observed mud-bricks only tentatively. Whether or not there was a physical division between 0CS and 1CS at this stage or ever before, it is clear that the two units differed substantially in the use of space: 1CS was a store-room, after earlier ovens had been demolished in phase 4.1, whilst there is no evidence that 0CS ever contained any storage jars *in situ* or any storage pits. Paving d.019 is marginally higher than the top of the storage jars and may have been laid whilst they were still in use or just after. It never extended into 1CS, a further sign that 0CS and 1CS were used differently, even if there is no certain evidence for a solid division. A paving consisting of brick fragments (d.026) may well have formed a basic threshold between the two rooms. Two parallel brick alignments (d.017) frame a slot of 1.20 m length and 10 cm width, south of d.026, already discussed in the context of room 1CS.[104] It might have held one side of a doorframe or, as there is no counterpart to this slot on the other side of d.026, perhaps a pipe channelling water out of the room under a mud-brick wall or threshold (similar to the gully in room 5CS).[105] The width of d.017 (of 1.20 m west–east) would be similar to mud-brick walls (in the original barracks at least), and it is interesting to note that in the east of paving d.019 there is a slightly wider north–south alignment of three and a half bricks. These may have formed the foundation of a hypothetical late mud-brick wall dividing rooms 0CS and 1CS (Figs 4.49 and 4.55), though this would have been in a different alignment to d.017. No traces of this postulated mud-brick wall built on d.019 survive. As the top of d.019 is less than 0.50 m below the modern surface, any mud-brick structures built on this solid foundation would inevitably have been destroyed through bioturbation, not to mention windborne erosion. In contrast to Fort 4, the last phase of occupation of the barracks in Fort 2 may be difficult or impossible to reconstruct, as relevant structures and deposits have probably been largely erased.

As in row 1, we found no spindle whorls. There are too few of them from Trench d (11 in total) to be certain that their absence ultimately proves that no textiles were ever produced in the western annexe. It seems likely, however, that wool was spun mainly in the more solidly built and habitable original barracks and the eastern annexe, whilst the western annexe was used mainly for food preparation and storage. Later, perhaps, room 0CS may have been intended for work that benefited from an easy-to-clean brick floor. Easy access to the main road would have facilitated storage and redistribution of goods or providing access to, or temporary shelter for, mounts or packhorses. Should there indeed have been no very solid wall in the west or none at all, such an open shed may have been suitable for work that was not unduly impeded by high or low temperatures. It would have offered better light conditions in daylight hours than back rooms, but similar protection from rain exposure.

4.1.4.4.3. THE EASTERN ANNEXE: ROWS 4 AND 5
4.1.4.4.3.1. THE WESTERN ROW OF ROOMS (4) IN THE EASTERN ANNEXE
To the east of row 3, there was a narrow row of rooms (4), mirroring the narrow row of rooms (1) west of row 2. Initially, however, this appears to have been an outdoor area. A small sondage in the south of the trench yielded finds down to 97.68 m, approximately 0.50 m deeper than at any other point of the trench (excluding only the four storage pits). The finds concentration was unusually high with just over a quarter of the pottery from row 4 coming from this small sondage of just 0.50 × 1.50 m (i.e. deposit d.250 under the later floor d.132). The sondage was dug at the end of the 2016 season, and more excavation would

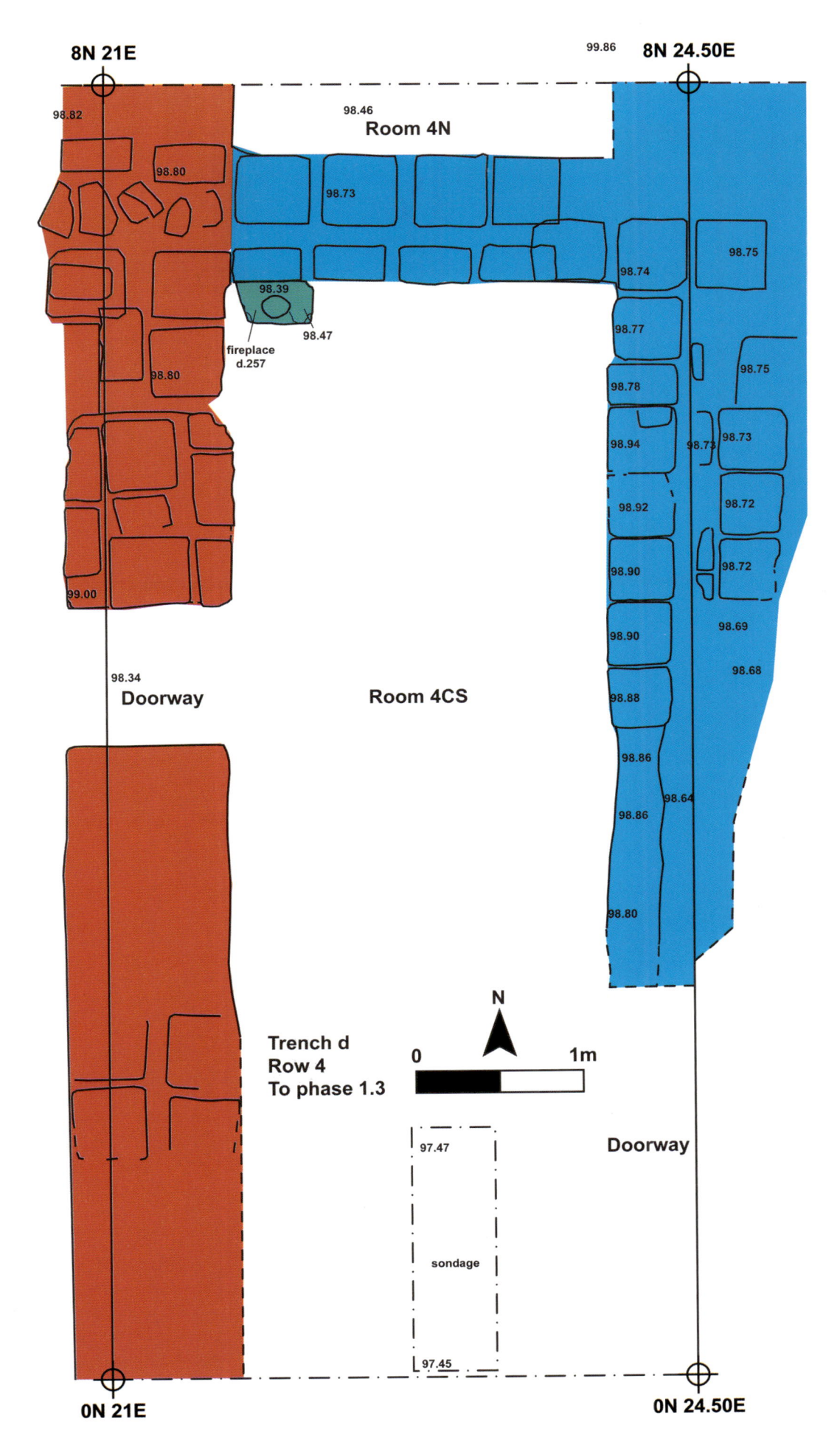

Fig. 4.57: Row 4 in the eastern annexe in phase 1.

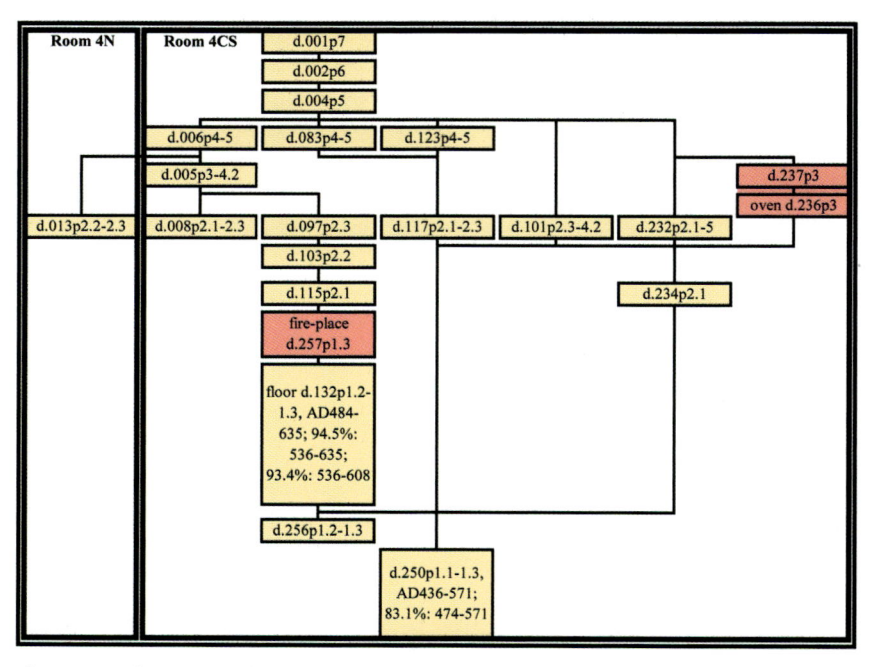

Fig. 4.58: Stratigraphic matrix for row 4. The matrix lists modelled radiocarbon dates. (For unmodelled dates, see Table 4.8.)

Table 4.20: Finds from the interior of room 4CS. Weights are in grams.

Room 4CS deposits	Bottom	Top	Depth	Phase	Pottery	Bone	Other finds
d.083 (N of room)	98.87	99.05	0.18	4–5	4,897	1,542	Iron blade? (7 g)
d.123 (S of room)	98.85	99.02	0.17	4–5	646	204	n/a
d.237 (fill of oven d.236, centre of room)	98.61	98.91	0.30	3	>0	>0	Eggshell, traces of unidentified charcoal
d.232 (centre of room)	98.46	99.02	0.56	2.1–5	5,298	395	Flint working debris (11 g) and iron (2 g)
d.101 (E of room)	98.80	99.00	0.20	2.3–4.2	851	690	n/a
d.097 (N of room)	98.69	98.87	0.18	2.3	1,270	3,710	n/a
d.117 (S of room)	98.40	98.85	0.45	2.1–2.3	6,885	573	n/a
d.103 (N of room)	98.60	98.69	0.09	2.2	1,355	20	n/a
d.115 (N of room)	98.40	98.60	0.20	2.1	1,391	152	Charcoal and eggshell (4 g)
d.234 (centre of room)	98.40	98.46	0.06	2.1	1,595	107	Worked stone (30 g)
d.132 (floor)	98.31	98.40	0.09	1.2–1.3	266	23	Charcoal
d.250 (S of room, but pre-dating annexe)	97.68	98.31	0.63	1.1–1.3	8,781	16	n/a
Total					33,235	7,432	Ratio, pot:bone: c. 4:1
Up to phase 2.2					13,388	318	Ratio, pot:bone: c. 42:1
Sondage, phase 1.1–1.3 (d.250)					8,781	16	Ratio, pot:bone: c. 549:1

be required to offer a certain interpretation, but a tentative explanation of the high concentration of finds may be offered here. We were not able to identify a cut, probably as d.250 is of similar colour to the natural soil. There was no trace of a storage pit here and as other such pits were identified without difficulty, it seems more likely that we found a soil extraction pit in which largely inorganic debris (more than 500 times as much of ceramics than bone) accumulated. This soil extraction pit may have been dug outside the original barracks to obtain the soil needed for supplementary mud-brick production (or potentially a raised floor). A sheep or goat rib (d.250/843) from near the base of the deposit yielded a radiocarbon date of c. AD 436–571. The sample falls into the radiocarbon calibration plateau and would be compatible with our hypothesis that this represents material deposited here at a very early stage of the occupation of the barracks (e.g. the fifth century) or at the time when the decision was made to build an annexe here (perhaps in the later fifth or early sixth century). If we are right in thinking that there were soil extraction pits in the area of the later eastern annexe that subsequently needed to be filled up, to create a level building platform, then this suggests that the workforce erecting the original barracks did not anticipate that the buildings would be extended subsequently – circumstantial evidence to suggest that the decision to add annexes was made later, rather than being part of a short-term or long-term plan from the start.

The eastern annexe was probably added at the same time as the western annexe, considering their broadly symmetrical arrangement, despite differing in many details. Fired bricks, as well as sun-baked mud-bricks, were employed in the wall dividing rooms 4CS and 5CS (as well as the eastern wall of room 5CS). Whilst the very wide wall between 4CS and 5CS may have been narrower originally and widened, the selective use of fired bricks in the annexe walls (absent from the walls of the original barracks) is a possible sign for a later date when less standardised construction techniques and the reuse of old building material became the norm. The doorway connecting rooms 4CS and 5CS will have been in the southern 2.40 m of the trench where we failed to find any continuation of the room division. Perhaps there was indeed a very wide doorway, as it connected two heatable internal rooms, perhaps (as elsewhere in the trench) walls were partially demolished at a later stage to widen entrances. In our hypothetical reconstruction (Fig. 4.15), we assume it was wide from the start and that its centre was in alignment with the outside entrance to room 5CS. If correct, the doorway connecting rooms 4CS and 5CS and the eastern door of 5CS may have been a little to the south of the axis of symmetry of the rooms. It is, of course, possible that the rooms were even larger than assumed (and that rooms 2S and 3S also extended further south, and were bigger than 2C and 3C, if their southern walls were to be in alignment with those of 4CS and 5CS). If so, the doors of 4CS and 5CS might have been in the centre of their eastern walls. Perhaps the assumption that the eastern entrances of rooms 5CS and 4CS were close to the centre of their eastern walls, but not perfectly so, is more likely. Room 3C's entrance certainly was slightly off-centre, evidence to suggest that functional symmetrical design prevailed in Sasanian military architecture, but no pointless perfectionism, not even when the original barracks were built.

After annexe construction, a trampled earth floor (d.132) of stiff mid-yellowish brown silty clay formed in the area of 4CS. Its top elevation (98.40 m) was within 1 cm of that (d.085) in barrack room 3C and the corridor (d.138). It was also within 3 cm of the floor (d.050) in room 2C. The four floor deposits were not only of virtually identical elevation but also strikingly similar composition, leaving little doubt that they all formed part of a walking surface in use at the same time. Our assumption that they are contemporary gains in strength by there being only a single recognisable earthen floor in any one room or corridor. A floor (d.167 = d.175) at a slightly lower level in row 5, and likely to be contemporary as well, will be discussed separately below.[106] A dicot herb (d.132/501) from the floor in room 4CS was radiocarbon-dated to c. AD 484–635, with a 94.5% probability that the date falls between AD 536 and 635, suggesting that the floor was in use as late as the AD 530s or beyond. Irrespective of its precise date, the trampled earth floor is not easy to explain. We encountered no such floor anywhere in the western annexes (i.e. rows 0–1). That it was at the same level as that in room 3C and the corridor connecting 3C and 4CS does not prove contemporary creation, but makes it a near certainty that their periods of use overlapped. No indoor deposits had evidently been allowed to accumulate on top of the floor in room 3C at the time row 4 was added in the east and provided with the same form of trampled earth floor. This does not necessarily mean that not much time passed between the erection of the original barracks (rows 2 and 3) and the addition of row 4 or indeed the entire annexes (rows 0–1 and 4–5). The makeshift style of the annexe walls, as opposed to the much more regular walls of the original barracks, points perhaps to a different construction date. One wonders if it was tidiness of the barracks' occupants that explains the virtually identical floor level in the original barracks (rows 2–3) and row 4 within the eastern annexe. The low rate of bone deposition, perhaps related to the garrison's Zoroastrian faith or military discipline,[107] suggests that tidiness played a part and that the same earthen floors formed a walking surface for decades or generations. Maybe it was regularly swept clean, maybe occupants avoided indoor rubbish disposal in the first place, maybe there were carpets or other organic floor coverings in the interior of the rooms in rows 2, 3, 4 and 5. Ultimately, however, we cannot be sure how much time passed between the construction of rows 2–3 and the addition of the eastern and western annexes (rows 4–5 and 0–1) and how long the phase 1 floors of the original building and the eastern annexe remained in use, though it seems not beyond around the mid-sixth century at the latest.

On top of floor d.132, there was a distinctly fire-reddened hearth (d.257). Following the pattern, also observed elsewhere in the trench, of ovens and hearths being located preferentially next to room partitions where they would have caused minimal obstruction, it was located in the north-west corner of room 4CS and will have been used for heating and preparation of meals. Like fireplace d.047 in row 1 and ovens d.114 and d.222, it belongs to the earliest occupation of the annexes.

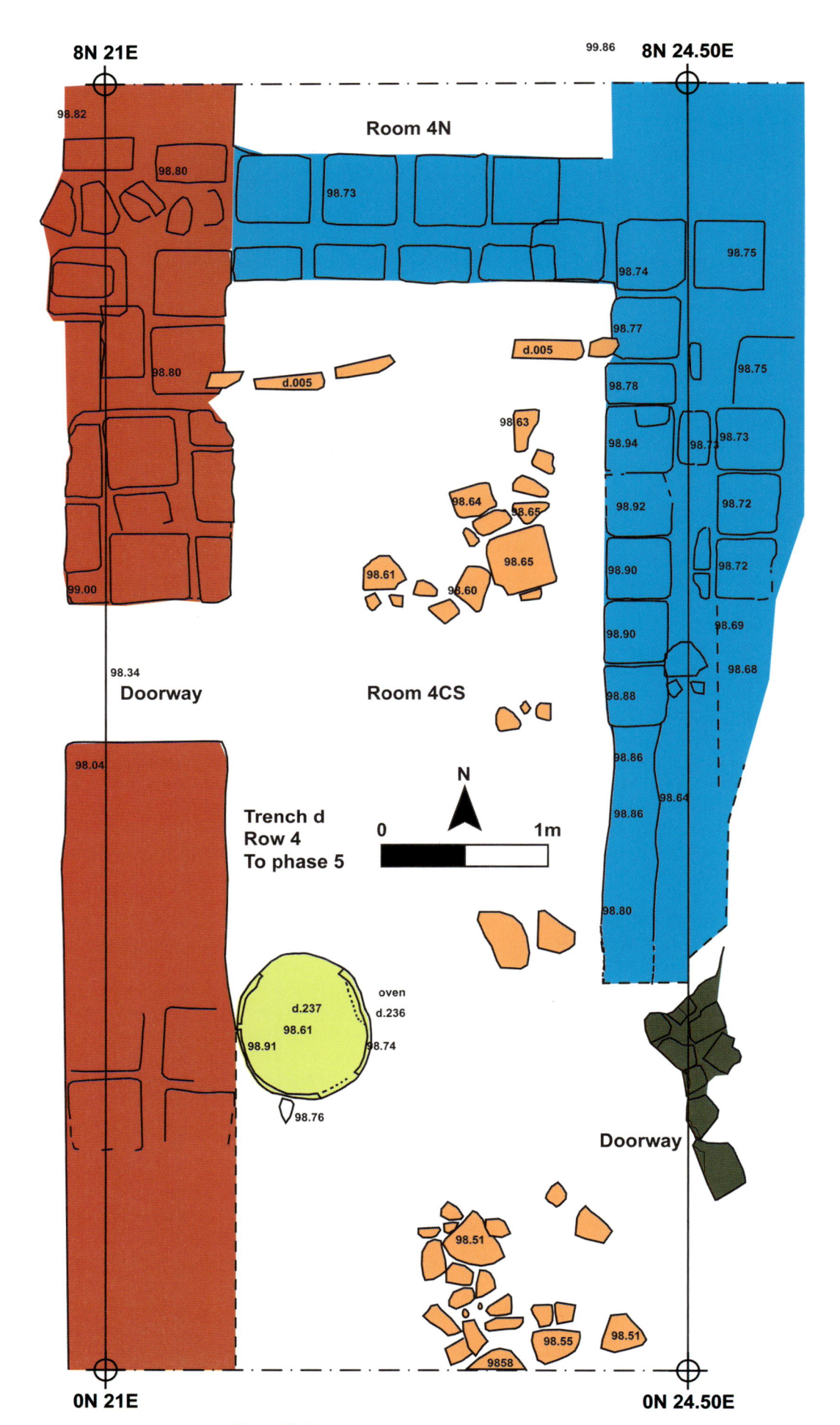

Fig. 4.59: Row 4 in the eastern annexe up to phase 5.

Table 4.21: Finds from the interior of the southern edge of room 4N. Weights are in grams.

Room 4N deposit	Bottom	Top	Depth	Phase	Pottery	Bone	Other finds
d.013	98.46	98.98	0.52	2.2–2.3	1,343	0	n/a
Total					**1,343**	**0**	

Over time, 50–60 cm of deposits built up in the interior of the room, and the ratio of bone to pottery increased on average over time (Table 4.20), pointing to changing habits of the garrison. There is much variation in the ratios within phase 2 deposits. This suggests, perhaps, that the floor was not everywhere raised rapidly or that it was patched up in places at a later date. In phase 3, an oven (d.236) was built abutting the room's western wall. Its top elevation was virtually identical to that of ovens d.028 and d.030 in row 1 and d.187 and d.169 in row 0, and we may assume that these cooking and baking facilities (all attributed to phase 3) are contemporary. Flotation of a ten-litre sample from the oven fill (d.237) yielded eggshells, suggesting that meals were prepared here. Unlike the ovens in row 1, their counterpart (d.236) in row 4 was not demolished to make way for storage facilities. Unlike room 1CS, there were no *in-situ* storage jars in room 4CS, perhaps as it was more cumbersome to access, from a back route rather than the central road, but there were fragments of such jars, notably from the earlier levels.[108]

No spindle whorls or unusual items were found in room 4CS. Given the smaller size of the room and that there were only 11 in total from the trench, this is not firm proof that no textile production ever took place in the room, notably as spindle whorls were found both west (four and three respectively in rows 2 and 3) and east (four in row 5)[109] of narrow row 4. A tanged iron blade of a dagger or combat knife (d.083/343) from a late deposit, or niche in the wall too close to the surface for mud-bricks to survive, between rooms 4CS and room 5CS is worth noting.[110] In a late phase (3 or 4) the northernmost part of the room was partitioned off via an alignment of reused Gorgan Wall fired bricks, placed in an upright position (d.005). Evidently some food preparation took place in row 4 and the compacted earth floor suggests heavy traffic or, more probably, prolonged use, at least during its earlier occupation. We do not know what other activities beyond food preparation the rooms in this row may have been used for. That there was additional accommodation here can neither be proven nor excluded.

The southernmost part of room 4N was also within our trench. Excavation down to 98.46 m site height yielded 1,343 g of pottery embedded in a deposit (d.013) of the usual composition. Due to the limited extent of our excavations, little certain can be said about the function or layout of the room. Even its precise west–east extent could not be ascertained, although we assume it was identical to that of 4CS.

4.1.4.4.3.2. The eastern row of rooms (5) in the eastern annexe

In Row 5, as in rows 2–4, we encountered a compacted earth floor (d.167 = d.175), but at a lower level of c. 98.12–98.25 m site height, some 20 cm below that in adjacent row 4. Such a stepped arrangement may have saved the efforts involved in raising all floors to an identical level and might have been advantageous in keeping the barracks dry. Underneath the floor, there was a levelling deposit (d.186), with a very early radiocarbon sample of c. AD 430–535. This belonged to a horse, comparable to modern horses. The animal must have perished before the eastern annexe was added to the barracks and proves that horses were present already during the earliest occupation of Fort 2.[111] Deposit d.186 contained more bone than pottery as well as a copper alloy (d.186/799) object of uncertain significance, perhaps an awl.[112] It is possible that levelling was required as a result of soil from this area having been used for making supplementary mud-bricks for, or raising the floor in, the original barracks. The high proportion of bone suggests that d.186 is an outdoor deposit pre-dating annexe construction. It is hard to tell why there was much more bone from this deposit than from the pre-annexe deposit d.250 (in the area of the later room 4CS); perhaps greater distance from the original barracks, where the smell and sight of rotting food remains may have caused less concern, might be part of the explanation.

There was no evidence of any early oven or fireplace on top of the floor anywhere in the row, suggesting that initially no baking or cooking took place here. An ashy deposit (d.177) in the east of the room at floor level (98.22 m site height) suggests, however, that fires were burning nearby. There was, of course, also no hearth or oven in the original barracks (rows 2–3). The compacted earth floors in the eastern annexe (rows 4–5) and the more solid construction of the walls forms a noticeable contrast to the western annexe and suggests that it would have offered a more comfortable space to live and engage in domestic activities. The precise function of two possible postholes (d.180 and d.182) is unknown.

Later, the floor was raised to c. 98.37 m site height (but there was no compacted earth floor at this level). An alignment of four small stake holes (d.157, d.159, d.161 and d.163) plus a posthole (d.154) may form part of a basic structure of unknown function. Two pits (d.216 and d.230) were also cut from this level. They may be contemporary to pit d.064 in row 1. Pit d.216 was roughly twice the depth of, and of a larger diameter than, d.230

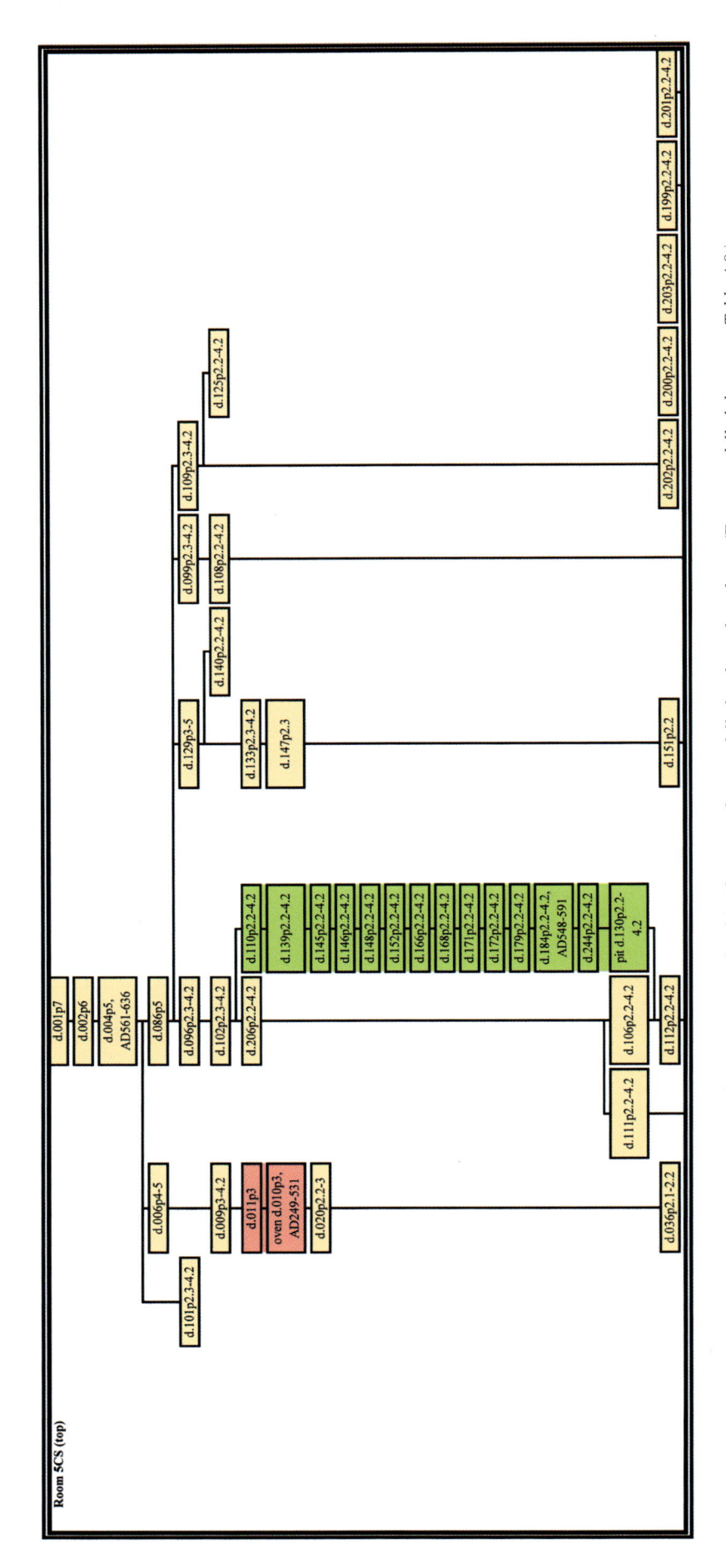

Fig. 4.60: Stratigraphic matrix for row 5 (upper levels). The matrix lists modelled radiocarbon dates. (For unmodelled dates, see Table 4.8.)

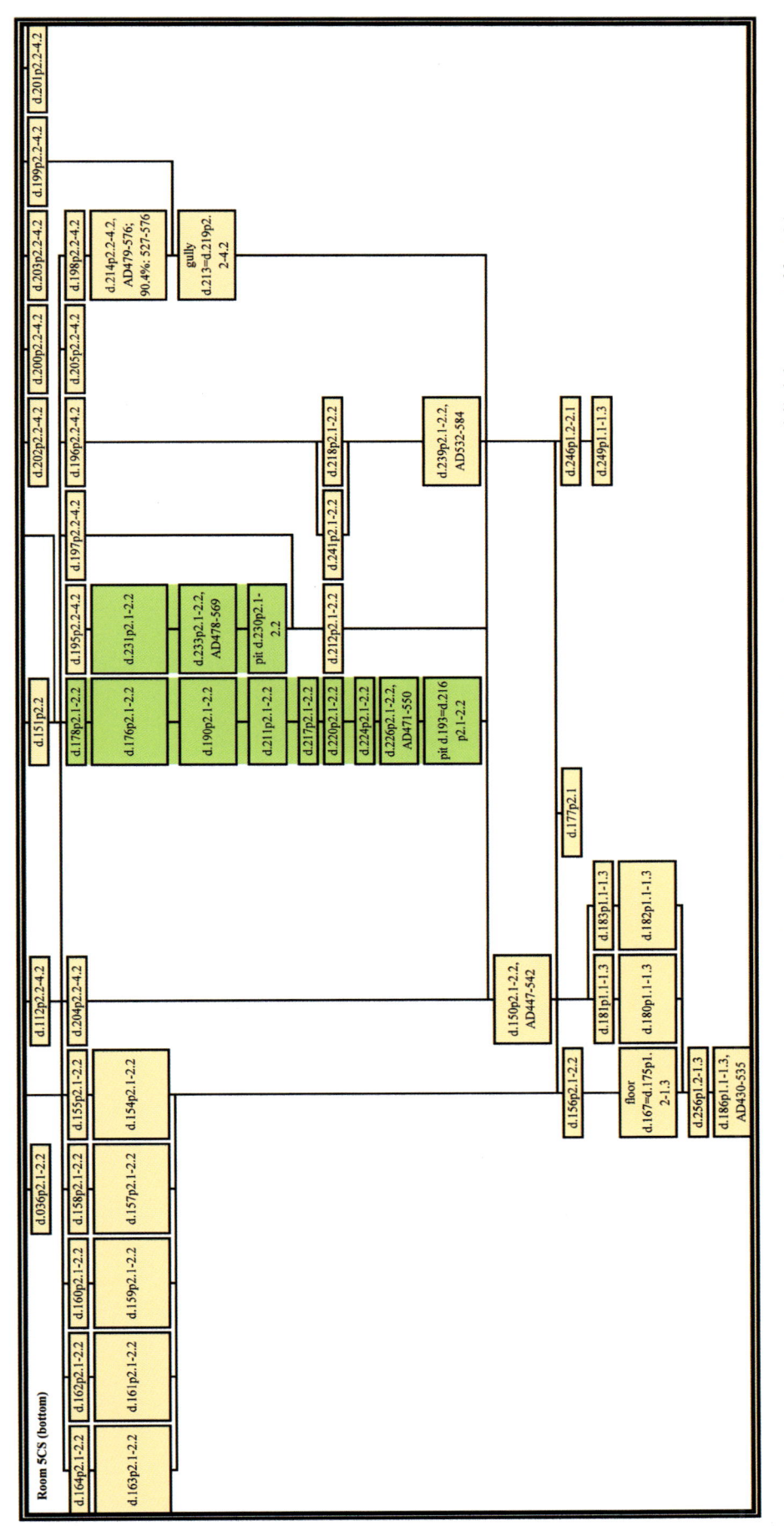

Fig. 4.61: Stratigraphic matrix for row 5 (lower levels). The matrix lists modelled radiocarbon dates. (For unmodelled dates, see Table 4.8.)

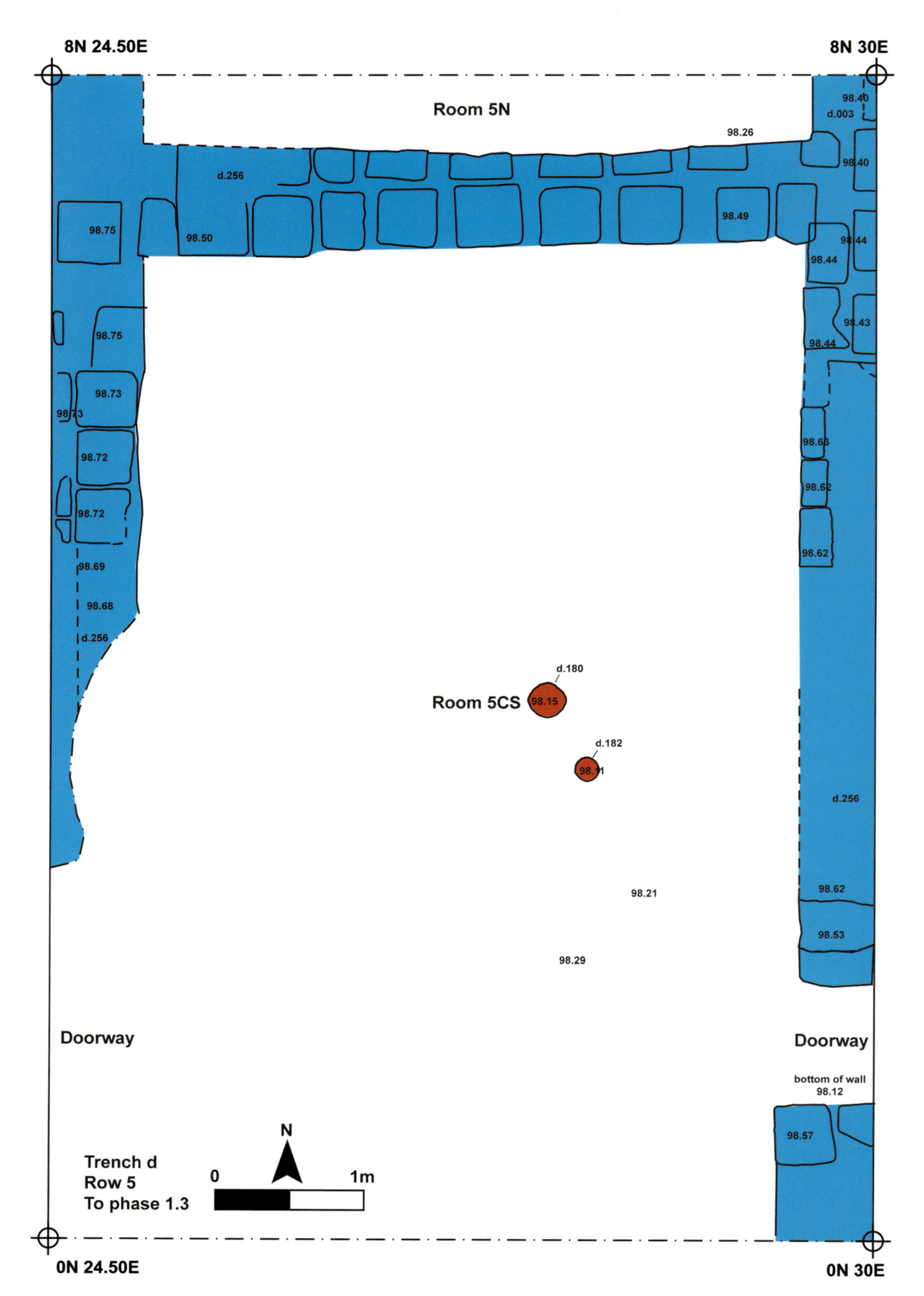

Fig. 4.62: Row 5 in the eastern annexe in phase 1.

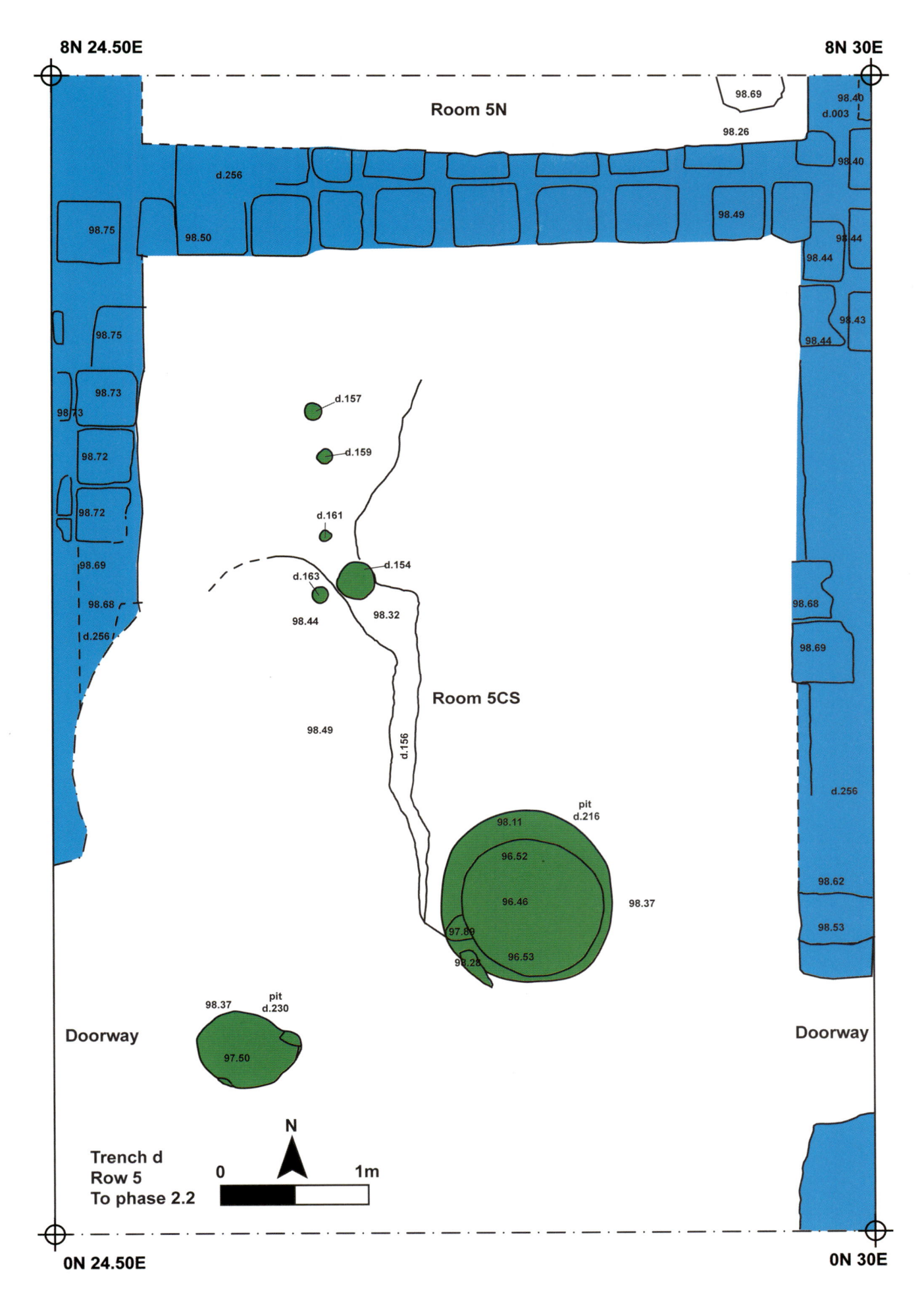

Fig. 4.63: Row 5 in the eastern annexe up to phase 2.1/2.2.

Table 4.22: Finds from within room 5CS. (Note that deposit d.009, assigned before the room units were recognised, extended from 5CS to the eastern outdoor area, and not all of the pottery and bone will be from 5CS.)

Room 5CS deposits	Bottom	Top	Depth	Phase	Pottery	Bone	Other finds
d.086	98.83	99.06	0.23	5	8,511	610	n/a
d.129	98.71	98.83	0.12	3–5	4,240	912	n/a
d.009	98.61	98.92	0.31	3–4.2	1,882	318	n/a
d.133	98.58	98.70	0.12	2.3–4.2	14,747	6,090	Glass (14 g)
d.099	98.66	98.88	0.22	2.3–4.2	1,769	445	n/a
d.109	98.64	98.84	0.20	2.3–4.2	430	35	n/a
d.096	98.67	98.86	0.19	2.3–4.2	4,510	539	Iron slag (26 g)
d.102	98.66	98.71	0.05	2.3–4.2	1,175	244	Worked flint? (22 g)
d.147	98.48	98.62	0.14	2.3	10,004	3,660	Charcoal
d.110 (fill of pit d.130)	98.23	98.61	0.38	2.2–4.2	2,100	1,275	Charcoal
d.139 (fill of pit d.130)	98.09	98.23	0.14	2.2–4.2	1,095	531	Charcoal
d.145 (fill of pit d.130)	97.98	98.09	0.11	2.2–4.2	424	271	Charcoal and eggshell (2 g)
d.146 (fill of pit d.130)	97.78	97.98	0.20	2.2–4.2	1,437	350	Charcoal
d.148 (fill of pit d.130)	97.63	97.78	0.15	2.2–4.2	1,457	717	Charcoal and prehistoric flint arrowhead (13 g)
d.152 (fill of pit d.130)	97.33	97.63	0.30	2.2–4.2	735	181	Charcoal
d.166 (fill of pit d.130)	97.27	97.33	0.06	2.2–4.2	493	8	Charcoal
d.168 (fill of pit d.130)	97.06	97.27	0.21	2.2–4.2	633	532	Charcoal and glass (<1 g)
d.171 (fill of pit d.130)	96.96	97.06	0.10	2.2–4.2	1,530	427	Glass (22 g)
d.172 (fill of pit d.130)	96.79	96.96	0.17	2.2–4.2	1,110	142	Charcoal
d.179 (fill of pit d.130)	96.56	96.79	0.23	2.2–4.2	1,417	108	Glass (10 g)
d.184 (fill of pit d.130)	96.34	96.56	0.22	2.2–4.2	2,580	353	Charcoal, glass and whetstone (71 g)
d.125	98.62	98.64	0.02	2.2–4.2	40	62	n/a
d.140	98.51	98.67	0.16	2.2–4.2	1,220	2,272	Bone spindle whorl (6 g) and iron sheet (9 g)
d.108	98.45	98.60	0.15	2.2–4.2	3,098	485	Charcoal
d.106	98.52	98.58	0.06	2.2–4.2	3,130	1,067	n/a
d.111	98.57	98.61	0.04	2.2–4.2	53	0	n/a
d.112	98.45	98.51	0.06	2.2–4.2	3,830	522	Charcoal and glass (2 g)
d.195	98.47	98.61	0.14	2.2–4.2	0	>0	n/a
d.196	98.45	98.51	0.06	2.2–4.2	233	0	n/a
d.197	98.45	98.48	0.03	2.2–4.2	0	>0	n/a
d.198	98.52	98.62	0.10	2.2–4.2	0	0	Glass
d.214 (fill of gully d.213)	98.33	98.56	0.23	2.2–4.2	0	27	n/a
d.151	98.37	98.48	0.11	2.2	3,731	152	Charcoal
d.241	98.21	98.41	0.20	2.1–2.2	3,489	573	Charcoal
d.218	98.36	98.43	0.07	2.1–2.2	783	100	Iron arrowhead (13 g)
d.231 (fill of pit d.230)	97.97	98.37	0.40	2.1–2.2	2,018	122	n/a
d.233 (fill of pit d.230)	97.50	97.97	0.47	2.1–2.2	342	25	Charcoal
d.176 and d.178 (fill of pit d.216)	98.06	98.37	0.31	2.1–2.2	3,468	173	n/a
d.190 (fill of pit d.216)	97.90	98.06	0.16	2.1–2.2	0	111	Charcoal and slag
d.211 (fill of pit d.216)	97.71	97.90	0.19	2.1–2.2	487	282	Charcoal and poss. worked stone (79 g)
d.217 (fill of pit d.216)	97.49	97.71	0.22	2.1–2.2	919	181	Charcoal
d.220 (fill of pit d.216)	97.17	97.49	0.32	2.1–2.2	938	311	Charcoal
d.224 (fill of pit d.216)	96.77	97.17	0.40	2.1–2.2	1,597	2,690	Charcoal
d.226 (fill of pit d.216)	96.63	96.77	0.14	2.1–2.2	241	579	n/a
d.212	?	98.37	≤0.10	2.1–2.2	2,785	28	Charcoal
d.239	98.30	98.34	0.04	2.1–2.2	175	21	Charcoal
d.150	98.26	98.36	0.10	2.1–2.2	2,584	963	Charcoal
d.156	98.15	98.46	0.31	2.1–2.2	1,230	868	n/a
d.177 ashy deposit	?	98.22	≤0.05	2.1	>0	0	n/a
d.246	98.06	98.29	0.23	1.2–2.1	5,005	1,268	Copper alloy sheet (2 g), charcoal and glass (6 g)
d.167 = d.175 (floor)	98.14	98.25	0.11	1.2–1.3	562	320	n/a
d.249	?	98.14	≤0.10	1.1–1.3	1,891	791	Copper alloy (2 g)
d.186	97.92	98.14	0.22	1.1–1.3	2,254	2,582	Pointed copper alloy implement (awl?) (8 g)

(Continued)

4. Forts on the Gorgan Wall

Table 4.22: (Continued)

Room 5CS deposits	Bottom	Top	Depth	Phase	Pottery	Bone	Other finds
Total					108,382	34,323	Ratio, pot:bone: c. 3:1
Up to phase 2.2					34,499	12,140	Ratio, pot:bone: c. 3:1
Up to phase 1.3					4,707	3,693	Ratio, pot:bone: c. 1:1
Pits					25,021	9,369	Ratio, pot:bone: c. 3:1
Other deposits					83,361	24,954	Ratio, pot:bone: c. 3:1
Up to phase 2.2 pits					10,010	4,474	Ratio, pot:bone: c. 2:1
Up to phase 2.2 other deposits					24,489	7,666	Ratio, pot:bone: c. 3:1

Fig. 4.64: Storage pit d.216.

Fig. 4.65: Storage pit d.130, with sterile clay lining (d.244). The horizontal and the two vertical scales (each red and silver segment measuring 50 cm) show its massive dimensions.

and had a greater storage capacity. They differed also in shape: pit d.216 (= d.193) was circular in plan and had almost vertical walls; pit d.230 was ovoid in plan and bulb-shaped in section. Both pits had flat bases (Fig. 4.84).

Both pits appear to have been filled up later and before another storage pit (d.130) was cut from a higher level, i.e. c. 98.64 m site height. It is interesting to note that the bottom spits (d.226 and d.224) of the fill of pit d.216 contained more bone than pot, which is unusual for Trench d. Most deposits in the trench yielded more pottery than bone. The fort's tidy garrison evidently did not normally leave rotting food remains lying around. The high bone content may suggest that the pit, once no longer in use, was deliberately chosen to dispose of potentially smelly rubbish. One observes a relatively high proportion of bone not only in pit fills, but also levelling and occupation horizons. Overall, in no other row within the barracks[113] is the proportion of bone to pot higher than in row 5. Only approximately a quarter of the finds from row 5 are from the fill of pits. Most of the finds and most of the bone is from levelling/occupation horizons. Some 27% of the bone and 23% of the pottery found in row 5 came from the fill of pits, the remaining 73% and 77% from other deposits. Even if the proportion of bone from the pit fills is slightly higher than that from occupation horizons, the difference is small. The distinct and often fairly consistent difference in the ratio of pot to bone between the different rows is a powerful argument for most of the material having been deposited by the occupants/users of the rooms in question. Had it been random material brought in from the outside, one would expect the ratio of pottery to bone to be similar in all rows or to fluctuate from one phase to another. The consistently high proportion of bone in all phases in row 5 points to functional continuity. Perhaps row 5, facing the back of the building, was an area where much food preparation and consumption and much domestic work may have taken place. Leaving aside a wall sherd from a late deposit in row 2 or 1, it was also exclusively in rooms 5CS and 0CS that fragments of vessel glass, including fragments of beakers, were found, both from the fill of pit d.130 and occupation layers.[114] This is perhaps further evidence for drinking and dining predominantly taking place at the entrances to the barracks rather than in the interior rooms.

The later pit d.130 was oval in plan and distinctly bell-shaped in section, widening from c. 1.45 m at the top, in its narrow west–east section, to c. 2.75 m at the base (Fig. 4.84). It was deeper (with a maximum depth of 2.30 m) than the two earlier pits (d.216 had been 1.91 m and d.230 just 0.87 m deep). That it was cut from a higher level (similar to that of oven d.010) shows that it is later. Interestingly, its bell-shaped profile matches that of the pits excavated in Fort 4.[115] Its sides were sealed with sterile soft mid-yellowish brown clayey silt (d.244). A sample from the bottom fill (d.184) of the pit yielded a date of c. AD 439–594 (prior to modelling). In theory, this would allow for the pit having been filled with debris as early as the AD 430s at the one end of the spectrum or long after the AD 590s at the other, if old material had been used to fill up the disused feature. One is inclined to think, however, that a date before the sixth century is unlikely, bearing in mind that the pit evidently post-dates the construction of the Gorgan Wall and of Fort 2, the construction of barracks within, the use of the earliest floors, the digging and probable disuse of two earlier pits and the subsequent raising of the surface within the room. Furthermore, the pit is likely to have been in use for some time before being filled up. Our attempt to create a Bayesian model for the radiocarbon samples from this room suggests a much narrower date for the sample of c. AD 548–591. This adds strength to our observation that it is unlikely that the pit would have been put out of use early. That the pit was filled with debris not before the 540s at the very earliest and quite possibly several decades later is credible.

Starting at some stage between phases 2.2 and 4.2, much reused Gorgan Wall fired brick was employed in room 5CS. Most interesting is perhaps a gully (d.213 = d.219) lined and covered with such reused building material. The area within the trench was almost 5 m in length. It leads through the eastern doorway and continues to the eastern edge of the trench in the outdoor area. Within room 5CS, it curves in a southerly direction in the west. There was no clear and consistent gradient over this short stretch, and we cannot decide for certain if the gully was designed to channel water out of or into room 5CS. Its fill, soft light-yellowish brown clayey silt (d.214), showed no obvious signs of alluvial sedimentation, nor was it lined with waterproof materials, perhaps suggesting occasional use. The only finds from the fill were two bones. One of these (d.214/789), a metapodial of a pig, was radiocarbon-dated to c. AD 479–576 (with an over 90% probability of a post-AD 527 date). It was found in a covered section of the gully 12–13 cm below the top of the bricks lining the sides of the gully. It may have been washed in or eroded out of earlier material at the base of the gully. The gully continues beyond the southern limits of the trench, suggesting that it was further south in room 5CS that an activity took place that required occasional water supply or drainage. If it was a supply channel, rather than a drain, the water would not have been clean and must have been intended for some industrial purpose. The cover remained mostly in place and the fill contained no finds other than the cited two bones. Whether or not the gully remained operational to the end of occupation, it was evidently never dismantled. Fired brick was also employed to widen the division wall with room 4CS, adding an alignment of fired bricks (d.206).

There is no evidence for baking or cooking in row 5 before an oven was installed in the north-east corner of the room. The location is unsurprising. Ovens and fireplaces were frequently positioned along walls and in corners of rooms where they caused minimum obstruction. The roundish, but not perfectly circular, oven (d.010) had a maximum diameter of 0.88 m internally and 0.92 m externally. The hard oven walls were c. 2 cm thick and, as usual, smooth on the fire-exposed inside and rough on the outside. A horizontal oven floor at the same level as the base of the walls was discernible, but showed no signs of fire-exposure. The oven's fill (d.011, very soft mid-greyish brown clayey silt) contained fragments of its collapsed (probably domed) superstructure. Its base was at the same level as that of the oven wall (d.010). We found no large charcoal fragments in the oven's fill (d.011), but flotation of a sample yielded many small fragments of charred wood, as well as of a fungus growing on tree and shrub roots and charred oat, barley and fruit shell fragments. These may be the remnants of meals cooked and/or bread baked in the oven and the fuel used. The sample from the deposit (d.020) from under the oven, however, contained cereals as well (including millet and wheat)[116] and we cannot exclude that the food remains from d.011 are secondary, but we may be sure that they relate to food prepared and consumed nearby. Similar questions arise concerning charred wood which may be oven fuel or secondary. Evidence for the use of tree or shrub roots may indicate that firewood was a precious commodity in steppe-land and none was wasted. It is possible that dung fuel may have been used as well, as is still common in the area today. Unlike the ovens in room 1CS, there is no evidence for its deliberate demolition. This need not indicate a later date, as the space in room 5CS (unlike room 1CS) was not needed for later storage facilities. Its oven walls survive to 98.64 m site height, 18–27 cm lower than ovens attributed to phase 3 in rows 4, 1 and 0. Yet, original floor levels were higher, too, further west. If we base phasing not on absolute height, but on how much the ground had risen above the original earth floors, phase 3 ovens are always found roughly 0.50 m above the original floor level. This also holds true for oven d.010 in room 5CS. We may thus assign oven d.010 to phase 3 and postulate that its creation is contemporary to that of ovens d.028, d.030, d.169, d.187, d.236 and d.240 further west, with the caveat that deposits do not tend to extend beyond a single room and there is no absolute certainty how the stratigraphy in one room relates to another. Interestingly, the walls of ovens d.010 in room 5CS and d.169 in or at the edge of room 0CS have yielded similar archaeomagnetic dates, with possible date ranges of AD 249–531 for d.010 and AD 418–520 for d.169.[117] Considering how much activity preceded oven construction and that the date may relate to the latest rather than the earliest use, perhaps an early

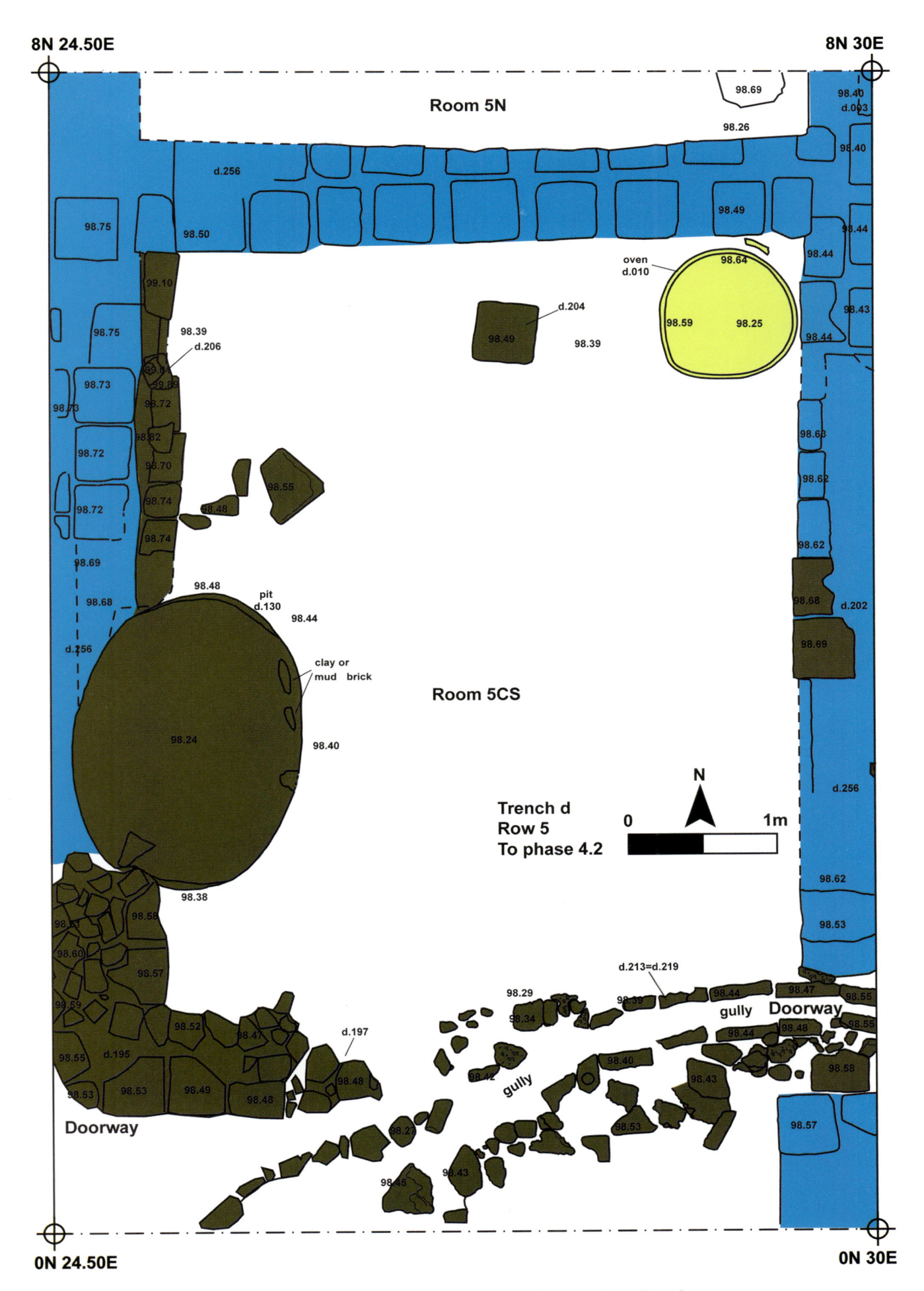

Fig. 4.66: Row 5 in the eastern annexe up to phase 4, featuring the gully without cover.

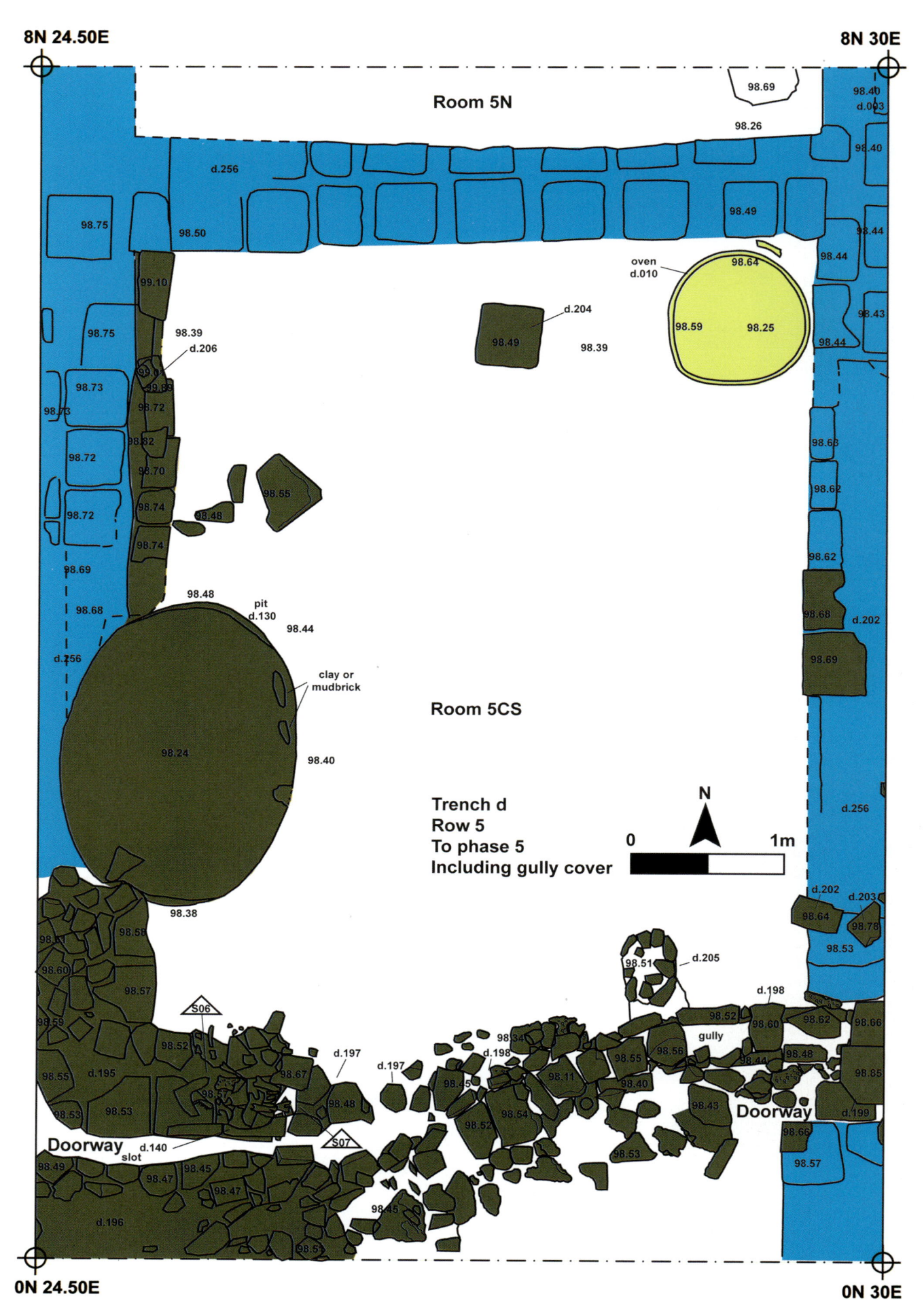

Fig. 4.67: Row 5 in the eastern annexe up to phase 4, featuring the gully with cover.

Fig. 4.68: The eastern annexe and the barracks, seen from the south-east corner of the trench at the end of the 2016 season.

Fig. 4.69: The eastern annexe and the barracks, seen from the north-east corner of the trench at the end of the 2016 season.

Fig. 4.70: The brick-covered and brick-lined gully (d.213 = d.219) running from room 5CS (left) to the outdoor area (right), used to channel water into or out of the building.

Fig. 4.72: Oven d.010.

Fig. 4.71: The brick-lined gully (d.213 = d.219) after the removal of the cover slabs (except for the cover slab in the eastern trench profile (right). Note the three storage pits in the background.

sixth-century date is plausible. And perhaps one should be cautious in using these dates for attempting precision-dating. Radiocarbon samples from earlier horizons in the annexes suggest that some phase 3 ovens are more likely to have been in use well beyond AD 520. We cannot, of course, be sure that all these ovens were installed at the same time, but their overall number suggests nonetheless that there was a considerable demand for food from phase 3 onwards, perhaps even more so than during initial occupation.

4.1.4.4.4. THE AREA OUTDOORS TO THE WEST OF THE BARRACKS

We were unable to pinpoint with certainty the precise western extent of the barracks. Assuming the western terminal of the mud-brick wall on the northern side of rooms 1CS and 0CS marks the extent of the building, only the westernmost 1.50 m of the trench (or even just over 1 m, if a single mud-brick *in situ* to the south-west of d.093 formed part of it) were outside the building. No attempt has been made to subdivide the bulk deposits between room 0CS and the western outdoor area. There was no recognisable division, perhaps as the western wall was lightly built or entirely demolished. It is even possible that no wall ever existed here, perhaps the western annexe forming a roofed shed without an outer wall in the west. As we were unable to neatly separate indoor from outdoor areas, all bulk deposits are discussed and listed under room 0CS as well as the oven (d.169) in the entrance area.

The thin strip of land between the likely western end of the building and the western trench edge contained, however, two significant structures: two geometric brick linings, one of rectangular shape internally (d.093), the other (d.253) probably too, even if only three sides were within the area excavated. These are strikingly similar to a brick lining (J.019) found in Fort 4, overlying a shaft (J.033) that widened towards the bottom, but has not been completely excavated. There was also a shaft (d.254) under d.093, but time constraints prevented us from excavating more than the top metre of its fill. There was no opportunity to explore whether there was a shaft under d.253 but, based on the cited parallels, it seems a near certainty that there was. In Fort 4 we had originally been undecided whether shaft J.033 and a second shaft (J.034) functioned as storage pits or wells, but the arguments for the former seemed stronger.[118] In the light of the parallels from Fort 2, it seems exceedingly unlikely now that any of the shafts served as wells. In Fort 2, certainly, well-digging down to the water-table (assuming this was at a similar level to the Sari Su River) would have been an almost impossible task, whilst the well-drained plateau would have been ideal for underground grain storage. Due to non-excavation of the postulated pit under d.253 and incomplete excavation of d.254, we do not know their profiles. Enough, however, has been excavated of shafts J.033 and J.034 in Fort 4 to suggest that they were bell-shaped, just as pit d.130 in room 5CS. Their similarity with other storage pits is further discussed below.[119] It is interesting to note that only the two outdoor pits had brick-lined access shafts, probably once covered, whereas none of the four indoor pits in Trench d were brick-lined. Perhaps brick-lined covers were thought necessary outdoors, to mark them more clearly near the central roadway, to prevent accidental contamination or accidents.

No unusual finds emerged from the fill of pit d.254. A compacted clay surface (d.095) west of it, maybe related to the nearby roadway, only produced an unidentified clay object. Worth noting, however, is that a bone (d.252/854) from the pit fill, dating to c. AD 429–544, is amongst the earliest dated samples. It suggests, even if the possibility of later redeposition of earlier material cannot be excluded, that the pit filled up with debris no later than the AD 540s and possibly well before.

4.1.4.4.5. THE AREA OUTDOORS TO THE EAST OF THE BARRACKS

Our trench extended just 70 cm beyond the eastern edge of the barracks, except for a 2 m-wide extension in the north that stretched 3.70 m beyond the eastern barrack walls. No mud-brick walls were found east of the barracks. We found a pit or ditch (d.259) in the eastern extension, reaching down to c. 97.71 m site height, some 40–50 cm below the floor level in row 5. It had probably been dug to obtain soil for mud-brick production for the annexe walls and was filled, from bottom to top, by d.149, d.134, d.127, d.104, d.105 and d.084. These deposits all consisted of clayey silt, suggestive of material accumulating under wet conditions in a depression. They proved very rich in bone, as did also later deposits on top. With a ratio of pottery to bone, of c. 1.5:1, bone accounted in terms of weight for a higher percentage of finds than in any other larger part of the trench.[120] No glass or metal was found, indicating that the area was used for deposition of debris without value. We have argued above that the high, though smaller, percentage of bone from row 5 suggests this was an area of food preparation and consumption. If so, this would explain the higher rate of bone deposition nearby, in the eastern outdoor area than in the west, even if admittedly less of the area outdoors in the west has been excavated.

At a later stage, brick fragments accumulated alongside the eastern barrack wall. We also observed a basic short brick and stone alignment in the area of the filled-up depression, centred on c. 32.30 m east. Its two courses were given separate context numbers (d.120 over d.141), but it appears to be a single structure, whose function is unknown.

Fig. 4.73: The western outdoor area in phase 1.

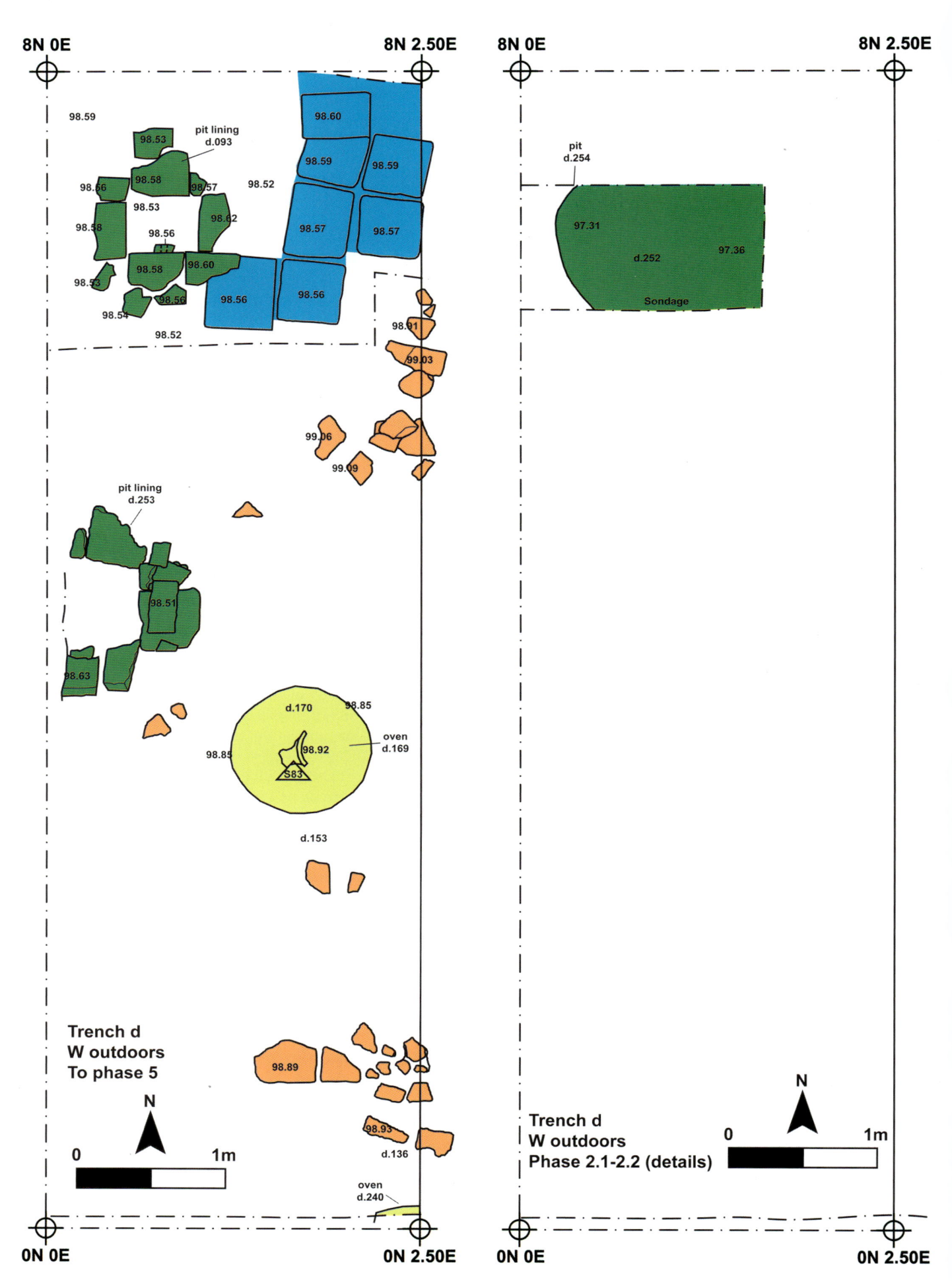

Figs 4.74–4.75: The western outdoor area up to phase 5 (left) and with partially excavated pit d.254 under brick lining d.093 (right).

Table 4.23: Finds from the western outdoor area. Note that, as a result of the poor preservation of walls, it was not possible to distinguish between bulk deposits in the western outdoor area and room 0CS. See Table 4.18 above for deposits that cover both areas. Weights are in grams.

Western outdoor area deposits	Bottom	Top	Depth	Phase	Pottery	Bone	Other finds
d.095	98.50	98.59	0.09	2.1–2.2	0	0	Clay object (3 g)
d.094 (fill of pit d.254)	97.77	98.53	0.76	2.1–2.2	21	0	n/a
d.252 (fill of pit d.254)	97.60	97.77	0.17	2.1–2.2	521	85	Charcoal
Total					542	85	Ratio, pot:bone: c. 6:1
Up to phase 2.2					542	85	Ratio, pot:bone: c. 6:1

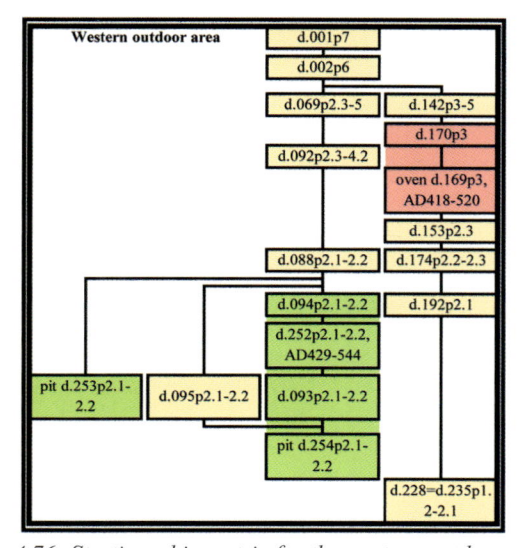

Fig. 4.76: Stratigraphic matrix for the western outdoor area.

Fig. 4.77: Brick lining d.093, top course, with scale over the north side (top) and west side (left), over pit d.254.

4.1.4.5. Life in Sasanian barracks on the Gorgan Wall

4.1.4.5.1. Heating and cooking in Sasanian barracks

With the sole exception of a fire-reddened patch with a semi-circular edge (d.258), probably a small oven of the final phase of occupation (as far as preserved), over the (partially demolished?) wall between rooms 2N and 2C, we found ovens and fireplaces exclusively in rows 0, 1, 4 and 5 (all part of the annexes), but none in the original barracks (rows 2 and 3). These indoor cooking or baking facilities, that could also have been used for heating in the cold season, are significant. We discovered several ovens of similar design in Fort 4 (in Trench J). They were certainly outside the original solidly built barracks, but their location allows for the possibility that they could have been just inside hypothetical annexes or (in part?) just outside.[121] In Fort 4, of course, we only excavated a small part of two rooms in the original barracks (in Trench H). If our above assumptions about the size of barracks in Fort 2 are correct, outdoor space would have been in short supply in Fort 2,

Fig. 4.78: Brick lining d.093, lower course, with scale over the north side (top) and west side (left), over pit d.254.

Fig. 4.79: View from the north-west corner of the trench over the western outdoor area and the barracks at the end of the 2016 season.

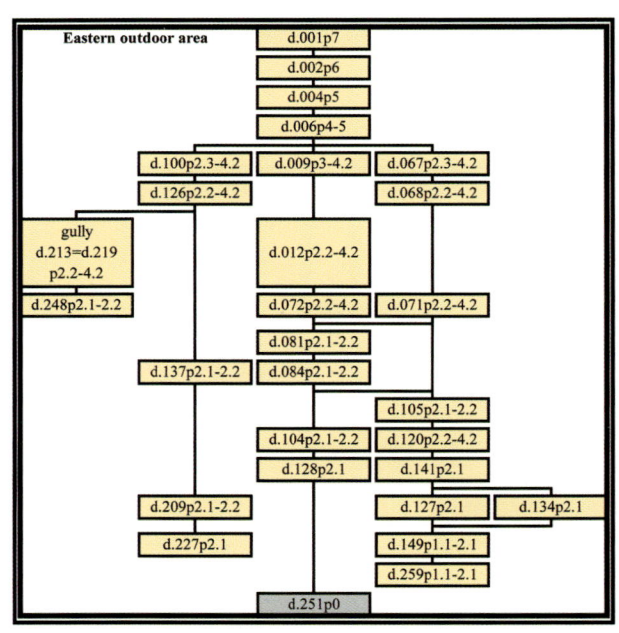

Fig. 4.80: Stratigraphic matrix for the eastern outdoor area.

and the same may be true for Fort 4, if there were annexes added to the original barracks. From our limited research, we have no evidence for *in-situ* heating or cooking facilities in the original barracks in either fort, perhaps suggesting that any living quarters were upstairs. If downstairs rooms in rows 2 and 3 served solely as bedrooms, thick blankets may have been sufficient to keep occupants warm on chilly nights. Redeposited cinders of fires, furthermore, make one wonder if there were untraceable, e.g. portable, heating facilities.

The combined number of ovens and fireplaces doubled from phase 1 to phase 3 (from four to eight, not counting the remains of an oven from robber pit d.229 which could belong to either phase). With the exception of the two ovens in room 1CS, cut by storage jar pits, the phase 3 ovens may have been in use until the end of phase 4 or the beginning of phase 5 and were only covered with sediments subsequently. The number of known fireplaces/ovens diminished to just two in the final phase of occupation, but as the latest levels were least well preserved, we cannot be sure whether or not this reflects

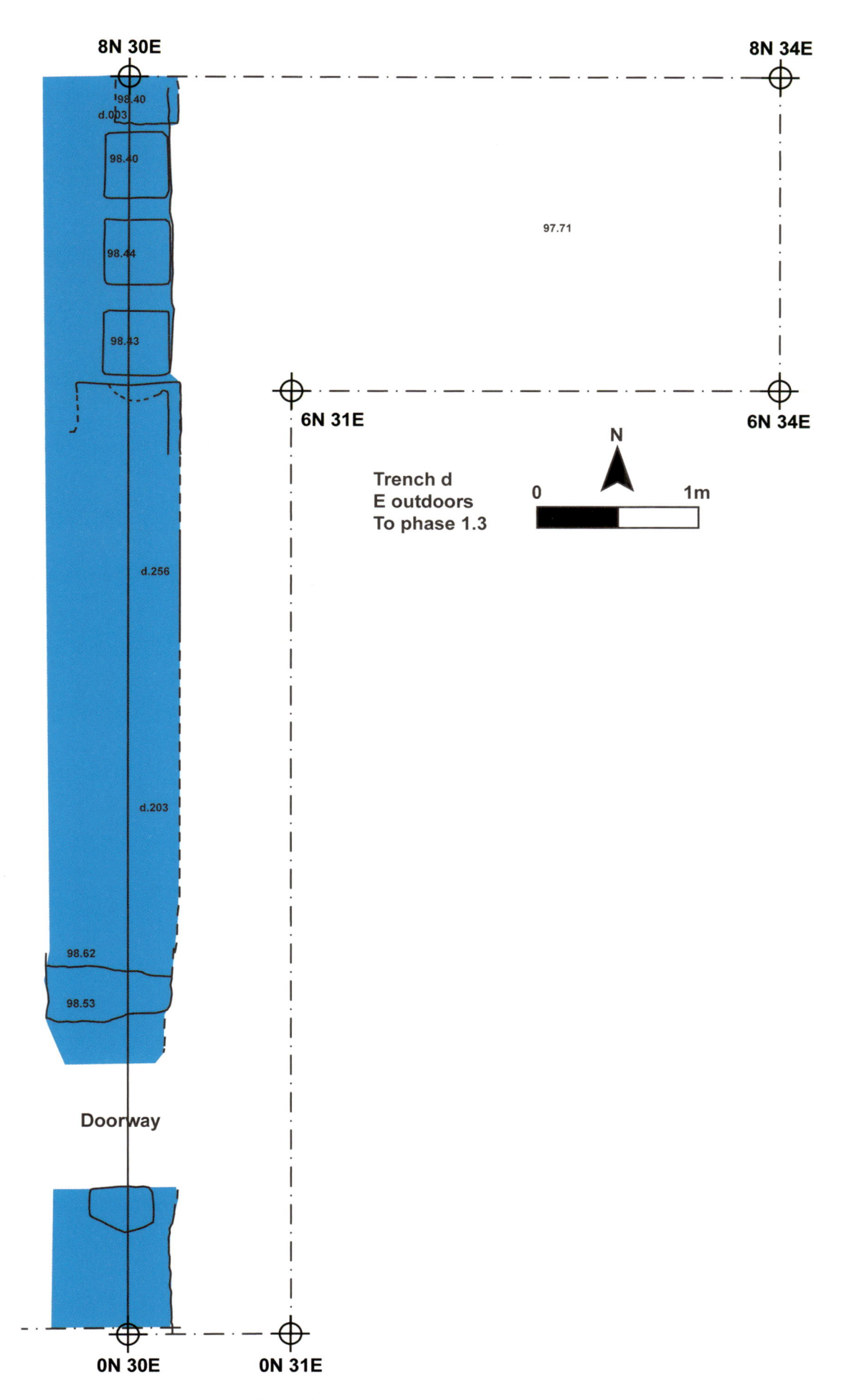

Fig. 4.81: The eastern outdoor area in phase 1.

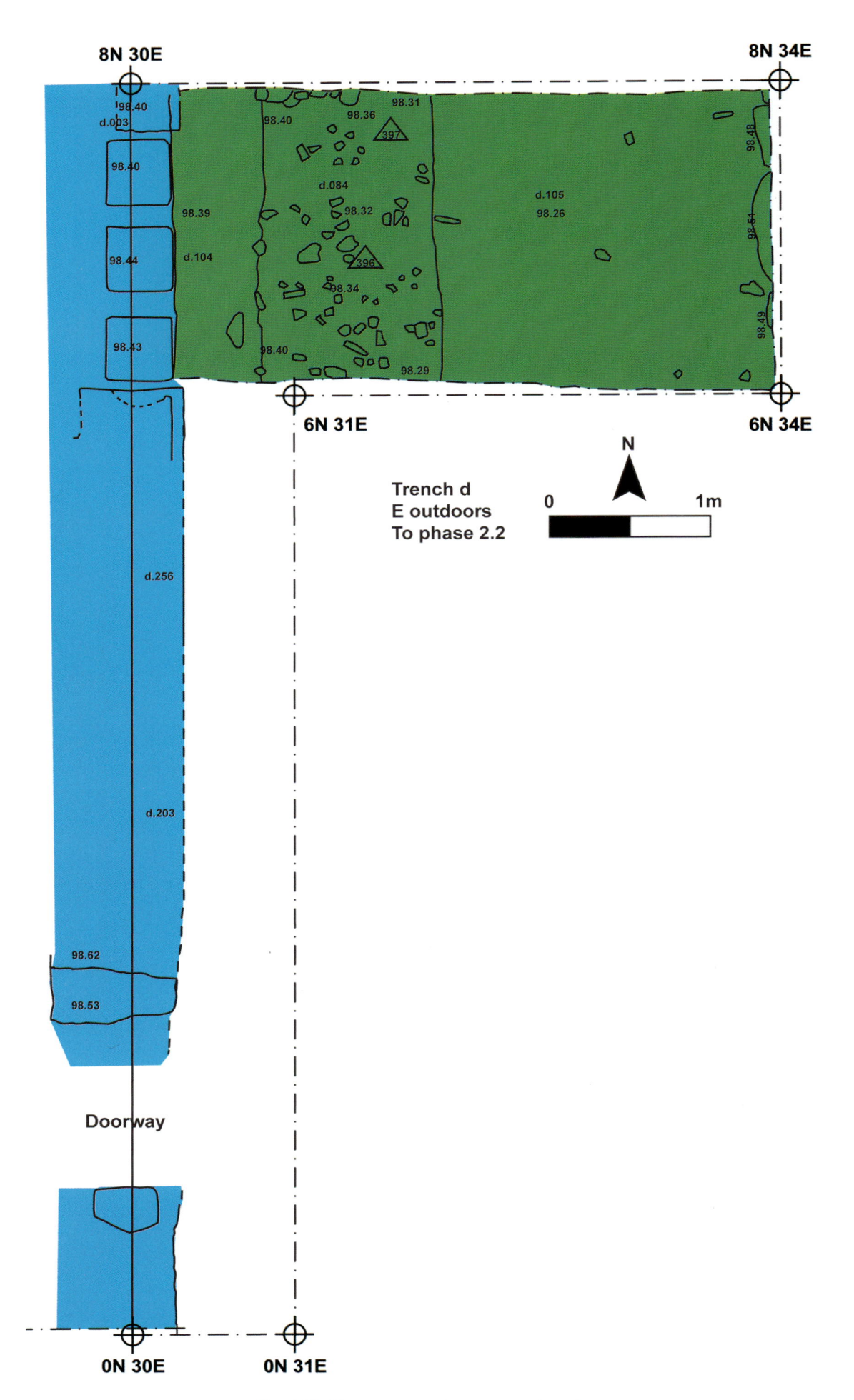

Fig. 4.82: The eastern outdoor area to phase 2.

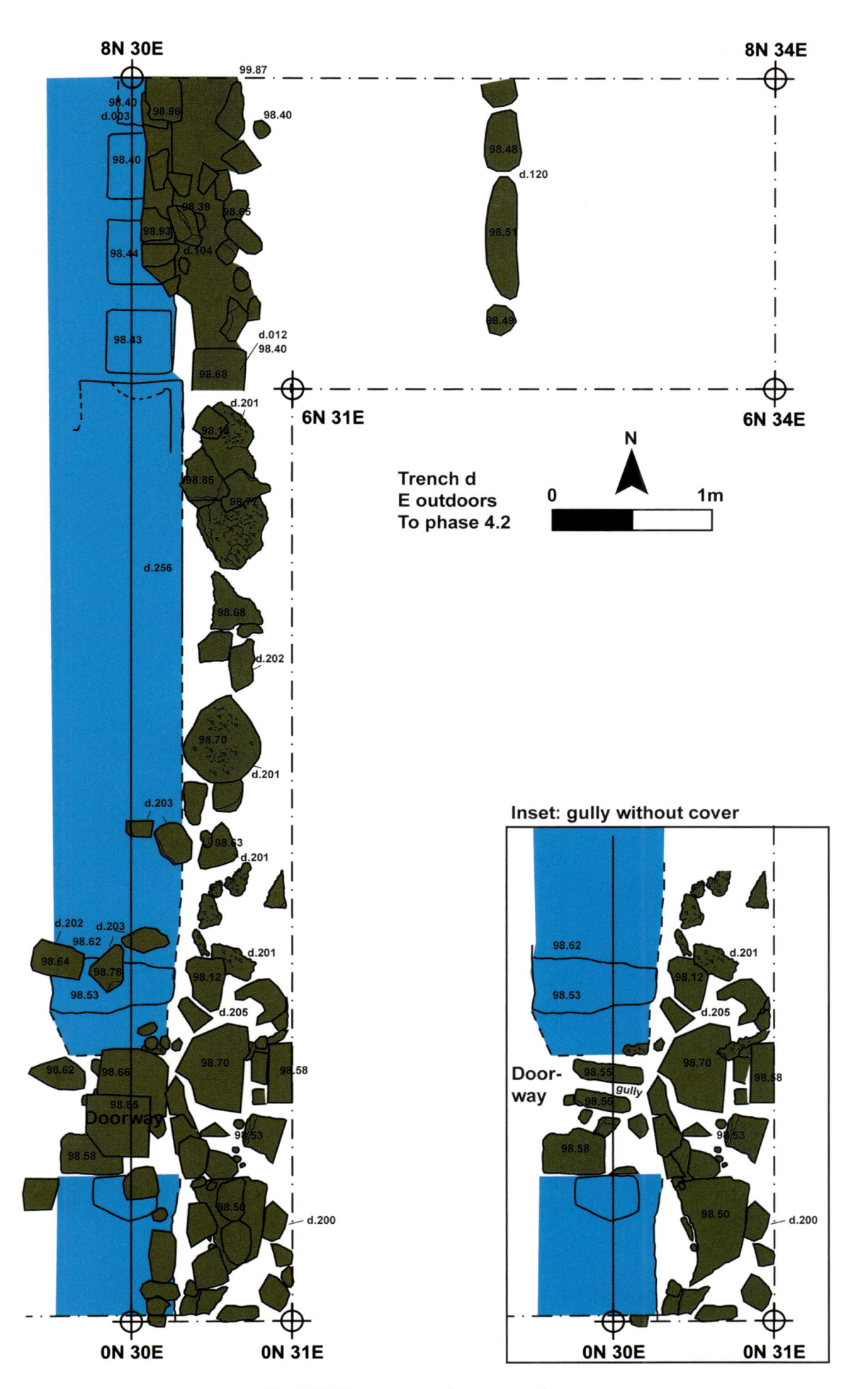

Fig. 4.83: The eastern outdoor area in phase 4.

Table 4.24: Finds from the eastern outdoor area. Weights are in grams.

Eastern outdoor area deposits	Bottom	Top	Depth	Phase	Pottery	Bone	Other finds
d.100	98.65	98.88	0.23	2.3–4.2	530	16	n/a
d.067	98.56	98.71	0.15	2.3–4.2	915	140	n/a
d.126	98.60	98.64	0.04	2.2–4.2	300	109	n/a
d.068	98.58	98.65	0.07	2.2–4.2	570	47	n/a
d.071	98.52	98.58	0.06	2.2–4.2	90	0	n/a
d.072	98.40	98.56	0.16	2.2–4.2	480	160	n/a
d.137	98.36	98.49	0.13	2.1–2.2	236	111	n/a
d.081	98.37	98.44	0.07	2.1–2.2	370	827	n/a
d.084	98.30	98.44	0.14	2.1–2.2	1,535	742	n/a
d.209	98.21	98.36	0.15	2.1–2.2	192	249	n/a
d.105	98.23	98.30	0.07	2.1–2.2	5,550	5,144	n/a
d.248	98.11	98.38	0.27	2.1–2.2	3,473	484	n/a
d.227	98.21	98.27	0.06	2.1	196	211	n/a
d.127	97.86	98.10	0.24	2.1	1,005	1,357	n/a
d.134	97.81	98.07	0.26	2.1	236	671	n/a
d.149	97.71	97.86	0.15	1–2.1	360	285	n/a
Total					**16,038**	**10,553**	**Ratio, pot:bone: c. 2:1**
Up to phase 2.2					**13,153**	**10,081**	**Ratio, pot:bone: c. 1:1**

Table 4.25: Ovens and fireplaces/hearths in the barracks. Those cut into or over one side of an earlier wall have been attributed the nearest room.

Feature	Function	Room	Over earlier wall	Phase	Terminus ante quem
d.222	Oven	0CS	no	1.3	2.1
d.114	Oven	0N	no	1.3	2.1
d.047	Fireplace or oven, cut by pit d.064	1CS	no	1.3	2.1
d.257	Fireplace	4CS	no	1.3	2.1
d.187	Oven	0CS	no	3	5
d.240	Oven	0CS	no	3	5
d.169	Oven	0CS or W outdoors	no	3	5
d.065	Fireplace	0N	no?	3	5
d.028	Oven, cut by pits for jars 8 and 9	1CS	no	3	4.1
d.030	Oven, cut by pit for jar 10	1CS	yes	3	4.1
d.236	Oven	4CS	no	3	5
d.010	Oven	5CS	no	3	5
d.229	Remains of destroyed oven, under pavement d.019, in a robber trench	0CS (or 1CS?)	?	1.3 or 3?	4.2
d.021	Fireplace	1CS	yes	4.2–5	6
d.258	Oven	2N	yes	4.2–5	6

Table 4.26: Ovens and fireplaces/hearths in the western and eastern halves of the barracks per phase.

Area	Western rooms (rows 0–2)	Eastern rooms (rows 3–5)
Phase 1.3	3 or 4	1
Phase 3 (prior to demolition of the two ovens in room 1CS)	6 or 7	2
Phase 4.2–5	2	0
Total	**12**	**3**

a real numerical reduction. Nor can we be sure if the spatial distribution, with both known late fireplaces being in the western half of the barracks, is meaningful. We should not necessarily assume that much of the barracks were unheated towards the end or that fewer meals were prepared. It seems safe to conclude, however, that the latest fireplaces still attest occupation, even if the barracks had been substantially modified at the time, some old walls had been partially demolished and others lined with basic brick structures.

It is interesting to note that the number of ovens and fireplaces in the western half of the building was in all phases at least three times as large as in the eastern half (Table 4.26). Whilst the much higher quantity of animal bones from the eastern rooms,[122] the somewhat larger number of cooking pots and bowls,[123] the more solid walls of the eastern annexe and the prominent presence of textile working implements[124] make one wonder if the eastern rooms were more heavily occupied, the ovens and fireplaces paint a different picture. They must have served mainly as cooking and heating facilities and there is no evidence that they were used for any industrial purposes. Cereal seeds from the fills of ovens d.010 and d.222 and eggshell from that of d.236 may be remnants of bread baked and meals prepared here. Small quantities of wood charcoal from some oven fills likely attest the use of firewood and there is a strong likelihood that dung fuel, as today, would have been used too.[125] Perhaps the concentration of cooking facilities in the west suggests that there were no fewer mouths to feed in the western half of the building than in the eastern half. Maybe the vicinity of the central road made it less acceptable to dispose of food remains here than in the backyard behind room 5CS and a little easier to reach extramural lands for rubbish disposal. One wonders if the cluster of ovens in row 0 next to the road served not just the needs of the occupants of adjacent rooms. Perhaps there was roadside catering here for other fort occupants. They may have taken meals away and consumed them elsewhere, which may explain in part the low number of bones found. At Qal'eh Kharabeh there were, of course, also catering/supply facilities lining the central road.[126] Even if there were probably central kitchen facilities or bakeries in campaign bases and (to a lesser extent?) in permanent forts, the presence of ovens in both halves of the building proves that there was also much self-catering in forts. Whilst we cannot draw any certain conclusions about the occupation density of different rooms units or the rank or status of those involved in any communal cooking and baking, the significant number and concentration of ovens, bones, cooking pots, storage jars and storage pits (not to mention food remains with a lesser chance of being preserved, such as charred grain or eggshells) leaves no doubt that the fort was permanently occupied by a substantial garrison.

4.1.4.5.2. FOOD STORAGE
4.1.4.5.2.1. STORAGE PITS
Four large pits were found within the barracks in Trench d and all were completely excavated. Two more pits appear to have existed in the western outdoor area. One of them was partially excavated, but no more than the cover of the second was exposed. It seems likely that we have found most or all pits in Trench d, but as we have not reached natural soil everywhere, notably in the western parts of the trench, one should allow for the possibility that we might have missed one or two. These pits served, no doubt, for storing supplies and help to explain why there are, as far as we know, no purpose-built storehouses in Sasanian forts. The commodities stored have left no traces. We found neither deposits whose colour is suggestive of decayed organic matter nor any other obvious traces. That the supplies were recovered prior to filling up the storage pits with debris is unsurprising. The storage pits in Trench d were exclusively in rows 5 and 1 as well as outdoors. The indoor storage pits all post-date the construction of the western and eastern annexes, suggesting that initially the garrison relied on outdoor storage pits or some other form of storage, e.g. in vessels placed on the ground or upstairs. The question also arises whether initially lower quantities of supplies were kept in the intramural area than later.

Excavation in Fort 4 had already unearthed two large bell-shaped pits in Trench J (J.033 and J.034). At least one of these (J.033) was provided with a remarkably similar cover (J.019) to d.093 and d.253 in Fort 2, suggesting that they were all of a similar design and served a similar purpose.[127] A variety of commodities could be stored in these pits, most probably grain. The clayey sealing (d.244) of the sides of the largest pit (d.130) adds strength to its interpretation as a grain store. Sealed grain can be stored underground for five years without deteriorating, but cannot be preserved for long once opened.[128] This suggests that the larger pits contained communal supplies rather than serving exclusively the needs of the occupants of the associated room or room units. Opening one large pit at a time and sharing its edible contents amongst the garrison would have minimised wastage. The pits could have been used multiple times. The pit linings in the western outdoor area (d.093 over pit d.252 and d.253 over an unexcavated postulated pit) next to the central road would have been more easily accessible, suggesting that they are even less likely to have contained the personal property of the occupants of the nearest rooms. It made sense to line pits in areas of heavy traffic where there may have been a greater risk of disturbance, e.g. by animals, than indoors. The design of the pits was functional and there are many parallels from prehistoric to modern times.[129] In addition to keeping food supplies safe from rodents, insects and microbes, pits were particularly advantageous in a military context: underground storage of supplies meant that more space was available for accommodation and essential activities whilst keeping the defensive perimeter small. It may also have been more difficult for hostile forces to detect and rob or destroy vital supplies during any temporary inroads and the hypothetical temporary deployment of fort garrisons away from their base. The latter, however, will not have been the principal motive. In the case of the pits with brick-lined covers, at least, there was evidently no attempt to conceal them. Some other

162   ANCIENT ARMS RACE

Table 4.27: Storage pits in and near the barracks. Note that the termini ante quos *for disuse are only approximate and based on pits no longer being traceable at a higher level, suggesting that they had been filled up at the time. Due to the lack of variation in colour and composition of most deposits, cuts and fills might not always have been recognised.*

Feature	Function	Top	Bottom	Depth in m	Room	Phase	T.a.q. for disuse: phase	Radiocarbon date of sample from secondary fill
d.254	Storage pit with brick-lined cover (d.093), partially excavated	98.62	<97.31	>1.31	W outdoors	2.1–2.2	4.2	AD 429–544
d.253	Brick-lined cover, probably over (unexcavated) storage pit	98.63	<98.25	>0.38	W outdoors	2.1–2.2	4.2	n/a
d.064	Storage pit, shaft	98.52	96.84	1.68	1CS	2.2	4.2	AD 441–560 (83.7%: 472-560)
d.216	Storage pit, shaft (= d.193)	98.37	96.46	1.91	5CS	2.1–2.2	2.2	AD 471–550
d.230	Storage pit, bulb-shaped	98.37	97.50	0.87	5CS	2.1–2.2	2.2	AD 478–569
d.130	Storage pit, bell-shaped	98.64	96.34	2.30	5CS	2.2–4.2	4.2	AD 548–591

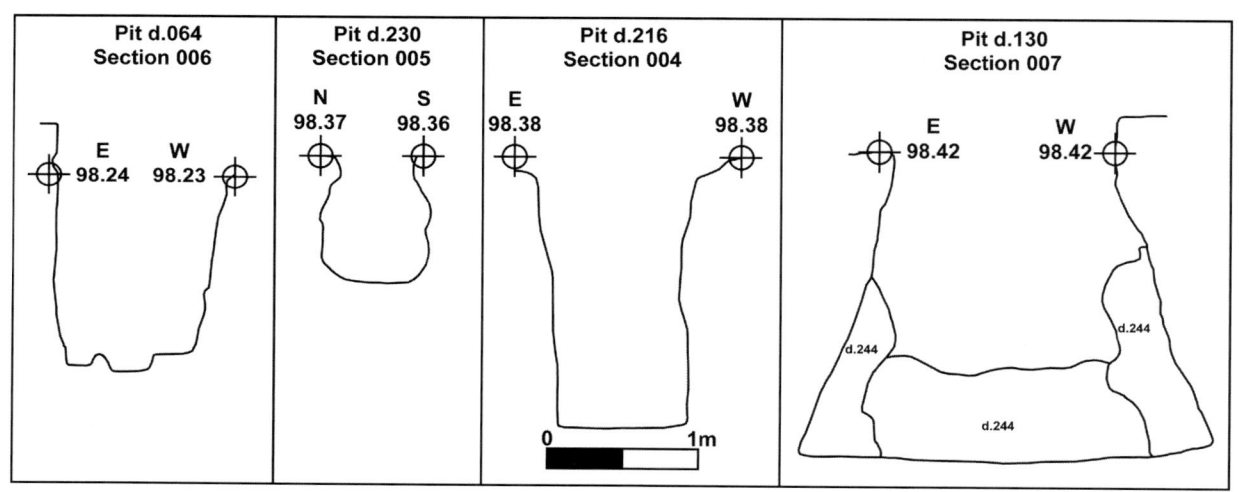

Fig. 4.84: Sections of the four storage pits within the barracks, all completely excavated and plotted at the same scale. Pit d.130 retained its original clay lining (d.244), whose extent in the east, south and west is recorded here. (Numbers refer to site height of the plotted profile nails.)

ancient, medieval and post-medieval grain pits far from Iran were provided with solid covers as well, sometimes also of square shape,[130] evidence that such covers proved effective in firmly sealing the contents and facilitating access. We found no traces of the actual covers. The two preserved linings in Fort 2 and the one in Fort 4 were all larger than a single Gorgan Wall brick. Perhaps the covers were wooden and weighted down with fired bricks.

In Trench d, storage pits were found exclusively in the annexes (in one row of rooms each: 1 and 5) and the western outdoor area (and with little of the eastern outdoor area excavated, it is perfectly possible that there were further such pits here, even if further from the road and less easily accessible than those west of the barracks). The level from which the storage pits were cut suggests that none of them is as early as phase 1. One should, however, add the caveat that, in the light of the almost imperceptible colour variations between deposits, we cannot rule out the possibility that the surface was raised around the top of the pits rather than them necessarily all having been cut from phase 2 levels or later horizons. If so, it is not beyond possibility that some of the five earlier pits might date back to phase 1. More probably, however, there were no storage pits in the area of Trench d prior to phase 2, neither within the original barracks (rows 2–3) nor in the contemporary outdoor area. Whilst we have allowed for the possibility that some phase 2 features or deposits could date back to the fifth century, as the floor does not appear to have been raised in some rooms at least before the 530s or so,[131] the most likely *terminus post quem* for digging of the pits is also around AD 530. If so, the storage pits in Fort 2 may have been used for a comparatively short period only, maybe for the final two thirds of the sixth century. Perhaps provisions were kept indoors (e.g. upstairs) at earlier times, perhaps there were pits outside the area of Trench d, perhaps the occupants benefited from regular deliveries and felt no need keep substantial supplies on the premises. In contrast to the ovens, which were replaced by ovens at a higher level on two or three occasions, pits appear to have been in use for longer periods. We see two phases only in row 5; small pit d.230 and large pit d.216 appear to have been replaced here by a very large pit, d.130, cutting into the earlier division wall between rows 4 and 5, around phase 2.2 or later.

We do not know for how long the pits served their intended purpose, but all, except probably d.216 and d.230, could have remained in use until phase 4.2. There is no evidence for the continued use of the pits in phase 5, their top all being well below phase 5 levels, nor for the excavation of new pits. One radiocarbon sample of bone or charred remains from the secondary fill of each of the five pits fully or partially excavated was processed. In theory these samples could all have been redeposited at a later date. The substantial differences in the frequency of finds between rooms cannot, however, be plausibly be attributed to the hypothetical redeposition of old material brought in from the outside; it seems much more probable that most or all of the samples came from nearby and date to just before the pits were filled up. If this assumption is correct, four of the five sampled pits appear to have been taken out of use by the 540s–560s at the very latest (but could also have been abandoned at earlier dates) and one by the 540s–590s. Only for the last (d.130), the largest pit, can we be confident that it was still open in the middle or second half of the sixth century. We found no later storage pits and one wonders if they were elsewhere in the fort, if the garrison was reduced, if other forms of storage (e.g. on upper storeys) replaced the pits or if occupants decided (reverted?) to regularly sourcing their supplies from the outside, in lieu of long-term storage. The two excavated storage pits in Fort 4, by contrast, both demonstrably remained in use beyond the mid-sixth century, one of them even into the seventh century.[132] The probably early dates of pit disuse at Fort 2 should not lead us to assume that garrisons had rapidly declined already by or before the mid-sixth century. Indeed, the very fact that much trouble was taken to fill up large pits clearly proves that there was no intention at the time to abandon the fort and that space was still at a premium, so much so that even the small area covered by pits was worth reoccupying. If, as we have argued, local waste was used to fill the pits, supplemented by soil, this would have facilitated rubbish disposal for a short period. It also suggests that people continued to live nearby, consuming meat and breaking pots. Pit-filling clearly did not mark fort abandonment, but occurred during continued intensive occupation.

How much storage was available across the fort as a whole? Trench d covered approximately a 47th of the intramural area of Fort 2. Assuming six pits per 254 m^2 is the average across the fort, we may hypothesise there may have been as many as 282. Needless to stress that there is much uncertainty in this estimate: with little of the outdoor area excavated in Fort 2 (and Trench J in Fort 4 having been excavated to sufficient depth only partially), we have no reliable way of estimating pit density, notably outdoors. If the four indoor pits are typical for one west–east row of the barracks in Fort 2, then there may have been 128 pits in the 32 rows in the two barracks alone. It seems exceedingly unlikely that the discovery of six pits in a single trench in Fort 2 and of another two in a far less completely excavated trench in Fort 4, with just one small deep sondage, is exceptional. In all probability, there were many more. Our hypothetical estimate of 282 storage pits (almost certainly differing greatly in storage capacity and not all in use at any one time) may be double or half the real number, but we may be confident that there would have been a three-digit number of pits in Fort 2 alone, though not necessarily all in contemporary use. This is further powerful evidence for permanent occupation by a sizeable garrison.

4.1.4.5.2.2. STORAGE VESSELS AND POSSIBLE REFORMS IN PROVISIONING THE ARMY

Not all supplies would have been stored in pits, as they were evidently unsuitable for fresh produce or liquids. In all probability, some of the food required would have reached the fort on a daily basis, notably during harvest seasons. We have already referred to the possibility of upstairs food storage. This is, of course, unprovable, just as any commodities stored at ground-floor level may not have left any traces, notably if stored in sacks, barrels or other containers made of perishable materials. In phase 4.1, however, we have firm evidence for ground-floor storage of supplies. Twelve large storage vessel were inserted in the floor in room 1CS. And we found, with the sole exception of row 3, fragments of storage jars also elsewhere in the barracks.[133] There is no certain evidence what commodities most of the large vessels in room 1CS contained. Parallels suggest that it may have been wine and, based on analysis, there may have been honey (-wine/mead) in one, and we cannot exclude other possibilities (e.g. oil or a variety of other products). These large jars have been discussed in the relevant chapter above,[134] but their potential broader significance merits further scrutiny here.

Were the provisions in room 1CS for the occupants of their respective back rooms (2C and 2S)? If so, it would be hard to explain why there is no evidence for any *in-situ* storage jars anywhere in the eastern half of the barracks within our Trench d; nor did we encounter any imprints of vessels removed at a later stage. The large jars in room 1CS are thus best interpreted as containing provisions for the garrison and not specifically for the occupants of adjacent rooms. Unequal size, number and distribution of storage pits in the two halves of the barracks (as discussed in the previous chapter), even if it should be noted that there may have been additional ones outdoors (including two west of the building), are also easier to explain by supplies being for the communal benefit of the garrison rather than the exclusive use of the group of occupants housed nearby. If we are right in suggesting that the cluster of ovens in row 0 may mark this out as a communal roadside kitchen and supply facility,[135] perhaps the jars in the room behind contained beverages for roadside distribution.

A few years ago, three similar large jars have been excavated in Fort 2, suggesting that rooms full of storage jars were not confined to Trench d, but may once have been more widely distributed across the fort. No plan of the location of these jars exists, but they appear to have been found in the northern part of the western barracks or their annexes.[136] Perhaps entire rows of rooms were devoted to storage, but more fieldwork is required to test this hypothesis.

When was room 1CS transformed into a storeroom, with 12 storage vessels placed in the area of this room unit alone (as far as excavated) and probably many more, perhaps hundreds, in the fort as a whole? Precision-dating of this phase (4.1) is unfortunately impossible. One is tempted, however, to date phase 4.1 to the mid-third of the sixth century or potentially even few years later. It evidently post-dates the construction of the main barracks (perhaps in the second or third quarter of the fifth century), the subsequent addition of annexes, the installation of ovens, their use, disuse, the raising of the floor surface, the installation of replacement ovens cutting into earlier walls and their use and partial disuse. Whilst the duration and date of none of these structural alterations and phases of occupation can be determined with precision, it is hard to imagine that it would not have taken a few generations, making a date in the fifth century or even the first third of the sixth century for phase 4.1 unlikely. Furthermore, in some rooms the raising of the floor surface in phase 2 appears to have occurred no earlier than the AD 530s at the earliest and probably not much after the mid-sixth century at the latest. If the pig bone (d.041/205) from the fill of jar 5 represents food waste from the period post-dating the use of the storage vessels, then phase 4 ended no later than the AD 580s at the very latest. Yet, the vessel could in theory have been filled with redeposited earlier debris at a later date. Differences in bone to pot ratios between different rooms suggest, however, that the material in each room consisted mainly of local debris – rather than material from soil extraction pits outside – making it likely that AD 585 is the approximate *terminus ante quem* for the filling of the disused storage jars with debris.[137] The subsequent phase 5, for which we have a radiocarbon date of c. AD 561–636, and which is not likely to have lasted beyond the first half of the seventh century, involved an extensive build-up of deposits and structural alterations of the building. We may hypothesise therefore that phase 5 lasted for at least a few decades and is unlikely to have started after the early seventh century at the very latest but, quite possibly, began already in the later sixth century.

In Fort 4 only one storage vessel (H-025) has been found *in situ* (broken in antiquity), in this case within the original barracks.[138] Excavations in Fort 4, however, covered far less indoor space than in Fort 2, and floor horizons were buried much deeper below the modern surface. Indeed, if storage vessels, as in Fort 2, were also stored in the inner rooms of a roadside annexe to the original barracks, they would be outside the excavated area in Fort 4 and further excavation is required to establish whether or not barracks and annexes in Fort 4, and the use of rooms within, mirror arrangements in Fort 2. It is thus perfectly possible that there were similar storage facilities in Fort 4 that still await discovery (but it is not inconceivable that the two forts differed in their use of space).

It is interesting to note that at Tureng Tappeh similar vessels have been found with similar lids (of stone, whereas there were both ceramic and stone lids represented at Fort 2), similarly in part cut into earlier walls. The jars at Tureng Tappeh were also found within a military compound. Three of them were in a row, their narrow spacing not unlike what we found in Fort 2. The similarities between Tureng Tappeh and Fort 2 are striking. They cannot be coincidence. The vessels at Tureng Tappeh were empty, except for soil deposits with grains or seeds, whether intrusive or original, at the bottom. The storage jars at Tureng Tappeh belong to phase VIIA/B, thought to date to the seventh or seventh to eighth century, but the chronology seems insecure and even the sixth century is not excluded. The excavators' tentative dating proposal appears to be based on the assumption that this phase is post-Sasanian and that it post-dates the abandonment of the Sasanian fort, whose internal walls (just as in the case of Fort 2) had partially been demolished.[139] Yet, radiocarbon dates and relative phasing in Fort 2 make clear that the storage vessels here are undoubtedly Sasanian, probably not even of the very end of the era, but likely the sixth century – and that partial demolition of walls occurred generations before the demise of the Sasanian dynasty. There must be a reason why the same types of storage vessels were used in a similar manner in two Sasanian military compound over 100 km apart. This cannot plausibly be explained with independent initiatives of local communities, but is likely to be the material manifestation of state politics. These considerations make a date in the Sasanian era more likely also for the jars at Tureng Tappeh than after the collapse of Sasanian rule, when the Gorgan Wall was within a small Turkish principality and reportedly abandoned.[140] Similarities in the ceramic repertoire between the forts on the Gorgan Wall and that of phase VIIA/B at Tureng Tappeh also suggest that the latter is broadly contemporary with the Sasanian-era occupation of the Gorgan Wall forts, as observed by Maria Daghmehchi.[141]

These similar storage facilities at Sasanian military sites are, almost certainly, the material traces of a new way of storing provisions for the army and/or tax revenues in kind for the state. Sasanian taxes may well mostly have been levied in kind,[142] rather than coinage, and it is possible that the large-scale storage of commodities at Fort 2 and Tureng Tappeh is an archaeological manifestation of this practice. It is interesting to note that, according to Tabari, Khusro I's land taxes were intended in part to feed the army and in part to provide reserves for a military emergency. In addition to wheat and barley and various other staple foods, grapes are specifically mentioned.[143] Alternatively, the similar vessels in Fort 2 and at Tureng Tappeh might represent part of a single bulk order by the army and do not necessarily prove on their own the introduction of a new system of army provision.[144] Whether the vessels were brought to the fort following the famous reform, or whether they simply represent one of many such bulk orders which we can trace archaeologically, they suggest that a well-organised military supply network was in operation at the time. In the Sasanian Empire of the sixth century, similar to the late Roman army,[145] commodities will have been stored in military compounds – and may have been systematically collected for the needs of the garrison or in part perhaps for redistribution. The latter is, however, less probable, as the jars were in part buried to the neck, to judge by the packing material, and there is no evidence for recuts – as one might expect had the filled vessels been tax revenue in interim storage intended for transport elsewhere. There is nothing to suggest that the garrison on the Gorgan Wall received any monetary stipend.[146] Instead, it may have been supplied with some of the necessities of life, collected as tax and redistributed in part directly to the army.

It is too early to tell whether such storage vessels were placed in all Sasanian forts on the wall and its hinterland or just some. It is also possible that there were collection centres elsewhere, e.g. in urban agglomerations. Recent excavations at Sasanian Tol-e Qal'eh Seifabad west of Lake Parishan in Fars, thought to be an administrative and commercial centre, have brought to light similarly huge storage vessels,[147] and they occur elsewhere.[148] It is worth noting that there appears to be a strip of higher magnetisation towards the front of the Fort 16 barracks.[149] Only excavation will allow us to tell whether this was a row of rooms filled with storage vessels, not far from the central road, or whether there is another explanation, e.g. brick-paved working surfaces as in Trench J in Fort 4 and Room 0CS in Trench d in Fort 2. Not all such storage facilities are as late as those in Fort 2. A much earlier example is found in Sasanian casemates (rooms alongside the wall) at the Paykand Fort near Bukhara, that has been attributed to the Sasanians and was perhaps built under Shapur I (r. c. 240–272). Two of the rooms have yielded numerous sherds of large storage vessels and pits for their placement and are thought to have served exclusively storage purposes.[150]

The storage jars will only have accommodated some of the supplies, and it is worth noting that the largest storage pit in the trench (d.130) cuts the earlier annexe room division between units 4CS and 5CS, which reminds one of some of the storage jars in row 1 having been inserted in pits cut into earlier mud-brick walls. The large pit d.130 is cut from the same level as phase 3 oven d.010 in the same room (5CS). Both the storage jars and the pit d.130 imply a major reorganisation of space. Whilst one needs to be careful in trying to make archaeological findings fit the little we know from historical sources, one wonders if the huge bell-shaped storage pits in Forts 2 and 4 and the storage jars found in Fort 2 and Tureng Tappeh might be related to Khusro I's reforms. The case, admittedly, is far from proven in the light of the lack of precision of radiocarbon dating in this period. It is hard to tell how long the jars remained in use, perhaps just for a few years, perhaps for several decades.

4.1.4.5.3. FINDS DISTRIBUTION OVER SPACE AND TIME
There is much more pottery from the western rooms (rows 0 to 2) than the separate eastern rooms (rows 3 to 5). Yet, one ought to bear in mind that excluding the 12 large *in-situ* storage jars (of 459,460 kg combined), there was just c. 215 kg of pottery, not massively more than the 185 kg from the eastern rooms.

Much more astonishing is the spatial distribution of bone, also examined in the context of our archaeozoological studies.[151] It is striking that far more bone was found in the eastern half than the western half of the barracks. It is worth stressing that the even higher concentration of animal bones in the eastern outdoor area (in terms of bone to pot ratio) is likely to represent, to a large extent, food remains discarded by the occupants of the eastern rooms. It is, of course, also worth noting that little of the western outdoor area was excavated and the storage pits in this area were never emptied of their lower fill. So,

Table 4.28: The spatial distribution of bone and pottery throughout Trench d. Weights are in grams.[152]

Row	WO	0	1	2	3	Corridor 3–4	4	5	EO	Total
Area in m²	12	29.565	18.63	20.33	23.385	0.8075	16.2	30.26	11.6	162.7775
Bone	85	2,810	360	532	6,326	1,225	7,432	34,323	10,553	63,646
%	0.13	4.42	0.57	0.84	9.94	1.92	11.68	53.93	16.58	100.00
Bone per m²	7.08	95.04	19.32	26.17	270.52	1,517.03	458.77	1,134.27	909.74	av. 391.00
Pottery	542	62,595	493,100	118,724	40,831	1,083	34,578	108,382	16,038	875,873
%	0.06	7.15	56.30	13.55	4.66	0.12	3.95	12.37	1.83	100.00
Pot per m²	45.17	2,117.20	26,468.06	5,839.84	1,746.03	1,341.18	2,134.44	3,581.69	1,382.59	av. 5,380.80

Area	WO	Western room units			Eastern room units			EO	Total
Area in m²	12		68.525			70.6525		11.6	162.7775
Bone	85		3,702			49,306		10,553	63,646
%	0.13		5.82			77.47		16.58	100.00
Bone per m²	7.08		54.02			697.87		909.74	av. 391.00
Pottery	542		674,419			184,874		16,038	875,873
%	0.06		77.00			21.11		1.83	100.00
Pot per m²	45.17		9,841.94			2,616.67		1,382.59	av. 5,380.80

WO = western outdoor area; EO = eastern outdoor area.
Note that little of the WO was excavated, that the separation between 0 and the WO was not well defined, and that some of the finds attributed to row 0 deposits may belong to the WO.
Area of rows excludes walls and refers only to excavated part of rooms (not all of which were excavated to the lowest levels, notably in the WO).

for purposes of comparison, the outdoor areas are best excluded. Comparing just the quantity of bones from the eastern rooms, it is more than 13 times greater than that from the western rooms (cf. Table 4.28). Does this imply that more food/meat was consumed in the eastern rooms, that occupants of the western rooms were tidier or that there were fewer people living here?

Row 5 contained three storage pits, including the largest of all pits excavated. Yet, their secondary filling up, once no longer needed (assuming disposing of food waste in disused pits was considered more acceptable than elsewhere), does not explain why there was much more bone from the eastern half of the building. Less than 30% of the bone from row 5 came from the pit fills. Furthermore, the difference to the finds recovered from pit d.064 in row 1 is telling: it yielded a mere 26 g of bone (and that there may have been a few grams more from the upper shaft, that was not recognised in time, is not likely to alter the picture). The extreme scarcity of bone from the fill of the pit in row 1 suggests that not much bone was available in the surrounding area when it was filled up – thus supporting our impression that there was far less bone discarded in the western half of the building than in the eastern half.

How did disposal patterns change over time? Little material remains from the earlier phases of occupation, due to the tidiness of the occupants, and it is harder to draw any firm conclusions from the finds about activities prior to the raising of floors in phase 2. Furthermore, some of the early material from the area of the annexes comes from material extraction pits which pre-date annexe

Table 4.29: The finds from pits in the barracks in Trench d.

Pit	Row	Pottery	Bone
d.064	1	2,437	26
d.130	5	15,011	4,895
d.216	5	7,650	4,327
d.230	5	2,360	147
Total row 1	1	2,437	26
Total row 5	5	25,021	9,369
Total	n/a	**27,458**	**9,395**

construction. In the later phases at least, much more bone was discarded in the eastern half, which might have been more heavily occupied whilst parts of the western half were transformed into storage areas and work spaces.

Important in this context are spatial differences in the distribution of facilities. We do not know for certain why there was better provision for heating and cooking in the western rooms (with four times as many ovens and fireplaces than in the eastern half and the west dominating over the east in all phases),[153] as opposed to overall better insulation, more evidence for textile working,[154] a slightly higher quantity of cooking pots and bowls[155] and a massively higher quantity of animal bones from the eastern rooms.[156] The distribution of textile working implements, notably spindle whorls, provides evidence for domestic activities in the western half of the building, though admittedly confined to row 2, whereas there is more evidence for textile working from the eastern half (in rows 3 and 5).[157] Indeed, an argument for less food being consumed in the western rooms is that in the later phases row 1 served as an exclusive storage area and the brick paving in row 0 (and the absence of clear traces of a western wall) may suggest that this may have been a draughty working area and kitchen facility rather than a living room. Yet, as discussed above, the cluster of ovens in row 0 suggests that much food was prepared here, though not necessarily for the exclusive use of occupants of nearby rooms.[158]

We may conclude that people lived in the western and eastern half of the building throughout its occupation, though there may perhaps have been a shift to more intensive domestic occupation of the eastern half in the later phases. Group dynamics are a further possible explanation for different disposal patterns.[159] Most probably, both halves were intensively occupied, but the groups occupying them differed in habits more than in numbers. Differences in the types of meat consumed, proportionally more mutton in the western rooms and more beef in the eastern rooms, might also reflect differences in status or dietary preferences. Whilst the simple design of the barracks may imply standardisation and equality, the groups occupying room units may have been far from uniform in practices, traditions, rank, status and areas of responsibility (e.g. in terms of involvement in any communal catering).

4.1.4.6. The chronology of Fort 2's occupation (Trench d)

4.1.4.6.1. THE START OF OCCUPATION

Apart from redeposited prehistoric flint and stone tools from Sasanian-era deposits,[160] there was no evidence for any pre-Sasanian activity on the plateau. The prominent hilltop may have served as a campsite several millennia before fort construction, but there is no evidence for permanent settlement on the spot at any stage other than during the fort's time of occupation. Nor was the site of the fort ever reoccupied in medieval or modern times. Not only do we lack any diagnostic finds for occupation in other eras or structures pre- or post-dating the fort, but also the scientific dating evidence corroborates single-phase occupation. Twenty radiocarbon samples from Trench d were processed, 19 of them Sasanian and one an intrusive rodent of the Late Middle Ages.[161]

The samples from Fort 2 allow for a start of occupation contemporary to that of Fort 4 (as well as, theoretically, for occupation to have started some time apart). Interesting is the high proportion of radiocarbon samples that belong to the fifth to sixth-century plateau (14, or 17 including three that might be as early as the fifth or as late as the early seventh century, out of 19, excluding the late medieval rodent sample), some of them high in the stratigraphy. Nine of the 19 samples have yielded likely *termini ante quos* between AD 539 and 570, the other ten falling between AD 591 and 646. This preponderance of early samples has added strength to the Gorgan Wall having been built in the first half of the possible date range (i.e. the AD 420s to the 470s or 480s) rather than the second half.

Admittedly, there is no doubt that traceable activity peaked in the sixth century, and we cannot exclude that the very intensive occupation of Fort 2 in the earlier sixth century accounts for the high proportion of early samples. Some might wonder if the fact that even the earliest samples could be as late as the late 530s may allow for the frequent attribution of the Gorgan Wall to Khusro I (r. 531–579) being possible after all. This seems unlikely. Firstly, we need to remember that, due to the plateau in the calibration curve, material from any date within the last three quarters of the fifth or the first third of the sixth century will normally produce a likely *terminus ante quem* in or after the AD 530s. The dates themselves only indicate that likely occupation could have started at any date between around the AD 420s and the 530s. For an informed estimate as to when traceable activity commenced within this century-long period, we need to examine the sequence of events that must have taken place during or before the first half of the sixth century. Phasing indeed adds support for the occupation of Fort 2 having started in the fifth century, as it is hard to imagine that the distinct early phases we could identify all belong to the early sixth century, let alone that all post-date Khusro I's accession to the throne in AD 531. Whilst the raising of floors in phase 2 may be as late as the 530s or even later, one is inclined to think that some of phase 1 dates back to the fifth century, even if, admittedly, the dating evidence also allows in theory for an early sixth-century construction of the barracks. That four of the pits have yielded samples from their fill not likely to be later than the AD 540s, 550s or 560s is significant. Whilst the bones and charred nutshell sampled could in theory be redeposited at a later date, such a hypothetical scenario is not likely to apply to four out of five pits. In all probability, several pits in Fort 2 had gone out of use in the middle third of the sixth century. This implies that they had been dug at earlier dates and that there were many mouths to feed in Fort 2 in the mid-sixth century (and perhaps already before). That in Room 3C 0.50 m of deposits on top of the original trampled earth floor had been built by or before the 540s (unless sample d.070/313 was redeposited later) is further circumstantial evidence for the barracks having been built well before – though the surface could have been raised rapidly and it is not easy to gauge how much time had passed between construction and raising of the floor.

Room 1CS provides a particularly interesting sequence: the storage jars appear to have been filled up with debris by the AD 580s at the latest. They will have been used for some time before. Earlier ovens had been demolished to create space for them. These earlier phase 3 ovens are also likely to have been used for some time. The ovens had been cut into earlier walls, signalling a major

Table 4.30: Comparison of radiocarbon samples at 95.4% confidence from Forts 2 and 4, sorted by terminus post quem *(earliest to latest). Note that 13 samples were processed from Fort 4, but two of them were from the same bone (J.009/247) and this is counted as a single sample, whose combined date is used here. The samples from Trenches H and J have all been recalibrated, using the 2020 version of the OxCal programme, and some dates thus differ slightly from those published. Note that all dates cited are unmodelled, as using a mixture of modelled and unmodelled dates could have led to unreliable results.*[162]

	Fort 2			
Find no.	*T.p.q.*	*T.a.q.*	*BP*	*±*
d.186/674	423	539	1597	18
d.226/739	423	539	1597	18
d.150/547	428	544	1584	18
d.252/854	429	544	1583	18
d.070/313	430	548	1576	18
d.090/S3	432	560	1566	18
d.045/251	432	566	1561	21
d.233/756	432	568	1560	23
d.250/843	433	570	1556	18
d.041/205	435	591	1543	21
d.214/789	436	591	1542	18
d.044/211	436	599	1534	21
d.184/862	439	594	1536	18
d.165/649	439	595	1535	18
d.239/797	442	605	1519	22
d.132/501	442	639	1511	26
d.223/S7	482	632	1515	22
d.024/103	540	640	1501	25
d.004/16	578	646	1456	21
d.040/183 (intrusive, rodent)	1396	1440	524	21
	Fort 4			
Find no.	*T.p.q.*	*T.a.q.*	*BP*	*±*
J.021/432	424	550	1579	25
J.002/198	440	640	1511	29
H.005/20	540	640	1501	26
H.005/27	546	641	1489	29
J.009/257	555	641	1482	26
J.030/490	563	648	1466	29
H.005/61	564	646	1468	27
J.027/496	583	655	1435	27
J.028/310	591	656	1430	26
J.009/247	598	651	1440 and 1429	25 and 27
H.005/96	602	664	1399	27
J.027/493	605	671	1384	25

Table 4.31: Summary of results.

Site	Earliest sample	Latest sample	Ratio t.p.q. 423–482:540–605	Ratio t.a.q. 539–639:640–671	Number of samples (excl. intrusive later sample)
Fort 2	AD 423/539	AD 578/646	17:2 (c. 89:11)	17:2 (c. 89:11)	19
Fort 4	AD 424/550	AD 605/671	2:10 (c. 17:83)	1:11 (c. 8:92)	12

reorganisation of space. They post-date a raising of the floor which, judged by the evidence from other rooms, may perhaps be dated to the 530s–550s. Before, a storage pit had been cut in the room which destroyed an earlier fireplace that will have been used for some time during the original occupation of annexe room 1CS. The higher base level and distinctly different construction imply that the annexes are later than the original barracks, probably by at least several years, more likely decades.

No precision estimate can be offered as to the duration of each of these developments but, if we allow for a decade or two for each, this would suggest that the

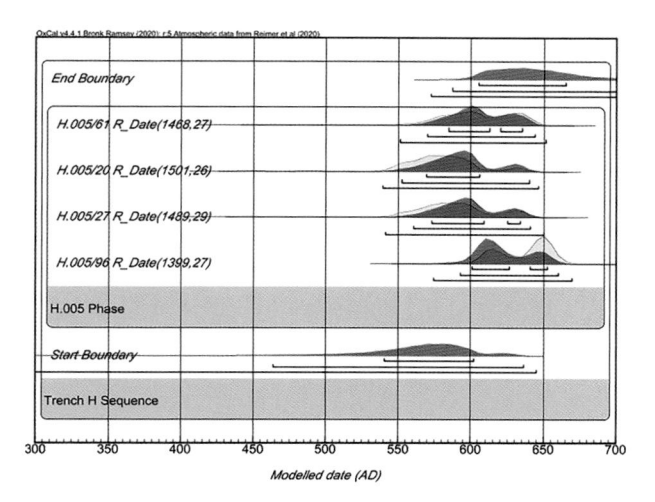

Fig. 4.85: Recalibration of radiocarbon samples from Trench H in the Fort 4 barracks. As all samples come from a single deep levelling horizon, with the most recent sample from the bottom of the sequence, it is clear that they represent no sequence, but probably material from one or more sources used on a single occasion to raise the indoor surface. Interestingly, the surface was probably only raised in the early seventh century – significantly later than in Fort 2. Modelling (dark grey graphs) may not be reliable, and we only cite unmodelled dates (represented by light grey graphs) in the tables.

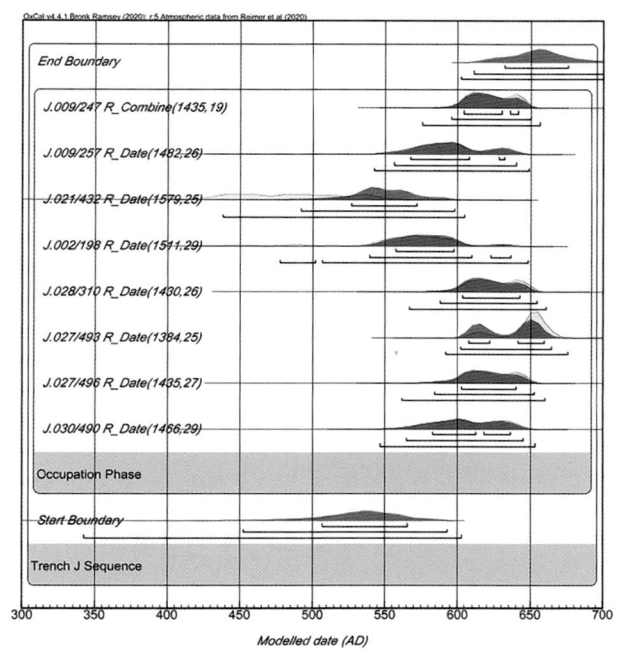

Fig. 4.86: Recalibration of radiocarbon samples from Trench J in Fort 4. The samples come from the fill of two pits and a gully as well as one from a working surface near an oven. The relative sequence of these features cannot be established with certainty, nor can we be sure whether the pits and the gully were filled up in a single phase or successively. It has therefore not been attempted to model the samples based on a purely hypothetical sequence. It is clear from the graph that the majority of the samples are later than the majority from Fort 2. There is, however, one sample (J.021/432) that is as early as some of the earliest samples from Fort 2. Attempted modelling (dark grey graphs) seems particularly unreliable, in the light of the range of dates, and we only cite unmodelled dates (represented by light grey graphs) in the tables.

original barracks at least will date to the fifth century (or the beginning of the sixth century at the latest). A start of construction under Khusro I (r. 531–579) is inconceivable, a start early in the reign of Kavad I (r. c. 488–496 and 499–531) possible, but in the light of the economic and military repercussion of the Hephthalite victory of AD 484 perhaps unlikely. If wall and fort construction started in the second or third quarter of the fifth century, there may have been enough time to largely complete it before this setback. Even disregarding historical developments, we may conclude that the strong representation of fifth- to early sixth-century samples and multiple successive phases of building, structural alteration and occupation make fifth-century origins of at least the narrow original barracks in Fort 2 likely and a start of construction much after the early sixth century highly improbable. There is no evidence for the fort having been empty initially and we are inclined to assign its defences to the same phase as its original barracks.

Also worth noting are the archaeomagnetic samples from ovens in Fort 2, with likely date ranges of AD 249–531 for oven d.010 and AD 418–520 for oven d.169. These both belong to phase 3 and the archaeomagnetic dating is likely to relate to their latest use. With archaeomagnetic dating still being a method in development for this region, perhaps we should not be overconfident that AD 520 and AD 531 are secure *termini ante quos* for the latest use of these phase 3 ovens, in particular as radiocarbon dating suggests that phase 3 is not likely to be earlier than the 530s at the earliest. They add, however, further circumstantial evidence to suggest that fort construction is likely to have taken place before the sixth century. Even leaving aside the archaeomagnetic dates, the new radiocarbon chronology for Fort 2 is significant. The new samples from Fort 2 have not altered the likely *terminus post quem* in the 420s for the construction of the Gorgan Wall, but they have added strength to the *terminus ante quem* also being in the fifth century, though sixth-century origins cannot be excluded with absolute certainty.

Interestingly, of all radiocarbon samples from the Gorgan Wall, the one with the earliest *terminus post quem* (c. AD 376 unmodelled and 394 modelled) comes from the Trench G brick kiln west of Fort 30, although a second sample from the same kiln (c. AD 430 unmodelled and 427 modelled) is no earlier than some of the samples from Fort 2. A sample from the Trench F kiln next to the Tammisheh Wall has also yielded an earlier *terminus post quem* (c. AD 416) than all samples from the forts on both walls.¹⁶³ We cannot tell whether this may indicate that the walls were built before the forts (or some of them) or perhaps that the walls and the associated forts in the west of the Gorgan Plain pre-date those in the east. Until there is independent dating evidence from more kilns and more forts, we also have to allow for the possibility that construction works started at multiple points simultaneously and that it is no more than coincidence that the two potentially earliest samples are both from the west and both from kilns. Irrespective of scientific dating, it is perfectly possible that the wall was built before some or all of the forts, some of which overlie brick kilns.¹⁶⁴ All forts on the Gorgan Wall abut the barrier and must be later than the stretch of wall next to them, though we cannot gauge by how much. As there is now clear evidence that some military bases in the hinterland are earlier than the Gorgan Wall,¹⁶⁵ the Sasanian army would already have been well protected and completing wall construction may have been a more urgent task than adding forts to an as yet incomplete and indefensible barrier. The entire (lowland?) wall might have been built first before any forts were added, or forts might have been added to completed sections of the wall whilst other stretches were still under construction or at the planning stage. We may conclude that it seems likely that Fort 2 and many other forts, and the original narrow barracks within, originated in the fifth century. The case for fifth-century origins of the Gorgan Wall itself is even stronger.

It was, however, without doubt in the sixth century that we see the heaviest deposition of material in Fort 2. This may be a result of tidiness with no indoor dumping of rubbish taking place initially. Most of our finds relate to later raising of floors and filling of pits, and the earliest occupation is far harder to trace. It cannot be excluded that the number of occupants increased in the sixth century and/or that it fluctuated over time, but, for the stated reasons, deposition rates of artefacts are no reliable indicator of occupation density over time. It certainly would have made no sense to build large barracks and add huge annexes later if there was no intention to occupy them fully. It is certainly inconceivable that the early ovens and fireplaces of phase 1.3, all with evidence of *in-situ* burning, were within an empty building. There must have been a standing army on the Gorgan Wall at the time the barracks were built, probably in the fifth century, and when the annexes were added, in the fifth or early sixth century. We cannot be sure, however, whether or not there were always units of similar nominal strength in the fort. Its garrison may well have fluctuated to some extent over time. There is no question, however, that there were long periods of heavy, dense and intensive occupation and no evidence for any temporary evacuation at any point.

4.1.4.6.2. THE END OF OCCUPATION
Whilst there are several samples with *termini post quos* in the early seventh century from Fort 4, no material that is certain to be similarly late has emerged at Fort 2. In contrast to Trenches H and J in Fort 4, there were no certain seventh-century samples from Fort 2. Find d.004/16 yielded the latest *termini post quem* and *ante quem* (AD 561 or 578 and AD 636 or 646, modelled and unmodelled at 95.4% confidence). Does this suggest earlier abandonment of the small Fort 2? Was the wall's garrison in its final phase of occupation concentrated on a smaller number of forts, including the large Fort 4 strategically located between two vulnerable river crossings? Perhaps, but one ought to remember that on the well-drained plateau of Fort 2 there was no need to raise floor levels by as much as in moat-enclosed lowland Fort 4. Shallower stratigraphy made deposits and structures in Fort 2 more vulnerable to modern disturbance and bioturbation than was the case at Fort 4. Fort 4 has furthermore not been ploughed recently whilst Fort 2 is heavily affected by modern agriculture. Its elevated location also resulted in greater exposure to windborne erosion. The possibility that at Fort 2 late horizons and structures, close to the modern surface, were disturbed and in part perhaps even swept away provides a possible alternative explanation for the absence of certain seventh-century samples from Fort 2 to the hypothetical scenario of earlier abandonment.

It is, however, worth noting that the samples from deep in the secondary fill of storage pits also show the same tendency, i.e. that those from Fort 4 are later than those from Fort 2 (Table 4.32). The earliest and latest likely dates and the median for all five samples from Fort 2 are earlier than those of the three samples from Fort 4. The samples from at least three (out of five sampled) pits in Fort 2 are almost certainly earlier (i.e. their entire likely date range is earlier) than all three sample from the two pits in Fort 4. All five excavated pits in Fort 2 have yielded samples that are clearly earlier than the latest sample from a pit in Fort 4. The latest pit in Fort 4 was definitely not filled up before the early to mid-seventh century; none of the pits in Fort 2 has yielded similarly late samples. It is worth noting that the above dates are all unmodelled, but even if one included the modelled dates (significantly later for d.184/862, i.e. c. AD 548–591), the same would be true.¹⁶⁶ Ploughing or erosion may have erased the latest occupation levels at Fort 2, but cannot have affected the fill of deep storage pits. The excavated storage pits in Fort 4 appear to have remained in use longer than at Fort 2, but it is far from certain that our sample is representative:

- Only five samples from five pits in Fort 2 were processed, and only three samples from two pits in Fort 4. Our sample is numerically small and need not be representative.

- In both forts, all pits were found in a single trench. We cannot be sure that the absence of early or late material from pits in a small area is representative for the fort as a whole, as pits of a different phase may have clustered elsewhere within the fort.

Table 4.32: Unmodelled dates of samples from the secondary fill of pits in Forts 2 and 4 (from earliest to latest).[167]

Fort	Pit	Sample	Earliest likely date (95.4%)	Latest likely date (95.4%)
2	d.216	d.226/739	AD 423	AD 539
2	d.254	d.252/854	AD 429	AD 544
2	d.064	d.090/s3	AD 432	AD 560
2	d.230	d.233/756	AD 432	AD 568
2	d.130	d.184/862	AD 439	AD 594
4	J.034	J.030/490	AD 563	AD 648
4	J.033	J.027/496	AD 583	AD 655
4	J.033	J.027/493	AD 605	AD 671

- All eight samples provide only a *terminus post quem*; it is possible in theory that as late as the seventh century pits were filled up with redeposited material from a much earlier phase of occupation. This, however, seems improbable for reasons stated.[168]

We may conclude that it is likely that the two excavated pits in Fort 4 remained in use longer than the five in Fort 2. We cannot, however, be sure that they are representative for all pits from the two forts in question. If future excavations increase the sample size, we may be able to see if there is a clear pattern.

Overall, two out of 12 dated organic samples from Fort 4 have yielded certain *termini post quos* in the early seventh century (of AD 602 and AD 605), as opposed to none out of 19 (not counting the intrusive late medieval rodent sample) from Fort 2 (all at 95.4% confidence). As to the preserved undisturbed layers from Fort 2, there is no positive evidence that they extend into the seventh century, even if there are some that may well do so. Is the lack of certain evidence for seventh-century occupation from Fort 2 evidence for earlier abandonment? Potentially, but poor preservation of later deposits at Fort 2 and the overall small sample size mean that the case is far from proven. Occupation in the two forts could have ceased simultaneously or decades apart. Fort 4 was certainly occupied, and probably heavily occupied, into the early seventh century, the (admittedly few) samples suggesting undiminished intensity of activity right to the end.

It is perhaps also worth considering if a hypothetical reduction of troop numbers on the Gorgan Wall in the late Sasanian era led to partial occupation of some or all forts. If so, parts of the barracks in both, Fort 2 and Fort 4, may still have been occupied in the first half of the seventh century and it may be coincidence that we happened to encounter rooms used to the end in Fort 4 as opposed to rooms potentially vacated a little earlier in Fort 2 – with parts of the barracks elsewhere in the fort perhaps frequented as long as those in Fort 4. At Buraq Tappeh the evidence suggests that phases when the fort was partially occupied, with the room in the area of our Trench g being abandoned, alternated with phases when more rooms, or all rooms, were in use. Is it possible that garrison sizes of the Gorgan Wall forts fluctuated as much as appears to have been the case at Buraq Tappeh? First, we should note that the strategic significance of the hinterland fort of Buraq Tappeh will have diminished after completion of the Great Wall, even if perhaps temporarily regaining importance at times of crisis. By contrast, the wall forts, disregarding potential outpost forts further north, formed the first line of defence and were arguably of more constant importance – making it less likely they would have been episodically denuded of troops. Assuming we are right in thinking that Buraq Tappeh had probably been built in the early fifth century and before the Gorgan Wall, that its occupation overlapped with that of the forts on the wall, but that it was abandoned before them, its history of occupation almost certainly differed in chronology and will also have differed in the degree of fluctuation of occupation density. Furthermore, whilst there were phases when the room explored at Buraq Tappeh was roofed and equipped with heating and cooking facilities, alternating with times when it was roofless and exposed to the elements,[169] there is no positive evidence that any part of the barracks excavated in Forts 2 or 4 was in a ruinous roofless state at any stage in the Sasanian era. The evidence from Buraq Tappeh demonstrates that occupation density of a Sasanian military site could vary greatly over time, but there is no reason to think that the forts on the wall experienced similar episodes of disrepair. Even if occupation density may well have changed over time, it appears that the barracks of the wall forts were maintained until eventually abandoned altogether.

We may conclude that a reduced garrison occupying only parts of Fort 2 is possible, but there will have been more than a token garrison, as an understaffed fort would have been hard to maintain and defend. More probably, raising the surface in Fort 4 has increased the quantity of late material, whilst disturbance of late layers near the surface in Fort 2 makes the latest phase of occupation hard to trace. The start and end of occupation of the two forts need not have differed and neither was there necessarily any difference in intensity of occupation over time.

A defensive chain is only as strong as its weakest link and the defensibility of the Gorgan Wall would have been compromised had a decision been taken to occupy only a selection of forts in a late phase (and also, if perhaps to a lesser extent, if the garrison of all forts had been reduced), considerations that perhaps add strength to both forts having been abandoned at a similar time. Recalibration of a bone sample deposited in the Gorgan Wall ditch north of Fort 9 points to a likely date of AD 533–607 (at 86.0% likelihood) and, with most bones from the ditch coming from stratigraphically higher levels, we may assume that Fort 9 continued to be occupied for decades beyond. This suggests that Fort 9 was occupied into the seventh century or at least to the late sixth century.[170] Whilst in theory Fort 2 could have been vacated already in the sixth century, it makes much more sense to assume that all forts along the defensive chain were either evacuated simultaneously or that their garrisons melted away over a short period of time when the Sasanian Empire disintegrated towards the mid-seventh century. This is admittedly a circular argument. Perhaps only a selection of forts was garrisoned to the end, perhaps still enough on all sections to counter low- and medium-level threats at least, perhaps the garrisons of some or all forts were reduced, but the barracks maintained, perhaps it was a result of disturbance of the upper levels that the latest occupation has not left a clear imprint in the area of Trench d and all forts were occupied similarly intensively to the end. No certain decision is possible without further fieldwork. Civil war in the 590s, westwards expansion in the 600s–620s and defence against the Arab invasions in the 630s–640s (not to mention the possibility of unrecorded crises at other frontiers) all provide possible scenarios for potential partial troop withdrawal and redeployment, whilst the northern threat provided a powerful incentive not to deplete the wall of its guardians. Our dating evidence proves that at least parts of the wall remained garrisoned certainly into the early and possibly to the mid-seventh century. Historically, it is hard to imagine it would have been abandoned completely before the 630s at the earliest.[171] Even if we cannot be sure if there were differences in the date, speed and manner of abandonment of the forts of the Great Wall over the last 60 years or so of Sasanian rule, there is no evidence as yet of any of them lasting into post-Sasanian times. There is no proof for any occupation then at Fort 2, an observation that similarly applies to Fort 4, and we are not aware of any surface finds or mounding in any other fort either that points to continued habitation. The Gorgan Wall appears to have been abandoned as a whole no later than the mid-seventh century.

4.1.4.6.3. Occupation density over time
It is hard to be sure how the occupation density of Fort 2 may have changed over time. The addition of the annexes certainly substantially increased indoor space available for accommodation and domestic activities. Yet, we cannot be sure whether the number of occupants increased and, if so, whether the additional space was for used for more troops or for accommodating their dependants and/or for the pursuit of other domestic activities. Neither can we gauge how much time exactly passed between the erection of the original barracks and their annexes. A number of observations (i.e. the existence of probable material extraction pits in the area of the annexes that later had to be filled up, the higher base of their walls and the substantial architectural differences between the original solid mud-brick barracks and the more lightly constructed annexe walls, often employing a mixture or mud-bricks and broken fired bricks) suggest that the annexes were not part of the original design and were probably added a few decades after erection of the original barracks.

It is interesting to note that amongst the few very early bones pre-dating annexe construction, there was a metacarpal of a large horse from the fill of a material extraction pit in the area of later room 5CS (with radiocarbon date of c. AD 423–539 and a modelled date of c. AD 430–535). Perhaps it suggests that the garrison was mounted or part-mounted, though other explanations, e.g. that it was the horse of a messenger or other visitor, cannot be ruled out. Horses may also have been kept within the fort during its latest occupation. The implications of these findings and where horses may have been kept (probably outdoors) are discussed below.[172] The open space outside the barracks will have been used for a variety of social, domestic and perhaps economic activities and probably also for military training and for tethering mounts.

It seems clear that indoor space was used for multiple purposes as well and not exclusively as accommodation. In the western annexe we found no compacted earth floors and, with the exception of one west–east wall, little in terms of clear mud-brick walls. Later, in phase 4, much of room 1CS was filled with storage jars. Front room 0CS, which anybody entering the barracks from the central road would have had to cross, was haphazardly paved with reused fired bricks. This was probably a work floor and there is nothing to suggest that there were bedrooms anywhere in the western annexe within Trench d. The much better insulated and perhaps quieter eastern annexe on the back side of the building, boasting like the original barracks trampled earth floors, may well have provided additional bedrooms and/or space for other domestic activities, even if initially there was little in terms of heating and cooking facilities (i.e. just one fireplace, in room 4CS, replaced by two ovens, in rooms 4CS and 5CS, in phase 3).

The doubling of the number of ovens and fireplaces from phases 1.3 to 3 and their substantial reduction in phase 5 make one wonder whether this reflects rising and falling numbers of occupants – or whether people in phase 3 simply lived in greater comfort than earlier or later generations of occupants. Alternatively, maybe it was only in phases 3 to 4 that there was roadside catering, and the smaller number of cooking facilities before and after does not reflect reduced population levels but a potential change from self-catering to central supply of some hot meals for a limited period of time. The state of repair of the barracks seems to have deteriorated in phase 5, and the latest levels are less well preserved. Some of the latest fireplaces may not have been preserved at all, and the fourfold decline from phases 3 to 5 may be deceptive. The creation of large storage pits in phases 2 to 4 and the placing of 12 large storage vessels in the barracks in phase 4 indicate an increase in food storage. If this is best explained by a rising number of occupants or changes in provision or storage (e.g. from bringing in the daily needs from outside to permanent storage of staple foods and special provisions, e.g. wine, in the intramural area) is impossible to decide. Any storage facilities on an upper storey or loft would, furthermore, be archaeologically untraceable. It is worth noting, however, that fragments of smaller storage jars from rows 2 and 0 and/or the outdoor area west of the barracks, from phases 1–2, and in row 5, from phases 2–5, prove that such vessels had been in use already at earlier phases of occupation and in multiple rooms.[173] This suggests perhaps that phase 4 was less anomalous than the large vessels *in situ* imply and that there was bulk storage or liquid commodities already available much earlier. Initially, most rooms may have been multifunctional, and it was probably not until phase 4.1 that room 1CS was used mainly or exclusively as a storeroom. We are not sure how intramural storage capacity changed over time and if the smaller size of the earlier vessels may perhaps suggest that it indeed increased in phase 4.1. Quantification of finds by phase is fraught with difficulties, as most of the pottery, bone and other finds seem to be from secondary deposits (to raise the surface or filling disused storage pits). Distinct differences in the ratio of pot to bone from room to room suggests that this may have been mainly material deposited by room users, rather than brought in from a common source from the outside, but we have to assume that local deposition of pot and bone occurred mainly at times when surfaces were raised or disused pits or storage vessels filled with debris; at other times, the tidy occupants must have disposed of broken pot and food waste outdoors; intensity of deposition therefore need not reflect intensity of occupation, and the number of finds per phase is no reliable yardstick at all as to the number of people present. The garrison indeed seems to have been very tidy and did not normally dump rubbish indoors – though perhaps less so in the latest phase of occupation. In short, despite various indicators for intensification or reduction of various activities, none of them is certain to reflect the number of occupants. It seems clear that already the original barracks were designed for a substantial number of occupants. There is much evidence for intensive occupation right to the end. We may be sure that Fort 2 was intensively occupied, probably from the fifth and certainly from the early sixth to at least the late sixth or, more probably, early or mid-seventh century. The number of occupants will have fluctuated to a greater or lesser extent over these one-and-a-half or two centuries, but we have no reliable way of reconstructing how.

4.2. Barracks in Fort 15

Already when writing up the first phase of our project, we had noticed that aerial imagery had the potential to show not just oblong mounds, representing collapsed military barracks, but individual rooms within barrack. This was first observed at Fort 26.[174] Research on drone and satellite images has since revealed traces of rows of barrack rooms also in Forts 15 and 25, and we will describe remains and dimensions of barracks in these forts, from east to west.

At Fort 15, drone and satellite imagery of October 2016 (Figs 4.87–4.88 and 4.109) shows rooms within the western two of the fort's four barracks and, less clearly, perhaps also in the third from the west. These were only recognised when examining the imagery and it has not been possible to verify on the ground what soil marks or vegetation patterns have made the room divisions visible. It is possible, as the fort is now arable land, that the plough has cut sterile fort walls and more organic deposits within rooms and that this process has brought to light differences in soil colour. It is also possible that the more fertile soil within rooms has attracted lusher plant growth.

Two rows of rooms in the western two buildings are very distinct, and their combined width including walls is c. 11–12 m. The buildings are well defined in the south of the fort, but not in the north. Assuming a broadly symmetrical arrangement, we may estimate the total length of the barracks at c. 110–130 m, each containing approximate 20–24 × 2 rooms, i.e. 40–48 rooms in total. In places, one sees clearly that rooms are provided with central door openings in the west and east outside walls, a pattern also observed in the geophysical survey plot of Fort 4[175] and during our excavations of the barracks at Fort 2.[176] There may be fainter traces of walls to the west and east of the clear two-row barracks, but we are not sure. It is certainly possible, though as yet unproven, that in Fort 15, just as at Forts 2, 25 and 26 (and probably Fort 16), lightly built annexes were added to more solidly constructed original barracks. Indeed, it is possible that annexes were added to the original barracks in all forts. There is no fort on the Gorgan Wall as yet where we can prove that there were two-row barracks without annexes, but the sample of well-explored forts is still too small to prove or disprove that this was a universal development.

4.3. Barracks in Fort 25

A similar pattern as in Forts 15 and 26 has also been observed in Fort 26's eastern neighbour (Fort 25), but it has as yet not been possible to examine this on the ground. Google Earth satellite imagery of 2014 and 2019 (Figs 4.89–4.90) shows parts of the barracks in Fort 25 very clearly, notably in the western half of the fort. This

Fig. 4.87: Google Earth image of Fort 15 of 2016, clearly showing traces of individual rooms within the western two of the fort's four barracks, with potential traces of walls also in of third barracks from the west (Image © Maxar Technologies).

Fig. 4.88: Drone image by Davit Naskidashvili and the joint team of Fort 15, taken on 22 October 2016, showing room divisions within the western two barracks as well as the eastern two barracks as long mounds and the outer walls of the fort. The track (top) runs parallel to the Great Wall. The outer walls, with visible traces of towers in the south, are also discernible.

Fig. 4.89: Google Earth image of Fort 25 of 2014, showing barracks in the west of the fort particularly clearly (Image © CNES / Airbus).

seems to be a result of the destruction of the upper layers, revealing walls in lighter colours (barren ridges?) and darker room units (probably again depressions covered in vegetation). The fort was clearly very densely built-up, and it is possible that the western two of the four barracks formed a single large block as there are neatly aligned rows of rectangular rooms without any clear traces of a lane separating them. The typical oblong mounds in the interior[177] suggest perhaps that there were originally four (two-storey?) barracks. Subsequent addition of (single-storey?) annexes may have resulted in the western two barracks (and perhaps also the eastern two barracks, but the imagery is less clear here) subsequently being joined and forming a single complex of over 60 m width, with the original barracks rising to greater height than the rooms added later. The easternmost six rows measure c. 33 m west–east, making them even wider than the Fort 2 barracks. It is hard to be sure about north–south extent, but it is possible that there were 25–28 rows of an average north–south extent of a room unit of c. 4.60 m, including room partitions and outer walls. Attempting to reconstruct the layout and architecture of buildings on the basis of aerial imagery involves, of course, an element of interpretation, and our conclusions should be considered tentative only as far as details are concerned. We may be sure, however, that what we see are the remains of substantial military-style accommodation filling a high proportion of the interior of Fort 25. There is certainly no doubt that the barracks exceeded those at Fort 2 in length and number of rows, and it seems clear now that barracks in larger forts often or always provided more indoor space than their counterparts in smaller forts. But even within larger forts, the pattern does not appear to have been uniform, and barracks probably differed in the number of rooms and the total indoor space they contained.

4.4. Barracks in Fort 26

On 26 November 2014, we visited Forts 26 and 27, inspired by Google Earth satellite imagery of Fort 26 (cf. Fig. 4.91) implying the existence of a remarkably orthogonal grid of possible narrow ridges of light grey colour, separating small rectangular plots of greenish brown colour. The dimensions, alignments and relative location of some of these rectilinear ridges and the plots in between were strikingly similar to those of the walls and rooms of the barracks in Fort 4.[178] Further units of this kind (even if less distinct or less regular) between our postulated two barracks cannot be explained with the hypothesis that ridges mark the location of walls and large and shallow pit-like features that of rooms of Fort 4-style narrow barracks. Were the barracks in Fort 26 perhaps much wider? The phenomenon seemed worth exploring.[179]

Both forts visited are full of pits or depressions. Those in Fort 27, the next fort west of Fort 26, vary in size and do not form neat alignments, and the barrack mounds were clearly targeted by pit-diggers (as opposed to the flat

Fig. 4.90: On this Google Earth image of Fort 25 of 2019 room divisions in the north of the compound show up distinctly (Image © CNES / Airbus).

ground around them).[180] Did people at Fort 26 in search of treasure, or even just fertile soil, excavate the interior of rooms, avoiding the sterile walls, and then continue to dig pits of similar size elsewhere? It appears that the fort may have been affected by some robbing or earth-moving operations around 2002.[181] In order to assess whether pit-digging is a likely explanation for the pattern observed at Fort 26, we should first briefly examine sites demonstrably affected by such operations: Fort 27 as well as one much further east, Fort 2A. Like Fort 27, Fort 2A appears to have been robbed unsystematically, but far more extensively. The entire surface of the plateau is densely covered in pits. We cannot be sure whether Fort 2A was confined to the northern parts of the plateau or whether it may have covered most of it, especially if erosion should have changed its shape and dimensions over the past one and a half millennia. On various visits to the fort, we observed a fair number of fired brick fragments on the ground, notably on the side of the Great Wall. Yet the concentration of fired brick was no greater than at other forts and not high enough to suggest that there were fired brick buildings, accounting for the numerous robber pits. Furthermore, had there been brick walls, one would have expected there to be linear robber trenches rather than random punctual pits. Can the dense concentration of the robber pits be explained with the immediate vicinity of a village?[182] Perhaps, but the pits need not be recent, to judge by them being cut by erosion channels. Furthermore, as this is not the only fort near a village, factors that are irrational and thus unknowable, such as potential past rumours of treasure, may have played a part. Indeed, there is no village currently near Fort 27 and we do not know why these two forts were affected disproportionately. It is worth noting that the pits at Forts 2A and 27 differ from very recent robber shafts, e.g. at Buraq Tappeh and Qalʻeh Kharabeh,[183] the latter being mostly round, of small diameter, but vastly greater depth (and sometimes leading to underground chambers or tunnels). It is likely that those at Forts 2A and 27 are older, partially silted up and need not, of course, necessarily have reached the same depth. The random pit digging in Forts 2A and 27 will have done extensive damage and has not revealed any significant information on the layout of buildings.

By contrast, the shallow depressions in Fort 26 follow in part at least a regular pattern, with depressions and the ridges separating them often being in, more or less, rectilinear alignments. It would be astonishing if robber pits had been dug with such military precision and if they never reached more than a shallow depth or silted up so regularly. Notably the eastern barracks are quite clearly recognisable on the ground, with rectangular room units of c. 7 m west–east by c. 5 m north–south, separated by shallow barren ridges. Two central rows are particularly distinct, and one is tempted to think that they formed the original barracks (c. 14 × 80 m, containing an estimated 16 rows of two rooms each). The less distinct rows of cells abutting them were probably later annexes – just as in Fort 2 and maybe most or all forts along the Great

Fig. 4.91: Google Earth Image of Fort 26 of 3 June 2013 (Image © CNES / Astrium).

Wall. An earlier hypothesis, forwarded before we knew about annexes to barracks, that there might have been four barracks in Fort 26,[184] should be disregarded, notably as there is no gap between the regular two-row building (i.e. the original barracks) and the less regular compartments (i.e. the annexe rooms). The interior of these cells, notably within the original eastern barracks, is in places of rectangular shape. Plants naturally grow predominantly within these shallow rectangular depressions and account for the greenish discoloration. Less clearly, similar patterns can be observed in the west of the fort. The depressions in the centre, whilst in part also following a north–south alignment are less regular in diameter, shape and depth. The same is true for depressions (annexe rooms) on the east side of the eastern barracks.

The principal explanation for the regular patterns observed at Fort 26 is not pit-digging, but undoubtedly occupation deposits within rooms being prone to greater subsidence than the mud-brick walls, thus creating depressions in the interior of rooms, separated by ridges formed by walls. The site is not currently ploughed, so the difference in height between walls and the subsided interiors of rooms has been preserved and maybe accentuated over the years. One wonders if potential topsoil stripping some time ago may explain why walls and rooms are visible above ground at Fort 26, but not at the equally unploughed Fort 4. Alternatively, a similar pattern in Fort 4 may have been erased through ploughing in the more distant past. Perhaps the once tall mud-bricks

Fig. 4.92: The north of the eastern barracks in Fort 26, visited on 26 November 2014. Remarkably regular depressions, with plants growing inside, may represent rooms and are separated by barren ridges formed by collapsed mud-brick walls.

walls at Fort 26 formed ridges when they collapsed, which have been preserved in areas where there was little or no plough damage. Subsidence affecting levelling and occupation deposits much more than mud-brick walls is certainly a phenomenon we observed at Buraq Tappeh; deposits building up within a room have subsided distinctly, and more so towards the centre of the room, whereas a mud-brick wall they abut has not suffered similar shrinkage (even if its uppermost sections suffered erosion and partial collapse).[185] Water naturally flows into these depressions enhancing plant growth, perhaps further boosted by the soil within rooms being more organic than the sterile decayed mud-bricks of the walls. Former rooms form plots covered in vegetation, separated by barren ridges, creating a pattern visible from space. In addition to the barracks, the eastern fort walls, as well as at least one tower, perhaps two, are also visible. One can also make out the western fort wall. The distance of fort defences to both postulated barracks is similar, adding much strength to our proposed identification of these features, as Sasanian forts tend to be remarkably symmetrical.

Drone and satellite images of Fort 26 and inspection of the pit-like features on the ground leave no doubt that many of the large shallow depressions mark the location of individual rooms. Subsidence and modern land-use, rather than pit-digging (even if there might have been some), have made the plans of buildings visible, and the walls are preserved as often rectilinear ridges which separate rooms. If the patterns are inevitably less clear than in the case of our excavations (of Trench d in Fort 2), our observations suggest that a broadly similar percentage of space was taken up by barracks in Forts 2 and 26 (and it cannot be excluded that it was even more at Fort 26). In both cases, there were probably two symmetrical barracks with substantial annexes.

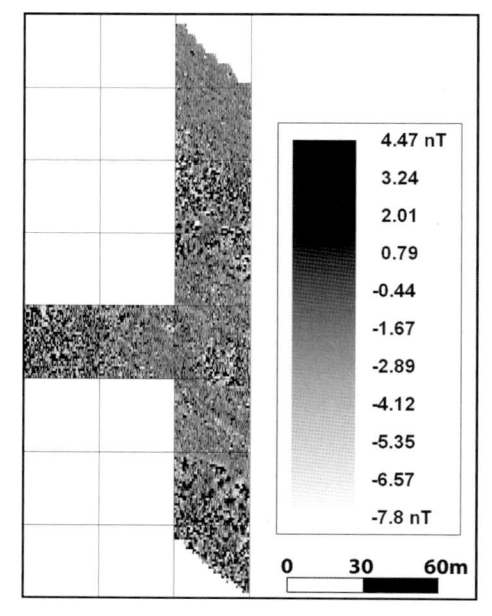

Fig. 4.93: GWS-65, surveyed by Mohammad Arman Ershadi, Julian Jansen Van Rensburg et al. Results processed by them and Roger Ainslie of Abingdon Archaeological Geophysics. Each grid measures 30 × 30 m.

4.5. Geophysical survey at a compound on the north side of the Great Wall: GWS-65 near Fort 28[186]

We carried out a magnetometer survey at site GWS-65 near Fort 28, a potential fort site abutting the wall on the north (Fig. 4.122), first explored by the landscape survey team.[187] Due to its close proximity to Fort 28, its broadly similar size, geometric plan (even if differing in shape from Fort 28) and its location on the Great Wall, although uniquely abutting or underlying its north side, the site is discussed in this chapter. The survey detected broad high magnetic anomalies, potentially in the right alignment for the fort walls, but not sufficiently well defined to prove or disprove the hypothesis. The significance of an oval feature in the interior is uncertain, but circular and roundish (medieval or modern?) burial enclosures on several fort platforms provide potential parallels.[188]

The geophysical survey has neither proven nor disproven the hypothesis that GWS-65 might have been a fort. Excavation is needed to gain certainty. Its location, abutting the north side of the wall, would, however, be most unusual – and it would have been more difficult to defend than any other fort on the Great Wall. If GWS-65 was a fort, one wonders if it might be earlier than the Gorgan Wall, perhaps part of a chain of forts that preceded wall construction and was replaced by Fort 28 thereafter. Perhaps at one stage the projected alignment of the Great Wall was meant to coincide with the fort's north side and it was marked out shortly before a decision was made to alter the wall's course, leading to the abandonment of the fort or building site. It seems unlikely that it was occupied at the same time as the forts abutting the south side of the wall and is likely to be earlier. Its potential significance is discussed in the context of the non-wall-related forts.[189] With no clear evidence that the hypothetical identification of the site as a fort is correct, even if satellite imagery suggests that this is a strong possibility, it is best not to speculate further, but the site would potentially merit further investigation in future. In the light of its state of preservation, little if anything is likely to survive above ground, but the fill of the moat/ditch surrounding the compound and any pits inside may hold the clues as to chronology and nature of its occupation.

4.6. Remote survey of forts along the Great Wall

4.6.1. Introduction

Whilst labour-intensive excavations were inevitably confined to just one fort during this phase of our project, we also studied satellite images more systematically than had been possible during the first phase of our project in 2005–2009. In 2016, we were able to conduct a systematic programme of drone photography covering all well-preserved forts on the Gorgan Wall. It was Davit Naskidashvili's idea to employ drone photography on the Great Wall on a larger scale, and he also took all the drone images in 2016, invariably in close collaboration with

Iranian archaeologists, notably Hamid Omrani Rekavandi, selecting the most suitable locations for taking photos. The drone photography team made every effort to reach sites in ideal light conditions in the early morning or late afternoon and produced a wealth of excellent images. Due to limitations of space, only one image is produced per fort, and we deliberately chose different photos to those selected for preliminary reports,[190] to make a larger selection available.

4.6.2. Satellite survey

Re-examination of satellite images has not only shed significant new light on the size, plan and internal layout of barracks,[191] but has also confirmed the conclusion presented before that all well-preserved forts on the Gorgan Wall appear to contain an even number of barracks: most commonly two, occasionally four or six and once only eight.[192] This suggests, even if barracks varied in size, that there was a significant degree of standardisation in Sasanian fort design and probably theoretical unit sizes (though we have to assume that the real numerical strength of units will have fluctuated). Satellite images of forts are discussed in detail elsewhere, where also the visual evidence is presented prominently. Little would be gained by repetition and the reader is referred to our separate report on this topic.[193]

4.6.3. Drone survey

Much satellite imagery is now easily accessible, so that there is no need for extensive reproduction. Our drone survey, however, has yielded new primary evidence not otherwise available. As mechanised agriculture is increasingly flattening once prominent forts, the images our team was able to take in 2016 may well show the remains more prominently and clearly for some of the sites than what future photographers will be able to capture. The drone images in this section, all taken by Davit Naskidashvili and the project team, are thus a unique record of the forts, often showing prominently the parallel barracks in the interior, the fort platforms, the defensive walls and the moats, and sometimes also the tower mounds dotted around the edges. In two cases (Forts 15 and 26) we can even see probable room divisions within barracks, in the former fort probably a result of soil marks in a ploughed field, in the latter a result of degradation of an unploughed site, with walls forming low banks between rows of rooms.[194] Drone images also corroborate satellite images in providing important evidence for barracks within forts. They sometimes do so more clearly than satellite imagery, as they have a much higher resolution and were often taken in ideal light conditions. This is particularly evident in the case of Fort 5, where our drone images (as well as recent Google Earth imagery) show the barrack mounds clearly, the remains of which had been less evident on earlier satellite imagery.[195] More often, however, the opposite is true, i.e. that the traces of barracks that can clearly be discerned on satellite imagery of the 1960s are now less prominent, or have vanished altogether, as a result of mechanised modern agriculture. The contrast is particularly stark in the case of Fort 28: its two barracks and outer walls were strikingly clear on CORONA imagery of 1969,[196] as were traces of possible extramural settlement.[197] All of this has been flattened since and no traces remain visible above ground. In addition to providing a record of current preservation and threats, the visual evidence for forts along the wall is important to place the results of our investigations at Fort 2 in a broader context. Aerial imagery proves that there are traces of symmetrically arranged barracks in all well-preserved forts, but also demonstrates that they differed in number and dimensions.

In this chapter, we will briefly summarise the result of the drone survey, following the wall from east to west. We have selected one photo of every fort visited and discuss the visible architectural features. Little remains of the forts east of the Pishkamar Rocks. The team photographed the location of postulated Fort -4, now under a village. Part of the fort defences have been tentatively identified, but we could not discern any clear archaeological features on the imagery and therefore excluded it from our selection of photos.[198] Poorly preserved Fort -3, -2 and -1 were not recorded, but the small compound of Qareh Doyub, perhaps serving a religious function as well as guarding the strategically important point where the Gorgan Wall crosses the Gorgan River,[199] was visited by the team.

To the west of the Pishkamar Rocks, the wall runs across the lowlands towards the Caspian Sea. It is lined here by substantial rectangular forts. Skirting the steppe margins north of the green and lush Gorgan River Valley, it guards the most prosperous lands and had to negotiate fewer river crossings than any alternative route south of the river would have done. Fort 1, a four-barracks fort, guarded the strategically significant easternmost part of the wall's lowland section. Surrounded by a substantial moat on the canal-lined Great Wall, it is likely that water was channelled into the moat and ditch – as is probably also true for the ditch/canal along all other lowland sections of the wall and all moats around forts. Fort 2, by contrast, was on a hilltop and there is no moat or canal. It was in an ideal position for surveillance, towering high above the surrounding landscape. Jointly with Fort 2A, it guarded the point where the Gorgan Wall crossed the Sari Su River. In the area of Fort 2A, on a loess cliff high above the river, the Gorgan Wall bifurcates, and the northern branch forms the north side of Fort 2A. The bridge on which the Gorgan Wall crosses the river is in alignment with the southern branch,[200] but the high loess cliff west of the bridge renders it doubtful that the wall ever ascended the steep slope. A continuous wall would not have been required here, as long as Fort 2A's garrison permanently guarded the top of the dangerously steep cliff.

Fig. 4.94: Qareh Doyub: a fire temple on the Gorgan Wall (foreground, centre) overlooking the Gorgan River, its banks now densely overgrown with reeds. A short section of the Great Wall, abutting the fire temple at an oblique angle, has been excavated. Beyond the excavations, the Gorgan Wall is visible as a bank in the same alignment as the excavated wall, running from the temple to the northern (left) terminal of the crest of the ridge in the middle ground. Towering over the valley (left), the wall was evidently built to facilitate area surveillance and/or defence and to minimise any exposure to flood damage.

Fig. 4.95: Fort 1, the easternmost fort in the lowland section of the Great Wall before its ascent to the Pishkamar Rocks in the east (background left). Four barracks in the interior and a substantial moat around the fort platform are clearly visible. It is possible that a substantial loess canyon (right) might represent an eroded canal channelling water into the moat. (Note, however, that it is less straight than its counterpart at Fort 4.) The wall protects the fertile Gorgan River Valley (in the background) and separates it from less prosperous land north (left).

Fig. 4.96: Fort 2, with our Trenches c and d on view, on a hilltop, overlooking the Sari Su River, with Fort 2A in the background (centre). One can see the towered walls and, despite substantial plough damage, can still make out the eastern of the fort's two barracks as an oblong mound.

Fig. 4.97: Fort 2A, strewn with robber pits, with the northern branch of the ditch-lined Gorgan Wall right and the Gorgan Wall bridge (centre left) in the Sari Su River Valley deep below. Note that pits extend right to the edge of the loess cliff, perhaps suggesting, as would defensive logic, that the fort too extended to the cliff edge. There may be faint traces of two long mounds (though the evidence is far from certain) parallel to the Great Wall, potentially the collapsed remains of barracks in an alignment that would have facilitated access to the vantage point above the cliff.

Fig. 4.98: Fort 4, with its eight barracks, two each in alignment, and later burial enclosures in the interior. The eroded canal (centre, right), once channelling water into the moat around the fort platform, and the canal-lined Great Wall (in the foreground) still form prominent landmarks today. Projecting tower-mounds are visible too, most clearly on this photo on the north-east (left) side of the platform and its shadow, shaped like a saw-blade.

Fig. 4.99: Fort 5A overlooks the Great Wall crossing the Kal Aji River. Like Forts 2 and 2A, Forts 5 and 5A form a functional unit, of two forts each guarding two opposite banks of a river. Like Fort 2A, it takes advantage of natural defences and is not of geometric shape, but there is a straight ditch in the north-east (right). The distinct line of robber pits (background left) proves that the wall once led across the valley.

Fig. 4.100: Fort 5, towering over the Kal Aji River (middle-ground, left), near its confluence with the Gorgan River (in the background). Like Fort 4, there appears to be an eroded canal on its south-west (right) side, once supplying the canal along the Great Wall (foreground) with water. The alignment of robber pits (foreground) marks the course of the brick-built wall, and there are traces of tower mounds at other sides of the fort platform, most clearly on the north-east (left) side. In the fort's interior, one sees two oblong barrack mounds, one of them dissected by a rectangular burial enclosure. Note also circular burial enclosures in the east of the fort (left), probably deliberately placed at this point that commands the best views. As in Fort 12 (and potentially in Fort 2A), but unlike all other forts with clearly traceable barracks, the oblong military housing complexes are parallel to the wall, probably to facilitate access to the strategically important river crossing.

Fig. 4.101: Fort 6 (centre), surrounded by walls and a substantial moat and with two barrack mounds inside, along the canal-lined Gorgan Wall (foreground, left to background, right) – straighter even than modern landmarks.

Fig. 4.102: Fort 7, now serving as a graveyard, with the Gorgan Wall in the foreground and possible bastions abutting it in the south-west (right) and north-east (left). Substantial robber pits (foreground) are all that remains of the Great Wall. In low sunlight, the tower mounds on the fort's south-west (left) side show up as distinct humps in the shadow of the platform. One can still make out slight mounding in the interior, the indistinct remains of the fort's two barracks.

Fig. 4.103: Fort 8 has been heavily damaged by modern agriculture, but is still clearly recognisable, as is the moat surrounding it and the canal along the Great Wall (right).

Fig. 4.104: Fort 9, despite later burial enclosures and modern pits on the platform, is still well preserved, and one can clearly discern its two barrack mounds (as usual, at a right angle to the Great Wall) and the canal along the wall (foreground, left to background, right). The fort's towered walls stand out, being of higher elevation and more barren than the interior. A band of dark soil along the outer edges of the platform marks the location of the moat.

Fig. 4.105: Fort 10, on the outskirts of Gonbad-e Kavus. Its two barrack mounds are recognisable and its outer walls survive well, with a burial enclosure prominently placed in the north-west corner (background, centre). One notices that the moat around the fort is marked in places by lusher vegetation, a result of water gathering in the depression and perhaps the more fertile soil washed in.

Fig. 4.106: Fort 12 was one of the strongest forts on the wall, boasting three long double-barracks (i.e. six barracks) parallel to the wall, the orientation perhaps designed to facilitate access to a hypothetical gate between Forts 12 (right) and 13 (left). Due to ploughing, these mounds are scarcely discernible now, but the fort platform and the outer walls are still prominently visible. The Great Wall is in alignment with the modern road north of Fort 12, but visible west of Fort 13 (left).

Fig. 4.107: Fort 13 incorporates a large earlier settlement mound, Qaravol Tappeh, in its north-east corner (foreground, right). The outer walls still form distinct banks.

Fig. 4.108: Fort 14, with distinct tower mounds on the west (left) side and the typical two oblong barracks on either side of a central roadway, abutting the Great Wall (top).

Fig. 4.109: Fort 15 has suffered much from ploughing which, however, has also made the neat rows of rooms (foreground) in the western two of the fort's four barracks visible. The outer walls still form a prominent bank, with tower mounds in the south (right). The fort guards the point where a minor stream (background, behind the fort platform) crosses the Great Wall.

Fig. 4.110: Fort 16, a typical two-barracks fort, guards another fairly straight section of the Gorgan Wall (right).

Fig. 4.111: Fort 17, with two barracks inside, one of them with later burial enclosures on top, and prominent fort walls. The fort is placed next to an old stream, now dammed to create large pools of water. The canal lining the Gorgan Wall still forms a depression and is in places (background, centre) filled with water.

Fig. 4.112: Fort 18, with two parallel barrack mounds, a central hollow-way and distinct fort walls, abutting the Great Wall (right). The water-filled ditch follows the ancient canal along the wall.

Fig. 4.113: Fort 19 (centre), along the Gorgan Wall (left), is now barely recognisable.

Fig. 4.114: *The well-drained platform of Fort 20 along the Great Wall stands out prominently over its moat and wider surroundings due to different vegetation cover. Two barrack mounds and the outer walls remain visible.*

Fig. 4.115: *An island in modern development: Fort 21 (centre) along the Gorgan Wall (right).*

Fig. 4.116: Now at the edge of a reservoir, the platform of Fort 22 (centre) rises well above the water table. There appear to be the typical two barracks perpendicular to the Great Wall (right) on both sides of a central roadway.

Fig. 4.117: Fort 23's two barracks, still prominent in the 1960s, have now been flattened, but the platform remains visible. The modern road runs parallel to the Gorgan Wall.

Fig. 4.118: Fort 25 is filled with the typical oblong barrack mounds, four in this large compound, perpendicular to the Great Wall (along the road, left). The fort is heavily damaged in places, but in places individual room units are visible on satellite imagery (but not on the drone image).

Fig. 4.119: Much of the interior of Fort 26 is filled with accommodation, and individual room units and decayed barrack walls are prominently visible. Arguably best preserved is a double row of rooms (foreground, left), perhaps the remains of the eastern original (two-storey) barrack block. A small fort with just two barracks (but extensive annexes), the cars on the road running along the Gorgan Wall provide an idea of scale. The fort walls are heavily damaged.

Fig. 4.120: Fort 27 has suffered much from pit-digging, whose shapes and distribution are not likely to reflect the original layout of its four barracks. Distinct tower mound survive on the west (right) side. The road runs along the Great Wall.

Fig. 4.121: (above) All clear above-ground remains of Fort 28 have vanished, powerfully demonstrating the threat modern agriculture poses to the Great Wall (along the track in the foreground, with Fort 28 once abutting it in the south, middle-ground).

Fig. 4.122: (right) Fort 28 on CORONA satellite imagery of 1969 (courtesy of the USGS), then still prominently surviving, with two barrack mounds in the interior, a moat and what appears to be extramural settlement. Note also a rectangular enclosure (GWS-65) north of the wall and north-east of Fort 28 (top, right), potentially a fort but in a most unusual position and unlikely to be contemporary with Fort 28.

Fig. 4.123: Fort 29, once filled with six barracks (i.e. three long double-barracks) was probably the strongest fort along the western Gorgan Wall (left, foreground, to centre, background), excluding any potential forts west of Fort 33 concealed under marine sediments. Evidently affected by ploughing, one can still make out the long mounds in the interior and the towered outer walls.

Fig. 4.124: It is now no longer possible to see (as on CORONA imagery) that Fort 30 once contained two oblong barracks, but the four projecting tower mounds on the east side (right), not counting a possible fifth where the compound abuts the Gorgan Wall (top) still stand out. A central projection in the south (bottom) of the fort platform probably represents a gate.

Fig. 4.125: Scarcely recognisable now, the extent of Fort 31 matches more of less the field in the centre of the photo. The Great Wall runs along the road (top).

Fig. 4.126: Modern settlement has encroached on Fort 32 (in the field above and left of the cars). The road leads along the Gorgan Wall.

We are not aware of any evidence for the existence of Kiani's postulated Fort 3, and the distance between Forts 2A and 4, of c. 10 km, is significantly greater than that between any other two forts on the lowland section of the Great Wall. (This is based on the assumption that Qizlar Qal'eh functioned as a fort; if not, Forts 29 and 30 are similarly far apart.[201]) Fort 4 had to guard a longer stretch of wall than any other single fort. It was between two vulnerable river crossings and probably intended to send reinforcement to either, in case of any enemy attempts to breach the wall following these unsealable water courses. This may explain why Fort 4 is the largest on the Great Wall and the only fort to contain as many as eight barracks. Forts 5 and 5A frame the point where the wall crosses the Kal Aji River. Fort 5A is unique on the Great Wall in being essentially a promontory fort, with artificial defences on one side only. There are no clear traces of barrack mounds in Fort 5A, and we do not know if it was ever completed and permanently occupied. Its barracks may have been erased by the plough or never existed. Even assuming it never contained permanent housing (and the case is neither proven nor disproven), it was clearly capable of providing a safe and well-defended campsite for troops whenever required.

Forts 6, 7, 8 and 9[202] all abut a largely straight, 20 km-long section of the Great Wall, and the drone images impressively visualise the evident 'military precision' in planning, surveying and constructing the defensive barrier. Fort 10 still survives well despite urban sprawl. There is no evidence for the existence of postulated Fort 11.

Forts 12 and 13 form a unique pair, spaced as little as c. 200 m apart (edge to edge) or c. 400 m (centre to centre), roughly a twentieth and tenth respectively of the average distance between forts and much closer than any other two forts, even those framing two opposite sides of river valleys.[203] It is possible that there may have been a gate in the wall between the two forts. Clustering of fortifications and hollow-ways may add strength to the hypothesis,[204] though traces of the postulated gate remain elusive. Built of sought-after fired bricks, most of the Great Wall has been demolished to ground level, a fate probably shared by associated gates and towers. It is possible that Fort 13 was deliberately designed to incorporate the old settlement mound of Qaravol Tappeh in its north-east corner, as an elevated observation post abutting the Gorgan Wall on the side facing Fort 12 (and the gateway?). The reuse of old settlement mounds for defensive advantage and/or area surveillance in the Sasanian era has also been observed at Qizlar Qal'eh and the citadels of Qal'eh Gug A and Dasht Qal'eh.[205] Fort 13 boasts typical defences and projecting towers, as well as mud-brick structures in the interior,[206] but no traces of barrack mounds have been detected.

Further west, the Gorgan Wall, built in long straight alignments, is abutted by a series of forts, often degraded by ploughing, but with the main features still visible. Forts 15 and 17 are placed next to stream crossings, and Fort 15, with four barracks, is the strongest in the area; Forts 14, 16, 17 and 18 only contain the usual two barracks each. Near Fort 14 there are two square forts, one south and one north of the wall, and near Fort 17 there is a third and there are further similar installations further west, including one near Fort 22. As none is on the Great Wall, contains barrack mounds or has produced any positive evidence so far for contemporary occupation, they are discussed in the context of the isolated forts on both sides of the wall.[207]

From Fort 19 westwards, the wall follows a more sinuous course, curving southwards and running roughly parallel to the Gorgan River from Forts 21 to 24. Preservation of forts is variable; Fort 20 is arguably the best preserved. Most other forts in this section have been affected by agriculture (Forts 19 and 23), flattening Fort 23's two barracks, or development (Forts 21, 22 and 24, the latter completely destroyed through settlement sprawl), and the drone photos tend to be less informative than the CORONA images of the 1960s. The oblique close-range pictures of Fort 22 show, however, more clearly than earlier satellite imagery that there were indeed two barracks, as we had assumed before.[208]

Forts 25 and 26 are of particular interest as individual room units are visible as soil marks, filling much of the interior of both forts.[209] The oblong mounds in the interior of Fort 25 suggest that there were originally four barracks of higher elevation than the annexes added later. Most forts further west have been heavily damaged, Fort 27 by extensive pit-digging; Fort 28 has been flattened;[210] Forts 29 and 30 have been degraded by agriculture, though some key features remain distinct. Fort 31 is little more than recognisable. Fort 32 has almost vanished. The outlines of Fort 33 stand out prominently, though it is dissected by a road and without clear traces of internal structures and little surviving of the defences. Old reports consider Gomish Tappeh a fort on the Great Wall, but our research indicates that the wall runs 2 km north of this large and complex settlement (without any remains of a fort identified to date).[211] The existence of

Fig. 4.127: Fort 33, diagonally dissected by a modern road, with the Great Wall (foreground, centre/right to middle-ground, centre) running west towards the Caspian Sea, whose shore is currently c. 18 km WSW of the fort. This is the westernmost known fort on the Gorgan Wall, but it is a near certainty that there are remains of further forts, now buried under post-Sasanian marine sediments.

Fig. 4.128: Old unconfirmed reports consider Gomish Tappeh (seen from the north), c. 12 km south-west of Fort 33, a fort on the wall as well as a harbour town.

Table 4.33: Number of barracks per fort, excluding forts along the eastern extension (which are all too poorly preserved for the identification of any potential barracks), as well as any still to be discovered, concealed under marine sediments, in the westernmost section.

Kiani's Forts, with additions	Barrack mounds of c. 80–130 m length (if c. 200 m long, counted as 2) visible on CORONA, Google Earth and drone images. Numbers marked with an asterisk (*) are those where the number of certain and/or postulated barracks differs from the numbers previously published.[1]	Orientation to the Great Wall
1	4	perpendicular
2	2	perpendicular
2A	potential faint traces: 2?	parallel?
3	no fort	n/a
4	8	perpendicular
5A?	none visible: 2?* [or empty?]	unknown
5	2*	parallel
6	2*	perpendicular
7	2*	perpendicular
8	2*	perpendicular
9	2	perpendicular
10	2	perpendicular
11	no fort	n/a
12	6	parallel
13	none visible: 4? [or other buildings?]	unknown
14	2	perpendicular
15	4	perpendicular
16	2	perpendicular
17	2*	perpendicular
18	2*	perpendicular
19	none visible: 2?	unknown
20	2	perpendicular
21	2	perpendicular
22	2*	perpendicular
23	2*	perpendicular
24	none visible: 2?	unknown
25	4	perpendicular
26	2*	perpendicular
27	4*	perpendicular
28	2	perpendicular
29	6*	perpendicular
Qizlar Qal'eh?	none visible: 2? [or other buildings?]	unknown
30	2*	perpendicular
31	none visible: 2?	unknown
32	none visible: 2?	unknown
33	none visible: 2?	unknown
Total	c. 92* [Incl. the likely holding capacity of forts without evidence for barracks.]	parallel: in 2 or 3 forts perpendicular: in 23 forts unknown: in 8 or 9 forts

[1] Sauer *et al.* 2013, 232 table 6:8. All changes to this table are marked with an asterisk (whether or not already corrected in Sauer *et al.* 2020e).

more than one branch of wall is, however, possible.[212] There may have been a medieval harbour here, but in Sasanian times the shoreline and any harbour must have been further west.[213]

The drone survey has created an invaluable record of the current preservation of the forts along the Great Wall, as well as adding new information on the interior structures and defences of some forts. Together with a re-examination of the satellite imagery, it has also allowed us to identify securely barracks at more forts than has been possible before, though by and large our earlier findings and estimates have been proven to be correct.

PS: We understand that, contrary to the hypotheses presented above (in chapters 4.1.4.4.2.2, 4.1.4.4.3.2 and 4.1.4.6.1), archaeomagnetic dates for ovens d.010 and d.169 need not relate to their latest use. Repeated reheating at similar or lower temperatures would not be detectable (Cathy Batt, pers. comm.). If the *termini ante quos* of AD 531 and AD 520 relate to any stage of oven use, they are compatible with other dating evidence, which indicates that installation of these two ovens of phase 3 may well have preceded these dates, but that they may have remained in use for perhaps up to a few decades beyond.

Notes

1. Wilkinson *et al.* 2013, 60–65.
2. Key points of the geophysics grid are as follows: SW: 0 m E/0 m N = 40S E 0369196, N 4151390, 204 mt; SE: 180 m E/0 m N = 40S E 0369374, N 4151419, 204 mt; NE: 180 m E/90 m N = 40S E 0369361, N 4151507, 205 mt; NW: 0 m E/90 m N = 40S E 0369184, N 4151478, 203 mt. The machine used was a Geometrics Magnetometer G-858. A 60 × 60 m area in the centre of the fort was re-surveyed in 2015 by Mohammad Arman Ershadi, Julian Jansen Van Rensburg and Mohammad Taghi Maleka. The results were processed by them and Roger Ainslie. This survey, in wet conditions, showed the central road across the fort quite clearly, but revealed nothing of significance that had not already been detected in 2014.
3. Sauer *et al.* 2013, 179 fig. 6:2, 184, 681 pl. 6:4.
4. See chapters 8 and 9.
5. See chapters 4.1.4.2.3 and 8.3.1.
6. Riesch 2017, 120–21.
7. Dr Christophe Benech, pers. comm., 3 March 2015. Prior to excavation, it seemed tempting to think that these are walls with arrow-slots, as frequently found in Sasanian defensive architecture, such as Tureng Tappeh. This Sasanian fort in the hinterland of the Gorgan Wall boasted projecting towers of 5 to 7 m diameter, with arrow-slots spaced at c. 1 m intervals and covering all angles. At Tureng Tappeh, the slots were only 13–20 cm wide, even if of substantial height: Boucharlat and Lecomte 1987, 32 fig. 7, 34, 36–37, 47–48 figs 8–10, pls 7–8, 12, 17, 20–21, 23, 109, 112–16. It is unlikely that any arrow-slots would have been much wider at Fort 2 than at Tureng Tappeh, since narrow slots offered greater protection. They enabled bowmen to discharge arrows from the safe interior of the towers to attack and deter assailants, without giving enemy archers a realistic chance to retaliate. Not just the narrowness (unless later widened through erosion) rules out an explanation of the anomalies as walls pierced with slots. More importantly, excavation (see section 4.1.3) has demonstrated that walls do not survive to the level at which one would expect slots. This neither proves nor disproves that they once existed, but suggests that no detectable remains of any slots survive at Fort 2.
8. See section 4.1.3 below. Prior to excavation, we had wondered if these positive magnetic anomalies were the result of fires lit inside the towers by their garrisons for heating and/or cooking, magnetic occupation debris accumulating inside or slow accumulation of waterborne sediments, e.g. liquid mud being washed into the interior as a result of the disintegration of mud-brick walls. No traces of fire exposure were, however, detected during subsequent excavation of Trench c. Furthermore, the magnetisation of the semi-circles is remarkably uniform and there is a band of similarly uniform magnetisation on the inside of the fort, notably along its southern wall (probably in the area of the wall-walk). Fires would not have caused such a regular effect.
9. For relevant aerial photos of Fort 7, see chapter 4.6.3 with Fig. 4.102 and Sauer *et al.* 2019, 135 fig. 9; cf. 2013, cover and pl. 6:1 and 2020e, 87 fig. 6.10 for satellite imagery of Fort 7 showing the corner bastions, but less clearly.
10. See chapter 3.2.6.
11. Sauer *et al.* 2013, 180 fig. 6:3, 184–85, 679 pl. 6:2.
12. Amin Pour 2012, 356 fig. 7; Sauer *et al.* 2013, 165 fig. 5:12, 677 pl. 5:3.
13. Sauer *et al.* 2013, 223–27 with figs 6:40–6:42, 684 pl. 6:11. We have argued that at the Bansaran Fort, near the Tammisheh Wall, there might have been an earth or mud-brick wall faced with fired bricks on both sides (Sauer *et al.* 2013, 275–76 with fig. 9:3, 688 pl. 9:2). Such a fort wall would, however, be without parallel so far in the area. The hypothesis is based on geophysics only and should be considered no more than a possibility unless and until verified by excavation.
14. Sauer *et al.* 2013, 218 with fig. 6:35, 220–21 with fig. 6:38.
15. Sauer *et al.* 2013, 182–84 with fig. 6:6, 680 pl. 6:3.
16. See chapter 4.1.4.
17. See Figs 4.1, 4.7 and 4.96 (tower mounds at Fort 2), 4.98 (Fort 4), 4.102 (Fort 7), 4.108 (Fort 14), 4.120 (Fort 27) and 4.124 (Fort 30). See chapter 4.6.3, *passim* for other less distinct photos of tower mounds along fort platform edges. The towers of Forts 2 and 14 are also clearly visible on the CORONA images (see Fig. 4.2 and Sauer *et al.* 2020e, 87 fig. 6.10).
18. Kiani 1982b, 19, fig. 10: tower c. 6 m wide and projecting c. 4.50 m. N.b. the scale is incorrect; but the distances alongside trenches appear to be correct. Cf. *ibid.*, fig. 12; *id.* 1982a, 76 fig. 2, pl. Ib. The tower in our Trench c was c. 7 m wide, with a 5.50 m projection: see chapter 4.1.3.
19. See Sauer *et al.* 2013, 223–27, 684 pl. 6:11.
20. The coordinates of Trench c were as follows (magnetometer survey grid coordinates followed by UTM, taken with a handheld GPS): SW: 54 m E/14 m N = 40S E 0369249, N 4151413, 200 mt; SE: 64 m E/14 m N = 40S E 0369259, N 4151414, 200 mt; NW: 54 m E/24 m N = 40S E 0369247, N 4151420, 203 mt; NE: 64 m E/24 m N = 40S E 0369256, N 4151423, 206 mt (height measurement unreliable).
21. Boucharlat and Lecomte 1987, *passim*, e.g. 26 fig. 5, pls 7–9.
22. At 0.36 m E, 5.26 m N, 97.02 m site height. See chapter 18.4.
23. The successful excavation of the complex mud-brick architecture of the trench owes much to Esmail Safari Tamak's unrivalled skills in the difficult task of unearthing such remains, often only revealed through higher compaction, and supervising the workmen in doing so. The trench team furthermore comprised Lana Chologauri, Ana Gabunia, Eve MacDonald and Mohadesseh Malekan, as well as temporarily the project directors, Bardia Shabani, Baygeldi Arteghi, Mohammad Mehdi Borhani, Claudia Caldeira, David Gagoshidze, Davit Naskidashvili and

others. The diligent recording of the contexts is the result of their joint efforts. Drawings were accomplished by Maryam Hossein-Zadeh and her team. They were subsequently edited and transformed into phase plans by Dr Silvia Perini, in collaboration with EWS.

24 Kiani 1982b, 19–22, figs 3, 10, 12–15, pls 4.2–4.3, 6–8; 1982a, 75–76, fig. 2, pls Ib, III.
25 The coordinates of the corner points of the Trench d by the end of the 2015 season were as follows: SW: 102 m E/48 m N; corner point: 112 m E/48 m N; corner point: 112 m E/54 m N; SE: 126 m E/54 m N; NE: 126 m E/56 m N; NW: 102 m E/56 m N. Measurements are in relation to the geophysical survey (see Figs 4.4–4.5).
26 The coordinates of the corner points of the extended Trench d by the end of the 2016 season were as follows: SW: 95 m E/48 m N; corner point: 126 m E/48 m N; corner point: 126 m E/54 m N; corner point: 129 m E/54 m N; NE: 129 m E/56 m N; NW: 95 m E/56 m N. Measurements are in relation to the geophysical survey (see Figs 4.4–4.5).
27 See Sauer *et al.* 2013, 193–94. Some of Trench J may have been covered by annexes (see chapter 4.1.4.2.3), but not all; all of Trench J will at least initially have been outdoors.
28 See chapter 18.9.
29 See chapters 4.1.4.4.1.1–4.1.4.4.1.2 for a detailed description and plans of these features.
30 See chapters 4.2–4.4 and 4.6.3 on Forts 15, 25 and 26.
31 See chapter 4.1.4.4.2.1 for a detailed description and plans of the storage jars in the area of the doorway.
32 See Sauer *et al.* 2013, 185–99, esp. 194.
33 Sauer *et al.* 2013, 679–80 pls 6:2–6:3.
34 Sauer *et al.* 2013, 178–89, 679–81 pls 6:2–6:4.
35 Sauer *et al.* 2013, 186 fig. 6:10, 188–89 with figs 6:14–6:15, cf. 680–81 pls 6:3–6:4 for the location of Trench H (in the barracks north-east of the central road and in the row of rooms on the side opposite to the central road).
36 See chapters 4.2–4.4.
37 See chapter 4.3.
38 See chapter 4.1.4.2.3.
39 Trench c has provided us with a clear idea of the plan of a tower and the width (or at least minimum width) of the fort walls. Models hypothesizing how many bricks would have been required for the towered walls were attempted, but seemed too speculative to merit publication. There are too many unknown variables: e.g. up to what height walls and towers were solid, from what height upwards towers may have contained chambers, what their overall height was etc.
40 Sauer *et al.* 2013, 144 table 4.2; cf. chapter 3.1 for a correction of the length estimate of the wall.
41 Aliev *et al.* 2006, 154, 156; Gadjiev 2017a.
42 See Sauer *et al.* 2013, 157, 255–56.
43 See Table 4.33 (cf. Sauer *et al.* 2013, 232 table 6.8) for the number of barracks per fort.
44 See Sauer *et al.* 2013, 180, 194, figs 6:3–6:4, 679 pl. 6:2.
45 See chapter 15.4.2.2.
46 Sauer *et al.* 2013, 194–99, 230–34.
47 See chapter 7.2.4.11.
48 See chapter 15.4.2.3, especially Table 15.6 (based on MNV, not sherd count, as some vessels were heavily fragmented). The assemblage from the annexe rooms was less dominant in some other vessel types.
49 See chapter 16.
50 See chapter 4.1.4.5.1.
51 See chapters 4.1.4.5.3 and 20.3.1.
52 See chapter 18.3.5.
53 For forts with tower spacing of approximately 30 m/100 feet (centre to centre) or with a side length of this distance or multiples thereof, see Al-Jahwari *et al.* 2018; Gadjiev 2008a, 31–32; Naumann 1977, suppl. plan 2, cf. 34–38; and Sauer *et al.* 2013, 184, 230; see also Gregory 1997a, 74–75, figs 3.60–3.61; Sauer in Priestman *et al.* 2022; and Whitehouse 1971, 265 fig. 2 and 2009, 10–11. For late Roman forts on the Anastasian Wall, it has been argued too that they employed multiples on 100 feet, if in this case 100 × 200 feet (Crow and Ricci 1997, 250–51 with fig. 9; Schuchhardt 1901, 112 with figs 5–6). Note, however, that there is a wide range of variations, e.g. in tower spacing, at campaign bases (see chapter 8.5), and towers on the Ghilghilchay Wall were spaced at a range of intervals, 38–40 m centre to centre, being the most common (Aliev *et al.* 2006, 156–59 with table 1). See also Bivar 2010 on the foot as a unit of measurement. See chapters 4.1.2.1 and 8.3.1 for further discussion.
54 It is perhaps prudent not to include the postulated length of the barracks in Forts 15 and 26 into our model unless and until verified by excavation.
55 See also Bivar 2010 on units of measurement in pre-Islamic Persia.
56 Wilkinson *et al.* 2013, 82 table 3:4; see also chapter 2.5 for further, if unfortunately inconclusive, survey of possible extramural settlement at Forts 2, 12, 13 and 16 and the somewhat more successful survey at Fort 28 (cf. chapters 4.5 and 4.6.3).
57 See chapter 4.1.4.5.2.2.
58 See Sauer *et al.* 2019 and 2020e and chapter 4.6.3 for the visual evidence.
59 See chapter 7 for some examples and further reading.
60 Oates 2005, 82–85; Sauer *et al.* 2013, 235–36.
61 Sauer *et al.* 2013, 223–27, 684 pl. 6:11.
62 See chapter 4.4.
63 See chapter 4.3.
64 See chapter 4.3.
65 See Sauer *et al.* 2013, 180 figs 6:3–6:4, 679 pl. 6:2.
66 Sauer *et al.* 2013, 185–215, 680–81 pls 6:3–6:4, 682–83 pls 6:6–6:7.
67 See chapter 4.2.
68 See chapter 4.1.4.6.
69 Radiocarbon dates kindly supplied by the Scottish Universities Environmental Research Centre (SUERC) and the Poznan Radiocarbon Laboratory. Bones were identified by Homa Fathi and Dr Marjan Mashkour. For archaeomagnetic dates, by Dr Cathy M. Batt, David Greenwood and Tehreem Kainaat, see chapter 22.
70 See chapter 18.9.
71 Differences in colour and composition between different deposits/spits tended to be indistinct and context boundaries diffuse, so that sequencing involves an element of subjective judgement and a risk of errors over an area as large as Trench d. It may, however, be possible to create more complex models, as some sequencing, e.g. the floor across all rooms being raised before new ovens were created in phase 3, seems secure.

72 See chapter 21, Table 21.3 for these archaeobotanic finds from this room and other rooms and areas in Trench d, as well as the other trenches; cf. Table 21.1 for charcoal samples.
73 As indicated, the quantities of bulk finds, notably pottery, in this and subsequent tables often differ from those cited in chapter 15, where only securely identified pottery is counted. By contrast, in this chapter we cite consistently quantities specified by the finds processing team after recovery. Citing both figures would have resulted in much confusion and there is no certain way to determine which weight is more accurate in each and every case.
74 See chapter 4.1.4.2.
75 Omel'chienko 2016, especially 81–82, 97 fig. 8, 99 figs 10.1–2. See also Kaim 2018, 455–56 with fig. II on benches lining walls at Merv.
76 See Herrmann *et al.* 2000, 4 on the archaeological traceability of dung fuel; see also chapters 21.1.4 and 21.2.3.3.
77 Wicke 2020, 466–67, 470, 475 fig. 5, 476 fig. 6, 478 fig. 9a–b.
78 It was found in the room 2C, at 12.20 m E, 5.94 m N and 99.01 m site height. See chapters 18.3.1 and 18.3.5 on these finds.
79 Sauer *et al.* 2013, 186–89.
80 See chapters 4.1.4.5.3 and 20.3.1 for further discussion.
81 See chapter 18.2.
82 See chapter 15.4.2.3 with Table 15.6.
83 See Tamm *et al.* 2018, 115 on heating and cooking in the small late Sasanian fortlet of Gird-i Kazhaw.
84 See chapters 4.1.4.5.3 and 20.3.1 for further discussion.
85 D.047 extended from the NE corner of the room 0.67 m west and 0.58 m south. At the corner, fire-reddening was observed from 98.55–98.84 m site height, penetrating c. 7 cm into the bricks.
86 See chapter 18.5.
87 It is far too shallow for a well, with the water table probably being at an extraordinary depth, perhaps of similar elevation as the Sari Su River. There is no waterproof lining as one might expect in case of a cistern, nor is there any evidence for standing water within, such as clay deposits, iron staining or greenish discoloration. The sharp edges of the round depression and slot at the base of the pit are further evidence that there was never standing water in the shaft.
88 Sauer *et al.* 2013, 200 fig. 6:22, 201 fig. 6:24, 206–09.
89 See chapter 4.1.4.2.3.
90 See Tables 4.28–4.29 for the data.
91 See chapter 4.1.4.3.
92 Johnson 1983, 166–76, with references; see Davison 1989, *passim*, e.g. 237–38 on storage pits not being confined to particular rooms.
93 See chapter 15.4.2.3 with Table 15.6.
94 See chapter 21.2.3.3.
95 Lordkipanidse 1991, 168. Kaim (2018, 457) cites the cooling effect of underfloor storage as an argument in favour of large jars containing liquids.
96 Cf. Simpson 2015b, 20–21.
97 See chapter 18.6. The Sasanian fort of Tureng Tappeh was provided with piped drainage, employing pipes of larger diameter: Boucharlat and Lecomte 1987, 27, 30–31 with fig. 6, pls 7, 20, 115b, 118a–19a. On the use of pipes in the Sasanian era, see also Mammadova and Hajiyeva 2013, 178; Sauer *et al.* 2020a, 166–71.
98 At 11.60 m E, 6.28 m N and 99.12 m site height.
99 It was found in room 1CS, between jars 6 and 9, but at a higher level, at 9.58 m E, 2.26 m N and 98.90 m site height: see chapter 18.5.
100 See chapter 7; cf. Sauer *et al.* 2013, 221, 227, 253, 275, 289, 291–92, 294, 322; Wilkinson *et al.* 2013, 124.
101 See chapter 21.1.3.2, Table 21.1.
102 See chapters 4.1.4.3, 4.1.4.4.3.2, 4.1.4.4.4 and 22.
103 Sauer *et al.* 2013, 200 fig. 6:22, 210; cf. chapter 4.1.4.2.3.
104 See chapter 4.1.4.4.2.1.
105 See chapter 4.1.4.4.3.2.
106 See chapter 4.1.4.4.3.2.
107 See also chapters 8.2.16, 9.2.2.1 and 18.2 with references.
108 See chapter 15.4.2.3 with Table 15.6.
109 See chapter 18.3.5.
110 See chapter 18.2.
111 See chapters 4.1.4.6.3 and 20.4.3.
112 See chapter 18.3.1.
113 See Table 4.28; this excludes the eastern outdoor area, as not within the barracks, and the corridor between rows 3 and 4, as the sample is small and hardly statistically viable.
114 See chapter 16.
115 Sauer *et al.* 2013, 201 fig. 6:24, 206–09.
116 See chapter 21.2.3.3.
117 See chapters 4.1.4.3 and 22.
118 Sauer *et al.* 2013, 200–01 figs 6:23–6:24; 206–09.
119 See chapter 4.1.4.5.2.1.
120 See Table 4.28; the corridor between rooms 3C and 4CS, with an even higher percentage of bone, forms an exception, but is small and the sample of finds may not be statistically viable.
121 See chapter 4.1.4.2.3 and Sauer *et al.* 2013, 200 fig. 6:22, 202 fig. 6:26, 209–10.
122 See chapters 4.1.4.5.3 and 20.3.1.
123 See chapter 15.4.2.3 with Table 15.6.
124 See chapter 18.3.5.
125 See chapters 4.1.4.4.1.1, 4.1.4.4.2.2, 4.1.4.4.3.2 and 21.2.3.3 and Table 21.1.
126 Sauer *et al.* 2013, 334–41.
127 Sauer *et al.* 2013, 200–01, 206–09.
128 Dunkel 1995; Franklin 2018, 79*; cf. Bossard 2019, 54–56. Pliny (*Naturalis historia* 18.306–07) and Varro (*De re rustica* 1.57.2) even claim that wheat could be stored for 50 years in underground pits.
129 See Sauer *et al.* 2013, 207 with examples and reference; see also previous note and Columella, *De re rustica* 1.6.83–86; Vigil-Escalera Guirado 2013. Poulter (2019, 55–58, 163–64) provides interesting parallels from the late Roman fort at Dichin.
130 Valls *et al.* 2015; Vigil-Escalera Guirado 2013, 132–34 with figs 7.8 and 7.10.
131 See chapter 4.1.4.3.
132 See chapter 4.1.4.6.2.
133 See chapter 15.4.2.3 with Table 15.6.
134 See chapter 4.1.4.4.2.1; cf. 21.2.3.3.
135 See chapter 4.1.4.5.1.
136 The vessels were spotted in 2007 and excavated at a later date (to avoid the risk of damage or loss due to agricultural activity or illegal digging), but we do not

know precisely when. There are photographs, but no plan or GPS measurement, but it should be easy to relocate the trench in future via topsoil stripping. The point as far as remembered was c. 30 m south of the northern fort edge/ Great Wall and c. 31 m east of the top of the western rampart ridge. It was c. 7 m south of the centre of the northernmost tower mound on the west side of the fort (not counting the postulated corner tower on the Great Wall). Plotted on the geophysics grid (Fig. 4.5), this would place the jars at c. 102 m north and 66 m east, i.e. the inner row of the western annexe of the western barracks. If correct, this may mean that there was no perfect (if any) symmetry in the arrangement of the jars and that they were not always on the road-facing side of the annexes. But it should be remembered that this is only an approximate location based on memory several years after excavations, and we cannot be sure in which room the vessels had been placed, though it seems very likely that they were from somewhere within the western complex of barracks plus annexes.

137 The rodent remains proved irrelevant to Sasanian chronology. The animal had perished in its burrow some 700–800 years after the fort's abandonment.
138 Sauer *et al.* 2013, 193–94 with fig. 6:21; Priestman 2013, 472 fig. 18:7.
139 Bouchariat and Lecomte 1987, 18–20, 22 table 5, 51, 72, 118–19, 197–98, pls 35, 132–33.
140 Baladhuri 336 = trans. Murgotten 1924, 42; Sauer *et al.* 2013, 4, 600–01.
141 See chapter 15.4.2.3 and 15.5.1. See, however, also Priestman 2013, 528–29 on the difficulties involved in trying to synchronise the ceramic chronologies of Tureng Tappeh and other Sasanian sites on the Gorgan Plain.
142 Altheim and Stiehl 1957, 7–8, 10–18, 35–49; Sárközy 2014, 707–09.
143 Tabari 1.960–63 = trans. Bosworth 1999, 255–62. See also Frye 1983, 153–54; Gariboldi 2015; Jackson Bonner 2011, 75–78; Lukonin 1983, 745–46.
144 We are grateful to Dr James Howard-Johnston for this valid observation.
145 Rizos 2015a and b; Sarantis 2019.
146 Sauer *et al.* 2013, 195; cf. Ammianus Marcellinus 23.6.83. Interestingly, the output of the Gorgan mint was relatively large for a frontier zone (Schindel 2015b, 123 table 6, 127–28), but coins were evidently not produced for paying frontier troops. See also chapter 18.7.
147 Noruzi *et al.* 2016.
148 See, for example, Ghasemi *et al.* 2020a, 279, 287; Khosrowzadeh *et al.* 2020, 224, 230; Whitcomb 1985, 94 fig. 30, 103, 111–17, 201–03 pls 35–39.
149 Sauer *et al.* 2013, 684 pl. 6:11.
150 Omel'chienko 2016, especially 81, 83, 85–86, 97 fig. 8, 98 fig. 9.2.
151 See chapter 20.3.1.
152 Note that the quantities are those initially recorded by the finds processing team and were taken prior to further analysis. They differ from those in chapters 15 and 20, recorded during analysis of the pottery and bone. We considered using only one set of data, but came to the conclusion that it was not always possible to explain discrepancies, even if often further cleaning or reclassification of initially falsely identified finds or the later misplacement of the odd finds bags may account for some of the difference. Both sets contain lacunae, but both appear to present a broadly accurate picture of the overall distribution, and we thus decided to keep the originally recorded data here.
153 See chapter 4.1.4.5.1.
154 See chapter 18.3.5.
155 See chapter 15.4.2.3 with Table 15.6.
156 See, in addition to this section, chapter 20.3.1.
157 See chapter 18.3.5.
158 See chapter 4.1.4.5.1.
159 On the spatial distribution of bone and pottery, see also chapters 15.4.2.3 and 20.3.1.
160 See chapter 18.9.
161 See chapter 4.1.4.3 with Table 4.8 and Figs 4.20–4.26.
162 Sauer *et al.* 2013, 192 table 6:1 and fig. 6:20, 212 table 6:4 and fig. 6:30.
163 See chapters 3.1 and 5.1.
164 See chapter 24.4 for further discussion of forts overlying kilns and the question whether some forts may be later additions.
165 See chapters 7 and 8.
166 See Table 4.8 above for the modelled dates from Fort 2. Sequencing of samples has not been attempted for the samples from Fort 4. The samples from Trench H came from bulk levelling horizons and most of the samples from Trench J from the secondary bulk fill of the two pits and a gully. This makes it impossible to establish a secure sequence for most samples from these trenches in Fort 4.
167 For the pits and samples from Trench J in Fort 4, see Sauer *et al.* 2013, 200–01, 206–09, 211–15.
168 See chapter 4.1.4.5.2.1.
169 See chapter 7.2.
170 See chapter 3.1.
171 See chapter 24.8.
172 See chapter 20.4.3; see also chapters 4.1.4.3 and 4.1.4.4.3.2.
173 See chapter 15.3.4.2.2.
174 Sauer *et al.* 2013, 233; 2020e, 83, 86 with fig. 6.9, 92; see also chapter 4.4.
175 Sauer *et al.* 2013, 178, 180 figs 6:3–6:4, 679–81 pls 6:2–6:4.
176 See chapter 4.1.
177 See chapter 4.6.3; cf. Sauer *et al.* 2020e, 87 fig. 6.11.
178 Sauer *et al.* 2013, 679–81 pls 6:2–6:4.
179 We had thought from the start, after first spotting this phenomenon, that this pattern was probably the result of barracks having been exposed through earth-moving operations: Sauer *et al.* 2013, 233. When presenting a lecture on this on 10 January 2014, Dr Jason Ur and Dr Dan Lawrence agreed and suggested that robber pits could have been dug within the room units (cf. Sauer *et al.* 2020e, 83, 86 with fig. 6.9, 92). In the light of our field observations since, it now seems more likely that subsidence is mainly responsible for the phenomenon.
180 See chapter 4.6.3.
181 Information by Dr Jebrael Nokandeh.
182 As suggested by Hamid Omrani Rekavandi.
183 See chapters 4.1.4.4.4.2 and 7 with references; Sauer *et al.* 2013, 322 with fig. 12:17.
184 Sauer *et al.* 2013, 232 table 6:8, 233.
185 See chapter 7.2.

186 Magnetometer survey carried out by Mohammad Arman Ershadi, Julian Jansen Van Rensburg and Mohammad Taghi Maleka. Results processed by Roger Ainslie, Mohammad Arman Ershadi and Julian Jansen Van Rensburg.
187 See also chapters 2.5 and 4.6.3 on this site.
188 See chapter 4.6.3 for drone images of round burial enclosures on Forts 4, 5, 7, 9, 10 and 17; cf. Sauer *et al.* 2013, 182–84 with fig. 6:6, 680–81 pls 6:2–6:3 on such a circular enclosure at Fort 4; see chapter 4.1.2.2 for a further possible parallel at Fort 2.
189 See chapter 7.4.
190 Sauer *et al.* 2019; 2020d; Naskidashvili *et al.* 2019.
191 See chapters 4.2–4.4.
192 Sauer *et al.* 2013, 230–34; 2020e.
193 Sauer *et al.* 2020e.
194 See chapters 4.2 and 4.4.
195 Sauer *et al.* 2013, 220–21, 232 table 6:8, pl. 6:10; 2020e, 90, 92.
196 Sauer *et al.* 2020e, 87 fig. 6.10.
197 Wilkinson *et al.* 2013, 80–82 with table 3:4; Sauer *et al.* 2013, 313 fig. 12:9.
198 Wilkinson *et al.* 2013, 64 fig. 3:42, 66; it is thought to be potentially as large as 4–5 ha, making it, if correct, by far the largest on the eastern extension of the wall. It may be on a terrace south of the Gorgan River and, most unusually, abut the wall on the enemy side. No images are reproduced here as no clear archaeological features were visible from the air.
199 Nokandeh *et al.* 2012, ۳۷۴–۳۷۷/374–77 [288–91].
200 Wilkinson *et al.* 2013, 60–63 with figs 3:37–3:41; cf. chapter 3.2.
201 Kiani 1982b, 15 fig. 9, general map, figs 1–8b; Sauer *et al.* 2013, 227–30.
202 See also Amin Pour 2012, 356 fig. 7 for a complete geophysical survey of Fort 9, showing clearly the Great Wall, the fort platform and two possible brick kilns underneath.
203 Average spacing c. 4,200 m from the centre-point of the wall-facing side of one fort to the next (Kiani 1982b, 15 fig. 9: c. 137 km split into 33 intervals, from Fort -1 on the Pishkamar Rocks to Fort 33; our figures: c. 144 km for the same distance, based on Google Earth distances, split into 34 intervals, omitting Forts 3 and 11 and adding Forts 2A and 5A and Qizlar Qal'eh).
204 Hopper 2017a, 134–38; Sauer *et al.* 2013, 20 no. 12, 234; 2020e, 89–90. See also chapter 2.5.
205 Sauer *et al.* 2013, 227–30, 357, 364, 400–01.
206 Kiani 1982b, 17–21, figs 12–14, pls 4–8.
207 See chapters 2.3.2–2.3.3 and 7.1.
208 See Sauer *et al.* 2020e, 87 fig. 6.10 and 2013, 232 table 6:8 on Forts 22 and 23.
209 See chapter 4.3–4.4.
210 See also chapters 2.5 and 4.5.
211 See chapters 11 and 13.
212 See chapter 11 with Fig. 11.10; cf. Sauer *et al.* 2013, 268, 271 no. 86, 272 no. 109, 636, 644 no. 71.
213 Sauer *et al.* 2013, 11–12, 14, 17–18, 21–23, 149, 152–54, 177, 234, 256, 265, 271–72, 305, 601–02, 630–36, 639–45, 647, with sources; cf. Hopper and Omrani Rekavandi 2020, 101–03; Jansen Van Rensburg *et al.* 2013, 430, 432 and chapters 11 and 13; Al-Muqaddasi 358 = trans. Collins 1994, 315–16; *Hudud al-'Alam* 32.5 = trans. Minorsky 1937, 133, cf. 386.

5

The Tammisheh Wall and associated forts

5.1. Introduction

Less fieldwork than in the first phase of the joint project[1] has focused on the Tammisheh Wall, a defensive barrier of similar architecture and chronology to the Gorgan Wall, but perhaps more speedily completed due to it being much shorter. Its location at the easternmost point of a narrow stretch of the Caspian coastal plain, along or close to the provincial boundary between Parishwargar in the west and Gorgan in the east,[2] was ideal for protecting the fertile coastal plain from incursions from the east that may have penetrated the Gorgan Wall (or perhaps any prior to its completion). It could also have shielded the Gorgan Plain from any invasions from the west, e.g. from across the Caucasus. This chapter summarises the results of our aerial and pedestrian surveys and diving operations. A sonar survey of the wall's submerged remains, tracing the wall further north and extending its known length to a little over 12 km (or close to 14 km, including 1.5 km of ditch in the south), and a study of the palaeo-environments near the wall terminals feature in a separate section.[3] The main focus of this chapter is our survey of the submerged fort in the Caspian Sea.[4]

In order to facilitate comparison with radiocarbon dates cited in other chapters of the report, we have also recalibrated radiocarbon samples from the first phase of the

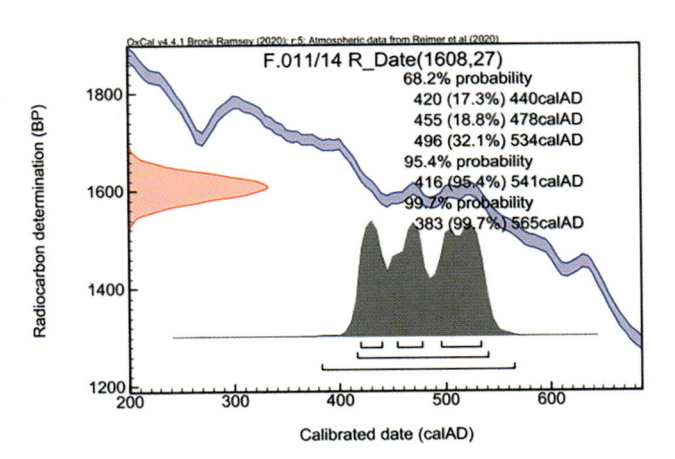

Fig. 5.1: Recalibration of a charcoal sample of fuel used in the kiln in Trench F on the Tammisheh Wall. It dates at 95.4% probability to c. AD 416–541.

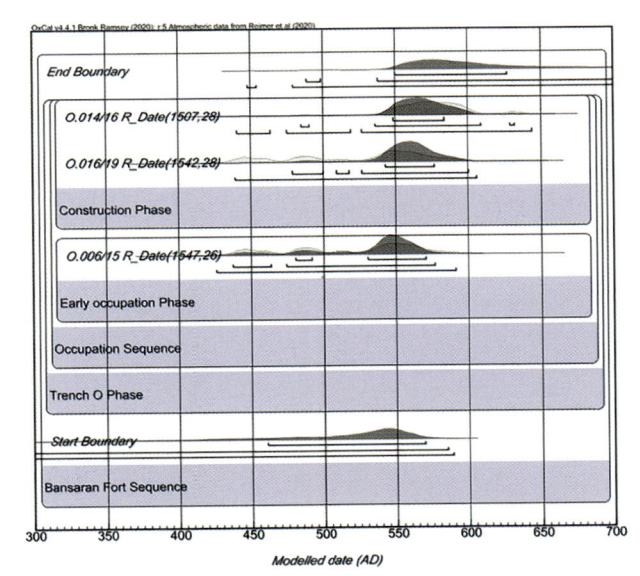

Fig. 5.2: Recalibration and model of three charcoal samples from Trench O in the Bansaran Fort. A sample (O.006/15) from an early occupation horizon dates at 95.4% probability to c. AD 433–588 (modelled date: 437–576; 87.3%: 474–576). One sample (O.016/19) from construction levels dates to c. AD 433–595 (modelled date: 479–600; 90.7%: 527–600), another (O.014/16), to c. AD 444–641 (modelled date: 485–632; 94.1%: 485–609; 94.6%: 536–632).

project using the latest version of the OxCal programme. This has only marginally changed the likely date range for a sample from a brick kiln excavated in Trench F on the Tammisheh Wall.[5] Perhaps more significantly, recalibration of three samples from Trench O in the Bansaran Fort[6] near the Tammisheh Wall has confirmed that it was occupied from the fifth and/or sixth century onwards. The construction of a pillared hall within the fort arguably also occurred in the Sasanian era, probably between the AD 530s and 600. Pillared halls were also erected at other Sasanian sites.[7] This tentative model assumes that the charcoal embedded in construction-related deposits is from fuel burnt at the time the hall was built. If the charcoal was embedded in redeposited soil from earlier occupation horizons, then we cannot be sure that the latter two samples are later than that from the early occupation levels. In this case, all three samples provide fifth-century *termini post quos*, and we cannot rule out that the hall might be post-Sasanian. That all three samples are without doubt of the mid- or late Sasanian era is, however, beyond doubt, suggesting that this was the main occupation phase of the fort.

5.2. Underwater survey of a submerged fort

Previous archaeological diving operations have established that the Tammisheh Wall runs into terrain that is today submerged under the waters of the Caspian Sea, but will have been dry land in the Sasanian era when the water table was much lower than it is today. An area of shallow water abutting the wall was identified as a probable submerged fort.[8] In 2014 further diving operations by Francesco Caputo and Davoud Taji, supported by Hamid Omrani Rekavandi and Bardia Shabani, aimed at further exploration of the submerged wall with the aim of quantifying the brick in the Tammisheh Wall's rubble heap. They also accomplished, jointly with Mohammad Bagher Bayati and Andrea Ricci, a topographical survey (Fig. 5.4) of the submerged platform thought to represent the fort. The water table in the Caspian Sea had dropped substantially since our surveys in 2007, 2008 and 2009, and tends to be lower in late autumn and winter than in summer,[9] so that the highest point of the platform, with its dense concentration of brick rubble on the surface, was now above the water. Even the deeper parts of the platform were covered by no more than about a metre of water. This facilitated surveying considerably, even if visibility under water was no better than it had been in the previous seasons.

We thought that, if it was possible to find a section of the submerged and collapsed wall not affected by robbing, then the quantity of bricks in the rubble heap should provide clues as to the weight of bricks used in any section of the wall and to the height of the wall. Local people have reportedly robbed brick from the submerged section of the Tammisheh Wall within living memory, but

Fig. 5.3: Topographical survey of the submerged fort in the Caspian Sea in progress on 28 November 2014. Due to the low water table, the fort platform was at a shallow depth and in places above water. Note the scatter of bricks in the foreground, which cover much of the platform.

it is not known where exactly. In our endeavour to gain insights into the likely quantity of bricks used, it thus seemed prudent not to focus our brick weighing survey on an area near the coast, where there was a risk of recovering an unrepresentative small sample. We eventually marked out a transect running from UTM 40S E 0233977, N 4078339 to UTM 40S E 0234048, N4078351, via UTM 40S E 0234007, N 4078343. The actual weighing exercise focused on the area of detectable brick scatter within the first four 2 × 2 m grids between the latter two points.[10] This survey line was in a similar location and alignment to a previous diving survey.[11] Additional diving transects further north proved barren.[12] Our divers also re-examined the rock alignment west of the wall, consisting of large dressed stones. The subsequent sonar survey by Richard Bates in 2015 established that this is likely to be a modern feature, perhaps to protect a pipeline or a cable (and not an ancient breakwater as hypothesised before).[13]

The diving team recovered 117 kg of bricks from the first (westernmost) 2 × 2 m grid along the survey line, 144 kg from a second grid, 50 kg from the third grid and 74 kg from the fourth grid (i.e. 385 kg in total). These were the bricks that could easily be lifted. More bricks seemed firmly stuck in sediments in some grids and could not be recovered. To test how many, if any, bricks were buried too deeply for easy recovery, the team dug the fourth grid to c. 40 cm depth, but found no more bricks. Each course of bricks of each 2 m long section of the wall should have employed 25 bricks of c. 500 kg combined weight, and a 2 m long section across a solid 2 m wide wall, of an estimated height of 80 courses (c. 8.80 m), should have yielded 40 tons of bricks,[14] even if considerably less in single squares. The material recovered from the four grids is astonishingly small in quantity and would not even have sufficed for a single course of wall. Of course, the

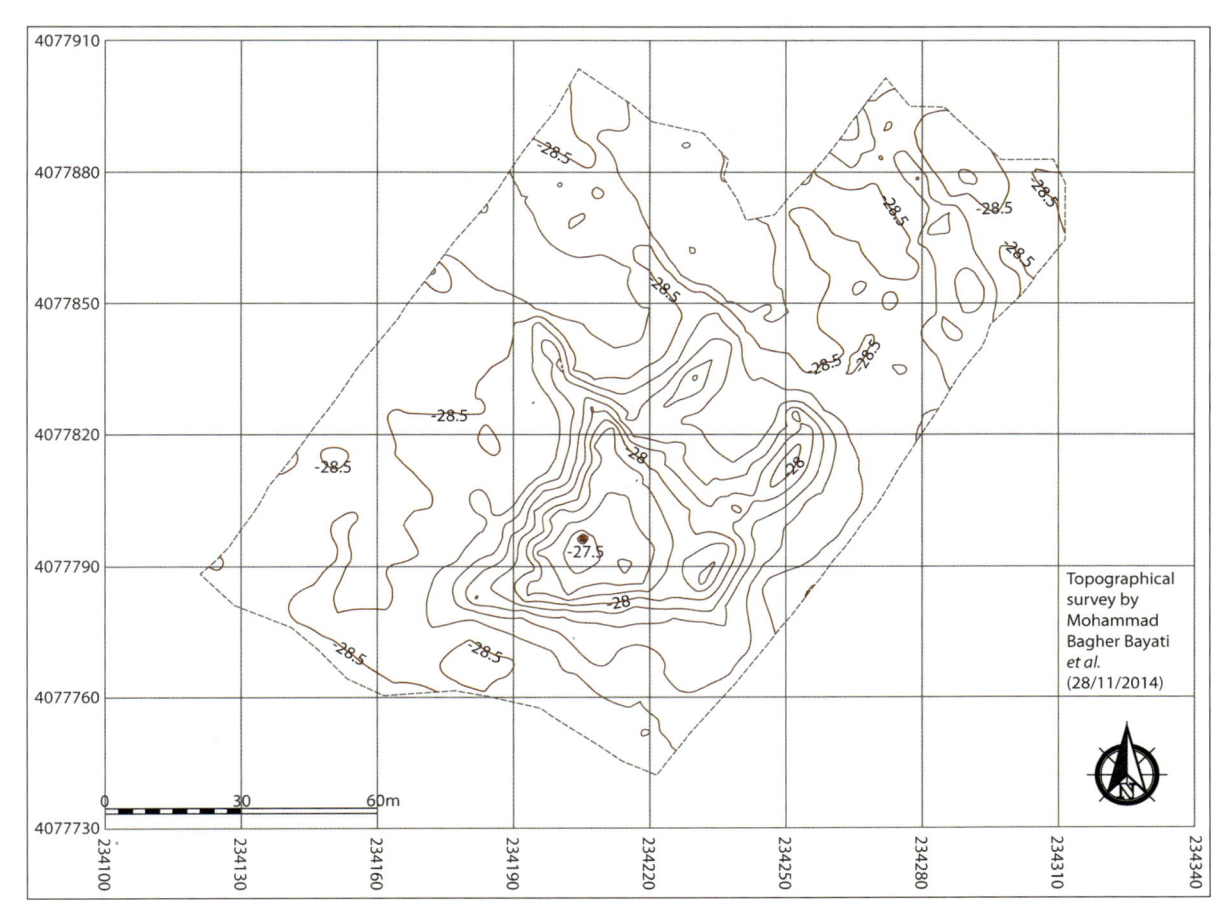

Fig. 5.4: Topographical survey of a probable submerged fort in the Caspian Sea by Mohammad Bagher Bayati, Francesco Caputo, Andrea Ricci et al. Note that relative heights are accurate, but absolute heights only approximate, but the error is likely to be under half a metre: a small heap of bricks on the platform was a few centimetres above the water table (at c. 27.47 m on the day of the survey).

weighing exercise covered only 8 × 2 m of the rubble heap and, especially in the light of the surprisingly variable number of bricks per grid, it is impossible to estimate how many bricks a complete transect may have yielded. Even allowing for as low as a 10 % recovery rate, the bricks would not even have sufficed for building a brick-faced earthwork of a noteworthy height. In all probability, unless there is indeed much further brick covered by a sterile layer of sediments, the wall had been heavily robbed at the point of our survey – probably at a time when the water table was much lower than it is today. Perhaps we should have anticipated this, bearing in mind that there were times when the now submerged section of the wall was on dry land and times when it was in shallow water and its sought-after bricks could easily have been salvaged. At such times, the collapsed wall will initially have formed a substantial bank all local people will have been well aware of until this source of high-quality building material had been exhausted.

Our topographical survey (Fig. 5.4) of the submerged postulated fort yielded interesting results, though not as clear as we had hoped. The submerged fort mound's dimensions (roughly 60 m north-west to south-east by 80 m south-west to north-east) correspond roughly to the area of shallow water seen on a CORONA satellite image, even if the latter suggests perhaps that it was a little larger.[15] These dimensions are approximate, however, as it is hard to be certain where on the shallow platform the fort walls would have been. Two linear ridges in the north-east of the platform are thought to be part of it. It is possible that surveying along a small number of parallel lines inadequately covered the area and gives the false impression that ridges and slopes are more rectilinear, and appear more parallel to the survey lines and to each other than they are in reality. This may also account in part at least for the sides of the platform not being parallel to its equivalent on the CORONA image. In the light of the likely slight distortion of the plot, and the platform having been levelled to less than a metre in height by waves and currents over more than a millennium, it is probably best not to speculate extensively as to the significance of individual ridges and hillocks within the platform.

Fig. 5.5: Two of the Sasanian bricks from the submerged fort. (The scale measures 4 × 10 cm.)

Collapsed barracks, walls or towers may account for the uneven surface. It should be noted that the subsequent sonar seafloor survey picked up a brick scatter that covers a substantially larger area (approximately 150 × 180 m and oval in shape), extending in all directions beyond the submerged mound (Fig. 12.20).[16] We assume that the mound, rather than the wider scatter of material, reflects the size of the fort.

The postulated fort appears to cover no more than roughly half a hectare, to judge by the topographical survey, making it potentially the smallest known fort on the main sections of the Gorgan and Tammisheh Walls.[17] The CORONA image, however, allows for it to have been somewhat larger, but probably also under a hectare. No other known fort on the Gorgan Wall west of the Pishkamar Rocks is quite so small, even if there are a few small fortlets or towers in the eastern extension of the Gorgan Wall and in its hinterland, as well as a fortlet or watchtower at the southern terminal of the Tammisheh Wall. Despite the atypical size, all other observations point to it indeed being a fort: the likely rectangular shape as well as a, for the seafloor, unusually steep slope at the edges of the features – probably corresponding to the fort platforms on land – and probably largely levelled through the waves of the Caspian Sea. It also abuts the wall and is covered in typical Sasanian bricks and fragments thereof. Furthermore, various pottery sherds, including much of the rim of a large storage vessel, buried in sediments for the past 1,500 years or so, were recovered from the platform, adding much strength to our hypothesis that it was a fort or in any case an occupied area. A complete square brick of 40 cm diameter was also found (Fig. 5.5) – as well as bricks of the slightly smaller size typical for the Tammisheh Wall. It is thus in all probability indeed a fort, even if an unusually small one.

The survey team spotted the highest brick concentration in the west of the fort, unsurprisingly so, as this is in alignment with the Tammisheh Wall on land. The Gorgan Wall consisted, of course, of solid fired-brick masonry and was abutted by mud-brick forts. Did the same apply to the Tammisheh Wall? The buildings inside the submerged fort and the other fort walls probably employed mainly unfired mud-brick, whose collapse created the platform. According to our previous underwater survey, however, the Tammisheh Wall may have changed alignment at the fort, the section from the SSE leading to the fort's WSW side, but continuing from the fort's ENE side to the NNW.[18] There was no similarly dense brick concentration on the east side, even if our previous mapping suggests that the northern continuation of the Tammisheh Wall is connected to the fort's northern corner. Perhaps, however, the wide scatter of bricks is related to waterproof fired bricks being employed more extensively on a fort not far from the shore at the time, whether from the start or in a later effort to shore up defences when the rising waters of the Caspian Sea began to encroach upon the stronghold. The topographical survey revealed a very shallow ridge running from the northern corner of the platform to the north-west or NNW. It is possible that this marks the Tammisheh Wall.

We do not know to date whether or not the fort was surrounded by a ditch. There is no trace of a ditch on the surface, but the sea could easily have filled it with sediments. As material would have been needed for the walls and buildings in the fort, we may assume that, as usual, a ditch or moat was dug to provide construction material whilst enhancing the defences at the same time. At the time of construction, the water table of the Caspian Sea would have been some 3 to 4.50 m below the current surface in the area of fort platform,[19] though, of course, the platform was higher in antiquity. Excavating a ditch should thus have been possible without having the dig deep into waterlogged layers. Subsequent sonar survey established that there was indeed a ditch to the east of the fort, but its traces are less clear on other sides. This ditch lined the Tammisheh Wall in the east, but its traceable dimensions are shallow (not exceeding 1.20 m and mostly well under 1 m in depth). In places there was also a less substantial ditch in the west.[20]

The fort may also have the potential to shed light on the environment. Dr Lyudmila Shumilovskikh took core samples form the northern slope of the fort and examined other samples from the edges of the fort, its interior being too clayey for sampling, as the ground could not be penetrated manually by our auger. Sediments unearthed were partially marine, but there were also layers without molluscs and with iron staining. The latter are probably terrestrial, but we do not know yet whether they are recent

5. *The Tammisheh Wall and associated forts* 207

Fig. 5.6: The Tammisheh Wall, with a modern track and road on top of it, runs from the left bottom corner of the image to the right top corner and into land now submerged in the Caspian Sea in the north.

Fig. 5.7: The Tammisheh Wall, followed by a modern track and with a white car on top and here still forming a substantial causeway, cuts across a narrow part of the coastal plain and runs towards the Alborz Mountains in the south (background).

Fig. 5.8: The southern section of the Tammisheh Wall has been flattened, but can still be traced as a brick scatter on the ground. It follows roughly the right (western) edge of the strip of woodland in the foreground (right) and runs from there to the first hilltop in the forest (middle ground near the right edge of the picture) where it terminates at a tower mound. A ditch follows the crest of the ridge left for a further one-and-a-half kilometres or so.

Fig. 5.9: The Bansaran Fort seen from the north-west. Its northern part (foreground) is now used as an orchard. The overgrown edge of the rectangular elevated fort platform is still prominently visible in the area of its north-west corner (foreground, centre–right). It extends in the south (background) into the forest.

or ancient and whether any of them date back to the time of the fort's occupation. The deposits are thin, suggesting that much of the (mud-brick?) architecture has been washed away, as well as probably occupation horizons.[21]

5.3. Remote survey of the Tammisheh Wall

On 3 October 2016, Davit Naskidashvili and the joint project took drone photographs of the Tammisheh Wall. By and large, its preservation had not deteriorated since our earlier fieldwork in 2005, 2007 and 2009.[22] The aerial photos (Figs 5.6–5.9) help to convey a visual idea of the topography of the monument and changing land-use patterns that may have an impact on its future preservation. The Bansaran fort platform still has a distinct edge in the north-west. As before, we are unable to discern any towers. We do not know whether these have been levelled through agriculture, perhaps unusually built of fired bricks and robbed, or whether there never were any.[23]

Notes

1. Sauer *et al.* 2013, 15–17, 244–87; Jansen Van Rensburg *et al.* 2013.
2. See Gyselen 2019, 93–95, 172–73 on the approximate boundaries of these provinces.
3. See chapters 12–13.
4. A case could have been made to include this subchapter in the section on 'Marine survey', but not only would this have reduced this chapter to one of the shortest in the volume, it also would have resulted in a less coherent structure. The focus of this chapter is on the architecture of the wall and associated forts whether on dry land or submerged in the sea now. The focus of the section on 'Marine survey', by contrast, is on the rising and falling water levels of the Caspian Sea, the marine environment and on tracing the course of the Gorgan and Tammisheh Walls where submerged under the waters of the world's largest inland sea or buried under past marine sediments.
5. Sauer *et al.* 2013, 245–50.
6. Sauer *et al.* 2013, 278–86.
7. In addition to parallels cited before (Sauer *et al.* 2013, 285), see also Tamm 2020, 426–27, 434 fig. 6 and Tamm *et al.* 2018, 120–23 for a Sasanian hall with square pillars near the late Sasanian fortlet of Gird-i Kazhaw, and Labbaf-Khaniki 2020 for a long building employing round columns at Bazeh-Hur.
8. Sauer *et al.* 2013, 266 fig. 8:2, 273–75; Jansen Van Rensburg *et al.* 2013, 424 fig. 15:2, 427–28, 691 pl. 15:1.
9. See http://hydroweb.theia-land.fr/hydroweb/view/L_caspian?lang=en_(accessed on 13 June 2020).
10. Starting at UTM 40S E 0234007, N 4078343 (or UTM 40S E 0234005, N 4078339 when measured in again) and progressing from this point eight metres to the east, towards UTM 40S E 0234048, N4078351.
11. From UTM 40S E 0233950, N 4078350 to 40S E 0234050, N 4078350; cf. Jansen Van Rensburg *et al.* 2013, with 691 pl. 15:1.
12. Transect 1 start: UTM 40 S 0233950 E, 4078600 N; end: UTM 40 S 0233800 E, 4078600 N; transect 2 start: UTM 40 S 0233950 E, 4078650 N; end: UTM 40 S 0233800 E, 4078650 N; transect 3 start: UTM 40 S 0233900 E, 4078700 N; end: UTM 40 S 0233750 E, 4078700 N; transect 4 start: UTM 40 S 0233900 E, 4078750 N; end: UTM 40 S 0233700 E, 4078750 N; transect 5 start: UTM 40 S 0233850 E, 4078800 N; end: UTM 40 S 0233700 E, 4078800 N; transect 6 start: UTM 40 S 0233850 E, 4078850 N; end: UTM 40 S 0233700 E, 4078850 N; transect 7 start: UTM 40 S 0233800 E, 4078900 N; end: UTM 40 S 0233650 E, 4078900 N.
13. See chapter 12.4.3; cf. Jansen Van Rensburg *et al.* 2013, 428, 691 pl. 15:1.
14. See Sauer *et al.* 2013, 144 table 4:2 for similar models.
15. Jansen Van Rensburg *et al.* 2013, 691 pl. 15:1.
16. See chapter 12.
17. We do not know, if these dimensions are correct, why it may have been so small, corresponding in size to a typical Sasanian hinterland fort, but covering only approximately 40% of the size of a typical two-barracks fort.
18. Jansen Van Rensburg *et al.* 2013, 691 pl. 15:1.
19. On 28 November 2014, the day of the survey, the water level in the Caspian Sea was -27.47±0.03 m (see http://hydroweb.theia-land.fr/hydroweb/view/L_caspian?lang=en (accessed on 13 June 2020)). The platform was some 0–1 m below the water level, i.e. at c. -27.50 to -28.50 m. It was probably at c. -31.50 to 32.00m OD in the sixth century: Kudrjavcev and Gadžiev 2002, 339–40; cf. Aliev *et al.* 2006, 152 (see also Naderi Beni *et al.* 2013, 1645 on the sea level at earlier times).
20. See chapter 12.
21. Paragraph based largely on information kindly supplied by Dr Lyudmila Shumilovskikh. The detailed results will be published in a separate study.
22. Sauer *et al.* 2013, 244–87.
23. Bivar and Fehérvári 1966, 40–41 fig. 2 shows indentations on the fort's east walls, making one wonder if remains of towers may have survived on this side in the 1960s. We have not yet examined any CORONA satellite imagery of this area.

6

Post-Sasanian barriers

6.1. The Jar-e Kulbad Earthwork: a basic clone of the Tammisheh Wall, decisive in modern warfare

The Jar-e Kulbad linear earthwork is 17–20 km west of the Tammisheh Wall and, like its Sasanian counterpart, cuts across the coastal plain. Both are located in a narrow section of the plain, which is today even narrower where dissected by the Jar-e Kulbad than in the area of the Tammisheh Wall. The documentary evidence has been summarised in our previous report,[1] but we had not inspected its remains at the time. Our team visited the earthwork on 11 January 2013,[2] and this chapter provides a brief description of the physical remains and an evaluation of the earthwork's significance.

The Jar-e Kulbad is probably of post-medieval origins, certainly no later than the eighteenth century and more likely as early as the late sixteenth or early seventeenth century.[3] Interestingly, there was a strong octagonal fort (Meyan Qal'eh), measuring some 155 m across, of the seventeenth century on the Ashuradeh Peninsula further north. It is thought to have been built to protect Safavid palaces further west from Turkmen raids. We do not know for certain if it was operational at the same time as the Jar-e Kulbad and functioned as part of the same defensive system, but one is inclined to think that it was, as it would not have been very effective in preventing raids from the east on its own and as long as the main land route remained open. The proposed attribution of both Meyan Qal'eh and the Jar-e Kulbad to Shah 'Abbas (r. AD 1588–1629)[4] may well be correct, but whatever the precise date of erection of the Jar-e Kulbad, it is likely to be Safavid. We may assume that the Tammisheh Wall, reportedly in use at least into the tenth century,[5] had been abandoned many centuries before. The robbing of its sought-after bricks would probably have commenced soon after it had been decommissioned, so that not much other than an eroded earth bank would have remained – not easy to restore to an effective defensive wall, short of complete reconstruction. The Jar-e Kulbad may have been built further west to take advantage of the even narrower coastal corridor at this point, so as to speed up construction, save labour and facilitate patrolling the barrier. Perhaps it was indeed mainly intended to protect royal palaces further west rather than securing the maximum expanse of arable land. It is also possible that the new alignment reflects a westward shift of the administrative boundary between the provinces of Parishwargar/Tabarestan/Mazandaran in the west and Gorgan in the east.[6] Furthermore, after the abandonment of the town of Tammisheh in the thirteenth century or after, protection of the easternmost part of the coastal plain from incursions by raiders inhabiting the steppes may have been a lesser priority. Despite the change in location, it is clear that the two walls reflect the same strategic concept. Both will have been used, successively, to control traffic and to serve as a defensive obstacle at points where it was impossible to bypass a gated barrier, short of venturing into difficult mountainous and densely forested terrain or taking the sea-route.

The southernmost part of Jar-e Kulbad earthwork still survives well, overgrown and protected by forest. We followed it from the northernmost well-preserved point, located south of its intersection with a west–east road.[7] From this point southwards, it still rises an estimated 4 to 5 m, and perhaps up to 6 m above the associated (silted-up?) ditch on its east side. There is no ditch in the west, but it still forms a substantial obstacle even if approached from this side. The earthwork appears to come to a terminal at the foot of the mountains, some 600 m beyond the intersection with the road. Its slopes are still very steep today, though no doubt less so than during its period of active use over two centuries ago. Reportedly, large and thick trees had been planted in the ditch so as

Fig. 6.1: The southernmost 600 m of the Jar-e Kulbad earthwork (behind the team members), here near the northernmost well-preserved point and its intersection with a road, looking south towards the mountains, still survive prominently today.

Fig. 6.2: The Jar-e Kulbad earthwork (left) is lined by a ditch in the east (right).

Fig. 6.3: The Jar-e Kulbad earthwork, with team members on its crest, forms a significant obstacle, especially if approached from the east (right).

to form a thicket,[8] and impenetrable vegetation would have made it much more difficult for humans or beasts of burden to climb over it.

Beyond the well-preserved section in the south, a modern track on top of the earthwork runs towards the coast. Despite being much flattened and widened, the Jar-e Kulbad still forms a distinct elevated causeway, the adjacent fields being on a lower level on both sides. We spotted no trace of any preserved associated fort. At the northern terminal point of the road and causeway, some 7 km beyond the earthwork's southern terminal, there is a modern water pool and no clear trace of the earthwork appears to be visible from a terrestrial perspective beyond. A linear feature, following the alignment of the track-topped causeway to the coast for another 1.1 km is, however, visible on Google Earth imagery, would merit further investigation and may well be the northernmost preserved part of the linear barrier.[9] Wherever the precise sea-side terminus was, it is hard to believe Hasan-e Fasaʻi's report that the ditched obstacle was once c. 24 km (four parasangs) long,[10] as the coastal plain at this point is only some 8 km wide today. Xavier Hommaire de Hell by contrast provides a much more credible length estimate of 6,000 paces. The earthwork was no more than 2.60 m high and lined by a 1.70 m deep (silted-up?) ditch in the section recorded, but the French geographer and engineer was sufficiently impressed to see in it the famous ancient wall against the Gog and Magog.[11]

That the ditch is in the east adds strength to Samuel Gottlieb Gmelin's testimony that the earthwork was erected as a protection against devastating Turkmen raids. When Gmelin visited the area in 1771, it was reportedly guarded by of total of 3,550 soldiers stationed in nine forts. We are not aware of any remains of these forts, but have not carried out pedestrian or aerial surveys, have not interviewed local people and have not systematically examined satellite imagery. Gmelin attests that their defences consisted of earthen ramparts with gates and accommodation for soldiers inside.[12] Their chances of survival in prime agricultural land must have been slim.

What makes this earthwork particularly fascinating, also for those interested in much earlier, Sasanian, barriers, is that it forms a close parallel, in most aspects other than construction method and date, to the Tammisheh Wall (and other Sasanian sea-side-to-mountain barriers on the Caspian coast). This suggests perhaps that it may have been inspired by its nearby earlier counterpart, whose prominent bank was still standing then (as in part it still does today). Furthermore, even if of much more basic construction, a tree-lined earthen rampart, as opposed to a wall built in part of

Fig. 6.4: A modern track (left) follows the Jar-e Kulbad earthwork, which still forms a causeway in places, to the mountains. Photo taken from near the northern terminal of the preserved causeway, a little over 1 km south of the present coastline and some 7 km north of the earthwork's southern terminal at the foot of the Alborz Mountains (in the background).

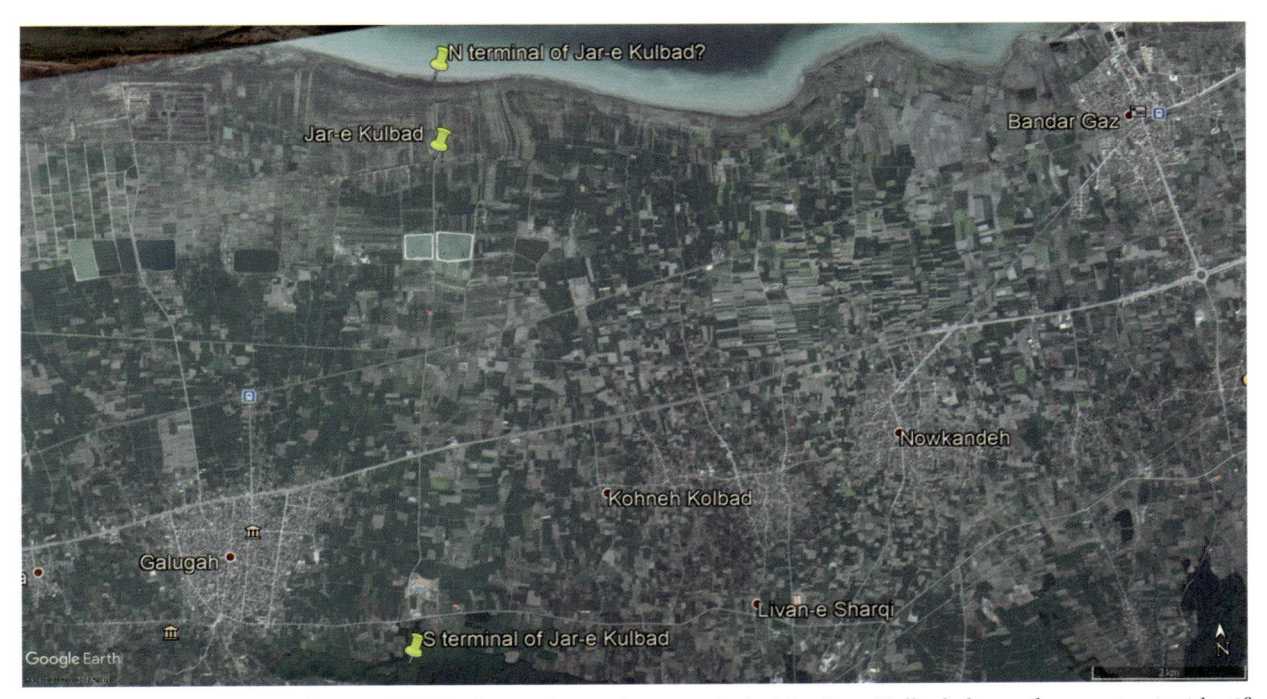

Fig. 6.5: Google Earth image of 13 April 2017, plotting the southern terminal of the Jar-e Kulbad, the northernmost point identified on the ground and the probable northern terminal of the preserved section as far as traced remotely (Image © CNES / Airbus).

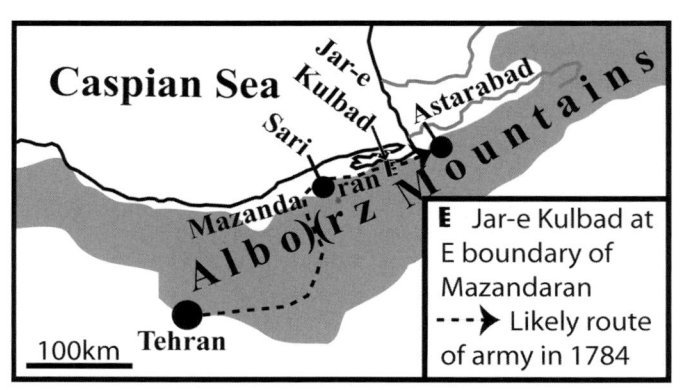

Fig. 6.6: The Jar-e Kulbad earthwork was decisive in the civil war of 1784, enabling the troops defending Astarabad to deprive a strong expeditionary force sent from Tehran of all supplies and to defeat and decimate it when eventually forced to flee.

fired bricks, it proved remarkably effective. Not only does Gmelin attest that it had been built to halt major Turkmen incursions, it even decided, a few years after Gmelin's visit, the outcome of a civil war in modern times, and paved the way for the rise of the Qajar dynasty. In 1784, all of Persia was ruled by 'Ali Morad Khan, with only Mazandaran and the Gorgan Plain being under renegade control. After the conquest of Mazandaran, troops were sent from Tehran to Astarabad (modern Gorgan) to quell the rebellion for good. This expedition army must have crossed the Jar-e Kulbad earthwork before laying siege to Astarabad, held by Aga Mohammad Khan. Conquest would have made 'Ali Morad Khan the undisputed Shah of Persia. Eventually, it was the Jar-e Kulbad earthwork that changed the course of history. Reoccupied by forces loyal to Aga Mohammad Khan, all supplies to the expedition force camped outside Astarabad were cut off, leading to famine and military defeat. Abandoning the siege of Astarabad, the soldiers fled and reportedly 10,000 perished when finding their escape route blocked by soldiers guarding the Jar-e Kulbad earthwork. Aga Mohammad Khan not only survived the siege of Astarabad, but later became Shah of Persia and the founder of the Qajar dynasty – the result of the effective use of a mere earthwork.[13] If such a basic installation could decide the outcome of a war in the age of firearms, how can it be doubted that the much more solidly built and moat-lined Tammisheh and Gorgan Walls could be militarily effective against foes armed with no more than bows and arrows and weapons for close combat?[14] Also in Europe, just as in Persia, large-scale earthworks were considered militarily effective as late as the eighteenth century.[15]

6.2. The Forud Wall near Kalat in Khorasan

Meysam Labbaf-Khaniki, Eberhard W. Sauer, Kristen Hopper, Davit Naskidashvili, Bardia Shabani and David Gagoshidze[16]

6.2.1. The Forud Wall

The Forud Wall follows the crest of a steep mountain ridge to the west and north-west of the town of Kalat in Khorasan (Fig. 6.7).[17] It was first explored and surveyed by Meysam Labbaf-Khaniki, who proposed the attractive hypothesis that it may form part of a system of barriers in continuation of the Gorgan Wall that originated over a long period of time, up to the reign of Nadir Shah (r. 1736–1747). Medieval and modern sources attest that it was widely believed that the Gorgan Wall continued much further east than the section known to date, to various postulated terminals in the area of Khorasan, modern Turkmenistan, Afghanistan, Uzbekistan or even China.[18] Evidently, the latter popular belief cannot literally be true. Apart from the Mongol Empire from the 1220s to its division in the 1250s, there never was a state that controlled land all the way from the Caspian Sea's south-eastern shore to northern China – and there is no evidence to suggest that the Mongols commissioned such a project. Even the geographically less outlandish theories must be incorrect at least in so far as there is no continuous wall. Perhaps, however, these reports contain a core of truth. It is possible that there was a discontinuous system of barriers, filling the gaps between natural mountain chains. Some of these could indeed be part of an effort to keep the northern frontiers of the Sasanian Empire secure. Alternatively, later travellers might have mistakenly concluded that a series of barriers of different date were all contemporary and part of a single wall.

How old was the Forud Wall and was it part of an extended defensive network or just a local feature? The historian Mirza Mahdi Khan Astarabadi attests that

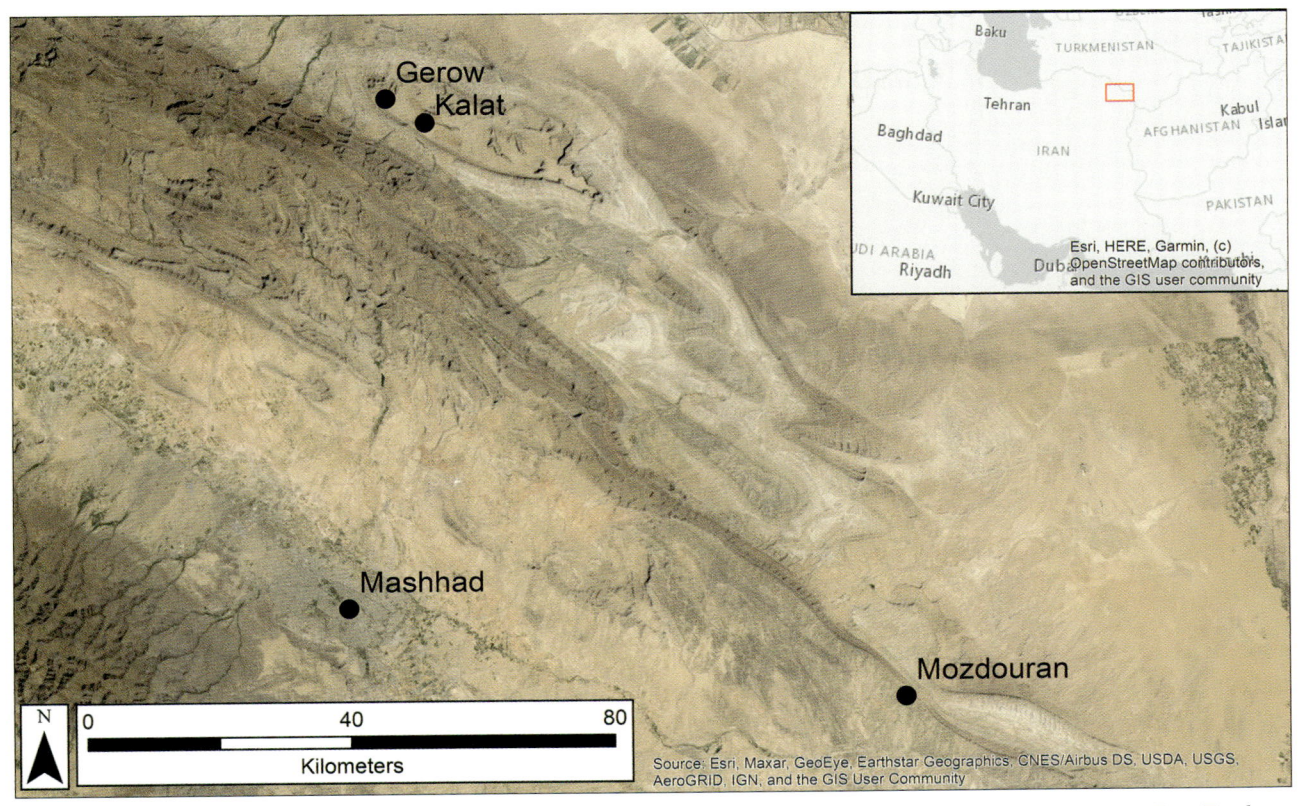

Fig. 6.7: Location of modern settlements mentioned in the text (map by Kristen Hopper; Image © Esri, Maxar, GeoEye, Earthstar Geographics, CNES/Airbus DS, USDA, USGS, AeroGRID, IGN and the GIS User Community).

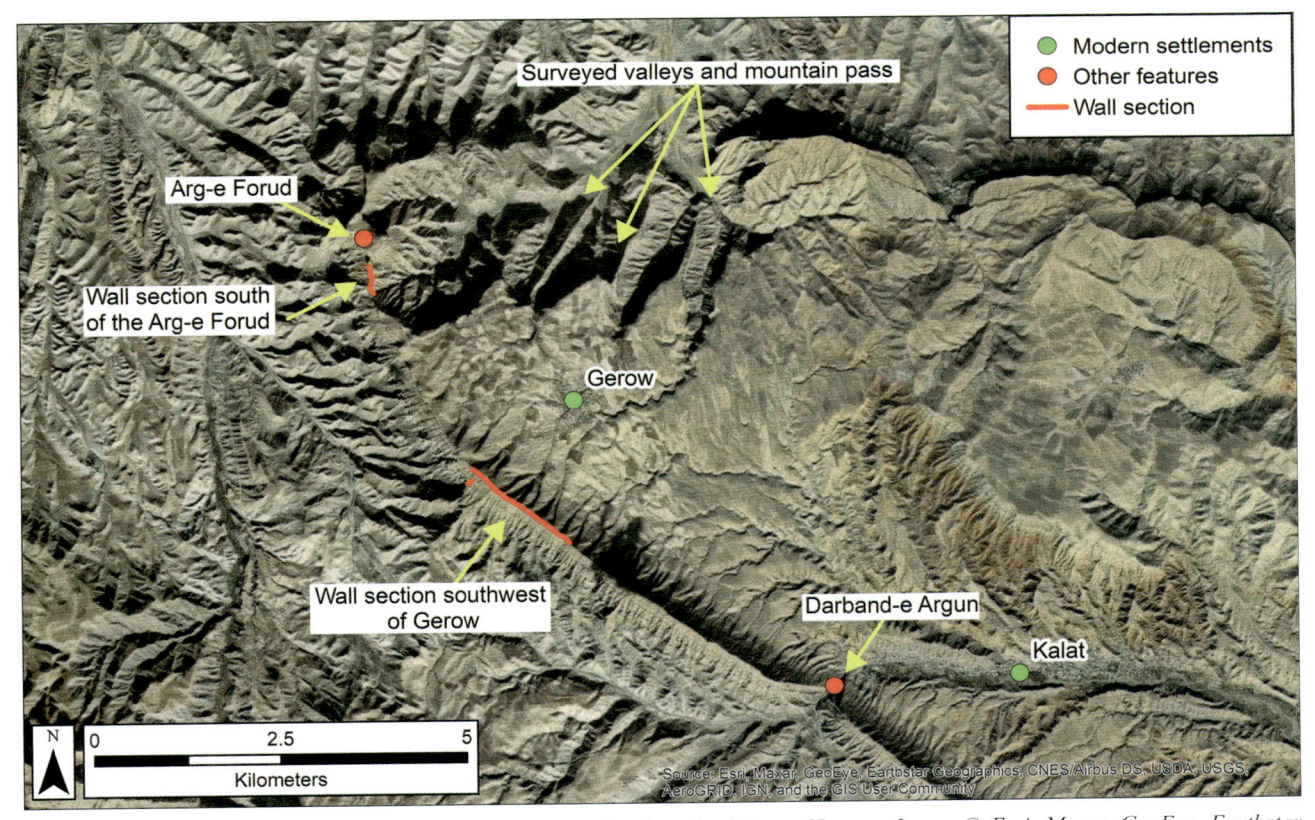

Fig. 6.8: Features visited or surveyed in the vicinity of Kalat (map by Kristen Hopper; Image © Esri, Maxar, GeoEye, Earthstar Geographics, CNES/Airbus DS, USDA, USGS, AeroGRID, IGN and the GIS User Community).

Fig. 6.9: Photograph (© Golestan Palace Photo Archive) of the Darband-e Argun of c. 1890: a medieval or post-medieval bridge with a Qajar parapet spanned the gorge at a narrow point. Note the remnants of masonry in the river bed in front of it, perhaps a bridge pier, employing large square bricks as typical for the Sasanian era – probably the remnants of an earlier bridge barrier to control access to the Kalat area via the gorge. Neither the bridge nor the remnants of its (pre-medieval?) predecessor survive today.

Nadir Shah had ordered the Kalat fortifications to be reinforced, implying that they had been built at an earlier date,[19] which raises the question as to when. The Ilkhanid ruler Argun Shah (r. 1284–1291) reportedly secured the southern access to Kalat via a narrow gorge (named after him, 'Darband-e Argun') with a defensive barrier. The Darband-e Argun (Fig. 6.10), despite its narrowness and travellers having to wade through the small river filling its full width, formed by far the easiest access route to Kalat as well as the one that was least difficult to control. It would have made sense for defensive efforts to be focused on the gorge first – and exclusively so at times of low threat levels or limited resources.

A Qajar photograph shows the remains of a collapsed ancient structure within the Darband-e Argun in front of the Argavan (i.e. Argun) Shah Bridge (Fig. 6.9).[20] It employed fired bricks whose dimensions, to judge by the photo, were similar or identical to typical pre-Islamic bricks, such as those from Sasanian Bazeh-Hur or the Gorgan Wall, suggesting perhaps that the earliest barrier within the gorge may have been built long before the reign of Argun Shah. A solid block of masonry in the riverbed, maybe a bridge pier, leaves no doubt it employed strong waterproof lime-mortar. The location between two cliffs of the gorge suggests it was not a bridge designed for ordinary traffic. This is certainly true for the medieval or post-medieval bridge succeeding it and not intended to enable people to cross the river. The legend of this photograph of around 1890 (Fig. 6.9) provides fascinating insights, presumably based on local oral traditions at the time, on how this bridge barrier was used. Based on this text, there had once been gates in the arches, closed by soldiers on duty overnight, designed to prevent trespass without impeding water-flow. After severe flood-damage,[21] the bridge had been partially rebuilt, but without the gates. The functional design of this bridge barrier, with strong flood breakers, may well have much in common with its pre-medieval(?) prototype. The bridge was reportedly 10 *zar'* (c. 10.40 m) high, 4.25 *zar'* (c. 4.42 m) wide and 25 *qadam*/paces (c. 25 m) long.[22] If its, probably pre-Islamic, predecessor was of broadly similar functional design, perhaps here, just as in Caucasian gorges and on the Gorgan and Ghilghilchay Walls,[23] it served as a bridge barrier. This specific barrier may have been built to control access to the natural cliff-enclosed Kalat fortress. Whilst little is known as yet about pre-Islamic settlement at Kalat, there has been no systematic survey. It seems perfectly possible to us that the earliest bridge barrier in the gorge was Sasanian, but with no more than circumstantial photographic evidence available, this dating proposal is tentative at best.

Whenever its natural defences were first enhanced by an artificial barrier, Kalat certainly was recognised as a virtually impregnable mountain stronghold in the second millennium. The local ruler of the naturally well-defended plateau of Kalat successfully resisted the powerful armies of Timur for two years in the 1380s. The natural fortress was of great strategic importance as late as the 1740s when Nadir Shah is reported to have re-fortified it. The 'Titanic fort of Kalát-Nádiri, which runs in an almost unbroken line as far as the eye can reach', as described by Major (later Sir) Percy Molesworth Sykes, was chosen by Nadir Shah as the safest place within his vast empire to house members of the royal family and to store the massive looted treasures, including a famous diamond, from his victorious invasion of India.

The cliffs and ridges surrounding the plateau would have been much harder to cross and much more arduous to secure against trespassers than the Darband-e Argun, the weakest link in defensive system. Parts of the tower-enforced ridge-top wall, reaching a height of up to 14 feet, were visited and described by Major C.O. Bruce in 1902.[24] The ridge-top wall, whose construction must have been inspired by serious security concerns, was thus likely to be of a later date than the gorge-blocking barrier, but it was hard to be sure how much later.[25]

6.2.2. The Arg-e Forud

The Arg-e Forud, a strong natural fortification at the northern terminal of the Forud Wall, may well have played a pivotal role in the system. It occupies an important strategic position in the mountains that separate the southern fertile plains from the northern steppes and deserts. A nearby valley, locally called Landar (Fig. 6.11), leads to the Karakum Desert and provides nomads with

Fig. 6.10: Drone photo by Davit Naskidashvili of the ridge, pierced by the Darband-e Argun gorge at Kalat, the only viable access to a natural fortress. A modern barrier may have replaced a much earlier bridge barrier.

Fig. 6.11: The location of the Arg-e Forud in north-eastern Iran, plotted onto Google Earth satellite imagery, showing the region's topography (Image © CNES / Astrium, DigitalGlobe and Google).

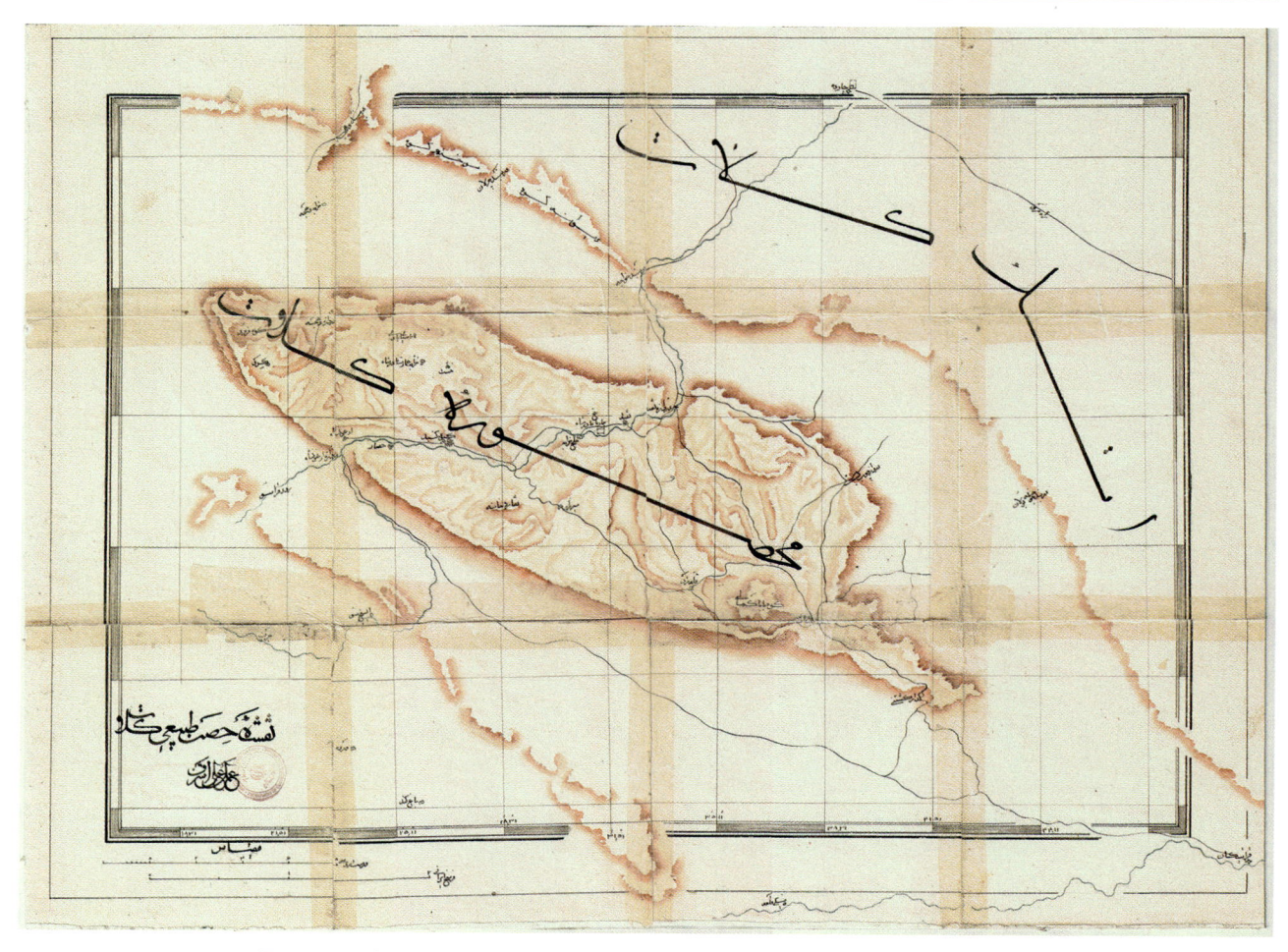

Fig. 6.12: The Forud Mountain on a Qajar map (Nazarahari et al. 2013, 50–51).

a path from the lowlands to the highlands of the Kopet Dag and Hezar Masjed, where they settle in spring and summer. The Arg-e Forud ('Forud's Fort') is named after a legendary figure. According to Ferdowsi's Shahnameh, Forud, son of Siavaksh of the Kayanian royal dynasty, resided at the fort and fought against his half-brother Kay Khusro's army, commanded by Tus son of Nowdar. Forud was finally defeated and his fort was captured by Tus.[26]

The Fortress of Kalat/the Arg-e Forud was mentioned for the first time in the Bundahishn,[27] a Pahlavi work that was probably compiled in the late Sasanian period and edited by Faranbaq Dadagi, a Zoroastrian priest, in the ninth century AD.[28] The fort features also at least once in the Dorrey-e Nadereh, a historical manuscript of the eighteenth century. According to Astarabadi, Nadir Shah (r. 1736–1747) visited the Qal'eh Forud and hunted wild birds.[29] In Qajar documents there is no mention of the Qal'eh or Arg-e Forud, but there are references to natural features whose names derive from the fort. For instance, in a diary written in 1892, Roshani Zafranlou refers to the Gardane-ye Forud (i.e. the 'Forud Pass').[30] On Qajar maps of the Kalat region, some landscape features near Kalat are plotted: Mowze'-e Forud ('the Place of Forud'),[31] Kuh-e Forud ('the Forud Mountain'),[32] Rah-e Forud ('Forud's Road')[33] and Gardane-ye Forud ('Forud's Pass').[34] In one map, the cartographer pointed out that 30 watchmen are required for guarding the pass. All these features were located at or near the Arg-e Forud.

The ancient site of Arg-e Forud occupies a plateau of more or less rectangular shape whose long axis is in a north-west to south-east alignment. The site measures approximately 500 m by 250 m and covers c. 12.5 hectares. There are low mounds all over the plateau, with a particular concentration in the southern part of the site. These mounds probably contain the remains of buildings. There are also several circular robber pits of 1 to 2 m diameter in the central area of the plateau. The site is currently used as a sheep pasture.

Two hills, in the north-west and south-east, with lower ground in between, dominate the fort. Worth noting are the ruins of a stone building on top of the north-western hill, near the north-western limits of the site. As far as one can make out, the building was square in plan, measuring c. 25 × 25 m, with a central 10 × 10 m courtyard surrounded by rectangular rooms. The precise dimensions of the rooms, separated by walls of c. 50 cm width, are not detectable,

Fig. 6.13: Aerial view of the Arg-e Forud from the south-west (drone photo by Davit Naskidashvili).

and illegal excavations have obscured the original plan of the building. A concentration of low mounds in the south of the plateau and traces of an access route from the fort's southern corner suggest that the main gate was probably in the south. There is no trace of a wall enclosing the Arg-e Forud, but none may have been required as the steep-sided cliffs make it difficult to gain access to the fort. A linear wall runs from the southern corner of the Arg-e Forud Fort along the crest of a mountain ridge to the south. This stone wall was furnished with at least three towers and forms part of the Forud Wall. To the north, the Arg-e Forud is connected via a narrow ridge to another mountain plateau, called locally 'Lokkeh' (Fig. 6.13).

6.2.3. Pedestrian and aerial survey of the Forud Wall

It seemed important to establish the facts and the date of the surviving barrier. A brief pedestrian survey of sections of the Forud Wall was carried out, on 24 and 25 October 2016, on the initiative of Meysam Labbaf-Khaniki, by Ali Hasanabadi, Kristen Hopper, David Naskidashvili, Eberhard Sauer and Bardia Shabani. The survey traced sections of a wall system along the cited ridgeline, arcing from the Arg-e Forud in the north-west to the south-east towards Kalat (Figs 6.7–6.8).[35]

During this survey, we observed that the section of the ridge immediately south of the Arg-e Forud (visited briefly on 24 October 2016) is guarded by watchtowers and a wall (see Fig. 6.8). Between the southern end of this wall section and the next recorded feature of the wall system there is a gap of over 2.5 km. It is worth noting that the section of the ridge within this postulated gap has not been surveyed, but investigation of at least the southernmost 600 m did not reveal any structures.

The mountain chain, part of the Kuh-e Hezar Masjed ('Mountain of the thousand mosques') Range,[36] is hard to cross in the section without wall and towers (Figs 6.8 and 6.14). No artificial defences were needed, as the ridge itself forms a sufficient natural obstacle that would have been virtually impossible to scale and insurmountable for mounted soldiers or raiding parties approaching it from the south-west. South-west of Gerow, a village in the valley to the east of the ridge, the near vertical cliff comes to an end (Fig. 6.8; NK-8 in Table 6.1). South-east of this point, the south-west flank of the ridge, whilst still very steep, can be scaled in places, and its crest is guarded by a wall and a chain of watchtowers (Figs 6.8 and 6.17). The wall with its towers is similar to that near the Arg-e Forud and in all probability part of the same system. Even these less forbidding sections of the ridge south-west of Gerow are not easy to access, and cliffs force those ascending the steep slope to make detours. Far fewer obstacles face those climbing the ridge on its north-eastern flank, but here too the ascent is arduous and time-consuming. No access to the ridge is entirely out of sight to those in control of the crest and any would-be trespassers could have been targeted with missiles, stones or, in modern times, guns.

The first feature encountered along this section of the wall system was a circular projecting tower (NK-8 in Table 6.1; Figs 6.15 and 6.17).[37] The next possible tower was located c. 100 m along the ridgeline (NK-10), but

Fig. 6.14: Section of the ridge without artificial barrier.

Fig. 6.15: Drone photo by Davit Naskidashvili of the north-western terminal (NK-8 in Table 6.1) of the central section of the Forud Wall, with a tower overlooking a sheer cliff.

Fig. 6.16: The Forud Wall built at the edge of an extremely steep, though not entirely inaccessible, slope.

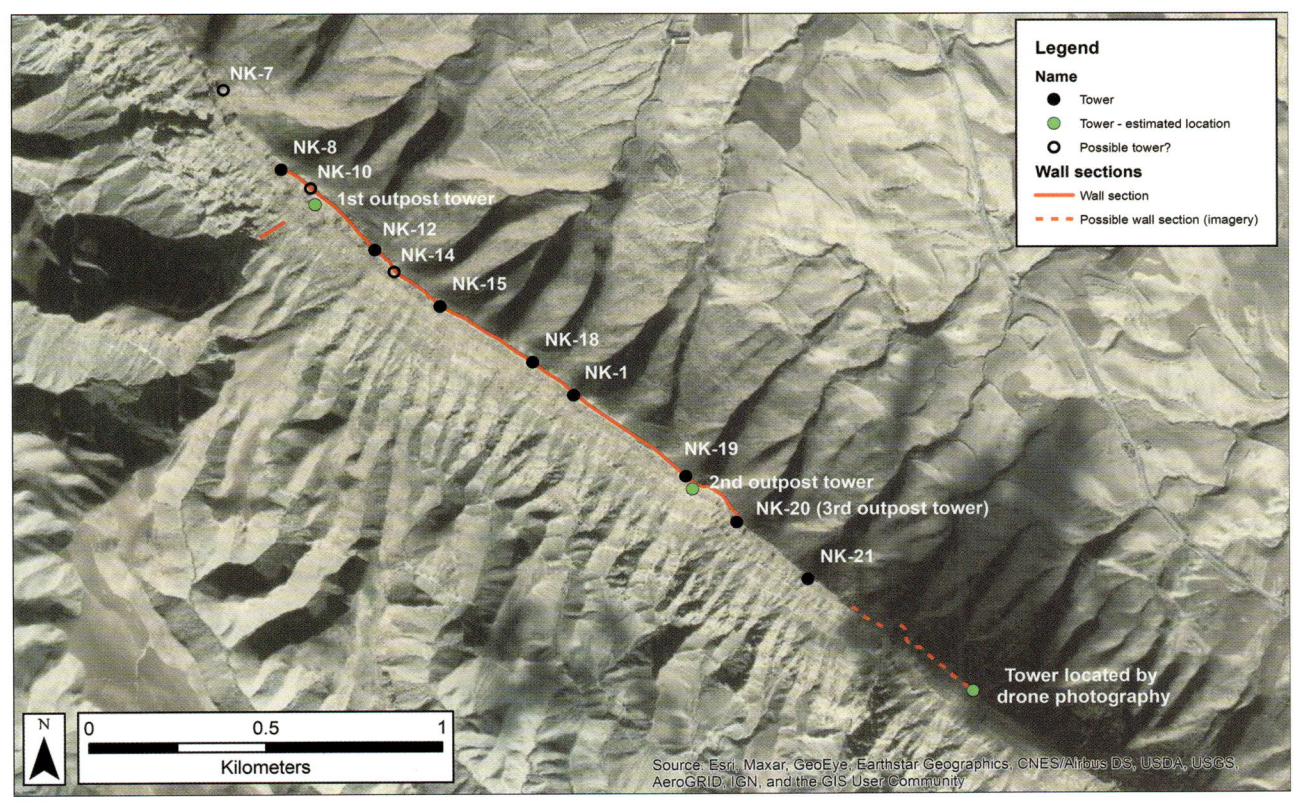

Fig. 6.17: Towers and wall sections located during pedestrian survey and via drone photography (map by Kristen Hopper; Image © Esri, Maxar, GeoEye, Earthstar Geographics, CNES/Airbus DS, USDA, USGS, AeroGRID, IGN and the GIS User Community).

it is uncertain whether this was indeed a tower or, more probably, just a projecting segment of the Forud Wall. A substantial round tower is located c. 50 m to the SSE (as the crow flies). This tower further downhill formed an outwork bastion beyond the line of the ridge-top wall. A short wall was built from the edge of a ravine towards the crest and towards the first outpost tower; its alignment is perpendicular to that of the ridge-top wall (Figs 6.17–6.20). This barrier would have blocked any sideways movement parallel to the crest. The tower overlooking it is the first of at least three outpost towers, placed downhill from the main wall, seen during our survey. Of these only the last was visited, the other two only inspected from nearby, due to the difficult terrain and time pressure (Figs 6.17–6.19 and 6.21–6.22).

Following the ridgeline to the south-east, the Forud Wall boasts further towers at irregular intervals (Table 6.1 and Fig. 6.17). Of these, the tower located at NK-15 was selected for excavation (Trench k).[38]

The best-preserved tower on the ridge-top wall (located at NK-18) stands some 2 m tall, above the surface level in its interior (Figs 6.23–6.25). The higher courses of the stonework on the inner face of the wall curve inwards, suggesting that it once had been covered by a domed roof. In the south-west, the outer wall of the tower measures 1.53 m across, on the opposite side 1.48 m; the interior diameter is c. 2.50 m, giving the tower an overall diameter of 5.51 m. A niche, window or door in the north-east is 0.51 m wide, at least 0.79 m high and at least 0.90 m deep. There is a suggestion of a wall at the end, perhaps supporting an interpretation as a niche.

The towers on the ridge are an integral part of the wall and were probably constructed at the same time. Stone collapse has sometimes obscured their plan and position in relation to the wall, but they tend to be round, often project beyond the line of the wall to the south-west and sometimes at least also in the opposite direction. The position of the watchtowers inspected during our survey is detailed in Table 6.1. The wall section inspected and discussed here appears to terminate in the vicinity of NK-20 where a circular outpost tower is located. A further tower was located at NK-21, another 256 m to the south-east.

The wall and towers are often built at the very edge of precariously steep precipices, evidently positioned here to ensure good views and maximum defensive advantage. The latter may have been more important, as the towers are often overlooked by rocky summits. Locating them on a saddle helped to secure the most likely crossing points whilst perhaps also reducing the risk of towers

Fig. 6.18: The first outpost tower, overlooking the sidewall, which is running perpendicular to the ridgeline Forud Wall.

Fig. 6.19: The sidewall (bottom left) overlooked by the first outpost tower (right).

Fig. 6.20: Drone photograph of the sidewall and the tower on the cliff, overlooking it, by Davit Naskidashvili.

being struck by lightning. The wall (like the towers) employs double-faced drystone masonry, bonded by mud mortar, with lime mortar spotted in one location only. One observes frequent large depressions lining the north-east side of the wall (e.g. at NK-17), probably material extraction pits (Fig. 6.30) dug when the wall was built. The wall survives in places to an estimated height of at least 3.50 m, but no attempt has been made

Table 6.1: Location of towers visited during our pedestrian survey, plus estimated location of two outpost towers nearby. All measurements were taken with a handheld GPS and there will be a small margin of error, notably as far as the elevation is concerned (coordinates are in UTM 40N). WP = waypoint.

WP no.	Structure	Elevation (m a.s.l.)	Easting	Northing	Distance to previous
NK-7	Small mound on ridge, potential tower, but far from certain	1669	737497	4100962	n/a
NK-8	Circular projecting tower, start of visible section of wall	1645	737659	4100727	285 m
NK-10	Hypothetical tower; more probably projection of Forud Wall following the edge of the slope	Unrecorded	737741	4100673	98 m
N/a	First outpost tower, estimated location	Unrecorded	737754	4100626	49 m
NK-12	Tower with robber hole in the interior	1665	737924	4100497	213 m
NK-14	Hypothetical tower	Unrecorded	737976	4100429	86 m
NK-15	Well-preserved tower and Trench k	1632	738107	4100328	165 m (249 m to NK-12)
NK-18	Best-preserved tower	1595	738370	4100167	308 m
NK-1	Well-preserved tower on steep rock cliff	1599	738484	4100068	151 m
NK-19	Internally projecting tower	1574	738799	4099831	394 m
NK-22	Point taken above a tower that was inaccessible; this is the second outpost tower; this tower may be aligned with the tower at NK-19	Unrecorded	738827	4099805	n/a
N/a	Second outpost tower, estimated location	Unrecorded	738818	4099792	43 m
NK-20	Third outpost tower in front of main wall, serving as a forward bastion	1554	738948	4099691	165 m
NK-21	Circular tower; appears to be built onto an outcrop	Unrecorded	739144	4099526	256 m (460 m to NK-19)
Average spacing, excl. hypothetical towers					**223 m**
Average spacing, excl. hypothetical towers and outpost towers					**313 m**

Table 6.2: Location of other architectural features and points of interest recorded by the survey (coordinates are in UTM 40N).

WP no.	Feature/point of interest	Elevation (m a.s.l.)	Easting	Northing
NK-9	Point along ridgeline from which a wall on the slopes, running perpendicular to the main wall on the ridgeline, is visible	Unrecorded	737701	4100709
NK-11	Point along wall line running along the ridge; from this point the lower tower SSE of NK-10 is visible	Unrecorded	737806	4100622
NK-53	Point where the wall is preserved to a height of c. 3.50 m, and where two sherds of pottery were found in front	1647	737876	4100540
NK-16	Location of a well-built drainage culvert outlet under the wall, on its south-west side	1646	737885	4100535
NK-13	Location where pottery was collected from the path along the wall	Unrecorded	737952	4100466
NK-55	Section of wall with two faces visible (reaching a width here of c. 2.10 m at the top)	1617	738219	4100264
NK-17	Point along wall alignment on ridgeline; possible material extraction pit located between wall line and large outcrop	Unrecorded	738281	4100227
NK-54	Section of wall employing lime mortar, to bond the stones, on top of a steep cliff	1582	738635	4099950

during our brief visual inspection to measure its height accurately, let alone in all sections surveyed or those only recorded from the air. We do not know how high it would have been originally, how much its height may have varied and whether or not there was a wall-walk and a parapet. As in places there is no level ground on either side of the wall, it seems probably that there was a wall-walk. This would certainly have facilitated effective surveillance and patrol. It would also have enabled more rapid deployment of reinforcements when needed. In the event of known or suspected enemies approaching the wall, easy access to all sections would have enabled its guardians to use long-range weapons or discharge a rock avalanche at any point.

The Forud Wall's construction date and period of use is likely to be identical to those of its towers and further discussed below. Repeated checking of the mud mortar revealed no trace of charcoal or bone suitable for radiocarbon dating. Along the wall, we found a moderate quantity of unglazed pottery on the surface.[39]

Fig. 6.21: The second outpost tower (near NK-22), seen from the third. The Forud Wall is on the crest of the ridge.

Fig. 6.22: Drone photograph of the third outpost tower (NK-20, bottom right) by Davit Naskidashvili.

Fig. 6.23: The best-preserved tower (at NK-18) with its inward-leaning wall and a possible niche. (As on the other photos, each red or white segment of the large ranging poles is 50 cm long, each segment of the small scales 10 cm.)

Fig. 6.24: The same tower (at NK-18) looking north-west: not built at the highest point with the best view, but at a more vulnerable section.

Fig. 6.26: Drone photo of a tower (NK-18) and the Forud Wall running north-west, by Davit Naskidashvili.

Fig. 6.25: The tower (at NK-18) seen from the outside, with stone collapse in front of the lower sections of the wall.

Beyond the section of the ridge accessible without major obstacles to pedestrian survey, the ridge running towards Kalat becomes very steep on both sides. The wall continues to follow its dangerously narrow crest, boasting a massive tower – well preserved perhaps as even harder to reach for stone robbers than the other towers. Whilst not visited on foot, this unnumbered additional tower and a substantial section of wall, beyond the terminus of the pedestrian survey at NK-21, has been surveyed and recorded in part via drone photography (Figs 6.17 and 6.31–6.37).

6.2.4. A sondage within the Arg-e Forud (Trench j)

On the plateau of the Arg-e Forud, in the area of the central saddle, one notices the remains of stone walls. Fortunately, illegal excavations, concentrated on the margins of the plateau, have not seriously disturbed the site. These excavations have unearthed some pottery sherds and building material, including gypsum and probably medieval bricks, measuring 23 × 23 × 5 cm, as well as unworked stone. The sherds are generally unglazed coarse wares and often belong to big jars, occasionally decorated with incised lines and thumb-impressed appliqué bands (Figs 6.39–6.40). Two of the robber holes have unearthed stone walls. The remains of these architectural structures were visible on the edges of these robber pits, cutting vertically through the walls. In order to gain a better understanding of these structures and the stratigraphy within the Arg-e Forud, we decided to expand and clean one of the pits dug by looters. We cleaned the eastern section of the eastern robber hole and recorded elevations in relation to a benchmark situated at the south end of the section (at 40S 736258 E 4103997, 1,360 m above sea level) with an automatic level. We recognised and recorded five contexts in the west-facing section of the trench and reached virgin soil at a depth of 1.26 m (c. 1.16–1.21 m below the surface) (Figs 6.41 and 6.43).[40]

The dark-brown topsoil (j.001), rich in humus and of c. 7–17 cm in depth, is overgrown by wild plants, and the area is nowadays used as a sheep pasture. The topsoil overlies contexts j.002, j.003 and j.004. Except for pottery sherds, sporadically found on the surface, j.001 contained no cultural material. Under j.001, and in vicinity of the northern end of the trench, the illegal excavations have cut through and thus revealed a wall (j.002) built of unworked stones, measuring mostly 0.10–0.30 m across, using mud mortar as a bonding agent. The southern vertical face of the wall is clearly visible in the profile. It appears that the wall ran probably in a north-east to south-west alignment. The base of the wall is at a depth of c. 1.03 m below the benchmark (c. 0.93 m below the surface), some 23 cm above the natural soil (j.005). The upper portion of the wall appears to lean to the south, perhaps suggesting that it eventually collapsed. The northern face of the wall is situated beyond the limits of the trench, and it is thus impossible to measure its precise width. Nevertheless,

Fig. 6.27: Drone photo of a tower (NK-18) and the Forud Wall running south-east, by Davit Naskidashvili.

Fig. 6.28: c. 3.50 m high section of the wall (NK-53).

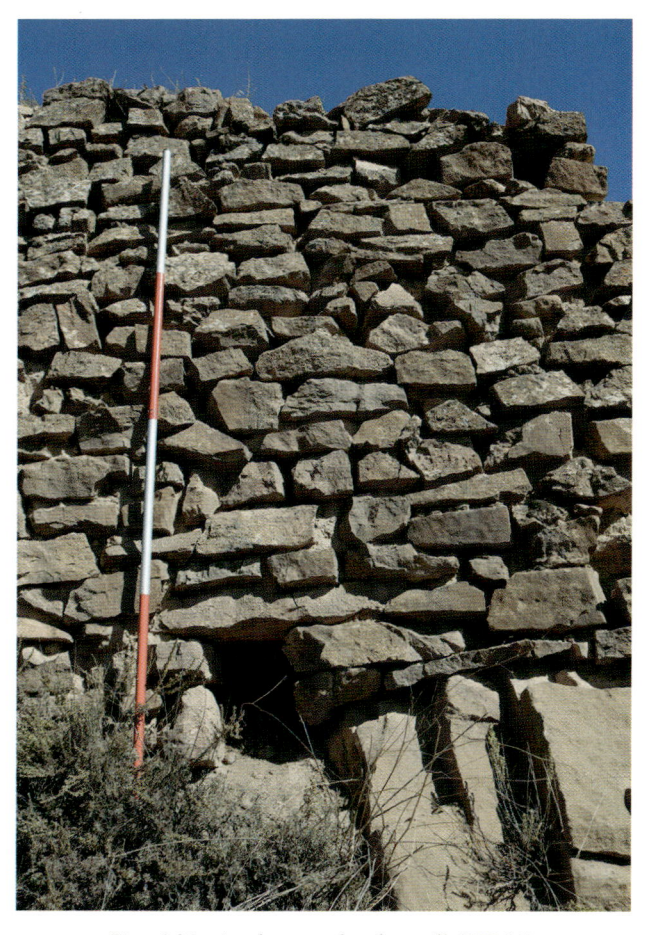

Fig. 6.29: A culvert under the wall (NK-16).

two facing stones, visible in the northern profile of the trench, suggest that it was c. 0.90 m wide.

In the south of the trench, we found another structure made of unworked stone (j.003). These varied in dimensions, with large blocks used at the northern face of this wall. Illegal digging has damaged this structure too and revealed its profile in the eastern section of the trench. The foundations are at a depth of 1.14 m (c. 1.09 m below the modern surface), not far above the level of the virgin soil. Like wall j.002, it was covered by topsoil (j.001), suggesting it is not recent. A stone accumulation to the north of wall j.003 is best explained as wall collapse. Unlike the distinct northern face, the southern face of the wall (j.003) is not well defined. The upper courses of the wall or an associated structure appear to continue beyond the southern limits of

Fig. 6.30: Drone photo by Davit Naskidashvili of the Forud Wall on the crest of the ridge running south-east, lined by material extraction pits.

Fig. 6.31: Drone photo of the Forud Wall, south-east of the section explored on foot, by Davit Naskidashvili. See Figs 6.32–6.37 for further images from various angles, showing the steep gradient of both flanks of the ridge and the substantial wall and tower on top.

the trench. Like j.002, the wall employs drystone masonry, using only mud mortar. Both walls (j.002 and j.003) are abutted by a deposit of soft mid-yellowish brown sandy clay (j.004), containing some gravel and larger stones as well as white particles. Deposit j.004 reaches from natural ground (j.005) to just under the modern topsoil (j.001). There was no noticeable variation in colour or composition, although the lower levels under the base of the walls must be earlier than the upper part of the deposit abutting them. Context j.004 contains significant quantities of stones, in part probably as a result of the collapse of walls j.002 and j.003. Only a single pottery sherd was found in deposit j.004, and the trench as a whole, sealed c. 25–30 cm under wall collapse. Evidently, it had been lost long before the wall collapsed, but after its construction. It was part of a brown undecorated jar (Fig. 6.42).

Under j.004, we encountered homogenous greyish brown clay (j.005), softer than j.004 above. J.005 contained no artefacts and appears to be natural soil, but deeper

Fig. 6.32: Drone photo of the Forud Wall, south-east of the section explored on foot, by Davit Naskidashvili.

Fig. 6.33: Close-up drone photo of the tower on this section, by Davit Naskidashvili.

Fig. 6.34: Inaccessibility may have contributed to good preservation, as shown by this drone photo by Davit Naskidashvili.

and more extensive excavations are required to verify that there are no further structures or cultural layers at a deeper level. We finished excavation at a depth of 1.35 m (1.25–1.30 m below the surface).

Cleaning of the eastern section of an illegal robber pit at the Arg-e Forud has shown that there are drystone structures, perhaps dwellings for the residents within the western area of the site. The bases of the walls were just some 13–23 cm above natural soil. No evidence for floors related to the walls was found. Any trampled-earth floors could easily have been destroyed via bioturbation. We cannot tell whether the buildings consisted entirely of stone or whether there might have been mud-brick superstructures that would not have lasted. There is no collapse mound, making it more likely that the upper sections of the walls were also stone-built and the stones perhaps reused. There are fired bricks on the surface. They may have been employed in these buildings.

Unfortunately, we found no *in-situ* diagnostic material. The pottery sherd from layer j.004, sealed well under the

Fig. 6.35: Drone photography (by Davit Naskidashvili) demonstrates how dangerously steep the cliffs on the outside were – although evidently a wall was still considered necessary.

Fig. 6.36: The narrow ridge with the towered wall on top; drone photo by Davit Naskidashvili.

Fig. 6.37: The Forud Wall protected a vast plateau (on the right); drone photo by Davit Naskidashvili.

Fig. 6.38: Drone photo by Davit Naskidashvili of the ridge running from Kalat to the north-west, without traces of a wall or of towers – perhaps not needed here, due to the steep gradient of the terrain.

Figs 6.39–6.40: Selection of surface finds from the vicinity of Trench j. The scale is 5 cm long.

Fig. 6.41: West-facing section of Trench j.

Fig. 6.42: The sherd found in Trench j (photos by Kristen Hopper).

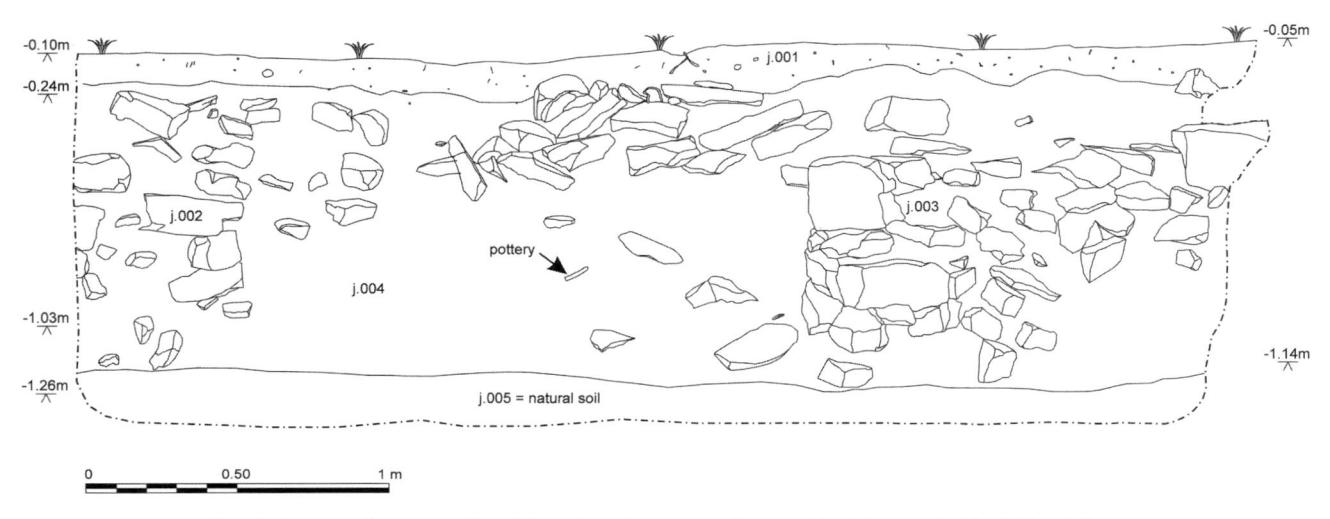

Fig. 6.43: West-facing profile of Trench j (drawn and digitised by Meysam Labbaf-Khaniki).

debris of the collapsed wall j.003, is the only artefact recovered. The sherd is in fabric and colour similar to late Sasanian and early Islamic pottery. No organic material suitable for radiocarbon dating has been recovered from Trench j. There is, however, circumstantial evidence for the chronology of the site's occupation. Surface pottery sherds show possible pre-Islamic characteristics, and the site name and Ferdowsi's allusions to the Arg-e Forud as a fort of the Kayanids imply that the fort has long been believed to be of pre-Islamic origins. Moreover, local people reported on the last day of our mission at Kalat that one of the illegal excavations, some 15 m to the south-west of Trench j, has reached an ash layer at a depth of c. 3 m. If this information is correct and accurate, this layer was more than 1.50 m lower than the postulated virgin soil in Trench j. The question arises whether this was part of a pit or cellar or whether there may be even earlier layers beneath the stone structures that we identified in Trench j. The Arg-e Forud is unlikely to have been left entirely unoccupied during more recent times when the Forud Wall was in operation and it is possible that there was multi-period occupation. These theoretical considerations, surface survey and excavations have, however, only proven that there were stone buildings on the strategic rock, but our conclusions on their chronology are tentative at best. In order to date the occupation of the Arg-e Forud, an archaeological excavation on a larger scale will be required.

6.2.5. A sondage within a watchtower on the Forud Wall (Trench k)[41]

Due to the absence of datable material from the Forud Wall, excavating a sondage within the interior of one of the associated towers seemed our best bet for obtaining dating evidence for this formidable barrier. It seemed likely that towers would have been at least temporarily occupied. Furthermore, organic material could have been lost during their construction. If these assumptions were correct, then dating evidence for the construction and/ or occupation was likely to survive. We opted for the tower NK-15, c. 1.5 km south-west of Gerow. This tower, of approximately 5 m diameter, is well preserved. It is (like other towers) round and employs drystone masonry. On drone imagery, we could see a drainage culvert on the cliff-side at its base. (Its small size and position at the base of the wall suggest that it is not a window and could not have been used effectively for rubbish disposal, surveillance of the approaches or for discharging stones, missiles or firearms against any would-be assailants.) The location of this feature at the precipice made any closer inspection impossible, but it gave us confidence that at least a metre of stratigraphy survived within the interior of the tower. There were no signs of a robber pit (unlike the NK-12 tower, with a distinct robber hole), suggesting that the deposits were undisturbed. Whilst the next tower (NK-18) in the system and already described above was even better preserved, its c. 2 m high overhanging drystone wall raised serious concerns that an excavation in the interior might destabilise the wall and put both the monument and excavators working inside at risk.

Within this tower, our team excavated a small sondage (Trench k) over two days (25–26 October 2016). It measured 2 m (SSW to NNE) × 1 m (WNW to ESE). This sondage was placed centrally within the tower and at no point did it reach the structure's circular wall. The reasons for this were as follows:

- Little would have been gained by exposing the inner face of the wall, already clearly visible at the next tower and preserved there to a higher level.

Fig. 6.44: The Trench k tower on top of a steep cliff and overlooked by higher ground.

- Exposing the drystone wall could potentially have destabilised the monument.
- Our main target was dating evidence for occupation and/or construction of the feature, more likely to be found in the interior.

Below c. 20 cm of topsoil (k.001, soft mid-brown sandy clay), we encountered a layer of wall collapse (k.002). The wall collapse forms a substantial, 90–96 cm thick, layer with an estimated 70% of stones of up to c. 45 cm diameter, in a matrix of very soft mid-yellowish brown clayey silt. We may assume that, just as the next tower to the south-east (to judge by its inward-curving upper wall), it had originally been covered with a domed roof. When the upper walls and roof collapsed, stones would inevitably have accumulated within the interior, if not necessarily exclusively so. Within the wall collapse, we found a pottery handle as well as one piece of charcoal (Rosaceae/Maloideae [apple subfamily], identified by Dr Lyudmila Shumilovskikh), both from the upper part of the collapse and near its interface with the topsoil. Under the wall collapse, we encountered a very stiff deposit of mid-yellowish brown clayey silt (k.003) containing, in sharp contrast to the densely stone-packed layer above, no more than an estimated 1% of, mainly small, stones. This may be a levelling horizon with a floor on top. Within k.003, we found a piece of undiagnostic pottery, as well as a total of 12 identifiable fragments of charcoal from three localities plus another from within a floated soil sample (12 dicot tree/shrub and one Rosaceae/Prunoideae [prune

Fig. 6.45: The Trench k tower.

Fig. 6.46: Drone photo of Trench k by Davit Naskidashvili, showing the small culvert at the base of tower NK-15.

Fig. 6.47: The Forud Wall with Trench k, commanding wide views in both directions, and material extraction pits on the left.

Fig. 6.48: Trench k: stone collapse in the interior of the tower, WNW-facing section.

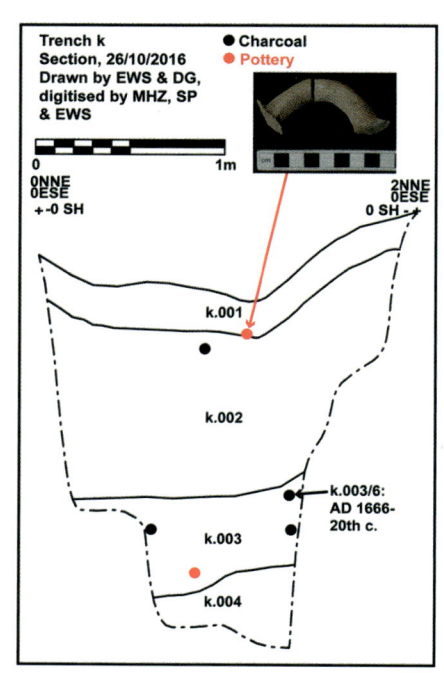

Fig. 6.49: Trench k, ESE-facing section, with finds distribution.

subfamily], identified by Dr Lyudmila Shumilovskikh).[42] The material for the levelling deposit and the mud mortar may well have been taken from substantial soil extraction/quarry pits nearby as well as perhaps some of the stones – and similar pits, as already pointed out above, line much of the wall. Perhaps the charcoal was from fires lit during the construction process. The workforce may have used fire to prepare food or simply to keep warm on the often windswept and chilly ridgetop. A sample of Rosaceae/Prunoideae charcoal (k.003/6), certain to be young, was submitted for radiocarbon dating and will be further discussed below. Underneath k.003, there was a very soft deposit of mid-brown clayey silt (k.004), its colour suggestive of more decayed organic matter than in the two deposits above. This may be the ancient topsoil, but only the very top of the deposit was excavated, and no finds were recovered, so that any conclusions about its significance are tentative at best.

Overall, the quantity of finds was small. Perhaps the tower's guardians, if it ever housed any occupants, tossed rubbish down the cliff rather allowing it to accumulate within the basement of the tower. The comparative scarcity of charcoal is harder to explain, as this would have been more difficult to remove systematically if ever present in substantial quantities. Perhaps this points to sporadic occupation in response to immediate signs of danger rather than the tower housing a permanent garrison. If so, where was the back-up force? The Arg-e Forud is an obvious site, if not necessarily the only one: it was naturally well defended, offered wide views over the approaches to the Forud Wall and was close enough for troops to reach rapidly, within a few hours at most, all sections of the wall whenever there were signs of danger. Furthermore, it formed a vital part of the defensive chain and cannot have been unoccupied whilst the Forud Wall was in active use without rendering the whole system ineffective. Villagers from the Gerow Valley could also have climbed up to guard the barrier within half an hour. With enough advance warning, reinforcements could have been dispatched from further afield, such as Kalat.

6.2.6. The date, historical context and function of the barriers around Kalat

One sample (k.003/6), taken from the upper part of the levelling horizon (k.003) immediately under the wall collapse (k.002), was submitted for radiocarbon dating (Table 6.3 and Figs 6.48–6.50). The piece of charcoal from the rose family, in what is thought to be the foundation level of the tower in Trench k, could date to any period between the final third of the seventeenth century and the very recent past. The absence of modern construction materials and debris makes a construction within living memory highly improbable, not to mention that Major C.O.

Table 6.3: Radiocarbon date of the sample from Trench k (SH = site height, below benchmark in relation to a benchmark for Trench k, set at an arbitrary height of 0 m.).[44]

Context and find no.	Location	Laboratory no.	Species	Date	Calibrated date at 95.4% confidence	Comments
k.003/6	0.44 m ESE, 1.33 m NNE, -1.55 m SH	Poz-89873	Charcoal, Rosaceae/Prunoideae (young)	158±21	AD 1666–20th c. (16.2%: 1666–1699; 34.3%: 1721–1784; 9.8%: 1795–1815; 13.9%: 1834–1887; 21.2%: 1909 or later)	d13C = -24.7

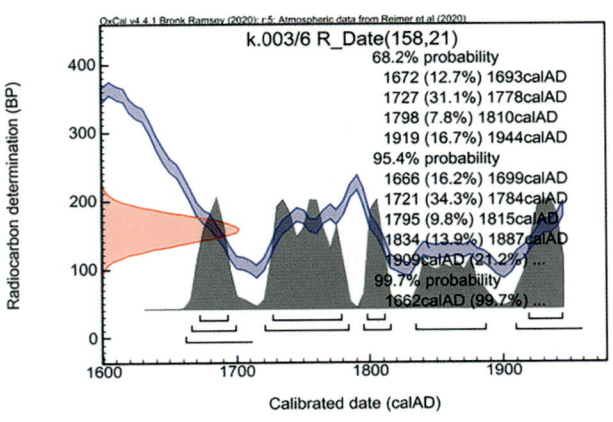

Fig. 6.50: Calibration curve of the radiocarbon sample from Trench k.

Bruce describes the towers as being in decay in 1902,[43] and we are also not aware of any local oral traditions as to the monument's origins. Furthermore, the drystone walls would not have been effective against modern artillery, let alone aerial bombardment. We may thus be sure that an erection in the twentieth century is inconceivable and even nineteenth-century origins seem unlikely. By contrast, the eighteenth century offers a strikingly obvious historical context and is perfectly compatible with the radiocarbon date (falling with a 34.3% probability between 1721 and 1784 – making this period at least as likely as any of the alternatives, even without taking the written evidence into consideration). Nadir Shah (r. 1736–1747), as already discussed, chose the natural stronghold to keep members of his family and the rich treasures amassed secure. The natural defences, whilst formidable, needed enhancing at a time when Kalat would have been the most rewarding target in the Shah's vast realm for those seeking wealth or wishing to spill the royal blood of likely pretenders to the throne. Muhammad Kazim, a contemporary author born in 1720 or 1721, attributes the erection of walls and watchtowers to Nadir Shah – a measure designed to further enhance the impregnability of the natural rock-wall circuit surrounding Kalat. Even the face of the natural precipitous cliffs was made smoother to make climbing them more difficult.[45] Whilst we have to allow for the possibility that the Forud Wall was built on another occasion in the late seventeenth or eighteenth century, which has left no trace in the historical sources known to us, a construction under Nadir Shah seems highly likely, being perfectly compatible with the written records and our scientific dating evidence.

It is worth noting that our conclusions on the age of the Forud Wall are based on a single date from a small sondage in one tower only. The sample is from underneath the wall collapse and from the upper part of what may well be a construction-related levelling deposit. We certainly found no evidence for earlier occupation underneath this deposit. As such it seems likely that this tower was built, rather than reconstructed or reoccupied, under Nadir Shah (or, solely based on the scientific date, rather than historical records, potentially a little earlier or later). Its similar construction to other towers suggests that this is also likely to be true for the other towers. Yet one should also note that the literary evidence points to Nadir Shah having re-fortified Kalat. May the Forud Wall have been rebuilt on this occasion or was it built from scratch? To date, there is no evidence for earlier origins, and Nadir Shah may well have re-fortified Kalat, probably including the Darband-e Argun access route, at the same time as fortifying parts of the natural fortress for the first time. The Forud Wall may have been built from scratch on this occasion. In the light of the small scale of our excavations, we must, however, allow for the possibility that future research may refine or alter the proposed chronology of the Forud Wall. It seems highly probable that elements of the system closer to Kalat originated in medieval or pre-medieval times and were rebuilt later.

It is interesting to note, assuming the proposed eighteenth-century date is correct, that the Forud Wall was mostly a drystone and mud-mortar construction at a time when much more advanced construction techniques were in common use. This should not imply that it could not have been built on royal orders and under the aegis of a well-organised and technically advanced state. The Gorgan Wall, built more than a millennium earlier, but also at a time when strong mortar was in common use for major monuments, similarly employs no more than mud mortar, except for points where a mud-mortar construction would not have lasted; when crossing the Sari Su River, the Gorgan Wall's bricks are bonded by solid concrete-like lime mortar.[46] It would have been even more difficult to produce and bring large quantities of lime mortar to the Forud Wall, as it would have required an arduous ascent from the valley. Even if probably less than three centuries old, the survival of sections of the Forud Wall to up 3.50 m height or so, and with vertical faces, proves the durability of the construction technique chosen (with the exception of the less stable domed watchtower roofs). This is all the more remarkable as it is in many sections built at the very edge of a steep cliff, where the risk of collapse (as a result of it slipping down the rocky slope) would have been greater than in the case of a wall built on level ground or with a deep foundation trench. The upper sections of the domed towers, of course, have collapsed, but one wonders to what extent the risk of collapse could have been reduced, during the wall's period of active use, via regular repairs of any frost cracks or washed-out mud mortar. The above-mentioned drainage culverts under the wall also suggests that the wall was designed to withstand the elements.

The towers are spaced irregularly, 151–460 m apart (394 m maximum if including the outpost towers), 223–313 m on average (centre to centre), in the section covered by the pedestrian survey.[47] They offer prominent views over both flanks of the ridge and the hinterland. The wall was designed for surveillance of any unauthorised approaches. It seems unlikely that the towers formed a signalling chain, although we have not as yet examined which towers may have been inter-visible, which would have depended also on their height and the location of any windows. The Trench k tower (NK-15) and other towers on the wall did not occupy the most elevated points on the ridge, nor do they appear to have reached great height, suggesting that the system was not designed for transmission of fire signals from one post to the next. There is no evidence of an observation platform, nor do we know whether they had window openings facing the next towers in the chain. If they did, this would have created a draughty and cold environment in the interior. In the light of the close proximity of the towers, relaying messages via a hypothetical signal post in the hinterland would have been faster, and along the viable sections of the ridge, pedestrian or mounted messengers could have been employed too. The very limited amount of material from our sondage (Trench k), two sherds and the odd piece of charcoal, as well as a thin scatter of pottery along the wall is clear evidence for human visits, even involving the use of fragile vessels on the top of the ridge. Yet, there is not enough material to suggest permanent occupation over a long period. Perhaps the Forud Wall was a back-up system, ready for use whenever there was a threat, but not with ever-present guardians in every tower. Whether this indicates that the strategy envisaged occupation only when enemies were approaching – or whether the system had not yet been completed when Nadir Shah was decapitated by his assassins (assuming it had indeed been built on the Shah's orders) – is unknown.

The efforts involved in building the wall were considerable. No attempt has been made as yet to calculate the quantities of stone and soil that were used, but the frequent large material extraction pits lining the wall may provide some idea of the efforts involved, despite, no doubt, having partially silted up. Not only was building the wall laborious, it would have been dangerous too. At many points, it is built right at the edge of steep cliffs, and those involved in erecting it would have been at risk of suffering severe or fatal accidents. One is inclined to think that this wall, an impressive piece of engineering built to make maximum use of the terrain, was erected in response to a real threat – indeed the case if intended to safeguard royal treasures and heirs to the throne. It makes little sense as a ruler's vanity project, as it cannot even be seen let alone appreciated until one gets close. Few other than its builders, guardians, shepherds and any daring (would-be?) assailants would ever have seen the mountain sections.

It is clear that nature made an approach from the outside of the gigantic natural ringfort[48] more difficult than from the inside (at least in the area explored during our fieldwork project). The architects of the system further enhanced these natural defences, by building the wall and towers at the very edge of the crest. They furthermore placed outpost towers and at least one side wall in front of the main barrier. There is no question that the system would have been most effective against assailants from the outside, even if guns, stones and missiles could have been targeted at suspect or hostile persons approaching it from both directions and surveillance need not have been confined to one side either.

The colossal construction efforts would fit with the scenario of massive investment into making a prime economic and dynastic asset impregnable. The scant evidence of occupation may be explained by the fortification's abandonment within a few years, or perhaps even before construction works were completed. After Nadir had been assassinated in 1747, Kalat was besieged for 16 days on the order of his assassins and then reportedly taken, a ladder the defenders had left on a cliff reportedly providing access. The sources are undecided whether negligence, the ladder having been left standing by garrison members one night after a sortie to fetch water from a stream outside the defences, or treachery[49] was behind this fatal security breach. In either case, it suggests that defensive efforts and surveillance were half-hearted at best – and perhaps not involving enough activity in

Table 6.4: Location and description of waypoints recorded during the survey. Coordinates are in UTM 40N.

WP no.	Description	Easting	Northing
NK-23	Watering place for animals; spring and stone/cement cistern	739470	4103457
NK-24	Place where passage has been widened	739482	4103924
NK-25	Gorge-blocking wall	739488	4104032
NK-26	Spring	739472	4104194
NK-27	Location of rectilinear depressions surrounded by lines of stones; likely associated with tents or foundations for other semi-permanent structures; circular storage pits located within each	739430	4104317
NK-28	Cemetery	739211	4104468
NK-29	Recently abandoned village	739280	4104499
NK-30	Tower overlooking village	739513	4104634
NK-31	Point in pass overlooked by towers on both the ridgeline to the NE and the SW	740796	4104655
NK-32	Part of a stone-built structure that may have at one point controlled movement through the pass: a gate, wall or bridge-barrier?	740907	4104426
NK-33	Grouping of stone-built structures	740952	4104362
NK-34	Northern end of extant portion of feature recorded as NK-32	740902	4104449
NK-35	Southern end of extant portion of feature recorded as NK-32	740928	4104427
NK-36	NK-36 may be a section of the feature recorded as NK-32 that has broken off; potentially part of an arch; likely washed down the gorge at some point in the past	740857	4104491

the Trench k tower, if occupied at all on the occasion, to leave physical evidence for the momentous events. After the slain Shah's treasures had been plundered and most of his closest relatives murdered, there would have been little incentive to attack Kalat, nor to invest major resources on its defence.

Whilst over a thousand years younger than the period at the heart of our project, the Forud Wall, just as other post-medieval barriers explored during our project, is of significant interest as to functional design and efficacy of such barriers. It is worth noting that even well into the age of firearms one of the best generals on the throne of Iran put his trust in a linear (or in this case, perhaps, vast circular) barrier, created by nature, but with its weak points sealed through human ingenuity. That it reportedly fell after only 16 days does not prove that it was militarily ineffective, notably if the sources are right in ascribing the besieging army's success to negligence of the garrison, if not outright treason. It is worth reiterating here that in the same century another linear barrier, the Jar-e Kulbad earthwork at the eastern borders of Mazandaran, far from being merely symbolic or obsolete, proved decisive in a war.[50] The long string of barriers at the southern edge of the Steppes of Eurasia, created over one-and-a-half millennia from Late Antiquity to the post-medieval era, can only be understood in the *longue durée*.[51]

6.3. The valley of Landar
Meysam Labbaf-Khaniki and Kristen Hopper[52]

A preliminary survey was conducted in a valley known as Landar to the east of the Arg-e Forud and to the NNW of Gerow on 26 October 2016 by Meysam Labbaf-Khaniki and Kristen Hopper. Local informants had alerted us to the presence of further archaeological features, including walls, in this area (see Fig. 6.8). Figure 6.51 indicates the location of the features recorded, while Table 6.4 lists these way points, their coordinates and provides a brief description. The valley was accessed via a steep pass that descends from the plateau to the north of Gerow. This route was difficult to traverse and only accessible on foot. We were informed that it was used to move animals to the valley below. Vehicular access to the valley can only be achieved from the north and involves a rather long and circuitous route.

Not far into the descent into the gorge we encountered a watering place for animals (Fig. 6.52). Here a spring, via a pipe, feeds into a cistern carved out of the rock and bordered by stone and concrete walls (NK-23). Descending further into the gorge a rough path continues along the eastern side of the gorge. Before the final descent down into the valley of Landar the path passes through a narrow opening between two nearly vertical rock faces (NK-24) (Fig. 6.53). It appears that this pass has been widened at some point in the past, as evidenced by the smoothing of the rock face on the west side of the pass.

Approximately 100 m (as the crow flies) further along the pass a gorge-blocking wall was encountered (NK-25) (Figs 6.54–6.55). This pass is one of two through which Gerow could be reached from the north (the other passes through the Darband-e Dehcheh where a massive barrier was constructed). The wall is locally called Divar (i.e. 'wall' in Persian). As it is more than 3 m in height and c. 1.5 m wide, and constructed of stones bound in *saruj* (ancient Iranian high-quality mortar),[53] it seems likely that it may have served not only to stop the movement of animals into or out of the valley, but also to impede

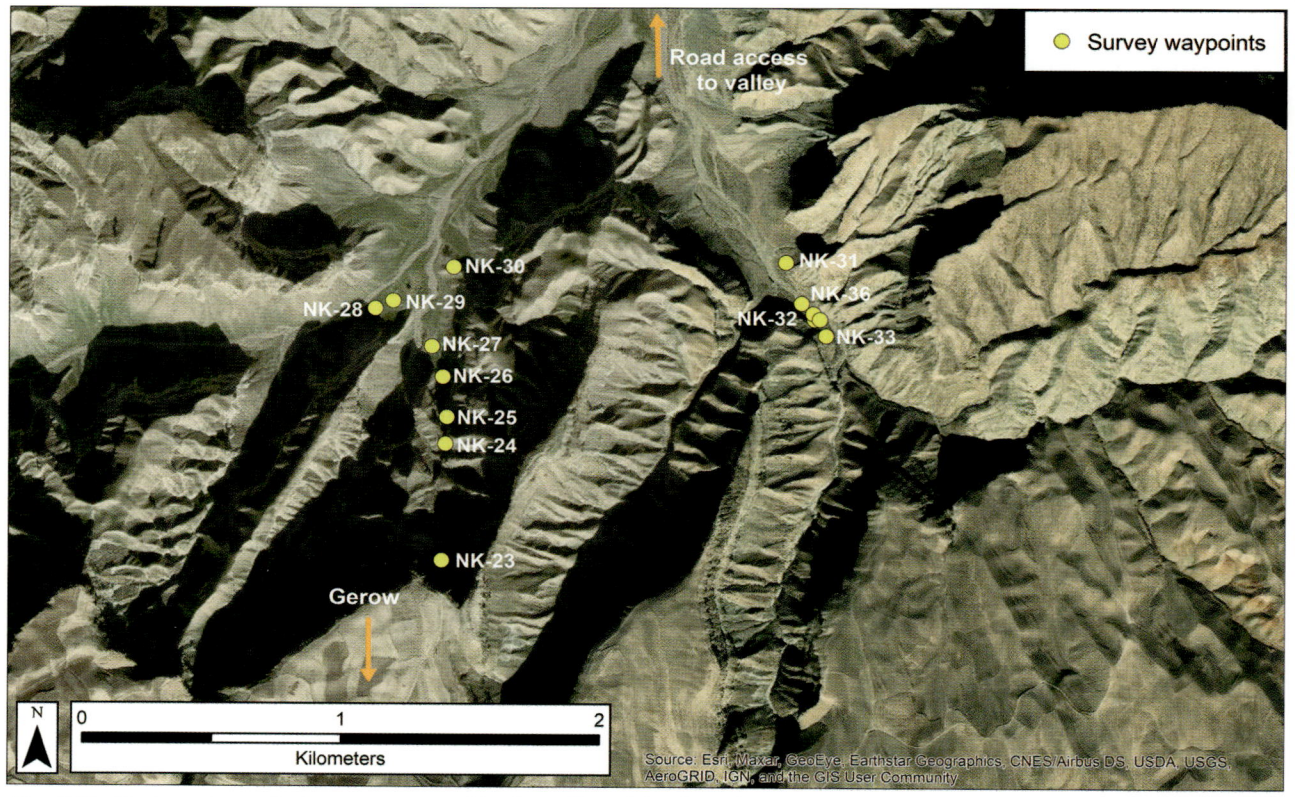

Fig. 6.51: Features located along a gorge and in the valley of Landar. The Darband-e Dehcheh is located near NK-32 (map by Kristen Hopper; Image © Esri, Maxar, GeoEye, Earthstar Geographics, CNES/Airbus DS, USDA, USGS, AeroGRID, IGN and the GIS User Community).

Fig. 6.52: NK-23, a watering place for animals.

Fig. 6.53: Place where the pass has been widened (NK-24).

raiders from the north from reaching Gerow or Kalat. After this, the gorge begins to open up considerably. A spring was noted another c. 160 m further north at the entrance to the valley proper (NK-26).

Located within the valley were numerous features that appeared to have been representative of at least seasonal inhabitation of the area in the recent past. They included several roughly rectangular features lined on the edges with stones that may have been associated with tents or other semi-permanent structures (NK-27). Within these

6. Post-Sasanian barriers

Fig. 6.54: Gorge-blocking wall (NK-25); location indicated with red arrow.

Fig. 6.55: The same gorge-blocking wall (NK-25), left.

Fig. 6.56: Storage pits.

Fig. 6.57: Foundations of structures (tents in a nomads' camp).

Figs 6.58–6.59: An abandoned village (NK-28).

features were pairs of circular pits that may have been used for storage (Figs 6.56–6.57).

Further into the valley we also found the remains of a recently abandoned village (Figs 6.58–6.60). The structures were constructed using traditional stone and

Fig. 6.60: Remnants of animal pens? (foreground) and circular tower (marked by red arrow) overlooking the village (NK-30).

Fig. 6.63: Possible wall, gate or bridge-barrier located at NK-32.

Figs 6.61–6.62: Towers overlooking the second valley surveyed. Near NK-31.

mud construction. A cemetery was also present in the vicinity. Overlooking the village to the north-east was a single round tower, c. 5–6 m in diameter, located on a steep ridge (NK-30). The tower was constructed of stone and mud without the use of mortar. Interestingly, the valley was visible, but not accessible, from the Arg-e Forud. Further north in the valley were several still inhabited buildings which are used seasonally by shepherds for grazing the sheep belonging to the village of Gerow.

A second valley, located east of and roughly parallel to Landar, was also visited. This valley, a local informant told us, formed the main passage between Gerow and Dehcheh. Upon entering the valley from the north, the first feature encountered was a round tower located on the ridgeline on the eastern side of the gorge (Fig. 6.61). Another tower (Fig. 6.62) on the opposite ridgeline was also spotted. Neither of these features were easily accessible and therefore were not visited. However, a GPS point was taken at a point in the gorge below these features (NK-31).

Approximately 200 m further into the valley a large brick and mortar structure was located on the western side of the gorge on a low outcrop. It has been interpreted as part of a possible gate that may have spanned the gorge at least by the Qajar period (see Figs 6.63–6.68). Estimating the date of this structure is difficult. A photograph taken c. 1890 (Fig. 6.68) indicates that by this time it was already in a state of ruin. Given the strategic importance of the pass, which connected Kalat and Gerow with Dargaz and Ashgabat, and the fact that the massive foundations appear to have been reinforced several times, it is possible that the structure may be earlier (pre-Safavid?). GPS points taken at the ends of the extant portion of the structure provided a measurement of at least 30 m (north-west to south-east). However, there may be some margin of error in this measurement due to the issues the narrow gorge was causing with the GPS signal. That this feature may have included arched gateways is suggested by no longer *in-situ* architectural remains located c. 60 m further north in the gorge (WP-36), which appears to be the destroyed pier of an arch that must have been washed down the gorge by water action at some point in the past. More

6. Post-Sasanian barriers 241

Fig. 6.64: Close-up view of the possible gate, wall or bridge-barrier spanning the gorge at NK-32.

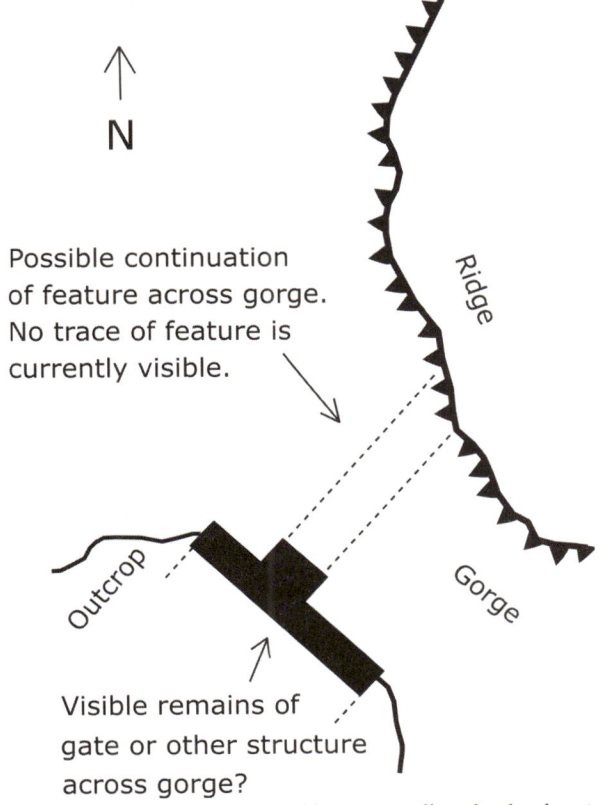

Possible continuation of feature across gorge. No trace of feature is currently visible.

Visible remains of gate or other structure across gorge?

Fig. 6.67: Sketch map of possible gate, wall or bridge-barrier feature in gorge at NK-32. Not to scale.

Figs 6.65–6.66: Destroyed pier.

Fig. 6.68: The ruins of Dehcheh Gate, Wall or Bridge-barrier in a photograph taken in c. 1890 by Abdollah Qajar (Nazarahari et al. 2013, 105).

recent temporary structures have been built on top of this possible gate/wall feature, and further structures of a far more ephemeral nature were located on low outcrops up to c. 70 m south (NK-33).

The abandoned settlements in the Landar Valley appear to have been occupied in the recent past, as clearly indicated by modern debris. Today, mobile pastoralists settle in the valley in spring to graze their livestock on

Fig. 6.69: Tower, explored by Meysam Labbaf-Khaniki in 2012, overlooking the gorge and modern route of Mozdouran–Serakhs; middle tower of the unlabelled three towers in the south (see Fig. 6.71).

Fig. 6.70: The north-western section of the southern wall, explored by Meysam Labbaf-Khaniki in 2012, looking south-east; background left: the northernmost of the unlabelled three towers in the south (see Fig. 6.71).

the land. However, seasonal use of this landscape may have occurred over a considerable period of time. The gorge-blocking wall encountered in the westernmost pass may have functioned to limit the movement of herd animals into or out of the valley. The difficulty involved in traversing this pass would have restricted movement to foot traffic, and does perhaps suggest that this was not the main route of access between Landar and the plateau on which Gerow sits. The second, more easterly pass, however, appears to have been a main route between the settlement at Dehcheh (and Turkmenistan) and Gerow. The remains of what may have been a gate in the pass, and further lookout towers, attest to an attempt to control movement along this route. As such, these features suggest, like the Forud Wall, that controlling access to the plateau may have been a recurring concern over the long term.

6.4. Walls, towers and a fort or caravanserai at Mozdouran

Meysam Labbaf-Khaniki, Kristen Hopper and Eberhard W. Sauer[54]

On 27 October 2016 a visit was made by Meysam Labbaf-Khaniki, Kristen Hopper and Eberhard Sauer to investigate a wall and towers[55] over 100 km to the southeast of Kalat (see Fig. 6.7). A line of four roughly circular towers is located on the lower edge of a ridgeline running north-west to south-east, north of the town of Mozdouran (or Mazdavand), located 80–85 km (as the crow flies or c. 100 km on terrestrial routes) east of Mashad, the capital of Khurasan-e Razavi province in north-eastern Iran (Figs 6.7 and 6.71; Table 6.5).

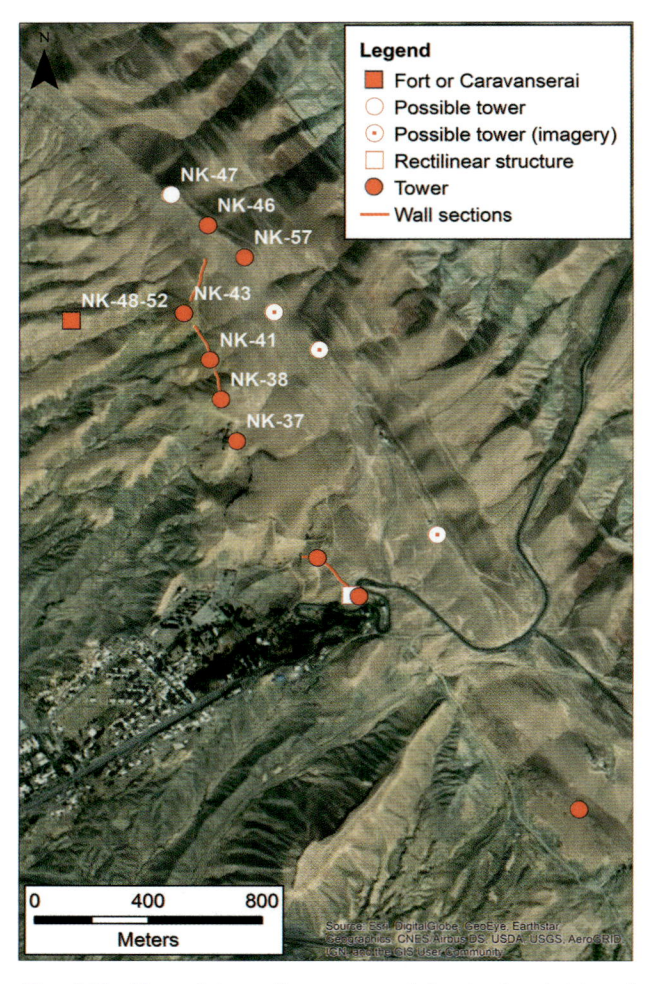

Fig. 6.71: Map of the wall, towers and fort in the vicinity of Mozdouran. Confirmed towers without waypoint numbers were recorded by Meysam Labbaf-Khaniki in 2012 (map by Kristen Hopper; Image © Esri, Maxar, GeoEye, Earthstar Geographics, CNES/Airbus DS, USDA, USGS, AeroGRID, IGN and the GIS User Community).

Table 6.5: List of features and locations noted during the survey. All coordinates are in UTM 41N. Towers and possible towers are highlighted in grey.

WP no.	Description	Easting	Northing
NK-37	Tower, collapsed on N side, with diameter of 6.25 m (NW–SE); stone construction with mortar	278228	4005073
NK-56	Start of wall section leading to second tower	278166	4005205
NK-38	Tower eroded and collapsed on S side, with diameter of perhaps up to c. 8 m maximum (SE–NW), but uncertain, as heavily eroded; brick and stone construction with mortar	278172	4005226
NK-39	Start of wall section	278171	4005248
NK-40	Gap in wall in gully; likely washed away	278149	4005333
NK-41	Tower, well preserved to at least 2.25 m height, with a diameter of c. 4.35 m; brick and stone construction with mortar; wall runs around the south-west side of the tower	278133	4005371
NK-42	Point where wall meets face of large rock outcrop	278074	4005495
NK-43	Tower, with diameter of c. 6 m; outer wall c. 1.40 m wide and interior c. 3.20 m diameter; mainly stone and mortar construction	278041	4005541
NK-44	Start of wall section	278065	4005585
NK-45	Terminal of wall section	278114	4005741
NK-46	Tower on ridgeline above wall system	278126	4005861
NK-47	Possible tower on ridgeline	277996	4005973
NK-57	Tower on ridgeline above wall system	278255	4005744
NK-48	Central mound of square fort	277653	4005517
NK-49	Corner of fort	277664	4005508
NK-50	Corner of fort	277633	4005496
NK-51	Corner of fort	277627	4005522
NK-52	Corner of fort	277655	4005535

A survey conducted by Meysam Labbaf-Khaniki in 2012 located two towers, a rectangular structure (perhaps a fort or a caravanserai), and a section of wall (appearing on the imagery to be at least 250 m in length) beginning c. 50 m north of the main road (Fig. 6.71). We were unable to visit this feature. As such, the first tower (located at NK-37) we visited in this survey is found on a ridge, c. 850 m north of the main road that runs through the town (Figs 6.72–6.73). A wall following the line of these towers is visible from near the second tower (NK-38) (Fig. 6.74) and runs, with several interruptions, to the third tower (NK-41) (Fig. 6.76). It continues for a further c. 130 m until it meets the southern edge of a high rocky outcrop. It measures 1.30–2.25 m at the base and 0.80–0.95 m at the top, as far as preserved (based on two sections only where we took measurements). Too narrow for a wall-walk, it was probably designed to function as a simple barrier and line of control. The fourth tower (NK-43) in this sequence sits atop this outcrop (Fig. 6.77). On the northern side of the outcrop, the wall again resumes and turns toward the NNE, heading up towards the crest of the ridgeline. The wall terminates c. 100 m below the crest. Pottery was found in the vicinity of all four towers and included brown-glazed ware that may be associated with the Qajar period.

The architecture and dimensions of the round towers (even if perhaps of more variable diameter) are similar to those on the Forud Wall, which can now probably be assigned to Nadir Shah (r. 1736–1747) and in any case

Figs 6.72–6.73: The first tower in the sequence from the south (NK-37).

Fig. 6.74: The second tower in the sequence (NK-38).

Fig. 6.77: The fourth tower (NK-43).

Fig. 6.75: The wall connecting the towers heading north.

Fig. 6.78: Ridge-top tower NK-46.

Figure 6.76: The third tower (NK-41).

Fig. 6.79: A possible tower (NK-47) along the crest of the ridgeline.

6. *Post-Sasanian barriers*

Fig. 6.80: The southernmost of the unlabelled three towers in the south (see Fig. 6.71).

Fig. 6.81: The fort or caravanserai viewed from the ridgeline.

Fig. 6.82: The fort or caravanserai on a Google Earth satellite image of 29 June 2010 (Image © Maxar Technologies).

to a period no earlier than the late seventeenth century at the earliest. Whilst we cannot be sure that the two tower-enforced barriers are contemporary, it would seem very likely they are of broadly similar date and most probably both post-medieval. The pottery assemblage, whilst not necessarily lost at the time of construction or occupation, clearly includes material of recent centuries as well. At two of the towers (NK-38 and NK-43) we saw square bricks of 31–32 × 31–32 × 7 cm, as also at the fort discussed below. This type of brick can occur in late Sasanian architecture,[56] but the small number of pieces, none of them seen in architectural context but perhaps employed in the collapsed higher sections of the towers, were probably just robbed from an earlier building and reused.

Along the crest of the ridgeline we identified a further two towers, at NK-46 and NK-57. Another possible tower was located at NK-47 (Figs 6.78–6.80). Further towers may exist to the south-east of NK-57 along this ridgeline, but were inaccessible to us. They have been tentatively identified on the satellite imagery (Fig. 6.71). As such, including the uncertain tower and those identified solely on the imagery, it appears that these towers are spaced between 172 m and 209 m, and an average of 195 m, apart. Another tower was located by Meysam Labbaf-Khaniki to the east of the Mozdouran Wall (east of the main road). The tower is located between two outcrops on a ridgeline. The ridgeline may have been used as a natural continuation of the wall system (Fig. 6.71). Further inspection of high resolution historical and modern imagery is being undertaken and may reveal further features in this chain. The relationship between the line of towers and the wall on the lower slopes and the towers along the ridgeline is difficult to determine at present.

To the west of the line of the wall, we visited what appeared to be a fort with projecting towers (Fig. 6.71: NK-48–52). This had previously been noted on the satellite imagery available on Google Earth by Meysam Labbaf-Khaniki. Investigation of the structure revealed a rectangular fort with projecting towers in each corner (Fig. 6.81). A mounded feature was also noted within the eastern half of the central courtyard. The compound measured approximately 29 m (north–south) by 31 m (west–east). These dimensions do not include the projecting towers, whose remains appear to extend a further 6–8 m from the corners, though the extent may be a consequence of how the structure has degraded.

Viewed on a high-resolution satellite Google Earth image from June 2010, the overall structure of the fort is quite clear (Fig. 6.82). A number of rooms are visible along the inside of the walls. Based on observations on the ground, there were at least five rooms on each of the two long sides, and the satellite image suggests that there were six each. Two more rooms (not double-counting the corner rooms) flanked each of the two gate openings, which are at the centres of the two short sides. Overall, there thus appear to have been 16 rooms. The mound in the eastern half of the courtyard, centrally on the long axis of the compound, has a maximum diameter of c. 11 m.

There was next to no surface pottery within the confines of the compound or in its immediate vicinity. Only two diagnostic sherds were retained as a sample, including one turquoise glazed sherd. The lack of pottery in the vicinity of the structure may indicate a limited period of use or burial of any occupation deposits at some depth. There were also a small number of fired brick fragments, at least two of them square and of similar size to those observed at the towers (c. 30–31 × 30–31 × 7 cm) or marginally smaller. This need not indicate that the fort and towers were contemporary, and it is worth noting that none of these fired bricks were seen in architectural context. They may have been robbed, perhaps on more than one occasion, from more ancient monuments and reused. Architecturally, rectangular forts with projecting U-shaped corner towers and rooms flanking a central courtyard could date to any period between the third and the nineteenth century, but our observations lead us to conclude that neither a very early nor a very late date within this range is likely. The mound, perhaps a decayed lookout post, would be unusual in Late Antique defensive architecture and might point to a medieval date. The glazed pottery similarly leads us to conclude that a medieval date of occupation is most probable, whilst the absence of modern debris suggests abandonment at least several centuries ago, rather than in the recent past. Its location on the summit of a small hill is advantageous from a defensive point of view. Being overlooked by much higher ground, it seems, however, that accessibility may have been as important to its architects as, or more important than, defensibility. Was it a short-lived medieval caravanserai? Plan[57] and surface finds would be consistent with such an interpretation, but it is at some distance to the main road, making it more likely that it was a fort than a caravanserai. Caravanserais, of course, needed to be defensible and it is unsurprising that they are often indistinguishable from military forts. It is indeed worth noting that many caravanserais strikingly resemble in plan smaller Sasanian and medieval forts[58] – and may be one of the lasting legacies of Sasanian architecture to the medieval world.

Notes

1. Sauer *et al.* 2013, 295–96.
2. Visited by Mohammad Arman Ershadi, Jebrael Nokandeh, Hamid Omrani Rekavandi, Bardia Shabani and Eberhard Sauer.
3. See discussion of sources in Sauer *et al.* 2013, 295–96. Kleiss (2015, 117, cf. 119 fig. 292) implies a belief in construction in the early Islamic or even Sasanian era, but there is, to our knowledge, no positive evidence for such an early date.
4. See Kleiss 1981b, 1982f, 347 and 1992, 69 on Meyan Qal'eh; see Hasan-e Fasa'i = trans. Busse 1972, 17–18 no. 78, cf. Dorn 1875, 103, on the attribution of the Jar-e Kulbad to Shah 'Abbas.
5. Sauer *et al.* 2013, 16–17 with sources.
6. Sauer *et al.* 2013, 295–96 with sources; cf. Gyselen 2019, 93–95, 172–73; Rahimi-Laridjani 1988, 45.
7. This point is at 36° 43.082' N, 53° 50.094' E (UTM 39S E 753196, N 4067340); the earthwork's southern terminal is at 36° 42.758' N, 53° 50.060' E (UTM 39S E 753163, N 4066739).
8. Hasan-e Fasa'i = trans. Busse 1972, 17–18 no. 78.
9. The causewayed track on top of the earthwork today terminates at 36° 46.490' N, 53° 50.566' E (UTM 39S E 753711, N 4073664). We followed a dam across waterlogged ground to 36° 46.818' N, 53° 50.493' E (UTM 39S E 753585, N 4074268), but could not spot any continuation of the earthwork beyond the end of the road. Based on Google Earth imagery, it may, however, continue to 36° 47.092' N, 53° 50.613' E (UTM 39S E 753749, N 4074779). According to Napier, the earthwork's terminal in 1874 was c. 300–400 yards from the sea-front then. The terminal observed by Napier (1876, 117) is likely to represent the furthest transgression of the Caspian Sea since the construction of the earthwork, as the sea would undoubtedly have washed away any section of the earthwork continuing beyond the shore for any length of time.
10. Hasan-e Fasa'i = trans. Busse 1972, 17–18 no. 78.
11. Hommaire de Hell 1856, 273, cf. 286–87 (here also referring to a second wall, which cannot be the Gorgan Wall, as just 15 minutes' distance from Astarabad/modern Gorgan); 1860, 405, pl. XXIII.9.
12. Gmelin 1774, 465–66, 457 (note that there appears to be a printing error in the work and the cited page numbers all are used twice; the relevant passage is found where page numbers 465 and 466 are used first, whereas page 457, after page 466, is the second such page). We have not yet examined CORONA imagery or carried out a systematic pedestrian survey. Any fort in forested land would have had a much better chance to be preserved.
13. Hasan-e Fasa'i = trans. Busse 1972: 16–19; cf. Hambly 1991.
14. See chapter 24.8 for a discussion on the purpose and effectiveness of linear barriers.
15. Hebert *et al.* 2019; Schwarzäugl and Tögel 2019.
16. Department of Archaeology, University of Tehran: Meysam Labbaf-Khaniki; School of History, Classics and Archaeology, University of Edinburgh: Eberhard W. Sauer; Department of Archaeology, Durham University: Kristen Hopper; Department of Archaeology, Tbilisi State University: Davit Naskidashvili and David Gagoshidze; Université Paul Valéry Montpellier 3: Bardia Shabani.
17. See chapter 6.2.2. for an explanation of the etymology of the name. See also Khaleghi-Motlagh 2001, Sykes 1906, 570–71 and Curzon 1892, 135. The same crest, crossed by a narrow gorge to the west of Kalat, continues in a south-easterly direction. From the distance, we spotted what looked like a wall on the ridge's southern slope to the south of Kalat, running at a right angle to the ridge. It is possible that this is a similar barrier to the one on the south-west side

of the ridge south-west of Gerow. Without closer inspection or aerial survey, we cannot be sure whether or not this is an ancient wall, nor do we know as yet whether or not there was a wall along the top of the crest also to the south of Kalat.
18 Labbaf-Khaniki 2013; Sauer *et al.* 2013, 14–15, with sources; cf. Kurbanov 2013, 153. See now also the useful summary of Central Asian Walls by Spring 2015, 201–08.
19 Astarabadi (= ed. Shahidi 2005).
20 This photograph, taken by Abdollah Qajar, is in the archives of Golestan Palace at Tehran. See also Labbaf-Khaniki 2013, especially 7 fig. 4; Nazarahari *et al.* 2013, 40. See below for further discussion of the history of Kalat, with sources. See also Mafi 2009, 276.
21 The date of this event is unknown. A later flood on 24 August 1905, attested by Abdulhosein Khan Sepehr (2005, 815), caused severe damage to the bridge.
22 Labbaf-Khaniki 2013, 7.
23 See chapter 3.2 with references.
24 Adamec 1981, 277–86, especially 281, citing Bruce; Sykes 1906, 569–76, especially 569, 572–75. On the history and archaeology of Kalat, see also Curzon 1892, 126–40, 193; Gerster 2008, 47; Le Strange 1905, 395; Lockhart 1938, 195, 254, 261, 263, 277; Planhol 2011; Roemer 1986, 49; Savory 1986; Tucker 2006; Wilkinson 2009b, 21 fig. 9.
25 Labbaf-Khaniki 2013, 2014 and personal comment; Planhol 2011, with sources.
26 Ferdowsi, *Shahnama* V.792– 847, V.871– 73 = ed. and trans. Mohl 1842, 590–671; 1846, 6–11 = trans. Warner and Warner 1908, 37–87, 111–13; cf. ed. Khaleghi-Motlagh 1992, 27–99. Note that Ferdowsi was from nearby Tus.
27 *Bundahishn* 9.38 (= ed. and trans. Dadagi and Bahar 2001, 73 = trans. Agostini and Thrope 2020, 60).
28 Tafazzoli, 2010, 141; cf. MacKenzie 1990.
29 Astarabadi (= ed. Shahidi 2005, 535).
30 Roshani Zafranlou 1982, 201.
31 Nazarahari *et al.* 2013, 54–55.
32 Nazarahari *et al.* 2013, 50–51, 60–61, 118–19, fig. 2.
33 Nazarahari *et al.* 2013, 66–67.
34 Nazarahari *et al.* 2013, 72–73, 88–89.
35 Waypoints of features and points of interest were taken with a handheld GPS and are listed in Tables 6.1 and 6.2. GPS points recorded by Kristen Hopper (with a Trimble Juno 3B) *et al.* are designated with the prefix NK (North Khorasan).
36 A name based on the shape of the mountain chain whose towering peaks resemble from afar the minarets of mosques, or a columned hall with a mihrab (Moein 1992, 2276; Mafi 2009, 274). According to E'temad al-Saltaneh (1843–1896), the mountains were called Hezar Majed because of the significant number of Sufi convents (kanaqah) located here (E'temad al-Saltaneh 1883–1885, 172). Some locals reportedly believe that the mountain range is holy and that there once had been many mosques (Kostka 2009, 268).
37 A possible tower feature (NK-7) was noted c. 300 m to the north-west of NK-8 along the ridge, but could not be confirmed; see Table 6.1.
38 See chapters 6.2.5–6.2.6.
39 We are grateful to Ali Hasanabadi for his observations on the pottery. We are unsure as to the chronology of the surface assemblage, not sufficiently diagnostic for secure classification. Perhaps all is post-medieval as the Forud Wall, perhaps it includes earlier sherds. It is, of course, possible and even likely that the ridges of the natural fortress would have been patrolled and guarded at times of danger long before the construction of the wall.
40 Trench j was excavated under the direction of Meysam Labbaf-Khaniki.
41 Trench k was excavated by David Gagoshidze, Davit Naskidashvili, Eberhard Sauer and Bardia Shabani.
42 See chapter 21.1.3.5–21.1.4 and Table 21.1.
43 Adamec 1981, 280–81.
44 Radiocarbon date kindly supplied by Professor Tomasz Goslar of the Poznan Radiocarbon Laboratory; charcoal identified by Dr Lyudmila Shumilovskikh.
45 Lockhart 1938, 254, citing Muhammad Kazim of Merv, vol. 3 (*Nadir-Nama*), 342; cf. Lockhart 1938, 296–99; Riahi 1985, 1089.
46 See chapters 3.2 and 19.
47 See Table 6.1; 460 m is the distance between NK-19 and NK-21.
48 Cf. Adamec 1981, 277–86, with sources.
49 Lockhart 1938, 263 with sources.
50 See chapter 6.1 and Sauer *et al.* 2013, 295–302, with sources. See Matthee 1999 on the use of firearms in post-medieval Iran.
51 See also Labbaf-Khaniki 2018; Labbaf-Khaniki *et al.* 2019; 2020.
52 Department of Archaeology, University of Tehran: Meysam Labbaf-Khaniki; Department of Archaeology, Durham University: Kristen Hopper.
53 Mazhari Motlagh 2010, 43; Sauer *et al.* 2013, 388, 405 no. 63; see also chapter 19.
54 Department of Archaeology, University of Tehran: Meysam Labbaf-Khaniki; Department of Archaeology, Durham University: Kristen Hopper; School of History, Classics and Archaeology, University of Edinburgh: Eberhard W. Sauer.
55 Also previously identified by Meysam Labbaf-Khaniki 2012.
56 Sauer *et al.* 2013, 388–91.
57 See Kleiss 1996, 1997, 1998, 1999, 2000, 2001 and 2015, 187–217 for a wide range of parallels. The site does not feature in Kleiss's work on caravanserais (cf. Kleiss 2001, 40–43 on caravanserais nearby) or in the local survey by Clevenger 1968. See also Mirzaakhmedov 2016.
58 See, for example, Kleiss 1982a, 385 fig. 11, 387; 1982b; Mousavi 2009, 150–51; Shokoohy 1983; Wordsworth 2019; see also La Vaissière 2004, 172–76, pl. VII.1.

7

Hinterland forts

7.1. Forts on the Gorgan Plain

Freestanding small and medium forts on the Gorgan Plain may have played an important role in the defensive network of this frontier zone and may provide vital clues as to its evolution before and after construction of the Great Wall. Our recent surveys and excavations have led to the discovery of more monuments of this kind and have shed significant new light on the architecture and chronology of a few. To place the results of our fieldwork in context, we will first summarise what we know about these installations and their purpose in the region and the late antique world more broadly.

Small forts are common across the late antique world. They tend to be heavily defended, with thick and tall walls and projecting towers, and the garrison often lived in rooms leaning against the outer walls around a courtyard in the centre. They are found across the Roman and the Sasanian Empires and in some neighbouring territories, but most research has been devoted to Roman forts and fortlets.[1] Although fewer small forts are known from the Sasanian world and fewer still excavated, it is clear that they sometimes formed networks, notably in interior territories, such as Fars[2] or the area of modern Iraqi Kurdistan,[3] or sparsely populated frontier zones, such as on the southern approaches to Mesopotamia.[4] Such installations could have offered safe night-shelters, sometimes spaced a day's march apart.[5] They could have fulfilled police functions, monitored the movement of groups and individuals, safeguarded roads and supply lines and offered space for the safe storage of provisions and perhaps valuables or taxes in kind. They also would have been an effective deterrent against any hostile raiding parties not strong enough to storm them. Venturing past them involved the risk of being ambushed from behind or on return and any supplies or messengers being intercepted.

The Gorgan Plain is unusual in containing the densest known concentration of medium to large forts and fortresses across the late antique world (certainly in terms of combined size), but only a few known small forts. All forts along the lowland section of the Gorgan Wall, from Fort 1 westwards, are over 1 ha in interior size. The smallest size category, with two barracks, was often just a little over 1 ha, such as Fort 2 (1.2 ha).[6] It is of interest to note that forts in its hinterland are sometimes significantly smaller than 1 ha. Amongst such small forts there is, of course, a considerable range in area and potential garrison size. Much has been written about the definition of, and distinction between, forts, small forts and fortlets in Roman military archaeology, notably of the early to high empire. Sometimes 'fortlets' are defined simply by area, e.g. any fort under 0.2 or 0.4 ha, sometimes this classification is applied to installations thought to have been occupied by temporary detachments rather than by a permanent, independent, self-administered unit.[7] There is no space here to explore these subtle distinctions, and no obvious logic to sub-classifying our forts into those falling above and below some arbitrary acreage. Little is known as to the permanency of their garrisons and their likely level of dependence on other installations, though we may note that, being sometimes a day's march from the nearest known counterpart, there must have been a degree of self-sufficiency; considering their small size there must, however, also have been a considerable level of interdependence. As there are not many small forts in our area, little would be gained by a sub-classification into size categories, topographical setting (hilltop versus plain/on riverbanks) or plan (geometric versus non-geometric). A more detailed discussion of small forts is offered in the context of our excavations of the Sasanian fort at Fulayj in modern Oman.[8] In the Gorgan Plain, we find small forts along the mountainous easternmost section of the

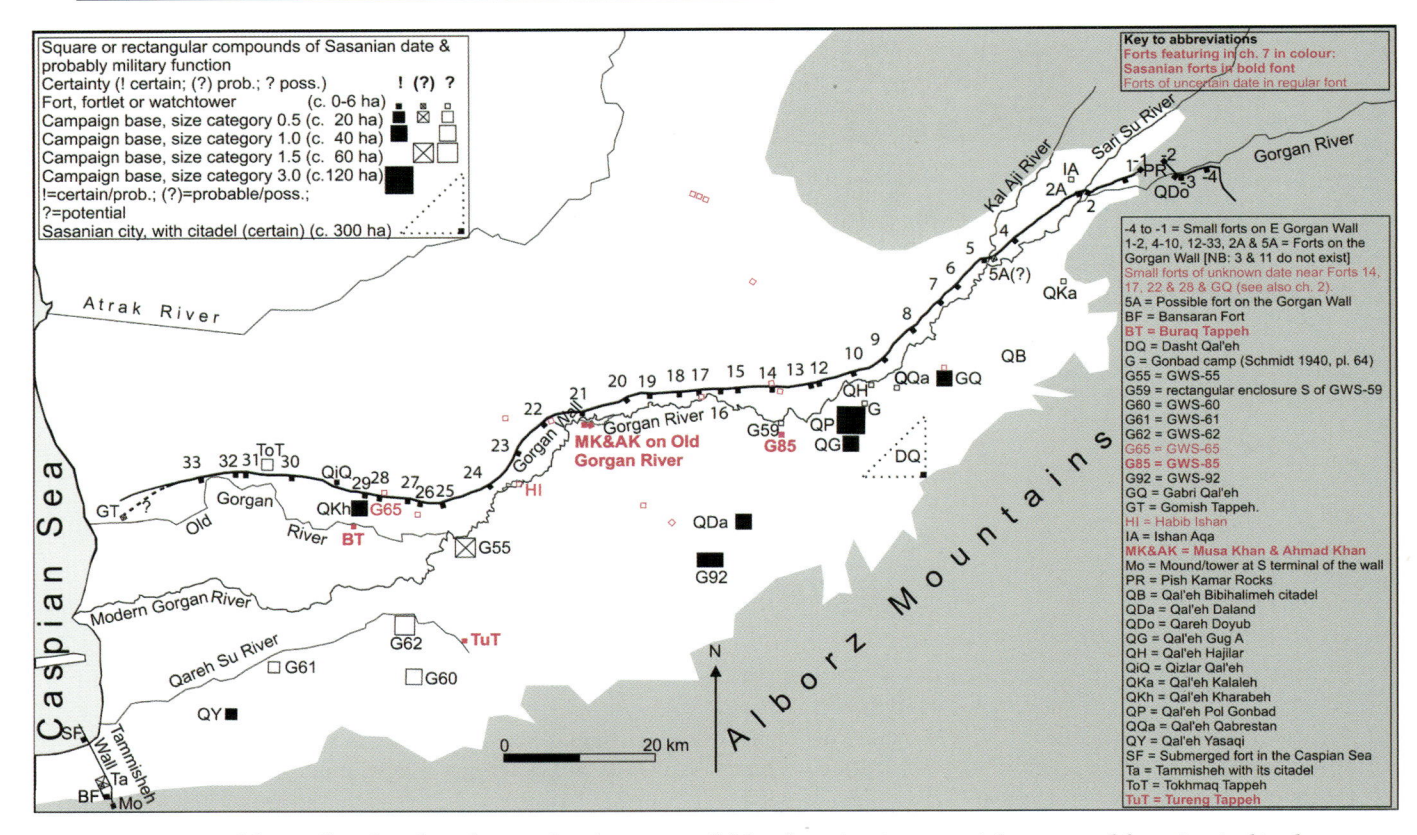

Fig. 7.1: Map of the small and medium forts explored via recent fieldwork, pedestrian or aerial survey and featuring in this chapter and chapter 2 and the Sasanian fort at Tureng Tappeh (in red) and of other certain and possible Sasanian-era fortifications on the Gorgan Plain (in black and white) by Kristen Hopper, Eberhard Sauer and the late Tony Wilkinson (based on Sauer et al. 2013, 305 fig. 12:2 and chapter 2, Fig. 2.19 with amendments). Note that sites have been plotted at an enlarged scale and that the 20 km scale only refers to distances, not to the absolute size of the compounds plotted. For all forts up to 6 ha, the same symbol is used, irrespective of size; for fortresses of over 6 ha, the relative size of the symbol reflects the relative size of the area enclosed. We also used the small symbol for a defended medium to large enclosure (Schmidt 1940, pl. 64) at Gonbad-e Kavus whose precise dimension are hard to estimate.

Gorgan Wall, some of them occupying prime strategic positions, such as the two terminal points of the wall on either side of the Pishkamar Rocks.[9] This interestingly matches the mountain section of the Derbent Wall, also protected by small forts.[10] The difficult terrain would have meant that the mountainous sections of the Gorgan and Derbent Walls were less likely to come under attack by a large force. Even if, any hostile army would not have been able to approach them at a similar speed as in the lowlands, giving the defenders more time to prepare and gather reinforcements. In the mountains, defensive forces could also have used the terrain to their advantage or their knowledge of the land to prepare an ambush on the approaches to the wall – making up to some extent for any numerical imbalance.

In the vicinity and hinterland of the northern edge of the fertile land, more or less corresponding to the alignment of the Gorgan Wall, there are small and medium-sized forts too. The chapter title 'hinterland forts' should not imply that they are all contemporary to the Great Wall, rather that they are in the hinterland of a non-static northern frontier, whether earlier or later than, or contemporary to, the wall. Forts on the Great Wall and large temporary campaign bases are discussed in separate chapters,[11] whilst this chapter focuses mainly on isolated fortified sites of a size no greater than the forts on the wall. Few such forts are known, some of them are certainly Sasanian, others are of as yet uncertain age, and it is hard to estimate how many more may once have existed. The small number of such installations, and the uncertain age of some, makes it more difficult to establish whether they formed networks or just guarded isolated key positions, a question further explored in the conclusion.[12]

The late Ghorban Abbasi has explored two forts south of Gorgan River, c. 1.7–2.1 km south to south-east of Fort 21. One of them, Ahmad Khan, is rectangular and surrounded by a substantial moat. The mound, including its substantial slopes, covers c. 1 ha, with an interior area of c. 0.5 ha (c. 80 × 60–70 m). Satellite imagery suggests that the eastern slope is steeper, and it is possible that

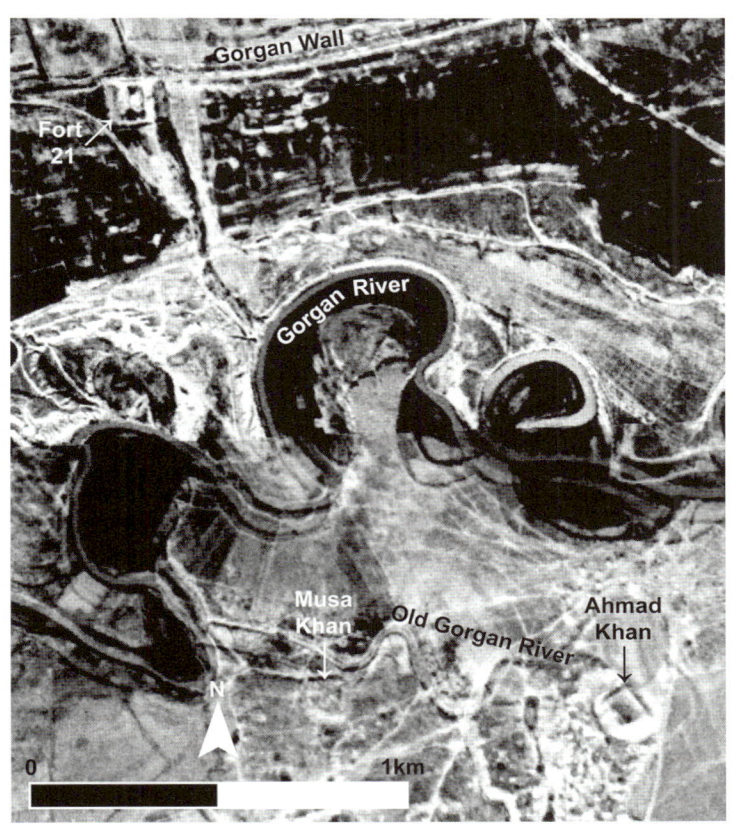

Fig. 7.2: CORONA Satellite image of 1969 of Fort 21 on the Gorgan Wall and the Musa Khan and Ahmad Khan forts on the Old Gorgan River further south: were the latter two forts perhaps part of an earlier river frontier? (Courtesy of the USGS).

Fig. 7.3: Google Earth image of 18 February 2019 of Sasanian Ahmad Khan and the substantial moat surrounding the rectangular fort (Image © CNES / Airbus).

this side along the Old Gorgan River suffered erosion. A substantial depression in the interior of the mound suggests that it was remarkably similar to Buraq Tappeh,[13] with buildings leaning against the fort walls and a courtyard in the interior. Ahmad Khan and Buraq Tappeh are also of similar size and shape and the eastern long side of both forts is very close and parallel to the river. There are traces of an indentation, close to the centre of the west side of Ahmad Khan. Like a hollow-way on the west side of Buraq Tappeh, it may well be modern, but it is also possible that it marks the position of the ancient gate. More probably, the gate was on the south side. There are possible traces of a hollow-way leading towards the centre of this side on satellite imagery (Fig. 7.3) and it would have been in a better position for patrolling the approaches to the river. Possible bulges in the corner may be the remnants of towers. There are no clear traces of preserved interim or gate towers. It should be noted,

Fig. 7.4: Drone image by Davit Naskidashvili and the joint team of Fort 17 on the Gorgan Wall (foreground) and a smaller square fort 0.5 km SSE (middle-ground, centre). Both forts are near a, currently dammed, small tributary (right) to the meandering Gorgan River (background).

however, that we had no opportunity to visit Ahmad Khan and that these observations are based solely on satellite imagery. At Buraq Tappeh we were only able to identify interim towers when inspecting the site, and we should allow for the possibility that there were interim towers at Ahmad Khan as well. The other fort, Musa Khan (which we also have not inspected on the ground), is less well preserved, but appears to be similar in plan, dimensions and location, just south of the Old Gorgan River. Sondages enabled Abbasi to attribute the defensive walls around both forts to Sasanian times, and the forts have yielded finds attributed to the Parthian and Sasanian eras.[14] The landscape team discovered a further fortified site (GWS-85) of c. 4 ha size occupied in Sasanian times and reusing an earlier settlement mound.[15]

The forts in the hinterland include also the arguably best-known of all Sasanian fortifications on the Gorgan Plain, Tureng Tappeh. This fort occupied the top of a prominent earlier settlement mound for defensive purposes and perhaps also to facilitate area surveillance and signal transmission. Due to its location, it takes advantage of the topography and, unlike most other Sasanian military fortifications discussed in this volume, does not have a geometric plan.[16] Buraq Tappeh, a small fort near Qal'eh Kharabeh and the site selected for excavations, in contrast to Tureng Tappeh (and GWS-85), does not reoccupy an existing settlement mound, but was built from scratch in the plain. Unsurprisingly, its plan is rectangular, as are those of Ahmad Khan and Musa Khan and all other purpose-built Sasanian forts on flat terrain in the lowlands known to us. It is worth noting that Buraq Tappeh, at c. 0.5 ha size excluding its walls, and Tureng Tappeh, at c. 0.2 ha,[17] were less than a half and approximately a sixth respectively of the size of the smallest forts on the lowland section of the Gorgan Wall. Even if densely occupied (and even allowing for Buraq Tappeh's initial garrison potentially having been as large as that of a two-barracks fort of more than twice its size[18]), they can only have operated as part of a network and/or dealt with low- to medium-level regional threats and/or regional

Fig. 7.5: Drone image by Davit Naskidashvili of the square fort, near Fort 17, with distinct walls, measuring some 85 m across. There are no traces of barracks and it does not abut the Great Wall. Like similar installations, of non-standardised dimensions, near Fort 14, it is likely to be of a different date. A typical burial enclosure inside, similar to one of the enclosures within Fort 17, at an oblique angle to the fort walls, is likely to be later; these enclosures tend to be placed on existing mounds or within existing enclosures rather than on flat ground.

administrative and policing tasks. Ahmad Khan and Musa Khan are just over 750 m apart (centre to centre), so that their garrisons could have supported each other. GWS-85 could potentially have housed a larger garrison.

A further possibly Sasanian site is worth noting. At Habib Ishan, there is a square enclosure with a corner citadel, and its plan is remarkably similar to Sasanian campaign bases, but it is vastly smaller. No excavations have taken place at the latter site and surface pottery points to heavy occupation or reoccupation in the Islamic era, though some sherds could be late Sasanian as further explored below.[19] It falls into the small fort category only if the size of its (perhaps permanently occupied?) corner citadel is considered. Habib Ishan's citadel and the larger enclosure combined fall within the size range of the Gorgan Wall forts. Even excluding Habib Ishan, the small number of known or probable hinterland forts on the Gorgan Plain display an astonishing variety in terms of plan, size and topographical location.

There are several further small to medium square forts in the immediate vicinity of the Gorgan Wall, mostly south and in some cases, e.g. one of those near Fort 14, north of it. They are mostly of unknown date. Like the cited certain and possible Sasanian hinterland forts, they differ in architecture from the forts on the wall and never contain barrack mounds. They vary in dimensions, and it is possible that some of them are medieval, to judge by surface material in one of them (a square fort, c. 100 m across and some 250 m centre to centre, north of Fort 14 and at a slightly oblique angle to it).[20] Worth noting is also an undated square compound of c. 1 ha, with possible regularly spaced tower mounds, some 800 m NNW of the citadel of Gabri Qal'eh.[21] The clustering of forts near the Great Wall is not likely to be coincidence. They make little sense as contemporary installations, least of all any forts in an exposed position north of the wall. They would have added little capacity to that of the more numerous and mostly larger forts on the wall. Those forts in isolated positions south of the wall would have been unsuitable for border zone surveillance. Do they mark an effort to reinstate the Gorgan Wall as a boundary marker at a later stage? Perhaps, but once the wall had been robbed out, it would no longer have formed an effective obstacle. As further explored in the conclusion,[22] there is a strong possibility that some may belong to a network of forts preceding the wall.

7.2. Buraq Tappeh

7.2.1. Buraq Tappeh: siting and research potential of a strategic guard-post

Buraq Tappeh[23] is located some 2 km south of the large campaign base of Qal'eh Kharabeh. It was first mapped as an unnamed settlement mound by Ture J. Arne's Swedish expedition in 1933.[24] Hiroshima University Scientific Expedition surveyed the area in 1974, correctly mapping the Old Gorgan River flowing past the east side of the Buraq Tappeh.[25] We examined the site briefly during the first phase of our fieldwork, and postulated already then that it was a Sasanian fort, perhaps guarding a crossing over the Old Gorgan River.[26] That the mound's eastern slope is narrower than any other is best explained by riverine erosion, circumstantial evidence for the river carrying water during and/or after the fort's construction, not to mention that it would be hard to explain why the fort would have been built next to an abandoned dry riverbed.[27]

There may have been a bridge, rather than a ford or ferries, as the Gorgan River in the past may have carried much more water than it does today, and attempting to cross it one reportedly risked one's life. The fourteenth-century author Hamd Allah Mustawfi describes the river as being 'very deep, its banks are steep, and for this reason it is very dangerous to ford, so that no day passes without somebody being drowned in its waters'.[28] It could be even more dangerous during periods of flooding, as Nadir Shah experienced, having already lost men during earlier crossings of the river, when in 1741 thousands of soldiers of his army, plus pack animals, drowned during a sudden flood.[29] Should the river have been similarly deep and dangerous 900 and 1,300 years before the times of Mustawfi and Nadir Shah, keeping bridges under tight military control would have provided an effective means of monitoring traffic between the steppe and the fertile lands south of the river. Even as recently as 2019, the modern Gorgan River (further south) caused a major flood in Golestan. On the other hand, Charles Edward Yate describes an uneventful crossing of the river, 30 yards (c. 27 m) wide in a 15 feet deep bed with steep banks, on a

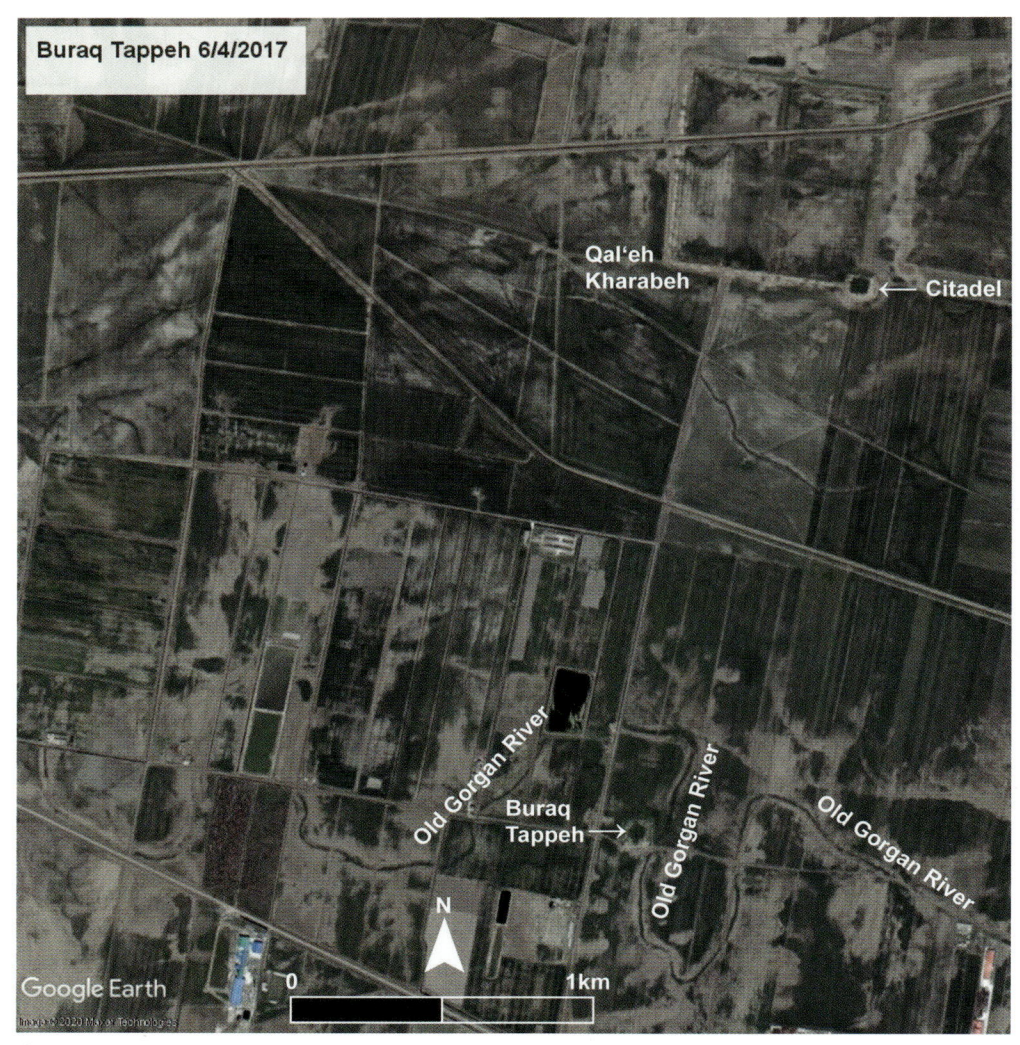

Fig. 7.6: Google Earth image of 6 April 2017 of Qal'eh Kharabeh and Buraq Tappeh, the latter overlooking the meandering Old Gorgan River and clearly surrounded by a moat in the east, north and west, a modern track obscuring any traces in the south (Image © Maxar Technologies).

firm ford near Aq Qala in the 1890s. The water reportedly reached no higher than the mules' girths,[30] suggesting that at times of normal or low water levels wading through the river at a ford need not have been unduly risky – nor was it necessarily without its dangers in case of rising water levels and/or travellers unable to swim. Excluding periods of severe flooding or seasonally shallow water, most traffic across the river will have taken advantage of easy and safe crossing points, where available.

The most logical position for a bridge would have been near the south-east or north-east corner of the fort, if its function was to guard the approaches to the crossing. As there are no signs of a gate or access route on the fort's north side, perhaps the gate was located in the south, where heavy plough damage might have erased any above-ground traces of tower mounds or any ancient hollow-way. We are not aware of the remains of a bridge, but this may of course have collapsed into the riverbed during a flood, if made of brick and mortar, and had no chance of survival if made entirely of perishable materials (such as timber, ropes and plant fibres). The postulated river crossing was just 2 km from the south gate of Qal'eh Kharabeh and will have been used by most travellers approaching the large campaign base from the south or departing from it in a southerly direction. Charcoal analysis, following our 2016 excavations, has added strength to the hypothesis that there was water in the adjacent bed of the Gorgan River at the time. The charcoal assemblage suggests that the Old Gorgan River may have been lined by elm and plane trees, in what is today a treeless landscape. Whilst we cannot exclude that firewood was brought from further afield, it seems much more likely that the charcoal recovered is fuel sourced in the vicinity of the compound.[31] The same may be true for fish, featuring prominently on the menu of the

Fig. 7.7: Buraq Tappeh, seen from the north, with the Alborz Mountains in the distant background.

fort's inhabitants and perhaps caught in nearby sections of the river or the moat.³²

As this strategically positioned small fortified compound represents a different type of monument to the forts on the Gorgan Wall and the large campaign bases in its hinterland, we felt it had the potential to shed light on the layout of small geometric forts. It furthermore promised to provide insights into the nature, evolution and chronology of military occupation in the hinterland of the Great Wall, e.g. whether the hinterland forts were built earlier or later than the Great Wall and, in the former case, whether they were still needed or were abandoned after wall construction.

Similar questions arise concerning the relative chronology of small forts and huge campaign bases. Intriguingly, Buraq Tappeh is in size, shape and elevation not dissimilar to the citadel of Qalʻeh Kharabeh. Whilst Qalʻeh Kharabeh's vast interior appears to have been occupied temporarily only,³³ both its citadel and Buraq Tappeh were small enough for permanent effective occupation.

Was Buraq Tappeh's construction contemporary to that of Qalʻeh Kharabeh or were they of different dates? In the latter case, which was earlier and did their periods of occupation overlap? It was clear, of course, that radiocarbon samples and artefacts were not likely to be datable to periods of less than a century or so, and that our chances of succeeding in obtaining full answers to all these questions were slim. Even partial insights into the relative and absolute chronology and the function and layout of military sites to the south of the Gorgan Wall, however, promised a much better understanding of how the network of military sites functioned and evolved over time.

7.2.2. Geophysical survey³⁴

In 2015, we carried out a magnetometer survey of Buraq Tappeh (Figs 7.8–7.10), with the aim of gaining a better understanding of the fort plan and providing us with the information needed for targeted excavation in the following year. The rectangular shape of the mound was remarkable, but there was little else to shed light on the compound's architecture. Whilst it is visible that there is a depression in the centre of the mound, the survey demonstrated that it is regular and must be a central courtyard. Interestingly, this matches our observations at the citadels of Qalʻeh Kharabeh and Gabri Qalʻeh where there is also a clear depression in the centre and a bank along the edges of the rectangular mounds – no doubt the remains of central courtyards (or, less probably, low-storey buildings) surrounded by substantial housing blocks

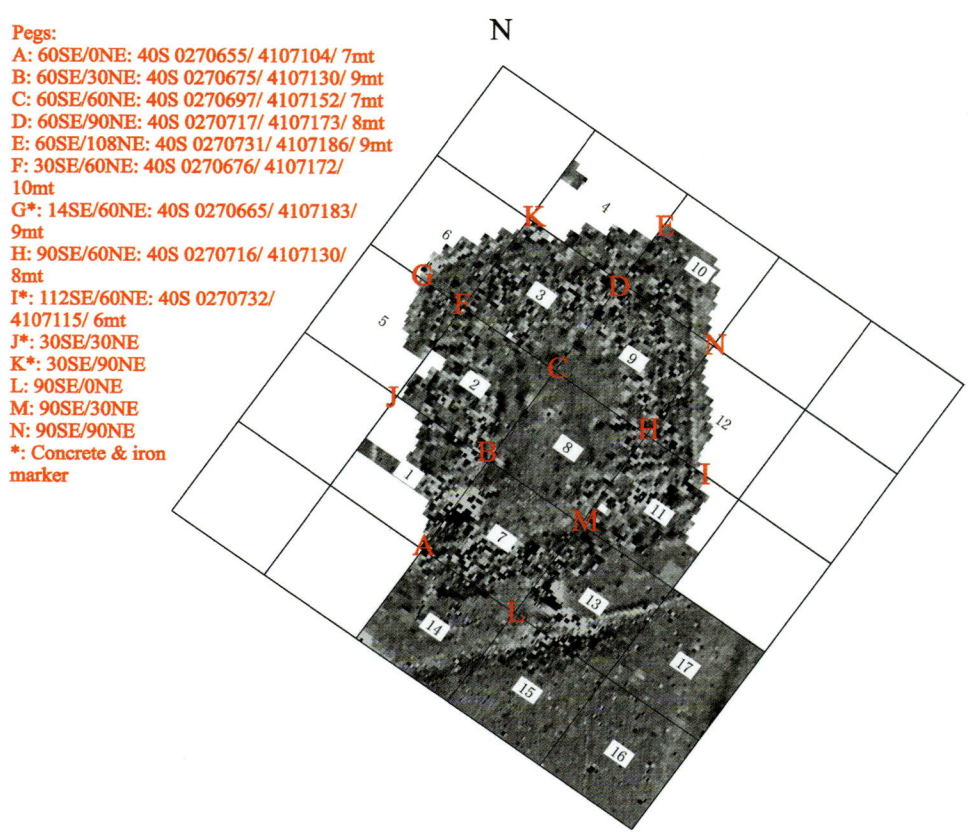

Fig. 7.8: Geophysics plot with the location of grids, temporary pegs and permanent markers. Each grid measures 30 × 30 m.

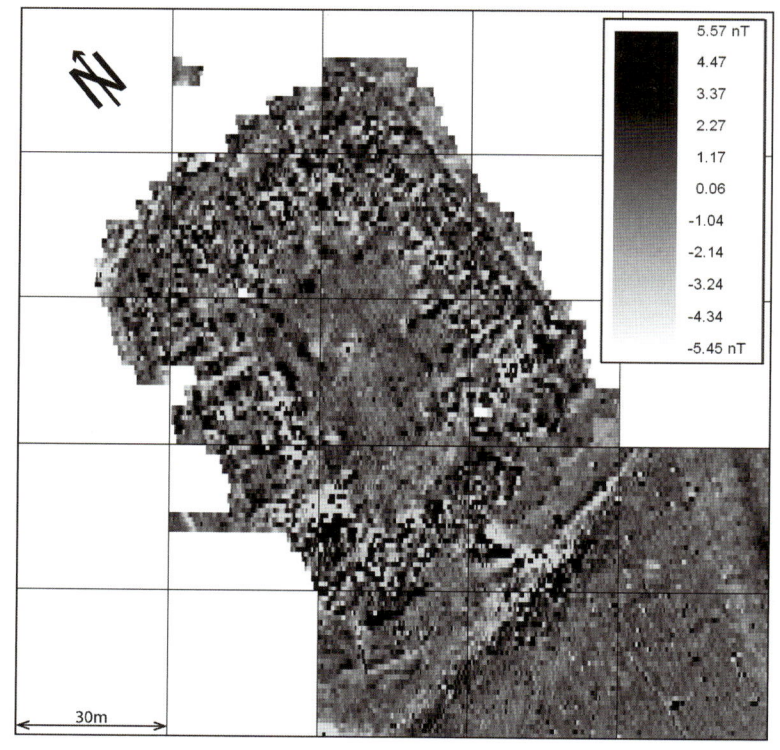

Fig. 7.9: Buraq Tappeh, magnetometer survey by Mohammad Arman Ershadi et al., further processed by Roger Ainslie of Abingdon Archaeological Geophysics. Each grid measures 30 × 30 m.

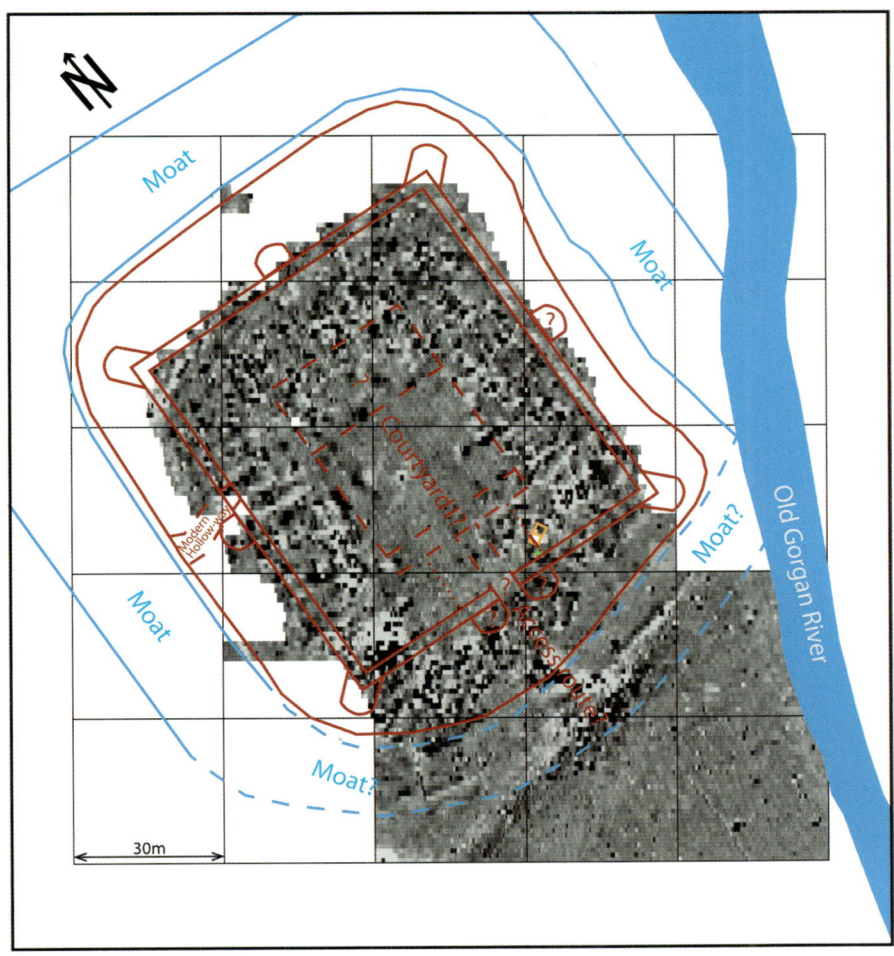

Fig. 7.10: Buraq Tappeh, interpretative plan, based on pedestrian and geophysical survey, satellite and drone images and excavations, superimposed over the magnetometer plot. The location of Trench g, centred on a robber pit with later extension to the north-east, is marked in yellow and that of a further nearby robber pit in green. The internal wall found in Trench g is plotted in red. It is parallel/perpendicular to the outer fort walls, but we do not know how far it extends to the south and north; it is possible that it connected the outer walls with the courtyard. Its possible continuation is plotted as a dotted line. It seems likely that there would have been a parallel wall on the other side of the postulated entranceway (also plotted as a red dotted line). Undoubtedly, there would have been many such walls between individual rooms and corridors. The hypothetical reconstruction of the fort walls and the approximate extent of the mound are also shown in red. Note that the mound, the plateau/fort, the modern hollow-way, the ancient moat and the Old Gorgan River have been plotted based on Google Earth imagery of 2016 and 2017, though the river bed, where surveyed, was also detectable as an anomaly. The approximate position of the towers is based on drone images and pedestrian survey; hypothetical towers are indicated with a question mark. The latter include the postulated gate towers. A scatter of magnetic debris might mark the access route and/or a bridge or causeway across the moat. The size of towers is unknown, as is the width of the outer wall, but the reconstruction assumes they are of the same dimensions as those of Fort 2. The extent of the courtyard has been plotted based on the magnetometer survey and seems quite well defined in the west and east, but uncertain in the south and north.

and towered mud-brick walls.[35] It appears that the Buraq Tappeh fort measured approximately 80 m north–south by 70 m west–east. It is hard to draw firm conclusions on the dimensions of the courtyard and the housing units lining it based on the magnetometer plot only; the survey may detect the extent of the original buildings or of wall collapse. The combined width of the outer wall and room units lining it was probably c. 20 m in the west and east, but is less well defined in the north (20–35 m?) and the south (15–20 m?). The fort essentially consists of a single building comprising four interconnected wings around a central courtyard, the latter measuring an estimated 30 m, west–east, and 25–45 m, north–south. This open space was symmetrically in the centre, west–east, but we do not know if the same is true, north–south. There are possible suggestions of lines parallel to the edges within the courtyard (perhaps further buildings or verandas?), but this is not clear. The prominent elevation of the mound of 4–5 m, reportedly even as high as 6.70 m in the recent past,[36] notably of the banks around the edges of the mound, suggests that the room units lining the fort walls would have risen to more than a single storey in height. Subsequent excavations have provided important information on the elevation of internal buildings. The question as to how many storeys there were will therefore be further explored in the context of this evidence.[37] Whilst questions remained as to the size and extent of indoor space within the fort, there can be little doubt that rooms lined the outer wall and that there was a, probably rectangular, courtyard in the centre. If so, the Buraq Tappeh fort differs in design from the Gorgan Wall forts, but has much in common with late antique forts elsewhere, where casemates abutting the inside of defensive wall are common.[38] It is also strikingly similar to the purpose-built citadels, which sometimes occupy one corner of a campaign base. The rooms and corridors embedded in Qal'eh Iraj's massive walls provide a further example for Sasanian military housing alongside defensive walls.[39] The reasons for accommodation units abutting the walls, especially often, if not exclusively so, in small forts, may be purely practical: it saved building material and offered additional protection from any enemy missiles. It created a larger contiguous protected outdoor space than would have been available between freestanding buildings. The large courtyard would have been easily accessible for all occupants and offered a safe space for tethering mounts of the garrison and official visitors and for outdoor activities at times of dry weather, e.g. communal meals or domestic work.

The geophysical survey also detected what must be magnetic debris accumulating in the old bed of the Gorgan River in grid 17. The riverbed is, however, much clearer on the satellite images. The west–east band of high magnetisation south of the fort is more likely related to the modern track and associated scatters of modern debris than any material from the moat around the fort. A band of magnetic material in a north to south alignment, roughly in the centre of the fort's southern slope, corresponds, however, to no known modern feature. Perhaps this marks the access route to a gate and/or the scattered remnants of a bridge or causeway across the moat, if this hypothesis is, admittedly, far from proven.

7.2.3. Aerial and pedestrian survey

On-site inspection in 2015 and 2016, and later examination of the drone images taken in 2016, added further information on the site. These were valuable in particular for the defences, as the mound's steep slopes in the west, north and east could not be geophysically surveyed; the more gentle surveyable south slope is heavily damaged and the terrain flattened by ploughing. About halfway on the north side of the tappeh, as well as, also centrally, on the west side, there is a suggestion of a projecting tower. Pedestrian survey in 2015 suggested there was also a central tower mound of the east side, although we could not discern any traces of it on the drone or satellite images. On the west side, one also observes a hollow-way next to the central bulge. Could this mark the position of the gate? This seems unlikely; the west side is closest to modern farmhouses and closest to the main modern north–south track, and there is a second less prominent hollow-way further south on the west side. These hollow-ways are probably modern and do not reflect the position of the gate. It is noticeable, however, that the main hollow-way is just to the north of the western slope's mid-point and just to the north the bulge, suggesting that people deliberately avoided the inconvenience of climbing up a steep tower mound, but chose the gentler slope next to it. The hollow-way, whilst probably post-Sasanian, thus adds strength to the interpretation of the bulge as the remains of an ancient interval tower. The fort's south side is too heavily ploughed for any potential interval tower or a gate flanked by towers to survive. It seems a near certainty, however, that there was either a gate or a central interval tower on this side, too, as the arrangement of towers on Sasanian forts tends to be broadly symmetrical and as not having an interval tower on one side would have weakened the defences. A gate seems more likely, as there is no firm evidence for a gate on the other three, steeply sloped, sides, not to mention the cited circumstantial evidence for an access route in the south. The eroded east side seems also an unlikely location for a gate, as it faced the river and there may not have been enough space here for a bridge and a roadway past the moated fort. If these assumptions are correct, then the tappeh had four corner towers, one interval tower each on the east, north and west sides and potentially two gate towers on the south side. In total, there thus would have been nine towers. Tower-spacing, excluding the postulated gate towers, may have been approximately 35–40 m, centre to centre. If so, it would be well outside the around 30 m (c. 100 feet) distance frequently observed elsewhere in Sasanian fort design.[40] Evidently, Sasanian architects did not always use neat round multiples of units of measurement, but more research is needed to establish what pragmatic considerations, or perhaps chronological developments or evolving regional practices, account for this being applied at some sites, but not at others.

Google Earth imagery, most clearly that of 6 April 2017 (Fig. 7.6), shows a broad band of lush green vegetation surrounding the fort in the east, north and west. This must be a band of fertile soil enhancing plant growth accumulating within a once water-filled moat around the fort. Its extent on, or even if it extended around, the south side of the fort is unclear as this area is obscured by a modern farm track. Moats also surrounded the lowland forts on the Gorgan Wall and most or all Sasanian campaign bases on the Gorgan Plain as well as the city of Dasht Qal'eh. At Buraq Tappeh, just as in the case of other Sasanian moated fortifications, the moat will have served the dual purpose of providing the material needed for the mud-bricks for

Fig. 7.11: Google Earth image of Buraq Tappeh of 27 November 2016, with Trench g clearly visible in the south-east, as well as the central depression, the disturbance created by modern pit digging in the south-west and two hollow-ways bypassing a probable central projecting tower in the west (Image © CNES / Airbus).

Fig. 7.12: Buraq Tappeh, drone image from the south by Davit Naskidashvili and the joint project. The projections on the left (west) side are likely to represent collapsed corner bastions and an interval tower. Note Trench g in the bottom right (south-east) corner and two recent robber trenches in the bottom left (south-west) corner.

the walls and internal buildings as well as to enhance the defences. In the case of Buraq Tappeh, water from the Old Gorgan River will have been channelled into the moat. One wonders, however, if this might have had the unpleasant side effect of creating a breeding ground for mosquitoes – or perhaps the opposite effect of creating a healthier environment. During our fieldwork, with far less water around, on some days mosquitoes were noticeably more troublesome in the area of Buraq Tappeh than at other sites explored. This phenomenon might be related to the current arid environment and scientific research showing that dehydration can increase aggressive blood-feeding of mosquitoes.[41] Plentiful availability of water around Buraq Tappeh in Sasanian times may have been a mixed blessing, but the benefits will have outweighed the drawbacks.

Fig. 7.13: Buraq Tappeh, drone image by Davit Naskidashvili and the joint project of the substantial recent robber pits and the associated spoil heap in the south-west of the fort.

There were recent robber pits in the south-west and south-east corners of the fort (in grid 7, at 62 m SE/17 m NE, and in grid 11, at 92 m SE/34 m NE plus a third shallower pit immediately NE). In the north of the fort (grid 3) there was a further such pit, but already filled with sediments more than the other shafts. It is quite clearly visible on Google Earth imagery of 24 February 2014, suggesting that it had been dug earlier in this year or the year before, and it is evidently of less recent date than the other pits. The first of the cited pits, dug it seems between 2014 and 2015, was c. 2.80–4.00 m deep, with mud-bricks visible down to c. 1.70 m below the surface;[42] the second was c. 2.00 m deep, with a small chamber dug at the bottom where mud-bricks had been exposed. A red carnelian bead was found near the latter robber pit and the later Trench g.[43] The pits seem to have targeted areas next to the mud-brick structures around the edge of the mound (but not the sterile walls themselves), although, given their moderate number, this may be coincidence. The mud-brick architecture exposed within the pits is preserved to a height of at least c. 1.50–2.00 m, but subsequent excavation established that it was almost as high as the mound itself. It seems that the robber pits have been dug in search of treasure, even if it remains doubtful that this endeavour yielded commercially valuable artefacts (judged by our own failure to unearth such finds at Buraq Tappeh or other Sasanian sites excavated). The site is evidently under threat from illegal digging and modern agriculture, but still survives well. Geophysical and pedestrian survey confirmed our impression that it merited excavations – as a representative of a so far unexplored category of site: a rectangular small hinterland fort.

7.2.4. A sondage at Buraq Tappeh (Trench g)[44]

7.2.4.1. Introduction

Based on the 2015 on-site inspection, we decided to excavate in 2016 a sondage centred on one of the robber

Fig. 7.14: Buraq Tappeh, drone image (by Davit Naskidashvili and the joint project) of Trench g, centred on a (at this stage invisible) robber pit. Another modern round robber shaft (top left) appears to form the access to an underground tunnel system extending metres beyond. We subsequently encountered parts of a tunnel, likely linked to the shaft, extending to the lower strata within our trench. We do not know if just this single tunnel or multiple modern tunnels emanate from this shaft. The photo, as the other drone images, was taken on 27 September 2016, prior to the extension of the trench, in a north-east-wards direction (i.e. towards the bottom of the picture) from 2 × 2 to 2 × 4 m.

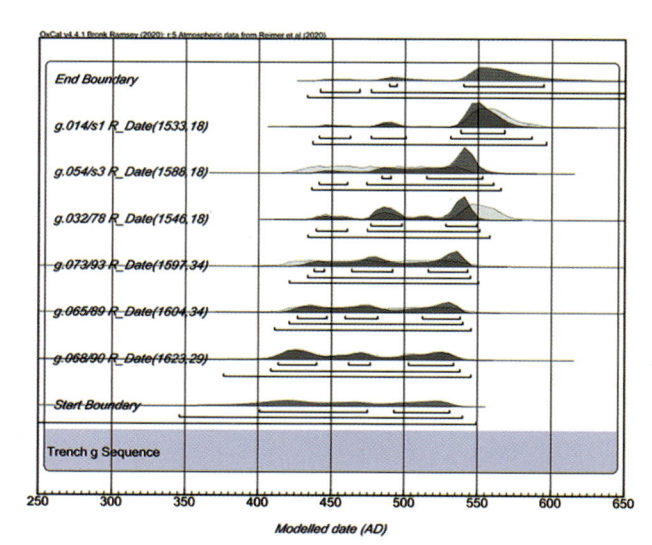

Fig. 7.15: Tentative Bayesian model of radiocarbon samples from Trench g. The deep stratigraphy of Trench g, with a clear relative sequence of contexts, enabled us to create a Bayesian model. Note, however, that the lowest three samples were not certain to be young, and the model should be considered hypothetical rather than certain.

Table 7.1: Radiocarbon dates of samples from Trench d.[45] (SH = site height in relation to a benchmark for Trench g set at an arbitrary height of 100 m.) On the tentative modelled dates, see Fig. 7.15 and the text. Considering that the three lowest samples are not certain to be young, it may be safer to use the unmodelled dates. The depth and complexity of the multi-phase stratigraphy unlikely to have built up in a short period, however, adds credence to our attempt at modelling.

Find no.	Location	Laboratory no.	Sample description	Date	Calibrated date at 95.4% confidence	Comments
g.014/s1	n/a	SUERC-71984	Bos (cf.), horn core fragments	1533±18	AD 440–597 → modelled date: 441–586 (90.9%: 477–586; 80.0%: 531–586)	d13C = -12.0
g.054/s3	n/a	SUERC-71986	Bird or reptile vertebra	1588±18	AD 428–541 → modelled date: 441–559 (90.1%: 473–559)	d13C = -19.8
g.032/78	2.23 m NE, 1.81 m NW, 99.71 m SH	SUERC-71985	Large mammal, rib	1546±18	AD 435–584 → modelled date: 439–551 (85.9%: 474–551)	d13C = -16.8
g.073/93	1.50 m NE, 1.15–1.60 m NW, 99.02 m SH	Poz-89934	Dicot charred wood	1597±34	AD 414–550+ → modelled date: 434–544+ (not certain to be young)	d13C = -23.1
g.065/89	1.18 m NE, 1.74 m NW, 98.02 m SH	Poz-89933	Dicot charred wood	1604±34	AD 410–550+ → modelled date: 421–540+ (not certain to be young)	d13C = -27.0
g.068/90	1.41 m NE, 1.65 m NW, 96.94 m SH	Poz-89936	Rosaceae/ Prunoideae charred wood	1623±29	AD 405–542+ → modelled date: 409–538+ (not certain to be young)	d13C = -25.9

trenches and to extend it. This decision was made both for reasons of practicality and preservation. Widening an existing modern robber trench, rather than excavating a new sondage from scratch, promised to enable us to reach deeper levels more rapidly, whilst at the same time minimising further loss of undisturbed archaeological layers. What we did not know, however, was that the underground system of vaulted robber trenches and tunnels was deeper and more extensive than was evident from the two substantial shafts in the south-east corner of the fort that were open and accessible – a result of eroded soil covering the bottom of the features, and us not exploring in detail, for obvious safety reasons, let alone clearing out, the underground vaults and tunnels. As we were to discover subsequently, the deep and extensive robber tunnel system had erased parts of the stratigraphy at the bottom of the sondage, so that our evidence for the earliest phases was more limited than we had hoped. It was also with the aim to recover as much information as possible from the illegal recent pit-digging that the substantial spoil heap, the upcast from the robber trenches in the south-west corner of the Tappeh, was systematically searched for finds.[46]

7.2.4.2. Fort construction and the architecture of interior buildings

In our 2 × 4 m large trench only a sondage of c. 2 × 0.70 m was excavated down to the lowest levels. A modern robber tunnel (g.040), filled in part with loose soil (g.005) and in part still open, had obliterated archaeological layers in the east of the deep sondage, but the west was undisturbed. This tunnel appears to be linked to the round access shaft south-west of the trench. At the bottom of this small sondage, we reached sterile soft mid-yellowish brown clayey silt (g.072). We spotted no charcoal, brick flecks or any artefacts, suggesting that this is the natural loess (phase 1). Above, there was similar material, but of greyish to reddish brown colour, with intensive iron-staining and blown-in charcoal, perhaps material deposited over a patch of wet ground (g.068). A sample of charred plants of the

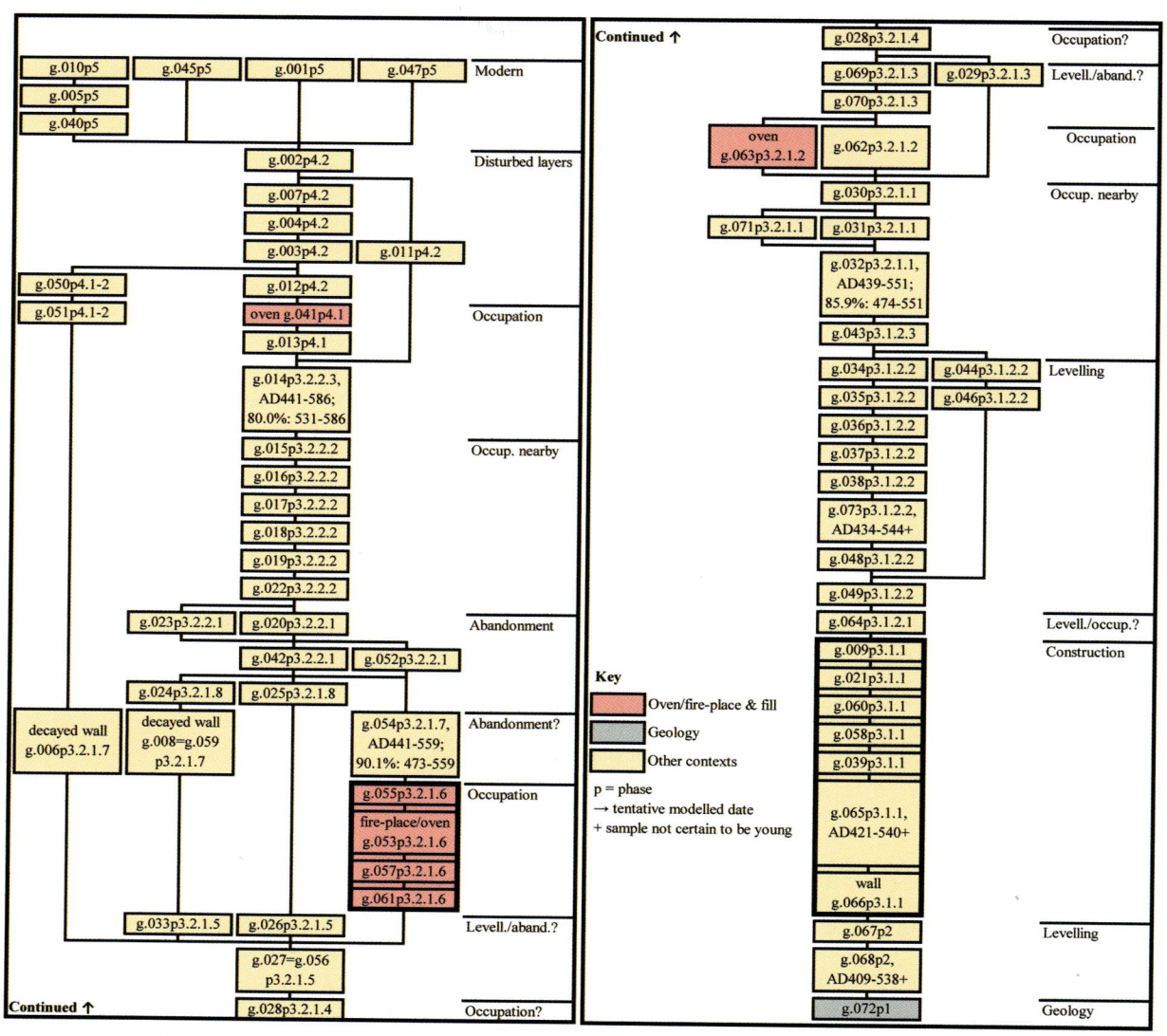

Fig. 7.16: Stratigraphic matrix for Trench g. The matrix lists modelled radiocarbon dates. (For unmodelled dates, see Table 7.1.) Note that the phases are site-specific and are not contemporary to phases of the same numbers at different sites. Phase 1 is geological. Phase 2 represents the earliest non-natural layers, which are probably part of a foundation platform and close in time to phase 3.1.1, which represents the earliest wall. Phases 3.1.2.1 to 4.1 represent successive phases of levelling and occupation, described in more detail in Table 7.2 and the text. Phase 4.2, whilst undated, is likely to be largely of Sasanian origins as well, but may contain later material, notably from g.003 upwards. Phase 5 represents the topsoil, the fill of animal burrows and modern robber trenches; it contains a small amount of modern material, but as there is no evidence to suggest that the mound was ever reoccupied in post-Sasanian times, most of the finds are likely to be Sasanian as well. As in other stratigraphic matrices, fireplaces/ovens and associated contexts are shown in red and geological horizons in grey (and all other contexts in light brown).

rose family could date to any time between the 400s and 530s or, bearing in mind that Prunoideae can reach an age of up 50 years,[47] even as late as the 580s in theory. Considering that there is younger material on top, a date in the later part of the spectrum seems, however, virtually impossible. G.068 was overlain by loess deposited in drier conditions and virtually sterile, except for further traces of charcoal (g.067). These two deposits (phase 2) had a combined depth of about 0.50 m. They seem to date to mid-Sasanian times and the complete lack of bone or pottery, even within a small sondage, indicates that they were not deposited at a time of heavy occupation. Perhaps they are levelling deposits to create a level surface on top of natural ground with water-filled puddles.

It was on top of g.067 that a mud-brick wall (g.066) was built (in phase 3.1.1). Individual mud-bricks were not always sufficiently distinct to enable us to record their dimensions, but it is clear that they were c. 8–11 cm thick and reached a width of at least 37 cm or more. It is unclear whether a fleck of fired brick was embedded

Table 7.2: Phasing. Due to the inaccuracy of radiocarbon dating in the fifth and early sixth century, precision-dating is impossible. The proposed dates for phases are based on radiocarbon dating (see Table 7.1), a comparison of the pottery assemblage from Buraq Tappeh to that from the Gorgan Wall forts[48] and guesstimates on the likely minimum duration of successive phases. The chronology is further explained in the text. Note that the same phases are used in the pottery and bone reports,[49] but with fewer sub-phases (e.g. phase 3.2 corresponds to all sub-phases from 3.2.1.1 to 3.2.2.3).

Phase	Date	Description
5	21st c.	Topsoil, modern robber trench and animal burrows; finds: mostly redeposited 5th–6th c. material.
4.2	Late 5th–20th c.	Disturbed horizons; finds: mostly or exclusively redeposited 5th–6th c. material.
4.1	Late 5th or 6th c.	Latest occupation, incl. construction and use of most recent oven.
3.2.2.3	Late 5th or 6th c.	Late occupation in dry conditions of (re-roofed?) room.
3.2.2.2	Late 5th or 6th c.	Room waterlogged (roofless?) and abandoned, but much bone and pottery deposited: fort occupied with a reduced garrison living nearby.
3.2.2.1 3.2.1.8	Late 5th or 6th c.	Room waterlogged (roofless?) and abandoned; no finds: fort temporarily abandoned?
3.2.1.7	5th or early/mid-6th c.	Room falling into a state of disrepair: erosion of walls and infiltration of water: loss of roof and probable abandonment?
3.2.1.6	5th or early/mid-6th c.	Construction and use of new large fireplace; spindle whorl points to wool-spinning nearby.
3.2.1.5	5th or early/mid-6th c.	Levelling to raise the surface or possibly temporary abandonment or neglect.
3.2.1.4	5th or early/mid-6th c.	Occupation or levelling horizon with (redeposited?) pottery and bone.
3.2.1.3	5th or early/mid-6th c.	Levelling to raise the surface or possibly temporary abandonment or neglect.
3.2.1.2	5th or early/mid-6th c.	Occupation, incl. construction and use of earliest oven found.
3.2.1.1 3.1.2.3	5th c. (or early/mid-6th c.?)	Occupation nearby and deposition of pottery and bone.
3.1.2.2	5th c. (or early/mid-6th c.?)	Levelling to raise the surface: entire ground floor filled up with largely sterile material.
3.1.2.1	5th c. (or early/mid-6th c.?)	Probably part of levelling horizon (as 3.1.2.2); deepest stratified pottery and bone: probably redeposited, possibly early occupation horizon. [Note that this deposit is c. 1 m above the base of the wall. There should be an earlier occupation horizon underneath which, probably due to the narrowness of the sondage and the heavy disturbance by the robber tunnel, has not been found.]
3.1.1	5th c.	Construction of internal housing within the fort.
2	(Early/mid-?) 5th c.	Levelling to raise the surface, probably to create a level and dry building platform for the fort.
1	Ice Age	Geological.

in mud mortar or in a decayed brick. We recovered a charcoal sample from g.065, a deposit consisting of redeposited loess abutting wall g.066, likely to date to the fifth century and in any case no later than the first half of the sixth century. This is based on radiocarbon dating to c. AD 421–540. One needs to add the caveat that the dated piece of charcoal could be from 'any dicotyledon plant including old trees or short-living shrubs'.[50] So even a date after the 540s is possible, though stratigraphically unlikely. There was no visible layering in g.065, and this deposit is overlain by what appear to be the upper sections of the wall (g.039, g.058, g.060, g.021 and g.009), suggesting g.065 was also part of the wall. Perhaps our inability to spot mud-bricks in g.065, as indeed in much of the upper sections of g.066, may have been a result of bricks of varying quality having been used, some perhaps more solidly sun-dried than others. The sample from g.065, the postulated core of the wall and in any case a deposit underlying the wall's upper sections, provides a likely *terminus post quem* for its construction. The fort's outer walls and internal buildings were probably erected in the fifth century, to judge by the radiocarbon samples and stratigraphy. The middle sections of the wall (g.039, g.058 and g.060), on top of the 1.42 m high mud-brick wall (g.066), were devoid of visible traces of mud-bricks. It is possible they were made of mud-bricks of poorer quality or of rammed earth. There were sparse lime inclusions, flecks of iron staining and charcoal in g.039. G.058 formed a thin band of soil whose colour (greyish as opposed to the yellowish brown of g.039) and composition (silty clay as opposed to clayey silt) was visibly different from g.039. Perhaps it represents an episode of rain dissolving the then top of the wall during construction. Above g.060 (similar to g.039), there were further courses of mud-brick (g.021) and what may be decayed mud-brick (g.009). Mud-bricks in g.021 were of a darker colour than the bands of mud mortar separating them. They were 8–11 cm thick and, whilst mostly not well-enough preserved for secure measurements, may have been up to c. 45 cm wide.

The bottom mud-brick section of the wall (g.066) is 1.42 m high, the middle (decayed mud-brick or

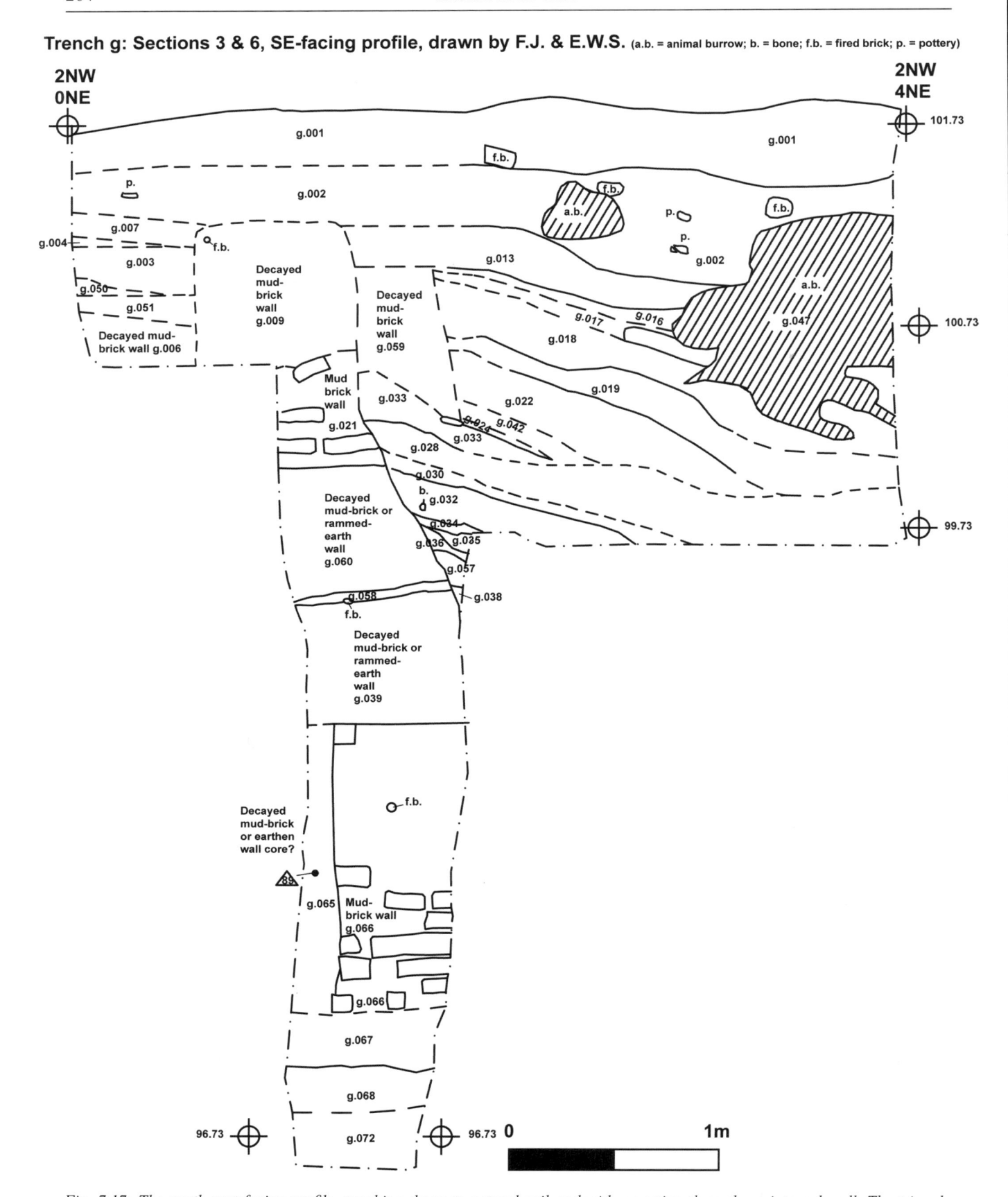

Fig. 7.17: The south-east-facing profile, reaching down to natural soil and with a section through an internal wall. The triangle symbol with the number 89 marks the location of radiocarbon sample g.065/89.

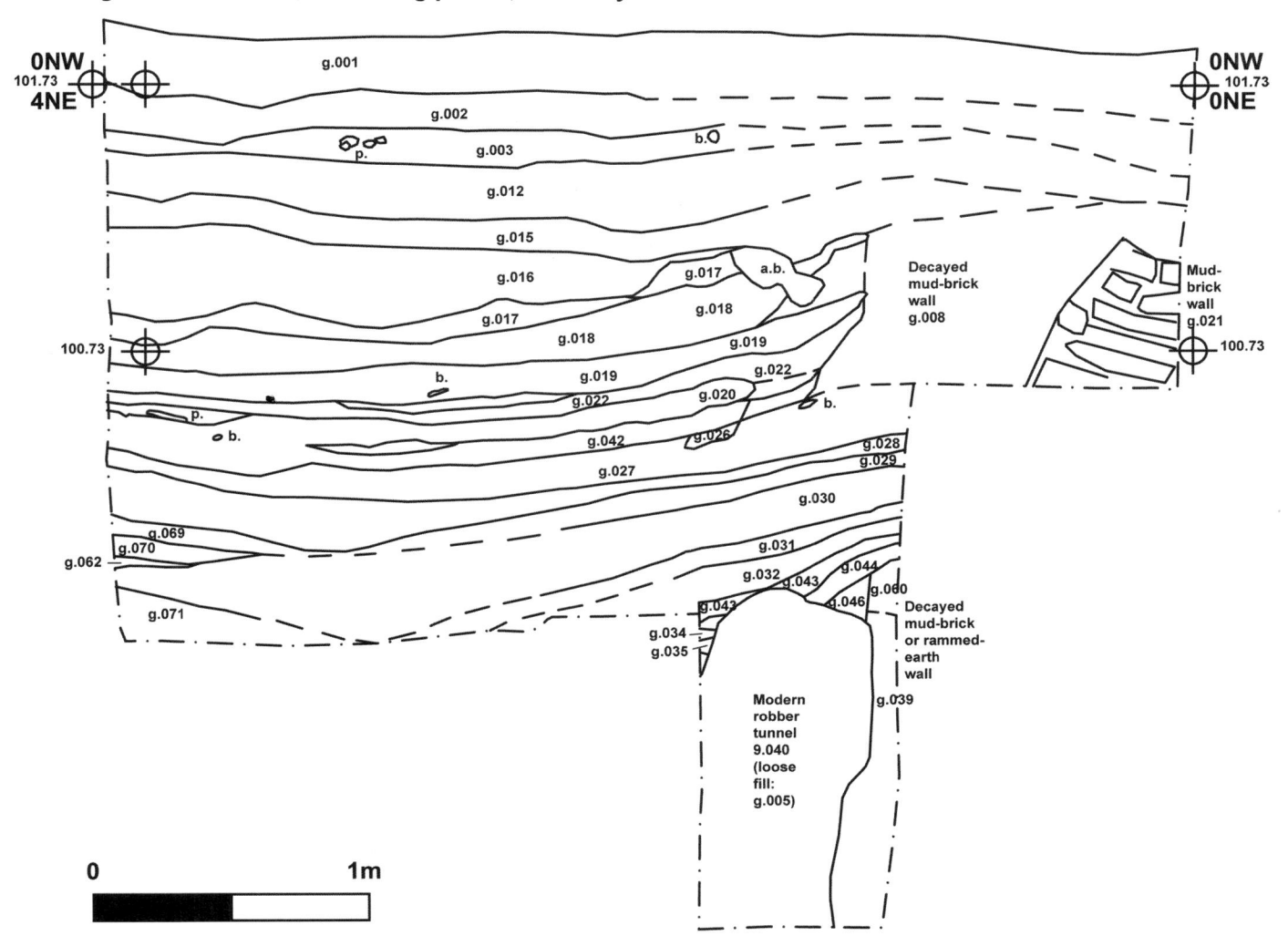

Trench g: Sections 4 & 7, NW-facing profile, drawn by F.J. & E.W.S. (a.b. = animal burrow; b. = bone; p. = pottery)

Fig. 7.18: The north-west-facing profile was heavily disturbed through a recent robber tunnel at its base. The sloping mud-brick wall formed the edge of the room.

rammed-earth?) section (g.039, g.058 and g.060) a further 1.28 m, the uppermost preserved parts of the wall in mud-brick (g.009 and g.021) 1.20 m. The total height of the wall, as far as preserved, is thus 3.90 m.[51] The wall's uppermost section may well have been destroyed through ploughing and bioturbation. If this internal wall reached the current surface within the Tappeh, some 0.57 m above the top of the discernible parts of the wall, this would increase its height to some 4.50 m minimum. It seems very likely that the internal walls would at least have risen to this height and probably well above. Had the internal walls been no higher than the 3.90 m preserved today, it would be hard to explain where all the material filling the interior of the fort, to the current height of the Tappeh of c. 4.50 m, had come from. This suggests that many of the internal walls, prior to the collapse of their uppermost courses and subsequent erosion and plough damage, would have risen to a height of well in excess of 3.90 m. And the fort's outer walls certainly are likely to have risen several metres higher.

Our excavation established that the base of cultural layers (i.e. the interface between g.068 and g.072) is about 4.95 m below the current surface in the area of Trench g. The mud-brick walls reach much deeper than what had been exposed in the robber trenches. Their base is c. 4.47 m below the present surface. It is worth noting that this was an internal wall, not the outer fort wall. Should we be right in thinking that g.068 and g.067 are levelling deposits of a foundation platform, as the dating evidence and the absence of finds suggest, we cannot be sure how extensive this platform was; it may have covered the entire building site or depressions only. Nor do we know whether it also formed

Fig. 7.19: The north-west-facing profile. Note that the photo was taken prior to complete excavation of the sondage, here heavily disturbed through a recent robber tunnel.

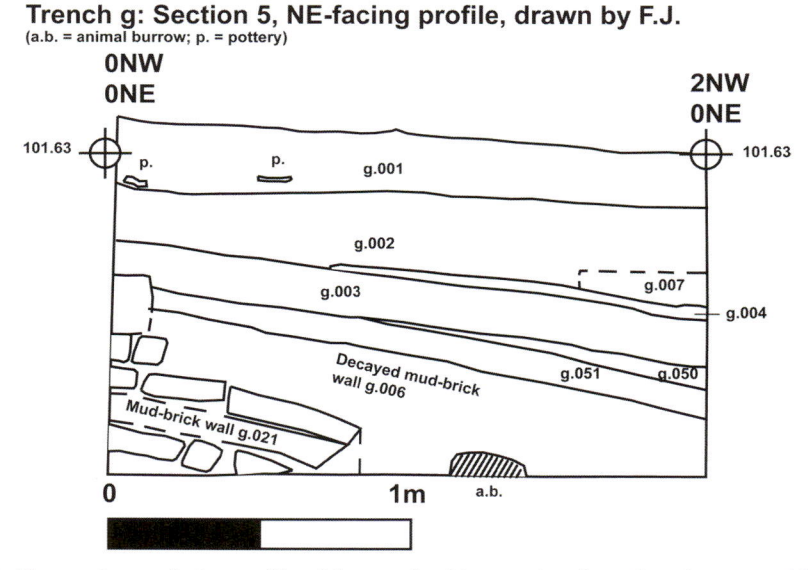

Fig. 7.20: The north-east-facing profile of the trench with a section through a sloping mud-brick wall.

the foundation of the fort's outer walls or whether it may have abutted them and only underlay the internal walls or some of them. The absence of pre-Sasanian layers suggests that the fort was built on virgin land. That the elevation of the earliest deposits corresponds roughly to the modern surface away from the Tappeh, not to mention the mound's remarkably rectangular shape, is further evidence for Buraq Tappeh being a single-phase Sasanian construction. The

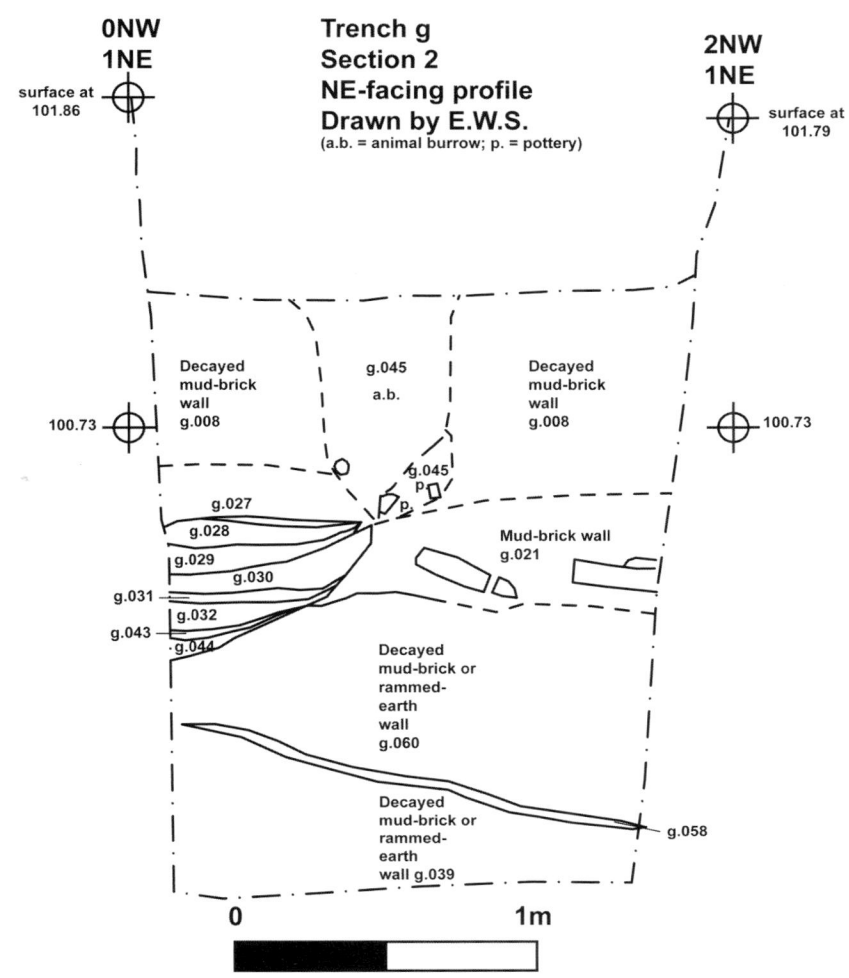

Fig. 7.21: The north-east-facing profile at 1 m north-east.

whole mound dates to this era; unlike Tureng Tappeh, it was not a fort built on an earlier settlement mound, but on virgin land in the plain.

The sectioned internal wall's height of 3.90 m at the very least implies, as we had assumed before, that internal housing was two storeys high (or potentially even more than two storeys). Two storeys seem most likely, but three storeys cannot be excluded, and it is worth noting that there is also evidence for two- or multi-storey accommodation elsewhere in Sasanian military architecture, such as at Fort 4 on the Gorgan Wall.[52] The precise elevation of the second storey is unknown. At Sasanian Dariali Fort, the lowest storey of the military casemates appears to have been about 2.40 m high and a slot in the wall, likely to have supported the floorboards of an upper storey, implies these may have been some 10 cm thick, so that the first floor would have been some 2.50 m above ground.[53] Whether such high ceilings were the standard or exceptional is unknown, but we may assume that it was the maximum likely height of a storey. There is nothing we observed in the structure of the wall to reveal the elevation of any interim floor. Yet, slots for timbers would be difficult or impossible to spot in a poorly preserved mud-brick wall, let alone in rammed earth layers. The top of the lower mud-brick section (g.066) seems, at 1.42 m height, too low for an interim floor, the bottom of the upper mud-brick component (g.021), at 2.70 m, perhaps rather high. One notices that the wall in the middle section (g.039, g.058 and g.060) gradually gets narrower. Perhaps it was somewhere within this section that the supporting timbers of an interim floor were slotted into the wall, but no trace of any voids or ledge were observed. As we will see, stratigraphy suggests that layers at this level overlie levelling deposits and the filling-up of the ground-floor. Nothing of the postulated original first floor appears to survive.

Considering Trench g's location, some 22.50–27 m west of the eastern edge of the plateau and some 5–8.50 m north of its southern limits – the latter harder to pinpoint precisely due to extensive plough damage – the presence of a substantial north–south mud-brick wall suggests that the building abutting the fort walls indeed

Trench g: Section 1, SW-facing profile, drawn by F.J.

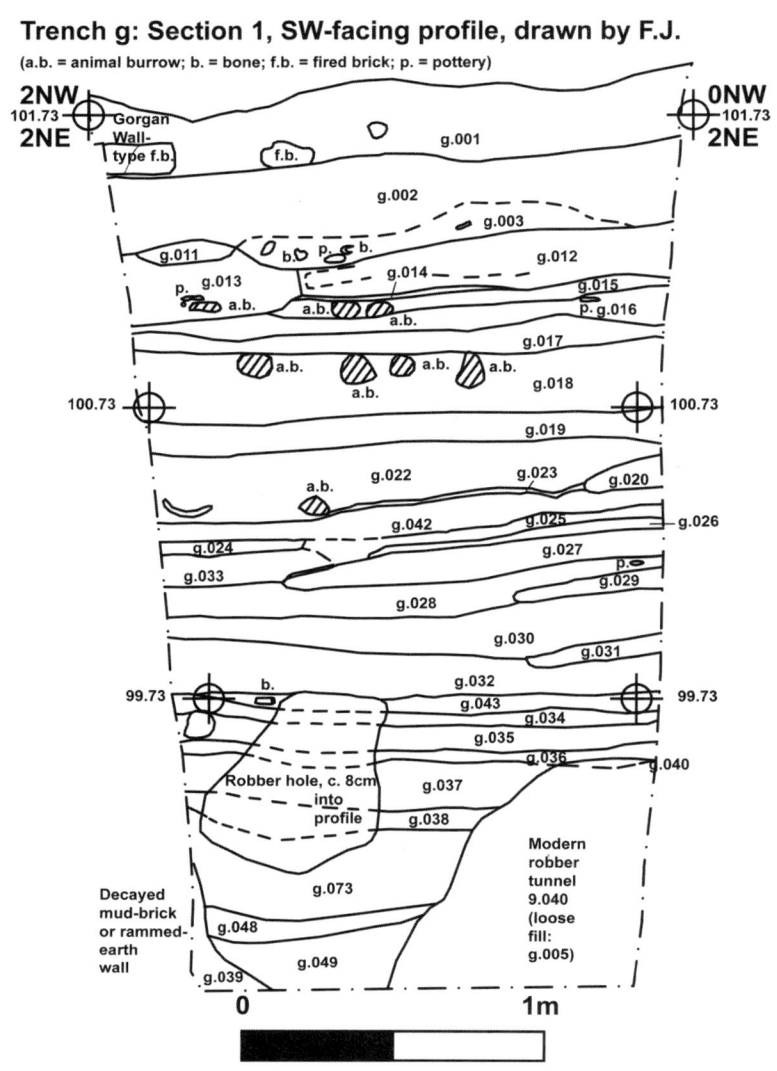

(a.b. = animal burrow; b. = bone; f.b. = fired brick; p. = pottery)

Fig. 7.22: The south-west-facing profile at 2 m north-east, also heavily disturbed by the recent robber tunnel.

extended for at least an estimated 8.50 m from the outer edge of the southern wall into the fort. Geophysical survey suggests that the wall and room units abutting it covered much more than the outermost 8 or 9 m and that there was more than a single narrow range of rooms lining the fort walls. Our trench was too small for reconstructing the size and position of individual rooms nor can division walls be clearly identified on the magnetometer plot. We found no second north–south wall in Trench g, indicating that the room was over 3 m wide (west–east). If our hypothetical reconstruction of the central gate and a corridor connecting the gateway with the courtyard (Fig. 7.10) should be accurate, then the room to the west of Trench g may have been some 7 m wide (if there was no subdivision), but this is far from certain. We have no means of estimating the north–south extent of rooms, except that the absence of any trace of a west–east wall in Trench g suggests that this room also extended over 3 m in a north–south direction (and rooms may, of course, have varied in size and plan).

7.2.4.3. Early occupation within the fort

Our deep sondage revealed little of the early occupation horizons. The earliest and deepest finds-bearing deposit was g.064 (phase 3.1.2.1), yielding 42 g of bone and 126 g of pottery, likely to be from an undisturbed early horizon. This deposit abutted wall g.066 at c. 98.35–98.45 m site height, a little over 1 m over the base of the wall (at c. 97.33 m). Considering the heavy disturbance caused by the robber tunnel and that parts of the narrow sondage were cut through the wall, no certain conclusions can be drawn from the dearth of evidence for early occupation. In the light of the elevation of the finds well above original ground-floor levels and the tidiness frequently prevailing in Sasanian military compounds, perhaps g.064

is a levelling deposit within a room rather than a horizon formed during actual occupation (and phase 3.1.2.1 is perhaps most plausibly interpreted as part of a single levelling operation, raising the surface by some 8 feet: phase 3.1.2.1–3.1.2.2). A larger future trench, away from modern robber shafts, has a good chance of providing us with a much better understanding of early occupation and levelling within the fort.

7.2.4.4. Levelling and living on higher ground

It is only much higher in the stratigraphy, towards the top of, and above, the narrow deep sondage, and above the robber tunnel, that we gain a better understanding of the successive build-up of deposits. Little would be gained by meticulous description of what appear to be successive levelling deposits (phase 3.1.2.2), from g.049 at the bottom to g.044 and g.034 at the top, and the reader is instead referred to the stratigraphic matrix (Fig. 7.16). They are mostly devoid of finds, except the odd charcoal fleck, and their colour and composition reveal that the main component tends to be redeposited loess. Iron-staining, green patches or clay in some of these levelling deposits suggest that some of the material was taken from areas temporarily under water, as must have been ubiquitous at a moated site next to a river. Indeed, it is possible that dredging the moat would have served multiple purposes: enhancing the defences, improving site drainage and providing a nearby source of material for levelling. A sample of charred dicot from g.073 implies that the levelling took place between AD 434 and 544 (or potentially more recently; the sample, like that from g.065, was from dicot and need not have been young). Stratigraphy would point to an earlier rather than later date.

It appears that the entire ground floor was filled up with soil. We cannot tell whether this happened soon after fort construction or maybe up to a century later. Why the effort was made to bring in substantial amounts of soil to raise the surface within the building, and thereby also to reduce significantly the space available for accommodation and storage, is unknown. Perhaps there were problems with water infiltration at ground-floor level at a moated site next to a river. We cannot tell whether this pre-dated or post-dated the construction of the Gorgan Wall and its associated forts. The construction of the Great Wall certainly provides a plausible scenario for parts of Buraq Tappeh's garrison being moved to the new forts. Considering the c. 200-year margin of error in our radiocarbon dates, it should be stressed that the assumption that this significant raising of the surface could be contemporary to the construction of the Gorgan Wall is no more than one of many possible hypotheses. The considerable efforts made to raise the surface by some two-and-a-half metres certainly suggests that there was no intention to abandon the fort at this stage. Instead, the massive earth-moving operations – assuming that these were not confined to one room, but that the surface was raised across the entire fort or at least the indoor space – prove that maintaining the fort was still considered worth considerable investment of labour.

The deepest deposit above g.064 to yield finds is g.043 (phase 3.1.2.3), with some 384 g of pottery and 28 g of bone, overlain by g.032 (phase 3.2.1.1), with 729 g of pottery and 434 g of bone. Little has been exposed of the deposits underneath, and a small quantity of finds would be easily explicable, but the complete absence suggests that the deposits sealed under g.043 are indeed, largely sterile, levelling deposits. G.043 and g.032, by contrast, have yielded clear evidence for occupation in the vicinity. Yet wet conditions may have prevailed, as suggested by frequent iron stains, but just occasional charcoal in both deposits. G.043 is very soft mid-reddish brown silty clay, g.032 very soft greenish grey silt, a colour also pointing to humid conditions. Perhaps this was a phase of occupation, but nearby rather than necessarily within the room. These deposits and, as far as we could observe, those underneath slope down away from the wall. This must be a result of subsidence of the substantial levelling deposits used to fill up the ground floor of the building. The tentative modelled date of a radiocarbon sample of a mammal rib from g.032 dates with an 85.9% probability to AD 474–551, though a mid-fifth century date is possible too. It was probably in the fifth century or the first half of the sixth century that, after the surface had been raised substantially, occupation continued. The brownish colour of the deposits above g.032 (g.031, g.071 and g.030) and an increased amount of charcoal suggest continued occupation in the vicinity (also assigned to phase 3.2.1.1). There was 127 g of pottery and 35 g of bone from g.030.

7.2.4.5. Oven construction

At the next level, we found the earliest cooking and heating facility within the trench. The absence of any earlier such remains, however, should probably be attributed to the very limited extent of the deep sondage rather than no cooking or heating having taken place within the fort at earlier times. In the northern corner of the trench, we encountered the distinctly fire-reddened edge of a round structure (g.063), evidently exposed to fire *in situ*, at a site height of 99.78 m. Whilst it extended only some 20 cm into the trench, there can be little doubt that this was an oven. Next to it, stretching from this structure to the south-east and rising from a similar level as g.063 to 99.95 m near the eastern trench corner, we encountered a deposit (g.062) with ash, 43 g of bone (including an unidentified fish bone)[54] and 48 g of pottery and traces of further *in-situ* burning. Oven g.063, its edge over 2 m east of the face of wall g.060/g.021, will have been used for cooking and heating, with related activities taking place in the area of g.062. The room abutting wall g.060/g.021 in

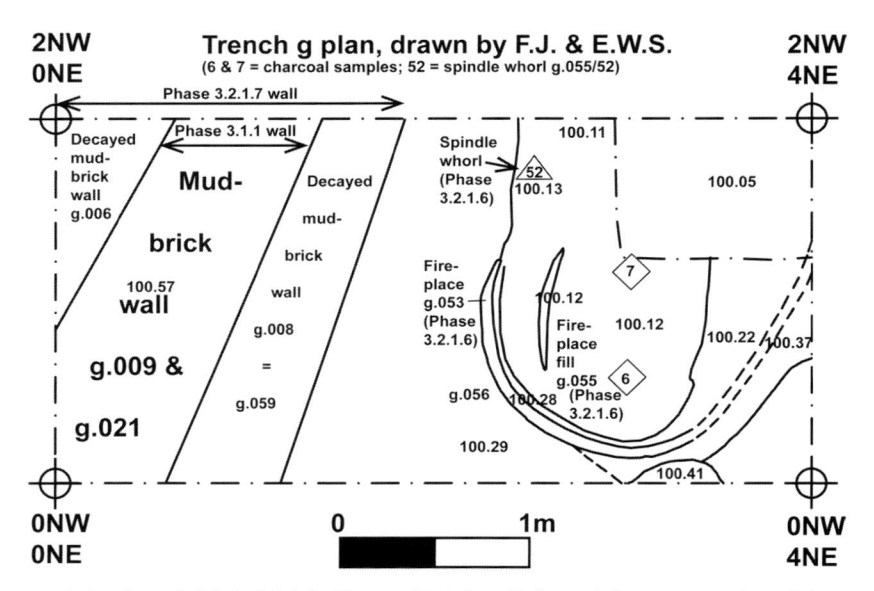

Fig. 7.23: Plan of the trench in phase 3.2.1.6–3.2.1.7. The mud-brick wall formed the western edge of the room. The spindle whorl suggests that domestic activities took place inside, next to the large fireplace. Subsequent decay appears to have widened the wall.

the east appears to have been used for domestic purposes in this new phase (3.2.1.2).

7.2.4.6. A new fireplace as a focus for domestic activities

Deposits g.070, g.069 and g.029 were sterile, except for lime and charcoal. Localised g.070 was soft mid-reddish brown clay, g.069, very soft mid-brown clayey silt and g.029, mid-grey to greenish brown clayey silt with iron stains and green flecks (phase 3.2.1.3), signifying wet conditions or levelling using alluvial material. Above, there was a further deposit with recorded finds (g.028), very soft mid-greyish brown sandy silt, yielding a moderate quantity of pottery (124 g), burnt clay lumps (24 g) and bone (61 g). Abutting wall g.021 and covering all of the interior of the room, this must be an occupation or, possibly, levelling horizon (phase 3.2.1.4). The ground was raised further subsequently in phase 3.2.1.5, represented by the sterile and localised deposits g.026, g.027/g.056 and g.033. The reddish brown to greyish colour of these clayey silt deposits and occasional green hue or iron stains in the latter two may point to washed-in material or levelling using alluvial material, prior to a further phase of activity. A small pit (g.061) was cut into g.027/g.056, with very soft mid-greyish brown clayey silt (g.057) at the bottom; it contained frequent charcoal and 45 g of bone. This shallow pit was dug to create a large fireplace or oven, whose curving wall (g.053) was fire-reddened. It was filled with very soft mid-greyish brown clayey silt and much charcoal (g.055) of plane tree and tamarisk.[55] Remarkably, almost half of the fish bones from Trench g, were found in association with this fireplace. The identified species belong to Cyprinidae, including carp, freshwater fish that will have been caught in the Old Gorgan River flowing past the fort and probably filling the moat surrounding it. Chicken bone was also found in area of the fireplace, evidently a place where the room's occupants once prepared a variety of meals.[56] This fireplace is evidently at a higher level and later than oven g.063 – evidence not just for multi-phase occupation of the room, but of occupation of an intensive nature involving structural alteration (phase 3.2.1.6).

There were also 21 g of pottery and 95 g of bone as well as a clay ball (g.055/53)[57] and a spindle whorl (g.055/52).[58] The precise point where the spindle whorl was found suggests that it may come from immediately west, rather than the fill, of the fireplace and the same might be true for the small quantity of pot and bone or some of it; the edge of the fireplace in the west was not well defined. The discovery suggests that next to the warmth of the fire, occupants spun wool (or potentially cotton) and maybe engaged in other domestic activities. As at Fort 2 in the late phases of occupation, and perhaps at an earlier time than at Fort 2, the occupants of Buraq Tappeh evidently produced some of their clothing and/or carpets themselves. With just a single such item found, little would be gained by speculating whether this was just for the garrison's own needs or potentially also for economic exchange. Neither can we gauge if the occupants of Buraq Tappeh or those of Fort 2 were more heavily involved in textile production, as 13 textile production implements from Fort 2 came from an over 30 times larger trench with shallower stratigraphy, but more fully excavated. Yet even a single spindle whorl from a small sondage proves that wool was spun at Buraq Tappeh whether on a small or a large scale. Evidently, not all occupants spent all their time on straightforward military duties. Perhaps members of, partially self-sufficient, military families occupied the fort and were engaged in the local pastoral economy. Herds of grazing sheep are not an uncommon sight around Buraq Tappeh today, and the bone assemblage suggests that mutton and goat meat featured prominently in the diet of the fort occupants one-and-a half millennia ago.[59] Wool for textile production would have been in plentiful supply.

7.2.4.7. Temporary site abandonment and decay?

On top of the fill of the fireplace (g.055), very sticky, soft greyish brown clayey silt (g.054) accumulated with charcoal and patches of green discoloration and iron-staining – probably a sign of rainwater infiltration at the time. This deposit contained 215 g of pottery and 20 g of bone. The latter included five fish bones, prominently presented, of course, also in the fill of the fireplace below, and perhaps suggesting that this layer engulfed this cooking facility and the remains of recent meals left behind by former residents. A bird or reptile vertebra produced a date of c. AD 473–559 (at a probability of 90.1%, though a mid-fifth-century date is possible), indicating that the fireplace may gone out of use as early as the fifth century or as late as the 550s.

The top of g.027/g.056 was the surface level when the fireplace was created and used, and it was on top of the same surface that substantial deposits accumulated on both sides of the western wall of the room (g.021 and g.009). What appears to be decayed wall (g.008/g.059), approximately 0.50 m in width, abutted mud-brick wall g.021/g.009 in the east and a deposit of similar composition and perhaps dimensions (g.006) in the west; g.006 was only present in the western corner of the trench and its extent and significance are far from certain. No individual mud-bricks were observed in these deposits. Were they wall extensions made of poorly burned and decayed mud-bricks or maybe rammed earth? Were the walls widened to improve insulation, keeping out the cold in winter and the heat in summer? Perhaps, but more likely g.006, g.008 and g.059 (phase 3.2.1.7) represent wall erosion. As we have seen, soon after the abandonment of the fireplace, water seems to have entered the room, to judge by the sticky nature of, and iron stains in, deposit g.054. If some or all of Buraq Tappeh was a roof-less rain-exposed ruin at the time, sterile material from the collapsing wall may have accumulated at the edge of the room. The sides of g.008/g.059 were not well defined, seemingly steep, but in places sloping at the bottom, perhaps pointing to wall decay. Near the southern corner of the trench, we also observed that the mud-bricks in wall g.021 were sloping in a distinctly westerly direction. If we are right in thinking that this is the upper part of a tall wall, then (unlike the occupation and levelling horizons in the room) this should not be a result of subsidence of deposits underneath. Admittedly, only the upper layers have been excavated in this part of the trench and there could be many explanations for the wall leaning westwards, e.g. the collapse of a hypothetical doorway underneath or simply localised water infiltration undermining parts of the west face of the wall. Whatever the cause, parts of the upper section of the wall became unstable, its top probably eroding, with wall collapse building up on both sides; what was left standing of the wall tilted to the west.

There may indeed have been a period of partial or complete abandonment of the fort at this time of structural decay. The layers that built up subsequently (g.025, very soft mid-yellowish brown clayey silt, g.024, firm mid-reddish brown clay with green stains, g.042, very soft clayey silt with green patches, g.023, very soft mid-greenish brown clayey silt and g.020, stiff mid-reddish brown silty clay) were devoid of finds, except for brick flecks and charcoal. The predominantly clayey nature of many of these layers and the patches of green discoloration is suggestive of waterborne erosion. The only deposit from this abandonment horizon (phase 3.2.1.8–3.2.2.1) to have yielded artefacts is g.052: yellowish brown clay with iron stains and green patches, it evidently also dates to a time when there was water in the room. It contained 1,200 g of pottery, probably of cooking pots, and was immediately to the east of the fireplace g.053. Its elevation (c. 100.19–100.47 m site height) was similar to other listed waterborne deposits. Perhaps it represents vessels left behind next to the fireplace when the interior of the derelict building was engulfed in washed-in material.

7.2.4.8. Reoccupation with a reduced garrison living nearby?

Increased finds concentrations in layers building up on top of these abandonment horizons imply reoccupation or intensified occupation. Yet, continued evidence for episodes of standing water suggests that the room itself remained roofless and abandoned and that people living nearby, perhaps a small garrison guarding the walls only, either deliberately dumped rubbish in the room or that it was accidentally washed in. The deepest horizon of this period of renewed activity nearby (phase 3.2.2.2) was g.022, soft mid-greenish brown clayey silt with occasional charcoal, 205 g of pottery, 145 g of bone and a clay ball weighing 11 g.[60] The deposits building up on top (g.019 and g.018, soft to very soft mid-greenish brown clayey silt with sporadic flecks of iron staining, charcoal, some 500 g of ceramics and 170 g of bone, and 1,140 g of pottery and 220 g of bone respectively), imply that debris from nearby occupation continued to accumulate in the wet interior of the abandoned room. The same is true for g.017, g.016 and g.015 (firm mid-reddish brown sandy clay, very soft mid-greenish grey clayey silt and very soft mid-greyish brown clay, the lower two of these horizons with iron-staining). These deposits, as well as g.022, g.019 and g.018 underneath, in places appear to slope distinctly away from g.008/g.059, adding strength to them being washed in from the outside. Due to their sloping nature, it was difficult to neatly separate finds by context, but the upper level yielded an additional 2,135 g of pottery and 945 g of bone.

7.2.4.9. Latest occupation and renewed oven construction

It was only on top of g.015 that we observe a return to drier conditions: g.014, very soft, dark greyish brown sandy silt, with much charcoal and ashy material and no trace of any waterlogging, may mark a reoccupation of the room (phase 3.2.2.3), facilitated by the ground now being level again. Pottery amounting to 1,260 g and 875 g of bone have been recovered from this deposit and the top of g.015 which could not be clearly separated. Cattle horn core fragments yielded a modelled radiocarbon date of c. AD 531–586 (at a probability of 80.0%, though the mid- to late fifth century is possible too). As unfortunately typical for the fifth to sixth century, radiocarbon dating can date this late horizon with a precision to one-and-a-half centuries only. Considering the multiple previous phases of occupation, levelling and site abandonment, it is hard to imagine, however, that g.014 is earlier than the later fifth century at the earliest and a date between the AD 530s and 580s is most likely.

We cannot tell whether the room had been re-roofed or whether g.014 marks a period of occupation or rubbish accumulation in the ruins during a dry spell. It is clear, however, from the continued deposition of both bone and pot, that humans continued to live nearby within Buraq Tappeh's walls. On top of g.014, there was soft mid-brown clayey silt (g.013) with sparse charcoal, 418 g of pottery and 50 g of bone – proving continued occupation, whether in the vicinity of the room excavated or within. This is the highest deposit to abut the top of the room division wall (g.009) in the east. In the west, if was abutted by very soft mid-yellowish brown (g.051), under mid-brownish grey (g.050), clayey silt.

Only in the north-eastern profile of the trench was a further oven (g.041) visible, its base at c. 101.26 m and its top at c. 101.63 m site height. Due to the poor definition of context boundaries, it is difficult to be certain, but the feature may well be above g.013 and may belong to the last phase of occupation within the room. It might be abutted by g.012 and it is certainly below the level of g.003. This was the final phase (4.1) of occupation we can trace and the third when the room was demonstrably provided with a new cooking and heating facility.

Fig. 7.24: The south-west-facing profile of the trench (at 4 m north-east). Only the edge of the latest oven (g.041) was within the trench, at the intersection of the uppermost white and red segments of the vertical scale.

7.2.4.10. Disturbed horizons above the abandoned fort

Dry conditions were not to last. On top of g.013, firm mid-greyish brown clayey silt with greenish/yellowish patches and iron-staining (g.012) built up, suggestive of renewed water infiltration and/or sewage deposition. G.012 contained some 1,100 g of pottery and 470 g of bone. This is the first deposit to overlie the wall, formed or spread after site abandonment (phase 4.2), but evidently still full of Sasanian-era material. Little would be gained by meticulous description of further deposits overlying g.012, evidently all formed or disturbed after site abandonment, but with nothing other than Sasanian-era finds, if any. Worth noting are g.003 and g.002, containing as much as 1,556 g of pottery and 1,032 g of bone, and 372 g of pottery, 165 g of bone and a copper alloy drawer handle weighing 4 g (g.002/20).[61] Both bulk deposits accumulated in dry conditions – probably a result of improved drainage on the hilltop once no walls were left standing. Embedded in the subsoil (g.002 and g.003) and topsoil (g.001) there were large fragments of reused fired Gorgan Wall bricks, including a cluster of them near the northern corner of the trench, not observed at deeper levels. We do not know whether these were brought to the site in Sasanian times or more recently, e.g. related to any potential short-lived and temporary nomadic reoccupation of the prominent mound. Fire-reddened patches in g.002 are best explained with campfires, perhaps lit by nomads and/or shepherds.

The modern topsoil (g.001) yielded a further 2,238 g of pottery and 135 g of bone. Animal burrows g.045 and g.047 contained 115 g of pot and 105 g of bone combined.[62] From the fill and spoil of the robber trenches (g.005 and g.010), we were able to retrieve 4,533 g of pottery and 1,626 g of bone. As there was no later occupation and as there is no pottery of distinctly different style, most of these finds from modern (phase 5) levels will be redeposited Sasanian material, although there might be the odd modern remain mixed in (notably plastic bottles from the modern robber tunnel fill, but no other recognisably modern artefacts). We found no glass at Buraq Tappeh. Amongst the surface finds, a carnelian bead is worth noting.[63]

7.2.4.11. Garrison size

Estimates for the number of occupants of any military compound are always fraught with difficulty (though arguably less so than for undefended civilian settlements where space tended to be less precious). Our attempt to reconstruct the possible garrison size of Buraq Tappeh is dependent on our interpretation of the geophysics and topography being correct and the results of the excavations of one sondage being broadly representative for indoor occupation in all postulated built-up areas. Based on these premises, the indoor space available to accommodate occupants at Buraq Tappeh may have changed considerably over time. Initially, there appear to have been two storeys (or, less probably, even three storeys) available to the garrison; later, this appears to have been reduced by one storey, to probably just a single storey upstairs. We know very little about the fort's occupation prior to the ground floor being filled up, reducing the indoor space to probably half of what had been available initially. Afterwards, as the discussion of its history of occupation has shown, occupation may have fluctuated considerably over time. At some stage, the fort may have been temporarily abandoned altogether, at other times it may have been guarded by a much-reduced garrison requiring only parts of the one storey, with parts of the building it seems roofless, exposed to the elements and filling up with debris. In at least three separate phases, however, the room we explored seems to have been fully occupied. A trench covering just 8 m² (including c. 6 m² indoors) need not necessarily reflect the history of occupation of a fort covering an estimated 700 times this area, i.e. c. 5,600 m² (excluding the projecting towers). Assuming the fort walls were as wide as postulated for Fort 2, i.e. c. 2.60 m, the intramural area would have encompassed c. 4,847 m², or 3,497–4,097 m², excluding the courtyard of 30 × 25–45 m. This suggests our trench covered more than a 400th and perhaps up to a 500th or so of the built-up intramural space of which a little less than the uppermost 50% was fully excavated. Despite the small size of our sample, and a random trench near the postulated gate not necessarily being representative of occupation throughout the much larger fort, it is still worth stressing that we found three successive ovens/fireplaces in such a small expanse of indoor space; this may well imply that at times the fort was densely occupied.

A comparison with Fort 2 on the Gorgan Wall and with small late Roman forts, for which estimates for the garrison have been proposed, may be of interest. Table 7.3 lists the intramural space as well as the estimated indoor space for all compounds as well as estimates for their garrison size. For Fort 2, we explained our estimate that there may have been a garrison of around 500 elsewhere.[64] We allow for an error of plus or minus 200. For Fort 2, it seems far more likely that the original barracks would have been double storey than single storey, but we allow for both possibilities. After the more lightly built annexes were added (which we assume were only one storey high) indoor space would have increased. For Buraq Tappeh, we ought to re-emphasise the uncertainty of our estimates of the available indoor space: there may have been a larger or smaller courtyard (and it is far from certain that the range for the built-up space indicated has been correctly estimated). There appear to have been initially two storeys, later reduced to one.

A comparison with the intramural occupation density of small late Roman forts (Tables 7.4–7.5; Fig. 7.25), notably the small fortlet of Qasr al-Gib in the Kharga Oasis in Egypt's Western Desert, produces figures of questionable reliability. It certainly seems impossible to believe Fort 2 or Buraq Tappeh ever housed several thousand occupants each, as the hypothetical scenario of it being occupied as densely as has been postulated (maybe wrongly) for the small Egyptian stronghold at Qasr al-Gib would imply. A comparison with En Boqeq and Tetrapyrgium in the Roman Near East produces more credible figures, though estimates for indoor occupation at the latter may perhaps be rather too low. Yet even they imply, assuming Fort 2's original barracks were two storeys high, that the garrison at both forts could easily have accommodated many hundreds of occupants. Perhaps the average indoor occupation densities of the latter two forts produces the most plausible figures, suggesting a garrison of c. 450–900 for Fort 2 and perhaps a holding capacity of c. 400–450 for Buraq Tappeh once occupation was confined to a single storey, and perhaps as many as 800–900 initially.

It is indeed significant that the data suggest that Buraq Tappeh may have initially offered as much indoor space as Fort 2 did after the addition of the annexes. Once the ground floor had been filled up, the indoor space in Buraq Tappeh may have been reduced by c. 50%. Whilst Fort 2's indoor area seems to have been increased over time, that of Buraq Tappeh appears to have been reduced. If our estimates of a garrison of 500 for Fort 2 should be in the right order of magnitude, a similar or even larger number could have been accommodated in Buraq Tappeh, despite the latter covering less than half the area. They would have had a similar amount of indoor living space, but considerably less intramural outdoor space for work or social interaction. An initial garrison of as many 500 or more in Buraq Tappeh would still have lived in arguably less cramped conditions than has been postulated for the average small late Roman fort. If indeed Buraq Tappeh pre-dates the Gorgan Wall and was a day's march from

Table 7.3: Estimated maximum and minimum garrisons of, and living space per person at, small to medium late Roman and Persian forts. Indoor space excludes internal walls and doorways. For Buraq Tappeh, we assume that rooms account for the same percentage of the area of the accommodation units as estimated for the original barracks in Fort 2 (c. 54.51%). Assuming the percentage was higher, though it seems unlikely it would have been as high as in the lightly built (single-storey?) annexes at Fort 2, this would allow for an even larger garrison to be accommodated or the occupants having each more space at their disposal.[65]

Fort (indoor space refers to the interior of rooms only)	Storeys	Intramural space (m²)	Postulated indoor space, all storeys (m²)	Hypothetical garrison (min.)	Hypothetical garrison (max.)	Space (m² per occupant)			
						Intramural (min.)	Intramural (max.)	Indoor (min.)	Indoor (max.)
Qasr al-Gib	2	132	78	60	60	2.20	2.20	1.30	1.30
En Boqeq, incl. towers	2?	335	189	46	56	5.98	7.28	3.38	4.11
Tetrapyrgium	2?	1,008	490	64	70	14.40	15.75	7.00	7.66
Fort 2 original barracks, 1 st.	1	11,935	1,114	300	700	17.05	39.78	1.59	3.71
Fort 2 original barracks, 2 st.	2	11,935	2,227	300	700	17.05	39.78	3.18	7.42
Fort 2 original barracks (2 st.) + annexes (1 st.)	1 & 2	11,935	4,465	300	700	17.05	39.78	6.38	14.88
Buraq Tappeh, large courtyard (30 × 45 m), 1 st.	1	4,847	1,906	100	500	9.69	48.47	3.81	19.06
Buraq Tappeh, small courtyard (30 × 25 m), 1 st.	1	4,847	2,233	100	500	9.69	48.47	4.47	22.33
Buraq Tappeh, large courtyard (30 × 45 m), 2 st.	2	4,847	3,812	100	500	9.69	48.47	7.62	38.12
Buraq Tappeh, small courtyard (30 × 25 m), 2 st.	2	4,847	4,467	100	500	9.69	48.47	8.93	44.67

Table 7.4: Possible garrison size of Fort 2 and Buraq Tappeh, based on the assumption of a similar intramural occupation density as postulated for late Roman forts.

Fort	Intramural occupation density as Qasr al-Gib	Intramural occupation density as En Boqeq (min.)	Intramural occupation density as En Boqeq (max.)	Intramural occupation density as Tetrapyrgium (min.)	Intramural occupation density as Tetrapyrgium (max.)	Average, excl. Qasr al-Gib
Fort 2	5,425?	1,639	1,995	758	829	1,305
Buraq Tappeh	2,203?	666	810	308	337	530

Table 7.5: Possible garrison size of Fort 2 and Buraq Tappeh, based on the assumption of a similar indoor occupation density as postulated for small late Roman forts (st. = storey).

Fort	Indoor occupation density as Qasr al-Gib	Indoor occupation density as En Boqeq (min.)	Indoor occupation density as En Boqeq (max.)	Indoor occupation density as Tetrapyrgium (min.)	Indoor occupation density as Tetrapyrgium (max.)	Average, excl. Qasr al-Gib
Fort 2 original barracks (1 st.)	857?	271	330	146	159	226
Fort 2 original barracks (2 st.)	1,713?	542	660	291	318	453
Fort 2 original barracks (2 st.) + annexes (1 st.)	3,435?	1,087	1,323	583	638	908
Buraq Tappeh, large courtyard (30 × 45 m), 1 st.	1,466?	464	565	249	272	387
Buraq Tappeh, small courtyard (30 × 25 m), 1 st.	1,718?	543	662	292	319	454
Buraq Tappeh, large courtyard (30 × 45 m), 2 st.	2,932?	928	1,129	498	545	775
Buraq Tappeh, small courtyard (30 × 25 m), 2 st.	3,436?	1,087	1,324	583	638	908

the nearest Sasanian fort, then it may have made sense to place a strong garrison in a heavily defended small fort. Of course, a much smaller garrison from the start (e.g. 250?) is perfectly possible too and fewer occupants would have had much more space available and would have lived in much greater comfort. Once the ground floor was filled up, the indoor space likely to have been available would have been reduced to about the same or less than what was available in the two barracks in Fort 2, if the latter rose to two storeys. After Fort 2's barracks had been provided with annexes, a single-storey Buraq Tappeh may still have provided half its holding capacity. There may well have been times when the garrison was substantially below its capacity. One hundred armed personnel may have been sufficient to defend the small fort or even substantially fewer, once shielded by the Gorgan Wall. This may explain episodes when the room in our trench may have been roofless with a small garrison living elsewhere within the fort, not requiring all of the indoor area.

There is much that we still do not know. Not all occupants need have been fighting men,[66] and soldiers may not have felt comfortable with their families (on the likely assumption that they did not all live on their own) living in unprotected housing somewhere outside the moated fort, notably if the fort was built in insecure times. There is furthermore no known evidence for extramural settlement around the tappeh, but lightly built structures would not be identifiable on aerial imagery. It seems likely that men, women and children were present at Buraq Tappeh and in the Gorgan Wall forts. Indeed, one wonders whether the annexes to the latter served to create more space for additional soldiers or, more probably, allowed them and their dependants to live in greater comfort. Little would be gained by speculating further. It is worth noting nonetheless that the above tables imply that there could have been a substantial number of occupants at Buraq Tappeh and Fort 2, without conditions being as cramped as has been postulated for some late Roman forts. Of course, whether the proportion of combatants was a low as 25% or as high as 100% may have major ramifications for unit sizes and effective strength of the garrisons – but we should also bear in mind that small children are not likely to have required as much space as adults. If there were 500 soldiers stationed at Fort 2 and initially at Buraq Tappeh, this does not mean that there was a permanent presence

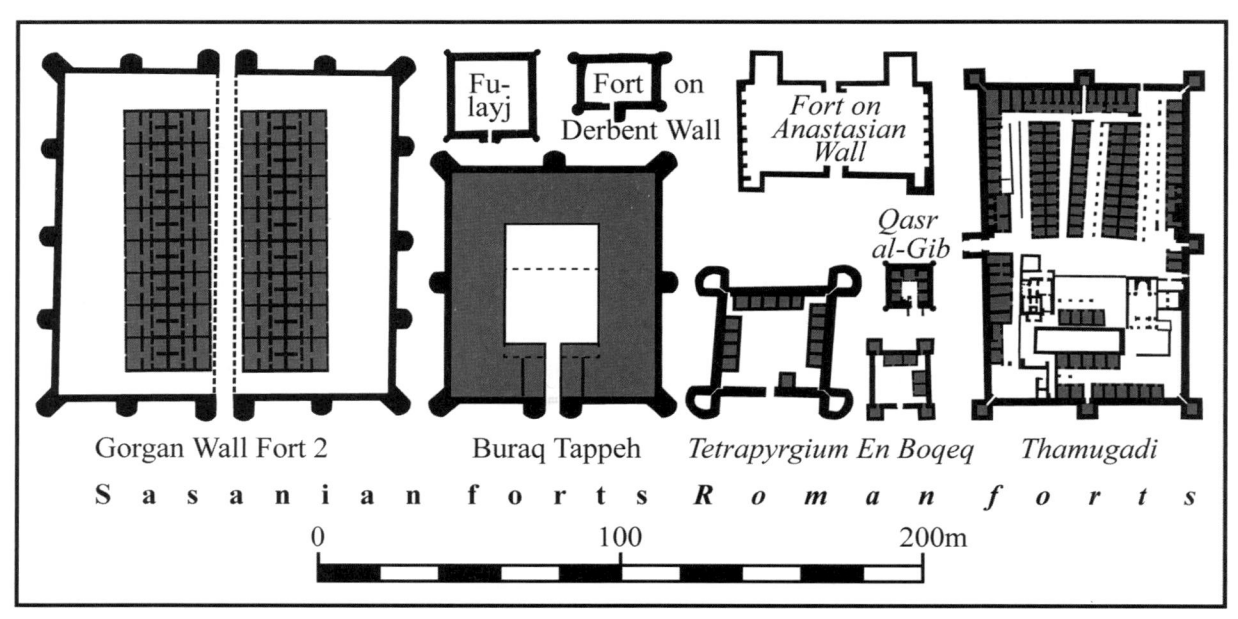

Fig. 7.25: Selection of four Sasanian forts (left) and five late Roman forts (right) in arbitrary orientation, but all on the same scale. Indoor areas thought to have been used as accommodation, or for other domestic activities or storage, are highlighted in grey. Note that the approximate extent of indoor space at Buraq Tappeh is based on geophysical survey; its courtyard is assumed here to measure 30 × 40 m, the most symmetrical and perhaps the most likely reconstruction, whereas the tables allow for it to be as large as 30 × 45 m (i.e. extending 5 m further to the dotted line at the bottom) or as small as 30 × 25 m (i.e. extending only to the dotted line across the courtyard). Whilst the extent of Sasanian-era intramural housing is unknown for the Fulayj fort and the forts on the Derbent and Anastasian Walls, it seems likely that there would also have been rooms lining the outer walls with a courtyard in the centre. This certainly was the case in a later, medieval, phase of occupation at the fort on the Derbent Wall that may well reflect earlier arrangements. The interior of towers has been shaded for the En Boqeq fortlet, as it has been specifically, and plausibly, postulated that they were occupied. It ought to be borne in mind, however, that larger towers in other Sasanian and Roman forts may well have been occupied too, even where the base was solid (as in the case of Fort 2); the diameter of the towers of Fulayj or Qasr al-Gib, of course, was small, and there would not have been space for rooms inside. Interior occupation may well have often been two storeys high; at the well-preserved fortlet of Qasr al-Gib, there is even evidence for a third storey. The comparison shows that Buraq Tappeh, whilst covering only half a hectare, may well have had the capacity to accommodate as many occupants as the 1.2 ha large Fort 2 or the 0.7 ha fort at Thamugadi and arguably many more than its smaller counterparts. Excluding Fort 2, where all accommodation detected so far is in freestanding buildings, one also sees similarities in Sasanian and late Roman fort design, e.g. in rooms lining fort walls, with a courtyard in the centre. (Sources: Sasanian forts: Buraq Tappeh: chapter 7.2; Fort 2: chapter 4.1; Fort on the Derbent Wall: Gadjiev 2008a, 31–32; Fulayj: Al-Jahwari et al. 2018; late Roman forts: En Boqeq: Gichon 1989; 1993, especially plan 4; Fort on the Anastasian Wall: Crow and Ricci 1997, 250 fig. 9; Qasr al-Gib: Rossi and Ikram 2018, 434–39; Tetrapyrgium: Konrad 2001, 23–43, 56–64, 68 fig. 41, 104–05, suppl. figs 6–7; Thamugadi: Lassus 1981; Pringle 2001, 232–36, 546–47 fig. 2.)

of 2,000; during daylight hours in peacetime many will have engaged in outdoor extramural economic activities.

In order to gauge the likely number of armed personnel, it may also be worthwhile to compare our compound with larger military bases whose garrison size is not quite as speculative as that of small compounds. The 0.67 ha Roman fort at Thamugadi in Numidia, completed in AD 539/540, was densely filled with buildings, notably accommodation units leaning against the fort walls and further freestanding barracks in the interior. These originally probably rose to a height of two or even three storeys; if they were all two storeys high, there would have been over 200 rooms in total of 9–16 m² each, not counting the basement and first-floor rooms in the seven large towers plus a chamber on the first floor of the eighth (gate) tower. Denys Pringle assumes that they were occupied by some 300 horsemen and their mounts, and that they were capable of sheltering 600 foot-soldiers – or 600 horsemen, if their mounts were kept elsewhere. The latter estimate is based on the assumption that all ground-floor units served storage purposes and that six soldiers slept in each of the rooms upstairs.[67] As there were probably well over 100 troughs, often two per ground-floor room/stables, it seems clear that at Thamugadi there was provision for horses to be kept in the intramural area and that there was a mounted or part-mounted garrison.[68] For the 4.57 ha late Roman legionary fortress of El-Lejjun a peak garrison of 2,000 fighting men has been proposed, i.e. just under seven times the estimated (cavalry) garrison for Thamugadi in a fortress of just over seven times the internal area of Thamugadi. The assumption of a similar intramural occupation density of Fort 2 and Buraq Tappeh as postulated for El-Lejjun and a cavalry garrison at Thamugadi would produce a garrison of just over 500 soldiers at Fort 2 and just over 200 at Buraq Tappeh (or over 1,000 and over 400 if compared to Thamugadi's postulated holding capacity of 600 foot-soldiers). A perhaps more plausible model based on a similar indoor occupation density at El-Lejjun, Fort 2 and Buraq Tappeh would produce a garrison of c. 450 soldiers at Fort 2 in the original two-storey barracks and c. 800 after the addition of the annexes and some 400–450 for single-storey Buraq Tappeh and as many as 750–900 for its postulated initial double-storey occupation – figures reassuringly close to our previous model.[69] Even if we assumed El-Lejjun never housed more than 1,000 fighting men, the minimum likely size of a late Roman legion, this would still imply a holding capacity of 400 soldiers after annexe construction at Fort 2 and 200–450 armed personnel at Buraq Tappeh, plus probably dependants.

A comparison with second-century Roman milecastles on Hadrian's Wall, with an estimated maximum garrison of 32 quartered within two barracks of perhaps 128 m^2 combined indoor space and a total interior area of c. 395 m^2, is interesting too.[70] Assuming Buraq Tappeh was similarly densely occupied, its garrison would have numbered around 400 (based on the same intramural occupation density) or as many as 900 occupants (based on a same indoor space available per person, single-storey occupation and a large courtyard) or even 2,000 (if both storeys were occupied and if the courtyard was small). It seems hard to believe that thousands could ever have guarded Buraq Tappeh, but a few hundred at peak occupation seems perfectly possible. If precision is impossible to achieve, it seems likely that Buraq Tappeh had the capacity to house more troops than its small size implies, at times perhaps as many or more than the much larger Fort 2, but numbers will fluctuated substantially over time.

7.2.4.12. History and chronology of Buraq Tappeh's occupation

All radiocarbon samples processed could fall within the plateau of the calibration curve in the fifth to early sixth century AD. The earliest could be as early as c. AD 409, but could date to any time in the fifth century (or, even if stratigraphically unlikely, as late as the 530s or even later if from an older plant). The sample above is most likely to date to between the 420s and 540s, but could again potentially be more recent if it was from an older tree; stratigraphy would point to a fifth-century date. It may be out of the matrix of an internal wall, which could be later than the outer walls of the fort, but is likely to pre-date the completion of construction works. It is interesting to note that the earliest samples are from flowering plants, shrubs or trees, and one wonders whether this could be vegetation set alight at the time of fort construction or from the fuel of campfires of the workforce building the fort. It is unfortunate that, due to the extreme scarcity of organic matter in the earliest deposits, we had no choice other than to date small charcoal fragments of uncertain age. If we consider the possibility that the earliest charcoal samples are from old wood and toward the end of the spectrum, all six samples could be of a similar date. The modelled dates, whilst perfectly plausible, should be considered tentative only. What is certain is that all six samples date to between the early fifth (or, with a very low probability, even the late fourth) to the sixth century and that Buraq Tappeh's occupation must fall within these parameters.

The latest sample is no likely to be earlier than c. AD 441, but could be as late as c. AD 586; modelling points to a four in five chance of a date between AD 531 and 586. There is certainly no positive evidence for occupation lasting into the seventh century, though no sample from the uppermost and not well-stratified phase 4 deposits has been processed.

Comparison of the pottery from Buraq Tappeh with the assemblage from the Gorgan Wall forts and other sites suggests that the Buraq Tappeh fort may have been established earlier than the forts on the Great Wall, that its occupation overlapped with the early phases of occupation of the forts on the wall, but that it was abandoned earlier.[71] This would point to fort construction starting early within the date range compatible with the radiocarbon dates, i.e. in the earlier fifth century, and that construction works were completed at some stage in the first half of the fifth century. It is hard to imagine that the fort could have been abandoned before the last quarter of the fifth century at the very earliest, if its occupation overlapped with that of the forts on the Gorgan Wall. Modelling suggests that abandonment was probably after AD 530. There is nothing to suggest that the fort remained occupied beyond the later sixth century, at the very latest. That it seems to end earlier than Fort 2, where most material also seems to be no later than the sixth century, points perhaps to abandonment in the first half or middle of the sixth century.

Whilst in theory all radiocarbon samples could be contemporary, not only the pottery assemblage, but also the substantial build-up of material and multiple phases of intense activity render it inconceivable that the tappeh was occupied for less than a few decades at least, more likely several generations. It is worth briefly summarising the stratigraphy to gauge the likely duration of occupation: following fort construction (phases 2–3.1.1), there must have been an initial phase of occupation at both ground-floor and first-floor level, even if we cannot trace this, let alone estimate how short or long this may have lasted, due to the small size of our sondage and the disturbance caused by the modern robber tunnel. It is tempting to think that the two-storey occupation might pre-date the construction of the Gorgan Wall, but there is no proof. Subsequently, the entire ground floor was filled with largely sterile soil (phases 3.1.2.1–3.1.2.2); a small quantity of bone and pottery (phase 3.1.2.1) represents perhaps redeposited material from the earliest phase of occupation rather than an additional phase of occupation half-way through this levelling operation. This was followed by a phase (3.1.2.3–3.2.1.1) of occupation nearby, when bone and pottery accumulated in the area. During the next phase of occupation (3.2.1.2) the room itself must have been occupied and an oven was built and used. Subsequently the ground was raised again either in a single phase, with some redeposited finds sandwiched between sterile levelling or alluvial deposits, or in two phases with an occupation phase in between (phases 3.2.1.3–3.2.1.5). Then a new fireplace was constructed at a higher level than the abandoned earlier oven, with evidence for occupation and textile production (phase 3.2.1.6). Water infiltration, wall erosion and lack of finds, excluding relic material from the previous phase, point to the building subsequently being a roofless and unoccupied ruin (phases 3.2.1.7–3.2.2.1). It is best not to speculate whether this may be related to bigger historical events, e.g. Peroz I's defeat in AD 484, as there could have been local factors at play. The subsequent build-up of several layers with pottery and bone in waterlogged conditions (phase 3.2.2.2) provide clear evidence for human habitation nearby, with occupation debris accumulating in a still abandoned and roofless internal room. Perhaps the garrison was smaller than before, now requiring only a part of the upper storey(s) and perhaps just guarding and occupying the walls. Reoccupation (and re-roofing?) of the room in dry conditions and the creation of another oven may imply that more of the interior was needed for a larger garrison later (phases 3.2.2.3–4.1). Perhaps this marks reinvigorated defensive efforts. The length of these phases cannot be estimated with any precision, but with so many changes, one would be more comfortable with the assumption that the sequence stretched over a century to a century and a half rather than just a few decades. The maximum possible period of occupation compatible with the radiocarbon dates could encompass up to almost two centuries at most, but it need not have been quite as long.

It is also important to note that heating and cooking facilities were installed during at least three distinct successive phases. As we probably only excavated a small part of a room and virtually none of the ground-floor level, there is a high probability that there were at least four occasions when ovens and/or fireplaces were created and quite possibly more – as opposed to just three occasions when ovens and/or fireplaces were installed or rebuilt at a higher level at Fort 2. Intervals of ground-raising and oven rebuilding could have been longer at Fort 2, which unlike Buraq Tappeh is in a well-drained hilltop location, and we should not take the frequent levelling and oven replacement at Buraq Tappeh as evidence for its

occupation lasting as long or longer than that of Fort 2. Neither, however, is the evidence easy to reconcile with an assumption of a short and transient occupation of Buraq Tappeh, notably as the three successive cooking facilities found are all on higher levels, and their replacement cannot be attributed to problems with groundwater.

In summary, we may conclude that, whilst a late fourth-century construction of Buraq Tappeh cannot be excluded, the probability is low and an early(?) fifth-century foundation or at least completion of building works is easier to reconcile with the samples. The site appears to have been abandoned earlier than the forts on the Gorgan Wall, but whether this was as late as the mid- (or even late?) sixth century or as early as the late fifth century or at some stage in between is unknown, but abandonment around the middle of the sixth century (plus or minus a few decades) seems most likely. There is no certainty either as to the relative chronology of Buraq Tappeh and Qal'eh Kharabeh, but it is worth noting that the uncalibrated dates from Buraq Tappeh start earlier and end later than the very homogenous four dates from Qal'eh Kharabeh.[72] One is inclined to think that their occupation may have overlapped. Buraq Tappeh may well have been occupied for longer – with the caveat that any potential short-lived episode(s) of reoccupation of Qal'eh Kharabeh by soldiers housed in tents and cooking outdoors need not be reflected in the small number of samples we were able to recover and process – nor do we know when and for how long Qal'eh Kharabeh's citadel housed a garrison.

7.3. Habib Ishan: a hinterland fortification with a corner citadel?

Habib Ishan, some 2.5 km south-east of the nearest section of the Gorgan Wall between Forts 23 and 24, is a c. 150 × 150 m large square enclosure, forming a platform, with a c. 50 × 50 m large square citadel in the south-east corner.[73] It is of a similar plan to several Sasanian campaign bases, even if only covering some 5% of their typical 40 ha size. It is at the south-eastern edge of a large archaeological site, which we had no time to survey. Today, it is on the right bank of the Gorgan River, but was at some stage on the left bank or on a, naturally well-defended, island, to judge by a partially dried-up old bed of the river further north. There are traces of a probable moat around the square mound. Now located at the confluence of the Gorgan River and the Qareh Su ('Black Water') stream, it probably already guarded a river crossing in antiquity. If so, it may have had much in common with Buraq Tappeh and maybe also the Musa Khan and/or Ahmad Khan forts, which probably guarded bridges further downstream and further upstream. Its architecture suggested possible Sasanian origins and, if correct, promised insights into Sasanian troop deployment in the hinterland of the wall. Should it date back to a time prior to the construction of the Gorgan Wall, as does Gabri Qal'eh with a similar plan though of much greater size, it

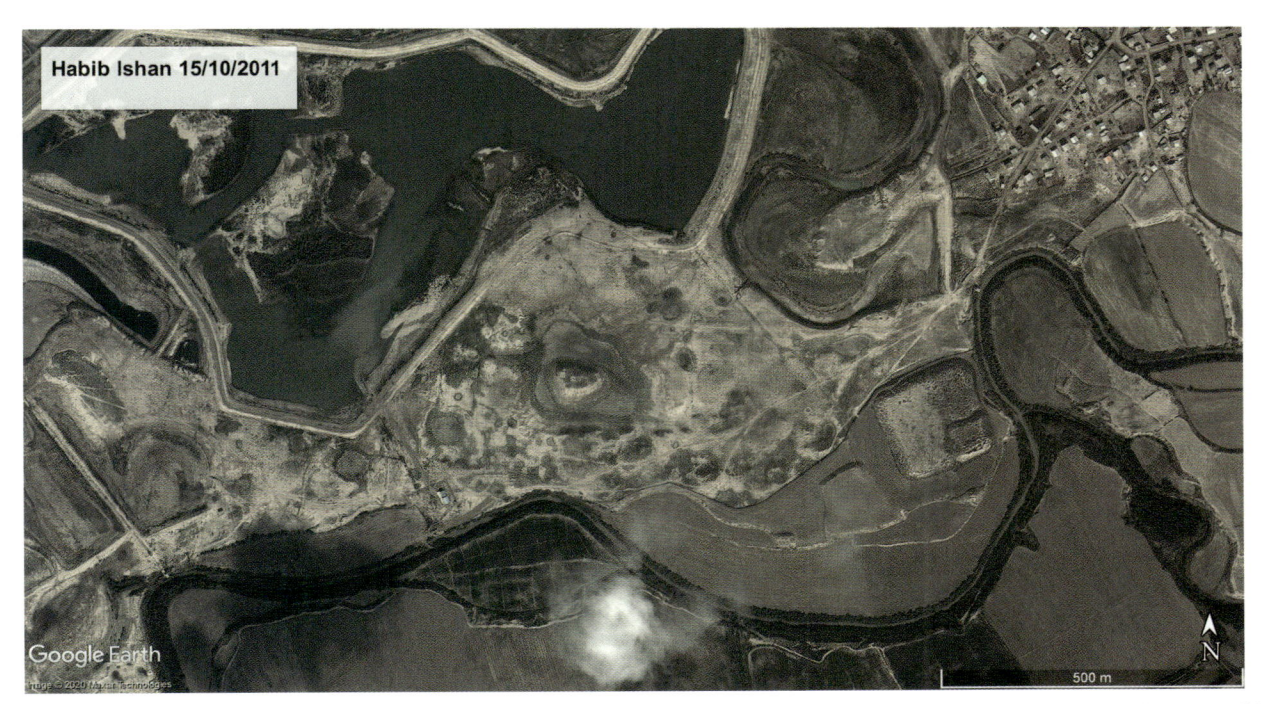

Fig. 7.26: Habib Ishan: a square compound with a corner citadel to the south-east of a large settlement. Google Earth image of 15 October 2011 (Image © Maxar Technologies).

might also offer further support for a Sasanian defensive network along the Gorgan River that might pre-date the Gorgan Wall as anticipated by the late Tony Wilkinson.[74]

On 9 November 2014, we visited Habib Ishan and collected pottery on top and on the slopes of the square mound and its corner citadel, keeping material from the citadel separate from that from the rest of the site.[75] According to the initial analysis of the pottery by Jebrael Nokandeh and Emanuele Intagliata,[76] there was much Islamic material, including of the Ilkhanid period, but there was also potential Gorgan Wall-era pottery and brick. Whilst the latter might have been reused, the former offers circumstantial evidence that the square compound with its corner citadel may have originated under Sasanian rule. Re-examination of the ceramics by the landscape team has confirmed that there is heavy Islamic occupation, with material of around the tenth to eleventh century being particularly prominent. There is also pottery that could be late Sasanian or early Islamic, including material that has parallels at Tureng Tappeh, phase VIIC, but the assemblage differs from Sasanian sites excavated as part of our project.[77] It hardly needs stressing that surface material, notably of sites densely occupied in Islamic times, need not include pottery of the earliest phase of occupation, notably if it should have been military and temporary (even if in this case there are earlier prehistoric finds). Indeed, excavation of part of an enclosure in the single-phase Sasanian campaign base of Qal'eh Kharabeh failed to unearth even a single artefact, evidence that

Fig. 7.27: The square compound overlooking the Gorgan River, seen from the north.

temporary military occupation need not be detectable by surface material, not even at single-phase, let alone heavily reoccupied, sites.[78] There were, however, some diagnostic Sasanian-era surface finds from Gabri Qal'eh (plus brick, whether reaching the site in Sasanian times or reused in the Middle Ages or in modern times). It appears, however, that Gabri Qal'eh may have been occupied more intensively than Qal'eh Kharabeh (bearing in mind the not insubstantial concentration of finds in Sasanian levels of Trench f, the site's location amidst fertile lands and its transformation into a town). Still, also at Gabri

Qal'eh there is vastly more Islamic-era surface material, with centuries of post-Sasanian reoccupation partially masking its proven Sasanian origins.[79] The same could be true for Habib Ishan. The surface assemblage may not prove Sasanian origins, but it is perfectly compatible with a Sasanian or early Islamic foundation. Strong similarities with Sasanian campaign base layout, if admittedly on a much smaller scale, may point to pre-Islamic design. We need to bear in mind, however, that Sasanian defensive architecture had a lasting influence on the Islamic era, and there were also post-Sasanian foundations of a similar layout.[80] Overall, we consider it perfectly possible that the square enclosure with corner citadel at Habib Ishan dates back to Sasanian times, and discuss it in this chapter as a possible representative of a hinterland fortification of this era. Excavation would be required to date the earliest phase of occupation and confirm or disprove the hypothesis.

The corner citadel is of a similar size to Tureng Tappeh and roughly half that of Qal'eh Kharabeh's citadel or Buraq Tappeh. It was perhaps designed for a smaller permanent garrison than Buraq Tappeh. The remainder of the compound, if as postulated for the campaign bases designed for the temporary accommodation of mobile forces, would have provided a safe shelter for a up to a few hundred troops en route. Excluding the citadel, the square mound at Habib Ishan covered roughly 2 ha. It was larger than an average two-barracks fort on the Gorgan Wall, but only one twentieth of the size of a typical 40 ha campaign base; it may well have been designed for a unit of the same size as the garrison of a four-barracks fort, but living in tents rather than mud-brick buildings. There is a ditch separating the citadel from the main compound. It seems likely that there would have been an outer wall connecting the two in antiquity. This hypothetical wall may have been slighted since (as in the case of the campaign bases) to enhance the defences of the citadel at a later time when the larger compound was no longer required.

GWS-85 with a central citadel and of c. 4 ha size may have functioned similarly and, whilst Habib Ishan's assignation to the Sasanian era is tentative and Islamic origins are possible, surface material from GWS-85 firmly points to Sasanian-era occupation, although the central mound at least appears to have been occupied already in pre-Sasanian times.[81] Both Habib Ishan, with its corner citadel, and GWS-85, with a central citadel, appear to have been inspired by earlier Central Asian architecture[82] and also resemble Sasanian campaign bases. There is a strong possibility they may be 'miniature' campaign bases, consisting of a small fortified mound, capable of accommodating a permanent garrison, and a larger enclosure perhaps also functioning as a safe base for mobile forces. If occupied similarly densely, as postulated for the large campaign bases (i.e. c. 250 men/ha), there may have up to 500 and 1,000 soldiers stationed inside when fully occupied, but far fewer at other times. And,

of course, whether Habib Ishan is of Sasanian or Islamic origins is still unknown.

7.4. Forts on the Old Gorgan River: parts of a Sasanian defensive network? The purpose of the Sasanian forts south of the Great Wall

The forts south of the Gorgan Wall are likely to have served a series of functions, ranging from possible control of human traffic between the steppe and the fertile agricultural land south, the potential levying of tolls in kind and possible policing duties, to being part of a military network, facilitating official travel and frontier defence.

If there were bridges across the Old Gorgan River next to Buraq Tappeh and perhaps also at some other river-side forts, such as Habib Ishan, Musa Khan and Ahmad Khan, these guard-posts would have been hard to bypass on any journeys from the steppe to the fertile land south or vice versa, except during dry spells when the river carried little water. We cannot know if even then there may have been rules regulating what routes travellers were permitted to use – though, of course, these would have only been relevant for Sasanian subjects and not for potential lawless or hostile groups. The duties of the fort garrisons may have included to keep an eye on those travelling along ancient roadways spanning both banks of the river. There is no positive evidence for a major trade route here nor have coins or precious items come to light from our excavations or the sieving of the spoil from robber trenches at Buraq Tappeh. The latter is not likely to have been searched so professionally by the treasure-hunters to enable them to recover all coins or other unusual small finds, had there been many. There is no evidence as yet for coins circulating here or at other Sasanian military bases on the Gorgan Plain, and they certainly cannot have circulated in significant numbers without any coming to light so far. No monetary customs or tolls will have been extracted from those crossing the river at Buraq Tappeh. If any levy was imposed on pastoralists from the north allowed to engage in barter trade on markets further south[83] at all, it may have been a small share of the herds or natural products they brought, rather than coinage or luxury goods.

Did the forts also function as safe staging posts/night-shelters for soldiers and/or other officials travelling in pursuit of their duties? It is worth noting that Buraq Tappeh, Habib Ishan and Tureng Tappeh were at a distance of a day's march from each other. The Musa Khan and Ahmad Khan pair of forts and GWS-85 were at more irregular intervals further east, which a pedestrian could also have covered within a day. It thus seems possible that they could all indeed have been used as safe overnight shelters, notably if they should pre-date Qal'eh Kharabeh and the Gorgan Wall forts. Afterwards, providing an additional night shelter just half an hour to an hour from other military bases is not likely to have been a key function, certainly as far as Buraq Tappeh is concerned. Buraq Tappeh, with its central courtyard, resembling the design of a medieval caravanserai, would certainly have been suitable to accommodate the camels, horses or packhorses of visiting officials or small groups of soldiers. Ahmad Khan, with a similar plan and south of the river, could have served a similar function. We do not know for certain whether Habib Ishan's citadel would have contained a courtyard, but it seems likely that it did; the outer enclosure certainly would have provided a large and safe campsite. Tureng Tappeh was smaller and appears to have been filled densely with buildings, but undoubtedly it could have accommodated travellers on official business, though perhaps in smaller numbers. Being much further from the steppe and amidst fertile lands, perhaps safety would have been a lesser concern, and in peacetime larger groups of official travellers may not have felt the need to seek shelter behind high walls. That there may have been an extramural road station or caravanserai near a Sasanian hinterland hilltop fort has also been suggested for Gird-i Kazhaw in the Sharizor Plain.[84]

Perhaps the late Tony Wilkinson was right in suggesting that Buraq Tappeh formed part of a Sasanian defensive system pre-dating the Gorgan Wall,[85] and now a strong case can be made that this river frontier extended in the east to Ahmad Khan or even the vicinity of GWS-85. The latter site recently discovered by the landscape team was a rectangular mound, set centrally within a square walled enclosure of c. 4 ha. There appears to be a gate in one side of the outer wall and it seems to have been surrounded by a moat. Even if 2 km south of the river (Figs 2.19–2.21; 7.1),[86] it may well have functioned as part of the system. The meandering river in the lowlands would not necessarily have been easy to patrol,[87] and it seems doubtful that regular inland navigation or even towing boats would have been possible.[88] If forts did not overlook fords or bridges or used river water for defensive purposes, it did not matter whether they were positioned on the river or on its approaches. Still, if the Gorgan River indeed carried more water in the past, it would have formed an obstacle to movement and if it filled the substantial moats around Buraq Tappeh, Habib Ishan, Musa Khan and Ahmad Khan with water, it would have considerably enhanced the defences of these small strongholds. It is worth noting that the Buraq Tappeh and Ahmad Khan forts, both dated via excavations to the Sasanian era, appear to be strikingly similar in dimensions, plan, moated defences and their location in relation to the river. It is tempting to assume that they both belong to the same building programme, adding strength to our assumption that the river at one stage functioned as a natural barrier under military control. The similarities between GWS-85 and Habib Ishan are less close (not to mention the uncertainties concerning Habib Ishan's date of foundation), but it is possible that they both represent a different site type along this frontier, i.e. small campaign bases with a citadel.

More research is needed to explore how much further this hypothetical frontier may have followed the river to the east. Forts in the eastern Gorgan Plain, south of the river, make one wonder if in the east the postulated early frontier was formed by a chain of forts behind the river. As yet, we know no Sasanian forts guarding the river or its southern approaches to the west of Buraq Tappeh. Further scrutiny of satellite imagery and fieldwork are required to establish whether the Old Gorgan River formed a watery boundary also from Buraq Tappeh to the Caspian Sea.

A further conundrum is how forts north of the river relate to this postulated riverine frontier. Were some of the forts near the Great Wall, but not physically connected to it, part of a separate chain of forts built before the linear barrier (and perhaps after the forts on the river)? The hypothetical chain of forts pre-dating the Gorgan Wall might include a possible fort (GWS-65) near Fort 28. This compound is in a unique position on the north side of the Great Wall, abutted or partially overlain by the (later?) wall or, less probably, abutting the (earlier?) wall.[89] Were GWS-65 and some of the other forts near the course of the wall outposts to the postulated riparian control line on the Old Gorgan River, built before the Great Wall? As there is no concrete evidence for their dates of construction as yet, little would be gained by extensive speculation how they may relate to certain Sasanian forts in the hinterland. Perhaps they post-date the establishment of the riparian and hinterland network of forts, or perhaps they form part of a single-phase multi-layered system (encompassing hinterland forts, guard-posts along the Gorgan River and a chain of forts north of it). Nor can we exclude the possibility that the isolated forts along the Gorgan Wall are all later, perhaps even much later, than the linear barrier.

The tradition of building rectangular forts in Iran appears to have started prior to the construction of the Gorgan Wall[90] and lasted into post-medieval times.[91] Until there is concrete evidence for the dates of construction and occupation of the forts near the Gorgan Wall with no physical connection to the great barrier, it is best to keep an open mind on their date, purpose and interrelation. They would certainly merit further investigation to establish if they, or some of them, could be early forts, partially perhaps reoccupied in the Middle Ages. They might shed light on a potential pre-wall chain of forts and/or a medieval network of forts around Gorgan/Jorjan. Most of the forts are south of the wall or just north of it, but the landscape team also discovered a chain of small forts on a possible route from Gorgan/Jorjan to the NNW. It is unknown whether they are medieval or perhaps Sasanian, along a route from a postulated gate in the wall between Forts 12 and 13 to Dehistan (Figs 2.8, 2.19 and 7.1).[92]

The case for a Sasanian defensive line along the Old Gorgan River is much stronger now than it was after the first phase of our joint project. Did they and a possible network of hinterland sites and outpost forts beyond the river indeed pre-date the wall? Unfortunately, due to the lack of precision of radiocarbon dating, we can neither prove nor disprove this hypothesis. The earliest radiocarbon samples from Buraq Tappeh could be contemporary to the earliest samples from the Gorgan Wall, a little earlier or a little later. What we can be sure of now is that Buraq Tappeh cannot be much earlier than the Gorgan Wall. Construction of the latter is not likely to have started before the AD 420s at the earliest and is likely have been largely completed by the early AD 480s at the very latest, and it will have taken some time to build. The earliest sample from Buraq Tappeh (g.068/90, dating to AD 409–538, at 95.4% confidence, or AD 377–545, at a probability of 99.7%) cannot be earlier than the late fourth century at the very earliest and is not likely to be later than the early sixth century at the latest. A fifth-century date seems most plausible. Buraq Tappeh could at most be three generations earlier than the Gorgan Wall, but it could also be later. If Buraq Tappeh was indeed part of an earlier defensive system, along the Old Gorgan River, it was likely to be short-lived. The system may have changed, within a relatively short period, beyond recognition: from a potential network of small forts taking advantage of the Gorgan River, at times supplemented by massive campaign bases, to a chain of (on average) much more narrowly spaced larger forts behind a defensive wall, probably still benefiting from the temporary support by mobile armies in campaign bases.

With Buraq Tappeh being the only independently dated Sasanian fort on the Old Gorgan River, we certainly cannot claim that there is proof that the river functioned as a border. Yet the evidence suggests that Ahmad Khan and Musa Khan were Sasanian too and remarkably similar to Buraq Tappeh. Habib Ishan, even if the surface material is mainly or exclusively Islamic, may well be of Sasanian origins as well; excavations would be needed to establish whether it was an Islamic-era foundation or a heavily reoccupied Sasanian site. It seems likely that at least some of the other geometric fortifications along the river (Fig. 7.1) are also of Sasanian origins.

If Buraq Tappeh, Ahmad Khan, Musa Khan, GWS-85 and Tureng Tappeh, as well as perhaps Habib Ishan, formed part of a Sasanian frontier defence system created a few years or decades before the Great Wall, and the case is far from proven, they certainly share, despite being very different in plan and size, some characteristics. They were all heavily defended: Buraq Tappeh's, Ahmad Khan's and Habib Ishan's defences (and probably also those of Musa Khan) were enhanced by substantial moats fed with Gorgan River water, those of Tureng Tappeh by its prominent hilltop location. The distances between some of the forts are remarkably similar. Three of them formed a triangle, with Buraq Tappeh located at c. 22 km distance from both Habib Ishan and Tureng Tappeh – which in turn were c. 23 km apart (all distances as the crow flies, but easily manageable for a fit walker or rider within daylight hours).

Whether or not there were any Sasanian posts north of the river at the time the Buraq Tappeh, Ahmad Khan, Musa Khan and Habib Ishan forts were built, we probably should not think of them as part of a linear riparian 'limes', but as an element in a multi-layered defensive system, potentially pre-dating the Gorgan Wall (or possibly supplementing it). Hinterland sites, such as Tureng Tappeh, are likely to have formed part of this system, whether created at once or over a few decades, perhaps in signal contact with the posts guarding the riverbanks.

It is interesting to note that we witness a potentially parallel, and similarly rapid, evolution of frontier defence in the Roman world some three centuries earlier. In Roman Britain, a network of forts was supplemented first by a chain of forts along the Stanegate road and then by Hadrian's Wall.[93] In southern Germany, chains of forts, first behind the Rhine and Danube and later beyond these rivers, preceded the construction the German 'Limes' (consisting in its final form of a continuous rampart, ditch and palisade in the province of Upper Germany and a thin wall in Raetia, both guarded by watchtowers and forts).[94] Developments in Roman Germany were broadly similar to those in northern Britain and perhaps the Gorgan Plain, though slower and culminating in the erection of a less formidable (but longer) barrier than Hadrian's Wall or the Gorgan Wall. In all three cases (if our hypothesis for a pre-wall chain of forts on the Gorgan Plain holds true), the erection of a continuous barrier was preceded by a control line guarded by a string of forts. Undoubtedly, these Romano-Persian parallels, far apart in space and time, do not reflect knowledge transfer, but similar situations triggering similar responses: concerns about border security were addressed first through a system offering limited protection, capable of being put into place rapidly with limited resources. Later, this was supplemented by a less permeable system requiring greater initial investment, but yielding higher returns in the long term. This was a logical sequence, as an incomplete and/or unmanned wall would have been wholly ineffective in controlling movement, whereas a chain of forts could have been effective in preventing major transgressions of such a line of control. Their garrisons could furthermore have overseen eventual wall construction. For similar reasons, it should not come as a surprise if defensive systems on the Gorgan Plain had also independently evolved in a similar manner, with a guarded riverbank (and potential chains of forts on roadways) being replaced by a linear barrier, with a chain of forts eventually abutting it.

How do the small forts relate to the large campaign bases? Might Qal'eh Kharabeh's citadel have originated as a Buraq Tappeh-style fort, and might it have formed part of the same early defensive system? Was it only at a later stage that the decision was taken to build a campaign base, reusing the citadel as a corner bastion? This seems unlikely. Being just 2 km from Buraq Tappeh, the citadel would have made little sense as a contemporary staging post. Most probably, Qalʻeh Kharabeh's citadel was built no earlier than the large campaign base. The similarity in plan and dimensions implies, however, that either Qalʻeh Kharabeh's citadel was inspired by Buraq Tappeh (if Buraq Tappeh was earlier) or potentially vice versa (if Buraq Tappeh was later).

At approximately a seventy-fifth of the size of Qalʻeh Kharabeh, Buraq Tappeh would not have offered much additional protection to this huge campaign base whilst fully occupied, nor are there reasons to think that the campaign base was likely to come under attack from the south. Guarding a bridge over which much of the supplies will have reached the Qalʻeh from potential sabotage might have been advantageous, however, notably if both compounds should pre-date the Gorgan Wall. It certainly should have been easy to transmit signals between Buraq Tappeh and Qalʻeh Kharabeh's citadel, perhaps explaining why the latter was in the south, the side facing Buraq Tappeh (Fig. 7.6).

What was the fate of the small forts after construction of the Great Wall? If Buraq Tappeh was part of an earlier defensive network pre-dating the Great Wall, its garrison may also have controlled (and taxed in kind) traffic across the river, it may have offered a safe shelter for official travellers and it may have guarded the southern supply lines to Qalʻeh Kharabeh. None of these duties may have been required once the wall was built and well guarded. An overlap in the pottery assemblage with the earlier material from the forts on the wall, however, suggests that it was not instantly abandoned but continued to be occupied for a few years, decades or even up to a century simultaneously with the Gorgan Wall.[95] There is no evidence that Buraq Tappeh continued to be occupied into the late sixth or seventh century. The creation of the big barrier may have not have made it instantly obsolete, but controlling hinterland traffic may indeed have been a lesser priority now, perhaps explaining the phases of partial occupation and neglect as revealed by our excavations. Phases of more intensive activity, as attested by repeated oven construction, may perhaps coincide with times of crisis when heavier troop concentration on the Gorgan Plain and/or concerns about security resulted in heavier occupation. One wonders whether, perhaps at a time when troops were needed elsewhere, a decision was taken to abandon the hinterland fort altogether and focus defensive efforts on the forts on the Great Wall – or perhaps eventually just some of them, if we bear in mind that there is far more evidence for late activity in the large Fort 4 than in the smaller Fort 2.[96]

There is much still to be learnt about the relative chronology and interrelation between the small hinterland forts, the large campaign bases and the Great Wall. Our recent research suggests, however, that there may have been more phases in the evolution of the multi-layered Sasanian defences across the Gorgan Plain than had been evident before. Perhaps there was a river frontier pre-dating the Great Wall, backed up by a network of fortifications in the hinterland. The chronology of most small forts is, however, unknown. Some may have formed contemporary or later chains or networks of forts. It seems that the system evolved relatively rapidly, with no positive evidence for any smaller installations of exclusive military purpose pre-dating the fourth century and most of the system probably being no earlier than the fifth century. Buraq Tappeh appears to have been maintained for some time, its late phases probably overlapping with the early phases of occupation of the forts on the Gorgan Wall. It thus will have been maintained until at least the late fifth or early sixth century, more probably, however, to the middle third of the sixth century; there is no evidence for occupation to the end of the century or beyond. Tureng Tappeh's much longer occupation suggests, however, that Buraq Tappeh does not reflect the history of the entire Sasanian military network in the hinterland of the wall. Perhaps it became dispensable due to its vicinity to the Gorgan Wall, or perhaps any potential temporary shortage of recruits (e.g. as a result of a hypothetical spread of the Justinianic Plague to the Gorgan Plain[97]) led to the abandonment of some of the strategically less crucial hinterland sites. Potentially, there might have been local factors we cannot know, such as riverine erosion or flooding damaging the fort defences and/or the postulated bridge.

Notes

1. See also chapter 24.2.
2. Ghasemi 2012; cf. Boucharlat 2015, 36–38; 2017a, 143 fig. 6, 146.
3. Tamm *et al.* 2018, especially 137–38; Tamm 2020.
4. Finster and Schmidt 1977.
5. See Cobb 2019 for chains of Roman forts in Egypt's Eastern Desert as a parallel. They were spaced around a day's march apart and probably intended to protect travellers and trade from banditry.
6. See chapter 4.1.
7. See recently Symonds 2018, 5–12.
8. Al-Jahwari *et al.* 2018; Sauer in Priestman *et al.* 2022. See also chapter 24.2.
9. Batt and Greenwood 2013, 435–36; Sauer *et al.* 2013, 14, 19, 215–17, 305; 2019, 130–31 with fig. 1; Wilkinson *et al.* 2013, 64–68. Qareh Doyub with its fire temple, next to the strategically significant point where the Gorgan Wall crosses the Gorgan River (Nokandeh *et al.* 2012, ۳۷۴–۳۷۷/374–77 [288–91]), may have been a primarily religious site as there is no evidence for a defensive wall on all sides, though a partial destruction of walls through flood damage may be possible.
10. Gadjiev 2008a.
11. See chapters 4 and 8.

12 See chapter 7.4.
13 See chapter 7.2.
14 Abbasi 2016, 189–95; cf. Kiani 1982b, fig. 5 and Google Earth imagery. Abbasi's survey suggested that Ahmad Khan was, like many Sasanian forts and fortresses, divided into four equal parts.
15 See chapters 2.2 Table 2.1 (GWS-85), 2.7 and 7.3.
16 Boucharlat and Lecomte 1987.
17 Boucharlat and Lecomte 1987, 25 indicate an approximate size of 0.25 ha, including it seems the 2.20–3 m wide walls. Pl. 6 implies the intramural area was indeed close to 0.2 ha; see also pls 4–7 and 8–9.
18 See chapter 7.2.4.11.
19 See chapter 7.3.
20 See chapter 2.3.2–2.3.3; Kiani 1982b, figs 3–4; Sauer *et al.* 2013, 306, 601; Wilkinson *et al.* 2013, 99, 131 no. 228.
21 See Wilkinson *et al.* 2013, 46 fig. 3:20.
22 See chapter 7.4.
23 A local farmer told Hamid Omrani Rekavandi that the name means 'white mound', as the soil looks white when cut. During excavation we found that some deposits contained lime.
24 Arne 1935, pl. I; 1945, fig. 3: an unlabelled mound some 2 km south of site 117 (Qal'eh Kharabeh: Arne 1935, pls I–II no. 117; 1945, 16 fig. 4, 27 and fig. 3 no. 117; cf. Sauer *et al.* 2013, 309) is almost certainly Buraq Tappeh.
25 Shiomi *et al.* 1976, map B4, plotting Buraq Tappeh as 'B4-No.8'.
26 Priestman 2013, 511, 526, 528; Sauer *et al.* 2013, 305, 311, 313, 318–19; Wilkinson *et al.* 2013, 30, 101–03, 113, 115.
27 In such a scenario it would also have been difficult to fill the moat around the fort with water, but it is, of course, not beyond possibility that it was a dry ditch.
28 Mustawfi 18 = trans. Le Strange 1919, 206; cf. Hopper 2017a, 132; Le Strange 1905, 376–77.
29 Lockhart 1938, 198–99.
30 Yate 1900, 259–60, cf. 221 on a crossing much further upstream.
31 See chapter 21.1.
32 See chapters 7.2.4.6 and 20.4.5.
33 See chapter 8.4 and Sauer *et al.* 2013, 312–53.
34 Carried out by Mohammad Arman Ershadi and Mohammad Taghi Maleka; results processed by Roger Ainslie and Mohammad Arman Ershadi.
35 See chapter 8.3.1 and Sauer *et al.* 2013, 312–30.
36 Shiomi *et al.* 1976, B4 no. 8. We have no means of verifying the accuracy of the height estimate in 1974 (Shiomi *et al.* 1976) and whether or not ploughing might indeed have reduced the height of the mound by as much as c. 2 m in just over three decades, until re-surveyed in 2007 (Wilkinson *et al.* 2013, 102; cf. Sauer *et al.* 2013, 318). Considering that some forts on the central and western section of the Gorgan Wall, as well as the walls of some campaign bases, have almost been ploughed flat, whilst others are preserved to a height of several metres, a height loss of 2 m in 33 years is far from inconceivable. We must consider, however, that only one slope is plough-damaged so far. Ploughing may well have flattened walls and tower mounds at the edges, but is not likely to have reduced the entire hilltop substantially in height. The CORONA image of the late 1960s (Sauer *et al.* 2013, 313 fig. 12:9), though perhaps not of sufficiently high definition for certain conclusions, may suggest that the walls formed more prominent features then, but provides no evidence that the shape and size of the hilltop been has altered massively since. We may tentatively conclude that 6.7 m height, if correct, can only relate to the walls and/or any tower mounds, not to the mound as a whole. We furthermore do not know what the reference point was for the 1974 height estimate. If the lowest point in the surroundings, then it is possible that further silting up of the moat may account for a small part of the difference between the 1974 and 2007 estimates.
37 See chapters 7.2.4.2 and 24.2.
38 E.g. Al-Jahwari *et al.* 2018; see also chapter 24.2.
39 See chapter 9 and Nemati *et al.* 2019/2020.
40 See chapter 4.1.2.1 with references.
41 Hagan *et al.* 2018.
42 Re-examination in 2016 suggests that there is a substantial vault under the rectangular pit, then estimated to be even of 4 m depth (as opposed to 2.80–2.90 m in 2015). There is a cylindrical pit nearby (see Fig. 7.13). The differences between our observations in 2015 and 2016 suggest that further illegal digging may have taken place between the two seasons.
43 Taghi Maleka found this red stone (carnelian) bead (BT/1; see chapter 18:4) near the second pit and there was also much pottery, identified as Sasanian by Hamid Omrani Rekavandi.
44 Friederike Jürcke and Majid Mahmoudi, supported by other team members, played a leading role in excavating and recording this trench. Without their diligent records and careful excavations, this chapter could not have been written.
45 Radiocarbon dates kindly supplied by the Scottish Universities Environmental Research Centre (SUERC) and the Poznan Radiocarbon Laboratory. Bones were identified by Homa Fathi and Dr Marjan Mashkour, charcoal, by Dr Lyudmila Shumilovskikh (see chapter 21.1).
46 The examination of the robber trench spoil was directed by the late Ghorban Ali Abbasi.
47 Lyudmila Shumilovskikh, email of 31 May 2020.
48 See chapter 15.4.3.
49 See chapters 15.4.3 and 20.
50 Lyudmila Shumilovskikh, email of 31 May 2020.
51 It should be stressed that this interpretation is tentative. The narrowness of the sondage, its partial disturbance through the robber trench and the uniformity of soil colour, so that despite repeated cleaning context boundaries could not always be securely identified, made the interpretation of the stratigraphy very challenging. Could g.066 be an early mud-brick wall, deposits g.039, g.058 and g.060 levelling deposits above the wall and g.021 and g.009 a later wall built on top of them? It is worth noting that there were clear layers of mud-brick in g.066 and g.021 and, to judge by the south-east-facing profile, their location is similar. Furthermore, the alignment of the edges of deposits g.039, g.058 and g.060, as far as visible, matches those of narrower wall g.021 above and they were abutted by much thinner, clearly distinguishable, occupation or levelling horizons. This would be hard to explain if they were levelling deposits, but makes perfect sense if they are part of the same wall as g.066 below and g.021 and g.009 above.

52 Sauer *et al.* 2013, 185–99.
53 Sauer *et al.* 2020a, 25–28.
54 See chapter 20.4.5.
55 See chapter 21.1.
56 See chapter 20.4.4–20.4.5.
57 See chapter 18.8.
58 See chapter 18.3.5.
59 See chapter 20.3.
60 See chapter 18.8.
61 See chapter 18.4.
62 One of the frequent animal burrows also contained small traces of plastic at the level of g.016.
63 See chapter 18.4.
64 See chapter 4.1.4.2.3 and Sauer *et al.* 2013, 194–99, 230–38.
65 Sources: see Gascou *et al.* 1979, 16–19, pl. VI; Ikram and Rossi 2004, 75–79; Rossi and Ikram 2018, 51–56, 434–37, 439 on Qasr al-Gib. Note that Rossi and Ikram 2018 (53 fig. 21, 54, 436, fig. 383) provide the most detailed description and plans of the fort, suggesting that there may have been c. 57 m² accommodation on the ground floor and 45 m² on the first floor, the upstairs rooms being mostly smaller (excluding internal walls, as well as corridors and the staircase). The area of rooms on a third storey, of which few traces remain, are hard to estimate. The figures in the table are only for six rooms at ground-floor and first-floor level (c. 44 m² plus 34 m² combined, totalling 78 m²). A poorly preserved larger seventh room at ground-floor level, its postulated counterpart on the first floor and the entire third storey has been excluded, as P.J. Grossmann's garrison estimate (in Gascou *et al.* 1979, 17–19) is based on the assumption that there were six men each in six rooms on the ground floor and four men each in six rooms on the first floor, so that it would be misleading to apply his estimate to more rooms than he had been aware of. Rossi and Ikram 2018, 451, doubt that the garrison consisted exclusively of soldiers. See Gichon 1989 and 1993 on En Boqeq, where the garrison estimate is based on the assumption that the four large towers were occupied too (which have not been included in the estimate for any of the other forts). Jęczmienowski 2017 applies similar estimates to *quadriburgia* in Moesia. See Konrad 1999, 400–02, and 2001, especially 56, 61–62, 98–99, 104–05, suppl. figs 6–7 on Tetrapyrgium and chapter 4.1.4.2.3 in this volume on Fort 2 and Table 4.5 (cf. Table 4.7) on extent of the indoor area at this fort. The above models do not take into account the model by Sidebotham and Gates-Foster 2019, 27–30, 39–43 table 1.2, 73–285, assuming that each occupant had as much as 58.265–79.32 m² intramural space at their disposal in Roman forts in Egypt's Eastern Desert, notably as the authors argue plausibly (p. 28) that due to 'limited water and food supply … there must have been far fewer dwelling in the *praesidia* than in their contemporary counterparts of equal sizes in more temperate climates or in regions with more abundant water and food supplies'. If applied to Buraq Tappeh, this would imply just 61–83 occupants. Garrison sizes of small forts are discussed also in Sauer in Priestman *et al.* 2022.
66 See Sauer *et al.* 2013, 195–96.
67 Pringle 2001, 83–89, 232–36, 403–05, 546–47 fig. 2; Lassus 1981, especially 235–37, 241–45, argues for a mounted garrison which could have been smaller. The internal area of the Thamugadi fort is based in the foldout plan in Lassus 1981; see Lassus 1981, *passim* on towers and internal buildings, cf. 182, 184–86, 237 on the height of buildings. Roblès *et al.* 2019, 203–06 assume the garrison could have numbered up to 1,000 soldiers.
68 Lassus 1981, 177, 235–37, 244.
69 These models are based on the assumption that the barracks (incl. walls) of El-Lejjun were two storeys high and covered 18,200 m² combined (Groot *et al.* 2006; Parker 2000; 2006b, 115; Sauer *et al.* 2013, 198 table 6:2), those of Fort 2, 4,086 m² and 7,227 m² with the annexes. The area covered by accommodation at Buraq Tappeh is estimated at 3,497–4,097 m² and twice these figures after the addition of the annexes. This model includes walls and doorways for the barracks at all three sites. The total number of soldiers, assuming a garrison of 2,000 for El-Lejjun, is rounded to the nearest 50. On the strength of late Roman army units, or estimated garrisons and the size of the forts they occupied, see also Duncan-Jones 1990, 110–14, 214–21, Franke 2012, 61; 2015, 371, Glaser 2008, 615–16, Konrad 2001, 104 with no. 507 and Mackensen 2013, 119.
70 Breeze, 2006, 66, 285–87; Breeze and Dobson 2000, 31–39, 41; Hodgson 2017, 88; Symmonds 2013; 2018, 113; note that garrison estimates for milecastles range from 12 to 48.
71 See chapter 15.4.3.
72 See chapter 8.4.3.
73 According to our hand-held GPS, the four corner points of the large square enclosure (the SE point being of course also a corner of the citadel) were as follows: SE: UTM 40S E 0292195, N 4112891; SW: UTM 40S E 0292067, N 4112843; NW: UTM 40S E 0292020, N 4112966; NE: UTM 40S E 0292157, N 4113020. There is, as usual, some inaccuracy, and the rounded corners result in the sides measuring 132–147 m, as opposed to c. 150 m. Google Earth indicates similar dimensions. Note that our measurements refer to the interior only and are therefore lower than those recorded by the landscape team (see chapter 2.3.2) for the entire mounds.
74 Wilkinson *et al.* 2013, 101–02.
75 See chapter 2.2 Table 2.1 (GWS-64) and 2.3.2. See also Hopper *et al.* 2022. Material from the citadel is recorded under GWS14/64.A, that from the remainder of the square enclosure under GWS14/64.B. See also Arne 1935, pls I–II and 1945, fig.3, 16 fig. 4, 29: DB = Dört Böurek, with Islamic surface pottery recorded.
76 See Sauer *et al.* 2020e, 90–91.
77 See chapter 2.3.2. On the chronology of Tureng Tappeh, phase VIIC, see also chapter 15.4.2.4 and 15.5.1.
78 Sauer *et al.* 2013, 341–46.
79 See chapters 2.2 and 8 and Hopper *et al.* 2022 (kind information Emanuele Intagliata and Kristen Hopper).
80 See chapter 24.9.
81 See chapter 2.2 Table 2.1 (GWS-85) and 2.7.
82 See chapter 24.3.
83 Interestingly, landscape survey has detected a Sasanian site (GWS-13) further south (Wilkinson *et al.* 2013, 115, cf. 31 fig. 3:7, 51 fig 3:26). Little would be gained by speculating where markets might have been, as little is known about Sasanian-era settlement in the Gorgan

Plain, due to incomplete survey, intensive agriculture and reoccupation. On coin circulation, or lack thereof, see also chapter 18.7.
84 Tamm 2020, 426–27, 429.
85 Wilkinson *et al.* 2013, 101–02.
86 See chapter 2.2 Table 2.1 (GWS-85) and 2.7.
87 See also Yate 1900, 260, 276 on the river being invisible until one had almost reached its deeply incised riverbed.
88 See chapter 7.2.1 on the dangers involved in crossing the river and the risk of catastrophic flash-floods.
89 This site has been discovered by the landscape team: see chapters 2.5, 4.5 and 4.6.3.
90 See also chapter 8.3.
91 See, for example, Fazeli *et al.* 2009; Kiani 1975; Kleiss 1993c; 1993d; 1993e; cf. 1975.
92 See chapter 2.3.3, 2.5 and 2.7.
93 E.g. Hodgson 2017.
94 See Kemkes 2020 for an up-to-date summary.
95 See chapter 15.4.3.
96 See chapter 4.1.4.6.2.
97 See also Jackson Bonner 2011, 86–87 on the potential effect of the plague on the Persian army.

8

Campaign bases

8.1. Introduction

'Campaign bases' is a term we have coined to describe vast and heavily fortified military compounds (of c. 10–210 ha size internally) without much or any permanent housing in the interior.[1] They are often as well defended as permanently occupied military fortresses or fortress cities, but are evidently not designed for comfortable permanent long-term occupation by a military garrison, let alone an urban community. Their massive defences could not have been erected in an evening as an overnight shelter, by an army en route, like earlier Roman marching camps. We have argued that they were occupied by field armies on campaign for one or more campaigning season(s), and they may well often have been reoccupied on several occasions. Evidence for permanent housing within the massive outer walls of Qal'eh Iraj, probably mirrored at some other sites, adds strength to this, as this would not have been required for compounds intended for single use – not to mention evidence for repeated architectural modification at Qal'eh Iraj. (We assume here that most other campaign bases also boasted permanent accommodation, either within their walls or their corner or central citadel (where present) or both, although this hypothesis admittedly has not been proven as yet.) Some may also have served as military assembly grounds where army units gathered and/or camped, in a state of readiness, to be dispatched to warzones or territories under threat. As the arguments have been presented in some detail before, there is no need for a repetition here.[2]

Fieldwork in 2014–2016 has, however, gone far beyond confirming our previous conclusions as to the chronology, architecture, purpose and spatial distribution of monuments of this category. We have been able to independently date the largest site of this type on the Gorgan Plain, Qal'eh Pol Gonbad-e Kavus. We now know that at least one campaign base in the Gorgan Plain (Gabri Qal'eh) appears to have been built earlier than the Gorgan Wall and the same is true for Qal'eh Iraj on the Tehran Plain. The landscape team has discovered a previously unknown 63 ha base at Miankaleh Fenderesk South (GWS-92) (Figs 2.1, 2.3.A, 2.4, 2.19 and 7.1).[3] Excavation and survey have shed important new light on the physical dimensions of defensive walls and ditches of some of these sites. We know much more about medieval reoccupation of selected installations and how Sasanian military investment boosted urbanism. Less significantly, we carried out further geophysical and aerial survey at Qal'eh Kharabeh and pedestrian survey at some other campaign bases. This chapter focuses on sites on the Gorgan Plain. Qal'eh Iraj, at c. 175 ha interior area one of the largest campaign bases, merited a separate chapter, due to its extraordinary dimensions and its location at one of the central crossroads of Persia – suggesting it played a pivotal role in the system, not to mention the discovery of unique written documents.[4]

8.2. Qal'eh Pol Gonbad-e Kavus: the largest Sasanian fortress on the Gorgan Plain

8.2.1. Introduction and comparative analysis of Qal'eh Pol Gonbad-e Kavus and other campaign bases

At an internal size of c. 1.25 km^2, one-and-a-half times the area of all known Gorgan Walls forts combined,[5] Qal'eh Pol Gonbad-e Kavus[6] is by far the largest of the quadrilateral compounds on the Gorgan Plain, and its construction will have required a formidable workforce. Geometric design points to original construction within a single phase. It shares several of the architectural features of smaller Sasanian campaign bases:

288   *Ancient Arms Race*

Fig. 8.1: CORONA Satellite image of 1969 of Qal'eh Pol Gonbad-e Kavus (courtesy of US Geological Survey), processed by Kristen Hopper, with location of significant features, surveys and Trench a added by EWS.

- It is of geometric shape, with rectilinear sides and four corners.

- It appears to be supplied with water via a raised canal.

- There are no traces of any permanent, let alone monumental, structures in its interior (other than the cited customary water supply canal and traces of a hollow-way).

- It appears to be surrounded by a moat.

- There are regularly spaced towers on the outside.

There are, however, also some characteristics which set it apart from some Sasanian campaign bases:

- The corner angles deviate more from a right angle than those of the majority of its counterparts.

- The raised canal does not follow an axis of symmetry of the compound.

- The width of the moat is at the lower end of the distribution range (c. 20–30 m, as opposed to 25–80 m at other campaign bases).

- The intervals between towers is smaller (c. 20 m, centre to centre, as opposed to 25–35 m in other Sasanian installations in the area[7]).

- There is no known corner or central citadel.

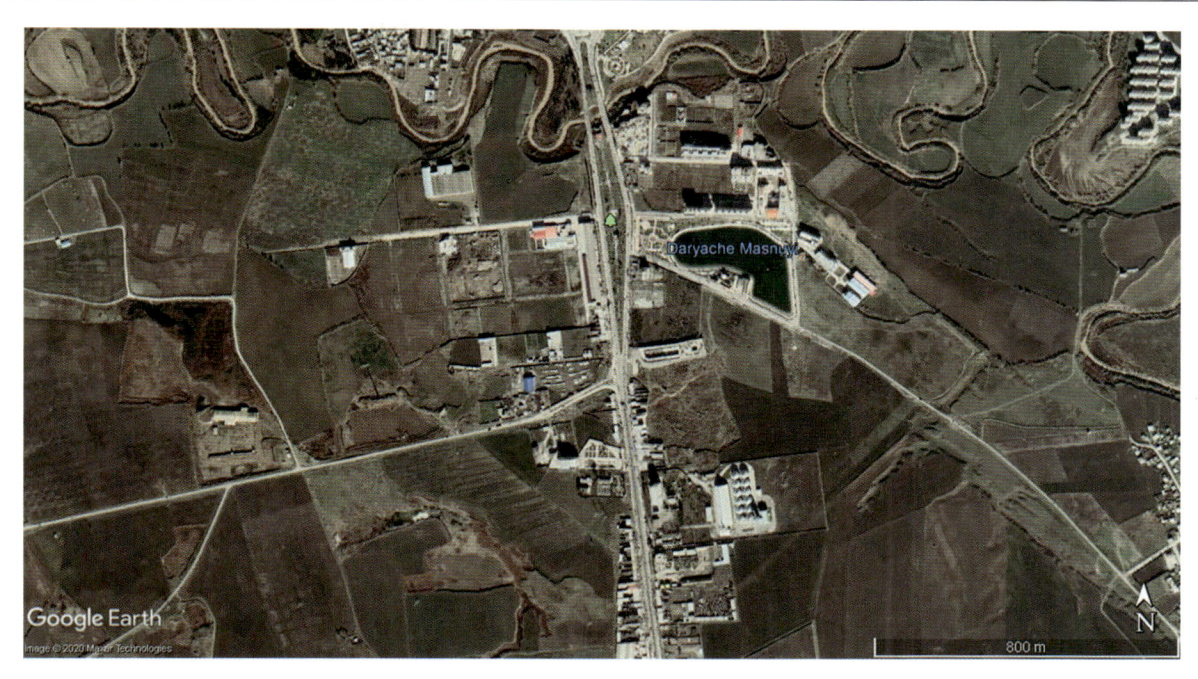

Fig. 8.2: Google Earth image of Qal'eh Pol Gonbad-e Kavus of 22 January 2020. Apart from a small area in the east, much of the mega-fortress has been destroyed by, or buried under, modern development (Image © Maxar Technologies).

– It is much larger than most of its counterparts (but there are some that are as large or larger further afield, as outlined below).

None of the latter observations proves that it belongs to a different tradition, all the more so if we bear in mind that the architecture of those compounds classified as certain Sasanian campaign bases[8] is far from uniform. Qal'eh Daland[9] and Miankaleh Fenderesk South (GWS-92),[10] for example, do not have a corner or central citadel either (and the same holds true for several other such sites further afield, namely Qal'eh Iraj and Leilan). Furthermore, Qal'eh Pol Gonbad-e Kavus was already heavily disturbed in the north when the CORONA satellite image was taken (Fig. 8.1), so that we cannot be absolutely sure whether it never had a corner citadel or whether a hypothetical corner citadel in the north might have been destroyed. The narrowly spaced towers may not belong to the original phase.[11] Even if some campaign bases have much wider moats, Qal'eh Yasaqi, Zal Tappeh (GWS-61/83) and Miankaleh Fenderesk South (GWS-92) are surrounded by moats of a similar width to that at Qal'eh Pol Gonbad-e Kavus.[12] Some other campaign bases, such as GWS-55 and Ghobal (discussed below), also lack right-angled corners and their plan also resembles a parallelogram.[13] Indeed, geometric perfection would have added little to the most effective use of space. Sasanian planners will have been pragmatists, and adapting fortifications as best as possible to the terrain and landscape features, such as rivers and stream channels, was more important than right-angled corners. Furthermore,

whilst Qal'eh Pol Gonbad-e Kavus is an outlier, in terms of the dimensions or spacing of some of the features listed above, a degree of variation can also be observed amongst other campaign bases. On architectural grounds, it seems clear that Qal'eh Pol Gonbad-e Kavus shares many of the traditions of the campaign bases.

The compound with its telling name Qal'eh Pol Gonbad-e Kavus, i.e. the 'Castle of the bridge of Gonbad-e Kavus', is located on the southern bank of the Chai Chai River and would, one assumes, once have controlled a river crossing. It may also have been positioned at this spot to guard the approaches of the central section of the Gorgan Wall. Later, it would have been positioned on the outskirts of medieval Gorgan/Jorjan. In Late Antiquity, one would have passed the massive camp en route from Dasht Qal'eh, the largest known city from this period, to the possible gate through the Gorgan Wall between Forts 12 and 13.[14] Not only was it strategically placed at a river crossing and the interface between the fertile plain and the steppe, its fairly central location also meant that it would have been easier to supply its large garrison with food or to deploy it speedily against any possible threat from the north; troops stationed at the western extremity of the plain would have taken much longer to reach any flashpoint in the north-east of the Gorgan Plain or the mountains beyond, whilst troops stationed at the eastern edge of the plain would have taken longer to reach the west. Qal'eh Pol Gonbad's location by contrast was ideal. That the largest known settlements of antiquity (Dasht Qal'eh) and of the Middle Ages (Gorgan/Jorjan) are both nearby shows that it was at very heart of the plain, even if it was east of its geometric centre (and it was more off-centre in the Sasanian era, when the Caspian Sea shore was further west than it is today). Furthermore, the east was probably more likely to come under attack from a major force than the west of the plain, the latter bordering on arid and thinly populated land.

Assuming the emptiness of its interior suggests, as in the case of the other campaign bases, that Qal'eh Pol Gonbad-e Kavus was intended to be filled with temporary shelters for a mobile field army, then its garrison is likely to have been substantial. Its occupation density may, however, have been not quite as high as that of the forts on the Gorgan Wall. The latter, filled with probably in part two-storey barracks, may have been even more densely occupied than Qal'eh Pol Gonbad-e Kavus. The temporary garrison of the Qal'eh may not have exceeded the permanent garrison of the nearby linear barrier by a factor of 1.5, even if its internal area exceeded that of all forts on the Gorgan Wall by approximately 50%. Neither was it necessarily smaller. Should our estimate of 40 ha compounds being intended for units of 10,000 horsemen each[15] be in the right order or magnitude, then this one compound alone could have comfortably accommodated some 30,000 mounted soldiers – numerically similar to our estimate for the entire garrison of the Gorgan Wall.[16] The occupation density of early imperial Roman marching camps is even thought to have been twice as high, with c. 5,000 soldiers requiring a marching camp of only c. 10 ha.[17] If similarly densely occupied, Qal'eh Pol Gonbad-e Kavus could have housed more than 60,000 soldiers, but there would have been little space for horses and thus our estimate of 30,000 may be more plausible. Even that would have allowed accommodating a formidable force, and a substantial proportion of the Sasanian field army deployed on the Gorgan Plain on any one occasion, in this one compound alone.

Sites of similar size, of over 1 km² and (more or less) rectangular shape without any major structures in the interior, existed elsewhere: there was an identically sized c. 125 ha fortress at Torpakh-Kala (Figs 8.3 and 24.1),[18] c. 20 km south of Derbent, a 175 ha mega-base at Qal'eh Iraj near Varamin[19] and a c. 210 ha fortress in northern Mesopotamia at Ghobal (Fig. 24.1), identified by Dr Anthony Comfort on satellite imagery. The latter shares several architectural characteristics with Sasanian campaign bases: it appears to be empty in the interior; its parallelogram-shaped plan resembles that of several campaign bases (notably Qal'eh Pol Gonbad-e Kavus, GWS-55 and Torpakh Kala); its size greatly exceeds that of all contemporary Roman and all pre-Sasanian and medieval empty military compounds known to us, whilst being only a little larger than Sasanian Qal'eh Iraj (and smaller than the outer enclosure of the Hatra siege camp). The following observations would also be compatible with this interpretation, if none of them is decisive: there appears to be a gate opening at the exact mid-point of the east side,[20] there may be faint traces of a moat or ditch outside the wall in places and possible remains of tower mounds (though too few and too indistinct for certain identification), spaced c. 30–40 m apart (centre to centre). Sir Aurel Stein estimated in the 1930s the height of the decayed walls, built of sun-dried mud-bricks, at 6–8 feet (c. 1.83–2.44 m) and their width at the top at 10–12 yards (c. 9–11 m). It is unclear how the top is defined, and it is impossible to deduce original dimensions from the description, but it seems that the walls were preserved to marginally lesser height than those of Qal'eh Pol Gonbad-e Kavus, were of similar or greater width and perhaps of similar dimensions overall.[21]

Not counting the larger and probably Sasanian camp at Hatra and similarly large and Sasanian and/or Roman camps at Dura-Europos,[22] we know thus at least three campaign bases of similar or larger size than Qal'eh Pol Gonbad-e Kavus. Torpakh Kala and Qal'eh Iraj may also have accommodated large field armies. The former would have made a perfect base for an army securing the hinterland of the Derbent Wall or operating beyond. The latter fortress was within the empire and at a crossroads and thus in an ideal position to dispatch troops against any major external forces threatening the north-eastern or north-western frontiers of the Sasanian Empire.[23] Radiocarbon samples and finds have now proven Qal'eh Iraj's Sasanian-era construction and occupation.[24] Torpakh-Kala (Fig. 8.3) has yielded late antique finds as well, including interestingly a bone or ivory pin with a head shaped like a human hand or fist.[25] The latter has a close parallels at several Sasanian sites.[26]

There are further large installations, which may have served as Sasanian campaign bases.[27] They include a large compound of over 50 ha internal dimensions at Leilan (Fig. 8.4) to the south-east of Lake Urmia. Survey by Wolfram Kleiss has revealed that it was protected by a mud-brick wall with projecting towers and, in places at least, also with a ditch.[28] It is polygonal, not far off a rectangle in the north-east, but more irregular in the south-west, measuring 600 × 800–1,000 m.[29] It employs mud-bricks of 40 × 40 × 11–12 cm size,[30] similar dimensions to those employed in Sasanian military installations on the Gorgan Plain. Kleiss attributed it to the Parthian (or in any case Partho-Sasanian) era, based on its architecture and pre-Islamic pottery.[31] The Leilan campaign base was probably intended for troops on their way to Armenia. Interestingly, it was not far from Leilan that a campaign base of similar design was built in the early AD 450s, according to the Armenian author Elishe:

> A few days later the Persian general set out with his whole heathen host, marched to Armenia, and reached the province of Her and Zarevand [located to the west of Lake Urmia]. Halting in that province, he pitched his camp, dug ditches, erected a rampart, surrounded it with a wooden palisade, and vigilantly fortified it like a city.[32]

Fig. 8.3: The Sasanian mega-fortress of Torpakh Kala, c. 20 km south of Derbent, with its distinct moat and tower mounds. Google Earth image of 25 October 2013. Like Qal'eh Pol Gonbad-e Kavus, corners are not right-angled and it is of virtually identical size (Image © CNES / Airbus).

Fig. 8.4: Possible Sasanian campaign base at Leilan: Google Earth image of 5 February 2012 (Image © Maxar Technologies).

The description of the camp, whilst composed or revised some two centuries after the events,[33] is unlikely to refer to Leilan, as the province of Her and Zarevand was to the west of Lake Urmia (Fig. 24.1) and did not extend as far as Leilan.[34] The passage does, however, confirm that such temporary fortresses were erected on the approaches to Transcaucasia.

It is possible that a large strategic response force was based at Qal'eh Iraj near Varamin, quite possibly the same that occupied, in times of crisis, either a compound of similar plan and some 70% of its size in the hinterland of the Gorgan Wall (i.e. Qal'eh Pol Gonbad) or the Derbent Wall (i.e. Torpakh Kala). Perhaps troops were indeed sent from Qal'eh Iraj to Qal'eh Pol Gonbad-e Kavus, perhaps sub-units were also dispatched to medium campaign bases (averaging 40 ha or 20 ha in area) on the Gorgan Plain, perhaps there were separate smaller units of the Sasanian field army sent from elsewhere to the medium campaign bases. The arrangements may have differed from campaign to campaign. Dating evidence, to be presented below, also allows for the possibility that Qal'eh Pol Gonbad-e Kavus is later than some other campaign bases on the Gorgan Plain and may have either replaced or supplemented them or may have replaced some of them.

There are probably also smaller campaign bases averaging 10 ha in area, approximately a quarter of the size of Qal'eh Kharabeh, Qal'eh Daland, Qal'eh Gug A and Gabri Qal'eh. These may include the Viranshar fortress

Fig. 8.5: Agriculture and industrial development encroach on Qal'eh Pol Gonbad-e Kavus: the south-eastern wall looking south-west.

Fig. 8.6: Modern development has destroyed much of the fortress. View from the northernmost preserved part of Qal'eh Pol Gonbad's eastern walls to the north-west. A vast modern pit has erased here the outer walls as well as all ancient to modern horizons within the fortress. The surface to the left and above the team members standing left (within the pit) and the top of the earth mound under the telegraph post mark the original land surface until recently.

in the Atrak Valley in northern Iran[35] and Qal'eh Garuna west of Kermanshah.[36]

In the light of Qal'eh Pol Gonbad-e Kavus's extraordinary dimensions and likely importance, establishing the date of this mega-fortress seemed of pre-eminent importance for the history of the Gorgan Plain and the wider Persianate world. Furthermore, not only is Qal'eh Pol Gonbad-e Kavus the largest installation of its kind on the Gorgan Plain, it is also amongst those under greatest threat. Little if anything of a raised canal visible on CORONA imagery, leading into the compound from the north-west, and probably channelling water raised from the stream bed via a water-lifting device to appropriate height, appears to survive.[37] This canal and traces of a hollow-way within the south-east gate (Fig. 8.1) are the only known archaeological features within the Qal'eh. Much of the defences have now disappeared under an industrial suburb of Gonbad-e Kavus. Some 15 years prior to our excavations, north-west of where we subsequently excavated Trench a, a vast pit was dug and the Qal'eh's wall, and the topsoil and ancient subsoil inside, machined off to furnish material for modern brick production.[38] Even parts of the compound so far spared from wholesale destruction have suffered damage. A c. 600 m-long section of wall on the south-east side of the Qal'eh, between an industrial complex and the compound's east corner, near a stream channel, are still visible. Notably west of the road, the plough is cutting heavily into the defences every year, and the wall will probably be flattened altogether within a few years (Fig. 8.5; cf. Figs 8.2, 8.7 and 8.9). Only a small part of the wall in the east, just over 160 m long, has as yet largely escaped modern development and here, too, deep holes have been dug into the wall. Its fate, in the light of likely further urban sprawl of Gonbad-e Kavus, is sadly predictable. Unless the little that is left of the Qal'eh is protected vigilantly, no remains are likely to survive above ground. It therefore seemed a task of great urgency to explore the last remnants of the greatest fortress on the Gorgan Plain.

8.2.2. The towered and gated walls

A topographical survey of the east of the Qal'eh was carried out by Mohammad Bagher Bayati, with a view of creating a permanent record of the little that was left visible above ground. Whilst tower mounds are often easier to make out by visual inspection than by topographical survey, notably if elevation and/or projection is reduced to decimetres, the survey showed some of the towers clearly. To judge by the survey plot (Fig. 8.7), the average distance of projecting towers was c. 20 m, less than our previous estimate of 22–23 m, based on visual inspection.[39] Since the earth bank in the area of Trench a is clearly bulging out, c. 40 m north-west of a clear hillock, it seems likely that there was a tower where the wall was sectioned in the trench or immediately next to it. There must have been also a tower some 20 m south-east of the trench, but this appears to have been erased by a hollow-way. From c. 40 m to 160 m south-east of Trench a one notices a clear or possible tower mound every 20 m or so. There must also have been a tower in the Qal'eh's east corner, some 180 m south-east of the trench, which does not survive.

The average distance of towers is less than that observed on the perimeter of Gorgan Wall forts or certain Sasanian campaign bases where the distance between towers (excluding more narrowly spaced gate towers), centre to centre, tends to be c. 25–35 m (and often c. 28–30 m). Such narrow spacing is unparalleled to our knowledge in Sasanian monuments on the Gorgan Plain. One wonders whether the narrow spacing of towers might point to Qal'eh Pol Gonbad-e Kavus being of a different date to other campaign bases on the Gorgan Plain. The one radiocarbon

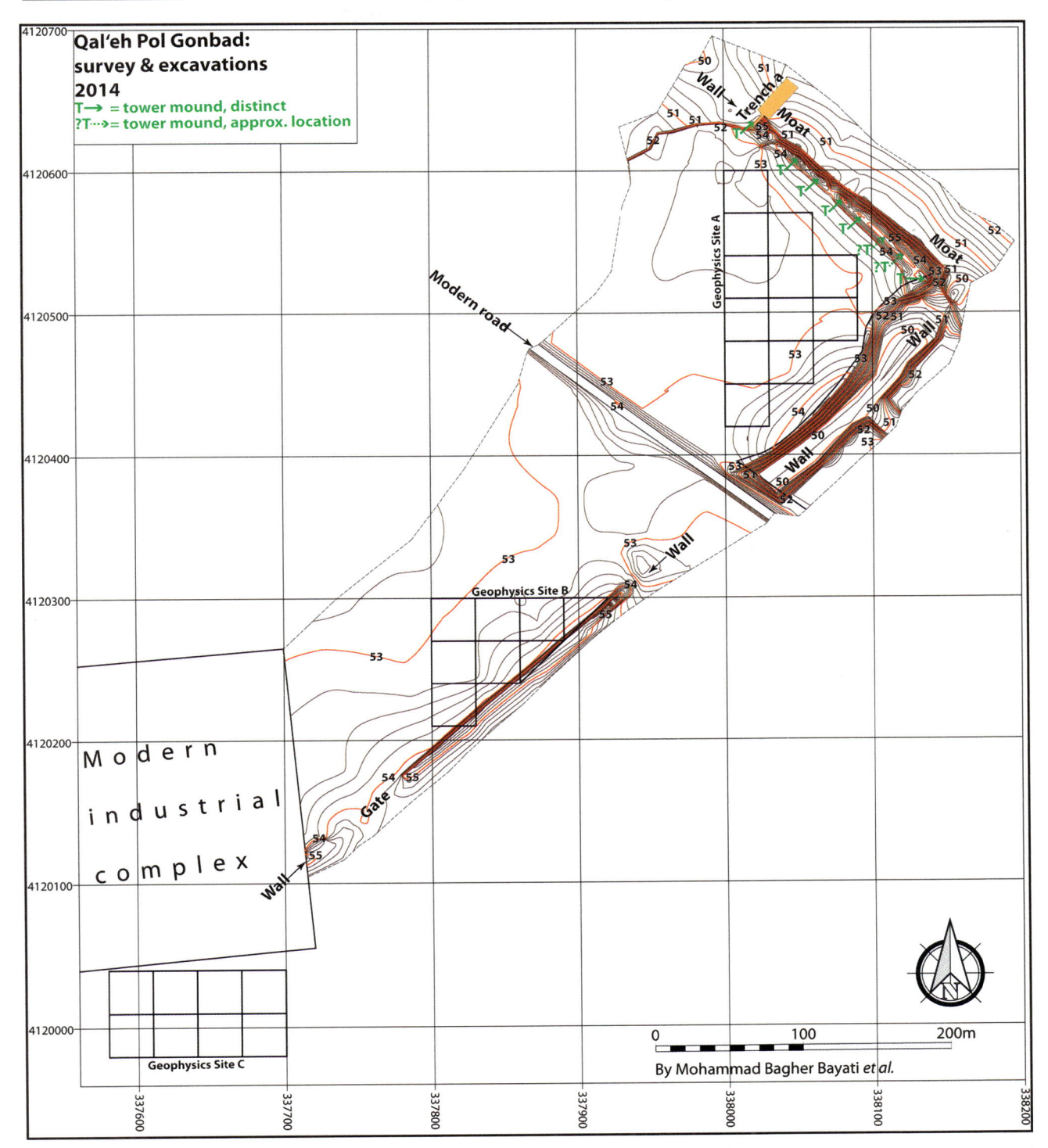

Fig. 8.7: Topographical survey of the south-east of Qal'eh Pol Gonbad-e Kavus by Mohammad Bagher Bayati et al. with preserved tower mounds marked with green arrows. The map also features other preserved archaeological structures and the location of the areas explored via magnetometer survey. The location of Trench a is marked in orange.

sample of charcoal sealed beneath the rampart points to the last three quarters of the sixth or the early seventh century as the most likely *terminus post quem* for its construction,[40] later than the dates for Qal'eh Kharabeh and much later than Gabri Qal'eh. Yet, the radiocarbon sample does not exclude a construction as early as the mid-fifth century. Not only may Qal'eh Pol Gonbad-e Kavus have potentially been established a few decades, or even a century or more, later than other campaign bases, its surviving towers may not belong to the original Sasanian walls at all. Our excavations revealed (as discussed below) that the ditch had been recut repeatedly; bearing in mind its considerable depth and c. 4.6 km length, each operation of this kind would have required a massive investment of manpower. Initially this may have involved creating an estimated 300,000 to 700,000 cubic metres of upcast (see Table 8.3). Evidently, there must have been a substantial workforce theoretically also capable of building and restoring the wall or its upper sections, and the ditch upcast would have provided plenty of material for mud-brick production. Judged by the quantity of upcast available, the original wall is likely to have been of substantially greater volume than the surviving bank, and one wonders whether erosion could have reduced it to a fraction of its former dimensions whilst neatly preserving all tower mounds. If the mounds represent the heavily eroded remains of the original Sasanian towers, we cannot decide whether their narrow spacing points to a different date of construction, when earlier traditions might have been abandoned – or simply reflects an *ad-hoc* decision of the architects or patron. More probably the tower mounds, spaced 20 m apart (centre to centre), belong to a medieval restoration of the wall.

The walls on the south-east side have been heavily damaged by ploughing, and we were unable to locate any preserved towers. Campaign base gates normally tend to be at, or close to, the mid-points of the walls on each side and need not be present on all sides.[41] One notices that there is a gap in the wall at the mid-point of the Qal'eh's south-east side. This is almost certainly one of the compound's gateways that must have been flanked by towers. On the CORONA image (Fig. 8.1) one sees traces of a hollow-way just inside of the gate which must be part of a central roadway. One also notices a distinct gap in the Qal'eh's south-west walls at their precise mid-point, no doubt a gate as well. There must also have been a gate on the north-west side, perhaps where the raised canal led into the fortress. If so, this gate would have been distinctly off-centre. Perhaps the architects preferred keeping a distance from the river flowing along the fortress's northern corner and/or the gate was placed where it was easiest to channel water into the fort or at the nearest point to a potential bridge over the river. The above-mentioned hollow-way some 20 m south-east of Trench a is likely to be modern and no ancient gateway, as it is nowhere near the mid-point of the north-east side. Furthermore, the CORONA image shows a linear anomaly (a modern track?) leading towards it at an oblique angle from the west, and a causeway across the ditch leading towards it from the north-east, pointing to it being a feature of modern date – or least in use until recently. There are gaps in the Qal'eh's north-eastern wall, including one near its mid-point. As there are no clear traces of ancient hollow-ways leading towards it (nor a causeway across the moat, though there need not have been one), it is perhaps safest to leave the question where the gate was on this side, or if there was one at all, undecided.

8.2.3. The moat

Whilst there are faint traces of what may be a moat (a band of darker discoloration), and/or a counterscarp bank beyond and parallel to the wall (a thin light line) surrounding the Qal'eh on all sides on the CORONA image (Fig. 8.1), it is on the Qal'eh's north-east side that these features can be identified most clearly. Was there a ditch or moat all around the Qal'eh or simply a canal along its east side?

Several observations suggest that the former hypothesis is far more plausible than the latter:

– The postulated traces of the ditch/moat and/or counterscarp bank on the other sides are sufficiently distinct, and their location and spacing similar, suggesting that they are part of the same feature surrounding the entire compound.

– The location of the ditch, parallel and close to the Qal'eh's outer wall, and the extremely steep gradient of the slope in phase 5 (Figs 8.14–8.15) make more sense if the function of the ditch was at least partially defensive.[42] If so, the ditch must have surrounded all of the Qal'eh; any gap would have rendered the efforts on the east side useless as any assailants would simply have targeted a more accessible spot.

– Material was needed to build the wall which, for similar reasons, is not likely to have varied substantially in height or width. By far the easiest means of obtaining the necessary soil would have been to excavate a ditch next to all sections.

– A canal on one side of the Qal'eh only, and with no known continuation, would have served no obvious purpose. If used for towing boats, the time saved would have been minimal, the efforts involved in building it very great. It would not have been needed for water supply (and its water, of course, would not have been drinkable), since there was a raised canal leading into the Qal'eh from the north-west. There was furthermore already access to the river in the north. (It is possible that the river bed has shifted its course marginally and cut into the edges of the compound, but it is surely no coincidence that the Qal'eh abuts the river and is likely to have done so already in antiquity.) There is a possible irregular supplier canal for the moat in the east (Fig. 8.1).[43] Given the direction of water flow, this is not likely to have been an overflow feature (as may have existed where the Qal'eh bordered on the river in the north). There is no trace of a canal beyond, and nothing to suggest that it was a ditch pre-dating the Qal'eh, reused and recut later.

Fig. 8.8: View of the land east of the Qal'eh, with telegraph posts on small hillocks, the area of the now indistinct and shallow moat on the Qal'eh's north-east side, looking north-west.

In short, there is no plausible explanation for the ditch other than as a defensive feature and elongated extraction pit for soil used to make mud-bricks for wall construction.

The clear visibility of the canal on the north-east side, as opposed to all other sides, is thus probably not a result of it being more prominent on, or confined to, this side, but related to its more recent history. On 11 November 2014 an old man, visiting the site, told us that his grandfather remembered that the Chai Chai River flowed past the north-east side of the Qal'eh, i.e. across the area of our Trench a, approximately one hundred years ago during periods of flooding. This suggests, most probably, that the canal bed, dug when the Qal'eh was erected and repeatedly recut since, still partially survived until the recent past. Indeed, it remains clearly visible as a distinct linear depression today, albeit one that is much wider than the original canal bed is likely to have been. Originally, at least during phases when the ditch was very deep, river water would probably have been channelled into the ditch, creating a defensive water-filled moat all around the Qal'eh. Naturally, water would have flowed more often and more rapidly along the north-east side, creating a canal connecting two bends of the river, whilst the other three sides would have dried up more rapidly. Perhaps this also meant that a proportion of the material eroding into the ditch, from the collapsing wall and the counterscarp bank, was swept downstream back into the river.

Today the ground is rising from south-west to north-east far beyond the point where we see the canal cut in the profile (Figs 8.8 and 8.13–8.16) and even far beyond the limits of our trench. One also notices that modern telegraph posts stand on small hillocks, even if not quite as tall as the hillocks under telegraph posts within the above-mentioned soil extraction pit. These hillocks bear witness to the level of the land surface at the time of their erection. Evidently, ploughing has massively accelerated the silting-up of the moat over the last two decades or so,

lowering the land surface away from the moat and raising it on top of it. The moat now forms a much shallower, but also wider, depression than even just a few years or decades ago.

8.2.4. Surface scatter of finds

Pottery was collected from the arable fields within the defences of the Qal'eh. The collection area extended from our Trench a to the east corner of compound and from there to an old trench excavated by a separate archaeological team through the Qal'eh's south-east wall some years ago.[44] In the north, the collection area extended to the edge of the 'Daryache Masnuyi', a modern concrete-lined lake (Fig. 8.2),[45] which forms part of a housing development. It focused on the area between this water-pool, the edge of a soil extraction pit (see above), the Qal'eh's defences and the modern north-west to south-east-running road. Pottery concentration across the area was similar, albeit with minor differences; there were fewer pieces on recently ploughed land, as opposed to areas exposed for longer to the elements. The sherds were mostly small, probably the result of fragmentation through prolonged ploughing and the prevalence of thin-walled vessels. Whilst the collection area did not encompass land outside the Qal'eh, there was no obvious scatter of pottery on the ground around Trench a. It needs to be borne in mind, of course, that the damp ditch probably could not be used for agriculture until it had largely silted up in the recent past. A more extensive survey is needed to establish whether or not there is a distinct difference in sherd density and chronology between the interior of the compound and the land outside.

The uniformity of the assemblage, and the scarcity of late or post-medieval sherds, may suggest that the pottery is related to the occupation of the compound or other settlement in the area, rather than manuring. Glazed pottery was scarce, as were thick-walled vessels, a distinct contrast to Gabri Qal'eh, where such pottery is abundant, pointing to more high to late medieval activity at the latter site. Whilst the analysis of the pottery by Emanuele Intagliata and Hamid Omrani Rekavandi, taking into account the pottery typology established by Seth Priestman, failed to reveal any certain Sasanian pieces, there is pottery thought to be either Sasanian or early Islamic. The small number of sherds and the strong fragmentation is worth noting, and the absence of Sasanian 'index fossils' does not necessarily prove that all is post-Sasanian. Activity in the Early to High Middle Ages, as also suggested by finds from the ditch to be discussed below, is what one might expect in close vicinity to a major medieval city.

No surface collection was carried out in any other part of the Qal'eh, where surface layers are now mostly buried under modern industrial complexes or housing or erased by soil extraction and the modern pool of water, but the regular spread of ceramic finds in ploughed land in the

Fig. 8.9: Areas surveyed via magnetometer at Qal'eh Pol Gonbad-e Kavus. Location map by Mohammad Bagher Bayati, with Trench a in red, plotted onto a Google Earth image of 16 September 2014 (Image © Maxar Technologies).

east of the compound is worth noting. What proportion of the finds might be related to actual occupation of the compound, as opposed to vanished unrelated settlements of other times, is impossible to establish. Fragile pottery would, of course, have been impractical for an army on campaign and may only have been used during any longer sojourns. However much or little, if any, of the pottery belongs to the compound's original occupation, it certainly would have made little sense to create such a vast compound and then only to occupy a part of it, and hypothetical partial occupation would have made effective defence much harder. Such logic need not apply to phases of reoccupation when fewer occupants may have taken advantage of existing defences, to save the considerable efforts of building a new compound from scratch. This, however, is only a likely scenario in the aftermath of the original creation or complete restoration of the defensive circuit – for as long as this remained in a condition to offer at least some protection. It also only makes sense if, at the time, there were enough adult occupants to effectively man 4.5 km of wall. A small group of people, whether peasants or military men, might as well have settled anywhere else. More research is needed to establish the nature of occupation. The absence of clear evidence for any mounding or other structures in the interior, not just now but also on the CORONA image, suggests that there were no monumental buildings. Like in other campaign bases, occupants will have lived in canvass, felt or leather tents, leaving few, if any, traces. Surface survey (if the finds relate to occupation) suggests that the area of the Qal'eh was occupied in similar density during one or several episodes between the Sasanian era and the High Middle Ages. It is clear that the heavily defended complex was never filled with any permanent housing, pointing to a temporary military establishment rather than a town.

8.2.5. Geophysical survey[46]

Whilst surface survey and examination of satellite imagery suggested that, as at other putative Sasanian campaign bases, there were no monumental structures in the interior, given Qal'eh Pol Gonbad's exceptional size and potential importance, it seemed worth testing

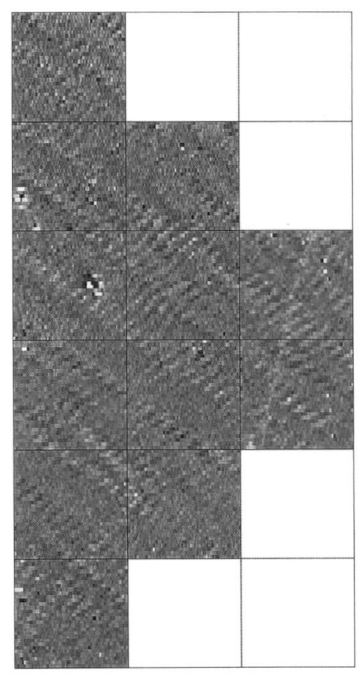

Fig. 8.10: Qal'eh Pol Gonbad-e Kavus, Site A, magnetometer survey by Mohammad Arman Ershadi, Julian Jansen Van Rensburg et al., processed by them and Roger Ainslie of Abingdon Archaeological Geophysics. North is at the top; see Figs 8.1, 8.7 and 8.9 for the exact location. Each grid measures 30 × 30 m.

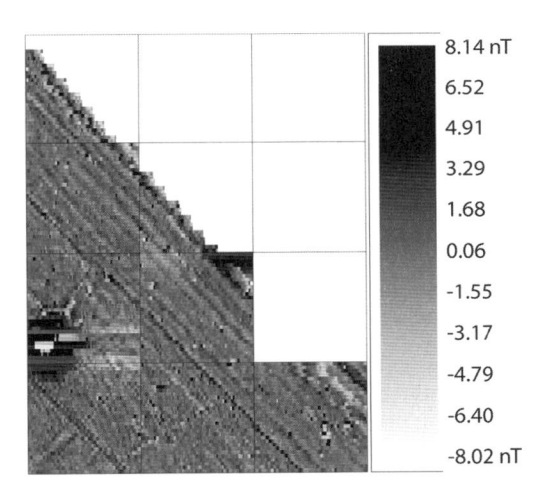

Fig. 8.11: Qal'eh Pol Gonbad-e Kavus, Site B, magnetometer survey by Mohammad Arman Ershadi, Julian Jansen Van Rensburg et al., processed by them and Roger Ainslie of Abingdon Archaeological Geophysics. North is left; see Figs 8.1, 8.7 and 8.9 for the exact location. Each grid measures 30 × 30 m.

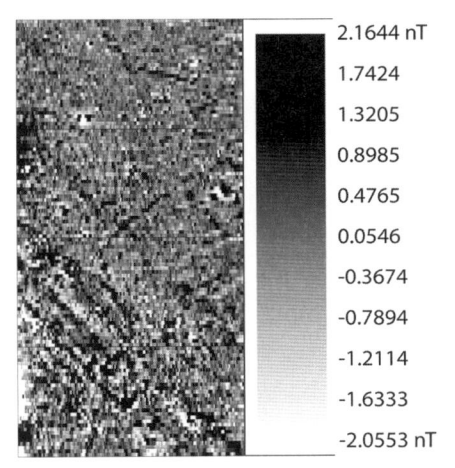

Fig. 8.12: Qal'eh Pol Gonbad-e Kavus, Site C, magnetometer survey by Mohammad Arman Ershadi, Julian Jansen Van Rensburg et al., processed by them and Roger Ainslie of Abingdon Archaeological Geophysics. North is left. The south-east wall of the Qal'eh are visible as a broad high magnetic linear anomaly; see Figs 8.1, 8.7 and 8.9 for the exact location. Each grid measures 30 × 30 m.

whether magnetometer survey had the potential to detect any structures in its interior.

The results were, perhaps predictably, disappointing. Except for showing the wall in the area of Site C (and unsurprisingly so, as also still visible above ground and on satellite imagery), no clear ancient features emerged, whilst modern ploughing and debris caused extensive disturbance. No clear traces of the hollow-way visible on CORONA imagery and crossing Site C emerged.[47] As other areas are either built over or even more heavily disturbed by earth-moving operations or covered with modern debris, it seems unlikely that further geophysical survey has the potential to trace any contemporary features in the interior. If much of them consisted of tented accommodation or yurts, such temporary occupation would almost certainly be impossible to detect. The detection of rectangular enclosure ditches, probably surrounding tents, in neat rows at Qal'eh Kharabeh in 2007 and 2008[48] was a windfall. Even if similar features should survive at Qal'eh Pol Gonbad-e Kavus, it is far less likely they could be detected here as ceramic and metallic debris, as well as potential pipes and cables, at the outskirts of a modern town could easily mask faint anomalies.[49]

8.2.6. *A section through the defences (Trench a)*[50]

With no known interior structures surviving, sampling the Qal'eh's defences seemed our best bet for dating this major site. Any material embedded within the wall would provide a *terminus post quem*, any from the ditch a *terminus ante quem*. In the case of multi-phase defences, these *termini* relate, of course, to the relevant phase and not necessarily the original construction.

We decided to section the defences where the wall is cut by the modern soil extraction pit (Fig. 8.6), to obtain a complete section across the ditch and the wall, whilst causing as little damage as possible to the little that is

Fig. 8.13: Trench a, with the multi-phase ditch showing up as a dark brown discoloration in the foreground, and the wall in the background.

left of the wall. Whilst the wall was carefully cut back manually, to create a section across, this was not a viable option for excavating a section across the huge moat. We first excavated by machine a 30 m long section across the ditch. We anticipated that the ditch would not only be deep but might reach under the water table, posing the risk that water infiltration might lead to the gradual collapse of sections. Shoring was not a viable option, due to the dimensions of the trench, the difficulty of obtaining suitable trench sheets and acrow props and the risks involved in taking down shoring at the end of operations. We therefore excavated a stepped trench. The four steps averaged 1.50 m in depth and width, so that the initial depth of the trench was c. 6 m below the present surface and its width 10.50 m (Figs 8.13–8.17 and 8.29).[51] The trench was dug very regularly by our skilled machine operators. The work was carried out under the direction and constant supervision of archaeologists. Due to the limited range of the JCB arm, and the technical difficulties posed for the machine to safely work its way out of the trench without causing damage, the steps were of lesser regularity in the north-east of the trench. Subsequently, the sections were manually straightened and cleaned, followed by drawing and photographic documentation, limited excavation, notably at the very base of the trench, and sampling. The scale of operations was considerable: in the ditch section alone we dug out an estimated 990 m^3 of soil, which took a large JCB two long days.

8.2.7. The stratigraphy of the ditch system

Cuts and context boundaries were often hard to identify. In the fairly arid surroundings of the northern Gorgan Plain natural soil and ditch fills, consisting largely of redeposited natural soil, often look almost identical. Whilst the team showed great skill in cleaning the sections, it was a constant battle against the elements. Faint differences in colour of adjacent deposits could quickly fade out when exposed to sunlight. Torrential downpours washed soil down the steps, repeatedly covering cleaned sections with a film of mud. Rising groundwater in the lower parts of the trench meant that every day and after each pause in pumping, sections had to be cleaned again, whilst groundwater infiltrating from the side caused the front part of the sections in step 4 to peel off and collapse. Notwithstanding these challenges, constant re-cleaning and re-examination of the sections, when wet and dry, when in sunlight or in the shadow, enabled us to spot more and more relevant deposits and

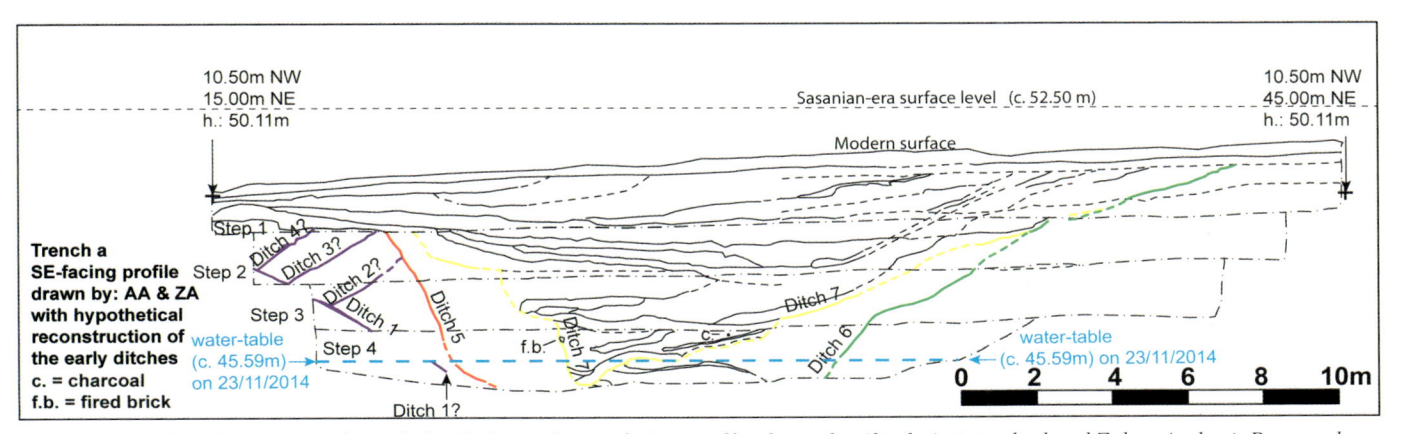

Fig. 8.14: Trench a, section through the ditch, south-east-facing profile, drawn by Aliyeh Amirinezhad and Zahra Asghari. Proposed phases: first to fourth ditches: purple; fifth ditch: red; sixth ditch: green; seventh ditch: yellow. Note that the Sasanian-era surface level (in this and the north-west facing profile) is based on the top of the cultivation horizon (a.063) sealed under the bank and relates to the time prior to Ditch 1. The ancient surface level is assumed to be level across the area of the trench. It shows how deep the ditches were and that a much more substantial wall than that surviving today could have been built from the upcast (see also Figs 8.15–8.16).

cuts over time. Sometimes these were amazingly clear and straight in one section, but untraceable on the opposite side, perhaps as a result of localised disturbances, e.g. through tree roots. Side erosion furthermore will often have gradually reduced the gradient of the slope, and plant growth will have obscured boundaries, making the original cuts hard to discern.

We observed a succession of probably seven major ditches (not counting the recent shallow field boundary ditches). Ditches 5 to 7 were dug a little further away from the wall, perhaps as a wider berm provided greater stability or perhaps just to save labour by recutting and widening the previous silted-up ditch. We cannot be sure, of course, that all ditches survive. Wide and deep ditches could easily have completely erased shallower and narrower precursors. Seven ditches are thus just the likely minimum number of major ditch cuts, each of them a massive undertaking, bearing in mind that the ditch was at least some 4 km long, not counting an additional 600 m or so where the river valley may have functioned as a defensive ditch. Even seven successive ditches are a remarkable number, all the more so as we had expected Qal'eh Pol Gonbad-e Kavus to be either a single-phase campaign base or one reoccupied repeatedly, but over a period not exceeding that of the permanent occupation of the Gorgan Wall. Now it appears it was a multi-phase installation, refortified repeatedly, quite possibly over many centuries and certainly until long after the Great Wall had fallen out of use.

8.2.8. The earliest ditches (1–4)

The earliest ditch is of particular importance. Even if in theory the original ditches might have been erased by later ditches of greater dimensions, the earliest preserved ditches would still be closest in time to the compound's foundation. Unfortunately, the earliest ditches are also those on which least is known. They have yielded no finds or other material suitable for dating. Only the south-west side of the earliest ditch is preserved, its upper part visible only in the north-west-facing profile (Fig. 8.16) and its lower part only in the south-east-facing profile (Fig. 8.14).[52] Despite such meagre evidence, in the south-east-facing profile, it is strikingly clear and remarkably straight. There is no question that it existed and that it was a human-made feature. The cut is very clear at the bottom south-west corner of step 2 as well as in step 3. No clear traces of it were visible in step 1 (perhaps unsurprisingly so, as the gradient of its slope, to judge by the opposite profile, suggests it would at this level be at the very edge of the excavations or potentially beyond the limits if irregular), nor were we able to spot at first a continuation in step 4. Under the water table we observed, however, that natural soil was washed out of the profile, but that a grey clay layer at the same level was unaffected. The edge of this probable ditch fill[53] was, more or less, in alignment with the cut in steps 2 and 3 (Figs 8.14 and 8.18), and it is possible that it was part of the ditch, even if also remarkably close to the alignment of the cut of Ditch 5. Even if we discount this probable continuation of the first ditch in step 4, revealed only by the fine-grained clay's greater resistance to erosion, the cut in steps 2 and 3 clearly underlies the steep cut of Ditch 5 and has to be earlier. The cuts of Ditches 5 or 6 will have destroyed the east sides of the first, second, third and fourth ditches. To judge by its angle and location, Ditch 5 may well also have erased some or all of the bottom of the earliest ditch. The opposite, north-west-facing, profile does not, unfortunately, show the lower parts of the early ditches clearly if at all. Whether deposits a.071, a.053 and a.052 belong to Ditch 5 or Ditch 1 is not certain (Figs

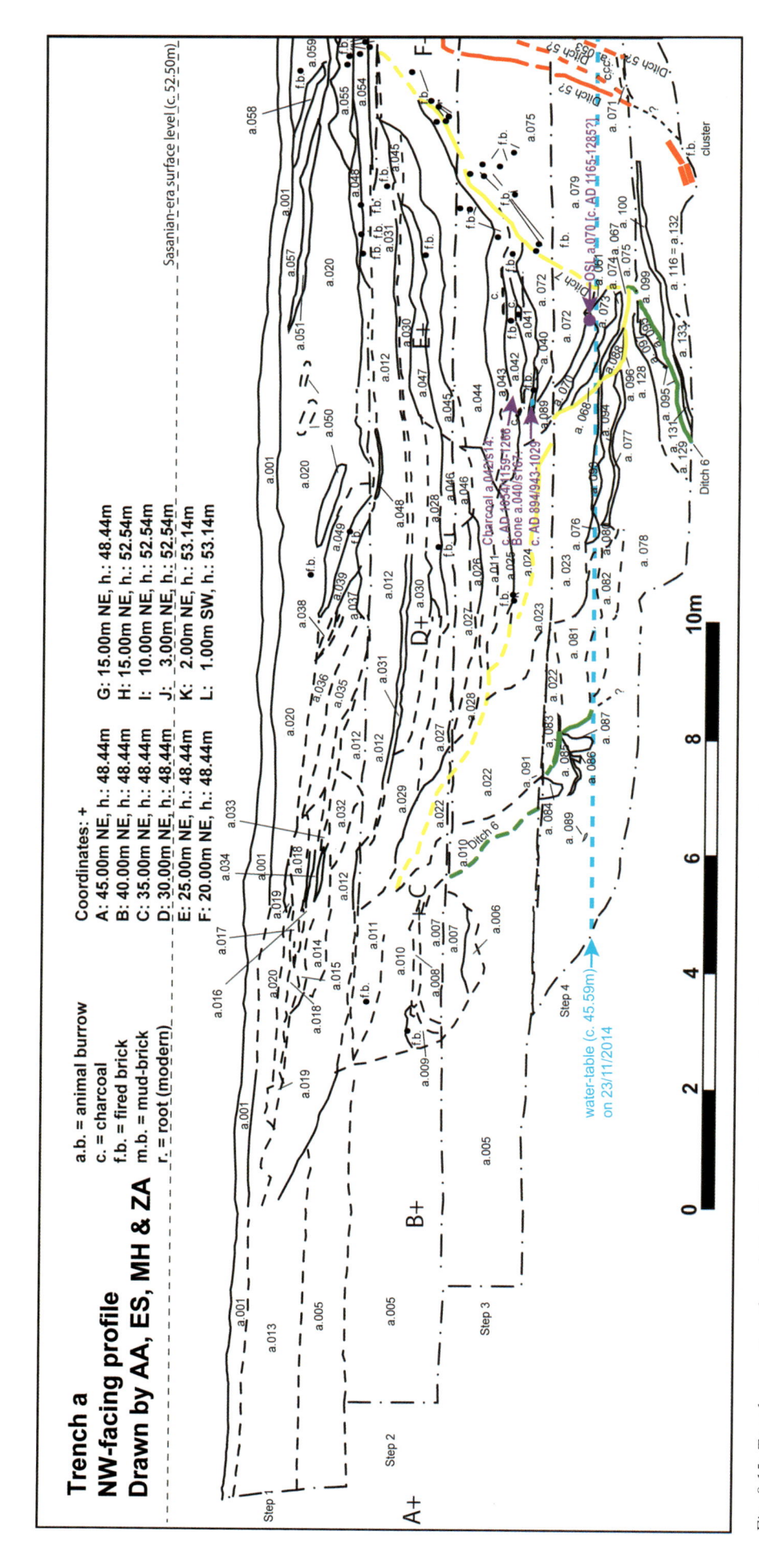

Fig. 8.15: Trench a, section through the ditch system and bank, north-eastern part of the north-west-facing profile, drawn by Marc Heise, Eberhard Sauer, Aliyeh Amirinezhad and Zahra Asghari. Proposed phases: first to fourth ditches: not visible; fifth ditch: red; sixth ditch: green; seventh ditch: yellow.

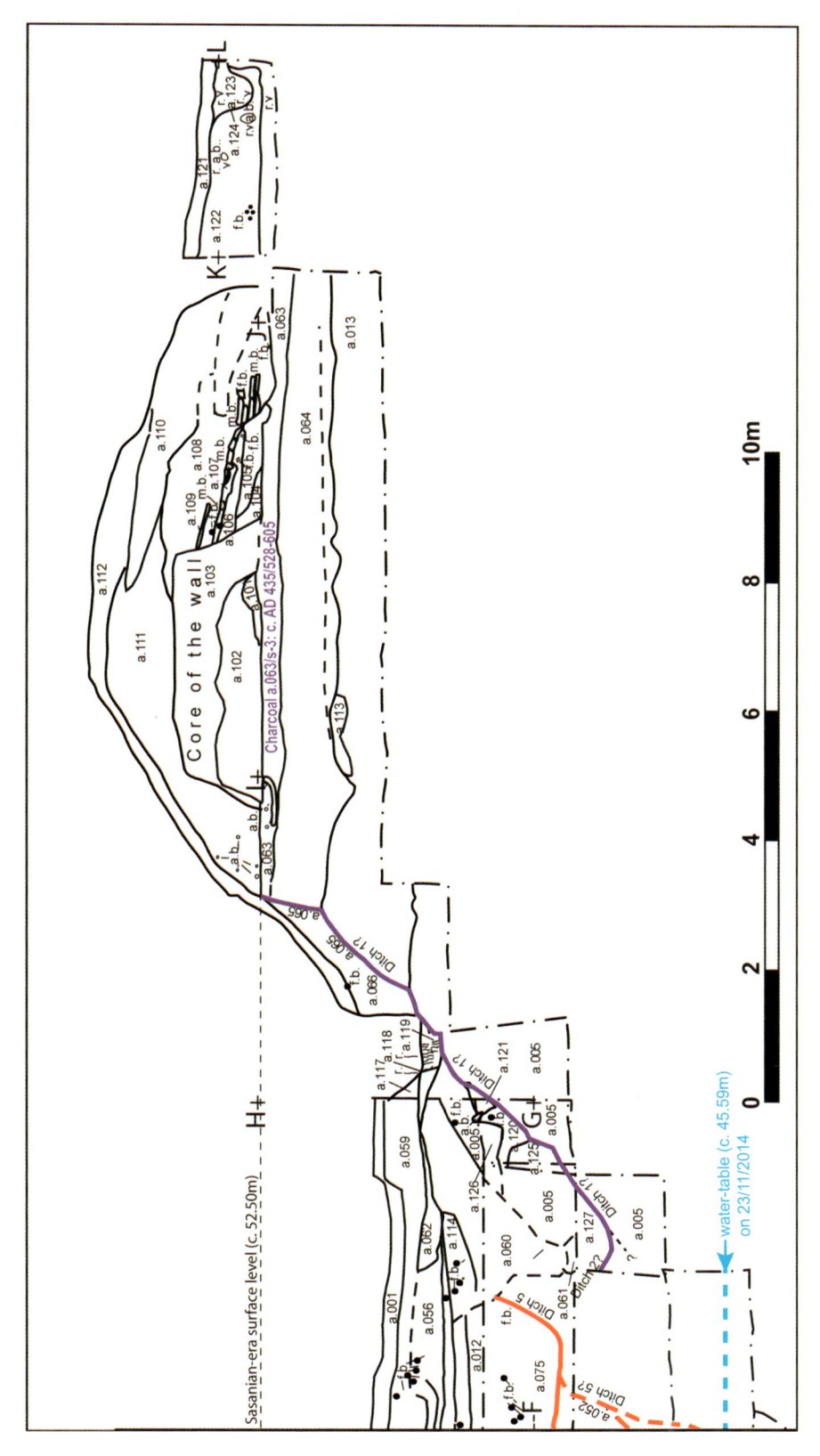

Fig. 8.16: Trench a, south-western part of the north-west-facing profile (continuation of Fig. 8.15). Proposed phases: first (and second?) ditch: purple; fifth ditch: red.

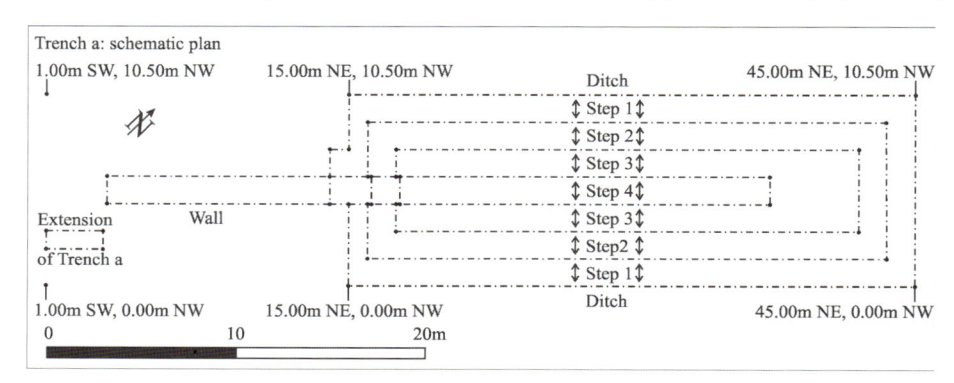

Fig. 8.17: Trench a, schematic plan showing the location of the steps (and the stepped sections).

Fig. 8.18: Postulated Ditch 1 was only visible through faint differences in soil colour between its fills and the natural soil, with rectilinear context boundaries, in the south-east-facing profiles in steps 2 and 3. Worth noting is the clayey ditch fill under the water-table in step 4 (to the right of the red bottom segment of the vertical ranging pole) perhaps part of its fill and, in contrast to the natural soil (bottom centre), not washed out by groundwater.

8.15–8.16). Their steep, though in places only tentatively identified, boundaries suggest that an attribution to Ditch 5 is more probable, and they will therefore be discussed in the next section.

Only the upper parts of the early ditch system were visible on the opposite, i.e. the north-west-facing profile (Fig. 8.16). We noticed a sharp cut (a.065) of the ancient topsoil (a.063), the subsoil (a.064) and natural soil (a.013) on the north-east side of the wall. The cut is very steep and likely to be part of the earliest ditch or a recut. It is overlain by a deposit (a.066) likely to consist of redeposited rampart material. The upper part of the earliest ditch in the north-west-facing profile is steeper and less regular and rectilinear than the lower part visible only on the opposite profile (Figs 8.14 and 8.18–8.19). The steeper gradient would have made it more difficult to scale, the

Fig. 8.19: Close-up of Ditches 1–4 in steps 2 and 3. (See Fig. 8.14 for a drawing of the section.)

lesser gradient of the lower section would have reduced waterborne erosion at the edge of a water-filled moat. It is hard to tell to what extent the irregular gradient of the upper slope was original and to what extent potentially the result of localised erosion, later recuts and trees or shrubs colonising the slope. In our reconstruction (Fig. 8.28) we assume it was originally straight. Whichever is true, however, minor irregularities would have made little difference to ditch dimensions or the difficulties involved in ascending the slope.

We observed three well-defined context boundaries to the north-east of Ditch 1 on the south-east-facing profile, the lowest of which (Ditch 2) has also been tentatively identified on the north-west-facing profile. These must be later cuts, as it is inconceivable that deposits filling Ditch 1 would have had such remarkably straight boundaries. It appears that the earliest ditch was recut three times, each subsequent ditch being narrower and shallower than its predecessor. This, of course, only applies to preserved ditches. Hypothetical ditches, deeper and wider than their predecessors, would have erased these, unless in a different position. It may seem odd that the inner side of the ditch should have been unaffected by the repeated recutting. If the top of the slope next to the Qal'eh had remained largely intact, then it should not have been difficult to follow the same gradient when removing sediments that had accumulated on top of the original cut. These ditches cannot be modern field boundary ditches, as the earliest two clearly run underneath the ditch attributed to phase five, not to mention that one would not expect the fill of modern ditches to be quite so sterile. That the third and fourth share the western edge of the first and second is unlikely to be coincidence. There is no attempt at denying, however, that there is some uncertainty about the interpretation of these sterile features. The slopes of these four ditches were not quite as steep as Ditch 5. This need not disprove a defensive function, as the ditches were still of formidable depth, as Table 8.1 demonstrates.

This is not to say that they were solely defensive features, as they will also have served to furnish the soil to build the wall inside, they will have marked the boundary of the compound and they will have facilitated drainage. It is worth noting that their depth was much greater than the average depth of ditches surrounding Roman forts and fortresses, let alone temporary marching camps. Judged by the north-west-facing profile, Ditch 1 came very close to the wall, c. 1.35 m from the edge of its core. There can have been no substantial berm in between, but a narrow berm is possible. Whilst less is known about the earliest ditches than their successors, it appears that

Table 8.1: Base level and depth of the earliest four ditches.

Ditch	Base	Depth below Sasanian-era surface = top of a.063 (at c. 52.50 m)
First	≤45.27 m (or 46.42 m minimum)	Probably ≥7.23 m (6.08 m minimum)
Second	47.07 m	5.43 m
Third	47.71 m	4.79 m
Fourth	48.06 m	4.44 m

these ditches were far from insubstantial. The first ditch reached a minimum width of 14 m, assuming we reached its bottom in step 3 and it was symmetrical. If the cut identified on step 4 is part of it, as seems likely, then its likely minimum width (if symmetrical) increases to over 18 m. More probably, if there was a flat-bottomed canal/moat in the centre, its width was well in excess of 20 m and perhaps c. 24–27 m, as further explored below (Fig. 8.28 and Table 8.3).[54] The dimensions of Ditches 2, 3 and 4 are unknown. We may be sure that Ditch 1 can only have silted up partially by the time Ditch 2 was cut, but we cannot know from what level it was cut. Ditches 2, 3 and 4 may well have been smaller V-shaped obstacles, dug within the much more substantial partially silted-up Ditch 1.

Whilst little survived of the ditch fills, which were remarkably sterile in so far as one can base a judgement on a profile of a machine-cut trench, it seems likely that at least the earliest was deep enough to be filled with water. A theoretical consideration may add strength to this hypothesis. Multiple factors may account for the Qal'eh's location next to the river. Its garrison may have controlled the river and probably a nearby bridge or ford across. Perhaps it was river water that was channelled into the interior of the compound via the raised canal. Reusing a section of the river valley as a defensive ditch and filling the deep moat with water may well have been one of the reasons for the Qal'eh's riverside location. Many other large Sasanian compounds on the Gorgan Plain were also surrounded by a moat. Should the admittedly hypothetical argument, that the choice of location may in part have been determined by a desire to channel water into the moat, be true, then the ditch around the compound will have been flooded with river water already in the earliest phase. The absence of clayey fills suggests that it may have been dry in phases 2, 3 and 4, but again filled with water in later phases.

No artefacts were recovered out of the earliest ditches, and we cannot be sure of their age. They are evidently earlier than the later ditches, thought to be early medieval. On the basis of general considerations on the architecture of the compound and the Sasanian-era radiocarbon sample sealed under the wall, it is tempting to think that Ditch 1 is Sasanian and contemporary to the earliest wall. The first ditch had apparently silted up to a considerable extent before Ditch 2 was cut, implying that more than a few years must have passed between the excavation of Ditches 1 and 2. As Ditches 2, 3 and 4 were not filled with water, they can only be defensive features. If so, they must date to a time when there were army units or well-organised local people in sufficient numbers to reinstate the defences and reoccupy the vast compound. One wonders whether this may point to repeated reoccupation of the vast compound. It is tempting to think that Ditches 1 to 4 are all of the Sasanian era, but there is no proof and the transitional era between the fall of the Sasanian Empire and the Islamic conquest cannot be excluded.

8.2.9. The fifth ditch

In the south-east-facing profile of the trench, the south-western cut of another ditch became strikingly clear as the soil had dried out. On the south-east-facing profile (Fig. 8.14), it is at 19.59 m north-east at the top of step 2 and at 20.43 m at the top and 20.95 m at the bottom of step 3, consisting of steep straight lines of similar gradient. Whilst less distinct and not rectilinear, it could also be identified in step 4, as well as on the bottom three steps of the opposite profile. In step 2 there is a step in the north-west-facing profile (Figs 8.15–8.16) as opposed to a regular steep cut in the south-east-facing profile, perhaps a result of the previous ditch having silted up irregularly. Below the step, alignment of the cut is not entirely clear and there are three possible cuts. The north-easternmost cut is in a similar position to the Ditch 5 cut on the opposite profile. The significance of deposits south-west of it, soft mid-brown silt with occasional charcoal flecks (a.071), firm mid-brown silt with charcoal flecks (a.053) and soft, mid-brownish clayey silt (a.052), is uncertain. Their boundaries were indistinct and identified only tentatively. It is possible that the cut of Ditch 5 is further south-west, and we plotted three possible cuts on the profile (Figs 8.15–8.16). Some or all of these three deposits may form part of the fill of Ditch 5. It is, however, also possible that they are part of the deep fill of Ditch 1. Their composition suggests that they may have formed as a result of parts of the wall disintegrating and eroding into the ditch.

Its extent in the north-east is not known, as it appears to be destroyed here by the sixth ditch. The north-eastern cut of the sixth ditch is at 37.10 m at the top of step 2,[55] evidently erasing the north-east sides of all earlier ditches. It follows that the fifth ditch cannot have extended any further in this direction, and its maximum possible width

Fig. 8.20: The fifth ditch in steps 2 and 3 of the south-east facing profile. (See Fig. 8.14 for a drawing of the section.)

at this level (c. 3.41 m below the ancient/ medieval surface) would have been 17.51 m and probably less. The very steep and straight cut on the Qal'eh's side, which would have been hard to scale, implies that it had been designed as a military obstacle. As the opposite side is not preserved, we cannot be sure whether or not it was symmetrical. It is worth noting that this (at least on the defenders' side) more steep-sided ditch was dug at a greater distance to the wall than previous ditches – perhaps just to save the considerable efforts involved in cutting back the silted-up previous ditch any further, perhaps also to prevent erosion and to enable digging a deeper ditch without risking that such an inherently unstable ditch might cause the wall to collapse.

Whilst it is hard to be sure without excavation of the lowest section of the ditch, it seems likely that the fifth ditch may have been the deepest. Deposit a.100, underlying the base of the seventh ditch and extending in the south-west well beyond a.077 or any other deposit deep within the fill of the sixth ditch, most probably belongs to the fifth ditch (Fig. 8.15). If this is correct, then all deposits underlying it are also likely to be part of the fifth ditch.

The argument, that the deepest deposits reached in this trench belong to the fifth ditch, gains in strength if we assume that a brick concentration (see Table 8.2) belongs to the fill of this ditch and was located near its edge, as the position of the individual pieces suggests, being just inside the alignment of the steep cut of phase five. This cluster of bricks is of considerable interest for the chronology of this ditch. As this cluster is from the stratigraphically deepest deposit (a.132) that we were able explore within our trench, it will be discussed first.

If these bricks should have formed part of the parapet, then this might explain the cluster at the edge of the ditch on the defenders' side. Hard and waterproof building material would have been best suited to withstand the weather and waterborne erosion. Such material may have been in short supply to judge by the reuse of broken old bricks alongside new bricks of much smaller size. The former were more fragmentary on average, and there was no complete specimen, perhaps due to them having been reused centuries after production and/or them being heavier and thus more fragile. Whilst old bricks break easily, it is also possible that some may have been deliberately cut into smaller blocks, for example if indeed used in narrow breastworks jointly with bricks of roughly half the diameter. It is worth noting that a.060/22 was a fairly regular half brick of similar width to the smaller and later bricks; a.132/20 had also been halved along its

Table 8.2: Bricks recovered from the ditch (those from a.132, attributed to the fifth ditch, are from a cluster, probably at the inner edge of the ditch, the brick from a.097 is from the fill of the sixth ditch, the brick from a.060 is from the fill of a cut of uncertain significance). All bricks appear to have been square prior to breakage. EHM = Early or High Medieval.

Find no.	Diam. in cm	Thickness in cm	Typological dating	Breakage	North-east	North-west	Elevation
a.060/22	38	8.5	Sasanian	Large fragment (half)	c. 16 m	c. 5.25 m	49.35 m
a.097/15	19–20	3	EHM	Complete	25.22–25.37 m	4.50–4.69 m	44.70–44.85 m
a.132/17	≥36	7	Sasanian	Large fragment	21.80–22.15 m	4.60–4.95 m	44.22–44.44 m
a.132/18	19–20	3	EHM	Large fragment	21.80 m (centre)	4.82 m (centre)	44.37 m (centre)
a.132/19	19–20	3	EHM	Large fragment	22.13 m (centre)	4.70 m (centre)	44.18–44.31 m
a.132/20	38	7	Sasanian	Large fragment (half)	22.22–22.51 m	4.65–4.87 m	44.15–44.24 m
a.132/21.1	19–20	3	EHM	Complete	Similar to 17a–20a	Similar to 17a–20a	44.04–44.09 m
a.132/21.2	19–20	3	EHM	Large fragment	As above	As above	As above
a.132/21.3	? (probably 19–20)	3	EHM	Small fragment	As above	As above	As above

Fig. 8.21: Bricks recovered from Trench a: early to high medieval pieces at the top, Sasanian brick fragments at the bottom. Each red or white segment of the scales is 10 cm in length.

axis, even if less regularly, whilst a.132/17 is not of cuboid shape. The sample is admittedly small, but that two out of three Sasanian brick fragments recovered are of, more or less, cuboid shape and of a width similar to the smaller bricks is worth noting. It adds strength to our hypothesis that some Sasanian bricks were deliberately cut in half, to facilitate use in a structure (probably the breastworks) built of reused Sasanian and (new?) medieval bricks. Reused Sasanian bricks were apparently employed, alongside much more recent bricks, in the wall, perhaps

Fig. 8.22: Brick a.097/15 in situ.

for its most rain-exposed elements on the top, e.g. for the battlements, paving of the walkway and/or the towers. The number of bricks is, however, small, even for a largely machine-cut trench. Perhaps they indeed formed part of a rebuilt parapet, perhaps, considering their small number, they had been employed in some basic makeshift structures nearby or perhaps they are just random losses.

Bricks a.132/17 and a.132/20 clearly sloped from south-west to north-east, following the gradient of the ditch. The same is true for a.097/15, also sloping down from south-west to north-east and found on its own at a higher level and further away from the wall. This isolated brick appears to have fallen off the wall or been redeposited at a later date. In all probability, the brick cluster near the base of the fifth ditch continues towards the north-east, following the slope of the ditch dipping beneath the base of our trench. The smaller type of 19–20 cm diameter, to judge by local parallels, is likely to be Islamic and might date to the eighth or ninth to early thirteenth centuries AD. Late Sasanian square bricks of the type found at Dasht Qal'eh of c. 31–33 cm side length and 6–8 cm thickness are not represented, but are generally less common. There appear to be no bricks from the Gorgan Plain whose manufacture can be attributed to the century following the end of the Sasanian era.[56] The chronology will be further explored below, but it seems safe to assign these bricks to post-Sasanian times and probably the early Islamic era rather than the transitional phase in between.

These bricks from the cluster in ditch fill a.132 were all recovered whilst partially submerged, as for technical reasons, and out of safety concerns, it was not possible to excavate deeper here without massively enlarging the whole stepped trench. Nor was it possible to drain the narrow trench to the bottom, as groundwater rose rapidly, turning soft sediments into liquid mud. The latter filled up sink holes and drainage channels, required for operating our pump, at an ever-increasing speed, making it difficult or impossible to see the boundaries of deposits or cuts. Whilst we thus cannot be absolutely certain that the brick concentration belongs to the fifth ditch, based on its location it is highly probable that it did. Even if the cut for the first ditch should have continued in a straight alignment beyond the section visible in the profile, and it may just as well have curved and continued at a reduced gradient, the brick concentration would have been beneath this line. The brick assemblage was thus deeper than the deepest likely base of the first ditch, but north-east of the projected edge of the fifth ditch and thus probably inside. It follows that the bricks, which evidently have to be attributed to one of the successive ditches, are part of the fill of the fifth ditch. If so, their location just inside the projected edge of the fifth ditch shows that the ditch cut continued at a similar inclination down to the level of the bricks and possibly beyond. The fifth ditch thus reached down to 44.04 m height, almost 8.50 m under the ancient or medieval surface level, and, to judge by the location and gradient of the deposits excavated, almost certainly well beyond. The virtual absence of bricks from higher levels within the ditch and the scarcity of finds from this ditch, with even charcoal flecks being far and few between, adds strength to our assumption that the bricks fell off the wall, rather being associated with other structures or activities. If the battlements were not restored, then the deposits filling the ditch, overlying the brick cluster, seem to post-date temporary abandonment of the Qal'eh.

Deposit a.132, soft mid-greyish brown clay, with a lens of mid-yellowish brown medium sand (a.133), was the stratigraphically deepest fill of the fifth ditch that we reached within our trench. With the exception of the brick cluster discussed above, it contained no artefacts or cultural material that we were able to spot, not even charcoal or brick flecks. It is worth noting that we excavated manually at this level, and the largely sterile nature of the ditch fill is thus not in doubt. The clayey ditch fill appears to have built up during a phase when there was little human activity in the area, perhaps shortly after the evacuation of the fifth-phase Qal'eh. In all probability, it overlies further ditch fills with a higher concentration of cultural materials. Indeed, the relatively low number of bricks found may be deceptive and perhaps a result not only of mechanical excavations of the upper fill, but also of the non-excavation of the bottom fill where one would expect the highest concentration of brick collapse. How much deeper the ditch may reach is impossible to tell without further excavation or coring. The location and layering of the successive fills, a.132, a.131, a.100 and a.075 (= a.099), suggests that the deepest point is somewhere beyond 26.95 m north-east where deposit a.100 dips beneath the bottom of the trench.

Did the ditch carry water at the time and how deep may this have been? It seemed potentially significant at first that the ditch, as far as excavated, yielded land snails, *Zebrina detrita* and *Xeropicta* (?)*mesopotamica*.[57] Radiocarbon dating of a representative of the former species to the thirtieth millennium BC suggests, however, that the molluscs were, in part at least, of a geological age. Perhaps some of them were washed in from the side where the crumbling wall stood, notably as the sample from deposit (a.132 = a.116) was taken from 21.30–22.10 m east at 44.28–44.45 m elevation, i.e. from the inner edge of the ditch. They thus do not allow us to decide whether the ditch was dry or contained stagnant or flowing water.

The various clay layers, however, indicate that there was standing or slow-flowing water in the ditch at least for some time. The colour and composition of the deposit (a.132 = a.116, soft mid-greyish brown clay) the sample was taken from is suggestive of waterborne sediments with washed-in humus. It is interesting to note that the ditch, as far as excavated at the deepest point of Trench a, reached c. 1.60 m below the water table in November and December 2014.[58] The current water level, however, may be influenced by modern hydraulic operations and irrigation. It may also fluctuate seasonally and provides no yardstick for ancient levels. It is clear that no ancient organic matter survived at any level – clear proof that not even at the deepest point of the trench were there permanently waterlogged strata.

The clayey layers in Ditch 5 leave no doubt that it carried water, even if we did not reach the bottom of the ditch and thus do not know its depth nor necessarily its earliest phases of silting up. Unlike the canal along the Gorgan Wall at Fort 9, where we can reconstruct, on the basis of greenish iron-stained deposits at the base and edge of the canal, that the water must once have been over 2 m deep,[59] we observed no similarly distinct indicators of water depth. We thus know the elevation of neither the bottom nor the top of the water-filled part of the ditch. There is a possible water channel linking the Chai Chai River with the moat at the east corner of the Qal'eh (Fig. 8.1), which verges on the same river in the north. Perhaps the water table corresponded to that in the river at the time, perhaps it was raised through dams. The considerable depth of some of the successive ditches is indeed perhaps best explained by such depth being required to fill the moat with river water. The clay deposits probably built up as a result of river water having been channelled into the moat, rather than the ditch being filled with groundwater, though medieval irrigation nearby is possible as well. Indeed, the river water could have been used for both irrigation and filling the moat. The ditches of the later phases (5, 7 and possibly 6) were extremely steep and hard to ascend on the defenders' side. Deep water at the base would have made a hostile crossing even more difficult and dangerous. They offer circumstantial evidence for temporary reoccupation of Qal'eh Pol Gonbad-e Kavus, as it is hard to see what other purpose the massive effort of recutting the ditch and channelling water into it would have served.

Deposit a.131 above a.132 consists of very soft mid-brownish yellow clayey silt. This silty deposit devoid of finds may have built up as a result of erosion of the steep-sided ditch (and potentially of the wall). This was followed by more stable conditions when a band of soft mid-grey clay (a.100) accumulated at the then base of the water-filled ditch. Deposit a.100 is the most extensive of the clayey fills, running from 22.10 m to 26.95 m north-east, gradually sloping down and almost certainly continuing further to the north-east, dipping beneath the bottom of our trench. Even on the basis of partial excavation, it is clear that a.100 is running underneath Ditches 6 and 7, filling a wider, deeper and earlier ditch. At a later stage, side-erosion increased massively, and a thick layer of soft mid-brownish yellow to mid-grey clay with a few brick fragments (a.075), perhaps material eroded into the ditch from the collapsing wall of the fifth phase, accumulated in the ditch.

The above-cited Islamic-era bricks (in addition to broken Sasanian bricks) from the very edge of the ditch prove that it was in Islamic times that Ditch 5 started to silt up, and it is hard to imagine that it could have been kept clean for long. We may conclude that Ditch 5, the deepest of all ditches, probably belongs to the early Islamic era, being evidently earlier than Ditches 6 and 7. It also appears to have been dug further away from the wall and differed substantially from recuts 2, 3 and 4, perhaps suggesting that some time had passed been the last recut (Ditch 4) of the original ditch and the excavation of Ditch 5. Perhaps the time when the Gorgan Plain came under Umayyad rule may provide a plausible historical context for the reinstatement of the vast fortification, but this is admittedly little more than an informed guess. The brick collapse occurred, of course, later, perhaps at a time of abandonment or neglect.

8.2.10. The sixth ditch

The sixth ditch cuts the fill of the fifth ditch. Its slopes are less regular than those of the preceding five ditches. In the north-east the cut is particularly steep in the fourth step (in the south-east-facing profile, but less clear on the opposite side where various features [a.084, a.085, a.086 and a.087] may be related to tree-growth at the edge of the ditch that caused disturbance). At a higher level,

Fig. 8.23: The north-eastern cut (between the ranging poles) of the sixth ditch in step 4 on the south-east-facing profile. (See Fig. 8.14 for a drawing of the section.)

further north-east, there may have been more trees lining the outside of the ditch. Deposits a.007 and a.009 may perhaps have formed as a result of tree roots penetrating the natural soil. It is possible that roots of plants growing in the ditch also account for the irregular base and diffuse context boundaries further south-west, in the area of deposits a.079, a.080, a.081 and a.082, which merit no detailed description. We were unable to see the bottom of the cut in this area. Perhaps the irregular profile was the result of lesser experience of the workforce, perhaps it was excavated more hastily or perhaps the gentler slopes were designed to prevent rapid erosion.

This ditch is cut in the south-west by the narrower Ditch 7. The distinct layers filling the sixth ditch (e.g. a.077) could not be seen in either profile beyond the point where they are cut by the seventh ditch. This observation suggests indeed that a.077 and the deposits above are not part of the fifth ditch, but of a separate sixth ditch whose opposite side has been erased by the seventh ditch. As from a.116 in the fifth ditch, there were also land snails from a.077 in the sixth ditch. They have not been dated. As the two dated molluscs from the trench were both of a geological to prehistoric date,[60] they may well also be much older than the ditch fills and provide no reliable indication for the environment. The band of soft mid-greenish grey clay (a.077) indicates that also this ditch at least temporarily carried standing or flowing water, even when already partially silted up. Charcoal flecks in a.077 prove unsurprisingly that there was human activity nearby – perhaps by the occupants of the Qal'eh or perhaps by peasants or shepherds dwelling or working in, or passing through, the area.

Interpretation of the deposits underneath a.077 is less secure, but it seems likely that a.078, a.129, a.097 and a.095 belong to the sixth ditch too. Like a.077, and unlike a.075, a.100 and a.132, none of them continues in the south-west beyond the alignment of the south-west cut of the seventh ditch. Yet they cannot be fills of the seventh ditch as they run underneath its north-eastern cut and are at a lower level than the base of the seventh ditch. If, on the other hand, a.078, a.129, a.097 and a.095 were fills of the fifth ditch, then it would be hard to explain why there is no trace of any of them beyond the cut for Ditch 6. It follows that they probably belong to the sixth ditch whose cut in the south-west appears to have been in a similar position to that of its successor or perhaps marginally further to the north-east and hence destroyed by the seventh ditch. If this admittedly tentative interpretation of partially excavated

Fig. 8.24: The south-western cut of the seventh ditch in step 4 of the south-east-facing profile, with a fragment of fired brick at its edge (to the right of the left vertical ranging pole). (See Fig. 8.14 for a drawing of the section.)

deposits, often with indistinct context boundaries, should be correct, then we may conclude that the deepest point of the ditch would have been to the north-east of the point where a.129 dips beneath the base of the trench. The sixth ditch appears to have been not quite as deep as its predecessor, the fifth ditch.

The stratigraphically oldest deposit of those thought to be part of the sixth ditch are a.129, a.097 and a.095. The latter was one of the most distinct layers, consisting of compact dark greenish yellow sand. Evidently, there was faster water flow at the time leading to the accumulation of sand, whilst the greenish hue suggests that waterlogged conditions prevailed. Immediately on top of it, but embedded in the next deposit, we found an early or high medieval brick (a.097/15). The steep angle, sloping down away from the Qal'eh, at which the piece from deposit a.097 was found (Table 8.2 and Figs 8.21–8.22), suggests that also this brick fell into the ditch from the side of the wall. We cannot be sure whether this is just a random loss or perhaps a redeposited brick originally employed in the rain-exposed top of the wall of the fifth phase – or a piece used in a hypothetical rebuilt wall, employing the same bricks.[61] Deposit a.097, very soft mid-yellow clay, built up in a waterlogged ditch at a time of reduced erosion. Waterlogged conditions prevailed when subsequently a more substantial layer of soft mid-reddish brown clay (a.129) was deposited, followed by the accumulation of a thick layer of sterile soft mid-brownish yellow clay (a.078). This was virtually identical, in colour and composition, to a.075, even if, unlike a.075, devoid of obvious inclusions. Like a.075 from the fifth ditch, thought to consist largely of material from the wall of the fifth phase washed into the ditch, the formation of a.078 may have been a result of the wall collapse.

Subsequently, layers suggestive of alluvial deposition and side erosion alternate: soft mid-greenish grey clay (a.077), sterile very soft clayey silt with a small quantity of sand (a.094), soft mid-brownish grey (a.093) and mid-greyish brown (a.076) clay and stiff mid-grey silt (a.023). An archaeomagnetic sample from deposit a.129 centred on 26.70 m north-east, 5.15 m north-west and 44.30 m height was tentatively dated to the tenth or ninth century BC.[62] Considering that there is medieval brick underneath, this seems impossible. More probably Ditch 6, evidently later than that of Ditch 5 and earlier than Ditch 7, may date to the eighth to tenth centuries AD, maybe the ninth century.

8.2.11. The seventh ditch

The last of the large defensive ditches was not as deep or wide as the fifth or sixth ditch had been. After the sixth ditch had partially silted up, Ditch 7 with a steep-sided bottom section was dug, representing the latest major ditch, probably associated with the final reinstatement of the Qal'eh as a defensive installation. Perhaps it was no more than a substantial recut of Ditch 6, notably at the bottom of its silted-up predecessor, involving lesser efforts than the previous two ditches. In the lowest step of the south-east-facing profile its edge is very clear in the south-west, where a brick fragment at a steep angle from the very edge of the ditch (Figs 8.14 and 8.24) gives an idea of the steep gradient of the cut. On the opposite side, the cut is also discernible.

The narrow ditch seems to have silted up whilst the wall remained intact, to judge by the material being washed in almost exclusively from the opposite side. A band of soft mid-yellowish grey clay at the base (a.096) and a layer of soft mid-brownish yellow clay (a.088) above seem to have formed in waterlogged conditions when largely sterile material accumulated within the ditch. The intensive green discoloration and frequent iron-staining of the soft greenish-grey clay (a.067) above indicates that the ditch still carried water, whilst there is little sign of erosion, suggesting that the slope will have reached a state of equilibrium. After a period when topsoil was washed into the ditch, forming a deposit of soft light-brown clayey silt (a.074), more stable waterlogged conditions prevailed again, and a deposit of soft greenish-grey clay (a.068), material similar to a.067, built up within the ditch. This was followed by another phase of increased side erosion, when soft mid-brownish yellow clayey silt (a.073) accumulated in the ditch. Up to this point, the deposits filling the ditch were sterile and contained no discernible traces of charcoal or brick. Presumably, the ditch silted up rapidly at the start. Subsequently, a layer of soft greenish grey clay (a.070) rich in snails and with charcoal fragments may suggest that more stable conditions prevailed then and that people were living and working in land nearby – probably in and around the Qal'eh – even if also this deposit was washed in from the opposite side into the still water-filled ditch. Firm mid-yellowish brown clay with charcoal flecks (a.072) above was the first deposit to be washed into the ditch from the Qal'eh's side. A small quantity of sheep or goat bones were recovered from deposit a.040 when the lowest part of the recut ditch had almost silted up. These belong to one, or possibly more than one, sheep or goat(s), dated to c. AD 894–1029, with about a four in five chance of it being no earlier than the AD 940s.[63] Perhaps it suggests that the Qal'eh was still occupied at the time, and the bones represent food waste the Qal'eh's occupants had disposed of. In the light of the small quantity of bone from this deposit and its virtual absence elsewhere[64] – even if much may have been missed in a machine-cut trench – it could also have been random refuse discarded by a passing shepherd or other peasant, and one perhaps should not read too much into this isolated find. There were also charcoal flecks in this thin band of soft mid-greyish brown clayey silt (a.040) pointing to human occupation nearby, debris of which were washed into the ditch. Charcoal from a.042 probably dates to between the mid-twelfth and mid-thirteenth century.[65] Recovered from just roughly one foot above the lower sample that was probably more than a century and possibly up to three centuries earlier, it suggests (assuming both samples represent contemporary activity rather than redeposited material) that there was little erosion during the early second millennium.

Little would be gained by meticulous description of all the undated deposits gradually filling up the ditch subsequently, but it is worth noting that they consisted mostly of redeposited natural soil and were largely or completely sterile, thus also not being datable with any precision. The clayey composition of many of the layers suggests that the ditch was still prone to occasional flooding. Whilst many context boundaries were diffuse and hard to see, barely differing in colour and composition, a.012, firm mid-brown clayey silt, stood out, being of darker colour and much richer in humus than most other deposits under the modern topsoil. This was an unusually thick layer, but nonetheless devoid of known finds, probably topsoil ploughed or washed into the depression. It is worth reiterating that the trench at this level was cut by machine. Whilst this will inevitably have led to a low recovery rate, the complete absence of even tiny fragments of fired clay in most deposits is telling. It appears that there was no settlement nearby when this ditch fill and others built up, but the land appears to have been in agricultural use at the time, to judge by the brown colour suggestive of organic matter and rapid erosion. A more detailed historical discussion is provided below,[66] but we may conclude that the seventh and last ditch cannot have been dug later than the tenth century (unless the bone was redeposited) and, as it was the third Islamic-era ditch, probably no earlier than the ninth century.

8.2.12. The Sasanian-era topsoil and land surface

Sealed under the wall of the Qal'eh (Fig. 8.16), we found a humus horizon (a.063). There were no finds from it other than shells (as well as small unidentified bones and four small fragments of what may be glass found during flotation).[67] No finds at all were recovered from the subsoil (a.064), firm mid-yellowish brown silt, and the natural loess (a.013) underneath. The flotation of samples in 2014 and 2015, however, revealed minute quantities of charcoal from the buried soil horizon (a.063). The colour and consistency of the soil horizon (a.063), firm mid-brown clayey silt, suggests it is ancient plough soil

Fig. 8.25: Section through the wall in Trench a. The humus layer (a.063), whose top is a few centimetres below the horizontal scales, is the buried topsoil with Sasanian-era charcoal. (See Fig. 8.16 for a drawing of the section.)

of land cultivated for some time. The complete absence of pottery and other artefacts or bones, even of charcoal flecks and brick fragments from the substantial topsoil and subsoil deposits, despite manually cutting the bank back by approximately 1.50 m at the base, suggests that there had been no settlement nearby when the geometric compound was first erected or at any time before.

Should this be the ancient ground surface, and it is hard to think of an alternative explanation, then the ditch would have been very deep and its volume would have greatly exceeded that of the surviving wall – perhaps partially destroyed, even if the eroded remains of the towers (of a late phase?) are still visible. It cannot be a levelling deposit, in the light of its depth, homogeneity and mid-brown colour in a region where the natural soil (a.005 and a.013) is mid-yellowish brown.

The remarkably level old surface, sealed under the bank at c. 52.50 m site height, is at a much higher level than the modern surface on top of the ditch section of our trench. The modern surface rises from 50.21 m at the south-western end of the south-east-facing profile to 51.51 m at north-eastern end, and from 50.53 m to 51.61 m from the deepest point (excluding the modern ditch a.118) near the south-western end to the highest point in the north-east on the opposite profile. The rise in the ground from south-west to north-east, of a little over 1 m over 30 m, suggests that the ditch still has not fully silted up. Indeed, as pointed out above, it may have been widened through modern ploughing and the level of the old surface is reached only well beyond the edge of the trench.

Whilst the charcoal sample from the cultivation horizon (a.063) taken during the 2014 season failed to yield a radiocarbon date, flotation of new samples taken in 2015 provided enough charcoal for dating. As discussed in more detail below,[68] the charcoal is certain to be of the mid-fifth to early seventh century and likely to date to the AD 520s to 600s. It is hard to imagine that an Islamic-era compound, of distinctly Sasanian-style military plan, had been erected on top of an undisturbed buried soil horizon of the Sasanian era. The charcoal may well derive from vegetation burnt down in the wake of wall construction – a wall that may have been rebuilt and modified later.

8.2.13. The wall

We carefully cut back the front part of the wall, in order to create a vertical profile (Fig. 8.16). This operation provided a clean section through the buried soil horizon (a.063), described in the previous chapter, and revealed the materials used to build the wall on top of it.[69]

Fig. 8.26: Fired and unfired mud-bricks at the back of the wall.

In the centre, there is a trapezium-shaped structure (Figs 8.16 and 8.25), consisting of a.101, a.102 and a.103, soft to very soft mid-yellowish brown and mid-brown clayey silt, remarkably barren with no clear traces of charcoal or brick flecks. The differences in colour may be due to more redeposited natural soil being at the bottom and more compacted plough soil or grass sods on the top and at the sides, perhaps to stabilise it. The south-west side of the trapezium has a much clearer and sharper boundary than the north-east side, probably as a result of disturbance caused by roots and animals in the north-east near the outer face of the bank. On the likely assumption that both slopes have been correctly recognised and plotted, the gradient of both slopes is remarkably similar. Symmetry and the distinct slope on both sides may suggest that it was a (rammed-earth?) foundation for the wall, rather than the soil core of a brick-faced wall.

The trapezium-shaped core of the wall is abutted at the back by a soil bank, made up of gently sloping layers of soft mid-yellowish brown clayey silt (a.104), firm light greyish brown sandy silt (a.105) and very soft light greyish brown clayey silt with numerous small fired brick fragments of up to 4 cm diameter (a.106). Behind there are at least four courses of mud-bricks and on top of a.106 there is one, in a matrix of very soft mid-greenish brown silty clay (a.107).[70] In addition to complete mud-bricks, there were also a few fragments of fired bricks in this structure. Like the soil bank beneath, the course of bricks on top rises at a gentle gradient from the south-west to the north-east. The mud-bricks were of c. 42 cm side length, a size also commonly used in the forts on the Gorgan Wall and other Sasanian construction projects.[71] The fragments of fired bricks were of c. 10 cm thickness and up to 26 cm preserved side length. There were no complete fired bricks, but shape and dimensions suggest that these are broken Gorgan Wall bricks, reused in the structure.

This brick-covered soil bank will have served the purpose of stabilising the back of the bank and of protecting it from erosion.[72] The deposit above (a.108) also forms part of the earth bank at the back of the wall and includes distinct sloping soil horizons within a.108, such as a.109 as well as several above (Figs 8.16 and 8.25–8.26). Evidently, layers of soil had been placed on top of the brick foundations. The main component of the deposits above the trapezium-shaped soil core and above the bank behind was clay,[73] in contrast to silt dominating the core of the bank. It is possible that these layers may consist of upcast from a recut waterlogged ditch and thus may not belong to the earliest phase. Clay, being less prone to erosion than silt, would not have been unsuitable material for the wall.

Whilst at one stage mud-bricks were also tentatively identified within the eroded front portion of the bank (a.111, firm mid-brown clayey silt), clear evidence failed to emerge. Distinctly visible recent animal burrows, and perhaps also plant roots, are likely to have erased any distinct traces of mud-bricks here. We certainly should not take the absence of evidence as evidence for non-existence. One would expect the front of the wall to have employed mud-bricks but, being at the edge of a deep ditch, it was also most vulnerable to erosion, followed by bioturbation of the little that remained. Quite possibly, the front of the postulated bank may have been stabilised by mud-bricks too. Alternatively, if there was a rammed earth wall, employing techniques for soil compression as on the ancient surface, no mud-bricks would have been required. No mud-bricks survived at the back of the wall in a.110 and in the topsoil above, a.112, the latter very soft light-yellowish brown silt.

The remains of the wall provide clues to its date of construction. Apart from the mud-bricks and the fragments of fired bricks, there were no artefacts in the wall, not even charcoal flecks or bone – suggesting that the surviving parts are early and were built on more or less virgin soil. The total absence of finds, except the possible small glass fragments cited, in the buried soil horizon (a.063) the wall was built upon adds strength to our assumption that there had been no previous settlement on the spot. There was no complete Sasanian fired brick, nor were there any bricks or brick fragments of non-Sasanian appearance. This indicates that Qal'eh Pol Gonbad-e Kavus dates to a similar time as the Gorgan Wall or later. The absence of complete Sasanian fired bricks from the trench, and the relatively sparse employment of fragments, may be of chronological significance. Obviously, the wall – or at least those parts of the wall containing Gorgan Wall-type fired brick fragments and the lower parts of the wall abutted by them – cannot pre-date the earliest manufacture of Gorgan Wall-style Sasanian bricks in the fifth century. Of significance for the chronology of the wall is also the use of complete mud-bricks of typical Sasanian size. Whilst fragments of Gorgan Wall-type fired bricks could have been reused much later, Sasanian sun-dried mud-bricks would not have stood the test of time. Since there is no evidence for the manufacture of mud-bricks of 42 cm diameter in post-Sasanian times, the lower sections of the wall must be Sasanian. Perhaps the walls of Qal'eh Pol Gonbad-e Kavus are later than the Gorgan Wall and date to later within the Sasanian era, when no new fired bricks of the Gorgan Wall type would have been available, but builders had access to old and broken material. Production of mud-bricks of 42 cm diameter, by contrast, may well have lasted for decades or generations beyond the construction of the Great Wall, to judge by the evidence from Fort 2 where they were employed in the original fort walls and the annexes.[74] That the Qal'eh's walls did not employ mainly or exclusively fired bricks is unsurprising, irrespective of their date. The manufacture of fired bricks was much more labour-intensive, and we know no ancient or medieval fort or fortress on the Gorgan Plain whose defences were built mainly of fired bricks. If even the side and back walls of forts on the Gorgan Wall were built mainly of unfired mud-brick, we should not expect that walls of fired brick would have been considered a worthwhile investment for a temporary installation of much greater scale. The use of Sasanian-style mud-bricks firmly points to a pre-medieval construction date for the lower sections of Qal'eh Pol Gonbad's walls. The complete absence in the body of the rampart of any medieval bricks, as found in the ditch, confirms that the lower parts of the wall are Sasanian and certainly not centuries later. These observations indicate that the Qal'eh was established in the Sasanian era. The astonishing scarcity of artefacts, and the total absence of any Islamic pottery, brick or other artefact, from the body of the wall and the buried soil (a.063) underneath (the latter with Sasanian-era charcoal), renders a post-Sasanian foundation date highly improbable, all the more so as there are no close Islamic parallels for this type of mega-fortress.

We may conclude that the lower sections of the wall at least (i.e. deposits a.101–107 and probably also a.108 and a.109) are Sasanian and are undisturbed. It is furthermore hard to imagine that in any later phase the trapezium-shaped earth bank or the slope behind, stabilised with layers of mud-bricks and fired bricks, could have been removed without cutting through the level and compacted surface underneath (the top of a.063). The undisturbed surface thus provides further circumstantial evidence that the lower parts of the wall are original, and any restoration must have been confined to the upper parts of the wall. There is no evidence for the top of the bank being post-Sasanian and deposits a.110 and a.111 may represent eroded Sasanian wall, but could also include disintegrated later structures on top, if built of sterile material.

The radiocarbon samples from the buried soil horizon (a.063) and the use of exclusively Sasanian-type mud-bricks and fired brick fragments prove that the earliest wall cannot be earlier than the fifth century and is not likely to be post-Sasanian. The charcoal sample from cultivation layer a.063, dating with an over 95% probability to AD 435–605 and with an over 75% probability to AD 528–605, suggests that construction at any stage between the 430s and the early

Fig. 8.27: The preserved wall (above the old topsoil horizon which is just under the horizontal scales) is small and will have been substantially higher when the Qal'eh was first built.

seventh century is possible, but the sixth to early seventh century is more likely than the fifth century.

If the wall, like the ditches, should have been rebuilt, restored or modified repeatedly or even just once, its height, width, tower spacing and architecture of the upper sections could have varied from phase to phase. It is clear, however, that the location of the wall has not shifted. If it was ever wider, it will have extended further to the back, but cannot ever have come much closer to the ditches – certainly not in the earliest phases; the gradient of the cut of Ditch 1 suggests that any berm in front of the wall (if existent, useful for its stability) was narrow. Tower spacing, as pointed out above, would be atypical for Sasanian installations in the area, perhaps suggesting that the preserved tower mounds are the collapsed remains of rebuilt rather than the original towers. The upper sections of the wall and the towers on top would have been most vulnerable to erosion, and it is indeed possible that they were rebuilt at least once and possibly repeatedly.

The surviving wall is, in all probability, no more than a mere shadow of its former self. Not only is its preserved height of approximately 2.50 m not much of a military obstacle, its volume is also no more than a small fraction of that of the ditch of any era. As there are no known mud-brick or rammed-earth buildings in the interior, most of the upcast of the original ditch will have been employed in the wall. The CORONA satellite image (Fig. 8.1) suggests that there was a counterscarp bank at least on the north-east side of the Qal'eh, with possible faint traces of such a bank also at other sides, and it seems likely that it would originally have been on all sides (even if what survived erosion until the satellite image was taken in 1969 has been ploughed flat since). Whilst substantial deposits were washed into the ditch, in Trench a, from both sides, the proportion of loess tends to be higher on the side of the Qal'eh, that of humus, higher on the opposite side. This observation suggests that more of the upcast loess was used in the Qal'eh's wall and from there washed back into the ditch, whilst less was used in the counterscarp bank and hence the greater proportion of redeposited plough soil on this side. Furthermore, unlike the Qal'eh's wall, a counterscarp bank served no purpose other than to reduce erosion and facilitate spoil removal when excavating the ditch at the side furthest from the Qal'eh. Stratigraphy and practical considerations suggest that the counterscarp bank would initially probably have been small and is not likely to have approached, let alone exceeded, the main wall in dimensions.

The upcast of the successive ditches must have been massive and is in striking contrast to the small volume of the preserved wall, if we are right in thinking that the humus-rich deposit (a.063) at a high level is the ancient topsoil. What happened to the remainder?

— Was the wall robbed? Unlikely, as it was built of unfired mud-brick or earth, not worth reusing. The survival of tower mounds certainly suggests that at least the latest phase did not suffer any systematic demolition.

— Was it ploughed into? Perhaps, but the architecture of the foundations of the wall (i.e. the intact trapezium-shaped core and brick-lined soil bank behind, with tower mounds on top, suggests that any plough damage will be small and can only have affected the back of the wall.

— Does the ditch reuse an earlier canal, so that only material from dredging would have been available for wall construction? Unlikely, as there is no known continuation nor obvious purpose of such a hypothetical canal pre-dating the Qal'eh.

— Was the soil used for mud-brick construction elsewhere? Improbable, as there are no traces of permanent buildings in the Qal'eh's interior and as the ubiquitous material would neither have been easy to transport far nor worth the effort.

— Did much of the wall and the towers of successive phases collapse and erode back into the ditch over time? Does much of the counterscarp bank perhaps relate to recutting of the ditch in later phases, as it would have involved a lot of effort to produce mud-bricks for heightening or restoring the wall or even piling up the upcast behind the wall?

Of all proposed explanations, the last seems by far the most plausible. The high proportion of redeposited loess in the ditch fills also points to the wall repeatedly being washed into the ditch, suggesting that the original wall would have been significantly higher than the bank today. Substantial deposits of redeposited loess with the odd fleck of fired brick or charcoal, likely to represent material eroding over a prolonged period of time from the wall into the ditch, include a.075 in the fifth ditch and a.044 in the seventh.

If we are right in thinking that much or all of the upcast of the earliest moat (Ditch 1) was used to build the wall, it will have been substantial. The walls of Gabri Qal'eh survive to a height of 8–14 m, three to six times the height of the walls of Qal'eh Pol Gonbad-e Kavus, and those of its citadel are even taller. Still most impressive today, undoubtedly, Gabri Qal'eh's walls were much higher prior to erosion.[75] Those of Qal'eh Iraj still reach up to 15 m today and will also have been even taller originally. Not all Sasanian campaign bases need to have had identically sized walls. Indeed, there is nothing to suggest that the fairly narrow walls of Qal'eh Pol Gonbad-e Kavus ever contained rooms and corridors, like those of Qal'eh Iraj.[76] It is, however, hard to imagine that Qal'eh Pol Gonbad's walls were as insubstantial, notably in terms of elevation, in the first phase as their preserved remains suggest. And it is perfectly possible that they were once as high as those of the cited parallels. Erosion must have affected them heavily and parts of the upper walls and towers will have collapsed into the moat. When the Qal'eh was brought back into use later, recutting the ditch would have been a massive undertaking – but not as great an effort as using all the upcast to rebuild the walls – not to mention that mud-brick production would have been difficult or impossible during winter or wet spells in other seasons. Perhaps later ditches (5–7) matched or exceeded the early ditches (1–4) in dimensions, but the walls may well have progressively diminished in scale. Any efforts to restore the wall, and not every dredging operation in the ditch need have involved wall repair or restoration, may have been on a smaller scale, focusing on erecting perhaps a parapet and/or small towers on top of what was left of the eroded wall.

8.2.14. Dimensions of the defences in phase 1

Can we make an informed estimate of the wall's dimensions, notably its height whilst upstanding, during

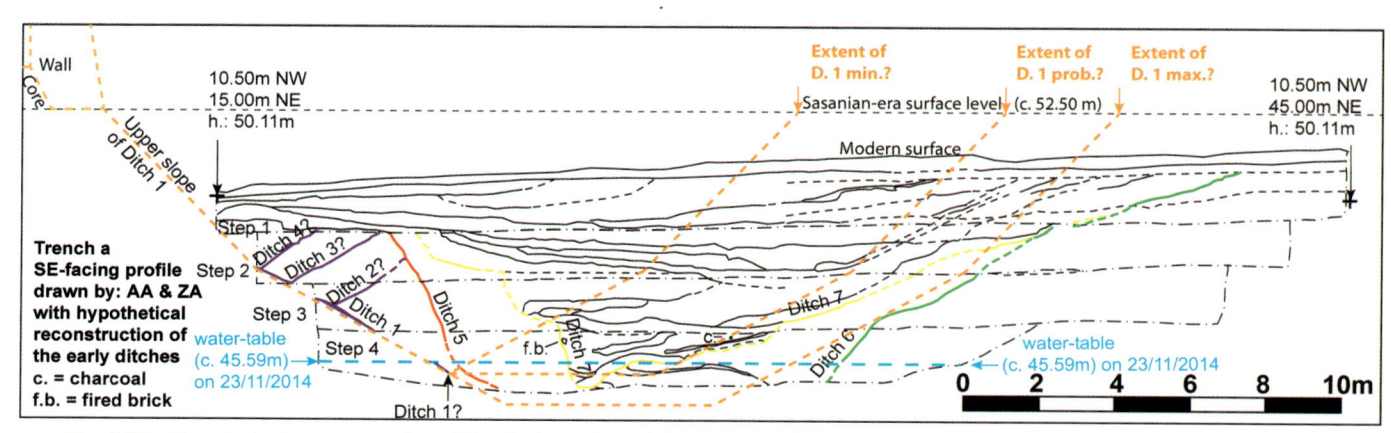

Fig. 8.28: Hypothetical reconstruction of the ditch in phase 1 (superimposed over the profile drawing), based on the assumption that the north-east side, destroyed by later ditches, was symmetrical to the south-west side. The minimum model assumes that the cut in step 4 forms part of the ditch and that it was more or less V-shaped. A perhaps more plausible model assumes that there was a flat-bottomed part, of similar width to that of the Gorgan Wall canal at Fort 9 (c. 5.50 m), in the centre. As in the case of the minimum model, the bottom of the cut identified on step 4 is assumed to be the base of the ditch. The maximum model assumes that the north-east side of Ditch 1 was just south-west of the widest later ditch and that the cuts on both sides continued at the same gradient to reach also a 5.50 m-wide flat-bottomed section in the centre.

one or more phases of occupation, based on the amount of ditch upcast available and the architecture of the preserved lower sections? The wall appears to survive to c. 9.10 m width at its base above the old topsoil (a.063). Its trapezium-shaped core was c.4.50 m wide at the base and 3.40 m at the top. It consists of soft to very soft clayey silt deposits of mid-yellowish brown to mid-brown colour (a.101, a.102 and a.103), and had evidently been built of redeposited natural material and topsoil. The top of a.103 is fairly level and may have formed the foundation of the main wall above, which may have had vertical sides. The gently sloping back of the wall, topped and abutted by mud-bricks and fragments of fired bricks, is 3.25 m wide, evidently designed to stabilise the core, whilst the front (parts of a.111) is only 1.35 m wide. It is possible that erosion may have reduced its width, but it seems unlikely that it reduced it significantly, as the earliest four ditches, judging by their location and the gradient of their slope, would have come very close to the edge of the surviving bank. If we are right in thinking that cut a.065 is part of the earliest ditch, the wall cannot have been wider than the bank today and must have had a very steep, if not vertical, face on the outside.

How high might the wall have been? The preserved remains allow us to establish its likely width at the base. It is more difficult to estimate the gradient of the inner and outer face of the wall at higher levels. We are also unsure how much material would have been available to build it in each phase, as we did not reach the bottom of the deepest ditches and have no complete profile for any one of the intersecting ditches, as later ones invariably destroyed earlier ditches at least in part. It is furthermore hard to estimate how much of the upcast might have been used for a counterscarp bank and how much for towers, breastworks etc., even if it seems likely, for reasons stated, that most of the upcast of the earliest ditch would have been used for wall construction. We do not know, however, how much, if any, of the upcast was used for wall repair when the ditch was dredged out later.

The ditches, of course, would have exceeded the c. 4.5 km wall in length, if dug on all sides. This means that if all ditch upcast had been used for wall construction, the volume of a section of the wall of fixed length should have slightly exceeded that of a section of ditch of identical length. In the case of a fortress the size of Qal'eh Pol Gonbad-e Kavus the difference is, however, small and perhaps negligible, all the more so as the counterscarp bank would have been of greater length than the ditch. Furthermore, some 600 m of the fortress perimeter follows the edge of the river today and probably already did so in antiquity. A ditch may not have been required here and/or was impossible to excavate. Should there have been no ditch here, upcast from other sections of the ditch may have provided the building material. Considering the weight and volume of the building material required, perhaps however the material for building the wall was taken from the edge of the river valley, thus perhaps also enhancing natural slopes and making the Qal'eh more defensive – whilst at the same time saving the efforts of bringing tens of thousands of cubic metres of soil over a distance of several hundred metres. As we do not know whether or not the wall along the river was built of material from nearby or from ditch upcast elsewhere, our model (Table 8.3) allows for a ditch of 4 km and 4.6 km length.

Fig. 8.29: A view from the much-eroded wall over the ditch demonstrates the dimensions of the defences – still impressive in the Middle Ages, though the original Sasanian wall may have been at least 8 m and perhaps up to 18 m higher than its remains today.

If, notwithstanding all these caveats and unknowns, it is permissible to venture a model, we may perhaps assume that the foundations were indeed 9.10 m wide at the base, as high as the surviving wall core (i.e. c. 1.30 m) with its sides sloping at a similar angle as those of the core, so that it would have been c. 8 m wide at 1.30 m above the ancient surface. The main wall on top may perhaps have been 8 m wide at the base and 3.40 m at the top, the latter corresponding to that of its solid rammed-earth foundations, i.e. an estimated 5.70 m on average. If a.103 formed the foundations of the main wall, then it was probably steeper on the enemy side than on the back. The postulated steeply sloping sides would have been more stable than a wall with vertical sides, but still unscalable. There probably would have been battlements on top. For the purpose of calculability, we estimate that these were perhaps 0.90 m wide and 1.50 m high on average. We do not know how high any towers and any counterscarp bank may have been, how tower spacing may have changed, if towers were completely rebuilt once or more than once, and how much material may have been needed for any ramps to provide access to the wall. We assume that a quarter of the upcast would have sufficed for all of these.

Initially, models were attempted, estimating the volume of ditch upcast in each of the seven phases and how high a wall could have been built with this quantity soil. Yet, it is hard to know how much or little the previous ditch had silted up by the time the next ditch was dug. And it is clear that the volume of the current wall amounts to a fraction of the ditch upcast. For these reasons, it is impossible to produce reliable models for wall height in the later phases, based on the dimensions of the ditch, nor can we be sure that every recutting of the ditch involved a partial, let alone complete, restoration of the wall. All we may tentatively conclude is that the upper sections of the wall were probably partially rebuilt at least once. Otherwise it would be hard to explain why regularly spaced small tower mounds are preserved, even though most of the original wall must have collapsed and been washed into the ditch, to judge by its minute dimensions in comparison with the volume of the larger ditches and the walls of well-preserved Sasanian campaign bases.

For the first phase, we may assume that the land surface was at the level of the top of Sasanian-era cultivation horizon a.063. It is more difficult to estimate the dimension of the ditch, as most of it has been erased by its successors. To judge by the virtual omnipresence of substantial moats around Sasanian-era lowland fortifications on the Gorgan Plain, we may conclude that it was likely to be wide and deep enough to be filled with water. It follows that the

Table 8.3: Model for possible dimensions of the ditch and the height of the wall in phase 1.

Model	Minimum	Probable	Maximum
Total width	18.36 m	23.86 m	26.86 m
Outer steep-sided sections, width	4.05 m	4.05 m	4.05 m
Inner section, width	5.13 m	5.13 m	6.63 m
Flat-bottomed central section, width	0.00 m	5.50 m	5.50 m
Depth, interface outer and inner section	4.38 m	4.38 m	4.38 m
Depth, centre	7.23 m	7.23 m	8.06 m
Ditch-fill/upcast, volume per metre	77.30 m³	117.06 m³	144.55 m³
Height of wall, incl. foundations and battlements	10.78 m	16.02 m	19.63 m
Volume of upcast for 4.6 km ditch	355,572 m³	538,491 m³	664,913 m³
Volume of upcast for 4.0 km ditch	309,193 m³	468,253 m³	578,185 m³
Volume of upcast for 4.6 km ditch in cubic feet	12,556,913 ft³	19,016,637 ft³	23,481,164 ft³
Volume of upcast for 4.0 km ditch in cubic feet	10,919,055 ft³	16,536,206 ft³	20,418,404 ft³
Worker hours for 4.6 km ditch at 3 cubic feet/hour	4,185,638 h	6,338,879 h	7,827,055 h
Worker hours for 4.6 km ditch at 5 cubic feet/hour	2,511,383 h	3,803,327 h	4,696,233 h
Worker hours for 4.0 km ditch at 3 cubic feet/hour	3,639,685 h	5,512,069 h	6,806,135 h
Worker hours for 4.0 km ditch at 5 cubic feet/hour	2,183,811 h	3,307,241 h	4,083,681 h

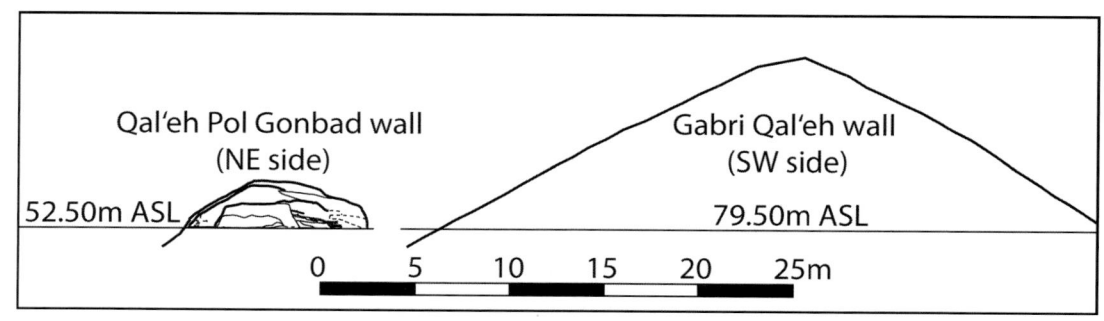

Fig. 8.30: The eroded wall of Qal'eh Pol Gonbad-e Kavus reaches only a little over a quarter of the width and the height and a tenth of the volume of that of Gabri Qal'eh (c. 18 m³ for Qal'eh Pol Gonbad's walls and c. 184 m³ for Gabri Qal'eh, assuming the surface was at c. 79.50 m a.s.l.). In part at least this difference is likely to be due to poorer preservation of the former. Both profiles are plotted on the same scale. The inside of the compound is in both cases on the right, the enemy/moat-facing side on the left. See Fig. 8.16 for details of the section across the wall of Qal'eh Pol Gonbad-e Kavus and Fig. 8.38 for the location of the height profile across the unexcavated wall of Gabri Qal'eh.

bottom of the cut attributed to Ditch 1 on step 4 is likely to represent its minimum depth. Assuming the ditch was symmetrical, the mid-point of Ditch 1 was probably further away from the wall than the deepest traceable point of this ditch (Fig. 8.28), and it cannot have been any closer. Even if, however, the bottom of the cut in step 4 should represent the mid- and bottom point, then Ditch 1 would have been quite substantial, i.e. 7.23 m deep and c. 18.36 m wide. This model implies a broadly V-shaped ditch profile, which seems unlikely for a water-bearing ditch and would have been more difficult to excavate than a ditch with a flat-bottomed section in the centre. If we assume the flat-bottomed centre was c. 5.50 m wide, like the Sasanian canal along the Gorgan Wall at Fort 9,[77] then the ditch would have been almost 24 m wide. If we assumed it was deeper and wider, but the gradients on both sides were identical to those observed in the south-west, the maximum likely dimensions would amount to just under 27 m width and some 8 m depth. Any greater width would have meant that the later ditches would not

have erased all of the opposite side and we should have found the opposite side of Ditch 1. Admittedly, ditch cuts were hard to identify, so these observations and estimates are tentative only, but are still useful in providing us with a rough idea of possible dimensions of the earliest ditch and wall.

The estimated wall height in the model is based on the assumption that 75% of the upcast of Ditch 1 was used for building the wall (the remaining 25% for towers, the counterscarp bank and any potential ramps). We assume the dimensions were as follows:

– Foundations: 8.55 m wide on average (9.10 m at the base, 8.00 m on top) × 1.30 m high = 11.115 m³ per m of wall.

– Battlements: 0.90 m wide × 1.50 m (high) = 1.35 m³ per m of wall.

– The height of main wall is calculated as follows: (ditch upcast × 0.75 minus foundations and battlements

(12.465 m³ per m of wall)) / 5.70 m average wall width (8.00 m at the base, 3.40 m on top).

A model based on so many assumptions and estimated variables is unlikely to produce reliable results, but will give an approximate idea of how high the original wall may have been. That the wall reached a height of over 10 m and perhaps up to 20 m or so is certainly perfectly possible. Even assuming Ditch 1 reached the dimensions of our maximum estimate, its volume per metre (let alone 75% of its volume) will still have been substantially below the volume of Gabri Qal'eh's walls (c. 184 m³). Gabri Qal'eh's walls may well have been wider, rather than necessarily taller, than those of Qal'eh Pol Gonbad-e Kavus. Perhaps there were rooms within the walls of Gabri Qal'eh, as was certainly the case at Qal'eh Iraj.[78]

Efforts would have been substantial. Experiments in rebuilding simple prehistoric earthworks in Britain have shown that one person can shift approximately 3–5 cubic feet (0.085–0.142 m³) per hour, equating to c. 2,000,000–8,000,000 working hours, depending which of the above models we follow – the equivalent of a workforce of 10,000 labouring for c. 27 to 98 eight-hour days.[79] These figures refer, of course, to a ditch and simple earth bank, and not a mud-brick wall, and thus are likely to substantially underestimate the amount of work. For the city walls of Hattusa it has been estimated that it would have required 2,154 workers four months to build 1 km of mud-brick wall, i.e. 10,000 approximately 117 days to build 4.5 km of wall.[80] This was a wider and more elaborate mud-brick wall with stone socle, but there was no ditch. Based on ethnographic data from Khuzestan provided by Behzad Mofidi-Nasrabadi, it has been estimated that it requires three workmen one day to build c. 0.7 m³ of wall. Applying this to a wall of an estimated volume of approximately 232,000–499,000 m³ (an estimated 75% of ditch upcast), a workforce of 10,000 would have had to labour for c. 99–214 days. Yet this figure does not include brick and mud mortar production and transport. Including this would mean that the time or workforce would have to be tripled, resulting in even higher numbers than the Hattusa estimate.[81] Based on modern ethnographic and experimental data, Mathilde Gelin postulates considerably faster construction. Based on her data, one mason could have built 1.5 m³ of mud-brick wall per day. In one eight-hour day a brick-maker would have produced almost 1.8 m³ of mud-bricks or potentially even up to 2.6 m³ in case of large mud-bricks of similar dimensions to those used in Sasanian Iran. Even taking the lower figure, this would mean that the average amount of wall built by a single worker in an eight-hour day, including producing the mud-bricks, would have averaged c. 0.8 m³. Based on Gelin's figures, a workforce of 10,000 would have laboured for 28–61 days to built Qal'eh Pol Gonbad's walls – i.e. a month or two. Whilst more research or experimental archaeology may be needed

Fig. 8.31: The modern ditch at the back of the wall.

to decide how long it might have taken to erect Qal'eh Pol Gonbad's defences, the models above suggest that it was no mean task, even assuming the last and lowest estimate is correct. Of course, transport efforts may have been less when extracting material out of a nearby ditch. Whatever the precise numbers, it would have required a workforce in their thousands working for many weeks, if not months, to build Qal'eh Pol Gonbad's defences.

A high and comparatively narrow mud-brick wall would have been particularly vulnerable to erosion and this may account for the distinct difference in volume between ditch upcast and volume of surviving wall. The multiple times the ditch was recut suggest that, whilst initially perhaps intended for single-phase use, the fortification was put back into use on several occasions. This is remarkable in the light of the major efforts needed to reinstate a defensive circuit of c. 4.5 km, even if efforts should have focused on recutting the ditch rather than restoring the wall to its original height.

The dimensions of the ditch provide the most powerful circumstantial evidence for a similarly massive wall inside, at least in the initial phase. Close examination of the wall offers further support for it being no more than a shadow of its former self. It is worth noting that the context boundary between the ancient topsoil (a.063) and the deposits above is strikingly sharp and level over 7.35 m and particularly so over the north-easternmost 4.55 m (Figs 8.16 and 8.25). It appears that this is not simply buried soil, but soil that has been artificially compacted, a technique still practised in local villages today.[82] Evidently, the ground was prepared for a wall of substantial height, hence the need to compact the surface, notably so on the enemy side where the main wall must have stood. There thus can be no serious doubt that there was a wall, rather than just an earth bank, and that it reached, or was at least intended to reach, formidable height. As mentioned above, there might also have been a (later?) projecting tower in the area of Trench a, as the bank reaches one of its high points at around 55 m a.s.l. (Fig. 8.7), but the compaction of the soil was more probably applied all along the wall; further trenches would be required, however, to test or disprove this hypothesis.

In order to establish whether or not the back of the wall extended further to the south-west, we excavated a 3 × 1 m large extension (1 m SW–2 m NE and 2–3 m NW: see Figs 8.16–8.17 and 8.31). The profile line of the extension is parallel to, but 2.50 m south-east of, the main profile line across the bank. It was not possible to extend the original profile as a footpath down into the modern soil extraction pit meant that no ancient layers were likely to be preserved in direct continuation of the profile line. The 3 m-long profile failed to reveal any ancient features or occupation deposits. In the south-west there was a 1.15 m wide and 0.50 m deep ditch (a.124) cut from the modern surface filled homogenously with humus (a.123, soft light-yellowish brown humus). Evidently a modern field boundary ditch, it was strikingly clear when first exposed (Fig. 8.31), probably a result of the humus being able to hold more moisture and its brown colour when wet, but it had almost completely faded away just a few days later and had become almost invisible. Whilst we cannot exclude that parts of the back of the wall have been ploughed away, the extension certainly yielded no positive evidence for the wall ever having reached the area of the extension.

8.2.15. The modern field boundary ditches

That the substantial earth bank formed a boundary for later fields can hardly come as a surprise. Initially, it will have done so only on the inside (as shown by ditch a.124 discussed above), whilst the former ditch will have been too wet for agricultural exploitation. This changed, when it silted up more and more. Parallel to the Qal'eh's wall and at the inner edge of the ditch, we find a modern field boundary bank (Fig. 8.16), consisting of soft mid-brown clayey silt (a.117). A ditch (a.118) alongside the bank is filled with soft mid-yellowish brown clayey silt (a.119). In step 1 and the top of step 2, one sees a ditch (or pit) in the south-western half of the south-east-facing profile, with a sterile fill sandwiched between two humus layers (Fig. 8.27). This feature appears to run at a distinctly oblique angle to the earlier ditches. There are no clear traces of this cut and associated fills in the north-eastern section of the same profile, and it is probably unrelated to, and of much more recent date than, Ditches 1 to 4. It is best interpreted as part of a modern field boundary pre-dating the current ditch. Its irregular alignment might have been dictated by trees.

8.2.16. The date of Qal'eh Pol Gonbad-e Kavus

The extreme scarcity of finds from the ditch in all phases and the complete absence of finds from some phases (notably Ditches 1–4) are worth noting and make it difficult to establish a precise chronology for the various successive ditches. Whilst a machine-cut trench will always yield far fewer finds than manual excavation of the same deposits, the sterility of the long and deep profile, repeatedly cleaned and closely inspected, leaves no doubt that very few objects were lost or intentionally deposited in the ditch. This cannot be just the result of excavation techniques. Even brick flecks of a few millimetres' diameter were far and few between, and charcoal flecks were even much scarcer than brick. Furthermore, manual excavation at the base of step 4 revealed similarly barren soil, even if sparse traces of cultural material increase in quantity toward the bottom of the trench. This increase must be the result of lower ditch fills being in part contemporary to the occupation of the interior. The contrast between the pottery scatter in the interior and the virtual absence of finds from the ditch may be due to a number of factors:

– Lack of human activity in the area of ditches difficult to cross.

– The wall preventing any material lost within the Qal'eh from being washed into the ditch.

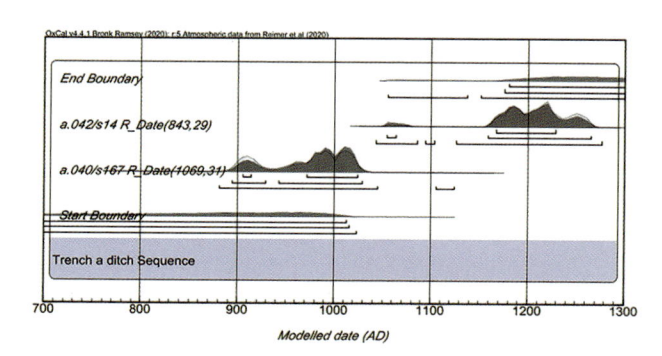

Fig. 8.32: Model of radiocarbon samples from the fill of Ditch 7, the latest phase of the moat around the Qal'eh, prove that it was still a substantial feature in the High Middle Ages.

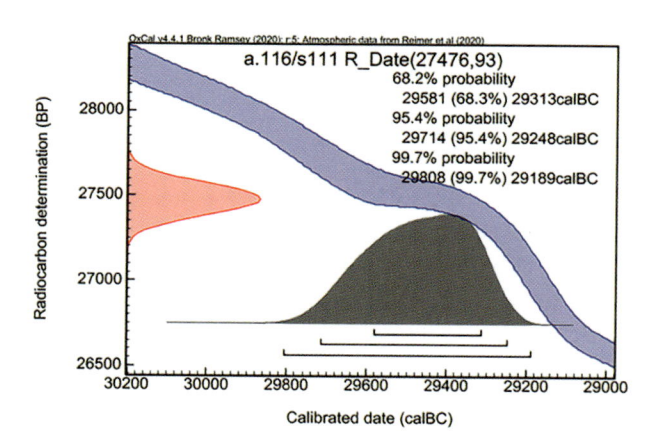

Fig. 8.33: A mollusc from Ditch 5 informs us about the chronology of Ice Age loess deposition, rather than that of the monument.

8. Campaign bases   321

Table 8.4: Radiocarbon and archaeomagnetic dates of samples from Trench a. Dates with a question mark and in square brackets are considered unreliable for dating the deposit, though in case of the Ice Age mollusc, the date is credible for the mollusc and the redeposited loess (a.s.l. = [approximate height] above sea level.).[83]

Find no.	Location	Laboratory no.	Sample description	Date	Calibrated date at 95.4% confidence	Comments
a.042/s14	Ditch 7, above a.040	SUERC-60043	Charcoal of monocots	843±29	AD 1161–1266 → modelled date: 1054–1266 (93.2%: 1159–1266)	d13C = -24.8
a.040/s167	Ditch 7, below a.042	SUERC-58114	Bone: *Ovis/Capra*, humerus	1069±31	AD 893–1027 → modelled date: 894–1029 (78.7%: 943–1029)	d13C = -19.2
a.070	Ditch 7, below a.040	OSL sample	Sediments	n/a	[AD 1165–1285?]	Date only tentative and earlier than radiocarbon samples above
a.129	Ditch 6, centred on 26.70 m E, 5.15 m N and 44.30 m a.s.l.	AM236	Sediments	n/a	[974–854 BC?]	Date incompatible with stratigraphy
a.116/s111	Ditch 5	SUERC-58116	Mollusc: *Zebrina detrita*	27476±93	[29714–29248 BC?]	d13C = -6.0; Ice Age mollusc from redeposited loess
a.063/s2–3	Cultivation layer under wall	Poz-80700	Charcoal of monocots	1525±29	AD 435–605 (87.2%: 474–605; 75.7%: 528–605)	d13C = -21.0; burnt vegetation at time just preceding wall construction?
a.063/s106	Cultivation layer under wall	SUERC-58115	Mollusc: *Xeropicta* spp.	3632±29	[2131–1898 BC (83.8%: 2046–1898)?]	d13C = -10.0; residual?

- No deliberate rubbish deposition in the ditches, in order not to lessen their depth and gradient of their slope, thus weakening them as defensive obstacles.

- Potential religious concerns not to contaminate the water,[84] even if this is only likely for any Zoroastrian occupants in the pre-Islamic era.

One ought to add the caveat that deposits were not always easy to recognise, especially at the very base of the trench when pumping made them visible for sometimes no more than a few minutes before they submerged again under rising groundwater. The proposed phasing of our not fully excavated trench is thus tentative, rather than each proposed context attribution established beyond all doubt. We succeeded in obtaining two radiocarbon dates from a sealed soil horizon (a.063) under the bank of the compound, as well as three from the ditch plus one archaeomagnetic date from the ditch.[85]

Two of these samples were molluscs, one was an animal bone. The shell from the bottom of the trench (as far as we were able to excavate the ditch) dates back to the Ice Age, just over 31,000 years ago. It provides a credible date for loess deposition in the Gorgan Plain and the geological age of the redeposited natural soil in deposit a.116. In the light of the sterility of the successive ditches, it should probably not come as a great surprise that some, and probably most, of the shells contained therein are geological rather than dating to the time when the ditch silted up.

The shell of c. 2000 BC from the plough soil (a.063), buried beneath the wall, is more difficult to explain and incompatible with the fifth- to early seventh-century

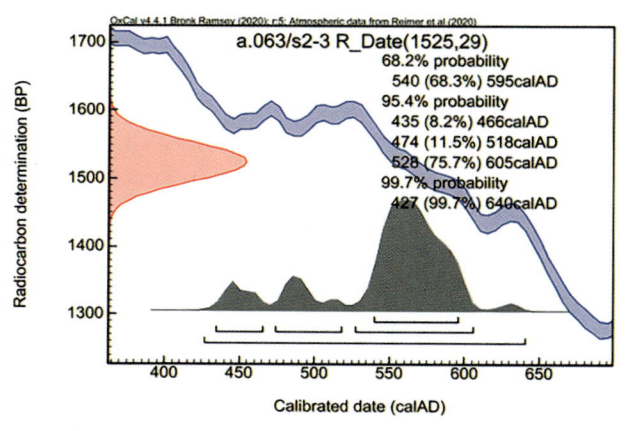

Fig. 8.34: Charred remains of grasses, herbs or reeds, sealed in a cultivation horizon under the wall, provide a credible terminus post quem *for its construction.*

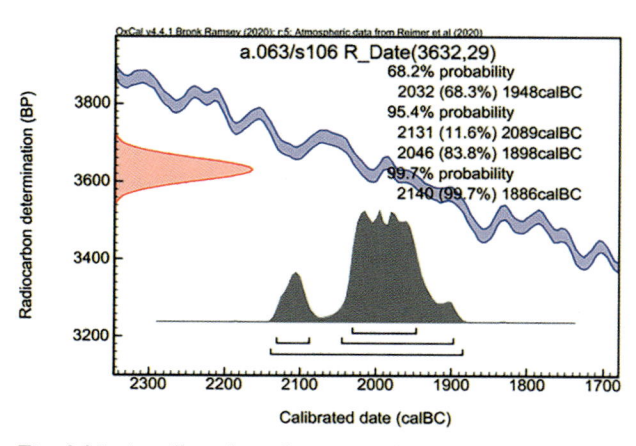

Fig. 8.35: A mollusc from the same cultivation horizon neither provides a credible date for the horizon nor for geological soil formation, demonstrating that radiocarbon-dating of molluscs is often problematic.

radiocarbon date of charcoal from the same context. It seems unlikely that the wall pre-dates the fifth century AD and inconceivable that it was built around or shortly after 2000 BC – as there is no known parallel for a compound of comparable plan and dimensions from this era. The following observations might explain the unexpectedly early date of the shell:

– The plough soil in the first millennium AD may still have contained such old shells, perhaps ploughed up or otherwise redeposited from a much older deposit.

– The phenomenon of shells sometimes producing older dates, due to their food intake, is also worth noting (but it seems unlikely that it could explain that the shell is two and a half millennia earlier than the deposit it was found in).[86]

Whilst the shells' radiocarbon dates do not provide any information relevant for the Qal'eh's chronology, our hypothesis that the earliest phase is Sasanian has gained much strength by the charcoal sample of c. AD 435–605 out of the buried plough soil (a.063), contemporary to the Gorgan Wall and its occupation. The sample could be attributed to monocotyledons (mainly grasses, herbs or reeds), but could not be identified to species, nor was it possible to determine its age with certainty.[87] Perhaps vegetation was burnt down just before the campaign base was constructed. It would be an unlikely coincidence if Sasanian charcoal had been sealed by chance under a much later wall, notably as not a single post-Sasanian artefact was found within the wall when cutting back the profile, not to mention the compound's architectural similarities to other campaign bases (i.e. the virtually identical size to Torpakh Kala, the emptiness of the interior, the substantial water-fed moat around it, the raised canal supplying it with water and the geometric plan). If

any date from the middle third of the fifth century to the early or mid-seventh century is possible, there is an over three-quarter probability of the sample dating to the time between the late AD 520s and the early 600s – making this not just the largest, but potentially also one of latest, Sasanian military compounds on the Gorgan Plain.

Some more general observations are worth noting. The material the wall was built of was remarkably sterile. Sasanian brick fragments of Gorgan Wall type provide a likely fifth-century AD *terminus post quem* for the construction of the preserved core of the wall. Mudbricks of typical dimensions for the Sasanian era provide evidence for the wall's likely pre-medieval construction. The absence of medieval bricks or other medieval finds or redeposited earlier pottery from the wall adds strength to its attribution to the Sasanian era, rather than a much later date. The absence of redeposited finds from the preserved core of the wall should not come as a surprise if it indeed belongs to the earliest phase and consists largely of upcast from a ditch cut into natural soil.

The nearby campaign base of Qal'eh Gug A provides further evidence for a remarkable cluster of activity in the area near later Gorgan/Jorjan. In addition to these two major bases, there may have been a third large rectangular compound visible on one of Erich Schmidt's aerial photographs, between the Gonbad-e Qabus Tower and a stream east of it, and already by the 1960s buried under the town's urban sprawl, perhaps a third large campaign base or a camp.[88]

If Qal'eh Pol Gonbad-e Kavus is Sasanian, then it is tempting to assume that large numbers of soldiers of the Sasanian field army were housed in this compound. It could have comfortably accommodated 30,000 if far fewer could have effectively defended it and more could have been squeezed in if required.[89] Repeated recutting of the ditch may well indicate that this happened on a number of successive occasions, some time apart, perhaps related to times of crisis when the Gorgan Plain was under threat from the Hephthalites or Turks and when it formed the launch-platform of offensive warfare against enemies in the north and north-east of the Sasanian Empire. If Ditches 2, 3 and 4 should be Sasanian, then it seems unlikely that Ditch 1 was as late as the seventh century. Perhaps the fortress was built in the second or third quarter of the sixth century, though fifth-century origins are also possible, but less likely. The considerable efforts invested in cutting and recutting the ditch suggests that the Qalʻeh saw one or more episodes of permanent occupation. If our estimate of 30,000 occupants should be in the right order of magnitude, then labour would not have been in short supply, not to mention that at times, when the area could supply army units of this size with food, a large civilian workforce should have been available too. Of course, whether the defences were built by garrison members, free or forced labour is impossible to tell. The massive investment in the Qalʻeh's defences and the raised water supply traced by satellite images suggest that it was intended to be occupied for some time, but not long enough to necessitate the construction of permanent barracks – perhaps for months, years or even a few decades, rather than as short as days or weeks or as long as generations or centuries. The size and prominent location certainly suggest that it housed a greater number of occupants than any other ancient or medieval military installation in the area. If it was here that the greatest number of soldiers was stationed during periods of ongoing or impending armed conflict, then it was probably here too that their commander-in-chief would have had his headquarters. It is thus perhaps not fanciful to suggest that major military commanders – perhaps including kings of Sasanian Persia – have been based temporarily at Qalʻeh Pol Gonbad-e Kavus.

Could this huge military establishment have been reoccupied in early Islamic times, maybe the eighth century, when the Caliphate was establishing control over the area, or the ninth century?[90] The presence of typically Islamic-style fired bricks already in the fill of Ditch 5, followed by Ditches 6 and 7, the latter perhaps half silted-up towards the turn of the millennium, certainly points to much activity in the Early Middle Ages.

Could the compound have been built, or substantially modified, by external forces of Central Asian, maybe Mongolian, origins? An intriguing parallel for various architectural features is provided by recent excavations at the Emgentiin Kherem fortress in Mongolia. The corners of this geometrical compound are also not right-angled, and the sides not of identical but of similar length. The rhombus-shaped compound is not dissimilar in plan to Qalʻeh Pol Gonbad-e Kavus, and it also lacks internal buildings. Whilst there are pottery sherds and other finds from the interior, the quantity is small. It has been persuasively interpreted as the base for a mobile

Fig. 8.36: The famous Gonbad-e Qabus Tower, with a building inscription of AD 1006–1007, a time when Gorgan/Jorjan was prosperous. It was around this time that bone was deposited in the last major ditch around nearby Qalʻeh Pol Gonbad-e Kavus. The tower was built of fired bricks of similar dimensions to several of those from the ditch around the Qalʻeh.

military garrison. A section through its wall provided a further close parallel: it has a trapezium-shaped core of similar height and only marginally lesser width. This core is also abutted at the back side with sloping layers of soil and stone (as opposed to brick in the stone-less Gorgan Plain). As at Qalʻeh Pol Gonbad-e Kavus, there is evidence for artificial soil compaction, and it was built of layers of rammed earth. Differences should not be overlooked: many horizontal layers could be seen in the core of Emgentiin Kherem, but as natural loess was used at Qalʻeh Pol Gonbad-e Kavus, layering may be invisible rather than non-existent. At 9.6 ha in size, Emgentiin Kherem was vastly smaller than Qalʻeh Pol Gonbad-e Kavus, but this does not disprove that it could have been a similar installation, merely for a much smaller garrison. Emgentiin Kherem has been attributed to the Khitan Empire (AD 907–1125),[91] which extended from Mongolia to the north-east of the Persianate world. Is it possible that Qalʻeh Pol Gonbad-e Kavus was designed by architects from Central Asia employing home-grown construction techniques? Despite the close parallels, it seems inconceivable that Qal'eh Pol Gonbad's walls were so late, let alone even later (e.g. the time of the thirteenth-century Mongol invasion), in the light of the cited evidence pointing to construction in the fifth to seventh, most probably perhaps the sixth century. This is not to imply that the close similarities between Qal'eh Pol Gonbad's Sasanian walls and those built centuries later in Mongolia are random and meaningless. It appears that there were long-term traditions in building geometric fortifications in the steppes of Eurasia which may explain similar defensive architecture thousands of kilometres and many centuries apart. Sasanian mega-fortresses may have been inspired by much earlier compounds in Central Asia and they may in turn have inspired early medieval fortifications in the steppes.[92] There may also have been multi-directional influences in wall construction techniques which are hard to disentangle.

Our Sasanian-era compound was reused, with substantial efforts devoted to recutting the ditch and making it steeper, in the Early Middle Ages. In contrast to the absence of medieval finds from the wall, medieval bricks were found in the ditch. Whilst the quantity was small (Table 8.2) and there were no other medieval objects, they do nonetheless provide a *terminus post quem* for Ditches 5 to 7. (Ditches 1 to 4 yielded no finds whatsoever, and the base of the earliest has, of course, probably been destroyed by the fifth ditch.) The early or high medieval bricks from the late ditches suggest that the ditch was recut repeatedly in the Middle Ages.

In addition to artefactual, there is also scientific evidence for medieval activity. The sheep or goat bone, dated to c. AD 894–1029 at 95.4% probability – the mid- to late tenth/early eleventh century being most likely – may well belong to the same or a similar time as the famous Gonbad-e Qabus Tower when the medieval city of Gorgan/Jorjan, at modern Gonbad-e Kavus, was at the height of its prosperity in the Middle Ages. It comes from deposit a.040, a cultural deposit from the latest ditch (of phase seven). Found c. 1.60 m above the base of the seventh ditch, it had already silted up quite substantially at the time of deposition. If the bone was discarded at the time, then it would suggest that the fortress was occupied, or more probably perhaps that there was intensive activity in this part of the countryside on the outskirts of the prospering city around AD 1000 and that all seven successive ditches had been dug before. Alternatively, it could be redeposited. Even if this were the case, this would still suggest that one of the phases of nearby activity dates to the tenth and/or early eleventh century. Whether the Qal'eh was occupied at the time or whether the find is unrelated, e.g. representing food waste from a local peasant's or shepherd's meal, is unknown. In the light of the virtual absence of other finds, and as several bones were found together, perhaps it indeed just points to nearby rural occupation or pastoral activity at a time when nearby Gonbad-e Kavus (medieval Gorgan/Jorjan) flourished around AD 1000. The scarcity of glazed pottery from the Qal'eh's interior would be consistent with there not being much occupation in the second millennium. There is, however, a small quantity of glazed ware from the topsoil, probably dating to between the eleventh and thirteenth century – unsurprising evidence for activity in the early second millennium at the outskirts of the largest city in the area.[93]

The substantial investment of manpower in recutting the deep ditch several times is worth noting and implies that Qal'eh Pol Gonbad-e Kavus played a major role on several occasions in early medieval history. This has come as a great surprise, as there are no other military compounds of this size known to us from the Early Middle Ages. Even its reoccupation and reinstatement are thus unexpected discoveries, perhaps best explained by nearby Gorgan/Jorjan providing the occupants – perhaps glad to take advantage of pre-existing nearby earthworks at times of insecurity.

The fertile Gorgan Plain was of course repeatedly under considerable threat, e.g. from the Mongols in the early thirteenth century, and Qal'eh Pol Gonbad-e Kavus was near a capital city. Perhaps the radiocarbon sample from a.040 of c. AD 943–1029 at 78.7% probability dates a late phase of occupation, whether of the vast compound or just peasant's hut and shepherd's tent or yurt, to around AD 1000. A charcoal sample from a higher level in the fill of the latest ditch (a.042), of AD 1159–1266 at 93.2% probability, is some two to three centuries more recent. Of course, either or both sample(s) might be redeposited, but this seems on the whole improbable. It is worth noting, however, that an OSL sample from deposit a.070 (below both samples) suggests a date of c. AD 1165–1285, but it should be noted that this date is tentative and a 'rough' estimate.[94] Should it be accurate, then at least the lower bone sample must have been redeposited. This, however, seems unlikely, as there was not just one bone but a small cluster (the only such cluster observed in the entire trench), all perhaps from the same sheep or goat.[95] In the light of the uncertainty concerning the tentative OSL date it is safer to consider the estimated OSL date as insecure. If both radiocarbon samples represent contemporary organisms, the ditch appears to have silted up slowly, some 20 cm in a quarter of a millennium. A.042, iron-stained soft mid-yellowish brown clay with flecks of charcoal throughout, but a higher concentration towards the bottom of the deposit, is evidently an alluvial deposit. The charcoal provides evidence for human activity, but not necessarily for occupation of the compound. It is worth noting nonetheless that the charred leaf may quite possibly date to the time of the Mongol invasion of AD 1220–1221 or its aftermath. This date makes one wonder whether the last reoccupation of the Qal'eh might be Mongol. Whilst little is known of the Mongol invasion, Gorgan/Jorjan appears to have been reduced to ruins and its population decimated.[96] A vast encampment of a Mongol army within the old mega-fortress next to the region's major city, perhaps in the course of a siege preceding its capture and sack, is a scenario that may account for these findings. Yet, there is no evidence that the ditch had been recut at the time. The date of the charcoal would, of course, also be compatible with a date of more than six decades prior to, or more than four decades later than, the Mongol invasion. In the light of Gabri Qal'eh's Ilkhanid-era occupation,[97] we certainly should not rule out a post-AD 1221 date, despite the reported devastation of Gorgan/Jorjan, though it seems improbable that the entirety of the 125 ha Qal'eh would have been occupied then. The evidence is unclear, and it is hard to decide whether the last phase of occupation dates to no later than the tenth or early eleventh century or perhaps to the time of the Mongol invasion. The small quantity of charcoal from ditch fill a.042 may attest no more than a camp-fire being lit nearby in the second half of the twelfth or the first half of the thirteenth century or perhaps a short-lived reoccupation around the time when disaster struck the flourishing city of Gorgan/Jorjan.

Evidence for activity in the twelfth or thirteenth century does not prove any major activity, let alone reoccupation of the vast compound. Yet, that there was much activity from the Sasanian era to late first millennium or beyond is clear. The evidence for multiple phases of reuse of Qal'eh Pol Gonbad-e Kavus has come as a surprise and forms a contrast to the Great Wall of Gorgan and its associated forts, occupied it seems continuously for a century or two, probably at least a century and a half, but never brought back into use in the Middle Ages. Of course, even the 4.5–4.6 km of defences of Qal'eh Pol Gonbad-e Kavus could have been restored more easily than the Great Wall and all associated forts. Whilst only a large number of people could have cleared out the ditch and reoccupied Qal'eh Pol Gonbad-e Kavus, it would not have required a similar level of manpower or organisation as reoccupying the Great Wall.

8.3. Gabri Qal'eh: from Sasanian campaign base to Ilkhanid town

8.3.1. Introduction and topographical survey

Unlike Qal'eh Pol Gonbad-e Kavus, Gabri Qal'eh is strikingly similar to Qal'eh Kharabeh. The latter compound originated probably in the fifth (or potentially in the early sixth) century AD and has been explored extensively already during the first phase of our project.[98] Gabri Qal'eh is arguably the best-preserved campaign base on the Gorgan Plain. Whilst Qal'eh Gug A and Qal'eh Daland have mostly been ploughed flat,[99] even if some sections of the walls remain recognisable, Gabri Qal'eh's walls survive to a height of c. 10–12 m above the current surface of the silted-up moat or an estimated 8–10 m above the current extramural surface beyond the moat. The width of well-preserved sections is 30–40 m at the base (Fig. 8.38). For one section, we drew a height profile (Fig. 8.30) and estimated the volume at c. 184 m^3 per metre of wall, assuming the ancient land surface was at c. 79.50 m above the sea level at this point.[100] This exceeds even the estimated maximum quantity of ditch upcast at Qal'eh Pol Gonbad-e Kavus,[101] suggesting that Gabri Qal'eh's walls were wider and/or higher than the original walls of Qal'eh Pol Gonbad-e Kavus. Originally, of course, Gabri Qal'eh's walls will have been even higher (and narrower at the base). Excavation is required to establish the original width of the walls. If as wide as 10 m on average, for example, they could easily have risen to 20 m or more, notably if we assume there were battlements on top. The elevated west, south and east corner towers even rise to a height of c. 12–14 m over the silted-up moat and c. 10–12 m over the terrain away from the moat. The tallest feature is the citadel, rising to some 18–19 m height over the edge of the silted-up moat and some 16–17 m over the landscape beyond the moat (Fig. 8.38). With the exception of some substantial depressions in the interior of the large enclosure (in part at least likely to represent qanat-related or other water-supply infrastructure, e.g. cisterns, wells or water basins), the land outside the Qal'eh, even beyond the moat, tends to be lower than on the inside. This is probably the result of substantial occupation deposits having built up in the intramural space, as also suggested by the results of our excavations in Trench e. The elevation of walls over the extramural area is thus a more reliable yardstick for their volume than their elevation over intramural land. Despite being at the heart of fertile lands, Gabri Qal'eh's walls are much better preserved even than those of Qal'eh Kharabeh, the latter in much more arid surroundings. Creating a permanent record of the best-preserved monument of its kind on the Gorgan Plain, notably in the light of the risk posed by modern mechanised agriculture, seemed of particular importance.

A complete topographical survey of Gabri Qal'eh was accomplished by Mohammad Bagher Bayati and his team between 14 November and 4 December 2014, creating an invaluable record of the monument (Fig. 8.38). Visual inspection of the monument in 2014 and 2015 provided further interesting insights into its architecture. It revealed features in sidelight, too indistinct to stand out on the survey plot. Whilst we had previously not spotted any towers, on-site inspection left no doubt that there have been projecting towers in similar numbers and spacing as at the other campaign bases. The eroded towers have left distinct equidistant ribs on the outside of the wall. Some of the ribs are very distinct (Figs 8.39–8.40), and we were able to identify most of them securely on the north-west and north-east side as well as a few on the south-east side and, even if tentatively only, also on the south-west side (Fig.

Fig. 8.37: Gabri Qal'eh with its impressive moat and the Alborz Mountains in the background, seen from the citadel. The team members at the edge of the moat (middle-ground left) help to visualise the scale of the monument.

8.46).[102] Poor preservation of towers on the south-west and south-east sides of the Qal'eh is likely to be the result of later destruction rather than only some sides having been provided with towers. It is worth noting that we could see no clear traces of tower mounds between the south-east gate and the east tower. The ruins of a modern village, abandoned only a few years ago, are on the inside of this stretch of wall, and we may conclude that earth-moving operations of the villagers and human and animal traffic will have erased the traces of towers here. One is inclined to think that the worse preservation of towers on the south-west and south-east sides may be a result of possible past cultivation of these sun-exposed slopes of the old Qal'eh. A re-examination of the CORONA and Google Earth imagery (Figs 8.43–8.44) also shows traces of projecting tower mounds, in both cases most clearly on the north-east side where their number appears to match that counted from a terrestrial perspective. The rib-like projections on both sides inspected seem regularly spaced and appear only on the outside, not the inside, and there is no doubt they are the heavily eroded remains of projecting towers of what must have been an extremely substantial wall. Walking along the crest of the wall one notices hillocks on average every 29 m, whose spacing corresponds to the highest points of the ribs. Based on these observations and the largely symmetrical plan, it is also possible to reconstruct the location of towers, which have left no traces, with a high degree of confidence. On the less regular citadel, however, towers can only be securely identified on the north-east side and the location of towers elsewhere is conjectural. Towers are often spaced 30±1 m (c. 100 feet) apart in Sasanian military architecture, much more so than one would expect in a random sample. It seems likely that also Gabri Qal'eh's architect(s) aimed at such a neat numerical spacing, even if campaign bases show perhaps a higher degree of variation in tower spacing than smaller forts, and some have towers spaced at greater intervals (centre to centre) than 100 feet.[103] We may conclude that Sasanian architects sometimes deliberately chose such a neat number, but were free to vary. Allowing for additional towers on the citadel and along the gaps in the wall of the large enclosure next to the citadel, where the wall may have been demolished in post-Sasanian times to transform the citadel into a stand-alone fortification, there appear to have been originally c. 91 towers in total. Previously, we counted 20–22 towers per side at other Sasanian campaign bases, and Gabri Qal'eh with 22 per side (and more in the north-west and north-east, if one includes the observed and

8. Campaign bases

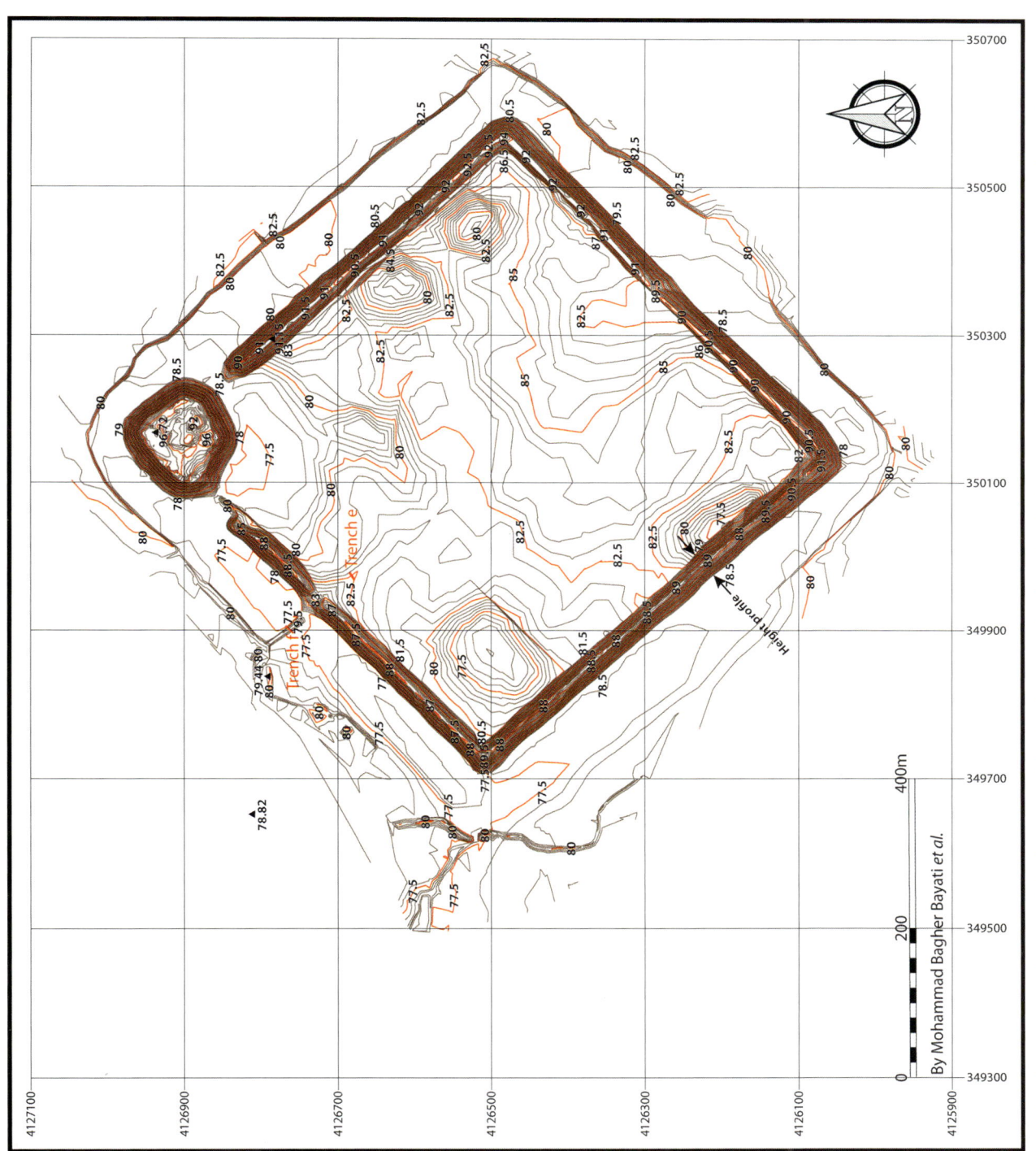

Fig. 8.38: Topographical survey of Gabri Qal'eh by Mohammad Bagher Bayati et al. Major height-lines (in red) are at 2.50 m intervals, minor height-lines (in brown), at 0.50 m intervals. Major height lines are labelled, except for those on the fortress walls. Due to the steepness of their slopes, there is no space to label major height lines here. Instead, height-lines (major or minor) at the base and top of the wall and citadel are indicated. Note that, as there is a height line for every 0.50 m, the nearest height line may thus be up to 0.49 m below the maximum elevation. For benchmarks (marked by triangle symbols), the exact height is indicated.

Fig. 8.39: Like at other campaign bases, there were regularly spaced projecting towers on the walls of Gabri Qal'eh, their eroded remains now shaped like ribs, as here on the north-east side of the compound, looking south-east.

Fig. 8.40: Eroded projecting towers on the walls of Gabri Qal'eh, shaped like ribs, on the south-western half of the north-west side of the compound, looking south-west.

Fig. 8.41: The raised causeway leading into Gabri Qal'eh from the north-west.

Fig. 8.42: Aerial photograph of Gabri Qal'eh taken by Erich Schmidt in 1937 (courtesy of the Oriental Institute of the University of Chicago), the earliest known photo of the site. The photo shows prominently the citadel, the walls, the moat and a swampy depression inside the west (bottom left) corner – perhaps the site of an ancient or medieval cistern. The ancient causeway running across the moat and from the north-west gate (left) to the south-east gate (right) stands out more clearly than on any of the more recent photos.

Fig. 8.43: CORONA satellite image of Gabri Qal'eh, edited by Kristen Hopper (courtesy of US Geological Survey). Note the causeway across the moat and its westwards continuation beyond. Clearly visible as dotted lines are also multiple qanats.

Fig. 8.44: Google Earth image of Gabri Qal'eh of 10 February 2006. Note the projecting towers on the north-east side of the main compound and the citadel (Image © Maxar Technologies).

Fig. 8.45: Drone image by Davit Naskidashvili and the joint project of Gabri Qal'eh, taken on 6 October 2016, clearly showing the substantial moat, the causeway across and its continuation into the interior.

postulated citadel towers) follows the pattern.[104] Evidently, campaign bases varied slightly in dimensions and design, but the similarities are striking: an even number of towers per side away from the citadel, mostly with a gate in the centre.

Gabri Qal'eh could only be accessed via three gates, in contrast to Qal'eh Kharabeh (and many other campaigns bases) boasting a gate on each of its four sides. At least there is no sign whatever for a gate in Gabri Qal'eh's south-west wall, whilst on all other sides there is a trough at the mid-point. With the exception of the north-west gate there is, however, no substantial depression marking the gateways, perhaps suggesting that the gateways across the substantial walls were narrow. The three gates were all at or near the centre of the respective side of the rectangle (disregarding the citadel). The depression in the centre of the Qal'eh's north-east side is less distinct than those in the centre of the north-west and south-east sides, perhaps suggesting that, despite identical tower spacing, the gate was narrower. Only excavation could reveal whether it is original or secondary and/or whether the gate was blocked at some stage. The preserved remains, and the causeway across the moat, suggest in any case that most traffic in and out of the Qal'eh passed via the north-west gate. Gate design at Gabri Qal'eh differed from that at Qal'eh Kharabeh. Gates at Qal'eh Kharabeh were flanked by massive towers projecting further beyond the wall than interval or corner towers. At Gabri Qal'eh, by contrast, there was no difference in dimensions between gate, interval and corner towers, at least none that was obvious from their eroded remains. All towers at Gabri Qal'eh were equidistant and it seems of similar size, including those flanking the gates. At Qal'eh Kharabeh and the forts on the Gorgan Wall towers flanking gates appear to be spaced at half the distance to that observed between towers elsewhere.[105] As we will see, Gabri Qal'eh was probably built earlier than Qal'eh Kharabeh and the Gorgan Wall, and the difference may reflect an evolution in defensive architecture. As far as one can tell on the basis of satellite images, all visible towers also appear to be spaced at similar intervals at Qal'eh Gug A and Qal'eh Daland.[106] This suggests that they are typologically closer to Gabri Qal'eh than Qal'eh Kharabeh and perhaps early too. We may thus tentatively suggest that these three campaign bases, all in fertile stretches of the Gorgan Plain, were built first. Qal'eh Kharabeh, in marginal arid land, and the Gorgan Wall are likely to be later in date (and Qal'eh Kharabeh perhaps a little earlier than the forts on the Gorgan Wall[107]). The later fortifications, i.e. Qal'eh Kharabeh and the forts on the Gorgan Wall, were furnished with gates whose towers were spaced at about half the distance of other towers. They would have been easier to defend than Gabri Qal'eh's gateways flanked by towers spaced much further apart, even if the gateways need not have been any wider. The sample of independently dated campaign bases is, however, small and our tentative conclusion that narrow spacing of gate towers may point to a later date than wide spacing remains to be confirmed or disproven.

We saw no traces of towers mounds or ridges during our survey at Gabri Qal'eh's citadel. Yet, Google Earth imagery (Fig. 8.44) shows four ribs on the citadel's north-east side spaced approximate 25–26 m apart (centre to centre), proving the existence of towers on the outer walls at least. The citadel's heavy reoccupation in the Middle Ages (as shown by a dense scatter of Islamic-era pottery, including glazed wares and roof tiles[108]) and later robber trenches may have erased the traces of other earlier towers. It seems likely that there would have been towers on all sides, probably at least four towers per side (including corner towers) and maybe five on

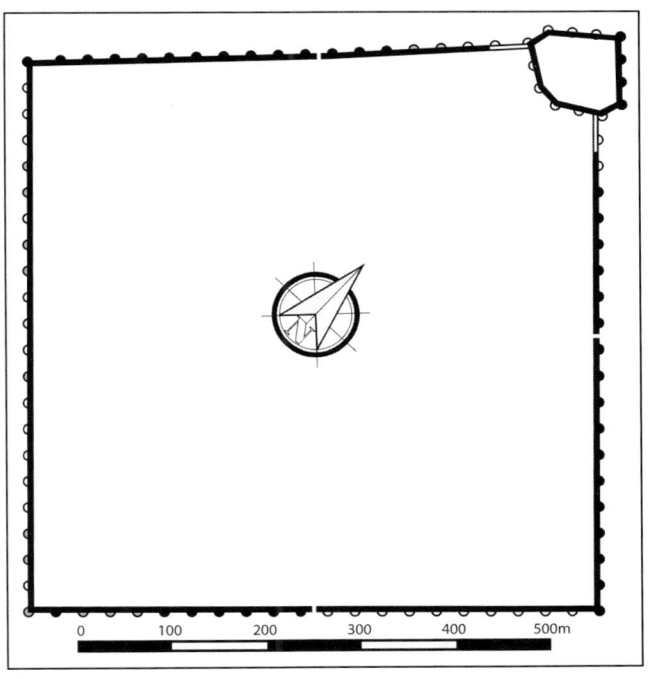

Fig. 8.46: Schematic plan of Gabri Qal'eh with its probable 91 towers, spaced c. 29 m centre to centre (and perhaps slightly more narrowly on the citadel), and its three gates. Towers and sections of wall with black fill: visible; towers with grey fill: possible indistinct traces; towers and sections of wall with white fill: conjectural; no visible traces remain. There are no substantial gaps or depressions in the walls in the area of the gates, notably on the north-east and south-east sides. This observation and defensive considerations suggest that the gateways were much narrower than the interval of the towers flanking them.

the longer north-west side, adding up to an estimated 13, including two at the postulated junctures with the walls of the main fortress. The citadel forms no square or rectangle; it is close to right-angled on the side facing the enemy, but its architects were 'cutting corners' on the inside. The citadel may have been built from scratch, and there is no positive evidence that it incorporates an earlier settlement mound, even if we cannot exclude that it did. One notices a distinct depression in the centre of the citadel mound. This undoubtedly is the result of high walls having collapsed, forming an earth bank, surrounding a central courtyard (or potentially low-rise buildings).

The ridge/causeway, initially thought to represent the central water supply canal for the Qal'eh, also still survives prominently (Figs 8.38, 8.41 and 8.43–8.45), another feature the Qal'eh shares with other campaign bases. This ridge is also distinctly visible on an aerial photograph taken by Erich Schmidt in 1937 (Fig. 8.42).[109] A subsequent section through the ridge (Trench f) yielded significant insights into its function and chronology.[110]

The surface in the intramural area is uneven, but higher on average than on the outside, in places perhaps

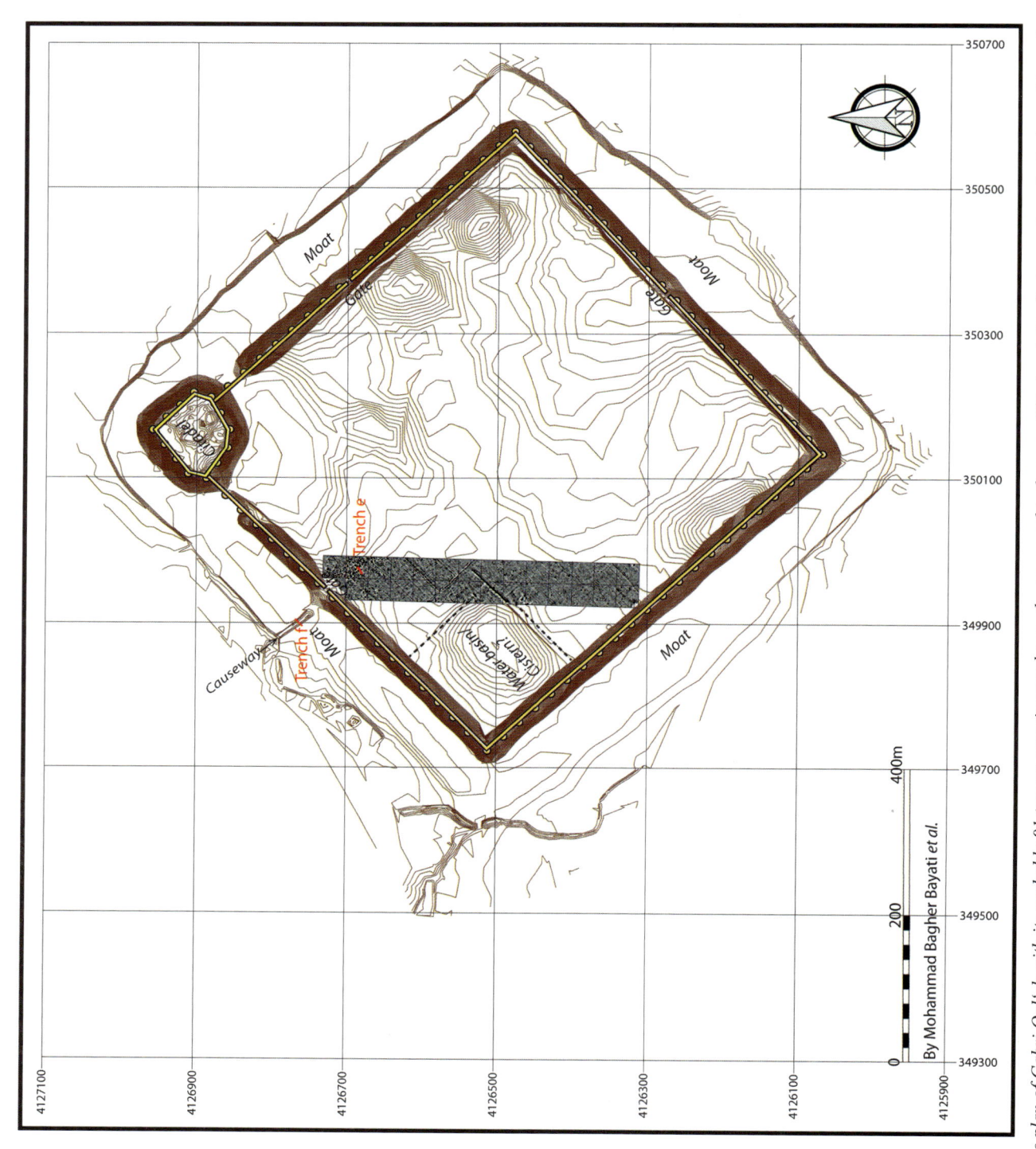

Fig. 8.47: Schematic plan of Gabri Qal'eh with its probable 91 towers superimposed over the topographical survey. This is admittedly in part hypothetical, notably as far as the three badly preserved sides of the citadel are concerned. The main compound seems remarkably close to a square. The map also plots the geophysical survey and the trenches.

rising by some 3 or 4 m above the natural surface beyond the moat. This must be a result of occupation deposits and collapsed mud-brick architecture building up in the interior of Gabri Qal'eh over the centuries. One wonders whether a remarkably rectangular depression in the west of the compound could be a large artificial water basin or cistern (Fig. 8.47). On Schmidt's aerial photograph of 1937 (Fig. 8.42), there appears to be a swamp in the area and no sign of modern settlement – suggesting it is of medieval or Sasanian origins. Without excavation we cannot date it.

Beyond these observations, there are several clues as to the date of the monument. Its telling name, 'Gabri Qal'eh', i.e. 'Zoroastrian Castle' attested already for the 1840s,[111] provides evidence for a local belief in pre-Islamic origins – a correct assumption, as now proven by radiocarbon dating and as also suggested by its striking similarity to Qal'eh Kharabeh, i.e. 'the Ruined Castle' (firmly dated to the fifth and/or early sixth century). Ruined fortifications elsewhere carry similar descriptive names, notably Qal'eh Iraj, also known as Qal'eh Gabri/Zoroastrian Castle.[112] Finds from within its interior[113] add strength to this hypothesis, but also provide evidence for intensive reoccupation, or continued occupation, later. On 15 November 2014, we carried out a surface collection of artefacts, in order to confirm and refine or correct the compound's proposed chronology. This survey focused on the citadel and the interior of the large compound (and within it exclusively on the north-west half), keeping the pottery from the two areas separate. The assemblages, differing from that from Qal'eh Pol Gonbad-e Kavus, contain a much higher proportion of glazed sherds and much larger and chunkier pieces on average. The site in its fertile surroundings was evidently heavily reoccupied in the Middle Ages, but some sherds have probable early/mid-Sasanian parallels.[114] There is much medieval as well as some Sasanian-style brick, the latter perhaps less significant than the pottery, as it is hard to be sure whether the Sasanian bricks were employed here already in antiquity or re-employed in the Middle Ages.

As in the case of Qal'eh Kharabeh, there are substantial gaps between the citadel and the walls of the large rectangular compound. These gaps are most probably a result of later occupants of the citadel, lacking the manpower to occupy and defend the whole site, strengthening the defences of the citadel by deliberately demolishing those parts of the defunct walls that were dangerously close. Eroded walls leading up to the citadels would have considerably facilitated any attempts to storm these small strongholds. Gabri Qal'eh's and Qal'eh Kharabeh's citadels would have formed attractive safe retreats for the local populations whilst the vast compounds would have been impossible to defend effectively for any force other than large military units or a later urban garrison or militia. We do not know when this happened. Any date between the late Sasanian era and recent centuries is possible. If wall demolition occurred after the last known occupation of the main compound in the late thirteenth or fourteenth century, it may explain why the site with its substantial walls proved attractive for settlers concerned about their safety; if walls had been demolished at an earlier date, safety concerns cannot have been the principal motive for continued occupation or reoccupation. The above-cited Islamic era surface pottery and roof tiles from the citadel, probably covering earlier occupation horizons, will hold the clue to the latest occupation. As a smaller number of occupants could have used the citadel as a defensible refuge, it is possible that its latest occupation might post-date that of the much more extensive area of the main fortifications.

Qanats in the surrounding of the Qal'eh will have provided water. One qanat, with a deep service shaft still surviving at the Qaleh's north-west gate and others cutting its silted-up moat, was according to an elderly local man still in use up to around the year 2000. We do not know when the earliest qanats at Gabri Qal'eh were created. These underground water supply channels would merit further research.

8.3.2. Geophysical survey[115]

We carried out a magnetometer survey of a 60 × 420 m strip, from the Qal'eh's north-west gate to its south-western walls (Figs 8.47–8.48).[116] The central causeway is visible as a distinct broad band of scattered high anomalies at the north (top) of the plot. The survey also revealed narrow linear features mostly parallel to the Qal'eh's walls. These are probably mostly modern field boundaries or older land divisions. No coherent picture emerges and no other structures of identifiable function were detected, with one probable exception. One wonders whether the distinct rectangular depression in the west (already discussed in the previous section) could have been a large water reservoir. One corner of this probable structure is within the survey plot and its limits are well defined. Contemporary field boundaries visible on Google Earth imagery (Fig. 8.44), however, run parallel to its edges and form much more prominent linear anomalies. This suggests that modern plot boundaries deliberately follow the edges of the deep and, until the 1930s (Fig. 8.42) or beyond, uncultivable depression. It is also possible that some of the land divisions within the Qal'eh are old boundaries maintained over a long period of time. Whilst ceramic material on the surface and modern ploughing may mask some faint anomalies, we may conclude that there were probably few, if any, substantial monuments built of fired bricks in the survey area, perhaps a result of mainly non-magnetic or not strongly magnetic building materials, such as sun-dried mud-brick, rammed earth or timber, being used. Subsequent excavations in Trench e, however, provided evidence for fired-brick structures,

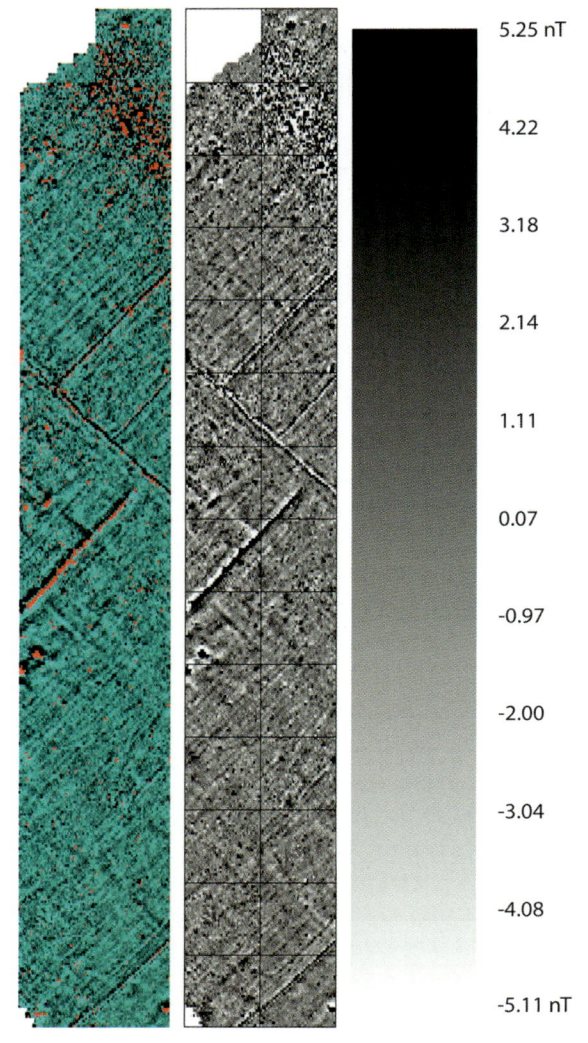

Fig. 8.48: The results of the magnetometer survey, by Mohammad Arman Ershadi et al., further processed by Roger Ainslie of Abingdon Archaeological Geophysics, in colour (left) and black and white (right). Each grid measures 30 × 30 m.

but these were basic, employing only small quantities of fired brick. Trench e along the central causewayed road was, furthermore, an area of high magnetism, and it seems likely that away from this intramural traffic axis fired bricks would have been used even more sparingly.

8.3.3. A busy bazaar street in a medieval town (Trench e)[117]

In order to explore the nature and chronology of intramural occupation, we excavated a trench of 3 × 12 m (Trench e) along the central causeway, running from the north-west to the south-east gate (Figs 8.49–8.51). Subsequently, we excavated a second trench (Trench f) across a stretch of the same causeway further north-west, where it bridges the moat on the approaches to the north-west gate. Two intersecting symmetrical causeways also provided access to Qal'eh Kharabeh, crossing the moat and each running from one central gate to another. At Gabri Qal'eh, the causeway from the north-west to the south-east gate survives prominently and there are traces of a less well preserved central roadway from the north-east gate towards the south-west. We assumed that also at Gabri Qal'eh these causeways were of Sasanian origins. At Qal'eh Kharabeh these earth banks formed raised canals as well as traffic lanes,[118] and it was tempting to assume that their counterparts at Gabri Qal'eh also served this dual function. The purpose and date of the original causeway will be explored in the next section, on Trench f. In Trench e, we never reached ancient layers and can only speculate what may be buried at deeper levels. The causeway just inside the north-west gate forms an impressively prominent ridge (Fig. 8.41). This is probably the result of settlement activity focusing over centuries on the main traffic route near the main gate. Most visitors and residents will have entered the town here, making the area a prime location to sell products and services.

The topsoil (e.001) proved rich in brick fragments and pottery, including glazed Islamic wares. The deposit underneath (e.003) contained square bricks of 19–21 cm diameter and 3–4 cm thickness, similar to those from the later ditch fills in Qal'eh Pol Gonbad-e Kavus (Fig. 8.21) and similar to those employed to build the early eleventh-century Gonbad-e Qabus Tower (Fig. 8.36). Brick size points to medieval manufacture, and subsequent scientific dating of associated material confirmed that it was indeed in the Middle Ages that these bricks were used. The trench revealed a series of structures which evidently belong to the latest phase of the Qal'eh's occupation in the area. Most notable amongst these was a round oven (e.004) of 1.40 m external and 1.24 m inner diameter (as far as excavated; only the south-eastern 53 cm, less than half, were within the trench). Similar ovens are known from other Islamic cities and were used to bake bread.[119] The 8 cm thick rim was fire-hardened and moulded ridges ran across its top at 5–8 cm intervals. Much of these survived, suggesting that much sediment built up over the feature before the area became agricultural land and that it is still under the plough horizon today. Its fill (e.005), reddish-brown silty sand containing charcoal, dates based on a bone sample to c. AD 1269–1386 (find e.005/62). The reddish hue is evidently a result of fire exposure. Cereals, i.e. barley, millet, common wheat and emmer, from the oven fill add much strength to the oven being used for bread-baking. The fuel used may have included dried dung or plants. Charred remains of barley, grape and walnut shells from deposit e.011 nearby provide further insights into medieval diet.[120] There was also much other burnt material, such as daub, south of the oven. The magnetometer plot corresponds nicely to the results of our excavations, both detecting much more magnetic material in the centre and north-east of the trench than in the barren south-west (Figs 8.48–8.51). It may have

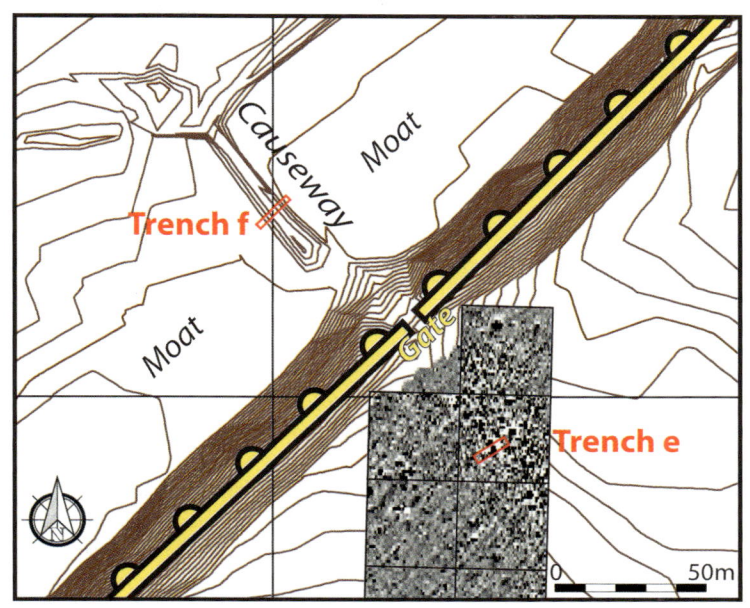

Fig. 8.49: Location plan of Trenches e and f.

Fig. 8.50: Trench e (foreground), revealing a medieval oven (left) and contemporary urban structures (centre), looking towards the north-west wall (background, left) and the citadel (background, centre).

Fig. 8.51: Trench e, plan by David Gagoshidze et al.

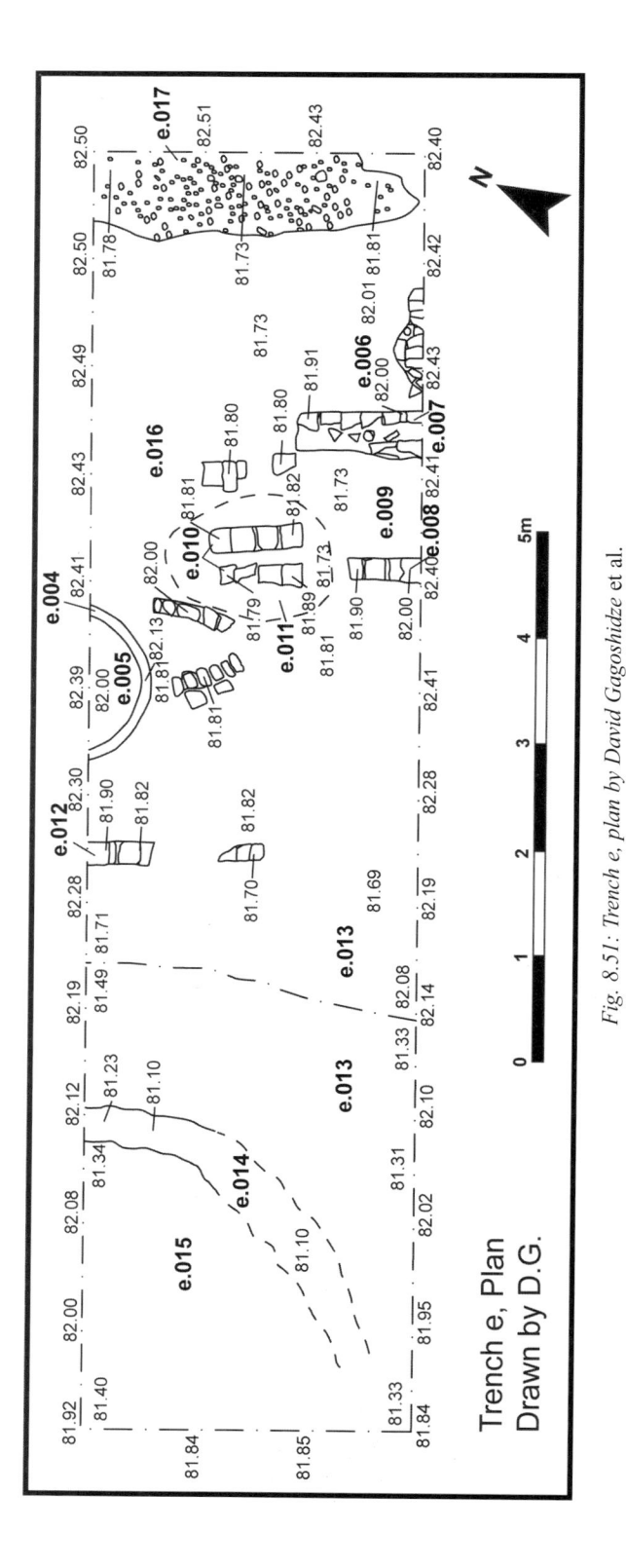

been features like this oven and related burning, as well as brick structures and ceramic debris, that the geophysics picked up rather than a canal, which, if present, will be much deeper (not to mention a possibly very deep and undetectable qanat tunnel).

We encountered a variety of short brick alignments (e.007, e.008, e.010 and e.012) within the trench, all consisting of the typical square bricks of 19–21 cm diameter, some 3–4 cm thick, the same type as also found in the subsoil (e.003). Little more than the surface of these alignments was exposed. They mostly run parallel/perpendicular to the Qal'eh's outer walls and must form part of basic structures, probably associated with medieval commercial facilities that might also have functioned as dwellings. It is possible that deeper excavation in future would expose more of these features, thus shedding further light on their function. It is possible the brick alignments formed the foundations of walls whose main construction material would have been sun-dried (and now largely decayed) mud-brick. Indeed, the failure of the magnetometer survey to reveal clear buildings of geometric shape suggests that there were no substantial walls of fired brick close to the surface, whilst the dense scatter of ceramics on the ground would mask any minor walls. A bone sample (e.009/54) of c. AD 1283–1394 from the deposit filling the space between brick alignments e.007 and e.008 suggests that these belong, like the oven, to the time of the Ilkhanid dynasty or the interlude between the Ilkhanid and Timurid eras.[122]

A worn pebble surface (e.017) in the east of the trench provides evidence for traffic and is likely to be part of the road leading from the north-west gate into the town. One coin (e.017/50) was found embedded in the track, as was a bone sample (e.017/57) of c. AD 1276–1389. As all three samples from Trench e are of the late thirteenth to fourteenth century, we may assume that a similar chronology also applies to most or all of the coins found

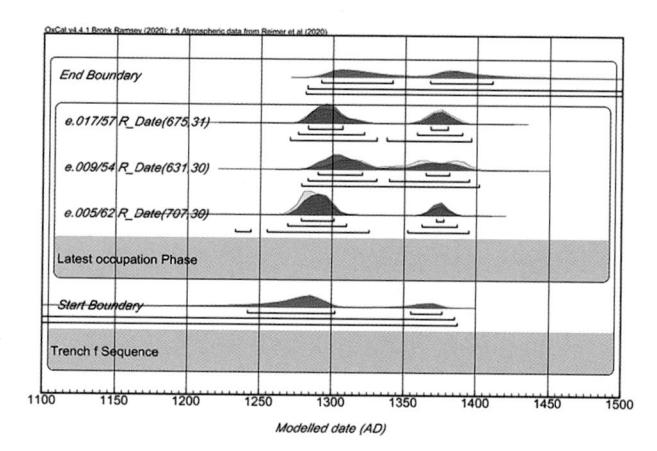

Fig. 8.52: Model of radiocarbon samples from Trench e showing that the latest phase of occupation dates to some time between the AD 1260s and 1390s.

Table 8.5: Radiocarbon dates of samples from Trench e (a.s.l. = [approximate height] above sea level in relation to a topographical survey benchmark for Gabri Qal'eh and probably close to real elevation above sea level).[121]

Find no.	Location	Laboratory no.	Sample description	Date	Calibrated date at 95.4% confidence	Comments
e.005/62	7.15 m E, 2.77 m N, 81.95 m a.s.l.	SUERC-65750	Bone: Small ruminant, long bone	707±30	AD 1264–1387 → modelled date: 1269–1386 (70.0%: 1269–1310)	d13C = -18.4
e.009/54	8.55 m E, 0.16 m N, 81.68 m a.s.l.	SUERC-65751	Bone: Small ruminant, long bone	631±30	AD 1292–1398 → modelled date: 1283–1394	d13C = -18.0
e.017/57	11.40 m E, 1.40 m N, 81.70 m a.s.l.	SUERC-65752	Bone: Caprini, femur, diaphysis	675±31	AD 1276–1392 → modelled date: 1276–1389	d13C = -19.5

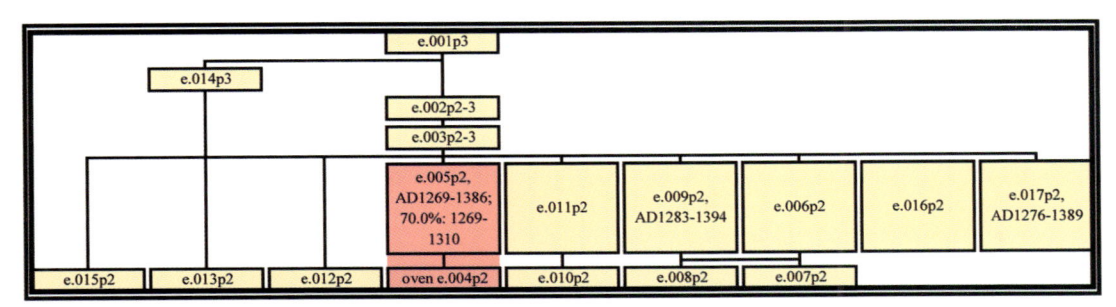

Fig. 8.53: Stratigraphic matrix for Trench e. As in other matrices, the oven and its fill are shown in red colour. The matrix lists modelled radiocarbon dates. (For unmodelled dates, see Table 8.5.) See Fig. 8.59 for the chronology of the phases (p) at Gabri Qal'eh.

in the trench. The pottery assemblage contains material datable to the first four centuries of the second millennium as well[123] and is consistent with the scientific dates. There were 17 coins from Trench e in total. Like four coins of similar design from Trench f and 21 surface finds from nearby areas within the Qal'eh, all were copper alloy issues of small module.[124] These, unlike precious metal, would almost certainly have been used for the purchase of everyday goods or services. Of the 17 coins from Trench e, 15 were found within the easternmost 3.30 m, two at 1.65 m and 3.30 m east of the western trench edge and none at all in the middle third of the trench. This may add strength to our hypothesis that paving e.017 was part of a busy road with much trade and commercial transactions taking place at its edge, be it in the open or along shopfronts or basic stalls lined up along the traffic axis.

The absence of coinage from the middle of the trench may suggest that the brick alignments formed part of domestic structures or, more probably, shop back rooms where no such transactions appear to have taken place. Oven e.004 may have formed part of a bakery where bread and maybe pastries were produced. In adjacent room units, perhaps stretching from wall foundation e.012 in the south-west to wall foundation e.007 in the north-east, the dough may have been prepared and the flour and other ingredients stored. The freshly baked bread may have been sold to passers-by, who did not need to enter the bakery, at the road-side shopfront. We cannot exclude, of course, that also more valuable products would have been on sale nor that there was more than a single store unit within the trench. The presence of much worked antler within the disturbed uppermost horizon (e.003) may signal that bone artefacts were produced and on sale here as well.[125] Meat, mainly of sheep and goat, was consumed, either by the shopkeepers, craftsmen and their families or the customers of potential catering facilities. The mutton on offer was often tender meat from younger animals, typical for an urban consumer society.[126] That the brick alignments/wall foundations in the trench are, however, parallel to the roadway may suggest that our postulated bakery, catering facility and/or shop extended to the south-eastern trench edge and beyond the north-western trench edge and beyond the partially excavated oven. Perhaps the only brick alignment perpendicular to the road (e.006) separated our bakery, food stall or multi-purpose store from the next such facility or shop. The two coins from the south-west of the trench may suggest commercial activity on a smaller scale and/or that some change or savings may have been kept away from the shopfront. Perhaps there was a backyard here, as suggested by the complete absence of any surviving structures at the levels we reached. A large animal burrow (e.014) is suggestive of intensive disturbance.

The systematic use of coinage is a strong argument that Gabri Qal'eh in the Ilkhanid era, and/or the time in the immediate aftermath of the collapse of Ilkhanid rule, was a centre of commercial exchange. Coins were not only frequent within our trench, but there were many surface finds too. These were mainly collected from the surroundings of the trench, mostly not by the team but by local visitors to our excavation. Their distribution is likely to reflect the area of operation of our visitors rather than ancient distribution. It is likely that coins would have been used much more widely, even if perhaps more so near Gabri Qal'eh's main gate. It is possible that the town's main bazaar was in this area. Whilst the trench was small, this suggests that intramural settlement at the time had an urban character, rather than us having found a small hamlet in an otherwise abandoned compound. The dense scatter of ancient and medieval pottery throughout much of the Qal'eh's interior, vastly in excess of what we found at Qal'eh Kharabeh, is also testimony to Gabri Qal'eh's much longer and more intensive occupation, not to mention that surface levels suggest that in places occupation deposits reach a depth of a few metres. It would be desirable in future to collect surface finds systematically across the Qal'eh, an exercise that would probably shed much light on the intensity of occupation of different quarters of the city throughout its history and notably the final phase of occupation.

That all three radiocarbon dates are of the Ilkhanid era or shortly after, and clearly later than Chingiz-Khan's invasion of AD 1221, is significant. The Mongols reportedly reduced Gorgan/Jorjan to ruins and it was tempting to think that nearby Gabri Qal'eh shared a similar fate. In some other cities at the southern margins of the steppe and desert belt, such as at Samarkand, Termez and Merv, the Mongol invasion appears to have had a devastating impact as well and to have led to a substantial drop in population levels and the abandonment of cities.[127] Evidently, however, urban life continued beyond the Mongol conquest, or resumed soon after. Our small trench does not, of course, allow us to reconstruct the events in the aftermath of AD 1221, and a variety of hypothetical scenarios might explain our findings. It is possible that the impact of Chingiz-Khan's conquest had been less severe than previously thought.[128] Alternatively, Gabri Qal'eh might have been spared because the smaller town did not dare to resist the Mongols. Or perhaps it severely suffered too, but was reoccupied by the remaining population later. What seems clear is that the Mongol invasion of AD 1221

did not involve genocide on a scale to wipe out urban life in the area for generations. Coin circulation and indeed local mintage similarly suggest that the Gorgan Plain in the Ilkhanid era retained some economic importance.[129]

We do not know what factors caused Gabri Qal'eh's eventual demise in the later thirteenth or fourteenth century. Whilst the dangers and pitfalls in trying to explain the fate of urban communities with the odd recorded climactic event are evident, it is worth noting that, to judge by the excavations of our small Trench e and surface finds, urban life flourished in the later thirteenth and/or fourteenth century, but did not survive beyond. A sudden and catastrophic end is certainly a possible scenario, even if far from the only one. The Black Death did not spare Iran, and various waves of the pandemic ravaged northern Persia from the 1340s onwards.[130] The plague will not have wiped out entire urban communities, but it could have reduced population levels massively and some settlement will been abandoned by those left behind. If still in existence at the time, Timur's campaigns in the late fourteenth century appear to have led to much devastation in the area and might have affected the town.[131] The economic repercussions of war and disease will have led to depopulation of settlements spared from the brunt of destruction. Until more evidence emerges as to the precise chronology and circumstances of the town's abandonment, it is best to refrain from further speculation and from any attempts to link it with specific events in recorded history.

8.3.4. The causewayed access to Sasanian and medieval Gabri Qal'eh (Trench f)[132]

Gabri Qal'eh's substantial moat is crossed by a causeway on one side only, the north-west. Whilst an elderly visitor remembered having already seen it 50 years ago, local workmen reported that an old man claimed to have built it just 40 years ago. The latter is evidently not credible as it features prominently already on the aerial photo (Fig. 8.42) taken by Erich Schmidt 78 years prior to

Fig. 8.54: Trench f sectioned the access causeway leading across the moat to Gabri Qal'eh.

our excavation in 2015. Excavation of Trench e had established intensive medieval reoccupation of the interior of the large compound. The highest point on the modern surface in Trench e was at 82.51 m elevation (Fig. 8.51), as opposed to the apex of the causeway in Trench f not rising beyond 78.82 m (Fig. 8.55). Assuming the causeway led at a similar level into the interior of Gabri Qal'eh, it would have required an at least 3.69 m deep trench just to reach the top of it in Trench e. The wealth of finds and structures in Trench e meant that there was little prospect of us being able to excavate rapidly through several metres of medieval occupation layers and structures. Whilst deeper excavations in Trench e or nearby may well have enabled us to gain insights into Gabri Qal'eh's occupation from its foundations to its abandonment, had unlimited time been at our disposal, there was no realistic prospect of us being able to accomplish this within the time available. Continuing the excavations of Trench e for a few more weeks or even months would only have shed light on the site's more recent phases of occupation, but not its origins. We therefore decided not to continue excavations in our intramural Trench e, except for small-scale operations, but to switch our main focus to the extramural area. Trench f promised to reveal earlier deposits much more rapidly and without the need of having to remove potentially significant medieval structures.

Trench f measured initially 10 × 2 m, but was later extended to 14 × 2 m. The uppermost deposits of the causeway yielded finds similar to those recovered from Trench e, including four, probably late medieval, coins, the second deepest (f.002/14) from c. 1 m below the present surface (Fig. 8.55).[133] We also found a fragment of a copper alloy finger ring (f.001/6) and some other small items of personal adornment that are likely to be of a similar age.[134] The bank appears to have been used as access route to the Qal'eh well into the second millennium. It should therefore come as no surprise that those entering or leaving the town occasionally dropped personal belongings here – or, less probably, potentially engaged in monetary transactions at hypothetical temporary stalls at the edge of the causeway. One copper alloy coin of just 10 mm diameter (f.010/51) proved the only distinct outlier, found 2.23 m below the top of the bank at this point. We were unable to identify the piece. It is of similar appearance to the other coins, but is the smallest and lightest of all 42 coins found at Gabri Qal'eh, and we cannot tell whether it is contemporary to the rest or earlier.[135] Below the subsoil (f.002), the material the bank was built of was remarkably uniform (yellowish brown to yellowish grey clayey silt) and separated into artificial spits (f.003 to f.013), as there were no clear context boundaries. The lowest

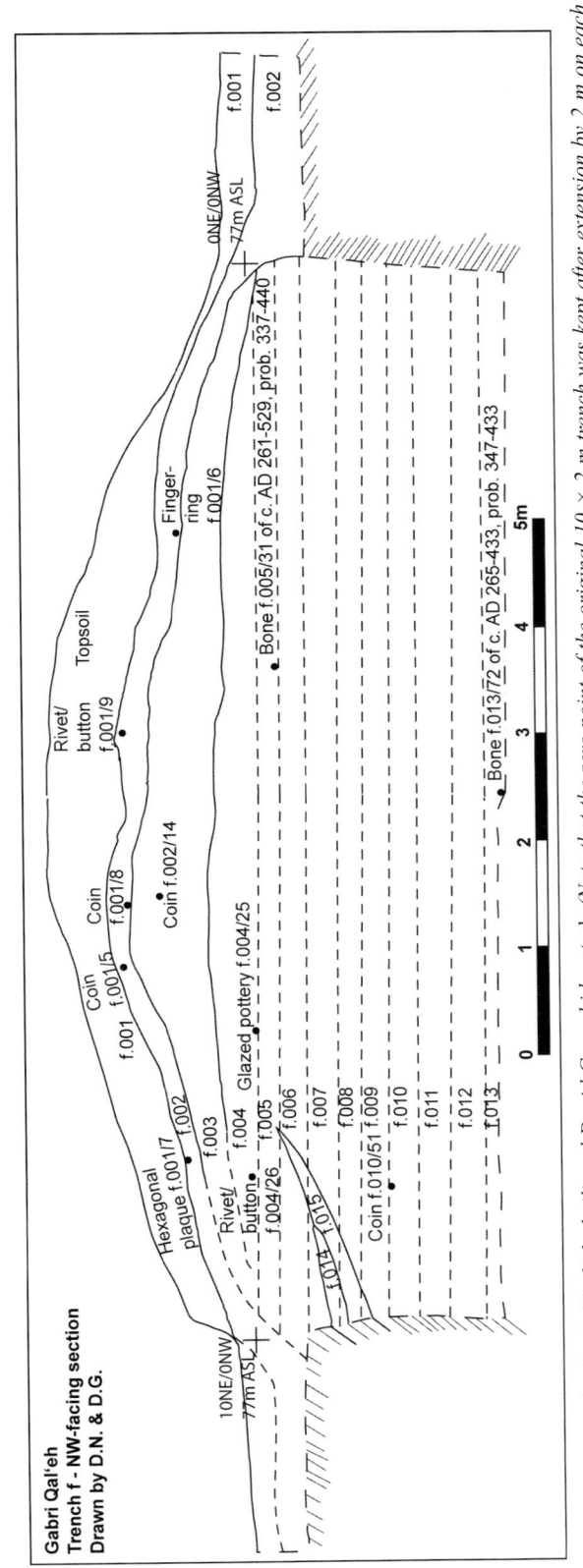

Fig. 8.55: Trench f, section by Davit Naskidashvili and David Gagoshidze et al. (Note that the zero point of the original 10 × 2 m trench was kept after extension by 2 m on each end to 14 × 2 m, so that the trench extended from -2NE to 12NE and 0NW to 2NW. As context boundaries were indistinct (and spit boundaries at arbitrary levels) and finds plotted onto the section found at up to 2 m north-west of it, the contexts recorded for the plotted finds do not always exactly match the extent of the contexts as plotted onto the section.)

Fig. 8.56: Trench f, view from the north-east, with Gabri Qal'eh's towered walls in the background.

Fig. 8.57: Trench f section, close-up of deposits f.014 and f.015.

spits (f.011 to f.013) appeared to contain least organic matter, to judge by their yellowish grey colour. The finds spectrum was remarkably uniform too, consisting mostly of Sasanian pottery.[136] The deepest glazed piece (f.004/25) was found at 1.47 m below the surface.[137]

Only when cleaning the profile did we discern a sloping deposit of firm mid-greyish brown clay, with less than 1% stones (f.015), overlain by soft mid-brownish yellow silty to sandy clay (f.014), with over 20% brick fragments, lime and stones. With clay being the main component of both deposits, albeit supplemented with much occupation debris in the upper, one wonders whether some of the material could have been dredged out of the moat. F.015 extends from spit f.009 to f.005, deposit f.014 from f.008 to f.007. It is possible that deposits f.014 and f.015 were placed here deliberately to stabilise the north-east side of the causeway which will have been wider here than the 10 m wide deep section of the trench. If so, they would mark the top of the causeway at one stage, and material above would belong to a later phase when the causeway was built up to a higher level. Alternatively, these two deposits may be no more than a load of different material piled up during the construction of the causeway. If so, material above could date to the same phase.

We stopped excavation at c. 74.67 m above sea level, some 4.15 m below the crest of the causeway, c. 2–2.50 m below the present surface level within the moat, for both logical and practical reasons. The base of the bank was likely to be at the same level as the base of the moat – or perhaps a little above if later. The moat, if fed with water by the nearby river, is likely to be over 10 m deep, to judge by the level of the deep river valley near the Qal'eh. Manual excavation to such a depth would have been difficult (and dangerous if digging beyond the current water table, likely to be well above the bottom of the causeway). It was also not likely to enable us to refine the chronology of construction. The uniformity of the deposits within the bank, in terms of soil colour and composition as well as finds assemblage, suggested that it consisted of redeposited soil, probably much of it, except for the uppermost deposits, built in a single phase. If so, little would have been gained by excavating it to its bottom; it was unlikely earlier finds would be yielded than already recovered.

Even if the core of the causeway was of a single phase, this evidently does not apply to the upper layers. Late medieval traffic in and out of the Qal'eh resulted in surface losses embedded in the uppermost deposits. The access causeway may have been increased in height then or restored. Is it possible that late medieval layers reached as deep as the deepest stratified coin cited above? Perhaps, but in the light of the absence of other diagnostic high or late medieval finds from a similar depth, it seems much more likely that the small metal item slipped down an animal burrow or may be earlier. We should remember the fourteenth- or fifteenth-century rodent remains from within a Sasanian storage jar at Fort 2.[138]

Assuming the purpose of the causeway was to provide access to the compound across a water-filled moat, then its crest must have been in all seasons above the water table. Already the earliest causeway thus should have been of substantial height. The uniformity of the soil and finds spectrum from the trench similarly point to a single-phase construction, except for possible later repair or disturbance of the uppermost deposits. Interestingly, the lowest spit reached (f.013) contained indicators of redeposited freshwater sediments.[139] The most obvious source of freshwater sediments would have been the moat itself, as there is no evidence for another body of water in antiquity in the vicinity of the trench. This might indicate that the moat pre-dates the causeway or at least its upper level as far as excavated. The compound may thus have been built first and water channelled into the moat, long enough for freshwater sediments to form. Only then was the causeway built across the moat or possibly raised in height. That the causeway (or the upper parts excavated) were not part of the original design is, of course, also evident from the ubiquity of bones and pottery throughout the causeway, inexplicable had it been built on virgin land.

Perhaps it was not before Gabri Qal'eh was transformed from a campaign base into a town that the causeway was added. If so, the finds embedded within would likely be redeposited material from the military phase and/or even the beginnings of the subsequent urban occupation. The similar, probably fourth- or early fifth-century dates of the two radiocarbon samples from the causeway would then provide a date for the likely occupation of the military compound and a *terminus post quem* for its transformation into a town or the time when it was felt necessary to facilitate access. The lack of medieval finds from the lower levels or even of late Sasanian samples suggests that the causeway was built in Sasanian times, perhaps in the fifth century – though, admittedly, the evidence for this precise dating proposal is circumstantial, and we cannot exclude later causeway construction. What is clear is that material was taken in part from Sasanian occupation horizons.

Initially we thought the causeway contained a Sasanian water supply channel, as proven for its intramural counterpart at Qal'eh Kharabeh.[140] It is worth noting that at other campaign bases in the Gorgan Plain causeways leading to gates across moats are not as prominent as at Gabri Qal'eh or are non-existent. There are no causeways leading to the gates of moat-enclosed forts on the Gorgan Wall. The presence of water canals at Qal'eh Kharabeh in alignment with canals leading towards the Qal'eh suggests that water was channelled into the compound either in canals embedded in a causeway, or a siphon or some other (wooden?) construction leading across the moat.[141] There is a clear causeway leading across the moat at the city of Dasht Qal'eh.[142] The lack of clear evidence for causeways across moats at most Sasanian military installations in the Gorgan Plain suggests that there were no such permanent access routes, for evident reasons: causeways would have enabled enemy forces to make their way across the water-filled moats and would have facilitated attempts to storm the gate or discharge missiles at close range.

The excavations at Gabri Qal'eh yielded no evidence whatever for the causeway representing a raised canal. Perhaps there was no water supply canal within the causeway or perhaps it is at a deeper level. We do not know the source of any water channelled into the Qal'eh nor from which direction it came. The nearby river provided a possible source of water, but not of drinking water, for both any supply canal and the moat.[143] A wide canal, clearly visible on the CORONA satellite image (Figs 2.15 and 8.43), leads from a palaeochannel of the river to the moat on the south-east side of the Qal'eh.[144] We may assume that this supplied the moat with water. If so, there must have been a dam to raise the water level to several metres' height in the valley, and the supplier canal and moat must have been significantly deeper than the water level in this postulated reservoir. Water for the garrison, of course, could have been channelled into the Qal'eh from the same direction and through the south-east gate which is closer to the river. The Trench f causeway would have been an access corridor, potentially containing a canal to channel excess water out of the fort. On the Qaleh's south-east side there is, however, no causeway visible on old photographs or on the ground today (but might in theory be buried in the silted-up moat).

Water from the river or moat would not have been fit for human consumption. It is possible that there was no water canal into the interior and that drinking water was drawn from wells instead or that some of the qanat system may be of ancient origins. The causeway within the Qal'eh, between the north-west and south-east gates, is distinctly raised. It features prominently on satellite and aerial photos, most notably the earliest by Erich Schmidt (Fig 8.42) where it appears to run right across the entire compound. It is much higher within the Qal'eh than in the area of Trench f, which, short of a siphon tunnel, would imply that the water cannot have been channelled into the compound via a raised canal from the north-west. Whether or not there is a Sasanian canal buried many metres beneath the crest of the causeway can only be decided by deep excavation or potentially drilling. Less probably, the

Table 8.6: Radiocarbon dates of samples from Trench f[145] *(a.s.l. = [approximate height] above sea level in relation to a topographical survey benchmark for Gabri Qal'eh and probably close to real elevation above sea level.)*

Find no.	Location	Laboratory no.	Sample description	Date	Calibrated date at 95.4% confidence	Comments
f.005/31	3.75 m NE, 0.70 m NW, 76.77 m a.s.l.	SUERC-65753	Bone: Equidae, tooth, P2, sup., complete	1662±30	AD 258–535 → modelled date: 261–529 (94.0%: 261–508; 93.3%: 261–476; 91.7%: 261–440; 88.9%: 337–440)	d13C = -19.9
f.013/72	4.95 m NE, 0.55 m NW, 74.75 m a.s.l.	SUERC-65872	Bone: Caprini, metacarpus, diaphysis	1663±22	AD 261–528→ modelled date: 265–433 (94.0%: 347–433)	d13C = -19.3

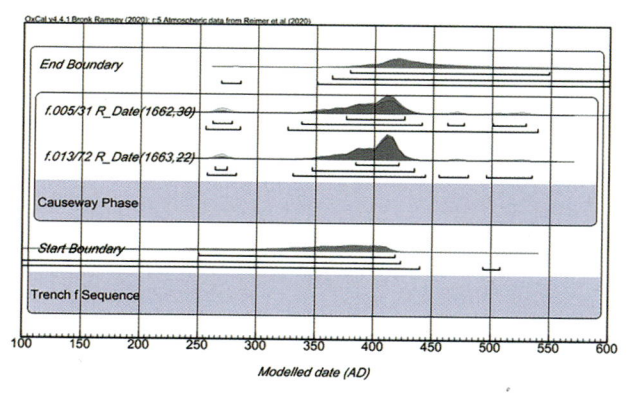

Fig. 8.58: Radiocarbon samples from Trench f. Note that, whilst it is certain that the deposition of sample f.005/31 is stratigraphically later than that of f.013/72, they may both be from a common source of material used to build, or raise the surface of, the causeway within a shorter period of time. We can therefore not be sure whether the equid, which the upper sample is from, perished at a later date than the sheep or goat whose bone is the stratigraphically earlier sample.

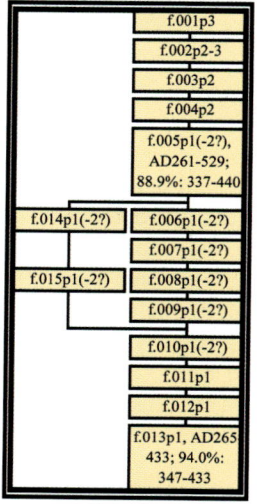

Fig. 8.59: Stratigraphic matrix for Trench f. The matrix lists modelled radiocarbon dates. (For unmodelled dates, see Table 8.6.) Note that due to unrecognisable context boundaries – the likely result of the causeway having been built or raised rapidly using similar material – much of the trench was excavated in spits. It should not be assumed that all material from one spit is later than all material from the spit underneath. Material towards either the south-western or the north-eastern trench limits in any one spit was closer to the surface and likely to be of more recent date than material from the centre of the causeway in the same spit. With one exception only (the small coin f.010/51) all certain or likely medieval finds came from the top 1.05 m of the causeway (deposits/spits f.001–f.004). It is likely that most material from underneath is Sasanian and belongs to a single phase of building/raising the original causeway. Key (also for Fig. 8.53): p = phase: p1: fourth–early fifth century; p1(–2?): fourth–early fifth century (or possibly to the thirteenth/fourteenth century?); p2: thirteenth–fourteenth century; p2–3: thirteenth/fourteenth century–modern; p3: modern.

canal could once have been at a higher level and destroyed through later erosion or the use of the bank as a road. We may conclude that there is no evidence that the causeway ever played a part in water supply, but even if it did, it was not its sole function. What is certain is that the causeway served as a traffic artery and access path and that it did so from early on to the town's abandonment or beyond.

If the above assumptions are correct, the material embedded in the causeway, except for the more recent upper layers, should provide clues as to the date of its probable construction and should not differ significantly from material from the base of the causeway, likely to be several metres below the base of Trench f. The two radiocarbon samples from the trench (Table 8.6) powerfully support this hypothesis. Whilst there was a difference of 2 m in elevation, the dates are virtually identical, suggesting that they belong to the same phase. Although it is clear that the upper sample is stratigraphically more recent, they were probably both taken from a similar source when the causeway was built. This may have happened a short time (e.g. a few days apart) and there is no way of establishing the likely relative age of the bones.

The concentration of finds was far too high to be explained with contemporary losses during the causeway's construction. Instead, the causeway must have been built out of reused debris that had built up within the Qal'eh before. The causeway cannot be an original feature, short of the improbable assumption that copious occupation debris of a different unknown site had been used as construction material. Had the material come from an earlier settlement mound, it seems unlikely it would have been so uniform, not to mention that there is no trace of earlier settlement from the vicinity of Trench f. Neither can causeway construction be assigned to the same phase as the Ilkhanid deposits recovered from Trench e. The prolific loss of diagnostic artefacts in this era, in Trench e and widely across the surface of the site, is in sharp contrast to their complete absence from the bottom 2.30 m of Trench f, i.e. over 40 m^3 of soil shifted manually, except for the one small and unidentified coin mentioned that may be intrusive or pre-Ilkhanid. The causeway is probably Sasanian, is undoubtedly earlier than any intensive Islamic-era activity and, irrespective of its exact date of construction, certainly attests Sasanian activity nearby.

8.3.5. Gabri Qal'eh's origins and significance

The material from Trench f (leaving aside only the late losses concentrated in the top layers) thus is likely to belong to the earliest intensive occupation of the Qal'eh. If so, the date is quite remarkable. The likely *terminus ante quem* of AD 433 provided by the lower radiocarbon sample (and perfectly consistent with the upper) suggests that the Qal'eh was already occupied in the early fifth century or before.[146] Could it have been built centuries before the Gorgan Wall, like some similar compounds with corner citadels in Central Asia?[147] Such a hypothesis would be hard to reconcile with the uniformity of the material.

We may conclude that it seems likely that Gabri Qal'eh dates back to probably no earlier than the fourth and no later than the early fifth century. As the Gorgan Wall has consistently yielded later radiocarbon dates, even if there is a small potential overlap in the AD 420s and early 430s, it was almost certainly later than Gabri Qal'eh, at least by a few years and at most by two centuries or so (if allowing for a construction as late as the early sixth century – or at most a little over a century if completed in the fifth century, as seems highly probable). Gabri Qal'eh is also likely to be earlier than Qal'eh Kharabeh, a campaign base dated via four samples to between the AD 410s and the 540s.[148] It would make sense for Qal'eh Kharabeh, in more marginal land, to be a later addition to the network of campaign bases than Gabri Qal'eh, at the very heart of the Gorgan Plain and close to its largest ancient and medieval towns. This proposed sequence is also consistent with the evolution of gate design discussed above: Gabri Qal'eh's gates were flanked by towers at the same distance as normal interval towers, as opposed to those at Qal'eh Kharabeh and the Gorgan Wall forts being at approximately half the normal interval. Narrow spacing of projecting gate towers made it easier to take effective action against assailants. Previously, we were not sure whether campaign bases or the Gorgan Wall had been built first or all simultaneously. Now it seems clear that at least two of the former (Gabri Qal'eh and Qal'eh Iraj) are earlier than the Gorgan Wall – and most probably several of them. An escalating security situation in the Gorgan Plain appears to have first led to the deployment of the Sasanian field army, requiring military fortifications like Gabri Qal'eh to keep it safe from surprise attacks and provide a secure launch platform for military expeditions. Only some time later was the decision taken to defend the area more systematically with a linear barrier.

Can we be sure that Gabri Qal'eh was a military campaign base or could it have been an urban foundation? We cannot rule out the possibility of urban origins with absolute certainty, but the evidence points strongly to military origins. For Qal'eh Kharabeh, a site that saw no later reoccupation, a military function has been established beyond reasonable doubt. The massive defences on the outside and the absence of urban architecture on the inside, not to mention the neat rows of small rectangular enclosures – circumstantial evidence for a tent city in the interior, leave no plausible alternative interpretation.[149] Gabri Qal'eh shows an overall similar design, sharing the following features with Qal'eh Kharabeh:

— A more or less rectangular plan of the main compound.

— A similar overall size.

— A substantial corner citadel.

— A similar number of towers per side (22 as opposed to 20).

— A similarly substantial moat.

— Gates (despite there being just three and with different tower spacing) also located in the main compound's axes of symmetry.

— A raised central causeway.

This, in conjunction with the two fortifications being located in the same region and their dates of first occupation probably being no more than a few decades to two centuries at most apart in time, cannot plausibly be dismissed as mere coincidence. Both originated probably as military foundations. What they differed in was arguably not their original function, but their later history. Gabri Qal'eh amidst fertile fields was a prime candidate for reoccupation, Qal'eh Kharabeh in the steppe was not. The semi-arid surrounding of the latter monument could not easily have sustained a large urban population.

The surface collection of pottery in 2014 has yielded potentially important circumstantial evidence for the site's Sasanian-era nature and intensity of occupation. Whilst dominated by Islamic material, there were sherds of possible 'early Sasanian' date from the interior of the large enclosure.[150] It is worth noting how little Sasanian surface pottery we found at Gabri Qal'eh's single-phase sister site of Qal'eh Kharabeh and that it was completely absent from a trench sectioning one of the (tent?) enclosures, even if there was more activity along the central causeways.[151] Even a small number of Sasanian sherds from Gabri Qal'eh are thus very significant. Bearing in mind that the average surface levels within the compound are a few metres above the area outside, there is every reason to assume that the site was occupied for a long period of time; any Sasanian sherds collected are likely to be redeposited material brought to the surface through medieval pit-digging and similar activities. The real proportion of Sasanian sherds is thus likely to be much greater than the surface assemblage suggests. Their presence offers much strength to our assumption that Gabri Qal'eh was occupied more intensively than Qal'eh Kharabeh already in Sasanian times. Perhaps, being located in more fertile land, it was a more heavily and/or frequently occupied campaign base. But it seems very likely that it was transformed into a town already in the Sasanian era and that this accounts for the presence of Sasanian material on the surface, despite heavy medieval occupation on top. That typologically 'early Sasanian' or mid-Sasanian pottery was found both on the surface within Gabri Qal'eh and redeposited in the causeway indicates a wide spatial distribution, no doubt the result of the material belonging to early occupation of the geometric fortification. It is hard to imagine that a hypothetical rural site buried under the compound would have produced so much pottery and spread over such a wide area, and it seems exceedingly unlikely that the Sasanian pottery from the surface collection and the Sasanian pottery and bones from the excavations of Trench f all happen to be redeposited material from an unrelated earlier hamlet. Furthermore, the fact that much Sasanian material was embedded in the causeway (Trench f) proves clearly that the causeway was only built after some reasonably intensive and longer prior occupation. It was evidently erected at a time when there was no intention to abandon the fortification, but instead to provide it with an easier access across the moat. The causeway across the moat would, of course, also have slightly weakened the defences, and it is possible that its construction marks the transformation of Gabri Qal'eh from a strongly fortified campaign base into a more easily accessible, but still well-protected, town. To judge by the material embedded in the lower parts of the causeway, it is likely to have been built in Sasanian times at some stage after the mid-fourth or early fifth century. It is safer not to speculate when precisely this occurred, but it is possible that this happened before the construction of the Great Wall or perhaps once it provided a protective barrier, so that making hinterland sites more easily accessible no longer posed a disproportionate risk.

There is much that is as yet unknown, as we have literally only scratched the surface in our excavations within the site (Trench e). We know that Gabri Qal'eh existed, and was probably established in, the fourth or early fifth century, almost certainly as a military site. There is no doubt that it was still (or was again?) occupied in the later thirteenth and/or fourteenth century, but we are ignorant as to its history between its Sasanian foundation and last occupation in Ilkhanid times or the transition from the Ilkhanid to the Timurid era. If little substantial architecture survives, a column base, discovered during an earlier site visit,[152] probably once formed part of a public urban building or colonnade. It is tempting to think the main north-west to south-east thoroughfare was a bazaar street lined by shops or stalls in the Ilkhanid era, as was typical for Islamic towns. At the Sasanian campaign base of Qal'eh Kharabeh, we found evidence for main traffic axes also being lined by small buildings, probably also supply facilities.[153] It is possible that Sasanian campaign base design inspired later Islamic town planning.[154] Only deep excavation might be able to reveal whether there were similar facilities lining Gabri Qal'eh's central roads already in the Sasanian era. And only deep excavation would enable us to tell whether there was continuity in the use of the central streets, indeed, whether the site was occupied continuously for almost a millennium or whether there were periods of abandonment. Whether or not it was inhabited continuously, we may be sure that it was occupied for centuries, not just in Sasanian times and not just in the earliest and latest phases we have found. Only a longer period of occupation can explain why the surface in many areas in the interior is a few metres above that of the surrounding landscape (beyond the moat).

If Gabri Qal'eh originated as a military compound and evolved into a town, it will not have been unique. Ören Qala and Ultan Qalasi also strikingly resemble campaign bases and are likely to have originated as military establishments.[155] Nishapur, whether an urban or military foundation originally, is a further example of a town of geometric plan, with a prominent citadel and a lower town. It may have, similarly to Gabri Qal'eh, originated in the late fourth or early fifth century and was also occupied until the Late Middle Ages (and succeeded by modern Neyshabur).[156] Qal'eh Timur at Zaranj is a further rectangular compound with a corner citadel thought to be of Sasanian origins to have evolved into a town.[157]

In the empire's north-eastern fringes the town of Kafyr Kala, whose origins have been assigned to the fourth, fifth or sixth century, or perhaps even as early as the second or third century, is strikingly similar to a Sasanian campaign base: it is almost square, has a prominent corner citadel, a distinct central roadway, central gates and regularly spaced tower mounds. The published plans suggest internal dimensions of c. 12 ha. Was it perhaps an eastern representative of such a military site evolving into a town – or a Hephthalite urban foundation inspired by Sasanian military or earlier Central Asian architecture? The similarly named and larger (c. 17 ha) rectangular Kafir Qal'a, further south-east, also shares some architectural characteristics of a campaign base, though the similarities may be less distinct, and it has no corner citadel. Jean-Claude Gardin observed projecting tower mounds spaced 30 m apart. Its walls still stand 4 m high (3 m on average), it is surrounded by a moat and it is of, more or less, rectangular plan. Surface finds suggest multi-period occupation from the sixth/fourth century BC to the tenth/thirteenth century AD. The occupation periods of both sites encompassed the era of Sasanian control.[158] It seems a near certainty that they were in the same architectural tradition as Sasanian military architecture, whether they were of earlier origins (as seems the case for Kafir Qal'a) and belonged a category of sites that inspired Sasanian campaign bases or whether they were inspired by Central Asian or Sasanian fortified compounds.

Whatever Kafyr Kala's role was in the evolutionary chain from pre-Sasanian Central Asian fortified compounds to Sasanian military foundations and Sasanian and early medieval fortified towns, it seems very likely that some Sasanian and medieval towns, including Gabri Qal'eh, originated as military foundations. In the Sasanian Empire, as in the early Roman Empire, dynamic military investment in frontier zones appears to have considerably boosted urbanism at times of security, stability and population growth. Sasanian military compounds, such as numerous parallels in Roman Europe (e.g. York, Exeter, Lincoln, Bonn, Mainz and Strasbourg, to name just a few), evolved into towns that lasted often much longer than the empire that had created them. Gabri Qal'eh, Ören Qala, Ultan Qalasi and Nishapur certainly all lasted long into the Middle Ages. In both cases, imperial armies paved the way for urban development in frontier territories. The difference lies in time: Sasanian military investment boosting urbanism occurred at a time when there were few urban foundations in the Roman world. Roman and Sasanian fortresses evolving into thriving towns are similar phenomena, even if they reached their peak centuries apart.[159]

8.4. Qal'eh Kharabeh

8.4.1. Geophysical survey[160]

In 2015 the opportunity arose to complement the 2007–2008 magnetometer survey of Qal'eh Kharabeh, a large Sasanian campaign base (Figs 8.60–8.61). Much of the south-west of this c. 42 ha large compound was surveyed. The survey traced the west–east causeway and canal very clearly. As in the areas previously surveyed, there was much activity alongside this traffic axis. It also established that a parallel west–east aligned boundary, dividing the south-western quarter of the Qal'eh into two symmetrical halves, continued to the western edge of the fortress. In places, the survey grids went beyond the Qal'eh's outer walls and showed the outline of the odd projecting tower mound, previously explored via topographical survey. As in 2007–2008 no trace of any rectangular enclosures, thought to have been dug around tents, were found in the western half of the compound. Perhaps the tent city, with enclosures in neat double rows in the eastern half (Fig. 8.61), was only half occupied in the phase when wet or windy weather necessitated drainage or securing the canvass with heavy clods of soil. Alternatively, perhaps those occupying the western half, for unknown reasons, dug no enclosure ditches. Distinct linear anomalies, criss-crossing the site at an oblique angle to the Qal'eh's walls, are probably modern. Drainage pipes may be a possible explanation. The survey added little to our previous exploration of this important site.[161]

8.4.2. Drone survey

Drone photographs of Qal'eh Kharabeh taken in 2016 provided powerful visual evidence for the state of preservation of this campaign base. The moat showed up clearly on the north and east side via dried-up water pools following the linear depression (Fig. 8.62). The raised roadways/canals dividing the compound into four quarters were visible as banks of lighter soil colour. Some of the projecting towers, notably on the eastern half of the north side, could also clearly be distinguished. The monumental projecting north gate still forms an impressive landmark. The projecting west and east gates are less well preserved but are clearly architecturally similar to the north gate. It is also evident that agriculture is taking its toll on the preservation of the site, and the south gate has almost vanished. Faint traces may suggest that it may once have been flanked by projecting gate towers as well, but this interpretation is tentative at best.

8.4.3. Recalibration of radiocarbon samples

To enable us to compare the chronology of Qal'eh Kharabeh with that of sites sampled during our excavations in 2014–2016, we recalibrated the four radiocarbon samples from the 2007 and 2008 excavations.[162] For Trench M, where all three samples are in neat stratigraphic sequence, we also produced a Bayesian model. Perhaps predictably, the results differ only marginally from those published, and modelling did not add much precision, with all samples falling into the fifth to early sixth-century plateau in the calibration curve. It is worth noting that the unmodelled *termini post quos* for all four samples are earlier than for the earliest of our 31 samples from Forts 2 and 4 on the Gorgan Wall, even if only marginally so. This adds strength to at least some of the hinterland campaign

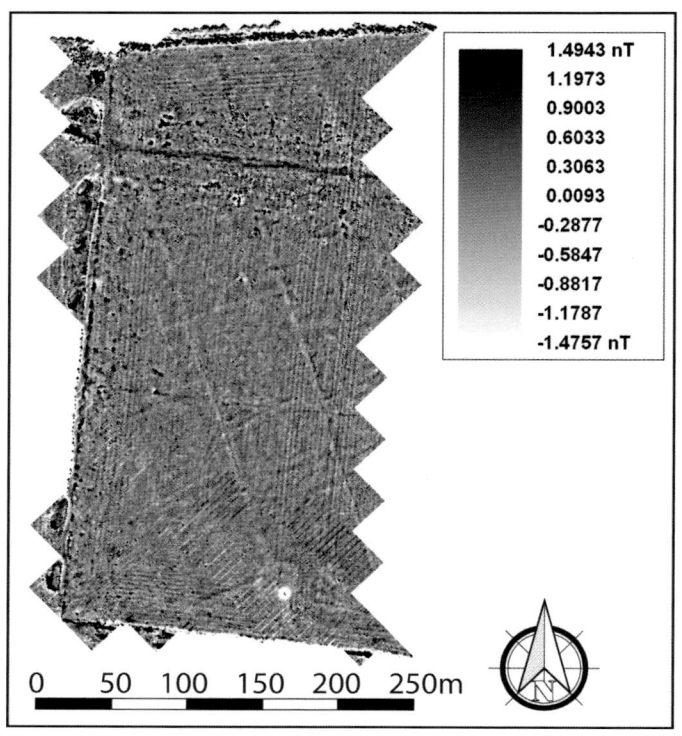

Fig. 8.60: The results of the 2015 magnetometer survey at Qal'eh Kharabeh by Mohammad Arman Ershadi et al., further processed by Roger Ainslie of Abingdon Archaeological Geophysics. (See Fig. 8.61 for location and interpretation.)

bases having been built before the Great Wall of Gorgan. Qal'eh Kharabeh was probably later than Gabri Qal'eh and more likely earlier than later than the Gorgan Wall, but there is no certainty as date ranges overlap.

8.5. Campaign bases on the Gorgan Plain

We have presented in this chapter the results of our geophysical surveys and the examination of drone and/or satellite at three campaigns bases, Qal'eh Pol Gonbad-e Kavus (GWS-37), Gabri Qal'eh (GWS-49) and Qal'eh Kharabeh (GWS-1), and those of excavations and topographical survey at the former two, in the 2014 to 2016 season. Four more potential or certain sites of this category, GWS-55, Zal Tappeh (GWS-61/83), Qal'eh Jigh (GWS-62/73) and Miankaleh Fenderesk South (GWS-92), were examined by the landscape team via pedestrian and remote survey. Our research on campaign bases in the Gorgan Plain added for some sites, including Qal'eh Kharabeh (GWS-1), GWS-55, Zal Tappeh (GWS-61/83) and Qal'eh Jigh (GWS-62/73),[163] new information, but no major breakthroughs. It is worth noting, however, that there was a mounded area centrally within GWS-55 with Parthian to early Sasanian material.[164] Mounded settlement within a large compound need not, of course, be contemporary to the geometric fortifications. Indeed, at Qal'eh Gug A and Dasht Qal'eh earlier settlement mounds seem to have been reused in the fifth or sixth century[165] and the same may well have happened at GWS-55. Furthermore, it is worth noting that typologically 'early Sasanian' pottery was found at Gabri Qal'eh and radiocarbon samples date early occupation of this compound to around the second half of the fourth/ early fifth century. This raises the question if activity at GWS-55, whether related to the campaign base or a site potentially pre-dating it, may in part at least be contemporary to Gabri Qal'eh's early occupation, starting probably at some stage between the AD 340s and the 430s. Survey at Qal'eh Jigh (GWS-62/73) yielded evidence for prehistoric, Parthian, Sasanian and Islamic occupation, whilst the now vanished, large geometric enclosure remains undated.[166] Similarly, the absence of Sasanian-era surface material from Zal Tappeh (GWS-61/83) and the presence of prehistoric and Islamic pottery from the central qal'eh does not disprove potential Sasanian origins. It does, however, suggest that any Sasanian-era occupation was comparatively short-lived and did not involve intensive use of pottery – unsurprising if it was indeed a campaign base occupied by mobile forces, who were not likely to have carried around heavy and fragile ceramic vessels; our excavation at a probable tent enclosure at Qal'eh Kharabeh did not even yield a single artefact.[167] Omnipresent Islamic-era pottery from the surface should not lead us to conclude that any of the large geometric sites under discussion were of post-Sasanian origins, certainly not until there is firm evidence that large empty

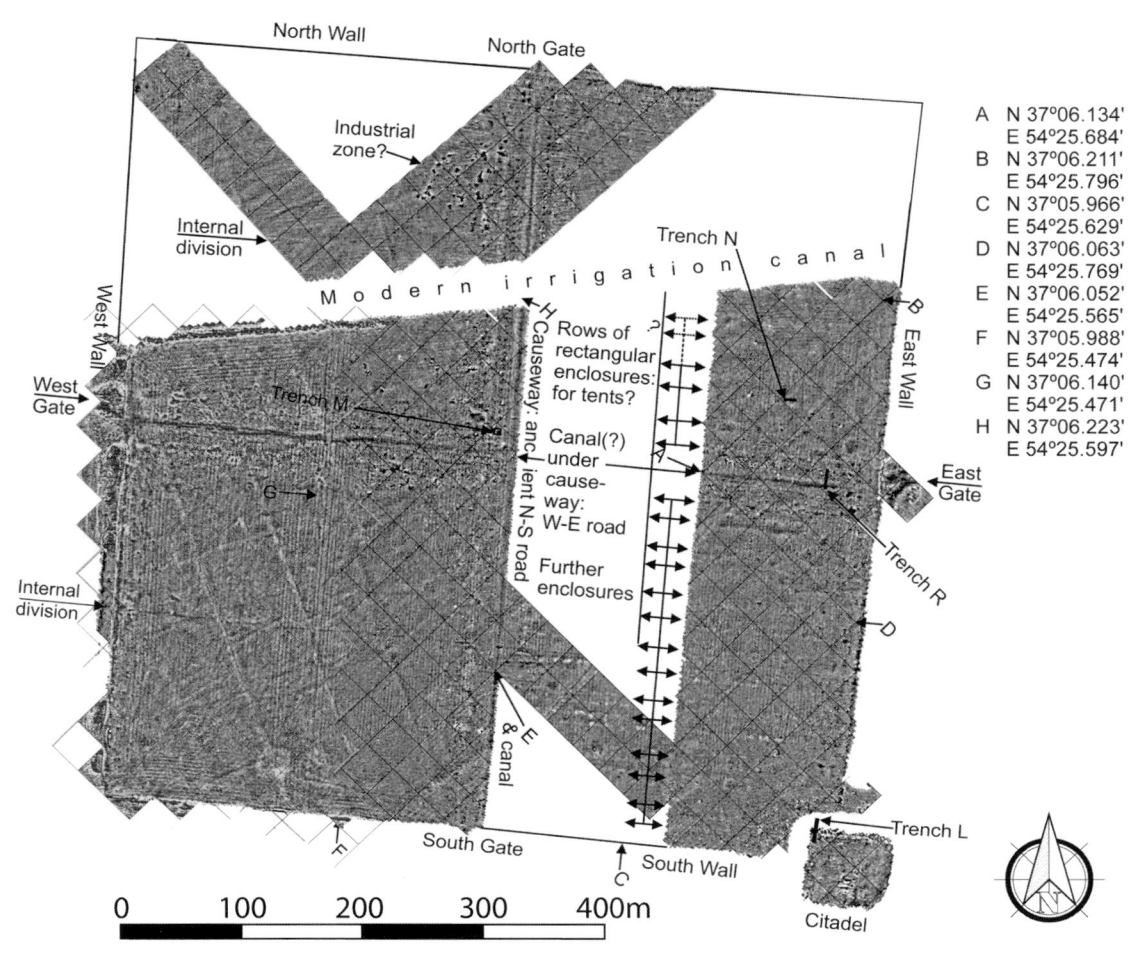

Fig. 8.61: The results of the 2015 magnetometer survey by Mohammad Arman Ershadi et al., plotted onto the 2007–2008 survey plan. Each grid measures 30 × 30 m.

enclosures were created and heavily fortified in the area in Islamic times – though there is no question that there were (much more heavily occupied) Islamic urban foundations in similar architectural tradition. Based on architecture and surface finds, GWS-55 was probably a campaign base, whilst Zal Tappeh (GWS-61/83) and Qal'eh Jigh (GWS-62/73) are no more than possible campaign bases; for none of the three do we have firm proof that the outer enclosure was Sasanian nor that it dates to a different era. We may, however, conclude that, irrespective of the exact date when the large enclosure were established, the associated qal'eh of Zal Tappeh (GWS-61/83) proved attractive for reoccupation in post-Sasanian times and the same holds true for GWS-55, Qal'eh Jigh (GWS-62/73) and other certain or possible campaign bases.

The recent discovery of a new monumental enclosure at Miankaleh Fenderesk South (GWS-92) by Kristen Hopper and the landscape team has been very important (see Figs 2.1, 2.3.A, 2.4, 2.19 and 7.1).[168] Whilst, admittedly, there is no dating evidence for GWS-92, it shares enough architectural features with Sasanian campaign bases (walls with regularly spaced prominent tower mounds, a moat, an empty interior and a possible raised canal/causeway leading across) that we are inclined to classify it as an almost certain representative of this category of site. At an internal area of c. 63 ha, similar to GWS-55, it is the second or third largest such site found to date on the Gorgan Plain. It is roughly half the size of Qal'eh Pol Gonbad-e Kavus, one-and-a-half times as large as Qal'eh Kharabeh, Qal'eh Daland, Qal'eh Gug A and Gabri Qal'eh and three times the size of smaller bases, such as Qal'eh Yasaqi. If our hypothesis that 40 ha bases were designed for c. 10,000 horsemen each is valid,[169] this site on its own could have accommodated some 15,000. Bearing in mind that not all such sites need have been occupied contemporaneously, it does not necessarily alter the size of the field army deployed on the Gorgan Plain at any one time, but it is further evidence for massive military investment, if one bears in mind the sheer scale of efforts involved in erecting a heavily fortified compound of some 1,050 × 600 m internal area, inside a massive towered wall and a moat. Unlike other, mostly square, almost square or

Fig. 8.62: Drone image by Davit Naskidashvili and the joint project of Qal'eh Kharabeh with its citadel, central causeways, outer walls and traces of the silted-up moat, taken on 27 September 2016, seen from the north, prominently showing its central projecting north gate (foreground, centre) and some of its projecting towers.

Fig. 8.63: In places, Qal'eh Kharabeh's towered walls are heavily eroded, and the tower mounds are more clearly visible from a terrestrial perspective: the western walls seen from the inside, with the car parked in the area of the west gate.

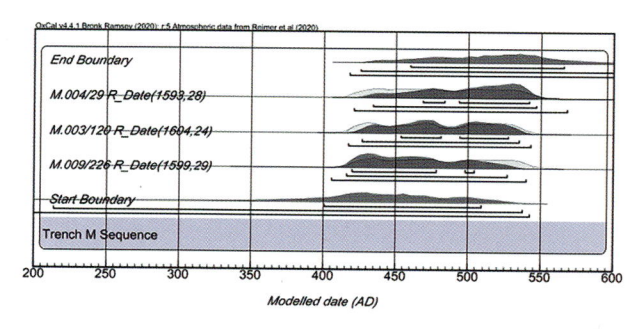

Fig. 8.64: Recalibration and model of three charcoal samples from Trench m in Qal'eh Kharabeh. The lowest sample (M.009/226) dates at 95.4% probability to c. AD 417–544 (modelled date: 416–527). The sample above (M.003/120) dates to c. AD 418–539 (modelled date: 426–535). The stratigraphically most recent sample (M.004/29) dates to c. AD 419–545 (modelled date: 434–547).

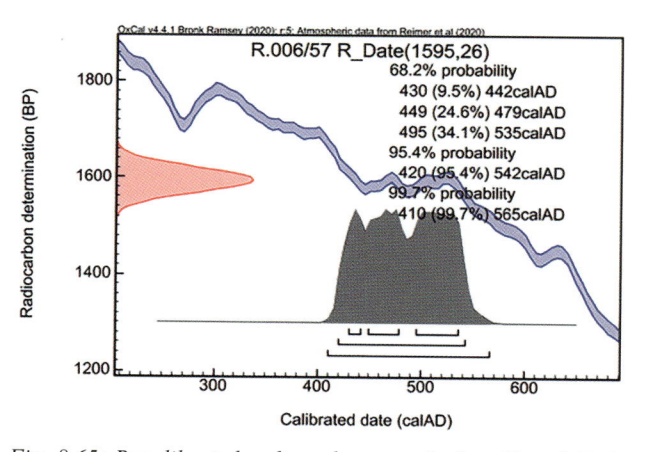

Fig. 8.65: Recalibrated radiocarbon sample from Trench R. It dates at 95.4% probability to c. AD 420–542.

Table 8.7: Dated campaign bases on the Gorgan Plain: architectural characteristics, excluding those they have in common (i.e. their geometric plan, their largely empty interior, their moat-lined towered and gated walls and their central causeways).

Site	Date	Tower spacing	Corner citadel	Gate-towers and spacing	Walls	Internal area
Gabri Qalʻeh	AD 340s–430s	29 m	Yes	Non-projecting, wide	Wide	36 ha
Qalʻeh Kharabeh	AD 410s–540s, prob. first half (maybe first quarter) of this range	34 m	Yes	Projecting, narrow	Wide	42 ha
Qalʻeh Pol Gonbad-e Kavus	AD 430s–600s, prob. 520s–600s	20 m (late phase?)	No(?)	Non-projecting?	Narrow	125 ha

almost equilateral parallelogram-shaped campaign bases, GWS-92 had a length to width ratio of c. 7:4. This unusual elongated rectangular shape might have been dictated by the landscape, e.g. the course of nearby streams, potential flood risk and/or the use of their water to fill the moat. A future topographical survey might help to explain the plan, although the landscape has changed beyond recognition. The even more irregular probable campaign base at Leilan (Fig. 8.4) shows that the design of such compounds could vary.[170] Located about an hour's walk south-west of Qalʻeh Daland at the heart of the plain, campaign base GWS-92 would have been ideally located to be supplied with food and sufficiently central to enable rapid redeployment of troops across the plain.

The dating of Qalʻeh Pol Gonbad-e Kavus and Gabri Qalʻeh has been a further major breakthrough. If we had suspected that Qalʻeh Pol Gonbad-e Kavus was Sasanian before, we have now scientific dating from buried soil under the wall to confirm this (and to suggest it may be one of the latest Sasanian fortifications in the area), which is significant as this compound exceeds all other ancient military fortifications north of the Alborz Mountains in scale. It has, in size, a close parallel in Sasanian Torpakh Kala to the west of the Caspian Sea. The scientific dating of Qalʻeh Pol Gonbad-e Kavus adds much strength to it being designed for the same purpose, and perhaps at a similar time, as Torpakh Kala, both serving as safe hinterland fortifications for large armies of similar numerical strength dispatched to the two opposite shores of the Caspian Sea at times of crisis. Whilst the mega-fortress of Qalʻeh Pol Gonbad-e Kavus may post-date the Gorgan Wall (though a similar or even marginally earlier date cannot be ruled out with certainty), Gabri Qalʻeh is probably earlier than the Great Wall – evidence for the gradual evolution of defensive architecture, and its build-up over generations or even centuries, on the Gorgan Plain.

Evidence has also emerged for variations in architecture. Average tower spacing was a little narrower at Gabri Qalʻeh (c. 29 m centre to centre) than at Qalʻeh Kharabeh (c. 34 m) or Qalʻeh Iraj (c. 37–38 m centre to centre),[171] whilst the very narrow spacing (c. 20 m) at Qalʻeh Pol Gonbad-e Kavus may relate to a later modification rather than the original walls. We observed a marked difference in gate design. Gabri Qalʻeh's gates were flanked by widely spaced non-projecting towers, whilst Qalʻeh Kharabeh's strongly projecting gate towers were narrowly spaced. With so few sites dated and examined in detail, it is hard to be sure whether this marks a chronological development, but the little one can see of Qalʻeh Pol Gonbad's gates on CORONA imagery suggests they were also non-projecting. On the likely assumption that Gabri Qalʻeh is the earliest and Qalʻeh Pol Gonbad-e Kavus the latest of the three, there may not be a uniform trend. It should be noted, however, that the walls of Qalʻeh Pol Gonbad-e Kavus are heavily eroded and may have been restored on a much-reduced scale in the Middle Ages. The preserved remains therefore only partially reflect the Sasanian phase, and we cannot be sure to what extent the little we know about its gates represents their Sasanian or medieval appearance. The fact that also at the Gorgan Wall forts, gate towers are spaced at around half the distance of that observed between other towers suggests that the shift from wide to narrow gate tower spacing may indeed be chronologically significant, but more research is required to prove or disprove the hypothesis.[172] It is worth noting that the gate towers of mid- to late Sasanian Takht-e Suleiman are spaced 18 m apart (centre to centre), much narrower (c. 60%) than the spacing of the other towers of c. 30 m on average.[173]

It is also interesting that enough is preserved of Qalʻeh Pol Gonbad's Sasanian-era core of the walls to suggest that they were narrow and almost certainly not designed to contain rooms (unlike the probably early fifth-century base of Qalʻeh Iraj). Gabri Qalʻeh's walls would need to be excavated to verify whether or not they contained also rows of rooms, but one is inclined to think that they did. The eroded walls are 30–40 m wide and 8–14 m high, with an estimated volume of 184 m^3 per metre for one section – enough material for a broad and tall wall with corridors and rooms inside. Qalʻeh Kharabeh's walls are less well preserved than those of Gabri Qalʻeh, but wide enough that they could also have contained rooms and corridors. Both Qalʻeh Kharabeh and Gabri Qalʻeh boast a corner citadel, whereas there was probably none at Qalʻeh Pol Gonbad-e Kavus. We may tentatively conclude that the former two campaign bases were intended to be maintained by a caretaker garrison stationed in their corner citadel and in probable accommodation within the wide walls. Qalʻeh Pol Gonbad-e Kavus, by contrast, was designed for a much larger temporary force, but not for a caretaker garrison. Perhaps presence and absence of permanent housing is more plausibly attributed to the massive difference in size between the bases, Qalʻeh Pol Gonbad-e Kavus being about three times larger than either of its smaller counterparts. It is also possible that a very specific event/crisis stimulated the construction of the mega-base of Qalʻeh Pol Gonbad-e Kavus (and perhaps also its identically sized counterpart at Torpakh Kala on the distant opposite shore of the Caspian Sea) whereas the bases of Gabri Qalʻeh and Qalʻeh Kharabeh, built probably before this mega-base, are part of earlier infrastructure specifically designed for the long term.

There is, as yet, not enough known about architectural development of campaign base design to establish a relative chronology of the undated campaign bases with confidence, nor are they all well enough preserved or documented to enable us to classify all of them into those with wide and narrow walls, those with narrowly and widely spaced gate towers and those with projecting and non-projecting gates. It is possible, however, that the change from wide gate tower spacing at Gabri Qalʻeh to narrow gate tower spacing at Qalʻeh Iraj, Qalʻeh Kharabeh and the Gorgan Wall forts reflects indeed a chronological evolution. Perhaps the development was as follows:

– First, in the fourth or early fifth century, campaign bases with widely spaced non-projecting gate towers were built in fertile lands. These include Gabri Qalʻeh and perhaps Qalʻeh Daland and Qalʻeh Gug A and some other campaign bases. (Qalʻeh Iraj, outside the Gorgan Plain, and with strongly projecting narrow gates, may have been built slightly later, probably in the early fifth century.)

– Second, probably in the fifth century, Qalʻeh Kharabeh (with similar monumental projecting gates as Qalʻeh Iraj,[174] but probably later radiocarbon dating) was built in marginal lands.

– Third, around the 420s–480s, the Gorgan Wall forts with their narrow gates (and likely later radiocarbon dating) were constructed.

– Fourth and last, probably in the sixth century, the massive fortress of Qalʻeh Pol Gonbad-e Kavus (with probably late Sasanian radiocarbon dating) was built.

It is interesting to note that campaign base GWS-92,[175] whilst also showing some of the typical features (empty interior, regularly spaced tower mounds (c. 36 m centre to centre) on the walls, a moat around the compound and a possible raised canal leading inside), lacks a corner citadel. We may observe that GWS-55 at an internal size of c. 63 ha (matching more or less the internal area of GWS-92) is the largest such site with a corner citadel (plus a second corner citadel and a central citadel) on the Gorgan Plain. The vast campaign base of Torpakh Kala, however, also boasts a prehistoric mound in its eastern corner that appears to have been reused as a corner citadel.[176] Similarly, the medium-size campaign base of Qalʻeh Gug A and the city of Dasht Qalʻeh reuse prehistoric mounds as corner citadels.[177] By contrast, the giant campaign bases of Qalʻeh Iraj and Qalʻeh Pol Gonbad-e Kavus lack citadels (and so does the large campaign base GWS-92). We may conclude that there is much variation amongst campaign bases, some of which have a corner and/or central citadel and some do not.[178] Thin walls and lack of a corner citadel may perhaps suggest that Qalʻeh Pol Gonbad-e Kavus was too large for permanent maintenance. This does not necessarily prove that all fortresses with citadels were designed for long-term use; where a prehistoric mound could easily be reoccupied as a corner bastion, it may well have been incorporated irrespective of whether the architects envisaged creating a fortification for single or long-term use.

Also significant is the post-Sasanian history of these large fortifications. There is nothing to suggest that Qalʻeh Pol Gonbad-e Kavus evolved into a town, but medieval finds and samples from deep in its moat, recut multiple times, suggest that the legacy of Sasanian military planning lasted much longer than the long-lived empire. The substantial efforts involved in recutting the massive moat must be related to temporary use as a safe retreat at the outskirts of the regional capital in the first centuries of the Islamic era. Gabri Qalʻeh, of smaller size than Qalʻeh Pol Gonbad-e Kavus and thus easier to reoccupy (and in more fertile land than Qalʻeh Kharabeh), evolved into a flourishing town, probably already in Sasanian times but in any case by the Islamic era. It may have been occupied for up to a millennium. The same is true for Sasanian foundations of likely military origins to the west of the Caspian Sea.[179] The Sasanian military in the north of the realm laid the foundations for urban growth that often lasted for many centuries or more beyond the end of the Sasanian era.

Notes

1. We are grateful to Dr Anthony Comfort for having drawn to our attention a CORONA image of a compound in northern Mesopotamia of approximately 210 ha interior dimensions that in our view is almost certainly a Sasanian campaign base and for his kind permission to refer to it. See Comfort 2021 and chapter 8.2.1 for further details.
2. Sauer et al. 2013, 303–81; Nemati et al. 2019/2020.
3. See chapters 2.2 Table 2.1, and 2.3.1.
4. See chapters 9 and 14.

5   See Sauer *et al.* 2013, 232 table 6:8.
6   See Sauer *et al.* 2013, 358–60, 367 table 12:7, 369–70; Wilkinson *et al.* 2013, 83, 89 fig. 3:70.
7   See chapters 8.3.1 and 8.5; cf. Sauer *et al.* 2013, 324, 364 table 12:6.
8   See Sauer *et al.* 2013, 364 table 12:6.
9   Sauer *et al.* 2013, 353–55; Wilkinson *et al.* 2013, 83, 86 fig. 3:67.
10 See chapters 2.2 Table 2.1, and 2.3.1.
11 See chapter 8.2.2.
12 Sauer *et al.* 2013, 364 table 12:6, 367 table 12:7; cf. chapter 2.2 with Table 2.1, and 2.3.1 with Fig. 2.3.A on GWS-92 with a perhaps 25 m wide moat; see also chapter 8.5.
13 Qal'eh Yasaqi is a further somewhat irregularly shaped campaign base. See Sauer *et al.* 2013, 367–69; Wilkinson *et al.* 2013, 87–88 figs 3:68–3:69, 121, 125.
14 See chapter 4.6.3 with references.
15 Sauer *et al.* 2013, 347–49, 370.
16 Sauer *et al.* 2013, 230–34, cf. 286–87.
17 Davies and Jones 2006, 39–45.
18 Gadjiev 2017b; Gadjiev and Magomedov 2008; Kazanski and Mastykova 2003, 99, 200–01; Lawrence and Wilkinson 2017, 110–11 with figs 5.5–5.6. The compound is very clearly visible on Google Earth imagery (Fig. 8.3). On its well-preserved west side there are 40 towers, including the corner towers. One gap is unusually wide and, allowing for a destroyed tower here, there would have been 41 towers, spaced on average 28.75 m apart. The spacing and semi-circular plan is typical for Sasanian installations. The size, c. 125 ha, is similar to that of Qal'eh Pol Gonbad-e Kavus too.
19 See chapter 9 and Nemati *et al.* 2019/2020; cf. Sauer *et al.* 2013, 372; Kleiss 1989; 1990; 2015, 119–20.
20 The location of gates at other sides is difficult to identify.
21 We are grateful to Dr Anthony Comfort for having drawn a satellite image of this important site, as well as its earlier exploration by Sir Aurel Stein (Gregory and Kennedy 1985a, 30–31), to our attention. Stein (Gregory and Kennedy 1985a, 30) also refers to a mound some 30 feet high towards the compound's north-west corner. One wonders if this might be a corner citadel, but there are no clear traces of such a citadel on the CORONA image. Several other Sasanian campaign bases (notably Qal'eh Daland, Qal'eh Iraj, Qal'eh Pol Gonbad-e Kavus and GWS-92), of course, also lack known citadels. There is, however, an irregular mounded area, as also observed by Sconzo *et al.* 2021, 167–68 with fig. 12B. See Comfort 2021 for further details.
22 See chapter 24.2 for a discussion of the Hatra and Dura-Europos camps and further references. See also Sauer *et al.* 2017, 250–51, 257, with references; cf. Edwell 2013, 843.
23 This heavily fortified compound was built in what was not normally a border zone. Its well-built massive fortifications render it unlikely that was erected in response to potential temporary internal security problems or a civil war. In the Roman Empire permanent military bases in the interior were as heavily fortified as those on the Empire's frontiers, but temporary marching camps, with archaeologically detectable defences, appear to have been erected only in enemy territory or insecure border zones (and normally only, it seems, up to the third century AD).
24 See chapter 9 and Nemati *et al.* 2019/2020.
25 Gadjiev and Magomedov 2008, especially 284, 297 fig. 11.7.
26 See chapter 18.5 with references.
27 A number of the sites compiled by Kleiss (1989, 301, 303–04, 306–07) are likely to belong to this category. See also Canepa 2018a, 127 fig. 6.2 for a large square enclosure of campaign-base dimensions (maybe 600 m across to judge by the plan) some 8 km south of Gur/Ardashir Khurrah. Not all such enclosures need have served a military function (Canepa 2018a, 362–63 with fig. 17.4).
28 Kleiss 1988; 1989, 301, 306 fig. 20; 1969, 9–10, pl. 2.1; cf. Minorsky 1964, 97, 103–05.
29 Without a site visit, it is hard to be certain, but satellite imagery implies that a stream course may have led to the less geometric shape of the compound in the south-west.
30 Kleiss 1988, 212–13.
31 Kleiss 1988, especially 217; 1990, 327–28.
32 Elishe 105 = trans. Thomson 1982, 157.
33 Thomson 1982, 22–29.
34 Hewsen 2001, 87–88.
35 See Sauer *et al.* 2013, 371 with references. An important new fieldwork project at Viranshar, under the direction of Meysam Labbaf-Khaniki and Rocco Rante, is in progress.
36 Kleiss 1976a, 127–28; 1989, 303–04, 306 fig. 20.
37 This raised water supply canal led into the compound from the north-west. Still prominently visible on the CORONA satellite imagery of the late 1960s, virtually all of this has been erased by modern development since. Hamid Omrani Rekavandi and Kristen Hopper succeeded in tracing a possible surviving section of the water supply canal under a modern brick wall. Behind the wall a shallow bank may survive. We cleaned a section through the putative raised canal at Qal'eh Pol Gonbad-e Kavus over 22.80 m. The results were ambiguous at best, and it seems that no well-preserved section of the canal survives. The left end of our section was at UTM 40S E 337107, N 4120621; the right end of our section was at 40S E 337085, N 4120616. A possible cut was observed to run from c. 3.10–17.30 m W. A clayey iron-stained deposit, c. 10 cm thick, with its base c. 1.23–1.33 m below the surface, was observed from 5.20–7.50 m W. This might be the canal bottom. Charcoal is visible in the section underneath, perhaps part of the raised bank. Its ephemeral nature may suggest that it was in use for a short time only. We cannot be sure whether this was at the start of occupation or later, but the frequent association of raised canals with Sasanian compounds renders it more likely that the canal is original. There were also sand lenses at its edge. The highest elevation of the shallow bank is currently from c. 5–15 m W, but its edge in the W is particularly unclear, obscured by recent activity. The apex of the bank and the centre of the putative bottom fill of the canal do not coincide, but this does not necessarily disprove the hypothesis that the iron-stained deposit is the fill of a raised canal. There were, however, pieces of charcoal beneath the canal bottom, as well as an undiagnostic piece of glass. Whilst the former is easy to explain, e.g. via burning vegetation prior to causeway construction, the presence of a piece of glass some 10 cm below the clayey water-stained fill is hard to reconcile with hypothesis of a raised canal on a virgin site. See also chapter 2.6 on this canal.

38 Information supplied by an old man, visiting the excavations on 11 November 2014.
39 Sauer *et al.* 2013, 358–60.
40 See chapter 8.2.16.
41 There is, however, a degree of variation: some of Torpakh Kala's gates are distinctly off-centre: Gadjiev 2017b, fig. 2; Gadjiev and Magomedov 2008, fig. 1.
42 Canals, however, can also have very steep sides: Graadt van Roggen 1905, 194 fig. 480, 196 fig. 481 (note that these profiles are drawn at different height and width scales, but even when this is taken into account, they are still very steep).
43 It is visible on CORONA and Google Earth (Figs 8.1–8.2). We are grateful to Andrea Ricci for his observations on this canal.
44 This trench was located at UTM 40S E 0337914, N 4120295 and a large fragment of a Sasanian-type fired brick lying nearby suggests that such brick was also used or reused in this section of the bank.
45 At UTM 40S E 0337664, N 4120910.
46 Carried out by Mohammad Arman Ershadi, Julian Jansen Van Rensburg and Mohammad Taghi Maleka. Results processed by Roger Ainslie, Mohammad Arman Ershadi and Julian Jansen Van Rensburg.
47 See chapter 2.6 with Figs 2.16 and 2.18; Fig. 8.1.
48 Sauer *et al.* 2013, 312–18, 341–46. See also Hopper and Omrani Rekavandi 2020, 103–06 on modern yurts in the area.
49 Modern debris and features may account for the lack of success of our survey of nearby Qal'eh Gug A: Sauer *et al.* 2013, 355–58.
50 Excavations were directed by Jebrael Nokandeh, Hamid Omrani Rekavandi and Eberhard Sauer. The trench was co-supervised by Marc Heise and Majid Mahmoudi, with the help of Baygeldi Arteghi and a team of dedicated workmen, with Jebrael Nokandeh, Hamid Omrani Rekavandi, Mohammad Reza and Eberhard Sauer very often taking part as well. Drawing and trench documentation were accomplished by Marc Heise, Aliyeh Amirinezhad, Zahra Asghari and Eberhard Sauer. The drawings, definition of context boundaries and interpretation is very much a joint effort of all. Our workmen did a wonderful job in cleaning sections and numerous other tasks.
51 The corner points of the ditch section were as follows: W (10.50 m NW/ 15 m NE): 49 mt UTM 40S E 338016, N 4120646; N (10.50 m NW/ 45 m NE): 51 mt UTM 40S E 338038, N 4120668; E (0 m NW/ 45 m NE): 51 mt UTM 40S E 338044, N 4120661; S (0 m NW/ 15 m NE): 49 mt 40S E 338024, N 4120639.
52 Deposits of very soft mid-brownish yellow clayey silt (a.060), yielding half a Sasanian brick (a.060/22), and firm mid-brownish clayey silt (a.114) with some brick fragments are intriguing, but hard to interpret. Their boundaries are diffuse and their significance uncertain, as are those of other relevant deposits (a.120, a.121, a.125, a.126 and a.127). They may form part of the fill of the postulated early ditches on the opposite profile and there may be later cuts. Tree roots may have obscured context boundaries here. Root or animal disturbance could easily have had different effects on the two opposite profiles.

53 The cut was observed from 20.80 m NE at c. 45.59 m height (the level of the water table on 23 November 2014). As elsewhere, height was established via a benchmark and corresponds to heights in the topographical survey, corresponding or close to the height above sea level. The cut was visible as the ditch fill, consisting of clay, was not affected by side erosion of water infiltrating through the section, whilst the natural deposits it was cut into differed in their physical properties and were washed out of the profile where under the water table. It is worth noting, however, that this only applied to this particular deposit in the ditch fill, whilst other (less clayey) deposits in the ditch fill were also affected by erosion through groundwater infiltration. It likely, but not certain, that the cut in step 4 was part of Ditch 1.
54 See chapter 8.2.14.
55 The sixth ditch, cut from beneath the topsoil in step 1, extended at this level to 40.95–41.65 m NE.
56 Assessment of brick chronology by Hamid Omrani Rekavandi.
57 See chapters 8.2.16 and 21.4 below.
58 The water table in Trench a, before first pumped out in the morning of 3 December 2014, was at 45.54 m; on 23 November it had been 5 cm higher, at 45.59 m.
59 Nokandeh *et al.* 2006, 143 with fig. 22; Sauer *et al.* 2013, 166–67 with fig. 5:15.
60 See chapters 8.2.16 and 21.4.
61 In what phase brick a.060/22 (see Table 8.2) had originally been used or lost is uncertain.
62 See chapters 8.2.16 and 22.
63 See chapters 8.2.16 and 20.3.4. Bones were identified by Antoine Ruchonnet. Based on his analysis, the minimum number of individuals is one, but there is no certainty that the bones all belong to the same animal. There was probably one ovine/caprine individual, most probably a sheep, and the identifiable fragments were from a humerus, a tibia and the os coxae. It was not possible to confirm the sex of the animal, nor to prove that all the fragments were from the same individual. Taphonomy suggests, however, that it may well be one individual.
64 We only observed a single bone in the spoil, despite continuously watching the JCB during excavation of the trench.
65 See chapter 8.2.16.
66 See chapter 8.2.16.
67 See chapter 21.2 Table 21.3.
68 See chapter 8.2.16.
69 The team excavating the wall was led by Majid Mahmoudi.
70 The greenish hue suggests perhaps that it contained material from already waterlogged levels of the ditch.
71 See chapters 4.1.3 and 4.1.4.2.2 and Sauer *et al.* 2013, 188–89 figs 6:12, 6:14–6:15, 322, 380 no. 335, 611; cf. Gadjiev 2017a.
72 That the wall does not bulge out at this point suggests that the sloping deposits do not form part of a ramp. It is possible that there were ramps on the defenders' side to facilitate access to the wall-walk, but no remains of any have been found.
73 A.107, very soft mid-greenish brown silty clay, a.108, very soft mid-yellowish brown clay, a.109, soft light yellowish brown silty clay and a.110, soft mid-yellowish brown clay.
74 See chapter 4.1.

75 See chapter 8.3.1.
76 See chapter 9 and Nemati *et al.* 2019/2020.
77 Sauer *et al.* 2013, 166 fig. 5:15, cf. 163–73.
78 See chapter 9 and Nemati *et al.* 2019/2020.
79 Jewell 1963, 50–58, pl. VIII; cf. Sauer 2005, 19, 21. See Gutjahr and Steigberger 2018, 457 (based on a 1907 mining manual inaccessible to us) for estimates of considerably faster progress in earth-moving operations, though perhaps using more modern tools.
80 Seeher 2007, 221. Note that there is a mistake, and the figures refer to 140 workers requiring 4 months (c. 121 days) to build 65 m of wall (not 56 m), i.e. c. 2,154 workers would have been able to build 1 km of wall within the same time.
81 Model based on Mofidi-Nasrabadi 2013, 326–27; multiplier based on 327 table 92.
82 We owe this observation and the modern ethnographic parallels to Hamid Omrani Rekavandi.
83 Radiocarbon dates kindly supplied by the Scottish Universities Environmental Research Centre (SUERC) and the Poznan Radiocarbon Laboratory. A further sample was submitted but proved undatable: *Xeropicta* sp., identified by Dr Catriona Pickard, from a.077, sample number 111. Bones were identified by Antoine Ruchonnet (see chapter 20.3.4), charcoal, by Dr Lyudmila Shumilovskikh (see chapter 21.1), molluscs, by Dr Catriona Pickard (see chapter 21.4). For the archaeomagnetic sample, see chapter 22. For the OSL sample, see chapter 23.
84 Bones were also absent from the lowest layers of the canal at Fort 9, and it was once suggested to us by a member of the audience at a lecture on the Gorgan Wall that religious reasons may have played a part: Sauer *et al.* 2013, 170–71; cf. Herodotus 1.138; Skjærvø 2013, 561. See also chapters 4.1.4.4.3.1, 9.2.2.1 and 18.2 with references.
85 See Table 8.4.
86 We are grateful to Professor Gordon Cook for having drawn our attention to this phenomenon, which provides perhaps the most plausible explanation for the unexpectedly early age, even if the age of small shells from loess can sometimes be remarkably reliable: Újvári *et al.* 2014.
87 Lyudmila Shumilovskikh, pers. comm. 10 February 2018.
88 Schmidt 1940, pl. 64. See also chapter 7.1 with Fig. 7.1. Spotted by EWS, who is grateful to Kristen Hopper for her advice on the compound's location.
89 Cf. Sauer *et al.* 2013, 365–71.
90 Bosworth 2003.
91 Kradin *et al.* 2014.
92 See chapters 24.3 and 24.9.
93 See chapter 15.4.4.
94 See chapter 23.
95 See chapters 8.2.11 and 20.3.4.
96 Bosworth 2003, 154 and Petrushevsky 1968, 488 with sources.
97 See chapter 8.3.3.
98 See also chapters 8.2 and 8.4 and Sauer *et al.* 2013, 312–53, 358–60 and 364–68 on these compounds and their chronology.
99 Sauer *et al.* 2013, 353–58.
100 This corresponds roughly to land surface west of the moat and seems a reasonable estimate. The volume would increase to c. 221 m³ if the land surface at this point had been at 78.50 m. The land surface within the Qal'eh provides no reliable clues as there may be substantial occupation horizons.
101 See chapter 8.2.14 with Table 8.3.
102 Counted by Eberhard W. Sauer, Hamid Omrani Rekavandi and Marc Heise in 2014 and by Eberhard W. Sauer, Hamid Omrani Rekavandi, Davit Naskidashvili and Richard Bates in 2015.
103 Sauer *et al.* 2013, 184, 230, 324, 358; Priestman *et al.* forthcoming 2022; cf. chapter 4.1.2.1. See also Gardin 1995, 87–88 with fig. 4, 104–05 Table 1 (cf. Gardin in Ball 1982a, 137–38 no. 487; 1982b, 451 fig. 35.2, 502 fig. 85 no. 487; Ball 2019a, 188–89 no. 487) for the rectangular fortification of Kafir Qal'a with projecting tower mounds spaced 30 m apart. See chapter 8.5 and Table 8.7 on tower spacing at campaign bases. See chapters 4.1.2.1 and 4.1.4.2.3 for further discussion.
104 Sauer *et al.* 2013, 364 table 12:6.
105 Sauer *et al.* 2013, 184, 318–24, 681 pl. 6:4.
106 Sauer *et al.* 2013, 354 fig. 12:37, 356 fig. 12:40.
107 See chapter 8.4.3.
108 Information by Emanuele Intagliata; see also Hopper *et al.* 2022.
109 Kindly provided by Dr Kiersten Neumann, Susan Allison and Thomas Urban (of the Oriental Institute of the University of Chicago).
110 See chapter 8.3.4.
111 Sauer *et al.* 2013, 637–38, cf. 309, 368, 372.
112 See chapter 9 and Nemati *et al.* 2019/2020; see also Rezaei Nia 2014 for an identically named site of pre-Islamic origins at Sapol-e Zahab.
113 Sauer *et al.* 2013, 364–68.
114 See chapter 2.2 and Hopper *et al.* 2022 (kind information by Emanuele Intagliata and Kristen Hopper).
115 Carried out by Mohammad Arman Ershadi, Julian Jansen Van Rensburg and Mohammad Taghi Maleka. Results processed by Roger Ainslie, Mohammad Arman Ershadi and Julian Jansen Van Rensburg.
116 From UTM 40S E 0349930–0349990, N 4126310–4126730.
117 Excavated under the supervision of Mohammad Mehdi Borhani, Davit Naskidashvili and David Gagoshidze.
118 Sauer *et al.* 2013, 312–18, 322–25, 330–41.
119 Eminli 2020, 284, 296 fig. 19; Nuriev 2020, 258, 268 figs 7–8.
120 See chapter 21.2.3.4.
121 Radiocarbon dates kindly supplied by the Scottish Universities Environmental Research Centre (SUERC). Bones were identified by Homa Fathi. See also chapter 20.3.3.
122 A rectangular post void (e.002) from 9.735–9.865 m east and 2.51–2.60 m N, surviving to 55 cm depth from 36–91 cm below the surface has not been plotted, as we cannot tell whether it is of medieval or modern date.
123 See chapter 15.4.5; pottery first identified by Hamid Omrani Rekavandi.
124 See chapter 18.7.
125 See chapter 20.6.
126 See chapter 20.5.
127 Ball 2021, 271–75; Leriche 2018, 146; Mantellini 2017, 335, 337, 339 fig. 4, 341; Kennedy 2008, 93; Sauer *et al.* 2013, 601, 619. See also Tolstov 1953, 332.

128 Sauer *et al.* 2013, 601, cf. 152, 619 with further references.
129 Kolbas 2006, *passim*.
130 Fazlinejad and Ahmadi 2018, especially 66–67.
131 Le Strange 1905, 370–73, 375–76; Petrushevsky 1968, 488; Roemer 1986, 62.
132 Excavated under the supervision of Mohammad Mehdi Borhani, Davit Naskidashvili and David Gagoshidze.
133 See chapter 18.7; the coin was attributed to deposit f.002, but to judge by the 3D, may perhaps be from f.003.
134 See chapter 18.5.
135 See chapter 18.7; the piece was found 3.05 m below the crest of the bank, but only 2.23 m below the surface of the bank above.
136 See chapter 15.4.5.
137 F.004/25, found 7.15 m NE, 0.40 m NW and 76.97 m a.s.l., 1.85 m below the crest of the bank, but only 1.47 m below the surface of the bank above.
138 See chapter 4.1.4.3.
139 See chapter 21.2.3.5.
140 Sauer *et al.* 2013, 313–17, 330–34.
141 Sauer *et al.* 2013, 314 fig. 12:10, 316–17 with fig. 12:13, cf. 351; see also 354–55 with fig. 12:37 for a possible causeway at Qal'eh Daland.
142 See chapter 10 with Figs 10.2, 10.4 and 10.14; Sauer *et al.* 2013, 383 fig. 13:1, 386–88, 399 with fig. 13:18.
143 A survey with a handheld GPS suggests that there may be a difference of c. 10 m between the current stream bed and the highest point in Trench f, but this is only an approximate figure. We also saw an ancient fired brick of 50 cm diameter at the edge of the stream, larger than the typical Gorgan Wall bricks.
144 See also chapter 2.6.
145 Radiocarbon dates kindly supplied by the Scottish Universities Environmental Research Centre (SUERC). Bones were identified by Homa Fathi. See also chapter 20.3.3.
146 It is also worth noting that, according to Homa Fathi's examination, pig bones are strongly represented in the lower levels of Trench f, further circumstantial evidence for the construction of the causeway into Gabri Qal'eh in the pre-Islamic era. See chapter 20.3.3 for details.
147 See chapter 24.3 and Sauer *et al.* 2013, 372–74 with references.
148 See Sauer *et al.* 2013, 349–53.
149 See chapter 8.4 and Sauer *et al.* 2013, 312–53.
150 Surface pottery from Gabri Qal'eh was dominated by Islamic material of around the tenth to fifteenth centuries (but these dates are, of course, approximate only). There were also a few indicators of possible early/mid-Sasanian material (kind information by Kristen Hopper and Emanule Intagliata; see also chapter 2.2 Table 2.1 and Hopper *et al.* 2022).
151 Sauer *et al.* 2013, 312–53, especially 342; Priestman 2013, 506–11.
152 Sauer *et al.* 2013, 366 fig. 12:52, 368.
153 Sauer *et al.* 2013, 314–15 with fig. 12:11, 334–41.
154 Sauer *et al.* 2013, 373, 392; on Islamic Anjar whose plan resembles a Sasanian campaign base see now also Chéhab 2018.
155 Alizadeh 2011; 2014; Alizadeh *et al.* 2021; Lawrence and Wilkinson 2017, 114–16 with fig. 5.9; Mammadova and Mammadova 2013, 14–18 with fig. 6, cf. 27–28 with fig. 10 on Ardabil; Mongait 1959, 254, 256; Morony 2013, 982–83; Sauer 2017a, 3; Sauer *et al.* 2017, 257–58 with fig. 11.8; Ur and Alizadeh 2013. Previous fieldwork points to Sasanian origins. We are grateful to Dr Andrea Ricci and Professor Barbara Helwing for having alerted us to Ören Qala, a square compound of similar size to the campaign bases in the Gorgan Plain with a large corner citadel, and having enabled EWS to visit it on 20–23 August 2012.
156 Rante and Collinet 2013, especially 53, 204; cf. Bosworth 2010; Mousavi 2009, 113–15; Rante 2016.
157 Gerster 2008, 70–71.
158 On Kafyr-Kala, see Baimatowa 2008, 298–307 and Kurbanov 2013, 52–53 with fig. 15; on Kafir Qal'a, see Ball 2019a, 188–89 no. 487; Gardin in Ball 1982a, 137–38 no. 487; 1982b, 451 fig. 35.2, 502 fig. 85 no. 487; Gardin 1995, 87–88 with fig. 4, 104–05 Table 1; Google Earth imagery (centred on 37°03'13" N, 69°10'08" E). See also Ball 2019a, 304–05 no. 892 on the large rectangular (c. 1,800 × 900 m) not precisely dated town of Qal'a-i Zal, whose outer walls and corner citadel both boast regularly spaced projecting towers.
159 See chapters 10.5 and 24.9 for further discussion of Sasanian and late Roman urban foundations.
160 Carried out by Mohammad Arman Ershadi and Mohammad Taghi Maleka. Results processed by Mohammad Arman Ershadi and Roger Ainslie.
161 Sauer *et al.* 2013, 303–53.
162 Recalibrated in 2020 using the OxCal programme. See Sauer *et al.* 2013, 349–53 for the original data and discussion.
163 All three were surveyed by the landscape team (see chapters 2.2, with Table 2.1, and 2.3.1), and the former sites were also visited by Jebrael Nokandeh, Bardia Shabani, Mashalah Rahmani and Eberhard Sauer on 13 January 2013. At GWS-61 (cf. Wilkinson *et al.* 2013, 92, 97 fig. 3:77, 128; Sauer *et al.* 2013, 305 fig. 12:2, 367 table 12:7, 370), the central tappeh is still a dominant feature, even if somewhat widened by ploughing. There is much pottery on this tappeh as well as some brick, most probably medieval, but some sherds and one thick brick fragment could be Sasanian and there might be potentially Parthian material as well (identification by Jebrael Nokandeh). The moat around the tappeh is also still partially preserved and was water-filled. Nothing obvious was visible of the larger enclosure wall. There was virtually no pottery on the surface outside the tappeh from within the larger enclosure – a characteristic GWS-61 has in common with other campaign bases, should it belong to this category of site. The GWS-55 (cf. Wilkinson *et al.* 2013, 83, 88 fig. 3:69, 125; Sauer *et al.* 2013, 305 fig. 12:2, 367 table 12:7, 369–70 with fig. 12:54) enclosure was largely destroyed, and we could not detect any remains of its outer walls in the south or east, nor of the SE and NW corner citadels. There were traces of what is probably the westernmost section of the compound's north wall. Near the central citadel, by contrast, mounding is still clearly visible, as is the surrounding moat, even if flattened by ploughing. Based on re-examination of the site by the landscape team, part of the mound may have been flattened and material spread westwards. There is a fairly high concentration of

8. Campaign bases

pottery (including unidentified red ware) on the central mounding. There was no pottery in the compound away from the centre, which might support the interpretation of GWS-55 as another geometric complex with transient occupation, quite possibly a campaign base.

164 See chapters 2.2 Table 2.1, 2.3.1 and 2.7.
165 Priestman *et al.* 2013, 521–24; Sauer *et al.* 2013, 357, 400.
166 See chapters 2.2 Table 2.1, and 2.3.1.
167 Sauer *et al.* 2013, 341–46.
168 See chapters 2.2 Table 2.1, and 2.3.1.
169 See Sauer *et al.* 2013, 347–49, 365–71.
170 See chapter 8.2.1 with references.
171 See chapter 9 and Nemati *et al.* 2019/2020, 197.
172 As the database of well-explored campaign bases grows, it may also be worth exploring whether there is any chronological development in gate number (three versus four) and location (perfectly central versus slightly off-centre). A larger database is required to see whether there are patterns, notably as due to poor preservation and/or potential later gate blockage, we cannot always be sure how many gates there were originally.
173 Naumann 1977, 34–38 with fig. 17, suppl. plan 2.
174 The zigzag alignment of the gateways at Qal'eh Iraj may also potentially be paralleled at Qal'eh Kharabeh: see chapter 9.2.2.1 and Sauer *et al.* 2013, 320.
175 See chapter 2.2 Table 2.1, and 2.3.1.
176 Gadjiev 2017b; Gadjiev and Magomedov 2008.
177 Sauer *et al.* 2013, 355–58, 382–406; cf. chapter 10.
178 See Sauer *et al.* 2013, 361–74 for parallels; cf. chapter 9 and Nemati *et al.* 2019/2020.
179 See chapter 24.9 and Sauer 2017a, 3. See also Gadjiev's (2017b; 2020, 112–14; Gadjiev and Magomedov 2008) important work at Torpakh Kala and his hypothesis that the site was a Sasanian urban foundation lasting into post-Sasanian times, though it seems likely to us that it was originally designed as a military fortification.

9

Qal'eh Iraj: a campaign base/command centre of the army's northern division?

Mahdi Mousavinia, Mohammadreza Nemati and Eberhard W. Sauer[1]

9.1. Introduction

Excluding fortified cities that housed sizeable civilian populations (and not mainly military personnel), the temporary siege camp at Hatra[2] and thinly occupied hillforts/mountain refuges, Qal'eh Iraj is the second-largest ancient fortress known to us in the south-west of Asia and the Western world as a whole. The only larger ancient non-urban fortress we are aware of is a probable Sasanian campaign base of c. 210 ha size in north-western Mesopotamia.[3] Enclosing an area of 175 ha, not counting its massive walls, Qal'eh Iraj (also known as Qal'eh Gabri) has attracted the interest of scholars since the 1860s. As the history of research has been presented in detail elsewhere,[4] there is no need for a repetition here. Worth noting in particular are the observations of Jane and Marcel-Auguste Dieulafoy, who visited the ruins in 1881 and concluded that it was of Sasanian origins and part of a system of defensive installations against invasions from Khorasan.[5] Other scholars preferred an interpretation as an urban site or royal hunting grounds and advocated a

Fig. 9.1: Drone image of Qal'eh Iraj by Davit Naskidashvili and the joint project.

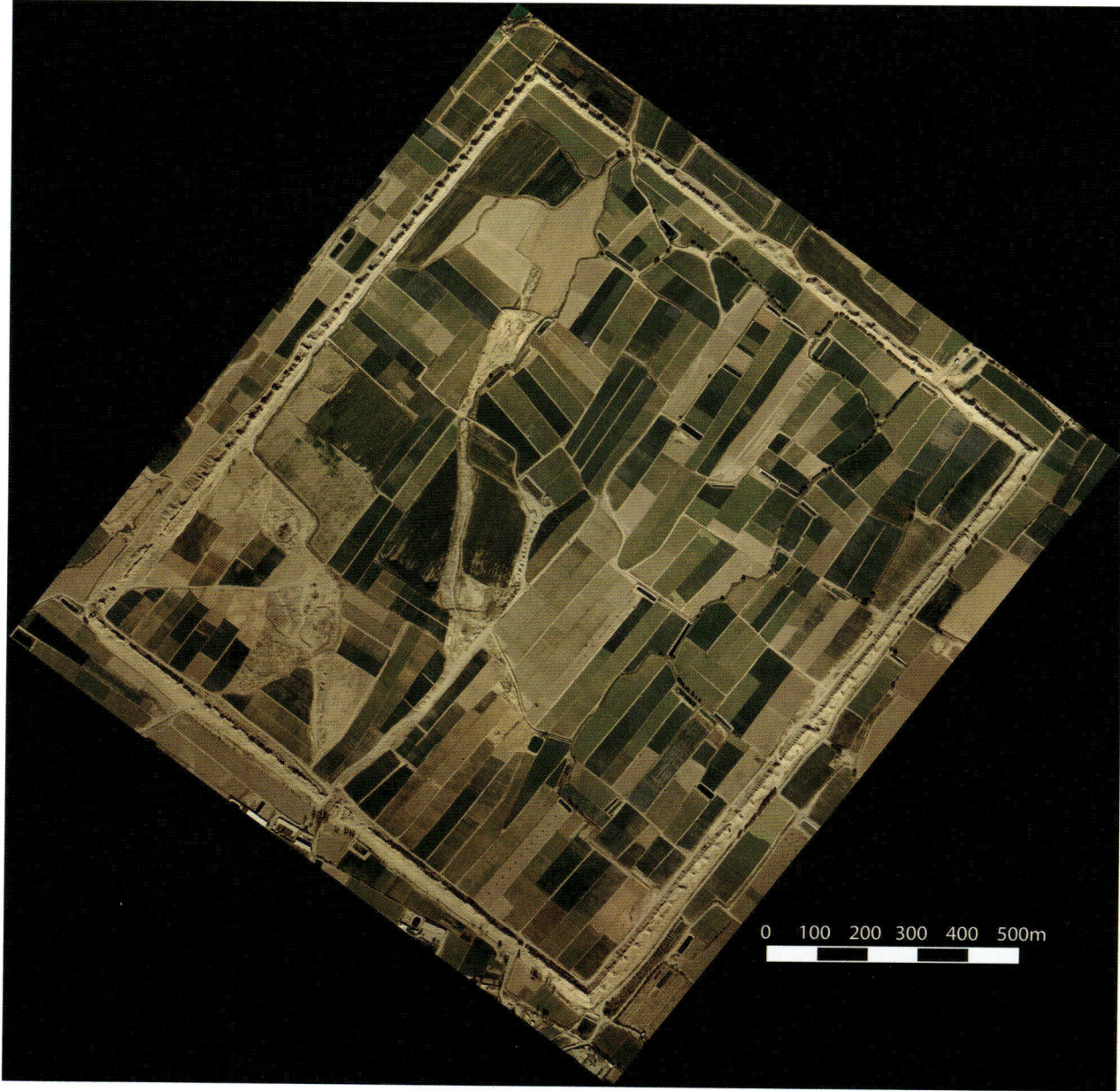

Fig. 9.2: Rectified composite drone image of Qal'eh Iraj by Eve MacDonald, Davit Naskidashvili and the joint project.

wide range of dating proposals, ranging from unspecified very ancient or Parthian to Islamic origins. Despite its extraordinary dimensions and obvious significance, there has been little fieldwork. Recent excavations and surveys by Dr Mohammadreza Nemati and Dr Mahdi Mousavinia have demonstrated that it was Sasanian.[6] Architectural parallels with Sasanian campaign bases led us to propose Sasanian origins too in the previous *Persia* report.[7]

Qal'eh Iraj is located some 45 km south-east of the centre of Tehran and 2 km north-east of the northern outskirts of Varamin, near Askar Abad village in the district of Pishva (Endpapers, back). Our surveys and sondages have failed to yield evidence for housing, urban amenities or any extensive permanent structures in the interior, except for a small area of mounding.[8] Scarcity or absence of interior buildings and the massive defences suggest that it was a military base.[9] It is of largely rectangular shape, measuring 1,278–1,285 m in width and 1,455–1,460 m in length, including its 22 m wide walls (reduced to 15 m width in the upper sections). In places, these survive to a height of up to 15 m. The fortress boasts four projecting gates, 148 towers and an estimated 828 rooms embedded in the massive walls.

It was not until 2006 that Dr Mohammadreza Nemati embarked upon the first systematic archaeological excavations at Qal'eh Iraj. So far, he has conducted six

Fig. 9.3: Google Earth image of Qal'eh Iraj of 18 October 2012, showing prominently the towered walls of the vast fortress (Image © Maxar Technologies).

seasons of excavations at the site. In spring 2006 he carried out excavations at the south-east gate, where he accomplished further work in autumn 2008, in summer 2012 and autumn 2015. Summer and autumn 2016 saw a further season of fieldwork. It involved geophysical survey and the excavation of sondages within the south-east gate, work carried out in part within the framework of the joint project. In the so far final season of excavations in autumn 2017, Dr Nemati's excavations focused on the southern parts of the fortification. Some of the earlier work has already been presented in some detail, but no more than a brief summary has as yet been published on our work in 2016 and on the ostraca and clay seals found in Dr Nemati's excavations; fieldwork in 2017 came too late for inclusion in previous reports, except for a plan showing some of the key results.[10] The reader is referred to these publications[11] for detailed discussion of earlier work. Here we will focus on the most recent fieldwork in 2016 and 2017, as well as on other important new insights, and discuss how they contribute to our understanding of the site as a whole.

9.2. Excavations within the south-eastern gate

9.2.1. The first field seasons

Of particular significance were excavations within the south-east gate, the best-preserved of the fortress's four gates, where a unique assemblage of Sasanian bullae and ostraca came to light.[12] These excavations are also of particular interest in the context of this report, as the two sondages (Trenches h and i) excavated by the joint project were also both within the gate area. These sondages, located based on Dr Nemati's advice, have yielded a series of samples that have provided absolute dates for structures and deposits within the gate area.

The excavations from 2006 onwards contributed much to our understanding of the architecture of this massive projecting gate. They succeeded in defining the precise dimensions and location of the towers, the gateway, a side chamber and the stairs that provided access, via corridors, to the towers and the rooms within the defensive walls. Excavations of the gateway yielded a particularly exciting discovery: a series of inscribed potsherds. These ostraca were found scattered widely within the gate area, and the approximate extent of their distribution is indicated in shading on the plan (Fig. 9.4). They were found in two successive layers: about half of them lay on a surface of silt and clay. The remainder were embedded in a deposit below, consisting of gravel, sand, pebbles and cobble stones, evidently a paved surface. The latter had either been brought here with material to pave parts of the heavily used gateway and raise the surface, or they may have been lost in the gaps between paving stones; the former appear to have been scattered across the area subsequently, perhaps having been stored nearby before. Interestingly, there thus may be two phases, or a longer period, of deposition. These were the highest undisturbed layers to survive in the gateway; deposits above had been damaged by machinery prior to the start of Dr Nemati's excavations.

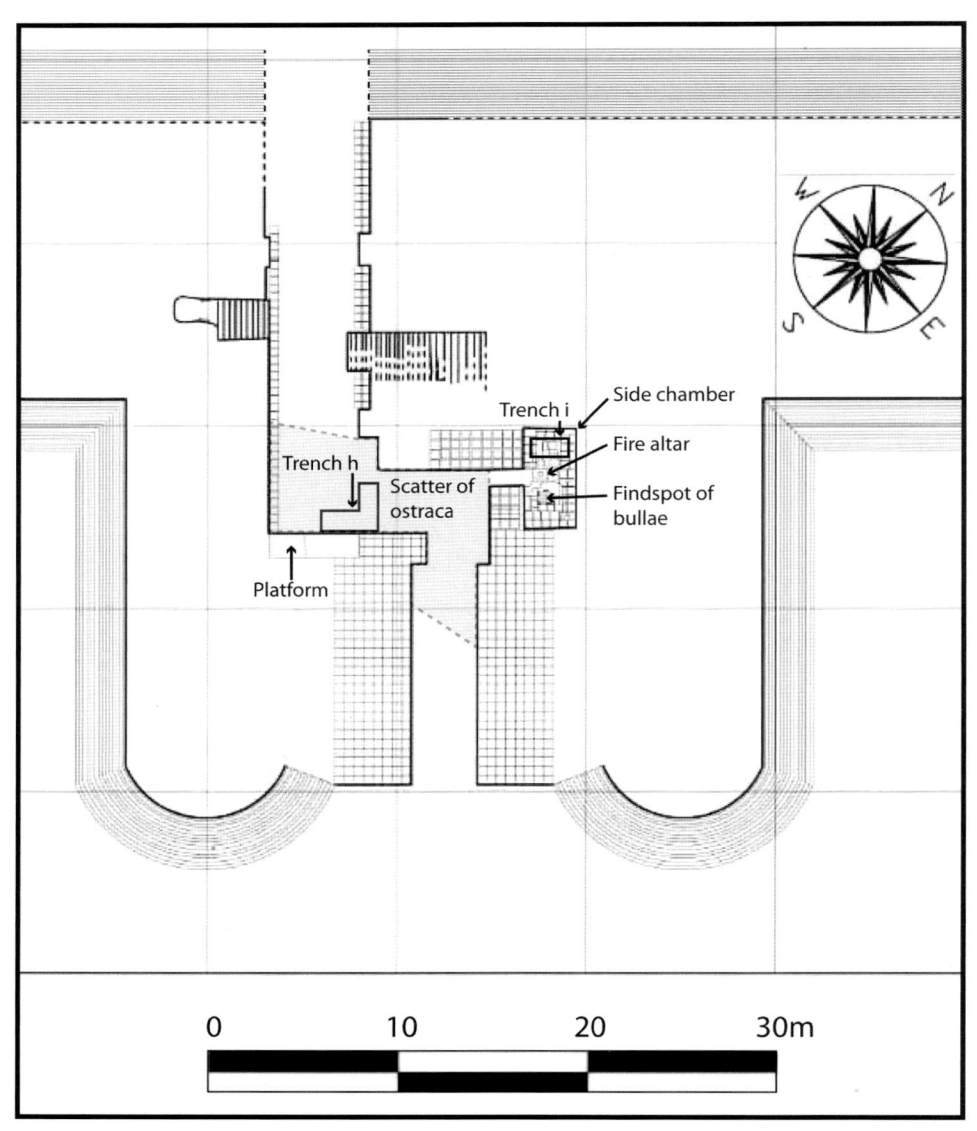

Fig. 9.4: The south-east gate, with the location of the ostraca and bullae and the 2016 Trenches h and i, plotted onto a plan by Dr Mohammadreza Nemati.

The bullae by contrast were found in the side chamber to the right of its entrance. The joint project subsequently excavated Trench i within the same side chamber, to the left of the entrance. Unlike the ostraca, there is nothing to suggest that the bullae (four in total, two of them identifiable)[13] had been discarded, and they certainly were found concentrated in one area and not widely scattered. Their location is marked on the plan, and they were found at an equivalent depth to deposit i.005. It is likely that they date to a similar time as the samples from i.005 and from i.008 underneath. These yielded dates of c. AD 442–564 and AD 440–592 respectively, the latter and lower sample dating with an over 80% probability to the AD 530s–590s (Table 9.2). The likely *terminus post quem* of c. AD 532 for this sample from i.008 arguably applies to all levels above. If a mid- to late sixth-century date for the context seems most likely, we cannot exclude an even later date, as we need to bear in mind that:

- The samples might be redeposited and other material from i.005 might be later.

- The bullae were found on the opposite side of the later fire altar. Whilst it seems highly probable that surface levels across the small chamber were similar at any date and the absolute dating for i.005 therefore applies to this level across the chamber, the case is not proven.

If a slightly later date is possible, the bullae must be Sasanian, as there is no evidence whatever for occupation continuing into the Islamic era.

Fig. 9.5: Excavation within the massive gate in progress (drone image by Davit Naskidashvili and the joint project). The excavators provide an idea of the scale of this monumental gate.

The fire altar, with traces of ash on top, in the side chamber may signal that the room served a religious function,[14] but not necessarily continuously or exclusively so. Its location next to the gateway made it an obvious place for a guard chamber, and it is possible that the room served both religious and secular functions. Excavations within the gate also led to the discovery of two burials. One of these is currently being examined and will be published separately in due course.

9.2.2. Dating the fortress: excavations within the south-eastern gateway in 2016

Whilst Dr Nemati's and Dr Mousavinia's research had already established that the vast fortress was almost certainly built, and certainly occupied, in the Sasanian era, contrary to earlier dating proposals to Parthian and Islamic times,[15] it seemed essential to scientifically verify and refine this dating proposal; a fortification of this magnitude at one of the major crossroads of Persia was likely to have played a pivotal role in the Sasanian defensive network, if we were correct in advocating Sasanian origins. The ERC Persia project had therefore hoped for some years that an opportunity would arise for joint explorations and was very grateful when permission was granted in 2016. The lack of firm evidence for permanent buildings in the interior, contemporary to the defences, meant that the walls, notably the gates, were our best bet for retrieving stratified material of the time of the fortress's occupation. The cited earlier excavations by Dr Nemati within the south-east gate had of course already unearthed Sasanian-era occupation layers as well as bullae and ostraca of the time. Based on his advice, two sondages were excavated within this gateway: Trench h in the passageway and Trench i in the side chamber to the north-west of the central fire altar.

9.2.2.1. Excavations in the gateway (Trench h)

Trench h covered an area of 4.8 m², centrally within the gateway (Figs 9.4–9.13).[16] Anybody entering the fortress via this gate would have had to pass this spot. The zigzag passageway was no doubt designed to make

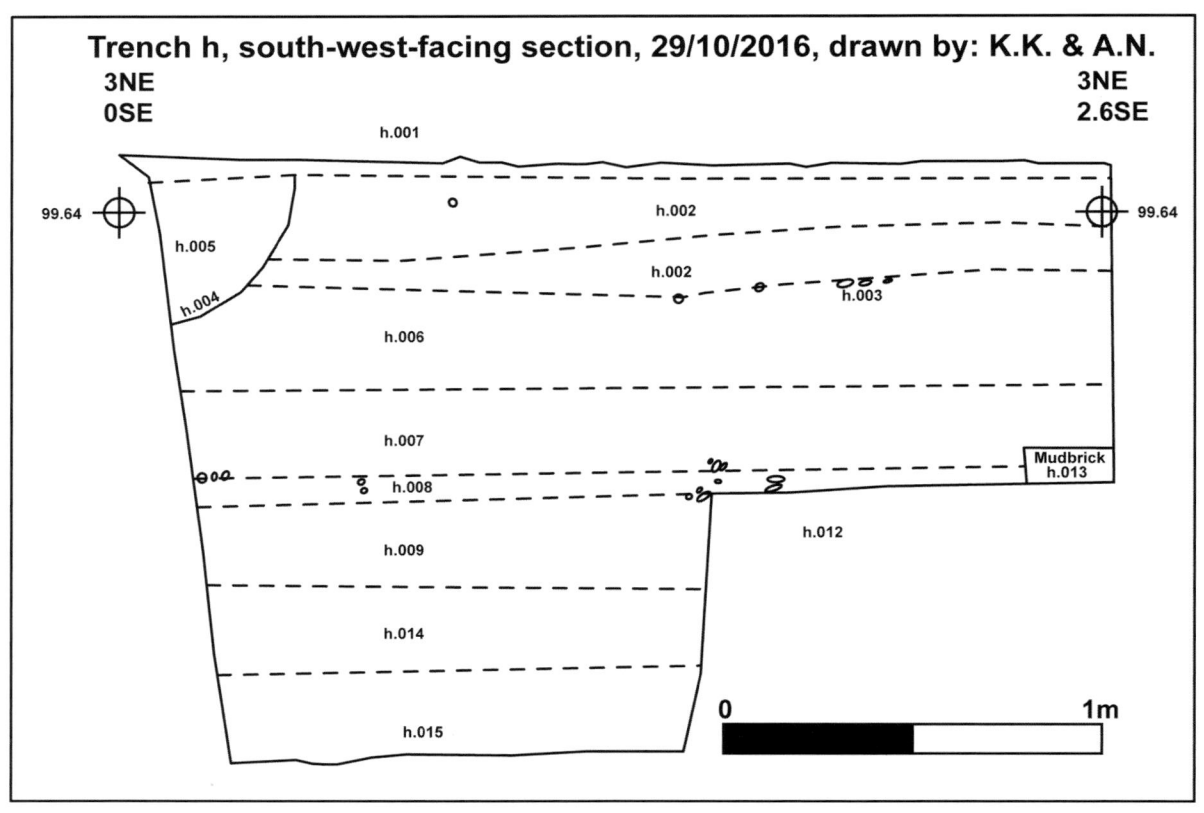

Fig. 9.6: Trench h: south-west-facing section through deposits in the gateway. Note that heights in this and all other sections, plans and tables refer to a benchmark for Trenches h and i, set at an arbitrary height of 100 m. They provide information on the relative elevation of all finds from, and structures in, these two trenches.

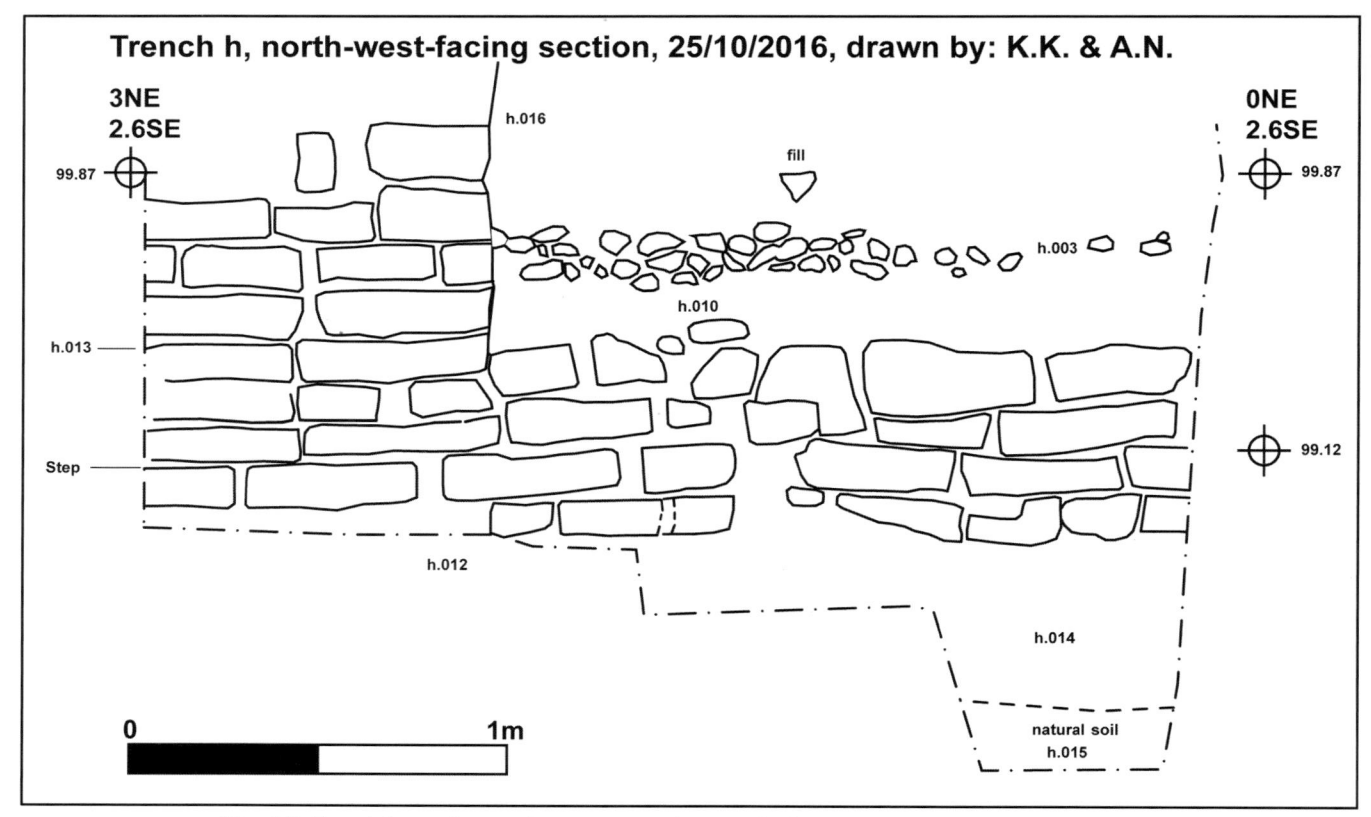

Fig. 9.7: Trench h: north-west-facing section showing the lower courses of the walls of the gate.

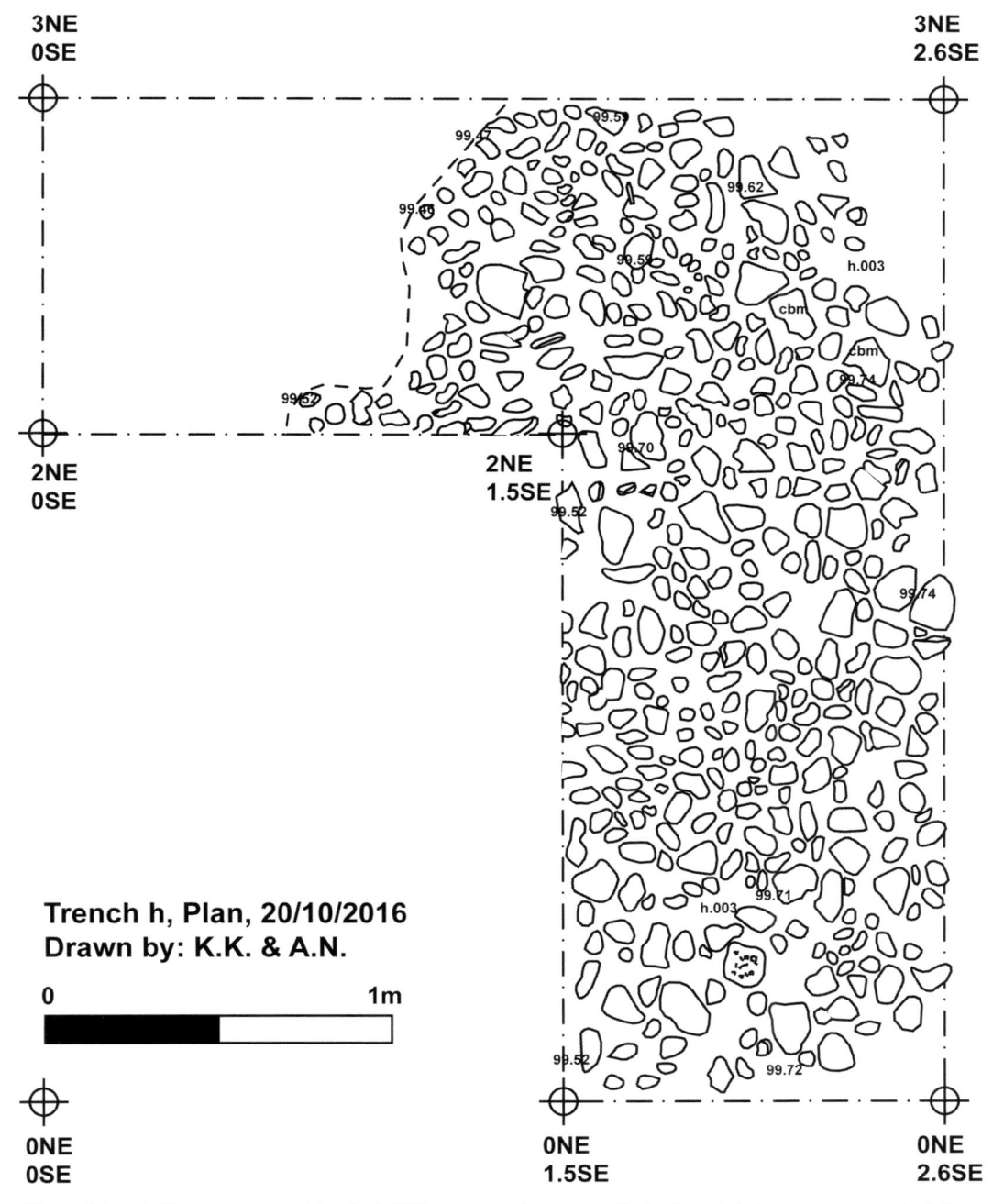

Fig. 9.8: Plan of the shallow stone-paved bank (h.003) abutting the gate walls in Trench h (cbm = ceramic building material).

it impossible for enemies to charge quickly through the gate and expose them for the maximum period of time to missile bombardment from above whilst approaching the gate or trapped in the narrow passage.[17] We do not know whether there ever was a successful breakthrough, but we can be sure that the gateways would have seen heavy traffic whilst the fortress was occupied, initially by the construction force and later by the garrison housed in the estimated 828 rooms within the walls (plus perhaps the interior of the 148 towers), estimated at 2,000–6,000. The vast interior could comfortably have accommodated an additional 40,000–50,000, living in tents, plus their mounts.[18] Whilst we assume that the fortress was only temporarily fully occupied, at such times thousands may have passed through each gate every day. Few places would have been more frequented, and one would not expect any structures or activity here obstructing traffic.

The earliest cultural level we found was h.014. It some 24–50 cm below the base of the gate's mud-brick wall (h.013). It contained 252 g of pottery and 14 g of bone, less than 5% of the pottery and less than 8% of the bone recovered from the most prolific deposit in

Fig. 9.9: The stone-paved bank abutting the gate walls in Trench h.

Fig. 9.10: The gate walls in Trench h, with stone paving h.003 visible in profile. Where the wall is lower (centre to right) there may have been an access to a platform at the edge of the gateway (and earlier excavations have unearthed a human burial here).

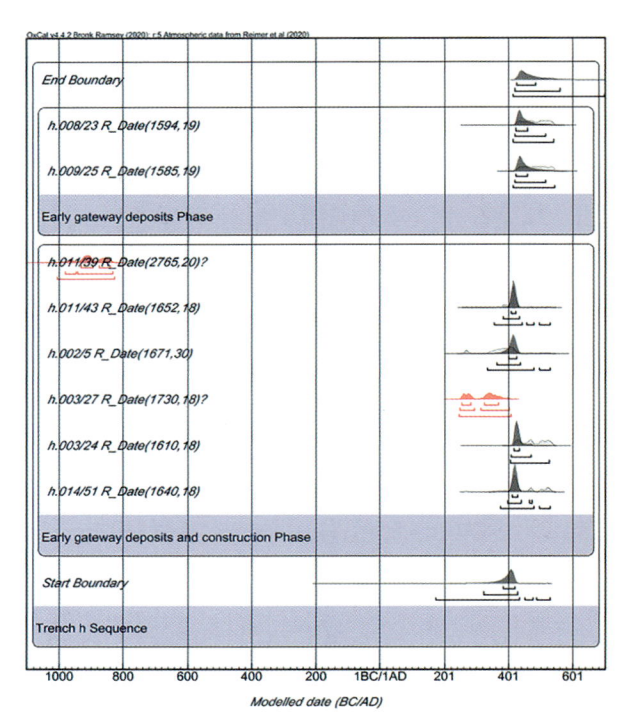

Fig. 9.11: Bayesian model of the radiocarbon samples from Trench h. This is a new model, based on the hypothesis that deposition of all material thought to be embedded in levelling horizons, mud-bricks and the stone-covered bank is construction-related, the bones being of animals slaughtered and consumed and pack-horses perished whilst the defences were erected, and from the early phases of fortress occupation prior to the erection of the stone bank. Material from within the gateway (deposits h.009 and h.008) may be later. As the difference in elevation between the latter two bone samples in minimal, we cannot be entirely sure in which sequence the animals in question perished and allow for all options.

the trench (h.003/h.010). It overlies sterile natural soil (h.015). Deposit h.014 may be a levelling deposit. There is nothing in the pottery spectrum to suggest that it is an earlier occupation layer, and the radiocarbon sample of c. AD 399–473, most likely of 399–440 (modelled or 382–535 unmodelled: Table 9.1), is close in age to those from deposits above. It probably forms the earliest phase of the construction project, rather than being an unrelated earlier horizon. The quantity of finds is large enough to render it improbable that these are random losses on unoccupied land. Nor is there any evidence for a marginally earlier site underlying the gate. The sampled bone belongs, most probably, to an animal consumed or perished during the construction works. If so, it is likely to provide an approximate date for the start of the building project. The mud-brick wall of the gate (h.013), with an opening (h.016) above the four bottom courses, was built on top of this levelling horizon. The trench exposed the face of this wall. It was built of sun-baked mud-bricks of c. 42–45 cm side length and a thickness of 12 cm, as well as half bricks.

A layer of mud-bricks (h.011), c. 50 cm thick, was found exclusively in the south-eastern part of the trench, extending from the edge of outer wall of the gate (h.013) approximately 1 m to the north-west. It overlay an unexcavated surface (h.012) at a similar level to h.008. Unlike deposits h.009 and h.008 further north-west, surface h.012 was buried under a bank consisting of the cited mud-brick layer (h.011) with a stone paving (h.003/h.010) on top. Despite the similar elevation, the last human traffic on surface h.012 is likely to be earlier than in the area of h.009 and h.008, which remained accessible after bank construction. H.011 contained a sizeable quantity of pottery (873 g), bone (389 g) and charcoal. Two bone samples yielded dates of c. AD 385–435 and 981–832 BC. The latter was evidently redeposited, and it is worth noting that there is also Iron Age pottery from surface surveys around the monument.[19] The use of soil dug up locally,

Table 9.1: *Radiocarbon dates from Trench h (location relates to the trench, its eastern corner being at 2.60 m SE and 3.00 m NE; SH = site height, relates to a benchmark set at an arbitrary height of 100 m used for both trenches at Qal'eh Iraj). Note that the unmodelled and modelled calibrated dates differ slightly from those published previously, as all were recalibrated via the updated 2020 version of the OxCal programme and a new revised model was compiled.*[20]

Find and context no.	Laboratory no.	Location	Sample description	Date	Calibrated date at 95.4% confidence (→ modelled date, taking into account stratigraphy and Bayesian statistics)	Comments
h.002/5	SUERC-87439	0.45 m SE; 2.40 m NE; 99.65 m SH	Bone: Caprini, rib, medial part	1671±30	AD 257–530 → modelled 366–438	d13C = -19.4
h.003/24	SUERC-71992	2.30 m SE; 0.10 m NE; 99.52 m SH	Bone: Caprini, left maxilla	1610±18	AD 417–538 → modelled 411–472	d13C = -12.2
h.003/27	SUERC-71993	2.30 m SE; 2.50 m NE; 99.36 m SH	Bone: Small ruminant, medial rib	1730±18	AD 250–403 (prob. outlier, redeposited?)	d13C = -19.2
h.008/23	SUERC-74174	0.67 m SE; 2.56 m NE; 98.95 m SH	Bone: Small ruminant, long bone	1594±19	AD 424–540 → modelled 419–517	d13C = -19.2
h.009/25	SUERC-74175	0.60 m SE; 2.27 m NE; 98.91 m SH	Bone: Small ruminant, long bone	1585±19	AD 427–544 → modelled 419–516	d13C = -19.2
h.011/39	SUERC-75254	1.73 m SE; 1.46 m NE; 99.27 m SH	Bone: Large mammal, rib	2765±20	981–832; 83.3%: 941–832 BC (outlier, redeposited)	d13C = -23.0
h.011/43	SUERC-71994	1.88 m SE; 1.40 m NE; 99.12 m SH	Bone: Equidae, right metacarpal	1652±18	AD 268–531 → modelled 385–435	d13C = -18.5
h.014/51	SUERC-71995	0.25 m SE; 2.80 m NE; 98.55 m SH	Bone: Small ruminant, long bone	1640±18	AD 382–535 → modelled 399–473; 94.6%: 399–440	d13C = -18.8

on land already occupied more than a millennium before, in mud-brick production and bank construction provides an obvious scenario for the presence of an Iron Age bone in a Sasanian-era deposit. The dense concentration of mud-bricks (h.011) abutting the mud-brick wall (h.013) leaves no doubt that this deposit post-dates the start of construction works. The brick fragments tended to be large and horizontal, suggesting that they were deliberately placed here against the base of the wall rather than having tumbled to the surface. The voids between may have been filled with redeposited soil, which may account for the high proportion of cultural material, including the bone sample pre-dating construction works by more than a millennium, as well as another likely to date to around the time of the construction works. It is tempting think that the latter sample, an equid bone of c. AD 385–435, belonged to a pack-animal employed during construction works, or a soldier's horse, perishing whilst the compound was being built. Sealed in the stone-paved bank, it is probably earlier than material in deposits h.008 and h.009,

Fig. 9.12: Stratigraphic matrix of Trench h. The matrix lists modelled radiocarbon dates. (For unmodelled dates, see Table 9.1. Crossed-out sample: clearly redeposited; ?: probably redeposited; redep.: sample from redeposited mud-brick, but with a plausible date for original mud-brick production; grey shading: natural soil.)

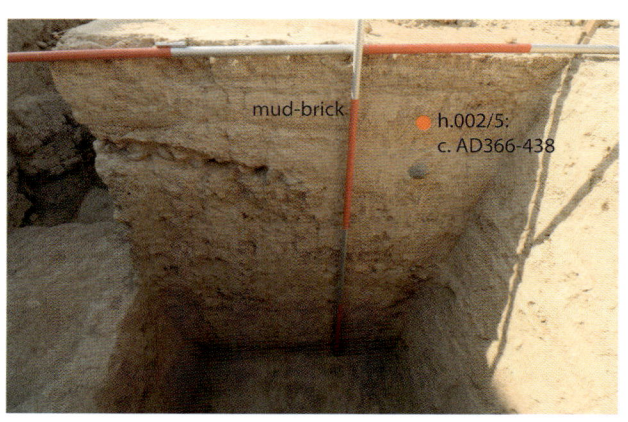

Fig. 9:13: Location of sample h.002/5, plotted on the nearest section, though found 40 cm away from it – suggesting that the sample might have been embedded in a decayed (and reused?) mud-brick, perhaps explaining its early date.

in the area of the causeway beyond the bank. Covered with a cobbled surface (h.003/h.010), with stones of up to 20 cm diameter packed densely, the bank was probably intended to prevent surface water from eroding the base of the wall. The cobbles were embedded in a matrix of soft mid-yellowish brown silty clay (h.003/h.010). The deposit was unusually rich in finds, containing 5,477 g of pottery, at least 184 g of bone, as well as glass, brick slag and charcoal. Bone samples from this deposit yielded dates of c. AD 250–403 and 411–472 (the latter a modelled date; without modelling the date range is c. 417–538). These two samples do not overlap in time.[21] Could they relate to construction works extending over a longer period of time, e.g. the earlier bone belonging to an animal slaughtered or otherwise perishing when the gate was constructed, and redeposited when the bank was added some time (perhaps a few decades?) later – and the later bone to a sheep or goat eaten shortly before bank erection? This is possible. Considering that the bone of c. AD 250–403 may only be a few years or decades earlier than the majority of samples, it seems improbable that it was a random loss on unoccupied land or belonged to an otherwise untraceable rural settlement. Perhaps it provides circumstantial evidence for activity prior to the start of construction works, e.g. that the site had functioned as an assembly area already some time before the massive defences were built.

The mud-brick and soil bank, covered with a stone paving (h.011 and h.003/h.010) and abutting the outer gate wall h.013, is evidently later than the wall, and one wonders whether it was built immediately after the wall or may have been added a few years or decades later. The later sample from h.003 provides a likely *terminus post quem* for this structure of c. AD 411. The observation that h.003 was, in terms of finds, the most prolific of all deposits from the trench suggests perhaps that it was not added shortly after gate construction but later, after the fortress had seen some occupation. Some of the material from the bank may well relate to early occupation of the fortress rather than exclusively the time of construction works.

The bank must be later than surface h.012, but not necessarily later than material embedded in, or trampled into, h.009 and h.008 that lay beyond the edge of the bank. Deposit h.009, above h.014, may post-date the wall in its entirety or may in part pre-date and in part post-date the wall. It contained c. 159 g of pottery and some bone. A sample (h.009/25) from the deposit from a similar level as the base of the wall, but 2 m from its edge and more likely to be later, dates probably to the AD 410s–510s. Deposit h.009 is sealed by a thinner layer, of light yellowish brown silty clay (h.008), its base at c. 98.89–98.91 m and its top at c. 98.93–98.99 m site height. A paving consisting of small pebbles on top indicates that this was a walking surface. It can hardly be coincidence that this was just above the base of the gate's mud-brick walls (98.91m), suggesting that this surface dates to the time after the erection of the gate and remained in use perhaps some time beyond. The sample from h.008, like the nearby sample from h.009 probably dating to the 410s–510s, is likely to belong to a period of occupation of the fortress and provides a probable *terminus ante quem* for gate construction.

Subsequently, deposits h.007, h.006 and h.002 formed within the gateway. H.007 and h.006 contained few finds (9 g of pottery in the former and 34 g in the latter, as well as a small quantity of bone, glass and charcoal) – perhaps unsurprising as rubbish dumping in the gateway would have impeded traffic, not to mention the general tidiness prevailing at many Sasanian military compounds with relatively small quantities of intramural finds overall (and most finds normally coming from make-up layers and/or pit fills and very few from surfaces).[22] Furthermore, bones on the surface had little chance of surviving unless buried in soil. H.002 contained a significant concentration of finds (2,248 g of pottery and 133 g of bone as well as some charcoal), perhaps from a time when keeping the gateways clear seemed less important or, more probably, when the surface was raised deliberately. One bone from h.002 submitted for radiocarbon dating yielded a surprisingly early date (1671±30 BP, i.e. c. AD 257–530 unmodelled, with a 91.9% probability of the date falling between AD 257 and 435). Stratigraphically well above the probably later samples from h.009 and h.008 (of 1585±19 BP and 1594±19 BP), it must be redeposited. There were mud-bricks embedded in h.002, one of them clearly visible in section, its base at a similar level to our sample (Fig. 9.13). Sun-baked mud-bricks are not always easy to spot during excavation. Any traces of those close to the surface often vanish as a result of bioturbation. We did not observe that this bone was embedded in a mud-brick, but it is tempting to think that it was. If so, we may assign it to the construction phase, suggesting a date of c. AD 366–438 (Table 9.1; Fig. 9.11). Its likely *terminus ante quem* of c. AD 438 (or AD 435 unmodelled) would match other samples pointing to a likely construction date of the fortress in the late fourth or, more probably, early fifth century, when most of the mud-bricks must have been produced. That our sample might have come from a largely disintegrated, reused construction-era mud-brick is no more than a possibility. Even if this hypothesis should be wrong, however, the sample provides further circumstantial evidence for activity in the first third of the fifth century or before. It is hard to imagine that the multiple samples not likely to be later than the early fifth century from the gate area belong to an earlier unknown site. They indicate, with a high degree of probability, that the fortress originated towards the very end of the fourth or, more probably, the early fifth century, perhaps between the late 390s or 400s and the 430s. Assuming that the deepest stratified sample from the probable levelling horizon h.014 is likely to be no earlier than AD 399, perhaps construction in the first third of the fifth century is most likely. H.002 was cut by a pit or potentially large posthole (h.004). Filled with h.005, soft mid-yellowish brown silty clay, i.e. material of similar colour and composition to other deposits within the trench and not noticeably more organic, we have no obvious clues as to the date and function of this feature. Any time between the late Sasanian occupation of the fortress and recent centuries is possible.

None of the samples from Trench h is later than the fifth to early or mid-sixth century and none need be later than the fifth. This need not indicate that the gate was used for a short period only, as all samples are embedded in construction-related deposits or early soil horizons within the gateway and, as we will see, some of the samples from Trench i are likely to be later. Indeed, no late deposits seem to survive in the gateway area. At a level just above our trench, Dr Nemati's earlier excavations had revealed a scatter of Sasanian ostraca, whose approximate extent is indicated in shading on our plan (Fig. 9.4). No further ostraca came to light in Trench h (or Trench i), adding strength to attributing their deposition to a phase after our radiocarbon sequence for this trench.

9.2.2.2. A side chamber of the south-eastern gate (Trench i)

Trench i in the north-west of the small side chamber of the gate (Figs 9.4–9.5, 9.14–9.26) covered just 2 m² (2 × 1 m).[23] The deepest deposit (i.029) was devoid of any finds or visible traces of organic material. The base of the deepest cultural layer (i.028) was interestingly more than 0.50 m higher than in Trench h (at c. 99.06 m as opposed to c. 98.43–98.51 m site height) and even above the base of the wall (h.013) in Trench h (c. 98.90 m). Whether topography alone explains the difference, despite the two trenches being only c. 11 m apart, centre to centre, and whether i.029 is natural soil or might be a sterile make-up layer is hard to decide. A sheep or goat bone (i.028/95) found c. 11 cm above the base of the layer yielded a modelled date of c. AD 410–539. This sample need not be later than some of the material from the stone-covered bank in Trench h. In addition to 49 g of bone, there was also pottery (47 g) and glass (9 g) from this earliest occupation layer.

The deepest structure to emerge was a stone block with a flat surface lined by bricks (i.024), with traces of lime (i.025) perhaps of a bonding agent on top, in a shallow pit (i.027). The deposit (i.026) under the stone and within the brick lining, soft mid-yellowish brown silt with charcoal of willow or poplar[24] and traces of ash, yielded no finds whatsoever. Perhaps the structure at the edge of the room was a fireplace, but this is far from certain. Unlike the later fire altar to the south-east of the trench, it was not raised or of geometric shape. It was covered by a possible levelling deposit (i.022), containing 11 g of pottery and 10 g of bone, and a clay floor (i.023) in the south-west of the trench. In addition to a small amount of pottery (14 g), bone (13 g) and glass (4 g), it contained an iron projectile (i.023/87) weighing 6 g. The latter was found embedded in the clay floor, some 8 cm below its surface, and is likely to be part of the material used to raise the floor rather than trampled into the floor. Perhaps crossbow ammunition,[25] it provides unsurprising evidence for the presence of armed personnel in the fortress. Whether it signals that

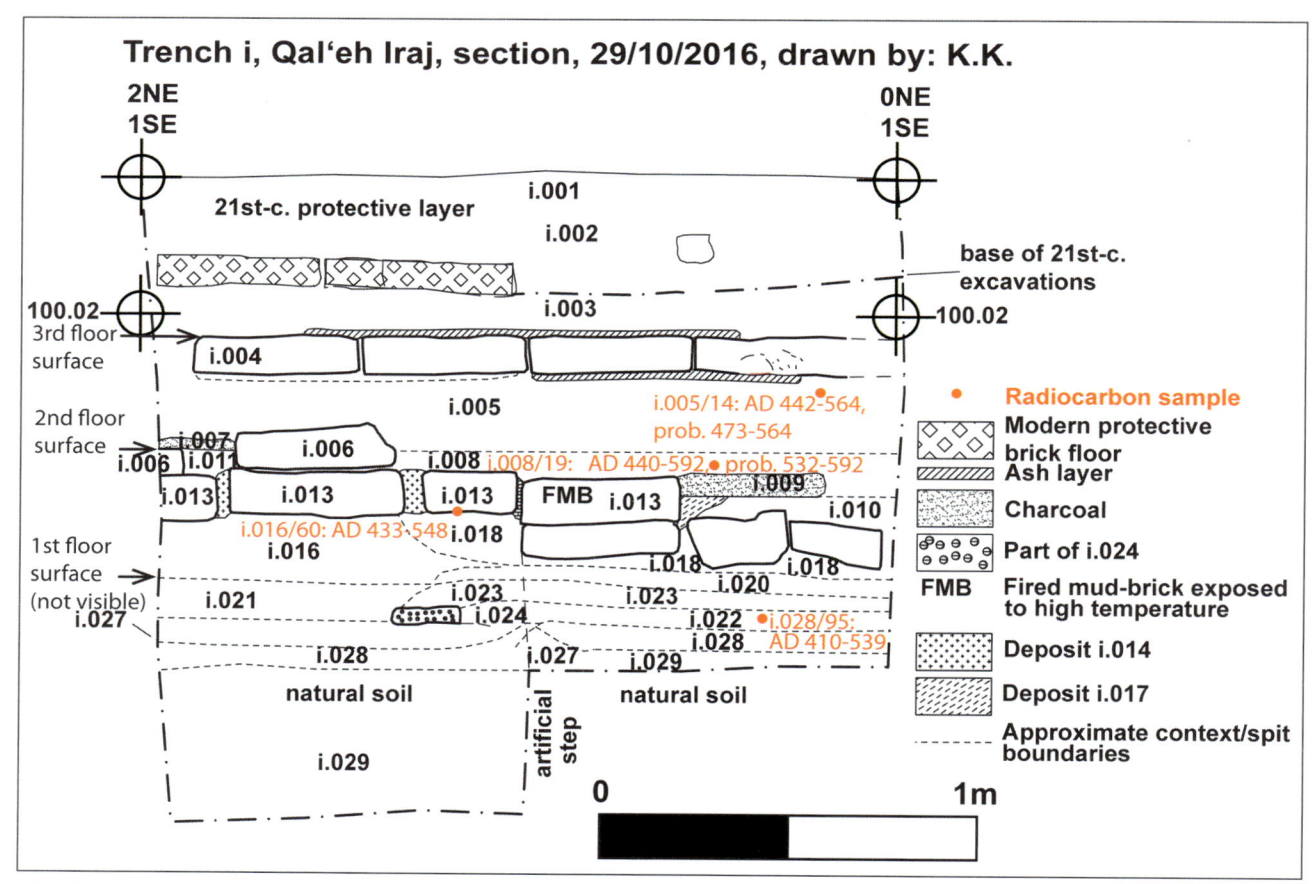

Fig. 9.14: North-west facing section of Trench i, with the four dated radiocarbon samples plotted onto the section. Note that the modelled dates (with a probability of 95.4%) are shown. See Table 9.2 for a list of the samples. Note that the lower mud-brick floor did not extend to the drawn section.

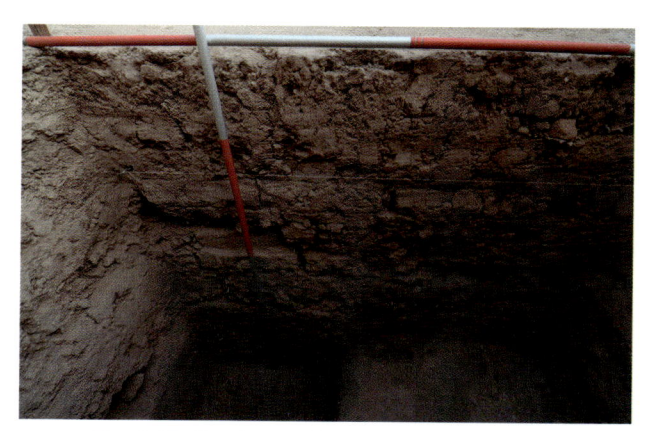

Fig. 9.15: North-west facing section of Trench i.

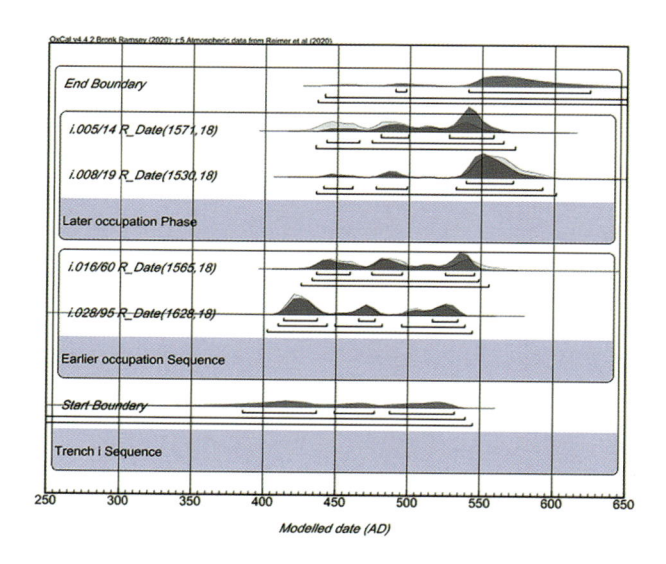

Fig. 9.16: Bayesian model of the radiocarbon samples from Trench i. All four samples were found in clear stratigraphic sequence, but the uppermost two might belong to a single raising of the floor surface and our new model therefore places them in the same phase rather than in a sequence.

the room may have been used as a guard chamber and/or an armoury at the time or whether the projectile was lost or discharged by a non-occupant is impossible to tell. On top of i.022 and abutting i.023, there was the deepest mud-brick floor (i.019) in the north of the trench. One of the bricks from this early floor features three finger imprints, evidently dating to a time when the brick was

Table 9.2: Radiocarbon dates from Trench i (location relates to the trench; SH = site height, relates to a benchmark set at an arbitrary height of 100 m used for both trenches at Qal'eh Iraj). Note that the unmodelled and modelled calibrated dates differ from those published previously, as all were recalibrated via the updated 2020 version of the OxCal programme. A new revised model was compiled. The new version of OxCal produces later date ranges for all samples from this trench than the previous version, notably shifting the likely terminus post quem *for the earliest sample by as much as a quarter-century, from AD 384 to 408 (unmodelled; from 386 to 410, modelled).*[26]

Find and context no.	Laboratory no.	Location	Sample description	Date	Calibrated date at 95.4% confidence (→ modelled date, taking into account stratigraphy and Bayesian statistics)	Comments
i.005/14	SUERC-71996	0.24 m SE; 0.21 m NE; 99.79 m SH	Bone: Caprini, proximal medial rib	1571±18	AD 431–553 → modelled 442–564; 88.0%: 473–564	d13C = -18.2
i.008/19	SUERC-73306	0.05 m SE; 0.49 m NE; 99.54 m SH	Bone: Caprini, rib	1530±18	AD 441–599 → modelled 440–592; 90.6%: 477–592; 80.4%: 532–592	d13C = -18.7
i.016/60	SUERC-72002	0.73 m SE; 1.17 m NE; 99.46 m SH	Bone: *Capra*, tooth (P4 Inf.)	1565±18	AD 433–560 → modelled 433–548	d13C = -18.6
i.028/95	SUERC-72003	0.85 m SE; 0.36 m NE; 99.17 m SH	Bone: Caprini, right femur	1628±18	AD 408–535 → modelled 410–539	d13C = -19.2

still wet and before it had been sun-dried and used to pave the room. This paving did not extend to the south-eastern edge of the trench, where we encountered deposits rich in finds: i.021, very soft dark to mid-brown silt, towards the eastern corner of the trench, with 490 g of pottery and 59 g of bone, and i.020 further south-west, soft mid-brown silty clay with 32 g of pottery, 9 g of glass and some charcoal. The most unusual find to emerge from the latter deposit, and the trench as a whole, was a bird-headed hair pin (i.020/71).[27] Found marginally above the level of the surface of the mud-brick floor (i.019) and a little south of it, perhaps it was an item used by, or kept for, a (female?) occupant of, or visitor to, the room. The glass and pottery were perhaps also used by the room's occupants. The brown colour of the two deposits may point to some decayed organic matter. It is in any case clear that people lived nearby, as it is hard to imagine that the material would have been brought over any great distance. Interestingly, the projectile and hair pin were both sealed under a second floor (i.013 and i.006), to be discussed below, and there are no equivalent unusual metal finds on top of the second floor. Were these two items ever used or stored in the side chamber or just brought in as part of an effort to raise the floor? Size and quality of the decorated pin renders random redeposition unlikely, and one is inclined to think that it belonged to a person stationed in, or visiting, the chamber. The number of metal finds is, however, too small to be statistically meaningful – and it is best not to speculate whether their deposition in this earlier phase might be explained by the room having initially served a different function than later; as we will see, it was only after a second floor had been laid, sealing these metal finds, that we have evidence for a rectangular fire altar being installed and used in the chamber. In the barracks in Fort 2 on the Gorgan Wall, distinct differences in finds spectra between adjacent groups of rooms strongly suggest that even material from levelling horizons was largely sourced from the same rooms, or their immediate vicinity, and not embedded in soil brought in from afar.[28] One is inclined to think that the same is likely to be true for the side chamber in our gate and that the hair pin (i.020/71) and projectile (i.023/87) had indeed been used or stored in the chamber.

Floors i.019 and i.023 and deposits i.021 and i.020 were covered by soft mid-brownish yellow sandy silt (i.016), which yielded 138 g of pottery, 37 g of bone, 4 g of glass, some charcoal and brick slag. Containing little organic matter, to judge by its colour, the latter deposit is best interpreted as a levelling horizon. A goat tooth (i.016/60) produced a modelled date of AD 433–548. This

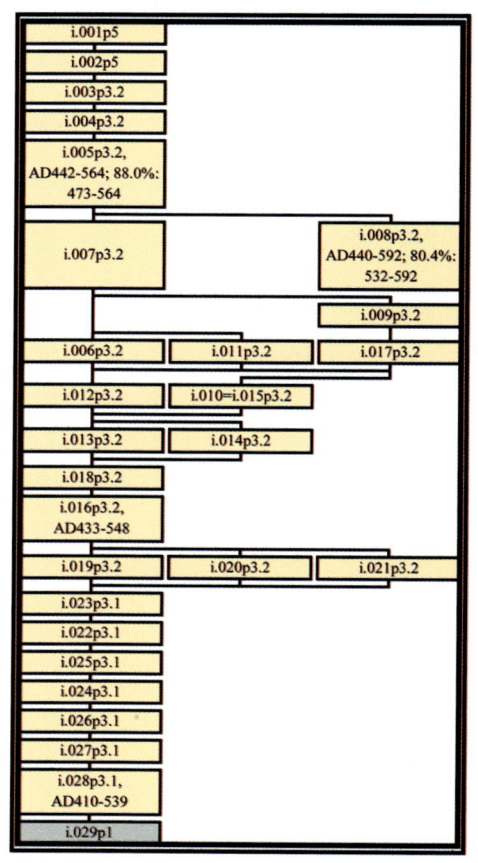

Fig. 9.17: Stratigraphic matrix of Trench i. The matrix lists modelled radiocarbon dates. (For unmodelled dates, see Table 9.2.)

Fig. 9.18: A stone block lined by bricks (i.024) (photo by Przemysław Polakiewicz).

Fig. 9.19: Brick-lining (i.024) after removal of the stone (photo by Przemysław Polakiewicz).

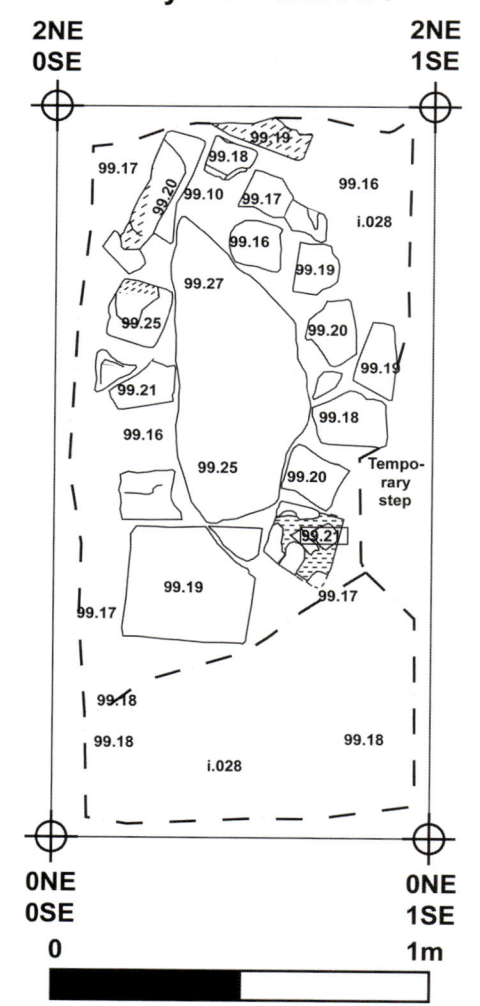

Fig. 9.20: Plan of brick lining i.024.

suggests that the indoor surface level was raised within the fifth century or in the first half of the sixth century, and deposits and finds sealed underneath, including the hair pin, also date to a similar time span. Levelling horizon i.016 was in the south-east of the trench and was covered

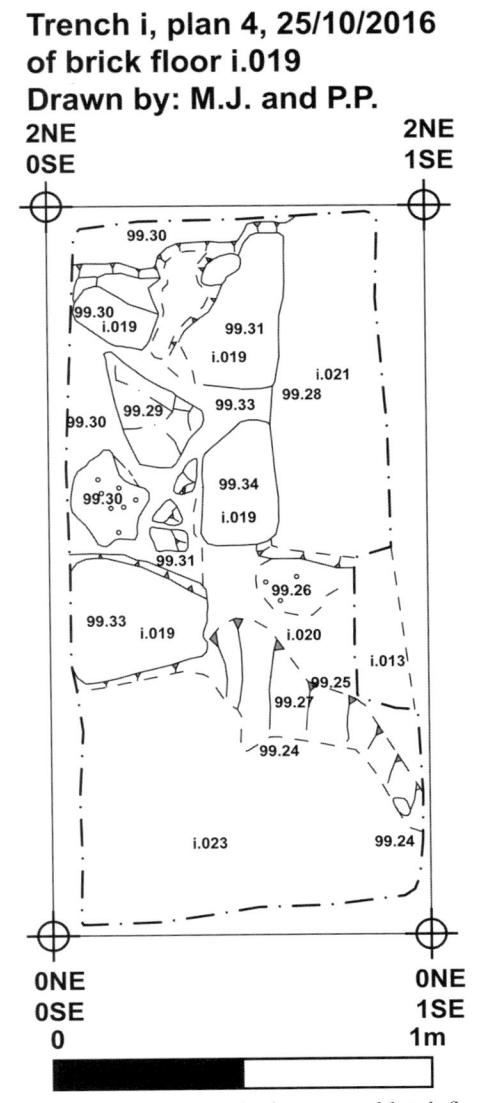

Fig. 9.21: Plan of the i.019, the lowest mud-brick floor in the side chamber.

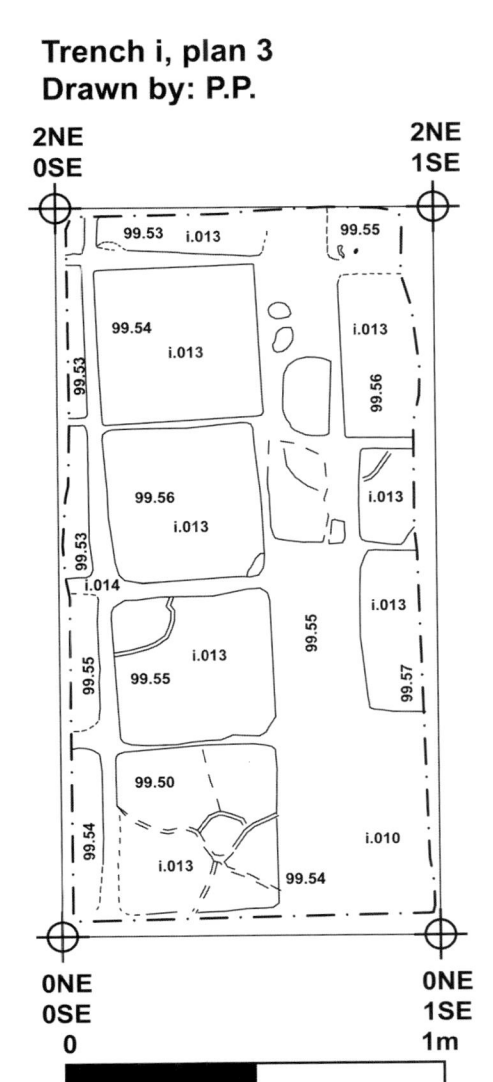

Fig. 9.22: Plan of the i.013, the lower course of the second mud-brick floor.

by mid-brown clay (i.018), devoid of finds except for a fragment of ceramic building material and charcoal flecks. These layers formed the bedding for a second mud-brick floor (i.013), some 20–30 cm above the previous floor (i.019) and covering more ground, as far as exposed in our small trench. The mud-bricks in i.013 contained 22 g of bone; mud mortar (i.014) filled the gaps between the bricks. In the south of the trench there was gap in the paving covered with light yellowish brown silty clay (i.010), with 4 g of pottery and 7 g of bone, which formed a part of the floor. In places there was a layer of mud mortar (i.012) with some charcoal on top and a further course of mud-bricks (i.006) with mud mortar bonding (i.011). It seems probable that the two courses of mud-bricks (i.013 and i.006), mud mortar and silty clay (i.014, i.019, i.012 and i.011) filling the gaps, were all part of a single raised floor, the top of the upper courses (i.006), only partially visible in section, forming the surface. The mud mortar filling the gaps did, unsurprisingly, produce few finds; in addition to charcoal, there was one sherd (11 g) of glass in i.014 and 26 g of pottery in i.011.

On top of mud-brick paving i.006, we encountered charcoal-rich ashy material (i.017, soft dark brownish yellow silty clay, with 24 g of pottery, i.009, very soft mid-greyish brown clayey silt, and i.007, soft mid-grey to blackish grey clayey silt with black and reddish brown patches), perhaps the cinders of fires burning on the nearby fire altar explored by Dr Nemati before. The charcoal came from a wide variety of species, including plane, willow, tamarisk, sandthorn, mulberry and grapevine, evidence for a rich and varied environment around the Sasanian fortress.[29] I.009 was overlain by a further thin layer of very

372 Ancient Arms Race

Fig. 9.23: The lower course of mud-bricks (i.013).

Fig. 9.25: Mud-brick floor i.006.

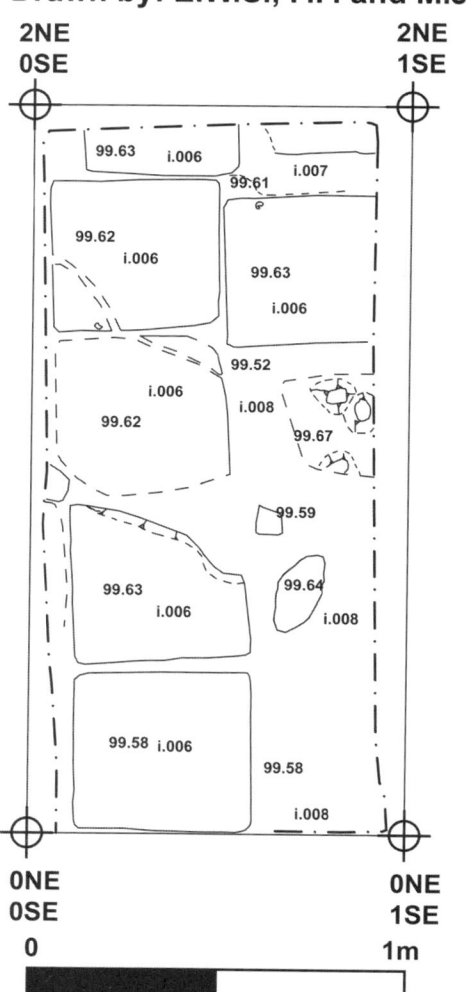

Fig. 9.24: Plan of the i.006, the upper course of the second mud-brick floor.

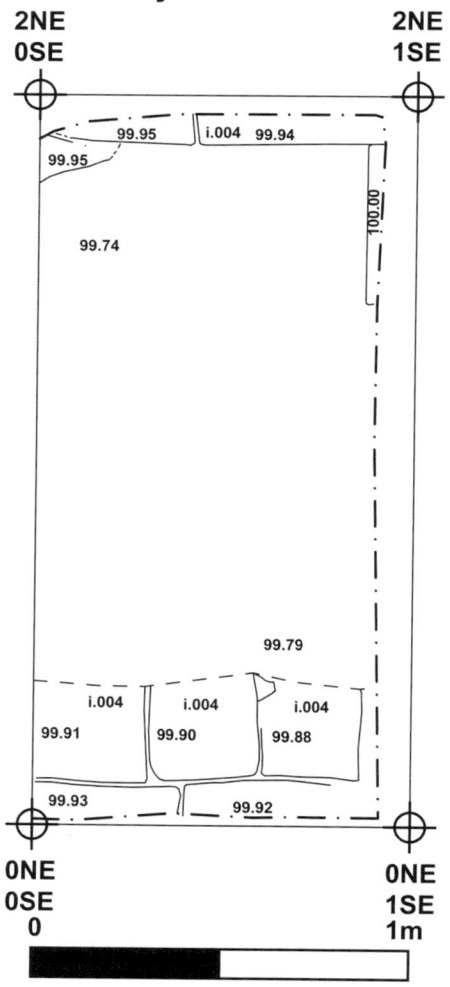

Fig. 9.26: Plan of the patchy traces of i.004, the third mud-brick floor.

soft mid-yellowish brown clay (i.008), a further make-up horizon and clay floor with 53 g of pottery, 2 g of glass and 49 g of bone. The few bones included a sheep or goat rib (i.008/19) with a modelled date of c. AD 440–592, most probably of 532–592.[30] If deposition of clay deposit i.008 was part of an effort to patch up and level the surface of the second floor, then we may conclude that this floor was probably laid and repaired in the sixth century. It is, however, also possible that deposits i.008 and i.005 were laid down in quick succession. The occurrence of ashy deposits only on top of the second floor surface suggests that there had been no fire altar prior to the laying of the second floor.

Deposits i.008 and i.007 were overlain by a substantial deposit of mid-yellowish brown clayey silt (i.005), with 165 g of pottery, but just 13 g of bone. The yellow colour, signalling that it contains little organic matter, suggests that this is a further levelling horizon, rather than occupation debris accumulating *in situ*. A radiocarbon sample of c. AD 442–564, probably 473–564 (and most likely not before the 530s to judge by the sample from i.008), provides a certain *terminus post quem* for this phase of levelling. On top, there was a third, patchy, mud-brick floor (i.004), much more distinctly visible in section than in plan (Figs 9.14 and 9.26). It is likely that i.005 (as well as i.008 underneath?) was a make-up layer intended as the bedding for this floor. The repeated raising of the floor may in part have been intended to make sure that it was well above that in the gateway, to prevent surface water from infiltrating during periods of rain. The presence of films of ashy material above and below i.004 is worth noting and perhaps a sign of continued use of the fire altar.

On top of i.004, we found a further bulk deposit of yellowish-brown clayey silt (i.003) with 262 g of pottery, some charcoal and no bone. This was covered by a modern protective brick layer and plastic sheeting, marking the bottom of previous excavations. Deposits i.002 and i.001 are clearly spoil of twenty-first-century date.

Trench i, with three floor surfaces and its radiocarbon sequence probably extending to a later date than the samples from Trench h in the gateway, has demonstrated that the side chamber of the gate was occupied for some time and probably until at least the mid- or late sixth century.

9.3. Geophysical survey

9.3.1. Introduction

In 2016, we surveyed selected areas within the fortress. The magnetometer survey was carried out by Mohammad Arman Ershadi and Mohammad Taghi Maleka. They and Roger Ainslie of Abingdon Archaeological Geophysics processed the results. Mohammad Bagher-Bayati produced a map of the survey areas, which we plotted onto a topographical survey of the Qal'eh commissioned by Dr Mohammadreza Nemati. As much of the interior of the fortress is in agricultural use, the choice of survey areas was determined by what land was accessible and uncultivated at the time of our fieldwork in October 2016. Furthermore, we avoided areas of extensive modern disturbance where survey does not normally produce clear results. The sample is thus random to a significant extent, but as (with the possible exception of the structure described below[31]) no Sasanian-era architecture had been identified in the interior of the compound before, this did not matter. Indeed, it had been our aim to randomly sample a few areas in the interior, with the following research questions in mind:

1. Were we right in thinking that the interior was largely empty, with few if any permanent buildings inside?

2. Were there any traces of temporary occupation, such as the rectangular drainage or enclosure ditches (probably each once with a tent placed in the interior) in neat double rows that we had found at the Sasanian campaign base of Qal'eh Kharabeh?[32]

Both questions were important for verifying the function of the monument: a massive defensive enclosure with housing and urban amenities inside is best explained as a city. Strong defences around an empty interior, by contrast, point to a semi-permanent military campaign base, with space for tented occupation for a large number of soldiers in the interior. In terms of prospects of success, the first question was much more likely to yield significant positive or negative evidence. Buildings within a densely occupied city were not like to have vanished without a trace, whether built of sun-dried mud-brick or, less probably, rammed earth, fired brick or stone. By contrast, the cited geophysical evidence for enclosure ditches that probably mark the location of tents is, to our knowledge, so far unique. At most sites, tents would probably not have been surrounded by shallow ditches. Even where they were, the signal would in most instances be faint and untraceable, notably in areas where modern debris or uneven ground mask minor anomalies. The survey encompassed four areas, sites A–D (Figs 9.27–9.33).

9.3.2. Site A

This sample area was in the western quadrant of the fortress and extended from the inside of the north-western defensive walls into the interior. Fifteen 30 × 30 m grids were surveyed, not all of them completely, notably in the north-west where the base of the steep-sided defensive wall itself formed a limit. In the south-east, the survey extended to the lower parts of a shallow irregular mound with brick debris on the surface. Earlier excavations by Dr Mohammadreza Nemati in the area had revealed a clay floor with cobblestones in the area and Sasanian pottery on top of it, approximately 35 m south of the limits of the survey, but no occupation layers. In the

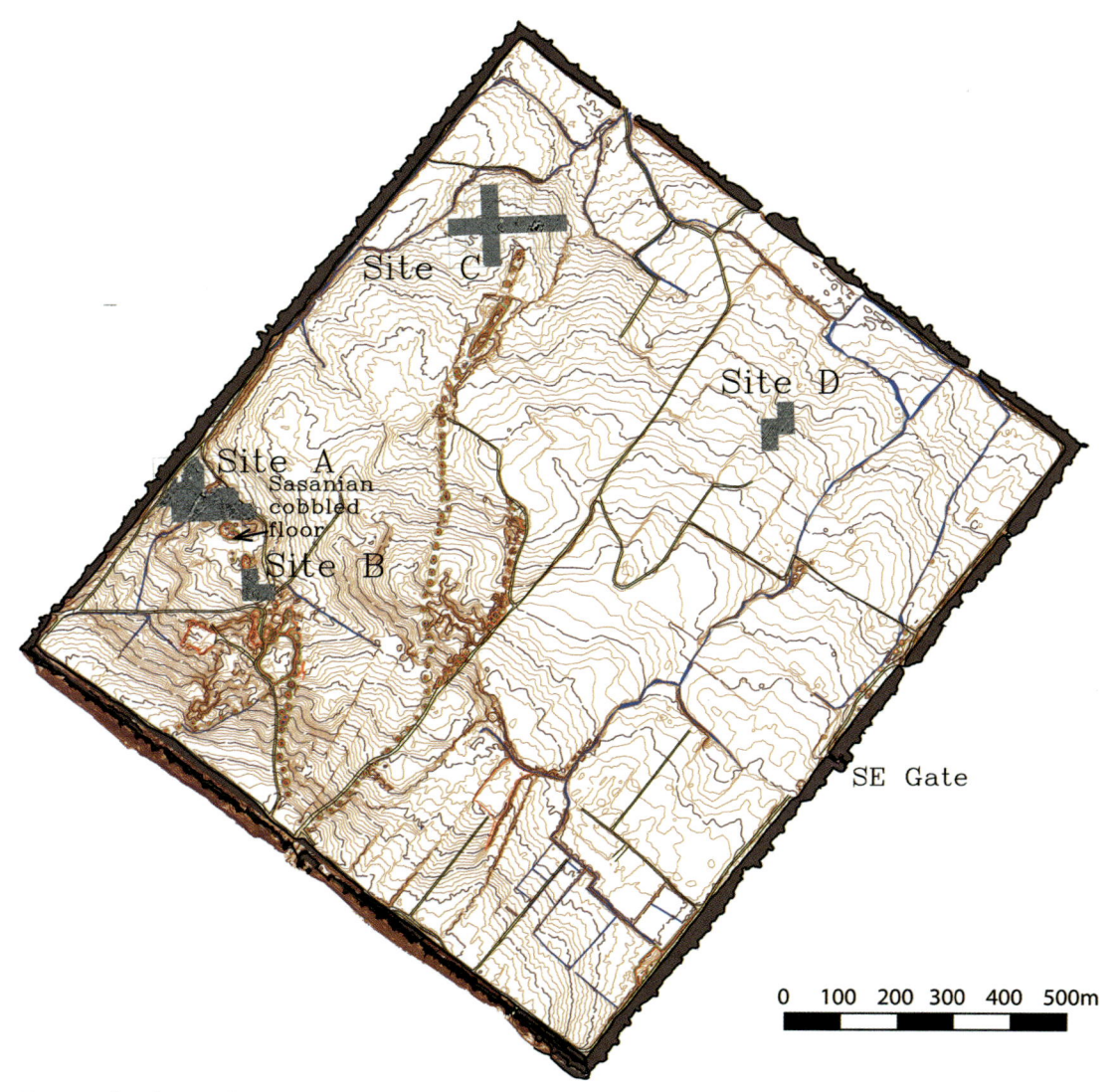

Fig. 9.27: Topographical map of Qal'eh Iraj, commissioned by Dr Mohammadreza Nemati, with the location of the qanat shafts, the four geophysical survey areas and the area where a cobbled floor was found in excavations, plotted by Mohammad Bagher Bayati and the joint project.

three south-easternmost grids there may be the northern corner of a large rectangular feature, whose edges roughly coincide with those of the brick-rich mound. Perhaps there was a building or walled enclosure here with the cobbled paving inside. The survey did not reveal any other obvious structures of possible ancient origins. The survey also detected magnetic anomalies next to the outer wall in the north-west as well as next to a modern tent. The former may be caused by debris dumped alongside a modern track on the inside of the wall and/or by debris from the wall itself. A modern ditch showed up too.

9.3.3. Sites B–D

We set up a further three grids to the east of the mound (site B) and 11 on two uncultivated fields in the north of the Qal'eh (site C). The grids at site C were arranged in a cross-shaped arrangement to maximise area coverage. At site C we saw debris of mud-bricks as well as the odd fired brick and pottery sherd on the surface. A fourth survey area (site D) was marked out in the north-east of the site and four grids were surveyed. No features of obvious significance emerged at sites B and D, and little would be gained by reproducing featureless plots (see Fig. 9.27 for small-scale plots of the results). Site C revealed, in addition to an L-shaped anomaly that is no more than a modern field boundary, one large distinct magnetic anomaly that was not visible on the surface (Figs 9.32–9.33). As it is precisely in the alignment of a qanat (Fig. 9.27), there can be no doubt that it is a qanat shaft filled with magnetic debris. The main qanat is entering through, or starting at, the south-west gate of the fortress before splitting into three separate branches, one of them once supplying the cited mounded sites in

9. Qal'eh Iraj: a campaign base/command centre 375

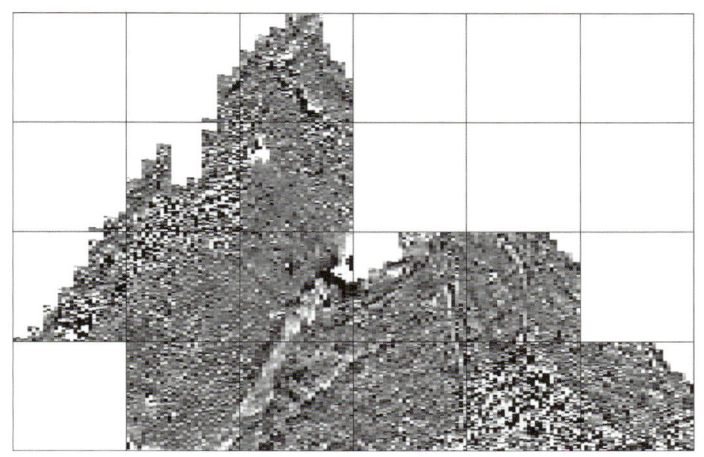

Fig. 9.28: Black and white plot of geophysical survey at Site A by Mohammad Arman Ershadi and Mohammad Taghi Maleka. Processed by them and Roger Ainslie of Abingdon Archaeological Geophysics. Each grid measures 30 × 30 m. Traces of the corner of a large rectangular structure may be visible in the south-easternmost grids (bottom, right). See Fig. 9.27 for the location of the survey area.

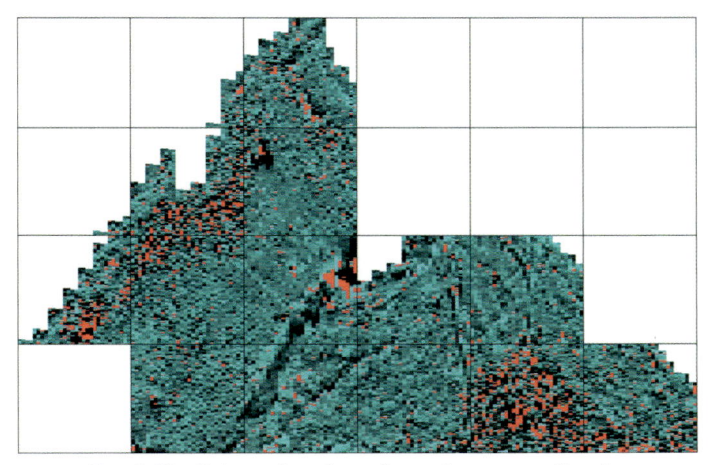

Fig. 9.29: Colour plot of geophysical survey at Site A.

Fig. 9.30: Parts of site A next to the north-western walls.

Fig. 9.31: View over parts of the survey area (Sites A and B) from the north-western walls with the area of shallow mounding in the middle ground.

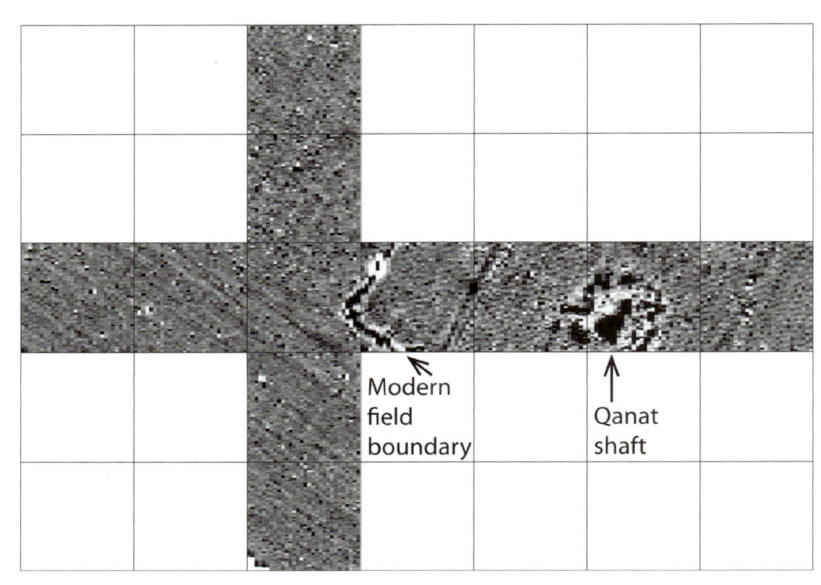

Fig. 9.32: Interpretative black and white plot of geophysical survey at Site C by Mohammad Arman Ershadi and Mohammad Taghi Maleka. Processed by them and Roger Ainslie of Abingdon Archaeological Geophysics. Each grid measures 30 × 30 m. See Fig. 9.27 for the location of the survey area.

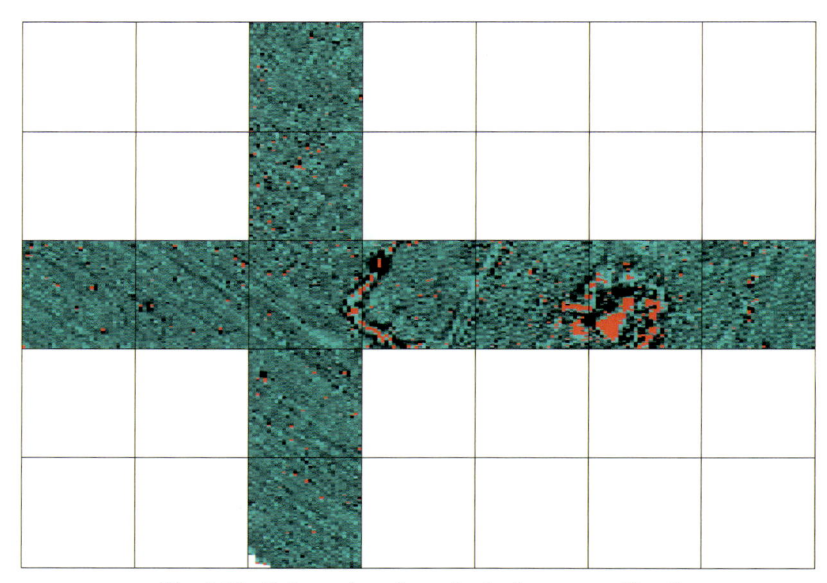

Fig. 9.33: Colour plot of geophysical survey at Site C.

the west of the fortress with water, another leading to the centre of the compound and a third as far as our site C in the northernmost part of the fortress. Perhaps the latter two branches provided water for irrigation in post-Sasanian times; they certainly do not lead to any known Sasanian structures. There is a further branch between the mounds and the mid-point between the south-west gate and the western corner of the fortress. No qanat shafts have as yet been identified outside the defensive perimeter (cf. Fig. 9.3). The qanat system was in use in the nineteenth century, when it reportedly provided clear and fresh water.[33] Parts of the qanat system are still in use today, with open shafts distinctly visible, though the access shaft at site C has evidently been filled up completely. The clear orientation of the qanat system towards the gate leaves little doubt that it post-dates fortress construction, but we do not know by how much. Sasanian as well as medieval or modern origins are possible, and it might have been expanded over time. Some qanats in Iran, such as this, have remained in use until very recent times, and this sophisticated system of underground water supply has a very long tradition in Iran, from the first millennium BC to modern times.[34]

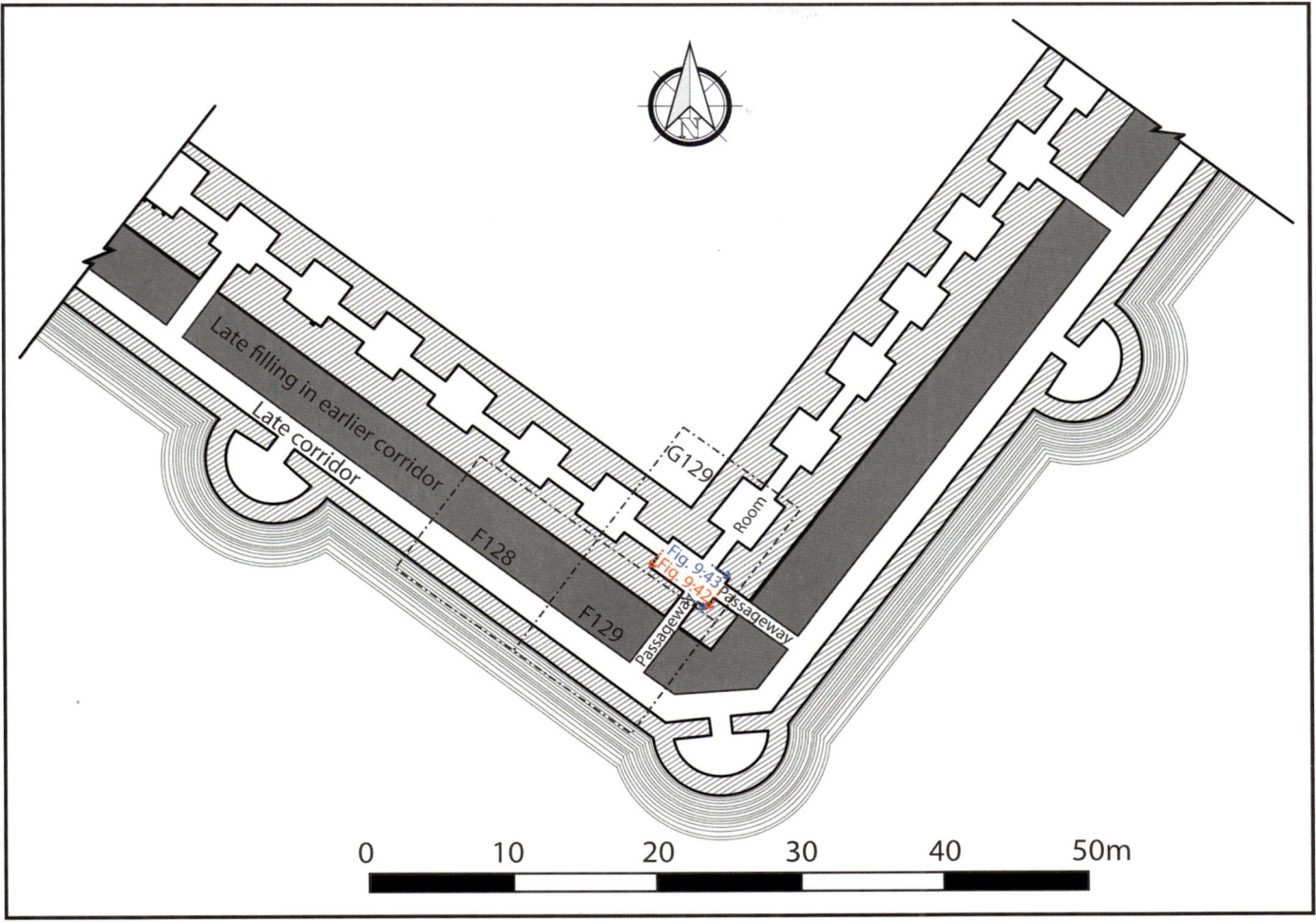

Fig. 9.34: Plan of the southern corner of the fortress, showing the location of rooms, corridors and late structural alterations as well as the three trenches excavated in 2017.

The survey produced no evidence for any permanent buildings in the interior of the fortress (other than those that may have existed in the area of mounding in the west of the compound), corroborating the results of prior pedestrian survey by Dr Nemati and Dr Mousavinia. Other than the cited building debris under the mounds in the west of the fortress and a monumental Qajar building with a large courtyard near the north-east gate, destroyed in 2010 and still visible on earlier satellite imagery, there are no traces of further ancient mounding or any interior structures on satellite and drone imagery.

9.4. New insights into the fortress's history of occupation: excavations on the southern fortress walls in 2017

9.4.1. Introduction

In the latest (sixth) season of archaeological fieldwork, Dr Mohammadreza Nemati and Dr Mahdi Mousavinia focused on the southern fortifications, which promised to shed significant new light on defensive architecture and the fortress's history of occupation. The area chosen included one of the corners of the fortress as well as substantial sections of the adjacent fortress walls. The southern defences have been less damaged than other parts of the huge complex, giving grounds for confidence that the structures inside were also better preserved than elsewhere, perhaps providing vital clues as to architectural phases. Furthermore, important questions remained unresolved as to the precise layout and arrangement of rooms, corridors and connecting doorways. The excavations focused on the upper parts of the wall and three trenches (F128, F129 and G129) were excavated, centred on rooms and the corridors (Figs 9.34 and 9.38–9.44). Each of the trenches measured 10 × 10 m.

9.4.2. Trench F128

This trench, located to the north-west of Trench F129, was centred on the long corridor within the fortress walls

Fig. 9.35: The southern corner of Qal'eh Iraj (drone image by Davit Naskidashvili and the joint project, taken on 21 October 2016).

Fig. 9.36: The southern corner of the fortress before the excavations (seen from the outside).

Fig. 9.37: The southern corner of fortress before the excavations (seen from the inside).

Fig. 9.38: Trench F128 after the end of excavations.

that provided access to the towers. Trenches F128 and F129 were excavated with the aim of exploring how this corridor was connected to individual rooms and other parts of the fortification, and how it was structurally modified over time. Our excavations established that the inner 4 m of the corridor had been filled up with mud-bricks of similar dimensions (of 42 × 42 × 10 cm and 43 × 43 × 10 cm). After removal of this late blockage, we could see clearly the width of the original long corridor: in the first phase, it measured 6 m across, reduced to 2 m in a later phase. As survey and excavation beyond the limits of Trench F128 demonstrated, the narrow corridor, just as the wide corridor before, was connected via side corridors with some of the rooms (and there were short corridors from each room to the next in the row). The late and narrow corridor also continued to provide access to the towers. Pottery sherds found in this trench confirm that the corridor was frequented during the Sasanian era.[35]

9.4.3. Trench F129

This trench, to the south-east of F128, focused on a short arched passageway, connecting the corridor with the rows of rooms, in the upper section of the defensive wall. Just as other structures within this section of the wall, it had been blocked with mud-bricks during the last phase of occupation. Our excavations of this passageway were confined to removing the mud-bricks (some measuring 40 × 40 × 10 cm, others 42 × 42 × 10 cm) used to block it. It proved to be 6 m long (in phase 2, after the outer corridor had been reduced in width), 1.25 m wide and initially 3.15 m high. In the second phase, however, the height of the arch was reduced to 2.37 m. In the third and final phase, the entire passageway was filled with mud-bricks

Fig. 9.39: Excavation of the arched passageway in Trench F129. Top left: prior to excavation; top right and centre left: details; centre right: the passageway after excavation, seen from the inside; bottom left: the lower arch of the second phase (foreground right and top) and the higher passageway of the first phase (background centre); bottom right: the passageway after excavation, seen from the outside.

Fig. 9.40: The room in Trench G129 with a section through the levelling, occupation and floor horizons in its interior.

and mud mortar. Embedded within this blockage, we found fragments of glass, animal bone and some Sasanian pottery.[36] Evidently, earlier occupation material had been redeposited, indicating that this reinforcement of the defences dates to a late phase and that it was preceded by a period of Sasanian-era occupation of the fortress. It should be noted that these three architectural phases refer to Trenches F128, F129 and G129 only. They do not correspond to the numbered phases in Trenches h and i.

9.4.4. Trench G129

This trench was located to the north-east of F129, and provided significant new insights into the architecture of the fortress walls:

1. It clarified how the rooms within the wall were connected to the long corridor.
2. It shed, for the first time, significant light on the life of the occupants of these rooms.

This trench was centred on rooms and the corridors connecting them. It was only partially excavated, but succeeded in unearthing stratified deposits in one room. We found levelling and occupation as well as two floor horizons within this room. These floor surfaces post-date blockage of the access passageway in architectural phase three, as they are well above the floor of the latter. Under these floor surfaces, we found a mud-brick surface as well as remains of thatch in places. These levelling and floor horizons demonstrate that Qal'eh Iraj was not abandoned after partial blockage of the corridors and that the rooms continued to be occupied. It is unknown how they were accessed after the passageways connecting them with the outer corridor had been blocked, probably from the inside of the fortress via stairs or ladders. Little is known about the occupants, as virtually nothing appears to have been discarded indoors even during these late phases of occupation. On top of the two late floors, however, Sasanian potsherds were found.[37] This suggests that even the latest phase of occupation of this room still dates to the Sasanian era.

9.4.5. Discussion

The sixth season of excavations at Qal'eh Iraj by Dr Nemati and Dr Mousavinia has succeeded in shedding much new light on the architecture of the defensive wall, later phases of structural modification and the occupation of the rooms within the fortress walls. These results are of significance not only for Qal'eh Iraj, but also for Sasanian defensive architecture more broadly, which we hope will stimulate comparative studies. We now have a very clear understanding of the layout of the rooms and how they were connected to each other and the long corridor. We can distinguish a series of successive phases: initially, a broad corridor was connected via doorways to the watchtowers as well as via passageways to the parallel row of rooms (architectural phase 1). In the second phase, the width of the long corridor was reduced from 6 m to 2 m. In the third and last architectural phase, all of the interior spaces within the wall, including the outer corridor and the passageways, except for the rooms and the corridors connecting them, were filled up with mud-bricks. The rooms must now have been accessed from the interior of the compound. Excavation in Trench G129 demonstrated that after this blockage, which made the walls much more impregnable and impermeable in the final phase, people

Fig. 9.41: Southern room in Trench G129, with a section through the occupation and floor horizons in its interior (right), and the narrow arched passageway connecting it to the corridor (left). Note that the preserved arch is of the second phase.

Fig. 9.42: Section through the occupation and floor layers (in white) in the southern room in Trench G129. (See Fig. 9.34 for the location of this section and Fig. 9.41 for a photo.)

Fig. 9.43: The blocked-up and plastered-over entrance of the passageway once connecting the southern room in Trench G129 with the outer corridor. (See Fig. 9.34 for the location.)

Fig. 9.44: Close-up of the blocked-up and plastered-over entrance. Seven successive coats of plaster were observed here, evidence for continued occupation of the room after the passageways, providing access from the disused corridor, had been walled up.

continued to occupy these rooms. We found multiple levelling deposits and floor horizons, as well as remains of thatch. Finds included pieces of glass, metal, animal bones and potsherds, but the overall quantity was very small. Some finds were from between mud-bricks used for blocking the corridor and there was also a small number of sherds from the excavated room in Trench G129. Indeed, the successive levelling and floor layers are powerful evidence that this room in Trench G129 – as probably most or all rooms within the walls – was still occupied. Even if parts of these late horizons are levelling rather than occupation deposits, cultural materials were clearly present, and it is worth remembering that there is little indoor deposition of cultural materials at other Sasanian military sites, such as the forts on the Gorgan Wall, Buraq Tappeh or Sasanian-era Dariali Fort in the Caucasus – a sign of tidiness rather than sporadic or low-intensity occupation.[38] Even if we cannot gauge the duration and intensity of late occupation at Qal'eh Iraj, there is no reason to think that there were few occupants. Indeed, the amount of effort invested in architectural modification and eventual blockage of the long corridors demonstrates that there was no shortage of labour.

9.5. The chronology of Qal'eh Iraj

Reuse of old material, maybe sometimes embedded in decayed mud-bricks, poses challenges for establishing a precise model for the phases of occupation of the fortress, encountered in the two sondages. It is worth noting, however, that 11 out of 12 radiocarbon samples are clearly of the Sasanian era. There is just one redeposited Iron Age bone, as there is the odd prehistoric sherd in the predominantly Sasanian assemblage from the surface (and Trenches h and i have yielded no diagnostic pre- or post-Sasanian sherds at all).[39] There were no finds of the Islamic era from our excavations. We may conclude that the fortress was occupied solely under Sasanian rule. Not counting the Iron Age sample, three of our seven other samples from Trench h are probably no later than c. AD 435–440 at the latest and no earlier than c. AD 366–399. It may be significant that the deepest sample from levelling deposit h.014, probably deposited before the gate was erected, is not likely to be earlier than c. AD 399, though a date as early as the 380s cannot be excluded. The first third of the fifth century is perhaps the most likely time for the erection of Qal'eh Iraj. The bank with stone-paving h.003 on top is not likely to have been added before the AD 410s at the very earliest and only after the Qal'eh had been occupied for some time, to judge by the quantity of redeposited finds from within the bank. Found in the gate area, with no evidence for any earlier architecture underneath, we may be sure that the bones are of animals consumed or otherwise used by the construction workforce and the early occupants. The quantity of material embedded in the stone-covered bank renders it unlikely that all material was discarded during construction works. It is likely to comprise also early occupation debris, suggesting that the bank is perhaps some years or decades later than the gate.

In addition to a redeposited Iron Age and two Sasanian samples of c. AD 385–435 and AD 411–472, there was also a bone of c. AD 250–403 from this bank. This sample is likely to be the earliest of our 11 Sasanian radiocarbon samples from both trenches, but need not be much earlier. Whilst probably pre-dating fortress construction, it seems unlikely that it belongs to an undiscovered nearby rural site coincidentally occupying the same ground as the later fortress gate. Perhaps the area served as an unenclosed or lightly defended military assembly area or camp already in the fourth century, before being transformed into a massive fortification in the early fifth century – though admittedly the fourth-century assembly area/camp is hypothetical.

The likely construction of the gate, and the fortress as a whole, perhaps in the late 390s/AD 400s–430s, almost certainly pre-dates that of the Gorgan Wall, dated by numerous samples, none earlier than the plateau in the radiocarbon calibration curve of c. the AD 420s–530s. In terms of its architecture, Qalʿeh Iraj's strongly projecting but narrow gates resemble those of Qalʿeh Kharabeh. A detailed comparison is impossible as none of the gates of Qalʿeh Kharabeh have been excavated, but topographical survey, satellite and drone images and *in-situ* observation show clearly that the gates of Qalʿeh Kharabeh project almost as strongly. Qalʿeh Kharabeh appears to be later than Qalʿeh Iraj, as all four radiocarbon samples (though admittedly none of them from the defences that might be earlier than the interior deposits sampled) point to activity in the fifth and/or first half of the sixth century. There is, however, some overlap of the radiocarbon sequence from these two fortresses, and the hypothesis that Qalʿeh Iraj is earlier than Qalʿeh Kharabeh is not proven beyond doubt.[40] Gabri Qalʿeh near Gonbad-e Kavus, perhaps established between the AD 340s and 430s, has wider gates without strongly projecting gate towers.[41] Radiocarbon dating suggests that Gabri Qalʿeh and Qalʿeh Iraj are both earlier than Qalʿeh Kharabeh. We cannot be sure to what extent there were empire-wide trends in defensive architecture and to what extent they may have varied from region to region. If there was little regional variation, it is possible that we see an evolution from Gabri Qalʿeh's wide non-projecting gates to monumental and more defensible narrow projecting gates at Qalʿeh Iraj and Qalʿeh Kharabeh. It is possible that Gabri Qalʿeh was built first, Qalʿeh Iraj second and Qalʿeh Kharabeh last, but the case is far from proven. The Gorgan Wall forts, which are almost certainly later than Gabri Qalʿeh and Qalʿeh Iraj and are broadly contemporary with, or more probably perhaps slightly later than, Qalʿeh Kharabeh, have narrow gates as well, but these are flanked by gate towers that do not project much further than the interim towers. Future fieldwork may provide precision-dating for more Sasanian forts and fortresses and enable us to refine the typological development of Sasanian defensive architecture. What seems highly likely already now is that Qalʿeh Iraj pre-dates the Gorgan Wall.

The earliest and lowest of the four Trench i samples, dating probably to the 410s–530s, may be broadly contemporary to the later samples from Trench h (h.003/24, h.008/23 and h.009/25) that may be related to bank construction and gateway use. If the preserved sequence from Trench h covers the time from prior to fortress construction to early occupation, that in Trench i appears to extend from early to at least mid-occupation levels. If none of the four samples from Trench i need to be later than the fifth century, there is an over 80% probability that deposit i.008 and the layers above date no earlier than the AD 530s – and they could be as late as the 590s.

The upper layers found in Trenches h and i date in part to the century-long phase in the fifth/early sixth century when radiocarbon dating cannot establish a precise chronology, and we cannot decide for certain whether the latest of our 12 samples is as early as the AD 440s or as late as the 590s – though an end date early within the range seems very unlikely, bearing in mind how many successive structures and deposits we have unearthed and considering that the most likely date for the sample from deposit i.008 falls between the AD 530s and 590s. Continued occupation of the fortress well into the mid- or late sixth century (and quite possibly, though not yet scientifically confirmed, beyond) would also be consistent with the proposed dating of the ostraca.[42] And it ought to be remembered that the ostraca were found at a level within the gateway above all samples excavated and scientifically dated from Trench h; they are thus arguably of more recent origins. How much of the late horizons in the gateway above the ostraca have fallen prey to earthmoving operations by modern machinery, prior to the earliest excavations, is impossible to tell. Furthermore, a busy gateway will not yield dating evidence unless repaved, as the odd bone on the surface would have disintegrated unless buried under soil or stones. Excavation of G129, for which no scientific dating is available, provides tantalising evidence for multiple occupation and floor horizons and prolonged occupation, ending, to judge by the ceramic evidence uncovered, within Sasanian times. Deposits within these rooms may well furnish organic material in future that may establish a precise chronology for the Qalʿeh's latest occupation, even if organic material was not represented well within the assemblage from Trench G129.

9.6. Qalʿeh Iraj: nerve centre of northern Persia's defensive network?

We have discussed the historical significance and context of the fortress already in our previous report.[43] Little would be gained by extensive repetition, and instead we will focus on supplementary aspects, not discussed in detail or at all before. Worth noting is the mounded site in the west of the compound, explored via survey and small-scale excavation. Its function is unclear. The discovery by Dr Nemati of a cobblestone paving and clay floor in the area, with Sasanian ceramics on top of it, and the presence of mounds suggests that there were buildings here. The detection of a potential corner of a large rectangular positive anomaly via geophysical survey at the northern edge of the mound may also point to the existence of more permanent structures here, but the results are far from clear and decisive. Whilst no recent layers were found during the excavations, we cannot exclude that there might also have been remains of farm buildings of recent centuries in the area as observed elsewhere within the Qalʿeh. The function of these mounds/possible buildings is unclear, and we cannot be sure whether they formed part of the military establishment or might signal (temporary?) reoccupation of parts of the fortress. The clear orientation of branches of the qanat system towards the mounds suggests that there was access to flowing water here at some stage. The mounded area covers only a minute part of the intramural area, far too little to suggest that the site was ever a town. The numerous guard chambers all along the massive towered walls and the projecting gates with narrow zigzag gateways also clearly point to it being a heavily fortified military base, not an easily accessible city with gates designed for heavy traffic. It ought to be remembered that there were also some permanent mud-brick structures in other Sasanian campaign bases, i.e. within the citadels present at several such fortresses which probably contained permanent room units. At Qal'eh Kharabeh, we found also rows of small mud-brick houses, probably functioning as supply facilities, lining parts of a central causeway, in addition to a prominent corner citadel.[44] At Torpakh Kala, there were also small Sasanian-era mounds in the interior of an otherwise largely empty huge campaign base.[45] It is possible that there may have been administrative buildings, central logistical facilities or a command centre in the mounded area at Qal'eh Iraj – perhaps mirroring the function of the citadels at other campaign bases. These conclusions are tentative. Perhaps future fieldwork will shed significant additional light on the purpose and function of the small cluster of structures in the mounded area.

Whilst there is no scientific dating evidence for the exact period of occupation of the mounded area, recalibration of our radiocarbon samples from the south-east gate, using the 2020 OxCal curve, has significant ramifications for the chronology of traceable activity at this access point to the fortress. Previously we had argued that the fortress had been built between the AD 380s and 420s. This entire date range is still possible, though perhaps now a date between the late 390s or 400s and the 430s seems more likely. One of the Sasanian radiocarbon samples, however, is likely to be no later than the fourth century, and it still seems probable that it was in this century that the site gained military prominence, even if probably only heavily fortified in the early fifth century.

It was also in the late fourth and early fifth century that there is evidence for a growing significance of Rayy. A (no longer extant) Sasanian rock relief near Rayy finds, according to Hubertus von Gall, its closest parallels in reliefs assigned to the period after the accession of Bahram IV in AD 388.[46] Such typological dating is neither very precise nor absolutely secure, notably in the light of the rarity of parallels. If correct, however, it may be a further piece of circumstantial evidence for the growing importance of Rayy in the later fourth century. Irrespective of the precise date, there are few Sasanian rock reliefs outside the dynasty's heartlands in Fars. The existence of such a royal work of art at Rayy is in itself a likely sign for political prominence.

Rayy and Qal'eh Iraj were undoubtedly located on one of the major crossroads of Persia.[47] Under Bahram V (c. AD 420–438) the 'Turks', perhaps the Kidarite Huns, reportedly advanced as far as Rayy. The specific mention of Rayy underlines the city's central strategic importance: it was an obvious destination or staging post for any major hostile force from the north-east that had succeeded in crossing the empire's mountainous frontiers. The events, reported by the tenth-century author Mas'udi, cannot be reconstructed in detail, and we do not know the precise year of the invasion, though it cannot have been late in the king's reign. Our radiocarbon dates suggest that Sasanian activity at Qal'eh Iraj commenced well before the king's accession to the throne in c. AD 420. The fortress may well already have been completed at the time, but we cannot exclude the possibility that construction works were still in progress or even that they had not yet started then. The fortress was in any case almost certainly largely completed prior to his death in c. AD 438. Why did the invaders not advance further south? If Qal'eh Iraj already existed as a heavily fortified base with a strong military garrison, such a force might potentially have repelled the invasion or provided a powerful deterrent against the enemies advancing beyond – risking being attacked from behind or on return. Bahram V reportedly assembled his army afterwards and defeated and killed the king of the 'Turks' in his own camp much further north-east, beyond Merv.[48] The events are proof that even a site far from the frontiers and to the south of the Alborz was not necessarily safe from attack and may explain why the fortress was well defended (though less heavily than in later building phases), whether in wise foresight or in response to these events.

After recalibration of our samples, it now seems likely that our latest sample is no earlier than the AD 530s and may be as late as the 590s. And this sample was not from the latest occupation horizon. The ostraca, whilst not datable with precision, most likely are of the sixth or seventh century. These administrative documents discovered by Dr Nemati and deciphered by Professor Carlo Cereti, unquestionably just a small part of the written documents once in existence at this massive fortress, have provided novel and unique insights into Sasanian military logistics and administration.[49] Multi-phase occupation and repeated structural alteration of the rooms and corridors within the fortress walls point also to a longer period of occupation, as do, of course, the historical sources. We cannot be sure what role Qal'eh Iraj may have played when the Turks reached the borders of Rayy and the province of Esfahan in c. AD 615. Perhaps it was not fully occupied at a time when Sasanian troops operated as far west as the Bosporus and Palestine, emboldening the Turkish invaders to venture past the Tehran Plain and towards Esfahan. But they may have been conscious of the danger that reinforcements might arrive in their rear, intercept messengers from the homeland (as reportedly indeed sent from the Turkish khagan), disrupt their supplies and attack them on return. Perhaps these risks deterred them from venturing further south towards the empire's heartlands or may have played a part in the khagan's decision to order his troops to withdraw from Persian lands.[50] Whatever role Rayy and Qal'eh Iraj may have played in AD 615, Rayy was certainly one of the last major military bastions of the Sasanian state as late as the AD 630s–640s.[51] It seems likely that Qal'eh Iraj played a key military role for more than two centuries. Representatives of the Mihran family, based at Rayy, are known to have been spahbeds in command of the north, one of the four major divisions of the Sasanian army – as well as on one occasion at least of the south. The military importance of Rayy, notably during Vistham's rebellion (AD 594/595–601/602), has been discussed before.[52] It is interesting to note that already Ohrmazd III (r. 457–459?) was allegedly based at Rayy during the civil war with his brother Peroz I (r. 457–484), and that Peroz I's victory was a result of him being helped by the powerful Rayy-based Mihran family. This may add further strength to our observation that Rayy was of pivotal military significance already in the fifth century.[53] Charcoal recovered from our trenches has yielded evidence for grapevine and mulberry and a wide range of tree species, unsurprising evidence for a rich and varied environment that may have facilitated feeding a large garrison.[54]

It is hardly fortuitous that one of the very largest military fortresses in the Persian realm was in the immediate vicinity of Rayy, the nerve centre of northern Persia in ancient and medieval times – a position inherited by Tehran, the modern capital of Iran. Qal'eh Iraj may well have formed the assembly ground and command centre of the northern division of the Sasanian army. And it is worth noting that the construction of the fortress pre-dates the accession of Khusro I by a century at least. This does not necessarily prove that the administrative quadri-partition of the empire goes back to such an early date, but may suggest that the Rayy area assumed a central military function already in the early fifth century or even before, and retained it probably until the mid-seventh century.

Notes

1. Department of Archaeology, University of Neyshabur, m.mousavinia@neyshabur.ac.ir: Mahdi Mousavinia; Iranian Center for Archaeological Research and Research Institute of Cultural Heritage and Tourism, mohamadreza1973@gmail.com: Mohammadreza Nemati; School of History, Classics and Archaeology, University of Edinburgh, eberhard.sauer@ed.ac.uk: Eberhard W. Sauer. Excavations of Trenches h and i and geophysical survey in 2016 were conducted jointly, with the generous support of the ERC Persia and its Neighbours project. Fieldwork and survey in all other seasons was directed by Dr Mohammadreza Nemati and Dr Mahdi Mousavinia. Trenches h and i were excavated and recorded by Mahdi Jahed, Koba Koberidze, Mohammadreza Nemati, Ali Nankali, Przemysław Polakiewicz and Eberhard W. Sauer.
2. Hauser and Tucker 2009; cf. Blois 2016, 37; Fisher 2020, 71–73; Foietta 2015, 300; 2018, 133–39, 463–64, 470; Hauser 2013b; Tucker 2010.
3. We are grateful to Dr Anthony Comfort for having alerted us to a satellite image of this site. See Comfort 2021 and chapter 8.2.1 for further details.
4. Nemati *et al.* 2019/2020, 190–93.
5. Dieulafoy 1887, 142–45.
6. Nemati *et al.* 2019/2020; Mousavinia and Nemati 2016. On probable Sasanian hunting reserves (much larger and not heavily fortified), see also Northedge 2007, 21 fig. 3, 72–77 with figs 27–30, pls 18–20; Northedge and Kennet 2015a, 14 fig. 4, 62, 150–51; 2015b, 535–37; 2015c, 722–25 maps 1–4; Sconzo *et al.* 2021.
7. Sauer *et al.* 2013, 321–22, 360, 372.
8. See chapter 9.3.2–9.3.3 and 9.6.
9. See Nemati *et al.* 2019/2020 for detailed discussion.
10. Nemati *et al.* 2019/2020, 205 fig. 17.
11. Mousavinia and Nemati 2016; Nemati *et al.* 2019/2020.
12. See chapter 14 and Cereti 2019/2020.
13. See chapter 14.
14. See Kaim 2004 for fire altars, though, unlike Qal'eh Iraj, the examples discussed are associated with the typical *chahar taq* structures.
15. See Nemati *et al.* 2019/2020, 190–93 for a discussion of earlier dating proposals.
16. This trench was excavated by Koba Koberidze, Ali Nankali, Mohammadreza Nemati and Eberhard W. Sauer.
17. For other examples of zigzag or bent gateways in Sasanian fortification, see discussion in Sauer *et al.* 2013, 320, cf. 314 fig. 12:10.
18. Nemati *et al.* 2019/2020, 214–15.
19. Nemati *et al.* 2019/2020, 193, 208.
20. Radiocarbon dates kindly supplied by the Scottish Universities Environmental Research Centre (SUERC). The bones were identified by Dr Marjan Mashkour, Homa Fathi and Roya Khazaeli. The Bayesian model was compiled using the OxCal programme (as were all other models in this report). See Nemati *et al.* 2019/2020, 208–11 for calibration via the 2017 version of the OxCal programme and an earlier model. Note that there is a typing error in *ibid.* 211 table 1: the date of sample h.003/27 is 1730±18, not '1710±18', but, using the calibration curve available at the time, it was correctly calibrated to c. AD 250–381.
21. Modelling was attempted without excluding h.003/27, yielding an imperfect, if perhaps acceptable, agreement of 60.3% and a modelled date of AD 331–412 and AD 411–474 for h.003/24. It seems more plausible to assign h.003/27 to a slightly earlier phase.
22. See also chapters 4.1.4.4.3.1, 8.2.16 and 18.2 with references.
23. This trench was excavated by Mahdi Jahed, Mohammadreza Nemati, Przemysław Polakiewicz and Eberhard W. Sauer.
24. See chapter 21.1.
25. See chapter 18.2.
26. Radiocarbon dates kindly supplied by the Scottish Universities Environmental Research Centre (SUERC). The bones were identified by Dr Marjan Mashkour, Homa

Fathi and Roya Khazaeli. See Nemati *et al.* 2019/2020, 208–11 for calibration via the 2017 version of the OxCal programme and an earlier model.
27 See chapter 18.5.
28 See chapters 4.1.4.5.3 and 18.2.
29 See chapter 21.1.
30 The sample was originally assigned to deposit i.005, but, on the basis of its location, is more plausibly attributed to i.008.
31 See chapter 9.3.2.
32 Sauer *et al.* 2013, 312–18, 341–49; see also chapter 8.4.1.
33 Dieulafoy 1887, 142.
34 Fragner and Rollinger 2020, 497–506; Rahimi-Laridjani 1988, 435–91, 538–42.
35 See chapter 15.8.
36 See chapter 15.8.
37 See chapter 15.8.
38 See Sauer *et al.* 2020a, 105 no. 44, 112, cf. 6, 42, 45–46, 52, 177, 181, 275; 2020b, 904, cf. 877, 879–80, 887, 897–98, 905, 960, 966 and chapters 4.1.4.4.3.1, 7.2, 8.2.16, 9.2.2.1 and 18.2.
39 Maria Daghmehchi, correspondence of 3 June 2019; see also chapters 15.4.6 and 15.8.
40 See chapter 8.4 and Sauer *et al.* 2013, 312–53.
41 See chapter 8.3.
42 See chapter 14.
43 Nemati *et al.* 2019/2020, especially 208–17.
44 Sauer *et al.* 2013, 314–15 with fig. 12:11, 324–27, 334–41.
45 Gadjiev 2017b; Gadjiev and Magomedov 2008.
46 Gall 1990, 36–37, pl. 14; cf. Canepa 2013, 859, tentatively attributing the relief to Shapur II.
47 See, for example, Yaqubi's (= trans. Wiet 1937, 65, 70, 76, 79, 80–81, 101) frequent references to distances from Rayy to other major cities of the early medieval Near East. See also Christensen 1944, 127, 289; Rante 2015, 4–6, cf. 123, 126–27.
48 Al-Mas'udi 24 = trans. Barbier de Meynard and Pavet de Courteille 1863, 190–91; cf. Dinawari 57.18–19 = trans. Altheim 1960, 47–50; Tabari 1.863–65 = trans. Bosworth 1999, 94–96; Marquart 1901, 52; Potts 2014, 133–34; 2018b, 290–91; Rezakhani 2017, 99; Sauer *et al.* 2013, 595; Schindel 2004, 365–66; Vondrovec 2014a, 47.
49 See chapter 14.
50 *History of Khusro* (attributed to Sebeos) 101–02 = trans. Thomson 1999, 50–51; see chapter 24.8 for further discussion.
51 See Nemati *et al.* 2019/2020, 216 with sources; cf. Morony 1987, 205–07.
52 See Nemati *et al.* 2019/2020, 215–16 for sources; see also Gyselen 2001, 28–29, 41, 44–45, cf. 12–13 on the north being considered a region of demons – maybe a reflection of the fear associated with the empire's northern enemies; Gyselen 2004; 2019, 177–80; cf. Christensen 1944, 104–05, 109, 238, 290, 295, 411, 443, 520; Daryaee 2005, 132. On Rayy's strategic key position, see Howard-Johnston 2012, 97 fig. 2, 114 fig. 3, 118, 126; 2021, xxvi map 4.
53 Tabari 1.872 = trans. Bosworth 1999, 109–10; Elishe 197 = trans. Thomson 1982, 242; cf. Lazar 108, 113 = trans. Thomson 1991, 159, 166; Jackson Bonner 2020b, 124; see also Schindel 2004, 388–89 with no. 1715, suggesting that it may be a confusion with Vistham's Rayy-based revolt.
54 See chapter 21.1.

10

A Sasanian city: fire temple, brick pillar avenues and residential quarters: geophysical and aerial surveys at Dasht Qal'eh

10.1. Introduction

The 3 km² large city of Dasht Qal'eh, some 10 km south-east of the centre of Gonbad-e Kavus (Endpapers, front, no. 54), with its 6.5 km long walls was the largest Sasanian city in the Gorgan Plain we know, and it was an urban foundation from scratch, though in part built over old settlement mounds. Its intramural area covers almost twice the size of the Western Roman Empire's capital, Ravenna, the latter some 166 ha large within its 4.8 km long early to mid-fifth century walls – perhaps built at the same time as those of Dasht Qal'eh and in any case not more than a few decades apart. Admittedly, if nearby Classe is included, the Western Roman Empire's capital boasted longer walls and may have approached almost the area of this large urban foundation on the Gorgan Plain. And, of course, Ravenna was chosen as a capital city not because of its size and prominence, but because it was protected by marshland and water, with an escape route available via the Adriatic – at a time when urban populations were in severe decline in Western Europe.[1] Yet, even bearing in mind that the Western Roman Empire was ruled from its new capital for three generations only, before Roman emperors were replaced by Germanic kings, the comparison is telling. A newly built Sasanian frontier city in the Gorgan region was larger than the capital city of the western half of what had been Europe's most powerful empire for half a millennium.

Whilst Dasht Qal'eh's overall plan differs distinctly from Sasanian military bases, which were mostly rectangular, it is also of geometric shape and boasts a corner citadel, a feature it has in common with many Sasanian campaign bases and some Sasanian cities.[2] Earlier research, including our own survey and excavation in 2008, chronology of occupation and historical context have already been discussed in our previous report.[3] Little would be gained by repetition, and the focus of this chapter is on the results of our more recent work.

As in the case of other sites explored already in 2005–2008, we recalibrated the samples from our earlier excavations (of Trench S),[4] to facilitate chronological comparison of the likely periods of occupation of the sites under investigation. Modelling and recalibration has not substantially altered the picture, but has added strength to occupation spanning a longer period of time in the mid- to

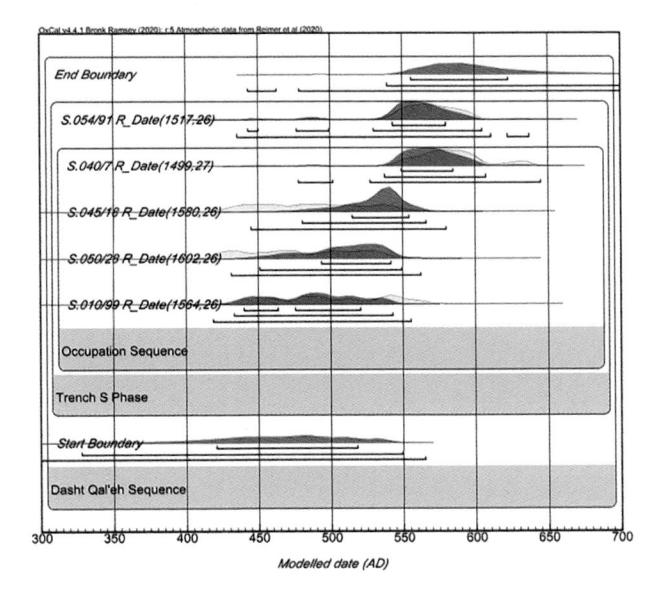

Fig. 10.1: Recalibration and model of the five radiocarbon samples from Trench S at Dasht Qal'eh. The earliest in the sequence (S.010/99) dates at 95.4% probability to c. AD 430–566 (modelled date: 433–543), the next (S.050/28), to c. AD 418–540 (modelled date: 451–549), the third (S.045/18), to c. AD 423–551 (modelled date: 480–566) and the uppermost (S.040/7), to c. AD 541–641 (modelled date: 537–607). A further sample (S.054/91) of a water buffalo bone, whose stratigraphic relation to the other three cannot be established securely, dates to c. AD 440–635 (modelled date: 443–605; 94.9%: 477–605; 90.7%: 530–605).

Fig. 10.2: Drone image (taken on 9 October 2016) of Dasht Qal'eh, seen from the east with the citadel in the foreground, by Davit Naskidashvili and the joint project. The mounds and ridges in the interior are remnants of monumental structures, including the raised supplier canals, brick pillar avenues and roadways, including a causeway leading to the city's northern quarters (right).

late Sasanian era. Whilst in theory a foundation as late as the early sixth century is possible, the observation that we obtained no datable samples from the earliest Sasanian levels – not to mention that it is hard to imagine that in the decades following the defeat of AD 484 the empire would have been resourceful enough to build a city of this scale from scratch – strongly points to fifth-century origins. The latest samples date to the mid- or late sixth to early seventh century, pointing to intensive occupation into the late Sasanian era, but the evidence is insufficient for precision-dating.

10.2. Remote surveys[5]

After the significant results of earlier surveys by Babak Amin Pour and the joint project (in 2008) followed by excavation, we felt that large-scale survey had the potential to yield significant new insights. The city's location amidst prime agricultural land ensured easy access to food for its urban population one-and-a-half millennia ago, but it also results in intensive arable use of its unoccupied interior today. Survey can only take place when land lies fallow and is only likely to yield good results when the ground is level. In autumn 2015 most of the intramural area was under cultivation already when we started. Our team tried, in a race against time, to set up grids and survey them whilst still in good condition for survey and before ploughing. Episodes of heavy rain making survey on wet grounds challenging, not to mention risking potential damage to seedlings, brought the survey temporarily to a standstill. On those days when survey was possible, what we could survey was dictated by land being accessible and unploughed, rather than us being able to choose areas of greatest potential based on satellite imagery. For practical reasons, and as it is often easier to see patterns in larger plots, we tended to survey more extensive contiguous areas rather than a multitude of small plots. Areas in the north of the Qal'eh where satellite imagery[6] shows impressive large rectangular structures were largely out of bounds. In 2016, we were able to fill much of this gap in the north and there was an opportunity to survey more land near the citadel in the south. The vastness of the Qal'eh means that it would take some 300 working days, if surveying one hectare per day, to cover the interior – and much longer if attempting to survey all fields when not under cultivation and in ideal weather and ground conditions. There is no claim that our sample is representative of all areas within the city, but it includes land near the citadel and areas up to c. 1,800 m away from this urban hub. It represents a genuinely random, if admittedly not scientifically selected, sample. The survey yielded important results, even if greatly varying in significance and clarity from area to area. The latter is in part also due to ground conditions, so that near the citadel results from the 2008 and 2016 surveys tended to be clearer than those from 2015, whereas in the north of the ancient city the results of 2015 were superior to those of 2016.

In 2016, Davit Naskidashvili and the joint team also took drone images of the entire city in oblique sunlight, clearly showing, in addition to the moat, walls and the citadel, the remnants of ancient causeways. Complete coverage of the whole city enabled Eve MacDonald and

Fig. 10.3: Drone image (taken on 8 October 2016) of Dasht Qal'eh, seen from the south-west, by Davit Naskidashvili and the joint project.

Davit Naskidashvili to produce a rectified image of the entire site.

10.3. A fire temple

Geophysical survey areas were labelled A, B, C and D. The latter three eventually joined and the former, at site A west of the citadel, complemented surveys of Babak Amin Pour and Roger Ainslie *et al.* (Figs 10.5–10.7),[7] showing clearly segments of colonnaded streets. Further north, the team made a particularly exciting discovery towards the end of the 2016 season, on 30 October: a square four-pillared structure, measuring approximately 7.50–8.00 m across, the pillars an estimated 2.50 × 2.50 m each with a gap of 2.50–3.00 m separating them. This was located centrally within a rectangular enclosure of c. 20 × 22 m outer diameter, the enclosure walls themselves perhaps 2 m across (Figs 10.6–10.11). Potential bulges in the north and south walls of the enclosure, in alignment with the four pillars, make one wonder if there might be two parallel rows of four pillars. If so, this would suggest that the building was an almost square (c. 22 m wide and just c. 20 m long) three-aisled hall. We are, however, not aware of any parallel for such an unusual structure, and it seems exceedingly improbable that there were indeed two rows of four pillars. The bulges may represent brick collapse, but only excavation could ultimately clarify their significance.

Whilst we are unaware of square halls, there are many parallels for square four-columned structures in the Sasanian Empire (Fig. 10.12). There can be little doubt that the building detected was a four-arched fire temple (*chahar taq*) and that it was built of strongly magnetic material, i.e. probably fired bricks (or, if there were sufficient quantities of combustible materials within the complex, potentially sun-baked mud-bricks affected by a conflagration). A linear anomaly running along the west side of the enclosure and continuing northwards raises the possibility that this was part of a larger complex. None of the potential adjacent structures are clearly defined, but there are potential traces of a west–east-aligned anomaly south of the temple. South-west of the temple a deep water-filled well prevented survey.[8] We do not know whether this feature is of modern or ancient origins. Sasanian fire temples are frequently found near springs, streams, rivers, lakes or pools of water,[9] and it is possible that a well was deliberately dug in the vicinity of the temple or that the temple was deliberately placed near a well.

Sasanian fire temples were of no standardised size. Many were bigger and some were smaller than the postulated temple detected at Dasht Qal'eh. Rectangular enclosures around the four-arched temples are not uncommon, even if the enclosure at Dasht Qal'eh provides more space than most of its counterparts.[10] The fire temple of Girre, located centrally within a square collapse mound,

Fig. 10.4: Rectified drone image of Dasht Qal'eh, by Eve MacDonald, Davit Naskidashvili and the joint project.

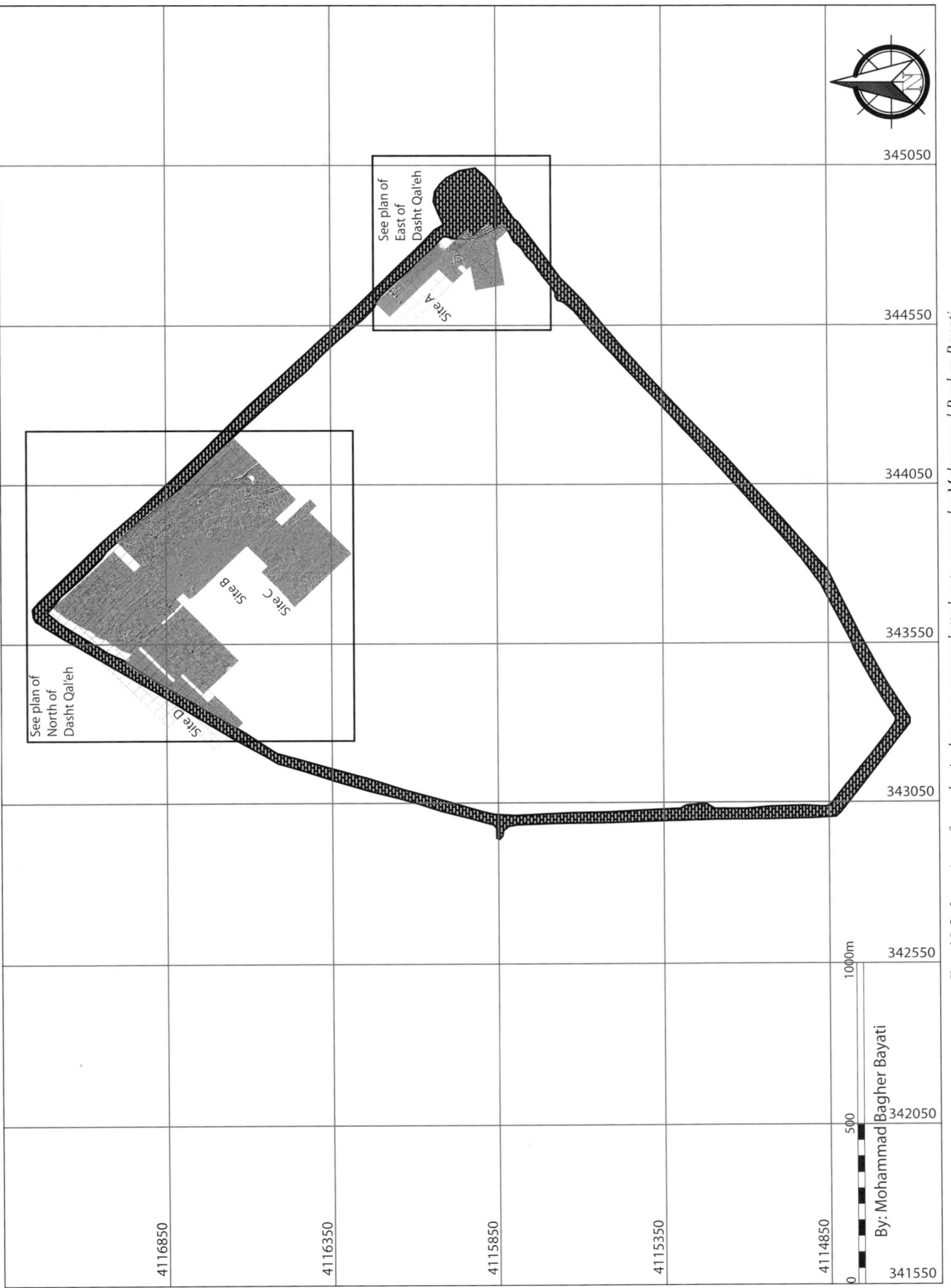

Fig. 10.5: Location of geophysical survey areas plotted onto a map by Mohammad Bagher Bayati.

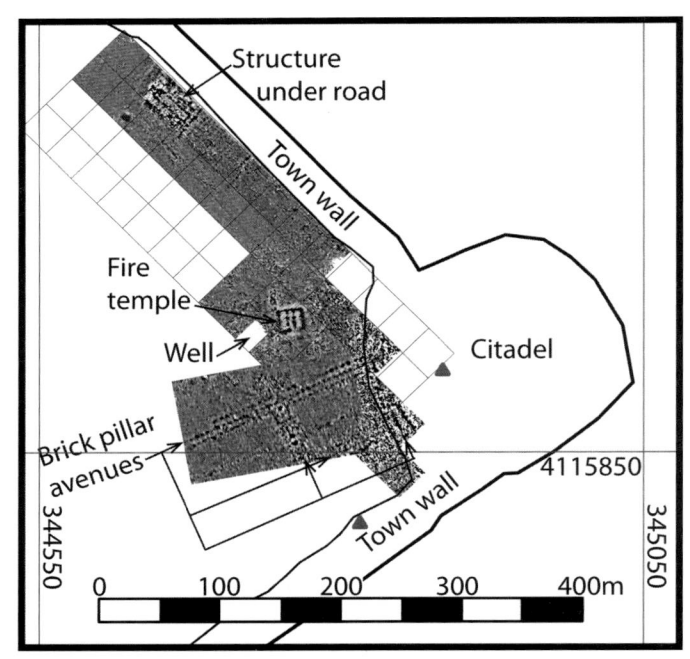

Fig. 10.6: Interpretative plot of the results of the magnetometer survey, in the east of Dasht Qal'eh near the citadel, of 2008, 2015 and 2016 by the ICHHTO and Abingdon Archaeological Geophysics (Mohammad Arman Ershadi, Roger Ainslie, Julian Jansen Van Rensburg and Mohammad Taghi Maleka). The triangles are modern benchmarks. It has not been possible to plot the earlier survey by Babak Amin Pour, which covered a little more of the southern WSW–ENE-running brick pillar avenue.

thought to represent a complex some 25–30 m across, may form a close parallel. Measuring c. 13.65 × 14.20 m, the arches 6.35–6.80 m wide, the central *chahar taq* is larger than its counterpart at Dasht Qal'eh. Dietrich Huff has argued persuasively that the larger complexes, within which fire temples stood, tended to be more thoroughly destroyed than the domed four-arched structures in the centre. Their demolition risked undermining the central cupola, making brick- or stone-robbing a potential suicide mission,[11] and potential respect for old sacred buildings might perhaps occasionally have played a part as well in the decision to spare them. More blurred readings in the southern part of the enclosure at Dasht Qal'eh may potentially suggest demolition to a great depth. Fire temples located centrally within rectangular or square outer enclosures/ambulatories, as at Dasht Qal'eh, may well have been more common than the surviving evidence suggests. In the Gorgan Plain, two other fire temples are known: at Tureng Tappeh and at Qareh Doyub. If our above estimates of the dimension of the *chahar taq* at Dasht Qal'eh are accurate, the pillars of its counterpart at Tureng Tappeh are of only marginally larger dimensions, but clearly spaced further apart.[12] The *chahar taq* at Qareh Doyub, measuring some 13 × 14 m, the pillars with a diameter of 4–5 m on average, was much larger.[13]

It is interesting to note that the (square) brick pillars in the three-aisled hall in the Bansaran Fort were of similar or slightly larger dimensions. Magnetometer survey had suggested a diameter of c. 3 m, dimensions subsequently confirmed for one of the pillars by excavations. The spacing, edge to edge, was c. 4 m in both rows and 6–7 m across the aisle.[14] They appear to have been spaced further apart than the pillars of the fire temple at Dasht Qal'eh. There is nothing to suggest that the fire temple was rebuilt or integrated into a later religious or secular structure. If it evidently has either collapsed or been destroyed, some of its lower courses appear to survive. These observations perhaps point to abandonment and eventual collapse at a time when there was no strong local demand for building material. Perhaps there was little, if any, post-Sasanian occupation in this quarter of the city.

10.4. Roads and residential quarters

Some 210 m (centre to centre) north-west of the fire temple, the survey detected an oblong positive magnetic anomaly (Figs 10.6 and 10.13), parallel to the town walls and probably just inside the point where a road leads into the Qal'eh and where already in antiquity a causeway and supplier canal led into the city (Fig. 10.14). Raised water supply canals under roadways are a frequent feature in Sasanian cities and campaign bases.[15] There must have been a gate in the town walls at this point, north-east of the anomaly. It appears that the rectangular structure, measuring c. 7 × 36–44 m with possible parallel walls, rows of pillars and/or aisles outside, was built here across

10. A Sasanian city

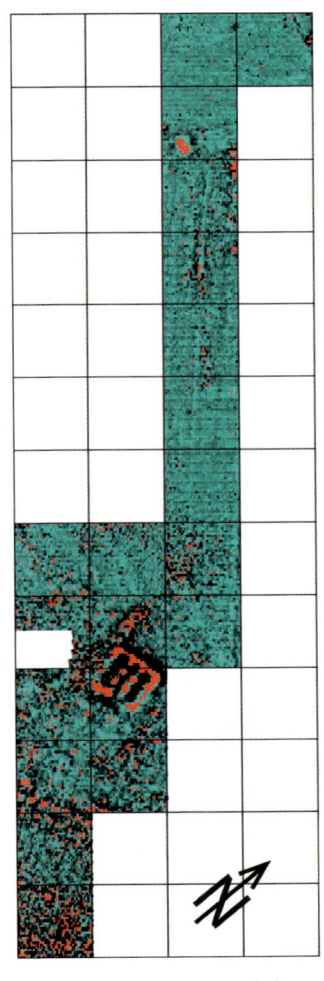

Fig. 10.8: The 2016 survey of the probable fire temple and a brick pillar avenue by the ICHHTO and Abingdon Archaeological Geophysics; first colour plot. Each grid measures 30 × 30 m.

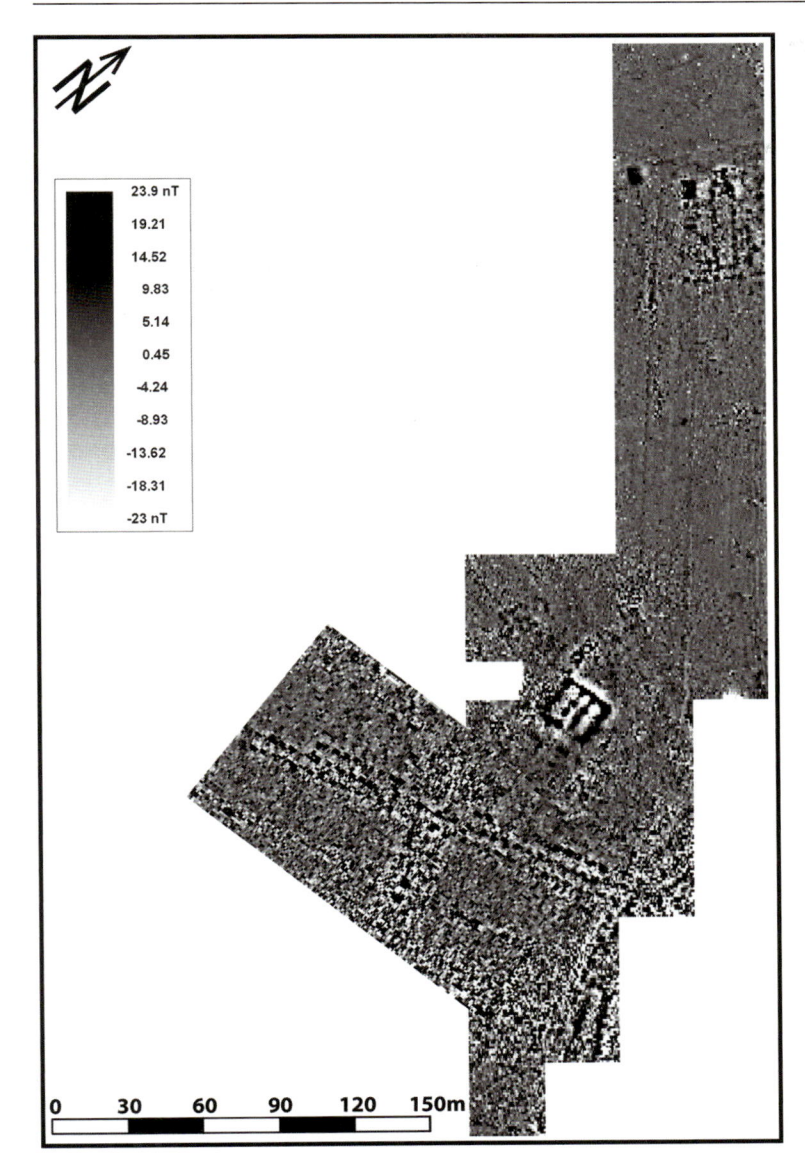

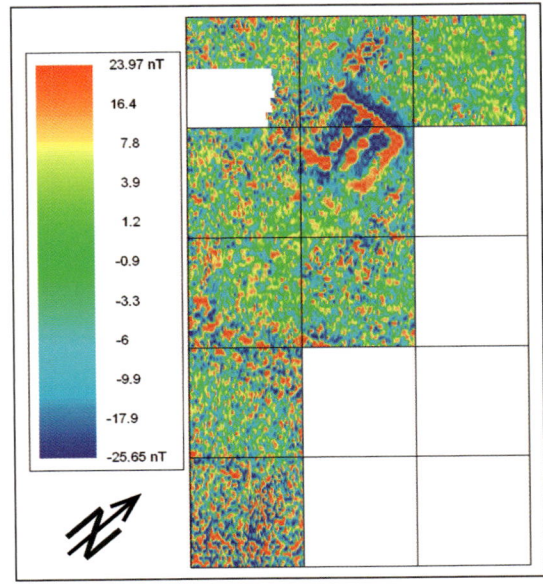

Fig. 10.7: (above) The magnetometer survey in the east of Dasht Qal'eh of 2008, 2015 and 2016 by the ICHHTO and Abingdon Archaeological Geophysics (Mohammad Arman Ershadi, Roger Ainslie, Julian Jansen Van Rensburg and Mohammad Taghi Maleka).

Fig. 10.9: (right) The 2016 survey of the probable fire temple and a brick pillar avenue by the ICHHTO and Abingdon Archaeological Geophysics; second colour plot. Each grid measures 30 × 30 m.

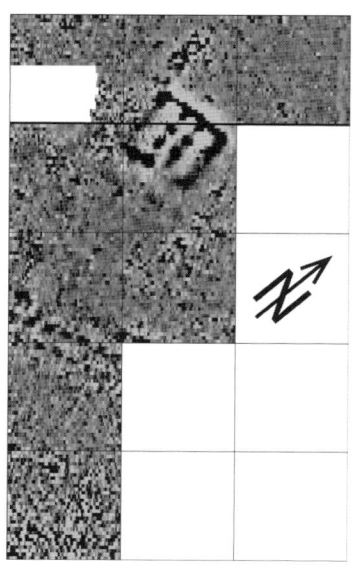

Fig. 10.10: The 2016 survey of the probable fire temple and a brick pillar avenue by the ICHHTO and Abingdon Archaeological Geophysics; black and white plot. Each grid measures 30 × 30 m.

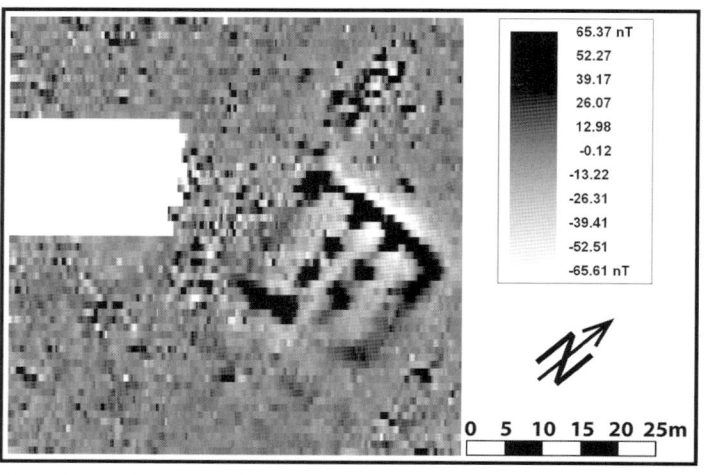

Fig. 10.11: Close-up of the 2016 survey of the probable fire temple by the ICHHTO and Abingdon Archaeological Geophysics; black and white plot.

Fig. 10.12: The restored Sasanian fire temple at Niasar was, at c. 11.30 m side length, larger than its counterpart at Dasht Qal'eh and built of stone not brick, but provides an idea what the central chahar taq *might have looked like.*

10. *A Sasanian city*   395

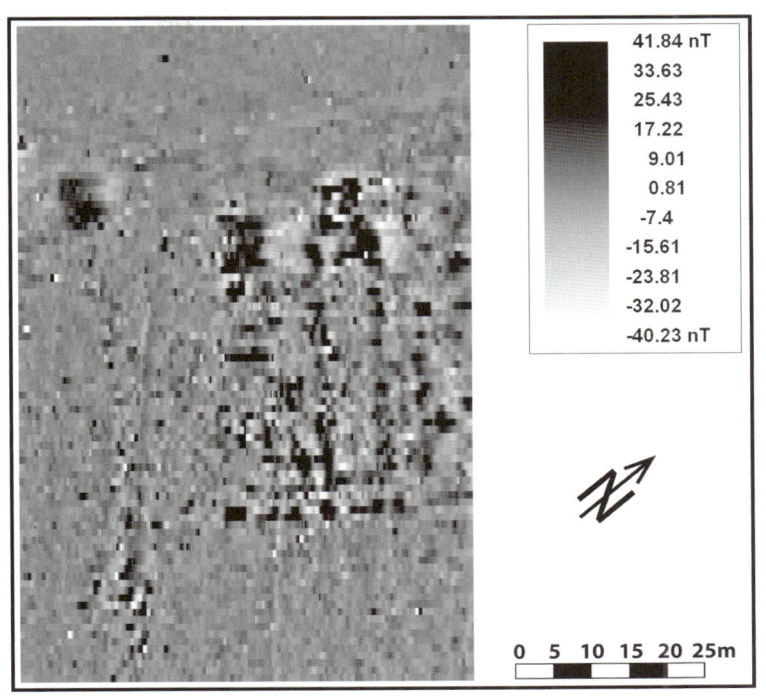

Fig. 10.13: Close-up of the 2015–2016 survey of an enigmatic structure under an ancient causeway by the ICHHTO and Abingdon Archaeological Geophysics.

Fig. 10.14: Dasht Qal'eh's town wall, moat and the raised canal/causeway across still functioning as a driveway, seen from the citadel.

Fig. 10.15: Interpretative plot of the results of the magnetometer survey, in the north of Dasht Qal'eh, of 2015 and 2016 by the ICHHTO and Abingdon Archaeological Geophysics (Mohammad Arman Ershadi, Roger Ainslie, Julian Jansen Van Rensburg and Mohammad Taghi Maleka). The triangles are modern benchmarks.

the road, but its significance is unclear. The regularity might point to a building, perhaps related to the gate, or perhaps a brick-lined cistern rather than a random pit, ditch or scatter of magnetic debris.

Sites B, C and D are contiguous and provide the largest plot surveyed so far with the city. Site B in particular yielded important and surprising results. There appears to be a road, also visible as a bank on satellite and drone imagery, some 10 m wide and perhaps with ditches filled with magnetic debris running alongside, at a c. 25-degree angle to the eastern town walls (Figs 10.5 and 10.15–10.17). This prominent road is lined by fired-brick structures, perhaps housing in residential quarters. The brick buildings appear to be arranged in strips at a right angle to the road, extending perhaps some 80 m beyond it on the west side of the road, matched by similar arrangements on the east side. The extent of buildings on the east side of the road is harder to reconstruct. In the west, fired brick seems to have been employed much more sporadically further away from the road. This need not imply that much of the city's interior was empty. More probably, cheaper building materials, such as sun-dried mud-brick, would have been used here. Surface scatter of finds and the activity of local people today, seemingly

Fig. 10.16: Survey areas B (right) and C (left), measuring 390 × 510 m, surveyed by Mohammad Arman Ershadi, Julian Jansen Van Rensburg et al. Results processed by them and Roger Ainslie of Abingdon Archaeological Geophysics. See Figs 10.5 and 10.15 for the location of the survey area.

searching for treasure, suggest that much of the interior of the compound saw dense occupation. The alignment of the road is intriguing. There may be faint traces of it on the CORONA imagery,[16] but not enough to reconstruct with certainty its course beyond the survey area. In oblique sunlight, it showed up distinctly as a causeway on drone imagery (Figs 10.2–10.4). In future, one may wish to explore whether there was a gate where it reached the town walls in the north and how it linked up with other roads further south. Might there have been roads radiating from a centre point further south? Roads radiating from a centre existed at Gur/Ardashir Khurrah near Firuzabad,[17] but in the light of the major differences in the shape, date and location of the two cities, one hesitates to draw any parallels – in particular as long as we know so little about the internal road network at Dasht Qal'eh.

Within Area D (Figs 10.5 and 10.15), just inside the city's north-western walls, the survey indicates perhaps

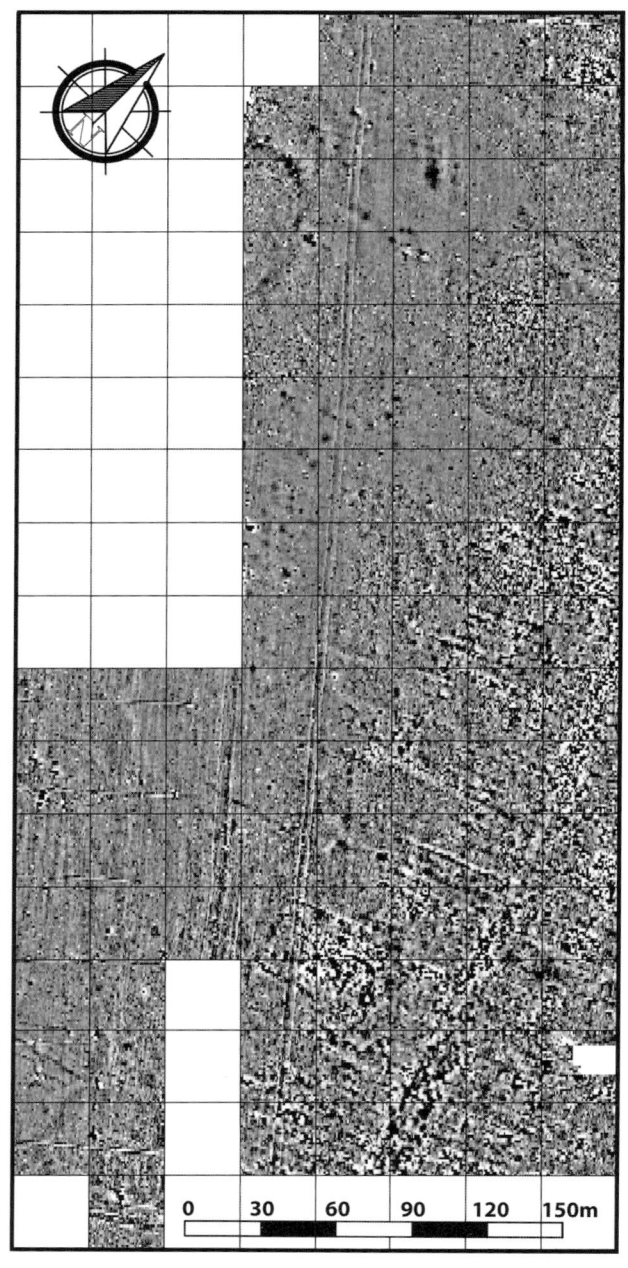

Fig. 10.17: Survey area B, surveyed by Mohammad Arman Ershadi, Julian Jansen Van Rensburg et al. Results processed by them and Roger Ainslie of Abingdon Archaeological Geophysics. See Figs 10.5 and 10.15 for the location of the survey area. Each grid measures 30 × 30 m.

unsurprisingly the presence of much magnetic ceramic material scattered along the city walls. The results of the survey towards the northern corner of the city were rather disappointing. Whilst the CORONA imagery[18] implies the existence of large square enclosures or buildings some 40 m across, the survey failed to reveal any trace of them.

We found in the northern quarters no equivalent to the brick pillar avenues and the fire temple dominating the east of the city. This suggests that monumental public buildings were not built across the vast intramural area, but cluster in the vicinity of the citadel, if not necessarily exclusively so. The CORONA image shows faint traces of linear features in light colour (negative cropmarks?) in alignment with the brick pillar avenues south and west of the survey area near the citadel, suggesting they continue, but perhaps not for far. Areas for survey had also been marked out in the west of the city, but ploughing and ground conditions following heavy rain prevented us from surveying them. Unless and until there is an opportunity for more extensive exploration, it is best not to speculate whether or not monumental structures were built exclusively in the east of the city.

We were also able to visually re-examine parts of the huge site. We observed that some of the monumental buildings on the citadel, explored by the late Mohammad Yusef Kiani,[19] consist exclusively of Sasanian, and possibly early Islamic-type fired bricks; despite a variation in size, there was none of the typical Jorjan type as found in high medieval levels at Gabri Qal'eh and Qal'eh Pol Gonbad-e Kavus, suggesting that the buildings are significantly earlier. Parts of the north-eastern and north-western town walls were inspected. In places they survive well, but ploughing has already destroyed much of the northern parts of the city's north-east walls. A topographical survey of the whole city would be an urgent desideratum, including mapping of any preserved tower mounds along the walls.

10.5. The region's capital?

Several Sasanian royal urban foundations are attested on the Gorgan Plain. Dasht Qal'eh's size, geometric plan and monumental architecture make it a very strong candidate for a city built from scratch on the orders of a king, perhaps one of those campaigning in the north. A fascinating passage in Hamza al-Isfahani on an urban foundation by Peroz I (r. 457–484) in the Gorgan area in the same paragraph that refers to a border wall built by the same king – quite possibly the earliest attribution of the Gorgan Wall to Peroz I – may be relevant.[20] But it is also perfectly possible that Dasht Qal'eh had been established already by one of Peroz I's predecessors. Being the largest known Sasanian city in the area, perhaps it was even Gorgan and the site of its mint. If so, however, this status must have been transferred to the city from an earlier regional capital, as there is no evidence that its foundation pre-dates the fifth century. Whilst built in part over long-abandoned earlier prehistoric settlement mounds, based on our limited fieldwork, the city's origins do not even reach back to the early Sasanian era.[21]

Our new research has added further evidence for the extent of its monumental architecture. Perhaps more importantly, it has shown that parts and maybe

Fig. 10.18: Dasht Qal'eh: view of the still well-preserved north-western town walls and moat, looking south-west, with the Alborz Mountains in the background.

Fig. 10.19: Dasht Qal'eh: view of the north-eastern town walls and moat from the northern corner, looking south-east, showing extensive plough damage to the wall.

most of the intramural land was densely occupied. It was not an urban foundation that failed before being completed nor a largely empty vanity monument. Dasht Qal'eh thus provides circumstantial evidence for population levels in the region being high enough to provide the spare workforce to build this vast urban foundation and to provide it with the necessities of life and with settlers. Originating probably in the fifth century, a time when there were no major wars with Rome or known deportations/resettlement programmes, its population is likely to have come from within the empire. Perhaps, however, it was so ambitious in scale that it flourished only under Sasanian rule. Probably the most populous city on the Gorgan Plain in mid- to late Sasanian times, there may not have been the economic or population surplus to sustain it beyond the empire's demise and to maintain and defend its vast urban space – or it may have made more economic sense then to redistribute its population. We have no new evidence for its administrative status and the reader is therefore referred to our earlier discussion,[22] as well as to more recent scholarly work. According to Rika Gyselen, Dasht Qal'eh may have been the capital of Warushag, one of the six districts of the Gorgan province known so far.[23] Remy Boucharlat considers it a certainty that it was the capital either of a district or the whole region/province as well as the military command centre.[24] In all probability, Sasanian kings will indeed have resided here often whilst on campaign on the empire's northern frontiers.

We may also assume that the city housed a permanent military garrison to guard its citadel and the 6.5 km long walls. In addition to protecting its population, urban infrastructure and valuables, such a garrison would have provided a useful back-up force in the hinterland of the Gorgan Wall and, depending on the city's date of foundation, perhaps earlier, in the hinterland of a network of forts that may have preceded the wall.[25] At times of war, there should have been space, even if it was densely occupied, to provide a refuge for civilians, livestock and portable assets.

Dasht Qalʻeh is not only the largest Sasanian city we know in the Gorgan Plain, it is also one of the largest urban foundations, notably outside of the heartland of the Sasanian Empire. Established probably in the fifth century, a period of peace in the west, it seems likely that it was populated by people from within the Sasanian Empire and quite possibly from the Gorgan Plain itself. It provides powerful evidence that at a period when we see few urban foundations in the Roman world, and most of them of much smaller size,[26] the Sasanian Empire had the economic resources to build vast cities from scratch and feed their population.[27]

It is interesting to note that within the Sasanian Empire urban foundations, some of them, it seems, as in the early Roman Empire evolving out of military establishments, appear to cluster in the northern frontier zones of the empire.[28] These new cities complemented early royal cities in the empire's heartlands. The emergence of new cities in the north may be a result of a number of factors, such as these frontier territories being as yet less saturated with urban foundations than the core territories of the empire, military investment creating fortifications attractive for civilian reuse and/or perhaps occupied by military/veteran families staying behind when the army moved on. Furthermore, security created the right conditions for urban growth. In contrast to cities evolving out of probable military fortresses, Dasht Qalʻeh will have been a city from the start,[29] and its size exceeded even that of the largest campaign bases.

Notes

1. Christie and Gibson 1988; Mauskopf Deliyannis 2010, 46–54; Snyder 2020a.
2. E.g. Qasr-i Abu Nasr: Whitcomb 1985. For a brief discussion of Dasht Qalʻeh, see now also Boucharlat 2015, 31–32; 2016, 3.
3. Amin Pour 2012, 353 figs 3–4; Amin Pour and Omrani Rekavandi 2007; Sauer et al. 2013, 382–406, 689 pls 13:1–3.
4. Sauer et al. 2013, 399–404.
5. The magnetometer surveys were carried out by Mohammad Arman Ershadi, Julian Jansen Van Rensburg and Mohammad Taghi Maleka. The results were processed by Roger Ainslie (who also contributed to the interpretation of the results), Mohammad Arman Ershadi and Julian Jansen Van Rensburg. Mohammad Bagher Bayati set up the grids. The drone survey was carried out by Davit Naskidashvili and the joint project, and the results were further processed by Eve MacDonald and Davit Naskidashvili.
6. Sauer et al. 2013, 383 fig. 13:1; Wilkinson et al. 2013, 84 fig. 3:65.
7. Amin Pour 2012, 353 figs 3–4; Amin Pour and Omrani Rekavandi 2007; Sauer et al. 2013, 383 fig. 13:1, 385–88, 689 pl. 13:2.
8. Sauer et al. 2013, 393 with fig. 13:10.
9. Schippmann 1971, pl. 3; Trümpelmann 1992, 70.
10. For parallels, see Schippmann 1971, e.g. 98–99 with fig. 13, 129–34 with fig. 18, 212–15 with fig. 28; Boucharlat 1999; Callieri 2014, 73–102, 239–47 figs 32–48; Ghanimati 2013, 882–83; Kaim 2004; Kaim and Hashemi 2010; Kaim et al. 2013; Khosravi et al. 2018, especially 286 pl. 9 (fire temple at Mil-e Milegeh of similar dimensions to its Dasht Qalʻeh counterpart); Kleiss 2015, 147–55; Labbaf-Khaniki 2017; Miri 2012, 111–17, especially 113–14, 139 fig. 11; Moradi and Keall 2020; Mortezaei and Zabanavar 2019, 332 fig. 11 (fire temple at Kermjgan of similar dimension to its Dasht Qalʻeh counterpart: c. 7 m across); Omelʼchenko 2013, 107 fig. 2; 2016, 80–81, 96 fig. 7; Vanden Berghe 1984; Zare 2019, 248–51.
11. Huff 1995, especially 75–76 with fig. 3, 84; cf. Mittertrainer 2020, 273.
12. Boucharlat and Lecomte 1987, 52–71, pls 29–32, 124–29.
13. Nokandeh et al. 2012, ۳۷۴–۳۷۷/374–77 [288–91].
14. Sauer et al. 2013, 275–86.
15. See chapter 8.2 and 8.5; Adams and Hansen 1972, 301; Mittertrainer 2020, 71–72, 80, 82–84, 208, cf. 268–69; Sauer et al. 2013, 383 fig. 13:1, 386–88, cf. 313–18, 330–34, 364, 367; Simpson 2017, 29–31.
16. Sauer et al. 2013, 383 fig. 13:1; Wilkinson et al. 2013, 84 fig. 3:65.
17. Huff 2009, 82–84; Mittertrainer 2020, 82–84; Rezaeian 2014, 130–41.
18. Sauer et al. 2013, 383 fig. 13:1; Wilkinson et al. 2013, 84 fig. 3:65.
19. Kiani 1982b, 48–52 with figs 33–35, pls 17.2–22.1, figs 30–31.
20. Hamza al-Isfahani 55 = trans. Hoyland 2018, 69 with nos 225–26, further discussed in chapter 24.7.
21. Sauer et al. 2013, 395–404.
22. Sauer et al. 2013, 382–406, especially 385 and 402. See also Schindel 2006, especially 677, 679, on the establishment of a mint in the Gorgan area in the early fifth century and the (later) foundation of a Sasanian city in the area under Yazdgerd II.
23. Gyselen 2019, 95, cf. 93, 294.
24. Boucharlat 2015, 31–32.
25. See chapter 7.
26. See Rizos 2017b for up-to-date surveys on late Roman urban foundations.
27. E.g. Simpson 2017; Whitcomb 2018.
28. See chapters 8.3.5 and 24.9 with references.
29. Note, however, that Hauser (2013b, 127) has pointed out that Dasht Qalʻeh's plan also bears similarity to the probably third-century Sasanian siege camp at Hatra. Both are polygonal, the two longest straight sides resembling an

'L', though the angles between the sides differ distinctly. Further research is required to determine to what extent the broadly similar shape may have been influenced by topography. Should future research add strength to the hypothesis that these similarities point to a common tradition, despite the two sites being far apart in space and time (Dasht Qal'eh is later and not likely to pre-date the early fifth century), then this may be a further indication that both sites were centrally planned rather than being the brainchildren of local architects. There is no evidence that Dasht Qal'eh evolved out of a Hatra-style camp, but in the light of how little we know about Sasanian camps, one should perhaps keep an open mind.

SECTION C

Marine survey

11

Discovering unknown sections of the Great Wall of Gorgan near the shores of the Caspian Sea

C. Richard Bates, Martin R. Bates and Hamid Omrani Rekavandi

11.1. Introduction

An electromagnetic geophysical survey was conducted to the north of the town of Gorgan (Fig. 13.1), with the purpose of investigating the western terminus of the Gorgan Wall. The survey was undertaken by the University of St Andrews and the University of Wales, Trinity St Davids. The geophysics consisted of an electromagnetic survey using a CMD Explorer and Mini-Explorer (GF Instruments) together with a limited ground truth/test pitting survey at key locations in order to calibrate the geophysics. The survey was undertaken over the period from 5 to 13 October 2016.

11.2. Aims of the survey

The geophysical survey had the following primary objectives:

- To map the extension of the wall beyond its last known position.
- To understand the relationship of the wall to the associated defensive ditch and to the kiln sites used for brick production.
- To sample for ground truth information on the environment surrounding the wall.

11.3. Methodology

The electromagnetic (EM) survey was undertaken using a CMD Explorer and a CMD Mini-Explorer[1] frequency domain ground conductivity meter together with positioning provided by a Leica 1200 differential GNSS. The CMD instruments both utilise the frequency domain electromagnetic (FDEM) technique to simultaneously measure ground conductivity and inphase (magnetic susceptibility) response of the ground. Both instruments are fitted with multiple coils and thus are capable of making recordings at different survey depths, as listed in Table 11.1. The multi-coil results can be displayed separately or used within inversion routines to create a simple 2-layer or complex multilayer Earth conductivity model. The Leica differential GNSS gives positional accuracy to better than 5 cm in x,y,z. Both instruments were hand carried (see Figs 11.1 and 11.2) with measurements made along survey lines separated by approximately 10 m and 5 m (for Explorer and Mini-Explorer respectively) across the site in a grid pattern. Additional survey lines were acquired across specific places of interest, for example at locations where possible archaeological material including scattered bricks were observed in the numerous modern ditches that cross-cut the site. These lines were treated as individual 2D geo-electric sections.

The acquisition began at the westernmost known section of the wall where a robber trench is clearly visible

Table 11.1: Effective exploration depths of CMD Explorer and CMD Mini-Explorer.

Instrument	Effective high/low depth range (m)	Dipole centre distance (m)
CMD Explorer	2.2/1.1	1.5
	4.2/2.1	2.8
	6.7/3.3	4.5
CMD Mini-Explorer	0.5/0.25	0.3
	1.0/0.5	0.7

Fig. 11.1: CMD Explorer, with the flat landscape, that is typical for the western section of the Gorgan Wall, in the background.

Fig. 11.2: Survey employing a CMD Mini-Explorer in the area of the westernmost preserved section of the Gorgan Wall robber trench.

Fig. 11.3: Concrete marker near the western end of the wall (as far as known prior to our survey in 2016), with a scattering of fragmented bricks on the surface (not visible on the photo).

and marked with concrete pillars. Scattered on the ground at this location are also numerous pieces of fragmented brick (Fig. 11.3). Once the signature of the ditch was established, the technique was then extended to the west where the wall and ditch were not evident at the surface. In all data acquisition a cycle time of 0.3 sec. was used for along-line station spacing which resulted in approximately 0.3 m separation between data points. Each instrument was calibrated on a daily basis at locations away from any metallic interference and in a position 1 m above the ground surface.

Following data acquisition, the geophysical results were downloaded to a PC for processing. Processing included filtering for bad navigation points/navigation jumps, uploading to Surfer (Golden Software Inc.) for gridding extrapolation using a Kriging routine and input to ArcGIS (ESRI Inc.) for comparison with other data sets. The line data surveyed along ground truth locations was processed using Res2DInv64 (Geotomosoft Inc.) as a series of 2D Earth resistivity pseudo-section models.

11.4. Results

The results of the geophysical survey are shown as a series of maps (Fig. 11.5). The ground conductivity varies from 200 to 600 mS/m across the site for the data acquired using the largest coil separation (4.5 m dipole separation) with the deepest penetration. Results for the 2D inversions are presented in Figure 11.5. The geophysical results are shown on a backdrop of the satellite image.

11.4.1. Survey results near the westernmost known location of the Gorgan Wall and the associated ditch (section 1)

The overall ground conductivity signature shows a number of linear and curved features that are associated with

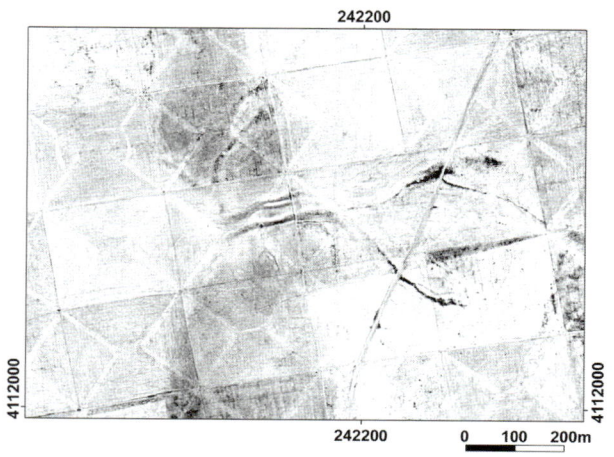

Fig. 11.4: Satellite image of field boundaries (diagonal markings on c. 200 m by 200 m fields) and palaeo-river channels (GAMBIT Imagery of 23 January 1966, courtesy of the USGS).

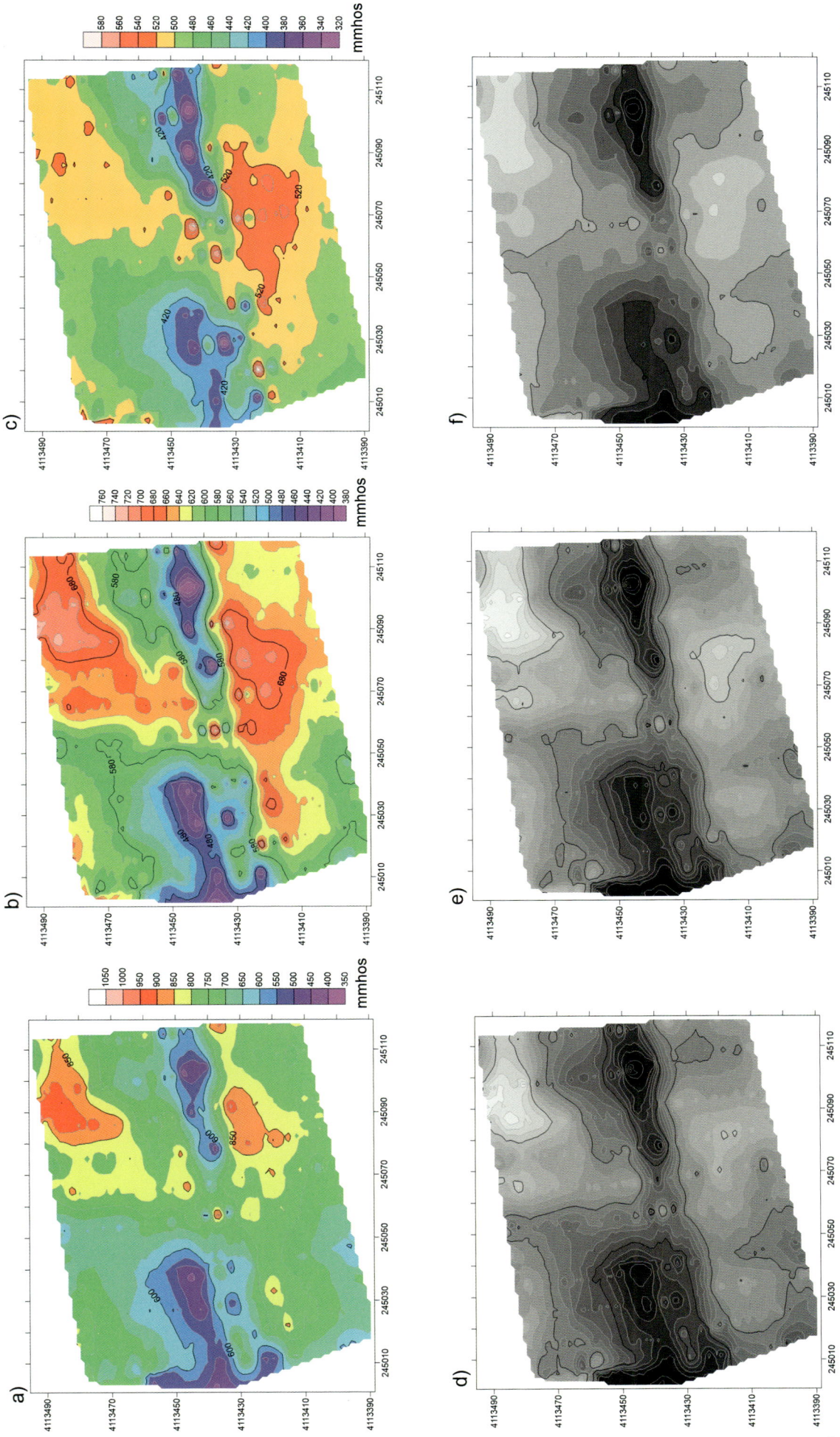

Fig. 11.5: Electromagnetic surface mapping at the eastern end of geophysics survey for conductivity in mmhos, a) shallow, b) medium depth, c) deep, and for inphase values in ppt d) shallow, e) medium depth, f) deep.

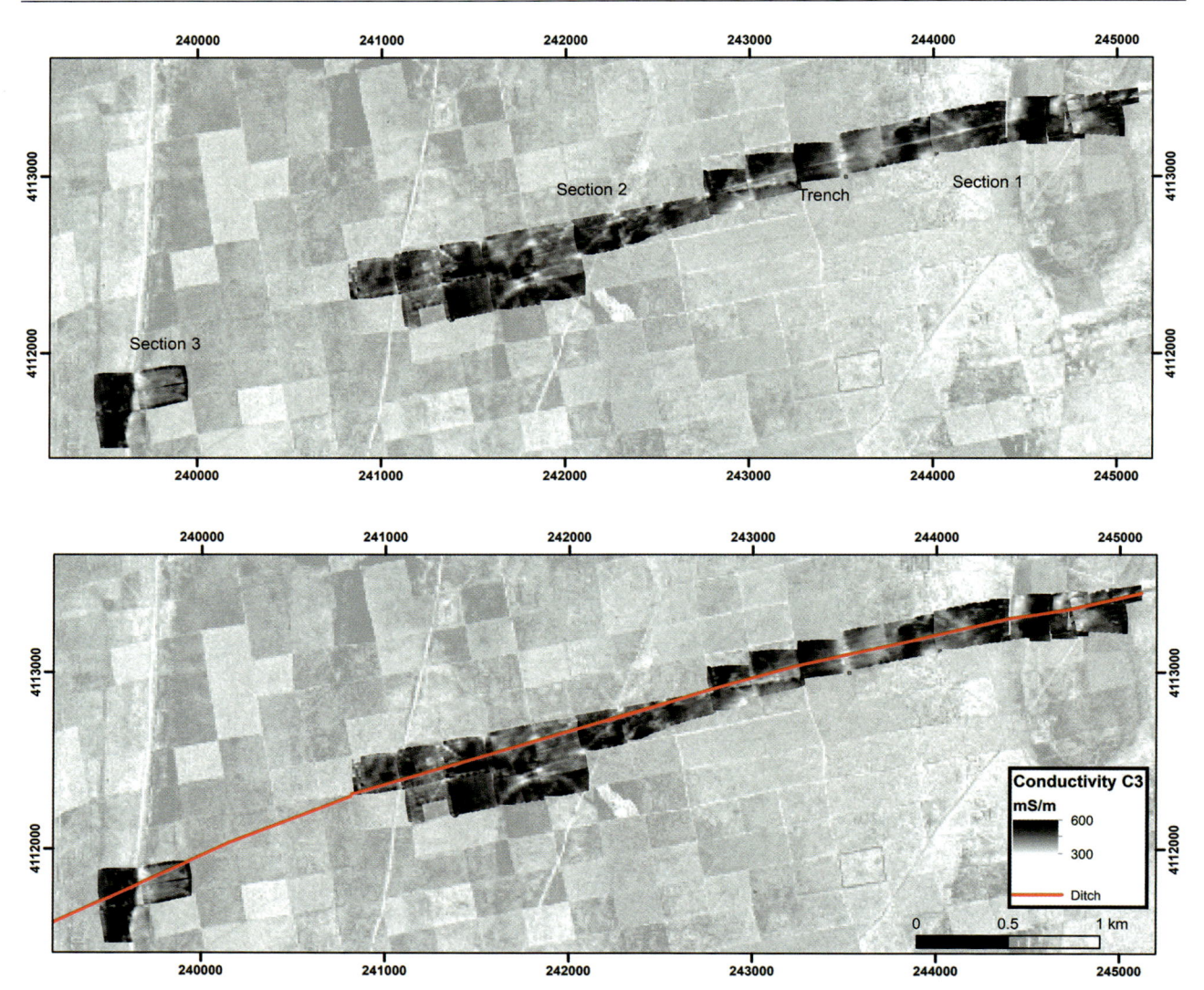

Fig. 11.6: Electromagnetic survey results showing un-interpreted (upper) and interpreted (lower) signatures superimposed on satellite imagery (GAMBIT Imagery of 23 January 1966, courtesy of the USGS).

recognisable noise sources that were identified at the site on remote sensing satellite images and from field walking. The most common noise source resulted from field boundaries and ploughing marks. The fields form a highly regular pattern typically in a 200 × 200 m grid pattern. Diagonal marks extending to the centre of each grid field square are a result of agricultural activity. Broad curved features crossing the site identified in the figures are interpreted as palaeo-river channels and old, abandoned shorelines of the Caspian Sea. The geomorphological and agricultural features are all evident on a range of satellite images (see Fig. 11.4 for comparison).

At the eastern end of the area explored via geophysical survey, the Gorgan Wall is marked and protected by a series of concrete pillars (Fig. 11.3). In places, the ditch has a distinct modern surface appearance and is approximately 1 m deep and 10 m wide, with a scattering of broken bricks extending over a distance of 20 m to the south. Numerous small pits and mounds are located to the south of the ditch and possibly represent places where the bricks were manufactured and fired, and also where bricks may have been robbed out of the wall (Fig. 11.5). The ditch here stands out as an area of generally lower electrical conductivity, likely as a function of the coarser-grained material that has subsequently filled in the ditch. The wall is likely to be of generally higher conductivity due to the increase in clay content resulting from its brick construction. This conductivity signature associated with the ditch and wall is seen in the results for all coil separations on both instruments. Both instruments also show an inphase signature associated with the bricks likely as a result of the changed magnetic response during the brick-firing process. The anomalous signatures are most prevalent in the greatest survey depths (widest coil

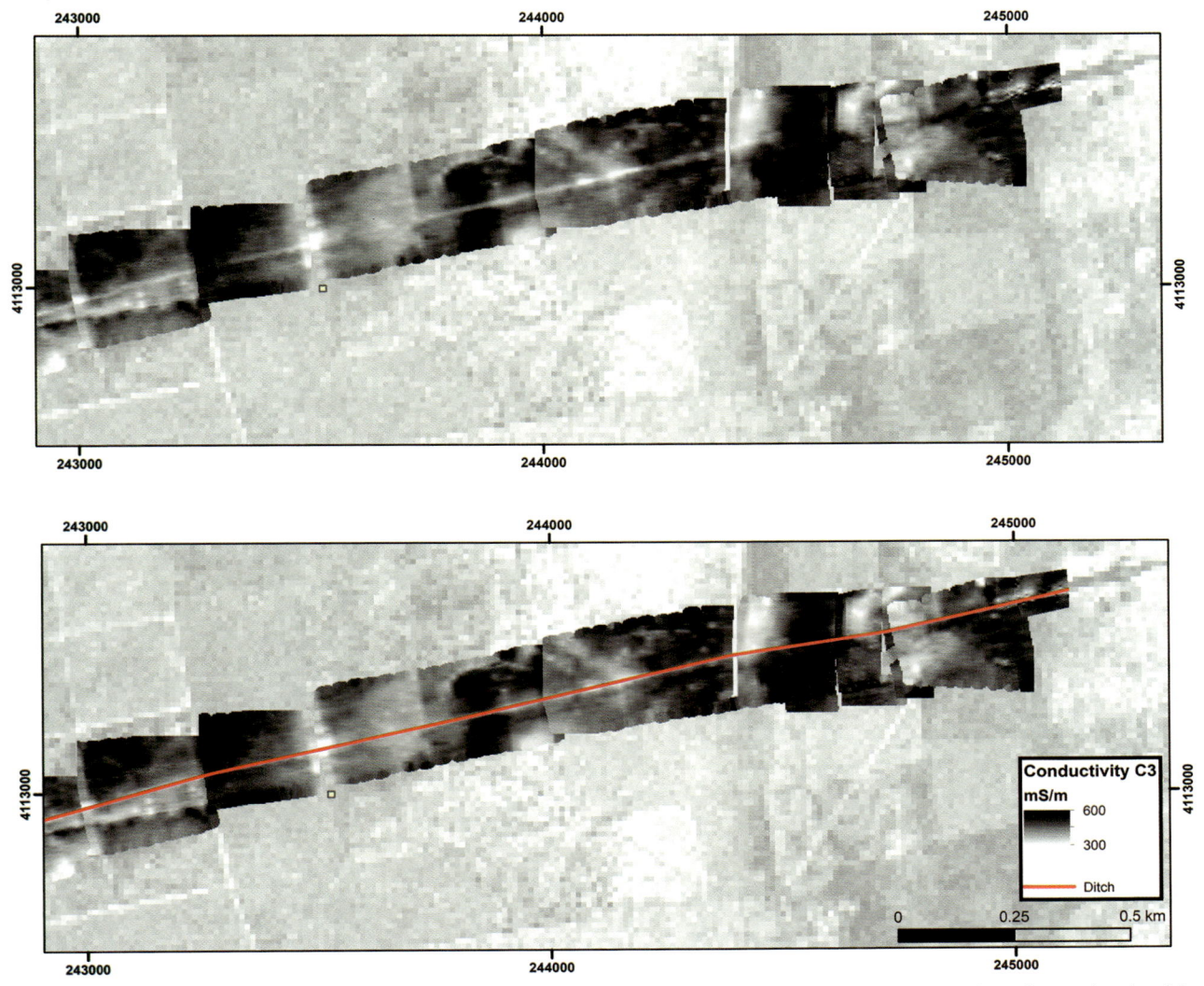

Fig. 11.7: Section 1 of electromagnetic mapping showing a linear (white) anomaly associated with the ditch on the north side of the Gorgan Wall (GAMBIT Imagery of 23 January 1966, courtesy of the USGS).

separations) where the largest amount of undisturbed subsurface material survives. For this reason, it is these data that have been used for interpretation and presentation of our results throughout. The mounds that contain fragments of brick also show generally higher conductivity and anomalous magnetic susceptibility compared to the surrounding landscape. To the west of the known extent of the wall, as far as marked by concrete pillars, there is a close correlation between traces of the wall detected by electromagnetic geophysical survey and those visible on satellite imagery. Where there is a break in the signature of the wall on the satellite images and geophysics, extensive brick robbing and concealment of its remains under sediments may have made it untraceable.

Further to the west of this location, the ditch and wall are traceable as distinct linear anomalies in the geophysics for approximately 2 km (see Fig. 11.6 for all geophysical results and Fig. 11.7 for details) until a point where they are crossed by a substantial irrigation trench and dirt roadway (UTM 40S 243518 E, 4113107 N). At this point, the ditch and wall can be clearly seen in the irrigation trench. This was further investigated through minor excavation which included the cleaning of the sides of the irrigation trench (as described in the next section). The area around the trench was also investigated with a more detailed geophysical survey (see next section).

11.4.2. Geophysical survey of remains of the Gorgan Wall and its associated ditch exposed in an irrigation trench

The landscape in this area is dissected by numerous irrigation trenches. Along one of the major north–south trenches the ditch and wall were exposed in the cutting and recognised by a change in sediment type with the

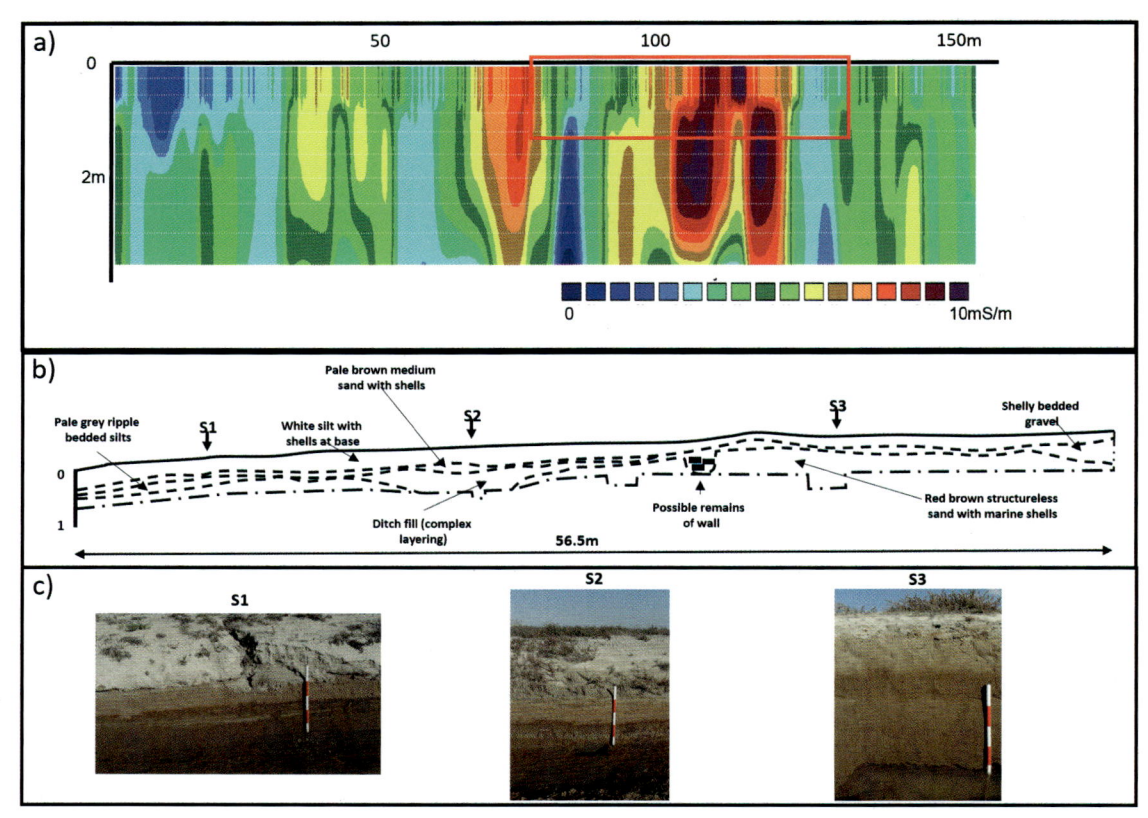

Fig. 11.8: Section through the Gorgan Wall and associated ditch, where cut by a modern irrigation trench: a) Res2DInv64 pseudo-resistivity section, b) sketch section of the west-facing side of the cleaned irrigation trench (location marked via a red rectangle on a), c) photographs of the west-facing side of the cleaned irrigation trench. (In all images, north is on the left and south is on the right. Each segment of the vertical photographic scale measures 10 cm.)

inclusion of brick fragments both in the trench and at the surface (UTM 40S 243518 E, 4113107 N). The irrigation trench was cleaned for further inspection that included the drawing of a section, photographic montage and also sediment sampling at specific places (Fig. 11.8). The sediment was subject to palynological analysis and radiocarbon dating of associated organic material.[2]

On either side of the trench high-resolution surface conductivity measurements were acquired with a reduced line spacing in order to map small changes in surface conductivity that might be associated with the ditch and the wall. In addition, individual line surveys were conducted parallel to the trench in order to invert the data for 2D electrical resistivity tomography modelling. The inversion was undertaken using RES2Dinv64 to produce an electrical 2D Earth model. Figure 11.8 shows the 2D electrical resistivity model. The central zone across the ditch correlates closely to the surface conductivity maps and suggests that the ditch extends to a depth of at least 2 m at this location. The sides of the features also correlate closely with the cleaned section in the trench. In the area where possible remains of the walls are visible in the irrigation trench, one notices a slight rise in the ground and high conductivity on the plot.

11.4.3. Survey results (section 2)

The geophysical survey to the west of the irrigation trench showed similar results as the survey on its east side, with a lower conductivity signature that is likely to represent the ditch and higher conductivity in the area of the postulated wall south of the ditch (Fig. 11.9). This pattern persisted for a further 2.5 km; however, after approximately 1.0 km there was an indication that the features may bifurcate into additional linear segments that trend south from the main line (Fig. 11.10). Further west, all linear geophysical anomalies become less apparent, due to background noise.

11.4.4. Survey results (section 3)

Time constraints prevented continuation of the survey; three additional fields were, however, surveyed at a point 1.3 km further west. Here the ditch and wall were observed once more where they are dissected by another deep modern irrigation trench (Fig. 11.11). Brick remains were noted as a scattered layer on a palaeo-landscape surface in the trench approximately 1.5 m below the present-day land surface. Electromagnetic conductivity mapping did not reveal any clear signature of the ditch

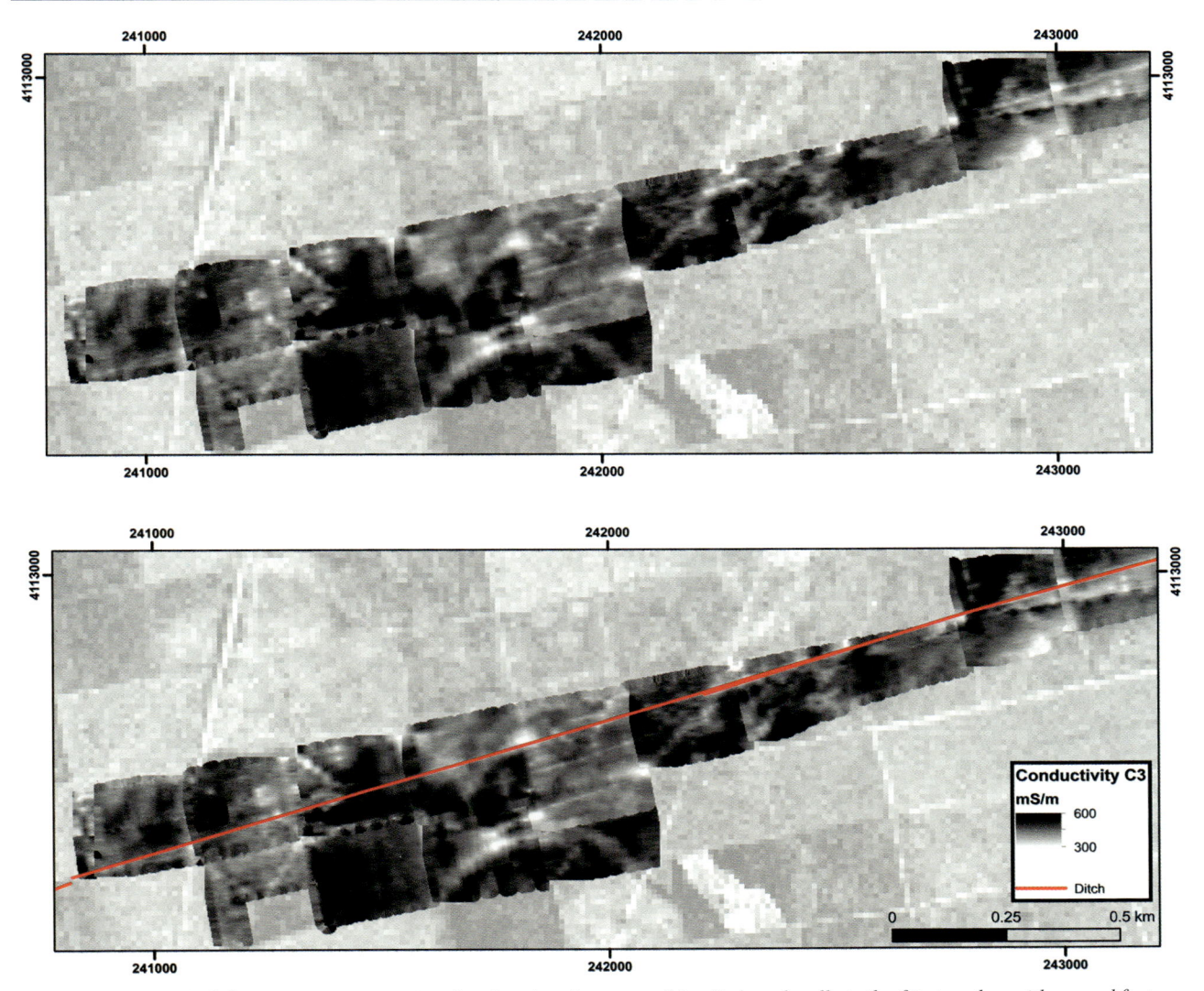

Fig. 11.9: Section 2 of electromagnetic mapping showing the alignment of the ditch and wall south of it, together with curved features associated with palaeo-rivers (GAMBIT Imagery of 23 January 1966, courtesy of the USGS).

and wall in the fields surrounding this location; the satellite background images, however, did suggest that a palaeo-shoreline was present, running approximately north–south through the survey area (and followed by the modern irrigation trench). The projection of the ditch and wall further to the west shows that at approximately 1.0 km further on the ditch would meet another palaeo-shoreline that was also clearly visible on the satellite images. This location is to the north of the modern village of Ishan Ova, and there is a maze of buried rectilinear ditches here that indicate a complex palimpsest of ancient shorelines.

11.5. A bathymetric and sub-bottom investigation in the Caspian Sea across the alignment of the Gorgan Wall

11.5.1. Introduction

Already in 2015, we conducted a sidescan sonar and sub-bottom sonar investigation across the expected alignment of the Gorgan Wall, in order to examine if any detectable traces of the wall continued beyond the current shore.[3]

The geophysical underwater survey had the following primary objectives:

- To map the seafloor along a zone extending from the known land positions of the Gorgan Wall on the east coast of the Caspian Sea.

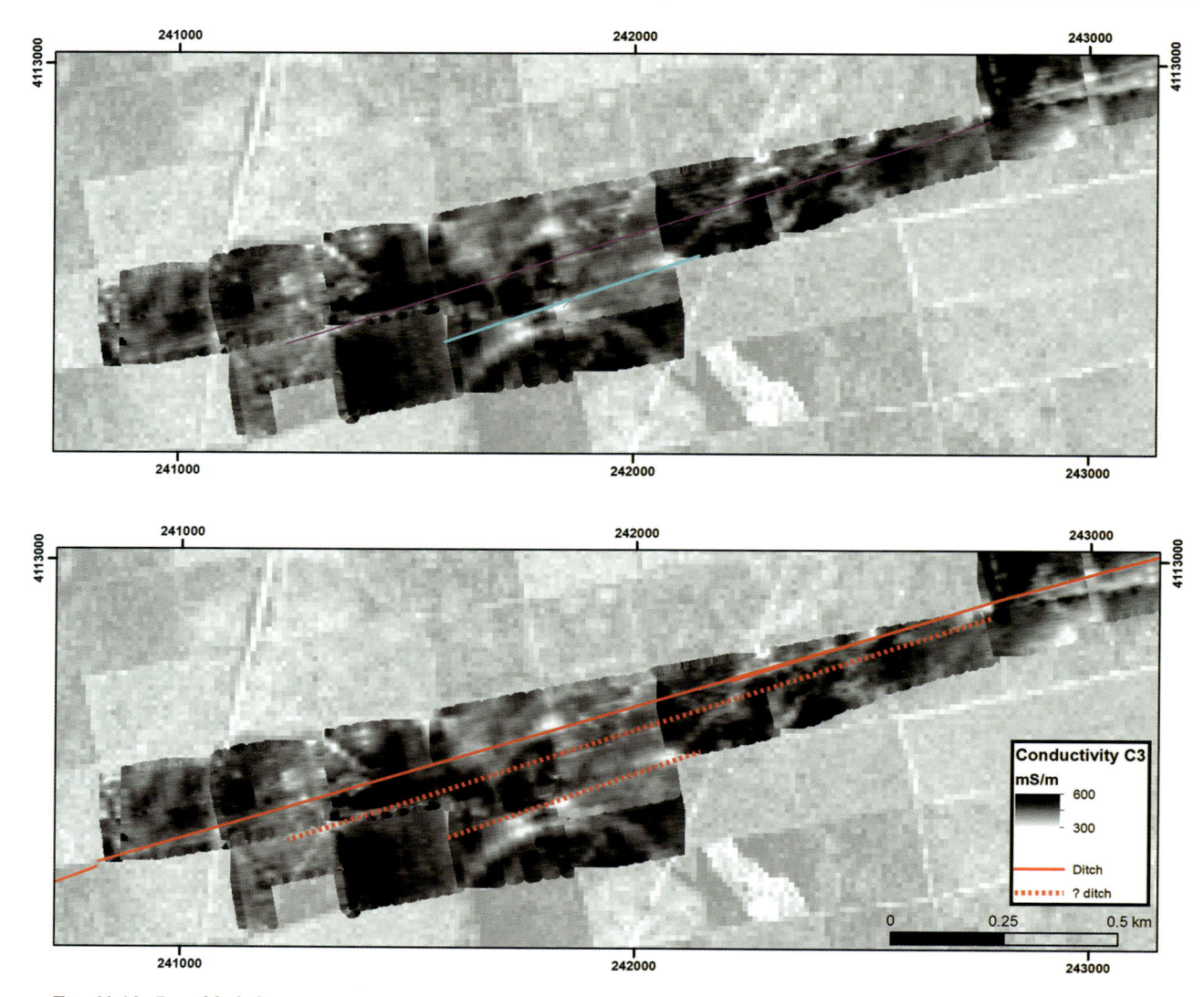

Fig. 11.10: Possible bifurcation or multi-phase wall building (GAMBIT Imagery of 23 January 1966, courtesy of the USGS).

- To map the sub-seafloor character of sediments along the projections of the wall.

A number of transects were made of this northern site with lines surveyed both parallel and oblique to the shore (Fig. 11.12). Acquisition of data along these lines was difficult as the fetch for waves impacting the shore is large and thus even on calm days there was a significant disturbance to the water.

11.5.2. Sidescan sonar

In comparison to the southern (Tammisheh) site, here at the northern site no features other than sand ripples were observed on the seafloor images derived from the sidescan sonar. There were no mounds of stone or piles of brick, unlike further south in the area of the Tammisheh Wall.[4]

11.5.3. Sub-bottom profiling

An example of the sub-bottom sonar data is illustrated in Figure 11.13. The records show the seafloor with sub-bottom reflection horizons parallel to the seafloor. These for the most part are continuous in nature; occasional discontinuities are, however, noted due to the presence of gas in the sediments. A similar issue was observed in the survey of the Tammisheh Wall to the south where gas is often present. However, as the main contribution of sediment load to this shoreline is from longshore drift, and thus is predominantly a coarse sand, extensive gas blankets often hamper survey. By contrast, gas occurs in patches in the relatively confined and sheltered bay in which the Tammisheh Wall projects into the sea. In contrast to the Tammisheh survey, the sonar data did not reveal any mound or ditch-like features.

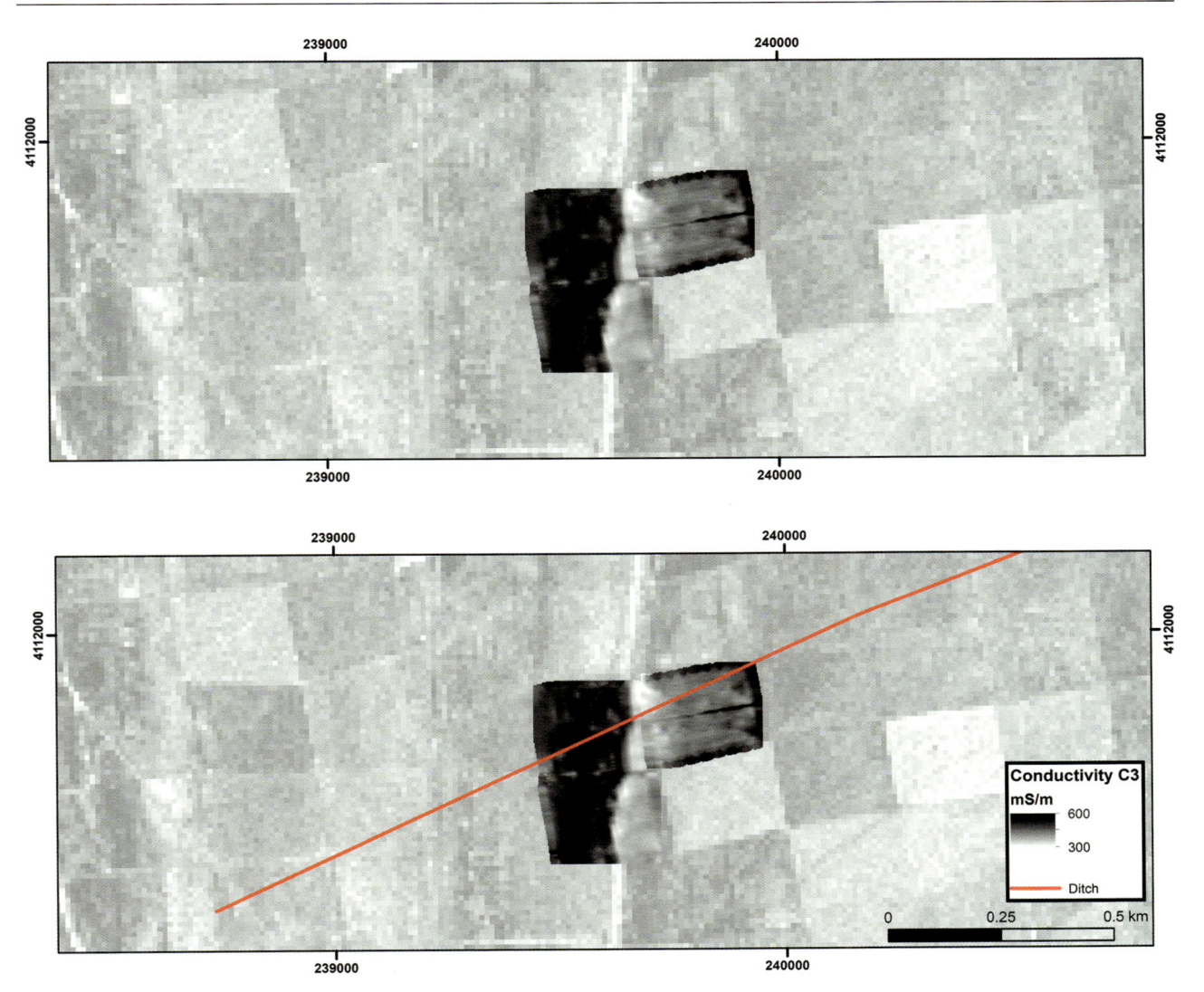

Fig. 11.11: Projection of the ditch (alongside the Gorgan Wall) crossing a further irrigation trench. Note that this trench follows a north–south-trending palaeo-shoreline (GAMBIT Imagery of 23 January 1966, courtesy of the USGS).

11.5.4. Results

Along this northern shoreline, the geophysical survey did not detect any features, either on the seafloor surface or buried in the sediments below, that could be interpreted as the remains of a wall or a ditch. However, because of the lack of penetration for the seismic energy into the sediments, likely a result of both, the coarse-grained nature of the sediment here and the presence of gas at deeper levels, it is not possible to rule out the existence of such features. Furthermore, any remains may be buried at some depth beneath the sediment so far to the west and would probably be beyond the penetration limits of the sonar. Our survey has neither proven that the Gorgan Wall ever crossed the boat transects nor proven that it did not.

11.6. Discussion

The preliminary results of the land-based electromagnetic geophysical survey showed a clear pattern of conductivity anomalies in a linear alignment that are best interpreted as the remnants of the buried wall and the associated ditch. These conductivity variations were mapped for a further 5 km beyond the westernmost point where the Gorgan Wall can be traced on satellite imagery.[5] The electromagnetic geophysical signature shows that the ditch has a low conductivity signature. This is likely due to the ditch infilling with coarser sediment material after its abandonment. The wall conversely is marked by a higher conductivity, and this is likely to be due to the presence of bricks, as clay often has higher conductivity values. Approximately halfway along the area examined via geophysical survey, there is an indication that the wall may either bifurcate or that it may have been rebuilt repeatedly in different alignments over time.

Marine geophysical surveys offshore in the Caspian Sea did not identify any clear signatures of the Gorgan Wall and the associated ditch similar to those identified to the south along the Tammisheh Wall. At the westernmost point of our terrestrial survey, the wall could be shown to intersect what appears to be the geomorphological signature of a (north–south-oriented) shoreline. The shoreline is evident on both the geophysics and the satellite imagery. The satellite data indicate two further shorelines to the west and suggest that the ditch and wall may extend as far as the palaeo-shoreline to the north and west of Gomish Tappeh, near modern Ishan Ova (Fig. 13.1). In order to verify this, it is recommended that further electromagnetic geophysics is carried out in this area together with trenching, to ground-truth the results.

Notes

1. GF Instruments: http://www.gfinstruments.cz/index.php?menu=gi&cont=cmd_ov (accessed on 30 July 2021).
2. See chapter 13.
3. See chapter 12 on this survey, especially 12.3 on the methodology.
4. See chapter 12.
5. Sauer et al. 2013, 149.

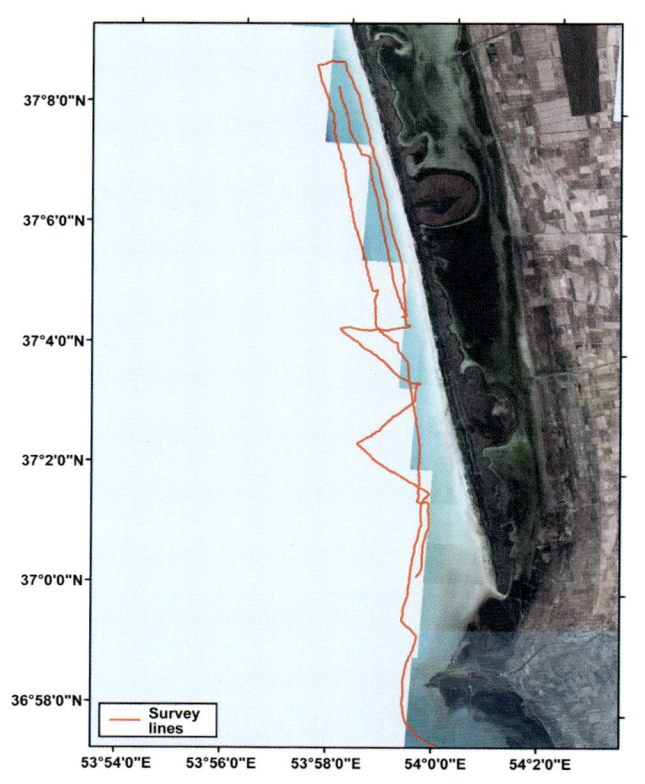

Fig. 11.12: Sonar track data for the northern survey area, from the current mouth of the Gorgan River in the south to well beyond the projected alignment of the Gorgan Wall in the north (Image © Landsat/Copernicus).

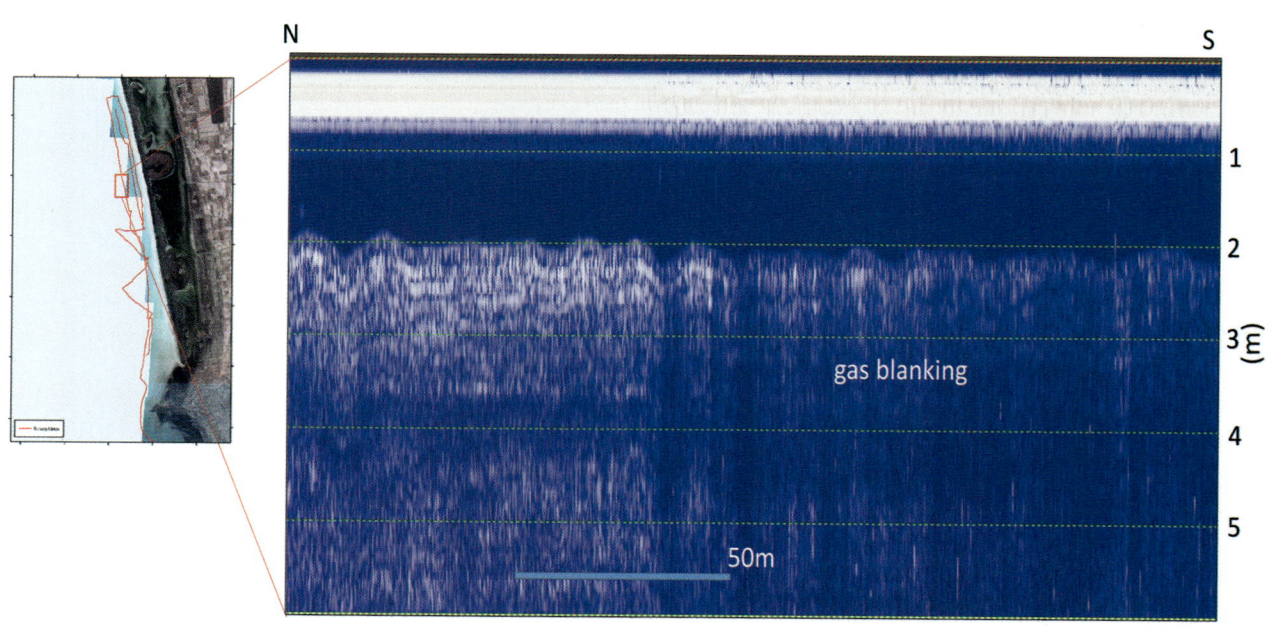

Fig. 11.13: Example of sub-bottom seismic data from the northern site, around the area of the projected alignment of the Gorgan Wall, showing sub-surface reflections and signature lost due to gas blanking.

12

A bathymetric and sub-bottom investigation of the Tammisheh Wall's northernmost section submerged in the Caspian Sea

C. Richard Bates, Hamid Omrani Rekavandi and Hossein Tofighian

12.1. Introduction

A geophysical survey was conducted in the Caspian Sea near the town of Gorgan, with the purpose of investigating the termini of the Gorgan and Tammisheh Walls where they project into the sea. The survey was undertaken by the University of St Andrews as part of the joint project. The survey consisted of a sidescan sonar and sub-bottom sonar investigation at two locations, namely north of the towns of Bandar Gaz and west of Bandar Torkaman (Figs 12.1–12.2 and 13.2). The northern survey, aimed at detecting whether the Gorgan Wall ran beyond the current shoreline into the area of the Caspian Sea, has already been discussed in a previous chapter.[1] The survey was undertaken over the period from 1 to 10 December 2015. This report describes the aims of the survey, the methodology used and the results.

Fig. 12.1: The southern Caspian Sea (Image © Landsat / Copernicus).

Fig. 12.2: Northern and southern field site areas offshore Gorgan (Image © Landsat / Copernicus).

12.2. Aims of the survey

The geophysical underwater survey had the following primary objectives:
- To map the seafloor along the known section of the Tammisheh Wall in the Caspian Sea.[2]
- To map the sub-seafloor character of sediments along the projection of the wall further NNW.
- To identify, record and interpret areas of potential archaeological significance with regard to the presence of the wall or other features that could be associated with it, for example forts, ditches and other buildings or structures.
- To produce maps of sediment for further ground truth-investigation using coring techniques.

12.3. Methodology

The survey was undertaken using a local vessel of opportunity. The vessel, a local tourist fishing boat, was fitted for survey with some minor adaptations in order that both sonar devices could be deployed on the vessel in a position where the least acoustic noise possible was apparent in the recorded data (Figs 12.3–12.4). The sidescan sonar data were acquired using a Tritech Starfish 900 kHz sonar.[3] This was deployed using the Starfish GPS capable of an absolute accuracy of 4 m positioning and relative accuracy of 0.50 m positioning along each survey line. The Starfish was mounted on the survey vessel rather than deployed in towed mode, as water depths within much of the survey area were less than 4 m. All data were recorded in the field in Tritech proprietary data format on a rugged laptop to ensure quality control on data acquisition and also to ensure that full coverage was obtained of the survey areas. The sub-bottom survey and bathymetric data were acquired using a Tritech SeaKing Parametric Sub-bottom profiler.[4] The parametric sonar operates at a primary frequency of 200 KHz with a sub-bottom penetration at 20 kHz. Data were acquired along transect lines oriented approximately parallel and perpendicular to the projection of the wall. Data processing for the sidescan and sub-bottom sonar was achieved using SonarWiz 5 (Chesapeake Inc.), ArcGIS (ESRI Inc.) and Fledermaus (QPS ltd.). The data processing included data filtering, trace balancing, seafloor picking, sub-lake floor reflector picking, extrapolation of horizons for map production and modelling of buried features.

Despite the near-shore and sheltered location of the survey sites, during the survey the weather and sea state varied considerably. On calm days with wind less than 10 kts and sea state less than 4 on the Douglas

Fig. 12.3: Vessel with sonar mount.

Fig. 12.4: Sonar mounted on starboard side.

Sea State scale, data quality was high. However, when environmental conditions increased above this, survey was abandoned in order to maintain high data quality. This chapter focuses on the Tammisheh Wall where it projects north into the Caspian Sea to an area of shallow water (sometimes forming an island when water levels are low) that has been interpreted as the remnants of a fort, and beyond.

12.4. Results

12.4.1. The site

The area was surveyed along lines oriented approximately parallel and perpendicular to the projection of the Tammisheh Wall. A bathymetric chart is presented for the site in Figure 12.5. This shows a gently dipping seafloor to the north from less than 1 m depth to over 3 m (elevations of just under -28 m to almost -32 m: Fig. 12.11). At the southern end, the shallowest part of the survey is exposed as a small island (partially above water at the time of the survey, but at times of higher water tables often completely submerged) that has previously been identified as the remains of a fort. This location is marked by a scatter of brick pieces, which had previously been identified by diver survey and mapped. The diver survey also succeeded in following a brick alignment, interpreted as the collapsed Tammisheh Wall, for c. 700 m beyond the fort to the NNW.[5]

12.4.2. Seafloor bathymetry

A map of seafloor bathymetry was produced from the seismic data and this is shown in Figure 12.5. The gentle dip of the seafloor to the north is evident in the survey and no manifestation of scour or sediment settlement as a result of buried features is shown on the seafloor.

12.4.3. Sidescan sonar

The results of the sidescan sonar survey are shown in Figure 12.6 for all lines conducted at the site. A single linear feature was mapped on the site extending for approximately 800 m to the north of the partially submerged fort platform (Fig. 12.7). The sharp nature of the returns from this feature would suggest that it is a hard object with a width of less than 1 m. Scattered along the feature is a narrow (less than 5 m wide) linear alignment of small rocks. These had previously been detected by divers and tentatively interpreted as an ancient breakwater to protect the wall. Based on signatures from other sites, however, this is likely to be a modern feature such as a pipe or cable. The rocks may have been placed on top to protect it and, contrary to the earlier hypothesis, it is not likely to be ancient.[6]

Extending in a line NNW from the shallow fort area, the sidescan sonar records showed rugged or rough seafloor in a wide band. The rough signature was associated with brick scatter that had also been mapped by the divers and stands out when compared to the surrounding soft silt/sand (Fig. 12.7). The feature is for the most part heavily covered in marine growth. The rough signature was mapped on the seafloor along the projection of the wall for approximately 700 m beyond the fort (Fig. 12.20).

12.4.4. Sub-bottom profiling

A number of sub-bottom profile transects were surveyed both parallel and perpendicular to the wall projection (Fig. 12.8). Seismic sub-bottom sonar works on the principle of acoustic impedance contrasts. These can occur between different sedimentary materials or between sediments and harder substrates such as rock or fired bricks or tiles. When a change in impedance is encountered, it causes a reflection in the subsurface that can either be mapped as a layer or as a point that causes diffraction patterns. For the southern site along the Tammisheh Wall, penetration of the seafloor with the seismic energy was achieved to depths of greater than 5 m. At the northern site, covering an area to the north and south of the projected alignment of the Gorgan Wall,[7] penetration was limited with few strong

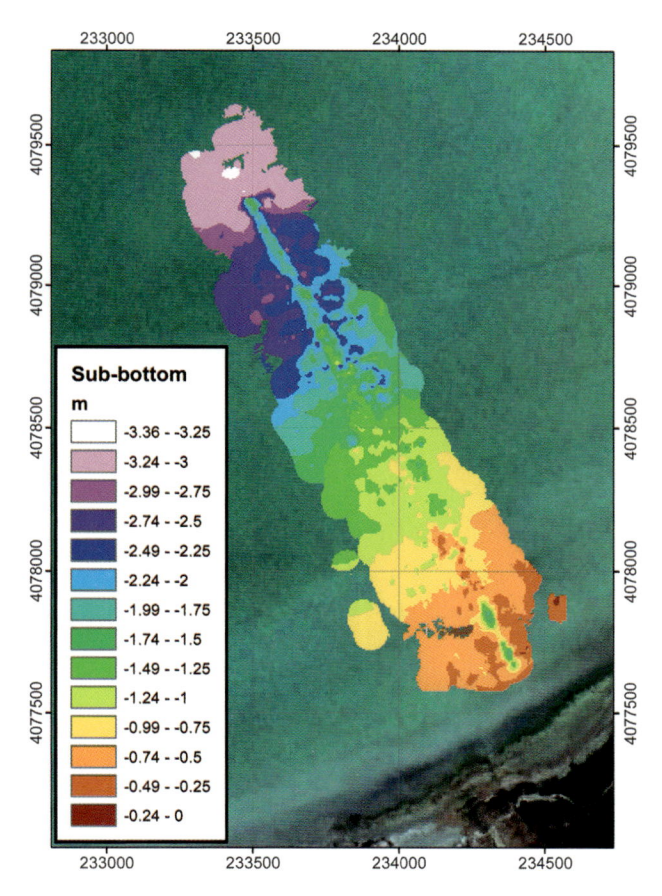

Fig. 12.5: Sub-seafloor surface (metres below sea level at the time of the survey in 2015) (background image: courtesy of Google Earth).

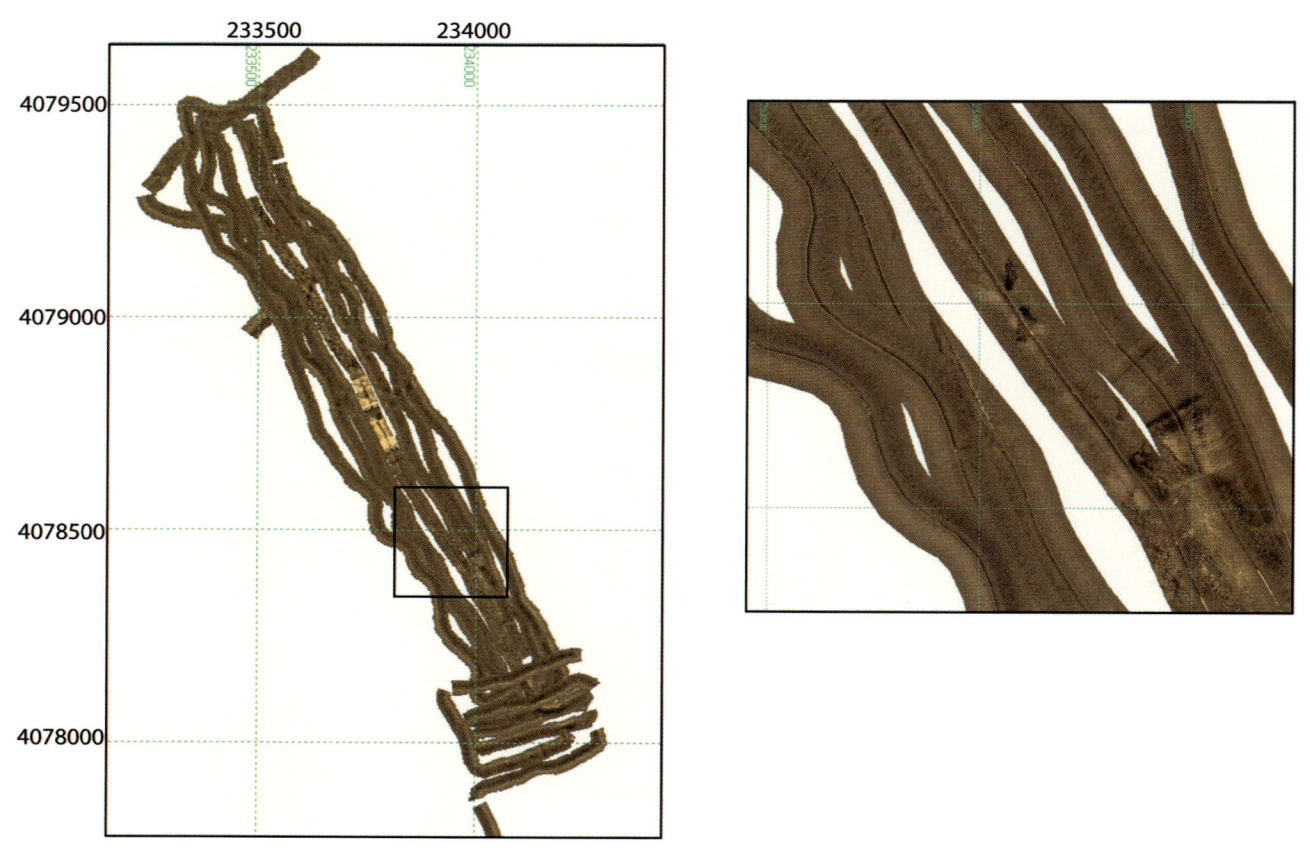

Fig. 12.6: Sidescan sonar track, southern site (left); sidescan sonar line tracks (right).

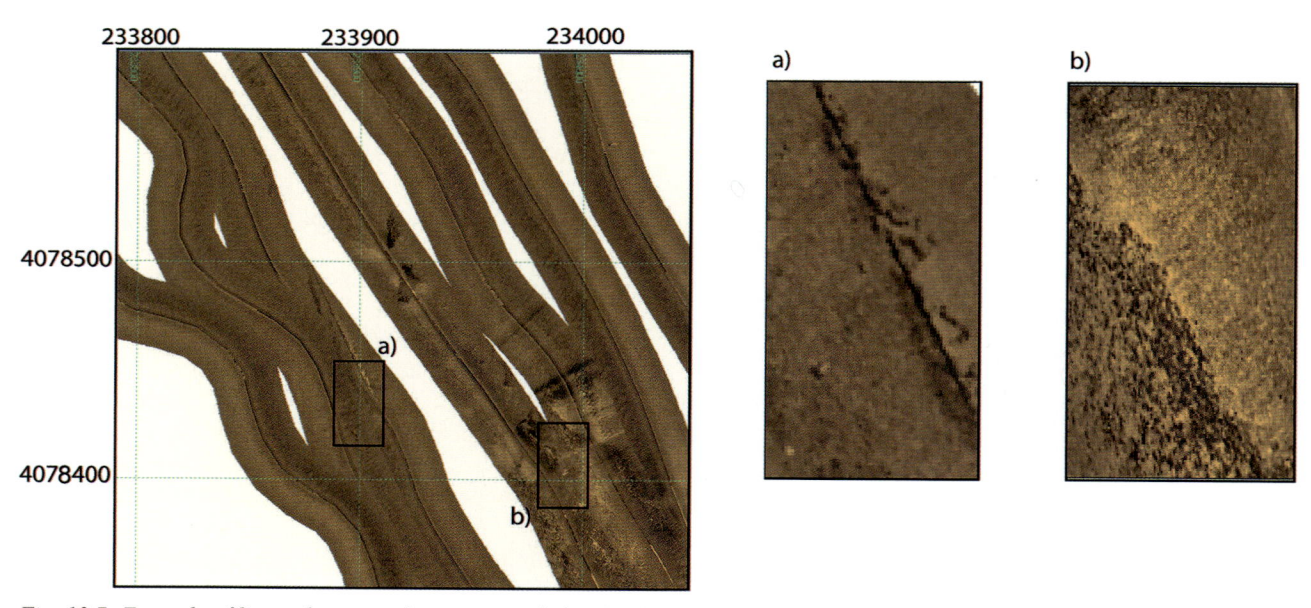

Fig. 12.7: Example of linear feature, sidescan sonar (left side of image); example of stony seafloor and soft sediment seafloor (right side of image).

reflection horizons identified. Three reasons for the lack of reflections or penetration are possible: either the acoustic properties of the sediments were such that no acoustic contrasts were evident, or the coarse-grained nature of the sediments resulted in little penetration, or, most likely, the sediments contained significant levels of gas. The latter is often the case in shallow water where there is a large organic input.

Along the Tammisheh Wall where penetration was good the seismic records of buried reflection horizons showed a topographic relief that was different from the seafloor, thus indicating that real old and buried surfaces exist at this location. Example records from the southern site are shown in Figures 12.9 and 12.10. In both records, submerged surfaces have been picked out to show depressions and ridges. The depressions have a maximum interpreted depth of 3 m with faint reflections seen in some of the depressions down to greater than 5 m beneath the present-day seafloor surface. Within the depressions multiple reflecting surfaces are evident; it is, however, difficult to determine if these signatures are artefacts of the data known as multiple reflections or represent real horizons. Nonetheless, the mapped depressions show a consistent signature across the site with surfaces extending away from the depressions that eventually become parallel to the seafloor. The width of depressions varies between 5 m and 30 m. Between the depressions the ridges in the buried surface (Fig. 12.9) have an elevation gain of

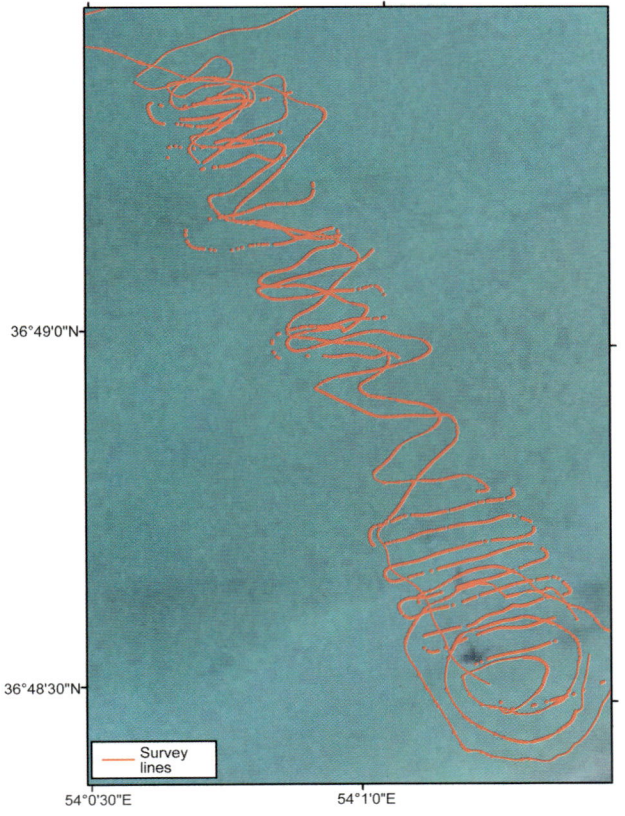

Fig. 12.8: Sub-bottom sonar track, southern site.

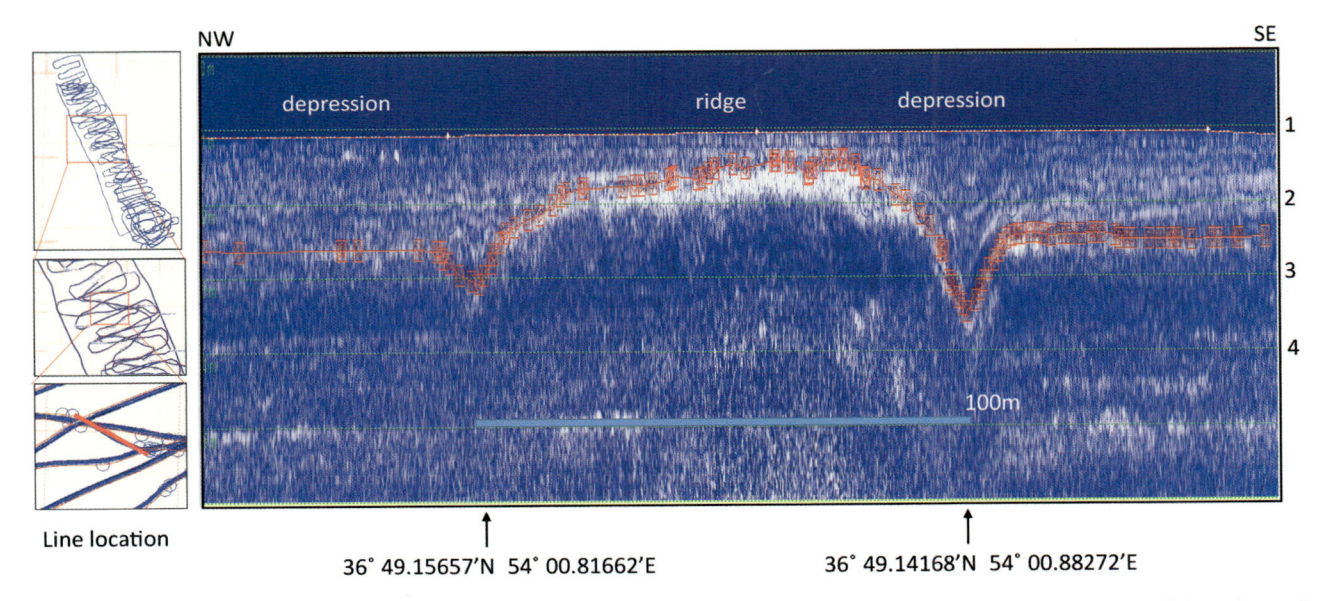

Fig. 12.9: Sub-bottom profile data showing depressions and a ridge: the Tammisheh Wall probably follows the top of the ridge and is flanked by ditches on either side. Note that the survey line cuts across the features at an oblique angle and that they are narrower than implied by the section.

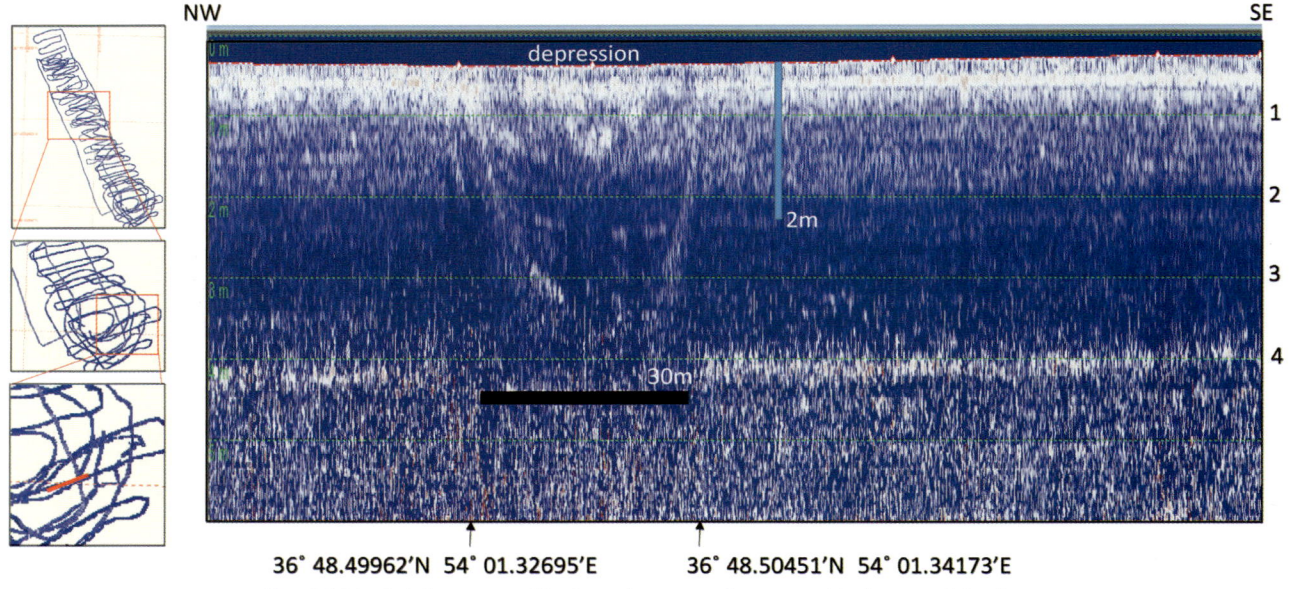

Fig. 12.10: Sub-bottom profile data showing a depression/ditch east of the fort.

approximately 1.5 m and the width of the ridges varies from 15 m to up to 100 m. Note, in Figure 12.9 the line direction is not perpendicular to the feature, rather it cuts the feature obliquely in a north-west–south-east direction and thus does not represent the true width. The depth of the ridge beneath the current seafloor shows an increase from the landward end of the features to sections further offshore in the north. No further reflection surface can be seen beneath the ridges. Once identified, mapping both the surfaces and edges of depressions was possible on each sub-bottom profile line. A map of the whole survey area could thus be extrapolated. There are traces of a series of possible parallel walls branching off the Tammisheh Wall on both sides at right angles (Figs 12.11 and 12.17–12.19). Their significance is unknown. One wonders whether they might be breakwaters and/or boat moorings maybe dating to the time when the wall became submerged in the late or post-Sasanian era.

Figure 12.10 shows an example of the sub-bottom profiles to the east of the fort (see also Fig. 12.20). At this location no ridge is seen but a shallow (less than 3 m deep) broad (approximately 30 m wide) depression was mapped. Beyond this to the east, deeper reflection surfaces were seen before the energy was absorbed by the gassy sediments. The full depth of acoustic penetration here was in excess of 5 m, suggesting a deep sediment sequence.

Maps of the sub-seafloor surface (Figs 12.5 and 12.11) show the top of the ridge and the base of depressions. We also produced a series of cross sections of the features from their northern seaward end towards the coast in the south (Figs 12.12–12.16). No traces of either depression or ridges were observed on records beyond a distance

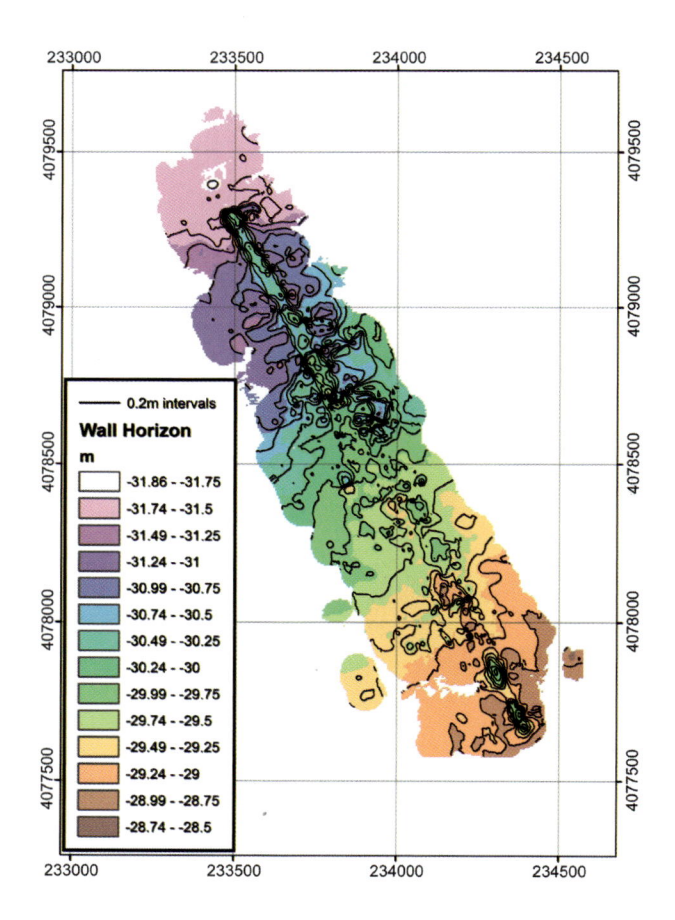

Figs 12.11: Contour map of sub-seafloor surface. Note that the terminal of the traceable wall is roughly at -31.50 m, corresponding to the approximate water level of the Caspian Sea in the late Sasanian era.

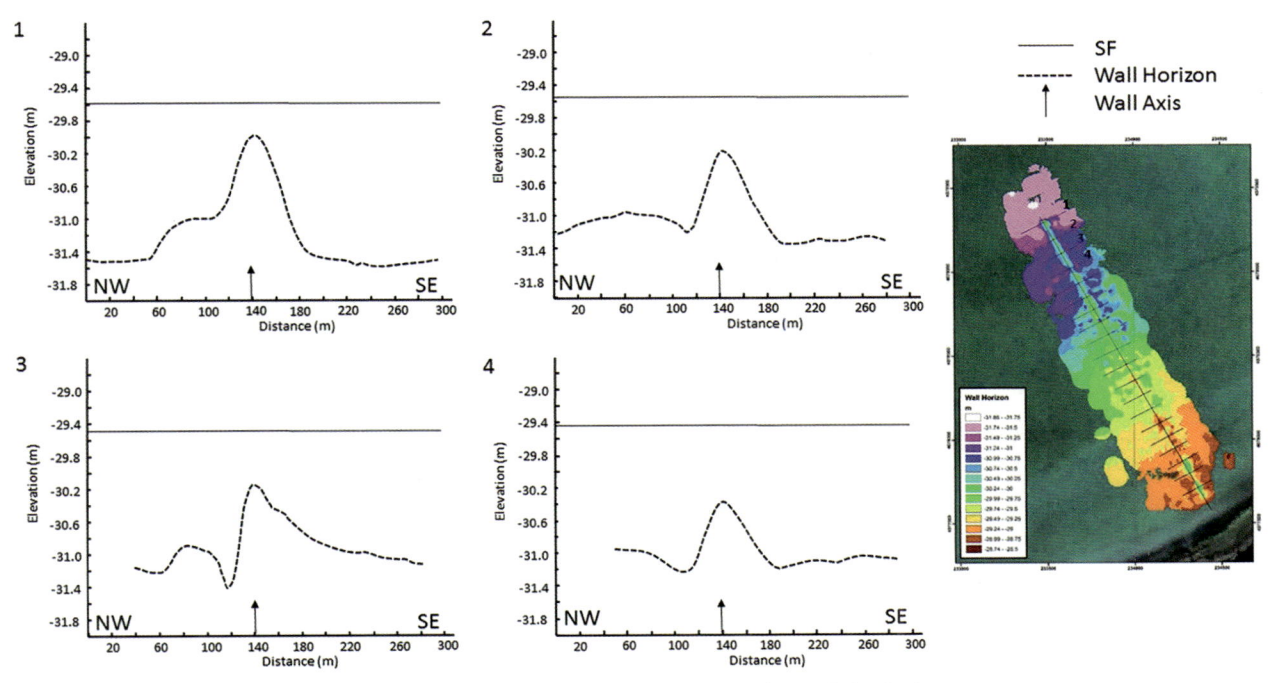

Fig. 12.12: Cross-sections 1–4 through the ridge and the ditches.

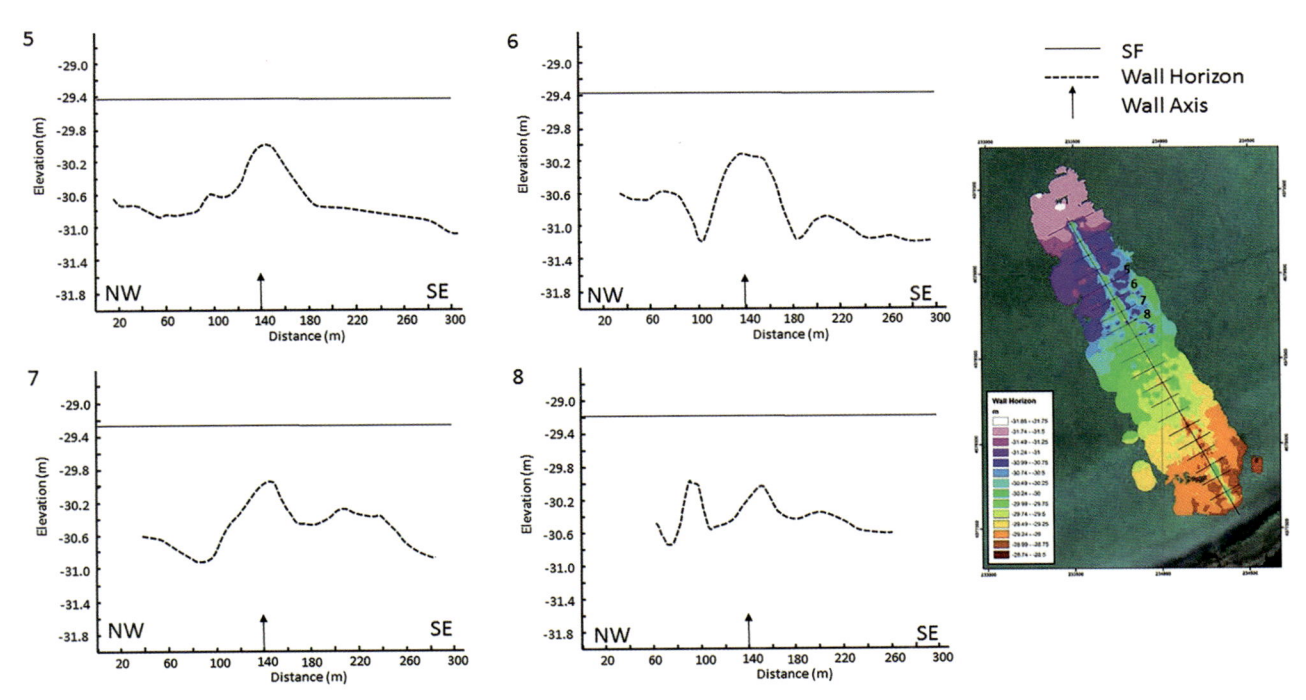

Fig. 12.13: Cross-sections 5–8 through the ridge and the ditches.

of approximately 1.75 km from the fort. A further brick accumulation on the seabed was, however, detected centred on UTM 40S 233399 E, 4079630 N (54°0'39" E, 36°49'30" N: Fig. 13.2). It is in alignment, if perhaps slightly offset to the east, with the ridge (terminating at UTM 40S 233467 E, 4079317 N) and some 320 m further NW. It may well form part of the wall and, if so, suggests that this continued for over 2 km beyond the fort. That it is in alignment with

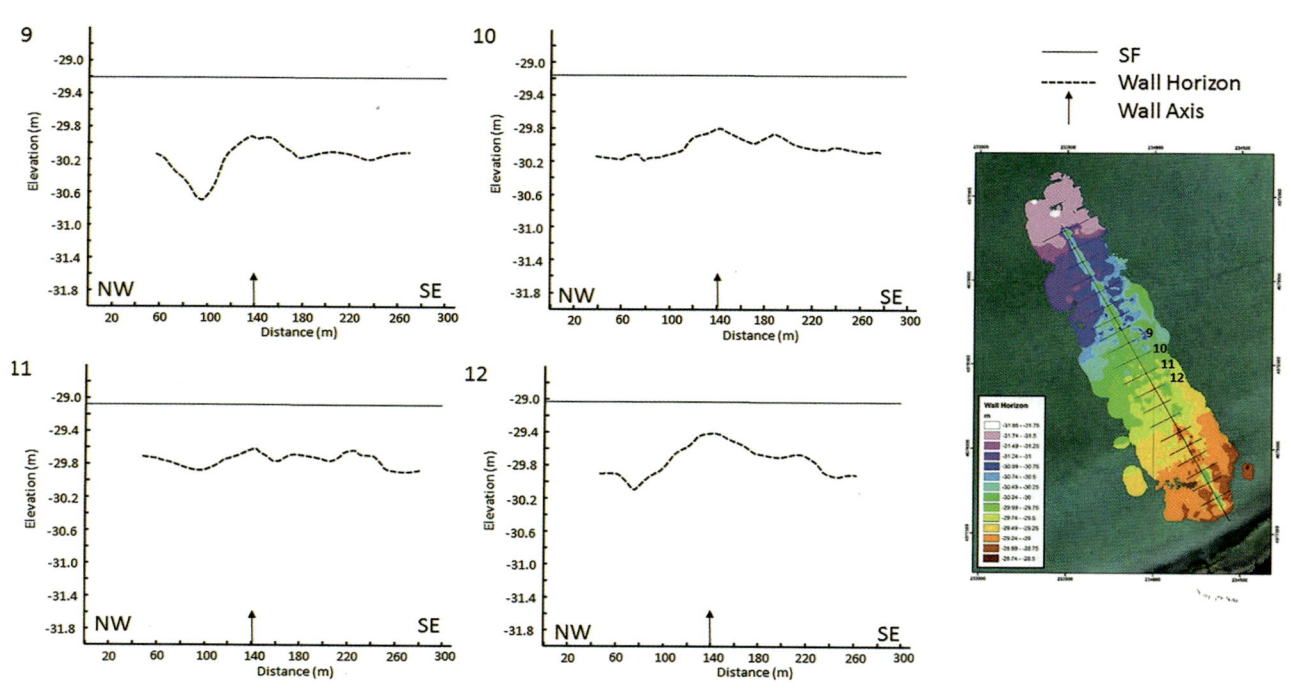

Fig. 12.14: Cross-sections 9–12 through the ridge and the ditches.

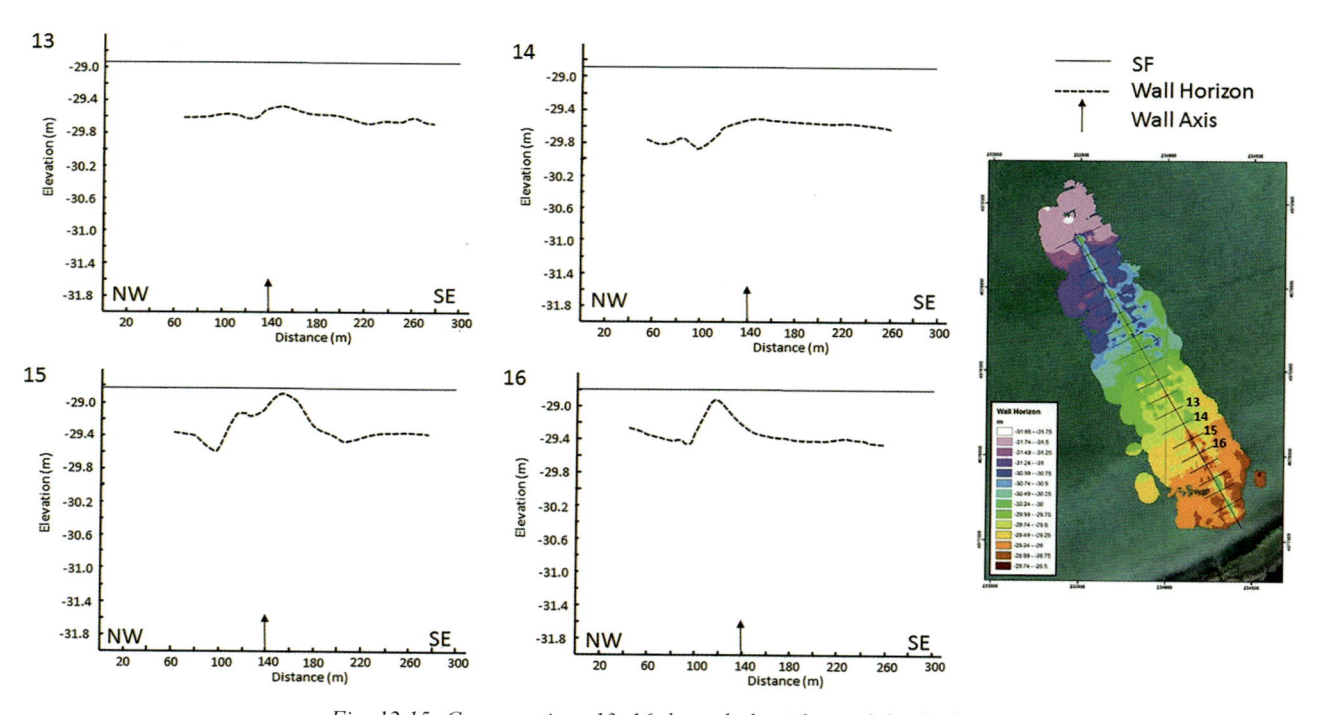

Fig. 12.15: Cross-sections 13–16 through the ridge and the ditches.

the wall suggests in any case that it is an installation that is associated with the wall (e.g. a part of a pier or perhaps even a small observation post or lighthouse at its end).

In summary, the ridge dips to the north (seawards) and the terminus at the seaward end of the features is abrupt at c. 1.75 km from the fort (Figs 12.5, 12.11 and 12.20). From the map and cross sections it is clear that ridges and depressions join to form a linear wall-like structure flanked by ditches. Figures 12.17–12.18 offer a three-dimensional view of these submerged features

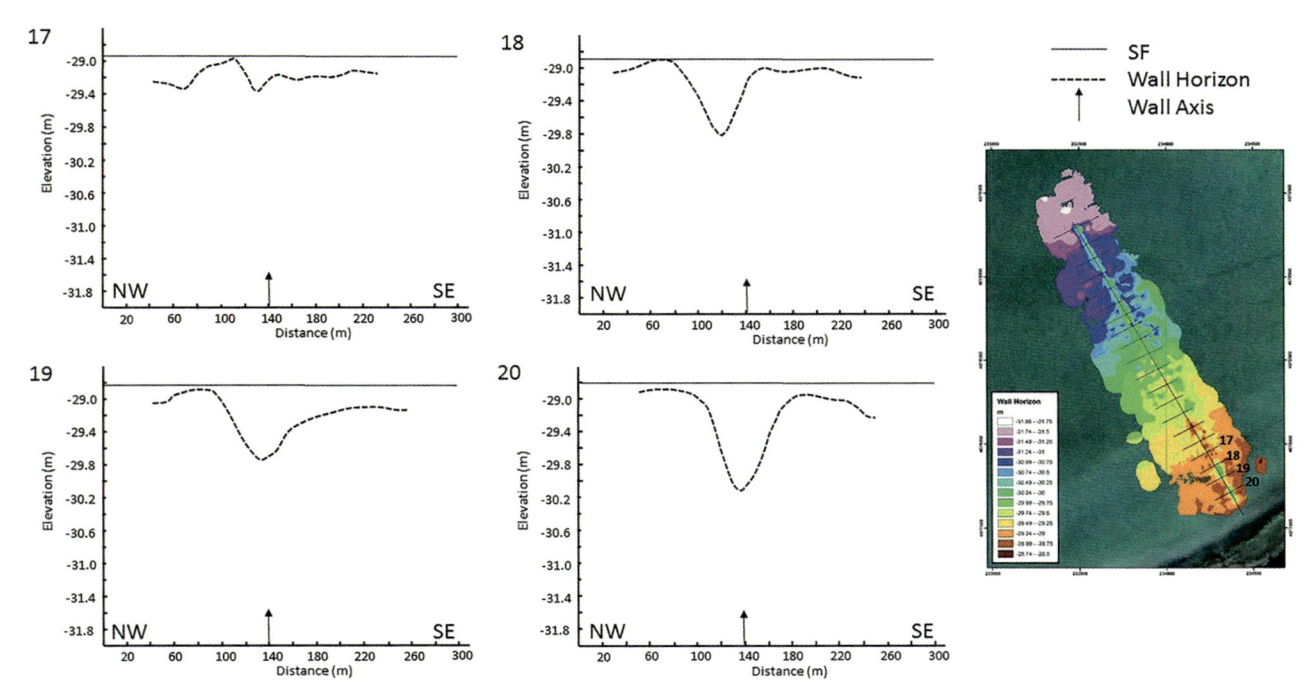

Fig. 12.16: Cross-sections 17–20 through the ridge and the ditches.

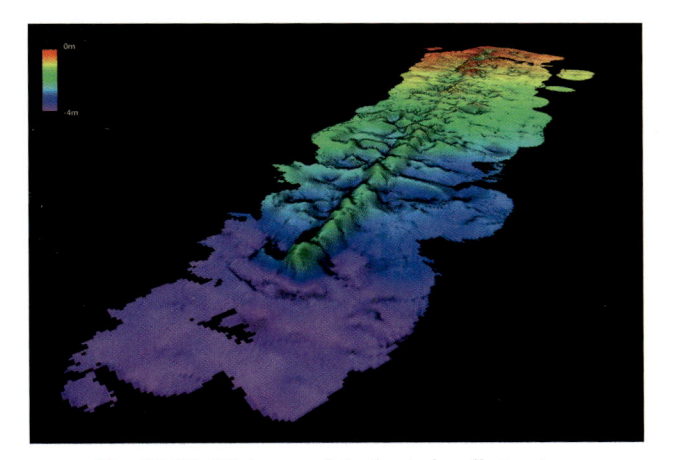

Fig. 12.17: 3D image of the buried wall structure.

with Figure 12.19 showing a cut-through version of the features with an example of the sub-bottom (seismic) profile data spliced into the seafloor and sub-bottom horizon.

12.5. Discussion

The map of sub-bottom sonar data for the southern site shows a broad linear feature extending along the projection of the wall line from the old fort for approximately 1.75 km north offshore (Fig. 12.20). At this distance, all evidence of the feature abruptly ceases. The isolated brick scatter some 320 m further NNW raises the possibility, however, that the wall may have continued beyond. Flanking either side of the linear ridge are two ditch-like features. In the southern

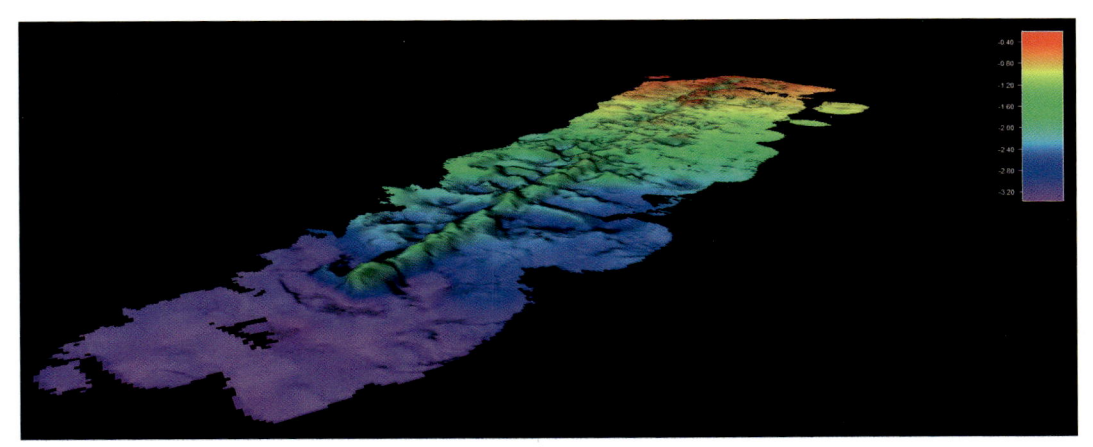

Fig. 12.18: 3D image of the buried wall structure.

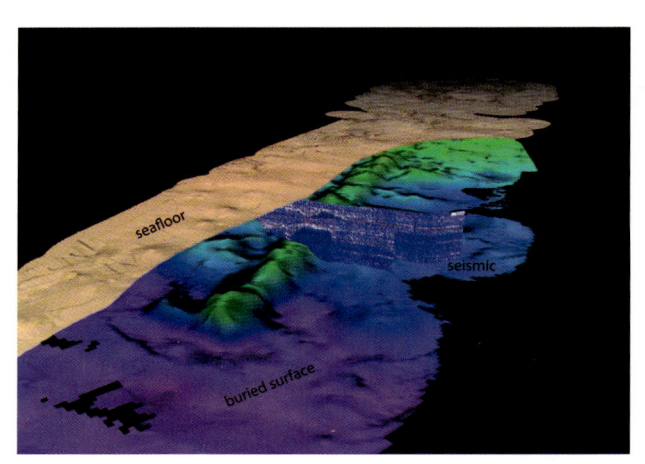

Fig. 12.19: 3D image of the buried wall structure, the seafloor and the cross-sections through the buried wall.

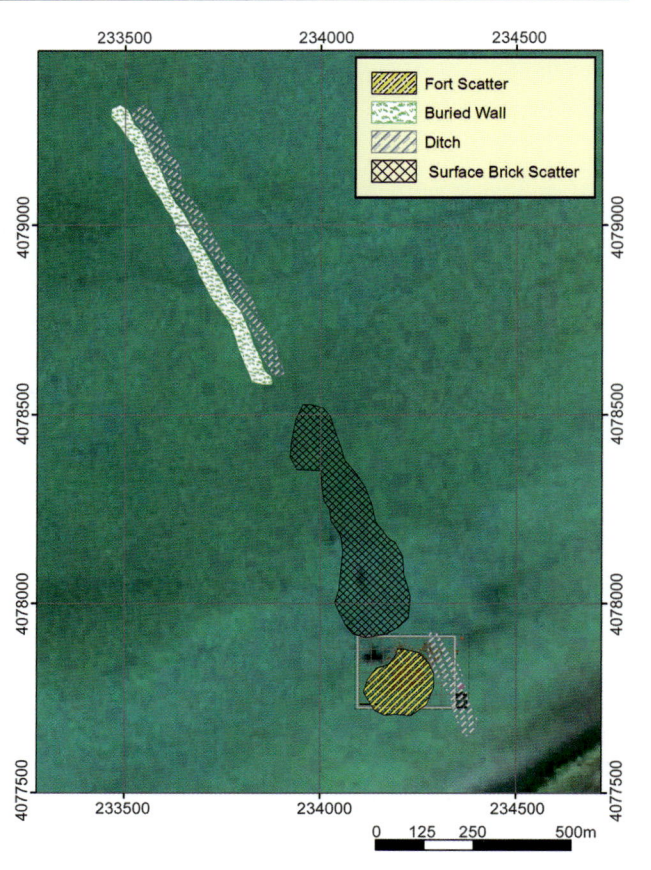

Fig. 12.20: Interpretative plot of the fort, the terminal section of the Tammisheh Wall and major ditches. The inset shows the location of the topographical survey of the fort in 2014 (see Fig. 5.4) (background image: courtesy of Google Earth).

end near the fort a main flanking ditch was identified on the eastern side but none on the west. However, a complex pattern of minor ditches is evident in the immediate fort vicinity. Further to the east of the fort, a deep (greater than 5 m) sequence of reflection surfaces was noted. This sequence likely exists throughout the area but is not penetrated by the seismic energy elsewhere. The ridge is shallowest at the southern (landward) end and deepest (to -2 m below the seafloor) at the northern (seaward) end. Near the fort the sidescan sonar data showed rubble on the seafloor, likely bricks (and/or stones), which extends along the line of wall projection for approximately 700 m to the north (Fig. 12.20). It is interpreted that these are the remnants of the collapsed wall which are covered further to the north by the present-day seafloor of soft mud and silt. The width of the feature associated with the collapsed wall is to be expected and is typical of features as they disintegrate under water, thereby causing a lateral spread many times greater than their original size. However, the width of the ridge may also imply that it was necessary to construct a foundation to the wall as it projected onto the softer sediments near the coast. The sea level has, of course, risen by at least 3 m since the wall was built on terrain that is now submerged under the waters of the Caspian Sea.

In order to investigate the Tammisheh Wall configuration further, it is recommended that additional diver survey is conducted along the line of the surface geophysical anomalies. Some core samples have already been taken and examined, and they shed interesting new light on the environment and sea level at the time.[8] In order to investigate the nature of the ditch on either side of the wall it is recommended that further coring is conducted in both west and east ditches, at the northern terminus and with additional cores in the ditch to the east of the fort.

Notes

1. See chapter 11.5 for the survey of the northern site across the projected alignment of the Gorgan Wall.
2. Sauer *et al.* 2013, 264–69; Jansen Van Rensburg *et al.* 2013.
3. See https://www.tritech.co.uk/product/starfish-990f-high-resolution-side-scan-sonar-shallow-water0 (accessed on 18 April 2020).
4. See https://www.tritech.co.uk/product/parametric-sub-bottom-profiling-seaking-sbp (accessed on 18 April 2020).
5. See chapter 5.2, Jansen Van Rensburg *et al.* 2013 and Sauer *et al.* 2013, 264–69.
6. Jansen Van Rensburg *et al.* 2013, 428, 691 pl. 15:1.
7. See chapter 11.5.
8. See chapter 13.

13

Palaeoenvironments at the Caspian terminals of the Gorgan and the Tammisheh Walls

Suzanne A.G. Leroy, François Demory, Françoise Chalié, Martin Bates, C. Richard Bates, Hamid Omrani Rekavandi, Eberhard W. Sauer and Paula J. Reimer[1]

13.1. Setting and aims

The Gorgan Wall in its western extremity runs across the Gorgan Plain. The wall sections known until recently stop at a point approximately 1 km west of a kiln explored by excavations in 2006 (Trench I) and c. 12 km before reaching the Caspian coastline in its 2016 position (Fig. 13.1).[2] Fieldwork in 2016 by Richard Bates *et al.* has detected another 5 km of wall in the westernmost section of the Gorgan Wall that shows a possible splitting into a series of different walls.[3] The southernmost tip of the Hassan Gholi (i.e. Lagoon of Hassan) reached close to Trench I. This lagoon existed until recently when it started drying out.[4] Nowadays it is still possible to detect the outline of this large bay by satellite imagery, such as Google Earth. It is possible that water-level fluctuations in this lagoon may have affected the stability of the wall and potentially necessitated its reconstruction on different alignments.

The northern terminal of the Tammisheh Wall is submerged under water in the Gorgan Bay, where it has been mapped by geophysical methods (Fig. 13.2).[5] This bay is separated from the Caspian Sea by the west–east Miankaleh Spit. In the last centuries with the highstand of the Little Ice Age (LIA), the number of openings of the bay to the Caspian Sea has increased and the spit was split into small islands.[6] It has been suggested that the spit did not exist during the previous highstand of 2600–2300 cal BP or 650–350 cal BC.[7] The eastern rivers extended further westwards (the Qareh Su and Gorgan Rivers) into the Gorgan Bay during the subsequent lowstand.[8] The Gorgan River began migrating northwards to its present position, perhaps only 500 years ago[9] or even more recently, if one considers that its delta started developing only since AD 1854 as proposed by Naderi *et al.*[10] Our main aim was to reconstruct palaeoenvironments before, during and after the construction of each of the two wall termini with a special focus on past relative water levels.

13.2. Previous palynological studies

Close to the sites studied here at the end of the Gorgan Wall, core TM (elevation estimated at -25.50 m) had been taken in a previous project at the south-west edge of the Hassan Gholi (Fig. 13.1).[11] It covers the last 20 millennia with a long depositional hiatus around 11 millennia ago.

In the Gorgan Bay, the sediment sequence at the Qareh Su (core Gha) and that of Shahkileh (core Sha) were studied. They are respectively 3 km east of the Tammisheh Wall and 37 km west of Tammisheh.[12] Their palynological diagrams cover approximately the last 21 millennia even though with some barren units and some hiatus. Although both sequences cover most of the last 2,500 years, only the sequence of the Gharasoo (i.e. the Qareh Su) has preserved pollen assemblages.

A surface sediment transect was made offshore the current mouth of the Gorgan River, i.e. the Gorgan transect.[13] These Caspian samples were studied by multiple proxies, including pollen and dinocysts. These modern data were used to support the palynological interpretation of the palaeo-sequences associated with the two wall terminals.

13.3. Material and methods

13.3.1. Fieldwork and core description

The infill of an old ditch north of the western end of the Gorgan Wall is crossed by a long north–south trench dug

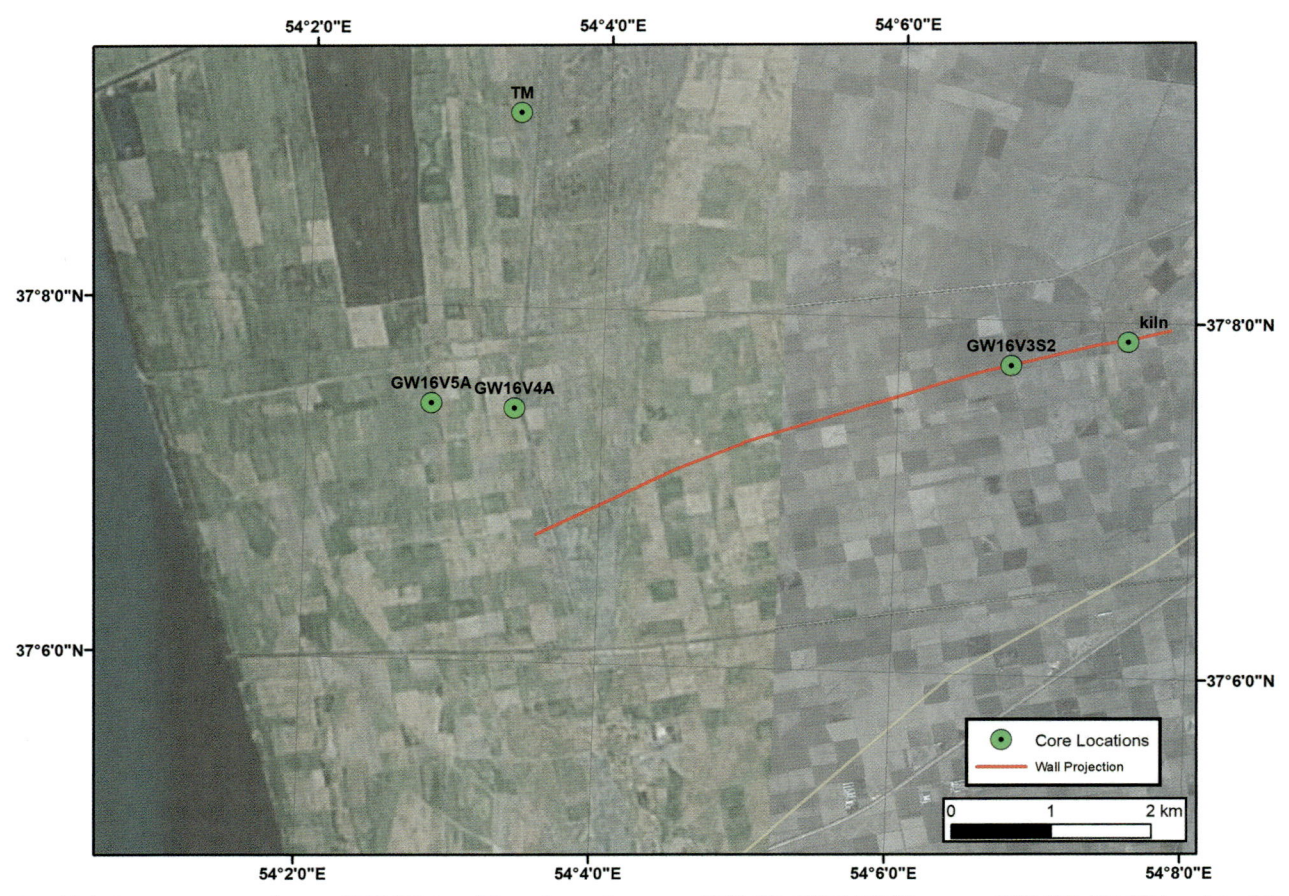

Fig. 13.1: Location map of cores GW16V3A and B and trench section GW16S2 (GW16V3S2), cores GW16V5, V4, TM and the kiln in Trench I in relation to the westernmost known section of the Gorgan Wall. Note that the 2019 coastline is another c. 3.5 km west of the lagoon coast shown on the satellite image. (Source of image: CNES/Airbus taken on 11 April 2019.)

by farmers and cleaned for the purpose of the investigation (Figs 11.6, 11.7 and 13.1). The trench is parallel to and west of a small north–south dirt road. In this trench, many brick fragments were found attesting to the presence of the wall, although no architectural remains survived *in situ*.[14] North of the brick accumulation, the stratigraphy slopes to a deeper level where a greenish-grey silt lens outcrops, that could originate from stagnant or slow-flowing water in a ditch. In this place, a section was cleaned, i.e. section S2 or in full GW16S2 (Figs 11.8 and 13.1). The absolute elevation of the nail indicating the top of section S2 has been measured by levelling from the nearest benchmark. It is at -23.40 m, which is 4 m above the Caspian water level in October 2016 (the latter exactly at -27.45 m on 10 October 2016[15]). A vibracorer was used to take a series of cores up to 5 m long. Two parallel cores (GW16V3A and B) were obtained next to Trench S2, on the east side of the road. Core GW16V5A was taken 5.8 km west of the trench, on a ridge separating the Hassan Gholi from the sea (Fig. 13.1). For comparative purposes, core TM was 3.2 km north of core V5 and 5.6 km NW of section S2 and core V3.

Near the terminal of the Tammisheh Wall, an improvised device (made of a drainpipe and a hand-made piston) was assembled to take cores in c. 1.80–2.10 m water depth (i.e. below water level) from a small motorboat. This allowed obtaining four cores that were up to 2 m long (GW16L1A, B and C and GW16L2A) in and close to an area where previously the end of the wall had been mapped.[16] The coring location is slightly over 2.5 km north of the south coast of Gorgan Bay in its 2016 position (Fig. 13.2).

The cores and samples were subsequently kept in a cool room. The cores were split into two lengthwise sections, photographed and visually described, before subsampling. For establishing the occurrence of diatoms, smear slides were made.

13.3.2. Magnetic susceptibility

Low field magnetic susceptibility measurements were performed using the MS2E Sensor (Bartington) at 2 cm resolution on the surface of one half of each split core. The magnetic susceptibility (MS) estimates the relative contribution of ferromagnetic (e.g. magnetite),

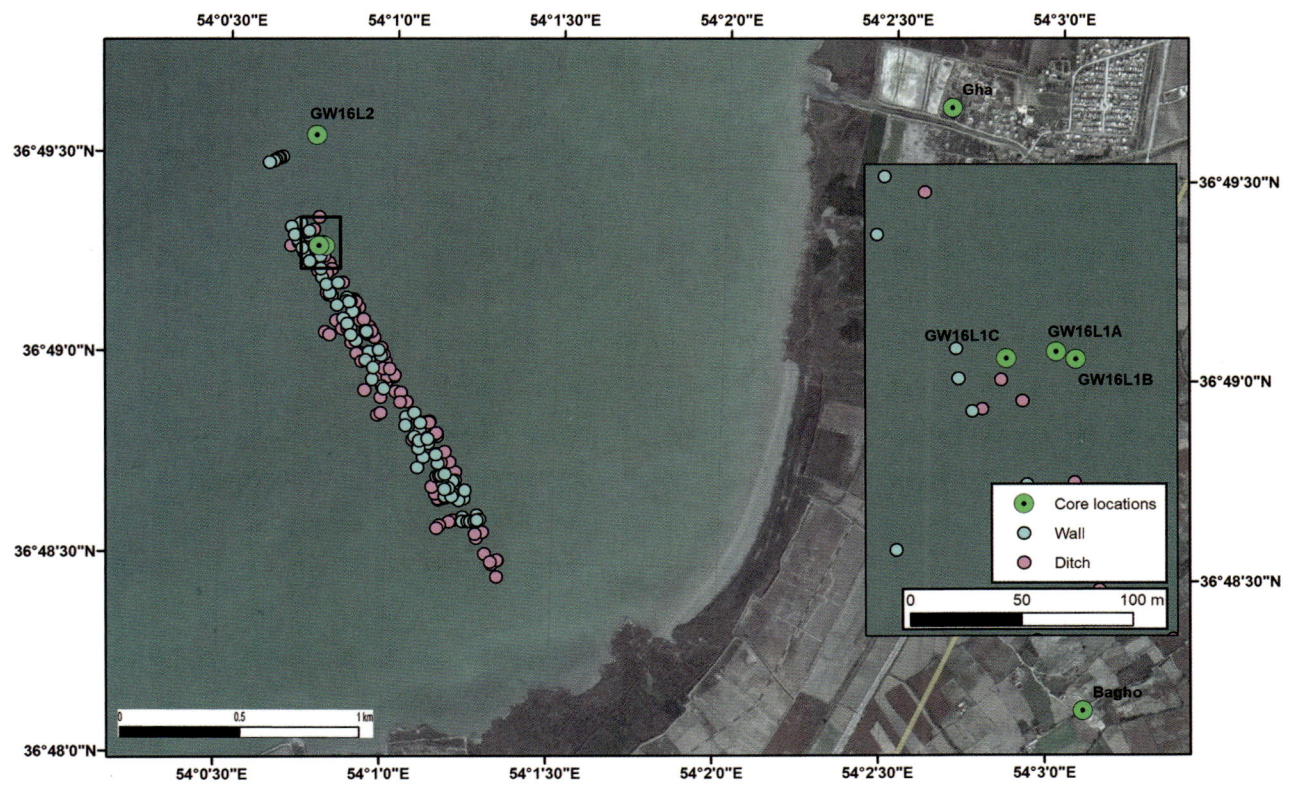

Fig. 13.2: Location map of cores GW16L1A, B, C and L2A (labelled L2), the Bagho outcrop and core Gha in relation to the now underwater terminal of the Tammisheh Wall. (Source of image: CNES/Airbus taken on 11 May 2019.)

paramagnetic (e.g. clay) and diamagnetic particles (e.g. quartz, carbonates or organic matter), ferromagnetic particles concentration being predominant in the signal variations. MS mostly reflects the detrital input but can also be influenced by diagenesis.[17] In the present study, most of the MS variations illustrate sedimentary changes.

13.3.3. Palynology

About 2 ml of wet sediment were examined for palynology, i.e. pollen, non-pollen palynomorphs (NPPs) and dinocysts. Initially tablets of *Lycopodium* were added in order to obtain an estimate of the concentration (in number of palynomorphs per ml). Then the samples were soaked in sodium pyrophosphate ($Na_4P_2O_7$), then cold HCl, followed by cold HF and cold HCl again. Only a few samples in more sandy horizons were treated with Sodium Polytungstate at a density of 2.4. In all cases, this was followed by sieving on 125 and 10 μm meshes. The residue was kept in glycerol before slide preparation.

Ninety-two samples were treated. Five samples from Trench S2 were processed, of which only two contained palynomorphs (dinocysts mostly). The proportion of samples yielding palynomorphs in core V3 was similar, i.e. only nine out of 24. Out of 18 samples from core V5, 12 samples contained palynomorphs, and out of 18 samples from core L1A, only nine were rich in palynomorphs. By contrast, all 27 samples of core L2A yielded preserved palynomorphs.

Minimal sums of 100 and 300 for the counts of dinocysts and of terrestrial pollen were reached respectively, these numbers being sufficient to build separately representative percentage diagrams. P/D represents the ratio between pollen and dinocyst concentration. The diagrams were plotted using psimpoll 4.27[18] and diagram zonation was obtained using CONISS after square root-transformation.

13.3.4. Radiocarbon dating

Samples for radiocarbon dating consisted of shells, and when possible, shells from complete bivalves, were selected. In one case only, organic remains visible by eye were found and dated. The samples were submitted to the Poznan radiocarbon laboratory. Then, the dates were corrected for a freshwater reservoir offset of 351±33 ^{14}C years and subsequently calibrated using the IntCal20 curve (Tables 13.1 and 13.2[19]). The results thus obtained are close to the marine calibration, but take into account that the Caspian Sea is not linked to the global ocean. The calibration is presented in more detail in a separate study.[20]

428   *Ancient Arms Race*

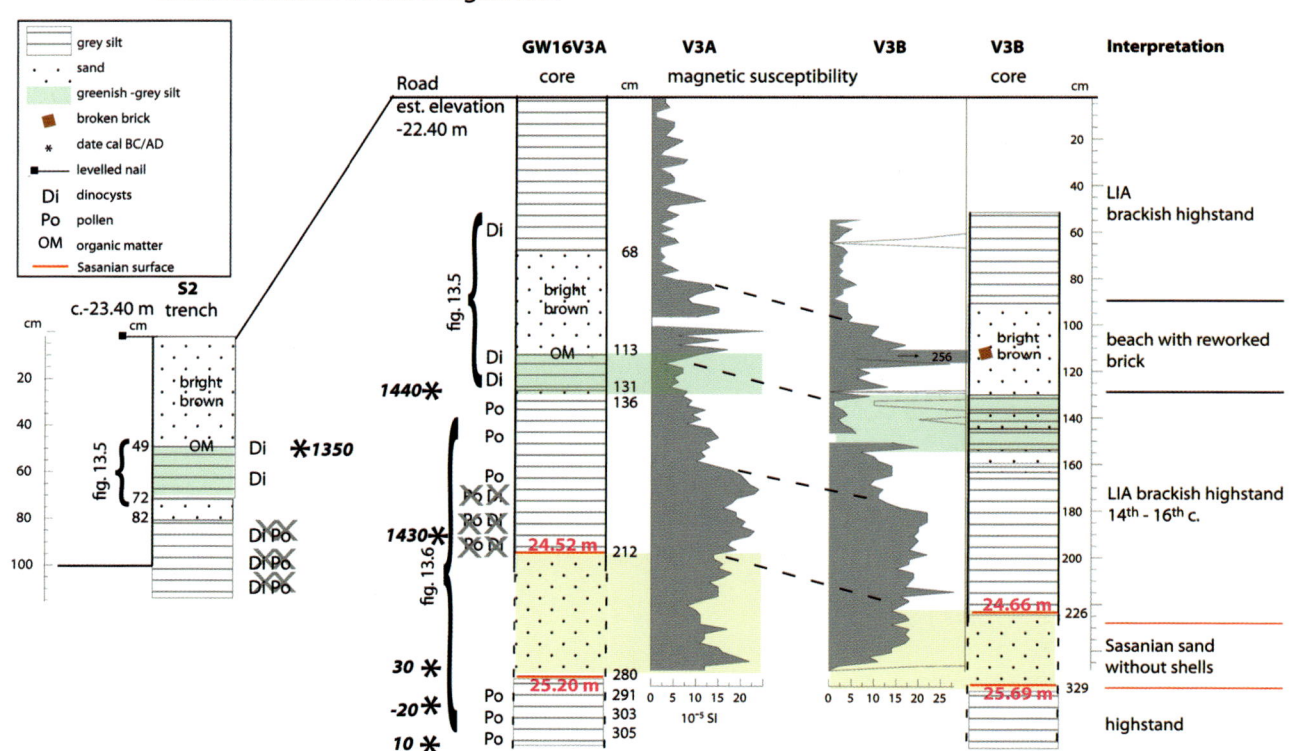

Fig. 13.3: Logs of Trench Section S2 and cores GW16V3A and B near the western section of the Gorgan Wall, with magnetic susceptibility of cores GW16V3A and B and interpretation. It should be noted that there is a ditch in the area (Fig. 11.8), which is likely to explain why we encountered the same deposits at different elevations. Dates shown (*) are the cal AD/BC median probability of the radiocarbon calibrated age range. For radiocarbon ages (*), see Table 13.1. LIA: Little Ice Age. Grey X symbols over Po and Di indicate the absence of microfossils at these depths.

13.4. Results

13.4.1. Western end of the Gorgan Wall

Trench S2 and core V3 are located east of the southernmost tip of the Hassan Gholi and in a ditch north of the presumed wall (as attested by the presence of bricks south of the ditch and the detection of these linear features via geophysical survey).[21] The top of the S2 trench has been levelled and reaches -23.40 m; the elevation of the top of core V3 has been estimated at -22.40 m. This is 8.10 m above the presumed water level of c. -31.50 m in the sixth century AD.[22] Core V5, south of core TM and directly west of core V3, is located between the Caspian Sea and the southernmost tip of the Hassan Gholi, at an elevation estimated to be 1 m lower than core V3.

SEDIMENT: The top of core V3 and the top of the section S2 in the trench (called the S2-V3 sequence) are estimated to be offset by c. 100 cm (Fig. 13.3). Starting from the top, one observes a 68 cm thick sediment disturbed by agricultural activities in core V3. It consists of grey silt with low MS values ($\sim 5 \ 10^{-5}$ SI). Then present in the S2 and V3 sequences, is a bright brown sand layer c. 45–49 cm thick, with some shells and intermediate MS values ranging from 10 to 15 10^{-5} SI with a high peak at 256 10^{-5} SI in its middle caused by the presence of a broken brick in core V3B. The sediment unit is separated from the bottom silt by a very thin grey sand layer rich in shells and additionally, in core V3A and trench S2, in black organic remains. Then a greenish grey silt layer between 23 and 18 cm thick is noted, which has low MS (below 5 10^{-5} SI). In core V3B, it contains a 1 cm thick orangey sand horizon. The greenish grey silt corresponds to a ditch infill (see Fig. 11.8). Then a thin layer of sand (5 to 10 cm) with many shells is found at the base of the S2 and V3 sequences, before turning to a bluish structureless silt with interspersed shells forming the base of the trench. This unit is rich in oxidation spots. It has generally high MS values around 20 10^{-5} SI.

Further down the information comes only from the cores. The sediment from 212 to 280 cm in core V3A is a brown sand unit with high MS (between 15 and 20 10^{-5} SI) and without shells. A combination of darker colour and low MS indicates a silt with less oxidation from 280

Western section of the Gorgan Wall, Core GW16V5A

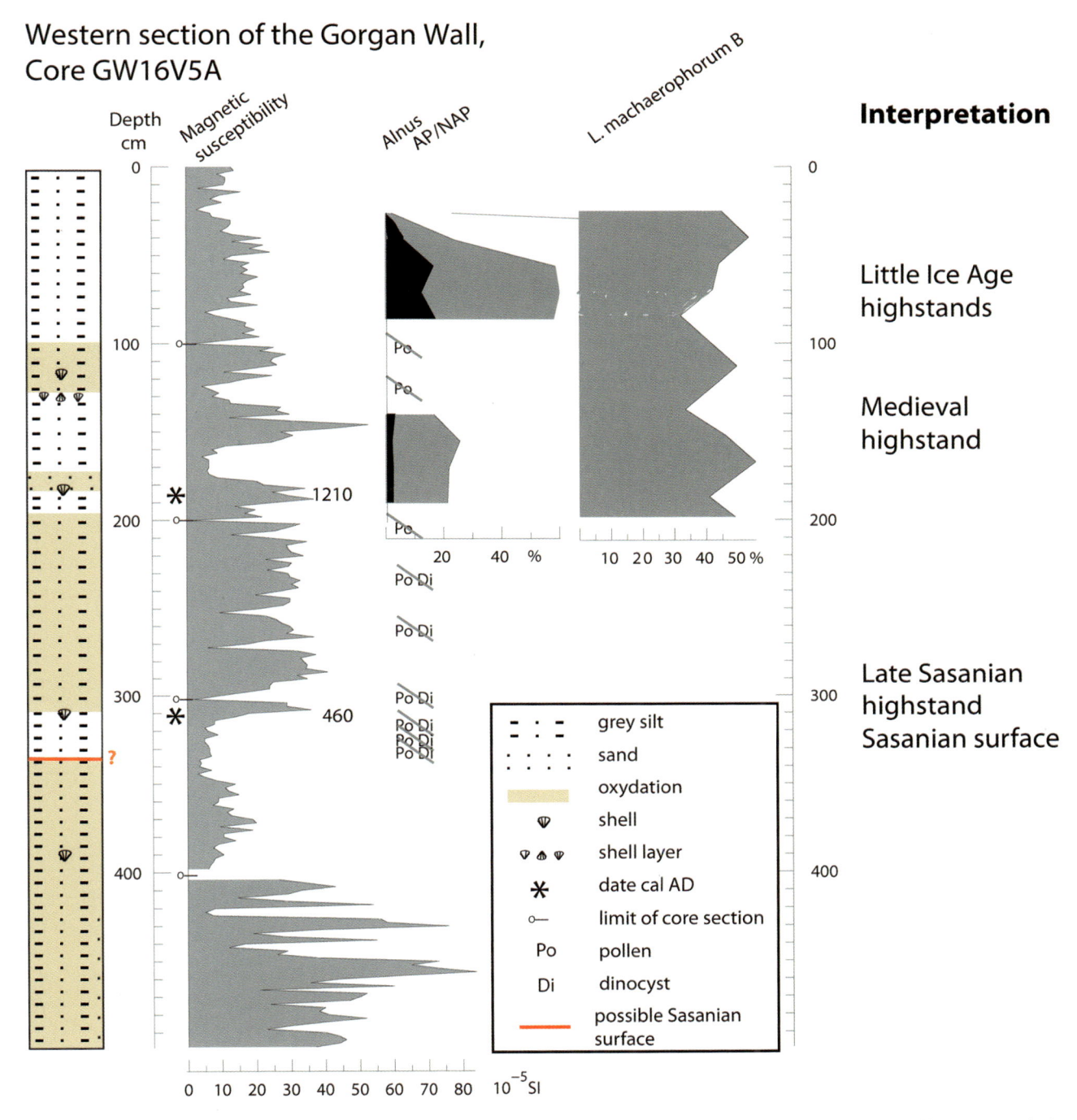

Interpretation

Little Ice Age highstands

Medieval highstand

Late Sasanian highstand
Sasanian surface

Fig. 13.4: Western section of the Gorgan Wall: Log, magnetic susceptibility, arboreal/non-arboreal (AP/NAP) pollen curve with (in black) an inset for Alnus %, and, on the right, the curve of Lingulodinium machaerophorum *for core GW16V5A. The slashed Po and Di indicate absence of microfossils, pollen and/or dinocysts respectively.*

to 334 cm depth. Below 334 cm, no shells are present in the greyish brown silt.

Core V5 is 480.5 cm long (Fig. 13.4). The upper part of the core is an olive silt down to 96 cm, then brown at 96–123 cm. An olive grey shell and silt layer occurs at 123–127 cm, then olive grey silt down to 195 cm, except at 176–184 cm where a brown sandy layer occurs with sharp boundaries and shells at its base. The lower part of the core (from 195 cm downwards) consists of brown silt, except at 298.5–323.5 cm where the silt turns light olive grey. The limit at 323.5 cm is sharp. The MS varies from 10 to 80 10^{-5} SI with strong fluctuations. These variations

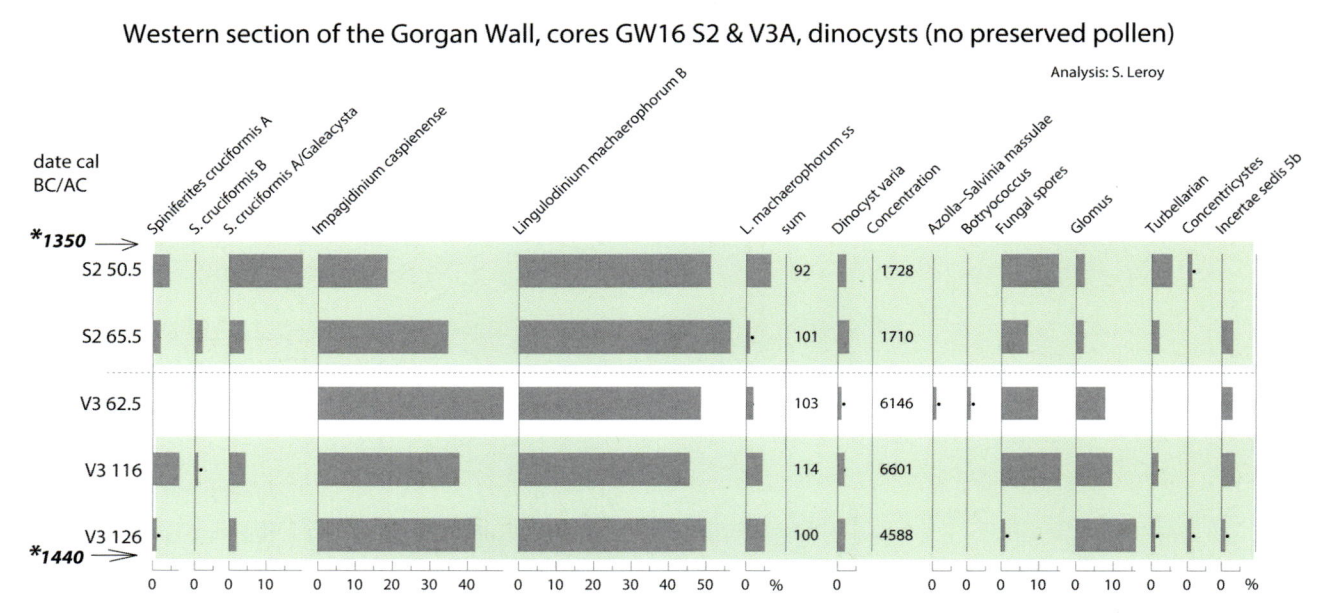

Fig. 13.5: Western section of the Gorgan Wall: Dinocyst assemblages in Trench section S2 and the top of core GW16V3A. Dots for values lower than 0.5%. For radiocarbon dates (*), see Table 13.1.

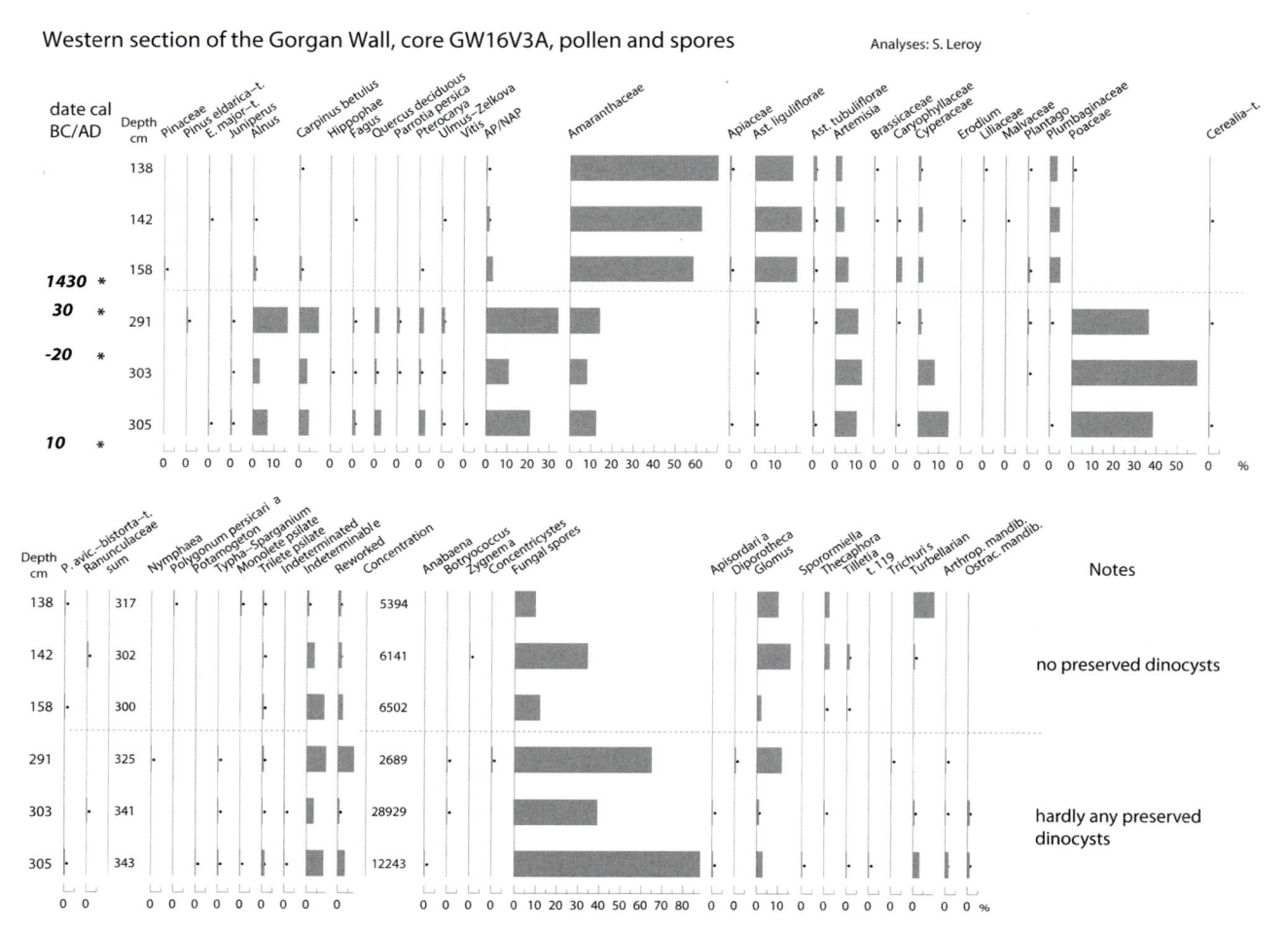

Fig. 13.6: Western section of the Gorgan Wall: Pollen assemblages of core GW16V3A. Dots for values lower than 0.5%. For radiocarbon dates (*), see Table 13.1.

Table 13.1: New radiocarbon samples from the vicinity of the westernmost section of the Gorgan Wall.[23] The date of the sample from just above the kiln in Trench I[24] has been recalibrated using the same method. The median probability dates are rounded to the nearest multiple of 10, and 5 is rounded up. Calibrated date at 95.4% confidence.[25]

Core and sample no.	Laboratory no.	Composite depth in cm	Sample description	Date (BP)	Calibrated date at 95.4% confidence	Median probability
S2 50	Poz-97351	50	Black organic remains	959±28	AD 1292–1410	AD 1350
S2 50	Poz-98161	50	3 *Theodoxus*	965±28	AD 1290–1408	AD 1350
V3A2 36.5	Poz-93406	131.5	1 valve of a double bivalve	817±28	AD 1397–1503	AD 1440
V3A3 5-6	Poz-106200	197.5	1 valve of a bivalve	845±30	AD 1393–1474	AD 1430
V3A3 75	Poz-93407	267.0	1 valve of *Dreissena*	2343±31	60 BC–AD 130	AD 30
V3A4 10.5	Poz-93408	297.5	Many small gastropods	2377±30	154 BC–AD 83	20 BC
V3A4 44.5	Poz-93409	331.5	1 valve of a double bivalve	2357±32	112 BC–AD 125	AD 10
V5A2 88.5	Poz-106203	184.5	1 valve of a bivalve	1190±30	AD 1151–1278	AD 1210
V5A4 19	Poz-106201	309.5	1 valve of a bivalve	1980±30	AD 348–550	AD 460
Other date						
Gorgan Wall, Trench I	OxA-17021	On top of kiln, c. 26 m b.s.l.	1 bivalve	933±26	AD 1300–1424	AD 1350

do not fit the oxidation state of the sediment but are more likely related to changes in the detrital input.

DINOCYSTS: These were present in the ditch samples of section S2 and in the top three samples of core V3 (upper 126 cm, i.e. ditch and above it) (Fig. 13.5). The concentration was low in section S2, i.e. around 1,700 dinocysts per ml of wet sediment, but clearly higher in core V3, i.e. around 6,000 dinocysts per ml. The five samples show similar assemblages dominated by *Lingulodinium machaerophorum* with abundant *Impagidinium caspiense*. It is worth noting the occurrence of *Spiniferites cruciformis* in most samples. A few other palynomorphs indicate the proximity of land with fungal spores and erosion indicators such as *Glomus* (especially in core V3) and *Concentricystes*. Pollen was not preserved in these five samples.

In core V5, the dinocysts are present down to 200.5 cm (Fig. 13.4). The spectra show no trend and are largely dominated by *I. caspiense* and *L. machaerophorum* (type B). No foraminifera were observed.

POLLEN: In the six pollen-rich samples of core V3A, hardly any dinocysts were observed (Fig. 13.6). In three samples around 150 cm depth, the assemblages are largely dominated by Amaranthaceae and Asteraceae liguliflorae. It is worth noting the continuous occurrence of Plumbaginaceae. The lower part of the diagram consists of three samples from around 300 cm depth, i.e. from the greyish horizon. These samples, rich in palynomorphs and totally different from those above, are dominated by Poaceae. *Alnus*, *Carpinus betulus*, *Artemisia* and Cyperaceae are abundant. A diverse range of trees and some aquatic plants are present. The other test samples in core V3A taken in the brown silt were barren.

In core V5, pollen is present down to 189 cm only (slightly less deep than for the dinocysts) with moreover an interruption of their preservation in the brown layer at 96–123 cm (Fig. 13.4). The lower spectra (between 139 and 189 cm) are dominated by Amaranthaceae (40–50%). In the upper part (25–85 cm), the spectra are dominated by tree pollen (*Carpinus betulus*, *Alnus*, *Quercus* and *Fagus*), with a significant amount of *Juglans* and *Vitis*. The topmost sample at 25 cm shows a dominance of Amaranthaceae (95%).

DIATOMS: Samples at 23 and 29 cm depth did not show any diatoms. The sample at 23 cm depth includes Bryozoan spicules.

RADIOCARBON DATES: Two dates were obtained from Trench S2 (Table 13.1, Fig. 13.3). They came from the same layer between the greenish clay and the bright brown silt. Although one consists of black organic remains and one consists of three *Theodoxus* gastropods, they yielded almost identical dates (i.e. between the very late thirteenth and very early fifteenth centuries, most likely in the fourteenth century), indicating that the black organic matter was affected by the same reservoir offset as the shells. In core V3, a sample from 131.5 cm depth, just below the greenish silt, is likely to date to around the fifteenth century (cal AD 1397–1503, median probability, cal AD 1440). A date at 197.5 cm depth (thus 66 cm

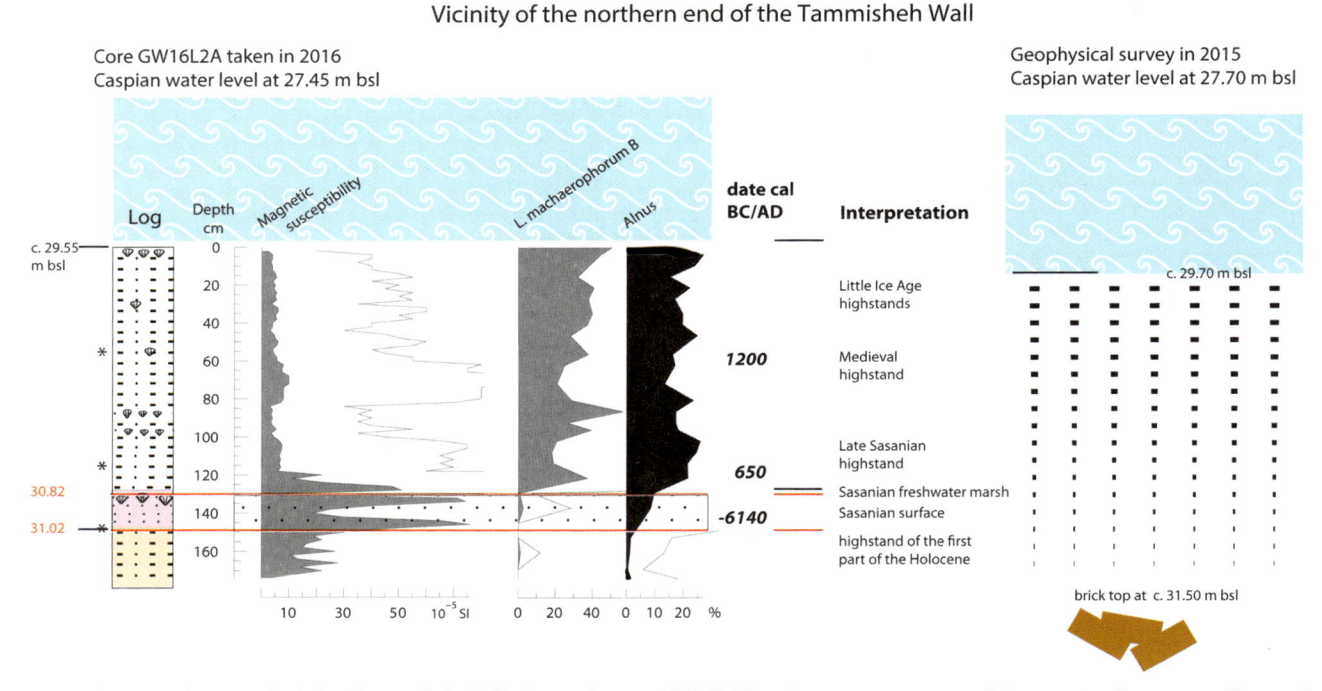

Fig. 13.7: Northern end of the Tammisheh Wall: Log of core GW16L2A with magnetic susceptibility, main dinocyst, pollen and interpretation. Core top 2.10 m below water level (-27.45 m in October 2016), i.e. at approximately -29.55 m. Legend: see Fig. 13.8. For radiocarbon dates (*), see Table 13.2.

deeper) shows a similar age (cal AD 1393–1474, median probability, cal AD 1430). Three further dates were obtained below a 69 cm-thick brown sand layer. This is at around 300 cm depth in core V3A from a grey silty sediment with low MS presumed to be formed during a highstand. The three dates show quite similar ages, all falling probably between the late second century BC at the earliest and the early second century AD at the latest (with approximate median probability at 20 cal BC, cal AD 10 and cal AD 30).

In core V5, a date of cal AD 1151–1278 (median probability, cal AD 1210) has been obtained at 184.5 cm depth corresponding to the base of the palynological diagram and just above the main change in sediment at 195 cm. At 309.5 cm, a date of cal AD 348–550 (median probability, cal AD 460) was determined in the light olive grey silt unit at 298.5–323.5 cm. This would lead to suggest that the top of the lowest oxidised unit at 323.5 cm depth may correspond to the Sasanian surface, but more information would be needed to refine this date (Fig. 13.4).

13.4.2. The vicinity of the northern end of the Tammisheh Wall

Core L2 was taken c. 170 m north-east of a probable brick accumulation (Fig. 13.2). The latter is in a near perfect alignment with the Tammisheh Wall and may mark its continuation, or it might be a separate structure.[26] Cores L1A, B and C were close to the terminal of the main wall and the ditch lining it in the east.

SEDIMENT: The base of core L2 shows a grey silty sediment with oxidation spots and without shells. It is topped by a shell-rich sandy layer from 127 to 147 cm depth (Fig. 13.7). The colour from c. 120 to 147 cm is grey with a light pink touch. From the core base to 127 cm, the magnetic susceptibility is high to very high, especially in the uppermost 30 cm with two spikes at ~80 10^{-5} SI. Upwards, the rest of the core is composed of grey silt with some shells and low MS (~5 10^{-5} SI). Specifically, two 1 cm-thick horizons of small broken shells are observed at 94–95 and 87–88 cm depth. The presence of shells above 127 cm and their complete absence below 147 cm clearly helps dividing the sequence into two distinct units, the depths of 127–147 cm representing a transition.

The logs of the other three cores (L1A, B and C) are presented in Figure 13.8. Cores L1A and C are the two longest and reach a c. 6 cm thick dark grey sandy silt horizon. It is followed upwards by 80 to 100 cm by silt, first grey, then grey with spots of oxidation. This is topped by a 2 cm-thick shell layer (at 79–81 cm depth in core L1C and at 121–123 cm depth in core L1A). Upwards from this, the sediment is a grey silt rich in shells. Core L1B is shorter and a shell-less grey silt with oxidation spots occurs at the bottom. In this core, no distinct shell layer separates this bottom unit from the upper unit of grey silt with shells. The MS is generally high in the oxidised silt and below it.

DINOCYSTS: The diagram from core L2 clearly indicates a main division at 130 cm depth, leading to separate zones

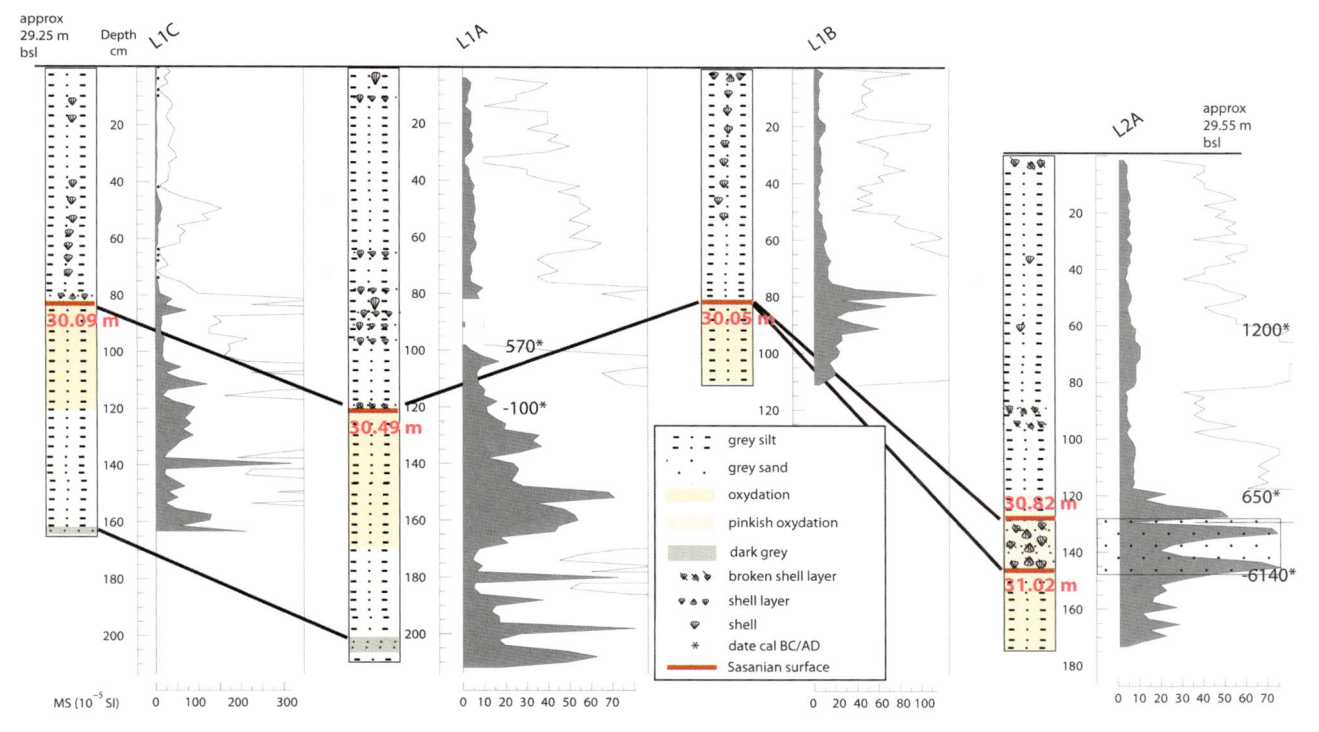

Fig. 13.8: Northern end of the Tammisheh Wall: Logs of cores GW16L1A, B and C and core L2A, with magnetic susceptibility and inter-core correlation. For radiocarbon dates (*), see Table 13.2. For cores L1AC, core top c. 1.80 m below water level (-27.45 m in October 2016), i.e. that was at approximately -29.25 m.

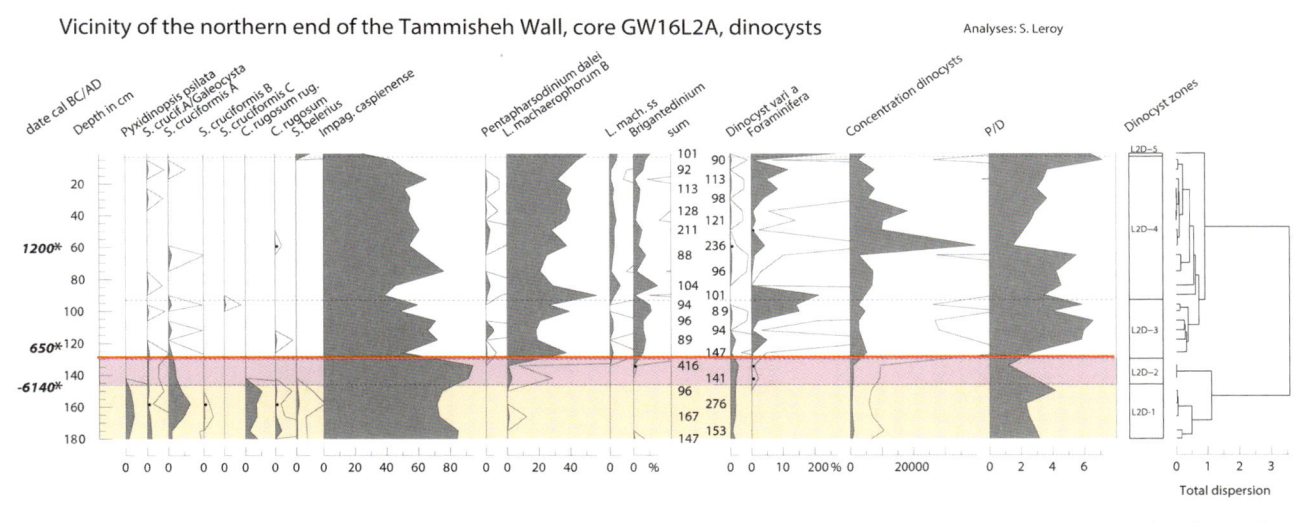

Fig. 13.9: The vicinity of the northern end of the Tammisheh Wall: Dinocyst diagram of core GW16L2A. Dots for values lower than 0.5%. For radiocarbon dates (*), see Table 13.2.

L2D1-2 and zones L2D3-4-5 (Fig. 13.9). Zones 1 and 2 are largely dominated by *I. caspienense*. A diverse range of other dinocysts is present: *S. cruciformis*, *P. psilata*, *Caspidinium rugosum* and *Spiniferites belerius*. The clear difference between zones 1 and 2 is due to the decline of these other taxa. A major change in the total dispersion clearly separates these two first zones from the rest of the diagram. In zones 3 to 5, *I. caspienense* has regressed slightly to give way to abundant *L. machaerophorum*, typical of the regional surface samples[27] and of the

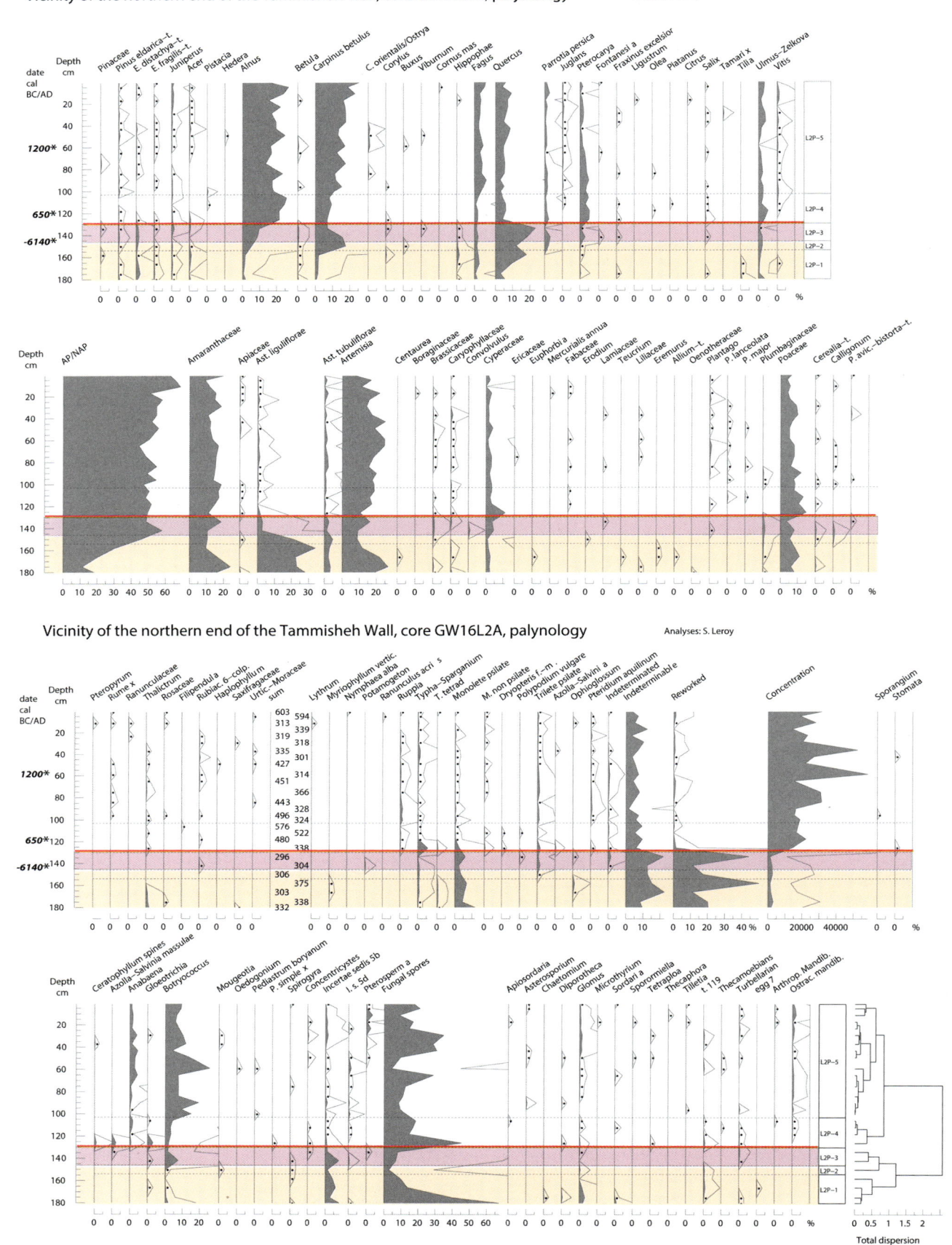

Fig. 13.10: Vicinity of the northern end of the Tammisheh Wall: Pollen diagram of core GW16L2A. Dots for values lower than 0.5%. For radiocarbon dates (*), see Table 13.2.

Table 13.2: *New radiocarbon samples from vicinity of the northernmost section of the Tammisheh Wall.*[28] *The date of the Bagho outcrop*[29] *has been recalibrated using the same method. The median probability dates are rounded to the nearest multiple of 10, and 5 is rounded up. Calibrated date at 95.4% confidence.*[30]

Core and sample no.	Laboratory no.	Composite depth in cm	Sample description	Date (BP)	Calibrated date at 95.4% confidence	Median probability
L1A2 97	Poz-119446	97	1 valve of Dreissena	1855±30	AD 529–647	AD 570
L1A2 121	Poz-119447	121	1 valve of a bivalve	2440±30	202 BC–AD 20	100 BC
L1A2 214	Poz-119448	214	1 valve of a bivalve	415±30	[modern]	[outlier; intrusive]
L2A1 58	Poz-93410	58	1 large bivalve	1200±29	AD 1048–1274 (86.3%: 1096–1274; 85.7%: 1126–1274; 84.0%: 1149–1274)	AD 1200
L2A2 118	Poz-93411	118	1 valve of Dreissena	1735±29	AD 588–773 (84.9%: AD 588–691)	AD 650
L2A2 144-147/8	Poz-98162	147	1 valve of a bivalve	7615±43	6229–6026 BC	6140 BC
Other date Bagho highstand	Poz-19943	22.06 m b.s.l.	Organic matter in Caspian Sea sediment	2380±35	163 BC–AD 83	20 BC

last 3,250 years.[31] *Pentapharsodinium dalei* is nearly continuously observed, as well as *Brigantedinium*. Foraminifera linings are also present, sometimes even very abundant (c. 200% of the dinocyst sum). The concentration in dinocysts is much higher than in the lower two zones, reaching nearly 40,000 cysts per ml of wet sediment. From zone 3 to 4, *I. caspiense* decreases and *L. machaerophorum* increases further. In zone 5 (one sample), *S. belerius* reappears.

In core L1, palynomorphs are nearly totally absent in the grey horizon with oxidation spots corresponding to the lower part of core L2 (132–167 cm, zone L1D-3), and completely absent below this horizon (206–214 cm, zone L1D-1) (Fig. 13.11). Zone L1D-2 is similar (but not identical) to zone L2D-1 and 2; amongst other differences more *Brigantedinium* are present in core L1. Zone L1D-4 resembles zones L2D-3, but has more *L. machaerophorum*.

POLLEN: In the diagram of core L2, as in the dinocyst diagram, a sharp change occurs at 130 cm depth (Fig. 13.10). The lower part (zones L2P-1-2-3) has abundant psilate monolete spores, unidentifiable and especially reworked palynomorphs. *Betula*, *Ephedra* and *Hippophae* are frequent, but occur in low percentages. Zone L2P-1 is dominated by A. liguliflorae, *Artemisia* and Amaranthaceae. The trees show an increasing curve of *Quercus*. Incertae sedis 5b (probably green algae) and fungal spores are abundant. In zones L2P-2 and 3, the arboreal pollen clearly increases. In particular, *Alnus* shows a steep rise. *Carpinus betulus* displays a bell-shaped curve. *Quercus* reaches a maximum. *Parrotia persica* and *Pterocarya* become quasi continuously present.

Zones L2P-4 and 5 are fairly similar with very high percentages of arboreal pollen dominated by *Alnus* and *C. betulus*. The zone limit is based on the increase in *Fagus* and the decrease (after high levels in L2P-4) of *Pterocarya*. Some possible indicators of human activity in zones 4 and 5 are *Pistacia*, *Juglans*, *Olea*, *Citrus* and *Vitis*; *Plantago* and *Rumex* may also indirectly point to the presence of humans.

Remarkably at 126 cm depth and to a lesser extent at 118 cm (i.e. the first two samples after the main diagram divide), a group of taxa reflects the temporary development of a freshwater marsh: a clear maximum in Cyperaceae and *Typha-Sparganium*, the occurrence of *Ceratophyllum*, *Azolla-Salvinia* and *Gloeotrichia* and peaks in *Pterocarya*, *Ulmus-Zelkova* and Poaceae.

In core L1A, pollen zone L1P-2, in comparison to zone L2P-1, has more Amaranthaceae, Poaceae and *Botryococcus*, and less A. liguliflorae and monolete psilate spores (Fig. 13.11). Pollen zone L1P-4 resembles zone L2P-4, but has less *Alnus*, *Carpinus betulus*, and more *Quercus* and *Pterocarya*. It also has quite a few palynomorphs indicating a freshwater environment.

DIATOMS: In core L2 two smear slide tests at 121 and 145 cm revealed an absence of diatoms.

RADIOCARBON DATES: Three dates (Table 13.2) are available for core L2. The age at the base of the sandy horizon is 6229–6026 cal BC (median probability, 6140 cal BC); while the age 29 cm above it dates to cal AD 588–773 (median probability, cal AD 650), with an almost 85% probability of the date falling between cal AD 588 and 691. A further 60 cm above, it is cal AD 1048–1274, most likely cal 1149–1274 (median

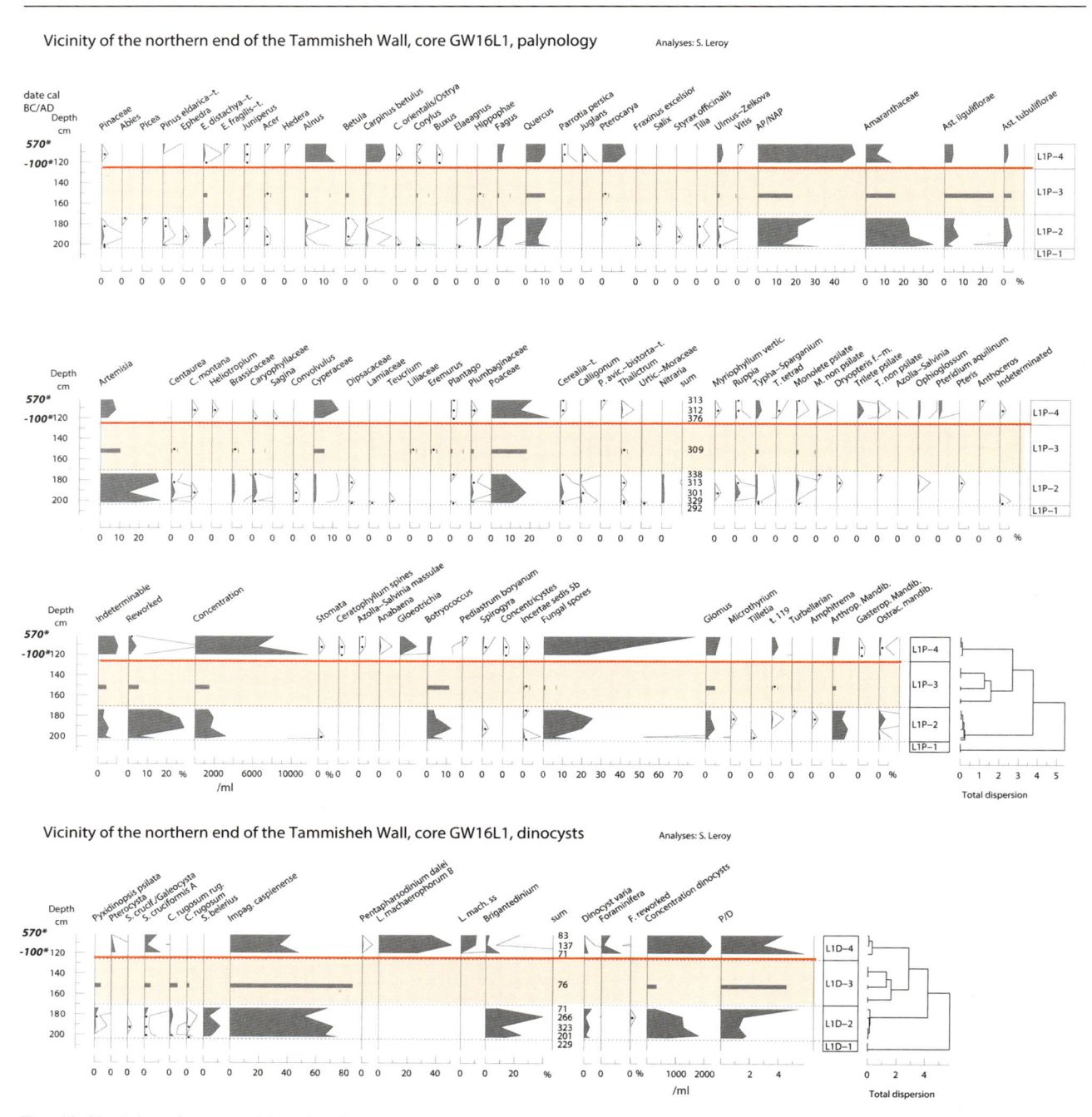

Fig. 13:11: A (top three panels) and B (bottom panel): Vicinity of the northern end of the Tammisheh Wall: Pollen (A) and dinocyst (B) diagrams of core GW16L1A. Dots for values lower than 0.5%. For radiocarbon dates (*), see Table 13.2.

probability, AD 1200). In core L1A, three dates were also obtained. That at 214 cm showing a recent age is rejected, as probably the shell was displaced during core section splitting. The dates at 121 and 97 cm are 202 cal BC–cal AD 20 (median probability, 100 cal BC) and cal AD 529–647 (median probability, cal AD 570) respectively.

13.5. Interpretation

13.5.1. Western terminal of the Gorgan Wall

LITHOLOGY LOG: Below the agricultural soil, the bright brown sand in core V3A may be interpreted as a beach interrupting a highstand. According to the three dates below the sand, the age is clearly the early Little Ice Age

(LIA) that is known to be an important highstand, although encompassing short periods at lower elevation.[32] The brick found at a depth of c. 110 cm in core V3B is probably redeposited. The sand layer around 200–300 cm in cores V3A and B differs from the other sands by the absence of shells. It is not dated directly. Based on its position in relation to dated samples in the sequence, it may correspond to the lowstand of the period when the Sasanians built the wall. If so, it is followed by a long hiatus.

DINOCYSTS: The dinocysts in the S2-V3 sequence just below the bright brown sands indicate a highstand. The three radiocarbon dates in this green-grey unit (Table 13.1) from cal AD 1290–1408 to 1397–1503 (median probability, cal AD 1350 to 1440) place it within the early LIA highstand, around the time and up to a century or two after the very high (historically attested[33]) level in AD 1304. The height of this flooding can be precisely estimated at 72 cm below the nail that is at 23.40 m b.s.l., thus 24.12 m b.s.l. at least. Note that either date places the S2 and V3 highstand elevation slightly above the curve by Naderi Beni *et al*.

POLLEN: Further down, below a 5 cm thick brown sand layer with many broken shells (most likely representing an erosional phase), the first three samples containing pollen in core V3 are at around 150 cm. The spectra are typical of an environment with saline soils. It is probable that a coastal marsh had developed with brackish water. This environment is dated by one sample of very similar age to that of the green-grey unit (when taking into consideration the very large confidence interval, Table 13.1), suggesting a rapid sedimentation.

In core V3 and still further down, below a sand layer without shells (68 to 103 cm thick), there was a bluish and grey silt layer. The pollen diagram in core V3 at around 300 cm depth reflects freshwater in a still environment, a grassland and, in the distance, the Hyrcanian forest. The bluish silt at the same depth in core V3A (three dates falling between the late second century BC and the early second century AD, with a median probability at 20 cal BC, cal AD 10 and cal AD 30) shows a highstand, younger than the end of the 650–350 cal BC highstand, attested elsewhere in the Gorgan Bay (see below). Due to the difference in elevation, age and dinocyst assemblage, it is uncertain that the two grey-green ditch infills in the S2 outcrop and the V3 core are the same (Fig. 13.3). What comes out clearly, though, is that they are not Sasanian.

In core V5, below 189 cm, the lack of palynomorphs and the oxidised colour suggest an environment that was shallow and regularly emerged. A calibrated date of cal AD 460 at 309.5 cm core depth has a wide age range, i.e. cal AD 348–550. It could pre-date or post-date (mid-fifth-century?) wall construction, but it certainly falls within the Sasanian era, and we may tentatively interpret the surface at 323.5 cm as a possible Sasanian-era surface (Fig. 13.4).

13.5.2. The vicinity of the northern terminal of the Tammisheh Wall

From bottom to top, the offshore cores provide the following information: in core L2A (the one furthest north), a hiatus is well marked at 127 cm depth (corresponding to c. 30.82 m b.s.l.) by sediment, pollen and dinocysts. Cores L1A, B and C (all from near the possible terminal of the wall) show the same change in sediment but at slightly shallower depths (124, 80 and 84 cm, i.e. c. 30.49, 30.05 and 30.09 m b.s.l. respectively: Fig. 13.8). The sediment below the hiatus in core L2A represents first a transitional zone (closer to the lower than the upper part of the core), and then further down, an old Caspian highstand, dated here at 6229–6026 cal BC (median probability, 6140 cal BC). The pollen and dinocyst assemblages of zones L2P-1 to 3 and L2D-1 and 2 are in agreement with such an old age, when compared to a diagram such as the TM sequence.[34] The absence of *L. machaerophorum* further confirms an age older than 3250 cal BP.[35] At that time (in the Early Holocene), one finds in zone TM-3 (from 7525 to 5280 cal BC) a similar vegetation and also the most marine/open water period of the TM sequence. Very similar spectra are also found in the pollen and dinocyst records of the Sha sequence in zone S-7, whose base is estimated at 6250 cal BC.[36]

The shell-rich sandy layer at 127–147 cm in core L2A is a disturbed high-energy horizon, probably a beach. The core top is at -29.55 m; thus the top of the beach is at -30.82 m and its base at -31.02 m. This beach unit is absent from the three L1 cores. The transition is dated from before cal AD 588–773 (median probability, AD 650). Based on the radiocarbon dates and palynology, this hiatus is possibly close to seven millennia long.

When the sedimentation starts again slightly before the date of cal AD 588–773 (median probability, cal AD 650) (in core L2A, at c. 127 cm core depth, i.e. -30.82 m b.s.l.), the environment is at first a freshwater marsh, and then later on turns into a brackish lagoon such as today. In comparison to this, core L1A shows a surface dated at 202 cal BC–cal AD 20 (median probability, 100 cal BC) with shells lying on it. The marine sediment overlying this hiatus is slightly older than cal AD 529–647 (median probability, cal AD 570). When comparing the chronology of the start of sedimentation near the wall (cores L1A) and further offshore (core L2A), only a small overlap exists. Perhaps the much more substantial build-up of sediments in the Sasanian era (or the Parthian and Sasanian eras) in the southern core L1A than further offshore in core L2A was a result of human intervention.

13.6. Caspian Sea level changes from pre-Sasanian to early modern times

13.6.1. The era preceding wall construction

The two walls were built on surfaces of completely different ages, corresponding to earlier highstands. Below the level of the westernmost section of the Gorgan Wall examined to date, the sediment from under 300 cm depth reflects a highstand of around 112 cal BC–cal AD 125 (median probability, cal AD 10). The elevation of the sand is 24.52–25.70 m b.s.l. (Fig. 13.3). Significantly, only a couple of kilometres south-east of the Gorgan Bay is the Bagho outcrop linked to a highstand at -22.06 m. The published calibrated age range is 541–389 cal BC[37] (Tables 13.1 and 13.2). Recalibration using the method outlined above,[38] however, suggests that it is later: 163 cal BC–cal AD 83 (median probability, 20 cal BC). The highstand at this site therefore has a similar age to that at a depth of c. 300 cm in core V3A.

At the terminal of the Tammisheh Wall, the first recognised highstand in cores L2 (below 147 cm, elevation 30.82–31.02 m b.s.l.) and L1A (below 124 cm, elevation 30.49 m b.s.l.) has palynological spectra very similar to those of the highstand from 7525 to 5280 cal BC in core TM. The highstand sediment at 650–350 cal BC (22.06 m b.s.l.) is thus missing in this core. This absence is unexpected as sediment from this highstand is widespread in the region, such as in the Larim and Neka Rivers, a few tens of kilometres west of the bay.[39]

13.6.2. Sasanian-period walls and the lowstand of the Caspian Sea

Near the westernmost known section of the Gorgan Wall, the Sasanian-era surface is most likely the shell-less sand unit crossed by cores V3A and B with an elevation of c. 24.52–25.69 m b.s.l. (Fig. 13.3).

Near the terminal of the Tammisheh Wall, the surface level is better defined: in core L2A at c. 31.02 m b.s.l. as marked by erosion and the emersion level at 127–147 cm (Fig. 13.8). Comparing core L2A (31.02 m b.s.l.) to cores L1A, B and C (30.49 m b.s.l. and above and thus shallower), it seems that the elevation of the Sasanian ground surface is lower further offshore. Moreover, a 20 cm thick pinkish sand layer rich in shells and with high MS is present in core L2A, but absent in the three other cores, and the postulated Sasanian surface is lower in L1A than in L1B and L1C. This may represent a lower elevation area filled in with sand. Several interpretations are possible. This low point

1. could be a result of erosion either by current around the end of the wall, as seen in groins or due to the Qareh Su that is at the same latitude eastwards and that would have extended westward during lowstands;

2. might be part of a larger area regularly trampled by people pulling their boats to the safety of a sandy beach;

3. might have been dug and regularly dredged for mooring purposes near the end of the Tammisheh Wall, perhaps related to structures linked to the main wall.[40]

The latter two hypotheses are preferred and are both possible as the south-east corner of the Caspian Sea has always been a place of exchange of goods transported from the north by boat and from the south by caravans, the rest of the south coast offering very little shelter.[41]

The various elevations of the sand units related to the Sasanian period reflect land management with perhaps dredging and basin maintenance, as the dynamic coast of the Caspian would constantly require. In addition to clay for bricks, timber for wood piling was plentiful owing to the proximity of the Hyrcanian forest. Continuous sedimentation has been observed elsewhere in the lagoon (as further discussed below).

The Sasanian surface, based on the current study, can be bracketed here between 202 cal BC–cal AD 20 (median probability, 100 cal BC) and before cal AD 529–647 (median probability, cal AD 570) (core L1A) and at an elevation of 30.05–31.02 m b.s.l. (cores L1A, B and C and L2A). This places the Sasanian floor close to the time of the Derbent Wall construction (in the sixth century) and in this location and time just slightly less low than that of the Derbent lowstand that is at c. 31.50 to 32.00 m b.s.l.[42]

The climate reconstructed from pollen diagrams do not show a dramatic change at that time: the Kongor Lake sequence inland along the Gorgan Wall,[43] the Mazgah Lagoon along the Caspian coast[44] and the Gomishan Lagoon with core TM point to similar climatic conditions.[45] In the latter, sediment with an age of cal AD 495 (transition pollen zones TM-7a to 7b, date estimated by age-depth modelling) is found at 4.20 m depth (i.e. c. 29.70 m b.s.l.) and shows a slight change from more steppic to more desertic vegetation. Variations between these three sequences seem to be mostly due to changes in human activities.

13.6.3. From the late Sasanian era to the Early Middle Ages

The grey-green silt filling a depression corresponds to a ditch infill (or more than one) of post-Sasanian age along the westernmost section of the Gorgan Wall, reflecting the later use of the Gorgan Plain for agriculture. Based on our investigations, four indications of flooding have been detected: three in the cores of the Gorgan Wall and one in the Tammisheh sequence.

THE LATE SASANIAN HIGHSTAND: An initial flooding is attested at the end of the Tammisheh Wall after the hiatus in cores L2 and L1 (Figs 13.7 and 13.8), as the Gorgan Bay is at a lower altitude than the westernmost section of the Gorgan Wall found so far. Sedimentation over the Sasanian surface started just before cal AD 588–773 (median probability, cal AD 650) or even before cal AD 529–647 (median probability, cal AD 570), i.e. perhaps towards, or just after, the end of the Sasanian era. The very first phase of sedimentation was under freshwater with some Caspian incursions indicating a general rise of the water table and the Caspian levels. The age of this flooding is in line with written evidence showing that the wall was already partially submerged by the ninth century.[46] In the TM sequence, at cal AD 590 and 640 (or at 390 and 380 cm depth, i.e. c. 29.40 and 29.30 m b.s.l., in core TM), a slight increase in dinocyst concentration occurs. This could be in line with the initial flooding over the Tammisheh Wall.

13.6.4. Medieval and Little Ice Age flooding

MEDIEVAL HIGHSTAND: As the western tip of the Gorgan Wall (as far as traced to date) is further inland, it allows distinguishing more easily small fluctuations of highstand water levels. The Sasanian shell-less sands are here followed by highstand silts of three separate phases, with intercalated sandy horizons. If the Little Ice Age (LIA) is taken to start at AD 1350, then two of them date from the LIA and one comes just before, i.e. in the High Middle Ages. The first one is of the mid-twelfth to late thirteenth century (with a median probability around the beginning of the thirteenth century) near the coast in core V5 at 184.5 cm and in core L2 at 58 cm (Figs 13.4 and 13.7). This may be the flooding that caused the disappearance of the nearby coastal harbour and town of Abeskun by AD 1260.[47]

LITTLE ICE AGE HIGHSTANDS: Flooding from the fourteenth century onwards reached further inland. This marine transgression is represented in section S2 at 50 cm depth, in core V3 at 131.5 cm, and over a brick kiln (Trench I) next to the Gorgan Wall (Fig. 13.3). The latter is found 1.1 km further inland of the S2-V3 site (Fig. 13.1). The kiln was covered by 1 m of marine sediment owing to transgressions of the Caspian Sea.[48] The radiocarbon dates of the shells were calibrated to cal AD 1300–1424 (median probability, cal AD 1350) (Table 13.1), remarkably close to the dates from section S2 and from core V3 of cal AD 1290–1408 and 1292–1410 to 1397–1503 and most likely all relating to the same initial transgression. Evidence for a last flooding is found at the top of all cores, but has not been independently dated. In general, the LIA is recognised as a period of highstand in the Caspian Sea,[49] although it was interrupted by several lower stands.

13.7. The coastal environment in Sasanian times

13.7.1. The Gorgan Wall west of the S2-V3 sequence

The westernmost point where the Gorgan Wall has been traced through excavation are in the trench with section S2 (Fig. 13.1: GW16V3S2). West of this site, the wall, as detected by geophysics, may have bent slightly southwards.[50] This is most likely to avoid the dynamic environments of Hassan Gholi and of the Gomishan Lagoon, as their shoreline fluctuates with Caspian level change amongst other factors.[51] If the preservation of palynomorphs and a fine-grained grey sediment are taken as acceptable proxies for permanent submersion, core TM in Hassan Gholi offers the most continuous palynological record over the last two millennia. This is explained by its position in a more lagoonal environment than cores V3 (east of Hassan Gholi) and V5 (west of Hassan Gholi) that are in more terrestrial locations and at slightly higher elevations.

13.7.2. Vegetation at the time of the walls and later

The wall construction period corresponds to a low water level, and no fine-grained sediment has accumulated in the GW16V and L cores, besides sand. Therefore information on the Sasanian vegetation have to be found either in the sediment of Hassan Gholi or offshore.

In core TM, the age-depth model suggests that four palynological samples fall in the Sasanian period.[52] The spectra are characterised by a peak of microcharcoal, that appears to be contemporary to a peak in microcharcoal at Lake Kongor in the eastern Gorgan Plain,[53] and high values of Amaranthaceae. It was suggested that human pressure was high with a transition from agriculture to grazing activities across the depths studied.

In previous investigations, charcoals from several trenches were analysed. Those closest to the coast in the Gorgan Wall area are Trenches I and G along the wall. Only Trench G has provided some poorly preserved charcoals and mostly of Chenopodioideae.[54] This result fits very well with the pollen spectra. Other trenches closer to the forest yielded more diverse charcoal taxa. Therefore, pollen and charcoal together suggest a very open, dry and halophytic vegetation in the area of the westernmost section of the Gorgan Wall during and just after the Sasanian era.

Post-Sasanian arboriculture is well represented at the northern end of the Tammisheh Wall. This activity was started most likely earlier as branches of *Juglans* were also used as fuel in an excavated Sasanian brick kiln next to the Tammisheh Wall (Trench F), and walnut is still cultivated in the area today.⁵⁵

Three pollen spectra in the V3A pollen diagram at around 150 cm depth, although poorly preserved and not directly dated, could represent the vegetation a millennium after the Sasanian era, around the fifteenth century. These spectra are clearly different from the grassland reconstructed at the start of our common era (at c. 300 cm depth). The reconstructed medieval to early modern vegetation (around 150 cm depth) shows a dry steppe, borderline desertic (60% of Amaranthaceae, a family including Chenopods often associated with desert or/and saline conditions). The soils are very saline, as attested by the presence of Plumbaginaceae. The occurrence of *Glomus* indicates soil erosion. The extremely low percentages of pollen from *Alnus* are worth noting. Nowadays this tree is still forming a coastal forest, although it is patchy due to agriculture. Modern pollen spectra reach 10–20% of *Alnus* offshore from the Miankaleh Spit⁵⁶ and 10% in the Gomishan Lagoon.⁵⁷ The suggested intense modification of the coast by the Sasanian-era, medieval and modern population of the area may largely explain the decline of the coastal alder forest.

13.8. Conclusion

Our multidisciplinary studies, centred on the terminals of the two Sasanian barriers, the Gorgan and Tammisheh Walls, have provided significant new insights into the changing marine environment. Both walls were obviously built at a time of lowstand. The estimated base of the Sasanian surface in the Gorgan Bay is at c. 31 m b.s.l., thus fairly similar to that of the Derbent Wall at 31.50 to 32 m b.s.l. Significant human management at the end of the Tammisheh Wall was found by the removal of substantial quantities of sediment, perhaps to create mooring for boats. The expected previous highstand sediment, dating from 650–350 cal BC and that should serve as the Sasanian surface, has been dredged and is absent from our sequences. The Sasanian floor is a sandy layer on top of deposits of an Early Holocene highstand.

Our studies yielded no new information on the vegetation for the Sasanian period, as it corresponds to a hiatus. The vegetation near the Gorgan Wall's western terminal during (as known from other studies) and after the Sasanian period was mostly likely very dry, as suggested by pollen and charcoal analysis. In the Gorgan Bay, the northern end of the Tammisheh Wall became submerged again already in the late Sasanian era or shortly after, and palynology reflects at first a brief period of freshwater before a return to fully brackish conditions, typical of the Caspian Sea.

Towards the western terminal of the Gorgan Wall, we have been able to examine a section of the wall and its environment 1.1 km west of the kiln in Trench I. The fill of the ditch north of the wall could be shown to be of a much more recent date than the Sasanian era and was flooded only approximately a millennium after wall construction. That the ditch had remained largely open before may be unsurprising, as also further inland the just partially silted-up ditch often survives as a depression to the present day.

The results of our examinations near the seaside terminals of the two walls complement each other. Traces of flooding are found in four phases: the first already during the highstand in the late Sasanian era, at cal AD 529–647 (median probability, cal AD 570), subsequently in the High Middle Ages, perhaps at the beginning of the thirteenth century, and finally twice during the Little Ice Age highstand in the Late Middle Ages to Early Modern Era.

Notes

1 Aix Marseille Univ, CNRS, IRD, INRAE, Coll. France, CEREGE, Aix-en-Provence, France: Suzanne A.G. Leroy, François Demory and Françoise Chalié; Aix Marseille Univ, CNRS, Minist Culture & Com, LAMPEA, 13094 Aix-en-Provence, France, suzleroy@hotmail.com and School of Environmental Sciences, University of Liverpool, L69 3GP Liverpool, UK: Suzanne A.G. Leroy; University of Wales Trinity Saint David, UK: Martin R. Bates; School of Earth & Environmental Sciences, University of St Andrews, UK: C. Richard Bates; Gorgan Wall Cultural Heritage Base, Iranian Cultural Heritage, Handcraft and Tourism Organization, Gorgan, Iran: Hamid Omrani Rekavandi; School of History, Classics and Archaeology, University of Edinburgh, UK: Eberhard W. Sauer; 14CHRONO Centre for Climate, the Environment and Chronology, Queen's University Belfast, Belfast BT7 1NN, UK: Paula J. Reimer.

    The vibracorer was kindly provided by INIOAS. We thank Naser Ghassemi (INIOAS) for his invaluable help in the field and Keyvan Kabiri (INIOAS) for the levelling. The palynological samples were treated at IMBE (France) and the School of Environmental Sciences at University of Liverpool (UK). We are grateful to Morteza Djamali, Dahvya Belkacem, Fabienne Marret and Jenny Bradley.

2 Sauer *et al.* 2013, 149–54.
3 See chapter 11.
4 Kakroodi *et al.* 2012.
5 See chapter 12.
6 Kakroodi *et al.* 2014.
7 Kakroodi *et al.* 2012.
8 Kakroodi *et al.* 2014.
9 Kakroodi *et al.* 2012.
10 Naderi Beni *et al.* 2014.
11 Kakroodi *et al.* 2015; Leroy *et al.* 2013a.
12 Leroy *et al.* 2019; note that the core name 'Gha' is based on a different transliteration of the Qareh Su, i.e. 'Gharasoo' (i.e. 'Black water').
13 Leroy *et al.* 2018.
14 See chapter 11.4.1–11.4.2.
15 See http://hydroweb.theia-land.fr/hydroweb/view/L_caspian?lang=en (accessed on 15 April 2020).
16 See chapter 12.

17　Dearing *et al.* 1997.
18　Bennett 2007.
19　Reimer *et al.* 2020.
20　Details in Leroy *et al.* submitted.
21　See chapter 11 with Fig. 11.8.
22　Kudrjavcev and Gadžiev 2002, 339–40.
23　Location of new cores: V3A: 37° 7.745' N, 54° 6.768' E; V4A: 37° 7.433' N, 54° 3.412' E; V5A: 37° 7.450' N, 54° 2.848' E.
24　Sauer *et al.* 2013, 152.
25　Stuiver and Polach 1977. Radiocarbon dates kindly supplied by the Poznan Radiocarbon Laboratory.
26　See chapter 12.4.4.
27　Leroy *et al.* 2018.
28　Location of new cores: L1A: 36° 49.278' N, 54° 0.797' E; L1B: 36° 49.277' N, 54° 0.801' E; L1C: 36° 49.277' N, 54° 0.784' E; L2A: 36° 49.555' N, 54° 0.665' E.
29　Kakroodi *et al.* 2012.
30　Stuiver and Polach 1977. Radiocarbon dates kindly supplied by the Poznan Radiocarbon Laboratory.
31　Leroy *et al.* 2013b.
32　Naderi Beni *et al.* 2013.
33　Naderi Beni *et al.* 2013.
34　Leroy *et al.* 2013a.
35　Leroy *et al.* 2013b.
36　Leroy *et al.* 2019.
37　Kakroodi *et al.* 2012.
38　See chapter 13.3.4.
39　Lahijani *et al.* 2009.
40　See chapter 12.4.4 and Figs 12.11 and 12.17–12.19.
41　See also chapter 24.8 and Sauer *et al.* 2013, 601–05 on potential Sasanian-era maritime trade on the Caspian Sea.
42　Kudrjavcev and Gadžiev 2002; Wilkinson *et al.* 2013, 35.
43　Shumilovskikh *et al.* 2016b and chapter 21.3.
44　Ramezani *et al.* 2016.
45　Leroy *et al.* 2013a.
46　Sauer *et al.* 2013, 16 with sources.
47　Naderi Beni *et al.* 2013.
48　Sauer *et al.* 2013, 151–52.
49　Haghani *et al.* 2016; Haghani and Leroy 2016; 2020; Kroonenberg *et al.* 2007; Leroy *et al.* 2011.
50　See chapter 11, cf. Sauer *et al.* 2013, 149, 153, 264–69.
51　Kakroodi *et al.* 2012 and Naderi Beni *et al.* 2013, fig. 3.
52　Leroy *et al.* 2013a.
53　See chapter 21.3.4.5 and Fig. 21.11.
54　Poole and Gale 2013, 582.
55　Poole and Gale 2013, 581–82; Sauer *et al.* 2013, 250; Shumilovskikh *et al.* 2017, 62–63; see also chapter 21.
56　Leroy *et al.* 2018.
57　Leroy *et al.* 2013a.

444 — Ancient Arms Race

تقدیم به زنده‌یاد پروفسور تونی ویلکینسون در پاسداشت نقش حیاتی وی در پروژه سال‌های ۲۰۰۵ تا ۲۰۱۴

تصاویر ۲ - ۱: تونی ویلکینسون در قلعه ماران در سال ۲۰۰۷.
(تصویر پایین نشسته از راست به چپ: محدثه منصوری رضی، تونی ویلکینسون و کوروش روستایی)

فهرست مطالب

فصل ۲۳. تاریخ‌گذاری لومینسانس و ارزیابی میکرو مورفولوژیکی ... ۷۳۹
لیزا اسنپ و ایان بایلیف
۲۳-۱. مقدمه ... ۷۳۹
۲۳-۱-۱. نمونه‌ها ... ۷۳۹
۲۳-۱-۲. سابقه OSL ... ۷۴۰
۲۳-۲. روش‌شناسی ... ۷۴۰
۲۳-۲-۱. نمونه‌گیری میدانی ... ۷۴۰
۲۳-۲-۲. اندازه‌گیری OSL ... ۷۴۱
۲۳-۲-۳. میکرومورفولوژی ... ۷۴۱
۲۳-۳. نتایج ... ۷۴۱
۲۳-۳-۱. سن OSL ... ۷۴۱
۲۳-۳-۲. میکرومورفولوژی ... ۷۴۲
۲۳-۴. بحث ... ۷۴۲

بخش E: تاریخ
فصل ۲۴. نگاه جدید به زیرساخت‌های نظامی ساسانیان ... ۷۴۷
۲۴-۱. مقدمه ... ۷۴۷
۲۴-۲. راهبردهای انعطاف‌پذیر: توزیع انواع مختلف از موانع دفاعی ... ۷۴۷
۲۴-۳. یادگیری از گذشته، پذیرش سنت‌های ولایتی: بزرگترین قلعه‌های جهان باستان، با الهام از معماری آسیای میانه ... ۷۵۲
۲۴-۴. تحول بزرگترین برنامه استحکامات جهان باستان ... ۷۵۵
۲۴-۵. تعداد و قابلیت‌های نیروهای ساسانی و رومی ... ۷۶۰
۲۴-۶. مسابقه تسلیحاتی در دنیای باستان ... ۷۶۵
۲۴-۷. حمایت سلطنتی از موانع دفاعی امپراطوری ... ۷۶۸
۲۴-۸. هدف و اثربخشی از مستحکم‌سازی امپراطوری ... ۷۷۰
۲۴-۹. میراث ارتش ساسانیان ... ۷۸۰
۲۴-۱۰. وضع صلح‌انگیز دولت ساسانی Pax Sasanica ... ۷۸۱

بخش F: نتیجه‌گیری و کتاب‌شناسی
نتیجه‌گیری ... ۷۹۳
- سپاسگزاری‌ها ... ۷۹۳
- مقدمات ... ۷۹۳
- کاوش‌ها و بررسی‌های میدانی ... ۷۹۳
- بررسی دریایی ... ۷۹۶
- اسناد مکتوب، یافته‌ها، مصالح ساختمانی، شواهد زیست‌شناختی و زیست‌محیطی و تاریخ‌گذاری علمی ... ۷۹۶
- تاریخ ... ۷۹۹
- فهرست منابع ... ۸۰۳
- بحث، سپاسگزاری، فهرست مطالب پروژه و عناوین به فارسی ... ۸۸۰

فهرست مطالب

۲-۳-۲-۲۱. پل دیوار گرگان بر فراز رودخانه ساری سو (ترانشه B)	۷۱۳
۳-۳-۲-۲۱. قلعه ۲ (ترانشه D)	۷۱۶
۴-۳-۲-۲۱. گبری قلعه (ترانشه E)	۷۱۸
۵-۳-۲-۲۱. گبری قلعه (ترانشه F)	۷۱۸
۶-۳-۲-۲۱. بوراق تپه (ترانشه g)	۷۱۸
۷-۳-۲-۲۱. قلعه ایرج (ترانشه i)	۷۱۸
۸-۳-۲-۲۱. دیوار فرود (ترانشه K)	۷۱۹
۳-۲۱. تاریخچه پوشش گیاهی دشت گرگان: شواهدی از تحلیل گرده‌شناسی در دریاچه کنگور	۷۱۹
لودمیلا شومیلوسکیخ	
۱-۳-۲۱. مقدمه	۷۱۹
۲-۳-۲۱. موقعیت جغرافیایی	۷۲۰
۳-۳-۲۱. پیشینه زیست‌بوم‌شناسی دیرینه از کنگور	۷۲۰
۴-۳-۲۱. تأثیرات انسانی، تغییرات اقلیمی و چشم‌انداز	۷۲۱
۱-۴-۳-۲۱. آب و هوا	۷۲۱
۲-۴-۳-۲۱. پوشش جنگلی	۷۲۲
۳-۴-۳-۲۱. زراعت و درختکاری	۷۲۳
۴-۴-۳-۲۱. چراگاه	۷۲۳
۵-۴-۳-۲۱. آتش	۷۲۴
۴-۲۱. نرم‌تنان	۷۲۵
کاتریونا پیکارد و لودمیلا شومیلویشیخ	

فصل ۲۲. مطالعات آرکئومگنتیک از عوارض حفرشده در امتداد دیوار گرگان   ۷۲۷

کتی بات، دیوید گرینوود و تریم کینات

۱-۲۲. چکیده	۷۲۷
۲-۲۲. مقدمه	۷۲۷
۳-۲۲. پیش زمینه	۷۲۸
۴-۲۲. نمونه‌برداری آرکئومگنتیک در دشت	۷۲۹
۱-۴-۲۲. قلعه پل گنبدکاووس	۷۲۹
۲-۴-۲۲. دره ساری سو	۷۲۹
۳-۴-۲۲. دره ساری سو	۷۳۰
۴-۴-۲۲. قلعه ۲	۷۳۰
۵-۴-۲۲. قلعه ۲	۷۳۰
۶-۴-۲۲. قلعه ۲	۷۳۱
۵-۲۲. اندازه‌گیری‌های مغناطیسی	۷۳۱
۱-۵-۲۲. آماده‌سازی نمونه	۷۳۱
۲-۵-۲۲. روند اندازه‌گیری	۷۳۲
۶-۲۲. نتایج	۷۳۲
۱-۶-۲۲. رسوبات	۷۳۲
۲-۶-۲۲. مواد حرارت‌دیده	۷۳۳
۷-۲۲. تفسیر نتایج آرکئومگنتیک و مقایسه آن با مدل میدان ژئومغناطیسی جهانی	۷۳۳
۸-۲۲. مطالعات آرکئومگنتیک پیشین در منطقه	۷۳۵
۹-۲۲. خلاصه و نتیجه‌گیری	۷۳۶
۱۰-۲۲. کار بیشتر	۷۳۷

فهرست مطالب

۶۶۵	۲۰-۴-۲. گرازها و وضعیت آن‌ها در قلعه ۲
۶۶۸	۲۰-۴-۳. بقایای اسب سانان
۶۶۸	۲۰-۴-۳-۱. دندان‌ها
۶۶۹	۲۰-۴-۳-۲. استخوان کف دست و زند زبرین
۶۷۰	۲۰-۴-۳-۳. بقایای اسب: شواهد بالقوه از سواره نظام در قلعه ۲؟
۶۷۱	۲۰-۴-۴. بقایای پرنده
۶۷۲	۲۰-۴-۵. بقایای ماهی
	والنتین رادو، مرجان مشکور و ابرهارد سوئر
۶۷۵	۲۰-۵. سن مرگ گوسفند و بز
۶۷۶	۲۰-۶. فعالیت‌های صنایع دستی
۶۷۶	۲۰-۷. نتیجه
۶۷۸	۲۰-۸. پیوست
۶۷۸	۲۰-۸-۱. پیوست ۱: اندازه‌گیری‌ها
۶۷۸	۲۰-۸-۱-۱. پیوست ۱.۱: اندازه‌گیری گوسفندان (جنس گوسفند)
۶۸۱	۲۰-۸-۱-۲. پیوست ۱.۲: اندازه‌گیری‌های بز (بز کوهی)
۶۸۴	۲۰-۸-۱-۳. پیوست ۱.۳: اندازه‌گیری گوسفند / بز (بزیان)
۶۸۴	۲۰-۸-۱-۴. پیوست ۱.۴: اندازه‌گیری گاو (گاوان)
۶۸۸	۲۰-۸-۱-۵. پیوست ۱.۵: اندازه‌گیری‌های خوک / گراز (گراز وحشی)
۶۹۰	۲۰-۸-۱-۶. پیوست ۱.۶: اندازه‌گیری اسب‌سان (اسب‌سانان)
۶۹۱	۲۰-۸-۲. پیوست ۲: محوطه‌های مقایسه‌ای
۶۹۴	۲۰-۸-۳. پیوست ۳: آنالیز آماری برای دندان‌های گرازان
۶۹۴	۲۰-۸-۴. پیوست ۴: انتساب سن دندان بزیان (جنس گوسفند/بز کوهی)

فصل ۲۱. محیط زیست پارینه

۶۹۹	
	لودمیلا شومیلوسکیخ، فلیکس بیتمن، بریژیت تالون، دنیئلا پاتزولد و کاتریونا پیکارد
۶۹۹	۲۱-۱. بهره‌برداری جنگل: شواهد حاصل از تحلیل زیست‌بوم‌شناسی پارینه
	لودمیلا شومیلوسکیخ و بریژیت تالون
۶۹۹	۲۱-۱-۱. مقدمه
۶۹۹	۲۱-۱-۲. مواد و روش‌ها
۶۹۹	۲۱-۱-۳. نتایج
۶۹۹	۲۱-۱-۳-۱. مقدمه
۷۰۰	۲۱-۱-۳-۲. قلعه ۲ (ترانشه D)
۷۰۰	۲۱-۱-۳-۳. بوراق تپه (ترانشه G)
۷۰۰	۲۱-۱-۳-۴. قلعه ایرج (ترانشه I)
۷۰۳	۲۱-۱-۳-۵. دیوار فرود (ترانشه K)
۷۰۳	۲۱-۱-۴. بحث
۷۰۵	۲۱-۱-۵. نتیجه
۷۰۵	۲۱-۲. مطالعات گیاه‌باستان‌شناسی در دشت گرگان
	لودمیلا شومیلوسکیخ، فلیکس بیتمن و دنیلا پاتزولد
۷۰۵	۲۱-۲-۱. مقدمه
۷۰۵	۲۱-۲-۲. مواد و روش‌ها
۷۱۳	۲۱-۲-۳. نتایج و بحث
۷۱۳	۲۱-۲-۳-۱. قلعه پل گنبدکاووس (ترانشه A)

فهرست مطالب

۴-۳-۱۸. ظروف فلزی	۶۰۸
۵-۳-۱۸. تولید نساجی	۶۰۹
۴-۱۸. مهره‌ها	۶۱۵

تیم پن

۱-۴-۱۸. مقدمه، مواد، سبک و گاهنگاری	۶۱۵
۲-۴-۱۸. توزیع فضایی، گاهنگاری و اهمیت	۶۱۷
۵-۱۸. اقلام دیگر از زینت‌های شخصی، لباس و اسباب و اثاثیه	۶۱۹
۶-۱۸. مصالح ساختمانی	۶۲۴
۷-۱۸. سکه‌ها	۶۲۵
۸-۱۸. اشیا متفرقه، سرباره و بقایای فلزات	۶۲۸
۹-۱۸. ابزار سنگی پیش‌ازتاریخ	۶۳۴

فصل ۱۹. هاون‌های آهکی از پل دیوار گرگان بر روی رودخانه ساری سو ۶۴۱

مارتینا آستولفی و ریلی اسنایدر

۱-۱۹. مقدمه	۶۴۱
۲-۱۹. مواد و روش‌ها	۶۴۱
۱-۲-۱۹. نمونه‌ها	۶۴۱
۲-۲-۱۹. تحلیل پتروگرافی از مقطع صیقل‌یافته	۶۴۳
۳-۲-۱۹. تحلیل فلورسانس اشعه ایکس	۶۴۴
۳-۱۹. بحث	۶۴۴
۴-۱۹. نتیجه	۶۴۵

فصل ۲۰. باستان‌جانورشناسی محوطه‌های ساسانی و اسلامی از دیوار گرگان تا دشت تهران ۶۴۷

مرجان مشکور، رویا خزائلی، سولماز امیری، هما فتحی، ساناز بیضایی دوست، آزاده محاسب، حسین داوودی، کارین دبو، آنتوان روونت، والنتین رادو، هایده لاله، جبرئیل نوکنده، حمید عمرانی رکاوندی، محمدرضا نعمتی و ابرهارد سوئر

۱-۲۰. مقدمه	۶۴۷
۲-۲۰. مواد و روش‌ها	۶۴۷
۱-۲-۲۰. تعیین خاصیت و تافونومی	۶۴۷
۲-۲-۲۰. زیست سنجی	۶۴۸
۳-۲-۲۰. تحلیل جمعیتی	۶۵۰
۳-۲۰. شیوه‌های مصرف و استفاده از جانوران در محوطه‌های ساسانی و محوطه‌های جدیدتر از گرگان تا دشت تهران	۶۵۰
۱-۳-۲۰. قلعه ۲	۶۵۰
۲-۳-۲۰. پل دیوار گرگان بر روی رودخانه ساری سو	۶۵۸
۳-۳-۲۰. گبری قلعه	۶۵۸
۴-۳-۲۰. قلعه پل گنبدکاووس	۶۵۹
۵-۳-۲۰. بوراق تپه	۶۶۱
۶-۳-۲۰. قلعه ایرج	۶۶۱
۴-۲۰. گونه‌های بیان‌شده	۶۶۱
۱-۴-۲۰. ریخت‌شناسی جمعیت گله گاو، بز و گوسفند	۶۶۱
۱-۱-۴-۲۰. مقدمه	۶۶۱
۲-۱-۴-۲۰. گوسفند	۶۶۴
۳-۱-۴-۲۰. بزها	۶۶۵
۴-۱-۴-۲۰. گاو	۶۶۵

فهرست مطالب

۵۶۳	۳-۴-۷-۱۵. تحلیل TGA-DTA و XRD
۵۷۰	۵-۷-۱۵. نتیجه
۵۷۰	۸-۱۵. پیوست: ظروف سفالی از فصل ۲۰۱۷ در قلعه ایرج
	محمدرضا نعمتی و مهدی موسوی‌نیا

فصل ۱۶. شیشه ۵۷۷

فیونا آنه موات و تیم پن

۵۷۷	۱-۱۶. مقدمه
۵۷۷	۲-۱۶. بررسی اجمالی مجموعه
۵۷۷	۳-۱۶. طبقات بافت
۵۷۷	۱-۳-۱۶. سبز آبی
۵۸۲	۲-۳-۱۶. آبی
۵۸۳	۳-۳-۱۶. سبز
۵۸۳	۴-۳-۱۶. زرد، کهربا و قهوه‌ای
۵۸۴	۵-۳-۱۶. بافت‌های مات
۵۸۴	۶-۳-۱۶. بافت‌های بی رنگ
۵۸۵	۷-۳-۱۶. بافت‌های نامشخص
۵۸۶	۴-۱۶. ظروف با اطمینان تاریخ‌گذاری‌شده
۵۸۷	۵-۱۶. موقعیت یافته‌ها و پراکنش آنها

فصل ۱۷. ظروف شیشه‌ای: یک دستیابی باستان‌سنجی ۵۹۱

محمدامین امامی و فرحناز بیات‌نژاد

۵۹۱	۱-۱۷. معرفی
۵۹۱	۲-۱۷. مواد و روش‌ها
۵۹۱	۱-۲-۱۷. روش‌های تحلیلی
۵۹۱	۱-۱-۲-۱۷. فلورسانس اشعه ایکس (WXRF)
۵۹۲	۲-۱-۲-۱۷. میکروسکوپ الکترونی روبشی (SEM)
۵۹۲	۳-۱-۲-۱۷. آنالیز حرارتی همزمان (STA)
۵۹۲	۲-۲-۱۷. نمونه
۵۹۲	۳-۱۷. نتایج و بحث
۵۹۲	۱-۳-۱۷. تحلیل فلورسانس اشعه ایکس از ترکیب شیمیایی حجم
۵۹۳	۲-۳-۱۷. تحلیل میکروساختاری از طریق میکروسکوپ الکترونی روبشی (SEM)
۵۹۶	۳-۳-۱۷. آنالیز حرارتی همزمان (STA)
۵۹۸	۴-۱۷. نتیجه

فصل ۱۸. اشیا کوچک و سایر یافته‌ها ۶۰۱

ابرهارد سوئر، سنت جان سیمپسون، مهدی جاهد، محدثه منصوری، مرضیه مصلحی، محمدرضا نعمتی، جبرئیل نوکنده، حمید عمرانی رکاوندی، تیم پن و علیرضا سالاری

۶۰۱	۱-۱۸. مقدمه
۶۰۱	۲-۱۸. جنگ‌افزار
۶۰۵	۳-۱۸. ابزارها
۶۰۵	۱-۳-۱۸. چاقو و ابزارهای شخصی دیگر
۶۰۷	۲-۳-۱۸. سنگ‌ساب‌ها
۶۰۸	۳-۳-۱۸. سنگ آسیاب

فهرست مطالب

۱-۳-۳-۱۵. ظروف خشن (بخش غربی دیوار گرگان و بوراق تپه)	۴۸۱
۲-۳-۳-۱۵. ظروف خشن (بخش شرقی دیوار گرگان، قلعه ۲)	۴۸۷
۴-۳-۱۵. مشخصات گونه شناسی سفال‌ها	۴۹۷
۱-۴-۳-۱۵. اشکال بسته در اندازه متوسط	۴۹۷
۱-۱-۴-۳-۱۵. کوزه‌های فاقد گردن	۴۹۷
۲-۱-۴-۳-۱۵. کوزه‌های فاقد گردن دارای بافت خشن	۴۹۹
۳-۱-۴-۳-۱۵. پارچه‌های دهانه شبدری	۵۰۰
۲-۴-۳-۱۵. اشکال بسته در اندازه بزرگ	۵۰۱
۱-۲-۴-۳-۱۵. کوزه‌های دارای یک دسته با گردن‌های بلند دراز و کشیده	۵۰۱
۲-۲-۴-۳-۱۵. خمره‌های ذخیره‌سازی	۵۰۱
۳-۲-۴-۳-۱۵. ظروف آشپزخانه‌ای	۵۰۳
۳-۴-۳-۱۵. اشکال باز در اندازه کوچک	۵۰۵
۱-۳-۴-۳-۱۵. کاسه	۵۰۵
۵-۳-۱۵. روش کمی متناوب	۵۰۶
۴-۱۵. محوطه‌های کاوش‌شده	۵۰۷
۱-۴-۱۵. پل ساری سو (ترانشه B)	۵۰۷
امانوئل اینتاگلیاتا	
۲-۴-۱۵. قلعه ۲ (ترانشه‌های سی و د، بخش شرقی دیوار بزرگ گرگان)	۵۰۸
۱-۲-۴-۱۵. مواد و روش‌ها	۵۰۸
۲-۲-۴-۱۵. مجموعه‌های سفالی از اتاق‌های سربازخانه‌ها (ترانشه D) نشانه‌ای از کارکرد آن‌ها در فضا و زمان	۵۱۰
۳-۲-۴-۱۵. تغییرات در مجموعه سفالی اتاق‌های سربازخانه‌ها (ترانشه D) با گذشت زمان	۵۱۵
۴-۲-۴-۱۵. نتایج و بحث	۵۱۸
۳-۴-۱۵. بوراق تپه (ترانشه G)	۵۳۴
۴-۴-۱۵. قلعه پل گنبد کاووس (ترانشهA)	۵۳۹
امانوئل اینتاگلیاتا	
۵-۴-۱۵. گبری قلعه (ترانشه‌های A و F)	۵۴۰
۶-۴-۱۵. قلعه ایرج	۵۴۲
۵-۱۵. مطالعات مقایسه‌ای	۵۴۲
۱-۵-۱۵. سفال‌های همزمان به‌دست‌آمده از قلعه‌های دیوار گرگان و استحکامات در مناطق داخلی	۵۴۲
۲-۵-۱۵. سفال‌های همزمان از مناطق همسایه	۵۴۸
۶-۱۵. نتیجه	۵۴۹
۷-۱۵. تحلیل‌های شیمیایی و طیف سنجی ارتعاشی از گونه‌های مشابه ظروف به‌دست‌آمده از قلعه‌های دیوار بزرگ گرگان و استحکامات در مناطق داخلی آن	۵۵۱
ماریا داغمه چی، بهروز کریمی شهرکی، هادی عمرانی، معصومه معدنی‌پور، آریانیت ریکا، جبرئیل نوکنده، حمید عمرانی رکاوندی، محمدامین امامی و ابرهارد سوئر	
۱-۷-۱۵. مقدمه	۵۵۱
۱-۱-۷-۱۵. طرح کلی	۵۵۱
۲-۱-۷-۱۵. پیش‌زمینه	۵۵۱
۲-۷-۱۵. مواد و روش‌ها	۵۵۲
۳-۷-۱۵. مشخصات پتروگرافی	۵۵۳
۴-۷-۱۵. ترکیبات شیمیایی ذرات کانی و بافت رسی	۵۵۴
۱-۴-۷-۱۵. تحلیل شیمیایی	۵۵۹
۲-۴-۷-۱۵. تحلیل FTIR	۵۵۹

فهرست مطالب

فصل ۱۳. محیط‌های پارینه در بخش انتهایی دیوارهای گرگان و تمیشه در کاسپی ۴۲۵

سوزان لروی، فرانسوا دیموری، فرانسوا شالیه، مارتین بیتس، ریچارد بیتس، حمید عمرانی رکاوندی و ابرهارد سوئر

۱-۱۳. زمینه و اهداف	۴۲۵
۲-۱۳. مطالعات پیشین پژوهش‌های گرده شناختی	۴۲۵
۳-۱۳. مواد و روش‌ها	۴۲۵
۱-۳-۱۳. کار میدانی و شرح مغزه‌ها	۴۲۵
۲-۳-۱۳. پذیرفتاری مغناطیسی	۴۲۶
۳-۳-۱۳. گرده‌شناسی	۴۲۷
۴-۳-۱۳. تاریخ‌گذاری رادیوکربن	۴۲۷
۴-۱۳. نتایج	۴۲۸
۱-۴-۱۳. انتهای غربی دیوار گرگان	۴۲۸
۲-۴-۱۳. محدوده انتهایی شمالی دیوار تمیشه	۴۳۲
۵-۱۳. تفسیر	۴۳۶
۱-۵-۱۳. بخش پایانی غربی دیوار گرگان	۴۳۶
۲-۵-۱۳. محدوده بخش پایانی شمالی دیوار تمیشه	۴۳۷
۶-۱۳. تغییرات سطح تراز آب دریای کاسپی از دوران پیش از ساسانیان تا اوایل زمان‌های اخیر	۴۳۸
۱-۶-۱۳. دوره پیش از ساخت دیوار	۴۳۸
۲-۶-۱۳. دیوارهای دوره ساسانیان و پسروی سطح تراز آب دریای کاسپی	۴۳۸
۳-۶-۱۳. از اواخر دوره ساسانیان تا اوایل قرون میانی	۴۳۸
۴-۶-۱۳. سیل‌زدگی قرون میانی و عصر یخبندان کوچک	۴۳۹
۷-۱۳. محیط ساحلی در زمان ساسانیان	۴۳۹
۱-۷-۱۳. توالی S2-V3 غرب دیوار گرگان	۴۳۹
۲-۷-۱۳. پوشش گیاهی در زمان دیوارها و بعد	۴۳۹
۸-۱۳. نتیجه	۴۴۰
فهرست مطالب، پروژه و عناوین در فارسی	۴۵۸

بخش D: همکاری‌های متخصصین: اسناد مکتوب، یافته‌ها، مصالح ساختمانی، شواهد محیطی و زیستی و تاریخ‌گذاری علمی

فصل ۱۴. استروکا و گل مهرها از قلعه ایرج ۴۶۱

کارلو چرتی، محمدرضا نعمتی و مهدی موسوی‌نیا

۱-۱۴. مقدمه	۴۶۱
۲-۱۴. کاتالوگ	۴۶۲
۳-۱۴. نتیجه	۴۷۲

فصل ۱۵. مطالعات مقایسه‌ای سفال‌های ساسانیان از قلعه‌های دیوار بزرگ گرگان و استحکامات در مناطق داخلی آن ۴۷۵

ماریا داغمه چی، ست پریستمن، گبریله پوشنیگ، جبرئیل نوکنده، امانوئل اینتاگلیاتا، حمید عمرانی رکاوندی و ابرهارد سوئر

۱-۱۵. مقدمات	۴۷۵
۱-۱-۱۵. چکیده	۴۷۵
۲-۱-۱۵. مقدمه	۴۷۵
۲-۱۵. مواد و روش‌ها	۴۷۶
۳-۱۵. طبقه‌بندی	۴۷۸
۱-۳-۱۵. مشخصات فیزیکی سفال‌های ساسانیان	۴۷۸
۲-۳-۱۵. گروه‌های پختی سفال‌ها	۴۷۹
۳-۳-۱۵. مشخصات پتروگرافی سفال‌ها	۴۸۰

فهرست مطالب

۵-۹. گاهنگاری قلعه ایرج	۳۸۱
۶-۹. قلعه ایرج: مرکز قدرت شبکه دفاعی شمال ایران؟	۳۸۲

فصل ۱۰. یک شهر ساسانیان: آتشکده، خیابان‌های آجرفرش و بخش‌های مسکونی: بررسی‌های ژئوفیزیکی و هوایی در دشت قلعه ۳۸۷

۱-۱۰. مقدمه	۳۸۷
۲-۱۰. بررسی سنجش از راه دور	۳۸۸
۳-۱۰. آتشکده	۳۸۹
۴-۱۰. جاده‌ها و بخش‌های مسکونی	۳۹۲
۵-۱۰. پایتخت منطقه؟	۳۹۸

بخش: C بررسی دریایی

فصل ۱۱. کشف بخش‌های ناشناخته دیوار بزرگ گرگان در نزدیکی سواحل دریای کاسپی ۴۰۵

ریچارد بیتس، مارتین بیتس و حمید عمرانی رکاوندی

۱-۱۱. مقدمه	۴۰۵
۲-۱۱. اهداف بررسی	۴۰۵
۳-۱۱. روش‌شناسی	۴۰۵
۴-۱۱. نتایج	۴۰۶
۱-۴-۱۱. نتایج بررسی در نزدیکی غربی‌ترین مکان شناخته‌شده‌ی خندق (مقطع ۱)	۴۰۶
۲-۴-۱۱. ژئوفیزیک ترانشه	۴۰۹
۳-۴-۱۱. نتایج بررسی (مقطع ۲)	۴۱۰
۴-۴-۱۱. نتایج بررسی (مقطع ۳)	۴۱۰
۵-۱۱. ژرفاسنجی و بررسی کف دریای کاسپی در امتداد دیوار گرگان	۴۱۱
۱-۵-۱۱. مقدمه	۴۱۱
۲-۵-۱۱. سونار روبش جانبی/سونار اسکن	۴۱۲
۳-۵-۱۱. نیمرخ کف دریا	۴۱۲
۴-۵-۱۱. نتایج	۴۱۳
۶-۱۱. بحث	۴۱۳

فصل ۱۲. ژرفاسنجی و بررسی کف (دریای کاسپی) به منظور شناسایی شمالی ترین بخش دیوار تمیشه فرورفته (مغروق) در دریای کاسپی ۴۱۵

ریچارد بیتس و حمید عمرانی رکاوندی و حسین توفیقیان

۱-۱۲. مقدمه	۴۱۵
۲-۱۲. اهداف بررسی	۴۱۶
۳-۱۲. روش‌شناسی	۴۱۶
۴-۱۲. نتایج	۴۱۷
۱-۴-۱۲. محوطه جنوبی	۴۱۷
۲-۴-۱۲. عمق‌سنجی کف دریا	۴۱۷
۳-۴-۱۲. سونار روبش جانبی/سونار اسکن	۴۱۷
۴-۴-۱۲. نیمرخ کف دریا	۴۱۷
۵-۱۲. بحث	۴۲۳

فهرست مطالب

۴-۲-۸. پراکندگی یافته‌های سطحی	۲۹۵
۵-۲-۸. بررسی ژئوفیزیک	۲۹۶
۶-۲-۸. یک برش در میان موانع دفاعی (ترانشه a)	۲۹۷
۷-۲-۸. چینه‌شناسی سیستم خندق	۲۹۸
۸-۲-۸. قدیمی‌ترین خندق‌ها (۴-۱)	۲۹۹
۹-۲-۸. خندق پنجم	۳۰۴
۱۰-۲-۸. خندق ششم	۳۰۸
۱۱-۲-۸. خندق هفتم	۳۱۱
۱۲-۲-۸. سطح زمین و خاک سطحی در دوره ساسانیان	۳۱۱
۱۳-۲-۸. دیوار	۳۱۲
۱۴-۲-۸. ابعاد موانع دفاعی در فاز ۱	۳۱۵
۱۵-۲-۸. عرصه امروزی سرحد خندق‌ها	۳۲۰
۱۶-۲-۸. تاریخ‌گذاری قلعه پل گنبد کاووس	۳۲۰
۳-۸. گبری قلعه: از دژ ساسانیان تا شهر ایلخانی	۳۲۵
۱-۳-۸. مقدمه و بررسی توپوگرافی	۳۲۵
۲-۳-۸. بررسی ژئوفیزیک	۳۳۳
۳-۳-۸. یک خیابان بازاری شلوغ در یک شهر قرون میانی (ترانشه E)	۳۳۴
۴-۳-۸. مسیر دسترسی به گبری قلعه ساسانی و قرون میانی (ترانشه F)	۳۳۸
۵-۳-۸. خاستگاه و اهمیت گبری قلعه	۳۴۳
۴-۸. قلعه خرابه	۳۴۵
۱-۴-۸. بررسی ژئوفیزیک	۳۴۵
۲-۴-۸. بررسی پهباد	۳۴۵
۳-۴-۸. کالیبراسیون مجدد نمونه‌های رادیوکربن	۳۴۵
۵-۸. دژ در دشت گرگان	۳۴۶

فصل ۹. قلعه ایرج: یک دژ / مرکز فرماندهی لشکر شمالی ارتش؟ ۳۵۷
محمدرضا نعمتی، مهدی موسوی‌نیا و ابرهارد سوئر

۱-۹. مقدمه	۳۵۷
۲-۹. کاوش‌ها در داخل دروازه جنوب شرقی	۳۵۹
۱-۲-۹. اولین فصل‌های میدانی	۳۵۹
۲-۲-۹. قدمت قلعه: کاوش‌ها در داخل دروازه جنوب‌شرقی در سال ۲۰۱۶	۳۶۱
۱-۲-۲-۹. کاوش‌ها در دروازه (ترانشه h)	۳۶۱
۲-۲-۲-۹. اتاق جانبی دروازه جنوب‌شرقی (ترانشه i)	۳۶۷
۳-۹. بررسی ژئوفیزیک	۳۷۳
۱-۳-۹. مقدمه	۳۷۳
۲-۳-۹. محوطه‌ی A	۳۷۳
۳-۳-۹. محوطه‌های B و D	۳۷۴
۴-۹. بینش‌های جدید درباره تاریخ اشغال قلعه: کاوش در دیوارهای جنوبی قلعه در سال ۲۰۱۷	۳۷۷
۱-۴-۹. مقدمه	۳۷۷
۲-۴-۹. ترانشه F128	۳۷۷
۳-۴-۹. ترانشه F 129	۳۷۸
۴-۴-۹. ترانشه G129	۳۷۹
۵-۴-۹. بحث	۳۷۹

فهرست مطالب

فصل ۶. موانع پس از ساسانیان ۲۱۱
۶-۱. سنگ خاکی جر کلباد: یک شبیه‌سازی اساسی از دیوار تمیشه، تعیین‌کننده در نزاع‌های دوره جدید امروزی ۲۱۱
۶-۲. دیوار فرود در نزدیکی کلات در خراسان ۲۱۴
میثم لباف‌خانیکی، ابرهارد سوئر، کریستین هوپر، داویت نسکیداشویلی، بردیا شعبانی و دیوید گاگوشیدزه
۶-۲-۱. دیوار فرود ۲۱۴
۶-۲-۲. ارگ فرود ۲۱۶
۶-۲-۳. بررسی پیمایشی و هوایی از دیوار فرود ۲۱۹
۶-۲-۴. یک گمانه در ارگ فرود (ترانشه j) ۲۲۵
۶-۲-۵. یک گمانه در داخل برج مراقبت در دیوار فرود (ترانشه k) ۲۳۱
۶-۲-۶. تاریخ، بافت تاریخی و کارکرد موانع اطراف کلات ۲۳۴
۶-۳. دره لاندار ۲۳۷
میثم لباف‌خانیکی و کریستین هوپر
۶-۴. دیوارها، برج‌ها و یک قلعه یا کاروانسرا در مزدوران ۲۴۲
میثم لباف‌خانیکی، کریستین هوپر و ابرهارد سوئر

فصل ۷. قلعه‌های در مناطق داخلی سرزمین ۲۴۹
۷-۱. قلعه‌هایی در جلگه گرگان ۲۴۹
۷-۲. بوراق تپه ۲۵۳
۷-۲-۱. بوراق تپه: جایگاه و ظرفیت‌های پژوهشی از یک پست نگهبانی راهبردی ۲۵۳
۷-۲-۲. بررسی ژئوفیزیک ۲۵۵
۷-۲-۳. بررسی هوایی و پیمایشی ۲۵۸
۷-۲-۴. یک گمانه در بوراق تپه (ترانشه g) ۲۶۰
۷-۲-۴-۱. مقدمه ۲۶۰
۷-۲-۴-۲. قلعه‌سازی و معماری ساختمان‌های داخلی ۲۶۱
۷-۲-۴-۳. سکونت اولیه در داخل قلعه ۲۶۸
۷-۲-۴-۴. تسطیح‌سازی و زندگی بر روی زمین بالاتر ۲۶۹
۷-۲-۴-۵. ساخت تنور ۲۶۹
۷-۲-۴-۶. یک اجاق /بخاری جدید به عنوان کانون فعالیت‌های داخلی ۲۷۰
۷-۲-۴-۷. ترک و خرابی موقت محوطه؟ ۲۷۱
۷-۲-۴-۸. سکونت مجدد و تقلیل به یک پادگان؟ ۲۷۱
۷-۲-۴-۹. آخرین دوره سکونت و ساخت مجدد تنور ۲۷۲
۷-۲-۴-۱۰. افق‌های بهم‌ریخته در بالای قلعه‌ی متروکه ۲۷۲
۷-۲-۴-۱۱. اندازه پادگان ۲۷۳
۷-۲-۴-۱۲. تاریخ و گاهنگاری سکونت بوراق تپه ۲۷۷
۷-۳. حبیب ایشان: یک نوع از استحکامات در مناطق داخلی ساسانی با یک ارگ در گوشه؟ ۲۷۸
۷-۴. قلعه‌ها در مسیر گرگان رود قدیم: بخش‌هایی از یک شبکه دفاعی ساسانیان؟ هدف از قلعه‌های ساسانی جنوب دیوار بزرگ ۲۸۰

فصل ۸. دژ/قلعه‌ها ۲۸۷
۸-۱. مقدمه ۲۸۷
۸-۲. قلعه پل گنبدکاووس: بزرگترین قلعه ساسانی در دشت گرگان ۲۸۷
۸-۲-۱. معرفی و تحلیل مقایسه‌ای قلعه پل گنبدکاووس و سایر دژها ۲۸۷
۸-۲-۲. دیوارهای دارای برج و دروازه ۲۹۲
۸-۲-۳. خندق ۲۹۴

فهرست مطالب

۸۴	۴-۱-۴. سربازخانه‌ها در قلعه ۲ (ترانشه D)
۸۴	۴-۱-۴-۱. مقدمه
۸۵	۴-۱-۴-۲. ساخت و طرح پادگان، فاز ۱ (ترانشه D)
۸۵	۴-۱-۴-۲-۱. سربازخانه‌های اصلی
۸۸	۴-۱-۴-۲-۲. تعیین خواص آجرهای مورد نیاز برای ساخت سربازخانه
۸۹	۴-۱-۴-۲-۳. گسترش سربازخانه از طریق الحاقات افزوده شده به بنا
۹۹	۴-۱-۴-۳. گاهنگاری ساخت و سکونت سربازخانه در ترانشه D
۱۰۶	۴-۱-۴-۴. تاریخ سکونت اتاق‌های سربازخانه
۱۰۶	۴-۱-۴-۴-۱. سربازخانه اصلی: ردیف‌های ۲ و ۳
۱۰۶	۴-۱-۴-۴-۱-۱. ردیف غربی اتاق‌ها (۲) در سربازخانه اصلی
۱۱۱	۴-۱-۴-۴-۱-۲. ردیف شرقی اتاق‌ها (۳) در سربازخانه اصلی
۱۱۶	۴-۱-۴-۴-۱-۳. مشخصات سربازخانه‌های اصلی (ردیف‌های ۲ و ۳)
۱۱۶	۴-۱-۴-۴-۲. الحاقات غربی: ردیف‌های ۰ و ۱
۱۱۶	۴-۱-۴-۴-۲-۱. ردیف شرقی اتاق‌ها (۱) در الحاقات غربی
۱۲۹	۴-۱-۴-۴-۲-۲. غربی‌ترین ردیف اتاق‌ها (۰) در الحاقات غربی
۱۳۶	۴-۱-۴-۴-۳. الحاقات شرقی: ردیف‌های ۴ و ۵
۱۳۶	۴-۱-۴-۴-۳-۱. ردیف غربی (۴) الحاقات شرقی
۱۴۱	۴-۱-۴-۴-۳-۲. ردیف شرقی (۵) در الحاقات شرقی
۱۵۲	۴-۱-۴-۴-۴. نواحی فضای باز تا غرب سربازخانه‌ها
۱۵۳	۴-۱-۴-۴-۵. نواحی فضای باز تا شرق سربازخانه‌ها
۱۵۵	۴-۱-۴-۵. زندگی در سربازخانه‌ها ساسانیان در دیوار گرگان
۱۵۵	۴-۱-۴-۵-۱. سیستم گرمایشی و پخت‌وپز در سربازخانه‌ها ساسانیان
۱۶۱	۴-۱-۴-۵-۲. ذخیره‌سازی مواد غذایی
۱۶۱	۴-۱-۴-۵-۲-۱. گودال‌های ذخیره‌سازی
۱۶۳	۴-۱-۴-۵-۲-۲. ظروف ذخیره‌سازی و بهسازی احتمالی برای تدارکات ارتش
۱۶۵	۴-۱-۴-۵-۳. توزیع یافته‌ها
۱۶۷	۴-۱-۴-۶. گاهنگاری سکونت قلعه ۲ (ترانشه D)
۱۶۷	۴-۱-۴-۶-۱. شروع سکونت
۱۷۰	۴-۱-۴-۶-۲. پایان سکونت
۱۷۲	۴-۱-۴-۶-۳. تراکم سکونت در طول زمان
۱۷۳	۴-۲. سربازخانه‌ها در قلعه ۱۵
۱۷۳	۴-۳. سربازخانه‌ها در قلعه ۲۵
۱۷۵	۴-۴. سربازخانه‌ها در قلعه ۲۶
۱۷۸	۴-۵. بررسی ژئوفیزیکی در محوطه‌ای در ضلع شمالی دیوار بزرگ
۱۷۸	۴-۶. بررسی سنجش از راه دور از قلعه‌ها در امتداد دیوار بزرگ
۱۷۸	۴-۶-۱. مقدمه
۱۷۹	۴-۶-۲. بررسی ماهواره‌ای
۱۷۹	۴-۶-۳. بررسی پهبادی

فصل ۵. دیوار تمیشه و قلعه‌های مرتبط با آن

۲۰۳	
۲۰۳	۵-۱. مقدمه
۲۰۴	۵-۲. بررسی زیر آب از یک قلعه غرق‌شده
۲۰۹	۵-۳. بررسی سنجش از راه دور دیوار تمیشه

فهرست مطالب

سپاسگزاری

بخش A: مقدمات

فصل ۱. مقدمه ... ۳
  ۱-۱. مسابقه تسلیحاتی باستان: از زمان شکل‌گیری تاریخ جهان تا به امروز ... ۳
  ۱-۲. زمینه و هدف پروژه ... ۵

بخش B: کاوش‌ها و بررسی‌های میدانی

فصل ۲. مناظر ساسانی دشت گرگان: بینش‌های جدیدی از سنجش از دور و بررسی میدانی ... ۱۱
کریستین هوپر، حمید عمرانی رکاوندی، آندره ریچی، لین ولتون، دن لارنس و گراهام فیلیپ
  ۲-۱. مقدمه ... ۱۱
  ۲-۲. بررسی دیوار گرگان ۲۰۱۶-۲۰۱۴ ... ۱۱
  ۲-۳. انواع محوطه ساسانیان: استحکامات هندسی ... ۱۱
    ۲-۳-۱. استحکامات هندسی با وسعت بیش از ۶ هکتار ... ۱۴
    ۲-۳-۲. استحکامات هندسی بین ۲ تا ۶ هکتار ... ۱۶
    ۲-۳-۳. استحکامات هندسی یک هکتاری یا کمتر ... ۱۸
  ۲-۴. سکونتگاه‌های روستایی ساسانیان ... ۱۸
  ۲-۵. بررسی عوارض در مجاورت قلعه‌های دیوار گرگان ... ۲۰
  ۲-۶. عوارض هیدرولوژیکی مرتبط با دیوار گرگان و استحکامات هندسی ... ۲۱
  ۲-۷. نتیجه‌گیری ... ۲۲

فصل ۳. دیوار گرگان ... ۲۷
  ۳-۱. مقدمه ... ۲۷
  ۳-۲. پل دیوار گرگان و یک مخزن آب ساسانیان بین قلعه‌های A۲ و ۲ ... ۲۹
    ۳-۲-۱. تاسیسات هیدرولیکی ساسانیان در دره رودخانه ساری سو ... ۲۹
    ۳-۲-۲. یک بخش جدید از دیوار گرگان، کشف‌شده توسط بررسی ژئوفیزیکی و پیمایشی، منتهی شده به سمت یک پل ... ۳۰
    ۳-۲-۳. پل دیوار گرگان (ترانشه B) ... ۳۴
    ۳-۲-۴. طرح پل ... ۴۹
    ۳-۲-۵. محافظت از پل در برابر فرسایش ... ۵۲
    ۳-۲-۶. رسوبات آبرفتی و شواهد ضمنی برای یک سد و مخزن ساسانیان در رودخانه ساری سو ... ۵۵
    ۳-۲-۷. گاه‌نگاری ... ۶۳
    ۳-۲-۸. هدف از مخزن آب ... ۶۶
    ۳-۲-۹. سرقت آجر و رسوب‌گذاری در زمان‌های پس از ساسانیان ... ۶۸
  ۳-۳. بررسی پهبادی از دیوار گرگان ... ۷۰

فصل ۴. قلعه‌های دیوار گرگان ... ۷۵
  ۴-۱. قلعه ۲ ... ۷۵
    ۴-۱-۱. مقدمه ... ۷۵
    ۴-۱-۲. بررسی سنجش از راه دور، پیمایشی، مغناطیس‌سنجی و توپوگرافی از قلعه ۲ ... ۷۶
      ۴-۱-۲-۱. موانع دفاعی قلعه ... ۷۶
      ۴-۱-۲-۲. اشغال داخلی ... ۸۰
      ۴-۱-۲-۳. نتیجه‌گیری ... ۸۲
    ۴-۱-۳. کاوش از یک برج فاصله‌ای قلعه ۲ (ترانشه C) ... ۸۲

الف

با همکاری

ریچارد بیتس،کتی بت، کارلو چرتی، ماریا داغمه چی، کریستین هوپر، میثم لباف خانیکی، سوزان لروی، مرجان مشکور، مهدی موسوی‌نیا، محمدرضا نعمتی، بردیا شعبانی، لودمیلا شومیلوسکیخ، مارتینا استولفی، محمد امین امامی، محمد (آرمان) ارشادی، رویا خزائیلی، ایو مک دونالد، فیونا موات، داویت نسکیداشویلی، تیم پن، ست پریستمن، اسماعیل صفری تمک، ست جان سیمپسون، ریلی اسنایدر، حسین توفیقیان، قربانعلی عباسی، سولماز امیری، بایگلدی آرتقی، محمد باقر بیاتی، یان بایلیف، مارتین بیتس، فرحناز بیات‌نژاد، فیلیکس بیتمن، محمد مهدی برهانی، فرانچسکو کاپوتو، لنا چولوگایوری، هما فتحی، آنا گابونیا، دیوید گاگوشیدزه، دیوید گرینوود، مارک هییسی، مریم حسین‌زاده، اما‌نوئل اینتاگلیاتا، مهدی جاهد، جولین جانسن فون رینسبورگ، فریدریکه یورکه، کوبا کوبیریدزه، دن لورینسی، مجید محمودی، محدثه منصوری رضی، کوروش محمدخانی، مرضیه مصلحی، علی نانکلی، کلودیا نونس کالدیرا، سیلویا پرینی، گراهام فیلیپ، پرزمیسلاو پولاکیویتس، گبریله پوشنیگ، ماشاالله رحمانی، اندریاس ریچی، علیرضا سالاری برکویی، لیزا اسنپ، بریژیت تالون، لینن ولتون، روجر اینسلی، مریم عجم حسینی، عالیه امیرنژاد، زهرا اصغری، ساناز بیضایی‌دوست، فرانسوا شالیه، حسین داوودی، کارین دبوو، فرانسوا دیموری، مرتضی حسنی، مونا حسین‌دوست، تریم کینات، بهروز کریمی شهرکی، فاطمه خواجوی، هایده لاله، معصومه معدنی‌پور، محدثه ملکان، مقداد میرموسوی، میلاد میرموسوی، آناهیتا میترترینر، سروش محمدخانی، آزاده محاسب، ناهید نظیفی، هادی عمرانی، دانیلا پایتزولد، کاتریونا پیکراد، مهدی پوربخت، والنتین رادو، محمدرضا رحیمی، مجید رمضانی‌فرد، آریانیت ریکا، آنتوان روشونت، سحر صفرزاده، محمدتقی ملکا، حامد طهماسبی‌فر و داود تاجی.

مسابقه تسلیحاتی در دنیای باستان:
بزرگترین استحکامات دفاعی دوره باستان
و شبکه‌های نظامی ساسانیان در شمال ایران

پروژه میدانی مشترک سازمان میراث‌فرهنگی، صنایع‌دستی و گردشگری ایران و دانشگاه ادینبورگ
(۲۰۱۴ - ۲۰۱۶)

موسسه مطالعات ایران‌شناسی بریتانیا
ویژه‌نامه‌ی پژوهشی باستان‌شناسی سری هفتم

ابرهارد سوئر، جبرئیل نوکنده و حمید عمرانی رکاوندی

OXBOW books
Oxford & Philadelphia

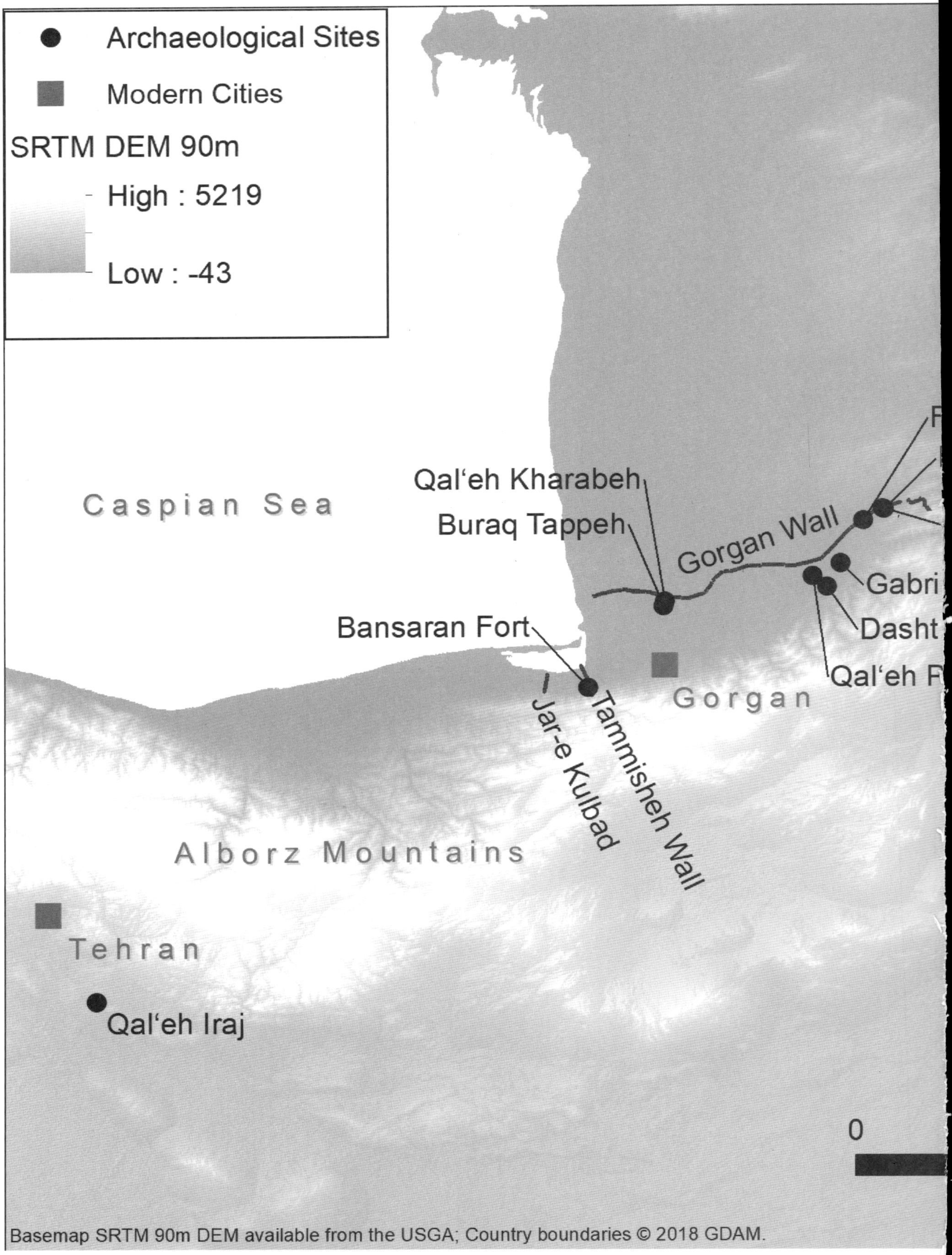
Archaeological Sites
Modern Cities
SRTM DEM 90m
High : 5219
Low : -43
Caspian Sea
Qal‘eh Kharabeh
Buraq Tappeh
Gorgan Wall
Bansaran Fort
Jar-e Kulbad
Tammisheh Wall
Gorgan
Dasht
Alborz Mountains
Tehran
Qal‘eh Iraj
0
Basemap SRTM 90m DEM available from the USGA; Country boundaries © 2018 GDAM.